CLOAK AND DAGGER FICTION

Recent Titles in
Bibliographies and Indexes in World Literature

Caribbean Women Novelists: An Annotated Critical Bibliography
Lizabeth Paravisini-Gebert and Olga Torres-Seda, compilers

Clockworks: A Multimedia Bibliography of Works Useful for the Study
of the Human/Machine Interface in SF
Richard D. Erlich and Thomas P. Dunn, compilers

Oscar Wilde: An Annotated Bibliography
Thomas A. Mikolyzk, compiler

Modern Verse Drama in English: An Annotated Bibliography
Kayla McKinney Wiggins, compiler

Children's Books on Ancient Greek and Roman Mythology
Antoinette Brazouski and Mary J. Klatt, compilers

The Proverbial Bernard Shaw: An Index to Proverbs in the Works of
George Bernard Shaw
George B. Bryan and Wolfgang Mieder, compilers

Bibliographic Guide to Gabriel García Márquez, 1986–1992
Nelly Sfeir de González, compiler

The Juvenile Novels of World War II: An Annotated Bibliography
Desmond Taylor

The Spanish Civil War in Literature, Film, and Art: An International
Bibliography of Secondary Literature
Peter Monteath, compiler

Africa in Literature for Children and Young Adults: An Annotated
Bibliography of English-Language Books
Meena Khorana

Indigenous Literature of Oceania: A Survey of Criticism and Interpretation
Nicholas J. Goetzfridt

Boccaccio in English: A Bibliography of Editions, Adaptations, and Criticism
F. S. Stych

CLOAK AND DAGGER FICTION

An Annotated Guide to Spy Thrillers

**Myron J. Smith, Jr.
and Terry White**

Foreword by Julian Rathbone

Preface by Joe Poyer

Third Edition

Bibliographies and Indexes in World Literature,
Number 45

GREENWOOD PRESS
Westport, Connecticut • London

Library of Congress Cataloging-in-Publication Data

Smith, Myron J.
    Cloak and dagger fiction : an annotated guide to spy thrillers. —
3rd ed. / Myron J. Smith, Jr., and Terry White ; foreword by Julian
Rathbone ; preface by Joe Poyer.
        p.   cm. — (Bibliographies and indexes in world literature,
ISSN 0742–6801 ; no. 45)
    Rev. ed. of: Cloak and dagger fiction / Myron J. Smith, Jr. 2nd
ed. Santa Barbara, Calif. : ABC-Clio, ©1982; without series.
    Includes bibliographical references and indexes.
    ISBN 0–313–27700–1
    1. Spy stories, English—Bibliography. 2. Spy stories, American—
Bibliography. 3. English fiction—20th century—Bibliography.
4. American fiction—20th century—Bibliography. 5. Spy stories—
Stories, plots, etc. I. White, Terry. II. Title.
III. Series.
Z2014.S64S54   1995
[PR830.S54]
016.823′ 087209—dc20   94–22017

British Library Cataloguing in Publication Data is available.

Library of Congress Catalog Card Number: 94–22017
ISBN: 0–313–27700–1
ISSN: 0742–6801

First published in 1995

Greenwood Press, 88 Post Road West, Westport, CT 06881
An imprint of Greenwood Publishing Group, Inc.

Printed in the United States of America

The paper used in this book complies with the
Permanent Paper Standard issued by the National
Information Standards Organization (Z39.48–1984).

10 9 8 7 6 5 4 3 2 1

Copyright Acknowledgment

In peace prepare for war, in war prepare for peace.
The art of war is of vital importance to the state.
It is a matter of life and death,
a road either to safety or to ruin.
Hence under no circumstances can it
be neglected.

> —Sun Tzu, *The Art of War*, 83

The man that hath no music in himself
Nor is not moved with concord of sweet sounds,
Is fit for treasons, stratagems and spoils.
The motions of his spirit are dull as night
And his affections dark as Erebus.
Let no such man be trusted. Mark the music.

> —Lorenzo's speech in Shakespeare's
> *The Merchant of Venice*,
> Act 5, Scene 1, Lines 83-88

Contents

Foreword by Julian Rathbone xi
Preface by Joe Poyer xiii
Preface to the Reader xv
Introduction xix
Acknowledgments and Bibliography xxix

Part 1: Early Spy Thrillers (to 1940)
         Introduction 1
         Bibliography: A to Z 7

Part 2: A Golden Age and Beyond (1940 to the Present)
         Introduction 57
         Bibliography: A to Z 63

Appendix A: Craft Notes 649
Appendix B: Guide to Pseudonyms 675
Appendix C: Guide to Characters in Series 685
Appendix D: Guide to Intelligence and Terrorist Organizations 703
Appendix E: Guide to the Jargon of Espionage (Spookspeak) 713
Author Index 737
Title Index 769

Foreword

THE GENRE OF crime writing has two axes, both bloody. The North-South axis runs from Mean and Real to Cozy and Escapist; East to West is Spies through Political, Terrorist, to Private Eyes, and Police Procedural ending with Miss Marples in the bland and balmy (barmy) West. *Cloak and Dagger* is THE work of reference covering the North-East quadrant (though it crosses the lines regularly enough), and as such is clearly indispensable for all who like their reading to be, however frankly enjoyable in itself, at least in part related to the world we live in: especially those parts of it that have to do with the *realpolitik* of nation-states with antlers perennially locked, corrupt politicians, drug barons and war-lords, oil and nuclear power, and, perhaps the least tapped by writers, but ultimately the most important of all, the economics and politics of food production. As Gerald Seymour says in one of the most cogent of the Craft Notes: "The genre has the capability of informing an audience, giving them more insight into the problems we are all talking about, than a forest of newspapers and a cloud of TV newscasts."

So what comprises *Cloak and Dagger*? The meat is an exhaustive but not exhausting list of authors and their work in the genre with perceptive and occasionally contentious (and that is as it should be) critical notes about the more major figures. And of course it is all done with the meticulous scholarship one knows one can rely on in a publication coming out of a major American university—but there is far more besides. Particularly, I should recommend to the criminally inclined serendipidist the appendices on Spookspeak and the Guide to Intelligence and Terrorist Organizations: I know I shall not only be relying on these for years to come, both as a reader and a writer, but I shall be browsing delicately on them much as an ancient seer might have nibbled at laurel leaves while waiting for a visitation from the Muse.

In short, and not to make too much of a mouthful of it, I am delighted that the editors have given me this opportunity to recommend this new edition of *Cloak and Dagger* to all aficionados of that branch of fiction which has more to say about the way we live now than any other.

Julian Rathbone

Preface

SPIES ARE PEOPLE who lie, cheat, steal, and occasionally kill other people for an ideology, a religion, a nation, or even a business. Some are driven by their beliefs, others by greed and like the most fanatical of nationalist or religious practitioners, they can justify their worst excesses in the name of a greater good. There is a fascination about this kind of person and perhaps that is what makes the "spy" novel so popular.

I personally find spy fiction an engrossing subject partly because of the type of personality that as an author I can explore, and partly because it concerns a real world that few are allowed to see first hand. In some respects, spy fiction is like science fiction; because few have been there, you can shape that world in any way you wish.

I number among my friends a past director of the Central Intelligence Agency. I have never discussed any operations with him nor sought to delve into specific matters because I respect the oath of secrecy that he took as director. But he has said enough at odd times concerning books and movies about intelligence work and espionage that lead me to believe that he is amused at the make believe, and grimly cognizant of the real world of spies.

Spy fiction requires the same skills as mainstream, romance, western, science or any other fiction. Writing is both a craft and an art. Until you have mastered the intricacies of developing plots, creating believable characters, setting and managing scenes, and producing a drama from the interaction of these elements, you will be unable to write a successful novel.

Several years of teaching novel writing taught me that all too often, new writers with the urge to write fiction, are not willing to master their craft. Too many feel that anything they write is divinely inspired and should not be changed, particularly by editors. Only with experience does one learn that a good editor is worth his or her weight in gold.

Dire predictions have been made regarding the demise of spy fiction now that the Soviet Union has collapsed and disappeared. Instead, I see spy fiction as breaking out of the straight jacket of East vs. West. The entire area of industrial espionage has been badly neglected. Few novels have been written about the intelligence activities that occur between friendly and allied nations. And the opening of the KGB/GRU and other East Bloc intelligence files should furnish authors with plentiful material for years to come for historical spy novels.

Writing fiction is the ultimate way to make a living as far as I am concerned. On the personal level, it allows you to arrange your life as you wish; on the emotional level, it allows that teacher-storyteller inside each of us to make contact with thousands of other human beings around the world.

Joe Poyer

Preface to the Reader

THE ARRANGEMENT OF this third edition follows its predecessor in most respects; we have kept the year 1940 as a benchmark for dividing espionage fiction in our century. Without arguing the point, one might say the twentieth century, or the so-called modern age that began with World War I and the October Revolution of 1917, ends with the fall of communism. The golden age of the spy thriller as we know it has clearly moved toward its closure. Certainly, as the reader will ascertain from a perusal of authors' commentary in our CRAFT NOTES section, the future of espionage fiction will undoubtedly provide us with new mirrors for the reality of what one scholar calls the new age of intransigent nationalism arriving in the wake of the Soviet Union's collapse. The shelling and slaughter of civilians in the former Yugoslavia—its rape camps and "ethnic cleansing" in Bosnia especially, where Muslim, Croat, and Serb oppose one another—sends us a chilling echo of the new rough beast slouching toward Bethlehem to be born in the very corner of the world that once provided the flashpoint to end one world order. Suffice it to say that the fictional world of espionage can be prophetic as well as entertaining.

Authors whose canons span the two eras are so noted, and the reader is advised to check a writer's production in the pre- or post-1940 part. An occasional exception is made whenever an author can be dealt with simply—that is, we have not included a separate entry for an author who overwhelmingly belongs to one section except for the happenstance of a dateline being crossed.

Moreover, in keeping with the plan already established, we have chosen to break the alphabetical ordering of books within a writer's canon whenever a certain work seems most representative of an author's work. This first annotation, then, is deemed the crucial one and may prove helpful to readers interested in a particular writer's themes. Biographical information, if any, will follow that annotation and the remainder of the works are listed alphabetically.

SPECIAL FEATURES

To assist the user, we have affixed several appendices. Appendix A, "Craft Notes," is alphabetically arranged by author. Appendix B, "Guide to Pseudonyms," provides in one place a listing of the pen names employed by spy-thriller writers, keyed to their real names. Appendix C, "Guide to Characters in Series," provides the user with quick access to particular authors by way of their characters or fictional organizations. Appendix D, "Guide to Intelligence and Terrorist Organizations," will provide the user with the formal identities of groups most often used by many spy-fiction writers; many of these occur by initials in citation annotations. The last appendix is Appendix E, "Guide to the Jargon of Espionage," which are real and fictional—terms familiar to most readers but certainly not all. We have included sources of the term where apt. Finally, each of the appendices has its own introduction that explains its purpose or details its usage. Three new sections have been added to this edition: first, a bibliography of articles and books that reflect recent popular scholarship have been added to the ACKNOWLEDGMENT; second, as noted above, we have included CRAFT NOTES, a section in which writers themselves speak to concerns of their own choosing, whether the craft of espionage fiction, its future directions and themes, or matters purely personal and idiosyncratic. The reader will find delightful tidbits here. Third, there is a glossary of terms in Appendix E on the fascinating and sometimes semantically bizarre language of spies and espionage. Veteran readers of spy fiction will recognize the majority of terms at a glance.

The decade that separates this edition has proved a rich one in terms of the expansions of the other appendices as well. The reader will find more pseudonyms in Appendix B (a few of which have been cracked, such as Rodney Whitaker as the celebrated author of the Trevanian novels. Hartshorne has graciously surrendered his alias and allowed the authors to recognize him as an esteemed Professor of Medicine at Stanford University; author of numerous scientific treatises and philosophical works). While the end of the Cold War may have signalled a decrease in the number of formally recognized intelligence communities in the world, it has seen an evil flowering of terrorist groups or organizations. Those can be located in Appendix D.

There has been an effort to include more paperbacks from the previous three decades in this edition, even though the ephemeral nature of these is obvious in some of their titles and intent, many of which have seen their reason for being lost in the changing political realities of the world or, simply, because no one much cares nowadays about spoofing the Cult of Bond. Contemporary paperback series heroes are a flourishing phenomenon in the pulp marketplace. Witness the Rambo imitators and spinoffs that proliferate the bookstore racks despite the fact that the Vietnam War ended two decades ago. A representative sampling has been taken for the sake of completeness, and so the reader will find a few mercenaries circulating among the rogue agents and traditional spies. Technothrillers need less apology and are amply represented in these pages despite the emphasis on hardware over human beings.

Some publishers and individuals have been especially valuable to this research, and we wish to thank them particularly, even though we provide a formal listing of sources in the bibliography. Special thanks go to Professor Alan Booth of Ohio University for course material from his syllabus, and to Mr. Norman Mailer for kind use of material from his Afterword to *Harlot's Ghost* (New York: Random, 1991) for use in CRAFT NOTES. We are grateful to Houghton, Mifflin for use of Alan Furst's diagram of the Opal Network in *Dark Star*. Also to Taplinger Press for allowing us use of Donald McCormick's *Who's Who in Spy Fiction* (New York, 1977). Donald McCormick's other work, a collaboration with Katy Fletcher, has also proven invaluable to our research, and we gratefully acknowledge *Spy Fiction: A Connoisseur's Guide*. Garland Press has also kindly allowed use of Bernard A. Drew's *Action Series & Sequels* (New York, 1988).

We acknowledge copyright permissions for use of terms from *Verbatim: The Language Quarterly*, as noted in the guide to espionage jargon. Former intelligence officer Donald R. Morris's article on le Carréisms was very helpful—we regret that we could not thank him personally; also to Scribner's for use of Ronald Kessler's *Spy vs. Spy* (New York, 1988), and Simon & Schuster for use of terms from Richard Marcinko & John Weisman's *Rogue Warrior II: Red Cell* (New York, 1994). By far, the genre's definitive source on espionage terminology is still Henry S. A. Becket's *Dictionary of Spookspeak*. Quotations of Sun Tzu's *The Art of War* follow the translation of Samuel B. Griffith (Oxford: Oxford U P, 1963). Lastly, we all owe much thanks to individuals who make espionage fiction a credible and outstanding field for reader and writer alike—to all sung and unsung heroes, from the inimitable Newgate Callendar of the *New York Times* to individuals like Saul Katz of New York, proprietor of The Corner Bookstore, who convinced editor Barry Lippman of Macmillan to publish its outstanding Spymaster series.

Cloak and Dagger Fiction is divided into two alphabetically arranged main sections, or "parts," each with its own introduction. Part 1 provides information on titles through 1939 and is the most selective. Part 2 focuses on the spy thriller after 1939, and it is here that you will find the bulk of the guide's citations. Citations in both parts are keyed to one sequential series of entry numbers that can be found in the single TITLE INDEX.

LEGEND

We continue the use of descriptive symbols for further assistance to the interested reader. As has been the case, no attempt is made to direct the reader's judgment about a writer's career or a particular book, but it may prove helpful for reference purposes. To summarize: P = exists exclusively in paperback; * = portrays no graphic sexuality; y = is suitable for a young-adult audience; H = humor is a major feature; HI = uses a historical plot, characters, or setting. Some symbols, of course, easily coexist for the same work.

Introduction

BACKGROUND

> Your surviving spy must be a man of keen intellect, though in outward appearance a fool; of shabby exterior, but with a will of iron. He must be active, robust, endowed with physical strength and courage; thoroughly accustomed to all sorts of dirty work. . . .
>
> —Sun Tzu, *The Art of War*, on the fifth class of spies, 80

SECRET AGENTS, MEANING here basically spies and counterspies, saboteurs, partisans, and commando-style regulars and irregulars, have been working undercover for thousands of years. Their profession has, rightly, been called the world's second oldest. Espionage, counterespionage, and covert action on behalf of church, state, or business probably began in pre-historic days when ice covered large portions of the earth, and Homo sapiens first conspired to "liquidate" competitors.

Throughout man's history, little known "secret wars" have raged over the gathering or safeguarding of information and the manipulation of officially denied clandestine interference by one group in the affairs of another. On the nation-state level, it would be very late before average citizens had any specific idea about what might really be transpiring in these quiet conflicts or any appreciation of their size or magnitude. In some cases, for example, such as those of Washington and Walsingham, much of our data come not from contemporary accounts, but through examination of expense accounts buried in dusty archives. Still, there have been some glimpses; we know that Chaucer spied for John of Gaunt and that Wordsworth was a spy in France. A number of prominent persons of the past have participated in or benefitted from what Rudyard Kipling first called "the great game" of intelligence operations.

The *Old Testament* (Num. 13) reveals that Moses dispatched agents on a forty-day mission into Canaan to gather data on the land and people, including rulers, of the Promised Land. Later, Joshua (Josh. 2) sent three operatives into Jericho on a similar mission, their rendezvous being the home of Rahab the Harlot, history's first recorded "safe house." Homer's Odysseus in Book IV of *The Odyssey* disguises himself as a beggar to spy in Troy. The Trojan Horse itself is one of history's first mentions of a "deception" scam, while Herodotus claims that Xerxes disregarded his spy's report on the status of Leonidas' defenses and so lost thousands in the Battle of Thermopylae.

Espionage and covert action techniques were employed and refined by others in the ancient world. Over and over, we are told by such writers as Plutarch, Josephus, Procopius, and Caesar himself of Greek, Roman, and Byzantine intelligence successes. Caesar, Hannibal, and Alexander the Great, to name only three important generals, profited handsomely from their espionage and deception apparatuses, which were as good in their world as anything the Allies had in World War II. In the Far East, Lo Kuang-chung's classic *San Kuo* (*The Romance of the Three Kingdoms*) devotes long passages to the exploits of agents during the Han Dynasty. In fact, it was in China that much of what we know of intelligence operations today was first systematically practiced—indeed, the level of ancient Chinese sophistication in this sphere might appear startling to modern students.

The premier student of early Chinese intelligence work was the philosopher Sun Tzu. Writing twenty-five hundred years ago in his "The Employment of Secret Agents," a chapter in his famous *The Art of War*, this early political scientist described several varieties of agents and operations, psychological warfare, counterintelligence and internal security, fabrication and deception (144-149).[1] He made the first written recommendations on how an intelligence service should be set up and run, giving it rules and a code of conduct for good measure. Counterespionage officers all around the world have mastered such precepts as these:

> Now there are five sorts of secret agents to be employed. These are native, inside, doubled, expendable and loving. When these five types of agents are all working simultaneously and none knows their method of operation, they are called 'The Divine Skein,'[*] and are the treasure of a sovereign... It is essential to seek out enemy agents who have come to conduct espionage against you and to bribe them to serve you. Give them instructions and care for them. Thus doubled agents are

---

[*]Also translated as "The Divine Manipulation of the Threads." Sun Tzu, *The Art of War*. Ed. James Clavell. (New York: Delacorte, 1983) 78. All display quotations are from this edition.

used... Secret operations are essential in war; upon them the army relies to make
its every move. (145-149)

Has the ancient world of espionage changed? Are not deep-penetration
agents (moles), double agents, and disinformation still the stuff of le Carré and
Deighton?

Intelligence operations in the West during the Middle Ages leave mainly
a record of failures and missed opportunities. Especially grave was the long-
standing underestimation by kings and popes of such groups as the Moslems and
the Mongols. The data brought back by merchants and some travellers, like
Marco Polo, was largely ignored as a source of intelligence due to the "infidel"
status of the subjects. Today the West continues to react to the complex
internecine politics of the Middle East without much success: witness the ham-
handed antics of Col. Oliver North and the taint on the Reagan-Bush
administration known as Iran-Contra. So complex is the issue of Palestinian
terrorism alone that many experts today believe that Abu Nidal's secret war
against the PLO and various Arab regimes is actually engineered by a ruthless
Mossad.[2]

Through the late Middle Ages, spies and assassins, often wearing cloaks
and usually employing daggers, were frequently busy in Renaissance Italy.
Indeed, it was the fifteenth-century Italians who made an important contribution
to the ease with which information could be collected when they established the
first permanent foreign embassies. The first real spymaster, however, was
certainly Sir Francis Walsingham, Secretary of State to Queen Elizabeth I of
England.

Walsingham was a practiced schemer who, according to some authorities,
established the world's first professional intelligence agency. It was his practice
to recruit gifted university students for foreign study in France or Italy—and a
bit of spying on the side. Some believe that Christopher Marlowe (alleged to
belong to the probably apocryphal Elizabethan School of Night along with
George Chapman and Sir Walter Raleigh) died cursing, a knife plunged into his
neck, in a Deptford tavern brawl as the end of one of his master's many plots.
Marlowe may have been murdered by Walsingham's own men because of his
involvement with Raleigh in a separate plot to depose of Queen Elizabeth. The
secretary was a fanatic about domestic security; he authorized the opening and
examination of diplomatic pouches and surveillance over the movements of
innocent and actual subversives among the outlawed Catholics. His work led
to the exposure of the ill-conceived Babington Conspiracy, evidence of
participation in which caused Mary, Queen of Scots, to lose her head. Later,
it was Walsingham's group who supplied a fresh stream of information on the
progress of the punitive but doomed expedition assembled by Philip II. In fact,
one of the secretary's agents is supposed to have interrupted Sir Francis Drake's
game of bowls to provide the famous seaman with his first "hard intelligence"

on the location of Spain's Armada in the English Channel. Although several others merit mention, it is generally safe to say that, before the mid-nineteenth century, only France's Cardinal Richelieu came anywhere near rivalling the exploits of Francis Walsingham.

Daniel Defoe, author of *Robinson Crusoe* and *Moll Flanders*, is sometimes called "the Father of the British Secret Service," because he admitted to having worked for Queen Anne "in several honourable, though secret services," though he never gave any details.[3] Aphra Behn, England's first important woman playwright, was also the first effective female agent, but she, like Defoe, remained silent about her adventures. We Americans, however, can claim James Fenimore Cooper as our first author of a spy-fiction work in his 1821 publication of *The Spy: A Tale of the Neutral Ground*, the background of which must have come from Cooper's days as a Navy midshipman on patrol in the Great Lakes area—quite likely having first-hand experience at espionage missions during his service.[4]

It was in Napoleon's France that a line was first drawn between the men charged with gathering foreign intelligence and those whose job it was to ensure internal security. The infamous Joseph Fouché, survivor and schemer of the French Revolution, served as Justice Minister and established the first large political secret police and counterespionage service. An Alsatian named Karl Schulmeister ran a large number of missions to gain information on the Austrian military establishment while at the same time deceiving it as to Napoleon's strength and intentions. So pleased was the emperor with the work of his intelligence officers that he was once heard to remark that a single spy in the right place was worth over twenty-thousand troops.

The Russians have been fond of spies and covert action since at least the time of the Tartars. Foreigners in Russia and Russians abroad have been "tailed" since the sixteenth century. In 1826, Czar Nicholas I established an organized political police under state control, a group later expanded into the Okhrana, or security section of the Interior Ministry. The czar's secret police were everywhere before 1917 and, with the assistance of large numbers of informants, tried to keep almost everyone under surveillance. Even Tolstoy was a subject of Okhrana attention. Lenin, during a stay in Prague in 1912, unknowingly had an Okhrana agent in his own household! This pales to insignificance, however, when one considers Stalin's NKVD and the ubiquitous KGB (Committee for State Security) which succeeded it. The Soviets used to employ more intelligence officers and spies than all of the other secret services of the world combined. Aleksandr Solzhenitsyn's *The Gulag Archipelago* remains a bitter triumph of those paranoid days when watchers watched the watchers of Soviet citizenry.

Except in time of war, the United States saw little official government intelligence activity until the advent of the Cold War in the late 1940s. Prior to that time, American intelligence work was almost always military—and often rather informal at that. Nathan Hale, Major John André, and Benedict Arnold are noteworthy examples of failed intelligence officers during the American Revolution; on a more positive side, Benjamin Franklin ran an apparently efficient network in France, though it was penetrated by a double agent named Dr. Edward Bancroft. Washington himself maintained a system of spies and dealt in secret codes (processed and analyzed by Alexander Hamilton) and from his expense accounts, we know that the "Father of Our Country" spent some $17,000 to pay for his information.

Though almost everywhere, spies and operatives apparently had little real impact on the events of the Civil War. Even so, espionage memoirists from both sides total nineteen men and five women, seventeen who served the North, seven the South.[5] True, there are many that suggest that Mrs. Rose Greenhow "spied" the Yankees into disaster at Bull Run in 1862, and that the "Great Locomotive Chase" was an example of a clandestine operation gone wrong, but on the whole, these sorts of exploits seemed to be limited and local in place and effect. More interesting and perhaps significant were two other developments of the conflict, both put forward by the North. Allan Pinkerton, the detective, established a security and counterespionage service which foreshadowed the work in that area today done by the Federal Bureau of Investigation (FBI). Professor T. Lowe used hot-air balloons in an effort to gain aerial reconnaissance objectives.

The first permanent peacetime military and naval intelligence groups in America were established during the 1880s. The Navy's Office of Intelligence has flourished since 1882, while the Army's Military Information Division became famous after 1903 as the Second Division, or G-2, of the General Staff. In 1962, the functions of these offices were combined with Air Force Intelligence and several sub-groups to form the Defense Intelligence Agency.

Although the State Department had performed some civilian intelligence tasks since its formation under Washington, a full-blown civilian intelligence agency had to await World War II. In 1941 as war threatened, President Roosevelt chose William Donovan to head the Coordination of Information groups which became the Office of Strategic Services in June 1942. While the FBI under J. Edgar Hoover provided domestic security (a task it would continue infamously in the Red Hunts of the McCarthy-Cohn hearings after V-J Day), Gen. Donovan's OSS, working closely with and modeled after British Intelligence, especially the Special Operations Executive, or SOE, was to become a formidable intelligence-gathering and covert-action agency. Briefly disbanded after the war, the functions of the OSS were reborn again in the National Security Act of 1947 and placed, together with many former disciples of "Wild Bill" Donovan, in the Central Intelligence Agency (CIA). The CIA, America's first permanent, civilian peacetime intelligence force is still a major source of information to the foreign-policy makers of the U.S. government. Indeed, the agency's 1992 budget request of $30 billion implies that the collapse of the Soviet Union into fragmented ethnic regions and the Berlin Wall's destruction have not altered its commitments abroad. Humint (human intelligence) is methodically processed at Langley even while the KH-11 satellite feeds video almost instantaneously to Washington, DC. As recent events in Iraq testify—one year after the victorious ticker-tape parades honoring Desert Storm veterans—the world is never at peace and humankind does not easily change its nature.

Of course, there have been many other intelligence developments in world history, which space does not permit us to review or list here. British exploits before, during, and after the World Wars are legendary as are those of the Russians, Germans, Chinese, Japanese, and lately the Israelis. Many in a variety of nations and settings have shown that the human agent, both as silent spy and activist commando, have been important in the constant and fast-moving secret wars conducted by states during both peace and war.

In short, actors in these silent battles have been charged with obtaining information, conveying it, safeguarding it, and sometimes spreading false versions of it in a fashion which, by the twentieth century, has evolved into a complicated process handled with similarity by most nations of the world. These same actors have also often been charged with conducting clandestine interference in the affairs of other states and in conducting secret guerrilla warfare in situations where regular forces might prove an embarrassment. Methods may change, but the trade in information-gathering and protection, as well as propaganda and covert action, continues as it has for centuries.

Prior to the invention and widespread use of electronic and photographic means of data collection, the intelligence profession was filled with danger for participants. Operatives working in the field have historically been beyond the honor code and regular rules of war. Every agent or commando, to say nothing of partisans, has always known that being unmasked and captured could be fatal. The 1771 first edition of the *Encyclopedia Britannica* was concise in its article on espionage: "when a spy is discovered, he is immediately hanged." This potential for execution is present in the world today; however, as all readers of le Carré know, at least in developed nations, captured agents are given long prison terms or exchanged for operatives held by "the other side."

The "secret wars" remained largely confidential through the centuries principally because of pride and the nonstrategic nature of the data involved. Leaders, writers, and thinkers simply did not like to admit that spies or assassins or partisans existed, let alone that they might be beneficial to the aims of great states. Generals, the most likely benefactors of secret war information, were caught up in their own rules of war, which paralleled society's general disdain of covert operators and concentrated instead on keeping the lines of their soldiers straight while on the march. War, throughout the eighteenth century, was still a "gentlemanly" affair, which meant agreeing to battle sites with the opposition, fighting only in daylight, and, most significantly, never involving civilians. In addition, the information sought was more often of a "tactical" or battlefield variety as opposed to "strategic," that which could directly affect the survival of a nation.

In the years following the Industrial Revolution, and as the weapons of war increased in potency, more secrets of strategic value became available. Everything from new kinds of warship armor through the theoretical physics of the atomic bomb to the latest spy satellite developed such an importance that a nation's fate could depend on its inventions and the confidentiality of those inventions. The theft or sabotage of such items or plans came to be appreciated as distinct strategic threats, especially in the middle of the twentieth century. As the atmosphere of concern generally intensified, so too did the attention of a larger audience become focused on the threat of espionage/sabotage and the need for security. Occasionally, a scandal, such as the Dreyfus Affair in France, would put the undercover business of spying before the public. If not such a flap, then the trickle of reminiscences or exposés by journalists or former agents or government officials, which foreshadowed the wholesale post-World War I memoir flood, served to remind citizens that all was not brass bands or dreadnoughts. The resistance and intrigues in such diverse areas as India, Ireland, the Philippines, and Cuba brought constant awareness that covert action was a possibility in even the most secure country or outpost.

What kind of people have taken up this life and what kept or keeps them at it? Again, we refer to Sun Tzu's *The Art of War* for a classic definition of the difference between field agents and enemy spies:

> We select men who are clever, talented, wise, and able to gain access to those of the enemy who are intimate with the sovereign and members of the nobility... [Enemy spies whom we employ] are sycophants and minions who are covetous of wealth... There are those who are two-faced, changeable, and deceitful, and who are always sitting on the fence. (145)

W. Somerset Maugham, now known to have been a crucial World War I operative in Russia, writes in the preface to his spy classic *Ashenden*: "There will always be men who from malice or for money will betray their kith and kin." "And," he continued, "there will always be men who from love of adventure or a sense of duty will risk a shameful death to secure information valuable to their country" (xiii).[6] Class consciousness has sometimes played a role for those employed by the intelligence services; in the early days of the British SIS and American OSS, ranks were often filled by rich men or their sons. The novels of Ted Allbeury and Len Deighton are frequently enriched by the wry, poignant social observations of their tough working-class operatives.

But public glory has never really been a drawing card, primarily because of the hush-hush aspect of the business. Frederic W. Winterbotham, who safeguarded the Ultra Secret during World War II, received in 1945 only a small medal and pension before retiring to his cottage, there, to wait until 1974 for the thirty-year security rule to expire before he could pen his memoirs.[7]

The life of a spy, as opposed to that of a partisan or a commando-operative, can be a very lonely or dull affair. Most real-life agents have been cogs in machines run from afar; whether that structure was Walsingham's or that of the XX Committee in World War II or of the KGB. The necessity of order and routine, especially in such counterespionage organizations as DI-5, have seldom left much room for James Bonds. Today, technology and overt sources provide much more intelligence than field operatives, whose importance has shrunk. The implications for future spy-fiction are serious, as Hartshorne comments in a letter to the editors: "There are fewer people attracted to high-tech agencies; as a country we are still paying for a Nixon years' then Carter years' decision to deemphasize Humint (human intelligence, i.e., good old-fashioned spies, agents who could report on intentions, or as in chaotic places, alignments, even houses where hostages are held), fewer in such assignments who will have flavorful experiences not spent in the photo lab or unscrambling microwaves."[8]

It was into such a world that certain writers first trod and began to pen tales which would eventually find a large readership. "The spy story owed its existence to awareness of the threat to national security implied in professionally organized spying," writes novelist-critic Julian Symons, "and also to the slow realization that the spy's activities may be both intricate and dangerous" (230).[9] Once the idea of secret agents was firmly established in the public eye—and that was largely accomplished by 1914—authors began to turn their attention to developing a literary genre and creating and fostering what would eventually become a spy thriller mania among readers.[10]

"Thriller" is so nebulous a term that it does not do justice to the variety or quality one finds in "entertainments," "spy fiction," "spy stories," "intelligence fiction," "suspense fiction"—whichever name it goes by.

Responding to our invitation to contribute commentary to our CRAFT NOTES section, esteemed novelist and former CIA operative, Charles McCarry writes: "I have never considered that I was engaged in writing 'thrillers,' a fact you might want to take into consideration before including me in your guide."[11]

"'Thriller' is so loose a word that it should really be abandoned as a form of description," Symons scoffs (230). Thrillers were in the past equated with the cheap sensationalism of the dime-novel. They were, as Eric Amber confided, "a dirty word."[12] Even today, many who fit espionage into their tales would never admit or subscribe to the description of work once advanced by E. Phillips Oppenheim: "I am a maker of stories while you wait" (Merry 3).

Others have, on the other hand, whole-heartedly adopted "thriller" when describing the literature of secret agents, choosing to categorize by calling it "spy thrillers" (Merry 1). "Techno-thriller," of course, is a term much in evidence today—especially on the dust-jacket blurbs of the novels of Tom Clancy, Dale Brown, Stephen Coonts, Douglas Terman, and Guy Durham.

Whatever one elects to call the fictional literature of clandestinism, its popularity has been on the rise ever since the days of William LeQueux and John Buchan. The World Wars, the Cold War and detente, and other real-life actions such as the Philby Affair, Bay of Pigs, and acts of terrorism in the skies and cities of Western Europe and the Middle East together with improved communications in what Marshal McLuhan once called the "global village" the world has become, have undoubtedly contributed to an unprecedented readership for spy thrillers.

Those interested in spy thrillers have, over the years, marvelled at the number of real-life operatives who have taken up the pen to write them. Many have used their background in "the game" to write in the genre: Compton Mackenzie, Buchan, LeQueux, Graham Greene, Ian Fleming, Dennis Wheatley, W. Somerset Maugham, David J. M. Cornwell (John le Carré), Ted Allbeury, E. Howard Hunt, William F. Buckley, Jr., Anthony Quayle, Stephen Coulter, David A. Phillips, Richard H. M. Clayton (William Haggard), Victor Marchetti, Alfred E. W. Mason, and John C. Masterman. There have been many others. Not surprising, given the impact of spy thrillers on the public imagination from the first appearance of Buchan's tuxedoed hero Richard Hannay through Fleming's suave James Bond to all those "agile, vigorous, hardy and brave" men and women of contemporary espionage fiction. We refer the reader to the bibliography section of the ACKNOWLEDGEMENTS for a listing of recent works that probe the social, literary, and philosophical underpinnings of this fascinating genre.

NOTES

1. Sun Tzu, "The Employment of Secret Agents," *The Art of War*, trans. Samuel B. Griffith (Oxford: Oxford U P, 1963). Other references will be cited in the text.

2. Patrick Seale, *Abu Nidal: A Gun for Hire* (New York: Random, 1992).

3. Donald McCormick and Katy Fletcher, *Spy Fiction: A Connoisseur's Guide* (New York: Facts on File, 1990) 4.

4. Donald McCormick, *Who's Who in Spy Fiction* (New York: Taplinger, 1977) 4.

5. Curtis Carroll Davis, "Companions of Crisis: The Spy Memoir as a Social Document," *Civil War History* 10 (1964): 385-401.

6. W. Somerset Maugham, *Ashenden; or, The British Agent* (Garden City, NY: Doubleday, 1941).

7. Peter Way, *Codes and Ciphers* (London: Aldus, 1977) 103.

8. Letter to Terry White, September 19, 1989.

9. Julian Symons, *Mortal Consequences: A History—From the Detective Story to the Crime Novel* (New York: Harper & Row, 1972) 230. Other references will be cited in the text.

10. George Siehl, "Cloak, Dust-Jacket, and Dagger," *Library Journal* 97 (1972): 377-383.

11. Letter to Terry White, September 14, 1992.

12. Quoted in Bruce Merry, *Anatomy of the Spy Thriller* (Montreal: McGill-Queen's University Press, 1977) 4. Other references will be cited in the text.

Acknowledgments and Bibliography

MOST THANKS TO Kelly Ingersoll for all her patience and skill. Much gratitude to Ms. Margee Zarriello of KSUAC's Library for solving our many problems in research, and to her Kent Campus colleagues, Diane Kovacs and Gladys Bell. We must also thank two DorothyL detectives: Joseph P. Browne, CSC, of University of Portland and Margaret F. Riley of Worcester Polytechnic.

Special thanks is offered to the authors who contributed their commentary to CRAFT NOTES—most especially, to Dick Blum in California—humanist, scholar, philosopher, espionage author, scientist, and gentleman—for his encouragement and the pleasure of his correspondence these past four years.

Kudos to the GET SMART GANG at the Ashtabula Campus: Dean John K. Mahan, Diana Anderson, Paula Brehl, Ron Brown, Kim Cook, Hal Dalrymple, Chris Dalheim, Irene Edge, Pat Flash, Mark Fratis, Claudia Greenwood, Kathy Heino, Ron Helms, Sue Krieg, Rog Lane, Rita Locke, George Matrisciano, Robin McDermott, Jeanne Novotny, Joyce Orth, Al Peck, Patsy Poncar, Charlie Poluga, Kerry Purkey, and Pam Urch. And more thanks yet to Sandy Branek of the Navajo Center for that privileged-character discount on those paperbacks—which does bring us to the end of the acknowledgments: Dumbos to the Professional Development Awards Committee (1988-1990) for delaying this book several years.

Students of spy fiction and espionage should find the following articles and texts helpful.

M.J.S.   *T.W.*

ARTICLES

Adams, Charles H. "'The Guardian of the Law': George Washington's Role in *The Spy*." James Fenimore Cooper: His Country and His Art 5. Ed. George A. Test. Oneonta: S U of New York, 1985. 49-59.

Auburn, Mark S. "The Pleasures of Espionage Fiction." *Clues: A Journal of Detection* 4.2 (1983): 30-42.

Bear, Andrew. "The Faction-Packed Thriller: The Novels of Frederick Forsyth." *Clues: A Journal of Detection* 4.2 (1983): 130-48.

Becker, Jens P. "John le Carré's Smiley-Saga: 'Nostalgia for a Lost Paradise.'" *Anglistik & Englischungterricht* 37 (1989): 99-111.

Bedell, Jeanne F. "A Sense of History: The Espionage Fiction of Anthony Price." *Armchair Detective: A Quarterly Journal Devoted to the Appreciation of Mystery, Detective and Suspense Fiction* 15.2 (1982): 114-18.

___. "Somerset Maugham's *Ashenden* and the Modernization of Espionage Fiction." *Studies in Popular Culture* 7 (1984): 40-46.

Behn, Noel. "Britannia's Bull Dog." *Armchair Detective: A Quarterly Journal Devoted to the Appreciation of Mystery, Detective, and Suspense Fiction* 17.4 (1984): 368-69.

Boyd, Mary K. "The Enduring Appeal of the Spy Thrillers of Helen MacInnes." *Clues: A Journal of Detection* 4.2 (1983): 66-75.

Brady, Charles A. "John le Carré's Smiley Saga." *Thought: A Review of Culture and Idea* September 1985: 274-96.

Buzard, James Michael. "Faces, Photos, Mirrors: Image and Ideology in the Novels of John le Carré." *Works and Days: Essays in the Socio-Historical Dimensions of Literature and the Arts* 7 (1989): 53-75.

Calendrillo, Linda T. "Cloaks and More Cloaks: Pynchon's *V.* and the Classic Spy Novel." *Clues: A Journal of Detection* 5.2 (1984): 58-65.

___. "Role Playing and 'Atmosphere' in Four Modern British Spy Novels." *Clues: A Journal of Detection* 3.1 (1982): 111-19.

Chace, William M. "Spies and God's Spies: Greene's Espionage Fiction." *Graham Greene: A Revaluation: New Essays.* Ed. Jeffrey Meyers. New York: St. Martin's, 1990. 156-80.

Colebatch, Hal. "Spies, Stinking Fish, and Dr. Bowdler's Headstand: What Has Happened to the Spy Novel?" *Quadrant* 30 (1986): 95-97.

Daleski, H. M. "*A Perfect Spy* and a Great Tradition." *Journal of Narrative Technique* 20 (1990): 56-64.

Donaldson-Evans, Lance K. "The Anatomy of a Spy Novel: Gerard de Villiers and the Modern French *Roman d'espionnage*." *Clues: A Journal of Detection* 2.2 (1981): 28-36.

___. "Conspiracy, Betrayal, and the Popularity of a Genre: Ludlum, Forsyth, Gerard de Villiers and the Spy Novel Format." *Clues* 4.2 (1983): 92-114.

Drew, Bernard A. "He Nails 'Em with Modesty: Peter O'Donnell's *Femme Fatale* Uses Everything to Fight Evil Forces." *Armchair Detective* 20.1 (1987): 26-30.

East, Andy. "The Spy in the Dark: A History of Espionage Fiction." *Armchair Detective* 19.1 (1986): 23-40.

Fletcher, Katy. "Evolution of the Modern American Spy Novel." *Journal of Contemporary History* 22.2 (1987): 319-31.

Follett, Ken. "The Spy as Hero and Villain." *The Murder Mystique: Crime Writers on Their Art.* Ed. Lucy Freeman. New York: Ungar, 1982. 74-81.

Giddings, Robert. "The Writing on the Igloo Walls: Narrative Technique in *The Spy Who Came in from the Cold.*" *The Quest for le Carré.* Ed. Alan Norman Bold. New York: St. Martin's, 1988. 188-210.

Griffiths, Gwen. "Individual and Societal Entropy in le Carré's *A Perfect Spy.*" *Critique: Studies in Contemporary Fiction* 31.2 (1990): 101-11.

Hammer, David L. "Sherlock Holmes: Secret Agent." *The Baker Street Journal: An Irregular Quarterly of Sherlockiana* December 1986: 231-34.

Handberg, Roger. "Know Thy Enemy: Changing Images of the Enemy in Popular Literature." *North Dakota Quarterly* 53.1 (1985): 121-27.

King, Holly Beth. "Child's Play in Le Carré's *Tinker, Tailor, Soldier, Spy.*" *Clues* 3.2 (1982): 87-92.

___. "George Smiley: The Reluctant Hero." *Clues* 2.1 (1981): 70-76.

Laity, Susan. "'The Second Burden of a Former Child: Doubling and Repetition in *A Perfect Spy.*'" *John le Carré.* Ed. Harold Bloom. New York: Chelsea, 1987. 137-64.

Laqueur, Walter. "Le Carré's Fantasies." *Commentary* June 1983: 62-67.

Lasseter, Victor. "*Tinker, Tailor, Soldier, Spy:* A Story of Modern Love." *Critique: Studies in Contemporary Fiction* 31.2 (1990): 101-11.

Lee, Thomas. "The Double Plot in John le Carré's *A Perfect Spy.*" *Notes on Contemporary Literature* 18.4 (1988): 5-7.

Monaghan, David. "John le Carré's England: A Spy's-Eye View." *Modern Fiction Studies* 29 (1983): 569-82.

Neville, John D. "Michael Innes." *Clues* 5.2 (1984): 119-30.

Newman, Judie. "Games in Greeneland: *The Human Factor.*" *Dutch Quarterly Review of Anglo-American Letters* 14 (1984): 250-68.

Noland, Richard W. "The Spy Fiction of John le Carré." *Clues* 1.2 (1980): 54-70.

O'Neill, Philip. "Le Carré: Faith and Dreams." *The Quest for le Carré*. Ed. Alan Norman Bold. New York: St. Martin's, 1988. 169-87.

Palmer, Jerry. "Thrillers." *Popular Fiction and Social Change*. Ed. Christopher Pawling. New York: St. Martin's, 1984. 76-98.

Ray, Philip E. "The Villain in the Spy Novels of John Buchan." *English Literature in Transition (1880-1920)* 24.2 (1981): 81-90.

Reynolds, William. "The Labyrinth Maker: The Espionage Fiction of Anthony Price." *Armchair Detective* 19.4 (1986): 350-58.

Sauerberg, Lars Ole. "Literature in Figures: An Essay on the Popularity of Thrillers." *Orbis Litterarum: International Review of Literary Studies* 38.2 (1983): 93-107.

___. "Secret-Agent Fiction: A Survey of Its Critical Literature with a Bibliography." *Clues* 7.2 (1986): 1-31.

Sarjeant, William A. S. "A Toast to the Secret Service: In Tribute to Manning Coles and Tommy Hambledon." *Armchair Detective* 15.2 (1982): 100-13.

Silverstein, Marc. "After the Fall: The World of Graham Greene's Thrillers." *Novel: A Forum on Fiction* 22 (188): 24-44.

Simons, John L. "Pynchon on Household: Reworking the Traditional Spy Novel." *Pynchon Notes* 16 (1985): 83-88.

Skene Melvin, David. "The Secret Eye; the Spy in Literature: The Evolution of Espionage Literature: A Survey of the History and Development of the Spy and Espionage Novel." *Pacific Quarterly* 3 (1978): 11-26.

Snyder, John R. "The Spy Story as Modern Tragedy." *Literature/Film Quarterly* 5 (1977): 216-35.

Stephensen-Payne, Phil. "Jack Higgins: An Annotated Checklist." *Million* July/August 1991: 39-43.

Stafford, David. "John Buchan's Tales of Espionage: A Popular Archive of British History." *Canadian Journal of History/Annales Canadiennes* 18.1 (1983): 1-21.

Tracy, Laura. "Forbidden Fantasy: The Villain as Cultural Double in the British Espionage Novel." *Clues* 9.1 (1988): 11-37.

Vaughn, Stephen. "Spies, National Security, and the 'Inertia Projector': The Secret Service Films of Ronald Reagan." *American Quarterly* 39 (1987): 355-80.

Winks, Robin. "The Sinister Oriental: Thriller Fiction and the Asian Scene." *Journal of Popular Culture* 19.2 (1985): 49-61.

BOOKS

Albert, Walter. *Detective and Mystery Fiction: An International Bibliography of Secondary Sources.* Madison, IN: Brownstone, 1985.

Atkins, John. *The British Spy Novel: Styles in Treachery.* London: Calder; New York: Riverrun, 1984.

Becket, Henry S. A. *The Dictionary of Espionage: Spookspeak into English.* Briarcliff Manor, NY: Stein & Day, 1986.

Benson, Raymond. *The James Bond Bedside Companion.* New York: Dodd, 1984.

Bold, Alan Norman, ed. *The Quest for Le Carré.* New York: St. Martin's, 1988.

Brosnan, John. *James Bond in the Cinema.* Rev. ed. New York: Barnes, 1981.

Buranelli, Nan, and Vincent Buranelli. *Spy/Counterspy: An Encyclopedia of Espionage.* New York: McGraw-Hill, 1982.

Cawelti, John G. *Adventure, Mystery and Romance: Formula Stories as Art and Popular Culture.* Chicago: Chicago U P, 1976.

___, and Bruce Rosenberg. *The Spy Story.* Chicago: Chicago U P, 1987.

Cline, Marjorie, *et al. Scholar's Guide to Intelligence Literature.* Baltimore: University Publications, 1983.

Cook, Michael L. *Mystery, Detective, and Espionage Magazines.* Westport, CT: Greenwood, 1983.

Craig, Patricia, and Mary Cadogan. *The Lady Investigates: Women Detectives and Spies in Fiction.* London: Gollancz, 1981.

Deacon, Richard, pseud. [Donald McCormick]. *Spyclopedia: The Comprehensive Handbook of Espionage.* New York: Morrow, 1988.

Denning, Michael. *Cover Stories: Narrative and Ideology in the British Spy Thriller.* London: Routledge & Paul, 1987.

Drew, Bernard A. *Action Series and Sequels: A Bibliography of Espionage, Vigilante, and Soldier-of-Fortune Novels.* New York: Garland, 1988.

Dulles, Allen, ed. *Great Spy Stories in Fiction.* New York: Harper & Row, 1969.

East, Andy. *The Cold War File.* Metuchen, NJ: Scarecrow, 1983.

Epstein, Edward Jay. *Deception: The Invisible War between the KGB and the CIA.* New York: Simon & Schuster, 1989.

Greene, Graham, and Hugh Greene. *The Spy's Bedside Book.* 2nd ed. 1985.

Harper, Ralph. *The World of the Thriller.* Cleveland, OH: Case Western U P, 1969.

Hibbin, Sally. *The New Official James Bond Moviebook.* New York: Crown, 1989.

Knightley, Phillip. *The Second Oldest Profession: The Spy as Bureaucrat, Patriot, Fantasist and Whore.* London: Deutsch, 1986.

Knudson, Richard. *The Whole Spy Catalog: An Espionage Lover's Guide.* New York: St. Martin's, 1986.

Lewis, Peter. *Eric Ambler.* New York: Ungar, 1989.

___. *John Le Carré.* New York: Ungar, 1985.

Magill, Frank, ed. *Critical Survey of Mystery and Detective Fiction.* Pasadena, CA: Salem, 1989. 4 vols.

McCormick, Donald, and Katy Fletcher. *Spy Fiction: A Connoisseur's Guide.* Oxford [NY]: Facts on File, 1990.

Melvin, David Skene, and Ann Skene Melvin, comps. and eds. *Crime, Detective, Espionage, and Thriller Fiction & Film: A Comprehensive Bibliography of Critical Writing through 1979.* Westport, CT: Greenwood, 1980.

Merry, Bruce. *Anatomy of the Spy Thriller.* Montreal: McGill-Queen U P, 1977.

Milward-Oliver, Edward. *The Len Deighton Companion.* London: Grafton, 1987.

Monaghan, David. *The Novels of John le Carré: The Art of Survival.* Oxford: Blackwell, 1985.

___. *Smiley's Circus: A Guide to the World of John le Carré.* New York: St. Martin's, 1986.

Panek, LeRoy L. *The Special Branch: The British Spy Novel, 1890-1980.* Bowling Green, OH: Bowling Green U Popular P, 1981.

Parish, James R., and Michael R. Pitts. *The Great Spy Pictures.* Metuchen, NJ: Scarecrow, 1974.

Payne, Ronald, and Christopher Dobson. *Who's Who in Espionage.* New York: St. Martin's, 1984.

Penzler, Otto. *The Private Lives of Private Eyes, Spies, Crime Fighters, and Other Good Guys.* New York: Grosset & Dunlap, 1977.

Rubinstein, Leonard. *The Great Spy Films.* Seacaucus, NJ: Citadel, 1979.

Sauerberg, Lars Ole. *Secret Agents in Fiction: Ian Fleming, John le Carré, and Len Deighton.* New York: St. Martin's, 1984.

Stafford, David. *The Silent Game: The Real World of Imaginary Spies.* New York: Viking, 1988.

Van Dover, Kenneth J. *Polemical Pulps: The Martin Beck Novels of Maj Sjowall and Per Wahloo.* San Bernadino, CA: Brownstone, 1993.

Winks, Robin. *Modus Operandi: An Excursion into Detective Fiction.* Boston: Godine, 1982.

Wolfe, Peter. *Corridors of Deceit: The World of John Le Carré.* Bowling Green, OH: Bowling Green U Popular P, 1987.

INTELLIGENCE JOURNALS AND FANZINES

Foreign Intelligence Literary Scene: A Bimonthly Newsletter/Book Review. Published by National Intelligence Study Center, 1800 K. St., Washington, DC 20006.

Intelligence and National Security. Published by Frank Cass & Co. Ltd., 11 Gainsborough Rd., London, E11 1RS, England.

International Journal of Intelligence and Counterintelligence. Published by International Journal of Intelligence and Counterintelligence, P.O. Box 188, Stroudsburg, PA 18360.

Intelligence Quarterly. Published by Michael F. Speers and Nigel West, P.O. Box 232, Weston, VT 05161.

Espionage. Published by Leo II Publications, 35 Roberts Road, Englewood Cliffs, NJ 07632.

First Principles. Published by Michael Macomber & based on the Yorkshire TV series "The Sandbaggers," created by Ian Mackintosh, #223 Linden Hills Apts., Lindenwold, NJ 08021.

It Couldn't Happen Then...It Couldn't Happen Now. Published by Sherri Fillingham & also based on "The Sandbaggers," P. O. Box 686, Washington Grove, NJ 20880.

Kuryakin File. Published by Lisa Brazdil & based on *The Man from UNCLE,* 916 Aintree Park Drive, Mayfield, OH 44143.

Stay Tuned: "The Missing Cases." Based on "The Avengers," P. O. Box 373, Archerfield, Qld 4108, Australia.

REFERENCE WORKS ON ESPIONAGE

American Traitors

Allen, Thomas B., and Norman Polmar. *Merchants of Treason: America's Secrets for Sale.* New York: Delacorte, 1988.

Corson, William R., Susan B. Trento, and Joseph J. Trento. *Widows: Four American Spies, the Wives They Left Behind, and the KGB's Crippling of American Intelligence.* New York: Crown, 1989.

Dulles, Allen, ed. *Great True Spy Stories.* New York: Ballantine, 1968.

Kneece, Jack. *Family Treason: The Walker Spy Case.* Briarcliff Manor, NY: Stein & Day, 1986.

Kwitny, Jonathan. *The Crimes of Patriots: A True Tale of Dope, Dirty Money, and the CIA.* New York: Norton, 1987.

Lindsey, Robert. *The Falcon and the Snowman: A True Story of Friendship and Espionage.* New York: Simon & Schuster, 1979.

Wise, David. *The Spy Who Got Away: The Inside Story of Edward Lee Howard*. New York: Random, 1988.

Autobiographies

Agee, Philip. *Inside the Company: A CIA Diary*. Harmondsworth, Middlesex: Penguin, 1975; Cambridge, MA: Stonehill, 1975.
___. *On the Run*. Seacaucus, NJ: L. Stuart, 1987.
Colby, William E. *Honorable Men: My Life in the CIA*. New York: Simon & Schuster, 1978.
Hunt, E. Howard. *Undercover*. New York: Putnam's, 1974.
Lonsdale, Gordon Arnold. *Spy: Twenty Years in Soviet Secret Service: The Memoirs of Gordon Lonsdale*. New York: Hawthorn, 1965.
McGehee, Ralph W. *Deadly Deceits: My 25 Years in the CIA*. New York: Sheridan Square, 1983.
Wright, Peter (with Paul Greengrass). *Spycatcher*. New York: Viking, 1987.

Biographies

Martin, David C. *Wilderness of Mirrors*. New York: Harper & Row, 1980.
Ranelagh, John. *The Agency: The Rise and Decline of the CIA from Wild Bill Donovan to Bill Casey*. New York: Simon & Schuster, 1987.
Troy, Thomas F. *Donovan and the CIA: A History of the Establishment of the Central Intelligence Agency*. Frederick, MD: Aletheia, 1981.
Winks, Robin. *Cloak & Gown: Scholars in the Secret War, 1939-1961*. New York: Morrow, 1987.

British Traitors

Deacon, Richard [Donald McCormick]. *The Greatest Treason: The Bizarre Story of Hollis, Liddell and Mountbatten*. Rev. ed. London: Century, 1990.
Page, Bruce, David Leitch, and Philip Knightly. *The Philby Conspiracy*. Garden City, NY: Doubleday, 1968.
Penrose, Barrie, and Simon Freeman. *Conspiracy of Silence: The Secret Life of Anthony Blunt*. London: Grafton, 1986.
Philby, Kim. *My Secret War*. London: MacGibbon & Mckee, 1968.
West, Nigel. *Mole-Hunt*. London: Weidenfeld & Nicholson, 1987.

Terrorism

Adams, James. *The Financing of Terror*. Sevenoaks, Kent: NEL, 1986.

___. *Secret Armies: Inside the American, Soviet and European Forces*. New York: Atlantic Monthly, 1988.

Cline, Ray S., and Yonah Alexander. *Terrorism: The Soviet Connection*. New York: Crane Russak, 1984.

Ford, Franklin L. *Political Murder: From Tyrannicide to Terrorism*. Cambridge, MA: Harvard U P, 1985.

Livingstone, Neil C., and Terrell E. Arnold. *Fighting Back: Winning the War against Terrorism*. Lexington, MA: Lexington, 1986.

Merari, Ariel, ed. *On Terrorism and Combating Terrorism: Proceedings of an International Seminar*. Tel Aviv, 1979. Tel Aviv: Jaffee Center for Strategic Studies, Tel Aviv Univ. Frederick, MD: Univ Publications, 1985.

Netanyahu, Benjamin, ed. *Terrorism: How the West Can Win*. New York: Farrar, 1986.

Rapoport, David C., and Yonah Alexander, eds. *The Rationalization of Terrorism*. Frederick, MD: University Publications, 1982.

Tremlett, George. *Gadaffi: The Desert Mystic*. New York: Carroll & Graf, 1993.

Yallop, David. *The Jackal: In Search of the World's Most Wanted Terrorist*. New York: Random, 1993.

Tradecraft

Casey, William. *The Secret War against Hitler*. New York: Berkley, 1987.

Cooper, H.A.A., and Lawrence Handlinger. *Making Spies*. Boulder, CO: Paladin, 1986.

Deacon, Richard, and Nigel West. *Spy!* London: BBC, 1980.

Krousher, Richard W. *Physical Interrogation Techniques*. Port Townsend, WA: Loompanics, 1985.

Masterman, J. C. *The Double-Cross System in the War of 1939 to 1945*. New Haven: Yale U P, 1972.

Phillips, David Atlee. *Careers in Secret Operations: How to Be a Federal Intelligence Officer*. Frederick, MD: Univ Publications, 1984.

Rapp, Burt. *Shadowing and Surveillance: A Complete Guidebook*. Port Townsend, WA: Loompanics, 1986.

Women in Espionage

Aline, Countess of Romanones [née Griffith]. *The Spy Wore Red: My Adventures as an Undercover Agent in World War II.* New York: Random, 1987.

Gleeson, James. *They Feared No Evil: The Woman[sic] Agents of Britain's Secret Armies, 1939-45.* London: Hale, 1976.

Miller, Joan C. *One Girl's War: Personal Exploits in MI5's Most Secret Station.* Dingle, Co., Kerry: Brandon, 1986.

CLOAK AND DAGGER FICTION

PART 1

Early Spy Thrillers (to 1940)

INTRODUCTION

> "Gentlemen do not open each other's mail."
> —*Henry L. Stimson*
> [The New England academic who declined a State
> Department request to establish a code-breaking unit]

LATE IN 1993, CZECH President Havel addressed the General Assembly of the
Council on Europe in Vienna. He spoke to the issue of Europe's new destiny
in the wake of communism's collapse. He warned:

> If various Western states cannot rid themselves of their desire for a dominant
> position in their own sphere of interests, if they don't stop trying to outwit history
> by reducing the idea of Europe to a noble backdrop against which they continue to
> defend their petty concerns, and if the post-Communist states do not make radical
> efforts to exorcise the ghosts their newly won freedom has set loose, then Europe
> will only with great difficulty be able to respond to the challenge of the present and
> fulfill the opportunities that lie before it.[1]

These words of hope and fear remind the reader of espionage fiction how much
has changed—and how little—since the spy thriller as we know it today began
to reflect the concerns and themes against the turbulent background of Europe.
Today, as in the pre-World War I era of German militarism and Russian
bolshevism, terrorists were looming large in the fiction of authors who would
themselves shape the imagination of their readers with tales of master criminals,
power-mad geniuses, secret weapons, missing documents, and bomb-wielding
anarchists. Moreover, the media saturates us daily with global horrors—so

much so that the Balkan atrocities of Bosnia-Herzegovena and Croatia are only two of many hot spots waiting to disrupt the stability of peoples and governments. Terrorists, authors of spy fiction remind us constantly, shape our imaginations nowadays, and we are constantly reminded of the seething of national factionalism beneath the surface in another assertion (by Leon Trotsky) that insurrection is a machine that makes no noise.

Before we turn to the first decades of the spy novel, let us, first, bypass various arguments put forward for this or that work being the first *real* spy novel. Such backtracking to antiquity we have attempted in the text's opening introduction; nor is this meant to disparage the usual claimants for distinction, such as Fenimore Cooper's *The Spy* (1821) or Poe's *The Gold Bug* and *Purloined Letter* (1843; 1845) or James's *The Princess Casamassima* (1885). They all speak well to the core of what interests us about the spy thriller today: international intrigue, mysterious documents, an "intelligence" analyst as opposed to an analytical policeman, political assassination, and so on. These are still the staple ingredients of spy fiction. Even though no less an authority than Eric Ambler described Cooper's book as unreadable and academics might wince at the thought of James's usual obsession with European treachery and intrigue linked nineteenth-century espionage fiction, there is the fact of the political assassination in *The Princess Casamassima* to be noted as evidence of more than topical matters at stake. Conrad, however, provides us with the best example why there is little to be gained in this kind of who-begot-whom search. As the editors of *Spy Fiction: A Connoisseur's Guide* note in their discussion of James's single foray into the "murky territory" of nineteenth-century espionage fiction, there was, at first, a very limited audience appeal.[2] Conrad shrugged off the failures of both *The Secret Agent* and *Under Western Eyes* (1907; 1911), but he never understood exactly why they failed. Yet Erskine Childers' *The Riddle of the Sands* (1903) clearly demonstrates why that is so: James and Conrad were writing for literate audiences; there is no spangle of romance or adventure to be found within their own dire warnings of a Europe about to explode and threaten English and American shores with their anarchist violence. (Conrad's use of the topical in *The Secret Agent*—that is, the real anarchist who hoist himself on his own petard in the sensation Greenwich Bomb Outrage of 1894—is all the more revealing for the loathsome portrait he draws of an actual "spy.")

Childers, on the other hand, subsumes a real fear of German militarism to an action story that appeals to a mass (and not necessarily masculine) audience. It may be safely argued that the modern spy novel became *modern* when the public ceased to perceive the spy as an odious, malevolent, bomb-wielding caricature and began to associate the persona of spy with those intellectual and moral qualities we associate with a contemporary "intelligence agent." In these early days, of course, American and English exposure to the apparatus of organized espionage was confined to newspaper images of tsarist police and subversives in cells and the multitudes of secret societies that emerged from the mid-nineteenth-century political and social chaos sweeping Europe in the aftermath of the Industrial Revolution. There were no real "intelligence agents," much less counterintelligence organizations to oppose them, but there was a public and popular appetite for the romance novel and the schoolboy adventure tale. It was inevitable that the spy story would come about in the face of such political realities as the machinery of insurrection accelerated across the falling Austro-Hungarian and Ottoman Empires in the days before the Great War. Such innocence was doomed on all fronts.

Inevitably, it would fall to a larger-than-life hero the task of saving his own society from the ruffians, international criminals and conspirators, and various bearded vandals of Bolshevism and their ilk. Those who did produced scores of "espionage" novels that would set the tone and pace for a generation until their cardboard heroes could be set aside for a new kind of spy, the true intelligence agent who works quietly for his country's goals in a realistic world. Most of these are tales are appalling in style, nationalistic in tone, and right-wing in politics. But the early monochromatic heroes never were spies or agents because they were, to a man, constrained to epic-like qualifications of heroism—such as we deem politically incorrect nowadays and therefore unpalatable for their representations of ethnocentric superiority—or their creators simply dipped them like teabags into the amateur business of espionage and allow their sterling qualities room to flex; once extricated from the evil forces surrounding them, their countries were saved from the sordid machinations of German spies, sinister organizations, and other manifestations of rotten European governments. Into this light step the heroes of the major names of this "Innocent Age": William LeQueux, E. Phillips Oppenheim, Sax Rohmer, and Herman C. ("Sapper") McNeile. Their characters are redblooded but boyish men whose deeds are festooned with public approval—if not paranoia. More importantly, they are valued for their virile looks and drawing-room charm, their physical and moral superiority over their foreign enemies, and because they are nearly all in one way or another saviors of the British Empire from the foreign scum who want to deprive good citizens of it.

Now, to be fair, this sameness of hero, villain, and plot is not as generic as one often hears. Not all heroes are chiseled from the same block of granite as Bulldog Drummond. Writes LeRoy Panek of one of the best products of the Sapper-LeQueux-Oppenheim tradition in his *The Special Branch*:

> Richard Hannay [John Buchan's protagonist] moves out of the ritzy, perfume-scented saloons of Oppy and LeQueux, and he shows, in the traditions of the schoolboy novel, the virtues of the healthy, responsible, active man.[3]

Hannay's escape from German spies *The Thirty-Nine Steps* (1915) alternates a great pace of rest between exciting exploits and escape, but Hannay does not distinguish himself markedly from other heroes of this first-generation of spy-fiction writers. Eric Ambler, of course, would later expand this motif of the bumbling amateur who takes on the concerted efforts of an organized enemy and, with sufficient pluck, outwits them. His *A Coffin for Dimitrios* [*A Mask of Dimitrios*] remains as readable and realistic as ever. The sophistication of the second-generation of writers is clear in their emphasis on across-the-board realism, their more sophisticated narrative structures, and their uses of varying points of view to "tell the tale." Multiple points of view to relay the events replaces unadulterated action/adventure. "The spy thriller," notes Bruce Merry in his *Anatomy of the Spy Thriller*, "like all popular art, must entertain but not frustrate the reader":

> The spy thriller finds its own esthetic filter between facts and their creative reformulation in the device of suspended narrative and messenger retelling of events to secondary members of the its cast of characters. The device also serves to provide a moment of stasis, a pause of the onward thrust which otherwise threatens to engulf the spy plot in an unrelieved sequence of exploits.[4]

Nor, of course, are the villains identical, even though their fears of anarchy or radical Bolshevism may be. George Valentine Williams, who undoubtedly belongs to the tribe of Sapper, opted for an evil figure known throughout his long series of tales as "Clubfoot" very much in the manner of Sapper's own Carl Peterson. It would take a world war and writers of "serious" literary persuasion little time to replace these two-dimensional heroes and villains with that familiar modern-day *Zeitgeist* of the agent-spy anchored to a few absolutes almost adrift in an amoral world. It is that familiar, gray world of modern espionage that has been passed down to Ted Allbeury, John le Carré, and Len Deighton; in this world new tactics would require an agent to defend the principle of good against new evils. Thus is it ever so, but until Eric Ambler, Graham Greene, and Somerset Maugham came along to show this spiritual transformation, there were endless spinoffs and variations of one of the twentieth-century's great themes in literature, the hunter and the hunted, being played out against very simple backdrops. The philosophical content of a Sapper novel's simplistic club-man philosophy would probably not fill in the circumference of a shot glass with a fat crayon.

Even the best of this lot, John Buchan, could only with difficulty comprehend real evil, according to one critic of the spy novel:

> Buchan could not understand the demonic and the sadistic; his mental world was too romantic and optimistic. There was something Edwardian about him: a Scot, not to the manner born, he admired an England that was vanishing.[5]

After World War I, the spy novel slowly began to move away from pure action and unadulterated jingoism toward a realistic approach that, as in Maugham's case, reflected actual war-time experiences in espionage. His *Ashenden* (1927) is a breakthrough novel, more so than Childers' *Riddle of the Sands*, because it explicitly confronts the gray moral issues of modern espionage tactics in securing its own ends. That latter phrase itself smacks of the duplicity inherent within the Great Game as it has been played in our times rather than LeQueux' or Buchan's where justifying murder—especially the murder of an innocent—is never an issue: things are black or white, never gray.

Another crucial point of difference between the first- and second-generation spy novel is in the techniques employed to tell the tale itself. Says Robin W. Winks in his *Modus Operandi*:

> The classic spy thriller of Kipling or Buchan is much like a game of chess—a comparison so often made as to be trite, the sacrifice of the pawn being part of the language of cliché so deeply rooted in the literature of duplicity—for it turns on repetition of situations that open lines to infinite variables.[6]

A new breed of writer after Maugham, however, would rarefy the idea of espionage as game and take an inward turning for their principal figures as significant as James himself once did for narrative fiction. Ambler, the authors of the Manning Coles series, and Greene would faintly resemble one another, as their own predecessors had once resembled one another in stock in trade, but the differences would be more striking than the similarities between the post-World War II group and the pre-World War I writers because of *how* they chose to write their narratives and the shifting of points of view used. Mainstream literature in America in the twenties is incredibly rich; its Lost Generation cadre formed in the cafe communities of Paris. For one thing, Ambler's characters fall into the dirty business of spying while minding their own business; Greene's clear-cut characters drag along with their human frailties and try to avoid falling into a moral pit that yawns in front of them, which hesitation usually forces a crisis of conscience at the end. During his long writing career until his death in 1990, Greene's characters emphasize the average person, someone who cannot escape from either impersonal, bureaucratic horror, such as in *The Ministry of Fear* (1943), or avoid becoming corrupted morally by it; the later novels reflect the squalid nature of espionage set in contemporary hot spots like Mexico, Central Africa, or Haiti. Too, there is always Greene's familiar stamp of an inward turning along the lines of a religious quest and moral choices that inevitably draw characters into webs of their own making.

This spiritual condition, as noted by Panek, characterizes Ambler in the thirties too: he cites Ambler's *Epitaph for a Spy* (1938) as evidence of the decisive reintroduction of "Conrad's stress on the little people who are the labor force of the espionage corporation."[7] The period between the wars did,

ultimately, sharpen this division between the Sappers and the Greenes but only
in retrospect; the emerging threats to world peace and the rise of police states
and dictators gave a brief resuscitation to the moribund Sappers still scribbling
exciting tales of brave Englishmen in flimsy plots about lost documents, secret
weapons, and nefarious spies lurking in shadows—for example, the "bubble-
brained concoctions" of the Dark books of Peter Cheyney.[8]

Yet at the end of the thirties—a decade that saw worldwide economic
depression and the rise of fascism—spy fiction had taken firm root in the soil of
verisimilitude and three-dimensional character development in the hands of
serious practitioners.   Although the same impulses that could create an
entertainment figure like Bulldog Drummond would still be there, the Red
menace more than ever a force of evil, but the spy novel had been opened to
serious exploitation for the new world coming into being after the Second World
War. A new breed of writers would build on that sturdy foundation as the Cold
War dominated the headlines and the lives of millions of the world's people.

Beginning with Eric Ambler, we will work our way through the big
names and some of the small of the period, providing details on good stories and
bad alike. Readers interested in a specific author should not forget to consult
Part 2 because many of these authors were active in the period after 1940.

NOTES

1.   Václav Havel, address, General Assembly of the Council of
Europe, Vienna, 9 October 1993; "How Europe Could Fail," trans. Paul
Wilson, *New York Review of Books* 18 November 1993: 3.

2.   Donald McCormick, and Katy Fletcher, *Spy Fiction: A
Connoisseur's Guide* (New York: Facts on File, 1990) 267.

3.   LeRoy Panek, *The Special Branch* (Bowling Green, OH: Bowling
Green U Popular P, 1981) 284.

4.   Bruce Merry, *Anatomy of the Spy Thriller* (Montreal: McGill-
Queen's U P, 1977) 167.

5.   Ralph Harper, *The World of the Thriller* (Cleveland, OH: Case
Western Reserve U P, 1969) 50.

6.   Robin W. Winks, *Modus Operandi* (Boston: Godine, 1982) 55.

7.   Panek, 285.

8.   Panek, 286.

Bibliography: A to Z

A

1. Ambler, Eric. *Background to Danger.* New York: Knopf, 1937. First published in England under the title *Uncommon Danger.* A British newsman gets mixed up in the fighting between European agents over possession of a file of secret documents of international importance. *

Born in 1909, Ambler is considered one of the fathers of the realistic spy thriller and the author principally responsible for changing it from a tool of upper crust nationalism into a vehicle through which writers could express concern over the lack of international morality and social justice. Ambler introduced ordinary people into his tales, mixing them up with agents from various lands who were both good and bad. Locales like Istanbul and Saigon were substituted for the better known such as Paris or London. Many additional Ambler yarns were told after 1940.

2. ___. *Cause for Alarm.* New York: Knopf, 1938. Aimed against what many Englishmen considered the villains of Munich, this novel concerns a quiet young English engineer named Nicholas Marlow, who serves as manager of the Spartacus Machine Tool Company in Milan, Italy, and how he succeeded in putting—as the book jacket had it—"a kink in the Rome-Berlin Axis." *

3. ___. *A Coffin for Dimitrios.* New York: Knopf, 1939. First published in England as *The Mask of Dimitrios*, this adventure tells us how an English writer tracked down the life story of a nondescript Greek fig-packer who turned up in a Turkish morgue. For two decades, it seems, the corpse had been involved in international intrigue—until one day it caught up with him. The huge, kindly Soviet agent Zaleshoff, who always seems to be disposed to help innocent Englishmen out of jams, is a major character employed by Ambler to demonstrate that all secret operatives of potential enemies are not evil. *

4. ___. *The Dark Frontier*. London: Hodder & Stoughton, 1936. In the introduction to the revised edition published by Mysterious Press in 1990, Ambler wrote that he had intended his first novel as a spoof "of the old secret service adventure thriller as written by E. Phillips Oppenheim, John Buchan, Dornford Yates and their crude imitators" (xii).

5. Annesley, Michael. *Fenton of the Foreign Service*. New York: Speller, 1937. First published in Britain by Harrap in 1935 as *Room 14: A Secret Service Adventure*. Lawne Fenton of the Secret Intelligence Service (SIS) is dispatched to Poland to deal with fascist plotters. *

Annesley, who tended to follow the Buchan-Oppenheim school with touches of Ambler realism, penned two more spy tales before World War II and a number afterwards. Those two are:

6. ___. *Spies in Action*. London: Harrap, 1937.

7. ___. *Spies in the Web*. London: Harrap, 1936.

Ashe, Gordon, pseud. *See* Creasey, John

B

Beeding, Francis, pseud. *See* Palmer, John Leslie and Hiliary Aiden St. George Saunders

8. Bindloss, Harold. *Brandon of the Engineers*. New York: Stokes, 1917. Published in England as *His One Talent*. A dismissed Royal Engineer working in South America discovers that the father of his girlfriend is the spy who stole the papers, the loss of which got him cashiered. *y

Blake, Nicholas, pseud. *See* Day-Lewis, Cecil

9. Blankfort, Michael. *I Met a Man*. Indianapolis: Bobbs-Merrill, 1937. The story of a World War I friendship between a German officer and an enlisted man who was, in fact, an American working for the British intelligence service. *y

10.   Blasco-Ibanez, Vincente. *Mare Nostrum.* Trans. from the Spanish. New York: Dutton, 1919. During World War I, a girl German spy uses the love of a Spanish sea captain to help U-boats refuel in the Mediterranean; when the man learns his son was killed in a torpedo attack on an Allied liner, he turns on his lover and attacks a German submarine, losing his life in the victory. *

11.   Bottome, Phyllis. *The Mortal Storm.* Boston: Little, 1938. A best seller at the time which employed espionage as a backdrop against which to reveal to the British public the inner workings of Nazi Germany.

     Bottome spent most of the years between her marriage in 1917 (to an army officer working in intelligence) and World War II moving on the fringes of "the game," in England, and abroad in cities like Vienna. During this time, she became a successful writer of mysteries, choosing not to employ her knowledge of secret agent affairs in her other stories. She and her husband are important to spy thrillers in another way. In his youth, Ian Fleming received tuition from the couple and it was she who encouraged him to write; under her mentorship, James Bond's creator wrote an unpublished story, "Death on Two Occasions."

12.   Bronson-Howard, George. *The Devil's Chaplain.* New York: Watt, 1922. American agent Keefe disperses a band of spies out to liquidate Balkan refugee Prince McIntosh; in the process, he wins the hand of Princess Faire. *y

13.   Buchan, John. *The Courts of the Morning.* Boston: Houghton, 1929. Richard Hannay, Buchan's hero and the first true progenitor of the modern agent, Arbuthnot, and company are drawn into a South American revolution against Castor, Dictator of Olifa. *y

     Born in 1875, John Buchan, master of the spy-adventure tale, product of the best schools and one who moved in the right political circles, is an important figure in the development of the spy thriller. During World War I, he was very much involved with British intelligence and propaganda activities which, when added to the knowledge gained in pre-war government work, gave him the background to create Richard Hannay, a landmark secret agent.

     "John Buchan was the first to realize," wrote Graham Greene in his 1941 essay "The Last Buchan" (in *Collected Essays* [New York: Viking, 1969], 223), "the enormous dramatic value of adventure in familiar surroundings happening to unadventurous men." Buchan's characters, upper-crust nationalists, were all romantics; the author was a master in describing the chase or escape—in keeping the action rapid and lively. His tales have paled a bit with time, but still make interesting reading. As Julian Symons put it, Buchan, who died as a baron and Governor General of Canada, "blended invention with material drawn from his own knowledge in these tales, which are notable for their sense of scenery and weather rather than for the plots," (*Mortal Consequences: A History—From the Detective Story to the Crime Novel* [New York: Schocken, 1972], 236).

14. ___. *Greenmantle.* New York: Doran, 1915. Richard Hannay and British agents in World War I Constantinople must foil a German effort to stir up a Holy War in the Middle East by manipulating an Islamic prophet. **y*

15. ___. *Huntingtower.* New York: Doran, 1923. A Glasgow grocer, recently retired, becomes involved with Bolsheviks, who have kidnapped an heiress and are holding her for ransom in a Scottish castle. With the help of a band of orphans, the quiet Scot effects a rescue. **y*

16. ___. *Mr. Standfast.* Boston: Houghton, 1919. Pretending to be a pacifist, agent Hannay works to thwart the activities of the German master spy Moxon Ivery (villain of *The Thirty Nine Steps*) who is posing as a liberal intellectual; the chase follows from Skye to a climactic finish in Switzerland, after which Ivery is taken to the Allied trenches and forced over the top where he is shot by his own countrymen. **y*

17. ___. *A Prince of the Captivity.* New York: Houghton, 1933. Adam Melfort serves with British intelligence in World War I and as a fighter for world peace thereafter. Spy thriller writer Nicholas Luard has called the first half of this book "one of the truest and most spell-binding accounts of an agent working in the field ever written." **y*

18. ___. *The Thirty Nine Steps.* New York: Doran, 1915. An informant who later turns up dead tells mining engineer Richard Hannay of a fantastic plot by the Black Stone organization to cause, through assassination, an Anglo-German war which will see Britain invaded. Under suspicion of murder, Hannay must avoid both the police and the nasties, while seeking intercession through high-placed friends. Learning of a secret meeting of defense officials, Hannay bursts in upon it warning of an imposter posing as the First Sea Lord. When his story is agreed upon, it becomes necessary to find the man by checking all ports of escape. Hannay comes upon a cove which leads by 39 steps up to a house, which he enters with police support. There three men, innocent-looking enough come to give themselves away as the enemy group and all are eventually taken in hand. **y*
    This story, which established Buchan's credentials as an early master of the spy thriller, was reprinted by the New York firm of Popular Library in

1974. It was also twice made into motion pictures, in 1935 and 1959, the first version being an important early vehicle for director Alfred Hitchcock.

19. ___. *The Three Hostages.* New York: Houghton, 1921. In a search through London and Norway, which involves him in murder and hypnotism, Sir Richard Hannay seeks three individuals who have mysteriously disappeared and eventually frustrates a revolutionary conspiracy by fanatics who are led by a master criminal. *y

C

20. Carter, John F. *Murder in the Embassy.* By "Diplomat," pseud. London: Cape, 1930. Dennis Tyler seeks the killer of Prince Hojo, a Japanese diplomat on a delicate mission to Washington. *

21. ___. *Murder in the State Department.* By "Diplomat," pseud. London: Cape, 1930. A detective investigates the murder of an Under Secretary of State and becomes involved with poison gas and two suspects: a rival Under Secretary and a villainous Bolshevik posing as a pacifist. Other "Diplomat" private eye thrillers with espionage-intrigue backgrounds include: *

22. ___. *The Brain Trust Murder.* New York: Coward, 1935. *

23. ___. *The Corpse on the White House Lawn.* London: Hurst, 1933. *

24. ___. *Death in the Senate.* New York: Covici, 1933. *

25. ___. *Scandal in the Chancery.* London: Cape & Smith, 1931. *

26. ___. *Slow Death in Geneva.* New York: Coward, 1934. *

27. Channing, Mark. *The Poisoned Mountain.* Philadelphia: Lippincott, 1936. In India, Colin Gray of British Intelligence must halt a native rebellion led by Lall Behari, who has discovered the secret of a lethal heliotrope gas in the Himalayas. *y

Charteris, Leslie, pseud. *See* Yin, Leslie C. B.

28.   Chesterton, Gilbert K. *The Man Who Was Thursday: A Nightmare.*
New York: Dodd, 1908. A poet named Syme, actually an undercover cop,
infiltrates a dangerous underground movement known as the Central Anarchist
Council in an effort to break it up before it can carry off its fantastic plot. This
story, according to Miles Copeland, has been described by some older
intelligence operatives as perhaps "the best spy book ever written." *y
        Chesterton is noted as both an essayist and as the writer of some
interesting detective fiction, much of it centering around the character of the
Jesuit, Father Brown. In this spy tale, Chesterton shows that he is no clone of
Buchan or Oppenheim, being more interested in the "romance of man" than in
any nationalism *per se*. To a certain extent, his fantasy and symbolism can be
said to foreshadow that of Graham Greene.

29.   Childers, Erskine. *The Riddle of the Sands: A Record of Secret
Service.* London: Nelson, 1903. Carruthers, a foppish Foreign Office official,
and his friend Davies, while on a yachting trip in the Frisian Islands, uncover
German plans for a cross-Channel invasion of England. The Englishman,
Dollman, a former naval officer working for the Germans, is the villain who is
properly denounced in the end. *y
        Reprinted by the New York firm of McKay in 1977, this tale, which
originally was aimed at drawing attention to pre-World War I German
militarism, is often considered to be the first spy thriller which can be
considered literature. The story, especially the matter of its sailing charts and
nautical escapes, led to a reorganization of British Naval Intelligence after two
of its operatives were caught using the Childers charts while on an actual
espionage mission in the Frisians in 1910.
        A Royal Navy officer during the Great War, this cavalier Irishman
opposed the Irish Treaty of 1919 and joined the Irish Republican Army battle
against the new Free State. Eventually Childers, who had done so much both
for literature and in warning the British about German potential, came to be
regarded as a traitor by the governments of England and Ireland. When
captured late in 1922, he was courtmartialed in Dublin and executed before a
firing squad.

30.   Christie, Agatha. *Secret Adversary.* New York: Dodd, 1922.
Tommy and Tuppence Beresford join forces with a young American to halt the
international conspiracy being pushed by the villainous Mr. Brown. *y
        Dame Agatha Christie, who died in 1979, is regarded as the first lady
of mystery fiction. Her character Inspector Hercule Poirot became the most
famous detective since Sherlock Holmes. Only occasionally did this writer
venture into spy thrillers and then mostly in the years after 1940.

31.   ___. *The Seven Dials Mystery*. New York: Dodd, 1929. It begins, innocently enough, on an English country weekend with a seemingly harmless prank staged by a group of "gay young things." Next morning, however, the victim of their practical joke is found dead in his bed. That development piques the interest of a plucky amateur sleuth named "Bundle" Brent, who is soon enmeshed in a web of murder and intrigue involving the British Foreign Office, an ambitious industrialist, and a mysterious secret society known only as "the Seven Dials." **y*

32.   Clouston, Joseph S. *Spy in Black*. New York: Doran, 1918. A beautiful Anglo-Irish girl thwarts the espionage plans of German Lt. von Belke, who is in England during World War I to ferret out Royal Navy secrets. ***

33.   Cobb, Humphrey. *Paths of Glory*. Athens: U of Georgia P, 1987. This 1935 novel's rediscovery is a boon to the war novel genre; it deals with a French regiment's retreat before a German entrenched position, and a general's vicious order of execution for that failure—one man from each company.

34.   Conde, Phillip. *The Case of the Crazy Pilot*. London: Wright, 1938. Conde wrote thrillers throughout the decade of the thirties; his novels are mysteries, mainly, that concern the aerial adventures of Dick Pemberty. Others:

35.   ___. *Death from the Air*. London: Wright, 1936.

36.   ___. *Death Laughs Aloft*. London: Wright, 1940.

37.   ___. *The Devil Has Wings*. London: Wright, 1937.

38.   ___. *The Mystery of the Vanishing Aerodrome*. London: Wright, 1939.

39.   ___. *The Secret of the Scarlet Bomber*. London: Wright, 1939.

40.   ___. *Spawn of the Hawk*. London: Wright, 1938.

41.   Conrad, Joseph. *The Secret Agent*. New York and London: Harper, 1907. An assistant Police Commissioner uncovers an anarchist plot to blow up the Greenwich Observatory in London's East End; reprinted by the Garden City, NY firm of Doubleday in 1953, this tale rather closely follows the details of an actual case. **y*

42. ___. *Under Western Eyes*. New York and London: Harper, 1911.
Having sold out his college roommate as a revolutionary, Razumov is recruited
into the Czar's secret service and is sent under cover to Geneva to spy on
Bolshevik plotters, but in the end turns out to be a double agent. *y
        Critics and scholars of straight literature and spy fiction have had
difficulty with these two tales ever since they were first published. Conrad
carefully develops his character and implies that revolution and the spies of
revolution are wholly evil. The importance of *Under Western Eyes* to students
of the spy thriller rests with the fact that it is the first tale in the genre to clearly
deal with the idea of a double agent and the difficulties and unpleasantries
associated with that calling. A useful collection of essays on Conrad's first
effort can be found in I. Watt, ed., *"The Secret Agent": A Selection of Critical
Essays* (London: Macmillan Casebook Series, 1973).

43.   Cooper, James Fenimore. *The Spy: A Tale of the Neutral Ground*.
Philadelphia: Carey, Lea & Carey, 1821. British officer Harvey Birch, out of
uniform and disguised as a pedlar, goes behind enemy lines during the American
Revolution in order to visit his family. Denounced, he is taken in hand by
Yankee forces and condemned to death. Birch survives in the end, a double
agent whose real allegiance, it turns out, is to the cause of General Washington.
*Hy
        Described by Julian Symons and others as the first spy thriller,
Cooper's tale is one of adventure and romance which views espionage and
double agents in purely military terms, peopled with characters which he does
not, like Conrad, flesh out. It would be the end of the nineteenth century before
readers would see tales about men similar in nature to Harvey Birch or Miles
Wallingford, one of Harvey's maritime counterparts. Between 1844 and 1846
Cooper published five novels, including *Afloat and Ashore* and its sequel *Miles
Wallingford*. In the latter, he challenged mindless subservience to country over
morality a century before John le Carré: "Our country, right or wrong is a
mark of spurious patriotism in that it subordinates God to country."

        Copplestone, Bennet, pseud. *See* Kitchin, Frederick

44.   Creasey, John. *The Death Mizer*. London: Long, 1933. Gordon
Craigie is named head of the counterintelligence Department Z, and employing
both patriotic and valiant agents, guards England's interests against foreign
espionage and criminal masterminds. Beginning in the early 1930s, this noted
author of mystery fiction turned his attention to the spy thriller and turned out
a number of Department Z tales before World War II. Most of these were
unavailable in the United States until the 1970s. All are rather straightforward
Buchan-Oppenheim style yarns with emphasis on action. *y The titles include:

45.   ___. *Carriers of Death.* London: Melrose, 1937. Reprinted by the New York firm of Popular Library in 1972. *y

46.   ___. *Days of Danger.* London: Melrose, 1937. Reprinted by the New York firm of Popular Library in 1972. *y

47.   ___. *Death by Night.* London: Long, 1940. Reprinted by the New York firm of Popular Library in 1972. *y

48.   ___. *Death Stands By.* London: Melrose, 1938. Reprinted by the New York firm of Popular Library in 1972. *y

49.   ___. *First Came a Murder.* London: Melrose, 1934. Reprinted by the New York firm of Popular Library in 1972. *y

50.   ___. *The Island of Peril.* London: Long, 1940. Reprinted by the New York firm of Popular Library in 1969. *y

51.   ___. *The Mark of the Crescent.* London: Melrose, 1935. Reprinted by the New York firm of Popular Library in 1972. *y

52.   ___. *Menace.* London: Long, 1938. Reprinted by the New York firm of Popular Library in 1972. *y

53.   ___. *Murder Must Wait.* London: Long, 1939. Reprinted by the New York firm of Popular Library in 1972. *y

54.   ___. *Panic.* London: Long, 1939. Reprinted by the New York firm of Popular Library in 1972. *y

55.   ___. *The Redhead.* London: Hurst & Blacket, 1934. *y

56.   ___. *The Terror Trap.* London: Melrose, 1936. Reprinted by the New York firm of Popular Library in 1972. *y

57.   ___. *Thunder in Europe.* London: Melrose, 1936. Reprinted by the New York firm of Popular Library in 1972. *y Creasey tales written under the pen names of Gordon Ashe and Norman Deane include:

58.   ___. *Dangerous Journey.* By Norman Deane, pseud. London: Hurst & Blacket, 1939. British agents Bruce Murdock and Mary Dell have been assigned to catch top Nazi spy Kurt Von Romain. Hot on his trail, they are

amazed to find that he has slipped away, necessitating their pursuit being carried ever more dangerously over onto the Continent. Reprinted by the New York firm of McKay in 1974. *y

59.   ___. *Death on Demand*. By Gordon Ashe, pseud. London: Long, 1939. Patrick Dawlish of MI-5 battles an evil Nazi plot against Britain. *y

60.   ___. *Death Round the Corner*. By Gordon Ashe, pseud. London: Melrose, 1935. Reprinted by the New York firm of Popular Library in 1969. Patrick Dawlish of MI-5 is drawn into a struggle with a master criminal of fascist bent who has plans for world conquest. *y

61.   ___. *Secret Errand*. By Norman Deane, pseud. London: Hurst & Blacket, 1939. Beautiful and dangerous! That was how British Intelligence rated actress Felice Damon when it ordered Bruce Murdock to find out what she was up to. Reprinted by the New York firm of McKay in 1974. *y

62.   ___. *The Speaker*. By Gordon Ashe, pseud. London: Long, 1939. Reprinted in the United States by the New York firm of Holt in 1973 under the title *The Croaker*. *y

D

63.   Davison, Gilderoy. *The Man with the Twisted Face*.   London: Jenkins, 1931. The hero, Major Peter Castle, is a spy in this series, opposed by the the "Man with the Twisted Face"—a "deformed, statanic creature with ghastly, hypnotic eyes"; these attempts are usually thwarted, as the copywriter of *The Prince of Spies* notes, "at the last minute." The series ended in 1940. Others:

64.   ___. *A Dog Fight with Death*. London: Jenkins, 1940.

65.   ___. *Exit Mr. Brent*. London: Jenkins, 1936.

66.   ___. *The Man with Half a Face*. London: Jenkins, 1936.

67.   ___. *The Prince of Spies*. London: Jenkins, 1932.

68.   Dawe, William Carlton Lanyon. *Leathermouth*. London: Ward, 1931. Between this publication's date and 1936, 10 more "Leathermouth" spy tales were cranked out. Half of the series:

69.   ___. *Fifteen Keys* London: Ward, 1932.

70.   ___. *Leathermouth's Luck*. London: Ward, 1934.

71.   ___. *A Royal Alliance*. London: Ward, 1935.

72.   ___. *Tough Company*. London: Ward, 1936.

73.   ___. *Waste Lands*. London: Ward, 1935.

74.   Day-Lewis, Cecil. *The Smiler with the Knife*. By Nicholas Blake, pseud. New York: Harper, 1939. The noted poet Day-Lewis wrote a large number of detective novels and some spy thrillers under his pen name. In this one, Nigel Strangeways and his wife Georgia expose a vast conspiracy to impose Nazism on England on the eve of World War II. *

Deane, Norman, pseud. *See* Creasey, John

"Diplomat," pseud. *See* Carter, John F.

75.   Dorling, Henry T. *The Longely Bungalow*. By "Taffrail," pseud. London: Hodder & Stoughton, 1930. A British naval officer and his girlfriend become involved in a desperate mission to halt the efforts of a Russian agent named Boris. *y
        "Taffrail" Dorling was a noted author of British naval literature in the period 1914-1940, turning only occasionally to the spy thriller. When he wrote of secret agents, he chose a nautical theme as his background, exploiting its scenery with mastery.

76.   ___. *Operation MO*. By "Taffrail," pseud. London: Hodder & Stoughton, 1938. A fascist agent works to uncover a British admiralty secret. *y

77.   ___. *The Shetland Plan*. By "Taffrail," pseud. London: Hodder & Stoughton, 1939. British fishermen are mixed up with a group of German spies who plan to seize one of the Shetland Islands when war breaks out with England. *y

78.   Doyle, Arthur Conan. "The Bruce-Partington Plans." [In *Great Spy Stories from Fiction*. Allen W. Dulles, ed., New York: Harper & Row, 1969. 119-44.] A short story of 1908, from that pre-Great War period when writers

like Erskine Childers and William LeQueux were attempting to draw England's attention to the menace of German agents and the Kaiser's imperial ambitions.

An unexpected culprit and an evil German spy attempt to obtain plans for a new English defense invention; the manner in which the operation is carried off so baffles the British Secret Service that it invites the illustrious Sherlock Holmes to investigate the matter, which, in a dazzling example of detection and analysis, he does to a successful conclusion. Also published in various editions of Holmes, including that introduced and given notes by William S. Baring-Gould, *The Adventure of the Speckled Band and Other Stories of Sherlock Holmes* (New York: Signet, 1965), 205-230. *y

A medical doctor, Arthur Conan Doyle turned his attention to fiction in the mid-1880s, publishing his first Sherlock Holmes adventure, "A Study in Scarlet," in the December 1887 edition of *Beeton's Christmas Annual*. His famous hero is more closely identified with the formation of the detective genre; however, he was involved, on a few occasions, with tales of espionage. The manner of detection and consideration which allowed these cases to be solved, particularly the matter of Holmes' disguises, served as inspiration for both contemporary, and later, exponents of espionage, writers and agents alike.

79.   ___. "The Naval Treaty." [In *The Adventure of the Speckled Band and Other Stories of Sherlock Holmes*. Introduction and Notes by William S. Baring-Gould. New York: Signet, 1965. 116-46.] Holmes and Dr. Watson are called in to solve the mystery of some important government documents which have been stolen and which are destined to be sold to a foreign agent. First published in 1894. *y

80.   ___. "A Scandal in Bohemia." [In *The Adventure of the Speckled Band and Other Stories of Sherlock Holmes*. Introduction and Notes by William S. Baring-Gould. New York: Signet, 1965. 39-59.] First published in 1891. Holmes portrays an agent of the Austro-Hungarian throne to deal with the difficulties put forward by the lady Irene Adler. *y

81.   Driggs, Laurence, L. T. *On Secret Air Service*. Boston: Little, 1930. Major Adair tells of a group of young World War I aviators who pledge themselves to do secret air service for the Allies. *y

F

82.   Fairlie, Gerald. *Bulldog Drummond on Dartmoor*. London: Hodder & Stoughton, 1938. The two-fisted right-wing hero becomes involved with thieves, a strangler, and the secret of Moreland Hall, where Cavaliers hid jewels

during the English Civil War. This title is significant to students of the spy thriller because it marks the changeover in Drummond authorship from "Sapper" McNeile, who died in 1937, to noted detective author Fairlie, upon whom the Drummond character was supposedly modeled. * Fairlie seemed to tire of Drummond and only one other appears before World War II:

83. ___. *Bulldog Drummond Attacks.* London: Hodder & Stoughton, 1939.

84. Faust, Frederick S. *The Bamboo Whistle.* By Frederick Frost, pseud. New York: Smith, 1937. American agent Anthony Hamilton travels to the Far East to battle a Japanese scheme to cause a quick war with the United States. *

Faust was the Michael Avallone of his day, writing over a hundred pulp thrillers under more than a dozen pseudonyms, including the immensely popular western novels as Max Brand (*Destry Rides Again* (1930), *Singing Guns* (1938), and *Danger Trail* (1940)). Faust lost his life in WW II as a war correspondent for *Harper's*.

85. ___. *Secret Agent Number One.* by Frederick Frost, pseud. New York: Smith, 1936. Hamilton uncovers and disposes of a fascist plot in Monte Carlo. *

86. ___. *Spy Meets Spy.* By Frederick Frost, pseud. New York: Smith, 1937. Agent Hamilton battles De Graulchier, Franco-Japanese head of the "Nipponese" espionage service, over secret dealings in Central Europe. *

87. Frankau, Gilbert. *Lonely Man.* New York: Dutton, 1933. Divorced twice, Marcus Orlando gives up on women only to fall in love with Alix Ingram, who, it turns out, is not pleased that he works for the British SIS. As much a love story as a spy thriller.

Frost, Frederick, pseud. *See* Faust, Frederick S.

G

88. Garth, David. *Eastward in Eden.* London: Kinsey, 1939. In Egypt, Faith Stirling accidentally gains admittance into the fellowship of a spy ring which is attempting to obtain a vital secret and must be saved by adventurer Jim Randall. *

89.   Gibbs, George. *The Yellow Dove.* New York: Appleton-Century, 1915. Planning to present the Kaiser's staff with false data, a British agent is nabbed by a German counterintelligence officer who has forced the Englishman's girlfriend to innocently betray him; playing up to the German, the girl maneuvers the British agent's escape on the eve of his execution and together the two flee to England in a stolen aircraft. *y

Graeme, Bruce, pseud. *See* Jeffries, Graham M.

90.   Grayson, Rupert. *Gunston Cotton: A Romance of the Secret Service.* New York: Nash, 1929. Though not technically espionage, and a dash of cowboy to boot, Gunston ("Gun") Cotton's adventures in the US Secret Service once sent him to Russia in this series, which ran the the decade of the thirties and concluded with: *

91.   ___. *Gunston Cotton: Secret Agent.* New York: Dutton, 1936. Cotton deals with a master criminal and his gang of murderers who have abducted a young European woman in America. *

92.   ___. *Gunston Cotton: Secret Airman.* New York: Dutton, 1939. Agent Cotton must thwart the plot of certain nasties to bomb various European capitals from the air thus starting a world war. *

93.   ___. *Secret Agent in Africa.* New York: Dutton, 1939. Gunston and his wife Toni fight an anti-British conspiracy in a central African colony on the eve of World War II. *

94.   Greene, Graham. *The Confidential Agent.* New York: Viking, 1939. A former professor of language in an unnamed country much like Franco's Spain, Mr. D. arrives in London to act as an agent in the obtaining of coal for his nation and is drawn into violence, theft, and love; successful in the latter, Agent D. eventually departs for home, his primary mission a failure. *y

　　　Greene is an important contemporary novelist whose tales, not exactly spy thrillers, always have some sort of corruption and/or espionage theme in them. The author has always had a fondness for examining the frailties of human nature and a suspicion of government smoothed over by a fine cynicism. Much of what takes place in his stories is symbolic. This writer would continue his "entertainments" in the post-1940 period, making them even better for having spent a period with British Intelligence in World War II.

95.   ___. *A Gun for Sale*. London: Heinemann, 1936. An English police inspector pursues a hired assassin who has gunned down a socialist minister of a European state—an act which almost plunges the Continent into war. **y*

96.   Greener, William O. *A Secret Agent in Port Arthur*. London: Constable, 1905. Jo Salis of the British Foreign Office examines the Russian position in the Far East in order to assist his superiors in taking a position during the Russo-Japanese War. **y*

97.   Gribbon, William L. *Devil's Guard*. By Talbot Mundy, pseud. Indianapolis: Bobbs-Merrill, 1926. Adventurer Jeff Ramsden and British agent Major James Schuyler Grim, known as "Jimgrim," depart India to seek a man supposedly lost in the wilds of forbidding Tibet. Under the Mundy penname, Gribbon turned out a large number of romantic spy-adventures during the first half of this century. **y*

   A bit short in character development as were other veterans of the Buchan school, Gribbon's tales exhibit interesting plots and fast-paced action. His locale is usually the Far East.

98.   ___. *East and West*. by Talbot Mundy, pseud. New York: Appleton-Century, 1936. A British officer on a secret mission in India is mixed up with a lovely American girl and an unscrupulous prince, heir of the Majarajah. **y*

99.   ___. *Jimgrim*. By Talbot Mundy, pseud. New York: Appleton-Century, 1931. British secret service agent James S. Grim is dispatched to India to resolve an intrigue centered high up in the Himalayas. **y*

100.   ___. *Jimgrim and Allah's Peace*. By Talbot Mundy, pseud. New York: Appleton-Century, 1936. Jimgrim is sent to the Holy Land to stop an Arab revolt against British authority. **y*

101.   ___. *Jungle Jest*. By Talbot Mundy, pseud. New York: Appleton-Century, 1932. Depicts the undercover work of English diplomat Cotswold Ommony during a Moplah uprising in Malabar. **y*

102.   ___. *King in Check*. by Talbot Mundy, pseud. New York: Appleton-Century, 1934. With the help of friends in Jerusalem, Jimgrim rescues the Arabian king Feisal from French mercenaries. **y*

103.   ___. *King—of the Khyber Rifles*. By Talbot Mundy, pseud. Indianapolis: Bobbs-Merrill, 1916. British agent Athelstan King is in India

when the Great War breaks out in Europe and soon finds himself involved with a beautiful woman who is assembling the tribes of Afghanistan near that famous pass for a revolt against British rule. 20th Century Fox released a movie version of this author's most famous yarn in 1954. *y

104.   ___. *Lion of Petra*. By Talbot Mundy, pseud. New York: Appleton-Century, 1933. Agent Grim needs the help of a band of thieves and two harem girls to make an unofficial treaty with a Bedouin chief. *y

105.   ___. *Mystery of Khufu's Tomb*. By Talbot Mundy, pseud. New York: Appleton-Century, 1935. Jimgrim assists a wealthy American girl in Egypt to solve the mystery of why a band of nasties covet her apparently worthless desert tract. *y

106.   ___. *Nine Unknown*. By Talbot Mundy, pseud. Indianapolis: Bobbs-Merrill, 1924. Jimgrim and eleven other adventurers seek nine books of black magic and become mixed up with an Indian secret society called the Nine Unknown and its spurious band of cutthroats, the Unknowns. *y

107.   ___. *Old Ugly Face*. By Talbot Mundy, pseud. New York: Appleton-Century, 1940. Jimgrim must thwart an evil group's plans to kidnap the young Dalai Lama of Tibet. *y

108.   ___. *The Thunder Dragon Gate*. By Talbot Mundy, pseud. New York: Appleton-Century, 1937. In London, British agent Tom Grayne meets a native of Tibet whose tale leads our hero into a series of amazing adventures which culminate in a monastery in the high Himalayas. *y

109.   ___. *The Woman Ayisha*. By Talbot Mundy, pseud. London: Hutchinson, 1930. Jimgrim of British Intelligence seeks an evil princess plotting skullduggery in the deserts of Arabia. *y

H

110.   Hamilton, Bruce. *Traitor's Way*. Indianapolis: Bobbs-Merrill, 1939. English fascists plot to involve Britain as an ally of Germany in a war with Russia. *

111.   Hardy, Jocelyn L. *Recoil*. Garden City, NY: Doubleday, 1936. Hauptmann Stranard of the German Abwehr is employed to discover and frustrate the plans of a rebel group in a German province annexed by the Soviets

after World War I. * One of the few English-language spy thrillers before 1940 to have a German agent as the hero.

112. Harvey, John H. *The Black Arab.* By "Operator 1384," pseud. New York: Rich, 1937. A British agent is dispatched to Palestine to counter an evil Holy Man attempting to ferment a revolution against British rule. * Other espionage tales by this student of the Buchan-Oppenheim school include:

113. ___. *The Catacombs of Death.* By "Operator 1384," pseud. London: Hutchinson, 1936. *

114. ___. *The Devil's Diplomats.* By "Operator 1384," pseud. London: Hutchinson, 1935. *

115. ___. *Jackals of the Secret Service.* By "Operator 1384," pseud. New York: Rich, 1938. *

116. ___. *Queen of the Riffs.* By "Operator 1384," pseud. London: Lane, 1937. *

117. ___. *The Scourge of the Desert.* By "Operator 1384," pseud. New York: Rich, 1936. *

118. ___. *Spies and Rebels.* By "Operator 1384," pseud. New York: Rich, 1939. *

119. ___. *The White Tuareg.* By "Operator 1384," pseud. New York: Rich, 1936. *

120. Hilton, James. *Without Armor.* New York: Morrow, 1934. How Ainsley Jergwin served as a British secret agent in pre-Revolutionary Russia. The author was best known for his book about Tibet called *Lost Horizon.* *

121. Horler, Sydney. *Miss Mystery.* Boston: Little, 1935. Diana Fordwyck, intimate of the sinister and dangerous Baron Serge Velessoffsky, becomes involved with the chief of the Monte Carlo secret police, a M. Jacquard, "Mademoiselle Mystery," who wants her to act as a double agent to trap the Soviet spy. *

Horler, who served as an intelligence officer with the Royal Air Force during World War I, went on to pen over 150 novels, which were in many ways similar to those coming from E. Phillips Oppenheim, with regard to wooden characters and high color.

122. ___. *False-Face.* New York: Doran, 1926. Introduces Baron Velessoffsky, called by agents the most dangerous man in Europe. **y*

123. ___. *The Secret Agent.* Boston: Little, 1933. "Bunny" Chipstead battles a nasty band of conspirators. ***

124. ___. *The Secret Service Man.* New York: Knopf, 1930. Martin Huish and Gerald Lissendale ape Miss Chipstead. ***

125. ___. *Tiger Standist Steps on It.* London: Hodder & Stoughton, 1940. The author's famous detective hero battles Nazis plotting against England's security. *** Others include:

126. ___. *The Curse of Doone.* London: Hodder & Stoughton, 1928. **y*

127. ___. *The Spy.* London: Hodder & Stoughton, 1931. ***

128. ___. *Terror on Tiptoe.* London: Hodder & Stoughton, 1939. ***

129. ___. *The Traitor.* Boston: Little, 1936. ***

130. Household, Geoffrey. *Rogue Male (Man Hunt).* Boston: Little, 1939. Spotted aiming his rifle at the mountain terrace of a certain unnamed European dictator (Hitler), a wealthy English big game hunter, Sir Robert Hunter, is pursued across the Continent and back to Britain, where he is denied help from agents of his own government and continues to be sought by secret police operatives from overseas. ***

The son of an English barrister, Household travelled the world in the 1920s and 1930s holding a variety of positions, including an eight-year stint as confidential secretary to the Bank of Rumania. After working in Spain for a few years in the printing and banana trades, he came to America in the early '30s where he wrote radio plays and married and divorced a New York City girl. Restless, he left the US to travel in the Middle East and South America before finally settling down in Britain.

In England, Household turned his talents to the production of fiction, but it was not until the 1938 publication of his *Rogue Male* that his mark was made. That story was one of ideas and suspense uncommon in an era of Sapper and Oppenheim. Its main character was a courageous and straightforward upper-class Englishman, whose unswerving and unswaggering pursuit of his goal was quite unlike the he-men then in vogue in most British spy thrillers. Well-plotted and well-written, *Rogue Male* would prove surprisingly fresh and readable many years later. After World War II, his output of tales was markedly increased (see Part 2).

131.   Hutchison, Graham S. *Eye for an Eye.* By Graham Seton, pseud. New York: Farrar, 1933. Agents become involved in an intrigue which eventually leads to a future war between Britain and Russia. *

J

132.   Jeffries, Graham M. *Madame Spy.* By Bruce Graeme, pseud. London: Allan, 1935. Journalist turned novelist, Jeffries introduced the detective hero "Blackshirt," a "gentleman crackshot." Usually running clear of espionage themes, he relented this time out to tell a tale about how a British female spy was employed to foil a fascist plot against England's safety.

K

133.   Kipling, Rudyard. *Kim.* Garden City, NY: Doubleday, 1901. An Irish soldier's derelict child born in Lahore, a precocious little vagabond journeys throughout India as a disciple of an old Lama and an incidental assistant to a disguised British secret service agent. Made into a 1951 MGM motion picture, this yarn treated espionage in a vein similar to Cooper's sixty years earlier as well as being an adventure and romance appreciated by many who would prepare spy thrillers early in this century. *y

134.   Kitchin, Frederick. *The Lost Naval Papers.* By Bennet Copplestone, pseud. London: Murray, 1917. Published simultaneously by the New York firm of E. P. Dutton. Captain William Dawson of Scotland Yard's CID traces the stories of various German spies infiltrating the British naval service through a series of short interconnected stories. *y

L

135.   LeQueux, William T. *At the Sign of the Sword.* London: Sully & Kleinteuk, 1915. Belgian Aimee de Neuville, who loves a young lawyer, is forced into a marriage arranged by her father with a business associate; when the war comes, Aimee suffers the atrocities of the German invasion, learns that her father's partner is a German operator and traitor, and is rescued from his

clutches by her lover, who returns from his regiment to help her get to England.
*y

William LeQueux was a father of the action school of spy thriller, who himself spent some time in secret agent work at the time of World War I. Like Erskine Childers, his early tales warn of England's peril, but they lack the literary gracefulness of the Irishman; however, tales like *At the Sign of the Sword*, filled as they were with both romance and sensationalism, made excellent propaganda. LeQueux's yarns reached a large readership, including British Conservative Party leader A. J. Balfour.

Picturing himself a patriotic gentleman, this journalist-turned-novelist was known to claim that his spy thrillers paid his expenses as a free-lance operator for the SIS. He also claimed that his life was threatened by German agents during the Great War, a melodramatic thought which gave him reason to carry a loaded pistol around with him during his travels.

Following World War I, LeQueux lectured frequently on the subject of "spys and spying," but always seemed to get a little fiction confused into his presentations along with the facts. He was also a keen fan of the new medium of radio, which he exploited in several of his yarns. Of his approximately 100 novels, something like a quarter qualify as spy thrillers and Julian Symons, quoting Richard Usborne, has said that LeQueux "mapped the guidelines for all subsequent British spy fiction." (*Mortal Consequences: A History—From the Detective Story to the Crime Novel.* [New York: Schocken, 1972], 232.) LeQueux is guilty of some of the worst writing and most padded plots in the entire history of the genre; however, his niche is secure because he redirected the romantic yarn toward the sensationalism of espionage and, along with Oppenheim and Buchan, prepared a foundation for the greater skills of Maugham and Ambler to exploit. The authors of *Special Branch* note: "Today it takes a determined will and a high tolerance for unrefined and unmitigated twaddle to get through many books by William LeQueux . . . " (5).

136.   ___. *Cipher Six.* London: Cassell, 1919. German agents are active in London's West End during Armistice negotiations in late 1918; the author claimed this yarn was based on actual events in which he participated "with the actors in the thrilling drama duly disguised." *y

137.   ___. *Crime Code.* London: Macaulay, 1928. Lionel Hipwell flees to London after an accident, is doped by persons unknown, loses his memory for two years during which time he is married, and is mixed up with titled criminals and traitors who employ a new kind of cryptography. *y

involving German agents who are attempting to obtain a shopping-list of British secrets; fascinating because a group of diagrams of items purported to be the secrets sought. *y Other spy thrillers by LeQueux include:

154.   ___. *Behind the Throne*. London: Methuen, 1905.

155.   ___. *Bolo, the Super Spy: An Amazing Exposure of the Traitor's Secret Adventures as a Spy in Britain and France Disclosed from Official Documents by Armand Mejan, ex-Inspector of the Paris Sureté Generale* [and] Edited by William LeQueux. London: Odhams, 1918. *y

156.   ___. *The Bond of Black*. New York: Dillingham, 1899. *y

157.   ___. *Double Nought; in Which Lionel Hipwell of His Majesty's Foreign Office Recounts His Exciting Adventures Following His Follies and Discloses the Truth Concerning the Most Amazing and Desperate Conspiracy, with World-Wide Ramifications*. London: Hodder & Stoughton, 1927. *y

158.   ___. *The Great Plot*. London: Hodder & Stoughton, 1907.

159.   ___. *The House of Whispers*. New York: Bretano's, 1910. *y

160.   ___. *No. 70 Berlin*. London: Hodder & Stoughton, 1916.

161.   ___. *Poison Shadows*. New York: Macaulay, 1927. [*The Chameleon*. London: Hodder & Stoughton, 1927]. *y

M

162.   McCulley, Johnston. *The Mark of Zorro*. New York: Grosset & Dunlap, 1924. El Zorro (the Fox) is the Scarlet Pimpernel of the California West in the days days of Spanish dominion. *HI* Resurrected in the 1980s by D. J. Arneson (*Zorro Rides Again*. New York: Bantam, 1986), this enduring hero has been adapted to screen and television—even spoofed (*Zorro the Gay Blade*. By Les Dean. New York: Leisure, 1981).

163.   MacIntyre, John T. *Ashton Kirk: Secret Agent*. New York: Penn, 1912. Part of a series in which Ashton Kirk examines various crime-fighting careers, e.g., detective, investigator, etc. *y

164.   McKay, Randle and R. J. Gerrard. *The "Intelligence" Game of Secret Service Cases and Problems.* New York: McBride, 1935. A collection of short stories, complete with a fold-out cipher puzzle. *y

165.   McKenna, Marthe. *Lancer Spy.* London: Jarrolds, 1937. A British World War I agent goes behind German lines to impersonate a baron imprisoned in England; the Kaiser's counter-espionage service sends a beautiful girl to trap the suspicious newcomer, but she becomes torn between duty and romance when she falls in love with her quarry. *y
          McKenna was an actual Great War British operative, who served behind the lines on the Continent. Despite this taste of realism, her novels accentuate the romance of the profession, with special attention to the role of women. McKenna's memoirs, *I Was A Spy* (London: Jarrolds, 1932), still make interesting reading.

166.   ___. *A Spy was Born.* London: Jarrolds, 1935. A German soldier, revolted by atrocities in World War I Belgium, secretly passes critical information to the Allies. *y

167.   ___. *Spying Blind.* London: Jarrolds, 1939. Writing in her introduction, McKenna suggested that: "In Book I, I have endeavored to forecast woman's role in espionage during peacetime. In Book II, by relating eight of my own active service experiences, I have tried to paint a picture of what may be expected under the searing conditions of war." *y Other spy thrillers include:

168.   ___. *Double Spy.* London: Jarrolds, 1938. *y

169.   ___. *Drums Never Beat.* London: Jarrolds, 1936. *y

170.   ___. *Hunt the Spy.* London: Jarrolds, 1939. *y

171.   ___. *My Master Spy.* London: Jarrolds, 1936. *y

172.   ___. *Set a Spy.* London: Jarrolds, 1937. *y

173.   Mackenzie, Compton. *Water on the Brain.* Garden City, NY: Doubleday, 1933. Published simultaneously by the London firm of Cassel, this spoof on the SIS is based on the author's World War I service; a henpecked returned British Army major is recruited to go undercover as an importer of tropical fruits. *Hy

Born Edward Montagu Compton, Compton MacKenzie saw a good bit of intelligence service with the British in the Great War Mediterranean-Near East theater and later wrote a number of titles, two of which, *Aegean Memories* (1940) and *Greek Memories* (1932, withdrawn and reissued in 1940), landed him in trouble with the SIS for alleged violations of the Official Secrets Act when he revealed that Mansfield Cumming was "C," head of the British Secret Service. In *Water on the Brain*, published as a novel because fiction could not be banned under the OSA, Mackenzie mixed his satire with so much realism that the American OSS in 1942 put it on the required reading list for trainees.

174.   McNeile, Herman C. *Bulldog Drummond.*   By "Sapper," pseud. Garden City, NY: Doubleday, 1920. [original title: *Bull-Dog Drummond: The Adventures of a Demobilized Officer Who Found Peace Dull*]. A "clean-limbed young Englishman," Hugh Drummond, together with his various associates, take on the infamous Carl Peterson and his gang, of whom it is learned that they are behind a giant conspiracy (involving important government officials) to overthrow the British government by means of a General Strike paid for with gold from Moscow. *

By today's standards, "crude," "unsophisticated," "right-wing," "cliché-ridden," and as Ambler suggests, even "fascist," are not adjectives too strong to employ when describing the xenophobic novels of a man possessed of possibly the most famous pseudonym in the genre's history.   The violent, ultranationalist, absurdly plotted, but exciting tales of this "sportsman and gentleman" were extremely popular with the reading public in the twenties and early thirties. Those who enjoyed Drummond did not seem concerned with the more sinister manner in which minorities, especially Jews, and foreigners were referred to and treated, the extremely violent fashion in which nasties were handled or dispatched, or the stilted manner in romance present in every tale. So popular was Drummond that movie-makers brought him to the silver screen in a dozen pictures between 1934 and 1947, some of which were better than the books upon which they were based. With the advent of Ambler realism, and the death of "Sapper" in 1937, Bulldog Drummond began an immediate decline which even the practiced Gerald Fairlie was unable to halt.

Despite these criticisms, spy thriller readers owe a certain debt to "Sapper" and Bulldog Drummond.   Certain of the more ugly features were sanitized, but many writers of the post-World War II James Bond period, including Ian Fleming and Nick Carter, can be said to employ the same violent, ultranationalist, exciting plotting to make their yarns successful.   For this reason, Bulldog Drummond deserves to be remembered—if not read.

175.   ___. *Bulldog Drummond at Bay.* By "Sapper," pseud. Garden City, NY: Doubleday, 1935. Hugh Drummond and his friends uncover a fascist plot against England which is hidden by prominent members of a group known as the Key Club. *

176. ___. *Bulldog Drummond Returns.* By "Sapper," pseud. Garden City, NY: Doubleday, 1932. [*Bulldog Drummond Returns.* By "Sapper," pseud. London: Hodder & Stoughton, 1932]. Hugh Drummond takes the law into his own hands to thwart a fiend's murderous plot. *

177. ___. *Challenge: A Bulldog Drummond Novel.* By "Sapper," pseud. Garden City, NY: Sun Dial, 1938. Drummond and Private Eye Ronald Standish thwart the plans of the "Russian financier," Menalin, to sabotage British factories and facilitate a poison gas attack on English cities. *

178. ___. *The Female of the Species.* By "Sapper," pseud. Garden City, NY: Doubleday, 1928. The late Carl Peterson's mistress snatches Drummond's bride and plays a maliciously protracted game of hide-and-seek until cornered by the hero. *

179. ___. *The Final Count.* By "Sapper," pseud. Garden City, NY: Doran, 1926. Carl Peterson seizes a scientist who has invented a lethal poison gas; when Bulldog Drummond encounters the villain, a violent death battle rages. *

180. ___. *Temple Tower.* By "Sapper," pseud. Garden City, NY: Doubleday, 1929. A pair of novelettes. In the first, Drummond investigates a closely guarded house in Romney Marsh where live an elderly recluse and a pugilist; in the second, he searches for the true identity of a "monster" called Le Bossu Masqué. * A few other Drummond titles are:

181. ___. *The Black Gang.* By "Sapper," pseud. Garden City, NY: Doran, 1922. *

182. ___. *Bulldog Drummond Doubleheader, Including Third Round and Final Count.* By "Sapper," pseud. Garden City, NY: Sun Dial, 1937. *

183. ___. *Bulldog Drummond Strikes Back.* By "Sapper," pseud. Garden City, NY: Doubleday, 1933. [*Knock-Out.* By "Sapper," pseud. London: Hodder & Stoughton, 1933]. *

184. ___. *Bulldog Drummond's Third Round.* By "Sapper," pseud. Garden City, NY: Doran, 1924. [*The Third Round.* By "Sapper," pseud. London: Hodder & Stoughton, 1924]. *

185. ___. *The Dinner Club Stories.* By "Sapper," pseud. Garden City, NY: Doran, 1923. *

186. ___. *Four Rounds of Bulldog Drummond.* By "Sapper," pseud. London: Hodder & Stoughton, 1929. *

187. Mandell-Essington, Francis. *The Lunatic at Large.* By J. Storer Clouston, pseud. New York: Appleton, 1900. [Authorized ed. New York: Brentano's, 1920]. An early spy series featuring "The Lunatic," who, besides being at large, in later novels is *"in Charge"* and *"in Love."*

188. ___. *Mr. Essington in Love.* By J. Storer Clouston, pseud. London: Bodley Head, 1927.

189. ___. *The Lunatic at Large Again.* By J. Storer Clouston, pseud. New York: Dutton, 1923.

190. ___. *The Lunatic Still at Large.* By J. Storer Clouston, pseud. New York: Dutton, 1923.

191. Marquand, John P. *Mr. Moto Is So Sorry.* Boston: Little, 1938. Our hero, an agent of Japanese Intelligence, sets up a war game to test the responses of a foreign power, but forgets to tell the leaders of his country's army, which takes what it observes so seriously that Moto is barely able to prevent a genuine conflict.
    Marquand was a major American writer during this period and afterwards, whose spy thrillers, often bordering on pure Charlie Chan-style detection, were relatively well received by the US public, especially in the period just before Pearl Harbor. Altogether, 20th Century Fox released five Moto movies in 1938-1939 in an effort to capitalize on the Oriental's popularity. Moto died as a literary character following December 7, 1941, with only one additional title (noted in Part 2) published.

192. ___. *No Hero.* Boston: Little, 1935. [*Mr. Moto Takes a Hand.* London: Hale, 1940]. A drunken American aviator in the Far East gets mixed up with an oil formula, a beautiful Russian, and Japanese operative Moto.

193. ___. *Thank You, Mr. Moto.* Boston: Little, 1936. In Peking, Moto assists a young American, whose life is endangered when a British Major is murdered by unknown forces.

194.   ___. *Think Fast, Mr. Moto.* Boston: Little, 1937. Moto helps young Wilson Hutchings clean up the Honolulu Branch of his father's Boston banking firm.

195.   Mason, Alfred E. W. *The Summons.* New York: Doran, 1920. While employed as a British agent in Spain, Harry Luttrell is able to clear his new love, Joan, of murdering his previous girlfriend. *y
    Mason was an important early exponent of the spy thriller, whose literary talent was better than either Oppenheim or LeQueux. Those reading Mason today will find both his characters and narration better than others writing in the genre early in the century. During the Great War, Mason was a very effective agent of British Naval Intelligence whose main beat was Spain and the Mediterranean. After World War I, Mason continued to operate for and have influence in the British intelligence community. Although his production of spy thrillers was limited, he remained constantly before the reading public of his day with a number of soundly developed detective novels.

196.   ___. *The Winding Stair.* New York: Doran, 1923. A British agent goes to Morocco to assist the French in putting down a rebellion fermented by the Germans. *y

197.   Mason, Francis Van Wyck. *The Cairo Garden Murders.* Garden City, NY: Doubleday, 1938. In Egypt, Captain Hugh North of G-2 Army Intelligence pursues the mysterious Mr. Armstrong, culprit in many political assassinations and the mastermind behind nefarious Mideast arms deals.
    Noted for his historical research and skillful use of background locale, Mason became one of America's most famous historical novelists. Beginning in the early thirties, he created the North character for his novels of intrigue and espionage and on into the post-World War II period advanced him in rank from Captain to Colonel. Writing these yarns often under the pseudonym of Geoffrey Coffin, Mason mixed detection, action, and intrigue with acceptable narration but sometimes rather wooden characterization.

198.   ___. *Military Intelligence-8: Captain North's Most Celebrated Intrigues.* 3 vols. in 1. New York: Stokes, 1940. Contents: *Washington Legation Murders*; *Hong Kong Airbase Murders*; and *Singapore Exile Murders.*

199.   ___. *Oriental Division G-2: Captain North's Three Famous Intrigues of the Far East.* 3 vols. in 1. New York: Reynal, 1942. Contents: *Sulu Sea Murders*; *Fort Terror Murders*; and *Shanghai Bund Murders.*

200.   ___. *Seven Seas Murders*. Garden City, NY: Doubleday, 1936. Four novellas—cases drawn from Captain North's secret files.

201.   ___. *Washington Legation Murders*. Garden City, NY: Doubleday, 1935.   Captain North must battle the continuous pilfering of top secret US military secrets by a sinister unknown party.   Other pre-World War II Hugh North tales include:

202.   ___. *The Branded Spy Murders*. Garden City, NY: Doubleday, 1932.

203.   ___. *The Bucharest Ballerina Murders*. New York: Stokes, 1940.

204.   ___. *The Budapest Parade Murders*. Garden City, NY: Doubleday, 1935.

205.   ___. *The Castle Island Case*. New York: Reynal, 1937. Revised and reissued by Doubleday in 1960 as the *Multi-Million Dollar Murders*.

206.   ___. *The Fort Terror Murders*. Garden City, NY: Doubleday, 1931.

207.   ___. *The Hong Kong Airbase Murders*.   Garden City, NY: Doubleday, 1937.

208.   ___. *The Shanghai Bund Murders*. Garden City, NY: Doubleday, 1933. Revised and reissued by Doubleday and Pocket Books in 1959 as *The China Sea Murders*.

209.   ___. *The Singapore Exile Murders*. Garden City, NY: Doubleday, 1939.

210.   ___. *The Sulu Sea Murders*. Garden City, NY: Doubleday, 1933.

211.   ___. *The Vesper Service Murders*. Garden City, NY: Doubleday, 1931.

212.   ___. *The Yellow Arrow Murders*. Garden City, NY: Doubleday, 1932.

213.   Masterman, John. *Fate Cannot Harm Me*. London: Gollancz, 1935. Besides this one, Masterman wrote one other novel, highly anticipatory of his important work to come in espionage:

214.   ___. *An Oxford Tragedy.* n.p.: n.p., 1933. [rpt. London: Dover, 1986].

215.   Maugham, W. Somerset. *Ashenden: or, The British Agent.* Garden City, NY: Doubleday, 1941. First published in Britain in 1928 and reissued by Arno Press in 1977, this volume is, in fact, a series of short interconnected tales concerning agent Ashenden's exploits from Geneva to Petrograd during the Russian revolutionary period. Scholars and others believe that the operative was modeled on the author himself, a British agent during World War I. *y

A master of the short story, Maugham penned only this one spy thriller during this period, but given its significance, it was sufficient. *Ashenden* is generally regarded as the finest example of the genre written before Ambler, and a little later, Graham Greene.

Maugham's tale represents a radical departure from the romantic, nationalist, right-wing, agent-as-hero school of Buchan, LeQueux, and Oppenheim. Ashenden in his travels reflects the realism encountered by the spy in almost any age—the boredom, the deceit, the mistakes, and the weaknesses of human nature. He was even nervous before a fellow operator "took out" a Greek spy. Ashenden wrote long reports, visited the market to receive instructions, and engaged in the patient work of counterintelligence. All of this is described in smooth, descriptive narrative made so plain as to serve as an instructor's manual—which, in fact, it did.

As noted in the introduction to Part 1, the reading public, while interested, was not quite ready for *Ashenden*, preferring its consumption of Oppenheim and "Sapper." Maugham prepared no further installments and only once, during World War II, did he write another tale with anything approaching an espionage theme. Having prepared the way for a new realism in the spy thriller, he turned his attention to other matters and left it for his disciples to carry on. In 1936, *Ashenden* was made into a movie, called *The Secret Agent*, which starred John Gielgud and was directed by Alfred Hitchcock. This British product was only mildly successful, both at home and in America.

Mundy, Talbot, pseud. *See* Gribbon, William L.

N

216.   New, Clarence H. *The Unseen Hand: Adventures of a Diplomatic Free-Lance.* Garden City, NY: Doubleday, 1918. An American free-lance agent moves around the globe in this interconnected series of tales, foiling the plans and plots of German operatives against England. *y

217. Newman, Bernard. *German Spy.* London: Gollancz, 1936. Purports to be the World War I memoirs of German spy Ludwig Grein, an ace agent in Britain. **y*

A grand-nephew of George Eliot and an ardent cyclist, Newman published a number of spy thrillers during the thirties. Researching his stories while cycling about Europe, Newman was, during the day, an official of the British Foreign Office. Following the success of his *The Spy*, Newman began to put forth a large number of titles, most involving the new realism as practiced by Maugham, Ambler, and Greene. The majority of those penned before September 1939 reflected his interest in the military prowess and possible secret weapons of Nazi Germany. During World War II, he served with the Ministry of Information and continued turning out tales, many involved with the intricacies of code and cipher. As in the previous decade, these were mixed in with a few travel books. Later during the Cold War, he would pen a number of secret agent yarns under the pseudonym of Don Betteridge.

218. ___. *The Mussolini Murder Plot.* London: Hutchinson, 1936. The League of International Amity, dissatisfied with the efforts of Il Duce, plans his assassination during the first day of the Abyssinian War; however, he is saved through the quick work of a secret agent. **y*

219. ___. *Papa Pontivy and the Maginot Murder.* New York: Holt, 1940. First published in Britain the previous year under the Gollancz title of *Maginot Line Murder*. A French operative is called in to quash a dangerous German plot against his nation's defenses. **y*

220. ___. *Secret Servant.* London: Gollancz, 1935. A British agent goes behind the scenes to ensure the success of the 1919 Versailles Conference. **y*

221. ___. *Spy.* New York: Appleton-Century, 1935. The authors of *A Connoisseur's Guide* call this one a "marvelous leg-pull" in spy fiction because it was taken as an actual account in its time, and it began Newman's espionage fiction career with gusto (196). The collapse of German commander Ludendorff in September 1918 is attributed to an enemy agent's infiltration of the German General Staff, as told to the "author" by this former British spy who discreetly and insidiously burrowed into the General's psyche and brought about his collapse. **y* Other pre-World War II tales include:

222. ___. *Armoured Doves, a Peace Book.* London: Jarrolds, 1931.

223. ___. *Cast Iron Alibi.* By Don Betteridge, pseud. London: Jenkins, 1939.

224.   ___. *The Cavalry Goes Through*. New York: Holt, 1930. [*The Cavalry Went Through*. London: Gollancz, 1930].

225.   ___. *Death of a Harlot*. London: Laurie, 1934.

226.   ___. *Death to the Spy*. London: Gollancz, 1939.

227.   ___. *Death under Gibraltar*. London: Gollancz, 1938.

228.   ___. *Lady Doctor-Woman Spy*. London: Gollancz, 1937. *y

229.   ___. *The Scotland Yard Alibi*. By Don Betteridge, pseud. London: Jenkins, 1938.

230.   ___. *The Siegfried Spy*. London: Gollancz, 1940.

O

"Operator 1384," pseud. *See* Harvey, John H.

231.   Oppenheim, E. Phillips. *Advice Limited*. Boston: Little, 1936. Clara, Baroness Linz, head of a secret service agency, solves eleven problems presented by her clients and superiors. *y
    Beginning his literary career in middle age, Oppenheim was a contemporary of LeQueux and Buchan who wrote in a very similar vein. Always fascinated by the world of secret diplomacy and espionage, Oppenheim was an early supporter of those who looked to England's preparedness in the days before World War I. It was Oppenheim who did the most to create early secret agent stereotypes such as the all-knowing spymaster, the muscle-bound, romantic, derring-do agent-hero, and the female seductress. His tales were weak in plotting and characterization, but like Buchan and others, strong in improbable action and questionable deduction which allowed agents to make the kind of simple mistakes which would have gotten Ashenden killed. Most of his spy thrillers took place in the world's great cities, which he knew well, and resorts which he favored. Sentiments expressed were always upper-class, right-wing, and nationalist in tone and flavor, although considerably more refined than "Sapper." In all, he penned 115 novels; or, at least, dictated them to his secretaries, who added the "polish." An exponent of the high life whose beginnings were those of the leather trade, Oppenheim was immensely popular on both sides of the Atlantic and often had his works serialized in such magazines as *The Saturday Evening Post*. The Germans were often the villains

in his pieces and in real-life, proved equally inconsiderate. This patriarch of spy thrillers was forced out of his Riviera home in 1940 when the Nazi Wehrmacht invaded and later from his home on Guernsey.

232.   ___. *The Box with Broken Seals*. Boston: Little, 1919. [*The Strange Case of Mr. Jocelyn Thews*. London: Hodder & Stoughton, 1919]. An English detective pursues a German agent suspected of conveying documents relative to German propaganda activities in the US during World War I. *y

233.   ___. *The Devil's Paw*. Boston: Little, 1920. An ex-soldier learns that his girlfriend is a ringleader in negotiations between German and British labor leaders designed to end the Great War and saves her from an SIS plot to capture her with incriminating papers. *y

234.   ___. *Envoy Extraordinary*. Boston: Little, 1937. A young English noble with a playboy cover works as Britain's SIS instrument in preventing another world conflict. *y

235.   ___. *Exit a Dictator*. Boston: Little, 1939. A Russian of noble birth, living in London, attempts to organize the overthrow of the Soviet government. *y

236.   ___. *Gabriel Samara, Peacemaker*. Boston: Little, 1925. Agent Catherine Borans convinces Russian strongman Gabriel, who has put down Bolshevism, that he is wrong in attempting to restore the nobility. *y

237.   ___. *The Great Impersonation*. Boston: Little, 1920. Reprinted by Dover Books in 1978. An English-educated German in East Africa meets an old friend and double, Sir Everard Dominez; when the former receives orders to proceed to Britain on a secret mission before World War I, he makes away with the Englishman and travels under his identity. This, the most famous Oppenheim tale, was made into a movie three times, by Paramount in 1921, Universal in 1935, and by the same firm, with a World War II bent in 1942. *y

238.   ___. *The Great Secret*. Boston: Little, 1907. Lord Leslie Wendover, alias Leslie Grant, a renowned English cricket player, and an American girl thwart a German conspiracy against Britain. *y

239.   ___. *The Illustrious Prince*. Boston: Little, 1910. An American girl and a Japanese prince unravel the plot behind the murder of a secret messenger enroute to England from the United States. *y

240.   ___. *The Kingdom of the Blind.* Boston: Little, 1916. British agent Hugh Thomson faces social ridicule and loss of his fiancée when he seeks to prove that a popular army officer and nephew of an important financier is, in fact, a German spy. **y*

241.   ___. *The Last Train Out.* Boston: Little, 1940. Through clever ruses, a Viennese philanthropist manages to outwit the Gestapo and escape Austria with his famous art collection. **y*

242.   ___. *The Light Beyond.* Boston: Little, 1928. American attaché Mark van Stratton of the London embassy seeks to upset the menace of a financier's pending deal with Germany. **y*

243.   ___. *The Lost Ambassador; or, The Search for the Missing Delora.* Boston: Little, 1910. A worthless brother snatches an Englishman's secret papers and the niece of a wealthy Brazilian in an effort to obtain two battleships under contract in a British shipyard. **y*

244.   ___. *The Maker of History.* Boston: Little, 1906. An English youth, who has witnessed an anti-English treaty-signing between the Czar and the Kaiser, is hidden away in Paris by British agents, who debrief him and hide him from agents of the Russian and German intelligence services. **y*

245.   ___. *Matorni's Vineyard.* Boston: Little, 1928. An SIS agent outwaits plans of an Italian Mussolini-type dictator intriguing with Germany for a war on France. **y*

246.   ___. *The Mischiefmaker.* Boston: Little, 1913. Having revealed a state secret to a black-velveted woman during an indiscreet moment, a young British under-secretary for foreign affairs is forced to resign and go into hiding until SIS agents can recover his paramour. **y*

247.   ___. *Mr. Billingham, the Marquis, and Madelon.* Boston: Little, 1929. Ten short tales concerning the Monte Carlo intrigues and crooked course of a New Yorker, who has teamed up with the Marquis de Felan and his lovely niece. **y*

248.   ___. *Mr. Grex of Monte Carlo.* Boston: Little, 1914. A British Member of Parliament and American Richard Lane work together to thwart the plans of assembled French, German, and Russian representatives, who are considering how best to remake the map of Europe. **y*

249. ___. *The Mysterious Mr. Sabin.* Boston: Little, 1905. An unscrupulous French royalist, Mr. Sabin aids in a German conspiracy against Britain by attempting to steal the secret plans of England's coastal defenses from a British admiral equally determined to safeguard them. *y

250. ___. *The Ostrekoff Jewels.* Boston: Little, 1932. An American outwits the Soviet secret police to smuggle out of Russia the jewels of a Russian princess who wants them delivered to her daughter in London. *y

251. ___. *The Pawns Count.* Boston: Little, 1918. An SIS agent and two Americans seek the formula of a terrible new German explosive. *y

252. ___. *The Profiteers.* Boston: Little, 1921. When a London syndicate corners the world's wheat supply, an American kidnaps three of the group's directors and holds them hostage in an effort to lower prices. *y

253. ___. *Secret Service Omnibus, Number One.* Boston: Little, 1946. Contents: *Mysterious Mr. Sabin*; *A Maker of History*; and *The Illustrious Prince.* *y

254. ___. *The Seven Conundrums.* Boston: Little, 1923. A trio of down-and-out entertainers are rescued by a mysterious philanthropist who turns them into secret agents and employs them in seven different cases, here related. *y

255. ___. *Spies and Intrigues: The Oppenheim Secret Service Omnibus.* Boston: Little, 1936. Contents: *Wrath to Come*; *The Great Impersonation*; *Gabriel Samara, Peacemaker*; and *Mr. Billingham, the Marquis, and Madelon.* *y

256. ___. *The Spymaster.* Boston: Little, 1938. A villain named Florestan and his enigmatic wife set up an espionage network in London to funnel secrets to Britain's enemies. *y

257. ___. *The Vanished Messenger.* Boston: Little, 1914. A crippled British master criminal, who has intercepted secret wireless messages, will blackmail England and America into war unless he can be stopped by a young US representative of The Hague. *y

258. ___. *The Wrath to Come.* Boston: Little, 1924. US agent Grant Slattery evades a charming woman spy while foiling futurish plots by Germany, Japan, and Russia to invade America. *y

259.   ___. *The Yellow Crayon.* London: Ward, 1903. Mr. Sabin returns in this adventure; he is playing golf in New England when a nefarious international secret society kidnaps his wife.

260.   ___. *The Zeppelin's Passenger.* Boston: Little, 1918. [*Mr. Lessingham Goes Home.* London: Hodder & Stoughton, 1919]. Amidst Zeppelin raids, one airship drops a passenger on England's North Sea coast; thus did the hatless Hamar Lessingham come to enter the home of Sir Henry Cranston. *y Other Oppenheim yarns include:

261.   ___. *Ambrose Lavendale, Diplomat.* London: Hodder & Stoughton, 1920. *y

262.   ___. *An Amiable Charlatan.* Boston: Little, 1916. *y

263.   ___. *Anna the Adventuress.* Boston: Little, 1904. *y

264.   ___. *The Avenger.* Boston: Little, 1908. *y

265.   ___. *The Betrayal.* New York: Dodd, 1904. *y

266.   ___. *The Black Box.* New York: Grosset & Dunlap, 1915. *y

267.   ___. *The Colossus of Arcadia.* Boston: Little, 1938. *y

268.   ___. *The Double Life of Mr. Alfred Burton.* Boston: Little, 1913. *y

269.   ___. *The Double Traitor.* Boston: Little, 1915. *y

270.   ___. *Expiation.* London: Maxwell, 1887.

271.   ___. *For The Queen.* Boston: Little, 1913. *y

272.   ___. *The Great Prince Shan.* Boston: Little, 1922. *y

273.   ___. *Havoc.* Boston: Little, 1911. *y

274.   ___. *The Long Arm of Mannister.* Boston: Little, 1908. *y

275.   ___. *A Lost Leader.* Boston: Little, 1907. *y

276.   ___. *The Magnificent Hoax*. Boston: Little, 1936. *y

277.   ___. *The Malefactor*. Boston: Little, 1906. *y

278.   ___. *Miss Brown of the X.Y.O.* Boston: Little, 1927. *y

279.   ___. *Mr. Marx's Secret*. Boston: Little, 1916. *y

280.   ___. *The Spy Paramount*. Boston: Little, 1935. *y

281.   ___. *The Traitors*. New York: Dodd, 1903. *y

282.   ___. *The World's Great Snare*. Boston: Little, 1913. *y

283.   Orczy, Emmuska Baroness. *The Scarlet Pimpernel*. New York: Putnam's, 1905. Sir Percy Blakeney is just another idle, bored aristocrat, a Sir Fopling Flutter by day; by night, rapier in hand, he is the brave enemy of the Reign of Terror, rescuing aristocratic victims from the guillotine in cavalier defiance of the revolutionary *canaille*. *yHI The film (GB, 1934) inspired an equally famous sequel and was resurrected for a made-for-TV movie in 1982.

284.   ___. *Pimpernel and Rosemary*. New York: Doran, 1925. The great-great-grandson of the Scarlet Pimpernel becomes involved in a Hungarian-Rumanian conflict and daringly rescues his rash young cousins from pending death. *yHI

285.   ___. *A Spy of Napoleon*. New York: Doubleday, 1934. Sentenced to death for treason by a court of Napoleon III, young Gerard is snatched by Secret Service chief Papa Toulon, who wants him to marry one of his most successful operatives. *y More Pimpernels:

286.   ___. *Eldorado: A Story of the Scarlet Pimpernel*. London: Hodder & Stoughton, 1913. *HI*

287.   ___. *The Elusive Pimpernel*. New York: Dodd, 1908. *HI*

288.   ___. *The First Sir Percy: An Adventure of the Laughing Cavalier*. London: Hodder & Stoughton, 1920. *HI*

289.   ___. *I Will Repay*. Philadelphia: Lippincott, 1906. *HI*

290.   ___. *Lord Tony's Wife: An Adventure of the Scarlet Pimpernel.*
London: Hodder & Stoughton, 1917. *HI*

291.   ___. *Mam'zelle Guillotine: An Adventure of the Scarlet Pimpernel.*
London: Hodder & Stoughton, 1940. *HI*

292.   ___. *Sir Percy Hits Back: An Adventure of the Scarlet Pimpernel.*
London: Hodder & Stoughton, 1927. *HI*

293.   ___. *The Triumph of the Scarlet Pimpernel.* London: Hodder &
Stoughton, 1922. *HI*

294.   ___. *The Way of the Scarlet Pimpernel.* London: Hodder &
Stoughton, 1934. *HI*

P

295.   Palmer, John Leslie and Hiliary Aiden St. George Saunders. *The Black
Arrows.* By Francis Beeding, pseud. New York: Harper, 1938. SIS agent
John Cowper is sent to Venice to study British fleet defenses and is mixed up
with a fascist plot of the evil Jiacomo Beruti's Society of the Black Arrows,
which is convinced that Mussolini's expansion plans are too slow, and plans to
take action by sinking a battleship of the British Mediterranean Fleet with a
privately owned submarine.
     How does the Beeding tandem differ from Buchan-Oppenheim style?
The Special Branch opines:

> If Beeding differs from other writers of the twenties in the cultural
> level of his [sic] books, he also differs in his doctrinal base. Although
> German villains spill over into the twenties . . . most espionage writers in
> Britain lost some of their focus. Most spy writers in the twenties and early
> thirties drifted among relatively vague concepts of decency, sanity, and
> individuality. Buchan resuscitated the Master Crook, as did Sapper and
> Horler, while Oppenheim moved to the international peace-maker. . . . Now
> Beeding, too, uses Master Criminals and spy detectives, but he has a surer
> doctrinal base. Both Palmer and Saunders worked for the Permanent
> Secretariat of the League of Nations from 1920 until the Second World War.
> Most of their early novels have concrete connections with Geneva and the
> League. (85-86)

296.   ___. *Five Flamboys.* By Francis Beeding, pseud. Boston: Little,
1929. In the Geneva of the League of Nations, Colonel Granby of the SIS sets

out to find the murderers of a British diplomat, who knew their identity and schemes and was about to give them away. *y

297.   ___. *The Four Armourers.* By Francis Beeding, pseud. Boston: Little, 1930. Granby attempts to help American plutocrat Hazelnig obtain a secret formula for a gas which could serve as a deterrent to war. *y

298.   ___. *Hell Let Loose.* By Francis Beeding, pseud. New York: Harper, 1937. The colonel becomes involved with spy-counterspy games in Spain during the early months of the civil war. *y

299.   ___. *The Hidden Kingdom.* By Francis Beeding, pseud. Boston: Little, 1927. The hero of *The Seven Sleepers* and his two French secret service friends set out to capture German superfiend Prof. Kreutzemark, who is out to establish the reign of an anti-Christ known as "the Lord of Fear." *y

300.   ___. *The League of Discontent.* By Francis Beeding, pseud. Boston: Little, 1930. In southern France, Colonel Granby seeks to thwart a plot to wreck the peace of Central Europe; to do so, he must uncover a nefarious secret at a forbidding chateau. *y

301.   ___. *The Nine Waxed Faces.* By Francis Beeding, pseud. New York: Harper, 1936. Again attempting to halt a war in Central Europe, Granby is mixed up with secret diplomacy and fascist double-dealing. *y

302.   ___. *The One Sane Man.* By Francis Beeding, pseud. Boston: Little, 1934. Granby is sent to halt the work of a madman who is employing secret powers to enforce on the world what he considers to be moral laws of universal redemption. *y

303.   ___. *Pretty Sinister.* By Francis Beeding, pseud. Boston: Little, 1929. Beginning in the middle and working both ways, the "author" details agent Granby's hunt for two groups of nasties who are seeking the same important prize. A difficult tale to follow. *y

304.   ___. *The Seven Sleepers.* By Francis Beeding, pseud. Boston: Little, 1925. Led by a famous field marshal, a new German conspiracy is unmasked by an English hardware salesman, who must then outwit the agents of the group calling itself "the Seven Sleepers" to alert his nation's leaders to their peril. *y

305.   ___. *The Six Proud Walkers.* By Francis Beeding, pseud. Boston: Little, 1928. Assisted by a veteran secret agent in the employ of the League of

Nations, a young Englishman seeks to thwart a horrific plot to embroil Europe in a new war. *y

306. ___. *Take It Crooked.* By Francis Beeding, pseud. Boston: Little, 1932. In order to rescue his new wife from her abductors, Colonel Granby must rout a group conspiring against England's security. *y

307. ___. *The Ten Holy Terrors.* By Francis Beeding, pseud. New York: Harper, 1939. Granby becomes involved with East European refugees, missing secrets, and Nazi spies. *y Three other pre-war Granby tales are:

308. ___. *The Eight Crooked Trenches.* By Francis Beeding, pseud. New York: Harper, 1936. [*Coffin for One.* New York: Avon, 1943.] *y

309. ___. *The Three Fishers.* By Francis Beeding, pseud. Boston: Little, 1931.

310. ___. *The Two Undertakers.* By Francis Beeding, pseud. Boston: Little, 1933. *y

311. Poe, Edgar Allan. *The Purloined Letter.* Philadelphia: Carey & Hart, 1844. The claim of some for Poe's being the father of the spy thriller rests on this tale in which French detective C. Auguste Dupin confronts a Minister of State, so high that he is untouchable by secret police, with evidence that it was he who stole a secret document from the royal apartments and instead of secreting it away, in fact, placed it in an obvious place that searchers missed when checking his flat. *y
    Another facet of Poe's contribution to the genre was his introduction in *The Gold Bug* (1843) of the cipher and cryptography, a major ingredient in many modern cloak-and-dagger tales. Both *The Purloined Letter* and *The Gold Bug* can be found in *The Portable Poe*, (Ed. Philip V. D. Stern. New York: Penguin, 1977).

312. Post, Melville D. *Walker of the Secret Service.* New York: Appleton-Century, 1924. An American agent foils a German plot against the US at the time of World War I. *y
    Post was a major contributor of short detective tales to American publishers and magazines and one of the first US writers to dabble in spy thrillers. His tales were not unlike those of Oppenheim in theme, action, and characterization.

313. Powell, Edward A. *Red Drums*. New York: Washburn, 1935. A young Washington diplomat named Remington Post is sent on an espionage mission to Latin America to uncover the reasons behind an outbreak of Communism. *

R

314. Reeve, Arthur B. *The Panama Plot*. New York: Harper, 1918. Working for Intelligence, detective Craig Kennedy goes to Panama to look in on a German plot against the Canal Zone. *y

315. ___. *The War Terror*. New York: Hearst's, 1915. Craig Kennedy runs down a band of anarchists in New York, who have killed an explosives inventor and as part of their plot to kill all militarists, have threatened the life of a German baron. *y

Rohmer, Sax, pseud. *See* Ward, Arthur Sarsfield

S

316. Sabatini, Rafael. *Scaramouche*. Boston: Houghton, 1921. During the First World War, Sabatini worked for British Intelligence; he wrote mostly costume romances, and this highly popular historical spy tale of Scaramouche, a nobleman who posed as a clown, during the time of the French Revolution—much in the style and manner of Baroness Orczy. *HI*

"Sapper," pseud. *See* McNeile, Herman C.

317. Sayer, Walter W. *The Adventures of the Albanian Avenger*. London: Amalgamated, 1925. Associated with the SIS, British detective Sexton Blake pursues an East European terrorist loose in London. *y
     In the annals of spy thrillers and detective stories, there have been a few of what we might call "house heroes," i.e., characters written about in a long series of tales by different authors. The most famous American character of this nature is Nick Carter; in Britain, it was Sexton Blake. Other pre-World War II Blake-as-agent tales by this writer include:

318. ___. *The Case of the King's Spy*. London: Amalgamated, 1920. *y

319.   ___.   *The Mystery of the Lost Battleship.*   London: Amalgamated, 1924. **y*

320.   ___.   *The Outlaws of Yugo-Slavia.*   London: Amalgamated, 1923. **y*

321.   ___.   *The Phantom of the Pacific.*   London: Amalgamated, 1922. **y*

322.   ___.   *The Secret of the Frozen North.*   London: Amalgamated, 1921. **y*

323.   Scott, John R.   *Cab of the Sleeping Horse.*   New York: Putnam's, 1916. Agents of British, French, German, and US intelligence seek to recover a cipher letter which, unbeknownst to them, was left in a deserted Washington, DC cab guarded only by a sleeping horse. **y*

324.   Scott, Reginald T. M.   *Ann's Crime—Still Another Adventure of "Secret Service Smith."*   New York: Dutton, 1926. Aurelius Smith and his associates seek to end a girl's depression by looking into its origins and find themselves mixed up in a World War I intrigue involving a mysterious English captain. **y*

325.   ___.   *"Secret Service Smith"—the Wanderings of an American Detective.*   New York: Dutton, 1923. While traveling the Subcontinent after World War I, an American detective finds himself working for British Intelligence against a nefarious plot by local terrorists who desire a separate nation. **y* One other spy thriller by this author is:

326.   ___.   *The Black Magician—Another Adventure of "Secret Service Smith."*   New York: Dutton, 1925. **y*

Seton, Graham, pseud.   *See* Hutchinson, Graham S.

327.   Stringer, Arthur J. A.   *Door of Dread: A Secret Service Romance.* Indianapolis: Bobbs-Merrill, 1916. Two men and a woman acting as agents of the Secret Service pursue German spies across the US to recover vital defense secrets. **y*

T

"Taffrail," pseud.   *See* Dorling, Henry T.

328.   Teilhet, Darwin L. *The Talking Sparrow Murders*. New York: International Polygonics, 1985. First published in 1934, Teilhet's novel is prophetically reviewed by classical scholar and mystery novelist Dorothy L. Sayers in the London *Sunday Times* of 10 June 1934: "There are sinister hints of intrigue, lurid flashes of light on the persecution of the Jews, grim little scenes of blood and squalor mingled with the glitter of nightclub life, and over it all hangs the atmosphere of suspicion and insecurity which is bound to accompany national upheavals" (qtd. on dust jacket; *see* Part 2 for a listing of his major work). Teilhet's murder mystery is also a spy story as the narrator, William Tatson, and the local police superintendent investigate high-ranking Nazis implicated in a series of murders in Heidelberg, a city in the grip of the New Order.

329.   Thurston, Temple. *Portrait of a Spy*. Garden City, NY: Doubleday, 1929. A biographical novel concerning the notorious dancer and spy Mata Hari, told by an English lover sent to draw her official portrait as she awaited her execution. **y*

330.   Tyson, John A. *Scarlet Tanager*. New York and London: Macmillan, 1922. In 1930, conspirators assemble to plot the overthrow of the US government, but are thwarted by daring Secret Service agents. **y*

U

331.   Upward, Allen. *The International Spy*. New York: Dillingham, 1905. Monsieur H. V. is posted to England by the Czar with a secret message designed to prevent war with Japan; too late, the hero travels on to Japan where he is adopted into the royal family but finding he cannot prevent conflict, elects to escape to Russia on a stolen German torpedo boat. **y* One other fantastic adventure by this hero is:

332.   ___. *On Her Majesty's Service*. London: Primrose, 1904. **y*

V

Valentine, Douglas, pseud. *See* Williams, Valentine

333.   Vance, Louis J. *Alias the Lone Wolf*. Garden City, NY: Doubleday, 1921. A gentleman jewel thief becomes involved with secret agents while smuggling diamonds, combatting competitors, and assisting a beautiful girl. **y*

W

334.   Wallace, Edgar. *The Adventures of Major Haynes (of the Counter Espionage Bureau), with Some Additional Stories.* New York: Ward, 1919. A series of pre-World War I stories about a British operative working against the Germans; all of these tales first appeared in *Thomson's Weekly News.* **y*
          Wallace was a journalist who penned most of his spy thrillers as articles for magazines and tabloids such as *Thomson's Weekly News* and *Strand* Magazine. To counter his British agent, he also created the German spy Hermann Gallwitz and for those who enjoyed mixing their espionage with sea stories, he gave us John Frazer and the submarine Z-1 in the series "Secret Service Submarine." His greatest contribution to the genre was the story "Code No. 2," which appeared in the April 1916 edition of *Strand* Magazine and which has been reprinted in various anthologies since then. In it, he anticipated a number of ingredients of later spy thrillers such as hidden cameras, infra-red photography, and computers. Wallace gave up spy thrillers just after the Great War.

335.   ___. *The Four Just Men.* London: Tallis, 1905. The author's first novel was reprinted by the London firm of Pan Books, in 1971. To save a foreign patriot from extradition, four Spanish secret service agents in Britain threaten the life of the British Foreign Secretary unless the provisions of the government's extradition law are quickly set aside. **y* Giving no details of the story's conclusion, Wallace offered a £500 prize to readers who could send in the correct solution. When several did, the claims, mounted on top of his own expenses in publishing and promoting the title, caused this journalist grievous financial loss.

336.   ___. *The Fourth Plague.* Garden City, NY: Doubleday, 1930. Mixing espionage into what would become by the 1970s a standard terrorist tale, Wallace details the workings of the Red Hand, an Italian terrorist organization which has demanded £10 million from the British government or else London will be victimized by the germs of a new Great Plague. **y*

337.   Walsh, J. M. [James Morgan]. *Black Dragon.* London: Collins, 1938. Oliver ("OK") Keene is the spy-hero of this series that ran from 1937 to the end of WW II (*see* Part 2 for more adventures of "OK" Keene).

338.   ___. *Bullets for Breakfast.* London: Collins, 1939.

339.   ___. *Dial 999.* London: Collins, 1938.

340. ___. *Island of Spies*. London: Collins, 1937.

341. ___. *King's Enemies*. London: Collins, 1939. Walsh also wrote eighteen novels about a spy named Timothy Terrel—under the pseudonym Stephen Maddock—and these also bridge the two sections of this book with a sampling of post-1940 listed after the Keene novels of the same period. Here are a few of the Terrel spy adventures:

342. ___. *Conspirators in Capri*. By Stephen Maddock, pseud. London: Collins, 1936.

343. ___. *The Forbidden Frontiers*. By Stephen Maddock, pseud. London: Collins, 1936.

344. ___. *Lamp-Post 592*. By Stephen Maddock, pseud. London: Collins, 1938.

345. ___. *Spies along the Severn*. By Stephen Maddock, pseud. London: Collins, 1939.

346. Ward, Arthur Sarsfield. *The Day the World Ended*. By Sax Rohmer, pseud. Garden City, NY: Doubleday, 1930. A French Sureté agent and two companions discover an Oriental plot for world domination which leads them into a desperate assault on the strangely guarded castle of Mme. Yburg at Felsenweir. *y

A free-lance journalist with an immense interest in Egypt and the Far East, Ward came into the genre at a time when the "Yellow Peril" of China had superseded the nefarious Germans and the villainy of Russia was confined to Bolshevik bomb-throwers. In creating the arch-nasty Fu Manchu, Ward helped to exploit Caucasian fears of easterners in a racist manner which can be said to have existed well into the Cold War period.

Ward's tales of the evil doctor were as improbable, crude, and violent in their way as were "Sapper's" accounts of Bulldog Drummond. For years, the evil plotter, who engaged in scheming the fall of the west with his spies and infiltrators, was pursued across the pages of ill-constructed stories by the daring English amateur detective Nayland Smith, who was also a Burmese Commissioner, a controller of the CID of Scotland Yard, and a spymaster of the SIS!

As our listing reveals, Ward also wrote a few other improbable novels of espionage and derring-do, which read very much like LeQueux. But it was the evil Dr. Fu Manchu which made the penname Sax Rohmer famous; indeed, no more sinister Chinaman existed until Wo Fat appeared on the scene to harass Steve McGarrett in the TV-series "Hawaii Five-O."

347.   ___. *The Emperor of America.* By Sax Rohmer, pseud. Garden City, NY: Doubleday, 1929. Commander Drade Roscoe battles a masked madman, who controls a complex criminal organization by means of a zone map hidden deep within his underground Manhattan headquarters. *y

348.   ___. *Fire Tongue.* By Sax Rohmer, pseud. Garden City, NY: Doubleday, 1922. A detective and a millionaire team up to expose the evil international conspiracy of a secret death-dealing Hindu society led by the mystic called Fire Tongue. *y

349.   ___. *The Hand of Fu Manchu.* By Sax Rohmer, pseud. New York: McBride, 1917. In London, Dr. Petrie and Nayland Smith battle the mysterious Si-Fan organization of the evil Chinese doctor which is employing strange weapons in a plot to slaughter the White race. *y

350.   ___. *The Insidious Dr. Fu Manchu.* By Sax Rohmer, pseud. New York: McBride, 1913. Nayland Smith pursues the archvillain to Britain and through a series of outrageous and improbable occurrences from which the Chinaman escapes. *y

351.   ___. *Moon of Madness.* By Sax Rohmer, pseud. Garden City, NY: Doubleday, 1927. An Irish secret service agent and an American girl track an international spy across Europe and into a death-fight in Madeira. *y

352.   ___. *The Return of Fu Manchu.* By Sax Rohmer, pseud. New York: McBride, 1916. The wily Chinaman returns to England with a new plan to subjugate the White race and is immediately engaged by Nayland Smith. *y Other examples of this writer's stories include:

353.   ___. *The Drums of Fu Manchu.* By Sax Rohmer, pseud. Garden City, NY: Doubleday, 1939. *y

354.   ___. *Fu Manchu's Bride.* By Sax Rohmer, pseud. Garden City, NY: Doubleday, 1933. Reprinted by Pyramid Books in 1962 and issued under the title, *The Bride of Fu Manchu.* *y

355.   ___. *The Golden Scorpion.* By Sax Rohmer, pseud. New York: Burt, 1920. *y

356.   ___. *The Mask of Fu Manchu.* By Sax Rohmer, pseud. Garden City, NY: Doubleday, 1932. *y

357.   ___. *President Fu Manchu.* By Sax Rohmer, pseud. Garden City, NY: Doubleday, 1936. *y

358.   ___. *Tales of Chinatown.* By Sax Rohmer, pseud. Garden City, NY: Doubleday, 1922. *y

359.   ___. *The Trail of Fu Manchu.* By Sax Rohmer, pseud. Garden City, NY: Doubleday, 1934. *y

360.   Wheatley, Dennis. *The Forbidden Territory.* New York: Dutton, 1933. Wheatley's first novel in a prolific writing career that lasted until his death in 1977 began with espionage, and it concerns three men in Soviet Russia in the dangerous, heady days of Communism's infancy: an American, a Jewish financier, and a French aristocrat, the Duc de Richelieu; the book was later filmed. (See Part 2 for a fuller listing of Wheatley's post-war production.) Two more:

361.   ___. *Black August.* New York: Dutton, 1934.

362.   ___. *Contraband.* London: Hutchinson, 1936.

363.   White, Ethel L. *The Wheel Spins.* New York: Harper, 1936. Returning to England aboard a train from the Balkans, a debutante befriends an elderly governess who disappears; seeking the old lady with the help of an itinerant musician, the girl learns that her new friend is a spy when the trio is sidetracked onto a spur line where enemy agents plan to liquidate them. Reprinted in 1966 by Paperback Library under the title *The Lady Vanishes.* *y

364.   White, Stewart E. *The Leopard Woman.* Garden City, NY: Doubleday, 1916. Leading a strange African tribe, a Hungarian countess sides with the Germans in World War I and seeks to thwart the designs of a British agent who is attempting to win the support of native chiefs. *y

365.   Williams, Valentine. *Clubfoot the Avenger, Being Some Further Adventures of Desmond Okewood of the British Secret Service.* By Douglas Valentine, pseud. New York: Houghton, 1924. Major Desmond Okewood must seal off the escape routes which allow the notorious-if-crippled German masterspy Adolf Grundt to constantly elude capture during his campaign of revenge against the SIS.

Like so many other spy thriller writers of this period, Williams was originally a journalist. During World War I, he was a decorated soldier and later represented the *London Daily Mail* so skillfully during the Versailles Conference that he was made that paper's foreign editor.

Although he wrote a few other spy thrillers and continued his craft through World War II, it was the sinister Clubfoot which won Williams a niche in the history of the genre. Adolf Grundt was perhaps the most well-rounded villain of the period, an infinitely more plausible character than either Carl Peterson or Fu Manchu. Williams' tales were at least quasi-realistic with regard to plot, locale, characterizations, and action.

366.   ___. *The Crouching Beast: A Clubfoot Story.* By Douglas Valentine, pseud. New York: Houghton, 1928. Grundt unsuccessfully attempts to prevent Olivia Dunbar from completing her work for British intelligence in a 1914 German town.

367.   ___. *The Fox Prowls.* By Douglas Valentine, pseud. New York: Houghton, 1939. SIS agent Don Boulton is dispatched to rescue an American tycoon and his beautiful daughter, who are being held hostage in a Bessarabian castle by a pack of scoundrels led by Alexis de Bahl, known throughout his native Rumania as "The Fox." *y

368.   ___. *The Knife behind the Curtain: Tales of Crime and the Secret Service.* By Douglas Valentine, pseud. New York: Houghton, 1930. Thirteen short stories, only a few of which deal with intelligence matters and none with Clubfoot. *y

369.   ___. *The Man with the Clubfoot.* By Douglas Valentine, pseud. New York: McBride, 1918. Ace Prussian operative Dr. Adolf Grundt does not allow his handicap to interfere with his nefarious scheme to do in England and the British Secret Service during World War I. This first Clubfoot tale was an instant success and led to the various sequels. *y

370.   ___. *The Mystery of the Gold Box.* By Douglas Valentine, pseud. Boston: Houghton, 1932. [*The Gold Comfit box.* London: Hodder & Stoughton, 1932]. When an American embassy official disappears with secret documents, his sister asks the aid of four adventurers in saving him from—what turns out to be—the clutches of the evil Clubfoot. *y

371.   ___. *The Secret Hand: Some Further Adventures of Desmond Okewood of the British Secret Service.* By Douglas Valentine, pseud. London: Jenkins, 1919. Published simultaneously by the New York firm of McBride

under the title *Okewood of the Secret Service*. A young British agent assumes Grundt's identity to learn about and thwart the plans of his London-based spy network. Sequel to the previous title. **y*

372. ___. *The Spider's Touch*. Boston: Houghton, 1936. In this Clubfoot adventure, young James Fane, diplomatic secretary, leaves London on a confidential mission to receive a packet of documents describing fortifications of a group of Pacific islands—and doesn't return. His twin sister engages some adventurers to rescue him.

373. ___. *The Three of Clubs*. By Douglas Valentine, pseud. New York: Houghton, 1924. During the intrigue-filled months just after World War I, a secret society called "The Three of Clubs" conspires to have the archduchess proclaimed Queen of Hungary. **y* Other titles by the author include:

374. ___. *The Red Mass*. Boston: Houghton, 1925.

375. ___. *Mr. Ramosi*. Boston: Houghton, 1926.

Y

376. Yin, Leslie C. B. *Avenging Saint*. by Leslie Charteris, pseud. Garden City, NY: Doubleday, 1931. Simon Templar, a playboy, lone-wolf detective known as "The Saint," gets mixed up with an archvillain who is out to start another World War. **y*

Starting out as a well-educated journeyman writer, Yin published his first "Saint" story in 1930; so successful was it, that Simon Templar has been a noteworthy standard for over half a century. Only occasionally has Yin strayed from the detective yarn, but especially during the World War II years, the unorthodox methods of his hero have given readers of spy thrillers some exciting, if somewhat improbable, action.

PART 2

A Golden Age and Beyond
(1940 to the Present)

INTRODUCTION

> "I hope you went hungry and thirsty, and I hope you were scared, every day. I
> hope you goddamn *suffered*! You ... *terrorist!*"
> —Robin Raleigh, fourteen, to his mother, Leila Hanif
> in John Trenhaile's *Blood Rules*, 421

THE SPY THRILLER came of age in England and America because of World War II. The amount and kind of espionage has filled not only books but libraries in the detailing of espionage activities that range from the British commando raids of the Special Operations Executive through MI-5's Double X Committee's counterintelligence against the German Abwehr through spectacular codebreaking developments such as the cracking of Enigma.[1] Spying, once the dirty business of foreign intrigue and seedy individuals, had been pressed into service on all sides as indispensable to the war effort. To quote former CIA Director Allen Dulles, the war "served to elevate the reputation of spying in the public mind."[2]

During the war, morale-building efforts kept spy writers busy—so busy that even traditional mystery writers like Agatha Christie, John Creasey, and Michael Hammond-Innes (writing as Michael Innes) lent their star sleuths to the noble cause. Today, perhaps, we smile at the mouth-filling, patriotic sentiments uttered by Basil Rathbone as Sherlock Holmes, anachronistically relocated to the present of war-time England, as he foils yet one more attempt by German saboteurs to steal the latest bomb-sight weapon or undermine the forces at home. Yet these were stirring times, fascism was a real evil, and invasion of the homeland was a continual threat to the average citizen. Unlike the class-conscious jingoism of Bulldog Drummond, this call to nationalism was directed to the common man and woman. Ultimately, as the war progressed, American writers would equal their British counterparts in sheer output. By the war's end, America's fledgling intelligence effort, pioneered by "Wild Bill" Donovan in association with Britain's organized intelligence divisions against threats at home and abroad, would result in the fledgling CIA under President Truman. The relationship between "the Friends" and "the Cousins" was begun in those short-lived days of euphoria after Hitler's defeat.

The Free World, however, awoke to new fears that, in some respects were, as terrifying as the old: now the Red Menace was real, not the product of spy thrillers. Faceless fears and anxieties disturbed the world's peace as the Cold War commenced even before the Red Army had taken Hitler's bunker in the last days of the war. Rampant inflation, scarcities of basic goods, nationalistic clamorings all across Europe, the self-inflicted wounds of red-baiting and McCarthyism, new technologies of mass destruction, "hot" little wars and revolutionary communism that resulted in "police actions" such as in Korea—many events and clashing ideologies threatened the stability of governments and disturbed peace. Covert action, or secret political intervention by one state in the affairs of another, was carried off in places as diverse as Eastern Europe and Latin America. Spies seemed to be everywhere swiping atomic secrets. The future of democracy in the world seemed greatly limited.

In fiction as in real life, the new evils cried out for containment by some order of good. Such was the situation when, in 1954, James Bond stepped forth from the pages of *Casino Royale*. Gathering a popularity and an intensity hard to imagine nowadays, Ian Fleming, and his lesser imitators, would make the spy and the intelligence agent a cult figure as romantically irresistible as the cowboy of the American West. In what we have called a golden age of spy thrillers, the first two decades were all but consumed in a rash of heroic adventures of agents like Bond or rogue agents of unheroic proportions that fascinated millions of readers. The public couldn't get enough of it, and the reader will see in these pages the hard- and paperback results from the Cult of Bond during the sixties and early seventies.

These superagents were all cruelly handsome men, like Bond, and adept at the latest gee-whiz weaponry, able to speak various dialects when needed, withstand torture, and were proficient love machines to boot. Farcical as they seem to us now, they could interpret a world that was baffling to the common person because they were all active interpreters of right in a world where evil was a throwback to the power-mad geniuses and villains of the early spy-fiction writers before Ambler, Maugham, and Greene. Even the organizations of evil were larger than life. Communist murder groups like SMERSH and criminal conspiracies like THRUSH abetted the individual dictators, scientists, traitor-agents, and terrorists who abounded in the pages of these thrillers to plague the superspy and threaten democracy—but never for long.

Whatever or whoever the adversary, Bond and the superagent-heroes of these days (some of whom continue to thrive in male-oriented paperback series, such as Nick Carter and "The Death Merchant") were seen as figures who "could act, could destroy [and] appeared to be free"—patriots "individually powerful" in a world where ordinary citizens, on their own, could do very little to change difficult situations.[3]

This total fascination with the glamorous superspy has abated considerably but is not gone; witness the popularity of Bond films into the present. But given the realities of social and political protest of the early to mid-sixties, people seemed to grow wary of what critic Julian Symons later called a "pipe dream."[4] When the reaction came, it was swift and dramatic. A new, much more accurate, more sophisticated, school of spy fiction emerged. By the time the Beatles sojourned to America, the Bondian spy novel was already the subject of spoof and satire. The time had come for a new, harder-edged realism and cynicism to emerge, one reminiscent of Ambler and Maugham. "These writers," argues espionage expert and writer Donald McCormick, "actually loathed Bond, seeing him as a Neo-Fascist, a propagandist of the Cold War, and an awful reminder of the nadir of racialist, right-wing 'Bulldog' Drummondism."[5] Some of them, he adds, "felt this instinctively on aesthetic grounds, while others reacted morally and politically."[6]

Of course, we refer here to the great writers of this era now, some would say, drawing to its close in the last days of communism where only North Korea and Castro's Cuba—if it survives the next few months—remain of the Cold War, the Berlin Wall, and the infamous Iron Curtain. To Ted Allbeury, John le Carré, and Len Deighton, principally, go the accolade of bringing new depth to spy fiction. They and their many disciples bring the message that espionage and covert action is indeed, as Kipling's young Kim once learned, a game—but a game where people, pretending to be what they are not, are often the victims of deceit and a non-benevolent authority (usually their own agencies and governments) that can crush them in an instant. Those working in this "game" may be weak or strong as characters, may in fact be evil by conventional standards of morality, but all are individuals whose ideas and feelings may or may not transcend or determine their success or failure. In other words, the "Innocent Age" of Sapper and LeQueux—and the inheritors of their mantle in the modern era like Fleming—is replaced by the "Age of Irony" in spy fiction.

Symons notes that the special quality of le Carré's fiction "[is] their sense of place, their sense of doom, their irony."[7] David J. M. Cornwell, better known to the world as John le Carré, gives us the anti-hero, the unheroic spy, the non-snobbish man of conscience who may be a simple civil servant. Such realism is a tonic to the sensationalism of the Bondian superspy. The cold, gray realism of *A Small Town in Germany* is a novel that could find a niche in a great contemporary novels class for other reasons than espionage, but we must acknowledge the superior quality of writing as literature without the academic's snobbery of affixing "spy fiction" as rubric.

Besides this battle in the marketplace for the dollars between the fans of Fleming versus the new reading public of Allbeury, Deighton, and Cornwell, a third force appeared on the scene and threatened to engulf them both and at its core was a central idea: action. Writers like Alistair Maclean, Raymond H. Sawkins—better known as Colin Forbes—and Henry Patterson, known most usually under his pseudonym Jack Higgins thrilled the reading public with tales of violent action that were built around heroes who were not so much beyond the pale of an ordinary individual's grasp; they were men of action, of course, but with that highly prized and salable commodity urged upon a readership familiar with the latest in self-help, pep-talk psychology: sensitivity. Writes one disciple of this school of these characters as people who "are sharply defined in their looks and mannerism and come across well without pages of historical background. No special gimmickry needed—and sometimes the plots are lacking in the plausible—but John Buchan would have acknowledged them proudly. Purists, perhaps, will be annoyed that we include a large number of such practitioners in these pages, but we believed that we could not be rigorously exclusive in a genre that refuses to limit itself to formulaic conventions.

What of the spy thriller today? Just a glance at the commentary in this guide's CRAFT NOTES Appendix will convince any reader that it is alive, flourishing, taking myriad forms and venues for future exploitation. No writer in those pages, who commented upon the future of the spy thriller—and many of them chose to—is anything but optimistic about its promise in the coming decade.   Reviewer and Senior Editor of the PBS foreign policy series *American Interests* Morton Kondracke chronicles the career of only one commentator of these pages in the light of our very recent history: Tom Clancy. Mr. Clancy's began with the exciting technothriller *The Hunt for Red October* in 1984 before the US-USSR relationship had altered significantly its usual stance from the Cold War days of the fifties. His *Red Storm Rising* in 1986 is a book that depicts how a nuclear war can evolve from the hotbed of the Middle East. In 1988, before Saddam Hussein had replaced Libya's Muammar el-Quaddafi as the principal mad man of that region, he showed America's susceptibility to terrorism in *Patriot Games*. He followed that book in 1989 with *Clear and Present Danger* with thaw between East and West formalized in the destruction of the Berlin Wall and communism's collapse in Eastern Europe. He turned to the drug cartels as the subject of his fiction. From there, in 1991, Kondracke notes, he moved to a subject that captures the fears of many observers of the world crisis:

> [*The Sum of All Fears*] is exactly that: a treasure trove of geopolitical terrors. The
> cold war is over and the Gulf war has made a Middle East settlement possible. Ah,

but what's peace for us good people is disaster and betrayal for the bad people, including Palestinian terrorists, European ultra-radicals and former East German secret police and military scientists. They get together, obtain a slightly damaged Israeli nuclear weapon and try to turn it into an H-bomb that, once exploded, will cause hard-liners in the United States and the Soviet Union to seize control from panicked leaders and plunge the good guys into all-out war.[8]

With his recent book *Without Remorse* (1993), Mr. Clancy returns to Vietnam, that old aching American wound, in a tale about the rescue of prisoners. Those themes, familiar to all readers of espionage fiction within the last decade, comprise an overwhelming number of the books annotated in Part 2. Clearly, the inspiration for ideas is not lacking; it remains to be seen whether the recent innovation of the technothriller, aviation, underwater, or otherwise is a path that will continue to be trod, but the writers in this sub-genre are numerous and as popular as ever, and several are represented in CRAFT NOTES, including Craig Thomas and Douglas Terman.

Perhaps the most encouraging sign of all is that the great writers continue to write excellent fiction. John le Carré and Len Deighton both published in 1993, and Ted Allbeury—the man credited with Len Deighton's inspiration—continues to write excellent fiction on a steady basis. Others as critically popular as Frederick Forsyth, who has recently turned toward historical thrillers, and John Trenhaile, who has completed his second trilogy on the Chinese Secret Service and Gerald Seymour, one of the finest of the school of Ambler, has returned—geographically speaking—to the setting of *Harry's Game*, his first great spy thriller. A year does not pass without a Jack Higgins thriller returning to the bestseller lists. Anthony Price's Dr. Audley and Jack Butler are, we hope, preparing themselves for yet another sojourn into the English countryside and a murky past that impinges on the present. And so too the other outstanding writers like Ken Follett, Julian Rathbone, and Gavin Lyall who give us varying glimpses of the secret and not-so-secret worlds in first-rate fiction. We savor their talents and express our debt to them, and most happily for the reader who faces such variety, it falls to our own choosing which novelists to follow.

The citations in this section are arranged alphabetically by author. We begin with David Aaron and move back through the big and small names of the post-1940 era, providing details on good and bad alike. Readers interested in a specific author should consult Part 1, for some of these writers were active in the years before World War II.

NOTES

1.   See, for example, Vol. 1 of Myron J. Smith, Jr.'s *The Secret Wars* (Santa Barbara, CA: ABC-Clio, 1980).

2.   Allen Dulles, ed., *Great Spy Stories from Fiction* (New York: Harper & Row, 1969) xi.

3.   Julian Symons, *Mortal Consequences* (New York: Schocken, 1972) 242.

4.   Symons 242.

5.   Donald McCormick, *Who's Who in Spy Fiction* (New York: Taplinger, 1977) 10.

6.   McCormick 10.

7.   Symons 244.

8.   Morton Kondracke, "A Missile for Every Occasion," rev. of *The Sum of All Fears*, by Tom Clancy, *New York Times Book Review* July 28, 1991, sec. 7: 9.

Bibliography: A to Z

A

377. Aaron, David. *Agent of Influence.* New York: Putnam's, 1989. Aaron has earned the Pentagon's highest civilian award and served as Deputy Assistant to the President for National Security Affairs until 1981; moreover, he has been a member of the National Security Council. Aaron puts his insider's experience on Wall Street to use in this tale of Wall Street investment banker Jason Lyman's investigation into a mysterious Frenchman's takeover of an American newspaper conglomerate, which masks a Soviet attempt to control Western press.

378. ___. *State Scarlet.* London: Macmillan; New York: Putnam's, 1987. Aaron's first novel was an immediate bestseller about the paranoid relations between the two superpowers when a nuclear device is stolen and both sides accuse the other; the plot thickens as the Americans move toward a pre-emptive first strike against the Soviets.

379. Aarons, Edward S. *Assignment: Afghan Dragon.* Greenwich, CT: Fawcett, 1976. Over forty titles have been published in this exclusively paperback series by Aarons and his son Will on daring CIA agent Sam Durell of "K" section. The emphasis in these tales is on action, with plot, characterization, locale, and pure romance secondary. In this outing, Durell, on a routine mission to the Iran-Afghanistan border, becomes involved with a feud between Soviet and Chinese secret agents. *P*

380. ___. *Assignment: Amazon Queen.* Greenwich, CT: Fawcett, 1974. Durell is sent to South America to uncover the nasties behind a Nazi plot and becomes involved—as usual—with a beautiful girl. *P*

381. ___. *Assignment: Angelina.* Greenwich, CT: Fawcett, 1958. Durell finds himself at the end of a list of murdered men, all of whom are mixed up with classified World War II files; her name meant "Little Angel," but she was an enemy agent. *P*

382. ___. *Assignment: Ankara.* Greenwich, CT: Fawcett, 1969. When his plan is deliberately lured off course and shot down on the Soviet-Turkish border, Durell knows the KGB is onto a hush-hush tape he is guarding. *P*

383. ___. *Assignment: Bangkok.* Greenwich, CT: Fawcett, 1972. Upon his arrival in Thailand to undertake a secret US government mission, Sam Durell is kidnapped and held in a prison in the city's sewer wondering who had betrayed him and why. *P*

384. ___. *Assignment: Black Gold.* Greenwich, CT: Fawcett, 1975. Durell must stay the hands of invisible terrorists who are using an oil secret in an attempt to take over the small African country of Lubinda. *P*

385. ___. *Assignment: Budapest.* Greenwich, CT: Fawcett, 1957. Sam Durell is dispatched to Hungary to find and rescue a beautiful freedom fighter before she is apprehended by the secret police. *P*

386. ___. *Assignment: Burma Girl.* Greenwich, CT: Fawcett, 1961. An ex-whore with $300 million-worth of influence arranges for Durell to be sent up the Irrawaddy to rescue two men from Communist guerrillas. *P*

387. ___. *Assignment: The Cairo Dancers.* Greenwich, CT: Fawcett, 1965. In Egypt, Durell tries to learn who is looting the world's best brains in order to create a superweapon. *P*

388. ___. *Assignment: Carlotta Cortez.* Greenwich, CT: Fawcett, 1959. Durell seeks to halt the employment of twenty hijacked A-bombs while a beautiful girl offers herself as a bribe to ensure his inactivity. *P*

389. ___. *Assignment: Ceylon.* Greenwich, CT: Fawcett, 1973. While chasing a defecting diplomat, Durell is suspected of being a double agent and must also outwit CIA killers sent to liquidate him. *P*

390. ___. *Assignment: Cong Hai Kill.* Greenwich, CT: Fawcett, 1966. Durell is sent to Southeast Asia to capture a sadistic killer-defector who has gone over to the Reds. *P*

391. ___. *Assignment: The Girl in the Gondola.* Greenwich, CT: Fawcett, 1974. Sam Durell is sent to Venice to track down a Russian traitor and is led to believe that a beautiful Italian girl can help him. *P*

392. ___. *Assignment: Golden Girl.* Greenwich, CT: Fawcett, 1971. Using an old train, Durell rushes to rescue the beautiful princess-leader of the African country of Pakuru before she can be captured by traitors and terrorists. *P*

393. ___. *Assignment: Helene.* Greenwich, CT: Fawcett, 1959. Durell must halt the unknown American who is helping rebels on Salangap wage a guerrilla war. *P*

394. ___. *Assignment: Karachi.* Greenwich, CT: Fawcett, 1973. An impetuous millionairess, whose life is in constant danger as she travels in the mountains of Pakistan, must be protected from harm by Agent Durell. *P*

395. ___. *Assignment: Lowlands.* Greenwich, CT: Fawcett, 1961. Notes keep coming into Langley about an impending disaster; then operative Durell is dispatched to Holland with orders to find someone named Cassandra within 47 hours. *P*

396. ___. *Assignment: Manchurian Doll.* Greenwich, CT: Fawcett, 1972. Durell pits his wits against those of a ruthless KGB agent—who suddenly decides to defect! *P*

397. ___. *Assignment: Nuclear Nude.* Greenwich, CT: Fawcett, 1970. Agent Durell must prevent a Red Chinese torture-queen from grabbing a secret atomic formula, which is hidden in an abstract painting of a nude woman. *P*

398. ___. *Assignment: Peking.* Greenwich, CT: Fawcett, 1969. They gave him another man's face and sent him into China on a terrifying mission—the one and only Sam Durell was now somebody else, his own worst enemy! *P*

399. ___. *Assignment: Quayle Question.* Greenwich, CT: Fawcett, 1975. Durell battles the infamous Dr. Sinn, who has masterminded a plot involving billions of dollars and the control of millions of minds. *P*

400. ___. *Assignment: Silver Scorpion.* Greenwich, CT: Fawcett, 1973. In the emerging African nation of Boganda, Durell must battle a group of female pirates in order to recover $300 million in American currency. *P*

401. ___. *Assignment: Star Stealers.* Greenwich, CT: Fawcett, 1970. In Morocco, Durell and a beautiful widow hunt a secret installation which has atomic weapons pointed at Chinese, Russian, and American satellites. *P*

402. ___. *Assignment: Stella Marni.* Greenwich, CT: Fawcett, 1957. Durell seeks answers to the fate of missing Hungarian refugees and only a beautiful blonde knows the full story. *P*

403. ___. *Assignment: Suicide.* Greenwich, CT: Fawcett, 1965. Durell must parachute into Russia, reach Moscow undetected, locate and assassinate the madman known only as "Comrade Z," before he can fire the missile which will surely plunge the world into nuclear war. *P*

404. ___. *Assignment: Sulu Sea.* Greenwich, CT: Fawcett, 1964. Durell is sent to Malaysia to trace an American nuclear submarine which disappeared off that nation's coast. *P*

405. ___. *Assignment: Sumatra.* Greenwich, CT: Fawcett, 1974. On a secret mission to the island nation, Durell finds he must trust his life to his lethal lady assistant while trying to get a government official safely to an international conference. *P*

406. ___. *Assignment: To Disaster.* Greenwich, CT: Fawcett, 1955. Difficulties on a US project to put a remote-controlled super bomb into orbit brings Agent Durell into the action. *P*

407. ___. *Assignment: Treason.* Greenwich, CT: Fawcett, 1973. Durell is taken captive by a known and trusted colleague in the complex brain of the CIA—a man who is a traitor and has ordered the assassination of a high European official as a way of starting World War III. *P*

408. ___. *Assignment: Unicorn.* Greenwich, CT: Fawcett, 1976. Assassins powered by a super drug murder Premier Shang of Palingpen and are being turned loose to kill every available CIA agent; Durell is sent in to solve the problem. *P*

409. ___. *Assignment: White Rajah.* Greenwich, CT: Fawcett, 1974. Durell is called upon to solve the mystery of who is hijacking American fighter planes in Southeast Asia. *P*

410. ___. *The State Department Murders.* Greenwich, CT: Fawcett, 1958. In Washington, DC, Barney Cornell knows too much about another man—a man who has dossiers on just about everyone. *P* Others in the Durell series by this author include:

411. ___. *Assignment: Argentina.* Greenwich, CT: Fawcett, 1964. *P*

412. ___. *Assignment: Black Viking.* Greenwich, CT: Fawcett, 1972. *P*

413. ___. *Assignment: Lili Lamaris.* Greenwich, CT: Fawcett, 1973. *P*

414. ___. *Assignment: London.* Greenwich, CT: Fawcett, 1963. *P*

415. ___. *Assignment: Madeleine.* Greenwich, CT: Fawcett, 1971. *P*

416. ___. *Assignment: Malta.* Greenwich, CT: Fawcett, 1966. *P*

417. ___. *Assignment: Maltese Maiden.* Greenwich, CT: Fawcett, 1972. *P*

418. ___. *Assignment: Mara Tirana.* Greenwich, CT: Fawcett, 1972. *P*

419. ___. *Assignment: Moon Girl.* Greenwich, CT: Fawcett, 1972. *P*

420. ___. *Assignment: New York.* Greenwich, CT: Fawcett, 1963. *P*

421. ___. *Assignment: Palermo.* Greenwich, CT: Fawcett, 1972. *P*

422. ___. *Assignment: School for Spies.* Greenwich, CT: Fawcett, 1970. *P*

423. ___. *Assignment: Sea Bird.* Greenwich, CT: Fawcett, 1969. *P*

424. ___. *Assignment: Sorrento Siren.* Greenwich, CT: Fawcett, 1973. *P*

425. ___. *Assignment: Tokyo.* Greenwich, CT: Fawcett, 1971. *P*

426. ___. *Assignment: Zoraya.* Greenwich, CT: Fawcett, 1972. *P*

427. Aarons, Will B. *Assignment: Death Ship.* New York: Fawcett, 1983. Durell faces the threat of global biological warfare when a Caribbean cruise ship is found adrift hundreds of miles north of Argentina with a thousand bloated corpses lying about her decks. *P*

428. ___. *Assignment: Mermaid.* Greenwich, CT: Fawcett, 1979. Durell searches for a vanished Russian atomic scientist amidst reports of women half human and half fish. *P*

429. ___. *Assignment: Sheba.* Greenwich, CT: Fawcett, 1977. On the Red Sea coast of Ethiopia, Sam Durell encounters terrorists and tracks down the cause of a mysterious atomic blast which had shattered the African wilderness. *P*

430. ___. *Assignment: Tyrant's Bride.* Greenwich, CT: Fawcett, 1980. Durell must rescue an African princess and transport her to the safety of her tribe, which is waiting to revolt against the evil dictator, Field Marshal Ausi. *P* Other Durell stories by this writer include:

431. ___. *Assignment: Thirteenth Princess.* Greenwich, CT: Fawcett, 1977. *P*

432. ___. *Assignment: Tiger Devil.* Greenwich, CT: Fawcett, 1978. *P*

433. Aasheim, Ashley. *Vulcan Rising.* New York: Dell, 1982. Former SS General Stahel allows himself to be used by both the Russians and the Americans because he intends to use them to create the Fourth Reich. *P*

434. Abbott, John, pseud. *Scimitar.* New York: Crown, 1992. Sonny Hemkar, a handsome Los Angeles doctor, is also an Libyan sleeper-agent and assassin who has been awakened to kill former head of state Margaret Thatcher and current President Bush at a meeting in New York.

435. Abrahams, Peter. *Red Message.* New York: Avon, 1986. A Chinese criminal society engineers the disappearance of a brilliant mathematician named Teddy Wu for the KGB but his fiancée refuses to believe US intelligence's verdict that Wu defected to Red China. *P*

436. Abro, Ben, pseud. *Assassination.* New York: Morrow, 1963. The radical right-wing OAS plots to kill Charles DeGaulle on Bastille Day; published in England simultaneously under the title *July 14 Assassination.* Compare with Frederick Forsyth's *The Day of the Jackal.*

437. Adams, Cleve F. *Sabotage.* New York. Dutton, 1940. Hard-boiled detective Rex McBride seeks those responsible for destroying a munitions plant and runs into a nest of Nazi spies. After the outbreak of World War II, a large number of fictional detectives were turned into counterespionage agents by their creators. **y*

438. Adams, Eustace L. *Death Charter.* New York. Coward-McCann, 1943. When a fishing yacht outward bound from Miami stops to assist three German flyers struggling in the water, it is almost taken over when the newcomers join a planted agent in turning on the crew. ***

439. Adams, Nathan M. *The Fifth Horseman.* Greenwich, CT: Fawcett, 1968. Kidnapped and turned by the Mossad, a former Nazi SS officer is forced to return to West Germany and penetrate a dangerous modern neo-Nazi underground movement. *P*

440. Adler, Warren. *American Sextet.* New York: Arbor, 1983. Det. Fiona Fitzgerald discovers a sex scandal that links a suicide to six prominent American officials and their blackmail.

441. ___. *The Casanova Embrace.* New York: Putnam's, 1978. To learn why a prominent Chilean exile was murdered, a maverick CIA agent must delve into the suave revolutionary's exotic past.

442. ___. *Trans-Siberian Express.* New York: Putnam's, 1977. American physician Alex Cousins is sent to Russia to treat the ailing Secretary of the Communist Party and is then trailed by the KGB as he returns to the West, streaking across the Soviet Union on the world's most opulent train.

443. ___. *We Are Holding the President Hostage.* New York: Macmillan, 1986. When a Mafia don's daughter and grandson are kidnapped by Arab terrorists in Cairo, Salvatore Padronelli, the Padre, creates a plan to get the United States government moving to free them: he and three associates hold the President and First Lady hostage at a state dinner by strapping liquid explosives to their bodies and infiltrating the dinner as waiters. Two more:

444. ___. *Immaculate Deception.* New York: Fine, 1991.

445. ___. *Senator Love.* New York: Fine, 1991.

446. Aellen, Richard. *The Cain Conversion.* New York: Fine, 1993. A member of the Secret Service's Protection Detail is actually a Soviet sleeper agent, whose personality has been engineered; now, in the collpase of the Soviet Union, a KGB man activates the assassin at the core of this Secret Service agent's personality, and he is compelled into murderous action, and self-discovery, against his own will.

447. ___. *Crux.* New York: Fine, 1989. A Vietnam vet returns from twenty years in captivity seeking revenge on the three men from his platoon who set him up—one of whom is a Presidential candidate and married to the wife he left behind.

448. ___. *Flash Point.* New York: Fine, 1991. A woman whose three children are blown up in the plane they are returning from vows revenge against the fanatic Muslim leader responsible.

449. ___. *Red Eye.* New York: Fine, 1988. A journalist publishes pulp thrillers on the side—the inspiration comes in his nightmares. The trouble is that the CIA want to know *how* Paul Stafford manages to write about the real names of its agents who are assassinated exactly in the manner his stories describe. Could there be an identical twin brother lost in the rubble of war-torn Berlin who is now an East German intelligence assassin?

450. Agel, Jerome and Eugene Boe. *Deliverance in Shanghai.* New York: Lorevan, 1983. Fictionalized treatment of the thousands of European Jews who, fleeing Hitler, wound up in the infamous Hongkew ghetto of Shanghai. *P*

451. Alan, Ray. *The Beirut Pipeline.* New York: Farrar, 1980. When his contact on Cyprus is killed, a British agent, under cover as a newsman, moves on to Aleppo where he is caught up in a drug-running operation which is being used to cover PLO terrorist activities.

452. Albert, Marvin H. *The Dark Goddess.* Garden City, NY: Doubleday, 1978. When his wife is kidnapped by the KGB, which thinks her a valuable source of information, a Presidential aide races the CIA to get her back before she is killed.

453. ___. *The Gargoyle Conspiracy.* Garden City, NY: Doubleday, 1975. US agent Simon Hunter must locate and eliminate Arab terrorist Bel Jahra and his band before they can bring off their bloodiest strike yet, the assassination of King Hussein of Jordan and Secretary of State Henry Kissinger.

Albrand, Martha, pseud. *See* Loewengard, Heidi H.

Aldanov, Mark, pseud. *See* Landau, Mark A.

Alding, Peter, pseud. *See* Jeffries, Roderic

454. Aldridge, James. *A Captive in the Land*. Garden City, NY: Doubleday, 1963. Englishman Royce saves an injured Russian in the Arctic, is invited to the Soviet Union to receive a medal; there he is trailed by SIS and CIA agents, but unknown to them, is on his own espionage mission for Naval Intelligence. *

455. ___. *The Last Exile*. Garden City, NY: Doubleday, 1961. British agent Royce attempts to assist his country's interests in Egypt during the ill-fated 1956 Suez invasion. *

456. ___. *The Statesman's Game*. Garden City, NY: Doubleday, 1966. Royce once more deals with the Soviets, trading British ships for Russian oil. *

457. Alexander, David. *Phoenix #1: Dark Messiah*. New York: Leisure, 1987. Post-nuclear mercs led by John Tallon and SCORF (Special Commando Retaliatory Force) enforce a new world order; opposing him is Phoenix, "grim-faced warrior of the Apocalypse," a Vietnam vet of the Special Forces. *P*

458. ___. *Phoenix #2: Ground Zero*. New York: Leisure, 1987. More nuclear-holocaust badasses and Phoenix-style justice with high-tech weaponry. *P*

459. Alexander, David M. *The Chocolate Spy*. New York: Coward-McCann, 1978. An FBI arson agent uncovers a computer, codenamed "Chocolate," which has been cloned from human brain cells as part of a Soviet plot against the United States.

460. Alexander, Patrick. *Death of a Thin-Skinned Animal*. New York: Dutton, 1977. When his cover is blown, SIS agent Richard Abbott spends two years in prison; when at last freed, he returns to London determined to carry out his original mission of assassinating an African dictator.

461. ___. *Show Me a Hero*. New York: Playboy, 1981. A conquered England struggles against the Party and its merciless TacForce patrols; however, there's a resistance movement afoot led by The Falcon.

462. Aline, Countess of Romanones. *The Spy Wore Silk.* New York: Putnam's, 1991.

463. Allbeury, Ted. *All Our Tomorrows.* London: Granada, 1982. In this antiutopian novel, British democracy degenerates under economic woes and subversive hooliganism to the point of civil war. The British Prime Minister feels compelled to ask the Soviet Union to intercede.

 Full name Theodore Edward le Bouthillier Allbeury, this former member of British Army Intelligence during World War II is widely believed to be the inspiration of Len Deighton's Harry Palmer; for a time, he also operated a pirate radio station, worked as an executive in advertising, became a member of a BBC advisory and wrote his first spy thriller in 1971 as a partial autobiography. (See his comments in CRAFT NOTES.) Allbeury is the perfect counterfoil to the excesses of contemporaries who may be better known, such as the introspection of le Carré or the outlandish plot excesses of a Robert Ludlum. His novels reflect much realism and attention to detail without undue attention to hardware. He convinces the reader that his stories are what they purport to be: accurate reflections of the intelligence business as played by modern professionals.

464. ___. *The Alpha List.* London: Methuen, 1980. An MI-5 agent must learn if a close boyhood friend, now a Labour member of Parliament, is actually a KGB agent.

465. ___. *Children of Tender Years.* Sevenoaks: NEL*, 1985. [New York: Beaufort, 1985]. Jake Malik, a Jewish survivor of Auschwitz, works for British SIS; his assignment to investigate a rash of anti-Semitic activities in Germany leads him to an incredible conspiracy of fanatic German and Israeli businessmen who have built and armed six nuclear missile silos and aimed at Soviet cities.

466. ___. *The Choice.* Sevenoaks: NEL, 1986. Allbeury's protagonist is David Collins, a working-class boy who went to war, came back, and made good in his profession but has to make choices between his wife and the woman he loves in this nonespionage novel.

467. ___. *A Choice of Enemies.* New York: St. Martin's, 1973. Practically blackmailed into intelligence work a quarter of a century after the end of the war, Ted Bailey soon comes up against a KGB agent whom he had first met in

*New English Library

Germany at the conclusion of the conflict and learns that, though the game may be played with computers now, its essential ruthlessness has not changed at all.

468. ___. *Codeword Cromwell*. By Patrick Kelly, pseud. London: Granada, 1980. Max Von Bayer, scion of a wealthy German baron, and Sadie Aarons, a Jewish girl of seventeen, meet and fall in love in England before war breaks out. When Bayer is rejected as Sadie's suitor, he returns to England with a raiding party of civilians and misfits after war is declared.

469. ___. *Consequence of Fear*. London: Granada, 1979. The intersections of three lives in espionage from WW II through the Cold War: Yuri Galitsyn, a KGB officer who saw his mother raped during the Siege of Leningrad; Otto Lemke, a German double agent, and his first handler, James Boyle, Intelligence Corps officer.

470. ___. *Deep Purple*. Sevenoaks: NEL, 1989. [New York: Mysterious, 1990]. Eddie Hoggart's task as MI-6 interrogator of defector Yakunin is to find out whether he is the genuine article and verify his claim that there's another supermole in SIS—that is, if Hoggart can keep his Lolita of a wife from destroying his career.

471. ___. *The Judas Factor*. Sevenoaks: NEL, 1984. [New York: Mysterious, 1984]. Tadeusz "Tad" Anders, SIS's "Dirty Harry," is brooding in his Soho nightclub (a covert intelligence set-up) about his newfound inactivity; it seems his bosses consider him too resourceful with violence lately. But the call comes in: an East German KGB thug is killing agents and SIS wants Anders to kidnap this man.

472. ___. *The Lantern Network*. London: Davies, 1978. When Nicholas Bailey, Special Branch Commander, casually interrogates a London businessman about a remote connection to a KGB drop site, the man commits suicide; behind the mystery man's suicide lay heroic resistance during WW II in the maquis and a singular betrayal that leads Bailey to the man's widow and daughter.

473. ___. *The Man with the President's Mind*. New York: Simon & Schuster, 1978. The CIA must prevent the introduction into the US of a man whom KGB psychologists have trained to think like the American President and who could predict that leader's reactions to any given event or crisis. When the time comes, the Russians do manage to sneak Andrei Levin into Washington, but then their plans go awry and the infiltrator becomes the object of a terrifying and brutal manhunt which leads right to the White House.

474. ___. *Mission Berlin.* [original title: *The Only Good German.* London: Davies, 1976]. New York: Walker, 1986. A friendship formed in the aftermath of World War II between an Intelligence Corps officer and an Abwehr colonel form the basis of an investigation twenty years later when a group of ex-Nazis resort to sabotage to undermine the Warsaw Pact.

475. ___. *Moscow Quadrille.* London: Davies, 1976. The "honey trap" set for the British ambassador in Moscow works too well when he marries his KGB "swallow" and returns to a key government post in London at a time when England is beginning to crumble under the pressure of communist sympathizers in government, the trade unions, and the press.

476. ___. *No Place to Hide.* Sevenoaks: NEL, 1984. John Rennie has been a lifelong patriot and fiercely loyal SIS dirty-tricks specialist until the kidnapping of a wealthy Arab's two children forces him to confront the question of where his loyalty lies.

477. ___. *Omega Minus.* New York: Viking, 1975. [*Palomino Blonde.* London: Davies, 1975]. British scientist James Hallet has invented a doomsday device called Omega Minus. Competition for it among British, Soviet, and American agents becomes vicious as word leaks out of this earth-shaking death ray.

478. ___. *The Other Side of Silence.* New York: Scribner's, 1981. Aging Kim Philby wants to come home, and a special SIS subcommittee investigates the pros and cons of Philby's return, apparently with the KGB's blessing. However, tough John Powell, the committee's elected investigator, begins to wonder whether it's a matter of a traitor coming home to die in peace—or a deep-cover agent coming in from the cold.

479. ___. *Pay Any Price.* London: Granada, 1983. The assassination of the Kennedys is a result of an ongoing experiment in deep hypnosis by a rogue CIA department. When the true identities of two psychiatrists are discovered by SIS in Northumberland, a dirty-tricks division decides to use the hypnotists to assassinate undesirables by the same means.

480. ___. *The Secret Whispers.* London: Granada, 1981. Seventeen years ago a young British captain "turned" an agent named Richter who is now in great danger when his cover is blown, and it is his responsibility to exfiltrate Richter from East Germany.

481. ___. *The Seeds of Treason.* Sevenoaks: NEL, 1986. [New York: Mysterious, 1987]. The focus of this work is on love and betrayal, a familiar Allbeury theme. The nexus of four couples' espionage activities is Berlin, and the focus is on Jan Massey's love for the wife of his KGB opposite.

482. ___. *Shadow of Shadows.* New York: Scribner's, 1982. SIS's James Lawler heads the interrogation of a defecting KGB colonel in London who is holding back on two years of vital information.

483. ___. *Snowball.* Philadelphia: Lippincott, 1964. Operation Snowball is the Soviet solution to destroy NATO by discrediting America in Britain and Europe. The KGB plans to exhibit a document proving that, during "her finest hour," President Roosevelt and the Canadian Prime Minister had exchanged memos agreeing to abandon the British to an imminent Nazi invasion in 1940. Tad Anders (like Ted Bailey, a team player when he has to be but mostly a maverick pressed into service when the work to be done is dirty) is assigned to retrieve that paper and liquidate the scheme and its enemy perpetrators.

484. ___. *The Special Collection.* London: Heinemann, 1975. The so-called Special Collection is an ongoing plan that calls for a first-strike against America; now, however, it's gone operational as the Red Army makes its move for dominance in Soviet power by ordering massive subversion in Great Britain on all fronts.

485. ___. *The Stalking Angel.* New York: Mysterious, 1989. Anna Simon, a beautiful, young German woman, meets and falls in love with a young scholar of medieval studies. When Paul is killed by a bomb planted outside their flat in Paris, she learns that he was tracking Nazis and decides to take up his cause and finds herself in a worldwide manhunt after dangerous Neo-Nazis.

486. ___. *A Time without Shadows.* New York: Mysterious, 1991. MI-6's Harry Chapman must decide whether Churchill betrayed to Stalin a French resistance unit when the surviving members are being murdered.

487. ___. *A Wilderness of Mirrors.* Sevenoaks: NEL, 1988. Directly based on his own experiences as an interrogation officer of Germans for possible war crimes with 21 Army Group (security services) after the surrender, Allbeury himself describes this novel: "*A Wilderness of Mirrors* is about an SIS officer who is efficient, loyal and patriotic, who is ordered by London to carry out the kidnapping of a girl from the other side of the Wall. When the operation collapses and he finds out what his superiors expect him to do with the girl, he decides that their solution is unfair and unjust . . . it is essentially the story of

what can happen when a good man decides to ignore the rules of the game."
Other Allbeury tales:

488. ___. *The Crossing*. Sevenoaks: NEL, 1987.

489. ___. *The Girl from Addis*. London: Granada, 1984.

490. ___. *Italian Assets*. By Richard Butler, pseud. London: Davies, 1976.

491. ___. *The Lonely Margins*. By Patrick Kelly, pseud. London: Granada,
1981.

492. ___. *The Reaper*. London: Granada, 1983.

493. ___. *The Twentieth Day of January*. London: Granada, 1980.

494. ___. *Where All the Girls Are Sweeter*. By Richard Butler, pseud.
London: Granada, 1975.

495. Allen, Ralph. *Ask the Name of the Lion*. Garden City, NY: Doubleday,
1962. In an effort to assist besieged Whites, a select band of mercenaries are
sent to the rescue during the Congolese Civil War of 1960.

496. Allingham, Margery. *Cargo of Eagles*. London: Chatto & Windus,
1968. Detective Albert Campion links up with MI-5 to investigate extortion and
smuggling in the Essex countryside. *y
    The daughter of a boys' fiction writer, Margery Allingham is famous as
the creator of the Campion figure, a sleuth "well bred and a trifle absent-
minded." As with many private-eyes, Campion occasionally was put onto an
espionage or security caper.

497. ___. *Pearls Before Swine*. Garden City, NY: Doubleday, 1945.
Detective Campion becomes involved with art treasures, artificial pearls, and a
champion sow, which are all linked in a mystery of crime and espionage. *y

498. ___. *Traitor's Purse*. London: Heinemann, 1941. Albert Campion is
temporarily attached to MI-5 in order to discover who is behind a plot to bring
down the British government with a cunningly conceived inflation scheme. *y

499. Ambler, Eric. *The Care of Time*. New York: Farrar, 1981. American
freelance writer Robert Halliday is coerced into negotiations between NATO and
a powerful Gulf sheik of questionable sanity known as "the Ruler."

Ambler is one of the giants of the spy thriller, credited along with W. Somerset Maugham with introducing realism and other facets to the genre (see Part 1). During World War II, he served as an officer in the royal Artillery and later as Assistant Director of British Army Kinematography in London. After the conflict he retired to Switzerland to continue his writing, turning out the many tales listed here. He also took time out here and there to write reviews, always being careful to point out inaccuracies in the spy tales of others. Although some of his earlier works may appear dated, they still read well and retain their somewhat ironic style. Ambler, more than any other practitioner of spy fiction ended the jingoistic extravagance, coarse sentimentality, and racist piffle of his predecessors "Sapper" and LeQueux by introducing flesh-and-blood human beings caught up in espionage against their will and forced to act against the dark forces of governments and groups for their own survival.

500. ___. *Dirty Story*. New York: Atheneum, 1968. Arthur Simpson attempts to flee Greece and ends up joining a mercenary army which has been hired to fight a dirty war in Africa. *

501. ___. *Doctor Frigo*. New York: Atheneum, 1974. Espionage and intrigue in Central America; a consortium is out to reap huge profits and spill blood. *

502. ___. *Epitaph for a Spy*. New York: Knopf, 1952. A prophetic volume in which the author hints that Western intelligence agencies might soon be plagued with defectors and infiltrators—just as occurred a few years later with Kim Philby. A timid language teacher, visiting Nice, is arrested as a spy and employed by British Intelligence to investigate Schimmler, a man converted from moderate socialism to Communism. *

503. ___. *The Intercom Conspiracy*. New York: Atheneum, 1969. Two intelligence agents from small NATO countries use secret information to embarrass America and Russia. *

504. ___. *Intrigue: Four Great Spy Novels*. New York: Knopf, 1960. Includes *Background to Danger*, *A Coffin for Dimitrios*, and *Journey into Fear*. The introductory material is quite valuable. *

505. ___. *The Intriguers: Four Superb Novels of Suspense*. New York: Knopf, 1965. Contains *Judgment on Deltchev*, *Passage of Arms*, *The Schirmer Inheritance*, and *State of Siege*. *

506. ___. *Journey into Fear.* New York: Knopf, 1940. German agents pursue an English engineer returning with intelligence from neutral Turkey. The last novel penned by the author before he joined the Royal Artillery in 1941. *

507. ___. *Judgment on Deltchev.* New York: Knopf, 1951. An English playwright reports on a trial from inside a Communist East European country and becomes involved in Cold War intrigue. *

508. ___. *A Kind of Anger.* New York: Atheneum, 1964. Piet Maas, something less than an ace reporter, is sent on a short assignment to find the beautiful, bikini-clad witness to the murder of an Iraqi politician. *

509. ___. *The Levanter.* New York: Atheneum, 1972. A radical breakaway group of Palestinian terrorists plan to wreak havoc in Tel Aviv. *

510. ___. *The Light of Day.* London: Heinemann, 1962. [*Topkapi.* New York: Bantam, 1964]. Arthur Simpson, a small-time thief, is drawn into a conspiracy plotting the world's most daring crime. *

511. ___. *Passage of Arms.* New York: Knopf, 1959. An Indian clerk, two Chinese brothers, and a middle-aged American couple become involved in a plot to smuggle arms to anti-Communist forces in Indonesia. *

512. ___. *The Schirmer Inheritance.* New York: Knopf, 1953. A lawyer searches for the lost heir to an American fortune among the displaced peoples of post-war Europe. *

513. ___. *The Siege of the Villa Lipp.* New York: Random, 1976. [*Send No More Roses.* London: Weidenfeld & Nicholson, 1977]. An arch criminal, whose international capers had been so perfect that he was an uncatchable legend, has had his network penetrated. He is now being blackmailed, not for money, but a confession and is holed up in a villa on the Italian Riviera fighting for time—time in which to save his criminal empire and his life. *

514. ___. *State of Siege.* New York: Knopf, 1956. First published in Britain as *The Night-Comers.* Two English civilians are caught in the crossfire in an attack on a Southeast Asian capital. *

515. ___, ed. *To Catch a Spy: An Anthology of Favourite Spy Stories.* New York: Atheneum, 1965. An anthology of excerpts from various leading spy thriller writers, past and present; note especially Ambler's introduction, which contains one of the best discussions of the genre by a practitioner. *

516. ___ and Charles Rodda. *Tender to Danger.* By Eliot Reed, pseud. Garden City, NY: Doubleday, 1952. A vacationing Scot is convinced that something sinister is about to happen in Belgium; rebuffed by the Belgian police, he returns to England where he learns he was correct. *

517. ___. *Waiting for Orders.* New York: Mysterious, 1991. The complete short stories.

518. Ames, Rachel. *Appointment in Vienna.* By Sarah Gainham, pseud. New York: Dutton, 1958. [*The Mythmaker.* London: Barker, 1957]. A British agent is assigned to track down one Otto Berger, who is rumored to have escaped Hitler's bunker during the last days of the Third Reich with a fortune in gold.

Rachel Ames is one of the three or four most important female practitioners of the modern spy thriller. An Englishwoman, she married a World War II British Army intelligence officer and later served in several "hot" posts in Eastern Europe as a journalist. Familiar with the intrigue of post-war Vienna, she was also on the scene during the 1956 Hungarian revolt. A devotee of realism, Gainham injected Ambler-like realism into her stories, trying to make them as close as possible to the real-life workings of various intelligence services she had become familiar with.

519. ___. *The Cold, Dark Night.* By Sarah Gainham, pseud. New York: Walker, 1961. Agents of various nationalities attempt to hinder the workings of a Big Power conference in 1954 Berlin.

520. ___. *Maculan's Daughter.* By Sarah Gainham, pseud. New York: Putnam's, 1974. A British businessman marries the boss's daughter to get at military secrets. When he dies, his records raise sufficient doubt that an agent posing as the company lawyer is called upon to unravel the threads of treason.

521. ___. *Night Falls on the City.* By Sarah Gainham, pseud. New York: Holt, 1967. Beautiful actress Julia Homburg must play her most challenging role in hiding her Jewish husband Franz from the Gestapo in wartime Vienna.

522. ___. *The Silent Hostage.* By Sarah Gainham, pseud. New York: Dutton, 1960. Agents must rescue a hostage held on the Adriatic coast of Yugoslavia.

523. ___. *The Stone Roses.* By Sarah Gainham, pseud. New York: Dutton, 1959. A Russian villainess attempts to prevent the escape of two defectors from Prague during the time of the Communist takeover in 1948.

524. ___. *Time Right Deadly.* By Sarah Gainham, pseud. New York: Walker, 1961. An elderly agent named Herr Mollnar solves the murder of a British journalist, who was found dead in the Russian Zone of Vienna in the early 1950s.

525. Amis, Kingsley. *The Anti-Death League.* New York: Harcourt, 1966. The noted satirist of *Lucky Jim* (1954) produced a witty examination of Bond's credentials, character, and adventures in *The James Bond Dossier* (London: Cape, 1965). Examines "Operation Apollo," a scheme which will visit death in a grisly manner on randomly selected Red Chinese.

526. ___. *Colonel Sun.* By Robert Markham, pseud. New York: Harper, 1968. Sequel to Fleming's Bond series; "M" is captured by Colonel Sun of the People's Liberation Army of China and held prisoner in Greece. 007 is sent to the rescue.

527. Andersch, Alfred. *The Redhead.* Trans. from the German. New York: Pantheon, 1961. Fleeing to Venice from her husband, a German woman becomes involved in a dangerous intrigue between agents of East and West.

528. Anderson, Jack. *Zero Time.* New York: Zebra, 1990. Noted investigative reporter Anderson's tale features an incredible plot to destroy America—straight from the Ayatollah Khomeini's deathbed.

529. Anderson, James. *The Abolition of Death.* New York: Walker, 1975. British agents locate within an Iron Curtain country a scientist, who has discovered an age-enhancing drug, and smuggle him out to the West.

530. ___. *The Alpha List.* New York: Walker, 1973. Agents must locate the persons listed on a mysterious document.

531. ___. *Assassin.* New York: Simon & Schuster, 1970. Awaiting execution in a Middle East jail, a man is offered his freedom if he will kill a head of state; to ensure his success and provide inspiration, the nasties give him an injection which will kill him in three months unless he returns to them for the antidote.

532. Anderson, John R. L. *Death in the Desert.* New York: Stein & Day, 1977. In Africa, Col. Peter Blair discovers a plot to monopolize the world's power sources.

533. Anderson, Patrick. *The President's Mistress.* New York: Simon & Schuster, 1976. A brother seeks to learn about his sister's death, only to find that she was on intimate terms with the President and under surveillance by various US government agents.

534. Andrews, Shelly. *Group Seven.* Mitcham, Eng.: Maiden & Budge, 1961. German underwater commandos, known as K-Men, attempt to sabotage Allied ships in the harbors of the Low Countries late in World War II. *y

535. Andreyev, Vladimir, pseud. *Gamailes, and Other Tales from Stalin's Russia.* Trans. from the Russian. Chicago: Regnery, 1963. The author, a defected KGB officer in real life, tells six tales of state suppression in pre-war Russia. *

536. Andric, Ivo. *Bridge on the Drina.* New York: Macmillan, 1959. During World War II, Yugoslav partisans must take out a vital German-held bridge in order to prevent the moving up of massive numbers of German troop reinforcements. Readers might want to compare this with Alistair MacLean's *Force 10 From Navarone.*

537. Angus, Sylvia. *Death of a Hittite.* New York: Macmillan, 1969. If David Gain, a newspaperman on assignment to cover an ancient dig in Turkey, had not deplaned at Athens, he would not have become a marked man when he reached intrigue-rich Istanbul.

538. Annesley, Michael. *An Agent Intervenes.* London: Paul, 1944. Lawnie Fenton and his colleagues in the SIS look into a Nazi scheme which could prove immensely embarrassing to the Allied offensive. *y
    Annesley penned three pre-war spy thrillers (see Part 1) which contained only a bit of realism mixed with much derring-do. During the war, his SIS character Fenton took on the Abwehr in these additional tales:

539. ___. *Spies Abounding.* London: Paul, 1945. *y

540. ___. *Spies against the Reich.* London: Paul, 1940. *y

541. ___. *Spy Corner.* London: Paul, 1948. Fenton and his colleagues turn their attention to fighting the Cold War against Russia. *y

542. ___. *Spy Counter-Spy.* London: Paul, 1948. **y*

543. ___. *Spy Island.* London: Paul, 1950. **y*

544. ___. *Suicide Spies.* London: Paul, 1944. **y*

545. ___. *They Won't Lie Down.* London: Paul, 1947. **y*

546. ___. *Unknown Agent.* London: Paul, 1940. **y*

Anthony, Evelyn, pseud. *See* Ward-Thomas, Evelyn B. P.

547. Appel, Benjamin. *Fortress in the Rice.* Indianapolis: Bobbs-Merrill, 1952. After the 1942 fall of Bataan, David McVay fights on as a guerrilla in the Philippines. **y*

548. Appleby, John. *Secret Mountains.* New York: Washburn, 1957. Agents of the East and West intrigue in the tiny country of Andorra, high in the Pyrenees. **y*

549. Archer, Charles S. *Hankow Return.* Boston: Houghton, 1941. Disgusted with the Chinese war, a US aerial mercenary is on his way home when events force him to return to the battle. **y*

550. Archer, Jeffrey. *Honor among Thieves.* New York: HarperCollins, 1993. Oxford-educated Archer has been distinguished in other arenas besides the mystery thriller; he has been a world-class sprinter, the youngest member of the House of Commons (1969) and was elevated to the House of Lords in 1992. This espionage thriller features Saddam Hussein, bristling with humiliation after the Gulf War débâcle and eager for revenge: the plot calls for a President Clinton look-alike, $100 million in cash, a Mafia boss—and the Declaration of Independence.

551. Arden, William. *Deadly Legacy.* New York: Dodd, 1973. Industrial spy Kane Jackson must solve several murders perpetuated by nasties who are taking over the component manufacturers of a rotary engine which is better than the Wankel of his employer.

552. Ardies, Tom. *Kosygin Is Coming.* Garden City, NY: Doubleday, 1973. Filmed as *Russian Roulette* in 1975, a brash, low-level agent named Charlie Sparrow is given the assignment of kidnapping a Latvian fanatic before the Soviet premier's visit to Vancouver. Sparrow also figures in two other Ardies novels. A former special assistant to the governor of Guam in the mid-sixties, Ardies turned to full-time writing and has shown, according to the authors of *Spy Fiction: A Connoisseur's Guide* (1990), an adroitness in creating colorful characters and even parodying his own plots.

553. ___. *In a Lady's Service.* Garden City, NY: Doubleday, 1976. In another bawdy, punning thriller featuring high-speed chases, double crosses, and murder, cowardly soldier-of-fortune "Slick" Buchanan is in the Mexican mountains in search of a ointment compound that cures everything. A third Ardies novel is:

554. ___. *Palm Springs.* Garden City, NY: Doubleday, 1976.

555. ___. *Pandemic.* Garden City, NY: Doubleday, 1973. Counterespionage agents look into the matter of a rich American who is preparing for an upcoming disaster by, among other things, seducing one leading female per month.

556. ___. *Their Man in the White House.* Garden City, NY: Doubleday, 1971. A free-lance journalist believes that he has uncovered a foreign plot to gain control of the President of the United States.

557. ___. *This Suitcase is Going to Explode.* Garden City, NY: Doubleday, 1973. Atomic bombs have been hidden around America in suitcases as part of a massive blackmail plot; agents of the Washington based agency known as ASPIRE must hunt them down. *

558. Ardman, Harvey. *Endgame.* New York: Avon, 1975. Three men and a woman fight for their lives and nations amongst Arab oil sheiks, atomic spies, and counterespionage agents. *P*

559. Arent, Arthur. *Gravedigger's Funeral.* New York: Grossman, 1967. An American playwright is off to West Germany to find an older brother, but a neo-Nazi group there does not want him to succeed. *

560. ___. *The Laying on of Hands.* Boston: Little, 1970. Similar to the previous entry. Fergus John and a friend set out to locate his parents and run smack into Israeli agents, who are hunting a former Nazi concentration camp doctor. Flying on to Vienna from New York, they learn about ODESSA, that group of ex-SS nasties about which Frederick Forsyth writes so well in *The Odessa File.*

561. Aricha, Amos. *The Flying Camel.* New York: Dutton, 1987. [Published in England as *Spymaster.* London: Allen, 1987]. Unassuming Daniel Kottler is a deep-cover CIA assassin who works for a New York law firm that does business in the Middle East. His current assignment is to kill the prominent Arab who,
his superiors say, is responsible for the Beirut massacre of US Marines.

562. ___. *Hour of the Clown.* New York: Signet, 1981. Aricha, who has had solo exhibitions of his paintings, is a former chief superintendent of the Israeli Police Force. A double agent is the key to a Soviet-backed terrorist plot to murder fifteen leading Americans. *P*

563. ___ and Eli Landau. *The Phoenix.* New York: Signet, 1979. Shadowy Middle East power figures contract with a professional killer, codenamed "the Phoenix," to make a $3 million hit on Moshe Dayan; the murder is calculated to destroy the Egyptian-Israeli Camp David Accords. *P*

Armstrong, Anthony, pseud. *See* Willis, Anthony A.

564. Armstrong, Campbell. *Agents of Darkness.* New York: Harcourt, 1991. An obscure cleaning woman dies and sets in motion an investigation that takes Charlie Galloway, burn-out LA cop, all the way to the White House and beyond to a vast international network of conspiracies.

565. ___. *Jig.* New York: Morrow, 1987. "Jig the Dancer" is the IRA's top assassin—so named because of his deftness in killing; he is in America to retrieve $10 million raised by the IRA, but Inspector Pagan of British counterintelligence is on his trail.

566. ___. *Mambo.* New York: Harper & Row, 1990. In this third novel of the trilogy featuring Inspector Pagan of Scotland Yard, a plot hatched by a West German terrorist known as "The Claw" seeks to unseat Castro in Cuba with the help of a hijacked nuclear missile. Two more:

567. ___. *Concert of Ghosts.* New York: HarperCollins, 1993.

568. ___. *White Light.* New York: Morrow, 1988.

569. Arnold, Elliott. *Code of Conduct.* New York: Scribner's, 1970. East German agent Wilhelm Kern and North Korean Army operative Chung catch and interrogate NSA official Quade, during which drilling they learn that the US spy ship *Pueblo* was set up for capture in 1968 in order that America could provide false information to the Communists.

570. ___. *The Commandos.* New York: Duell, Sloan & Pearce, 1942. Examines the training and deployment of British clandestine military groups for and against Norwegian targets early in World War II. *y

571. ___. *A Night of Watching.* New York: Scribner's, 1967. In 1943 a German informs the head of the Danish underground that 8,000 Jews will be rounded up on Yom Kippur for transport to concentration camps; acting quickly, the underground smuggles the bulk of the appointed to safety. *y

572. ___. *Proving Ground.* New York: Scribner's, 1973. An American-born Albanian partisan and his band come upon the wreckage of a US C-47 downed while transporting Yugoslav wounded to hospital; gallantly the guerrillas assist the survivors to elude capture by the Nazis. *y

573. Arnothy, Christine. *The Captive Cardinal.* Trans. from the French. Garden City, NY: Doubleday, 1964. When in 1976 the entire world is Communist except for England, Canada, and the United States, a number of Americans at the Budapest consulate devise a plan to free a Catholic Cardinal who has been a volunteer prisoner there for twenty years. *y

574. Arvay, Harry. *Operation Kuwait.* New York: Bantam, 1975. Introduces a new paperback team from the Israeli Security Branch which here attempts to break up a terrorist skyjack training encampment in the desert. P

575. ___. *The Piraeus Plot.* New York: Bantam, 1975. Israeli agents work to foil a plot against Yasser Arafat. P Three others in this series are:

576. ___. *Eleven Bullets for Mohammed.* New York: Bantam, 1975. P

577. ___. *The Meirovitz Plan.* London: Corgi, 1975. P

578. ___. *The Moscow Intercept.* New York: Bantam, 1975. P

579. Ash, William. *Ride a Paper Tiger.* New York: Walker, 1969. When Kyle Brandeis flees to a small South African nation, he immediately becomes involved with espionage and guerrillas.

580. ___. *Take-Off.* New York: Walker, 1970. While searching for a publisher to print the prose of his revolutionary friend Ortiz, Kyle Brandeis

becomes involved with financiers and arms merchants and has to play the FBI off against the CIA in order to ensure his friend's safety.

Ashe, Gordon, pseud. *See* Creasey, John

581. Ashford, Jeffrey. *A Conflict of Interest.* New York: St. Martin's, 1990. In the manner of Ambler, a quiet, ordinary civil servant named Bowles, whose work for HMG is routine, finds himself in a conflict of interest between duty and doing the right thing. A recent Ashford mystery:

582. ___. *Deadly Reunion.* New York: St. Martins, 1992.

583. Asprey, Robert B. *Operation Prophet.* Garden City, NY: Doubleday, 1977. American intelligence suspects that the defecting Soviet Nobel laureate Nikolai Kubiatshev may be a KGB imposter and asks top agent "Echo" to locate the real Kubiatshev.

584. Astrup, Helen and B. L. Jacot. *Oslo Intrigue.* New York: McGraw-Hill, 1954. Norwegian underground fighters battle the Gestapo tyranny during World War II. **y*

585. Atkinson, Hugh. *The Man in the Middle.* New York: Putnam's, 1973. A penniless interpreter is pitted against the oil interests of Russia and the Arabs; when he translated secret documents, he can no longer be permitted to live. *

Atlee, Philip, pseud. *See* Phillips James Atlee

586. Atwater, James D. *Time Bomb.* New York: Viking, 1977. A World War II demolitions expert, David Thomas begins to lose his nerve under stress of a stepped up IRA bombing attack on London and the potential disaster in his challenge to terrorist Patrick Reilly to build a bomb which cannot be defused. *

August, John, pseud. *See* DeVoto, Bernard A.

587. Avallone, Michael A., Jr. *Assassins Don't Die in Bed.* New York: Signet, 1968. Like Upton Sinclair's Lanny Budd series, Ed Noon is the President's "private spy," who here plays red herring to a killer. *P*
     This creator of the famous Ed Noon detective series has spawned hundreds of books and published thousands of pieces altogether in every conceivable genre—indeed, he is rightly acknowledged as the "The Fastest Typewriter in the East." Of the almost 40 Noon books, those written during the

seventies show the influence of the Cult of Bond most; in fact, Ed Noon takes his secret-agent instructions from the President alone. Beginning with *The Man from UNCLE: The Thousand Coffins Affair* (New York: Ace, 1965), he produced several novels that would form the basis of that popular series (the next year he added Napoleon Solo's female counterpart to the series title). A stonemason's son, born in 1924 as one of 17 siblings whose parents were ruined in the Depression, Avallone is one of the world's most frequently read authors with nearly 200 novels written under dozens of pseudonyms. That figure includes three from his days as Nick Carter house author. (See Michael "The Av" Avallone's commentary in CRAFT NOTES.)

588. ___. *The Doomsday Bag.* New York: Signet, 1969. The President's "bagman" is the man who carries the satchel containing nuclear attack codes; when he turns up missing, Noon is commissioned to get him and them back—fast! *P*

589. ___. *The February Doll Murders.* New York: Signet, 1968. Agent Noon tackles a Communist spy ring and its ingenious plan to sabotage the U.N. *P*

590. ___. *The Flower-Covered Corpse.* New York: Signet, 1969. To expose the underground movement which is foiling the youth revolution, Ed Noon takes the ultimate trip into the depths of Greenwich Village. *P*

591. ___. *The Girl from UNCLE: The Birds of a Feather Affair.* New York: Signet, 1966. April Dancer, the Girl from UNCLE, who must rescue a fellow agent from THRUSH. *PH*

592. ___. *The Girl from UNCLE: A Blazing Affair.* New York: Signet, 1966. April travels from Budapest to Johannesburg on the trail of a Fourth Reich organization dedicated to the building of a super race. *PH*

593. ___. *Hawaii Five-O.* New York: Signet, 1968. Steve McGarrett, head of the islands' special police force, is kidnapped by Communist agent Wo Fat. *P*

594. ___. *Hawaii Five-O: Terror in the Sun.* New York: Signet, 1969. Sequel to the McGarrett series. *P*

595. ___. *The Living Bomb.* New York: Signet, 1963. Agent Ed Noon races a silky assassin to find missing scientist Homer Conroy. *P*

596. ___. *The Man from UNCLE.* New York: Ace, 1965. Introduces readers to the print exploits of TV hero Napoleon Solo and his sidekick Illya Kuryakin, agents of the United Network Command for Law Enforcement, as they seek a deadly new plague weapon developed by a band of international scum known as THRUSH [Technological Hierarchy for the Removal of Undesirables and the Subjugation of Humanity].

597. ___. *Missing.* New York: Signet, 1969. The President-elect has disappeared (not an Ed Noon caper, however). *P* Other Ed Noon titles include:

598. ___. *The Alarming Clock.* New York: Curtis, 1972. *P*

599. ___. *The Bedroom Bolero.* New York: Belmont, 1963. [*The Bolero Murders.* London: Hale, 1972]. *P*

600. ___. *The Case of the Bouncing Betty.* New York: Ace, 1957. *P*

601. ___. *The Case of the Violent Virgin.* New York: Ace, 1957. *P*

602. ___. *Charlie Chan and the Curse of the Dragon Queen.* Los Angeles: Pinnacle, 1981. *P*

603. ___. *The Crazy Mixed-Up Corpse.* New York: Fawcett, 1957. *P*

604. ___. *Dead Game.* New York: Holt, 1954. *P*

605. ___. *The Fat Death.* New York: Curtis, 1972. *P*

606. ___. *London, Bloody London.* New York: Curtis, 1972. [*Ed Noon in London.* London: Hale, 1974]. *P*

607. ___. *Lust Is No Lady.* New York: Belmont, 1964. [*The Brutal Knock.* London: Hale, 1972]. *P*

608. ___. *The Man from UNCLE: The Thousand Coffins Affair.* New York: Ace, 1965. *PH*

609. ___. *Meanwhile Back at the Morgue.* New York: Fawcett, 1960. *P*

610. ___. *The Spitting Image.* New York: Holt, 1953. *P*

611. ___. *The Tall Dolores.* New York: Holt, 1953. *P*

612. ___. *There Is Something about a Dame.* New York: Belmont, 1963. *P*

613. ___. *Violence in Velvet.* New York: Signet, 1956. *P*

614. ___. *The Voodoo Murders.* New York: Fawcett, 1957. *P* Avallone tales under the Nick Carter pseudonym include:

615. _____. *China Doll.* By Nick Carter, house pseud. New York: Award, 1969. In China on a hush-hush mission, Carter finds himself the first white man in the "Forbidden City" of Peking. *P*

616. _____. *Saigon.* By Nick Carter, house pseud. New York: Award, 1970. The black depths of the Indochina underworld forms the background of N-3's attempt to halt a mastermind from wreaking destruction on the many Americans present in that carefree wartime city. *P* One other:

617. ___. *Run, Spy, Run.* By Nick Carter, house pseud. New York: Award, 1964.

618. Ayer, Frederick. *The Man in the Mirror.* Chicago: Regnery, 1965. The President's special assistant is kidnapped by the Reds, who have substituted a double for him; all of those who come upon the secret are also eliminated. *

619. ___. *Where No Flags Fly.* Chicago: Regnery, 1961. A refugee scientist agrees to go behind the Iron Curtain to find out for American Intelligence when the Soviets will launch their missile attack on the United States. *

B

620. Bachmann, Lawrence P. *The Bitter Lake.* Boston: Little, 1970. A "guest" aboard a freighter stranded in the Suez Canal during the Six Day War of 1967 is busy gathering data for British Intelligence. *

621. Backus, Jean L. *Fellow Traveler.* By David Montross, pseud. Garden City, NY: Doubleday, 1965. An American agent tries to protect a young girl while on a dangerous Mediterranean cruise.

622. ___. *Traitor's Wife.* By David Montross, pseud. Garden City, NY: Doubleday, 1962. Della Borden, a Berkeley, California, housewife, meets a Communist agent who helps her join her defecting scientist husband in Moscow.

623. ___. *Troika.* By David Montross, pseud. Garden City, NY: Doubleday, 1963. A KGB agent attempts to spirit a Russian girl into the home of a US Army major.

624. Baddock, James. *The Dutch Caper.* New York: Walker, 1990. [*The Radar Job.* London: Malvern, 1986]. Likened to Higgins, Baddock introduces two series characters—Royal Marine Commando Captain Alan Cormack and RAF Flight Lieutenant Tony Woodward—whose mission is to work with the Dutch Resistance in stealing a German bomber with the latest radar aboard.

625. ___. *The Faust Conspiracy.* New York: Walker, 1989. Late in the war Hitler authorizes Operation Faust, an assassination attempt against the King, to be carried out by SS Major Karl Vogel; however, Admiral Canaris of the Abwehr sends his own man to London to stop Vogel.

626. ___. *Piccolo.* New York: Walker, 1992. Piccolo is the codename of a top-secret project involving nuclear submarines. Inspector Steven Redmond of the Yard's Special Branch is assigned to investigate the apparent suicides of computer experts working on the project. One more:

627. ___. *Emerald.* New York: Walker, 1991.

628. Bagley, Desmond. *The Enemy.* Garden City, NY: Doubleday, 1978. SIS agent Malcolm Jaggard searches for a missing genetic researcher who is the father of his girlfriend. *

Favoring action-adventure over espionage, Bagley, who died in 1983, spent time in Africa and wrote for the *Rand Daily Mail* in Johannesburg in the early sixties.

629. ___. *The Freedom Trap.* Garden City, NY: Doubleday, 1972. A counterintelligence agent who has been sentenced to prison is freed along with a Soviet spy; the plan to tail the Russian to the source of some secret goodies is airtight—until someone betrays it. *

630. ___. *The Golden Keel.* Garden City, NY: Doubleday, 1964. Operatives uncover Mussolini's missing treasure and plan to smuggle it out of Italy. *

631. ___. *High Citadel.* Garden City, NY: Doubleday, 1965. When Communist insurgents force down the plane of a South American president, the survivors must hold off guerrilla attacks with improvised weapons. *

632. ___. *Running Blind.* Garden City, NY: Doubleday, 1971. Someone is trying to kill agent Alan Stewart before he can deliver a secret electronic unit to an unknown pickup in Iceland. *

633. ___. *The Spoilers.* Garden City, NY: Doubleday, 1968. The father and doctor of a dead girl become involved in intrigue as they seek the source of Middle East drugs and the killer. *

634. ___. *The Tightrope Men.* Garden City, NY: Doubleday, 1973. Giles Denison agrees to serve as a decoy scientist while British agents find some secret papers which will reveal how laser beams can be projected by X rays. *

635. ___. *Windfall.* New York: Summit, 1982. The action moves from the West Coast to England to Kenya in this thriller about a p.i. conducting his own investigation surrounding the missing son of a South African client.

636. ___. *Wyatt's Hurricane.* Garden City, NY: Doubleday, 1966. As a tropical storm flashes down on a Caribbean vacationland, only one man can save the inhabitants from the winds and a pending revolution. * Three other Bagley novels are:

637. ___. *Landslide.* Garden City, NY: Doubleday, 1967.

638. ___. *The Vivero Letter.* Garden City, NY: Doubleday, 1968.

639. ___. *The Snow Tiger.* Garden City, NY: Doubleday, 1975.

640. Bahr, Jerome. *Holes in the Wall.* New York: McKay, 1970. A State Department official is captured by the East Germans for spying; an attempt to secure his release leads to a tank confrontation at the Berlin Wall. *

641. Bailey, Anthony. *Making Progress.* New York: Dial, 1959. Vacationing at a Swiss resort, Englishman Slater meets an agent from an Arab country and is offered a secret mission to Poland, which a friend from SIS subsequently asks him not to undertake. *

642. Baker, Charlotte. *House of the Roses.* New York: Dutton, 1942. Nazi spies are involved with buried treasure in a Mexico City haunted house where a mysterious Austrian has died. *

643. Baker, Elliott. *Pocock & Pitt.* New York: Putnam's, 1971. A spy farce in which the bored hero, Wendell Pocock, ditches his family and emerges as the superspy Winston Pitt. The Jekyll and Hyde of espionage. *H*

644. Baker, Ivon. *Grave Doubt.* New York: McKay, 1973. The Heinkel aircraft was another salvage job; when the grave of a Luftwaffe airman is opened, yesterday's question becomes today's murder—with international complications. *

645. Baker, Peter. *A Killing Affair.* Boston: Houghton, 1971. When a female British attaché in Geneva falls in love with a Communist double agent, he obtains secret data from her; outraged, she determines to get it back.

646. Baker, W. Howard. *The Rape of Berlin.* New York: Prestige, 1965. OSS agent Richard Quintain is sent to Berlin in April 1945 to beat the rampaging Russians and the NKVD to a German military secret. *P* Other Richard Quintain tales include:

647. ___. *Destination Dieppe.* London: Mayflower, 1965. *P*

648. ___. *Drums of the Dark Gods.* London: Mayflower, 1966. *P*

649. ___. *The Judas Diary.* New York: Lancer, 1968. *P*

650. ___. *Night of the Wolf.* New York: Lancer, 1967. *P*

651. ___. *No Place for Strangers.* London: Consul, 1965. *P*

652. ___. *Strike North.* New York: Lancer, 1968. *P*

653. ___. *Unfriendly Persuasion.* London: Consul, 1964. *P* Besides Quintain, Baker wrote:

654. ___. *Secret Agent: Departure Deferred.* New York: Macfadden, 1965. Introduces readers to the print exploits of British SIS agent John Drake. As portrayed by Patrick McGoohan in the British made series, *Secret Agent* appeared in the United States as a summer replacement then became a regular network offering in the fall of 1965, opening the way for a large number of

English productions, including the famous "Avengers." *P* Two other Drake tales by this writer are:

655.   ___. *Secret Agent: The Exterminator.* New York: Macfadden, 1966. *P*

656.   ___. *Secret Agent: Storm over Rockall.* New York: Macfadden, 1966. *P*

657. Baker, William A. H. *The Man Who Knew Too Much.* London: Amalgamated, 1955. On vacation in Morocco, an American couple meet a British couple and a mysterious, dying Frenchman who details a London assassination conspiracy; the daughter of the Americans is kidnapped by the Britishers, who turn out to be double agents, and the Yanks move on to Britain to recover the little girl and halt the pending murders. This much-used title was originally released as a 1934 Hitchcock film from a script by Charles Bennett and D. B. Wyndham-Lewis. **y*

Baldwin, Alex, pseud. *See* Butterworth, W. E. [William Edmund III]

Ballard, K. G., pseud. *See* Roth, Holly

658. Ballard, Willis T. *The Spy Catchers.* By Neil MacNeil, pseud. Greenwich, CT: Fawcett, 1963. An anthology of stories chosen to reflect a theme of counterespionage. *P* See also* Carter, Nick (1047, 1112).

659. Ballinger, Bill S. *Beacon in the Night.* New York: Harper & Row, 1959. A large number of criminal agents seek to obtain a map to Balkan oil fields. ***

660.   ___. *The Carrion Eaters.* New York: Putnam's, 1971. An international band of nasties is caught with its victims in a bloody war between Moslems and Hindus on India's Northwest Frontier.

661.   ___. *The Chinese Mask.* New York: Signet, 1965. CIA agent Joaquin Hawks must rescue three scientists held in a Red Chinese prison fortress. *P*

662.   ___. *The Spy at Angkor Wat.* New York: Putnam's, 1965. Hawks is sent to Cambodia to uncover a mysterious plot emanating from the ruins of an ancient civilization.

663. ___. *The Spy in Bangkok.* New York: Signet, 1965. Hawks is detailed to reclaim a cache of stolen US nuclear arms before they can be sold to the Red Chinese. *P*

664. ___. *The Spy in the Java Sea.* New York: Putnam's, 1965. All of his extraordinary linguistic skill, his strength, and his mastery of disguise come into play as agent Hawks strives to locate a computer expert in Djakarta and get him to repair a crippled submarine in the Java Sea before the Communists discover its whereabouts.

665. ___. *The Spy in the Jungle.* New York: Putnam's, 1965. Hawks battles Communist guerrillas in the jungles of Laos.

666. Bamford, James. *The Puzzle Palace: A Report on America's Most Secret Agency.* New York: Penguin, 1983.

667. Banks, Carolyn. *The Darkroom.* New York: Viking, 1980. When Thomas Holland disappears and his family is murdered, CIA agent Al Amatucci is ordered to ensure that no connection exists between the agency and Holland, once an unwilling subject of its drug experiments.

668. Bar-Zohar, Michael. *The Secret List of Heinrich Roehm.* By Michael Barak, pseud. New York: Morrow, 1976. Dr. Michael Bar-Zohar comes to espionage writing with military and writing credentials; in fact, he was a member of Israeli's elite Air Force Intelligence and Paratroopers, holds a doctorate from the University of Paris, and authored several nonfiction works, including the 1964 bestseller *Suez-Ultra Secret*, an account of the 1956 Sinai campaign—in which he saw service as well as the 1967 Six-Day War. In this novel Lt. Col. Joe Gonan of Air Force Intelligence endures great physical torture to discover the Arab plot which resulted in the Yom Kippur Arab-Israeli conflict.

669. ___. *The Deadly Document.* New York: Delacorte, 1980. A graduate student working in the Public Records Office in London comes across a 1910 document marked "classified" and takes it home to show to his girlfriend; when he is murdered by the KGB shortly after, the CIA must send its best agent to find her and the document.

670. ___. *Double Cross.* By Michael Barak, pseud. New York: Signet, 1981. The Jewish state depends upon finding and stopping Alfred Mueller, trained assassin and terrorist, whose plan is to kill a single important man in Jerusalem. *P*

671. ___. *The Devil's Spy.* By Michael Hastings, pseud. New York: Scribner's, 1988. Based on the life and espionage adventures of Sarah Aaronsohn, a woman who set up NILI, the Jewish espionage network in Palestine during WW I and who paid with her life by spying on the Turks for the British. The heroine of this fictional account is Ruth Mendelson, who is convinced that helping the British at war with the Ottoman Empire may lead to a Jewish state; she reports on the activities of Turkish officers to Saul Donsky, a former Russian revolutionary, now a Zionist, working for British Intelligence.

672. ___. *The Unknown Soldier.* By Michael Hastings, pseud. New York: Macmillan, 1986. A CIA analyst wants to halt the burial of an "unknown soldier" at Arlington after the Vietnam conflict when his own investigation turns up three possibilities for the dead soldier's fate: he may have been "fragged" by his own men, he may have been a hero—or he may have been a traitor. Others:

673. ___. *Brothers.* By Michael Barak, pseud. New York: Fawcett, 1992.

674. ___. *Enigma.* By Michael Barak, pseud. New York: Morrow, 1978.

675. ___. *The Phantom Conspiracy.* By Michael Barak, pseud. New York: Morrow, 1980.

676. ___. *The Spy Who Died Twice.* Boston: Houghton, 1975.

677. ___. *A Spy in Winter.* By Michael Hastings, pseud. New York: Macmillan, 1984.

678. ___. *The Third Truth.* By Michael Hastings, pseud. London: Hodder & Stoughton, 1973.

Barak, Michael, pseud. *See* Bar-Zohar, Michael

Bannerman, David, pseud. *See* Hagberg, David

679. Barber, Rowland. *The Midnighters.* New York: Crown, 1970. Based on the memoirs of Jewish hero Martin Allen Ribakof, this is a "nonfiction novel" which shows how an "air force" was smuggled into Israel in 1948.

680. Bark, Conrad Voss. *See the Living Crocodiles.* New York: Walker, 1968. The British government's top scientific advisor for defense disappears

just before an important Cabinet meeting and the Prime Minister's top security man, William Holmes, is ordered to locate him. *

681. ___. *The Shepherd File.* New York: Dutton, 1966. Assigned to investigate an unusual chemical factory in the Libyan desert, one of MI-5's best agents is found dead in the Thames River.

682. Barker, Albert. *The Apollo Legacy.* New York: Award, 1971. Actor-turned-agent Reefe King is drawn into a conspiracy involving a group of nasties out to damage America's moon-landing missions. *P*

683. ___. *The Gift from Berlin.* New York: Award, 1969. A bizarre drug is twisting American movie stars into mindless sex machines and agent Reefe King is called upon to learn who is causing this frightful problem. *P*

684. Barker, Dudley. *Arafat Is Next!* By Lionel Black, pseud. New York: Stein & Day, 1975. When an innocent bystander is killed by a Palestinian terrorist bomb, his brothers vow to kill Arafat in vengeance.

685. ___. *The Life and Death of Peter Wade.* By Lionel Black, pseud. New York: Stein & Day, 1974. Johnny Trott is assigned to write a biography of a recently deceased actor whose life was, in fact, a bore. Not so disappointing is the life of Trott's ex-wife, the actor's agent, who reveals a link with a new African nation where East-West power plays are in motion.

686. Barker, Joseph. *Fourth at Junction.* New York: St. Martin's, 1980. Enemy agents lock into an undercover battle over a plot to kill the President of the United States when he visits Britain.

687. Barlay, Stephen. *In the Company of Spies.* New York: Summit, 1981. The CIA versus the KGB against the historic backdrop of the Cuban Missile Crisis of 1962.

688. Barley, Rex. *Cross to Bear Proudly.* New York: Signet, 1963. A girl seeks romance and ends up battling the Gestapo as a member of the French Resistance during World War II. *Py*

689. Baron, Stanley W. *All My Enemies.* New York: Ballantine, 1953. A Soviet agent is sent to New York City on a secret mission, but botches everything up by falling in love with the manicurist at his hotel. *PH*

Barrington, Maurice, pseud. *See* Brogan, Denis W.

690. Barron, Donald G. *The Man Who Was There*. New York: Atheneum, 1969. The Canfield Institute establishes ideological links in nonaligned nations as a cover for its espionage operations; a chance meeting with an old friend in Beirut starts its top operative, teacher Michael Locke, on a dangerous Middle East chase.

691. ___. *The Zilov Bombs*. New York: Norton, 1963. Depicts the growing effectiveness of a resistance group in a futuristic Britain occupied by the Soviets.

692. Bartholomew, Cecilia. *The Risk*. Garden City, NY: Doubleday, 1958. A family is torn apart when the father is declared a security risk during the McCarthy era. *y

693. Barton, Donald R. *Once in Aleppo*. New York: Scribner's, 1955. A young American vice-counsel in Turaq becomes involved with two female spies—one American and one Russian.

694. Bartram, George. *The Aelian Fragment*. New York: Putnam's, 1976. A book collector purchases a manuscript in a Turkish shop only to discover it is badly wanted by the KGB due to its containing the names of prisoners held in Siberian prisons.

695. ___. *A Job Abroad*. New York: Macmillan, 1975. Off overseas to conduct research for a book, a middle-aged US college professor is asked to undertake a one-time spy job. One more:

696. ___. *Under the Freeze*. New York: Pinnacle, 1984. *P*

697. Barwick, James. *The Hangman's Crusade*. New York: Coward-McCann, 1981. After Franklin D. Roosevelt, Winston Churchill, and the Pope refuse to help, Reinhard Heydrich elects to mount his own coup against Hitler.

698. ___. *Shadow of the Wolf*. New York: Coward-McCann, 1979. Hauptmann Alfred Horn crash lands in Scotland with Rudolf Hess early in World War II and escapes to carry a peace mission to the Americans. *

699. Basile, Gloria Vitanza. *Global 2000: Eye of the Eagle*. New York: Pinnacle, 1983. A nuclear explosion in the Middle East sends the President's trusted advisor, General Brad Lincoln, ex-CIA, to investigate the causes before the world plunges into global genocide. *P*

700. Bass, Ronald. *The Emerald Illusion.* New York: Morrow, 1984. "Emerald" is the codename of the SS's best English spy; he also happens to be MI-5's best German agent. The secret of D-Day hangs in the balance when Emerald feeds the Germans information about a phony invasion exercise that turns out to be the real thing.

701. Battye, Gladys S. *A Light in the Window.* By Margaret Lynn, pseud. Garden City, NY: Doubleday, 1967. In this cross between a romance and a spy thriller, Rosanne seems to be more disturbed about her husband's leaving her for another than she is about his treason.

Bax, Roger, pseud. *See* Winterton, Paul

702. Bayne, Spencer. *Agent Extraordinary.* New York: Dutton, 1942. An American archaeologist in Syria impersonates a missing British agent in order to locate his records and halt Nazi infiltration of that country's government. **y*

703. Beach, Edward L. *Cold is the Sea.* New York: Holt, 1978. Having been sent on a secret mission to the Arctic Ocean, a US nuclear submarine becomes incapacitated while a suspicious Soviet sub lurks in the vicinity. **y*

704. Beare, George. *The Bee Sting Deal.* New York: Harper & Row, 1972. Residents of the island of Jarma are unhappy because their government has entered into a deal with Iran for the construction of a road between the island and the mainland; an investigative-adventurer and his girlfriend seek to get to the bottom of the agreement.

705. ___. *The Bloody Sun at Noon.* Boston: Houghton, 1971. British officials, agents, and expatriates nursing secret pasts become involved in a revolution in an oil rich Middle East sheikdom.

706. Beatty, Elizabeth. *The Jupiter Missile Mystery.* New York: Airmont, 1960. A young secretary at Cape Canaveral is immersed in espionage and kidnapping, eventually going on trial for the abduction of her glamorous roommate. **P*

707. Becher, Ulrich. *The Woodchuck Hunt.* Trans. from the German. New York: Crown, 1977. During World War II an Austrian noble escapes the Gestapo by fleeing on skis into Switzerland.

708. Beck, K. K. *Without a Trace.* New York: Jove, 1988. Sunny Sinclair searches for her ex-lover Alex Markoff, a spy who had been pronounced dead years before.

709. Becker, Stephen W. *The Chinese Bandit.* New York: Random, 1975. Forced to desert, a US Marine becomes a brigand in China during the days just before Mao took over the mainland.

710. ___. *The Last Mandarin.* New York: Random, 1979. Major Jack Burnhan has only a few days of 1949 left to catch a notorious Japanese war criminal called Kanamori in Peking.

Beckingham, Bruce, pseud. *See* Lilley, Peter and Anthony Stansfeld

Beech, Webb. *See* Butterworth, W. E. [William Edmund III]

Beechcroft, William, pseud. *See* Hallstead, William Finn III

711. Beecher, William. *Mayday Man.* McLean, VA: Brassey's, 1990. Two prominent Egyptians, a general and a nuclear physicist, plot to destroy Israel by stealing a Russian plane, arming it with a nuclear device containing stolen plutonium from South Africa, then sending it on a mission against Moscow.

Beeding, Francis, pseud. *See* Palmer, John L. and Hilary Aiden St. George Saunders.

712. Beevor, Antony. *The Faustian Pact.* London: Cape, 1983. Career diplomat David Raynor has been demoted to a desk job with the Friends (British SIS) because of his wife's erratic behavior. When the Prime Minister is kidnapped by a terrorist group calling itself Red Vanguard, Raynor discovers evidence of sabotage that suggests a right-wing conspiracy—by the British Secret Service itself!

713. ___. *For Reasons of State.* New York: Macmillan, 1981. Former British army officer Brooke Hamilton joins an anarchist group that plans to kill a hated South American dictator recuperating at Hamilton's mother's villa in France.

714. Behn, Noel. *The Kremlin Letter.* New York: Simon & Schuster, 1966. A Navy officer is taught all the new espionage techniques and is then sent off to Moscow to recover a message outlining secret agreements for detente between the West and a Politburo faction.

715.   ___. *The Shadowboxer*. New York: Simon & Schuster, 1969. In 1944 Europe a man is so completely the lone wolf agent in disguise that he can successfully smuggle concentration camp prisoners off the Continent.

716.   Behr, Edward. *Getting Even*. New York: Harper & Row, 1980. A French counterintelligence agent is romantically thwarted in his love affair with a Chinese defector by his own government and vows to get even.

717.   Beinhart, Larry. *American Hero*. New York: Pantheon, 1993. Darkly satirical thrust at the Bush Administration as the dying Lee Atwater, Republican campaign genius, entrusts the secret of his re-election scam concerning Desert Storm to Jim Baker.

718.   ___. *Foreign Exchange*. New York: Harmony, 1991. Cynically elegant spoof of the CIA's agents in action.

719.   Bekessy, Jean. *Devil's Agent*. By Hans Habe, pseud. Trans. from the German. New York: Fell, 1958. A satirical tale involving an operative who spies on both the Russians and Americans and who comes to believe it might be a good deal healthier if he can somehow "drop out" of the game. *H*

720.   Belhancourt, T. Ernesto. *Doris Fein: Superspy*. New York: Holiday, 1980. In New York City on vacation, a girl discovers she is under surveillance by mysterious strangers and enlists the aid of a handsome private eye to learn the reason why. *y*

721.   Bellow, Saul. *The Bellarosa Connection*. New York: Penguin, 1989. The Nobel laureate's "entertainment" features an underground anti-Nazi movement and one Billy Rose, its organizer. *P*

722.   Benchley, Nathaniel. *Catch a Falling Spy*. New York: McGraw-Hill, 1963. A funny caper concerning an apparently ordinary young American couple who earn their living spying for the Communist government of Albania. *H*

723.   Bennett, Dorothea. *The Jigsaw Man*. New York: Coward-McCann, 1976. When KGB agent Philip Kimberly learns of a plot to kill him in London, he attempts to defect to the British with the aid of his daughter.

724.   Bennett, Jack. *Ocean Road*. Boston: Little, 1967. A charter fisherman undertakes a British assignment to organize a counter-revolution against a group of Red Chinese-trained Africans who have assassinated a sultan and taken over his island kingdom.

725. Bennett, Ken. *Devil's Current*. Garden City, NY: Doubleday, 1953. Someone does not want a young engineer to reach Egypt where he is to install a hydroelectric plant. *y

726. ___. *Passport for a Renegade*. Garden City, NY: Doubleday, 1955. At the height of the Cold War, agents of Russia and Britain cross swords over a defector.

727. Benson, Eugene P. *The Bulls of Ronda*. London: Methuen, 1977. A Canadian journalist becomes involved in the terrorism of Spain's Basque Separatist movement.

728. Benton, Kenneth. *A Single Monstrous Act*. London: Macmillan, 1976. Left-wing anarchists, led by Professor Thaxton, plan a series of terrible crimes to pave the way for a revolutionary takeover of England; Peter Craig is sent to quash the plot.

729. ___. *Sole Agent*. New York: Walker, 1974. Agent Craig must locate a British girl involved with a left-wing group planning the overthrow of the Portuguese government.

730. ___. *Spy in Chancery*. New York: Walker, 1973. A Russian spy is detected at work in Britain's Rome embassy and agent Craig must ferret out the person's identity. Benton's other fictional works include:

731. ___. *Craig and the Jaguar*. New York: Walker, 1974.

732. ___. *Craig and the Living Dead*. Milan: Mondadori, 1979.

733. ___. *Craig and the Midas Touch*. New York: Walker, 1976.

734. ___. *Craig and the Tunisian Tangle*. New York: Walker, 1975.

735. ___. *Death on the Appian Way*. London: Chatto & Windus, 1974. *HI*

736. ___. *The Red Hen Conspiracy*. New York: Macmillan, 1977.

737. ___. *The Twenty-Fourth Level*. New York: Dodd, 1970.

738. Berent, Mark. *Eagle Station*. New York: Putnam's, 1992. Technothriller author Berent frequently writes about adventure during the Vietnamese conflict between 1960 and 1970. Three more by Berent:

739. ___. *Phantom Leader*. New York: Putnam's, 1991.

740. ___. *Steel Tiger*. New York: Jove, 1990. *P*

741. ___. *Storm Flight*. New York: Putnam's, 1993.

742. Bergamini, David. *The Fleet in the Window*. New York: Simon & Schuster, 1961. A young man becomes a guerrilla fighter and courier after the Japanese invade the Philippines in December 1941. **y*

Bernard, Jay, pseud. *See* Sawkins, Raymond H.

743. Bernard, Joel. *The Man from UNCLE: The Thinking Machine Affair*. New York: Ace, 1970. Napoleon and Illya set out to destroy a machine bent on conquering the world for THRUSH. *PH*

Bernard, Robert, pseud. *See* Martin, Robert B.

744. Bernhardsen, Christian. *The Fight in the Mountains*. Trans. from the Danish. New York: Harcourt, 1968. Two brothers escape from the Gestapo and join the Norwegian resistance in battling the Nazi occupation. **y*

745. Bernau, George. *Promises to Keep*. New York: Warner, 1988. A JFK conspiracy "what-if" with a twist: What if JFK recovered from his wounds in Dallas, stepped down in favor of Lyndon Johnson in 1964, and returns for a second term?

746. Bernstein, Ken. *Intercept*. New York: Coward-McCann, 1971. When a US reconnaissance plane is downed near the Crimean coast, the two surviving crewmen are picked up by the KGB and must begin plotting their escape.

747. ___. *The Senator's Ransom*. New York: Coward-McCann, 1972. A US Senator is kidnapped in Brazil by terrorists who attempt to convince him of their cause's validity while the CIA seeks his release.

748. Berrassi, Mark. *The Thor Option*. New York: Dell, 1980. An African dictator threatens to use a stolen US nuclear missile unless America grants him unlimited foreign aid. *P*

749. Beste, R. Vernon. *The Moonbeams*. New York: Harper & Row, 1962. Agent Maltby is parachuted back into German-occupied France charged with

finding the traitor in his little band of Maquis saboteurs. First published in Britain as *Faith Has No Country.* *y

750. ___. *Next Time I'll Pay My Own Fare.* New York: Simon & Schuster, 1970. A combination spy-detective tale concerning a Scotland Yard sleuth's mission to get a former Nazi out of Spain.

751. ___. *Repeat the Instructions.* New York: Harcourt, 1968. A British civil servant is used as a pawn by the SIS, being ordered to "defect" to the Russians while actually serving as a double agent.

Betteridge, Don, pseud. *See* Newman, Bernard

752. Bickers, Richard T. *Volunteers for Danger.* London: Brown, Watson, 1960. Employing swift boats, British Special Operations officers engage in counterespionage activities in and off North Africa during World War II. *y

753. Bickham, Jack M. *Breakfast at Wimbledon.* New York: St. Martin's, 1991. Ex-tennis pro, former journalist and CIA man Brad Smith is assigned to play Wimbledon because an Irish player may be targeted by IRA killers.

754. ___. *Dropshot.* New York: TOR[†], 1990. When Brad Smith's court nemesis, Al Hesser, is killed, Smith is asked by Washington to check out swank Court College. Smith discovers high-tech espionage involving a computer chip, smuggling and the malodorous presence of the KGB. Other Bickham novels are:

755. ___. *Overhead.* New York: TOR, 1991. The evil KGB assassin, codename Sylvester, is Brad Smith's nemesis once again as he takes another part-time assignment for the CIA.

756. ___. *The Regensburg Legacy.* Garden City, NY: Doubleday, 1980. CIA agent Joe Dugger links several unusual murders to a master plan to establish a Fourth Reich by means of a secret weapon buried in Africa. * Two more:

757. ___. *Ariel.* London: Severn, 1980.

758. ___. *Tiebreaker.* New York: TOR, 1990.

[†]Tom Doherty Associates

759. Bingham, John M. W. (Lord Clanmorris). *The Double Agent.* New York: Dutton, 1968. An Englishman is blackmailed while visiting Moscow into supplying data to the Russians; upon his return home, he tells all to British Intelligence which immediately recruits him for a return mission to the Soviet Union.

Before his Ducane and Brock series, Bingham wrote *Murder Plan Six* (London: Gollancz, 1958), *Night's Black Agent* (London: Gollancz, 1961), and *A Fragment of Fear* (London: Gollancz, 1965). He also wrote *God's Defector* (London: Macmillan, 1976), which was retitled in America as *Ministry of Death* (New York: Walker, 1977).

Before his death in 1988, Bingham added to his espionage series of Ducane and Brock with:

760. ___. *Brock.* London: Gollancz, 1981.

761. ___. *Brock and the Defector.* London: Gollancz, 1982.

762. ___. *Vulture in the Sun.* London: Gollancz, 1977.

763. Binyon, T. J. [Timothy John]. *Swan Song.* Garden City, NY: Doubleday, 1982. An ambitious KGB man embroils a Moscow literature professor, his estranged wife, and the CIA in a plot to further his career by inspiring mass rebellion among the people through a religious cult called White Swan.

764. Bischoff, David. *WarGames.* New York: Dell, 1983. Novelization of the film based on the screenplay by Lawrence Lasker and Walter F. Parkes about a high-school hacker who taps into "Joshua," America's computerized defense system; young David Lightman has no idea that Joshua is playing the game of Global Nuclear Warfare, with him as an opponent, for keeps. *P*

765. Black, Campbell. *Asterisk Destiny.* New York: Morrow, 1978. Project Blue Book, it seems, is Project Whitewash as far as UFO activity is concerned, and two men risk their lives to discover the truth in the Arizona desert.

766. ___. *Brainfire.* New York: Morrow, 1979. An American agent seeks the cause of his brother's death, unaware that he will become entrapped in a plot to slay the President.

767. ___. *Death's Head.* Philadelphia: Lippincott, 1972. As the only witness to his concentration camp atrocities, Gruenwald the Jew is sought by an SS doctor in dying Berlin, 1945. Three more:

768. ___. *Assassins and Victims.* New York: Harper's, 1969.

769. ___. *Letters from the Dead.* New York: Villard, 1985.

770. ___. *Raiders of the Lost Ark.* New York: Ballantine, 1981.

Black, Gavin, pseud. *See* Wynd, Oswald

771. Black, Ian S. *Journey to a Safe Place.* New York: St. Martin's, 1979.
SIS agent Peter Munro must first outwit KGB ace Chikin before a famous Soviet
scientist and his daughter can be helped to defect.

772. ___. *The Man on the Bridge.* New York: St. Martin's, 1976. A
repatriated spy is asked to return to the bridge on the Greek-Albanian border
where he was captured.

Black, Lionel, pseud. *See* Barker, Dudley

773. Blackburn, John. *Broken Boy.* New York: Morrow, 1962. A young
woman found brutally murdered in Britain appears to have been a Soviet spy.

774. ___. *Dead Man Running.* New York: Morrow, 1961. A man must
prove that not only is he no traitor but that he did not murder his wife.

775. ___. *The Gaunt Woman.* New York: Morrow, 1964. Russian defector
Vanin is kidnapped by East German agents and driven back through
Brandenburg Tor in a box marked "radio spare parts."

776. ___. *Packed for Murder.* New York: Morrow, 1964. [*Colonel Bogus*.
(London: Cape, 1964)]. An eccentric old Russian woman is mysteriously
murdered while on a train trip to Edinburgh. Other Gen. Kirk spy tales are:

777. ___. *A Ring of Roses.* London: Cape, 1965. [*A Wreath of Roses*. New
York: Morrow, 1965].

778. ___. *A Scent of New Mown Hay.* London: Secker & Warburg, 1958.
[*The Reluctant Spy*. New York: Morrow, 1958].

779. ___. *A Sour Apple Tree.* London: Secker & Warburg, 1958.

780. Blacker, Irwin R. *The Kilroy Gambit.* Cleveland, OH: World, 1960.
The Russians uncover a "Genops" group in Afghanistan and unless the agency's

agents can reach that remote country in time to cover the situation, it will be exposed and destroyed.

Blacker has taught at the University of Southern California and worked as a writer, producer, and story consultant of television and film.

781. ___. *Search and Destroy.* New York: Random, 1966. Gen. Richard LeGrande, head of GENOPS [General Operations], learns from air reconnaissance photos that Hanoi is building up with installations, bridges, and an airfield in a month's time. Against advice, he decides to send in a GENOPS team—always subject to disavowal by their government if caught—headed by an old West Point classmate to destroy five crucial targets.

782. Blagowidow, George. *Last Train from Berlin.* Garden City, NY: Doubleday, 1977. Having failed on his own to kill Hitler at Berchtesgaden, a traitor is employed by a faction of the Gestapo to do the job on *Der Führer* when his special train reaches Sterbfritz, a town located between two tunnels.

Blair, Eric. *See* Orwell, George, pseud.

Blake, Nicholas, pseud. *See* Day-Lewis, Cecil

Blake, Patrick, pseud. *See* Egleton, Clive

783. Blakenship, William. *Tiger Ten.* New York: Putnam's, 1976. Riley Stone, roughest of General Chennault's Flying Tigers, accepts a British request to swipe a Zero fighter from a Japanese airbase behind the lines in 1942 Burma. *

784. Blankfort, Michael. *The Widow-Makers.* New York: Simon & Schuster, 1946. When Elliot Green is killed on assignment in Lisbon, his three children become unwitting possessors of his fatal secret. *y

Bleeck, Oliver, pseud. *See* Thomas, Ross

785. Block, Thomas H. *Airship Nine.* New York: Putnam's, 1984. After a bizarre electromagnetic disturbance triggers an all-out nuclear war between the US and the USSR, seventeen survivors from the American dirigible *Airship Nine* confront the few remaining survivors from a Soviet motorship at a South Pole station in Antarctica.

786. ___. *Forced Landing.* New York: Coward-McCann, 1983.

787.   ___. *Mayday.* New York: Marek, 1979.

788.   ___. *Orbit.* New York: Coward-McCann, 1982.

789.   ___. *Skyfall.* New York: Jove, 1987. *P*

790.   Blum, Richard H. A. [Hosmer Adams]. *The Mexican Assassin.* By Hartshorne, pseud. New York: Scribner's, 1978. Richard Hosmer Adams Blum would remain one of the most versatile of scholars and humanists writing today even if he had not turned a hand toward espionage fiction. His entry in *Who's Who International* covers a spectacular career in several professions and lists accomplishments that include Stanford Professor of Medicine (also a member of its prestigious Law School), recipient of numerous awards stemming from his service in the Korean War to accomplishments in research on such issues as bio-behavioral research, espionage, surveillance, drug addiction, and numerous public health issues. He has also written for science and poetry journals and authored dozens of texts on contemporary international socio-political concerns. He began publishing fiction with *The Late Lt. Dessin and Other Stories* in 1967, followed by *Death and Festivals* in 1968.

His black-humored collection of short stories *The Medical School* (By G. P. Hosmer, pseud. Chevy Chase, MD: Claycomb, 1988) has been described as a breakthrough of a new kind of science fiction. His first spy novel compares well with Graham Greene's *The Power and the Glory* in theme, tone, and style. CIA agent Barbour, a veteran of agency-sanctioned killings, is sent to a remote section of Mexico to help quash a Soviet-sponsored populist revolution. The Mexican assassin is actually a priest who forsakes the collar for the machine gun as an instrument of social change, and is based on the life and violent death of Fr. Camillo Torres of Columbia. "My effort," writes the author, "is to present the spy novel within the context of actual cultures, including the bureaucratic, with sensitivity to the Janus-like nature of the heroes and villains on both sides . . . The humanity of those involved is not to be ignored."

791.   ___. *Codename Starlight.* By Hartshorne, pseud. London: Hale, 1978. An exciting story line balances out the hard, insightful look at, as the author describes it, the "pointlessly ugly environments in which people on either side of the Iron Curtain work."

792.   ___. *Whisper of Treason.* By Hartshorne, pseud. London: Hale, 1981. The author describes his third espionage venture as being about the "treachery of the bureaucrat." Ben Cornelius arrives in Yugoslavia hoping to purchase icons for his art shop in Oregon, but he discovers his true talents as a spy-agent

when he volunteers to assist a Soviet general's defection from a top-secret military intelligence center.

793. Bobker, Lee R. *Flight of a Dragon.* New York: Morrow, 1981. The second-highest man in China is going to defect, or so the Americans think, and an all-out race to acquire him at any cost commences.

794. ___. *The Unicorn Group.* New York: Morrow, 1979. Years after the establishment of a 25-man intelligence group, it becomes clear that one of seven survivors is eliminating the others.

795. Bocca, Geoffrey. *The Fourth Horseman.* New York: Rawson Wade, 1980. Tagged as a scapegoat for the failures of others in Northern Ireland, cashiered SAS officer "Ginger" Brownlow seeks revenge.

796. Boland, John. *Counterpol in Paris.* New York: Walker, 1965. Kim Smith and his group, who form an answer to INTERPOL, become involved with a megalomaniac French policeman named Mapoix, who seeks power by stealing the crown jewels of France.

797. ___. *The Gentlemen at Large.* New York: Award, 1968. "The Gentlemen" are an unlikely task force of ex-Commando officers in the pay of British Intelligence who, in this outing, work to smash a ruthless Communist spy ring. *P*

798. ___. *The Gentlemen Reform.* New York: Award, 1968. "Operation Jailbreak" has "the Gentlemen" freeing a prisoner from a maximum security British prison. *P*

799. Bolton, Alexander. *Ladies of the Dark: The Lives, Loves, and Daring Exploits of Famous Female Spies.* New York: Monarch, 1961. A series of fictionalized biographies based on fact. *P*

800. Bolton, Melvin. *The Softener.* New York: Watts, 1986. In this first Peter Lawson novel of intrigue, this smooth burglar becomes the subject of a manhunt involving both British and Soviet intelligence agencies. Two more Lawson tales are:

801. ___. *The Offering.* London: Gollancz, 1988.

802. ___. *The Testing.* London: Gollancz, 1987.

803. Bond, Larry. *Cauldron.* New York: Warner, 1993. A futuristic look at a world sharply divided as a result of rampant nationalism after the Soviet Union's collapse. France and Germany are opposed by factions of the old USSR—now about to fall under a neo-Stalinist regime—and the US-Britain backed Eastern European nations, which must now go to war against an attacking Franco-German armored division.

804. ___. *Red Phoenix.* New York: Warner, 1989. A superb storyteller and former naval officer, Bond presents gripping tableaux of war rooms and fighting men—especially his tough-minded commanding general in this tale of a "second" Korean war, one ignited by the son of an aged North Korean dictator and abetted by the aide to a sleazebag Congressman.

805. ___. *Vortex.* New York: Warner, 1991. A white supremacist government takes over when the African National Congress assassinates the entire staff of his predecessor; the subplot involves a Cuban invasion in the midst of the internal chaos.

806. Bond, Raymond T., ed. *Famous Stories of Code and Cipher.* New York: Rinehart, 1947. Sixteen tales ranging from Poe to Agatha Christie. **y*

807. Bonfiglioli, Kyril. *After You with the Pistol.* Garden City, NY: Doubleday, 1980. Charlie Mordecai, a crooked art dealer, marries an heiress who orders him to kill the Queen. *H*

808. Bonnecarrère, Paul and John Hemingway. *Rosebud.* New York: Morrow, 1974. Five girls of wealthy parents are kidnapped and held for ransom aboard the *Rosebud*, a luxury yacht; their captors are PLO terrorists. The film (US, 1975) was directed by Otto Preminger and starred Peter O'Toole and Richard Attenborough. Two more suspense thrillers by Bonnecarrére:

809. ___. *The Golden Triangle.* Trans. Oliver Coburn. Henley-on-Thames, Eng.: Ellis, 1977.

810. ___. *The Lost Victory.* Trans. Abigail Israel. Henley-on-Thames, Eng.: Ellis, 1979.

811. ___. *Ultimatum.* Paris: Fayard, 1975.

812. Bonner, Paul. *SPQR.* New York: Scribner's, 1952. The First Secretary of the American embassy in Rome finds himself hunting a Communist spy. ***

813. Bontly, Thomas. *The Giant's Shadow.* New York: Random, 1988. An American poet who defects to Moscow at the height of the Cold War possesses a ms. that, if smuggled to the West, could end *glasnost.* One more:

814. ___. *Celestial Chess.* New York: Ballantine, 1980. *P*

815. Borden, Mary. *Catspaw.* New York: Longmans, 1950. Published in Britain as *For the Record*, this first person narrative reveals the growing revulsion of a young secretary to a European prince, whose Soviet masters demand he betray his adopted country. *

816. Bornemark, Kjell-Olof. *The Messenger Must Die.* Trans. Laurie Thompson. New York: Dembner, 1986. [*Legat Till en Trolös.* Stockholm: Norstedt, 1982.] Greger Tragg is a freelance writer in Stockholm who is also the intermediary between East German Intelligence and a high-ranking government official known as Alex, but Greger finds himself in great danger as Swedish security starts to close in on him—not only from Swedish security but from Alex and his East German masters.

817. Bosse, M. J. *The Incident at Naha.* New York: Simon & Schuster, 1972. An unscrupulous CIA agent forces a Black scholar to begin sifting clues behind the death of a fellow teacher, a White who may have information on a Mylai-like massacre.

818. Bottome, Phyllis. *Life Line.* Boston: Little, 1946. The SIS persuades a young Eton professor of Austrian background to go to work as a courier in wartime Innsbruck; operating under the cover of confinement in a mental hospital, the Englishman is eventually caught and tortured by the Gestapo. *

819. Boulle, Pierre. *Ears of the Jungle.* Trans. from the French. New York: Vanguard, 1972. The "jungle" is Southeast Asia, but the "ears" belong to the American espionage system that North Vietnam's agents turn to their own advantage.

820. ___. *A Noble Profession.* Trans. from the French. New York: Vanguard, 1961. The author of *Planet of the Apes* and *Bridge on the River Kwai* here entertains us with the story of Cousin, an intellectual writer, who enters the secret service during World War II and grimly achieves his end of becoming a hero.

821. ___. *Not the Glory.* Trans. from the French. New York: Vanguard, 1955. A novelist-journalist who is a decorated veteran of Dunkirk is suspected by MI-5 of being the top Nazi agent in Britain. *

822. Bova, Ben and Bill Pogue. *The Trikon Deception.* New York: TOR, 1992. Sci-fi author Bova and Skylab astronaut Pogue combine skills to render a sci-fi thriller with espionage themes: Trikon is a space station orbiting the earth in 1998, which is doing research that can save the planet from ecological destruction—that is, if Commander Dan Tighe can keep his crew of scientists from sabotaging the mission.

823. Bowen, Elizabeth. *Heat of the Day.* New York: Knopf, 1948. In wartime London, a woman's lover turns out to be a Nazi sympathizer. A British agent, in turn, attempts to bring the two—innocent and guilty alike—to book.

824. Boyer, Bruce H. *The Solstice Caper.* Philadelphia: Lippincott, 1979. A US Army major, who has been assigned in early 1944 to choose the invasion beaches for D-Day, is secretly parachuted into German-held territory for a clandestine meeting with Field Marshal Rommel, who is now plotting against Hitler.

825. Boyington, Gregory "Pappy." *Tonya.* Indianapolis: Bobbs-Merrill, 1960. The real-life leader of the USMC "Black Sheep Squadron" draws on his experience as a "Flying Tiger" to tell us about the nymphomaniac wife of an American pilot who has become involved with a group of aerial mercenaries in Burma at the time of Pearl Harbor.

826. Boyle, Kay. *A Frenchman Must Die.* New York: Simon & Schuster, 1946. After the 1944 Liberation, a former Resistance fighter seeks out a collaborator responsible for the deaths of many innocents in the village of Savoyard. *

827. Boyne, Walter J. and Steven L. Thompson. *The Wild Blue.* New York: Crown, 1986. Saga of six fearless pilots at home, on the job, and in combat.

828. Braddon, Russell. *The Finalist.* New York: Atheneum, 1977. Unless a ransom is paid, terrorists threaten to kill the Queen of England and the winner of this year's Wimbledon men's tennis match.

829. ___. *The White Mouse.* New York: Norton, 1957. French Maquis irregulars battle the Germans in southern France. *

830. Bradshaw-Jones, Malcolm H. *The Crooked Phoenix.* By Bradshaw Jones, pseud. London: Long, 1963. Jones authored a series of novels of intrigue about a security force of the British government; his later novels, also set in England, concern the activities and investigations of Interpol.

831. ___. *The Deadly Trade.* By Bradshaw Jones, pseud. London: Long, 1967. The mysterious death of a night club owner leads Detective Chief Inspector Arthur Carson on an investigation of two respected men, one of whom is the Chief of Police. Others:

832. ___. *Death on a Pale Horse.* By Bradshaw Jones, pseud. London: Long, 1964.

833. ___. *A Den of Savage Men.* By Bradshaw Jones, pseud. London: Long, 1967.

834. ___. *The Hamlet Problem.* By Bradshaw Jones, pseud. London: Long, 1962.

835. ___. *The Embers of Hate.* By Bradshaw Jones, pseud. London: Long, 1966.

836. ___. *Private Vendetta.* By Bradshaw Jones, pseud. London: Long, 1964.

837. ___. *Testament of Evil.* By Bradshaw Jones, pseud. London: Long, 1966.

838. ___. *Tiger from the Shadows.* By Bradshaw Jones, pseud. London: Long, 1963.

839. Brady, Michael. *American Surrender.* New York: Delacorte, 1979. The best friend of the US President is, in fact, a female KGB agent who, in the last move of the Cold War as masterminded by Soviet intelligence chief Zimov, holds America in checkmate.

840. Brain, Leonard. *It's a Free Country.* New York: Coward-McCann, 1966. Charlie Howard is released from his job in an electronics firm because he is believed to be a security risk. He investigates his investigators and learns that the same case can truthfully be made against them.

841. Braine, John. *The Pious Agent.* New York: Atheneum, 1976. Xavier, a devout Catholic and ruthless British killer-agent, is assigned to kill President Kennedy at the instigation of the CIA.

842. Branon, Bill. *Let Us Prey.* Carlsbad, CA: Black Seal, 1992. One man's revenge against the Internal Revenue Service.

843. Brelis, Dean. *The Mission.* New York: Random, 1958. A fictional account, based on fact, of how the OSS organized a native Kachin guerrilla force to oppose the 1944 Japanese retreat from Myitkyina, Burma. *y

844. Brennan, Frederick H. *Memo to a Firing Squad.* New York: Knopf, 1943. In Lisbon, an unemployed American journalist with the help of a Polish girl infiltrates an underground anti-Nazi group and eventually foils a German conspiracy to create a phony peace. *

845. Brennan, John, ed. *Best Secret Service Stories.* By John Welcome, pseud. London: Faber & Faber, 1965. Eleven tales, including one each by Maugham, Fleming, Haggard, and LeQueux. *y

846. ___. *Beware of Midnight.* By John Welcome, pseud. New York: Knopf, 1962. A tale of international intrigue involving necromancy and neo-Nazis in Ireland, the Cotswolds, and southern Spain.

847. ___. *Run for Cover.* By John Welcome, pseud. New York: Knopf, 1960. A Soviet spy ring attempts to make off with a stolen manuscript via the French Riviera.

848. Brent, Peter. *Cry Vengeance.* By Ludovic Peters, pseud. New York: Walker, 1961. When a goodwill ambassador of a small Balkan country is assassinated, the peace is endangered until Inspector Ian Firth of Scotland Yard's Special Branch puts matters right.

849. ___. *Riot '71.* By Ludovic Peters, pseud. New York: Walker, 1967. Post-Bondian gore abounds in this British spy thriller which recounts Inspector Firth's attempt to find the mysterious killers who are inciting a riot in the midst of a terrible local depression.

850. ___. *Tarakian.* By Ludovic Peters, pseud. New York: Walker, 1963. When a footloose American saves the life of an elder statesman in Paris, he is introduced into the world of agents and intrigue.

851. ___. *Two After Malic.* By Ludovic Peters, pseud. New York: Walker, 1967. A Communist agent is commissioned to return escaped scientist Zoran Malic back behind the Iron Curtain, but when he is thwarted in his first attempt by Inspector Firth, the Red learns the truth of the title. Other Inspector Firth tales are:

852. ___. *Double Take.* By Ludovic Peters, pseud. London: Hodder & Stoughton, 1968.

853. ___. *Fall of Terror.* By Ludovic Peters, pseud. London: Hodder & Stoughton, 1968.

854. ___. *The Killing Game.* By Ludovic Peters, pseud. London: Hodder & Stoughton, 1969.

855. ___. *No Way Back from Prague.* by Ludovic Peters, pseud. London: Hodder & Stoughton, 1970.

856. ___. *Out by the River.* By Ludovic Peters, pseud. New York: Coward-McCann, 1964.

857. ___. *A Snatch of Music.* By Ludovic Peters, pseud. New York: Abelard-Schulman, 1962.

858. ___. *Two Sets to Murder.* By Ludovic Peters, pseud. New York: Coward-McCann, 1964.

859. Breslin, Patrick. *Interventions.* Garden City, NY: Doubleday, 1980. US State Department functionary Paul Steward accepts a desperate espionage mission to Chile during the final days of the Allende government.

Bridge, Ann, pseud. *See* O'Malley, Mary D.

860. Brierley, David. *Cold War.* New York: Summit, 1979. Educated in South Africa and a former copywriter in London, Brierley's novels feature tough, brainy ex-spy Cody who is now a freelancer. In this first novel, she must extricate herself from a cold-war plot to discredit the French Communists in the presidential election. Brierley, in an interview quoted in McCormick & Fletcher's *Spy Fiction*, says: "I am a novelist. I am not interested in James Bond fantasies . . . My books show the larger world impinging on smaller people" (39).

861.   ___ . *Blood Group O.* New York: Summit, 1984. Blood Group O is the name of an anti-fascist terrorist group Cody must take on—along with scheming Crèvecoeur of the Sûreté and various street criminals—when she agrees to help find the kidnapped daughter of a wealthy diamond merchant. Other Cody novels are:

862.   ___ . *Big Bear, Little Bear.* New York: Scribner's, 1981.

863.   ___ . *Czechmate.* London: Collins, 1984.

864.   ___ . *One Lives, One Dies.* London: Collins, 1987.

865.   ___ . *Shooting Star.* New York: Scribner's, 1983

866.   ___ . *Skorpion's Death.* New York: Summit, 1985.

867.   ___ . *Snowline.* London: Collins, 1986.

868.   Briley, John. *The Traitors.* New York: Putnam's, 1969. An American patrol in Vietnam is ambushed and captured by the Viet Cong. While the survivors are being herded back toward the prison cages, they are lectured on the "true" history of the conflict by a Yankee defector. All of this is, however, an elaborate setup . . .

869.   Brinkley, Joel. *The Circus Maker's Mission.* New York: Fawcett, 1990. *New York Times* foreign correspondent Brinkley puts his expertise to work in this first novel about Nicaragua and the Contras.

870.   Brochet, Jean A. *Trouble in Tokyo Bay.* By Jean Bruce, pseud. Trans. from the French. Greenwich, CT: Fawcett, 1965. CIA agent OSS 117 is sent to Japan to defeat a secret group planning to destroy US treaties designed to secure Pacific island fortifications. These rather impossible yarns spawned a number of poorly made French spy thriller movies during the height of the 1960s spy boom. *P* Other Brochet OSS 117 adventures are:

871.   ___ . *Photo Finish.* By Jean Bruce, pseud. Trans. from the French. London: Corgi, 1965. *P*

872.   ___ . *Pole Reaction.* By Jean Bruce, pseud. Trans. from the French. London: Cassell, 1965.

873. ___. *Short Wave.* By Jean Bruce, pseud. Trans. from the French. London: Cassell, 1964.

874. ___. *Soft Sell.* By Jean Bruce, pseud. Trans. from the French. London: Corgi, 1965. *P*

875. ___. *Strip Tease.* By Jean Bruce, pseud. Trans. from the French. London: Corgi, 1968. *P*

876. ___. *Top Secret.* By Jean Bruce, pseud. Trans. from the French. London: Corgi, 1967. *P*

877. Brodeur, Paul. *The Sick Fox.* Boston: Little, 1963. An American agent fails to kill a fox which bites him one day while he is guarding a secret underground nuclear storage site in the remote German countryside. His failure leads to all sorts of consequences.

878. Brogan, Denis W. *Stop on the Green Light.* By Maurice Barrington, pseud. New York: Harper, 1942. Held up by a young American female agent after entering the wrong New York City hotel room, an Oxford professor becomes forcibly involved in an effort to flush out a Nazi sabotage-espionage network. **y*

879. Brome, Vincent. *The Ambassador and the Spy.* New York: Crown, 1967. A desperate man who can prove his British citizenship is given sanctuary in Britain's legation in a Soviet satellite nation; several times the ambassador's "guest" attempts to escape, but each time he fails.

880. Brook-Shepherd, Gordon. *The Eferding Diaries.* Philadelphia: Lippincott, 1967. Published in England as *The Lion and the Unicorn.* Stephen Lane discovers secret documents which the Soviets want in exchange for incriminating evidence against him.

881. Brothers, Jay. *Ox.* Indianapolis: Bobbs-Merrill, 1975. Oxford Pomeroy of the British SIS is being used—but for what?

Brown, Carter, pseud. *See* Yates, Alan Geoffrey

882. Brown, Dale. *Chains of Command.* Putnam's, 1993. Major Daren Mace, radar navigator, finds himself in internal exile within the Air Force because he aborted a mission during Desert Storm; now, however, the new

political realities of factional wars, particularly a nuclear strike by Russia against the Ukraine, have thrust him back into action.

883. ___. *Day of the Cheetah*. New York: Fine, 1989. A pilot, who happens to be the KGB's own sleeper agent, is given command of America's most advanced weapon.

884. ___. *Hammerheads*. New York: Fine, 1990. The President takes a hardnosed admiral's suggestion to close off the US borders to all unidentified flights to defeat the drug cartel, but children are put aboard the flights delivering the drugs and aboard the ships picking up the cocaine.

885. ___. *Night of the Hawk*. New York: Fine, 1992. American pilots undertake a joint operation with Marines to save a serviceman in Lithuania.

886. ___. *Sky Masters*. New York: Fine, 1991. This technothriller concerns a confrontation between China and the US when a Chinese fleet commander detonates a nuclear bomb over a dispute in the oil-rich chain of islands in the South China Sea. Two others:

887. ___. *Flight of the Old Dog*. New York: Fine, 1987.

888. ___. *Silver Tower*. New York: Fine, 1987.

889. Brown, Dee A. *They Went Thataway*. New York: Putnam's, 1960. In this spoof of TV westerns and spy shows, the librarian author of *Bury My Heart at Wounded Knee* shows how a college instructor's PhD dissertation is confused with espionage and enemy intelligence by an over-zealous secret agent. *H*

890. Browne, Gerald. *Hazard*. New York: Arbor, 1973. Agents attempt to foil an Arab scheme to use a bacteriological super-weapon against Israel.

891. Broxholme, John F. *Black Camelot*. By Duncan Kyle, pseud. New York: St. Martin's, 1978. A Nazi commando, set up as a pawn in a last ditch effort by the SS against the Allies, eludes his betrayers and comes to discover the devastating secrets within Himmler's hidden castle. *See also* Meldrum, James.

892. ___. *A Cage of Ice*. By Duncan Kyle, pseud. New York: St. Martin's, 1971. Take one innocent-looking envelope postmarked Moscow that contains an unimportant paper on hydroelectricity and deliver it by mistake to a surgeon

in New York. What do you have besides poor mail service? Naturally, the outline of a sinister plot against world peace.

893. ___. *Flight into Fear*. By Duncan Kyle, pseud. New York: St. Martin's, 1972. John Shaw is a freelance pilot who occasionally works for British Intelligence; this time, he is set up as a pawn en route to San Francisco with a mysterious package.

894. ___. *The Honey Ant*. By Duncan Kyle, pseud. London: Collins, 1988. John Close is an estate lawyer in Perth, Australia who is handling the Green Estate, a tract of very valuable land in Western Australia, but the man who inherits the property, as well as solicitor Close, is soon involved in violence.

895. ___. *The King's Commissar*. By Duncan Kyle, pseud. New York: St. Martin's, 1984. City of London banker Laurence Pilgrim goes to Switzerland on a routine investigation unaware that his prestigious firm is linked to the historic events of the execution of the Romanov dynasty and the disappearance of their vast fortune in gold bullion.

896. ___. *The Semenov Impulse*. By James Meldrum, pseud. New York: St. Martin's, 1976. Having failed to capture a Nazi war criminal, agents of the Israeli Mossad kidnap a Russian Olympic star and demand the German as ransom.

897. ___. *The Suvarov Adventure*. By Duncan Kyle, pseud. New York: St. Martin's, 1974. [*A Raft of Swords*. London: Collins, 1974]. The Russians wish to obtain a long-immersed, but still lethal, missile from the depths near Vancouver Island and to do the work, they kidnap a British torpedo recovery expert.

898. ___. *Terror's Cradle*. By Duncan Kyle, pseud. New York: St. Martin's, 1975. A correspondent acting as an unwilling courier for both the KGB and the CIA seeks to locate a tiny piece of microfilm which holds the fate of several governments.

899. ___. *Whiteout!* By Duncan Kyle, pseud. New York: St. Martin's, 1976. [*In Deep*. London: Collins, 1976]. In a desolate outpost in Greenland, Harry Bowes uncovers mysterious circumstances surrounding massive failures of equipment and many deaths among soldiers and engineers. Other Duncan Kyle novels are:

900. ___. *The Dancing Men.* By Duncan Kyle, pseud. New York: Holt, 1986.

901. ___. *Green River High.* By Duncan Kyle, pseud. New York: St. Martin's, 1980.

902. ___. *Stalking Point.* By Duncan Kyle, pseud. New York: St. Martin's 1981.

Bruce, Jean, pseud. *See* Brochet, Jean A.

Brust, Harold, pseud. *See* Cheyney, Reginald Southouse

903. Bryant, Peter. *Dr. Strangelove.* New York: Bantam, 1963. Basis of the Stanley Kubrick black-comedy film in 1963. Kubrick, Terry Southern, and Bryant (using the pseudonym Peter George) collaborated on the script, which received an Academy Award nomination. Although seemingly based on *Red Alert*'s plot of a scenario of events occurring when the failsafe network fails, the madcap antics of the principal characters—a German-American scientist, mainly—there is little of the nightmarishness of *Fail-Safe*, a film directed by Sidney Lumet on the same theme (see Burdick, Eugene and Harvey Wheeler). *HP*

904. ___. *Red Alert.* New York: Bantam, 1963. In a chillingly authentic script on nuclear brinksmanship—"burgh bargaining"—the US President is forced to expose New York to Soviet nuclear bombs when an errant B-52 mistakenly flies past its failsafe point with orders to bomb Moscow. The publishing history of this novel is complex. When it was first published in England in 1958 under the title *Two Hours to Doom*, it was suppressed by MI-5 under the Official Secrets Act. The book was then reissued under this title, but the author was forced to employ the pseudonym Peter George.

905. Bryers, Paul. *Target: Plutex.* Garden City, NY: Doubleday, 1976. A Scotland Yard Special Branch detective must halt a group of militants who are bombing the London facilities of a large, but evil, oil company.

906. Buchan, John. *The Island of Sheep.* London: Hodder & Stoughton, 1936. This final Hannay novel was published in America under the title *The Man from the Norlands* (Boston: Houghton, 1936).

907. Buchan, William. *Helen All Alone.* New York: Morrow, 1962. Helen Clark is sent to Senj, the capital of a tiny Central European country, to keep an

eye on the children of the British ambassador—and check out his activities for the intelligence boys. The author was the second son of John Buchan, one of the fathers of the spy thriller genre.

908. Buchanan, James D. *The Professional.* New York: Coward-McCann, 1972. Guerin, a professional spy for a semi-official US intelligence agency known as "The Firm," is sent to Cuba to retrieve some documents and a female agent.

909. Buchard, Robert. *Thirty Seconds over New York.* Trans. from the French. New York: Morrow, 1970. A deranged Chinese colonel places an atomic bomb on a converted 707 jetliner, shoots down the regular Paris-to-New York flight, and substitutes his "bomber" for an "under the doormat" attack on Fun City.

910. Buckley, Christopher. *Wet Work.* New York: Knopf, 1991. More satire than thriller, a man plots revenge against the system responsible for his granddaughter's fatal overdose. Another:

911. ___. *The White House Mess.* New York: Knopf, 1986.

912. Buckley, William F., Jr. *Saving the Queen.* Garden City, NY: Doubleday, 1976. Top CIA agent Blackford Oakes' first assignment in the early 1950s takes him to England to learn who has been funneling state secrets to the Russians—the Queen or a member of the Royal Family.
      Buckley, articulate editor of the *National Review*, long-time conservative spokesman, and internationally known columnist and commentator, came to the spy story late, but his tales have been well-received. During the early 1950s, Buckley served as a contract CIA agent in Mexico City, reporting to the chief of the Agency's covert action desk in that nation, E. Howard Hunt. The work, Buckley recounted for *60 Minutes*, was most boring.

913. ___. *Marco Polo, If You Can.* Garden City, NY: Doubleday, 1982. Eisenhower's second administration and the Francis Gary Powers U2 spy-plane incident provides the backdrop for perennial preppie agent Oakes' adventure in which the scandal is a smokescreen for the US's attempt to alter Sino-Soviet relations and expose the mole operation from within the State Department.

914. ___. *Mongoose R.I.P.* New York: Random, 1987. Mongoose, as aficionados know, is the infamous operation of joint CIA and Mafia forces that were combined to assassinate Castro with exploding cigars and poisoned wet suits. In this, the eighth "Blacky" Oakes adventure, Buckley sends his alter ego to Cuba and weaves five separate stories into this tableau of a critical time in American foreign policy and reveals, finally, a sympathetic portrait of Castro.

915. ___. *Stained Glass*. Garden City, NY: Doubleday, 1978. Blackford Oakes plays a high stakes card game with the KGB over the matter of a well-heeled German count who, as a budding independent political leader, threatens to be a thorn in the side of the Americans, the Russians, and the West German government.

916. ___. *Tucker's Last Stand*. New York: Random, 1990. Blackford Oakes is dispatched to the Gulf of Tonkin in that dangerous year of 1964. Assignment: focus on the Vietnamese coastline and slow down the transport of military aid from North Vietnam.

917. ___. *A Very Private Affair*. New York: Morrow, 1994. This time the year of crisis is 1985 for Blackford Oakes, although the story opens in the near future (1995) when Oakes, retired CIA chief of covert operations, is being compelled by a Senate investigation to reveal what he knows about a plot to assassinate Mikhail Gorbachev by a dissident faction of Soviet veterns of Afghanistan. What Blacky knows—and tells—may be the end of the CIA.

918. ___. *Who's on First*. Garden City, NY: Doubleday, 1980. Sent to France to kidnap a Soviet scientist who possesses data critical to the early American space program, Agent Oakes experiences a crisis of conscience—which means trouble for his superiors as well as a beautiful Hungarian freedom fighter. Other Buckley novels featuring Oakes are:

919. ___. *High Jinx*. Garden City, NY: Doubleday, 1986.

920. ___. *See You Later Alligator*. Garden City, NY: Doubleday, 1985.

921. ___. *The Story of Henri Tod*. Garden City, NY: Doubleday, 1984.

922. Buckmaster, Henrietta. *The Lion in the Stone*. New York: Harcourt, 1968. The UN Secretary General, who has recently settled the Vietnam conflict, must act to prevent a nuclear confrontation between Russia and China over Mongolia.

923. Bulliet, Richard. *The Sufi Fiddle*. New York: St. Martin's, 1991. Castle Winter becomes enchanted by a madcap young woman, and when she is kidnapped and taken to an Arab country, he pursues her with the help of a DEA agent. *H*

924. ___. *The Tomb of the Twelfth Imam.* New York: Harper & Row, 1979. American scholar Ben Gross becomes involved with the effort of dissident Iranians to outwit SAVAK and bring down the Shah.

925. Burdick, Eugene and Harvey Wheeler. *Fail-Safe.* McGraw-Hill, 1962. A breakdown at SAC sends a plane to bomb Moscow in this controversial book, which many readers and critics have called the "ultimate man vs. machine" novel. The movie version with Henry Fonda as the US President also stirred controversy when Columbia Pictures released *Dr. Strangelove: Or How I Learned to Stop Worrying and Love the Bomb* in 1964 and litigation was threatened against the authors of *Fail-Safe* and the producers of the film version because of its identical theme (see Bryant, Peter).

Burgess, Anthony, pseud. *See* Wilson, John A. B.

926. Burke, John F. and George Theiner. *Echo of Treason.* By Jonathan Burke, pseud. New York: Dodd, 1966. When a wartime traitor is released from prison, he decides he ought to write his memoirs; some very powerful men, who would rather that he not, decide his journalism should be halted—permanently.

927. ___. *The Kill Dog.* By Jonathan Burke, pseud. Garden City, NY: Doubleday, 1970. In Prague during the 1968 Soviet invasion, a professor and an English businesswoman seek to solve the riddle posed by a mysterious map.

Burke, Jonathan, pseud. *See* Burke, John F. and George Theiner

928. Burkhardt, Robert F. and Eve. *Love Comes Flying.* New York: Phoenix, 1940. Sent to catch a suspected spy in an aircraft plant, Ellen Anvers falls in love with her suspect, but manages to save both her life and her reputation as a crime fighter. *y

929. Burkholz, Herbert. *The Sensitives.* New York: Atheneum, 1987. Burkholtz, a former bartender, ski instructor and writer-in-residence at William and Mary College, collaborated with Clifford Irving (see his entry) on the nonfiction *Spy: History of Modern Espionage* (New York: Macmillan, 1969) and *The Sleeping Spy* (New York: Atheneum, 1983). This first of two novels features the "sensitives," a group of people sequestered by opposing intelligence agencies and who can read minds but are doomed to die before thirty-five; the group's most gifted member, Ben Slade, is sent by Pop, the man he trusts most and the group's leader, on a mission to convince a Swedish scientist to bring his new microchip to the American side.

930. ___. *Strange Bedfellows*. New York: Atheneum, 1988. The sensitives are again featured in this one about a plot to kill Mikhail Gorbachev at the moment of his signing a major treaty. Like the first, the sci-fi element is made believable—compares with Richard Condon's *The Manchurian Candidate*. Other Burkholz novels are:

931. ___. *The Snow Gods*. New York: Atheneum, 1985.

932. ___. *The Spanish Soldier*. New York: Charterhouse, 1973.

933. Burmeister, Jon. *The Hard Men*. New York: St. Martin's, 1978. Ex-CIA agent Quayle leads a mercenary band against Cuban soldiers in Angola who have murdered his sister.

934. ___. *Running Scared*. New York: St. Martin's, 1973. African President "Tiger" Lunda, a dying man, is kidnapped by a man who, being also in a fatal condition, plans to leave the ransom to his wife.

935. Burnett, Hallie. *Watch on the Wall*. New York: Morrow, 1965. While visiting Berlin, an American girl becomes involved in a scheme to help an East German escape over "the Wall."

936. Burt, Katharine. *Captain Millett's Island*. New York: Macrae Smith, 1944. An ex-Nazi officer, acting as a butler, together with his henchmen hold hostage the owner of an island off the Carolina coast until an intrepid American arrives on the scene. *y

937. Burton, Anthony. *The Coventry Option*. New York: Putnam's, 1976. While on assignment in London in 1940, an IRA gunman forms an alliance with the German Abwehr and agrees to show Luftwaffe bombers the route to Coventry via a radio transmitter which he will set up in the town cathedral.

938. ___. *Embrace of the Butcher*. New York: Dodd, 1982. An American reporter travels to Ireland, despite a D-Notice put on the press, to discover the circumstances of his brother's death at the hands of the IRA.

939. Busch, Nivan. *The Titan Game*. New York: Random, 1989. High-tech weaponry and the cynical means of procurement is the real subject of this explosively written novel about a young man's inheritance of his father's company—one that has produced a super-sophisticated robot tank that attracts the cynical might of the Pentagon's power brokers.

940.   Butler, Jimmie H. *The Iskra Incident.* New York: Dutton, 1990. Ex-Air Force Colonel Butler (Air Force, Ret.) delivers some fine flying sequences in this tale of rising tensions between the Soviet Union and America on the verge of signing a non-aggression pact, when a plane carrying Soviet V.I.P.s is shot down by an American fighter as it approaches San Francisco. Another:

941.   ___. *Red Lightning—Black Thunder.* New York: Dutton, 1991.

Butler, Richard, pseud. *See* Allbeury, Ted

942.   Butters, Dorothy Gilman. *The Amazing Mrs. Pollifax.* Garden City, NY: Doubleday, 1970. In this sequel to *The Unexpected Mrs. Pollifax* cited below, Emily is sent to Turkey to aid in the escape of a famous double agent. **H*

943.   ___. *The Elusive Mrs. Pollifax.* Garden City, NY: Doubleday, 1971. While ancient Emily is watching her garden grow, Carstairs and Bishop of the CIA are in a Harlem hotel room wondering whom they can persuade to smuggle some desperately needed passports to their man trapped in Sofia. **H*

944.   ___. *Mrs. Pollifax and the Golden Triangle.* New York: Doubleday, 1988. Mrs. P. and hubbie are visiting Bangkok to deliver a mysterious package to an agent when he is unceremoniously snatched. **H*

945.   ___. *Mrs. Pollifax on Safari.* Garden City, NY: Doubleday, 1977. After a coded message provides a clue on the whereabouts of a terrorist leader, Emily is asked to photograph her fellow travellers on a Zambian safari. **H*

946.   ___. *Mrs. Pollifax and the Second Thief.* New York: Doubleday, 1993. Emily and Kate Rossiter venture to Sicily to aid a former CIA man's request for assistance; it seems that he was helping himself to a document supposed to bear Julius Caesar's signature and found instead a list of mysterious names that nearly proved fatal to him.

947.   ___. *Mrs. Pollifax: Three Complete Mysteries.* New York: Barnes & Noble, 1993. Contains *The Amazing Mrs. Pollifax, The Elusive Mrs. Pollifax,* and *The Unexpected Mrs. Pollifax.* **H*

948.   ___. *A Palm for Mrs. Pollifax.* Garden City, NY: Doubleday, 1973. Emily's mission is to check into a Swiss hotel and try to trace some stolen plutonium with a miniature Geiger counter. **H*

949. ___. *The Unexpected Mrs. Pollifax.* Garden City, NY: Doubleday, 1966. In this first of the "Pollifax Series," lonely widow Emily Pollifax, a lady in her sixties, is tapped by the CIA for a simple but important courier assignment. Unfortunately, the unpredictable heroine is kidnapped to Albania. *H* One more Mrs. Pollifax:

950. ___. *Mrs. Pollifax and the Whirling Dervish.* New York: Fawcett, 1991. *H*

951. Butterworth, Michael. *Remains to Be Seen.* Garden City, NY: Doubleday, 1976. When a rich old Russian emigre dies, his children, all members of different intelligence services, are faced with difficult problems.

952. Butterworth, W. E. [William Edmund III]. *The Assassin.* By W. E. B. Griffin, pseud. New York: Jove, 1993. The Philadelphia police must stop a plot to kill the visiting Vice President. *P*

Butterworth is an incredibly prolific writer who at one point had sixteen consecutive books on the *New York Times* best seller lists (*Contemporary Authors*. New Ser. Vol. 40: 54). Butterworth has written under a number of aliases including several volumes of the M*A*S*H series with Richard Hooker:

953. ___ and Richard Hooker. *M*A*S*H Goes to Moscow.* New York: Pocket, 1974. *P*

954. ___ and Richard Hooker. *M*A*S*H Goes to Paris.* New York: Pocket, 1974. *P*

955. ___ and Richard Hooker. *M*A*S*H Goes to Vienna.* New York: Pocket, 1976. *P* Butterworth wrote four books in a series called *Men at War*:

956. ___. *The Fighting Agents.* By Alex Baldwin, pseud. New York: Pocket, 1988. *P*

957. ___. *The Last Heroes.* By Alex Baldwin, pseud. New York: Pocket, 1985. *P*

958. ___. *The Secret Warriors.* By Alex Baldwin, pseud. New York: Pocket, 1986. *P*

959. ___. *The Soldier Spies.* By Alex Baldwin, pseud. New York: Pocket, 1987. *P* In the early to mid sixties, Butterworth wrote four tales of military adventure under the pseudonym Webb Beech:

960. ___. *Article 92: Murder-Rape.* By Webb Beech, pseud. Greenwich, CT: Fawcett, 1965. *P*

961. ___. *Make War in Madness.* By Webb Beech, pseud. Greenwich, CT: Fawcett, 1966. *P*

962. ___. *No French Leave.* By Webb Beech, pseud. Toronto: Gold Medal, 1960. *P*

963. ___. *Warrior's Way.* By Webb Beech, pseud. Greenwich, CT: Fawcett, 1965. *P*

964. ___. *Close Combat.* By W. E. B. Griffin, pseud. New York: Putnam's, 1993. Here, in Volume 6 of the saga of the Marine Corps, the action is Guadalcanal, and the heroes are twenty-one-year-old combat pilot William Dunn and hot-headed Sergeant Thomas McCoy. Griffin is the authory of two military series *Brotherhood of War* and *Badge of Honor* (a police procedural series). Tales in the *Brotherhood of War* series:

965. ___. *The Berets.* By W. E. B. Griffin, pseud. New York: Putnam's, 1986.

966. ___. *The Captains.* By W. E. B. Griffin, pseud. New York: Putnam's, 1986.

967. ___. *The Colonels.* By W. E. B. Griffin, pseud. New York: Putnam's, 1986.

968. ___. *The Generals.* By W. E. B. Griffin, pseud. New York: Putnam's, 1987.

969. ___. *The Lieutenants.* By W. E. B. Griffin, pseud. New York: Putnam's, 1986.

970. ___. *The Majors.* By W. E. B. Griffin, pseud. New York: Putnam's, 1986. Tales in the *Corps* series include:

971. ___. *Battleground.* By W. E. B. Griffin, pseud. New York: Putnam's, 1991.

972. ___. *Call to Arms.* By W. E. B. Griffin, pseud. New York: Jove, 1987. *P*

973. ___. *The Corps*. By W. E. B. Griffin, pseud. New York: Jove, 1986.
P

974. ___. *Counterattack*. By W. E. B. Griffin, pseud. New York:
Putnam's, 1990.

975. ___. *Line of Fire*. By W. E. B. Griffin, pseud. New York: Jove,
1993. P

976. ___. *Semper Fi*. By W. E. B. Griffin, pseud. New York: Jove, 1986.
P *Badge of Honor* series:

977. ___. *Men in Blue*. By W. E. B. Griffin, pseud. New York: Jove,
1988. P

978. ___. *Special Operations*. By W. E. B. Griffin, pseud. New York:
Jove, 1989. P

979. ___. *The Victim*. By W. E. B. Griffin, pseud. New York: Jove, 1991.
P

980. ___. *The Witness*. By W. E. B. Griffin, pseud. New York: Jove,
1992. P Additional books in these series:

981. ___. *The Aviators*. By W. E. B. Griffin, pseud. New York: Putnam's,
1988.

982. ___. *Honor Bound*. By W. E. B. Griffin, pseud. New York:
Putnam's, 1994.

983. ___. *The New Breed*. By W. E. B. Griffin, pseud. New York:
Putnam's, 1987. One final work under the pseudonym Jack Dugan:

984. ___. *The Deep Kill*. By Jack Dugan, pseud. New York: Charter, 1984.
P

985. Byrd, Max. *Target of Opportunity*. New York: Bantam, 1988.
Gilman, a California p.i., witnesses his brother-in-law's shocking murder in a
convenience store; however, he learns that the motive for the murder isn't so
senseless—in fact, as he untangles a skein of events and murders from California
to Boston, he encounters a famous Harvard activist and World War II hero

whose past and whose dark secret about a Resistance fighter named Colonel Verlaine killed over forty years ago is about to come to light.

986.   Byrne, Robert. *The Tunnel.* New York: Harcourt, 1977. IRA terrorists attempt to destroy construction of the first England-France tunnel being built under the Channel.

C

987.   Caidin, Martin. *Almost Midnight.* New York: Morrow, 1971. Five nuclear bombs of multi-kiloton force are missing and five major American cities will mushroom up in smoke unless $100 million is paid to the gang who stole them.   An enterprising Air Force/intelligence team sets out to catch the perpetrators and halt the explosions.

988.   ___. *The Cape.* Garden City, NY: Doubleday, 1971. Someone is out to sabotage the launching of an American space platform scheduled to beat the Russians into orbit.

989.   ___. *Cyborg.* New York: Arbor, 1972. A US Air Force test pilot crashes and is put back together with artificial parts at a top secret installation; when he has recuperated, Colonel Steve Austin, the "Six Million Dollar Man," finds himself a member of the OSI and is sent on an underwater search for nuclear subs off South America and on an anti-Arab mission with a female Israeli agent.

990.   ___. *Cyborg IV.* New York: Arbor, 1975. Bionic marvel Steve Austin finds himself dispatched in a space vehicle to find the source that is rendering American spy satellites inoperative.

991.   ___. *The Final Countdown.* New York: Bantam, 1980. A freak electrical storm causes the world's largest aircraft carrier to be transported back through time to Pearl Harbor, where it arrives three days before the December 7, 1941, Japanese attack. *P*

992.   ___. *The God Machine.* New York: McKay, 1968. An agent must halt the government's secret computer, which has gone berserk and threatens to take over the world.

993. ___. *High Crystal.* New York: Arbor, 1974. Austin becomes involved in a race to find the hidden source of a mysterious laser high in the Andes and to uncover the secret behind the "Chariots of the Gods."

994. ___. *Operation Nuke.* New York: McKay, 1973. The "Six Million Dollar Man" must uncover some tactical nuclear weapons which a group of nasties is using to blackmail the American government. A variation on the theme of the author's *Almost Midnight.*

Caillou, Alan, pseud. *See* Lyle-Smythe, Alan

995. Cairns, Robert. *The Two O'Clock Sun.* New York: Random, 1964. While working for Radio Free Europe, a broadcaster decides to find a way to abolish the conflicts between the world's current political systems.

996. Calder-Marshall, Arthur. *Way to Santiago.* New York: Reynal, 1940. A young newsman in Mexico is accidentally plunged into an abortive revolution run by a Nazi mastermind. *

997. Calin, Harold. *Genesis in the Desert.* New York: Norden, 1977. A veteran of desert fighting becomes a forceful anti-Arab mercenary leader. *P*

998. ___. *Mercenary.* New York: Norden, 1977. A modern soldier-of-fortune battles terrorists in the Arabian desert. *P*

999. Callas, Theo. *The City of Kites.* New York: Walker, 1964. Western agents battle the Russian NKVD in 1946 Vienna. *

1000. Callison, Brian. *An Act of War.* New York: Dutton, 1977. British Naval Intelligence officer Brevet Cable is sent aboard a freighter to take it into a test of the Soviet closing of the Baltic, not knowing that his ship is equipped with a sophisticated and undetectable H-bomb.

1001. ___. *Dawn Attack.* New York: Putnam's, 1973. Depicts the training activities of a group of 1941 British Royal Marine Commandos and their subsequent attack on a German held Norwegian port. Should be compared with Elliott Arnold's 1942 novel *The Commandos.*

1002. ___. *A Plague of Sailors.* New York: Putnam's, 1971. An agent must learn who has stolen a new brand of killer germs for use against Israel. All of the action takes place at sea.

1003. ___. *Trapp's War.* New York: Saturday Review, 1976. While minding his own affairs, Captain Trapp, a veteran of piracy, gunrunning, and World War II special operations for the Royal Navy, has his vessel taken over by Arab terrorists who suggest at gunpoint that his specialized services are needed to further their aims.

1004. Calmer, Ned. *Bay of Lions.* New York: Arbor, 1980. On vacation in the African country of Luanga, American TV correspondent Gayle Marchant becomes involved with a guerrilla hero and a Rhodesian mercenary and is torn between the two.

1005. Cameron, Lou. *Before It's Too Late.* Greenwich, CT: Fawcett, 1970. Returned war hero Steve Warren gets mixed up with a female Mossad agent, a terrified biology teacher who is watching over a cache of deadly germs, and a coroner with his own private crematorium. *P*

1006. ___. *The First Blood.* New York: Prestige, 1971. Two dozen American paratroops are dropped into the North African desert to capture the German-held Fort Wadi Gemal and thus gain control of Rommel's southern defense line. **P*

1007. ___. *Sky Riders.* Greenwich, CT: Fawcett, 1976. Mercenary pilot Jim McCabe and a troop of hang glider acrobats rescue the kidnapped wife of an American businessman from a Greek mountain fortress. *P*

1008. Campbell, Alice. *Ringed with Fire.* New York: Random, 1942. British Ministry of Domestic Security official Mark Chaney and his girlfriend are suspected by MI-5 of being caught up in a fifth column plot designed to ease the way for a German invasion. **y*

Campbell, Keith, pseud. *See* West-Watson, Keith Campbell

1009. Campbell, R. Wright. *The Spy Who Sat and Waited.* New York: Pocket, 1975. An undistinguished German clerk changes his identity and as the Swiss, Will Hartz, is sent to the Orkneys after World War I as a sleeper agent of the Abwehr; in 1939, he is "awakened" to send information on the Scapa Flow naval base and its defenses which allow a U-boat to enter and sink a British battleship. *P*

This little paperback is an excellent example of realism in the spy thriller with accuracy built upon fact that a Nazi submarine, the *U-47* under Lt. Guenther Prien, did, in fact, sink H.M. battleship *Royal Oak* in Scapa on October 14, 1939. In the years after, a story was current that a certain sleeper agent, who had changed his identity to that of a Swiss, sent the harbor defense plans to the Reich. In recent times, however, the tale of the "Watchmaker of Kirkwall" has been discredited.

1010. ___. *Circus Couronne.* New York: Pocket, 1979. A small travelling circus harbors a conspirator with a maniacal plot to wreak havoc on the Western world. *P*

1011. Canning, Victor. *Birdcage.* New York: Morrow, 1979. Sister Luiza, born Sarah Branton, is rescued by an agent destined to become her lover; as the story develops, we see that Bellmaster, the girl's father, wishes her to destroy a diary given to her by her mother which shows the surviving parent's intelligence misdeeds. *

Victor Canning began writing in the 1930s with a series of travelogs and served with the Royal Artillery during the Second World War. Following that conflict, Canning branched out to the novel, choosing to center his attention on the preparation of stories with espionage themes ("I hate labelling them," he once said). In many of his yarns, Canning has chosen, like Ambler, to build his plots around non-intelligence personnel (teachers, engineers, etc.) who must cope with nasty situations just to survive. In addition to spy thrillers, Canning has penned a large number of pure mystery adventures.

1012. ___. *Black Flamingo.* New York: Sloane, 1963. In Central Africa, a down-on-his-luck man assumes the identity of a dead pilot and gets mixed up in a sinister political situation. *

1013. ___. *The Doomsday Carrier.* New York: Morrow, 1977. A monkey escapes a Ministry of Defense research lab carrying a plague bacillus which will threaten the lives of millions if not recovered within the next twenty-one days. *

1014. ___. *Doubled in Diamonds.* New York: Morrow, 1967. A British agent must prevent the exchange of stolen industrial diamonds for Chinese opium. *

1015. ___. *The Dragon Tree.* New York: Sloane, 1958. An English major is involved with intrigue and nationalism on the South American island of Cyrenia. *

1016. ___. *The Finger of Saturn.* New York: Morrow, 1974. An Englishman receives word that his missing wife is alive and well and with the help of an SIS agent sets out to rescue her. *

1017. ___. *Firecrest*. New York: Morrow, 1972. In order to prolong his life, a research scientist must hide a new and rather reasonable secret weapon from agents of "The Department." *

1018. ___. *Forest of Eyes*. New York: Mill, 1950. A British engineer engineers the escape of an important anti-Communist VIP from post-war Yugoslavia. This was Canning's first true spy thriller whose hero, Robert Hudson, does not want to play "the game." *

1019. ___. *The Golden Salamander*. New York: Mill, 1949. Canning's first successful mystery adventure involved an English scholar caught up in murder and intrigue in the North African desert. *

1020. ___. *The Great Affair*. New York: Morrow, 1971. A defrocked clergyman and superspy uses the funds he gathered from knocking off enemy agents to build a home for crippled children. *

1021. ___. *A Handful of Silver*. New York: Sloane, 1954. A British schoolmaster agrees to work for the SIS. His mission is to kidnap and hold the son of an Eastern potentate until an oil concession is safe. *

1022. ___. *The Limbo Line*. New York: Sloane, 1964. First published in *Ladies' Home Journal* under the title *Margin of Peril*. A retired British agent is reinstated to find Limbo, the French location of a reverse underground railway in which Soviet refugees are kidnapped and returned to Russia. *

1023. ___. *The Mask of Memory*. New York: Morrow, 1975. SIS agent Tucker fights a trade unionist conspiracy to take over the British government. *

1024. ___. *Panther's Moon*. New York: Mill, 1948. A pair of circus panthers have escaped and in the collar of one is an important microdot which British agent Catherine Talbot must recover before it falls into Soviet hands. *y

1025. ___. *The Python Project*. New York: Morrow, 1968. A private eye becomes involved with the British SIS, a gang of kidnappers, a foreign government, the London police, and murder. *

1026. ___. *Queen's Pawn*. New York: Morrow, 1969. A bitter aristocrat, a beautiful woman, and a big-time thief are all employed as pawns by a man named Sarling, who has a peculiar dream. *

1027. ___. *The Rainbow Pattern.* New York: Morrow, 1973. In Book I, a likeable British con artist tries to help an old woman trace a long lost illegitimate nephew; in Book II, agents, track down a man who kidnaps VIPs and provide the connection with Book I. *

1028. ___. *The Scorpio Letters.* New York: Sloane, 1964. American Joe Christopher is enlisted by the SIS to take up where a murdered agent left off and infiltrate a blackmail ring led by Scorpio while, simultaneously, learning what a group of former French Resistance men, calling themselves "the Bianeri," know about the criminal's band. *

1029. ___. *The Whip Hand.* New York: Morrow, 1965. Rex Carver follows a sadistic German blonde, who plans to reactivate German nationalism, and winds up trapped in a theatrical schloss in the Bavarian Alps. * Two more Canning novels with espionage themes are:

1030. ___. *The Boy on Platform One.* London: Heinemann, 1981. [*Memory Boy.* New York: Morrow, 1981]. *

1031. ___. *Vanishing Point.* New York: Morrow, 1983. *

1032. Cannon, John. *Intersect File: Death Cruise.* North Hollywood, CA: American Art Enterprises, 1980. When Black September terrorists take over a cruise ship and demand a huge ransom, a crack commando team is sent to take care of the situation. *P*

1033. Cape, Tony. *The Cambridge Theorem.* New York: Doubleday, 1989. Det. Sgt. Derek Smailes is called in to investigate the death of a Cambridge student who just happened to be investigating the identity of the notorious "Fifth Man" in the British spy line. Another:

1034. ___. *The Last Defector.* New York: Doubleday, 1991.

1035. Caputo, Philip. *Horn of Africa.* New York: Holt, 1980. Three mercenaries are chosen to smuggle arms to non-Communist forces in the primitive wasteland of Somalia.

1036. Carey, Constance. *The Chekhov Proposal.* New York: Putnam's, 1975. CIA agents must determine if Presidential candidate Hoffman is a Soviet "sleeper" agent.

1037. Carney, Daniel.   *The Wild Geese.*   New York: Bantam, 1978. Mercenaries, who in the movie version were led by Richard Burton, free a White politician being held hostage in Africa. **P**

1038. Carpenter, Scott.   *The Steel Albatross.*   New York: Pocket, 1990. Former astronaut Carpenter, who became the second man to orbit the earth in 1962, draws upon his own Navy experiences in this tale of an elite force, a secret submarine-glider, and an underwater project of the Soviets named Temnota, an underseas power plant that can knock out all US computers.

1039. Carroll, Gerry. *Ghostrider One.* New York: Pocket, 1993. Aviation technothriller about a fighter squadron of Skyhawks off the coast of Vietnam.

1040. Carroll, James. *Firebird.* New York: Dutton, 1989. Young Chris Malone is swept up in treachery and betrayal, both political and sexual in postwar Washington, DC, as the Soviets attempt to steal America's atomic secrets. **P**

1041. ___. *Madonna Red.* Boston: Little, 1976. Like his better-known first novel that mixes theology and intrigue, this one opens with the attempted assassination of a British ambassador before settling back to its real thesis: the problems of Catholicism in the modern world.

1042. ___. *Mortal Friends.* Boston: Little, 1976. Colman Brady, Irish rebel, lands in Boston with his infant son and is soon embroiled in politics and intrigue.

1043. ___. *Supply of Heros.* New York: Dutton, 1986. About the Troubles during the second decade of the twentieth century. Two more:

1044. ___. *Family Trade.* Boston: Little, 1982.

1045. ___. *Memorial Bridge.* Boston: Houghton, 1991.

1046. Carter, Lin. *The Nemesis of Evil.* Garden City, NY: Doubleday, 1975. Prince Zarkon and his Omega organization are pitted against the arch-nasty Lucifer in this combination spy thriller and horror story. *

Carter, Nick, house pseud. *See* Nick Carter, pseud.; Michael A. Avallone, Jr.; W. T. Ballard; Marilyn Granbeck; Ralph E. Hayes; Jeffrey M. Wallman & a hundred others.

1047. Carter, Nick, pseud. *Agent Double-Agent.* New York: Award, 1973. Superspy narrator Nick Carter, called "N-3" or "Killmaster," has survived more capers (over 100) than any other secret operative in spy fiction. In this tale, a threat to American sovereignty catapults him into a mind-bending game of wits and nerves with a notorious KGB agent. *P*

The character "Nick Carter" first saw the printed page as a detective at about the same time that Conan Doyle was inventing Sherlock Holmes. Carter was (and is) a "house name," that is, a hero written about by many authors. The present agent retains the same name as his predecessor, but has been transformed from a rather harmless private eye into an oversexed, super-good guy. According to Joan Rockwell, in her essay "Normative Attitudes of Spies in Fiction," "Killmaster" is the product "of an entrepreneur named L. Kenyon Engel [who] employs 64 writers to fill in the outlines of plots and characters as directed by him" (Bernard Rosenberg and David M. White, eds. *Mass Culture Revisited* [New York: Van Nostrand, 1971], 339). According to information provided by Ms. Karen E. Goff, Reference Librarian, West Virginia Library Commission, Charleston, the following authors have written under the Carter pseudonym: W. T. Ballard; Marilyn Granbeck; Ralph E. Hayes; Jeffrey M. Wallman. *See also* Avallone, Michael A. Jr.

1048. ___. *Amazon.* New York: Award, 1969. Carter goes on a death hunt in the South American jungle with a guide who is both a lady and a tigress—which could be fatal in a climate of sudden death! *P*

1049. ___. *Amsterdam.* New York: Award, 1970. A wanton blonde whom the enemy has pledged to kill is Carter's only lead to stolen American atomic plans and the international diamond cartel that has set up a private spy network—complete with a spy school. *P*

1050. ___. *And Next the King.* New York: Ace-Charter, 1980. In Spain, "N-3" must find the kidnapped General Rodrigues and halt a bizarre assassination plot by the El Grupo Febrero terrorists against King Carlos—all of which hinges on a single night at the opera. *P*

1051. ___. *The Arab Plague.* New York: Award, 1970. Carter is exposed to a mind-altering drug and gets mixed up in an Arab slave trader's plot to sabotage the hair-trigger machinery of international politics. *P*

1052. ___. *The Asian Mantrap.* New York: Ace-Charter, 1978. Masquerading as a Vietnamese peasant, Killmaster attempts to halt a vengeance-minded US POW hero who is killing off high-ranking North Vietnamese officials. *P*

1053. ___. *Assassin: Code Name Vulture.* New York: Award, 1974. N-3 must stop the bloody coup-masters led by an international assassin known only as "the Vulture." *P*

1054. ___. *The Assassination Brigade.* New York: Award, 1973. Killmaster faces an army of kamikaze slaves and a mad super genius bent on world conquest. *P*

1055. ___. *Assault on England.* New York: Award, 1974. Carter is pitted against an ingenious assassin prepared to wipe out the entire British Cabinet—one by one—unless he receives a ransom of ten million pounds sterling. *See also* Hayes, Ralph E. (2524-2531) and Carter, Nick (1047). *P*

1056. ___. *Assignment: Intercept.* New York: Award, 1977. N-3 traces a Chinese scientist who is armed with a diabolical weapon that can trigger flaming death anywhere in the world. *See also* Granbeck, Marilyn (2240-2243) and Carter, Nick (1047). *P*

1057. ___. *Assignment: Israel.* New York: Award, 1974. A deranged Nazi threatens revenge and destruction in the Middle East; Carter is called in to deal with him. *P*

1058. ___. *The Aztec Avenger.* New York: Award, 1974. A deranged Inca holds the secret key to an endless supply of free heroin—for sale to the highest bidder on the black market. *P*

1059. ___. *Beirut Incident.* New York: Award, 1974. Killmaster infiltrates the Mafia to stop the number one Don and destroy the syndicate's new army of killers. *P*

1060. ___. *Berlin.* New York: Award, 1970. Killmaster must destroy the fanatic leader of Germany's neo-Nazi underground—a man wearing a known and trusted face, but hell bent on becoming the next Fuehrer. *P*

1061. ___. *The Black Death.* New York: Award, 1969. Voo-doo zombies guard a secret missile complex in Haiti and by the time Carter arrives on the scene, the countdown for launching has already started. *P*

1062. ___. *A Bullet for Fidel.* New York: Award, 1970. The Doomsday weapon in Cuban hands ignites the fuse of war and N-3 is called upon to snuff it out. *P*

1063. ___. *The Butcher of Belgrade.* New York: Award, 1973. The mysterious mastermind of a brutally powerful intelligence network involves Killmaster in a dangerous chase aboard a highballing express train, which is hurtling through Europe with a cargo of top secret electronic equipment. *See also* Hayes, Ralph E. (2524-2531) and Carter, Nick (1047). *P*

1064. ___. *The Cairo Mafia.* New York: Award, 1972. Tracking down secret plans for a deadly Russian secret weapon, Carter fights the New Brotherhood in the shadow of the pyramids. *See also* Hayes, Ralph E. (2524-2531) and Carter, Nick (1047). *P*

1065. ___. *Cambodia.* New York: Award, 1970. Assigned to penetrate the Cambodian jungles and accidentally aligned with a sensuous guide, Killmaster faces native terrorists primed to kill. *P*

1066. ___. *Carnival for Killing.* New York: Award, 1969. A fantastic espionage plot turns laughter to horror at the Carnival in Rio. *P*

1067. ___. *Casbah Killers.* New York: Award, 1969. Carter is sent to Casablanca to locate Karminian, who sent a cable to say he was onto something big; on the scene, N-3 finds his man missing and the Russians in pursuit. *P*

1068. ___. *Checkmate in Rio.* New York: Award, 1970. N-3 heads for a vacation on the beach and ends up caught in a deadly snare laid by the top agents of the world's two most super secret spy organizations. *P*

1069. ___. *The Chinese Paymaster.* New York: Award, 1970. Killmaster must halt the payoff being made by a double agent who is the vital link between Peking and a world wide network of spies. *P*

1070. ___. *Cobra Kill.* New York: Award, 1971. In Malaysia to prevent a Communist takeover, Carter's efforts lead him to an ancient temple with a secret which has lain buried since the end of World War II. *P*

1071. ___. *The Code.* New York: Award, 1973. The dead AXE agent (Carter's outfit) could tell no tales, but N-3 must track his murderers through a maze of Syndicate subterfuge, dirty tricks, and sensuous, treacherous women. *P*

1072. ___. *Code Name Werewolf.* New York: Award, 1974. Killmaster matches wits and nerves with a ruthless Spanish assassin bent on Franco's death and the takeover of American bases. *P*

1073. ___. *Counterfeit Agent.* New York: Award, 1975. Carter faces a hydra-headed army of assassins that threaten to turn an international peace conference into a bloody massacre. *P*

1074. ___. *The Coyote Connection.* New York: Ace-Charter, 1981. Carter must halt a group of Middle East terrorists who are infiltrating assassins into the US disguised as Mexicans via the illegal alien route from Mexico across to Brownsville, Texas. *P*

1075. ___. *Danger Key.* New York: Award, 1973. N-3 masquerades as a vulnerable CIA agent to thwart the detestable plans of the CLAW, an insidious Chinese secret society. *P*

1076. ___. *The Day of the Dingo.* New York: Ace-Charter, 1980. When a new agent turns up dead in Tokyo, Killmaster follows a trail of intrigue which leads to a mysterious killer. *P*

1077. ___. *Death Message: Oil 74-2.* New York: Award, 1975. An obscure coded message holds the key to a lethal outbreak of sabotage that is destroying America's vital oil supply lines. *P*

1078. ___. *Death of the Falcon.* New York: Award, 1974. Arab fanatics launch a harrowing terror campaign that threatens to trigger a world wide holocaust. *P*

1079. ___. *Death's Head Conspiracy.* New York: Award, 1973. America's largest cities are doomed to nuclear destruction unless Killmaster can disarm the elusive human fuse. *P*

1080. ___. *Death Strain.* New York: Award, 1970. N-3 must find the maddened scientist who threatens to unleash a lethal virus. *P*

1081. ___. *The Defector.* New York: Award, 1974. Carter obeys the whims of a beautiful spy to keep the US from being blown sky high. *P*

1082. ___. *The Devil's Cockpit.* New York: Award, 1969. N-3 infiltrates a pornographic propaganda mill pledged to pervert the West. *P*

1083. ___. *The Devil's Dozen.* New York: Award, 1973. Killmaster walks a tightrope of disguise and double-cross when he infiltrates the American Mafia. *P*

1084. ___. *The Doomsday Formula.* New York: Award, 1972. When the Japanese terrorists threaten to sink Hawaii to the bottom of the sea in a plot which is a dazzling, inventive work of black art, the call goes out for Carter. *P*

1085. ___. *The Doomsday Spore.* New York: Ace-Charter, 1979. N-3 battles the Red Swineberg Gang, which threatens to unleash the D-S, a deadly virus picked up on a space mission. *P*

1086. ___. *Double Identity.* New York: Award, 1969. Killmaster must eliminate the deadly double who matches him in every skill. *P*

1087. ___. *Dragon Flame.* New York: Award, 1969. Hong Kong—a nerve-scorching inferno for an agent who smuggles generals. *P*

1088. ___. *The Ebony Cross.* New York: Ace-Charter, 1978. In Budapest to direct the escape of a scientist who had solved the cost factor of an alternative energy force, N-3 discovers that his cover has been blown by a trusted, but unknown, double agent. *P*

1089. ___. *Eight Card Stud.* New York: Ace-Charter, 1980. When the chief scientist of a critical testing area near Las Vegas is found dead, Killmaster knows that an enemy is onto Project Eight Card. *P*

1090. ___. *The Executioners.* New York: Award, 1973. A scientifically perfect espionage plot to destroy America's defense network is fueled by crazy revenge and clouded by friend killing friend. *P*

1091. ___. *The Eyes of the Tiger.* New York: Award, 1965. Carter and a beautiful blonde must prevent a neo-Nazi organization from claiming a Japanese treasure secreted in a Swiss vault. *P*

1092. ___. *The Fanatics of Al Asad.* New York: Award, 1977. Israel has the atomic bomb and unless N-3 can intervene, a handful of Arab terrorists may make her use it. *P*

1093. ___. *The Filthy Five.* New York: Award, 1967. Killmaster races to prevent the assassination of the President of the United States by a power-hungry mercenary. *P*

1094. ___. *Fourteen Seconds to Hell.* New York: Award, 1968. A deranged master of Peking's death factory plots to destroy the US and Russia on voice command. *P*

1095. ___. *Fraulein Spy.* New York: Award, 1970. N-3 is on the trail of Hitler's right hand man, Martin Bormann. *P*

1096. ___. *The Golden Serpent.* New York: Award, 1972. Armed with only a suicide pill, Killmaster must stop the ruin of America's economy. *P*

1097. ___. *The Green Wolf Connection.* New York: Ace-Charter, 1979. Middle East oil is the name of the game and the sheiks are masters of torture; Carter stands alone against a daring corporate conspiracy to seize world power starting in that area and with those people. *P*

1098. ___. *Haiti.* New York: Award, 1970. A half-mad fanatic unleashes the power of black magic and the might of modern weaponry in a bid for world domination, opposed only by N-3 and a beautiful revolutionary. *P*

1099. ___. *Hanoi.* New York: Award, 1968. Impersonating a German scientist, Killmaster crawls deep into North Vietnam on a mission vital to American security. *P*

1100. ___. *Hawaii.* New York: Ace-Charter, 1979. Carter must locate the surfer son of a Vice-Presidential candidate who is missing in Hawaii's jungles and also defuse a crop of dangerous toxic mushrooms being grown by a group of nasties within the depths of a dead volcano. *P*

1101. ___. *Hood of Death.* New York: Award, 1970. The bait—six beautiful women; the plot—to destroy every powerful official in America. Each time N-3 comes near to finding the "Chicom" agent behind it all, an attempt is made on his life. *P*

1102. ___. *Hour of the Wolf.* New York: Award, 1973. Killmaster gambles against desperate odds to save a deadly nuclear secret from falling into enemy hands. *See also* Carter, Nick (1047). *P*

1103. ___. *Human Time-Bomb.* New York: Award, 1970. Carter is faced by a master army of men and women—programmed assassins—who are neither dead nor alive. *P*

1104. ___. *Ice-Bomb Zero.* New York: Award, 1974. N-3 must destroy an evil colonel and the electronic weaponry with which he is threatening to create a twentieth-century ice age. *P*

1105. ___. *Inca Death Squad.* New York: Award, 1972. Killmaster must survive a three-handed death trap as he is cornered by "Chicoms," pursued by Chilean guerrillas, and hounded by a fiendishly cruel and powerful Soviet minister. *P*

1106. ___. *Istanbul.* New York: Award, 1971. Ace spy Nick Carter finds sultry love and sudden violence in Turkey's ancient capital. *P*

1107. ___. *The Jerusalem File.* New York: Award, 1975. N-3 battles Arab terrorists who have kidnapped the world's ten wealthiest men. *P*

1108. ___. *Jewel of Doom.* New York: Award, 1969. Killmaster must steal the most heavily guarded ruby on earth, inside of which is a nuclear secret America desperately needs. *P*

1109. ___. *Judas Spy.* New York: Award, 1968. Carter is trapped in the jungles of Indonesia by Mr. Judas—a man of incredible cruelty and savagery who is master of a bloodthirsty terrorist army. *P*

1110. ___. *The Katmandu Contract.* New York: Ace-Charter, 1978. Killmaster will safeguard the fate of Asia, if he can locate a billion dollars in diamonds held by Chinese terrorists in the Himalayas, the roof of the world. *P*

1111. ___. *Korean Tiger.* New York: Award, 1967. Carter must recover stolen nuclear plans that can crush America to dust. *P*

1112. ___. *The Kremlin File.* New York: Award, 1973. Russian missiles on a Caribbean island pose a threat that can trigger a world crisis unless N-3 takes them out. *See also* Ballard, Willis T. (658) and Carter, Nick (1047). *P*

1113. ___. *The Liquidator.* New York: Award, 1973. The KGB officer was ready to defect, but when Killmaster tries to engineer his escape, he triggers a blazing battle between spy and counterspy. *P*

1114. ___. *The List.* New York: Award, 1976. An evil Chinese princess guards a list of US agents in the Orient—men who are dying at a rapid rate; Carter's job: recover the list before all the operatives are dead. *P*

1115. ___. Living Death. New York: Award, 1969. A hideous destruction-machine is stealing the minds of the world's most brilliant scientists and N-3 must find and destroy it. *P*

1116. ___. Macao. New York: Award, 1970. To save the US from destruction at the hands of a Red Chinese madman, Killmaster must lure a beautiful girl into suicide. *P*

1117. ___. The Man Who Sold Death. New York: Award, 1974. Carter must deal with a madman's plot to corner the gold market through murder, theft, and international sabotage. *P*

1118. ___. The Mark of Cosa Nostra. New York: Award, 1971. N-3 is involved in a grisly Mafia manhunt—an assignment exploding with sex, savagery, and revenge. *P*

1119. ___. Massacre in Milan. New York: Award, 1974. In Italy, Killmaster is mixed up with Arab terrorists, Nazi spies, and Mossad agents who are all colliding in a deadly game of oil diplomacy and espionage. *P*

1120. ___. The Mind Killers. New York: Award, 1970. They were all-American heroes—scientifically programmed to assassinate; Nick Carter's orders: stop them before they reach the President of the United States. *P*

1121. ___. The Mind Poisoners. New York: Award, 1971. N-3 must quash an international plot to hook American college kids on violence drugs and use them to destroy their country. *P*

1122. ___. Mission to Venice. New York: Award, 1971. A missing H-bomb triggers a game of global blackmail. *P*

1123. ___. Moscow. New York: Award, 1970. AXE sends Killmaster inside the Kremlin to meet a gorgeous Russian double agent and ferret out and destroy a new super secret weapon. *P*

1124. ___. The N-3 Conspiracy. New York: Award, 1974. Carter fights for survival in Africa against white slavers, rebel commandos, and vicious mercenaries. *P*

1125. ___. Nepal. New York: Award, 1969. N-3's job is to uncover a mythical abominable snowman who is frightening the locals into accepting Red Chinese rule. *P*

1126. ___. *Night of the Avenger.* New York: Award, 1973. In India, Killmaster combats a chilling stratagem to build a private empire on the smoldering ruins of the world. *P*

1127. ___. *The Omega Terror.* New York: Award, 1972. An American defector plans to unleash a deadly microscopic bug that would render the entire US lifeless, unless Carter can destroy both before the appointed day. *See also* Hayes, Ralph E. (2524-2531) and Carter, Nick (1047). *P*

1128. ___. *Operation Che Guevara.* New York: Award, 1969. The dead guerrilla leader is kept strangely alive in a secret kept by two beautiful, treacherous women. *P*

1129. ___. *Operation Hi-Jack.* New York: Award, 1970. When a Russian SST disappears from Kennedy Airport and the Soviets accuse the US of duplicity, N-3 must deliver the plane in order to maintain world peace. *P*

1130. ___. *Operation Moon Rocket.* New York: Award, 1970. Killmaster must become human bait to flush out one of five men suspected of being the Red Chinese agent behind the death of four American astronauts. *P*

1131. ___. *Operation Snake.* New York: Award, 1969. A nightmare mission pits Carter against a power-mad monk with a programmed abominable snowman and a Chinese-backed scheme to take over Nepal; compare with the author's *Nepal* above. *P*

1132. ___. *Operation Starvation.* New York: Award, 1966. N-3 battles a heinous plan for world domination predicated on a nasty's ability to control world food supplies. *P*

1133. ___. *Our Agent in Rome is Missing.* New York: Award, 1973. The ultimate psychopath has the means to trigger World War III and Killmaster must penetrate his fantastically deceptive cover in order to avert the final Armageddon. *P*

1134. ___. *The Peking Dossier.* New York: Award, 1974. Carter must find the mysterious Chinese mastermind who has been dispatching an endless wave of programmed assassins to eliminate American officials. *P*

1135. ___. *The Red Guard.* New York: Award, 1967. Unless N-3 acts fast, the monsters of the Cultural Revolution will blow up the world with a superbomb more lethal than any ever built by America or Russia. *P*

1136. ___. *Red Rays.* New York: Award, 1969. A bizarre new "sex" ray is being used by the Red Chinese to launch a global death game. *P*

1137. ___. *Red Rebellion.* New York: Award, 1970. Carter is called upon to end the menace caused by Red Chinese operatives working with radicals on American college campuses. *P*

1138. ___. *Redolmo Affair.* New York: Ace-Charter, 1979. Under cover of his forced retirement, Killmaster's mission is to break a Southeast Asian drug operation, headed by a mad scientist name Redolmo, which is crippling the West. *P*

1139. ___. *Reich Four.* New York: Ace-Charter, 1979. With only two clues and a dead man's musician daughter, N-3 must locate the missing Dr. Karl Nordheim and uncover a savage enemy bent on reestablishing Nazi glory. *P*

1140. ___. *Rhodesia.* New York: Award, 1970. A revenge-crazed Nazi brings Zimbabwe to the brink of race war. *P*

1141. ___. *Safari for Spies.* New York: Award, 1970. In Africa, Carter finds that the underworld has been alerted to the purpose of his mission and so, in Casablanca—the international crossroads of sex and espionage—he faces a death trap. *P*

1142. ___. *Sea Trap.* New York: Award, 1972. Killmaster faces a madman genius and must deal with the problem of US subs trapped beneath the sea. *P*

1143. ___. *Seven Against Greece.* New York: Award, 1973. Seven men join Princess Electra—whose evil beauty cannot be resisted—in a deadly duel with Carter. *P*

1144. ___. *Sign of the Cobra.* New York: Award, 1974. The back alleys of India explode with violence as N-3 collides with the invincible might of a secret organization known as SHIVA. *P*

1145. ___. *The Sign of the Prayer Shawl.* New York: Award, 1976. Within 48 hours, airliners will crash into the world's major financial centers—unless Killmaster can halt the men working for the mad Japanese plotter Aki Shintu. *P*

1146. ___. *Six Bloody Summer Days.* New York: Award, 1975. Carter is sent to retrieve or destroy a nuclear missile which has been snatched by the military strongman of a North African republic. *P*

1147. ___. *The Snake Flag Conspiracy.* New York: Award, 1976. The KGB has planted an agent in one of the oldest families in Boston in order to manipulate its vast financial power and wreck the US economy by forcing the largest banks to dump all of their stocks at the same time. *P*

1148. ___. *The Spanish Connection.* New York: Award, 1973. The Syndicate's drug network will crumble if N-3 can battle his way to an ex-mobster on the run. *P*

1149. ___. *Spy Castle.* New York: Award, 1971. British Intelligence is infiltrated and subverted for world conquest. *P*

1150. ___. *Strike Force Terror.* New York: Award, 1974. Impersonating a sadistic police chief, Killmaster infiltrates Russia's most notorious slave labor camp to obstruct an electrifying kidnap attempt against a Soviet leader. *See also* Hayes, Ralph E. (2524-2531) and Carter, Nick (1047). *P*

1151. ___. *Strike of the Hawk.* New York: Ace-Charter, 1980. The new terrorist cartel known as NOTCH wants to expose AXE and contaminate the West with bubonic plague. *P*

1152. ___. *Tarantula Strike.* New York: Ace-Charter, 1980. When the KGB's top agent is terminated, Carter joins his beautiful replacement in searching for the assassin. *P*

1153. ___. *Target: Doomsday Island.* New York: Award, 1973. A treacherous nuclear arsenal is concealed on a billionaire's island paradise and the US is targeted for invasion. *P*

1154. ___. *Temple of Fear.* New York: Award, 1970. N-3 assumes the identity of a man long dead in his fight to stop KGB killers in the Orient. *P*

1155. ___. *The Terrible Ones.* New York: Award, 1968. "Operation Blast" will move from Dominica to destroy the US unless Killmaster can do something about it. *P*

1156. ___. *The Thirteenth Spy.* New York: Award, 1970. Carter masquerades as Ivan Kiroschka, who is intent on writing a new novel, meeting a ballerina from the Bolshoi—and preventing World War III. *P*

1157. ___. *Thunderstrike in Syria.* New York: Ace-Charter, 1979. With the help of double agent Miriam Kamel, N-3 must infiltrate the desert camp of the terrorist Syrian Liberation Army and destroy it together with its fanatical leader, known only as "the Hawk." *P*

1158. ___. *Time Clock of Death.* New York: Award, 1968. The Soviet super spy jet had been hijacked and the Kremlin blamed America; Killmaster's mission: find the plane before the Russians decide to attack. *P*

1159. ___. *Triple Cross.* New York: Award, 1976. While doing a routine favor for MI-6 in the Trieste area, Carter encounters a group of murdering schemers and his new mission becomes immediately clear: stop the outbreak of political assassinations before they reach America. *P*

1160. ___. *The Turkish Bloodbath.* New York: Ace-Charter, 1980. N-3 is asked to locate a secret formula for a new weapon before the IRA, KGB, or PLO. *P*

1161. ___. *The Turncoat.* New York: Award, 1977. A top scientist seeks to defect from the USSR, but mobsters stand between him and freedom until Killmaster moves in to help. *P*

1162. ___. *The Ultimate Code.* New York: Ace-Charter, 1979. Carter delivers a decoding machine to Athens—and finds himself in a CIA trap that threatens world disaster. *P*

1163. ___. *The Vatican Vendetta.* New York: Award, 1974. N-3 works with Italian intelligence to stop the mad scheme of the evil, amoral Judas, who is out to murder the Pope. *See also* Hayes, Ralph E. (2524-2531) and Carter, Nick (1047). *P*

1164. ___. *The Vulcan Disaster.* New York: Award, 1976. When AXE "vanishes," Killmaster is alone in war-torn Southeast Asia to find a roll of explosive microfilm which a dozen agents had already been brutally murdered for. *P*

1165. ___. *War From the Clouds*. New York: Ace-Charter, 1980. Carter attempts to eliminate guerrilla leader Don Carlos Italla who, together with his followers, is holed up in a mountain fortress on a Caribbean island. *P*

1166. ___. *The Weapon of Night*. New York: Award, 1971. Total annihilation is threatened under the cover of paralyzing power failures. *P*

1167. ___. *Web of Spies*. New York: Award, 1971. N-3 is ordered to smash Spain's notorious espionage group called "the Spiders." *P*

1168. ___. *The Z Document*. New York: Award, 1975. A power-hungry Italian traitor, hiding out in the Ethiopian desert with missiles stolen from Egypt and Israel, will stop at nothing in his mad plan to dominate the globe. *P* Other Nick Carter tales include:

1169. ___. *Australia*. New York: Award, 1970. *P*

1170. ___. *Death Mission: Havana*. New York: Ace-Charter, 1980. *P*

1171. ___. *Ice Trap Terror*. New York: Award, 1974. *See also* Carter, Nick (1047). *P*

1172. ___. *Paris*. New York: Award, 1970. *P*

1173. ___. *Peking and the Tulip Affair*. New York: Award, 1969. *P*

1174. ___. *The Suicide Seat*. New York: Ace-Charter, 1980. *P*

1175. ___. *Typhoon Ray*. New York: Ace-Charter, 1980. *P*

1176. Carter, Youngman. *Mr. Campion's Farthing*. New York: Morrow, 1969. MI-5 seeks a Soviet scientist who has disappeared in England and is known to have KGB agents hounding him. *H

1177. Cartwright, Justin. *The Horse of Darius*. New York: Macmillan, 1980. The impending fall of the Shah brings a scurry among intelligence agents from East and West who are concerned over what kind of government will replace him.

1178. Cassell, Stephen. *The Final Voyage of the S.S.N. Skate*. New York: Pinnacle, 1989. The *Skate* is a nuclear attack sub on her way to the scrapyard until an incredible act of underwater piracy forces her, and her inexperienced crew, into action against the best of the Soviet fleet. *P* Two more:

1179. ___. *Deadpoint*. New York: Pinnacle, 1993. *P*

1180. ___. *Strike of the China Falcon*. New York: Pinnacle, 1992. *P*

1181. Cassidy, John. *A Station in the Delta.* New York: Scribner's, 1979. A failure in West Germany, CIA agent Toby Busch is reassigned to South Vietnam where he uncovers evidence of an impending large scale Communist attack on US positions.

1182. Cassill, R. V. *Dr. Cobb's Game.* New York: Geis, 1970. A man has a mission to save a scandal-ridden Britain; as much a look at the occult as a spy thriller.

Castle, John, pseud. *See* Payne, Ronald and John Garrod

1183. Catano, James V. *The Spy Who Was Vertically Challenged.* Baton Rouge, LA: Minette, 1993. An arrogant academic twit is mistakenly appointed to a government position in a war-scenario think-tank; he manages to convince his colleagues to pursue a policy that will lead to nuclear annihilation. *H*

1184. Catto, Max. *The Banana Men.* New York: Simon & Schuster, 1967. Hurricane Hannah blows a helicopter carrying the President into the middle of a Cuban swamp.

1185. Cave, Peter. *Foxbat*. New York: Jove, 1978. Project Cuckoo is CIA head Frank Hayman's operation to liberate from the Soviets its new fighter plane capable of blasting out enemy satellites in orbit. *P*

1186. Cerf, Bennett, comp. *Three Famous Spy Novels*. New York: Random, 1973. Contents: *The Great Impersonation*, by E. Phillips Oppenheim; *Journey Into Fear*, by Eric Ambler; and *The Confidential Agent*, by Graham Greene. *

1187. ___ and Michael K. Frith. *Alligator*. By I*n Fl*m*ng, pseud. New York: Vanitas, 1962. A parody, naturally, of Fleming's James Bond stories. *H*

Chaber, M. E., pseud. *See* Crossen, Kendell F.

1188. Chacko, David. *Gage.* New York: St. Martin's, 1974. An agent attempts to destroy an espionage outfit involved in domestic political assassinations. Two more:

1189. ___. *The Black Chamber.* New York: St. Martin's, 1988.

1190. ___. *Brick Alley.* New York: Delacorte, 1981.

1191. Chamales, Thomas. *Never So Few.* New York: Scribner's, 1957. Col. Reynolds leads OSS-sponsored Kachin guerrillas against the Japanese in 1944 Burma. **y*

1192. Chamberlain, William. *Red January.* New York: Paperback, 1964. A plot is hatched by the Soviets which would force the United States to surrender or be destroyed. *P*

Chambers, Dana, pseud. *See* Leffingwell, Albert

1193. Chandler, David. *The Masters Connection.* New York: Arbor, 1981. A young woman, employing a fortune in diamonds amassed by her father and his friend, will attempt to avenge her father's murder by that partner by kidnapping the ruthless wretch from his sanctuary in a North African fortress.

1194. Chantler, David T. *The Casablanca Opening.* New York: St. Martin's, 1977. The US consul general in a Latin American city is abducted by Soviet-backed urban guerrillas and must be freed by the local CIA station chief.

1195. Charbonneau, Louis. *The Lair.* New York: Fawcett, 1979. An advertiser's son is kidnapped by a crazed Nazi and an ex-GI. *P*

1196. ___. *Psychedelic-40.* New York: Bantam, 1965. Agents battle a power mad syndicate which is tyrannizing the world through the use of a super drug. *P*

1197. ___. *Stalk.* New York: Fine, 1992. One rogue CIA agent hunts another who is retired from the agency; they meet in a face-off with guns blazing. Two more:

1198. ___. *The Ice.* New York: Pocket, 1993.

1199. ___. *The Brea File.* Garden City, NY: 1983.

1200. Charles, Martin. *The Bent Hostage.* London: Trafalgar Square, 1992. A young American corporate executive gets kidnapped by a slovenly band of terrorists in Central America. *H*

Charles, Robert, pseud. *See* Smith, Robert C.

Charteris, Leslie, pseud. *See* Yin, Leslie C. B.

Chase, James H., pseud. *See* Raymond, René B.

Chase, Glen, pseud. *See* Fox, Gardner

Chase, Philip, pseud. *See* Friedman, Phillip

1201. Chesbro, George C. *The Cold Smell of Sacred Stone.* New York: Atheneum, 1988. Mongo, dwarf private investigator and criminologist, brings his brother out of a coma—only to discover that he can perform miracles. Two more Mongo mysteries:

1202. ___. *An Incident at Bloodtide.* New York: Mysterious, 1993.

1203. ___. *In the House of Secret Enemies.* New York: Mysterious, 1992.

Cheyney, Peter, pseud. *See* Cheyney, Reginald Southouse

1204. Cheyney, Reginald Southouse. *Dark Hero.* By Peter Cheyney, pseud. Dodd, 1946. An ex-Chicago mob triggerman is converted into an OSS agent and is sent to Europe during World War II to employ his old talent against the Nazis. *

Unsuccessful in several pursuits before World War II, Cheyney was, until 1939, a member of the British Union of Fascists. Turning to novels in 1936 he created the detective Lemmy Caution who, in a departure from many British crime heroes, investigated wrongs not in high society, but in low. During the War, Brust penned a number of highly successful tales involving the espionage theme and by the late 1940s was one of the world's best known crime writers by the name Peter Cheyney.

Cheyney was often panned by reviewers for spurious dialogue between his characters and a degree of violence reminiscent of Bulldog Drummond. Nevertheless, his tales, especially the Dark series, were imaginative and exciting and toward the end, he was even able to cure many of the dialogue difficulties of his earlier works. According to Donald McCormick, "Fleming was not only an avid reader of Cheyney, but studied the latter's books most carefully before creating Bond" (*Who's Who in Spy Fiction* [New York: Taplinger, 1977], 45).

1205. ___. *Dark Interlude.* By Peter Cheyney, pseud. New York: Dodd, 1947. The post-war murders of British agents in France by an unquenchable Nazi are finally halted by SIS operator O'Mara and his loyal assistants. *

1206. ___. *Dark Omnibus.* By Peter Cheyney, pseud. 3 vols. in 1. New York: Dodd, 1952. Contents: *Sinister Errand, Dark Street,* and *Stars Are Dark.* *

1207. ___. *Dark Street.* By Peter Cheyney, pseud. New York: Dodd, 1944. Peter Quayle of British Intelligence battles Nazi agents in Britain and later assists the French Resistance against the Gestapo. *

1208. ___. *I'll Say She Does.* By Peter Cheyney, pseud. New York: Dodd, 1946. Private eye Lemmy Caution assists the French counterespionage service to put paid to the account of a master spy. *

1209. ___. *Sinister Errand.* By Peter Cheyney, pseud. New York: Dodd, 1945. An amateur courier fumbles his way through a sophisticated caper to obtain the Russian timetable for a projected invasion of Yugoslavia. *

1210. ___. *Stars Are Dark.* By Peter Cheyney, pseud. New York: Dodd, 1943. Led by agent Quayle, MI-5 operators thwart a group of Nazi fifth columnists working in England. *

1211. ___. *Your Deal, My Lovely.* By Peter Cheyney, pseud. London: Collins, 1941. Lemmy Caution travels to the Middle East to uncover the reason behind a female agent's death and to recover a mission scientist, who turns out to be the leader of a Nazi spy network. * Two other Cheyney spy thrillers are:

1212. ___. *The Counterspy Murders.* Published originally under the title *Dark Duet.* By Peter Cheyney, pseud. New York: Avon, 1944. *P*

1213. ___. *The Killing Game.* By Peter Cheyney, pseud. New York: Belmont-Tower, 1975. First published in Britain in 1954 as *The Adventures of Julia and Two Other Spy Stories.* *P*

1214. Chevalier, Paul. *The Grudge.* New York: St. Martin's, 1981. A Luftwaffe pilot, who has refused to execute a particularly onerous order, takes refuge with an unwitting British family in order to escape the agents of MI-5 and Himmler.

1215. Childers, James S. *Enemy Outpost.* New York: Appleton-Century, 1942. American newsman Mike Kilpatrick must fight for his life in the Canadian wilderness to prevent members of a Nazi spy ring from obtaining the secret he has recently uncovered by accident. **y*

1216. Childs, Marquis. *The Peacemakers.* New York: Harcourt, 1961. The Big Four leaders meet in Vienna to stave off an immediate threat of nuclear war, but agents of their intelligence services continue to work to each's disadvantage.

1217. ___. *Taint of Innocence.* New York: Harper & Row, 1967. A recent CIA recruit—from Harvard—finds himself off on his first mission—to keep the oil rich sheikdom of Sibai out of the Russian orbit.

1218. Christian, John. *Five Gates to Armageddon.* New York: St. Martin's, 1975. Arriving in London with a cryptic message, a British SIS agent is shot while he deplanes from a commandeered Israeli airliner; British Intelligence moves to learn why their man was shot and discovers that a new Arab secret weapon will soon be ready to imperil world peace.

1219. Christie, Agatha. *N or M?* New York: Dodd, 1941. Much better known for the murder mysteries she penned during the 1920s, Dame Agatha, like Leslie "Charteris" Yin, was prone from time to time to involve her detective characters Hercule Poirot and the Beresfords in espionage themes. In this outing, Tommy and Tuppence Beresford, retired World War I agents, are called on once more to enter service, this time to locate a Nazi masterspy operating in England early in World War II. **y*

1220. ___. *Passenger to Frankfurt.* New York: Dodd, 1971. The ageless Beresfords, who made their first counterespionage appearance in 1922 (see Part 1), are asked by the SIS to look into the matter of "Project Benvo," a sinister plot against international peace. **y*

1221. ___. *The Patriotic Murders.* New York: Dodd, 1941. Poirot is mixed up with a munition magnate's murder and Nazi agents, arriving at a hair-raising solution after a third man is killed. Published in Britain as *One, Two Buckle My Shoe.* **y*

1222. ___. *Postern of Fate.* New York: Dodd, 1973. The Beresfords set off on a dangerous trail that leads from the mysterious death of a World War I spy to intrigue in the present. *y

1223. ___. *So Many Steps to Death.* New York: Dodd, 1955. A famous European scientist's disappearance leads the Beresfords to Morocco. *y

1224. ___. *Spies among Us.* New York: Dodd, 1968. Contents: *They Came to Baghdad* (1951), *Murder in Mesopotamia* (1938), and *N or M?* (1941). *y

1225. ___. *They Came to Baghdad.* New York: Dodd, 1951. Victoria Jones, fired from her London job, journeys to Baghdad and there becomes a key figure in an espionage plot against world peace. *y

1226. Christie, William. *The Warriors of God.* Novato, CA: Presidio, 1992. Happy-to-die Iranian terrorists attempt to capture the White House.

1227. Clancy, Leo. *Fix.* New York: Knopf, 1979. Quinn, a resourceful IRA leader, escapes assassination and leads the police and MI-5 on a merry London chase.

1228. Clancy, Tom. *The Hunt for Red October.* Annapolis, MD: Naval Institute, 1984. To Tom Clancy belongs the distinction of ushering in the boom of the technothriller in this account of a Soviet submarine commander's decision to defect—with the most sophisticated nuclear submarine in the world, the Red October. Despite the plethora of technical details, Clancy's background is civilian, including an English major's degree from Loyola in 1969; in fact, he purchased the insurance agency he went to work for in Baltimore after leaving The Hartford Insurance Company. Clancy's fiction does not engage the moral complexities of espionage, such as one finds in Allbeury, Deighton, and le Carré; instead, he prefers a black-and-white world—notably one filled with action for his protagonist "Jack" Ryan. The film starred Sean Connery. (See Mr. Clancy's commentary in CRAFT NOTES.)

1229. ___. *The Cardinal of the Kremlin.* New York: Berkley, 1989. Jack Ryan must save Cardinal—America's agent-in-place inside the Kremlin and the only man besides Ryan with information on the Soviet satellite defense system—from KGB killers.

1230. ___. *Clear and Present Danger.* New York: Putnam, 1989. Newgate Callendar quotes David Wise's review of this Clancy novel about the US government's unofficial war on the Medellín drug cartels and the crisis of conscience this provokes in CIA analyst John Patrick ("Jack") Ryan: "He [Clancy] lovingly describes the hardware of death; he is an indecent docent in a gallery of horrors. Heads roll (literally), body parts fly, blood flows."

1231. ___. *Patriot Games*. New York: Berkley, 1986. In this third novel featuring Ryan, who is visiting London with wife and child, a rogue branch of IRA terrorists decides to kill the Prince of Wales; as gunfire erupts, Ryan manages to save the royal and kill a terrorist, only to bring down the wrath of the dead man's brother. The 1993 film starred Harrison Ford.

1232. ___. *Red Storm Rising*. New York: Putnam's, 1986. The Soviets plunge into a conventional war with the US when Muslim fundamentalists destroy their Siberian oil production, triggering an energy crisis, and precipitating an invasion of their forces into Western Europe.

1233. ___. *The Sum of All Fears*. New York: Berkley, 1992. This time, Jack Ryan goes into action when an Israeli nuclear device fall into the hands of a formidable conspiracy of rabid Palestinians, European extremists, East German secret police and renegade scientists.

1234. ___. *Without Remorse*. New York: Putnam's, 1993. The Pentagon selects John Kelly as its man to head a rescue of prisoners held in North Vietnam.

1235. Clark, Eric. *Black Gambit*. New York: Warner, 1977. A dissident Russian scientist, under house arrest by the KGB, is the object of a bait-and-switch operation that will smuggle him to Israel and replace him with an impersonator.

1236. ___. *Send in the Lions*. New York: Atheneum, 1981. Several years from now, retired CIA agent George Singleton is given the impossible task of outwitting or meeting the demands of a detestable band of international terrorists who have hijacked a Concorde packed with all kinds of important people.

1237. ___. *The Sleeper*. New York: Atheneum, 1980. A disaffected Soviet "mole" is commissioned by MI-5 to compromise the Prime Minister's top advisor, who is suspected of leaking state secrets to Moscow.

1238. Clark, William. *Number Ten*. Boston: Houghton, 1967. A power struggle breaks out in the British government, sparked by a crisis in Africa.

1239. ___. *Special Relationship.* Boston: Houghton, 1969. In a futuristic 1977, the new US President agrees to a CIA plan for unseating the Indian government and replacing it with a military junta.

1240. Clavell, James. *Noble House.* New York: Delacorte, 1981. The KGB, CIA, and Chinese Intelligence Service all have a stake in the fate of Struan's, "the Noble House," oldest of Hong Kong's trading firms.

1241. Clayton, Richard. *The Antagonists.* By William Haggard, pseud. New York: Washburn, 1964. An important Yugoslav scientist in England is wanted dead-or-alive by certain Russian, British, and American agents, despite the fact that Colonel Charles Russell of the Security Executive has been charged with his safety. **y*

Clayton, a long-time employee of the Indian and British civil services, was intimately involved with intelligence matters throughout his career.

Clayton's Russell has been described as "Buchanish" and his tales a bridge between the unrealistic pre-Ambler school and the spy thrillers of the James Bond era. Throughout his many exploits, Russell is made to act correctly in all matters and even with his opposite numbers in the KGB. Clayton's tales are filled with action and are all, as he once described them, "political novels" of romantic derring-do.

1242. ___. *The Arena.* By William Haggard, pseud. New York: Washburn, 1962. The Security Executive must see if a huge financial deal in London is a danger to the state. **y*

1243. ___. *Closed Circuit.* By William Haggard, pseud. New York: Washburn, 1961. Colonel Russell becomes involved with British Foreign Office meddling in the South American republic of Candoro. **y*

1244. ___. *The Conspirators.* By William Haggard, pseud. New York: Walker, 1968. Russell looks for the second of two atomic bombs accidentally dropped off the coast of Devon and is charged with finding it before anti-American elements in Britain learn of it. **y*

1245. ___. *A Cool Day for Killing.* By William Haggard, pseud. New York: Walker, 1968. Agent Russell works to overcome the effects of a political assassination and a military coup in a far-off Malay kingdom. ***

1246. ___. *The Hard Sell.* By William Haggard, pseud. New York: Washburn, 1966. Industrial espionage and murder during the production of a

British aircraft engine, which could mean millions for a Britain in competition with America, brings Colonel Russell in to investigate. *y

1247. ___. *The Hardliners.* By William Haggard, pseud. New York: Walker, 1971. After his retirement from the Security Executive, Russell is asked to dissuade a prominent author from writing a book about a Central European nation. *y

1248. ___. *The High Wire.* By William Haggard, pseud. New York: Washburn, 1963. An indiscreet remark leads an innocent into involvement with enemy spies; Russell saves the day in a climactic battle atop a cable car stranded high above the Alps. *y

1249. ___. *Notch on the Knife.* By William Haggard, pseud. New York: Walker, 1973. [*The Old Masters.* London: Cassell, 1973]. Russell travels to a Balkan country where bloody violence and ancient customs are widely accepted.

1250. ___. *The Powder Barrel.* By William Haggard, pseud. New York: Washburn, 1965. Colonel Russell must work together with a Soviet agent to prevent an explosive crisis in a Middle East oil sheikdom ripe for anarchy. *y

1251. ___. *The Power House.* By William Haggard, pseud. New York: Washburn, 1967. Colonel Russell's favorite nephew brings word that his girlfriend's father, a left wing member of Parliament, is planning to defect. *y

1252. ___. *The Protectors.* By William Haggard, pseud. New York: Walker, 1973. Stolen from the safe of a rich American who has been buying secrets from a top British official, a document ends up on Cyprus from whence Colonel Russell must retrieve it. *y

1253. ___. *Slow Burner.* By William Haggard, pseud. Boston: Little, 1958. The first Colonel Russell tale in which he joins a physicist in a search for a nuclear device which is emitting strange rays from a modest private building in a London suburb. *y

1254. ___. *The Telemann Touch.* By William Haggard, pseud. Boston: Little, 1959. The British have discovered oil beneath a Caribbean island and send Colonel Russell to protect it for the Commonwealth, unaware that a KGB competitor is already on the scene. *y

1255. ___. *Too Many Enemies.* By William Haggard, pseud. New York: Walker, 1972. [*The Bitter Harvest.* London, Cassell, 1971]. An incorruptible Member of Parliament and an Arab agent and assassin cross swords with Colonel Russell. *y

1256. ___. *The Unquiet Sleep.* By William Haggard, pseud. New York: Washburn, 1962. Cypriot terrorists steal a British-made tranquilizer with unpredictable properties for use in unseating a minister opposed to their activities; Colonel Russell is called upon to recover the drug and quash the plot. *y

1257. ___. *Venetian Blind.* By William Haggard, pseud. New York: Washburn, 1960. Colonel Russell is asked to halt the flood of secrets leaking out of a British industrial plant. *y

1258. ___. *Visa to Limbo.* By William Haggard, pseud. New York: Walker, 1979. On vacation in Israel, Colonel Russell is caught up with the schemes of a Palestinian youth, an Israeli admiral, and the politically troubled Sheikh of Alidra. *

1259. ___. *Yesterday's Enemy.* By William Haggard, pseud. New York: Walker, 1976. Russell moves to halt the mad plans of the rich fiend Belami Clark, who is plotting to cause war between Russia and the United States. * Four more Clayton novels are:

1260. ___. *The Doubtful Disciple.* London: Cassell, 1969.

1261. ___. *The Median Line.* New York: Walker, 1981.

1262. ___. *The Poison People.* New York: Walker, 1979.

1263. ___. *The Scorpion's Tail.* By William Haggard, pseud. New York: Walker, 1975.

1264. Cleary, Jon. *The High Commissioner.* New York: Morrow, 1967. A cross between a spy and detective thriller: an Australian sleuth is sent to arrest the High Commissioner for murder but, upon finding him in London, must protect him while he is involved in negotiations to end the Vietnam War.

1265. ___. *The Long Pursuit.* New York: Morrow, 1967. Having missed their chance to escape Sumatra in early 1942, a group of survivors from besieged Singapore join native guerrillas in fighting the Japanese invaders.

1266. ___. *Peter's Pence.* New York: Morrow, 1974. A British agent is called upon to rescue the Pope, who has been kidnapped by IRA terrorists.

1267. ___. *The Pulse of Danger.* New York: Morrow, 1966. An English expedition in the Himalayas discovers Red Chinese troops advancing on India's Northwest Frontier.

1268. ___. *Season of Doubt.* New York: Morrow, 1968. An American embassy official in Lebanon attempts to dissuade a friend in the gunrunning business.

1269. ___. *A Very Private War.* New York: Morrow, 1980. Two New Britain coastwatchers, an expatriate American baseball pitcher and an Australian youth, are sent on a desperate mission against a Japanese installation in the Solomons early in 1942.

1270. Cleeve, Brian T. *Dark Blood, Dark Terror.* New York: Random, 1966. British Intelligence assists the South African Special Branch to locate a band of terrorists who are sabotaging various installations.

1271. ___. *Death of a Bitter Englishman.* New York: Random, 1967. "The Agency" has had a recent change in command and the former Director asks Sean Ryan to investigate the death of an agent—a death officially listed as a suicide.

1272. ___. *Vice Isn't Private.* New York: Random, 1966. Ryan arranges the escape of a convicted murderer planning to blackmail the British Home Secretary and then pursues him in an effort to prevent the plan's success.

1273. ___. *Vote X for Treason.* New York: Random, 1964. Agent Ryan must foil the plot of the neo-Fascist group, called The New Party, which is planning to rig the British general election. One other Ryan story is:

1274. ___. *Escape from Prague.* New York: Random, 1970.

1275. Clements, Eileen H. *Cherry Harvest.* London: Messner, 1944. An RAF intelligence officer breaks a German espionage ring operating out of an English girls' school. **y*

1276. ___. *Let Him Die.* New York: Dutton, 1940.

1277. Clewes, Howard. *Epitaph for Love.* Garden City, NY: Doubleday, 1953. An English resident of Italy meets a girl years after their short love affair and joint work in the wartime Resistance; unfortunately, they meet as enemies in an espionage plot.

Clifford, Francis, pseud. *See* Thompson, Arthur L. B.

1278. Clive, John. *Barossa*. New York: Delacorte, 1981. Two former Nazi scientists plotting in the Australian desert to change the world balance of power are uncovered by American TV reporter Harry Brockway, who is there investigating a series of sensational child kidnappings.

1279. ___. *The Last Liberator*. New York: Delacorte, 1980. To hide his Nazi past, Koessler races a Dutch businessman and a Jew to reclaim the wreck of an American bomber, now in ruins in the Zuider Zee, that he piloted in 1945 in an effort to transport a top German leader to Ireland.

1280. *Cloak-and-Dagger: Ten Thrilling Stories of Espionage*. Intro. by Robert Arthur. New York: Mayflower, 1967. An anthology including these stories: "From a View to a Kill," by Ian Fleming; "The Hut," by Geoffrey Household; "High Tide," by John P. Marquand; and "The Hairless Mexican," by W. Somerset Maugham. *P*

Clyde, Allison, pseud. *See* Knowles, William

Cody, James P., pseud. *See* Rohrbach, Peter T.

1281. Coen, Franklin. *The Plunderers*. New York: Coward-McCann, 1980. At the end of World War II, agents of the OSS seek the lost treasure of Hermann Goering with the help of his chief aide.

1282. Cohen, Arthur A. *A Hero in His Time*. New York: Random, 1976. A minor Russian Jewish poet is forced to become a KGB courier and is dispatched to the United States.

1283. Cohen, Stanley. *330 Park*. New York: Putnam's, 1977. Using tactics learned in Vietnam, Larry Devereau and his private platoon capture a New York City building and hold 600 hostages.

Coles, Manning, pseud. *See* Manning, Adelaide F. O. and C. Henry Coles

1284. Collin, Richard O. *Imbroglio.* New York: St. Martin's, 1980. An introverted American diplomat in Rome must act forcefully when the future of Italy is suddenly thrust into his modest hands.

1285. Collingwood, Charles. *The Defector.* New York: Harper & Row, 1970. The veteran CBS correspondent tells us of the adventures of a "colleague," who was persuaded by the CIA to make a trip to North Vietnam and contact a Hanoi official rumored to be interested in defecting to the Americans. *

1286. Collins, Larry. *Fall from Grace.* New York: Simon & Schuster, 1985. Born John Lawrence Collins, Jr., this versatile writer of a half dozen bestsellers with Dominique LaPierre is a former *Newsweek* editor who earned an international reputation for the exacting research behind his works. Based on Operation Fortitude (which kept the German High Command preoccupied at Pas-de-Calais after the Normandy landings); Catherine Pradier is dropped into France on a mission of sabotage, unaware that she has been betrayed by her own OSS masters as the final piece of disinformation about the coming invasion. (See Mr. Collins' commentary in CRAFT NOTES.)

1287. ___. *Maze.* New York: Simon & Schuster, 1989. The "maze" is an intricately timed plot that links a murdered psychic, who was capable of pinpointing a Soviet sub, an embittered head of CIA's Behavioral Sciences Division, a brilliant Soviet brain researcher, the new US Prseident, Moslem terrorists, sleeper agents, and the man who manipulates all: KGB Director Feodorov; extra-low frequency signals are pulsed into the President's brain—and send him into uncontrollable spasms of rage.

1288. ___ and Dominique LaPierre. *The Fifth Horseman.* New York: Simon & Schuster, 1980. [*Le Cinquieme Cavalier.* Paris: Laffont, 1980]. The Collins-Lapierre team produces a meticulously explored scenario of our modern urban nightmare: this is what happens when Palestinian terrorists, orchestrated and bankrolled by the mad Libyan leader Muammar al-Qaddafi himself, announce they are going to explode a nuclear bomb in three days from its obscure location within New York City. Other Collins-LaPierre books include these highly acclaimed historical and biographical efforts:

1289. ___. *Freedom at Midnight.* New York: Simon & Schuster, 1975. [*Cette Nuit la Liberte.* Paris: Laffonte, 1975].

1290. ___. *Is Paris Burning?* New York: Simon & Schuster, 1965. [*Paris Brule-t-Il?* Paris: Laffont, 1964].

1291. ___. *Mountbatten and the Partition of India.* New Delhi: Vikas, 182.

1292. ___. *O Jerusalem!* New York: Simon & Schuster, 1972.

1293. ___. *Or I'll Dress You in Mourning.* New York: Simon & Schuster, 1968. [*Ou Tu Porteras Mon Deuil.* Paris: Laffont, 1967].

1294. Collins, Norman. *The Bat That Flits.* Boston: Little, 1953. Agents vie for the secrets of a top-secret laboratory hidden in a remote part of Cornwall, England. *

1295. Coltrane, James. *Talon.* Indianapolis: Bobbs-Merrill, 1978. When he discovers a suspicious aberration in a series of spy satellite photos, CIA analyst Talon is marked for death by the plotters on the rightist fringe of the intelligence body. Two more Coltrane works are:

1296. ___. *The Blind Trust Kills.* New York: Bobbs-Merrill, 1978.

1297. ___. *The Nirvana Contracts.* New York: Bobbs-Merrill, 1977.

1298. Condon, Richard. *The Manchurian Candidate.* New York: McGraw-Hill, 1959. Raymond was Red China's deadliest weapon—an All-American hero programmed to assassinate upon command. This work was said by some to have provided inspiration for the killing of President Kennedy. *
     A former movie press agent and Broadway odd-jobsman, Condon began his literary career at the age of forty-two. In the years since 1958, he has written various novels, plays, essays, and non-fiction titles. *The Manchurian Candidate*, his first spy thriller, was written from climactic ending backwards to the beginning. Never connected with any intelligence agency, Condon's espionage yarns all demonstrate a fascination with mind control and are tense, exciting, and well-charactered.

1299. ___. *Emperor of America.* New York: Simon & Schuster, 1990. Charismatic Chay Appleton, the nation's first six-star general, becomes its first monarch. *H*

1300. ___. *An Infinity of Mirrors.* New York: Random, 1964. Condon's novel spans the turbulent decade between the early thirties and early forties and shifts from Paris to Berlin and back to Paris during the Occupation; a French Jew and a Prussian military officer meet, fall in love, and marry in Berlin just as Hitler comes to power.

1301. ___. *The Star-Spangled Crunch.* New York: Bantam, 1974. A satire in which a power-mad but wacky gang of schemers plot the slickest takeover of the world. *PH*

1302. ___. *The Venerable Bead.* New York: St. Martin's, 1992. *H*

1303. ___. *The Whisper of the Axe.* New York: Dial, 1976. A beautiful Black Maoist terrorist devises a plan to wreck America by setting loose a Chinese-trained urban guerrilla band in thirty cities on July 4, 1976; when the intelligence community learns of this plot, a Defense Intelligence Agency (DIA) operative and a brother-sister CIA team are ordered to halt it.

1304. ___. *Winter Kills.* New York: Dial, 1974. The family of President Tim Kegan is forced by a deathbed confession to reopen the investigation into his assassination and the ensuing trail leads almost everywhere including inside the CIA. The tale is obviously modeled on the Kennedy tragedy.

1305. Conly, Robert L. *Report From Group 17.* By Robert C. O'Brien, pseud. New York: Atheneum, 1972. A biologist is recruited to look into reports of unspeakable genetic experiments being performed at a Soviet villa by a former Nazi scientist.

1306. Connable, Alfred. *Twelve Trains to Babylon.* Boston: Little, 1971. A CIA agent must answer the question, "Is the Mafia planning to take over a secret Communist espionage organization operating inside this country?"

1307. Conners, Bernard F. *Don't Embarrass the Bureau.* New York: Avon, 1976. Recently appointed to the FBI, two new agents become the protagonists in a KGB effort to take it over. *P*

1308. Connolly, Cyril. "Bond Strikes Camp." In his *Previous Convictions.* London: Harper & Row, 1963. 354-372. First published in *London* magazine for April 1963, this story is aimed at the Bond Mania and remains the ultimate satire upon it.
     "M" orders James to disguise himself as a woman in order to trap a visiting KGB general, who in the end turns out to be "M" himself having a little fun with 007.

1309. Connolly, Ray. *Newsdeath.* New York: Atheneum, 1978. The PUMA urban terrorist gang begins setting off bombs in London as it wages war against the British mass media.

1310. Conrad, Brenda. *The Stars Give Warning.* New York: Scribner's, 1941. US Army G-2 agents battle Nazi spies in the Panama Canal Zone during that period of twilight war between America and Germany prior to Pearl Harbor. **y*

1311. Cook, Bob. *Disorderly Elements.* New York: St. Martin's, 1986. Michael Wyman is a middle-aged man who loses his teaching fellowship first and his job at MI-6 second. Worse yet, his girlfriend is pregnant and there's a mole in his department that his former superiors refuse to believe exists. *H*

1312. ___. *Fire and Forget.* New York: St. Martin's, 1991. Based on the former President Reagan's gaffe about bombing Russia during his weekly radio broadcast, a US President makes a preposterously indiscreet joke over the radio which triggers a Star War satellite's reaction to imminent war with the Soviet Union. *H*

1313. ___. *Paper Chase.* New York: St. Martin's, 1990. Four retired British agents, all paper pushers, decide to pen their memoirs, after being treated with contempt by a tough new agent; when they exaggerate their careers and capers *a la* James Bond, a crazed American officer decides to kill them all. *H*

1314. ___. *Questions of Identity.* London: Gollancz, 1987. Michael Wyman returns as a visiting professor of philosophy in Rome—only to become embroiled in espionage again when the Red Brigade captures a bacteriologist whose knowledge will enable them to destroy massive numbers of people. *H*
One more:

1315. ___. *Faceless Mortals.* London: Gollancz, 1988.

1316. Cook, Nick. *Angel, Archangel.* New York: St. Martin's, 1990. Aviation editor for the prestigious *Jane's Defence Weekly*, British author Cook creates a plot for the end of WW II as he combines Luftwaffe jets and a Russian plot to conquer the world.

1317. ___. *Aggressor.* New York: St. Martin's, 1993. A recent suspense adventure set in the Persian Gulf region.

1318. Cook, Sly. *The Child and the Serpent.* New York: Seaview, 1980. A Polish boy with murderous psychic powers is still under the control of South American Nazis.

1319. Cooke, David C. *Care of American Embassy*. New York: Dodd, 1967. A likeable CIA agent is sent to New Delhi to find out why a recently deceased beggar had a number of perfect counterfeit tenrupee notes.

1320. Cooney, Michael. *Doomsday England*. New York: Walker, 1966. The Queen's Investigator is the hereditary head of HM Secret Service, at least according to the ground rules of this tale. Using the tools of his trade—money, sex, and violence—he must find and disarm a monster cobalt bomb planted somewhere in England by the Russians.

1321. Coonts, Stephen. *Final Flight*. New York: Doubleday, 1988. International terrorist Colonel Qazi plots to loot America's nuclear weapons. (See Mr. Coonts' commentary in CRAFT NOTES.)

1322. ___. *Flight of the Intruder*. Annapolis, MD: US Naval Institute, 1986. His first aviation technothriller featuring Jake Grafton.

1323. ___. *The Minotaur*. New York: Doubleday, 1989. Navy pilot Jake Grafton makes his third appearance in this technothriller of a Pentagon mole stealing secrets for the Soviets and threatening the security of top secret "Athena," the next generation of tactical aircraft.

1324. ___. *The Red Horseman*. New York: Pocket, 1993. Jake Grafton, a Rear Admiral attached to Defense Intelligence, is sent to Moscow to stop the surreptitious sale of tactical nuclear weapons to the Middle East in the wake of the Soviet Union's collapse. However, rogue CIA agents and Moscow hardliners want him dead and his mission to fail.

1325. ___. *Under Siege*. New York: Pocket, 1990. Chano Aldana, the "big banana of the Medellín cartel," is captured and extradited to the US for trial. Assassins severely wound Bush in reprisal, Vice President Quayle assumes command, and Jake Grafton, working for the Joint Chiefs, joins the fight against Aldana's thugs [the real "Aldana," Pablo Escobar was killed by Columbian police while fleeing from his hideout across rooftops on December 6, 1993].

1326. Cooper, Alfred Duff. *Operation Heartbreak*. New York: Viking, 1951. A fictitious account, barely disguised from the real "Operation Mincemeat," of how British Intelligence used a corpse to lure the Germans into believing that a 1943 Mediterranean invasion would be in Sardinia rather than in Sicily.

    The Cooper novel led to a series of London newspaper exposes by Ian Colvin and to a temporary lifting of the Official Secrets Act which allowed

Ewen Montagu to reveal the full story of "Major Martin" in *The Man Who Never Was*.

1327. Cooper, Brian. *A Touch of Thunder.* New York: Vanguard, 1962. An intelligence officer in the old Indian Army seeks to prevent Gandhi's less-peaceful followers from blowing up a section of the Calcutta-Peshawar railway.

1328. ___. *The Van Langeren Girl.* New York: Vanguard, 1961. In India toward the close of World War II, a beautiful Eurasian girl is suspected by British Intelligence of being a Japanese spy.

1329. Cooper, Tom. *War*Moon.* Toronto: Worldwide, 1987. Natasha Smirnova is the Soviet's brilliant design engineer of an orbiting battle station. The US sends its own engineer, Chris Carmichael, to seduce her and bring her over to the Americans. *P*

1330. Copeland, William. *Five Hours from Isfahan.* New York: Putnam's, 1975. An OSS agent in 1943 Teheran is mixed-up in the real-life German plot to assassinate Roosevelt, Churchill, and Stalin.

1331. Copp, DeWitt. *The Pursuit of Agent M.* New York: Mill, 1961. A Western agent finds unexpected allies as he attempts to escape from behind the Iron Curtain after an espionage mission.

1332. Coppel, Alfred. *The Apocalypse Brigade.* New York: Holt, 1981. After meeting at a Peace Corps outpost in the Arabian desert, Egyptian physician Amira Shallai and US foreign correspondent Michael Rivas find themselves embarked on a desperate mission which could change the face of the earth.

1333. ___. *Between the Thunder and the Sun.* New York: Harcourt, 1971. A terrorist seizes an inflight Miami-bound airliner and directs it into the path of a hurricane.

1334. ___. *The Burning Mountain: A Novel of the Invasion of Japan.* New York: Harcourt, 1983. The author turns from international thriller, to present a detailed "what-if" saga that considers what might have happened if the dropping of the A-bomb had been delayed.

1335. ___. *The Dragon.* New York: Harcourt, 1977. A coup attempt in the USSR threatens war with a laser equipped Red China unless the US President can successfully and personally intervene.

1336. ___. *The Hastings Conspiracy.* New York: Holt, 1980. While transporting a secret document, a CIA agent disappears behind the Iron Curtain and becomes involved in a conspiracy which American and British operatives must untangle.

1337. ___. *Show Me a Hero.* San Diego: Harcourt, 1987. Major K. C. Quary, US Army combat assault specialist takes a team into Tunisia. Object: free the US ambassador to Lebanon and eleven hostages by pretending to be part of a film crew making a war epic in the Libyan desert.

1338. ___. *Thirty-Four East.* New York: Harcourt, 1974. The dusty desert of the Sinai Peninsula is the locale of an unexpected superpower confrontation, which is eventually defused by American and Soviet generals working together in a spirit of cooperation not shared by their governments. Another Coppels:

1339. ___. *A Land of Mirrors.* New York: Ivy, 1989.

1340. ___. *Wars and Winters.* New York: Fine, 1993. Spy fiction written under the A. C. Marin pseudonym:

1341. ___. *The Clash of Distant Thunder.* By A. C. Marin, pseud. New York: Harcourt, 1968. CIA agent John Wells is ordered to Paris to see why the local station chief has been missing his contacts.

1342. ___. *Rise with the Wind.* By A. C. Marin, pseud. New York: Harcourt, 1969. A disillusioned American CIA operative of the le Carré school is sent to a South American dictatorship to spirit out a gibbering drunk believed to be a former top Nazi who skipped Germany at the close of the war with millions in Jewish gold.

1343. ___. *A Storm of Spears.* By A. C. Marin, pseud. New York: Harcourt, 1971. A disaffected teaching assistant is blackmailed into stealing a secret document from the research institute of a California university.

1344. Corley, Edwin. *The Hanged Men.* By David Harper, pseud. New York: Dodd, 1977. A former CIA agent discovers three corpses among the Halloween dummies marking the mountain roads of the Adirondacks.

1345. ___. *Hijacked.* By David Harper, pseud. New York: Dodd, 1970. When a threatening note is found aboard the plane, the crew of a Trans-America flight begins a desperate search for the identity of their unknown hijacker. More:

1346. ___. *Air Force One*. New York: Dell, 1979. *P*

1347. ___. *The Genesis Rock*. Garden City, NY: Doubleday, 1980.

1348. ___. *Long Shots*. Garden City, NY: Doubleday, 1981.

1349. ___. *Sargasso*. New York: Dell, 1978. *P*

1350. ___. *Shadows*. New York: Stein & Day, 1975.

1351. ___. *Siege*. New York: Stein & Day, 1969.

1352. Cormier, Robert. *After the First Death*. New York: Pantheon, 1979. Terrorists in New England hold a busload of children and demand the dismantling of a secret government agency known as Inner Delta.

1353. Cornford, Philip. *Catalyst*. New York: Bantam, 1991. Colonel Klimenti Amalrik of the KGB is assigned to work with a CIA man in their investigation of a terrorist group calling itself Vigilantes for Peace—a group that is systematically killing off high-ranking Cold Warriors, Russian and American.

1354. Cornwell, Bernard. *Crackdown*. New York: HarperCollins, 1992. A charter skipper in the Caribbean becomes a marked man when he reports a bullet-riddled derelict to the Bahamian authorities.

1355. Cornwell, David J. M. *Call for the Dead*. By John le Carré, pseud. New York: Walker, 1962 [*The Deadly Affair*. New York: Penguin, 1966]. Agent George Smiley is concerned with the death of a British Foreign Office clerk who has just received security clearance.

An Oxford educated teacher, David Cornwell joined the British foreign service at the height of the Cold War in the late 1950s and served as Second Secretary of the British Embassy in Bonn from 1960-1963 and as Consul in Hamburg in 1964. This was, as the reader will remember, a period of intense East-West conflict over Berlin and divided Germany and a period when the operations of rival intelligence services in that arena—never slow—were in high gear.

Cornwell's work in Germany brought him intimate, first-hand knowledge of the "game" as it was then being played and provided him with the background against which he was to pen his many tales, stories which have made him the favorite of both professional intelligence officers and lay readers alike.

As his first three spy thrillers were written during the time he was in the Queen's employ, Cornwell found it necessary to adopt a pen name. When the KGB discovered later that le Carré had been a British Foreign Office official in Germany and had this fact published in the Russian *Literary Gazette*, Cornwell stepped in from "the cold" to reveal his true identity. As time wore on and his reputation increased, he spoke freely of his opinions on espionage and intelligence services, including a perceptive introduction to *The Philby Conspiracy* (1968) and a series of PBS interviews (which really should be published) before each installment of the dramatization of his *Tinker, Tailor, Soldier, Spy* on American television early in 1981.

Cornwell's writings were and are a reaction to the James Bond mania, descendent as it was from the pre-war melodramas of such writers as LeQueux, Oppenheim, and "Sapper." Indeed, his tales represent the logical and progressive continuation of the "realism" school of W. Somerset Maugham and Eric Ambler, flavored with dismay over the workings of intelligence services as he saw them in Germany and which he felt, along with others, over the revelations concerning George Blake, Burgess and Maclean, and Kim Philby.

The message of le Carré is that espionage is a game, a game in which people, pretending to be what they are not, are often the victims of deceit and a non-benevolent authority which may destroy them at a whim. Those working in intelligence may be good or evil, may be possessed of weak character or strong, but are all individuals with tastes, ideas, and feelings which may or may not transcend and/or determine their success or failure as agents. "The special quality of le Carré's books," wrote Julian Symons, "are their sense of place, their sense of doom, their irony" (*Mortal Consequences: A History—From the Detective Story to the Crime Novel* (New York: Schocken, 1972), 244. Cornwell gives us the anti-hero—unheroic men and women, unheroic spies, and non-snobbish characters who do the dirty work of espionage. Sometimes, like the short, fat, ill-dressed Smiley, they are beguilingly simple civil servants of a clandestine world with problems like unfaithful wives, but they do all try to cope in the same murky, unfriendly—but altogether common—everyday world.

Cornwell said in an interview that there are thirty-two wars going on in the world of one kind or another—despite the fact that the Cold War is over. He disputes as "wishful thinking" a *New Yorker* editor's remark about him that, with Communism defeated, there is nothing for him to write about: "Spies are more in demand than ever," he insists.*

His most recent novel, *The Night Manager*, (New York: Knopf, 1993) is about a former undercover agent who once worked for British Intelligence in Northern Ireland but is now a night manager at the Hotel Meister Palace in

---

*Hillel Italie, "LeCarre [sic] Speaks on Spying, Writing," *Star Beacon* [Ashtabula, OH] July 20, 1993, sec. C: 3.

Zurich. Jonathan Pine, the protagonist, gets involved with Richard Onslow Roper, international arms dealer with a past that connects him to Pine:

> Vowing to "treat himself to a little chaos," Pine accepts an offer from a splinter group of British [I]ntelligence to spy on Roper. A fake kidnapping of Roper's son is staged and Pine comes to the rescue. He soon becomes friends with Roper and meets some of his friends, veterans of "every dirty war from Cuba to Salvador to Guatemala to Nicaragua."

Obviously, from this small excerpt, readers of John le Carré will have scented out his themes of betrayal, honor, loyalty—the irruption of sudden violence into an ordinary character's drab life, and the excruciating tension of public demands versus private conscience—quintessential le Carré. Noting the "Conradian complexity" that sometimes obscures plotline in le Carré, Julian Symons asks whether it measures up to the best of his canon and answers with an equivocal yes: "Mr. le Carré sometimes surrenders to the inescapably sensational nature of the espionage thriller, and also to a romanticism about women that leads to the creation of a pipe-dream fantasy rather than a character in Jed, Roper's mistress" (29).*

Only Ted Allbeury and Len Deighton can claim equal standing with le Carré in reputation on the points of writing skill and realistic depiction of the convoluted, intricacies of modern espionage—especially in dealing with the human core of this complex world of spies and agents. Le Carré's has shown less interest in the kind of realism that made *A Small Town in Germany* such a stunning portrayal of the gray world of espionage, and he has expanded his characterizations in the novels after *Tinker, Tailor* to consider wider issues such as the social underpinnings of an individual's betrayal, for example, in *A Perfect Spy*. Plot tends to dissipate in the smoke of these convoluted reflections and digressions. But like his two great contemporaries, he is always concerned with the universal themes of betrayal and trust and the rocky terrain of the human heart. Thus, Cornwell's attention to detail may lack the scrupulous realism favored in the professional worlds of Allbeury and Deighton (he freely coins espionage jargon to suit his plot), but he is as adept as they at introducing everyday problems into the lives of his men and women.

1356. ___. *The Honourable Schoolboy.* By John le Carré, pseud. New York: Knopf, 1977. Having found the mole in *Tinker, Tailor, Soldier, Spy* (q.v.), George Smiley becomes involved in an intelligence fiasco and must relentlessly

---

*Julian Symons, "Our Man in Zurich," rev. of *The Night Manager*, by John le Carré, (New York: Knopf, 1993), *New York Times Book Review* 27 June 1993, sec. 7: 1+.

backtrack the facts of the disaster, thus uncovering the fact that it emanates from a Communist money supply to a rich Hong Kong banker. *

1357. ___. *The Incongruous Spy: Two Novels of Suspense.* By John le Carré, pseud. 2 vols. in 1. New York: Walker, 1964. Contents: *Call for the Dead* and *A Murder of Quality.* Cornwell's first two less successful novels were reissued in this form to take advantage of the success of his third, *The Spy Who Came in from the Cold.* *

1358. ___. *The Little Drummer Girl.* New York: Knopf, 1983. A young woman agrees to enter the espionage business to help her country by posing as the girlfriend of a terrorist.

1359. ___. *The Looking Glass War.* By John le Carré, pseud. New York: Coward-McCann, 1965. The death of a courier, who had been sent to Finland to collect films taken by a commercial pilot over East Germany, results in the recruitment of an agent to be planted in that northern country; when it is understood that the man's slow transmittal over an old radio will result in his capture, his intelligence chief cold-bloodedly disavows him. *

This is an extremely realistic piece of writing, as no less an authority than former CIA Director Allen W. Dulles has testified. "To anyone who has ever been associated with an intelligence service, its jumble of unusual personalities, their speech and behavior, their daily business, and even the awful scheme which carries them in their enthusiasm far from reality," he wrote in 1969, "all ring true" (*Great Spy Stories From Fiction.* [New York: Harper & Row, 1969], 347).

1360. ___. *A Murder of Quality.* By John le Carré, pseud. New York: Walker, 1963. Agent Smiley is dispatched to an exclusive British girls' school to solve what appears to be a senseless murder and uncovers an East German agent running amuck. *

1361. ___. *A Perfect Spy.* New York: Knopf, 1986. Le Carré's twisting, meditative memoir is an autobiography of the soul of a spy.

1362. ___. *The Quest for Karla.* New York: Knopf, 1982. Contains *Tinker, Tailor, Soldier, Spy, The Honourable Schoolboy,* and *Smiley's People.*

1363. ___. *The Russia House.* New York: Knopf, 1989. Le Carré splices humor into this espionage novel of a reluctant spy, a bookseller attending the Moscow Book Fair in the age of *glasnost,* dragooned into a search for Dante, a Soviet physicist whose treatise on the missile capabilities of his country reveals it to be farcically inadequate to its pretensions. Sean Connery played the lead role, the boozing but audaciously clever Barley, in the film version.

1364. ___. *The Secret Pilgrim.* New York: Knopf, 1991. A retiring British agent, known to the reader only as Ned, reviews his thirty years as a spy for his government during a night of reverie at Sarratt, the spy school where his long-time colleague in the espionage business, George Smiley, has come as guest lecturer.

1365. ___. *A Small Town in Germany.* By John le Carré, pseud. New York: Coward-McCann, 1969. The first spy thriller published by Cornwell after leaving government service. Agent Alan Turner arrives in Germany to find the crucial Green File and other stolen papers taken from the very British embassy offices in Bonn where Cornwell formerly worked. The obvious villain is a disaffected Second Secretary (Cornwell's old post) who has disappeared, apparently a defector to the East. *

1366. ___. *Smiley's People.* By John le Carré, pseud. New York: Knopf, 1980. Aging spymaster George Smiley shuffles out of retirement to look into mysterious Soviet spy activities in Western Europe and perceives an opportunity to employ his colleagues in a scheme to trap his Russian alter ego, Karla, in Berlin. *

1367. ___. *The Spy Who Came in from the Cold.* By John le Carré, pseud. New York: Coward-McCann, 1964. Alec Leamas, a fifty-year-old professional British spy, has become a bit stale, but is offered one more assignment before his retirement. He lets himself be seduced into a pretended defection, thereby providing the East Germans with data from which they can establish that the head of their own intelligence establishment is really a double agent. At the same time, it becomes apparent that his own people have set Leamas up to be brutally discarded as part of a seamy orgy of deceit and double-crossing. *

The Spy established Cornwell as a major author of spy thrillers and won critical acclaim from nearly every quarter, including old master Graham Greene, who called it the best spy story he had ever read. Superbly constructed with style and literary fastidiousness, the authenticity of *The Spy* would have made Ambler and Maugham proud and, indeed, it won Cornwell the Somerset Maugham Award. This volume was immensely popular and did much to dampen public interest in the easy-fix derring-do of James Bond. Not everyone jumped on the band wagon, however. Two old agents did not consider *The Spy* to be all that great: Allen Dulles and Kim Philby. Dulles preferred *The Looking Glass War* while Philby, in a letter to his wife, remarked: "The whole plot from beginning to end is basically implausible, at any rate, to anyone who has any real knowledge of the business (Allen Dulles, ed., *Great Spy Stories From Fiction* [New York: Harper & Row, 1969], 347). On the other hand, one cannot imagine the MI-5 traitor as a great fan of le Carré after what the latter had to say in his introduction to Bruce Page, David Leitch, and Phillip Knightley, *The Philby Conspiracy* (Garden City, NY: Doubleday, 1968), "I have no . . . affection for Philby and no admiration."

1368. ___. *Tinker, Tailor, Soldier, Spy.* By John le Carré, pseud. New York: Knopf, 1974. Himself suspect, George Smiley, retired after a power play in "the Circus," is called upon to search out and destroy one of four top British agents, who was planted at the top of the British intelligence establishment as a "mole" years before by the Russians. *

Although Cornwell steadfastly maintained in his PBS interviews done before the American six-part TV serialization of this story that *Tinker, Tailor* was not a disguised version of the Philby case, most critics and students assume that it is. Nowhere in spy fiction does an author dissect as closely the relationship between the SIS and such old schools as Oxford and Cambridge. Incidentally, Sir Alec Guiness portrayed Smiley in the TV story so convincingly that his caricature now adorns many paperback editions of le Carré and to many who saw that production, he is as much Smiley as Robert Vaughan was Napoleon Solo.

1369. Cort, Ned. *Alpine Gambit.* Boxer Unit—OSS, No. 2. New York: Warner, 1981. The specially trained Boxer Unit of OSS is sent deep into the Bavarian mountains to eradicate a secret Nazi fortification. *P*

1370. ___. *French Entrapment.* Boxer Unit—OSS, No. 1. New York: Warner, 1981. Boxer Unit, the OSS multilingual kill team, races to destroy a special German radar installation on the French coast. *P*

Cory, Desmond, pseud. *See* McCarthy, John L.

1371. Cotler, Gordon. *The Cipher.* By Alexander Gordon, pseud. New York: Simon & Schuster, 1962. An expert at cuneiform deciphers a diplomatic message from a Middle East nation to earn a little cash on the side; he is soon, however, in great danger from a sinister international gang anxious over his extracurricular activities.

1372. Couch, Dick. *Pressure Point.* New York: Putnam's, 1992. Arab terrorists in Washington State steal a nuclear submarine and threaten to detonate it at the touch of a finger. The President calls Delta Force and Navy Seals (the author is a former member of this elite unit) into action. His other Seal Team adventures:

1373. ___. *Seal Team One.* New York: Avon, 1991. *P*

1374. ___. *Seal Team Two.* New York: Putnam's, 1993.

1375. Coulter, Stephen. *Embassy.* New York: Coward-McCann, 1971. The US embassy in Paris is a lively place, what with defecting Russians, mad assassins, traitorous staff members, tourists, reporters, anti-war demonstrators—and the French. Could a Soviet turncoat be smuggled out through that mob?

A newspaperman before World War II, Coulter served as an intelligence officer at General Eisenhower's SHAPE headquarters during World War II, charged with work on France and Scandinavia. After the war, he returned to newspaper work in the Paris bureau of a London chain. According to Donald McCormick, it was Coulter who provided Ian Fleming with the background necessary to draw the casino scenes in *Casino Royale*, which launched the Bond books (*Who's Who in Spy Fiction* [New York: Taplinger, 1977], 58). Seeing how successful Fleming was becoming, Coulter elected to pen spy thrillers on his own, writing some Bond-like tales under the pen-name of James Mayo and other, less flashy yarns under his true name.

1376. ___. *Hammerhead.* By James Mayo, pseud. New York: Morrow, 1964. A British agent probes the secrets hidden aboard a luxury yacht off the French Riviera.

1377. ___. *Shamelady.* By James Mayo, pseud. New York: Morrow, 1966. Published in England the previous year as *Let Sleeping Girls Lie.* CIRCLE agent Charles Hood tries to prevent a master criminal from hijacking an important cargo aboard a Soviet airliner and battles an electronic brain, named Lulu, which is programmed to take care of executions.

1378. ___. *A Stranger Called the Blues.* London: Heinemann, 1968. A tale of love and espionage set on the borders of Chinese-held Tibet.

1379. ___. *Threshold.* New York: Morrow, 1964. Crippled by an unexplained explosion, a British nuclear submarine becomes the center of international concern. More Charles Hood novels:

1380. ___. *An Account to Render.* London: Heinemann, 1970.

1381. ___. *Asking for It.* By James Mayo, pseud. London: Heinemann, 1971.

1382. ___. *Let Sleeping Girls Lie.* By James Mayo, pseud. New York: Morrow, 1966.

1383. ___. *The Loved Enemy.* London: Deutsch, 1962.

1384. ___. *The Man above Suspicion.* By James Mayo, pseud. London: Heinemann, 1969.

1385. ___. *Offshore!* New York: Morrow, 1966.

1386. ___. *Once in a Lifetime.* By James Mayo, pseud. London: Heinemann, 1966. [*Sergeant Death.* New York: Morrow, 1968].

1387. ___. *The Soyuz Affair.* London: Hart-Davis, 1977.

1388. Courter, Gay. *Code Ezra.* New York: Signet, 1987. Mixes five characters—a master spy, three women agents, and a traitor—in this intrigue that stretches from the Holocaust to the near-future of nuclear annihilation. *P*

1389. Cox, Richard. *Hartman's Game.* New York: St. Martin's, 1989. A son discovers clues about his father's secret past in Germany before WW II when the wealthy man disappears over Africa in his private plane.

1390. ___. *SAM-7.* New York: Crowell, 1977. In reprisal for a Mossad raid on one of its strongholds, PLO terrorists down an Israeli airliner over London with a Soviet supplied anti-aircraft guided missile. Four more:

1391. ___. *Ground Zero.* New York: Stein & Day, 1985.

1392. ___. *The Ice Raid.* New York: Berkley, 1988. *P*

1393. ___. *The KGB Directive.* New York: Viking, 1981. *P*

1394. ___. *Operation Sea Lion.* San Rafael, CA: Presidio, 1977.

1395. Coxe, George H. *Assignment in Guiana.* New York: Knopf, 1942. An FBI agent gets mixed up with mysterious deaths which force him into a number of dangerous escapes while seeking a Nazi spymaster in wartime South America. **y*

1396. ___. *Murder in Havana.* New York: Knopf, 1943. An American engineer in Cuba finds that almost everyone wants the papers in his briefcase. *y

1397. Coyle, Harold. *Bright Star.* New York: Simon & Schuster, 1990. A technothriller set in the near future between Egypt and Libya when the Soviet Union and the US confront each other in imminent nuclear annihilation after an attempted assassination by a Libyan terrorist. Other military technothrillers:

1398. ___. *Sword Point.* New York: Simon & Schuster, 1988. WW III military technothriller in which the US and USSR lock horns in the Iranian desert; meanwhile, to complicate matters, Iranian fanatics have the nuclear bomb.

1399. ___. *Team Yankee.* Novato, CA: Presidio, 1987. NATO forces are under attack when Soviet tanks sweep across West Germany; Captain Sean Bannon leads "Team Yankee" in defense against the Soviet armored assault.

1400. ___. *Trial by Fire.* New York: Simon & Schuster, 1992. In this high-tech look at warfare, Coyle returns Lt. Col. Scott Dixon and his lover, reporter Jan Fields, to combat—this time on US soil as the 2,000-mile border erupts in violence in the aftermath of the Mexican Revolution. One more:

1401. ___. *Ten Thousand.* New York: Simon & Schuster, 1993.

1402. Coyne, Joseph E. *House of Exile.* Milwaukee: Bruce, 1964. A deserted monastery is reopened in Massachusetts to house a group of monks who have escaped Eastern Europe with secret information vital to several governments.

Craig, David, pseud. *See* Tucker, Allan J.

1403. Craig, John. *In Council Rooms Apart.* New York: Putnam's, 1971. Frank Ridley is drawn out of retirement to discover why the Nazis are allowing the huge troop liners *Queen Mary* and *Queen Elizabeth* free passage across the war torn Atlantic.

1404. Craig, M. S. *To Play the Fox.* New York: Dodd, 1982. Two Soviet sleeper agents are activated; one must be eliminated.

1405. Craig, William. *The Strasbourg Legacy.* New York: Crowell, 1975. After members of the SS regroup following World War II and a blueprint for their restoration to power begins to unfold in late 1973, the Mossad, CIA, and KGB work to quash the plot with tough American operative Corcoran taking the lead.

1406. ___. *The Tashkent Crisis.* New York: Dutton, 1971. In this doomsday spy story, the President is dialed up on the hotline by the Soviet Premier and ordered to surrender America in 72 hours—or Washington will be destroyed by a Soviet laser weapon.

1407. Craik, Roger. *The Rabelais Ms.* London: Chittenden, 1993. A scholar working in an obscure library in Turkey uncovers an ancient sect of worldwide assassins who plot to destroy the US; they have already infiltrated the eastern ivy league schools. *P*

Crane, Robert, pseud. *See* Sellers, Connie L., Jr.

1408. Creasey, John. *The Black Spiders.* New York: Popular, 1975. First published by the London firm of Hodder and Stoughton in 1957. Gordon Craigie employs the agents of Department Z to guard Britain's interests against an international band of nasties intent upon taking over the country. **P*

John Creasey began his writing career in 1932 and by the time of his death had penned over 560 novels. Julian Symons, in *Mortal Consequences*, argues that Creasey's best work was done in crime fiction under the pseudonym J. J. Marric—actually as a pioneer of the modern-day police procedural, which marries detection to forensics: "The sum of the books . . . has given us an informative and never-boring account of police procedure, some good puzzles, some excellent chases, occasional psychological insights, much variety of plot and incident" (206). Creasey was prone to use pseudonyms such as Gordon Ashe, Norman Deane, and Anthony Morton and was an expert in both the detective and spy thriller genre. It usually took him about a fortnight to grind out a tale and the number of his characters is so extensive that no one has ever counted them all. In order that we might better differentiate between his various series, we shall begin with the Department Z and Dr. Palfrey tales written under his own name before venturing on to describe titles from several series penned under various alphabetically arranged pseudonyms.

1409. ___. *A Blast of Trumpets.* New York: Holt, 1976. An organization whose insignia is a golden trumpet is busily knocking off Britain's top scientists. ***

1410. ___. *Dangerous Quest*. New York: Walker, 1974. Department Z is alerted to capture a beautiful Nazi spy. First published by the London firm of Long in 1944. *

1411. ___. *Dead or Alive*. New York: Popular, 1974. When the possessor of vital defense secrets and his daughter are abducted, Gordon Craigie and the men of Department Z move to effect a rescue. First published by the London firm of Evans in 1951. *P

1412. ___. *The League of Dark Men*. Rev. ed. New York: Popular, 1965. Criminal assassins of the Council of Three attempt to wreck a U.N.-sponsored summit conference in London and it falls to Gordon Craigie's Department Z to find the men behind the plot—men whose wealth and industrial monopolies make them as powerful as the nations they seek to destroy. Originally published by the London firm of Hodder and Stoughton in 1954. *P Other Department Z tales include:

1413. ___. *Dark Peril*. New York: Popular, 1975. First published by the London firm of S. Paul in 1942. *P

1414. ___. *The Day of Disaster*. London: Paul, 1942. *

1415. ___. *The Department of Death*. London: Evans, 1949. *

1416. ___. *The Enemy Within*. New York: Popular, 1977. First published by the London firm of Evans in 1950. *P

1417. ___. *Go Away Death*. New York: Popular, 1976. Originally published by the London firm of S. Long in 1942. *P

1418. ___. *A Kind of Prisoner*. New York: Popular, 1975. First published by the London firm of Hodder and Stoughton in 1954. *P

1419. ___. *No Darker Crime*. New York: Popular, 1976. First published by the London firm of S. Paul in 1943. *P

1420. ___. *The Peril Ahead*. New York: Popular, 1974. Originally published by the London firm of S. Paul in 1946. *P

1421. ___. *Prepare for Action*. New York: Popular, 1975. Originally published by the London firm of S. Paul in 1942. *P

1422. ___. *Sabotage.* New York: Popular, 1976. First published by the London firm of Long in 1941. **P* Next series:

1423. ___. *The Blight.* New York: Walker, 1964. Dr. Palfrey leads an inter-Allied intelligence agency into action against various no-goods and plagues. In this outing, he must confront a strange Christmas tree disease that will soon threaten all plant life on earth. *

1424. ___. *The Dark Harvest.* New York: Walker, 1977. Dr. Palfrey and his agents battle an international criminal organization scheming to hold the world to ransom with a deadly crop destroying chemical. *

1425. ___. *The Famine.* New York: Walker, 1967. The staff of Dr. Palfrey's Z-5 international intelligence agency must find some man-eating, rabbit-like creatures that an evil genius has turned loose on the world. *

1426. ___. *Legion of the Lost.* New York: Dayne, 1944. Allied agents led by Dr. Palfrey rescue scientists in Norway and Denmark who are being liquidated by the Gestapo. *

1427. ___. *The Mists of Fear.* New York: Walker, 1977. While trying to learn why people the world over are vanishing in a mysterious mist, Dr. Palfrey confronts a resourceful and deadly adversary. *

1428. ___. *The Plague of Silence.* New York: Walker, 1961. Someone has purposefully loosed a dangerous epidemic on the world and Dr. Palfrey must find out who is responsible and effect a cure. *

1429. ___. *The Sleep.* New York: Walker, 1964. An African blackmailer attempts to use a form of sleeping sickness for world domination. Dr. Palfrey is needed . . . *

1430. ___. *The Terror.* New York: Walker, 1966. Dr. Palfrey attempts to halt the evil General Mildmay's plot to hold Britain at ransom against a threat of detonating nuclear devices. *

1431. ___. *The Touch of Death.* New York: Walker, 1969. A terrible ore, which affects all who come in contact with it, can be controlled by a mysterious enemy who will use it to gain world control unless Dr. Palfrey and the agents of Z-5 can stop him. *

1432. ___. *The Unbegotten.* New York: Walker, 1972. Dr. Palfrey must learn what evil force is behind the fact that women can no longer have babies. *

1433. ___. *The Voiceless Ones.* New York: Walker, 1974. Palfrey looks into an inexplicable disease which strikes down men in different parts of the world and is caused by a mysterious drug called Silena. *

1434. ___. *Wings of Peace.* New York: Walker, 1978. Palfrey proves to be the link between a woman hunted in London and a prince in India who is bent on a terrible mission. * Other Palfrey spy thrillers include:

1435. ___. *Dawn of Darkness.* London: Long, 1949. *

1436. ___. *Death in the Rising Sun.* New York: Walker, 1976. First published by the London firm of Long in 1945. *

1437. ___. *The Inferno.* New York: Walker, 1966. *

1438. ___. *The League of Light.* London: Evans, 1949. *

1439. ___. *The Man Who Shook the World.* London: Evans, 1950. *

1440. ___. *The Prophet of Fire.* London: Evans, 1951. *

1441. ___. *Traitor's Doom.* New York: Walker, 1970. Originally published by the London firm of Long in 1942. *

1442. ___. *The Valley of Fear.* London: Long, 1943. Reprinted by the New York firm of Walker in 1973 under the title *The Perilous Country.* * Next series:

1443. ___. *The Crime Haters.* By Gordon Ashe, pseud. Garden City, NY: Doubleday, 1960. An international committee is formed to wipe out transnational crime; its first mission is to discover who has planted a bomb aboard a plane at London's Heathrow Airport. *

1444. ___. *Death in Flames.* By Gordon Ashe, pseud. London: Long, 1943. Patrick Dawlish is parachuted into France to assist local patriots in ferreting out a traitor in their resistance unit. *

1445. ___. *Death in High Places.* By Gordon Ashe, pseud. London: Long, 1942. MI-5 investigator Dawlish is called upon to find out the reasons behind the deaths of several important British government functionaries. *

1446. ___. *Who Was the Jester?* By Gordon Ashe, pseud. London: Newnes, 1940. Agent Dawlish looks into the matter of a German operative given to working in and leaving riddles. * Other Dawlish tales include:

1447. ___. *Murder Most Foul.* By Gordon Ashe, pseud. London: Long, 1942. *

1448. ___. *Rouges Rampant.* By Gordon Ashe, pseud. London: Long, 1944. *

1449. ___. *The Secret Murder.* By Gordon Ashe, pseud. London: Long, 1940. *

1450. ___. *Terror by Day.* By Gordon Ashe, pseud. London: Long, 1940. *

1451. ___. *There Goes Death.* By Gordon Ashe, pseud. London: Long, 1942. *

1452. ___. *Two Men Missing.* By Gordon Ashe, pseud. London: Long, 1943. *

1453. ___. *'Ware Danger.* By Gordon Ashe, pseud. London: Long, 1941. * Next series:

1454. ___. *I Am the Withered Man.* By Norman Deane, pseud. New York: Washburn, 1973. First published by the London firm of Hurst in 1941, continuing the Withered Man series begun before World War II (See Part 1). Nazi agent Kurt von Romain is sent to Vichy France to kidnap a French journalist. The mission will also give him a chance to get revenge on British operatives Bruce Murdock and Mary Dell who plagued him earlier. *

1455. ___. *Where Is the Withered Man.* By Norman Deane, pseud. New York: McKay, 1974. A close friend of Hitler's, Kurt von Romain is discovered to be alive, and well, and plotting against the British government from within. First published by the London firm of Hurst in 1942. *

1456. ___. *The Withered Man.* By Norman Deane, pseud. New York: McKay, 1974. Agents Murdock and Dell must once again halt the plans of von Romain, who is working in England to assist the planned German invasion, "Operation Sealion." First published by the London firm of Hurst in 1940. One other Withered Man saga is: *

1457. ___. *The Unknown Mission.* By Norman Deane, pseud. New York: McKay, 1972. Originally published by the London firm of Hurst in 1940. * Next series:

1458. ___. *Affair for the Baron.* By Anthony Morton, pseud. New York: Walker. 1968. Agents seek both the Baron and a girl he is protecting—a girl holding a secret potentially damaging to mankind. *

1459. ___. *The Baron and the Chinese Puzzle.* By Anthony Morton, pseud. New York: Scribner's, 1966. While attending a Hong Kong exhibition of art treasures, the Baron becomes involved in the plotting of an international crime. *

1460. ___. *The Baron and the Mogul Swords.* By Anthony Morton, pseud. New York: Walker, 1966. In London the Baron must find the other half of a matched pair of Mogul victory swords and unravel the plot concerning them. *

1461. Crichton, Michael. *Congo.* New York: Knopf, 1980. A California scientist, a ruthless corporation agent, and a mercenary hunter search for diamonds in the lost city of Zing.

1462. ___. *The Terminal Man.* New York: Knopf, 1972. Against the advice of his psychiatrist, a team of surgeons successfully connects the brain of Harry Benson to a computer. The operation has unforeseen side effects, however, and by this terrifying miscalculation, a relentless human time bomb is unleashed.

1463. Crisp, N. J. [Norman James]. *In the Long Run.* New York: Viking, 1987. After Stephen Haden, who smuggles people out of Iron Curtain countries for a living, is nearly assassinated in his elegant house in Zurich, he begins a lone investigation across Europe for his assailant.

London playwright Crisp has written for television, including the successful *The Man Who was Hunting Himself.*

1464. ___. *The Odd-Job Man.* New York: St. Martin's, 1979. Former SAS commando George Griffin, now a small-time conman, is offered a mission in which he becomes the hunter instead of the hunted and looks into the matter of an IRA plot. N. J. Crisp, an ex-RAF pilot during the war, has also written:

1465. ___. *The Brink.* New York: Viking, 1982.

1466. ___. *A Family Affair.* London: Macdonald & Jane's, 1979.

1467. ___. *The Gotland Deal.* New York: Viking, 1976.

1468. ___. *The London Deal.* New York: St. Martin's, 1979.

1469. ___. *The Ninth Circle.* New York: Viking, 1988.

1470. ___. *Yesterday's Gone.* New York: Viking, 1983.

1471. Crook, William. *Four Days.* New York: Atheneum, 1980. Downed in Burma, reconnaissance pilot Neil Roget has only 96 hours to reach base with word that the Japanese control the landing points selected by the Allies for an airborne invasion.

1472. Crosby, John. *An Affair of Strangers.* New York: Stein & Day, 1975. Israeli agent Ferenc is assigned to discover how Arab terrorists are financed from France while PLO beauty Chantal tries to disrupt the Geneva peace talks.

1473. ___. *The Company of Friends.* New York: Stein & Day, 1977. Sascha Nagy is a world-famous pianist whose wife may be conspiring with another government to have him murdered.

1474. ___. *Contract on the President.* New York: Dell, 1973. One of those combination Mafia-hunting/secret agent yarns much in vogue in paperback. *P*

1475. ___. *Party of the Year.* New York: Stein & Day, 1979. An ex-CIA agent in New York is hired to protect a 12-year-old Contessa from a rumored planned kidnapping by the Italian Red Brigade terrorist organization. Another:

1476. ___. *Nightfall.* New York: Stein & Day, 1976.

1477. Cross, Gilbert B. *Berlin Fugue.* By Jon Winters, pseud. New York: Avon, 1985. According to source "Badger," someone high up in the British government is responsible for agents dying "too soon, too often, and too easily"; Joshua Davies of HMG must find, and terminate, the traitor. *P* (See Mr. Cross's comment in CRAFT NOTES.)

1478. ___. *The Catenary Exchange.* By Jon Winters, pseud. New York: Avon, 1983.

1479. ___. *The Drakov Memoranda.* By Jon Winters, pseud. New York: Avon, 1979.

Cross, James, pseud. *See* Parry, Hugh J.

1480. Crossen, Kendell F. *The Gentle Assassin.* By Clay Richards, pseud. Indianapolis: Bobbs-Merrill, 1964. Kim Lock of Army G-2 is assigned to help the CIA get two State Department defectors out of Cuba.

1481. ___. *The Splintered Man.* By M. E. Chaber, pseud. New York: Rinehart, 1955. Former US Army major, turned private eye, Milo March is sent to Berlin by the CIA to locate a politically important defector.

1482. ___. *Wanted: Dead Men.* By M. E. Chaber, pseud. New York: Holt, 1965. Milo March tracks a mystery man through Europe in order to solve a case involving a missing missile device and bloody murder.

1483. ___. *Wild Midnight Falls.* By M. E. Chaber, pseud. New York: Holt, 1968. Acting for the CIA, insurance investigator Milo March takes on the Soviets in a fast-paced professional espionage job for which he really has no training.

1484. Crowder, Herbert. *Ambush at Osirak.* New York: Jove, 1989. Iraq is building its nuclear war facility at Osirik with Russia's help, and again, the Israelis are planning to bomb it; however, there's a complication because of a mole, and David Llewellyn, veteran operations officer in the American Embassy in Jerusalem, must ferret him out or annihilation ensues. *P*

1485. ___. *Scimitar.* New York: Jove, 1992. Previously published as *Missile Zone. P*

1486. ___. *Weatherhawk.* New York: Jove, 1991. This technothriller involves a sexy new US Air Force fighter plane called the F-22 Weatherhawk with its revolutionary radar system called JAWS. When JAWS is stolen during a flight, ex-fighter jock Mark Muldoon answers the call. *P*

1487. Cudlip, David R. *Comprador.* New York: Dutton, 1984. Former Wall Street banker, Cudlip's first "economic" thriller won rave reviews for its sex-leavened plot about international commodities trading. Rushton Culhane tries to manipulate a deal to save the US economy when the government defaults on paying him three tons of gold. (See Mr. Cudlip's CRAFT NOTES commentary.) One more:

1488. ___. *Strangers in Blood*. New York: Warner, 1986.

1489. Cullen, Robert. *Soviet Sources*. New York: Ivy, 1992. An American journalist is the pawn in a KGB disinformation plot when he reports that Soviet Premier V. P. Ponomaryov is dying or already dead. Soon he and his lover, a Russian actress who wants to help him clear his name, are fleeing across Russia in a wild chase from Moscow to Finland.

Cunningham, E. V., pseud. *See* Fast, Howard

1490. Cunningham, Richard. *A Ceremony in the Lincoln Tunnel*. Kansas City, MO: Sheed, Andrews & McMeel, 1978. To prevent an Israeli-American accord, PLO terrorists plant bombs in a New York City highway tunnel timed to go off when a famous general of the Israeli Army passes through.

1491. Curtis, Jack. *Crows' Parliament*. New York: Dutton, 1987. Simon Guerney is a freelance solider-of-fortune who, in seeking to rescue a kidnapped son of an Italian millionaire, stumbles onto a global conspiracy.

1492. Cussler, Clive. *Dragon*. New York: Simon & Schuster, 1993. Dirk Pitt takes on a Japanese extremist determined to rule the world. Cussler's action adventures are proof that the Cult of Bond thrives into the present, albeit with an aquatic twist and without the polish of 007. In his most recent, *Inca Gold* (New York: Simon & Schuster, 1994), Dirk Pitt comes to the rescue of archaeologists on an expedition for lost Inca treasure in the Andes of Peru.

1493. ___. *Iceberg*. New York: Dodd, 1975. The failure of a deep-sea probe leads NUMA (National Underwater and Marine Agency) investigator Dirk Pitt to a worldwide conspiracy based in Iceland.

1494. ___. *The Mediterranean Caper*. New York: Pyramid, 1973. Dirk Pitt of NUMA searches for the cause behind the sabotage of a United States research vessel. *P*

1495. ___. *Night Probe*. Garden City, NY: Doubleday, 1981. Agent Dirk Pitt searches the dangerous ocean depths in a desperate bid to find a lost treaty which will restore his nearly bankrupt homeland to superpower status.

1496. ___. *Raise the Titanic.* New York: Viking, 1976. A hurricane and two KGB agents hinder Dirk Pitt's efforts to raise a famous passenger liner and thereby save for a secret American defense system the world's only supply of a rare metal.

1497. ___. *Sahara.* New York: Simon & Schuster, 1992. Dirk Pitt and NUMA sidekick Al Giordino are brought in when a World Health Organization team disappear after detecting a toxic "red tide" that threatens the world.

1498. ___. *Vixen 03.* New York: Viking, 1978. African terrorists plan to release a virulent organism, obtained from a thirty-year-old aircraft wreck, upon Washington, DC. Other Dirk Pitt tales, and deep-sea thrillers translated around the globe, are these:

1499. ___. *Cyclops.* New York: Simon & Schuster, 1986.

1500. ___. *Deep Six.* New York: Simon & Schuster, 1984.

1501. ___. *Mayday!* London: Severn, 1985.

1502. ___. *Pacific Vortex!* New York: Bantam, 1983.

1503. ___. *Treasure.* London: Grafton, 1988.

1504. Cutler, Roland. *The Gates of Sagittarius.* New York: Dial, 1980. In 1939, Vanderlys, the top MI-5 agent in the Caribbean, is called upon to eliminate the Austrian fiancée of a rich Cuban industrialist before she can deliver him and his power to the Nazi cause.

D

1505. Da Cruz, Daniel. *The Captive City.* New York: Ballantine, 1976. Ape Swain is a government agent in this paperback series of three novels published in the mid-1970's and concluding with this one. *P*

1506. ___. *Vulcan's Hammer.* New York: Signet, 1967. Lincoln Blackwood was the almost anonymous brain behind the MITRE anti-ballistic missile system, but was he worth the $5 million his kidnappers were demanding in exchange for his safe release? One more:

1507. ___. *Mixed Doubles.* New York: Ballantine, 1989. *P*

1508. Dan, Uri and Peter Manor. *Carlos Must Die*. New York: Leisure, 1976. An Israeli Mossad agent swears to rid the world of the dreaded terrorist Rameirez Sanchez. *P*

1509. ___. *Ultimatum: PU 94*. New York: Leisure, 1977. Terrorists will detonate a nuclear bomb unless they can be stopped by a maverick Mossad operative. *P*

1510. Daniel, David. *Ark*. New York: St. Martin's, 1984. The discovery of Noah's Ark at the bottom of a lake in eastern Turkey could become a priceless ideological weapon, or it could mean Armenian independence from Turkey—if CIA-backed Armenian commandos have their way. But it certainly meant one thing to its archeologist discoverer when daughter Eve and troubleshooter Jeff Rivers discover his floating corpse inside the Ark.

1511. ___. *The Tuesday Man*. New York: Dutton, 1991. A charismatic but dangerously disturbed President tries to wreak havoc.

1512. Daniels, J. R. *Firegold*. New York: Coward-McCann, 1975. Mercenary John White helps Indonesian troops track Communist rebels to their hideout in an extinct volcano.

1513. Daniels, Max. *Passport to Terror*. New York: Avon, 1960. An American journalist, who is hiding a female refugee somewhere in Italy, is sought by a killer, a crime mob, the police, and the CIA. *P*

1514. Daniels, Norman. *The Avengers: Moon Express*. New York: Berkely, 1969. John Steed and Tara King infiltrate a group involved in a project to sell lunar real estate. The well-dressed and suave agent Steed, as portrayed by Patrick McNee, had several female assistants during his popular TV series of the late 1960s and together these British operatives looked into the most unimaginable of capers. *P* One other Steed tale by this writer is:

1515. ___. *The Avengers: The Magnetic Man*. New York: Berkely, 1968. *P* Daniels is also the author of the John Keith series:

1516. ___. *Operation "K."* New York: Pyramid, 1966. John Keith, the "Man from APE"—super secret American agent—is pitted against Red China in an extraordinary effort to preserve world peace. *P*

1517. ___. *Operation "SL."* New York: Pyramid, 1971. Keith is sent to Sierra Leone to find the reason behind a sudden and strange influx of Red Chinese. Other Keith tales are: *P*

1518. ___. *The Baron of Hong Kong.* New York: Pyramid, 1966. *P*

1519. ___. *The Hunt Club.* New York: Pyramid, 1964. *P*

1520. ___. *Operation "N."* New York: Pyramid, 1966. *P*

1521. ___. *Operation "T."* New York: Pyramid, 1967. *P*

1522. ___. *Operation "VC."* New York: Pyramid, 1967. *P*

1523. ___. *Overkill.* New York: Pyramid, 1964. A US agent courts danger and women as he moves on a secret intelligence mission from Moscow to Albania. *P*

1524. ___. *The Spy Ghost.* New York: Pyramid, 1965. *P*

1525. Dark, James. *Assignment Tokyo.* New York: Signet, 1965. "Intertrust" agent Mark Hood unravels the plot of a power-hungry genius to infiltrate the Japanese nerve center of a vital secret operation in the Anglo-American defense system. Most of this author's Hood series was originally published by the Australian firm of Horowitz.

1526. ___. *The Bamboo Bomb.* New York: Signet, 1964. Mark Hood travels to the Far East to uncover a plot designed to convert a small, backward nation into a super nuclear power.

1527. ___. *Come Die With Me.* New York: Signet, 1965. Hood goes up a Brazilian mountain fortress to battle a fiendish madman and halt his plan—only to be captured and forced to join in its execution.

1528. ___. *Sea Scape.* New York: Signet, 1970. A brilliant but evil genius plans to steal the West's most deadly nuclear weapon—until Mark Hood learns of the scheme and interferes.

1529. ___. *Spying Blind.* New York: Signet, 1959. Interthrust operative Hood is assigned to hijack a Russian moon-probe. Other Mark Hood tales include:

1530. ___. *Assignment Hong Kong.* New York: Signet, 1966.

1531. ___. *The Invisibles.* New York: Signet, 1969.

1532. ___. *Operation Ice Cap.* New York: Signet, 1969.

1533. ___. *Operation Octopus.* New York: Signet, 1968.

1534. ___. *Operation Scuba.* New York: Signet, 1971.

1535. ___. *Sword of Genghis Khan.* New York: Signet, 1967.

1536. ___. *Throne of Saturn.* New York: Signet, 1967.

1537. Davenport, Gwen L. and Gustav J. Breuer. *Stranger and Afraid.* By Michael Hardt, pseud. Indianapolis: Bobbs-Merrill, 1943. An Austrian nobleman, who escaped his country to join the US Army is posted to the OSS, which trains him for a dangerous espionage mission to Vienna. *y

1538. Davey, Jocelyn. *Treasury Alarm.* New York: Walker, 1980. Western intelligence agents become concerned over rumors of the impending theft of a Donatello painting by a wealthy art collector.

1539. Davidsen, Leif. *The Russian Singer.* Trans. Jorgen Schiott. New York: Random, 1991. A Danish clerk from the embassy investigates the sordid murder of two women in a Moscow hotel room and finds evidence embarrassing to Denmark and Russia, which evidence everyone but him wants covered up.

1540. ___. *The Sardine Deception.* Seattle: Fjord, 1986. A Danish lawyer's quiet life is turned upside down when his journalist wife is killed in a terrorist bombing in post-Franco Spain; soon after retrieving her body, he finds himself embroiled in the conspiracy that cost her her life.

1541. Davidson, Lionel. *Night of Wenceslas.* New York: Harper & Row, 1961. Nicholas Whistler, an unemployed British writer, obtains a new employer via the Labor Exchange and is catapulted out of his mundane London life on a goodwill mission to Prague; only after he is in Czechoslovakia and finds the secret police after him does the author learn that he has innocently become an agent and naive carrier of secret nuclear data.

Davies, Frederic, pseud. *See* Ellik, Ron and Frederic Langley

1542. Davies, John E. W. *The Achilles Affair*. By Berkeley Mather, pseud. New York: Scribner's, 1959. Peter Feltham's life is in danger because, years ago, he met and presently knows the identity of a top Middle East Communist agitator known only as "Achilles."

1543. ___. *The Break*. By Berkeley Mather, pseud. New York: Scribner's, 1970. [*The Break in the Line*. By Berkeley Mather, pseud. London: Collins, 1970].

1544. ___. *The Pass beyond Kashmir*. By Berkeley Mather, pseud. New York: Scribner's, 1961. Idwal Rees, a Welshman, searches for secret papers which will reveal the location of huge oil deposits in the mountains of Kashmir.

1545. ___. *Snowline*. By Berkeley Mather, pseud. New York: Scribner's, 1973. Agent Rees works to crack the "Snowline," the trail of heroin moving via Bombay, the Seychelles, and North Africa to France. These Rees tales are about as much detective as spy, having considerable elements of both genres.

1546. ___. *A Spy for a Spy*. By Berkeley Mather, pseud. New York: Scribner's, 1968. [*The Springers*. By Berkeley Mather, pseud. London: Collins, 1968]. Using a banking job as his Hong Kong cover, SIS operative John Wainwright must arrange the exchange of a Russian held in England for a Britisher held in Communist China. Published in England as *The Springers*.

1547. ___. *The Terminators*. By Berkeley Mather, pseud. New York: Scribner's, 1972. Rees is ordered to India, there to uncover evil doing and rescue friends in a country lousy with secret sects.

1548. ___. *With Extreme Prejudice*. By Berkeley Mather, pseud. New York: Scribner's, 1976. SIS agent Feltham is assigned to watch a pair of terrorists operating around the Suez Canal to learn the identity of their leader.

1549. Davis, Bart. *A Conspiracy of Eagles*. New York: Bantam, 1984. An investigative reporter in Mississippi stumbles upon the *Adlerkinden*, "the Children of the Eagle," neo-Nazis with links to the diamond kings of South Africa who are masterminding a plot to take over the world. *P* Others:

1550. ___. *Atlantic Run*. New York: Pocket, 1993. *P*

1551. ___. *Blind Prophet*. Garden City, NY: Doubleday, 1983.

1552. ___. *Destroy the Kentucky*. New York: Pocket, 1992. *P*

1553. ___. *The Doomsday Exercise.* New York: Bantam, 1989. *P*

1554. ___. *Full Fathom Five.* New York: Bantam, 1987. *P*

1555. ___. *Raise the Red Dawn.* New York: Pocket, 1991. *P*

1556. Davis, Clyde B. *Playtime Is Over.* Philadelphia: Lippincott, 1949. After settling down on an Arkansas farm, an ex-soldier-of-fortune reviews his past exploits.

1557. Davis, Dorothy S. *Enemy and Brother.* New York: Scribner's, 1967. Set in Greece, the prosecutor and the man he jailed unjustly for murder join forces to find the answer to an even larger miscarriage of justice threatening the security of their nation.

1558. ___. *The Habit of Fear.* Toronto: Worldwide, 1989. A newspaper columnist in search of her father, an Irish poet, is confronted with violence in the form of IRA terrorists.

1559. ___. *The Pale Betrayer.* New York: Scribner's, 1966. After a brilliant young English teacher at a New York City university delivers her best friend, an important physicist, into the hands of enemy agents, the scientist is killed and it falls to an NYPD detective to locate the killers. An early novel:

1560. ___. *Black Sheet, White Lamb.* New York: Scribner's, 1963.

1561. Davis, Franklin M., Jr. *Kiss the Tiger.* New York: Pyramid, 1961. American agent Quinn is sent into Indochina to locate a Communist agent. *P*

1562. ___. *Secret: Hong Kong.* New York: Pyramid, 1962. While eluding capture, Quinn must uncover the Red Chinese mastermind scheming to take over the British Crown Colony. *P*

Davis, Gordon, pseud. *See* Hunt, E. Howard, and Leonard Levinson

1563. Davis, J. Madison. *Bloody Marko.* New York: Walker, 1991. The life history of an 82-year-old partisan from former Yugoslavia told in increments from his present trial as a war criminal and traitor to the year 1915.

1564. Davis, Maggie. *Rommel's Gold.* Philadelphia: Lippincott, 1971. Four young Americans are sent to explore Tunisia for a fabled cache of gold buried by the "Desert Fox" in 1942-1943.

1565. Dawson, James. *Hell Gate.* New York: McKay, 1967. A scientist, who has developed a revolutionary electronics device capable of changing the Cold War balance of power, is sought by his brother and enemy agents.

1566. Day, Gina. *Tell No Tales.* New York: Stein & Day, 1968. A female agent trails a handsome traitor and must avoid falling in love with him.

1567. Day-Lewis, Cecil. *The Sad Variety.* By Nicholas Blake, pseud. New York: Harper & Row, 1964. Nigel Strangeway is assigned the task of watching a scientist, vulnerable to enemy agents, and his daughter during a Christmas holiday at an English guest house.

This British poet wrote a number of detective novels and a few spy thrillers under his pseudonym both before World War II (see Part 1) and after.

Deacon, Richard, pseud. *See* McCormick, Donald

1568. Dean, Elizabeth. *Murder a Mile High.* Garden City, NY: Doubleday, 1944. Emma Marsh tails Nazi agents in wartime Colorado. *y

1569. Dean, Robert G. *Pinned Man.* By George Griswold, pseud. Boston: Little, 1955. SIS and CIA operatives cooperate in tracking down a dangerous Communist agent in Switzerland. *

1570. ___. *Red Pawns.* By George Griswold, pseud. New York: Dutton, 1954. Super spy Mr. Groode becomes involved in an anti-Communist espionage caper in the Middle East. *

1571. DeAndrea, William L. *Atropos.* New York: Mysterious, 1990. Allan Trotter, heading a counterespionage agency since his return from an operation that left him seriously hurt, must find a way to circumvent a Soviet plot to take over the US.

1572. ___. *Azrael.* New York: Mysterious, 1987. A top American agent is opposed by "Azrael," Angel of Death in a plot involving sleeper agents in the US.

1573. ___. *Cronus.* New York: Mysterious, 1984. Cliff Driscoll works, albeit against his will, for the Agency.

1574. ___. *Killed on the Ice.* Garden City, NY: Doubleday, 1984. A political activist is killed on a skating rink used by Matt Cobb's network. Two more:

1575. ___. *The Lunatic Fringe: A Novel Wherein Theodore Roosevelt Meets the Pink Angel.* New York: Evans, 1980.

1576. ___. *Snark.* New York: Mysterious, 1985.

Deane, Norman, pseud. *See* Creasey, John

1577. DeFelice, Jim. *Coyote Bird.* New York: St. Martin's, 1992. The Coyote is America's most sophisticated stealth plane; however, a Japanese consortium, financed by a billionaire who hates the US, has developed a counterpart that he intends to destroy American aircraft with unless stopped.

1578. Deford, Frank. *The Spy in the Deuce Court.* New York: Putnam's, 1986. Sports maven Deford (*Sports Illustrated* editor and football commentator) does the hat trick with a novel about the shady side of pro tennis—even the CIA is involved when an agent makes a proposition to enroll a journalist covering the tour.

1579. DeGramont, Sanche. *Lives to Give.* Trans. from the French. New York: Putnam's, 1971. Four Maquis fighters are summoned to a secret meeting in Paris—only to be met at the door by the Gestapo.

1580. Deighton, Len. *Berlin Game.* New York: Knopf, 1983. The first part of the first Bernard Samson trilogy.
    The son of a chauffeur, Len Deighton was educated as an artist and spent much of his life in ad agency and illustrator work. In the early 1960s, he penned his first spy thriller, *The Ipcress File*, which was a vast success and led to his writing the others listed here. Some call him the CIA's favorite spy novelist.
    Deighton is a master of intricate plotting, shifting tone, and locale. His prose is elliptical. The obscurities and ambiguities generated by his sentence structure force many to read his pages slowly and over to catch their full meaning. Deighton's characters are much like those of Ambler and David (le Carré) Cornwell. For example, the anti-hero Harry Palmer is thrust out of his environment and forced to act in a strange, intrigue-filled world peopled by a different class with which he can neither identify nor trust. "There is something almost lyrical about his recreation of the dangerous and transitory lives of agents, as well as something sharp and knowing," writes Julian Symons in admiration. "Writing of this quality, combined or contrasted with the constant crackle of the dialogue, makes Deighton a kind of poet of the spy novel" (*Mortal Consequences: A History—From the Detective Story to the Crime Novel* [New York: Schocken, 1972], 245-246).

Above all, Len Deighton has become noted for his fascination with technical minutiae, which is far more extensive than Fleming's ever was. In each outing, he provides the reader with insight on various forms of gadgetry and organizations, even to the extent of adding footnotes and appendices. Authenticity in this sort of detail is a hallmark which his public has come to expect and which newer practitioners in the genre have come to imitate. Deighton's two trilogies, and his fact-limned war novels have made him a writer who, as Julian Symons says in *Contemporary Authors* (NR Ser. Vol. 19) is "determined not to stay within the intentional pattern of the spy story or thriller" (167). Adding to this prestige are *Goodbye, Mickey Mouse* (New York: Knopf, 1982) and the nonfictional *Fighter: The True Story of the Battle of Great Britain* (New York: Knopf, 1978), and *Winter* (New York: Knopf, 1987, a saga of a German family leading up to WW II. Of this latter work, Deighton comments in an interview in *The Len Deighton Companion* by Edward Milward-Oliver (London: Grafton, 1987): "The style of the dialogue is quite different from *Game, Set & Match* but since I'd always intended *Winter* to be written in the third person this didn't make it incompatible with the other books" (24).

Deighton's latest work (he is called the world's hardest-working writer for good reason) adds yet another excellent historical tome to his already superb canon of WW II nonfiction in his informative and entertaining account of the successes and failures of strategy of the six great battlefronts of the Second World War (*Blood, Tears, and Folly: An Objective Look at World War II.* New York: Harcourt, 1993).

1581. ___. *The Billion Dollar Brain.* New York: Putnam's, 1966. An intricately plotted spy thriller in which a rather dull-witted double agent named Harvey Newbigin is recruited into a computer-based espionage unit presided over by a rich, but evil Texan, General Midwinter, an ultra-rightwinger who is out to destroy Moscow by sending saboteurs and plague-carriers into the USSR.

1582. ___. *Catch a Falling Spy.* New York: Harcourt, 1976. [*Twinkle, Twinkle, Little Spy.* London: Cape, 1976]. SIS and CIA agents recover the defecting Soviet electronics expert Bekuv in the Sahara Desert and take him to the US for a debriefing and to join his beautiful wife; soon, Western agents must begin plugging leaks through which the KGB is receiving data on American computer and other scientific secrets.

1583. ___. *City of Gold.* New York: HarperCollins, 1992. Rommel is receiving secret information from a source in Cairo about the disposition of the British 8th Army, its supply lines, troop placements, and even morale. So good is the information that in the waning months of 1941, he has thrown back the allies three hundred miles and sits poised to take back Cairo itself. Jimmy Ross is heading for a military prison in Cairo when fate interrupts his journey and, suddenly, he is the man whose job it will be to track down Rommel's spy.

1584. ___. *An Expensive Place to Die*. New York: Putnam's, 1967. An anonymous British agent is made personally responsible for heading off a catastrophe born of an American lie and rapidly maturing into the imminent explosion of a Red Chinese hydrogen bomb.

1585. ___. *Funeral in Berlin*. New York: Putnam's, 1965. In what is probably this author's most famous work, an anonymous SIS agent (named Harry Palmer in the Michael Caine movie version) smuggles a Russian scientist out of East Berlin with the connivance of a Soviet security officer.

1586. ___. *Game, Set, & Match*. New York: Knopf, 1989. The first trilogy: *Berlin Game*, *Mexico Set*, and *London Match*. Deighton notes in the Preface: "At first I'd planned to begin my story after the betrayal [Fiona's defection to East Berlin] . . . but as my planning continued it became obvious that more description was needed. I decided that the story needed a prologue. The 'prologue' draft got longer and longer and eventually became *Berlin Game*."

1587. ___. *Horse under Water*. New York: Putnam's, 1968. Against various opposition, an SIS operative attempts to salvage Nazi forged currency from a German submarine sunk off the Portuguese coast during World War II.

1588. ___. *The Ipcress File*. New York: Simon & Schuster, 1964. Harry Palmer (unnamed in the book, but titled in the Michael Caine film) is introduced to the world of espionage and participates in the rescue of a biochemist who has been kidnapped in Lebanon.

1589. ___. *London Match*. New York: Knopf, 1985. In this conclusion to the first trilogy, Samson shuttles between his home in England and Berlin, between both sides of the Wall, where he tries to avoid the fate of the pawn he has now become in an elaborate plot to destroy him and checkmate British Intelligence.

1590. ___. *MAMista*. New York: HarperCollins, 1991. MAMistas are Marxist rebels in Spanish Guiana who are trying to overthrow a government already corrupted by cocaine; now that oil reserves have been discovered, America's interest in "saving" the country grows keen. Into this heady broth of violence, politics, and revolution are three characters whose lives intertwine with a CIA agent and a dangerous march through the rain forest.

1591. ___. *Mexico Set*. New York: Knopf, 1985. Samson is sent to Mexico to arrange the defection of Erich Stinnes, a KGB major, but things go wrong so fast—including murder—that Samson is unable to keep London Central informed, and he falls under their suspicion as a result of internecine office politics.

1592. ___. *Spy Hook*. New York: Knopf, 1988. The first of Deighton's second trilogy details the maverick investigation of former field agent Bernard Samson as he comes upon information suggesting that millions of pounds have disappeared within the service. Implicated are Bert Renssselaer, his former boss—-presumed dead but alive and well in California—and Fiona, Samson's former wife, chief intriguer for the East German secret police.

1593. ___. *Spy Sinker*. New York: HarperCollins, 1990. Ties all six previous novels of this and the earlier trilogy together by answering the question: Why did Fiona, Samson's beautiful, brilliant wife and colleague, ruin his career and leave him and their two children behind when she fled to East Berlin?

1594. ___. *Spy Story*. New York: Harcourt, 1974. A British agent is assigned to the employ of a joint Anglo-American naval warfare committee. His orders provide for a bit of spying for his old employer and giving assistance to a defecting Russian admiral.

1595. ___. *Spyline*. New York: Knopf, 1989. In this second part of the Samson trilogy, Samson is on the run in Berlin when London Central calls him home to his desk. But things are not what they seem: when he's sent to Vienna without a briefing to meet with the KGB, he discovers Fiona instead and learns the bitter truth of her defection as a deep-cover agent—and now she must come home.

1596. ___. *SS-GB: Nazi-Occupied Britain, 1941*. New York: Knopf, 1979. In a 1940 Britain occupied by the Germans, Police Superintendent Douglas Archer of the Gestapo-controlled Scotland Yard is plunged into an earthshaking espionage struggle with resistance fighters over atomic secrets as the result of a routine murder investigation. Now considered a classic of the "What-if?" genre.

1597. ___. *Winter: A Novel of a Berlin Family*. New York: Knopf, 1987. Follows Germany's three crucial decades between between the Wars through the lives of the Winter family, especially the brothers Peter and Pauli.

1598. ___. *XPD.* New York: Random, 1981. Based on the codeword for "expedient demise." Top agents of Britain, West Germany, Soviet Russia, and the US are off on a desperate and violent pursuit of a film which depicts the wartime theft of top secret British documents.

1599. ___. *Yesterday's Spy.* New York: Harcourt, 1975. A dashing World War II spy in the age of the computer, SIS operative Steve Champion is to be liquidated by his old friend Charlie Bonnard.

1600. Dekker, Anthony. *Temptation in a Private Zoo.* New York: Morrow, 1970. In this Cold War Bondish yarn, a British public relations man is enmeshed at Bear Garden, ostensibly a management training school run by the German Gersachs Group for its English staff.

1601. Delaney, Laurence. *The Triton Ultimatum.* New York: Dell, 1977. Ten terrorists suddenly and brutally commandeer a Triton submarine with its two dozen Poseidon missiles and threaten to raze the world unless their ransom demand for $4 billion is met. *P*

1602. DeLillo, Don. *Libra.* New York: Viking, 1988. Another fictional account of those infamous six seconds in Dallas on November 22, 1963. Reviewer Anne Tyler writes in the *New York Times Book Review* (24 July 1988) that the "herringbone plot line serves to make the most humdrum occurrence seem suddenly meaningful, laden with a dark purpose" (1).

1603. ___. *Mao II.* New York: Viking, 1991. Loosely inspired by the circumstances of the Rushdi Affair: on 14 February 1989, the Ayatollah Ruholla Khomeini condemned Salman Rushdie to death for his *Satanic Verses* on the charge that it blasphemed Islam. DeLillo's novel features a writer, Bill Gray, who first attempts to give a reading in London in honor of a poet held captive in Beirut and finds himself fatefully moving toward a sharing of the captive's fate.

1604. Delman, David. *The Last Gambit.* New York: St. Martin's, 1991. Chess and espionage combine in this tale by mystery writer Delman and his series character Jacob Horowitz, Chicago homicide lieutenant when an American grand champion is murdered at a Philadelphia chess tournament.

Delving, Michael, pseud. *See* Williams, Jay

1605. Dembo, Samuel. *Kalahari Kill.* New York: Morrow, 1964. First published in England as *The Sands of Liliput.* SIS agent Brady is ordered to the

South African desert to locate the notorious Otto Hulsenbeck, a Gestapo death camp commandant who escaped the Allies at the close of World War II. *

1606. DeMille, Nelson. *By the Rivers of Babylon.* New York: Harcourt, 1978. A group of Israeli negotiators must struggle against the odds in the desert after their airliner is downed by PLO terrorists.

Vietnam vet, bronze star recipient, DeMille has been publishing novels since 1974 with over half a dozen police procedurals to his credit. He wrote *Hitler's Children* (New York: Manor, 1976) under the pseudonym Kurt Ladner and co-wrote *Mayday*, a suspense novel with Thomas H. Block. (See Mr. DeMille's comments in CRAFT NOTES.)

1607. ___. *Cathedral.* New York: Delacorte, 1981. On St. Patrick's Day, IRA terrorist seize St. Patrick's Cathedral in New York City and demand the release of inmates held in Ulster's Long Kesh prison.

1608. ___. *The Charm School.* New York: Warner, 1988. An American tourist in Russia learns that hundreds of Americans are being held captive in a top-secret Soviet plot.

1609. ___. *The General's Daughter.* New York: Warner, 1992. A general's daughter, herself an officer, is murdered and a military scandal is exposed.

1610. ___. *The Talbot Odyssey.* New York: Delacorte, 1984. A "what-iffer" based on the idea that the OSS has never been disbanded but still exists covertly through the children of the original members; now their help is needed more than ever because the traitor within the OSS thrives and is about to mastermind a coup with the help of a fanatical super-patriot dupe that will leave the US disarmed on the Fourth of July.

1611. ___. *Word of Honor.* New York: Warner, 1985. A respected businessman was once a young lieutenant in Vietnam in 1968 whose men committed an atrocity; now that secret is coming to light, and unless one woman tells the truth, his life, career, and family will be destroyed. One more:

1612. ___. *The Gold Coast.* New York: Warner, 1990. *P*

1613. Dempsey, Al. *The Stendhal Raid.* New York: Lorevan, 1985. Based on an historical incident in which Irgun-trained Zionists attempted to assassinate the Grand Mufti of Jerusalem at Stendhal Castle when the Nazis began provoking the leader to declare a jihad (holy war) against the Jews of Palestine.

1614. ___. *Pika Don.* New York: TOR, 1993. A recent political thriller concerning the A-bomb.

Denning, Mark, pseud. *See* Stevenson, John

1615. Dennis, Ralph. *MacTaggart's War.* New York: Holt, 1979. In 1940, eight US mercenaries invade Canada to obtain a giant gold shipment sent there from England for safekeeping.

1616. Denny, Robert. *Aces.* New York: Fine, 1990. WW II technothriller about B-17's versus Messerschmitts.

1617. ___. *Night Run.* New York: Fine, 1992. A bomber pilot shot down over the Eastern Front in WW II winds up assisting the Soviet Air Force and a regiment known as "Night Witches," young women who bomb the Germans at night flying old biplanes.

Derby, Mark, pseud. *See* Wilcox, Harry

1618. Derrick, Lionel. *Mardi Gras Massacre.* New York: Pinnacle, 1974. Mark Harden, the Penetrator, is in New Orleans to stop the plot of Mafia boss Marcel Bouchet to ruin the US economy with billions of counterfeit dollars which have been printed in Cuba on Russian supplied paper. *P*

1619. De St. Jerre, John and Brian Shakespeare. *The Patriot Game.* Boston: Houghton, 1973. A British agent is ordered to halt IRA terrorist strikes in England and Northern Ireland.

1620. DeStefano, Anthony. *Dachau Treasure.* New York: Manor, 1976. A generation after The Holocaust, a deadly game of vengeance is played against international greed as agents seek a fortune which once belonged to concentration camp inmates. *P*

1621. Deutermann, P. T. *Scorpion in the Sea: The Goldsborough Incident.* Fairfax, VA: George Mason U P, 1992. A Libyan submarine and an aging US destroyer play cat-and-mouse off the coast of Florida.

1622. Deverell, William. *Mindfield.* New York: Simon & Schuster, 1989. A hardnosed Montreal cop, Kellen O'Reilly, takes on the CIA—and becomes their next target.

1623. DeVilliers, Catherine. *Lieutenant Katia.* Trans. from the French. London: Constable, 1964. Traces the triumphs and sufferings of a woman officer of the World War II French Maquis resistance.

1624. DeVilliers, Gerard. *Malko: Angel of Vengeance.* Trans. from the French. New York: Pinnacle, 1974. Malko is one of the CIA's most daring and effective "special" agents—the man who gets the impossible missions, the dirty jobs, and the secret operations that demand the coolness of a million dollar caper and the finality of a commando hit. Reading on, other interesting aspects concerning the background of this paperback hero begin to pop out. Item: Agent Malko is, in fact, an Austrian nobleman, Prince Malko Linge. Item: Malko works on contract for the CIA in order to obtain enough cash to restore his ancestral castle. Item: In this tale, Malko must hijack a helicopter from the Uruguayan Army, disguise its markings, and force the pilot to fly him into a prison courtyard where he can rescue an important political hostage. *P*

This Malko series reads very much like imitation James Bond, which, indeed, it is. It is interesting to note that the French author chose to have his hero work for Uncle Sam instead of the SDECE.

1625. ___. *Malko: The Belfast Connection.* Trans. from the French. New York: Pinnacle, 1976. Malko is assisted by a beautiful terrorist in infiltrating a new IRA group, which has sinister connections to KGB sponsored sympathizers in New York City. *P*

1626. ___. *Malko: Checkpoint Charlie.* Trans. from the French. New York: Pinnacle, 1975. After two successful rescue missions behind the Berlin Wall, every Vopo east of Checkpoint Charlie is determined to trap Malko as he goes in a third time, occasioned by the necessity of saving a Nobel Prize-winning physicist. *P*

1627. ___. *Malko: The Countess and the Spy.* Trans. from the French. New York: Pinnacle, 1974. At a birthday party for a friend, Malko is forced to participate in a weird sale when a beautiful adventuress auctions off her captive, formerly the KGB's most dangerous official, to the highest bidding agent present. *P*

1628. ___. *Malko: Death in Santiago.* Trans. from the French. New York: Pinnacle, 1976. Malko is dispatched into revolution torn Chile to rescue a left-wing leader from the secret police of the post-Allende junta. *P*

1629. ___. *Malko: Death on the River Kwai.* Trans. from the French. New York: Pinnacle, 1975. In the shadow of the famous World War II bridge,

Malko seeks to solve the disappearance of a Bangkok CIA agent and the mystery behind a series of secret transactions in which millions of dollars are exchanged for shiploads of modern arms. *P*

1630. ___. *Malko: Hostage in Tokyo.* Trans. from the French. New York: Pinnacle, 1976. Malko is rushed to Japan to save the US ambassador and the American embassy, which has been taken over by United Red Army terrorists. *P*

1631. ___. *Malko: Kill Kissinger.* Trans. from the French. New York: Pinnacle, 1974. Terrorists will kill the American Secretary of State, who has been negotiating in Kuwait, unless Malko can infiltrate their group and destroy it. *P*

1632. ___. *Malko: Man From Kabul.* Trans. from the French. New York: Pinnacle, 1973. Malko is sent to Afghanistan to break up a Red Chinese plot against the sovereignty of that nation. *P*

1633. ___. *Malko: Operation New York.* Trans. from the French. New York: Pinnacle, 1973. Rudi Guern, former SS leader at Treblinka, is sought by the Russian GRU and the Israeli Mossad, but when the man claims to be a special CIA agent, Malko enters the lists to check out his story. *P*

1634. ___. *Malko: The Portuguese Defection.* Trans. from the French. New York: Pinnacle, 1977. Malko must rescue Natalia Grefanov, wife of a high KGB official, who is willing to defect and tell all she knows, from the Soviet embassy in Lisbon and get her safely out of the country and away from her husband's agents. *P*

1635. ___. *Malko: Que Viva Guevara.* Trans. from the French. New York: Pinnacle, 1975. Malko mixes it up with Cuban guerrillas in an effort to prevent the assassination of the American Vice President during his Latin American tour. *P*

1636. ___. *Malko: Versus the CIA.* Trans. from the French. New York: Pinnacle, 1974. Malko must halt a revolution in Iran whereby the Shah is to be assassinated and replaced by a CIA stooge. *P*

1637. ___. *Malko: West of Jerusalem.* Trans. from the French. New York: Pinnacle, 1973. When a top CIA official leaps to his death from a Washington, DC, building, Malko is drawn into a nasty plot against the national security of Israel. *P*

1638. DeVoto, Bernard A. *Advance Agent*. By John August, pseud. Boston: Little, 1942. A soldier and a journalist expose a secret Nazi sabotage organization. *

1639. ___. *Rain Before Seven*. By John August, pseud. Boston: Little, 1940. Hope Shaler, daughter of a prominent Wallisport, Massachusetts, manufacturing family, joins forces with a former Spanish Loyalist soldier to prove that a friend, who is a CIO organizer, did not sabotage a local defense factory. *

1640. DeWeese, Thomas G. and Robert S. Coulson. *The Man from UNCLE: The Invisibility Affair*. By Thomas Stratton, pseud. New York: Ace, 1967. THRUSH's most baffling weapon, an invisible and undetectable bomb, threatens world safety. One other UNCLE from these two is: *P*

1641. ___. *The Man from UNCLE: The Mind-Twisters Affair*. By Thomas Stratton, pseud. New York: Ace, 1967. *P*

1642. Dickey, Fred. *Burial in Moscow*. Don Mills, Ontario, Canada: Worldwide, 1988. CIA agent Jude Miller is called back for the biggest assignment of his life: bring back Nikita Khrushchev in Moscow. Yes, the ex-premier's death in 1971 was a hoax and now, embittered in exile, he wants to defect to the West. One more:

1643. ___. *Blood of the Eagle*. New York: Zebra, 1985. *P*

1644. Diehl, William. *Chameleon*. New York: Ballantine, 1981. A mash of industrial espionage, Oriental-style murder, and a globe-trotting assassin named Chameleon, whose trail is hounded by two reporters who discover a "nightmare empire" of greed and murder in an oil consortium named AMRAN. *P*

1645. ___. *Thai Horse*. New York: Villard, 1987. Christian Hatcher, the Shadow Warrior, is a free-lance agent who follows the trail of his best friend who has disappeared into the heroin pipeline from Hong Kong to Bangkok to Vietnam.

1646. ___. *27*. New York: Ballantine, 1990. Within the SS is a secret commando force assembled by Professor Vierhaus for the most sensitive assignments. Assignment to agent "27" is to slaughter the twenty-seven most powerful Americans at one time. *P*

Dietrich, Robert, pseud. *See* Hunt, E. Howard

1647. Diment, Adam. *The Bang, Bang Birds.* New York: Dutton, 1969. Philip McAlpine of British Intelligence is ordered to help his American colleagues check out the Aviary Club of Sweden—sort of an advanced Playboy Club for spies.

1648. ___. *The Dolly, Dolly Spy.* New York: Dutton, 1968. Assigned to fly an ex-Nazi out of Egypt and hand him over to the Americans, SIS agent McAlpine finds others interested and retires to Greece to bargain for the best price.

1649. ___. *The Great Spy Race.* New York: Dutton, 1968. McAlpine travels to a tiny island in the Indian Ocean where resides a retired spymaster. From the old man, he learns of "The Great Spy Race," in which he will participate with "contestants" from all over the world in a trial derring-do in which the one who outwits all the rest will receive the prize: a secret microfilm and a cash fortune.

1650. ___. *Think, Inc.* London: Joseph, 1971. McAlpine gets mixed up with an institution ostensively involved in advanced scientific research.

1651. DiMercurio. *Voyage of the Devilfish.* New York: Fine, 1992. An American sub tangles with the pride of the Soviet submarine fleet, while a fanatic Russian admiral sends a fleet of nuclear subs to attack the East Coast of the US.

1652. DiMona, Joseph. *The Benedict Arnold Connection.* New York: Morrow, 1977. Deputy Assistant Attorney General George Williams is temporarily assigned to the Office of the Joint Chiefs of Staff in order to learn who was responsible for the theft of three nuclear warheads.

1653. ___. *Last Man at Arlington.* New York: Morrow, 1973. A top Justice Department official, a Hollywood director, a beach bum, a socialite nymphomaniac, a corrupt Congressman, and a hardbitten football coach are all marked for death in the wake of President Kennedy's assassination.

1654. ___. *To the Eagle's Nest.* New York: Morrow, 1980. Hollywood's biggest names are on the set as the crew is filming the last days of Hitler at Berchtesgaden when terrorists abduct them all. DiMona also wrote a biography of the mobster Frank Costello and, with H.R. Haldeman, *The Ends of Power.*

1655. Dinallo, Greg. *Final Answers.* New York: Pocket, 1992. When a Vietnam vet stumbles across his own name on the Memorial Wall, he believes it to be a mere bureaucratic foul-up; soon, real attempts are made on his life, and he finds himself linked to a woman whose own husband was shot down in Nam.

1656. ___. *Rockets' Red Glare.* New York: St. Martin's, 1988. To America, the Cuban Missile Crisis of 1961 had been a decisive diplomatic win over Soviet militarism, but to a tiny number of Soviet elite, that was the beginning of Project Slow Burn, which is designed to leave America defenseless against a nuclear missile strike. This dangerous secret comes to light when Soviet Minister Deschin sends a fake Van Gogh to venal capitalist and conglomerate founder Theodor Churcher. Another:

1657. ___. *Purpose of Evasion.* New York: St. Martin's, 1990.

1658. Dipper, Alan. *The Golden Virgin.* New York: Walker, 1973. A physicist is working on a secret project for Britain when saboteurs try to grab his accumulated data.

1659. ___. *The Paradise Formula.* New York: Morrow, 1970. Drawing on his experience with the French Resistance, James Halfdan, head of a New York research firm, seeks to recover a stolen formula for the ultimate tranquilizer.

1660. Disney, Doris C. *17th Letter.* New York: Random, 1945. A husband-and-wife detective firm is mixed up in a wartime espionage caper in Canada. *y

1661. Divine, Arthur D. *Tunnel from Calais.* By David Rame, pseud. New York: Macmillan, 1943. A Royal Navy intelligence officer and a civilian engineer work to block the Germans from tunneling under the Channel. *y

1662. Dixon, H. Vernor. *Guerrilla.* New York: Monarch, 1963. An American soldier is called upon to defend five civilians in a Malayan jungle infested with Communist irregulars. *P*

1663. Dixon, Mark. *Deadly Force.* New York: Berkley, 1987. Luke Simpson is founder and president of Deadly Force, Inc.—a company which uses gee-whiz technology to combat world terrorism. *P* Number 6 in the Deadly Force series:

1664. ___. *Battle Zone.* New York: Berkley, 1989. *P* Another Dixon novel:

1665. ___. *Special Delivery.* New York: Berkley, 1987. *P*

1666. Doctorow, E. L. *The Book of Daniel.* New York: Random, 1971. Daniel Isaacson recalls the political, social, religious, and economic views of his late parents who were arrested and tried for espionage. Based on the 1950s Rosenberg spy case.

1667. Dodge, David. *Hooligan.* New York: Macmillan, 1969. Treasury Department agent John Abraham Lincoln is dispatched to Hong Kong to find out why so many claims for damage caused by a typhoon are being paid in American greenbacks; on the scene, he becomes involved in a Red Chinese plot to damage the US economy.

1668. ___. *Lights of Sharo.* New York: Random, 1954. Once inside a certain Communist nation, Western newsmen are not permitted to leave—alive!
*

1669. ___. *Troubleshooter.* New York: Macmillan, 1972. Two stories involving Treasury agent Lincoln. In the first, he is investigated after returning from three years' imprisonment in China; in the second, he is dispatched to South Africa where a black insurrection is planned against that nation's white rulers.

1670. Dodson, Daniel B. *The Man Who Ran Away.* New York: Dutton, 1961. An American expatriate unknowingly assists in a man's abduction from the US to the torture chambers of Dictator Torillo in the Caribbean.

1671. Doherty, Kevin. *A Long Day's Dying.* London: Sidgwick & Jackson, 1988. Nikolai Serov is the head of the First Chief Directorate of the KGB. But in the sweeping changes after Gorbachev's fall from power, he is also one of the leading black marketeers and drug lords of Moscow. When he comes across information in his official capacity that threatens the new world order, he must use all his wiles to keep from being snared in the murder and treachery that such knowledge brings.

1672. Doherty, P. C. *The Masked Man.* New York: St. Martin's, 1991. A rogue named Ralph Croft attempts to fathom the mystery of the Man in the Iron Mask. *HI*

1673. ___. *Spy in Chancery.* New York: St. Martin's, 1990. King Edward I commissions Hugh Corbett to find the traitor in his court. *HI* Two medieval suspense mysteries:

1674. ___. *Murder Wears a Cowl.* New York: St. Martin's, 1994.

1675. ___. *The Prince of Darkness*. New York: St. Martin's, 1993. *HI*

1676. Dolinger, Roy. *On the Edge*. New York: Viking, 1978. Former CIA agent Jack Sullivan comes into the possession of certain documents and after trying to sell them, must employ every trick he knows to stay alive when the agents of a big conglomerate are set on his trail.

1677. ___. *The Orange Air*. New York: Scribner's, 1961. Ex-baseball player Hank Easter travels to Castro's Cuba and there is mixed up in an espionage plot against the regime.

1678. ___. *Sandra Rifkin's Jewels*. New York: Signet, 1966. In this overly sex-laden parody of a secret agent yarn, Joel Bayside is commissioned by Castro to recover some ex-Cuban jewels. *H*

1679. ___. *The Thin Line*. New York: Crown, 1980. What happens to three CIA covert action specialists who are fired after the Agency withdraws its support of a Southeast Asian ruler in the early 1960s?

1680. Donald, Miles. *Boast*. New York: St. Martin's, 1980. With his son held hostage, Alistair Henry reluctantly agrees to work for the SIS against Rastafarian forces plotting a revolution in the West Indies.

1681. ___. *Diplomacy*. New York: St. Martin's, 1987. A polish prince living in England has lost faith in the Polish Resistance Movement until his best friend dies under mysterious circumstances, and he begins to investigate.

1682. Donner, Kyle. *Polar Day 9*. New York: Diamond, 1993. Environmental technothriller about a second ice age triggered by a secret experiment on climate control. *P*

1683. Donoghue, P. S. *The Dublin Affair*. New York: Fine, 1988. A young man inherits his father's business, which does highly secret work for the Defense Department, and makes changes to prevent someone inside from leaking that work to the Russians; soon, attempts are being made on his life.

1684. Donoso, José. *Curfew*. Trans. Alfred MacAdam. London: Weidenfeld & Nicholson, 1988. [*La Desesperanza*. Barcelona: Seix Barral, 1986]. One day in January of 1985 in the life of a Nobel Prize-winning poet in Pinochet's Chile.

1685. Dorling, Henry T. *The Jade Lizard.* By "Taffrail," pseud. London: Hodder & Stoughton, 1951. A British naval officer and a Greek girl join a resistance group fighting the Nazis on a Mediterranean island.

1686. Douglas, Richard. *The Rig.* London: Futura, 1975. While Big Tex Watson battles the North Atlantic to obtain an oil strike from his rig before a seven-day deadline expires, a particularly vile competitor hires an international saboteur/assassin to halt the American efforts. *P*

1687. Downes, Donald C. *The Easter Dinner.* New York: Rinehart, 1960. Italian anti-Fascists plus a pair of OSS agents sit down to a 1944 Easter dinner. Unknown to the spies, the main course consists of the carrier pigeons they employ to send messages to higher headquarters. *

1688. ___. *Red Rose for Maria.* New York: Rinehart, 1960. Jules Dellman, an OSS operative, makes use of a homely Italian schoolmistress to gather intelligence for the World War II Salerno and Monte Cassino offensives. *

1689. Downes, Hundon. *The Compassionate Tiger.* New York: Putnam's, 1960. An American mercenary is involved fighting the Viet Minh in 1954 Indochina.

1690. ___. *The Opium Strategem.* New York: Bantam, 1973. Through 256 pages of ceaseless violence, you will see the CIA, the Mafia, the Kuomingtang, local bandit rules, Communist and American officials all fighting in a warless Southeast Asia for control of the Golden Triangle, that real-life greatest source of the white poppy. *P*

1691. Doyle, David W. *An Accurate Watch.* New York: Morrow, 1990. A CIA officer is assigned to an African nation ruled by a king whose own son is planning a coup to turn the country over to Communism; complicating matters is a mole back at Langley.

1692. Driscoll, Peter. *The Barboza Credentials.* Philadelphia: Lippincott, 1976. Black nationalist guerrillas battle Portuguese troops in colonial Mozambique, while an ex-policeman uncovers the truth behind a massacre of black civilians.

1693. ___. *In Connection with Kilshaw.* Philadelphia: Lippincott, 1974. Posing as a reporter, a British agent is off to Ulster to eliminate a militant Protestant extremist leader.

1694. ___. *Pangolin*. Philadelphia: Lippincott, 1979. The intervention of Chinese and Philippine agents hampers the plot of a former crack British journalist to kidnap the CIA's top man in the Far East.

1695. ___. *Spearhead*. Boston: Little, 1989. Based on the experiences of ANC leader Nelson Mandela, a South African hero of the People's Congress and embarrassment to the government has been in prison for twenty-five years when plotters concoct a scheme to have him "discreetly" killed; however, an inmate overhears part of the conspiracy to kill Lincoln Kumalo and gets word out. An SAS officer is hired to lead a band of mercenaries to rescue him and get him out of South Africa.

1696. ___. *The White Lie Assignment*. London: Macdonald, 1971. British Intelligence asks a free-lance photographer to get some shots of a new super-secret missile base in Albania.

1697. ___. *The Wilby Conspiracy*. Philadelphia: Lippincott, 1972. A falling out among diamond thieves gets a man named Keough mixed up with a murderous South African policeman and a revolutionary named Wilby Xaba, who wants the diamonds to finance more violence along the Zambian border. The film starred Michael Caine and Sidney Poitier.

1698. Drummond, Ivor. *The Necklace of Skulls*. New York: Dell, 1980. SIS agent Colly Tucker must battle a murderous Indian cult trafficking in drugs. *P*
    Drummond also created espionage capers for an unlikely trio of characters consisting of a wealthy Italian named Count Alessandro di Ganzarello, a British aristocrat, Lady Jennifer Norrington, and—of course—an American playboy from a prominent family—Coleridge Tucker III.

1699. ___. *The Frog in the Moonflower*. New York: St. Martin's, 1973.

1700. ___. *The Jaws of the Watchdog*. New York: St. Martin's, 1973.

1701. ___. *The Power of the Bug*. New York: St. Martin's, 1974.

1702. ___. *A Stench of Poppies*. New York: St. Martin's, 1978.

1703. ___. *The Tank of Sacred Eels*. New York: St. Martin's, 1976.

1704. Drury, Allen. *The Hill of Summer: A Novel of the Soviet Conquest*. Garden City, NY: Doubleday, 1981. Best known as the author of the *roman a clef Advise and Consent* (Garden City, NY: Doubleday, 1959), Drury's recent novels incorporate more pronounced strains of espionage, although the insider's view of power politics in Washington, DC is still much in evidence. Despite the giveaway in this novel's subtitle, it suspensefully details the brilliant planning of Soviet Premier Yuri Serapin to conquer the world—an event set into motion when Hamilton Delbacher ascends to the US Presidency.

1705. ___. *The Promise of Joy: The Presidency of Orrin Knox.* Garden City, NY: Doubleday, 1975. Orrin Knox ascends to the Presidency after the assassination of President Jason (and Mrs. Knox) at a time when the US is mediating a nuclear war between China and the Soviet Union.

1706. ___. *A Shade of Difference.* Garden City, NY: Doubleday, 1962. Sort of a U.N. "Advise and Consent," in which the Harvard educated ruler of a small African country makes trouble for America when he is involved in a racial incident in Charleston, South Carolina.

1707. ___. *The Throne of Saturn: A Novel of Space and Politics.* Garden City, NY: Doubleday, 1970. America's race to Mars and passionate conflicts between astronauts are only part of the story as Soviet agents are lurking about attempting to put monkey wrenches into the Yankee endeavor. Other Drury novels:

1708. ___. *Come Ninevah, Come Tyre: The Presidency of Edward M. Jason.* Garden City, NY: Doubleday, 1973.

1709. ___. *Decision.* Garden City, NY: Doubleday, 1983.

1710. ___. *God against the Gods.* Garden City, NY: Doubleday, 1976.

1711. ___. *Mark Coffin, U.S.S.: A Novel of Capitol Hill.* Garden City, NY: Doubleday, 1979.

1712. ___. *Pentagon.* Garden City, NY: Doubleday, 1986.

1713. ___. *Preserve and Protect.* Garden City, NY: Doubleday, 1968.

1714. ___. *The Roads of Earth.* Garden City, NY: Doubleday, 1984.

1715. Dryer, Bernard V. *Image Makers.* New York: Harper, 1958. Dr. Adams, a renowned plastic surgeon, feels sorrow for certain deaths he believed he caused in his family. Flying to Paris for peace and reflection, he is swept into a dangerous adventure with the rebel leaders of French Algeria and Morocco.

1716. Duane, Allan. *The Hadrian Ransom*. New York: Putnam's, 1979. Enraged when her father and a churchman keep her from her seminarian lover, Rosella Asti and three terrorists plot to kidnap the Pope and hold him for a $4 million ransom.

1717. Duffy, Margaret. *Death of a Raven*. New York: St. Martin's, 1989. A small British firm is working on top-secret military hardware for both the Canadians and the British, but the Ministry of Defence believes the KGB has infiltrated the company. Langley and Gillard are sent to Canada to investigate.

1718. ___. *Man of Blood*. New York: St. Martin's, 1992. Piers Ashley belongs to F.9—a police unit so hush-hush that its members are often sentenced to prison with the gangs they have penetrated and helped convict; such is Piers' fate, just released from prison, and now someone is stalking him.

1719. ___. *A Murder of Crows*. New York: St. Martin's, 1988. A British agent joins his ex-wife in an investigation of her second husband's suspicious death. *P*

1720. ___. *Rook-Shoot*. New York: St. Martin's, 1991. Langley and Gillard on their honeymoon encounter murder and terrorism.

1721. ___. *Who Killed Cock Robin?* New York: St. Martin's, 1990. Langley and her husband are coached by MI-5 to investigate the death of their friend and discover that another friend's death is related. One more:

1722. ___. *Brass Eagle*. New York: St. Martin's, 1989.

Dugan, Jack, pseud. *See* Butterworth, W. E. [William Edmund III]

1723. Duggan, Ervin S. *Against All Enemies*. New York: Avon, 1979. A US President responds to an Angola-like situation in a South American country by sending in troops and spies. *P*

1724. Duke, Madelaine. *The Bormann Receipt*. Briarcliff Manor, NY: Stein & Day, 1978. A young Austrian woman's search for the paintings stolen from her family by the Nazis brings her to the attention of ODESSA.

1725. ___. *The Bormann Report.* New York: Charlter, 1977. A woman seeking to restore paintings to her family stolen by the Nazis comes across a receipt signed by Martin Bormann that begins a bloodbath by Nazis in hiding. *P*

1726. Dulles, Allen, ed. *Great Spy Stories from Fiction.* New York: Harper & Row, 1969. Allen Dulles, former OSS and CIA operative and official, is a legend in intelligence circles, who was forced to retire by the Bay of Pigs fiasco. Before his death, he penned a valuable memoir on espionage and his involvement with it as well as two anthologies of spy stories, one of fact and the other of fiction. It is the latter which concerns us here. **y*

In eleven sections following his introduction and appreciation of the spy thriller genre, Dulles presents thirty-two examples of what he considers to be the finest tales available, giving each a prefatory examination. These headnotes and critical comments are important reading for students of the literature and should be compared with those made by Eric Ambler in his anthology, *To Catch a Spy.* Among the authors included are: Leon Uris, Joseph Conrad, Baroness Orczy, Conan Doyle, Erskine Childers, Manning Coles (pseud.), Peter Cheney (pseud.), Rudyard Kipling, James Leasor, Eric Ambler, E. Phillips Oppenheim, Helen MacInnes, Duff Cooper, Len Deighton, Richard Condon, John le Carré (pseud.), Ian Fleming, W. Somerset Maugham, David St. John (pseud.), Compton MacKenzie, and Graham Greene.

1727. Duncan, Lee. *Fidel Castro Assassinate.* New York: Monarch, 1961. Five operatives plot to kill the Cuban leader. *P*

1728. Duncan, Robert L. *Brimstone.* By James H. Roberts, pseud. New York: Morrow, 1980. Working with three clues, Cameron attempts to prevent the US military from carrying out a plan so catastrophic that anyone who stumbles upon its devastating secret must, by official order, be immediately liquidated.

1729. ___. *China Dawn.* New York: Delacorte, 1988. A woman flees Shanghai in the turbulent thirties and, with Dawn, her half-Western daughter, opens a fashion house in Paris; however, events from her past are the cause of someone's sabotaging the House of Dawn.

1730. ___. *The Day the Sun Fell.* By James H. Roberts, pseud. New York: Morrow, 1970. Three American soldiers are dropped near Nagasaki shortly before the second A-bomb is scheduled to be dropped in August 1945 with orders to persuade the local Catholic bishop to evacuate the city.

1731. ___. *Dragons at the Gate.* By James H. Roberts, pseud. New York: Morrow, 1975. A CIA operative in Japan attempts to find a former Japanese government's treasure trove in order to foil an ill-conceived American espionage operation and save his own life.

1732. ___. *The February Plan.* By James H. Roberts, pseud. New York: Morrow, 1967. Arriving in Tokyo to investigate the US Army's official version of his son's death, a well-known American writer stumbles onto a monstrous plot by Yankee superpatriots to launch an unauthorized attack on Communist China.

1733. ___. *The Q Document.* By James H. Roberts, pseud. New York: Morrow, 1964. A blend of James Bond and the Bible in which agents of various nations attempt to obtain a document potentially damaging to the faith of millions.

1734. ___. *The Queen's Messenger.* London: Sphere, 1983. Originally published under the name W. R. Duncan (London: Joseph, 1982).

1735. ___. *Temple Dogs.* New York: Morrow, 1977. William Corbett is a troubleshooter and experienced agent who works for a multinational company, but now it seems that someone is setting him up for a fall. One more:

1736. ___. *The Serpent's Mark.* New York: St. Martin's, 1989.

1737. Dunham, Donald. *Zone of Violence.* New York: Belmont-Tower, 1962. Details the difficulties encountered by an American diplomat, pursued by secret police agents while behind the Iron Curtain. *P*

1738. Dunmore, Spencer. *Means of Escape.* New York: Coward-McCann, 1974. A downed British airman and a renegade German officer both stumble into the 1944 Battle of the Bulge and plan a startling escape.

1739. Dunne, Lee. *The Ringmaster.* New York: Simon & Schuster, 1980. A deadly game between British Intelligence and the IRA ends with the assassination of a top IRA official and an end to a truce called to work out a finish to "the Troubles."

1740. Dunne, Thomas L. *The Scourge.* New York: Coward-McCann, 1978. The US President orders a top security investigation of why the cancer death rate has suddenly escalated worldwide, except in Russia and among America's underprivileged.

1741. Dunnett, Dorothy. *Murder in Focus.* Boston: Houghton, 1973. Three scientists photographing the stars find themselves with film that somehow includes secret messages wanted by certain nasties.

1742. Durand, Loup. *Daddy.* Trans. J. Maxwell Brownjohn. New York: Villard, 1988. During WW II a banker who has secreted Jewish fortunes in coded accounts dies under torture before revealing the secret codes; the Nazis now must find the man's brilliant eleven-year-old son (who happens to be the real son of an American playboy financier).

1743. ___. *Jaguar.* Trans. from the French. New York: Villard, 1991. Candido Cavalcanti is a millionaire playboy who goes AWOL from the Brazilian Army and flees to Germany; he meets and falls in love with an American woman and decides to impress her by creating an identity for himself—the "Jaguar," fearless anarchist. What he does not know is that he will be manipulated into becoming the world's most feared terrorist by a brilliant Russian spymaster.

1744. Durham, Guy. *Extreme Prejudice.* New York: Putnam's, 1991. A US spy satellite picks up peculiar signals from a Soviet military installation.

1745. ___. *Stealth.* New York: Putnam's, 1991. A technothriller of espionage with high-tech military aviation.

1746. Durrell, Lawrence. *White Eagles Over Serbia.* New York: Criterion, 1957. A veteran British agent discovers the secret of an outlaw Royalist band which is attempting to overthrow Yugoslavia's Tito.

1747. Dwiggins, Toni. *Interrupt.* New York: TOR, 1993. A terrorist whose codename is "Interrupt" plots to destroy the telephone system of the US.

1748. Dwyer, K. R. *Dragonfly.* New York: Random, 1975. A Chinese youth, whose body is filled with bubonic bacilli by rightwingers plotting to destroy both Russia and China, must be stopped before a nuclear response is unleashed.

1749. Dye, Dale. *Outrage.* Boston: Little, 1988. Ex-marine captain and technical advisor to Oliver Stone's *Platoon*, Dye's third novel consists of a young marine corporal's involvement with a beautiful Arab in the days leading up to the bombing of the US Marine headquarters in Lebanon in 1983. Another:

1750. ___. *Conduct Unbecoming.* New York: Berkley, 1992. *P*

E

1751. "E-7," pseud. *Romance of a Spy.* London: Hurst & Blackett, 1947. A fictional detailing of the work of a British agent among resistance fighters and Nazis in Occupied France.

1752. Eachus, Irving. *Raid on the Bremerton.* New York: Viking, 1980. When terrorists seize control of the power plant of the US cruiser *Bremerton*, the ship's reactor technician must plan his strategy. *

Easterman, Daniel, pseud. *See* MacEoin, Denis

1753. Eastwood, James. *The Chinese Visitor.* New York: Coward-McCann, 1966. A resourceful and beautiful American-Hungarian girl, Anna Zordan, is so deeply mixed up in efforts to learn who killed a pro-Western Chinese VIP during his London visit that when the boys from MI-5 catch up with her, they have no choice but to take her into partnership and follow her leads.

1754. ___. *Diamonds Are Deadly.* New York: Coward-McCann, 1970. [*Come Die with Me.* New York: Macmillan, 1970]. SIS agent Anna Zordan is tracking the conspirators who are employing plots from stolen television spy shows to effect real headlines.

1755. ___. *Little Dragon from Peking.* New York: Coward-McCann, 1970. [*Seduce and Destroy.* New York: Dell, 1968]. Agent Zordan becomes involved with a Chinese terrorist group called "the Family."

1756. Ebert, Virginia. *Broken Image.* New York: Morrow, 1951. While awaiting her trial for treason, an American woman reveals how she became involved with a plot to sell a secret code. *

1757. Eckert, Allan W. *The Hab Theory.* Boston: Little, 1976. A ninety-four-year-old scientist is on his way to assassinate the US President to dramatize his theory that the Antarctica ice mass is about to start moving toward the equatorial bulge and destroy all life.

1758. Edelman, Maurice. *A Call on Kuprin.* Philadelphia: Lippincott, 1960. An English-educated Russian scientist is lured to Russia to help put a Soviet cosmonaut in space; a little later, a Member of Parliament travels to Moscow to persuade the defector to return home, but the politician is compromised in his hotel room by a KGB-controlled movie camera.

A British MP who received the Office of the Legion of Honor in 1960 and the Médaille de Paris in 1972 for his work on Anglo-French diplomacy, Edelman began in 1932 as a researcher into the uses of plastics in aircraft and during WW II put his language fluency skills to work as a reporter for *Picture Post* in North Africa and France.

1759. ___. *A Dream of Treason.* Philadelphia: Lippincott, 1955. The superiors of a Foreign Office agent order him to plant some misleading data in the French Communist press; they then inconsiderately die in an airplane crash, leaving the operative to face alone the problems resulting from his instructions.

1760. ___. *The Fratricides.* New York: Random, 1963. During the last days of the OAS campaign to keep Algeria French, the terrorist group is infiltrated by an agent working for de Gaulle.

1761. Eden, Matthew. *Conquest before Autumn.* New York: Abelard-Schuman, 1973. A journalist is due for lunch with his old friend, the recently resigned American Defense Secretary, but the diplomat has been kidnapped and US strategy for an upcoming conference with the Russians is endangered.

1762. ___. *Flight of Hawks.* New York: Abelard-Schuman, 1971. When an American bomber with nuclear weapons aboard crashes in Russia, retired CIA agent Mark Savage is called back to work with the KGB in recovering the death-sticks.

1763. ___. *The Gilt-Edged Traitor.* New York: Abelard-Schuman, 1972. Mark Savage is asked to intervene after money and idealogy weaken an agent into changing sides. Two early spy thrillers:

1764. ___. *Countdown to Crisis.* London: Hale, 1968.

1765. ___. *Dangerous Exchange.* London: Hale, 1969.

1766. Edwards, Anne. *Miklos Alexandrovitch Is Missing.* New York: Coward-McCann, 1970. During the 1968 Paris spring, filled as it was with riots, a general strike, and peace talks over Vietnam, a touring Soviet ballet star thinks no one will notice if he defects—but is he wrong.

1767. Edwards, Paul. *Expeditor: The Glyphs of Gold.* New York: Pyramid, 1974. In Yucatan, John Eagle, an Apache warrior who is also an American agent, must locate a lost city of gold, which is guarded by Mayan warriors and run by a neo-Nazi. *P* Other titles are:

1768. ___. *Expeditor: The Brain Scavengers.* New York: Pyramid, 1972. *P*

1769. ___. *Expeditor: The Fist of Fatima.* New York: Pyramid, 1973. *P*

1770. ___. *Expeditor: The Laughing Death.* New York: Pyramid, 1973. *P*

1771. ___. *Expeditor: Needles of Death.* New York: Pyramid, 1972. *P*

1772. ___. *Expeditor: Valley of Vultures.* New York: Pyramid, 1974. *P*

1773. Egleton, Clive. *Backfire.* New York: Antheneum, 1979. Under psychedelic drug experiments in Scotland during which an illusion of being in Siberia is created, a British SAS agent escapes and plots to destroy the hospital he thinks is enemy. Mjr. Robert Donaldson is called in to stop the deranged member of his organization. *
  Clive Egleton brings real-life experience to his spy thrillers. A member of the British Army from 1944 until his retirement in 1975, Egleton was employed in Persian Gulf intelligence matters as well as working in the Cyprus and East Africa counterinsurgency campaigns in the late 1950s and early 1960s. Much of his material and locale is based on first-hand knowledge drawn from years of travel and service around the globe. Egleton's tales are all action-oriented.

1774. ___. *The Bormann Brief.* New York: Coward-McCann, 1974. [*The October Plot.* London: Hodder & Stoughton, 1974]. A daring attempt is made by a band of Anglo-American commandos to assassinate Hitler's infamous deputy and thereby throw the already faltering Wehrmacht-SS High Command into total disarray. Reads very much like an Alistair Maclean tale. *

1775. ___. *The Clauberg Trigger.* By John Tarrant, pseud. New York: Atheneum, 1979. Professor Erwin von Clauberg's perfected atomic detonator must be retrieved from deep inside the Soviet zone of defeated Germany by an SIS agent and a dedicated US Army major.

1776. ___. *A Conflict of Interests.* New York: Atheneum, 1983. What do the KGB, CIA, and British Intelligence have in common? Answer: a dead prostitute. Detective Inspector Coghill must investigate the connection.

1777. ___. *A Different Drummer*. Chelsea, MI: Scarborough House, 1990. Irish terrorists penetrate a bureau of British Intelligence and escape time and again, leaving the officer in charge a scapegoat.

1778. ___. *A Double Deception*. New York: St. Martin's, 1992. A quarter-century after his disappearance when the Nazis invaded Warsaw, a young woman comes to London to find him; the search leads her—and MI-6's Campbell Parker—on a deadly spy hunt.

1779. ___. *The Eisenhower Deception*. New York: Atheneum, 1981. [*The Winter Touch*. London: Hodder & Stoughton, 1981]. Determined to advance the successful Anglo-Israeli invasion of Suez in 1956, Charles Winter manufactures evidence concerning the President and threatens to release it unless Eisenhower halts his efforts to stop the fighting.

1780. ___. *Escape to Athens*. By Patrick Blake, pseud. New York: Berkley, 1979. An Allied POW commando squad is sent to destroy a V-2 rocket station and to thwart a Nazi plot to loot the art treasures of Greece. *P*

1781. ___. *Hostile Intent*. New York: St. Martin's, 1993. British agent Peter Ashton investigate's a colleague's death, an agent handler, whose spy was a woman Soviet Army officer—now disappeared.

1782. ___. *In the Red*. New York: St. Martin's, 1990. Harry Freeland is an agent during those dark years (1949 - 1954) in British espionage when the Maclean-Burgess-Philby conspiracy had everyone under a cloud of suspicion. Harry's missions in China and West Germany fall through, and his superiors begin to suspect him; finally, on a dangerous mission in New York, he must clear himself completely.

1783. ___. *The Judas Mandate*. New York: Pinnacle, 1975. In the near future when England has been conquered by the Soviets, David Garnett becomes leader of an underground resistance movement. In this, chronologically the last of three tales, the British resistance must release Russian-held political prisoners so that they can escape to the US to form a government-in-exile. **P*

1784. ___. *Last Post for a Partisan*. New York: Pinnacle, 1973. Five years after the Soviet conquest, a split in England's underground resistance is threatening the entire movement; David Garnett is called in to find and eliminate the traitor who is fermenting the difficulties and there ensues a deadly game of intrigue in which every partisan is suspect. **P*

1785. ___. *The Mills Bomb.* New York: Atheneum, 1978. A former SIS agent is released from prison where he has served time for supposedly taking a bribe meant for a Soviet defector and is immediately pursued by British agents and IRA gunmen. *

1786. ___. *Missing from the Record.* New York: St. Martin's, 1989. [*Gone Missing.* London: Hodder & Stoughton, 1988]. The wife of an intelligence officer disappears, and he tracks her to Hong Kong.

1787. ___. *A Piece of Resistance.* New York: Pinnacle, 1974. Chronologically, the first in Egleton's British Resistance trilogy, which in the near future finds England occupied by Soviet troops after Bristol is destroyed by an A-bomb. When the assassin of a high Russian official is captured, he is sent to a maximum-security prison, from whence he must be rescued by David Garnett's partisans. *P

1788. ___. *The Rommel Plot.* By John Tarrant, pseud. Philadelphia: Lippincott, 1977. An MI-6 agent assists dissident German Wehrmacht officers in their plot to blow up Hitler at Berchtesgaden and replace the dead Fuehrer with Field Marshal Erwin Rommel. *

1789. ___. *Seven Days to a Killing.* London: Hodder & Stroughton, 1973. SAS Major John Tarrant receives a ransom demand for £500,000 in exchange for the life of his son, but while MI-5 is prepared to play a dangerous game of bluff with the terrorists, Tarrant elects to risk everything, including his own life, on a rescue attempt. *

1790. ___. *Skirmish.* New York: Coward-McCann, 1975. The Chief of the British SIS's Department of Subversive Warfare in London contemplates the signing of documents in a "safe house" which will give him a toehold in a Middle East country; suddenly, the situation is changed, the signators are dead, and it becomes necessary to learn who has penetrated the closely guarded arrangements. * Other Clive Egleton thrillers are:

1791. ___. *China Gold.* By John Tarrant, pseud. London: Macdonald & Jane's, 1982.

1792. ___. *Death of a Sahib.* London: Hodder & Stoughton, 1989.

1793. ___. *Double Griffin.* By Patrick Blake, pseud. New York: Jove, 1981. P

1794. ___. *A Falcon for the Hawks.* New York: Walker, 1984.

1795. ___. *The Last Act.* New York: St. Martin's, 1991.

1796. ___. *Picture of the Year.* London: Hodder & Stoughton, 1987.

1797. ___. *The Russian Enigma.* New York: Atheneum, 1982.

1798. ___. *State Visit.* London: Hodder & Stoughton, 1976.

1799. ___. *Troika.* London: Hodder & Stoughton, 1985.

1800. Ehrlichman, John. *The Company.* New York: Pocket, 1977. A CIA Director holds an ugly secret over the head of a US President who wants the Agency to perform some illegal "dirty tricks." *P*
    Ehrlichman was one of President Nixon's closest advisors and confidants, until he was forced out by Watergate. After serving time in prison for his role, Ehrlichman took up residence in New Mexico and began writing thrillers.

1801. ___. *The China Card.* New York: Simon & Schuster, 1986. A naive young idealist working in President Nixon's law firm is marked as a mole by Chinese Communists and targeted for assassination by the two nations he strove to bring to accord.

1802. ___. *Dorothy Rigby.* London: Hodder & Stoughton, 1989.

1803. ___. *The Whole Truth.* New York: Popular, 1979. White House aide Robin Warren is forced to choose between truth and expediency as the President of the United States covers up his involvement in a Latin American coup. *P*

1804. Eisenberg, Hershey. *The Reinhard Action.* New York: Morrow, 1980. While seeking a necklace stolen from his mother by the Nazis, David Davidowitz uncovers a neo-Nazi plot and works to assist the lovely Mossad agent out to quash it.

1805. Elder, Mark. *The Prometheus Operation.* New York: McGraw-Hill, 1980. A beautiful Abwehr agent assists a Nazi intelligence effort to infiltrate and sabotage the wartime US A-bomb project at Los Alamos.

1806. Elegant, Robert S. *A Kind of Treason.* New York: Holt, 1966. A best-selling author and syndicated columnist has run out of ideas. A group called QUEST hires him to learn "the truth about Vietnam," but he must do a little spying for the CIA on the side.

1807. Ellik, Ron and Frederic Langely. *The Man from UNCLE: The Cross of Gold Affair.* By Frederic Davies, pseud. New York: Ace, 1968. Napoleon and Illya are called upon to halt a THRUSH scheme aimed at the world's gold supply. *P*

1808. Ellis, Scott. *The Borzoi Control.* New York: St. Martin's, 1986. About another KGB plot to destroy the US.

1809. Elman, Richard. *The Breadfruit Lotteries.* London: Methuen, 1980. Wrongly accused of being an CIA assassin out to get the "PM," a Columbia University professor considers an unusual offer from Jamaican officials.

1810. Elon, Amos. *Timetable.* Garden City, NY: Doubleday, 1980. In 1944, courier Joel Brand of the Jewish Rescue Committee takes a message from SS official Adolph Eichman to Jewish leaders in Palestine: a hundred Jews will be released from concentration camps for every truck delivered to the Third Reich.

1811. Elwood, Roger and Sam Moskowitz, ed. *Great Spy Novels and Stories.* New York: Pyramid, 1965. Includes excerpts from six previously published tales. *P*

1812. Emmett, Robert. *Beat a Distant Drum.* New York: Signet, 1982. A paperback spy series featuring secret agent Mike McVeigh as hero. *P* Other titles:

1813. ___. *The Devil's Finger.* New York: Signet, 1982. *P*

1814. ___. *King, Bishop, Knight.* New York: Signet, 1982. *P*

1815. ___. *Trojan Horses.* New York: Signet, 1982. *P*

1816. Engel, Alan. *Variant.* New York: Fine, 1989. A mix of sci fi and espionage thriller as the Russians have discovered one of the secrets of genetic engineering—almost: the eight-year-old child the American Intelligence learns of does have superhuman powers, be he is also eight going on eighty in terms of bodily decrepitude.

1817. Engstrand, Stuard D. *Spring 1940.* Garden City, NY: Doubleday, 1941. Away from home in Germany for ten years, Norwegian Ralph Johanssen returns to his town ostensibly for his health, but actually as a Nazi spy; found out, he betrays his family, but weakens in the last moment. *

1818. Epstein, Edward Jay. *Cartel.* New York: Putnam's, 1978. "Faction" (half-fact, half fiction) about a Harvard professor who happens to be an expert on coup d'etats and governments, and who designs a scenario for the CIA that overthrows the Iranian government by assassinating its leader and installing a Shah friendly to the US and to Big Oil. Now he's in a desperate race across Europe to warn the Iranians.

1819. Erdman, Paul E. *The Billion Dollar Sure Thing.* New York: Scribner's, 1973. An international finance thriller featuring a multitude of agents, including some from the Mafia, a US-Soviet gold struggle, and an American plan for a new idea in money.

1820. ___. *The Crash of '79.* New York: Simon & Schuster, 1976. The Shah decides to take control of all OPEC resources, which leads to a Middle East war and the collapse of Western economies.

1821. ___. *The Panic of '89.* New York: Garden City, NY: Doubleday, 1987. Top financial writer Erdman's tale involves two Venezuelan brothers who engineer a scheme involving Swiss and Russian banking houses to make themselves vastly wealthy by inducing global financial panic which, triggered by defaults of massive amounts of short-term deposits, cause the Dow to plunge 150 points overnight.

1822. ___. *The Swiss Account.* New York: TOR, 1992. Erdman presents an inside look at Swiss banking during WW II in this tale in which CIA chief Allen Dulles sends three agents to Bavaria to stop Nazi profiteering and its ultimate goal: the purchase of military hardware necessary for an atomic bomb. One more:

1823. ___. *Zero Coupon.* New York: Forge, 1993.

Esdaile, David, pseud. *See* Walker, David Esdaile

1824. Estey, Dale. *A Lost Tale.* New York: St. Martin's, 1980. In his efforts to prevent the Nazis from stealing the secrets of the A-bomb, British spymaster William Stephenson is aided by the Druids of the Isle of Man.

1825. Estridge, Robin. *W.I.L. One to Curtis.* By Philip Loraine, pseud. New York: Random, 1967. The Western Intelligence Liaison, made up of agents from Britain and America, attempts to forestall the advent of a new leader in an unnamed country by manipulating five of his intimates into influencing his withdrawal—permanently if necessary—from political life.

Evans, Jonathan, pseud. *See* Freemantle, Brian

1826. Evans, Kenneth. *Oasis of Fear.* New York: Roy, 1968. Thirty years after the Western Desert Campaign, a British construction engineer supplements his income by aiding the Arabs in various dangerous smuggling operations.

1827. Evelyn, John M. *Reward for a Defector.* By Michael Underwood, pseud. New York: St. Martin's, 1974. An East German diplomat elects to defect and asks the aid of an old barrister friend who is already engaged defending a spy on trial.

1828. ___. *The Shadow Game.* By Michael Underwood, pseud. Garden City, NY: Doubleday, 1969. A London barrister, who has agreed to serve as a witness to an intelligence ploy, is kept hopping during a tedious bus trip from Munich to Istanbul.

1829. ___. *The Unprofessional Spy.* By Michael Underwood, pseud. Garden City, NY: Doubleday, 1965. A London barrister accepts a job to check out a Berlin woman he had loved thirty years before. During his assignment, he bitterly reaches the firm conclusion that "spying is strictly for professionals."

1830. Everett, Peter. *A Death in Ireland.* Boston: Little, 1981. About Ireland in the violent Black-and-Tan days, the IRA, and a hired American killer.

F

1831. Fairbairn, Douglas. *Street 8.* New York: Delacorte, 1977. Bobby Meade, a "Gringo" used car dealer in Miami, becomes involved with an anti-Castro commando squad.

1832. Fairlie, Gerald. *Bulldog Drummond at War.* London: Hodder & Stoughton, 1940. Hugh Drummond, hero of a series first began by "Sapper" McNeile, is once again faced with combating the evil and alluring Irma Peterson, who is now working for the Nazis against England.

Fairlie's treatment of the Drummond character during World War II and after does not seem quite so chauvinistic or contrived as the "Sapper" original. Fairlie served at the British Commando Training School and as a radio link with the French Maquis, even dropping into occupied territory James Bond style. Bulldog has had an extraordinary cinema career on two continents as well from the silent *Bulldog Drummond* (GB, 1925) through *Deadlier than the Male* (GB, 1967) to *Some Girls Do* (US, 1971).

1833. ___. *Hands Off Bulldog Drummond.* London: Hodder & Stoughton, 1949. Drummond continues to combat the evil Irma Peterson, who is now working for the Communist effort to take over England. Additional post-1940 Drummond tales, all involving Peterson, are:

1834. ___. *Bulldog Drummond Stands Fast.* London: Hodder & Stoughton, 1947.

1835. ___. *Calling Bulldog Drummond.* London: Hodder & Stoughton, 1951.

1836. ___. *Captain Bulldog Drummond.* London: Hodder & Stoughton, 1945.

1837. ___. *The Return of the Black Gang.* London: Hodder & Stoughton, 1945.

1838. ___. *They Found Each Other.* London: Hodder & Stoughton, 1946. A Breton aristocrat and an American girl named Micheline form a French resistance group. A non-Drummond adventure, this tale is based on Fairlie's actual World War II work in France.

1839. Fairman, Paul W. *The Man from STUD in the Solid Gold Screw.* By F. W. Paul, pseud. New York: Lancer, 1968. The first of Fairman's series of a half dozen spinoffs of the UNCLE books. *PH*

Falkirk, Richard, pseud. *See* Lambert, Derek

Fallon, Martin, pseud. *See* Patterson, Harry

1840. Farr, Finis. *The Elephant Valley.* Fort Wayne, IN: Arlington, 1967. A top CIA agent is assigned to discover who has blown up an atomic plant in New York and may want to start World War III.

1841. Fast, Charles. *Presidential Agent: Ride the Golden Tiger.* New York: Lancer, 1973. The activities of a German-born ex-professor who gets sent on secret missions by a President with bushy eyebrows: Curt Messinger resolves a monetary crisis with his computer brain and saves the life of Chou En-lai by outshooting four assassins in the Chinese premier's private conference room. *P*

1842. Fast, Howard. *The Assassin Who Gave Up His Gun.* By E. V. Cunningham, pseud. New York: Morrow, 1969. Richard Breckner is the top liquidator on the staff of "The Department," a secret international organization with its own plans for the world's future. While involved in a unique hunt for his latest victim, he falls in love and this "new experience" proves to be his professional undoing.

1843. Faur, Michael P., Jr. *A Friendly Place to Die.* New York: Signet, 1969. The CIA must chance trusting an American returned from thirteen years in the interior of Red China, because only he can supply invaluable data needed to forestall a world-shaking Communist plot. *P*

1844. Faust, Ron. *In the Forest of the Night.* New York: TOR, 1993. A doctor working in a violent, corrupt Central American nation witnesses a mass execution and for that reason he is imprisoned awaiting execution. He conspires with the daughter of the head of the secret police to escape and exact vengeance when he knows that his own wife has been put in a brothel.

1845. Feakes, G. J. *Moonrakers and Mischief.* New York: Washburn, 1962. Set in the English countryside and involving the failure of a secret weapons project.

1846. Feegel, John R. *The Dance Card.* New York: Dial, 1980. Ordered to fake the autopsies of Americans killed at the Bay of Pigs, a US Navy pathologist secretly records their real identities, which later creates a war of nerves between himself and the CIA.

1847. Fennell, George. *Killer Patrol.* New York: Pinnacle, 1970. A group of CIA-backed mercenaries are thrown into almost certain death when they are sent to stop a revolution and prevent a Communist takeover in a small Latin American country. *P*

1848. Fenner, Phyllis, ed. *Danger is the Password: Stories of Wartime Spies.* New York: Morrow, 1965. Ten short stories based on real-life adventures. **y*

1849. Fergusson, Bernard E. *Rare Adventure.* New York: Rinehart, 1954. A Scotsman visits a North African island and finds himself drawn into an uprising against its French administration. *

1850. Ferris, Paul. *Talk to Me About England.* New York: Coward-McCann, 1979. Released after imprisonment for trading secrets, an English newsman learns from Kim Philby that his wife had been having an affair and is offered a chance to get revenge on her and "the system."

1851. Fick, Carl. *The Danziger Transcript.* New York: Putnam's, 1971. Peter Danziger is a foreign correspondent living on the edge who runs afoul of military intelligence when he makes an excursion into the Cambodian jungles to report on the war effort of Vietnam against America.

1852. Fickling, G. G. *Honey on Her Tail.* New York: Pyramid, 1971. A mysterious international organization known as MAD is out to destroy lady superspy Honey. *P*

1853. Finch, Phillip. *Sugarland.* New York: St. Martin's, 1991. An insurance investigator encounters, amidst poverty and corruption in the Philippines, revolutionaries when he investigates a man's death.

1854. Finder, Joseph. *The Moscow Club.* New York: Viking, 1991. Charlie Stone is a CIA analyst with a murky family past: his father was disgraced during the McCarthy witch hunts of the fifties, and he's the godson of the mysterious Winthrop Lehman, a Cold Warrior of F.D.R. and Truman. His mission to Moscow will take him even deeper into his family past, which is linked to a mystery woman and to a disturbing group within the Kremlin, known as the Moscow Club, who are determined to topple Gorbachev and rekindle the Cold War.

1855. Fish, Robert L. *Always Kill a Stranger.* New York: Berkley, 1967. José da Silva of the Brazilian police must prevent an assassination during an OAS meeting. *P*

1856. ___. *The Diamond Bubble.* New York: Simon & Schuster, 1964. Da Silva and American agent Wilson work to break up a Rio tourist racket which has trapped US Senator Joseph P. Hastings.

1857. ___. *The Gold of Troy.* Garden City, NY: Doubleday, 1980. Golden artifacts from Troy, believed taken by the Russians in the onslaught of Berlin at the end of World War II, have been in CIA hands, but now the treasure is missing, and someone wants $15 million for its return.

1858. ___. *The Pursuit of Benjamin Grossman: A Novel about a Nazi War Criminal Who Posed as a Jew.* Garden City, NY: Doubleday, 1978. [*Pursuit.* New York: Berkley, 1979. *P*] ODESSA tries to gain nuclear material from Israel by blackmailing a man who once changed sides in a concentration camp and fought with Israeli forces in post-war Palestine.

1859. Fisher, David E. and Ralph Albertazzie. *Hostage One.* New York: Random, 1989. That baddie Qaddaffi is at it again; this time he has sent his loonies to kidnap President Bush aboard Air Force One thirty-thousand feet above the Rockies. The authors commanded and piloted Air Force One from 1968 to 1974.

1860. ___. *The Wrong Man.* New York: Random, 1993. Mossad agent David Melnik must stop an assassination in the US by a Nazi hunter who intends to kill Gottfried Waldner, the German Chancellor, because he believes him to be part of a conspiracy to restore the Third Reich. Other Fisher thrillers:

1861. ___. *Crisis.* Garden City, NY: Doubleday, 1971.

1862. ___. *A Fearful Symmetry.* Garden City, NY: Doubleday, 1974.

1863. ___. *Katie's Terror.* New York: Morrow, 1982.

1864. ___. *The Last Flying Tiger.* New York: Scribner's, 1976.

1865. ___. *Variation on a Theme.* Garden City, NY: Doubleday, 1981.

1866. Fisher, Norman. *Walk at a Steady Pace.* New York: Walker, 1972. Agent Nigel Morrison must outrace other spies to recover the payload of a Russian satellite which has crashed in Italy. Two other Morrison tales are:

1867. ___. *The Last Assignment.* New York: Walker, 1973.

1868. ___. *Rise at Dawn.* New York: Walker, 1971.

1869. Fitzmaurice, Eugene. *The Hawkeland Cache.* New York: Simon & Schuster, 1980. A Wall Street banker, who doubles as an assassin, the head of the Chinese intelligence service, and a Jesuit priest each seek a mysterious formula which can control the world's oil supply.

1870. Fitzsimons, Christopher. *Early Warning.* New York: Viking, 1978. An unemployed businessman comes to realize that he must act alone on his knowledge that an OPEC meeting is about to be attacked by terrorists.

1871. ___. *Reflex Action.* New York: Atheneum, 1980. Twelve years after his retirement from the SIS, a London insurance executive learns that his former chief is out to kill him.

Flannery, Sean, pseud. *See* Hagberg, David

1872. Fleischman, A. S. *Counterspy Express.* New York: Ace, 1954. When a Russian scientist escapes to the West, he is shadowed by two men who plan to sell his location to US agents and another who will bargain his future to the highest bidder. *P*

Fleming, Ian, pseud. *See* Cerf, Bennett and Michael K. Frith

1873. Fleming, Ian. *Bonded Fleming.* New York: Viking, 1965. This James Bond omnibus contains the following novels (cited with annotations below): *For Your Eyes Only, The Spy Who Loved Me,* and *Thunderball.*

Like many practitioners in the genre, Ian Fleming served as an active participant in "the game." Rear Admiral John Godfrey, Director of British Naval Intelligence, "recruited Fleming . . . over lunch at the Carlton Grill in May 1939" (David Wise and Thomas B. Ross, *The Espionage Establishment* [NY: Random, 1967], 83). Throughout World War II, the young officer, formerly a Reuters journalist, engaged in clandestine operations and a number of adventures which would later provide grist for his spy thrillers.

Following V-E Day, Fleming returned to journalism, enjoying his work as a foreign correspondent and manager for London's *Sunday Times*, posts he would hold until the success of James Bond allowed him to quit in 1959. During his newspaper career, he often retired to a Jamaican retreat, Goldeneye, which he had constructed in 1946. It was here in 1951, "horrified by the prospect of [an impending] marriage and to anesthetize my nerves, I sat down, rolled a piece of paper into my battered portable, and began." The book which resulted from this confession was *Casino Royale*, but, as he later wrote, "when I got back to London, I did nothing with the manuscript. I was too ashamed of it. No publisher would want it, and, if one did, I would not have the face to see it in print." Finally, Fleming's friend William Plomer persuaded him to submit the volume for publication—and the rest is history (Henry A. Zeiger, *Ian Fleming: The Spy Who Came In from the Cold—A Biography* [New York: Duell, Sloane & Pearce, 1965], 88-89).

The hero of *Casino Royale* was a British agent named James Bond, who subsequently became the most famous operative (technically, counterespionage) in the annals of intelligence fiction. The actual name Bond was chosen by Fleming almost as an afterthought, the result of his reading a book on ornithology by a scholar of that name. For a long time, there was conjecture upon whom, in real life, the hero might have been modeled after and which writers may have influenced the author's slam-bang, action-oriented style.

James Bond appears to be a character based upon several actual operatives, not the least of whom was Fleming himself. We know that Fleming and many others of British Intelligence in World War II were entranced by tales of the legendary ace-spy Sidney Reilly, who disappeared on a mission inside the Soviet Union during the late 1920s. By his own admission, Fleming's Bond was also heavily influenced by "Tricycle," the XX Committee's daring World War II agent whose real name was Dusko Popov. In his memoirs, *Spy Counter-Spy* (New York: Grosset & Dunlap, 1974), Popov tells of various encounters with Fleming, including a big bet the latter watched Popov place in a Lisbon casino in 1941.

"Fleming is the heir of Buchan and 'Sapper,' and James Bond was a more sophisticated version of Bulldog Drummond," wrote Julian Symon "in essence, the Bond pipedream was the 'Sapper' pipedream tuned to a mood of the fifties" (*Mortal Consequences: A History—From the Detective Story to the Crime Novel* [New York: Schocken, 1972], 242). Fleming never outwardly professed admiration for Drummond, preferring to suggest that Bond was, in fact, "a 'believable' hero, after the pattern of Raymond Chandler's and Dashiell Hammett's heroes." Other writers of whom Fleming was fond and to whom he felt indebted were once listed by him as "Edgar Allan Poe, Eric Ambler, and Graham Greene . . . [and] I supposed, if I were to examine the problem in depth, I'd go back to my childhood and find some roots of interest in E. Phillips Oppenheim and Sax Rohmer" (Ziegler, 93-96).

According to Symon and other students of the spy thriller, Fleming's Bond was successful at first only in Britain, where the difficulties of the post-war readjustment and the Cold War required an action hero, particularly a successful *English* one, who could provide an antithesis to the welfare state. In 1961, *Life* magazine published a list of President Kennedy's favorite books and among them was *From Russia with Love*. This acknowledgment gave Fleming's product a tremendous push in America. The US reading public, shockingly reminded of the realities of espionage by the recent romantic fiascos of the U-2 and Bay of Pigs, seemed to develop an appetite for a daring Western hero who was successful in both physical agility and clandestine warfare. Although most knew that the spy heroes of Fleming and his imitators rarely existed in actual intelligence agencies, a literary taste and desire for them became almost universal. "The spy story became the literature of the times . . . appealing alike to teenie-boppers and college professors, commoners and kings" (Wise and Ross, 262-263). This fever was heightened by the immense success of "Dr. No," the first Bond movie, which was released in 1962, and came to be reflected in everything from cigarettes to TV programs.

Interestingly enough, one of those upon whom Fleming made a lasting impression was spymaster Allen W. Dulles. Dulles was introduced to the British author's work by reading a copy of *From Russia with Love* given him by First Lady Jacqueline Kennedy in 1962. Thereafter the two men met and were in communication until Fleming's death in 1964. In reading the Bond tales, which were by now approaching an end, Dulles noticed two factors. First, Fleming had used up his Cold War fascination with the Soviets as opponents and was attempting to "internationalize" his titles by having Bond fight such crime syndicates as SPECTRE. Second, the number of references to CIA were increasing, some of whose personnel "even joined James Bond in his exploits—in a subordinate role of course!" (*Great Spy Stories from Fiction* [New York: Harper & Row, 1969], 361). Surely this was an effort to make Bond even more palatable to American readers.

Dulles, like other aficionados, was also struck by a Fleming hallmark, later carried to an extreme by Len Deighton: that of gimmicks and "secret gadgets." Every novel seemed to feature new and fascinating tools for the hero to employ against the villains. One of these, a radio homing device installed by Bond on an enemy car thus allowing it to be tracked over the Alps, particularly fascinated the CIA Director. The Langley labs were ordered to make such a contraption for field use, but unfortunately, they could not. In practical use, when the "tapped" vehicle of a suspect reached an urban area, the signal of the bug became lost in interference (*Great Spy Stories*, 362-363). Despite such real-life failures, Fleming went to immense expense to check facts such as these and to research locales, even travelling far afield to such places as Istanbul and Japan.

Fleming died of a heart attack in 1964 at the age of fifty-six. The dozen or so Bond novels which he authored had a profound effect on the development of the spy thriller in the years of his lifetime and after. Action, sex, violence, and gadgets created a picture of "the game" in real life and fiction. Fleming's niche as one of the two most important spy-fiction writer of the post-World War II era seemed secure right into the 1990s (le Carré being the other). However, the overwhelming sophistication of the espionage novel, as Allbeury and Deighton matured their craft, and with a host of outstanding authors led by Follett and Forsyth right behind, can only mean that Fleming's reputation in the aftermath of the Cult is diminished to a more realistic appraisal, and he is regarded nowadays as a minor writer of the genre he once dominated.

1874. ___. *Casino Royale.* New York: Macmillan, 1954. In Fleming's first Bond tale, agent 007, authorized to kill for Great Britain, declares war on LeChiffre, French Communist and paymaster of the Soviet murder organization SMERSH. The battle begins when Bond engages the nasty in a fifty-million-franc game of baccarat in a casino in the south of France, gains momentum in 007's fiery love affair with a sensuous lady spy, and reaches a chilling climax with fiendish torture at the hands of a master sadist. The David Niven-Woody Allen movie version of the same title bears no relationship whatsoever to this plot.

1875. ___. *Diamonds Are Forever.* New York: Macmillan, 1965. A fabulously wealthy racketeer has been spiriting vast quantities of diamonds out of South Africa and "M," the head of British Intelligence (whom Fleming modelled upon real-life spymaster Sir Maurice Oldfield, who died in March 1981), assigns 007 to look into this so-called "Spangled Mob." The trail leads from Amsterdam to Los Angeles and Las Vegas, where it turns out that the mastermind behind these huge thefts is Bond's old enemy, Ernst Blofeld. The evil genius and his girlfriend Tiffany Case are using the facilities of a nutty casino operator named Willard Whyte to gather in the stones and thereby construct a powerful laser satellite which can be orbited over Washington and used to blackmail America into surrender.

1876. ___. *The Diamond Smugglers.* London: Gildrose, 1957. Reprinted by the New York firm of Dell Books in 1965 during the height of the Bond craze, this non-Bondian tale was an effort by Fleming to produce a conventional detective-spy thriller devoid of his famous hero. A carefully organized private intelligence army and the mastermind who ingeniously commanded it smuggle diamonds from South Africa to Ireland and on to the Soviet Union.

1877. ___. *Dr. No.* New York: Macmillan, 1958. Ace agent James Bond goes to the Caribbean to find out why a secret service team has mysteriously vanished. There on an exotic tropical island, he meets a beautiful nature girl and discovers the hideout of Doctor No, a six-foot-six power-mad maniac with a lust for murder, a mania for torture, and a fantastic scheme to halt American rocket flights from Cape Canaveral.

1878. ___. *For Your Eyes Only.* New York: Viking, 1960. Five Bond novelettes, including: "From a View of a Kill," "For Your Eyes Only," "Quantum of Solace," "Risico," and "The Hildebrand Rarity."

1879. ___. *From Russia with Love.* New York: MacMillan, 1957. SMERSH wants to liquidate troublesome James Bond in a fashion which will embarrass

England and so lines up its best team to pull off the job: Tatiana
Romanova—an alluring brunette KGB seductress who looks like Greta Garbo;
Red Grant—a psychotic Irish hired assassin who likes to kill for kicks; and Rosa
Klebb—head of Otydell II, the department of torture and death, a hideous
woman with a lust for inflicting excruciating torment.

The conspirators' ploy works like this: Romanova "agrees" to defect
with a Lektor cipher machine in Istanbul, *if* James Bond, with whom she has
supposedly fallen in love from a photograph, is sent to pick them up.   "M"
dispatches 007, who is then forced into a perilous journey from Istanbul to Paris
via the lush Orient Express, a trip on which Bond makes passionate love to
Tatiana who then really does fall for him, while fighting desperately to protect
his life from Grant and Klebb.

Dulles, the Kennedys, and many others considered this to be the best of
Fleming's output.   The movie version varies somewhat from the book, but in
the main remains faithful.

1880.   ___.   *Gilt-Edged Bonds*.   New York: MacMillan, 1961.   Omnibus
containing *Casino Royale, Dr. No,* and *From Russia With Love*.

1881.   ___.   *Goldfinger*.   New York: MacMillan, 1960.   Bond has been
warned to stay away from Mr. Aurio Goldfinger, but the supercriminal's latest
obsession is too strong, too dangerous—he has to be stopped.   Enlisting the aid
of the top criminals in the United States, including a bevy of beautiful thieves
from the Bronx, and possessing a seemingly foolproof plan, Goldfinger
determines to take possession of half the supply of mined gold in the world—to
rob Fort Knox!   It takes all of Bond's unique talents and a measure of luck to
halt the madman's dangerous enterprise.

1882.   ___.   *Live and Let Die*.   New York: MacMillan, 1954.   "M" assigns
007 to crush Mr. Big, the master criminal whose network of Caribbean-Harlem
terror is reaping rich profits for the Kremlin.   Enlisting the help of a dangerous
French beauty, Bond seeks out his quarry on a mysterious yacht off the island
of Jamaica—a yacht guarded by savage sharks and blood-maddened
barracuda—where voodoo drums beat out a rhythm of death.

1883.   ___.   *The Man with the Golden Gun*.   New York: Signet, 1965.   The
final Bond adventure.   007 returns to London as a homicidally brainwashed
stooge of the KGB.   He is immediately taken in hand, rewashed, and sent on his
merry way to hamstring one of his mortal enemies, Francisco Scaramanga—the
world's deadliest assassin.   Aided by his sex-galore confederate Mary
Goodnight, Bond battles the nasty in a bloodcurdling death-duel from a native

bordello to a deluxe Jamaican hotel to a cobra-infested swamp. The movie was not altogether faithful to the book. *P*

1884. ___. *Moonraker*. New York: Macmillan, 1956. Bond has less than four days to discover the secret motive that is driving the mysterious Hugo Drax to build "Moonraker," a new super rocket that can blow the world sky high. Is the redhaired man a national hero out to save England and the universe, or a diabolical fiend bent on destruction? 007 must find the answer before zero hour when "Moonraker" will be finished and ready for use!

      Despite its beautiful special effects, the 1979 movie version of this title was extremely loose in its adaptation of the original novel's plot.

1885. ___. *More Gilt-Edged Bonds*. New York: Macmillan, 1965. Another anthology of novels, this one contains: *Diamonds Are Forever, Live and Let Die,* and *Moonraker*. It is probably not necessary to remind readers that all of the Fleming novels are in constant reissue by various paperback publishers.

1886. ___. *Octopussy*. New York: Signet, 1966. The last three James Bond short stories, reprinted from *Playboy* and *Argosy* under a single cover. Two are worth of annotation here: *Octopussy* concerns the last hours of a secret service agent who has gone to seed in Jamaica on some ill-got Nazi gold; *The Living Daylights* tells how Bond was sent to pick a sniper off the Berlin Wall. *P*

1887. ___. *On Her Majesty's Secret Service*. New York: Signet, 1964. The Special Executive for Counter-Intelligence, Terrorism, Revenge, and Extortion, otherwise known as SPECTRE (the godfather of THRUSH as faced by TV's Napoleon Solo in "The Man from UNCLE"), is headed by the evil Ernst Stavro Blofeld. In a closely guarded bastion of evil high in the Swiss Alps, he is putting the finishing touches to a most fiendish plot involving ten beautiful and ingenuous girls—to a most diabolical plot for murder by plague on a mass scale. Only one man can stop him and that man is secret agent James Bond, who has fallen in love with the gorgeous Tracy, daughter of Marc-Ange Draco, head of the Union Corse. *P*

      This novel is unusual on two counts. First is author Fleming's account of heraldry as employed by Bond as a cover to enter Blofeld's castle. The other is Bond's marriage to Tracy and the girl's demise at the tale's conclusion.

1888. ___. *The Spy Who Loved Me*. New York: Viking, 1962. If it were not for the movie version, which bears no plot relationship at all to the title, this would be the least known, least favorably reviewed, and most "different" of the Bond novels: Vivienne Michel's first-person account of a night of terror in the

Dreamy Pines Motor Court in the Adirondacks as she shared it with James Bond, 007.

1889. ___. *Thunderball.* New York: Macmillan, 1961. Emilio Largo is the scion of a famous and wealthy Roman family, an international charmer with an entrée to café society on four continents, and as No. 1 in SPECTRE, has nerves of steel, a heart of ice, and the ruthlessness of a Himmler. Largo and his confederates have put together Plan Omega, an operation of such fantastic magnitude that it threatens all humanity, when they steal a pair of nuclear bombs and threaten to detonate them unless the President and the Prime Minister give in to ransom demands.

       James Bond is sent to ferret out and crush Largo's evil plan. He has only one lead, one person who can help him if she will: Domino, the fiercely independent, fiery blonde who was Largo's mistress.

1890. ___. *You Only Live Twice.* New York: Signet, 1965. A condensed version appeared earlier in *Playboy.* Bond arrives in Japan to take on Dr. Guntrum Shatterhand, who has set up a suicide park on a volcanic island, and in the process falls into the arms of the delightful Kissy Suzuki and the trap of his old enemy, Ernst Blofeld. All this occasioned by 007's having gotten amnesia. *P*

1891. Fleming, Joan. *When I Grow Rich.* New York: Washburn, 1962. A novel of suspense and intrigue set in Istanbul and involving a young Turkish philosopher, a teen-aged English girl, and an elderly harem woman. **y*

1892. Fleming, Nichol. *Counter Paradise.* New York: Dell, 1970. A second-generation 007 runs the gamut of adventure from a gunfight on skis in the Swiss Alps to a ship-to-air combat in the Mediterranean. *P*

1893. Fletcher, Lucille. *Blindfold.* New York: Random, 1960. The CIA employs a New York City playboy-psychologist named Snow to treat a neurotic scientist, blindfolding the former on each visit to a secret Southern bayou hideaway, which soon becomes the subject of an enemy spymaster's attention.

1894. Flynn, Jay. *A Body for McHugh.* New York: Avon, 1960. McHugh is a hardnosed secret agent in a paperback series begun in 1959. *P* One more:

1895. ___. *Viva McHugh.* New York: Avon, 1960. *P*

1896. Follett, James. *Churchill's Gold.* London: Weidenfeld, 1980. Britain is facing bankruptcy in 1940 unless her last gold reserves can be shipped from

South Africa, a fact which German economists are all too well aware, so when Captain Robert Gerrard is commissioned to carry the bullion home, the Germans send U-boat skipper Kurt Miliand, Gerrard's former first mate, to track and destroy him.

1897. ___. *Dominator*. Garden City, NY: Doubleday, 1986. Follett is a marine engineer, underwater treasure hunter, and power-boat designer who turned to writing screenplays and novels. *Dominator* is an early technothriller about two men, an American astronaut and an Israeli Army officer (both in internal exile and disgrace from their colleagues and countries) who combine to thwart a brilliant Arab terrorist scheme.

1898. ___. *Swift*. London: Methuen, 1986. SWIFT is the built-in security system which monitors interbank transactions between London and New York. An unlikely trio consisting of a wealthy gangster, a *Tass* correspondent, and a wacky computer hacker have plans to break in, override the system, and make their fortunes. Other espionage-technothrillers:

1899. ___. *The Beam*. London: Methuen, 1989.

1900. ___. *Crown Court*. New York: St. Martin's, 1978.

1901. ___. *The Doomsday Ultimatum*. London: Weidenfeld & Nicholson, 1976.

1902. ___. *Ice*. New York: Stein & Day, 1978.

1903. ___. *Mirage*. London, Methuen, 1988.

1904. ___. *The Tiptoe Boys*. London: Transworld, 1982.

1905. ___. *U700*. London: Weidenfeld & Nicholson, 1979.

1906. ___. *The Wotan Warhead*. New York: Stein & Day, 1979.

1907. Follett, Ken. *Eye of the Needle*. New York: Arbor, 1978. *Der Nadel*, Hitler's handpicked favorite Abwehr agent, attempts to escape London with the real secret of D-Day.

   A London-educated journalist, Follett became a publishing executive and minor author, writing under the pseudonym of "Symon Myles." After getting an advance from a publisher to try something "new" in espionage fiction, Follett published *The Shakeout* in 1975 employing the seldom-used idea of industrial spying. Follett's formula for successful spy fiction is to keep his protagonists one step ahead of disaster—whether bad guy (*Der Nadel* or Alex Wolff) or good guy—Nat Dick Dickstein, for example—even though we always know how the events must inevitably turn out historically. Much of Follett's inspiration, in fact, is historical or headline occurrence, as in the examples *The Man from St. Petersburg* or *Triple*, inspired by the actual theft of tons of uranium at sea in 1968. Though his plots would seem ready-made, Follett is widely praised for his handling of one of espionage literature's most common conventions of shifting from hunter to hunted and back again. He has, in addition, an expert ear for dialogue and a skillful eye at painting in the scenery, whether historical or actual, that make his narratives full of tension.

1908. ___. *The Bear Raid.* London: Harwood-Smart, 1976. This is the second novel featuring the audacious rascal and industrial spy, Piers Roper, who takes on the Mafia.

1909. ___. *A Dangerous Fortune.* New York: Delacorte, 1993. Late-Victorian saga of a powerful family known as the Pilasters and a scheming ne'er-do-well named Micky Miranda whose manipulations of the family's finances could destroy the British economy.

1910. ___. *The Key to Rebecca.* New York: Morrow, 1980. The outcome of World War II could be affected when Abwehr agent Alex Wolff in Egypt steals General Montgomery's El Alamein plans and prepares to radio them in code to Rommel; British Major William Vandam must destroy Wolff before the information transfer can be made. Loosely based on an actual Big War espionage event.

1911. ___. *Lie Down with Lions.* New York: Morrow, 1986. A CIA agent is sent to Afghanistan to organize the guerrillas under the leadership of the charismatic Masud. Complicating matters there are his ex-lover, now married to a doctor who is spying for the Soviets, and Anatoly, the KGB man assigned to bring the rebellion to a halt.

1912. ___. *The Man from St. Petersburg.* New York: Morrow, 1982. Two men from Russia have it in their power to change the course of history in 1914 as the world prepares for war: Prince Orlov's goal is to seal a secret agreement with young Winston Churchill in Mayfair, whereas the other Russian's goal is assassination and anarchy.

1913. ___. *Night over Water.* New York: Morrow, 1991. About privileged characters fleeing England on the eve of the Second World War, including a

Fascist English lord, a German scientist, a jewel thief, and an attractive American widow aboard a 25- to 30-hour a trans-Atlantic flight after WW II breaks out.

1914. ___. *The Pillars of the Earth*. New York: Morrow, 1989. This historical saga of cathedral building, warfare in the violent Middle Ages, love and betrayal opens with the hanging of an innocent man. *HI*

1915. ___. *The Shakeout*. London: Hodder & Stoughton, 1975. Piers Roper, a withdrawn and inhibited upper class Englishman, is an expert marketing executive who joins various firms to rip off their industrial secrets for resale to the highest bidder.

1916. ___. *Triple*. New York: Arbor, 1979. British expatriate Nat Dickstein, now an agent of the Mossad, must shake a dangerous KGB operative in order to penetrate the control bureau of Euratom to steal uranium oxide for Israel.
 Besides "heist" mysteries (*The Modigliani Scandal*. By Zachary Stone, pseud. New York: Morrow, 1985 & *Under the Streets of Nice* with Rene Louis Maurice. Bethesda, MD: National, 1986), mysteries under the pseudonym Symon Myles, and film scripts, Follett has told the nonfictional "espionage" tale of Presidential candidate and Texas billionaire Ross Perot's liberation of some of his company officers held captive in Iran in *On Wings of Eagles* (New York: Morrow, 1983).

1917. Footman, Robert. *Always a Spy*. New York: Dodd, 1986. An ex-CIA man joins a British Intelligence woman agent, literally and figuratively, to find a missing Yugoslav. *P*

1918. ___. *Once a Spy*. New York: Dodd, 1980. Junius Oakland of the US State Department picks his old adversary Harry Ryder to rescue two political prisoners being held by terrorists in the Philippines.

1919. Forbes, Bryan. *The Endless Game*. New York: Random, 1986. Former British Intelligence officer, biographer of Dame Edith Evans, author of children's stories, novelist, and film director Forbes has created in his first espionage work a most cynical view of a nation in decline. The British want to know why the KGB would be interested in killing Caroline Oates—an agent who had been captured, tortured, and reduced to a vegetable. Her lover and fellow agent from the Austrian network, Alec Hillsden, is assigned to find out. This novel, and its sequel, compares well with le Carré's *The Spy Who Came in from the Cold* because of the rich mix of characterization, the inward turning to present a spy's motivations and, especially, the bittersweet residue of an agent's tainted victory at the end.

1920. ___. *A Spy at Twilight.* New York: Random, 1989. Originally published in London as *A Song at Twilight*, this sequel to *The Endless Game* opens with "defector" Alec Hillsden in Leningrad plotting to smuggle a manuscript exposing Control's betrayal of England—now on the verge of collapse and takeover by Control's GRU master.

Forbes, Colin, pseud. *See* Sawkins, Raymond H.

1921. Forbes, Stephen. *False Cross.* New York: Signet, 1989. US scientists attempt to retrieve a downed satellite in the frozen Antarctic wasteland—before a contingent of the Soviet Army can get to it first. One more:

1922. ___. *Neptune's Lance.* New York: Signet, 1992.

1923. Ford, John M. *The Scholars of Night.* New York: TOR, 1988. Thomas Hansard, Renaissance drama professor at Valentine College in the Northeast US, doubles as a strategic analyst for the ultrasecret White Group in Washington, DC. When Hansard exposes his friend berenson as a Soviet agent, the think tank enlists his help to find the key to another mystery—one that involves the answer to a code lost in a play of Christopher Marlowe.

Forrest, David, pseud. *See* Forrest-Webb, Robert

1924. Forrest-Webb, Robert. *And to My Nephew Albert I Leave the Island What I Won Off Fatty Hagan in a Poker Game.* By David Forrest, pseud. New York: Morrow, 1969. One of the most humorous "spy" stories ever written, this tale concerns a little speck of land (70 x 150 yards) off the coast of England. When Albert takes over, he discovers the frequent presence of Victoria, who loves to sunbathe. Just as the two are getting to know one another, a Soviet spy trawler runs aground nearby—and about an hour later, the US Marines start landing . . . *H*

1925. ___. *One of Our Dinosaurs Is Missing.* By David Forrest, pseud. New York: Avon, 1975. The print version of a Disney screenplay in which five British nannys swipe bones which contain a secret microdot from an American museum. *P*

1926. Forrester, Larry. *A Girl Called Fathom.* London: Heinemann, 1967. Douglas Campbell, head of NATO Intelligence, abducts amateur spy Fathom

Harvill and persuades her to help find "The Fire Dragon," a nuclear trigger device lost when a bomber crashed in the Mediterranean.

1927. Forsyth, Frederick. *The Day of the Jackal.* New York: Viking, 1971. Written in only thirty-five days and approved by President de Gaulle's Culture Minister André Malraux, this volume was an international hit and catapulted its author into preeminence among modern spy thriller writers. Sort of a "documentary" novel, all but a few of the volume's characters were real-life people and the plot was based on actual events. *

By the spring of 1963, the right-wing OAS in France, infuriated by de Gaulle's withdrawal from Algeria, had failed in six known assassination attempts on the President. Now it sought to hire an outsider, a professional killer who would be unknown to French police and intelligence. In Vienna, a blond-haired Englishman takes on the job. His code name: Jackal; his price: $500,000; his terms: total secrecy, even from his employers.

A multi-language journalist, Forsyth was both a print and BBC-TV reporter before going off to cover the Biafran civil war as a freelance investigator. After leaving Biafra in 1969, he had a little time to kill between jobs and so spent a month penning the novel which would turn out to be *Jackal.* The success of that novel was indeed sensational—so much so that controversy exists even today about the existence of such a mercenary killer as the Jackal. Forsyth immediately became a best-selling practitioner of the spy thriller, and every title he publishes is successful. There still exists, in addition to the *Jackal* controversy, much conjecture on the actual role Forsyth played or may have played in events chronicled in his best-selling *Dogs of War.*

Forsyth's contribution to the genre is multifold. His forte is not only the realism of Deighton, but the action of Maclean and suspense of MacInnes. Moreover, his novels are filled with real-life names, who are often important to the plot and build-up of his adventures. (See Mr. Forsyth's CRAFT NOTES comments.)

1928. ___. *The Deceiver.* New York: Bantam, 1991. Four interlocking short novels featuring fifty-one-year-old British spy Sam McCready, the Deceiver, and his exploits from the early days of the Cold War to the Persian Gulf era.

1929. ___. *The Devil's Alternative.* New York: Viking, 1980. The rescue of an unconscious man from the Black Sea in 1982 sets off a sequence of events which takes officials in various world capitals to the brink of global disaster.

1930. ___. *The Dogs of War.* New York: Viking, 1974. A London financial wizard and an Irish mercenary leader plot the takeover of Zangaro, a small West African dictatorship with a secret source of platinum.

1931. ___. *Forsyth's Three.* New York: Viking, 1980. An omnibus containing *The Day of the Jackal, The ODESSA File,* and *The Dogs of War.*

1932. ___. *The Fourth Protocol.* New York: Viking, 1984. John Preston is a hardnosed, resourceful agent who is held in contempt by his smarmy Oxbridge superiors and forced to work border security; what he discovers on the job is that the Soviet Union is violating the so-called Fourth Protocol and a nuclear device is being constructed piece by piece somewhere in England in time for a planned "accident" near an American air base.

1933. ___. *The Negotiator.* New York: Doubleday, 1989. A global conspiracy of Soviet military, a deranged Houston oil tycoon and his greedy cohorts, and Islamic fundamentalists is spearheaded by Col. Easterhouse, a computer expert now working for the Saudis; its plan: smash the House of Sa'ud and its stranglehold on oil by exterminating the Saudi line. Spy writer Richard Condon, in his *NYTBR* (16 April 1989) review of the novel writes: "Frederick Forsyth establish[es] *The Negotiator* as the Mount Everest of high-tech novels, taking a tack that produces a tech so high as to threaten its hero and villains alike with nosebleeds" (11). In his latest novel, Forsyth focuses upon the events that culminated in the Gulf War against Saddam Hussein in *The Fist of God* (New York: Bantam, 1994), which concerns an SAS major who must venture in disguise to Baghdad to find a former Mossad source known as "Jericho" within the Iraqi government and activate this mole for information about Hussein's war plans.

1934. ___. *No Comebacks.* New York: Viking, 1982. A versatile collection of short stories.

1935. ___. *The ODESSA File.* New York: Viking, 1972. In the fictional literature of spies, "ODESSA" is a group set up to protect former Nazi SS officers now living under new identities. This same organization is encountered in some of the other stories cited in this compilation. Forsyth's account is by and large the most gripping of the ODESSA tales and concerns a young German reporter, Peter Miller, who, having read about a particularly infamous Nazi death camp, attempts to penetrate ODESSA to find its commandant, one Eduard Roschmann. Roschmann is alive and well and as one of ODESSA's top leaders, is up to his eyebrows in the Arab missile program. He orders his confederates to stop Miller before anything damaging can be learned by the journalist.

1936. Forvé, Guy. *Ofanu.* New York: Carlyle, 1979. A CIA agent, a nimble explosives expert, and a Hollywood stuntman are tapped by American government leaders to go to Japan and retrieve a vital secret hidden in a nearly impregnable mountaintop fortress known as Ofanu. *P*

1937. Fournier, Pierre. *Lambs of Fire.* By Pierre Gascar, pseud. Trans. from the French. New York: Braziller, 1963. A number of French "organization" men obtain explosives to get back at the de Gaulle government for "betraying" the army in Algeria. Sort of an early *Day of the Jackal.*

1938. Fowlkes, Frank. *Majendie's Cat.* San Diego: Harcourt, 1986. About a plot against the US economy by a clever swindler.

1939. ___. *The Peruvian Contracts.* New York: Putnam's, 1976. Agents of Peru, the CIA, and the KGB seek a man who has been hired by the Peruvian government to speculate in US grain futures.

1940. Fox, Anthony. *Kingfisher Scream.* New York: Viking, 1981. To encourage the defection of a Soviet naval official, Paul Harvester must take the place of an SIS agent known to have been caught in a KGB mind-control scam.

1941. Fox, Gardner. *The Sexecutioner: Tong in Cheek.* By Glen Chase, pseud. New York: Leisure, 1972. A spy/crime-spoof series starring Cherry Delight, agent of NYMPHO [New York Mafia Prosecution and Harassment Organization]. *PH* The red-haired Ms. Delight's other tales include:

1942. ___. *The Sexecutioner: Silverfinger.* By Glen Chase, pseud. New York: Leisure, 1972. *PH*

1943. ___. *Chuck You, Farley!* By Glen Chase, pseud. New York: Leisure, 1973. *PH*

1944. ___. *Fire in the Hole.* By Glen Chase, pseud. New York: Leisure, 1974. *PH*

1945. ___. *Mexican Standoff.* By Glen Chase, pseud. New York: Leisure, 1975. *PH*

Fox, James M., pseud. *See* Knipscheer, James M.

1946. Fox, Victor J. *The Pentagon Case.* New York: Freedom, 1958. An ex-Marine and his wife are harassed when the former attempts to expose a Communist underground cell in the Defense Department during his tour as special assistant to a high official. *

1947. Frabutt, Paul. *The Spy Who Loved Married Blood.* Youngstown, OH: Porcine & Vixen, 1990. A lusty choir director goes undercover, literally, with many Washington, DC wives to gain their husbands' secrets—so he can sell them to the KGB. *PH*

1948. Frances, Stephen. *The Ambassador's Plot.* New York: Award, 1968. SIS agent John Gail faces a high-speed journey into terror and death as he attempts to end a deadly new twist to the game of espionage, blackmail, and seduction as ordered by a foreign representative of the British government. *P*

1949. ___. *The Caress of Conquest.* New York: Award, 1968. Gail's dirty job is to destroy a narcotic ring after other British agents have been turned into junkies trying to sabotage it. *P*

1950. ___. *Hate Is for the Hunted.* New York: Award, 1970. The fifth novel in a series about John Gail, amateur sleuth and sometime operative for British Intelligence. *P*

1951. ___. *To Love and Yet to Die.* New York: Award, 1968. Gail faces his most terrifying assignment as he takes on a madman's challenge—in a mission that marks him as a target for both the SIS and the KGB. *P* One other Gail title is:

1952. ___. *This Woman Is Death.* New York: Award, 1969. *P*

1953. Francis, Clare. *Wolf Winter.* New York: Morrow, 1988. A prodigy who was admitted to the Royal Ballet School at thirteen, Francis entered London University at seventeen and earned a degree in economics. An adventurer as well, she set the trans-Atlantic speed record for a solo crossing by a woman and documented her experiences in a bestseller *Woman Alone: Sailing Solo across the Atlantic* (New York: McKay, 1977). She broke into the US market with her first thriller, *Night Sky* (New York: Morrow, 1984) followed the next year by *Red Crystal* (London: Heinemann, 1985), before publishing this well-received espionage novel set in Scandinavia. It's the early 1960s and Russia is making overtures to neutral Norway via blackmailing an unscrupulous reporter with a secret to keep NATO, and strategic US missiles, from Lapp country. The murder of two spies will begin a complex chain of events that will set two men, one a traitor to his country, on a trek across the bleak Arctic wastes of the Scandinavian plateau.

1954. ___. *The Killing Winds.* New York: Simon & Schuster, 1992. A rock star and an environmentalist join to fight a multinational chemical corporation responsible for the death of the musician's wife.

1955. Francis, Dick. *Blood Sport.* New York: Harper & Row, 1967. On vacation from "the Agency," Gene Hawkins decides to employ his "talents" to help a friend recover his precious racehorse, the third to recently disappear. As much a detective as a spy thriller from the renowned writer of racetrack-mysteries.

1956. Frank, Patrick. *Forbidden Area.* Philadelphia: Lippincott, 1956. A Russian plot to annihilate America in the near future will succeed unless it can be broken up by a few dedicated agents. *

1957. Frankel, Sandor. *The Aleph Solution.* Briarcliff Manor, NY: Stein & Day, 1978. PLO terrorists take control of the UN General Assembly and demand the immediate dissolution of Israel.

Franklin, Charles, pseud. *See* Usher, Frank H.

1958. Franklin, Max. *Good Guys Wear Black.* New York: Signet, 1978. After surviving a Viet Cong trap, a retired Black Tiger Commando discovers he is earmarked for death by his own US government. *P*

1959. Franklin, Steve. *The Malcontents.* Garden City, NY: Doubleday, 1970. The Eastern Maritime Computer Company sends industrial spy Bill Stern to Venice to obtain a superior insulation formula developed by a rival firm. Compare with Ken Follett's *The Shakeout.*

1960. Fraser, Antonia. *Your Royal Hostage.* New York: Bantam, 1990. This seventh tale involving sleuth Jemima Shore and a spoiled British princess kidnapped by a band of crazies on the eve of her nuptials to a European prince. *P*

1961. Frayn, Michael. *A Landing of the Sun.* New York: Viking, 1992. A narrative that mixes fable with satire (on bureaucracies) and becomes, finally, a spy thriller with an twist. *H*

1962. ___. *The Russian Interpreter.* New York: Viking, 1967. A British graduate student in Moscow is bored; then one snowy day, a shadowy industrial magnate shows up and engages him as his interpreter.

1963. Frazer, Steve. *The Sky Block.* New York: Rinehart, 1953. A country lad aids agents in their search for the "Weather Wrecker," a machine causing drought over wide areas. **y*

1964. Freadhoff, Chuck. *Codename: Cipher.* New York: Walker, 1991. Terrorists grab a munitions depot with nuclear devices and demand the release of an Arab terrorist imprisoned in Germany.

Frede, Richard, pseud. *See* Frederics, Macdowell

1965. Frederics, Macdowell. *Black Work.* By Richard Frede, pseud. New York: Crowell, 1976. An extremist group plans to kill America's first Black Vice President.

1966. ___. *The Coming Out Party.* By Richard Frede, pseud. New York: Random, 1969. When he goes on assignment for the CIA to a Writer's Association Conference to uncover some nasties, an author finds he is faced with losing either his pen name or his life.

1967. Freed, Donald. *The China Card.* New York: Arbor, 1980. In 1984 a lover tries to halt a man who unconsciously leads the world into the path of nuclear destruction when he plays "the China Card."

1968. ___. *The Spymaster.* New York: Arbor, 1979. Nearing retirement, Vivian T. S. Prescott does not enjoy the prospect of a Congressional committee unraveling his career in covert action which led to his post as CIA Director.

1969. Freedgood, Morton. *Man in Question.* By John Godey, pseud. Garden City, NY: Doubleday, 1951. Peter Manning comes to America from behind the Iron Curtain to help in the anti-Communist resistance and is nearly done in by the opposition. Not a bad McCarthy-era yarn. *

1970. Freedman, John. *The False Joanna.* Indianapolis: Bobbs-Merrill, 1971. A lush of a spy is sent by his superiors in "the Fourth Agency" to find a girl whom the KGB has succeeded in smuggling into Britain.

1971. ___. *The Fourth Agency.* Indianapolis: Bobbs-Merrill, 1960. Our alcoholic operative is ordered to commence a dialogue with the GRU; the talks take place between Las Vegas and Mexico and are replete with unusual implications.

1972. Freeling, Nicholas. *The Dresden Green.* New York: Harper & Row, 1968. The senior French-Russian translator at Europaus, an organization devoted to peace and brotherhood, finds a strange diamond—the Dresden Green—under a quince tree. His discovery forces him to resume the role he played twenty years earlier in the French Resistance.

1973. Freemantle, Brian. *Charlie M.* Garden City, NY: Doubleday, 1977. [*Charlie Muffin.* London: Cape, 1977]. A scruffy SIS agent, Charlie Muffin, must outwit the KGB to secure the defection of one of its agents. Shunted aside by his superiors, snobs all, Charlie watches them bungle the biggest defection in the history of the British Intelligence when the head of the KGB wants to come over—until, at the last moment, they ask him to take on the assignment and save the day.

This well-respected spy thriller practitioner is exceptionally well read and regarded in the US despite his British origin. A foreign correspondent widely travelled to world trouble spots, Freemantle gave up a prestigious editorship on a London paper in the mid-1970s to devote full time to his writing. Freemantle, like Len Deighton devotes considerable research to his yarns and his writing and plotting is meticulously and intelligently accomplished. To a certain extent, Freemantle's work is similar to that of Frederick Forsyth in that, with some disguise, much of what is related actually took place at some point in the secret dirty-tricks conflict of the Cold War. Freemantle has traveled and worked in dozens of countries including the former USSR, and told an interviewer that he was "once ambushed on Vietnam's Highway One at the moment peace was supposed to come into being" (*Contemporary Authors*. New Ser. Vol. 16: 124).

Freemantle's nonfiction includes: *Sean Connery: Guilt-Edged Bond* (By Richard Gant, pseud. London: Mayflower, 1967), *The Lost American* (New York: TOR, 1984) and *The Vietnam Legacy* (New York: TOR, 1984). (See the BIBLIOGRAPHY to this edition for his two nonfiction works on the CIA and KGB, both of which were lauded by no less an expert than Miles Copeland.)

1974. ___. *Betrayals.* New York: TOR, 1991. Janet Stone is the only one who can, or cares to, rescue her fiancee, a CIA man held hostage in Lebanon.

1975. ___. *The Blind Run.* New York: Bantam, 1987. Charlie is languishing in Wormwood Scrubbs on a frame-up, ignored by his bosses until the Russian mole Edwin Sampson convinces him to escape with him to the USSR. Charlie does, with the approval of his bosses, who want him to pose as a defector and bring back a mole operating in the KGB. Sounds easy but Charlie falls in love behind the Iron Curtain.

1976. ___. *The Button Man.* New York: St. Martin's, 1993. An FBI man and a Moscow investigator reluctantly team up to find a serial killer in Moscow when a US Senator's daughter is murdered.

1977. ___. *Charlie Muffin U.S.A.* Garden City, NY: Doubleday, 1980. [*Charlie Muffin's Uncle Sam.* London: Cape, 1980]. Charlie gets in the crossfire of the mob and the FBI when he takes on the assignment of arranging security for a priceless stamp collection.

1978. ___. *Comrade Charlie.* New York: St. Martin's, 1992. Charlie, desk-bound because of his superior's animosity, is going to become the victim of a plot by the Russian enemies he has outwitted during his career even as the Soviet Union is about to collapse. This time, it's a frame-up, seemingly foolproof, and one that involves the American "Star Wars" program.

1979. ___. *Face Me When You Walk Away.* New York: Putnam's, 1974. A Russian diplomat, helped and hindered by the KGB, must babysit a daffy Russian writer who is a Nobel Prize candidate as the result of a blackmail campaign against the Swedish committee which awards the prizes.

1980. ___. *Goodbye to an Old Friend.* New York: Putnam's, 1973. A top Russian space scientist decides to defect, leaving his family to possible reprisal. The Western Allies want to put the man Pavel to work immediately, but an unprepossessing British operative, Adrian Dodds, believes the man may be a plant and sets out to prove his suspicions.

1981. ___. *Here Comes Charlie M.* Garden City, NY: Doubleday, 1978. [*Clap Hands, Here Comes Charlie M.* London: Cape: 1978]. Charlie Muffin, a scruffy SIS agent, is hunted by the CIA, which needs his services, and the KGB, which wants him dead. *H*

1982. ___. *The Man Who Wanted Tomorrow.* Briarcliff Manor, NY: Stein & Day, 1976. Now disguised, Soviet scientist Vladimir Kusnov is, in fact, an ex-Nazi doctor "worse than Mengele," who is wanted by Israel as a war criminal, by his ODESSA colleagues for his theft of concentration camp loot, and eventually by the KGB; following chapters of intricate maneuvers around the hunt by the pursuers for the incriminating contents of a box being auctioned off in Berlin, the Russian is finally run to ground by the Mossad.

1983. ___. *O'Farrell's Law.* New York: TOR, 1990. Charles O'Farrell has been doing the dirty work as a killer for a hush-hush agency for many years; his real crisis of faith comes when he is ordered to kill a Cuban diplomat in London—and kills the man's wife by mistake.

1984. ___. *The Run Around.* New York: Bantam, 1989. In this third Charlie Muffin "Run" novel, the rogue British agent must try to foil an assassination plot of an important Western politician in Switzerland with the help of an American and Israeli agent.

1985. ___. *See Charlie Run.* New York: Bantam, 1987. Charlie is in Japan where he is arranging the British end of the defection of a husband and wife team; he also foils his CIA opposite in the venture who is handling the American side and is, again, targeted by the KGB just on general principle.

Other Freemantle spy tales of Charlie Muffie, thrillers penned under his own name or with the Jonathan Evans alias include these:

1986. ___. *The Bearpit.* London: Century, 1987.

1987. ___. *Chairman of the Board.* By Jonathan Evans, pseud. New York: Viking, 1982.

1988. ___. *Charlie Muffin and Russian Rose.* London: Century, 1985.

1989. ___. *The Inscrutable Charlie Muffin.* Garden City, NY: Doubleday, 1979.

1990. ___. *The Kremlin Connection.* By Jonathan Evans, pseud. New York: TOR, 1984.

1991. ___. *The Kremlin Kiss.* London: Century, 1986.

1992. ___. *Little Grey Mice.* New York: St. Martin's, 1992.

1993. ___. *Madrigal for Charlie Muffin.* London: Hutchinson, 1981.

1994. ___. *The Midas Men.* By Jonathan Evans, pseud. New York: Viking, 1981.

1995. ___. *Misfire.* By Jonathan Evans, pseud. Mt. Kisco, NY: Futura, 1982. *P*

1996. ___. *Monopoly.* By Jonathan Evans, pseud. New York: Viking, 1984.

1997. ___. *The November Man.* London: Cape, 1976.

1998. ___. *The Sagomi Gambit.* By Jonathan Evans, pseud. New York: TOR, 1983. *P*

1999. ___. *The Solitary Man.* By Jonathan Evans, pseud. New York: TOR, 1983.

2000. ___. *Takeover.* By Jonathan Evans, pseud. New York: TOR, 1982.

2001. ___. *The Touchables.* London: Hodder & Stoughton, 1968.

2002. French, Richard P. *A Spy Is Forever.* Rutland, VT: Tuttle, 1970. Peter Layton must kill a National Intelligence Agency colleague who has defected—only first he must be found.

2003. Frentzen, Jeffrey. *Star of Egypt.* By Buck Sanders, pseud. New York: Warner, 1981. Ben Slayton is an agent for the Treasury Department in this co-authored series. (See Adcock, Thomas L.) *P*

2004. Freshman, Bruce J. *The Master Plan.* Indianapolis: Bobbs-Merrill, 1981. A child of a secret Nazi Bund grows up to be President of the United States, having been pursued throughout his career by a super-secret sleuth who has the politician pegged as the son of Adolf Hitler.

2005. Freund, Philip, ed. *The Spymaster.* New York: Washburn, 1966. Two novellas and a pair of short stories.

2006. Frey, James N. *The Armageddon Game.* New York: Zebra, 1985. A deadly strain of microbe is stolen from a top-secret US lab and is going to be sold to the Russians unless one agent can stop it from happening.

2007. ___. *Winter of the Wolves.* New York: Holt, 1992. An American agent is called out of retirement against his will to pursue a defecting agent—his best friend.

2008. Friedman, Phillip. *Termination Order.* New York: Dial, 1979. Having finally persuaded a top Russian agent to "come over," CIA operative Gregory Moore finds himself under suspicion of treason and marked for liquidation. Friedman also penned several novels about two counterintelligence operatives of the Special Unit, Bill Kendall and Ron Eisenberg, published by Dell under a pseudonym in the mid-1970's.

2009. ___. *Betrayal in Eden.* By Philip Chase, pseud. New York: Dell, 1977. Bill Kendall and Ron Eisenberg of the Joint Chiefs of Staff's Special Unit must halt a KGB effort to sabotage an underwater base in the Indian Ocean. *P*

2010. ___. *Defame and Destroy.* By Philip Chase, pseud. New York: Dell, 1976. The Special Unit of the JCS has its cover blown and the group is being used as an instrument of destruction by enemies of the US; SU leader, Col. William Kendall faces the agonizing choice of hunting out the unknown adversary or causing the band to self-destruct. *P*

2011. ___. *Merchants of Death.* By Philip Chase, pseud. New York: Dell, 1976. Kendall's Special Unit is the only group which can halt the mad terrorists led by an ex-Army officer, James Rivera, who is holding an entire city hostage against a huge ransom demand. *P*

2012. Frizell, Bernard. *The Grand Defiance.* New York: Morrow, 1972. Even locked up in an impregnable mountain fortress and guarded by the SS day and night, General de Forge was the embodiment of the French Resistance, which even now was sending agent-commando Maudet to effect his rescue.

2013. ___. *Ten Days in August.* New York: Simon & Schuster, 1957. The German occupiers of Paris and the French Resistance battle one another as both sides prepare for the Allied Liberation of 1944, due any moment.

2014. Frost, Mark. *The List of 7.* New York: Morrow, 1993. In 1884 young physician Arthur Conan Doyle has gained a certain notoriety for his anti-occultist writings. He is nearly killed at a séance in London's East End, and his rescuer, Jack Sparks, who is Queen Victoria's own secret agent, tells him of a coven of Satanists called the Dark Brotherhood that not only engineered his own near-fatal mishap but also have dangerous designs against the Crown.

Fry, Peter, pseud. *See* King, Clifford

2015. Fuentes, Carlos. *The Hydra Head.* Trans. from the Spanish. New York: Farrar, 1978. Mexican agent Felix Maldonado attempts to foil an Israeli-Arab plot against Mexico's oil reserves. A unique tale because this hero is the only Mexican secret agent we have ever uncovered.

2016. Fuller, Jack. *Convergence.* Garden City, NY: Doubleday, 1982. A CIA operative working with a double agent, discovers he is being used in a game of wits against a Soviet masterspy.

2017. Furst, Alan. *Dark Star*. Boston: Houghton, 1991. Young Andre Szara, a Polish Jew, becomes a spy by chance when he does a "favor" for the NKVD in the dark days before WW II. In the course of it, he acquires documentation of the most dangerous kind: proof that Stalin was a double agent working for the Czar's secret police before the Bolshevik Revolution. The reviewer in the *Washington Post* (4 June 1991) wrote of his first novel: "Furst . . . is . . . successful at controlling a complicated web of information, events, and characters . . . even the bit players come alive."

2018. ___. *The Caribbean Account*. New York: Delacorte, 1981. Having blown his drug proceeds on a bar which he then loses in a bet, Roger Levin turns p.i., and acquires a "simple" assignment: take half a million dollars to an individual in Miami as ransom for an heiress of the powerful DeScodellaire family.

2019. ___. *Night Soldiers*. Boston: Houghton, 1988. With laudable historical detail, Furst sweeps the reader across the European continent from the beginnings of Fascism in Bulgaria through the Spanish Civil War to WW II and beyond as we follow the career of Khristo Stoianev, torn from his native country and indoctrinated into Russian communism via the NKVD's ruthless espionage apparatus.

2020. ___. *The Paris Drop*. Garden City, NY: Doubleday, 1980. In this second Levin thriller, the ex-marijuana dealer is steeped in the world of commercial espionage, but something feels wrong about the Paris drop, where he is supposed to deliver $100,000, and he suspects it has to do with the simple delivery of a class ring for his uncle.

2021. ___. *Shadow Trade*. New York: Delacorte, 1983. When Guyer is dismissed from intelligence work for the CIA in June of 1977, he returns to the only work he knows by setting himself up in clandestine operations within the ruthless world of corporate espionage of New York. Another:

2022. ___. *Your Day in the Barrel*. New York: Atheneum, 1976.

G

2023. Gadney, Reginald. *The Cage*. New York: Coward-McCann, 1977. [*The Champagne Artist*. London: Hutchinson, 1976]. A retired FBI agent is asked to go to England to look into a murder at a super-secret USAF intelligence center.

2024. ___. *Drawn Blanc*. New York: Coward-McCann, 1971. Czech refugee O.B. Blanc will be forced to return home where authorities want him for killing a KGB man during the 1968 "unpleasantness"; British Intelligence steps in and makes an offer; if Blanc will do a little job for them, his visa will be extended.

2025. ___. *Nightshade*. New York: St. Martin's, 1988. SIS officer John Mahon is investigating his own father's death when he discovers a WW II secret so shocking that it is certain to poison relations between America and Britain forever. Other Gadney novels:

2026. ___. *Seduction of a Tall Man*. London: Heinemann, 1971.

2027. ___. *Something Worth Fighting For*. London: Heinemann, 1973.

2028. ___. *Somewhere in England*. New York: St. Martin's, 1972.

2029. ___. *Victoria*. New York: Coward-McCann, 1975. [*The Last Hours Before Dawn*. London: Heinemann, 1974].

2030. Gaines, Robert. *The Invisible Evil*. New York: Walker, 1963. Patriotic Orangemen conspire to hide a bomb in the British House of Commons where the Prime Minister is speaking on a plan for the unification of Ireland.

Gainham, Sarah, pseud. *See* Ames, Rachel

2031. Gallagher, Stephen. *Oktober*. New York: TOR, 1989. Jim Harper's skiing "accident" almost kills him; while recuperating, he discovers that is was the guinea pig for a conglomerate's experimental superdrug. Three more:

2032. ___. *Chimera*. New York: St. Martin's, 1982.

2033. ___. *Down River*. New York: TOR, 1990.

2034. ___. *Nightmare with Angel*. New York: Ballantine, 1993.

2035. Gallery, Daniel J. *The Brink*. Garden City, NY: Doubleday, 1968. In the Arctic an American nuclear submarine confronts a Soviet destroyer and World War III is on the brink. Compare with Mark Rascovich's *The Bedford Incident*.

2036. Gallico, Paul. *The Hand of Mary Constable.* Garden City, NY: Doubleday, 1964. Alexander Hero of the (British) Psychical Research Society is called upon to prevent Professor Constable from turning over to the Russians the secrets of a new missile defense system. The Soviets, not to be outdone, produce a wax hand bearing the fingerprints of the scientist's missing daughter and promise her safe return in exchange for his expert knowledge.

2037. ___. *Trial by Terror.* New York: Knopf, 1952. An American reporter purposefully delivers himself into the hands of Communist agents behind the Iron Curtain to discover why a group of men in America confessed to crimes they did not commit. *

2038. ___. *The Zoo Gang.* New York: Coward-McCann, 1971. In this funny espionage-detective tale, a gang of former French Resistance fighters turn their talents to halting the assorted crimes taking place on the glamorous Riviera. *H*

Galway, Robert Conington, pseud. *See* McCutchan, Philip

2039. Gandley, Kenneth Royce. *Assassination Day.* By Oliver Jacks, pseud. Briarcliff Manor, NY: Stein & Day, 1976. When a ruthless and successful London assassin pledges to kill Leonid Brezhnev during his British tour, chief superintendent Len Wilson of Special Branch comes out of retirement to get him. Like *Day of the Jackal* but better.

2040. ___. *The Autumn Heroes.* By Oliver Jacks, pseud. New York: St. Martin's, 1978. When a royal couple is captured by terrorists while on safari, Agent Todd and several old commandos with local wartime experience stage a dramatic rescue attempt.

2041. ___. *Bustillo.* By Kenneth Royce, pseud. New York: Coward-McCann, 1976. A former CIA agent is hunted by his ex-employer, who wants to end his knowledge of "Company" corruption, and by an old friend whom he should not have seen in a certain place.

2042. ___. *Code Name: Woodcutter.* By Kenneth Royce, pseud. New York: Simon & Schuster, 1975. [*The Woodcutter Operation.* London: Hodder & Stoughton, 1975]. An ex-paratrooper who deserts in Belfast comes up against five men who have taken over a London hospital with a VIP in a private wing—the Secretary of State.

2043. ___. *The Concrete Boot*. By Kenneth Royce, pseud. New York: McKay, 1971. Spider gets involved with London thugs and Special Branch doublecrossing designed to catch a traitor.

2044. ___. *Man on a Short Leash*. By Oliver Jacks, pseud. Briarcliff Manor, NY: Stein & Day, 1976. After interviewing a wanted man named Kuhn, MI-6 security officer Todd is arrested and imprisoned on a frame-up; in jail, the agent knows he must escape—even if he needs KGB assistance to bring it off.

2045. ___. *The Mosley Receipt*. By Kenneth Royce, pseud. London: Hodder & Stoughton, 1985. In this Spider tale, the "ex-creeper" teams up with the tough Inspector Bulman to investigate a retired police officer's "suicide"; however, some powerful men in HMG want the investigation terminated—that goes for Spider too.

2046. ___. *Patriots*. By Kenneth Royce, pseud. New York: Crown, 1988. The President, the First Lady, and the Soviet Ambassador are aboard Air Force One when it explodes in pieces off the Irish coast. But who are the traitors? The real patriots?

2047. ___. *My Turn to Die*. By Kenneth Royce, pseud. London: Barker, 1958. Royce's first espionage novel is set in France.

2048. ___. *The Third Arm*. By Kenneth Royce, pseud. New York: McGraw-Hill, 1980. SIS Captain Ross Gibbs is ordered to infiltrate a band of international terrorists who are planning to converge on London.

2049. ___. *The XYY Man*. By Kenneth Royce, pseud. New York: McKay, 1970. Willie ("Spider") Scott makes his first appearance in this novel, which led to a Granada TV series in 1976. The character of Inspector Bulman, incidentally, also appears in this thriller, and his persona ultimately led to the longest-running series featuring a detective in the history of British television. Kenneth Royce, as he is best known, was a captain in WW II in the King's African Rifles. Spider has just been released as one of HMG's guests at Wormwood Scrubbs Prison, and he knows that the next stint behind bars will cost him ten years of his life; however, this talented former B & E man will have to put his talents in the service of his country—a fact various shadowy intelligence figures will from time to time ensure. Spider gets enmeshed in a conspiracy that involves the Chinese Legation, South Africa's BOSS agents, who give him a thorough beating, and subject him to death threats from an enforcer for the Free Zimbabwe movement. (See Mr. Gandley's commentary in CRAFT NOTES.) Other Kenneth Royce novels:

2050. ___. *10,000 Days*. By Kenneth Royce, pseud. New York: Carroll & Graf, 1984.

2051. ___. *The Angry Island*. By Kenneth Royce, pseud. London: Cassell, 1963.

2052. ___. *Bones in the Sand*. By Kenneth Royce, pseud. London: Cassell, 1967.

2053. ___. *Channel Assault*. By Kenneth Royce, pseud. New York: Carroll & Graf, 1984.

2054. ___. *The Crypto Man*. By Kenneth Royce, pseud. Briarcliff Manor, NY: Stein & Day, 1984.

2055. ___. *The Day the Wind Dropped*. By Kenneth Royce, pseud. London: Cassell, 1964.

2056. ___. *Exchange of Doves*. New York: Pinnacle, 1992. *P*

2057. ___. *Fall-Out*. London: Hodder & Stoughton, 1989. [*Fallout*. New York: Crown, 1989.]

2058. ___. *The Long Corridor*. By Kenneth Royce, pseud. London: Cassell, 1960.

2059. ___. *The Masterpiece Affair*. New York: Simon & Schuster, 1973. [*Spider Underground*. London: Hodder & Stoughton, 1973].

2060. ___. *The Miniatures Frame*. By Kenneth Royce, pseud. New York: Simon & Schuster, 1972.

2061. ___. *The Night Seekers*. By Kenneth Royce, pseud. London: Cassell, 1962.

2062. ___. *No Way Back*. By Kenneth Royce, pseud. London: Hodder & Stoughton, 1986.

2063. ___. *A Peck of Salt*. By Kenneth Royce, pseud. London: Cassell, 1968.

2064. ___. *The Satan Touch.* By Kenneth Royce, pseud. London: Hodder & Stoughton, 1977.

2065. ___. *Single to Hong Kong.* By Kenneth Royce, pseud. London: Hodder & Stoughton, 1969.

2066. ___. *The Soft-Footed Moor.* By Kenneth Royce, pseud. London: Barker, 1959.

2067. ___. *The Stalin Account.* By Kenneth Royce, pseud. London: Hodder & Stoughton, 1983.

2068. ___. *Trapspider.* By Kenneth Royce, pseud. London: Hodder & Stoughton, 1974.

2069. ___. *A Wild Justice.* By Kenneth Royce, psued. Bath, Eng.: Chivers, 1992.

2070. Garbo, Norman. *Cabal.* New York: Dell, 1980. When a secret international network of prominent people dedicated to Jewish survival learns of an impending Arab attack on Israel, planned in cooperation with the President of the United States, it moves to ensure victory to the Star of David. *P*

2071. ___. *The Spy.* New York: Norton, 1980. When the US government begins a search for a retired intelligence agent who has assumed a new identity, the lives of the few people who have known him are jeopardized.

2072. ___ and Howard Goodkind. *Confrontation.* New York: Harper & Row, 1966. A nationally known news commentator, who has been subpoenaed to testify before the Subversive Activities Committee in 1952, confesses to being a Soviet agent and names the Under Secretary of State as his collaborator.

2073. Gardiner, Wayne J. *The Man on the Left.* New York: Ace-Charter, 1980. After Vietnam, David Mitchell returns home to Chicago where US Army Intelligence notifies him that he had been chosen for a highly confidential mission so secret that the President of the United States would be the only person to know its objective. The operation would take Mitchell to Germany to assassinate an unknown target. At stake: the fate of democratic government in Europe—and possibly the world. *P*

2074. Gardner, Alan. *Six-Day Week.* New York: Coward-McCann, 1966. SIS agent David Troy must break up a plot by Chinese and Italian Communists to kill a British princess who is visiting Italy to join with the Pope in dedicating a new orphanage. Three other Troy tales not published in the United States are:

2075. ___. *Assignment: Tahiti*. London: Muller, 1965.

2076. ___. *The Escalator*. London: Muller, 1963.

2077. ___. *The Man Who Was Too Much*. London: Muller, 1967.

2078. Gardner, John. *Air Apparent*. New York: Viking, 1970. [*The Airline Pirates*. London: Hodder & Stoughton, 1970]. Boysie Oakes of British Intelligence is put in charge of an air transport firm and becomes involved with air pirates and an African coup. *H*

A former journalist and ordained minister, Gardner was for a time in the early sixties the only full-time drama critic employed by a British newspaper. Like David (le Carré) Cornwell, he had little use for the James Bond character, then highly in vogue. The challenge of a novel-writing career and the chance to help "liquidate" Fleming's popularity, led to his entering the lists as a spy thriller practitioner.

Instead of developing his character and plots a la le Carré or Deighton, John Gardner elected to bypass gloom and tragedy in favor of humor and complete impossibility. Thus the character Boysie Oakes was not an anti-hero in the sense of George Smiley, but a complete spoof of James Bond himself. The Oakes approach was very successful for Gardner and a number of books and movies followed based on the agent's fumbling accomplishments. In a most remarkable turnabout, however, Gardner was chosen to undertake the continuation of Fleming's Bond, in much the same fashion that Gerald Fairlie earlier undertook to continue the Bulldog Drummond hero of "Sapper."

2079. ___. *Amber Nine*. New York: Viking, 1966. Agent Brian I. "Boysie" Oakes is ordered to liquidate a left-wing member of the British Parliament at a quiet resort hotel on Lake Maggiore. Oakes, the official murderer of the Department of Special Services, is a meek man, who cannot bring himself to kill and is even afraid of riding in airplanes. To accomplish his task, he sublets his assignment to a gangster from London's Soho district. *H*

2080. ___. *Brokenclaw*. New York: Putnam's, 1990. Fu-Chu "Brokenclaw" Lee is a brutal, half-Sioux, half-Chinese San Francisco gangster who intends to deliver secrets to the Chinese government, which 007 must stop at all costs.

2081. ___. *The Dancing Dodo*. Garden City, NY: Doubleday, 1978. In England, a mysterious fever virus spreads among investigators who have found a crashed World War II bomber with six bodies—all bearing dogtags of men yet alive.

2082. ___. *Death Is Forever*. New York: Putnam's, 1992. Despite the end of Soviet Communism, Bond and sidekick Easy St. John must race across Europe trying to save agents of a disintegrating American-British network operating in Eastbloc countries when two of their officers are murdered.

2083. ___. *For Special Services*. New York: Coward-McCann, 1982. Bond teams up with the daughter of old friend Felix Leitner, Cedar, when SPECTRE rears its ugly head again.

2084. ___. *Founder Member*. London: Muller, 1969. Boysie Oakes is out of espionage, but as director of the private security organization, Grimobo Enterprises, becomes involved with a crazy named Solomon, who had purloined a rocket to an island stronghold which he rules with a female pirate called Constanza Challis. *H*

2085. ___. *The Garden of Weapons*. New York: McGraw-Hill, 1981. In a tale strikingly reminiscent of le Carré, Gardner tells the story of British spymaster Bernie Kruger, who learns that his carefully planted East German network is about to be rolled up. Taking personal charge of the effort to extract his agents before they are caught, he is compromised by an old love affair, and loses both his ebullience and reputation in the resulting fiasco.

2086. ___. *Icebreaker*. New York: Putnam's, 1983. Bond's mission is to destroy a neo-Nazi enclave in northern Finland.

2087. ___. *A Killer for a Song*. London: Muller, 1975. In the final Boysie Oakes tale, the timid agent and his ruthless chief, Mostyn, become involved in an SIS plot to obtain revenge for the 1964 murder of a British agent in Mexico. *H*

2088. ___. *The Last Trump*. New York: McGraw-Hill, 1980. [*Golgotha*. London: Allan, 1980]. After the Soviets have employed Tito's death to quell a rebellious Yugoslavia and have gone on to take over Western Europe, the President of the United States prepares for a showdown international summit meeting with Russia's leaders.

2089. ___. *License Renewed.* New York: Richard Marek, 1981. 007 battles a super villain who holds nuclear plants for ransom all over the world. First in a new series of James Bond adventures written with the approval of the estate of the late Ian Fleming.

2090. ___. *License to Kill.* New York: Charter, 1989. A friend's wife is murdered by a cocaine drug lord and Bond vows to help him revenge her. The film starred Timothy Dalton; the most recent to inherit Sean Connery's mantle is Irish actor Pierce Brosnan.

2091. ___. *The Liquidator.* New York: Viking, 1965. In the first Boysie Oakes yarn, a man past forty, timid, terrified of violence and prone to air sickness, is recruited into the Department of Special Services and is charged with "removing" individuals who have become embarrassing to the crown. Ordered to liquidate operatives regarded by their higher-ups as security risks, he subcontracts the "hits" to London gangsters. *H*

2092. ___. *Madrigal.* New York: Viking, 1967. Oakes temporarily changes his shy personality after learning the facts of life about Red Chinese agents and "cooperating" with the KGB. *H*

2093. ___. *Maestro.* New York: Penzler, 1993. "Big Herbie" Kruger is assigned to interrogate orchestra conductor Louis Passau, who is about to celebrate his ninetieth-year on the podium before a crowd at Lincoln Center, because there is evidence he may have spied for Hitler and aided the KGB during the Cold War.

2094. ___. *The Man from Barbarossa.* New York: Putnam's, 1991. Bond meets a new breed of terrorism when he comes face to face with the Scales of Justice.

2095. ___. *Never Send Flowers.* New York: Putnam's, 1993. Bond and Swiss agent "Flicka" von Grüse investigate the murder of a colleague in the service and discover a startling fact at the woman's funeral linking her murder to four others of prominent personalities: a white rose with blood-tipped petals and a mysterious note accompanying a wreath.

2096. ___. *No Deals, Mr. Bond.* New York: Putnam's, 1987. James Bond must face the Soviet Union's top agent when ritualized murders, too much alike, commence.

2097. ___. *Nobody Lives Forever.* New York: Putnam's, 1986. Who dares offer ten million Swiss francs for anyone who will bring in the head of James Bond? None other than Tamil Rahani, archvillain from *Role of Honor.*

2098. ___. *The Nostradamus Traitor.* Garden City, NY: Doubleday, 1979. An intelligence agent seeks the link between an aging German beauty and various plots in wartime France and Germany.

2099. ___. *Role of Honor.* New York: Putnam's, 1984. Could it be? James Bond in the employ of SPECTRE?

2100. ___. *Scorpius.* New York: Putnam's, 1988. James Bond meets Father Valentine, cult leader secretly funneling arms to terrorists.

2101. ___. *The Secret Families.* New York: Putnam's, 1989. The third of the "Secret Generations" trilogy. The Railton family discovers that the late Caspar Railton, who had served with such distinction in British Intelligence, may have been a traitor.

2102. ___. *The Secret Generations.* New York: Putnam's, 1985. The Railtons-Farthings trilogy begins with the setting up of "Tarot," the Railtons' secret operation as Hitler and the Nazis rise to power in Germany.

2103. ___. *The Secret Houses.* New York: Putnam's, 1987. The second in the trilogy featuring the British Railtons and the American Farthings. The Railtons' spying operation is betrayed to the Gestapo, and the evidence points to a Railton as the traitor.

2104. ___. *Traitor's Exit.* London: Muller, 1970. With the assistance of Boysie Oakes, a British spy thriller writer is recruited to remove from Moscow a rather noted English defector. *H*

2105. ___. *Understrike.* New York: Viking, 1965. A carefully trained Russian double from the KGB is sent to California to take the place of a British agent and in San Diego, pits his skill against Boysie Oakes in hopes of obtaining the results of a hush-hush submarine trial. *H*

2106. ___. *The Werewolf Trace.* Garden City, NY: Doubleday, 1977. MI-5 agent Vincent Cooling attempts to discover if a naturalized British citizen is, in fact, the son of Reich Propaganda Minister Joseph Goebbels.

2107. ___. *Win, Lose or Die.* New York: Putnam's, 1989. Bond is assigned to active duty aboard an aircraft carrier, engaged in naval exercises with British, American, and Soviet fleets, as a terrorist hijacking plot unfolds.

Gardner, a writing machine, has produced two collections of short stories: *Hideaway* (London: Corgi, 1968) and *The Assassination File* (London: Corgi, 1974). One other:

2108. ___. *The Quiet Dogs.* London: Hodder & Stoughton, 1982.

2109. Garfield, Brian. *Deep Cover.* New York: Delacorte, 1973. For over twenty years, Russians trained "to be Americans" by the KGB have been settling around an Arizona missile base, where, upon orders of their controller, they have gradually taken over, extending their influence far afield even to Washington, DC. Sensing that all is not right, Senator Alan Forrester risks his life and career to look into the matter.

Garfield began his career not as a writer but as a professional musician, but once he turned his talents to publication, he rapidly achieved prominence and is presently one of the most favored American practitioners of the spy thriller. His tales are excellent in locale (Garfield is also a well-regarded writer of westerns), plotting, and character with sufficient action to hold the various story lines together.

2110. ___. *Hopscotch.* Philadelphia: Lippincott, 1975. A CIA man, whom some critics believe was modelled after real-life agent Miles Copeland, no longer wants to caper, but neither does he want to defect. Instead, he brings the international intelligence community to a standstill by writing an exposé. Aghast, agents from all over the world gang up to do him in before he can mail back to his publisher the final batch of "proof."

2111. ___. *Kolchak's Gold.* New York: McKay, 1975. Five hundred tons of gold, hidden by the Whites after the Russian Civil War, was stolen by the Nazis and is now wanted by agents of the Soviet and Western governments.

2112. ___. *The Last Bridge.* New York: McKay, 1966. An eight-man US Special Forces team is sent on a suicide mission inside North Vietnam. *

2113. ___. *Line of Succession.* New York: Delacorte, 1972. In the North African desert, a terrorist band and a worldweary "FSS" agent are locked in a brutal contest for the drugged half-dead body of the President-elect of the United States.

2114. ___ with Christopher Creighton. *The Paladin*. New York: Simon & Schuster, 1979. This colaboration based on fact recounts the real-life spy adventures of the agent codenamed "Christopher Robin," a 15-year-old boy who reported personally to Churchill, and who later, graduated to the role of agent and assassin.

2115. ___. *The Romanov Succession*. New York: Evans, 1974. A White Russian is released from duty with the US Army and with the tacit consent of the Allied governments, plots to overthrow Stalin, put a puppet prince in power, and wipe out the Communists. Based on the real-life adventures of the turn-coat Russian general, Vlasov, who fought for the Germans against his countrymen and who, having been captured by the Americans, was turned over to Stalin for execution shortly after V-E Day. *

2116. ___. *Target Manhattan*. By Drew Mallory, pseud. New York: Putnam's, 1975. Piloting his vintage B-17 bomber over New York City, a legendary aircraft designer, now on hard times, demands a $5 million ransom or he will start dropping 500-pounders. One more:

2117. ___. *Check Point Charlie*. New York: Mysterious, 1981.

2118. Garforth, John. *The Avengers: The Passing of Gloria Munday*. New York: Signet, 1967. With Steed locked behind steel doors, Mrs. Peel furthers her career as a lady spy by becoming a top pop singer idolized by millions. *P*
   During the mid-late 1960s, a highly popular British import TV series was "The Avengers," which featured derby-and-cane John Steed (impeccably portrayed by Patrick McNee), who favored old cars, and the glamorous and deadly Mrs. Peel (equally well played by Diana Rigg), addicted to sports cars and mod clothes. These two battled all sorts of nasties through intricately plotted (for TV) episodes to the delight of English and American audiences every week. These four titles are all print tie-ins to that series:

2119. ___. *The Avengers: The Floating Game*. New York: Signet, 1967. *P*

2120. ___. *The Avengers: Heil Harris*. New York: Signet, 1967. *P*

2121. ___. *The Avengers: The Laugh was on Lazarus*. New York: Signet, 1967. *P*

2122. Garn, Jake and Stephen Paul Cohen. *Night Launch*. New York: Morrow, 1989. The Utah Senator was the first member of Congress to go into space, and he uses this experience to detail a joint American-Soviet launch of a space shuttle, which an East german attempts to hijack for terrorists.

2123. Garner, William. *The Deep, Deep Freeze.* New York: Putnam's, 1968. Mike Jagger is forced out of retirement to help an East German defect and expose a double agent in the pay of British Intelligence.

2124. ___. *The Mobius Trap.* New York: Putnam's, 1978. When a scientist, who has refused to share his knowledge of his ultimate security system with the British Prime Minister, breaks down, an enigmatic man named Worthington takes it over and then vanishes.

2125. ___. *Overkill.* New York: Signet, 1966. Driven by a compulsive hunger for violence, the unemployed Mike Jagger answers a British newspaper ad and soon finds himself on the payroll of British Intelligence, working alone to undo a plot against the international peace. *P*

2126. ___. *The Us or Them War.* New York: Putnam's, 1969. When a naive scientist succeeds in crossing an X-ray with a laser beam, Jagger is called upon to protect Britain's interest. Four other agent Jagger stories are:

2127. ___. *The Big Enough Wreath.* New York: Putnam's, 1975.

2128. ___. *Ditto, Brother Rat.* London: Collins, 1972.

2129. ___. *The Manipulators.* Indianapolis: Bobbs-Merrill, 1970.

2130. ___. *Strip Jack Naked.* Indianapolis: Bobbs-Merrill, 1971.

2131. Garrett, George. *Entered from the Sun.* New York: Doubleday, 1990. Garrett's novel deals with the mysterious circumstances and characters surrounding the death of playwright Christopher Marlowe, who died in a drunken tavern brawl. Was he a spy, a member of the so-called School of Night? Was his death a well-plotted execution for his espionage activities? *HI*

2132. Garrett, Robert. *Spiral.* New York: Atheneum, 1972. A private eye investigates a right-wing revolutionary plot and runs into clandestine arms, subversion, and a terrorist group linked to old Nazis.

2133. Garrison, Jim. *The Star-Spangled Contract.* New York: McGraw-Hill, 1976. The former New Orleans DA who often held President Kennedy's assassination to be the result of a plot here tells us how ex-agent McFerrin must protect a US President from assassination by six rival government organizations.

2134. Garside, Jack. *The Barrabas Sweep*. By Jack Hild, house pseud. Toronto: Worldwide, 1990. Terrorists calling themselves the Realm are assassinating numbers of people with the intent of "freeing" Europe from the superpowers. Colonel Barrabas and his crack commando team are summoned to destroy this nefarious organization. *P*

2135. ___. *Desert Strike*. By Don Pendleton, house pseud. Greenwich, CN: Fawcett, 1989. *P* Garside told *Contemporary Authors* that he became a "world-class growth analyst in [his] late forties . . . and retired at the age of fifty-six to write full-time" (Vol. 127: 153). He writes adventure thrillers under three house pseudonyms: Nick Carter, Jack Hild, and Don Pendleton. Other Garside novels:

2136. ___. *Afghan Intercept*. By Nick Carter, house pseud. New York: Jove, 1988. *P*

2137. ___. *Alaska Deception*. By Jack Hild, house pseud. Greenwich, CN: Fawcett, 1987. *P*

2138. ___. *Canadian Sanction*. By Nick Carter, house pseud. New York: Jove, 1989. *P*

2139. ___. *East of Hell*. By Nick Carter, house pseud. New York: Jove, 1987. *P*

2140. ___. *Pacific Outcry*. By Nick Carter, house pseud. New York: Jove, 1989. *P*

2141. ___. *Pressure Point*. By Nick Carter, house pseud. New York: Jove, 1987. *P*

2142. ___. *Sakhalin Breakout*. By Jack Hild, house pseud. Greenwich, CN: Fawcett, 1987. *P*

2143. ___. *Singapore Sling*. By Nick Carter, house pseud. New York: Jove, 1989. *P*

2144. ___. *Sukhumi Destruction*. By Nick Carter, house pseud. New York: Jove, 1989. *P*

2145. Garth, David. *Bermuda Calling.* New York: Putnam's, 1944. American lawyer and OSS agent Zachery T. Rowland must interrupt his West Indian vacation in order to crack a Nazi spy plot on the British island of Bermuda. **y*

2146. ___. *The Road to Glenfairlie.* New York: Kinsey, 1940. A young US foreign service officer gets mixed up with Nazi spies and the lost heiress of a Scottish earldom. ***

2147. ___. *Tortured Angel.* New York: Putnam's, 1948. A former US Army officer is dispatched to France by the State Department to track down some missing documents vital to world peace. **y*

2148. ___. *The Watch on the Bridge.* New York: Putnam's, 1959. Agents prepare for a covert exchange of spy prisoners. ***

Garve, Andrew, pseud. *See* Winterton, Paul

2149. Garvin, Richard M. and Edmond G. Addeo. *The Fortec Conspiracy.* Los Angeles: Sherbourne, 1968. When the US Air Force buries Barney Russom's twin brother in a locked coffin and when they pay Bob's widow full insurance benefits, Barney decides to find out why. His search leads him to a small building at Wright Patterson AFB labeled simply Foreign Technology—FORTEC. Inside are . . .

2150. ___. *The Talbott Agreement.* Los Angeles: Sherbourne, 1967. With his appearance altered by plastic surgery to enable him to pass as a native, America's top agent in Red China discovers the significance of "TA," a bizarre Communist super weapon that combines nuclear force with mankind's power of ESP.

Gascar, Pierre, pseud. *See* Fournier, Pierre

2151. Gash, Jonathan. *Jade Woman.* New York: St. Martin's, 1989. Gash is the creator of the Lovejoy adventures about a slightly disreputable antique art appraiser with an expert eye for fakes. In this one, Lovejoy runs afoul of the Triad in Hong Kong.

2152. Gaskin, Catherine. *The File on Devlin.* Garden City, NY: Doubleday, 1965. A Nobel Prize winner is thought to have defected and a British agent carries the investigation to a grim Swiss chateau.

2153. Gates, Natalie. *Hush, Hush Johnson*. New York: Holt, 1969. In a spy spoof worthy of Gardner's Boysie Oakes, a plump British secretary is duped into smuggling some secret code-tapes. *H*

2154. Gavin, Catherine. *None Dare Call It Treason*. New York: St. Martin's, 1978. Jacques Brunel goes to France in the winter of 1941 to organize a network of guerrilla fighters determined to drive the German enemy from their native soil.

2155. Gazzaniga, Donald A. *A Few Good Men*. New York: Signet, 1988. Lt. Colonel William Baronne, USMC, takes on the enemy in the jungles of Vietnam. *P*

2156. Geddes, Paul. *Goliath*. New York: St. Martin's, 1986. A government official is sent to Majorca on a strange errand that soon entangles him as a pawn in what becomes a vast conspiracy.

2157. ___. *Hangman*. New York: St. Martin's, 1977. Scotland Yard enlists Paul Venniker to infiltrate an organization that combines political bombings and terrorism with drug trafficking.

2158. ___. *The Ottawa Allegation*. New York: Coward-McCann, 1973. Unsavory English agents attempt to prevent a Canadian from blowing the whistle on Whitehall's ministerial corruption.

2159. ___. *A Special Kind of Nightmare*. New York: St. Martin's, 1990. Detective Ludovic Fender is called out of retirement to investigate a prostitute's murder, one with ties to important members of the British Government.

2160. Geller, Stephen. *Gad*. New York: Harper & Row, 1980. Oliver Gad is recruited to put his psychic ability to work for British Intelligence.

George, Jonathan, pseud. *See* Burke, John F. and George Theiner

2161. George, Peter B. *The Big H*. By Bryan Peters, pseud. New York: Holt, 1963. English agent Anthony Brandon flies to America to help his Yankee colleagues frustrate a Soviet plot to smuggle huge amounts of heroin into Los Angeles.

2162. ___. *Hong Kong Kill*. By Bryan Peters, pseud. New York: Washburn, 1959. The SIS dispatches Brandon to Hong Kong to deal with an insidious plot co-sponsored by the Red Chinese and the KGB.

2163. Gerson, Jack. *Death Squad, London.* New York: St. Martin's, 1990. Ernst Lohmann is a former German police officer who has fled the Nazi regime like many others in 1936. In his second appearance, Lehman investigates a young emigre's death and exposes a conspiracy in the highest circles.

2164. ___. *The Back of the Tiger.* New York: Beaufort, 1984. Assassination fiction about J.F.K.

2165. ___. *Death's Head, Berlin.* New York: St. Martin's, 1989. Lohmann of the Berlin Criminal Police must infiltrate the Nazi Party at the dawn of the Third Reich in 1934 Germany to solve a series of murders.

2166. ___. *Deathwatch '39.* New York: St. Martin's, 1991. Lohmann, a Berlin police inspector, must protect a man on a hush-hush mission for Great Britain—the same man who is a prime suspect in a double murder Lohmann is investigating! One more:

2167. ___. *The Whitehall Sanction.* New York: Beaufort, 1984.

2168. Gerson, Noel B. *Neptune.* New York: Dodd-Mead, 1976. American agents seek to raise a sunken Russian submarine to get at its atomic device and secret codes.

2169. Gethin, David. *Wyatt and the Moresby Legacy.* New York: St. Martin's, 1984. A Soviet double agent known as Alpha is being hunted while the half-brother of a ruler of an Arab oil state attempts a coup.

Gibbs, Henry, pseud. *See* Rumbold-Gibbs, Henry St. John Clair

2170. Gibbs, Tony. *Landfall.* New York: Morrow, 1992. A terrorized caribbean island is the setting for this novel that mixes a demented US Army officer and a woman charter boat skipper—and terrorists. Two more:

2171. ___. *Dead Run.* New York: Random, 1988.

2172. ___. *Shadow Queen.* New York: Mysterious, 1992.

2173. Gibson, Frank E. *Cloak-and-Doctor.* New York: Exposition, 1974. A short look at the zany adventures of a CIA doctor in Washington and Europe. *H*

2174. Gifford, Thomas. *The Assassini*. New York: Bantam, 1990. The brother of a murdered sibling—a nun murdered at her prayers—from a prominent Catholic family is shocked when the Church fails to investigate; he soon uncovers evidence of a sordid history of papal assassins—still operating.

2175. ___. *The Glendower Legacy*. New York: Putnam's, 1978. A sentry frightened out of his wits at Valley Forge in 1778 witnesses three murders and high treason—George Washington signing an incriminating piece of paper—that the modern-day KGB would, and does, kill to get its hands on.

2176. ___. *Praetorian*. New York: Bantam, 1993. Operation Praetorian is a British plan to kill the Desert Fox in North Africa, but the ambush has been betrayed. Correspondent Rodger Godwin vows to discover the traitor.

2177. ___. *The Wind Chill Factor*. New York: Putnam's, 1975. A gigantic Nazi conspiracy is afoot with bases around the world. Can it be halted by the agent-grandson of a top Reich leader thought long dead?

2178. Gigga, Kenneth. *The Ampurias Exchange*. By Angus Ross, pseud. New York: Walker, 1977. MI-6 agent Mike Farrow works alone to assist in British government negotiations with Basque terrorists for exchange of political prisoners in Spain.

2179. ___. *The Greenham Plot*. By Angus Ross, pseud. Milan: Mondadori, 1984. *Spy Fiction: A Connoisseur's Guide* explains the unusual publication circumstance: "*The Greenham Plot* was based upon real events, but because of what happened there, the book was considered 'too sensitive' to be published in Britain—however, it was published abroad" (226).

2180. ___. *The Hamburg Switch*. By Angus Ross, pseud. New York: Walker, 1980. Agent Farrow aids an elderly scientist to escape East Berlin while other factions seek to kidnap the old man for a ransom.

2181. ___. *The Manchester Thing*. By Angus Ross, pseud. London: Long, 1970. Drawn into a murder investigation, newsman Marcus Aurelius "Mike" Farrow endures the murky world of espionage to solve the crime, whereupon he is recruited into the SIS. Other Farrow tales, none of which were published in the United States, include:

2182. ___. *The Aberdeen Conundrum*. By Angus Ross, pseud. London: Long, 1977.

2183. ___. *The Amsterdam Diversion.* By Angus Ross, pseud. London: Long, 1974.

2184. ___. *A Bad April.* By Angus Ross, pseud. London: Firecrest, 1988.

2185. ___. *The Bradford Business.* By Angus Ross, pseud. London: Long, 1974.

2186. ___. *The Burgos Contract.* By Angus Ross, pseud. New York: Walker, 1979.

2187. ___. *The Congleton Lark.* By Angus Ross, pseud. London: Long, 1979.

2188. ___. *The Darlington Jaunt.* By Angus Ross, pseud. London: Long, 1983.

2189. ___. *The Dunfermline Affair.* By Angus Ross, pseud. London: Long, 1973.

2190. ___. *The Edinburgh Exercise.* By Angus Ross, pseud. London: Long, 1975.

2191. ___. *The Huddersfield Job.* By Angus Ross, pseud. London: Long, 1971.

2192. ___. *The Leeds Fiasco.* By Angus Ross, pseud. London: Long, 1975.

2193. ___. *The Leipzig Manuscript.* By Angus Ross, pseud. London: Firecrest, 1989.

2194. ___. *The London Assignment.* By Angus Ross, pseud. London: Long, 1972.

2195. ___. *The Luxembourg Run.* By Angus Ross, pseud. London: Firecrest, 1985.

2196. ___. *The Menwith Tangle.* By Angus Ross, pseud. London: Hale, 1982.

2197. ___. *The Tyneside Ultimatum.* By Angus Ross, pseud. London: Firecrest, 1988.

Gilbert, Anthony, pseud. *See* Malleson, Lucy B.

2198. Gilbert, Harriett. *Given the Ammunition*. New York: Harper & Row, 1976. The unhappy daughter of a shady businessman becomes a willing convert to the cause of an Irish terrorist. Modelled on the Patty Hearst case.

2199. Gilbert, Michael. *After the Fine Weather*. New York: Harper & Row, 1963. A bishop is assassinated in a small Austrian province and an English eyewitness is sought by enemy agents.

2200. ___. *The Danger Within*. New York: Harper & Row, 1990. British POWs in an Italian camp during WW II are ready to break out, but they discover a traitor in their midst.

2201. ___. *Game without Rules*. New York: Harper & Row, 1967. Eleven short spy stories concerning Messers. Calder and Behrens, a pair of middle-aged agents working for the External Branch of Britain's Joint Services Standing Intelligence Committee, specializing in unorthodox methods. Something of a Bondian parody. *H*

2202. Gill, Bartholomew. *McGarr at the Dublin Horse Show*. New York: Scribner's, 1979. Chief Detective Peter McGarr of the Irish Police searches for clues to prevent a terrorist strike during the grand pageant of the Dublin Horse Show.

Gilman, Dorothy, pseud. *See* Butters, Dorothy Gilman

2203. Gilman, J. D. and John Clive. *KG-200*. New York: Simon & Schuster, 1972. Eluding Allied intelligence agents and employing captured American aircraft, the leader of a crack Luftwaffe unit attempts to mount a spectacular daylight raid on London. Modelled after the fact that every wartime air force maintained units of captured aircraft for use in teaching fighter pilots the best means of attack and defense. Even the Japanese flew a few B-17s!

2204. Gilroy, Dan. *Sight Unseen*. New York: Carroll & Graf, 1989. A submarine disaster off the coast of California in 1954 is linked to a reconnaissance satellite blunder that brings two specialists into an investigation.

2205. Gimpel, Erich. *Spy for Germany*. Trans. from the German. London: Hale, 1957. The fictionalized account of the activities of a World War II German Abwehr agent; reminiscent in form of the "edited" memoirs made a spy thriller form by William LeQueux (See Part 1).

2206. Giovannetti, Alberto. *Requiem for a Spy.* Trans. Frances F. Lanza. Garden City, NY: Doubleday, 1983. [*Requiem per Una Spia.* Rome: Bietti, 1978]. Monsignor Giovannetti, a native Roman, has been a member of the Vatican's diplomatic corps for many years. His novel involves a switching of identities and a crisis of conscience when a KGB colonel impersonates a kidnapped papal envoy to the UN.

2207. Gladilin, Anatoly. *Moscow Racetrack.* Trans. R. P. Schoenberg and Janet G. Tucker. Ann Arbor, MI: Ardis, 1990. Less an espionage tale than an incisive and sad portrait of contemporary Russia, Gladilin's hero is a lowly humanities instructor with a penchant for betting on the ponies and a writer of *samizdat* articles in the days before Gorbachev. When he hits big at the Moscow trotting track, the Politburo confiscates it and sends him to Paris to win money for the Soviet Union. *H*

2208. Glaskin, G. M. *The Man Who Didn't Count.* New York: Dial, 1967. Hunted in London by Russian agents who presume him to be a defected nuclear scientist, Morton Thomas escapes to Amsterdam only to be found once again.

2209. Goble, Neil. *Condition Green: Tokyo.* Rutland, VT: Tuttle, 1966. CIA agents must thwart a Japanese Communist coup attempt scheduled for May Day, 1970.

2210. Goddard, Harry. *The Silent Force.* New York: Popular, 1971. An incredible group of secret agents is turned loose on organized crime in the United States. *P*

2211. Goddard, Ken. *Prey.* New York: TOR, 1992. A secret office in Washington, DC is staffed by German, American, and Japanese hit men and dedicated to the violent dissolution of all environmental and conservation groups. *P*

2212. ___. *The Alchemist.* New York: Bantam, 1985.

2213. ___. *Balefire.* New York: Bantam, 1982.

Godey, John, pseud. *See* Freedgood, Morton

2214. Golan, Matti. *The Geneva Crisis.* New York: A & W, 1981. The chief of the Israeli Mossad refuses to release his PLO prisoners even though he knows that terrorists are holding a pleasure boatload of American tourists.

2215. Goldberg, Marshall. *Karamanov Equations.* Cleveland, OH: World, 1972. A Russian scientist, about to discover how to put his nation ahead in the missile race, is suddenly stricken and the best man for the surgery needed to help him is an American. The Russians send their patient to Paris where they hope to convince the Yanks he is an unimportant Frenchman, but the CIA is on top of the game and works out an arrangement to foil the Soviet goal.

2216. Goldman, James. *Waldorf.* New York: Random, 1966. In a forgotten village in Costa Rica, agents of five nations are busy attempting to snatch a fugitive Latin dictator. Waldorf Appleton, a painter and the only non-affiliated male in town is mistaken for the quarry and leads his pursuers on a merry chase. *H*

2217. Goldman, William. *Marathon Man.* New York: Delacorte, 1974. A young man who wants nothing more than to be a top runner and good student gets mixed up with the New York plans of Nazi war criminal Szell, who has recently flown in from exile in Paraguay.

2218. Goodfield, June. *Courier to Peking.* New York: Dutton, 1973. The President of the National Academy of Sciences visits Red China in the summer of 1971; on the side, he bears an important message from the President of the United States.

2219. Goodman, George J. W. and Winthrop Knowlton. *A Killing in the Market.* Garden City, NY: Doubleday, 1958. A Wall Street broker, ensnared unwittingly into buying shares in a missile corporation for an unknown European client, is held to the deal by the kidnapping of his daughter.

Gordon, Alexander, pseud. *See* Cotler, Gordon

Gordon, Donald, pseud. *See* Payne, Donald G.

2220. Gordon, Mildred and Gordon. *Power Play.* Garden City, NY: Doubleday, 1965. A daring plot erupts to seize control of the FBI.

2221. ___. *Tiger on my Back.* Garden City, NY: Doubleday, 1960. An American female CIA agent is drawn into a counter-spy deal in North Africa.

2222. Gottfried, Theodore M. *The Man from ORGY.* By Ted Mark, pseud. New York: Lancer, 1965. A US agent mixes sex and espionage on a dangerous Middle East assignment. *P*

2223. ___. *The Man from ORGY: The Nine-Month Caper.* By Ted Mark, pseud. New York: Lancer, 1965. A dangerous mission takes our hero into the bedrooms and spy dens of Latin America. *P*

2224. ___. *The Man from ORGY: The Real-Gone Girls.* By Ted Mark, pseud. New York: Lancer, 1966. The amorous agent seeks three prostitutes who have disappeared after inheriting a large fortune. *P*

2225. ___. *Where's Your ORGY?* By Ted Mark, pseud. New York: Berkley, 1969. *PH* Another of the many short-lived, spy-spoof series inspired by the commercial success of the UNCLE books include:

2226. ___. *The Girl from PUSSYCAT.* By Ted Mark, pseud. New York: Lancer, 1965. *P*

2227. ___. *Pussycat Transplant.* By Ted Mark, pseud. New York: Berkley, 1968. *PH* Gottfried, under the same alias, wrote humorous spy spoofs about an agent named Relevant after the fashion of the UNCLE books. One of these:

2228. ___. *The Man from CHARISMA.* By Ted Mark, pseud. New York: Dell, 1970. *PH*

2229. Gough, Laurence. *Sandstorm.* New York: Viking, 1992. Espionage and drugs combine in this tale of mercenaries working for the CIA in Egypt and Columbia.

2230. Gould, Heywood. *Glitterburn.* New York: St. Martin's, 1981. A greedy, cynical reporter has a story that no one will print: a militant group is killing and blackmailing the super-rich, who exert their influence to spike the story at every turn. *H*

2231. Gowing, Nik. *The Wire.* New York: St. Martin's, 1989. Gowing was an Eastern European correspondent during the Solidarity movement's most intense struggles. He based his story on first-hand experiences in Warsaw and insider knowledge gleaned from top-level sources, including one inside the Polish Secret Police. *The Wire* concerns an attempt to topple ailing Premier Brezhnev on the part of KGB head Yuri Andropov, who plans to discredit Brezhnev by having General Jaruzelski assassinated and the blame fixed on the CIA. Bogdan is the dedicated Solidarity activist, and Sulecki is the KGB's sleeper inside Solidarity reporting back to his masters.

2232. Grace, Alexander M. *Coup!* Novato, CA: Presidio, 1992. Ex-Foreign Service officer Grace takes a harsh look at corruption in Bolivia in this tale of drug cartels and an engineered coup to restore democracy to a corrupt country.

2233. Grady, James. *River of Darkness*. New York: Warner, 1991. Jud Stuart was already a legend with Special Forces before he became one of the CIA's top black operations men, but now, after years of loyal service against his country's enemies, someone has decided that he must be terminated.

2234. ___. *Shadow of the Condor*. New York: Putnam's, 1975. Acting as a decoy while his superiors check on the death of a US Air Force intelligence man whose body turns up at a Montana missile base far from his European assignment, CIA agent Ronald Malcolm uncovers an extraordinary double-cross operation directed at both the Americans and the Russians.

2235. ___. *Six Days of the Condor*. New York: Norton, 1974. Ronald Malcolm, the only survivor of a wiped-out branch of the CIA, tries to stay ahead of agents from the police, FBI, NSC, and "the Agency" itself as he seeks the double agent who sold out and murdered his comrades.

2236. Grady, Ronan C., Jr. *Pay on the Way Out*. By John Murphy, pseud. New York: Scribner's, 1975. A CIA trainee is assigned to work with Kit Moore, chief of Plans Blue Team Five, in the investigation of three apparently unconnected murders—one in Spain, one in London, and one in Washington, DC.

Graeme, Bruce, pseud. *See* Jeffries, Graham M.

Graham, James, pseud. *See* Patterson, Harry

2237. Graham, Mark. *The Harbinger*. New York: Holt, 1989. Chief Inspector Nigel Mansell of the Port Elizabeth police begins an investigation into the murder of a union official and soon becomes convinced there is more to it: a conspiracy of vast proportions is shaping up and prominent men are implicated. This novel evokes the South African landscape, apartheid, characters, and forensics in a manner similar to *Gorky Park*. As in Renko's case with his own superiors, the South African Security Branch tries to thwart Mansell at every turn. A recent one:

2238. ___. *The Fire Theft*. New York: Penguin, 1993.

2239. Graham, Winston. *Night Journey.* Garden City, NY: Doubleday, 1968. When the formula for a new kind of poison gas falls into the hands of a Nazi agent, British Intelligence determines to stop his dash back to Berlin—even if it means sacrificing a beautiful American agent and a brilliant British scientist to do it. *y

2240. Granbeck, Marilyn and Allen Moore. *The Peacemaker: The Wyss Pursuit.* By Adam Hamilton, pseud. New York: Berkley, 1975. Barrington Hawes-Bradford, chairman of the board of the multinational HG corporation, masquerades as a free-lance secret agent, "the Peacemaker." In this outing, he travels to the Indochinese country of Balabar to save a young king threatened by a coup at the hands of opium-dealing supporters of his late father. *See also*, Carter, Nick. *P*

2241. ___. *The Peacemaker: The Yashar Pursuit.* By Adam Hamilton, pseud. New York: Berkley, 1974. "The Peacemaker" travels to the Far East to find some nasties who have stolen a lot of dangerous nerve gas. *See also*, Carter, Nick. *P*

2242. ___. *The Peacemaker: The Xander Pursuit.* By Adam Hamilton, pseud. New York: Berkley, 1974. *See also*, Carter, Nick. *P*

2243. ___. *The Peacemaker: The Zaharan Pursuit.* By Adam Hamilton, pseud. New York: Berkley, 1974. *See also*, Carter, Nick. *P*

2244. Granger, Bill. *The British Cross.* New York: Crown, 1983. Devereaux is in Helsinki awaiting contact from a Russian would-be defector who has information to convince the Americans to take him in.

2245. ___. *Burning the Apostle.* New York: Warner, 1993. Devereaux has to stop a man intent on burning down a nuclear power plant in the Midwest.

2246. ___. *Henry McGee Is Not Dead.* New York: Warner, 1989. The November Man practices his dangerous craft in the frozen wilds of Alaska.

2247. ___. *The Infant of Prague.* New York: Warner, 1987. The November Man's assisting another seemingly routine defection—this time a Czechoslovakian cultural liaison; simultaneously, however, a miraculously weeping statue in Chicago triggers the defection of a famous Czechoslovakian child actress traveling in America who announces she will remain in America for freedom and Christ. Devereaux' job is to sniff out the connection and expose the conspiracy in the making.

2248. ___. *The Last Good German.* New York: Warner, 1991. Tired and broken by years of violent service, Devereaux wants to be left alone, but of course his superiors nix that. There's a piece of old, unfinished business in the character of a former Stasi member that Devereaux was supposed to exfiltrate from East Germany in 1976.

2249. ___. *League of Terror.* New York: Warner, 1990. Another in the November Man series; this time, the "pewter-eyed" killer Devereaux crosses swords with another assassin who has had the temerity to shoot the hero's girl friend to make him suffer.

2250. ___. *The Man Who Heard Too Much.* New York: Warner, 1989. In this tenth November Man novel, Devereaux is in Sweden where a low-level defection by a Russian sailor he's assisting coincides with missing tapes of a high-level Soviet-American conference in Malmö—at stake is a sophisticated computer virus.

2251. ___. *The November Man.* New York: Fawcett, 1979. Granger began his November Man series with this tale of Devereaux against the IRA—a book that became a sensation because of the assassination of Lord Louis Montbatten.

2252. ___. *The Shattered Eye.* New York: Crown, 1982. The Frunze War College computer in Moscow is playing another variation of a mock invasion of Western Europe when bad things begin happening: a blown covert operation, three murdered US agents in Europe, the CIA's own computer system "won't compute," and French President François Mitterand is marked for assassination; it's time to call in that R Section rogue agent and enforcer Devereaux.

2253. ___. *There Are No Spies.* New York: Warner, 1986. The November man has gone to ground in Switzerland when a message from Hanley, his R Section control, activates him just in time: "Nutcracker," a ploy that makes him a dangerously exposed pawn in a bid to lure a Soviet spy, is just about to go into effect. Other Devereaux adventures in the spy trade:

2254. ___. *Drover.* New York: Morrow, 1991.

2255. ___. *The El Murders.* New York: Holt, 1987.

2256. ___. *Hemingway's Notebook.* New York: Warner, 1986.

2257. ___. *Queen's Crossing.* New York: Fawcett, 1982.

2258. ___. *Schism*. New York: Crown, 1981.

2259. ___. *The Zurich Numbers*. New York: Crown, 1984.

Grant, David, pseud. *See* Thomas, Craig

2260. Grant, Edward. *The Ultimate Weapon: From the Log of the U.S.S. Devilfish*. New York: Pinnacle, 1976. Despite all risks, Russian agents attempt to capture or destroy the latest American nuclear submarine. *P*

2261. Grant, James. *Island of Gold*. New York: Walker, 1978. Down on his luck, Stanway is forced to search for a treasure which consists of millions of pounds of gold bullion from Nazi vaults.

2262. Grant, Pete, pseud. *Night Flying Avenger*. South Windsor, CT: Newmark, 1990. WW II technothriller by an ex-Navy combat pilot who flew an *Avenger* torpedo bomber.

2263. Graves, Richard L. *The Black Gold of Malaverde*. New York: Stein & Day, 1973. A bereaved father hires Wolfram, a demolitions expert, and his international gang to rub out a South American country where his son was brutally murdered.

2264. ___. *C.L.A.W.* Briarcliff Manor, NY: Stein & Day, 1976. CIA and KGB agents combine forces to halt a terrorist group which is planning to use a secret weapon against the candidates in a US presidential election.

2265. ___. *Cobalt 60*. Briarcliff Manor, NY: Stein & Day, 1975. Before an Arab terrorist group can spread death in Washington, DC, a multinational underground security agency moves to destroy its impregnable Red Sea island base.

2266. ___. *The Platinum Bullet*. Briarcliff Manor, NY: Stein & Day, 1974. American forces plan to frustrate plans by schemer DePrundis to corner the international platinum market for Russia.

2267. ___. *Quick Silver*. Briarcliff Manor, NY: Stein & Day, 1976. The CIA sends explosives expert Hugo Wolfram into the Guatemalan jungles to dispose of the Cuban-run Cinabre Corporation, which is taking in large amounts of mercury for a renegade Soviet scientist.

2268. Gray, Rod. *The Lady from LUST: Five Beds to Mecca.* New York: Belmont-Tower, 1974. Her name is Eve Drum, the Lady from LUST [League of Underground Spies and Terrorists], whose codename is Oh Oh Sex and whose not-so-secret weapon is her luscious body. In this outing, she must stop a Holy War in the Middle East. *P*

2269. ___. *The Lady from LUST: Kiss My Assassin.* New York: Belmont-Tower, 1973. Eve Drum is sent to a gorgeous villa on Italy's Amalfi coast to put a neo-Nazi group out of business. *P*

2270. ___. *The Lady from LUST: Lay Me Odds.* New York: Belmont-Tower, 1973. Eve proves that a tumble with her can be a gamble with death for a deadly, if zany, enemy operative. *P*

2271. ___. *The Lady from LUST: Lust Be a Lady Tonight.* New York: Belmont-Tower, 1972. A super-villain wants to wreck NATO and heat up the Cold War to the flash point; Agent Drum is asked to apply her own brand of heat. *P*

2272. ___. *The Lady from LUST: Skin Game Dame.* New York: Belmont-Tower, 1972. Eve Drum is in Denmark where she finds the porno-film business a convenient cover for some dirty intrigue. *P*

2273. ___. *The Lady from LUST: The 69 Pleasures.* New York: Belmont-Tower, 1974. They needed an undercover agent in Hong Kong—and nobody's better in that situation than secret agent Eve Drum. *P* More Eve Drum adventures:

2274. ___. *The Big Snatch.* New York: Belmont-Tower, 1969. [*Sock It to Me.* New York: Tower, 1974]. *P*

2275. ___. *Kill Her with Love.* New York: Tower, 1975. *P*

2276. ___. *The Poisoned Pussy.* New York: Belmont-Tower, 1969. *P*

2277. Greatorex, Wilfred. *Button Zone.* New York: Macmillan, 1984. Calvin Rudge works for British Intelligence, but his latest job—arranging the defection of a KGB officer and his stepdaughter—points him toward a high-ranking traitor close to the US President and a plot that puts a finger on the trigger of the US-USSR nuclear arsenals when that President is assassinated.

2278. ___. *Three Potato, Four.* New York: Coward-McCann, 1977. [*Crossover.* London: Weidenfeld & Nicholson, 1976]. A defecting KGB agent with a fortune in diamonds is hunted in England by his Russian colleagues, MI-5, and ruthless members from an international diamond cartel. Other Greatorex novels are:

2279. ___. *The Power Game.* London: Pan, 1976.

2280. ___. *The Freelancers.* London: Weidenfeld & Nicholson, 1975.

2281. ___. *Quicksand.* London: Weidenfeld & Nicholson, 1979.

2282. Green, Frederick L. *Ambush for a Hunter.* New York: Random, 1953. What happens when a lovely but false Czech refugee arrives in England to effect the undoing of a noted chemist, is given shelter by Charles, a middle-class businessman on the way up, and is discovered by Edna, the Englishman's wife?

2283. Green, Stagg. *Commando Escape.* London: Heinemann, 1943. Following an unsuccessful British commando raid, a combined forces soldier eludes capture by the Nazis.

2284. ___. *Fortress of the Marquis.* London: Heinemann, 1943. An English agent assists a well-emplaced French resistance group against a determined assault by Wehrmacht soldiers.

2285. Green, William M. *The Man Who Called Himself Devlin.* Indianapolis: Bobbs-Merrill, 1978. A soldier-of-fortune is hired by Petrolux Oil to infiltrate and destroy a terrorist group holding the company's Iranian oil-storage depot.

2286. ___. *The Romanov Connection.* New York: Beaufort, 1984. Englishman Charles Aldonby is invalided out of action on the home front, but when a dying messenger at the War office reveals the growing menace to the Romanovs, to whom he is distantly related, he vows to free them from the remote Siberian town where they are being held while the Red Guard consolidates its power in 1918 Russia.

2287. ___. *See How They Run.* Indianapolis: Bobbs-Merrill, 1976. Why were top secret government papers on leading US personalities hurriedly mailed to a remote Massachusetts hotel—which burned down years ago? Another:

2288. ___. *The Salisbury Manuscript.* Indianapolis: Bobbs-Merrill, 1974.

2289. Greene, Graham. *The Comedians*. New York: Viking, 1966. A number of foreigners or "comedians" stroll across the story line as native Haitians endure or rebel against "Papa Doc" and his dreaded secret police, the Tontons Macoute.

Greene was an important factor in the modern development of the spy thriller, having begun his work in the years just before the outbreak of the Second World War (see Part 1). During World War II, Greene served in the British SIS in West Africa, watching the activities of the Vichy French. Interestingly enough, his section of the intelligence service was at that time controlled by the arch-traitor Harold "Kim" Philby, a fact not known until many years later. In his memoirs, *My Secret War* (New York: Grove, 1968), Philby confessed that he could not remember anything about Greene's West African service. "I do remember, however, a meeting held to discuss a proposal of his to use a roving brothel to frustrate the French and two lonely Germans suspected of spying on British shipping in Portuguese Guinea," an idea which the spymaster remembered as having been "discussed quite seriously," but which had to be abandoned as it "seemed unlikely to be productive of hard intelligence."

Greene's wartime experiences, like those of Fleming and other writers, provided a great amount of grist for his later writings. After the war, Greene turned to serious authorship, and some film work. In 1948 while examining Vienna for a film, he became involved in the secret war between the SIS and the Soviets, being actively shadowed by the latter. The espionage theme, together with an understanding of human failings and a liberal dose of cynicism, flowed throughout his later product.

As always Green's penmanship continued to lean strongly toward intrigue, usually with just enough violence to make the story stand up. Despite and maybe because of an early influence by John Buchan later tempered by actual "field work," Greene's espionage tales border between the ironic for irony's sake and realism spiced with romanticism.

Greene died at La Providence Hospital in Vevey near Lake Geneva on 3 April 1991; the publications of his final novels included espionage fiction, nonfiction, a continuance of his autobiography, and, of course, what he once called "entertainments" (Greene told writer Anthony Burgess in a 1982 interview in *Saturday Review* (May 1982: 44-47): "The big Catholic verities like good and evil—you won't find these in my later work" (47).

2290. ___. *The Captain and the Enemy*. New York: Penguin, 1988. A boy named Baxter is spirited off to the Panamanian jungles by a mysterious figure known as the Captain. *P*

2291. ___. *The Honorary Consul.* New York: Simon & Schuster 1973. A priest joins the radical underground and a minor British functionary near Argentina's border with Paraguay is kidnapped. Greene's conversion to Catholicism and subsequent wrestling with that faith show forth in this work of intrigue.

2292. ___. *The Human Factor.* New York: Simon & Schuster 1978. Senior SIS officers move to plug a leak by eliminating a junior colleague, unheedful for the warnings of a veteran intelligence analyst.

2293. ___. *The Last Word.* London: Reinhardt, 1990. Short story collection contains the espionage tale "A Branch of the Service," published for the first time.

2294. ___. *Ministry of Fear.* New York: Viking, 1943. Probably the author's least remembered work, one showing the Buchan influence most clearly. A group of Fifth Column Englishmen attempt to corner and murder a neurotic fellow countryman who possesses a piece of military intelligence they want to pass on to Berlin. *

2295. ___. *Our Man in Havana.* New York: Viking, 1958. A satirical novel considered by many to be Greene's best spy thriller. An Englishman accepts a secret agent post in Cuba with no real intention of actually doing "the job." When the silly reports on guerrilla successes he has been making up and sending off to London start turning out to be true, he is precipitated into a rather nasty intrigue. *y

2296. ___. *The Quiet American.* New York: Viking, 1955. Anti-hero Alden Pyle, sublimely innocent of intrigue and espionage except for what he was able to read in books, accompanies a British journalist to French Indo-China during that earlier war with the Viet Minh in order to perform a secret job for the State Department. The character Pyle, according to some, was based on CIA covert-action specialist Edward Lansdale and the plot begs comparison with William J. Lederer's *The Ugly American.* In fact, the book reflects a former intelligence operator's unachieved hope that common sense could prevail in an area where history would yet bring much tragedy. *y

2297. ___, ed. *The Spy's Bedside Book.* Sevenoaks: NEL, 1962. An anthology of short stories reflecting the editor's preference.

2298. ___. *The Tenth Man.* New York: Simon & Schuster, 1985. This forgotten 1944 screenplay by Greene lay in the MGM archives until its discovery. It concerns a man who, along with nine others in a Gestapo prison in Occupied France, draws lots to see which three will be executed; after choosing one of the death ballots, he buys his life by offering all his possessions to a poor man among the others.

2299. ___. *The Third Man*. New York: Viking, 1950. A relentless manhunt through postwar Vienna after one Harry Lime, supposed witness to a brutal murder, forms the background for this author's most famous yarn, which is, in fact, not quite a spy thriller. As much a mystery tale or more than an espionage caper, this work, noteworthy for its portrayal of spy-filled Vienna, was made into an Orson Wells award-winning motion picture. *

2300. ___. *Travels with My Aunt*. New York: Viking, 1969. A retired London bank manager volunteers to accompany his aunt on a trip to Istanbul where he starts a new life in crime and encounters an ill-assorted group of travellers on the Orient Express, including an American girl hippie whose father is a CIA agent.

2301. Greene, Harris. *Inference of Guilt*. London: Hale, 1982. This highly praised spy novel tracks the intra-agency maneuverings within the CIA; it concerns several old hands at the CIA who are facing the moral and legal implications resulting from their exfiltration of a vicious Romanian Iron Guard head many years before. The man is now a successful, wealthy California businessman.

2302. ___. *The Thieves of Tumbutu*. Garden City, NY: Doubleday, 1968. A small African sheikdom is suddenly brought into the twentieth century with spies and intrigue everywhere. More Greenes:

2303. ___. *Cancelled Accounts*. Garden City, NY: Doubleday, 1972.

2304. ___. *FSO-1*. Garden City, NY: Doubleday, 1977.

2305. ___. *The Flags at Doney*. Garden City, NY: Doubleday, 1964.

2306. ___. *The Mozart Leaves at Nine*. Garden City, NY; Doubleday, 1961.

2307. Greenfield, Irving. *Barracuda*. New York: Dutton, 1979. A missing American nuclear missile submarine, operated by a crew unaware of its officers' terrible mission, is sought by both the United States and the Soviet Union.

2308. ___. *High Terror.* New York: Popular, 1978. A CIA agent posing as an art student looks into a mysterious power controlling the French police. P

2309. ___. *Tagget.* New York: Arbor, 1979. Searching Europe for World War II Maquis information, a historian encounters a spy net run by the same agent who betrayed him thirty years ago.

2310. Greenland, Francis. *The Misericordia Drop.* London: Davis-Poynter, 1976. British army veteran (1942-49) and Civil Servant until his retirement in 1971, Greenland's first spy novel mixes a Director of an old-boy network, a young economist, and a hard field agent into this tale of a stolen government document discovered in an old manor house in Portugal.

2311. Greenlee, Sam. *The Spook Who Sat by the Door.* New York: Dutton, 1969. Dan Freeman, the first black CIA man, attempts to organize a Chicago ghetto gang into a guerrilla band.

2312. Grey, Anthony. *The Chinese Assassin.* New York: Holt, 1979. According to a Chinese defector, Lin Piao did not die in a 1971 plan crash, but was murdered by the same radical faction now trying to take out Mao Tse-tung himself. Some more:

2313. ___. *The Bulgarian Exclusive.* New York: Dial, 1977.

2314. ___. *Hostage in Peking.* Garden City, NY: Doubleday, 1971.

2315. ___. *Peking.* London: Weidenfeld & Nicholson, 1988.

2316. ___. *The Prime Minister Was a Spy.* London: Weidenfeld & Nicholson, 1983.

2317. ___. *Saigon.* Boston: Little, 1982.

2318. Griffin, John. *The Camelot Conundrum.* London: Hale, 1979. Richard Raven is a freelancer agent in this violent series of counterespionage capers. Others:

2319. ___. *A Flame from Persepolis.* London: Hale, 1981.

2320. ___. *The Florentine Madonna.* London: Hale, 1979.

2321. ___. *The Midas Operation.* London: Hale, 1976.

2322. ___. *St. Catherine's Wheel*. London: Hale, 1978.

2323. ___. *Seeds of Destruction*. London: Hale, 1977.

Griffin, W. E. B., pseud. *See* Butterworth, W. E. [William Edmund III]

2324. Griffiths, John. *The Good Spy*. New York: Carroll & Graf, 1991. Oxford-educated Griffiths served in the diplomatic service and turned his experiences into espionage fiction. Here, he tells a deft story of a reluctant spy in Klaus Becker, who has come to the US after the Soviet invasion of Czechoslovakia in 1968 and worked hard to become a successful computer software entrepreneur. But his real name is Nicolai Beranski, he's a KGB sleeper who's been awakened by his masters, and he wants out of the spying game. *H*

2325. ___. *A Loyal and Dedicated Servant*. New York: Playboy, 1981. While investigating the suspicious death of a CIA analyst, former counterespionage ace Morgan Sullivan discovers evidence pointing to a mole in "the company." Three more:

2326. ___. *The Last Spy*. New York: Carroll & Graf, 1992.

2327. ___. *The Memory Man*. New York: Playboy, 1981.

2328. ___. *Snake Charmer*. New York: Jove, 1989.

Griswold, George, pseud. *See* Dean, Robert G.

2329. Groom, A. J. Pelham. *Mohune's Nine Lives*. New York: Liveright, 1944. Published in Britain as *Where are Your Angels Now?* A downed RAF pilot escapes the Gestapo and contrives to reach England with news of an upcoming invasion attempt. *

2330. Gross, Martin L. *The Red Swastika*. New York: Berkley, 1992. A Fourth Reich has sprung up in Germany and is backed by the Neo-Nazi organization called Red Swastika, which, if it succeeds, will impose its will on the new world order by providing neutron bombs to America's greatest enemy in North Africa.

2331. ___. *The Red President*. Garden City, NY: Doubleday, 1987. It's finally happened: a sleeper agent climbs the ladder of political success right to the Oval Office. Compares well with similar "what-ifs," such as *Seven Days in May* and *The Spike*. One other tale by this author is:

2332. ___. *The Red Defector*. New York: Berkley, 1991.

2333. Gross, Sheldon. *Havana X*. New York: Arbor, 1978. A wealthy American, whose past life as a hitman is known only to a few, is visited by a Mafia don and a CIA agent shortly before he is infiltrated into Cuba.

2334. Gruber, Frank. *Little Hercules*. New York: Dutton, 1966. In Africa and Yugoslavia, Harvey Fraser searches for a top secret nuclear grenade which may have fallen into Russian hands.

2335. Guenter, C. H., pseud. *Death in Aqaba*. Trans. from the German. New York: Manor, 1976. West German agent Robert Urban goes to Israel to help a fellow national only to discover the man is dead at the hands of certain PLO terrorists, who have stolen $10 million worth of rubies which will enable the Russians to expand their laser warfare program. *P*

2336. ___. *Max Galan: Hunter of Men*. Trans. from the German. New York: Pinnacle, 1975. [*Schlaf Mein Tuefel, Schlaf Ein*. n.p.: Erish Pabel, 1972.] The hero is Robert Urban, a West German BND agent. *P* Six other Urban tales were published in the US in paperback. One of these:

2337. ___. *A Swinger Named Zefano*. Trans. from the German. New York: Manor, 1979. *P*

2338. Guerard, Albert. *Gabrielle*. New York: Fine, 1992. An American diplomat in Paris looking for a night on the town winds up in the thrall of his chambermaid. *H*

2339. Guild, Nicholas. *Chain Reaction*. New York: Berkley, 1986. A battle-weary Prussian aristocrat (with a doctorate in nuclear physics) allows himself to be sent to New Mexico to get the atom bomb secret from a scientist mole planted by the SS years before. FBI agent George Havens must follow a trail of corpses to Los Alamos.

2340. ___. *The Favor*. New York: St. Martin's, 1981. An East German agent asks an assassin to save his daughter after she is kidnapped in a counterespionage operation in Amsterdam.

2341. ___. *The Linz Tattoo*. New York: McGraw-Hill, 1986. Inar Christiansen, a Norwegian cellist, is tracking and killing all members of a certain SS unit in search of its leader, Colonel Hagemann, who was responsible for the deaths of his parents and most of the townspeople in Kirstenstad, Norway.

2342. ___. *The Summer Soldier*. New York: Simon & Schuster, 1978. A retired CIA agent returns home to find his wife dead and himself the target of a KGB officer, now defected, whose own wife had been accidentally killed by the agent. A few more:

2343. ___. *The Assyrian*. New York: Atheneum, 1987.

2344. ___. *The Berlin Warning*. New York: Putnam's, 1984.

2345. ___. *The Blood Star*. New York: Atheneum, 1989.

2346. Guillou, Jan. *Enemy's Enemy*. Trans. Thomas Keeland. New York: Knopf, 1992. Swedish author Guillou's character is known to his enemies as Coq Rouge (to his enemies) and to his colleagues in Swedish counterintelligence he is Navy Commander Carl Hamilton—aristocrat, computer expert, and licensed to kill.

2347. Gulyashki, Andrei. *The Zakhov Mission*. Trans. from the Bulgarian. Garden City, NY: Doubleday, 1968. Ace Soviet operative Avakum Zakhov is assigned by the KGB the task of finding a top secret plan which has been stolen from the official Geological Survey. The map, which shows the location of strategic minerals in an area not far from the border of a hostile country, was snitched by no less than the infamous capitalist agent James Bond, whom Zakhov attempts to liquidate in between courses of cabbage and noodles!

    Beginning in the realm of memoirs, the KGB in the middle 1960s attempted to improve its image at home and abroad with a campaign to highlight the efforts of Russian spies like Rudolf Abel and Richard Sorge. Noting the tremendous popularity of Fleming's character, which it labelled "this supreme example of imperialistic espionage," the Soviet intelligence service approached portly Bulgarian author Gulyashki asking for a similar character who would fit in with Chairman Vladimir Semichastny's effort to portray the KGB as protector and not villain in Russian life.

    Gulyashki, in writing his tale, attempted to obtain copyright permission to use Bond's name or "007," but was unable to do so. Thus when his serialized yarn appeared in *Komsomolskaya Pravda* in September 1966, it ran with one zero less, "Avakum Zakhov versus 07." The series and other Russian efforts such as memoirs and movies were immensely successful throughout the Eastern Bloc and did much to blunt the propaganda success the Soviets actually believed the British had scored with the creation of Bond and similar characters (Donald McCormick, *Who's Who in Spy Fiction* [New York: Taplinger, 1977], 93-94 and David Wise and Thomas B. Ross, *The Espionage Establishment* [New York: Random, 1967] 280-281).

2348. ___. *Sedemte Dni Na Nashiia Zhivot.* Sofiia: Bulgarski, 1966.

2349. ___. *Vedrovo.* Sofiia: Bulgarski, 1959.

2350. ___. *Zlatnata Zhena.* Sofiia: Bulgarski, 1980.

2351. Gunther, John. *Troubled Midnight.* New York: Harper, 1945. While working in Constantinople for the Lend-Lease office, American Leslie Vattracts becomes romantically involved with both a German and a British agent, who end up pitted against one another in the final act of their intelligence war. *

2352. Gurewich, David. *Travels with Dubinsky and Clive.* New York: Viking, 1987. Oleg Dubinsky works at the Afro-Asian Proletarian Movement Institute—until the CIA overthrows the People's Republic of Pizdo, that is. Now he and his sidekick Slava, a blackmarketeer, are destined for the USA. *H*

2353. Gurr, David. *Troika.* London: Methuen, 1979. Close friends, SIS agent Peter Dravin and KGB spook Alexey Yanov receive orders from their respective governments to encourage one another to defect.

2354. ___. *A Woman Called Scylla.* New York: Viking, 1981. American journalist Jane Montigny seeks to learn the true fate of her mother, who was a widely travelled secret agent during World War II.

2355. Gutteridge, Lindsay. *Cold War in a Country Garden.* New York: Putnam's, 1972. A British scientific experiment shrinks a group of secret agents down to 1/4" in size and then Intelligence employs the little operatives in the espionage game in a big way.

2356. ___. *Killer Pine.* New York: Putnam's, 1973. One of the little agents shrunk in the previous citation uncovers a bizarre plot engineered by a Russian mastermind in the wilderness of the Rocky Mountains.

H

Habe, Hans, pseud. *See* Bekessy, Jean

2357. Hackforth-Jones, Gilbert. *Fish Out of Water.* London: Hodder & Stoughton, 1954. A British naval officer gets mixed up in a ruthless shore-based duel with a determined but unknown German saboteur in wartime England. * Two more novel is:

2358. ___. *Chinese Poison.* London: Hodder & Stoughton, 1969.

2359. ___. *All Stations to Malta.* London: Hodder & Stoughton, 1971.

2360. Haddad, C. A. *The Academic Factor.* New York: Harper & Row, 1980. Enroute by plane overseas to deliver a paper, a sociology professor meets an attractive man and, once in West Germany, becomes involved in a complicated murder case which forces her to match wits with spies and double agents.

2361. ___. *Bloody September.* New York: Harper & Row, 1976. A clumsy American wife, convinced her husband is up to no good, but not exactly sure what his profession is, makes life difficult for Mossad agent David Haham.

2362. ___. *The Moroccan.* New York: Harper & Row, 1975. A Moroccan-born Jew, Judah Biton, volunteers to lead an Israeli Intelligence penetration of an Arab terrorist band.

2363. Hagberg, David. *Broken Idols.* By Sean Flannery, pseud. New York: Charter, 1984. CIA agent Wallace Mahoney and his son John, ex-field agent and now a writer, team up to solve the mysterious disappearance of the missing Chair of NATO's Nuclear Defense Affairs Committee. Missing, too, is Genesis—a top-secret plan detailing NATO's new war scenarios. *P*

2364. ___. *Countdown.* By Sean Flannery, pseud. St. Martin's, 1990. The Soviets and the Americans square off in the form of a merciless KGB assassin and a top American agent.

2365. ___. *Counterstrike.* By Sean Flannery, pseud. New York: Morrow, 1990. Psychotic killer Donald Morgan is told to back off when the hit on Soviet Premier Mikhail Gorbachev is canceled by the contractors—high-level Russian officials, but it's too late: Morgan enjoys his work too much.

2366. ___. *Critical Mass*. New York: TOR, 1992. A man who lost his parents in the Nagasaki A-bombing and was horribly burned vows revenge on America, and half a century later has the wherewithal to effect it with nuclear devices planted in Los Angeles and San Francisco as the targets.

2367. ___. *Crossed Swords*. By Sean Flannery, pseud. New York: Jove, 1989. The world's fate hangs in the balance as two agents, one CIA and one KGB, confront each other as lifelong enemies for the final time. *P*

2368. ___. *Crossfire*. New York: TOR, 1991. Russian liberals versus hardliners and a KGB plot to shift the balance by hijacking a US gold shipment. *P*

2369. ___. *Desert Fire*. New York: TOR, 1993. Terrorists working for Saddam Hussein threaten to blow up a nuclear power plant in Germany; opposing that nefarious scheme is a good German cop whose murder investigation of two women by an Iraqi will bring him face-to-face with the terrorists. *P*

2370. ___. *False Prophets*. By Sean Flannery, pseud. New York: Charter, 1983. Wallace Mahoney and son John return in this spy thriller as Mahoney fakes his own death aboard an Israeli airliner. Just as John learns of a network of insiders within CIA that his father had come to suspect shortly before he was "killed," his own family is blown up in an attempt to tie up this loose end too. *P*

2371. ___. *Heartland*. New York: TOR, 1983. The Soviets are determined to crush America by acquiring its vast grain reserves—unless tycoon Kenneth Newman can foil the plot. *P*

2372. ___. *The Kremlin Conspiracy*. By Sean Flannery, pseud. New York: Charter, 1980. Two top agents find themselves pawns in an espionage game being played against the background of a US President's visit to Moscow. *P*

2373. ___. *Moscow Crossing*. By Sean Flannery, pseud. New York: Berkley, 1988. A Bolshoi ballerina, dying of leukemia, tries to get word to her lover in America, but the courier is killed in Finland. That unleashes teams of CIA and KGB hit men, among which former group is Jack Horn, who knows there has to be a mole operating freely in Washington somewhere. *P*

2374. ___. *The Zebra Network*. By Sean Flannery, pseud. New York: Morrow, 1989. Abducted, then tortured by the KGB, CIA agent David

MacAllister is no longer trusted by his superiors. More pseudonymous thrillers by Hagberg:

2375. ___. *Eagles Fly.* By Sean Flannery, pseud. New York: Charter, 1980. P

2376. ___. *The Gamov Factor.* By David Bannerman, pseud. New York: Zebra, 1984. This, and the two below, are espionage tales featuring the Magic Man. P

2377. ___. *The Hollow Men.* By Sean Flannery, pseud. New York: Charter, 1982. P

2378. ___. *The Kummersdorf Connection.* By Eric Ramsey, pseud. New York: Playboy, 1978.

2379. ___. *The Magic Man.* By David Bannerman, pseud. New York: Zebra, 1983. P

2380. ___. *Moving Targets.* By Sean Flannery, pseud. New York: TOR, 1992.

2381. ___. *Pipeline from Hell.* By David Bannerman, pseud. New York: Zebra, 1984. P

2382. ___. *The Trinity Factor.* By Sean Flannery, pseud. New York: Charter, 1981. P

2383. ___. *Without Honor.* New York: TOR, 1989. P

Haggard, William, pseud. *See* Clayton, Richard

2384. Haig, Alec. *Sign on for Tokyo.* New York: Dodd, 1969. The author "reveals" his role as an industrial spy for Instecon Steel and how he had to cross swords with his counterpart from Japan's Mitziguichi Steel over a stolen British process for making phosphorous-free metal.

2385. Hailey, Arthur. *In High Places.* Garden City, NY: Doubleday, 1962. A Canadian Prime Minister, bent on a political union with the US designed to prevent a possible nuclear war, is tripped up by his own imperfect past and by the plight of a stateless refugee.

2386. Hale, John. *The Whistle Blower*. New York: Atheneum, 1985. Frank Jones' son is a Russian linguist planning to quit his post at British Intelligence's complex at Cheltenham; his father is convinced that his son's death is no accident and is furthermore linked to the ongoing investigation of a traitor named Dodgson, but all the father's attempts to gain information are stonewalled by the myriad forms of subterfuge of a vast intelligence agency that conspires to keep its secrets.

2387. Halkin, John. *Hantu*. London: Bodley Head, 1981. In 1950 South Korea, British agent Peter Ross goes undercover inside Communist China. Another Halkin:

2388. ___. *Fatal Odds*. New York: Leisure, 1981.

Hall, Adam, pseud. *See* Trevor, Elleston

2389. Hall, Andrew. *Frost*. New York: Putnam's, 1967. Thomas H. Stern returns home every Friday from his London civil service job to his house in Essex. This Friday, however, spies kidnap him.

2390. Hall, Patrick. *The Power Sellers*. New York: Putnam's, 1969. The Buro Fletzer is an international armaments syndicate operating out of Zurich and dedicated to death in any spot on Earth. The more secret agent Griffiths becomes involved with it, the more he wants out.

2391. Hall, Roger. *19*. New York: Norton, 1970. Colonel Jabez Sparhawk sets up 19, an anonymous unofficial counterespionage group that operates within the official intelligence apparatus and is designed solely to safeguard it from penetration in this country. Soon its agents are on the track of a sick patient who has escaped from the CIA's funny farm.

2392. Hall, Warner. *Even Jericho*. New York: Smith, 1944. Major Matt Frayne of US Army G-2 investigates Japanese espionage in Alaska just before the 1942 Rising Sun attack on Dutch Harbor. *

2393. Hallahan, William H. *Catch Me, Kill Me*. Indianapolis: Bobbs-Merrill, 1977. Boris Kotlikoff is a minor Russian poet, now living in New York who is kidnapped—for no reason he can understand—by members of the Russian staff at the UN.

2394. ___. *Foxcatcher*. New York: Morrow, 1986. Charlie Brewer is framed, imprisoned and released—all due to the internal treachery of one highly trusted man, Robert McCall, and it looks as though he will have to become a real traitor to survive.

2395. ___. *The Trade.* New York: Morrow, 1981. Kathe Dorten, daughter of a German nationalist, and Colin Thomas, a brilliant arms merchant, seek to recover a cache of German secret documents known as the Doomsday Book.

2396. ___. *Tripletrap.* New York: Morrow, 1989. A Soviet-backed operation headed by a mysterious Russian steals the US's technological secrets with computer wizardry. Charlie Brewer is sent to stop him and uses a psychological profile to entrap his foe to turn him against the KGB's interests. Other novels are:

2397. ___. *The Dead of Winter.* Indianapolis: Bobbs-Merrill, 1973.

2398. ___. *The Ross Forgery.* Indianapolis: Bobbs-Merrill, 1973.

2399. Halliday, Brett. *Count Backwards to Zero.* New York: Avon, 1971. Private Eye Mike Shayne becomes involved with a beautiful Mossad agent, who is seeking an A-bomb scientist held by a group of Arab operatives. *P*

2400. Hallstead, William Finn III. *Position of Ultimate Trust.* By William Beechcroft, pseud. New York: Dodd, 1981. A conspiracy to assassinate the US President involves an order for the murder of six Florida tourists, all potential witnesses to the plot. Other Hallstead novels written under the Beechcroft pseudonym are:

2401. ___. *Agent of Evil.* By William Beechcroft, pseud. New York: Dodd, 1985. A mix of medical thriller and espionage as a masterspy uses a brain-switching technique to retrieve information from the mind of one of his dying agents.

2402. ___. *Chain of Vengeance.* By William Beechcroft, pseud. New York: Dodd, 1986.

2403. ___. *Image of Evil.* By William Beechcroft, pseud. New York: Dodd, 1985.

2404. ___. *Pursuit of Fear.* By William Beechcroft, pseud. New York: Carroll & Graf, 1989.

2405. ___. *The Rebuilt Man*. By William Beechcroft, pseud. New York: Dodd, 1987.

2406. ___. *Secret Kills*. By William Beechcroft, pseud. New York: Dodd, 1988.

2407. Hamill, Pete. *The Deadly Piece*. New York: Bantam, 1979. A New York City newspaper columnist aids his cousin, who has obtained a priceless breastplate wanted by a Puerto Rico mobster and a pretty Israeli killer. *P*

Hamilton, Adam, pseud. *See* Granbeck, Marilyn and Allen Moore

2408. Hamilton, Donald. *The Ambushers*. Greenwich, CT: Fawcett, 1963. Secret agent Matt Helm works his way from an assassination in Costa Verde to the pursuit of an ex-Nazi fanatic who is attempting to smuggle a Russian missile from Cuba into northern Mexico. *P*
    American author Hamilton has been writing detective and spy thrillers since the end of World War II. His character Matt Helm is a cross between James Bond and Nick Carter and proved one of the favorites with US readers during the spy craze of the 1960s. Singer Dean Martin portrayed Helm in several motion pictures loosely based on the Hamilton series. (See Mr. Hamilton's comment in CRAFT NOTES.)

2409. ___. *The Betrayers*. Greenwich, CT: Fawcett, 1966. Two lovely women complicate Helm's mission: dealing with a rogue agent in Hawaii. *P*

2410. ___. *Date with Darkness*. New York: Rinehart, 1947. While on leave at the close of World War II, a US Navy officer is captured by a beautiful French woman, her pro-Vichy father and collaborationist husband whose plot he has stumbled upon.

2411. ___. *Death of a Citizen*. Greenwich, CT: Fawcett, 1960. *P*

2412. ___. *The Devastators*. Greenwich, CT: Fawcett, 1973. Matt Helm must halt the plot of a mad Scottish scientist who is about to unleash a world-wide epidemic of bubonic plague. *P*

2413. ___. *The Interlopers*. Greenwich, CT: Fawcett, 1972. Helm takes over another man's identity, fiancée, and fate in a desperate attempt to decoy a Presidential assassin's wild dream. *P*

2414. ___. *The Intimidators*. Greenwich, CT: Fawcett, 1974. Agent Helm is pitted against a Caribbean rebel group which specializes in hijacking American planes and ships. *P*

2415. ___. *The Intriguers*. Greenwich, CT: Fawcett, 1972. Political schemers try, but fail, to assassinate Helm and wipe out his agency as a step towards taking over the US. *P*

2416. ___. *Line of Fire*. New York: Dell, 1955. Gunsmith Paul Nyquist's firearms expertise involves him in gangland violence.

2417. ___. *The Menacers*. Greenwich, CT: Fawcett, 1968. Helm goes to Mexico to find and escort a woman wanted by the KGB—a woman who claims to have viewed a flying saucer. *P*

2418. ___. *The Mona Intercept*. Greenwich, CT: Fawcett, 1980. Veteran CIA agent Philip Martin is sent to halt master terrorist Jimmy Columbus, who operates from a base in the Florida Keys. *P*

2419. ___. *Murderers' Row*. Greenwich, CT: Fawcett, 1962. Helm becomes involved with a kidnapped scientist's daughter while on a mission to rescue the man, or silence him before he can be forced to reveal the important military invention on which he is working. *P*

2420. ___. *The Poisoners*. Greenwich, CT: Fawcett, 1971. Helm is ordered to California to foil the evil Warfel, who is planning to smuggle a large quantity of dope into the US. *P*

2421. ___. *The Ravagers*. Greenwich, CT: Fawcett, 1964. Helm must learn who used acid to kill an American agent in Canada; the most likely suspect is a woman he has orders to protect—no matter what the cost. *P*

2422. ___. *The Removers*. Greenwich, CT: Fawcett, 1961. During a brutal journey into the bitter, silent world of official government assassins, where calculated killing occurs in subtle ways and strange places—and where wracking torture is a predictable rule of the game, Matt Helm finds himself torn between the neurotic urges of a gangster's headstrong daughter and a threat to the life of his own ex-wife. *P*

2423. ___. *The Retaliators*. Greenwich, CT: Fawcett, 1976. Agent Matt's bank account is mysteriously increased by someone out to make it look as though he is a traitor on the take; suddenly, word arrives that another agent, who also received a sudden cash surplus, has been murdered and Helm must find his "benefactor" before he is similarly retired. *P*

2424. ___. *The Shadowers*. Greenwich, CT: Fawcett, 1964. Helm marries a stuffy lady scientist in order to be able to protect her, respectably, from the assassins who are systematically stalking her, and others. *P*

2425. ___. *The Silencers*. Greenwich, CT: Fawcett, 1962. Helm becomes involved with a headstrong Texas beauty while tracking down a foreign agent trying to misdirect a dangerous test missile for his own purposes. *P*

2426. ___. *The Steel Mirror*. New York: Rinehart, 1948. Having given away her associates under Gestapo torture during the war, a woman joins a young scientist, suspected of spying, in seeking their joint postwar vindication.

2427. ___. *The Terminators*. Greenwich, CT: Fawcett, 1975. Sent along to ride shotgun on a secret mission to Norway—an assignment the goal of which he is not permitted to know—Matt Helm swings into murderous action after his partner and main agent—the woman who was supposed to be his "mistress"—is killed by unknown assassins. *P*

2428. ___. *The Terrorizers*. Greenwich, CT: Fawcett, 1977. Matt Helm recovers from amnesia just in time to undo a group of Canadian political terrorists. *P*

2429. ___. *The Threateners*. New York: Fawcett, 1992. Matt Helm is between the horns of a dilemma: one side is a South American drug lord and his cartel; the other is a group of dedicated, rogue agents who intend to wipe out the kingpin and his cocaine cowboys and remove this threat to US security. *P*

2430. ___. *The Vanishers*. New York: Fawcett, 1986. Matt returns from an assignment in Mexico to learn that Mac, his chief, is missing and Bennett, a powerful government figure Helm tried to destroy, is running the show; Helm's new assignment smells like a set-up—track Mac and other "vanishers" into the Scandinavian wastelands. *P*

2431. ___. *The Wrecking Crew*. Greenwich, CT: Fawcett, 1960. Helm tracks a deadly Russian spy through the bleak wastes of northern Scandinavia. *P* More recent Matt Helm series adventures:

2432. ___. *The Annihilators*. New York: Fawcett, 1983. *P*

2433. ___. *The Detonators*. New York: Fawcett, 1985. *P*

2434. ___. *The Frighteners*. New York: Fawcett, 1989. *P*

2435. ___. *The Infiltrators*. New York: Fawcett, 1984. *P*

2436. ___. *The Revengers*. New York: Fawcett, 1982. *P*

2437. Hammon, Henry. *Lapis*. Chicago: Academy, 1984. Petroleum geologist Joe McCandless is working in Pakistan when a group of Afgan rebels approach him to exchange their lapis stones for his greenbacks.

2438. Hammond-Innes, Ralph. *Attack Alarm*. By Hammond Innes, pseud. New York: Macmillan, 1942. A Nazi spy group attempts to cripple the RAF during the Battle of Britain. **y*

2439. ___. *Blue Ice*. By Hammond Innes, pseud. New York: Harper, 1949. A wild chase after a fugitive possessing secrets is carried on by yacht and overland into the rugged mountains of Norway. **y*

2440. ___. *High Stand*. By Hammond Innes, pseud. New York: Atheneum, 1988. A millionaire playboy disappears into the Yukon and his lawyer investigates.

2441. ___. *Isvik*. By Hammond Innes, pseud. New York: St. Martin's, 1992. An Anarctic adventure story involving a frigate locked up in the ice for two centuries and a British search party. Another:

2442. ___. *The Black Tide*. By Hammond Innes, pseud. Garden City, NY: Doubleday, 1983.

2443. Hamrick, Samuel J. Jr. *The Ants of God*. By W. T. Tyler, pseud. New York: Dial, 1980. McDermott is an American pilot embittered because of his USAF court martial during the Vietnam war; now he's a bush pilot running guns along the Sudanese-Ethiopian border in the 1970's. (See Mr. Hamrick's commentary in CRAFT NOTES.)

2444. ___. *The Man Who Lost the War*. By W. T. Tyler, pseud. New York: Dial, 1980. Ex-CIA agent David Plummer is now a businessman employed by a British firm in Berlin in the early 1960's. The plot concerns his attempt to uncover the identity of Solo, a double agent who has infiltrated British intelligence.

2445. ___. *Rogue's March.* New York: Harper & Row, 1982. Colonel N'Sika, commander of paramilitary forces in a small African nation, overthrows his corrupt government in this tale of intrigue, but the coup plotters have not reckoned on American Intelligence officer Andy Reddish, who treks across the Congo's interior in search of the answers behind the coup.

2446. ___. *The Shadow Cabinet.* By W. T. Tyler, pseud. New York: Dial, 1984. A so-called Washington novel set during the first year of Reagan's Presidency, this novel was praised by Michael Kernan of the *Washington Post* for its incisive portrayal of the "nether world of Washington, with its dealers and connivers, its social pretenders and high-placed lunatics, its cynics and has-beens and lost souls" (qtd. *Contemporary Authors.* Vol. 120: 158). Two more:

2447. ___. *Last Train from Berlin.* By W. T. Tyler, pseud. New York: Holt, 1994.

2448. ___. *The Lion and the Jackal.* By W. T. Tyler, pseud. New York: Linden, 1988.

2449. Hanlon, Sean. *The Big Dark.* New York: Pocket, 1989. A reporter and his girlfriend move to Baranov, Alaska and discover vestiges of the ancient sect of Czarist peasants known as Old Believers when one of them turns up beaten to death with an ancient Russian weapon. One more:

2450. ___. *The Cold Front.* New York: Pocket, 1989.

2451. Hanson, Dirk. *The Incursion.* Boston: Little, 1987. A technothriller with a computer-terrorist slant when a presumed foolproof computer security system—linking everything from banks to intelligence agencies—is penetrated.

2452. Harcourt, Palma. *Clash of Loyalties.* London: Collins, 1984. With her husband Jack Trotman (under the joint pseudonym John Penn), Harcourt has written over a dozen mysteries—many of which touch upon espionage or the "diplomatic" thriller. Alexis Dolkov, an escaped Russian prisoner during the German occupation, fathers a son in Jersey. The boy's secret is safe until Vladimir Dolkov, Alexis' brother in the KGB, discovers him and decides to recruit him for the Soviet espionage in the British Foreign Office.

2453. ___. *A Fair Exchange.* New York: McKay, 1975. A career diplomat's wife has a shadowy past that exposes her to blackmail and espionage and threatens US-Soviet détente at his new posting in Norway. More Harcourts:

2454. ___. *Agents of Influence*. New York: Walker, 1978.

2455. ___. *At High Risk*. New York: Walker, 1978.

2456. ___. *Climate for Conspiracy*. London: Collins, 1974.

2457. ___. *A Cloud of Doves*. London: Collins, 1985.

2458. ___. *Cover for a Traitor*. London: Collins, 1989.

2459. ___. *Dance for Diplomats*. London: Collins, 1976.

2460. ___. *The Distant Stranger*. New York: Beaufort, 1984.

2461. ___. *Double Deceit*. New York: Doubleday, 1991.

2462. ___. *Limited Options*. New York: Beaufort, 1986.

2463. ___. *A Matter of Conscience*. New York: Beaufort, 1986.

2464. ___. *The Reluctant Defector*. South Yarmouth, MA: Curley, 1992.

2465. ___. *Shadows of Doubt*. New York: Beaufort, 1985.

2466. ___. *A Sleep of Spies*. London: Collins, 1979.

2467. ___. *Tomorrow's Treason*. London: Collins, 1980.

2468. ___. *A Turn of Traitors*. New York: Scribner's, 1981.

2469. ___. *The Twisted Tree*. London: Collins, 1982.

Hardt, Michael, pseud. *See* Davenport, Gwen L. and Gustav J. Breuer

2470. Hardy, Ronald. *The Face of Jalanath*. New York: Putnam's, 1973. Six men are chosen and trained to climb a peak between Kashmir and China to take out China's nuclear potential.

2471. Harling, Robert. *Endless Colonnade*. New York: Putnam's, 1960. Dr. Rupert Frost finds himself in possession of H-bomb secrets one of his colleagues was about to turn over to Communists in Italy.

2472. ___. *The Enormous Shadow*. New York: Harper, 1955. A London reporter works to expose a British Parliament member and a big-name mathematician as members of a Communist spy ring.

Haroldson, William, pseud. *See* King, Harold

Harper, David, pseud. *See* Corley, Edwin

2473. Harper, Richard J. *The Dragonhead Deal*. New York: Warner, 1975. Employing a converted U-boat, Mossad agents attempt to safeguard an illegal arms shipment. *P*

2474. Harrington, Denis J. *The Silent Pursuits*. New York: Major, 1976. A West German agent and a former Nazi prisoner seek war criminal SS Colonel Erich Steidel. *P*

2475. Harrington, Kent. *The Gift of a Falcon*. New York: McGraw-Hill, 1988. Two men with a common past—one was a pilot who saved the other's life after a downing in 1972 in Laos—meet up agian in the present on opposite sides when one, now an FBI agent, uncovers a plot to assassinate an Arab ruler. Another:

2476. ___. *A Brother to Dragons*. New York: Fine, 1992.

2477. Harrington, R. E. *Death of a Patriot*. New York: Putnam's, 1979. A desk-bound CIA agent, Thomas Hobbs, suddenly is cast into the role of double agent when a traitor, who is a dead ringer for Hobbs, is killed without the knowledge of his Soviet contacts.

2478. ___. *Quintain*. New York: Putnam's, 1977. A timid systems analyst plagued by paranoid delusions, Alexander Quintain finds himself involved in a real-life intelligence-sponsored assassination conspiracy.

2479. Harrington, William. *Endgame in Berlin*. New York: Fine, 1991. Espionage industrial-style in this US versus USSR conflict.

2480. ___. *The English Lady*. New York: Seaview, 1982. Lady Nancy Hilary Alexandra Brookeford is known in Germany as *die Engländerin*—the English lady—who happens to be the only person allowed in the Führer's presence without being searched for weapons. She asks Winston Churchill: "Do you want me to kill Hitler?"

2481. ___. *The Jupiter Crisis*. New York: McKay, 1971. A reporter risks his life to follow a trail that leads across Europe from a Soviet-captured US spy satellite to Washington, DC, and the President of the United States himself.

2482. ___. *Columbo: The Grassy Knoll*. New York: Forge, 1993. Lt. Columbo and the J.F.K. assassination. Creator of the well-known TV series character (played by Peter Falk), Harrington has written other mystery/thrillers:

2483. ___. *The Cromwell File*. New York: St. Martin's, 1986.

2484. ___. *Mister Target*. New York: Delacorte, 1973.

2485. ___. *Oberst*. Toronto: Worldwide, 1989. *P*

2486. ___. *Scorpio 5*. New York: Coward, 1975.

2487. ___. *Skin Deep*. New York: Seaview, 1983.

2488. ___. *Virus*. New York: Morrow, 1991.

Harris, Brian, pseud. *See* King, Harold

2489. Harris, Harry. *The Daleth Effect*. New York: Putnam's, 1972. CIA and KGB agents attempt to steal a Danish secret formula which can provide for either quick space travel or an ultimate war weapon.

2490. ___. *Queen Victoria's Revenge*. Garden City, NY: Doubleday, 1975. US, Israeli, and British agents work to counter a rash of skyjackings by Cuban, Palestinian, and Scot revolutionaries.

2491. Harris, John. *A Killer for the Chairman*. By Mark Hebden, pseud. New York: Harcourt, 1972. A part-Chinese British secret agent is sent after a deranged spy who hates the Communist Chinese and plans to murder Mao Tse-tung.

2492. ___. *March of Violence*. By Mark Hebden, pseud. New York: Harcourt, 1970. Two of 100,000 students who march on a German city are not interested in education or government reform; they have in mind blowing up a British missile base.

2493. ___. *A Pride of Dolphins*. By Mark Hebden, pseud. New York: Harcourt, 1975. Someone wants ex-Navy men for an about-to-be-hijacked submarine and James Venner infiltrates the crew for MI-5 just as the Royal Navy discovers the sub in question is carrying dangerous nerve gas.

2494. Harris, Leonard. *The Masada Plan*. New York: Crown, 1976. When Israel is attacked by enemy forces on all sides and faces defeat, she threatens to set off A-bombs in various world cities unless the US agrees to pressure the Arabs into holding back their combined offensive.

2495. Harris, MacDonald. *Yukiko*. New York: Strauss, 1977. When their submarine is wrecked, four Yankee sailors land on one of the Japanese home islands late in World War II and try to blow up a hydroelectric plant.

2496. Harris, Richard. *Enemies*. New York: Marek, 1979. After a newspaper columnist wakes up in an alley next to the body of a dead woman, he is forced to flee from mysterious killers who maintain a terrible secret that could end the world.

2497. Harris, Robert. *Fatherland*. New York: Random, 1992. The author of *Selling Hitler: The Story of the Hitler Diaries* begins his novel in 1964 and Hitler is about to celebrate his seventy-fifth birthday. Life in the Third Reich—twenty years after Hitler wins WW II—and Xavier March, homicide investigator, does all he can to keep himself free in a regimented society where his own son will not hesitate to inform on him.

2498. Harris, Thomas. *Black Sunday*. New York: Putnam's, 1975. The Black September Palestine terrorist movement employs a psychotic ex-POW blimp commander in a mad scheme to drop a huge anti-personnel bomb on the Super Bowl, killing the US President and 80,000 spectators, in an effort to stop American support for Israel. Mossad agent Major Kabokov, with a minimum of aid from American intelligence agencies, must disrupt the plot before it is too late.

2499. Harrison, Harry and Marvin Minsky. *The Turing Option*. New York: Warner, 1992. A top scientist working on artificial intelligence at a secret installation in California is attacked by gunmen in his laboratory and left for dead with a bullet in his skull, but other scientists reconstruct his brain with the techniques of machine intelligence the victim himself had discovered.

2500. Harrison, Payne. *Storming Intrepid*. New York: Crown, 1989. Russia confiscates a US cargo that will make the "Star Wars" system functional.

2501. ___. *Thunder of Erebus*. New York: Crown, 1991. The US and the new "Soviet Confederation" have joined to form a symbolic mission of cooperation in Antarctica; however, beneath the glaciers, below Mt. Erebus, is a mining site of rubidium-96 that would mean world supremacy for the owner.

2502. Harrison, William. *Africana*. New York: Morrow, 1977. Three men lead a clandestine mercenary army into Central Africa during the 1960s in order to overthrow a dictatorial regime.

2503. ___. *Savannah Blue*. New York: Marek, 1981. The President of the United States orders an agent called "the Little Buddha" to look into the case of a deranged Englishman in Nairobi who is killing off all American businessmen interested in exploiting Africa's natural resources.

2504. Hart, Gary and William S. Cohen. *The Double Man*. New York: Macmillan, 1985. The Senators from Maine and Colorado teamed up to write this political thriller about a naive senator who discovers that Soviet agents are manipulating terrorists to destroy various capitalist enterprises.

2505. ___. *The Strategies of Zeus*. New York: Morrow, 1986. This plot centers on weapons negotiations with an underlying theme that sets patriotism and honor in opposition with greed and profit.

2506. Hart, Roy. *A Position of Trust*. New York: St. Martin's, 1986. This mole's-eye view of espionage concerns a spy recruited by the Soviets from Oxford University has been quietly betraying his country for a long time; now he must frame a colleague and scramble to avoid detection when word gets out of a traitor in their midst.

2507. Hart-Davis, Duff. *The Heights of Rimring*. New York: Atheneum, 1981. Led by a bitter SIS man, a secret expedition struggles through the Himalayas seeking to rescue an American general and to retrieve a vital document important to the West's future.

2508. Hartenfels, Jerome. *Doctor Death*. New York: Hill & Wang, 1970. A British bank clerk is recruited by a weird group calling itself the Experimental Institute of Psychocontrol, which is headed by the mysterious Doctor Death—an ex-Nazi scientist guilty of all sorts of grisly war crimes.

2509. Hartland, Michael. *Down among the Dead Men*. New York: Macmillan, 1983. Series character David Nairn of MI-6 is an expert on Chinese affairs, so when a Chinese agent is murdered in the Himalayas before he could seek asylum in Katmandu, he is sent to investigate.

2510. ___. *Seven Steps to Treason.* New York: Macmillan, 1984. Hartland's second series character is Sara Cable, daughter of a Viennese diplomat, who is kidnapped and used as a pawn to induce her father to provide secrets to the Russians. Two others:

2511. ___. *Frontier of Fear.* New York: Walker, 1992.

2512. ___. *The Third Betrayal.* New York: Macmillan, 1986.

2513. Hartley, Norman. *The Viking Process.* New York: Simon & Schuster, 1976. A multinational corporation uses sexual blackmail to get an agent, a terrorist expert, to assist techno-guerrillas ("Vikings") against corporate America. A couple more:

2514. ___. *Quicksilver.* New York: Atheneum, 1979.

2515. ___. *Shadowplay.* New York: Atheneum, 1982.

2516. Hartmann, Michael. *Days of Thunder.* New York: St. Martin's, 1981. A native scout and a missionary priest attempt to thwart the plan of Cuban mercenaries to snatch ore deposits in a newly independent African nation.

2517. ___. *Leap for the Sun.* New York: St. Martin's, 1977. While searching for a treasure, an English mercenary-adventurer becomes involved in a plot to depose the dictator of Uganda.

2518. Hartov, Steven. *The Heat of Ramadan.* New York: Harcourt, 1992. This veteran Israeli agent, member of its elite Parachute and Intelligence Corps, exposes the inner workings of Israeli security in this tale of an Israeli agent who tries to capture an Arab terrorist. Complicating matters is the fact that an Israeli hit team has killed the wrong man, and the right man could destroy Israel during the coming most sacred month of the Muslim year.

Hartshorne, pseud. *See,* Blum, Richard H. A. [Hosmer Adams]

Harvester, Simon, pseud. *See* Rumbold-Gibbs, Henry St. John Clair

Hastings, Michael, pseud. *See* Bar-Zohar, Michael

2519. Hauser, Thomas. *The Beethoven Conspiracy*. New York: Macmillan, 1985. A New York detective must learn the connection between a stranger's offering a violist $10,000 to learn and play a piece of music in Europeand the murder of three musicians in Lincoln Center.

2520. ___. *The Hawthorne Group*. New York: TOR, 1992. A woman, a former actress, takes a job with an international corporation headed by a billionaire; when a hush-hush agency asks her to spy on her company, she accepts and is ultimately caught between loyalties: to her employer or her country. *P*

2521. Hawkey, Raymond and Roger Bingham. *Wild Card*. Briarcliff Manor, NY: Stein & Day, 1980. In a divided America of the future, a President under constant threat of assassination, decides to mount a diversion to create unity—a diversion involving the deaths of ten thousand Los Angeles citizens.

2522. Hawkins, John and Ward. *Pilebuck*. New York: Dutton, 1943. FBI agents investigate Nazi sabotage in an American shipyard. *

2523. Haycraft, Howard, ed. *Five Great Spy Novels*. Garden City, NY: Doubleday, 1962. Contents: *The Great Impersonation*, by E. Phillips Oppenheim; *Greenmantle*, by John Buchan; *Epitaph for a Spy*, by Eric Ambler; *No Surrender*, by Martha Albrand, pseud; and *No Entry*, by Manning Coles, pseud. *y

2524. Hayes, Ralph. *Agent for COMINSEC: The Bloody Monday Conspiracy*. New York: Belmont-Tower, 1974. Formerly a Mafia hitman, Taggart goes to work for the Committee for International Security—formed by five major Free World nations to combat terrorism—and battles a depraved Arab plot to start a nuclear war by using a kidnapped Russian brain surgeon against Chinese Communist leader Mao Tse-tung. *P See also* Carter, Nick (1047, 1055, 1063-64, 1127, 1150, 1163).

2525. ___. *The Bloody Monday Conspiracy*. New York: Belmont-Tower, 1974. Hayes also authored this paperback series about an agency called Cominsec and Agent Taggart, responsible for securing world peace. *P* One more from this series:

2526. ___. *The Death-Makers Conspiracy*. New York: Belmont-Tower, 1975. *P*

2527. ___. *Check Force.* New York: Manor, 1975. A renegade CIA agent named Chance and KGB defector Karlov join forces to take on the fanatical criminal organization Force III, which is dedicated to seizing world power by forcing the superpowers into a nuclear world war. *P*

2528. ___. *Check Force: 100 Megaton Kill.* New York: Manor, 1975. Unless Chance and Karlov can intervene quickly, Force III plans to fire the first missile for Russia—or so it will seem—to which the US will respond bringing on Armageddon. *P*

2529. ___. *Check Force: Clouds of War.* New York: Manor, 1975. Force III plans to assassinate a brilliant US Secretary of State and lay the blame on the USSR—a deadly spark which could cause conflagration unless Chance and Karlov strike first. *P*

2530. ___. *Check Force: The Peking Plot.* New York: Manor, 1975. Unofficial agents Chance and Karlov must bust up a Force III scheme to cause nuclear war between Russia and China. *P*

2531. ___. *Check Force: Seeds of Doom.* New York: Manor, 1976. With a food shortage so critical that millions of people are threatened with starvation, Force III plots to wipe out the US grain crop—a spark in a tinderbox which could force the superpowers to blast the world apart. *P*

2532. Hayes, Roy. *The Hungarian Game.* New York: Simon & Schuster, 1973. An American counterespionage agent seeks a colonel of the Hungarian secret police, long believed dead, who surfaces at a ski resort with a group of Albanians bankrolled by a rich Californian.

2533. Heald, Timothy V. *Unbecoming Habits.* New York: Stein & Day, 1973. Simon Bognor of the British Board of Trade investigates an Anglican friary in Oxfordshire where he discovers the monks are smuggling state secrets to Eastern Europe hidden in jars of honey.
    Tim Heald's writing career includes both journalism and novels. He has edited *The Newest London Spy* (London: Muller, 1988) and *The Rigby File* (London: Hodder & Stoughton, 1989), but he has long been famous as the creator of Simon Bognor of the Board of Trade, bungling detective and wordsmith by inclination who, on occasion, crosses over to foray in matters of espionage in his sleuthing adventures. (See Mr. Heald's commentary in CRAFT NOTES.)

2534. ___. *Murder at Moose Jaw*. Garden City, NY: Doubleday, 1981. Bognor investigates the bathtub murder of womanizing rake Sir Roderick Farquhar.

2535. ___. *Red Herrings*. Garden City, NY: Doubleday, 1986. British Board of Trade sleuth Bognor investigates a man who is pinned to a tree with arrows sticking out of his stomach.

2536. ___. *A Small Masterpiece*. [*Masterstroke*. London: Hutchinson, 1982]. Garden City, NY: Doubleday, 1982. Bognor investigates the death of the Master of Apocrypha College at his alma mater when someone puts poison in the man's raspberry liqueur. Some of his other mysteries include:

2537. ___. *Blue Blood Will Out*. Briarcliff Manor, NY: Stein & Day, 1974.

2538. ___. *Brought to Book*. New York: Doubleday, 1988.

2539. ___. *Business as Usual*. London: Macmillan, 1989.

2540. ___. *Caroline R.* By David Lancaster, pseud. New York: Arbor, 1980.

2541. ___. *Class Distinctions*. London: Hutchinson, 1984.

2542. ___. *Deadline*. Briarcliff Manor, NY: Stein & Day, 1975.

2543. ___. *Just Desserts*. New York: Scribner's, 1979.

2544. ___. *Let Sleeping Dogs Lie*. Briarcliff Manor, NY: Stein & Day, 1976.

2545. Hearne, John and Morris Cargill. *Fever Grass*. By John Morris, pseud. New York: Putnam's, 1969. Peter Blackmore, a wealthy Jamaican and marijuana user, is lured into a sort of unofficial local CIA complete with its own native targets.

2546. Heath, Layne. *The Blue Deep*. New York: Morrow, 1993. Set in May of 1954 when the French were being pounded at Dienbienphu, a contingent of American troops arrives in Vietnam to train French helicopter pilots.

2547. Heatter, Basil. *The Einstein Plot*. New York: Dell, 1982. Hess' desperate flight to the Scottish countryside in May 1941 is part of a complex plot to obtain the secret of the A-bomb from the genius behind it all—Albert Einstein. *P*

2548. ___. *The Mutilators*. Greenwich, CN: Fawcett, 1962. An American and his girlfriend become involved in an OAS plot in Algeria aimed at keeping that province a part of France. *P*

    Hebden, Mark, pseud. *See* Harris, John

2549. Heberden, Mary V. *The Fanatic of Fez*. By Charles L. Leonard, pseud. Garden City, NY: Doubleday, 1943. Paul Kilgerrin goes to North Africa to retrieve an American-hating professor who has invented a formula to transmute coal to petroleum and along the way must battle the Gestapo, Italian undercover operatives, and the French police. *

2550. ___. *Secrets for Sale*. By Charles L. Leonard, pseud. Garden City, NY: Doubleday, 1950. Kilgerrin, always the sardonic detective, sallies forth to do battle with American traitors who are passing state secrets to agents of a Communist power.

2551. ___. *Treachery in Trieste*. By Charles L. Leonard, pseud. Garden City, NY: Doubleday, 1951. In Yugoslavia, Kilgerrin is caught up in an intrigue which would deliver that state more firmly into Moscow's orbit. Other Heberden adventures of Paul Kilgerrin:

2552. ___. *Deadline for Destruction*. By Charles L. Leonard, pseud. Garden City, NY: Doubleday, 1942.

2553. ___. *The Fourth Funeral*. By Charles L. Leonard, pseud. Garden City, NY: Doubleday, 1948.

2554. ___. *Pursuit in Peru*. By Charles L. Leonard, pseud. Garden City, NY: Doubleday, 1946.

2555. ___. *The Secret of the Spa*. By Charles L. Leonard, pseud. Garden City, NY: Doubleday, 1944.

2556. ___. *Sinister Shelter*. By Charles L. Leonard, pseud. Garden City, NY: Doubleday, 1949.

2557. ___. *The Stolen Squadron*. By Charles L. Leonard, pseud. Garden City, NY: Doubleday, 1942.

2558. Heckstall-Smith, Anthony. *The Man with Yellow Shoes.* New York: Roy, 1958. A middle-aged Englishman dresses himself up as an Arab to foil an Egyptian plot against the diminishing British interests in the Middle East.

2559. Heffernan, William. *Corsican Honor.* New York: Dutton, 1992. In this sequel to his 1983 novel *The Corsican*, Heffernan gives readers a mix of espionage and organized crime. Alex Moran is the Defense Intelligence Agency chief in Marseilles who locks horns with a terrorist and who must conspire, as his own father did in WW II when he allied interests with the Corsican crime network, to save his wife who is kidnapped by the terrorist. Another:

2560. ___. *Blood Rose.* New York: Dutton, 1991.

2561. Heim, Michael. *Aswan.* New York: Knopf, 1972. An international effort is mounted to keep Egypt from being swept into the Mediterranean after the crumbling of the high dam at Aswan. The question for Western agents is: did someone blow it?

2562. Heinrich, Willi. *The Crack of Doom.* Trans. from the German. New York: Farrar, 1958. In 1944 Czechoslovakia, Wehrmacht Sergeant Kolodzi and his unit are forced into a dirty war against the partisans.

2563. Helitzer, Florence. *Hans, Who Goes There?* New York: Harper & Row, 1965. A German survivor of Dachau and underling in American Intelligence leads a rather comfortable life until the day his boss sends him back to his old hometown to ferret out ex-Nazi Siegfried Gomul, who is suspected of collusion with East German agents.

2564. Helwig, David. *Old Wars.* New York: Viking, 1989. A missing Soviet agent is linked to a Canadian Mountie undercover agent's WW II past in Greece. *P*

2565. Hempstone, Smith. *A Tract of Time.* Boston: Houghton, 1966. In 1963 Vietnam, US Special Forces team members attempt to enlist mountain tribesmen as allies against the Viet Cong.

2566. Henaghan, Jim. *Azor.* New York: St. Martin's, 1976. When a close friend is killed, retired CIA agent Jeff Pride reenters "the game" to find the assassin, a mysterious killer known only as "the Gypsy."

2567. Henderson, James. *Copperhead.* New York: Knopf, 1971. Twelve people are infected with a new germ, but as they wander, they keep it under control with a special antidote carried on a penny, or "copperhead." When two go to Russia the Soviets accuse the West of attempting biological warfare and their agents, in cooperation with men from the CIA, must locate the other ten to end the experiment—only they are now missing.

2568. Henderson, Laurence. *The Final Glass*. Chicago: Academy, 1990. A woman joins the IRA as an idealist, marries one of its leaders, and becomes disillusioned with its violence and politics. Another:

2569. ___. *Sitting Target*. New York: St. Martin's, 1972.

2570. Henissart, Paul. *Margin of Error*. New York: Simon & Schuster, 1980. A CIA agent must halt the determined plan of a terrorist to assassinate Anwar Sadat when that Egyptian leader visits a Swiss clinic.
      Henissart was a foreign correspondent for *Time* magazine and later a radio/TV reporter before turning his attention to the writing of spy thrillers.
      Henissart is a disciple of David (le Carré) Cornwell and Len Deighton who believes that "like all superior fiction, good spy stories have one major asset—strong characters." "Far from being strapping James Bonds," he has written, "real-life spies and agents not only are short (to render surveillance more difficult), but they are also frequently grubby and, by accident or design, unimpressive." Realism and precision are required in high degree for today's espionage yarns and as this author has warned aspiring practitioners, they require "familiarity with intelligence services and their foibles, the deft rendering of place, atmosphere, and language [and] the witty reporting of human fallibility." Many of Henissart's characters are based on real-life counterparts he has known from his various postings in Europe and Africa, including stints at the CIA-funded Radio Free Europe, Vienna and Paris bureaus. Henissart also wrote a nonfictional summary of the OAS underground war and the end of French rule in *Wolves in the City: An Account of the Death of Algeria* (New York: Simon & Schuster, 1970).

2571. ___. *Narrow Exit*. New York: Simon & Schuster, 1974. The first time Arab militant Al Houaranni leaves the Middle East, the Israeli Mossad sends its top man, Alex Gauthier, to kidnap him.

2572. ___. *The Winter Spy*. New York: Simon & Schuster, 1976. Formerly published under the title *Winter Quarry*. Dr. Robert Wood is an American political scientist, a genius at global diplomacy, and advisor to two Presidents; he is also an agent whose contact Rappaport is a colonel in the Hungarian secret police. Ana Pecs, head of Hungarian Intelligence, intends to rid herself of her competition in Rappaport and sabotage treaty negotiations by assassinating Wood in Hamburg.

2573. Henrick, Richard P. *Sea of Death*. New York: Zebra, 1992. A conspiracy of Ninja warriors and scientists working in a biohazard facility will culminate in the release of a deadly toxin that will destroy America; opposing this mad scheme, codenamed "Deathwind," is a rustbucket of a submarine manned by computer-trained submariners. *P* Henrick's other technothrillers all feature submarine technology:

2574. ___. *Beneath the Silent Seas*. New York: Zebra, 1988. The Red Chinese send the *Red Dragon*, their latest supersub against the Soviets and the US. *P*

2575. ___. *Counterforce*. New York: Zebra, 1987. A Soviet killer sub is opposed by the USS *Triton*. *P*

2576. ___. *Dive to Oblivion*. New York: Zebra, 1993. Nuclear sub USS *Lewis and Clark* is on a routine training exercise in the Bahamas when it vanishes—and then, moments later, reappears in the Pacific, and the secret of Einstein's WW II experiment is exposed to the world. *P*

2577. ___. *The Golden U-Boat*. New York: Zebra, 1991. A fugitive SS officer salvages a deadly cargo from a German U-boat sunk in the North Sea in the hope off resurrecting the Third Reich. *P*

2578. ___. *The Phoenix Odyssey*. New York: Zebra, 1986. The USS *Phoenix* does not obey its recall order from the President, and it appears that it may be ready to unleash its nuclear payload on the unsuspecting Soviets. *P*

2579. ___. *Silent Warriors*. New York: Zebra, 1990. A *Red October-*influenced plotline in this tale of a Soviet sub skipper, commander of the most sophisticated sub in the Red fleet, opens his sealed orders prematurely and discovers his vessel and crew must spearhead a nuclear attack on the US. *P* More Henrick sea-sub adventures:

2580. ___. *Cry of the Deep*. New York: Zebra, 1989. *P*

2581. ___. *Flight of the Condor*. New York: Zebra, 1987. *P*

2582. ___. *Sea Devil*. New York: Zebra, 1990. *P*

2583. ___. *Under the Ice.* New York: Zebra, 1989. *P*

2584. ___. *When Duty Calls.* New York: Zebra, 1988. *P*

2585. Henriques, Robert D. Q. *The Commander.* New York: Viking, 1968. Picturing the training, waiting, and quick, bloody raids led by a British Commando captain in 1940-1941.

2586. Herbert, James. *The Spear.* New York: Signet, 1979. While investigating the disappearance of a young Mossad agent, Harry Steadman uncovers a bizarre cult of neo-Nazis with a terrible plan to unleash an age-old diabolical power on an unsuspecting world. *P*

2587. Herlin, Hans. *Grishin.* Trans. J. Maxwell Brownjohn. Garden City, NY: Doubleday, 1987. German-born Herlin's novel concerns British Intelligence's top agent in 1918 whose task is momentous: assassinate Vladimir Ilyich Lenin, leader of the Bolshevik Revolution.

2588. Herman, Richard, Jr. *Call to Duty.* New York: Morrow, 1993. Pirates capture a yacht in the China Sea with a US Senator's daughter aboard.

2589. ___. *Firebreak.* New York: Morrow, 1991. Major Richard Herman (USAF, Ret.) bases his technothriller on what happens after the Persian Gulf War. A fighter jock's career from his silver spoon infancy (his grandfather is a US President) to fighter-pilot manhood is paralleled with geopolitics as the Arabs plot yet another move against Israel.

2590. ___. *Force of Eagles.* New York: Fine, 1990. Two groups of Americans are being readied for an assault on Iran to free 300 prisoners. Which will go? Two more:

2591. ___. *Mosquito Run.* New York: Morrow, 1993.

2592. ___. *The Warbirds.* New York: Fine, 1988.

2593. Hernandez, Arnaldo. *Blind Conspiracy.* New York: Zebra, 1988. Trained from birth as a KGB agent, Andrea Hendrick is sent to the Silicon Valley to seduce a lonely computer expert who works in the top-secret "Blue-Cube." *P*

2594. ___. *The Moscow Sacrament.* New York: Zebra, 1988. Andrea Hendricks emerges from three years in a "reorientation" clinic to receive her

new orders: go to the US with a KGB killer and terminate her own husband.
P

2595. Herrick, William. *Love and Terror*. New York: New Directions, 1982.
A young German terrorist confronts his own ideology when his gang takes three
aged Communist revolutionaries hostage.

2596. Herron, Shaun. *The Hound and the Fox and the Harper*. New York:
Random, 1970. [*The Miro Papers*. London: Hale, 1972]. Miro, after twenty-
five years of working for the Americans, is close to burn-out; however, he and
his wife are on the lam from his former employers—and Soviet agents—in
Ireland over his whistleblowing.

2597. ___. *Miro*. New York: Random, 1969. Tough agent Miro, then
employed by "the Firm," is sent to Canada to find out who is behind a rash of
unique political murders.

2598. ___. *Through the Dark and Hairy Wood*. New York: Random, 1972.
Miro, now peacefully retired to a farm in southern Ireland, runs up to Ulster for
livestock; while there, he stays with a Protestant leader. When an attempt is
made on his host's life, Miro is asked by MI-5 to serve as the man's bodyguard.
Two other Miro tales not published in America are:

2599. ___. *The Bird in Last Year's Nest*. London: Evans, 1974.

2600. ___. *The Whore-Mother*. London: Evans, 1973.

2601. Hershatter, Richard L. *Fallout for a Spy*. New York: Ace, 1969.
Rand Stannard is coerced into working, as Agent 6-X, for the Defense
Intelligence Agency. *P* Two others:

2602. ___. *The Spy Who Hated Fudge*. New York: Ace, 1970. *P*

2603. ___. *The Spy Who Hated Licorice*. New York: Signet, 1966. *P*

2604. Herst, Roger E. *Status 1 S.Q.* Garden City, NY: Doubleday, 1979.
An nuclear submarine in Soviet Arctic waters is ordered to fire its cruise
missiles, triggering a top-level power struggle.

2605. Hesky, Olga. *A Different Night*. New York: Random, 1971.
Somebody wants to assassinate an American presidential assistant enroute to a

conference in Israel. A Mossad agent assists his CIA colleague in finding out who the nasty may be.

2606. ___. *The Serpent's Smile*. New York: Dodd, 1967. A top secret Israeli security agency, GAG, is established under Papa Barzilai and charged with rooting out terrorism which threatens the state.

2607. ___. *Time for Treason*. New York: Dodd, 1968. When a body is found hanging on a meat hook in a Tel Aviv slaughter house, Papa Barzilai and Tami Simoni of the top-secret GAG agency must learn the connection between it and a fire in a secret laboratory at the Weitzmann Institute at Rehovot.

2608. Hewitt, Kathleen D. *Mice Are Not Amused*. London: Jarrolds, 1942. Glenda Blake of MI-5 takes a head porter's position in a large London apartment house in order to mount surveillance over suspected Nazi agents and fifth columnists. *

2609. Heydenau, Friedrich. *Wrath of Eagles*. New York: Dutton, 1943. An American officer fights with Chetnik guerrillas in Yugoslavia. During the early part of World War II, it was widely believed that the Chetnik movement, as opposed to Tito's partisans, were the most efficient and loyal Yugoslav guerrilla fighters. Only later was it learned that the Chetniks were, if not actually assisting the Axis, extremely inefficient and nonaggressive. *

2610. Heym, Stefan. *Hostages*. New York: Putnam's, 1942. In Prague, Reinhardt Heydrich attempt to cover a German officer's suicide by blaming his death upon a group of hostages whom he orders executed. *

2611. Heywood, Joseph. *The Berkut*. New York: Random, 1987. A "what-if?" tale based on the possibility of Hitler's planned escape from the rubble of Berlin. When word reaches Stalin that a "Herr Wolf" is one of those not accounted for in the bunker's final days, he puts a special team led by a man called the Berkut to track him down and bring him back alive. Another:

2612. ___. *The Domino Conspiracy*. New York: Random, 1992.

2613. Hiatt, Fred. *The Secret Sun*. New York: Pantheon, 1992. Piper, a reporter working in Tokyo, uncovers a shocking secret—the Japanese are working on an atomic bomb project of their own.

Higgins, Jack, pseud. *See* Patterson, Harry

Highet, Helen *See* MacInnes, Helen

2614. Highsmith, Patricia. *Ripley's Game.* New York: Knopf, 1974. American Tom Ripley plays a dangerous game with the fate of a mild-mannered Englishman and his French wife.

Hild, Jack, house pseud. *See* Garside, Jack

2615. Hill, John. *The Man from UNCLE's ABC of Espionage.* New York: Signet, 1966. A look at the "ways and means" of spying as taken from the file of the famous TV organization. *P*

2616. Hill, Peter. *The Fanatics.* New York: Scribner's, 1978. After killing a political leader, two terrorists take hostages in London and await the repercussions spreading through Whitehall and the Kremlin.

2617. Hill, R. Lance. *The Doctor.* New York: Time, 1978. A woman whose family has been ravaged hires Holland, an international assassin, to find and kill the Doctor, the most demonic master of torture since the Nazis, who now lives deep in the Guatemalan jungle, shielded by the CIA.

2618. Hill, Reginald. *The Spy's Wife.* New York: Pantheon, 1980. After discovering she is married to a KGB agent who has used their union as a deception, Molly Keatley retreats to Yorkshire where she meets an overly solicitous British agent named Monk.

2619. Himmel, Richard. *Lions at Night.* New York: Delacorte, 1979. CIA agent Ross Edgerton looks into a Russian plot to stage an anti-Castro invasion of Cuba.
2620. ___. *The Twenty-Third Web.* New York: Random 1977. An American mathematical genius creates a computerized blackmail network which is employed by Arabs to cut off Jewish-American funds to Israel.

2621. Hirschfeld, Burt. *The Masters Affair.* New York: Arbor, 1971. The assassination of a top American intelligence official starts off the action as various agents attempt to find the perpetrator—or protect him.

2622. Hirschhorn, Richard C. *Target Mayflower.* New York: Harcourt, 1977. During the final days of World War II, Abwehr agents free Afrika Korps POWs in Maine in a plot to hijack a uranium shipment from a Boston held hostage by at-the-ready V-2 rockets.

2623. Hitchcock, Raymond. *The Canaris Legacy.* New York: St. Martin's, 1981. During World War II, British agents pursue Simon Manning, the one man who could halt the German extermination of Polish Jews.

2624. Hoch, Edward D. *The Spy and the Thief.* New York: Davis, 1971. Includes seven of the author's thirty-three short stories about Rand, a code-expert who works for the Department of Concealed Communications, a mythical branch of British Intelligence. The remaining yarns have all been published in *Ellery Queen's Mystery Magazine* at various times after 1965.

Hoch has written mostly mysteries in his long career (including over 700 short stories, of which at least 60 feature Rand's espionage adventures between 1965 and 1989). Of particular interest to espionage fans are two collections of tales (totalling fifteen) in *The Spy and the Thief* (New York: Davis, 1971) and *Tales of Espionage* (New York: Castle, 1989). Other series characters from his publications in *Ellery Queen's Mystery Magazine* include Carl Crader and Earl Jazine. Like Kenneth Royce's ex-thief-hero "Spider" Scott, Hoch's Nick Velvet is a professional thief who takes commissions that result in intrigues of various kinds; his stories were collected in 1978: (See Mr. Hoch's commentary in CRAFT NOTES.) A collection of American detective and mystery stories:

2625. ___ and Francis M. Nevins. *The Night, My Friend: Stories of Crime and Suspense.* Athens, OH: Ohio U P, 1992.

2626. ___. *The Quests of Simon Ark.* New York: Mysterious, 1984.

2627. ___. *The Thefts of Nick Velvet.* New York: Mysterious, 1978.

2628. Hoffenberg, Jack. *17 Ben Gurion.* New York: Putnam's, 1976. In order to find and eliminate a PLO terror group threatening the existence of Israel, Mossad agents fan out through Libya, Iraq, and Lebanon taking out potential members.

2629. ___. *A Thunder at Dawn.* New York: Dutton, 1965. Agents Jim Gerard and Alec Fletcher with an all-star CIA cast attempt to prevent a Castro-like takeover on the island of Liberté.

2630. Hogan, James P. *The Proteus Operation.* New York: Bantam, 1985. In this "what-if?" novel, the world in 1974 is bleak: the US, led by President Kennedy, is surrounded by Fascist governments in all directions (Hitler won the war), and the only hope is the Proteus Operation—return to 1939 and change history. Two others:

2631. ___. *Endgame Enigma.* New York: Bantam, 1988. *P*

2632. ___. *The Mirror Maze.* New York: Bantam, 1989. *P*

2633. Hogstrand, Olle. *The Debt.* New York: Pantheon, 1975. The murder of an employee of Sweden's Psychological Defense Department throws suspicion on three men.

2634. ___. *On the Prime Minister's Account.* New York: Pantheon, 1972. A fanatical leftist has assassinated the American ambassador to Sweden. In what appears to be retaliation, the daughter of the Swedish PM is kidnapped and the world learns that she will be released only when the diplomat's killer is caught.

2635. Holland, William E. *Moscow Twilight.* New York: Simon & Schuster, 1992. A Moscow militia investigator investigates what looks at first to be a routine murder in a night spot frequented by Mafia, Japanese businessmen and their hookers, and black marketeers in the Moscow underworld of the post-Gorbachev era; however, the corpse turns out to be the CIA station chief of the US embassy, and the investigation leads to an insidious plot of widespread corruption between the government and criminal enterprise. Compares well with Cruz Smith's *Red Square* in ambience and plot twists. Another:

2636. ___. *Let a Soldier Die.* New York: Delacorte, 1984.

2637. Holbrook, Marion. *Crime Wind.* New York: Dodd, 1945. Newly arrived in a South American republic as guardian of a mysterious package, a State Department clerk finds herself the central figure in a series of spy plots designed to relieve her of her charge. *

2638. Holles, Robert. *Spawn.* Garden City, NY: Doubleday, 1978. The Mossad tracks a rich German art dealer who has impregnated a woman with the frozen sperm of Adolf Hitler.

2639. Holt, Robert L. *Good Friday.* New York: Signet, 1987. Tensions between the US and the USSR boil over and battles erupt in the world's hot spots; the crisis approaches critical mass as a Soviet fleet of aircraft heads for the Saudi oil fields. *P*

2640. ___. *Havana Heat.* Carlsbad, CA: Pacific Rim, 1993. About Castro and Cuba.

Holly, J. Hunter, pseud. *See* Holly, Joan C.

2641. Holly, Joan C. *The Man from UNCLE: The Assassination Affair.* By J. Hunter Holly, pseud. New York: Ace, 1967. THRUSH launches all-out war on UNCLE's top enforcement agents with Napoleon Solo and Illya Kuryakin its first targets. *P*

2642. Holzer, Erika. *Double Crossing.* New York: Putnam's, 1985. About a man's struggle to the freedom of the West via the Glienicker Bridge separating East and West Berlin.

2643. Home, Michael. *Attack in the Desert.* New York: Morrow, 1942. A British flyer takes an SIS agent deep into Libya where they are to assist Free French and native troops in mounting a raid on an Italian outpost. *

2644. ___. *House of Shade.* New York: Morrow, 1942. The mysterious British agent Brice is asked to rescue a Vichy French admiral who is being held hostage by the Nazis near Tripoli. *

2645. Homewood, Charles H. *A Matter of Priority.* New York: O'Hara, 1976. A retired CIA agent is called back to service to halt a KGB plot to kill the President of the United States.

Homewood, Harry, pseud. *See* Charles H. Homewood

2646. Hone, Joseph. *The Oxford Gambit.* New York: Random, 1980. [*The Flowers of the Forest.* London: Secker & Warburg, 1980]. When a retired section head of the British Secret Service goes missing, Peter Marlow takes up the search and follows a trail of murder that leads from Scotland to Eastern Europe.

2647. ___. *The Private Sector.* New York: Dutton, 1972. A Cairo teacher named Marlowe becomes an SIS agent and as such spies out Arab defenses during the June 1967 Six-Day War.

2648. ___. *The Sixth Directorate.* New York: Dutton, 1975. Praised by Anatole Broyard of the *New York Times* as one of the best spy novels of the decade. Peter Marlow, framed by his own Department, has served four years in prison; now released, he is supposed to team with American agent McCoy when McCoy's operation to expose an English double agent in Moscow uncovers a far more sinister operation by five powerful agents operating out of Cheltenham (known as the "sixth directorate") who are plotting to overthrow their government before Moscow destroys them first. Two more:

2649. ___. *The Paris Trap*. London: Secker & Warburg, 1977.

2650. ___. *The Valley of the Fox*. London: Secker & Warburg, 1983.

2651. Hood, William. *Cry Spy*. New York: Norton, 1988. Hood has had a career in US Intelligence that extends from the OSS to the modern CIA; he has been Operations Chief of CIA's station in Vienna and "handled" one of the most famous spies in modern history, Major Pyotr Popov of the GRU, who exposed Russian operatives in the US and Europe for six years until his arrest and execution in 1958. In this second tale of Alan Trosper's activities, the agent returns to the game when his friend and former colleague is murdered with a weapon favored by the KGB.

2652. ___. *Mole*. New York: Norton, 1982. Hood records the daily affairs of GRU spy Major Popov (the CIA approved the book before its release), and he speculates via the fictionalized agent-handlers who might have betrayed Popov to the Soviets.

2653. ___. *Spy Wednesday*. New York: Norton, 1986. Another "true" spy story: Alan Trosper is blackmailed by "the Firm," a rogue chapter of CIA which splintered from the CIA after the Church Oversight Committee Hearings of the seventies, and sent back to Moscow—where his last mission had proved a catastrophe.

2654. Hoover, Thomas. *The Moghul*. Garden City, NY: Doubleday, 1983. Captain Brian Hawksworth (based on Captain William Hawkins, who sailed for the East India Company) is sailing for India, but his mission to dislodge the Portugese from the wealthy spoils of India is sabotaged when he finds armed Portugese galleons awaiting him at every turn. *HI*

2655. ___. *Project Cyclops*. New York: Bantam, 1992. About laser weapons in the Aegean Sea. *P*

2656. ___. *Project Daedalus*. New York: Bantam, 1991. The Japanese Yakuza and a renegade faction of Soviet military conspire to obtain "Daedalus," a high-tech superplane that flies in the Mach 20's and can shift the balance of power back to the hardliners in a collapsing Soviet Union. *P*

2657. ___. *The Samurai Strategy*. New York: Bantam, 1988. A high-finance thriller. *P*

2658. Hopkins, Robert S. *The D'Artagnan Signature.* By Robert Rostand, pseud. New York: Putnam's, 1976. After the OAS defeat in Algeria, its former chief executioner seeks a secret document which will unlock the Swiss vault holding the terrorist group's wealth, estimated at $4 million.

2659. ___. *The Killer Elite.* By Robert Rostand, pseud. New York: Delacorte, 1973. An expendable spy is unofficially assigned to protect a deposed prime minister from assassination.

2660. ___. *A Killing in Rome.* By Robert Rostand, pseud. New York: Delacorte, 1977. The KGB attempts to prevent a former Russian leader from defecting while he is on a visit to the Italian capital.

2661. ___. *The Viper's Game.* By Robert Rostand, pseud. New York: Delacorte, 1974. Mike Lochen, an ex-CIA man, must get fifty people off the Portuguese island colony of São Tomé—or at least keep them one step ahead of machete-carrying, white-hating native tribesmen. An early novel is:

2662. ___. *The Raid on Villa Joyosa.* New York: Putnam's, 1973.

2663. Horler, Sydney. *The Man Who Used Perfume.* London: Wingate, 1952. Robert Wynnton is involved with a British dandy who is selling state secrets to the Russians.
    Horler wrote a number of novel-adventures with espionage themes in the period before World War II (see Part 1). Full of color and excitement, they were modelled after those of E. Phillips Oppenheim.

2664. ___. *They Thought He Was Dead.* London: Hodder & Stoughton, 1949. The last adventure of secret agent Tiger Standish of British Intelligence.

2665. Hornig, Doug. *Stinger.* New York: Signet, 1990. First, a covert operation goes awry when a shipment of Stinger missiles destined for the Contras is hijacked; then a terrorist named Javier Vega uses one from the stolen cache to blast an Aer Lingus 747 out of the skies as it takes off from Logan Airport in Boston. CIA Agent Steven Kirk has just buried his wife and child, but he has to find and stop the terrorist, even though it seems powerful figures in his own government are mixed up in it. *P*

2666. ___. *Waterman.* New York: Mysterious, 1987. Scott Craik is a man in hiding, but the former covert operations agent has run to the wrong place in quiet Brawlton, Virginia, where the local judge is running guns to Latin

America, with the backing of the CIA, and a cocaine syndicate is using that operation as a cover for its own.

2667. Horton, Forest W., Jr. *The Technocrats.* New York: Leisure, 1980. When the President of the United States begins acting strangely during an international crisis, a member of the White House computer staff must ferret out and destroy the enemy within. *P*

2668. Hossent, Harry. *Memory of Treason.* London: Long, 1961. A cynical airman and World War II RAF Squadron Leader, Max Heald was posted to an unnamed SIS department following the conflict and asked to use his varied talents to crack difficult cases. In this outing, Heald looks into the matter of a treason by a prominent Englishman which occurred in the past and which has implications for the present. Other Heald tales, none of which were published in the United States, include:

2669. ___. *Gangster Movies.* London: Long, 1976.

2670. ___. *The Great Spectators.* London: Long, 1975.

2671. ___. *No End to Fear.* London: Long, 1959.

2672. ___. *Run for Your Death.* London: Long, 1965.

2673. ___. *Spies Die at Dawn.* London: Long, 1958.

2674. ___. *Spies Have No Friends.* London: Long, 1963.

2675. ___. *The Spy Who Got Off at Las Vegas.* London: Long, 1969.

2676. Hostovsky, Egon. *The Midnight Patient.* Trans. from the Czech. New York: Appleton-Century, 1954. The head of a financially strapped clinic accepts a government offer to secrete an important atomic scientist away in his hospital for a few days, only to discover that the man is the target of several new staff members who are, in fact, enemy agents. *

2677. Household, Geoffrey. *Arabesque.* Boston: Little, 1948. Not to be confused with the Gregory Peck movie based on Gordon Cotler's *The Cipher.* British Intelligence gives Armande Heine a new purpose in life as she drifts from Beirut to Jerusalem—an agent in the Palestine mandate spying on Jew and Arab alike. *

Household made his mark on the genre with his 1938 classic *Rogue Male* (See Part 1). In the years since, he has continued to turn out competent, suspense-filled tales which have been well-crafted and which are highly readable. The best of his prose style has been compared favorably with that of Eric Ambler.

2678. ___. *Doom's Caravan*. Boston: Little, 1971. An English spy who can pass for an Arab deserts British Intelligence during World War II and our hero-narrator catches up with him in Lebanon and forces the man to help forestall a Nazi plot to take over the entire Middle East.

2679. ___. *Fellow Passenger*. Boston: Little, 1955. Howard Wolferstan burgles a government think-tank disguised as a hostel and soon the British police and Russian security begin hunting him down; he must keep running, and changing disguises—from elephant trainer to Indian guitarist—to keep alive! *H*

2680. ___. *The High Place*. Boston: Little, 1950. A British Intelligence officer in Syria attempts to disperse a band of international anarchists. *

2681. ___. *Hostage-London: The Diary of Julian Despard*. Boston: Little, 1977. The fictional journal of a member of the fictional Magna terrorist group, which plans to cause a revolution in Great Britain with a hidden nuclear bomb.

2682. ___. *The Last Two Weeks of Georges Rivac*. Boston: Little, 1978. A French businessman becomes involved in an intelligence plan for the potential defection to NATO of various East European military units.

2683. ___. *The Lives and Times of Bernardo Brown*. Boston: Little, 1974. In this Household novel of political intrigue involving yet another picaresque character, Bernardo Brown, must go through a series of comic misadventures while being chased by the authorities, and he too dons various disguises as a fugitive: engineer, pimp, concierge, and stage manager. *H*

2684. ___. *Olura*. Boston: Little, 1965. British Intelligence works in the Middle East to stem the rising tide of Arab terrorism against Israel.

2685. ___. *Red Anger*. Boston: Little, 1975. A retired agent becomes involved with operatives from the KGB, CIA, and MI-5 as he seeks safety from false charges.

2686. ___. *Rogue Justice*. Boston: Little, 1982. "Scarred and half blind" from his 1938 attempt to assassinate Hitler, the anonymous hero of *Rogue Male* returns in this 40-year hiatus between novels. Another shot at *der Führer* fails, and he must escape to Sweden, where he is turned away by the British Embassy; now an operative without a country, he returns to Europe and fights his way across the Carpathians with a band of Polish guerillas in a lonely war against the Third Reich.

2687. ___. *A Rough Shoot.* Boston: Little, 1951. Roger Taine aids a Polish patriot in foiling the attempt of a fascist organization to take over Great Britain. *

2688. ___. *Tales of Adventure.* Boston: Little, 1952. Thirteen of the author's short stories in which his agents in separate accounts battle the Gestapo in Vienna, seek uranium in the Iranian desert, and smuggle Europe's best chef out of Soviet-dominated Budapest. *

2689. ___. *A Time to Kill.* Boston: Little, 1951. Sequel to *A Rough Shoot.* Roger Taine's children are kidnapped by Russian agents after he has raised the hue and cry against a scientist whom he believes is plotting biological mischief against England. *

2690. ___. *Watcher in the Shadows.* Boston: Little, 1960. During World War II a Vietnamese served in the SIS as a double-agent appearing to be a Nazi; now in Southeast Asia, he is pursued by a man still thinking that his cover as a German sympathizer long ago was real. * Another:

2691. ___. *Arrows of Desire.* Boston: Atlantic Monthly, 1986.

2692. Houston, Robert. *The Fourth Codex.* Boston: Houghton, 1988. Quintus Paz is a special agent for the US Customs Service who tangles with bandits, various bad guys, and ghosts of the pre-Mayan sort when he goes in search of a priceless Mayan parchment. Two others:

2693. ___. *Ararat.* New York: Avon, 1982. P

2694. ___. *Blood Tango.* New York: Avon, 1984. P

2695. Hoving, Thomas. *Masterpiece.* New York: Simon & Schuster, 1986. As director of the Metropolitan Museum of Art, Hoving supervised the acquisition of half a billion dollars worth of art. His novel pits two directors who battle for, and then fall in love over, one priceless art work—Velázquez' *Marchesa*; meanwhile the Soviets and the CIA are battling it out for the same prize.

2696. Howard, Clark. *The Doomsday Squad.* New York: Weybright & Talley, 1970. Fugitive US Army Sergeant Stoner leads six volunteers in a suicidal mission on a World War II Pacific island.

2697. ___. *Summit Kill.* New York: Pinnacle, 1975. A plot is afoot to assassinate the world's five most important leaders meeting "at the summit." *P*

2698. Howard, Hampton. *Friends, Russians, and Countrymen.* New York: St. Martin's, 1988. Ed Stuarti is a seventy-year-old agent runner and former forger who operates out of his New York safe house, and he enjoys outwitting Congressional oversight committees as much as he does Soviets. His newest target is a traitor somewhere in the upper echelon of the powerful US Nuclear Strategy Council, and Stuarti intends to find "him," and use him to run a disinformation game on the East German operative known as "Andreas."

2699. ___. *War Toys.* New York: Avon, 1983. An ex-CIA agent whose career is sacrificed by the agency decides to use his skills to exact revenge for his humiliation. *P*

Howard, Hartley, pseud. *See* Ognall, Leopold H.

2700. Howe, George. *Call It Treason.* New York: Viking, 1949. Three German POWs in the pay of US Army G-2 are parachuted as saboteurs into Nazi Germany. The tale follows their pre-mission training and the progress of one of them through part of the Reich. Sort of a scaled down, one quarter *Dirty Dozen.* *

2701. Howlett, John. *The Christmas Spy.* New York: Harcourt, 1975. Low-key SIS agent "Railway Joe" Morgan patiently works to crack an international drug network.

2702. ___. *Murder of a Moderate Man.* Toronto: Worldwide, 1987. The secret services of several countries conduct a covert counterterrorist war among one another when an Iranian dissident and his followers are stalked by assassins. *P*

2703. Howley, Brendan. *The Third Circle.* New York: Viking, 1990. A mysterious canister containing documents and a photograph of four men is passed to a Russian in an SS work camp in 1944; almost thirty years later the Russian, a Red Army major and double agent, wants out of the game. The secret of the canister comes to light in the wake of murder and a frenzied chase across the French Alps to discover its connection to a forthcoming American Presidential election.

2704. Hoyt, Richard. *Trotsky's Run*. New York: Morrow, 1982. Compares well to Richard Condon's classic *The Manchurian Candidate* with its similar theme of an "obsessed" contender for the US Presidency, Hoyt's man is a Soviet mole who believes he is the reincarnation of Trotsky.

    A former member of Army Intelligence in the early sixties, Hoyt brings both humor, numbers of wacky characters, and keen sardonic insight to his espionage fiction. Other suspense novels:

2705. ___. *30 for Harry*. New York: Evans, 1981.

2706. ___. *Bigfoot*. New York: TOR, 1993.

2707. ___. *Cool Runnings*. New York: Viking, 1984.

2708. ___. *Decoys*. New York: Evans, 1980.

2709. ___. *The Dragon Portfolio*. New York: TOR, 1986.

2710. ___. *Fish Story*. New York: Viking, 1985.

2711. ___. *Head of State*. London: Severn, 1987.

2712. ___. *The Manna Enzyme*. New York: Morrow, 1982.

2713. ___. *The Siskiyou Two-Step*. New York: Morrow, 1983.

2714. ___. *Whoo?* New York: TOR, 1991.

2715. Hubler, Richard G. *The Chase*. New York: Coward, 1952. Foreign and American spies, a mysterious mad scientist, and an innocent girl reporter cross paths as they hot-foot it through the mountains near the coast of California.

2716. Hughes, Dorothy B. *The Blackbirder*. New York: Duell, Sloan & Pearce, 1943. A young refugee from Occupied France leads the FBI to Nazi agents on the Mexican-American border. *

2717. ___. *The Davidian Report.* New York: Duell, Sloan & Pearce, 1952. The FBI, CCI, and Red agents are all interested in a strange scientific exposé. *

2718. ___. *The Fallen Sparrow.* New York: Duell, Sloan & Pearce, 1942. Returning to the US, an American who had fought for the Loyalists in the Spanish Civil War, captured and released, receives Inspector Tobin's assistance in triumphing over shadowing fascist agents and his own mental fears. *

Hughes, Zachery, pseud. *See* Zachary, Hugh

2719. Hugo, Richard. *Farewell to Russia.* New York: Pinnacle, 1989. A KGB agent plans to acquire nuclear technology, but he's in a race against time after a terrifying nuclear accident. *P*

2720. ___. *Last Judgment.* Braircliff Manor, NY: Stein & Day, 1987. Former SAS member James Ross vows vengeance against the terrorists responsible for the murder of his brother and his family. One more:

2721. ___. *The Gorbachev Version.* New York: Zebra, 1991.

2722. Huie, William B. *In the House of Night.* New York: Delacorte, 1975. The circumstances surrounding a public servant's psychological collapse as they relate to government security in the age of atomic secrets is investigated by a maverick agent.

Humana, Charles, pseud. *See* Jacobs, Joseph

2723. Humes, H. L. *The Underground City.* New York: Random, 1958. An American agent works with the French Resistance and after the war becomes the center of interest in the trial of an accused collaborator.

2724. Hunt, E. [Everette] Howard. *The Berlin Ending.* New York: Putnam's, 1973. CIA agent Thorpe tries to save the daughter of a treacherous West German foreign minister who is secretly in league with the Russians.

The son of a New York attorney, Howard Hunt served in the covert action arm of the Central Intelligence Agency for twenty-one years prior to his retirement in 1970. During that time he was assigned to Europe, the Far East, and Latin America, where at one time in the early 1950s he headed Covert Action in Mexico. One of his agents was William F. Buckley, Jr. Hunt was involved in both the CIA's 1954 success in Guatemala and its 1961 fiasco, the Bay of Pigs. After retiring from the agency, he became a Washington public relations executive and part-time consultant to White House Special Counsel Charles Colson who introduced him to G. Gordon Liddy. On Nixon's orders they recruited the Cuban team that ransacked the office of Daniel Ellsberg's psychiatrist and broke into Democratic headquarters at the Watergate in 1972. Hunt pled guilty to Watergate charges, was imprisoned for thirty-three months and heavily fined. Since his release in 1977, Hunt has been lecturing and writing and has recently resided in Mexico.

E. Howard Hunt is an example of the intelligence officer who writes under a pseudonym because of CIA requirements. He chose several pseudonyms, the most noteworthy of which was David St. John. Drawing on his intelligence experiences, Hunt penned eight St. John titles during the 1960s, and currently has produced over forty espionage novels. (See Mr. Hunt's commentary in CRAFT NOTES.)

2725. ___. *Chinese Red*. New York: St. Martin's, 1992. Spy stories with a neuroscience twist.

2726. ___. *Diabolus*. By David St. John, pseud. New York: Weybright & Talley, 1971. Vacationing in the Caribbean, CIA agent Peter Ward is involved in voodoo and a Red Chinese plot to take over the French islands of the West Indies.

2727. ___. *Festival for Spies*. By David St. John, pseud. New York: Signet, 1966. Agent Ward foils an insidious plot to bring Cambodia into the Red Chinese orbit.

2728. ___. *The Gaza Intercept*. Briarcliff Manor, NY: Stein & Day, 1981. [*Hazardous Duty*. London: Muller, 1966]. When Arab terrorists steal a US neutron warhead CIA and Mossad combine to prevent the destruction of Israel.

2729. ___. *Give Us This Day*. By David St. John, pseud. Fort Wayne, IN: Arlington, 1973. Hunt's personal memoirs of the CIA's Bay of Pigs operation. P

2730. ___. *The Goering Treasure*. By Gordon Davis, pseud. New York: Zebra, 1980. Two enterprising pimps from Berlin vie for Goering's massive pile of stolen loot with the Allies and *Der Spinne*—high-ranking Nazis who plan to survive the war and plan for the future of the cause. P

2731. ___. *The Hargrave Deception*. Briarcliff Manor, NY: Stein & Day, 1980. After agreeing to meet a former top US intelligence chief who had defected to the Russians, agent Morgan enters the car with the man Hargrave, a driver, and an escort—and is the only one to merge alive.

2732. ___. *The Judas Hour.* By David St. John, pseud. New York: Fawcett, 1951. CIA agent Jake Webb moves from Munich to Prague to assist a high Czech official who wants to defect. *P*

2733. ___. *The Mongol Mask.* By David St. John, pseud. New York: Weybright & Talley, 1968. The CIA has no reliable data on China's only missile base and Ward is sent to Mongolia to obtain it.

2734. ___. *Murder in State.* New York: St. Martin's, 1990. A buffoonish Washington, DC lawyer, retired from the State Department, gets kidnapped by the KGB and nearly triggers a nuclear confrontation.

2735. ___. *Murder on Her Mind.* By Robert Dietrich, pseud. New York: Dell, 1960. Hunt wrote a number of detective stories under this pseudonym. In this outing, Washington Private Eye Steve Bentley becomes involved with the problems of an exiled South American government leader. *P*

2736. ___. *On Hazardous Duty.* By David St. John, pseud. New York: Signet, 1965. [*Hazardous Duty.* By David St. John, pseud. London: Muller, 1966]. Two men's careers are at stake—dedicated CIA agent Peter Ward and a top Soviet scientist on the verge of defecting. *P*

2737. ___. *One of Our Agents Is Missing.* By David St. John, pseud. New York: Signet, 1967. Ward goes to Tokyo to investigate the disappearance of a top American spy and the ensuing manhunt leads him to the biggest sell-out in history.

2738. ___. *Return from Vorkuta.* By David St. John, pseud. New York: Signet, 1965. Agent Ward travels to Spain to quash a KGB plot to put a Russian imposter on that country's throne.

2739. ___. *The Sorcerers.* By David St. John, pseud. New York: Weybright & Talley, 1970. A Russian attempt to spread Communism by corrupting Black African students is thwarted by Ward's quick action.

2740. ___. *The Towers of Silence.* By David St. John, pseud. New York: Signet, 1966. Agent Ward is ordered to block a plot which would attract India into the Soviet sphere of influence. *P*

2741. ___. *Undercover: Memoirs of an American Secret Agent.* New York: Putnam/Berkley, 1974. Hunt's autobiography. Includes his career with the CIA.

2742. ___. *The Venus Probe.* By David St. John, pseud. New York: Signet, 1966. Ward sets out on a world-wide manhunt to find the thread which links the disappearances of seven internationally known scientists involved in space science research. *P*

2743. ___. *Whisper Her Name.* New York: Fawcett, 1952. A former agent is in Castro's Cuba seeking a pretty girl who has disappeared and a shipload of Czech farm implements which have turned out to be advanced machine guns. *P* Several more:

2744. ___. *The Black Yacht.* New York: Jove, 1982. *P*

2745. ___. *Bloody Bastogne.* New York: Bantam, 1981. The eighth book in a series called *The Sergeant.*

2746. ___. *Body Count.* New York: St. Martin's, 1992.

2747. ___. *The Counterfeit Kill.* New York: Pinnacle, 1975. Originally published by Fawcett, 1963 under Gordon Davis pseudonym.

2748. ___. *The Coven.* By David St. John, pseud. New York: Weybright & Talley, 1972.

2749. ___. *Cozumel.* Briarcliff Manor, NY: Stein & Day, 1985.

2750. ___. *Doom River.* New York: Bantam, 1981. Another in the *Sergeant* series.

2751. ___. *Guadalajara.* Chelsea, MI: Scarborough, 1990.

2752. ___. *Hammerhead.* New York: Bantam, 1982. *The Sergeant* No. 9.

2753. ___. *The Kremlin Conspiracy.* Briarcliff Manor, NY: Stein & Day, 1985.

2754. ___. *Mazatlan.* New York: Fine, 1993.

2755. Hunter, Evan. *The Sentries.* By Ed McBain, pseud. New York: Simon & Schuster, 1965. Right-wing extremists develop an almost fool-proof plan to force America's hand in the Cold War.

2756. Hunter, Jack D. *The Expendable Spy.* New York: Dutton, 1965. An agent is sent on a desperate mission knowing that, should he fail, his presence will not be missed.

2757. ___. *Florida Is Closed Today.* New York: Leisure, 1982. A military convoy en route to its West German base is hit by terrorists who steal a nuclear bomb; what the terrorists don't know is that, unless the fuse is adjusted every two weeks, this doomsday bomb automatically triggers. *P*

2758. ___. *One of Us Works for Them.* New York: Dutton, 1967. One night a US Army agent discovers a leak in his outfit in Heidelberg and is assigned to plug it by framing a fellow officer.

2759. ___. *Spies, Inc.* New York: Dutton, 1969. A tale of industrial espionage which starts off in a small chemical company in Pennsylvania and spreads as spies work their way into larger plants in Delaware and Maryland.

2760. ___. *The Terror Alliance.* New York: Leisure, 1979. CIA agent Roger Wagner has ten days in which to find a group of terrorists plotting the death of the US President. *P*

2761. ___. *The Tin Cravat.* New York: Time, 1981. A defector who has obtained stature within the OSS, Bruno Stachel is sent back into Germany in early 1945 to thwart Nazi plans for last-ditch guerrilla warfare. A few more:

2762. ___. *The Potsdam Bluff.* New York: TOR, 1992.

2763. ___. *Sweeney's Run.* New York: TOR, 1992.

2764. ___. *Talespin.* New York: TOR, 1991. *P*

2765. Hunter, Robin. *The Fourth Angel.* New York: Arbor, 1984. Two hundred passengers are slaughtered inside a burning airliner at the airport in Athens, including the wife and young daughters of Simon Quarry, a British publisher. He vows revenge and tracks the terrorists across Europe. Two more:

2766. ___. *The London Connection.* New York: Morrow, 1990.

2767. ___. *Quarry's Contract*. New York: Morrow, 1989.

2768. Hunter, Stephen. *The Day Before Midnight*. New York: Bantam, 1989. The countdown to WW III begins at an MX missile silo on a hilltop in Maryland. Shock troops, *spetznaz*, led by a charismatic Russian general have captured the site but failed to secure the launch key in time. Opposing them: a tough Delta Force colonel named Dick Puller (no pun), the compound's brilliant architect and wargames analyst Dr. Peter Thiokel, an FBI man, a convict, a Vietnam vet, and a Vietnamese refugee (herself a "tunnel rat"), and assorted National Guardsmen.

2769. ___. *The Master Sniper*. New York: Morrow, 1980. A German assassin ordered to kill one last time before the collapse of the Third Reich is pursued to a final confrontation by an unshakable American OSS officer.

2770. ___. *Point of Impact*. New York: Bantam, 1993. Bobby Lee Swagger of Blue Eye, Arkansas was known in Vietnam as "Bob the Nailer" for his 87 kills; He is recruited by a musterious company known as RamDyne Security, with CIA ties, for one more hit for his country—too late he learns that he is, as Oswald once said, just a patsy.

2771. ___. *The Spanish Gambit*. New York: Crown, 1985. David Sampson, an Etonian, is spying on the British Secret Service.

2772. ___. *The Second Saladin*. New York: Morrow, 1982. A secret code ("Fetch the shoe that fits") known only to Paul Chardy is finally broken by Miles Lanahan. Another espionage thriller is:

2773. ___. *Target*. New York: Warner, 1985.

2774. Hurd, Douglas. *Vote to Kill*. London: Collins, 1975. SIS agents become involved in an Irish campaign to get British troops out of Ulster.

Rt. Hon. Douglas Hurd, MP (for mid-Oxfordshire) has held a number of prestigious positions for his Conservative Party: private secretary to Prime Minister Heath, Home Secretary (1985), and Secretary of State for Foreign Affairs.

2775. ___ and Andrew Osmond. *Scotch on the Rocks*. London: Collins, 1971. An outbreak of revolutionary Scottish nationalism must be put down by agents of MI-5.

2776. ___. *The Smile on the Face of the Tiger*. New York: Macmillan, 1970. When the Red Chinese place an ultimatum on the future of Hong Kong, agents of SIS are sent in to defuse it and its originator, Communist official Chiang Li-shih. Five other Hurd novels are:

2777. ___ and Stephen Lamport. *Palace of Enchantments*. London: Hodder & Stoughton, 1985.

2778. ___ and Andrew Osmond. *Send Him Victorious*. New York: Collins, 1968.

2779. ___. *Truth Game*. New York: Collins, 1972.

2780. ___. *War without Frontiers*. London: Hodder & Stoughton, 1982.

2781. Hurwood, Bernhardt J. *The Man from TOMCAT: The Dirty Rotten Depriving Ray*. By Mallory T. Knight, pseud. New York: Award, 1968. From Scandinavia, the world's worst MOM-ZA launches his most fiendish scheme—to make sex impossible throughout the Western world! Agent Timothy O'Shane is a hapless victim of the dread force which he alone can destroy. *P*
       This paperback series about Tim O'Shane, agent of TOMCAT [Tactical Operations Master Counterintelligence Assault Team], is similar in content—and intent—to Rod Gray's The Lady from LUST series.

2782. ___. *The Man from TOMCAT: The Dozen Deadly Dragons of Joy*. By Mallory T. Knight, pseud. New York: Award, 1968. O'Shane prowls the secret alleyways of the world to tangle with twelve brainwashed beauties who can make men sterile! *P*

2783. ___. *The Man from TOMCAT: The Million Missing Maidens*. By Mallory T. Knight, pseud. New York: Award, 1968. To prevent a GRAVE international incident by a wild orgiastic cult, Agent O'Shane dutifully fights for peace by deflowering every virgin he can find. *P*

2784. ___. *The Man from TOMCAT: The Terrible Ten*. By Mallory T. Knight, pseud. New York: Award, 1968. Nothing can stop the power-mad GHOSTS from taking over the country, except Tim O'Shane, who must follow a trail which leads from dalliance to disaster. *P*

2785. ___. *The Man from TOMCAT: Tsimmis in Tangier*. By Mallory T. Knight, pseud. New York: Award, 1968. The arch fiend Merdalor sets out to conquer the world while Agent O'Shane is waylaid by the fleshpots of Casbah! *P* One more:

2786. ___. *The Man from TOMCAT: The Malignant Metaphysical Menace.* By Mallory T. Knight, pseud. New York: Award, 1968. *P*

2787. Hyde, Anthony. *China Lake.* New York: Knopf, 1992. A retired intelligence officer and a brilliant physicist whose career was shattered by accusations of spying are forced to flee Europe and run for their lives because of a murky secret that culminates in a chase across the Mojave Desert to China Lake, site of the ultrasecret US Naval Weapons Center.

2788. ___. *The Red Fox.* New York: Random: 1985. Robert Thorne wants to help May Brightman find her father, a millionaire fur dealer. Thorne's search takes him from Paris to Russia, a country that Harry Brightman had once spied for. Hyde and his brother Christopher wrote *Locksley* (New York: St. Martin's, 1983 *H HI*) under the joint pseudonym Nicholas Chase.

2789. Hyde, Christopher. *Hard Target.* New York: Morrow, 1991. An FBI man joins forces with an unlikely ally, a brilliant Soviet GRU agent, to stop an assassination of the President and Vice President.

2790. Hyland, Henry S. *Green Grow the Tresses-O.* Indianapolis: Bobbs-Merrill, 1959. A spy spoof involving the boys from MI-5 who are seeking the recovery of a missing secret formula. *H*

2791. ___. *Top Bloody Secret.* Indianapolis: Bobbs-Merrill, 1969. As the result of the first murder in the House of Commons since 1812 and the loss of vital atomic secrets, British agents are sent forth on a dangerous chase after the perpetrators which leads through Belgium, Germany, Greece, and Turkey.

2792. Hyman, Tom. *Prussian Blue.* New York: Signet, 1992. A journalist doing an unauthorized biography of the CIA Director comes under the murderous scrutiny of the Director's personal network called Night Watch. *P*

2793. ___. *Seven Days to Petrograd.* New York: Viking, 1988. Agent Harry Bauer has an assignment from Winston Churchill. The year is 1917 and the German government has conceived a scheme to knock Russia out of the war before America gets into it: Bauer is chosen to infiltrate a group of revolutionaries whose leader is about to embark on a fateful train ride from Zurich—Lenin, of course.

2794. Hyman, Vernon T. *Giant Killer.* New York: Marek, 1981. Unlike the book delivered by the hero in Brian Garfield's *Hopscotch*, the manuscript memoirs of an ex-CIA bigwig are found by the publisher in this tale to be less-than-exciting. In an effort to "spice them up," editor Jay Thompson farms them out to political correspondent Harriet Mitchell—and about that time the author is found dead and Thompson and Mitchell are drawn into a secret power plot codenamed "Zodiac."

2795. Hynd, Noel. *False Flags.* New York: Dial, 1979. Six small silicon chips taken from a US intelligence agency computer show up blank when they are located in the London flat of a Soviet diplomat.

2796. ___ and Christopher Creighton. *The Kruschev Objective.* Garden City, NY: Doubleday, 1987. A "true" spy story, the novel is based on two mutually occurring historical episodes that produced a scandal known as the "Crabbe Affair" that has not to this day been satisfactorily explained. In 1956 Party Chairman Kruschev and Politburo President Bulganin arrived in Portsmouth, England for a much-heralded visit. But when a Navy frogman, Commander Lionel Crabbe (Ret.) was caught spying on the war vessels of the Russians, an international incident was provoked. (Crabbe later turned up dead under mysterious circumstances.) Creighton was privy to information from no less a source than the Admiral of the Fleet, and used his knowledge to tell the story of how this incident dovetailed with others even more violent to bring the West into a potential nuclear confrontation with the Soviets.

2797. ___. *Revenge.* New York: Dial, 1976. Richard Silva finds his arch enemy who had tortured him in Vietnam and begins to track him through Paris—not knowing that the killer is waiting for him.

2798. ___. *The Sandler Inquiry.* New York: Dial, 1977. A master forger who flooded the British Exchequer with pound notes during World War II is turned by the Russians for a similar venture against the West.

2799. ___. *Truman's Spy.* New York: Zebra, 1990. The FBI's Tom Buchanan begins a routine investigation of a powerful Philadelphia banking family and ends up uncovering a mole within the Truman Presidency. Others:

2800. ___. *Flowers from Berlin.* New York: Star, 1986.

2801. ___. *Zigzag.* New York: Zebra, 1992. *P*

I

2802. Iams, Jack. *Into Thin Air*. New York: Morrow, 1952. An official of the Voice of America is drawn into a Communist espionage plot. *

2803. Ignatius, David. *Agents of Innocence*. New York: Norton, 1987. CIA's Tom Rogers is stationed in perennial hot-spot Beirut and is assigned to infiltrate the PLO after its expulsion from Jordan in 1970. The other "agent of innocence" is a young Fatah Palestinian who teams up with Rogers.

2804. ___. *Siro*. New York: Farrar, 1991. Anna Barnes is bored with her profession as an historian of the Ottoman Empire, so she joins the CIA and in various Third-World hot spots between the years of the fall of the Shah of Iran and the Soviet invasion of Afghanistan, she acquires first-hand experience of how, between them, the CIA and the KGB make history.

2805. Iles, Greg. *Spandau Phoenix*. New York: Dutton, 1993. Deputy Führer's bizarre flight to England in 1941 is the basis for this tale about Prisoner No. 7 behind Spandau prison walls; however, police sergeant Hans Apfel discovers papers hidden behind after Hess's death in 1987 and concludes that Hess's mad flight belies the boldest move Hitler made—one that will rock Germany, the Soviet Union even in its collapse, and most especially, an Israel fated for destruction.

2806. Ing, Dean. *Butcher Bird*. New York: TOR, 1993. Former research aerospace engineer Ing details a suspense adventure about a high-tech terminator known as "Butcher Bird," a nuclear-powered, flying death machine in the hands of the fanatical ruler of Syria and which is now targeting its enemies in America.

2807. ___. *The Nemesis Mission*. New York: St. Martin's, 1990. The Nemesis is a solar-powered plane which will get its first real test against druglord Simon Torres, who has plans to scuttle off with a plane full of hostages, and $1 billion, from Las Vegas to Mexico.

2808. ___. *The Ransom of Black Stealth One*. New York: St. Martin's, 1989. A hijacker, who also happens to be the aircraft's designer, gets his hands on the super-secret Black Stealth One fighter—and a beautiful hostage—and triggers an all-out manhunt by the KGB, CIA, GRU, and NSA.

2809. ___. *Soft Targets*. New York: Ace 1980. PLO terrorist Hakim Arif holds America hostage to his demands following a deadly example given the title

"The Colorado Incident." *P* Ing's prolific writing includes a mix of science fiction, fact, and espionage thriller:

2810. ___. *Anasazi.* New York: Ace, 1980. *P*

2811. ___. *The Big Lifters.* New York: St. Martin's, 1988.

2812. ___. *Blood of Eagles.* New York: TOR, 1988.

2813. ___. *Cathouse.* New York: Baen, 1990. *P*

2814. ___. *Firefight 2000.* New York: Baen, 1987. *P*

2815. ___. *Single Combat.* New York: TOR, 1983. *P*

2816. ___. *Wild Country.* New York: TOR, 1985. *P*

Innes, Hammond, pseud. *See* Hammond-Innes, Ralph

Innes, Michael, pseud. *See* Stewart, John I. M.

2817. Irving, Clifford. *The Thirty-Eighth Floor.* New York: McGraw-Hill, 1965. The successful running of the UN suddenly falls upon the shoulders of an American Black. All John Burden has to do to be successful is to follow his conscience, avoid enemy agents, and tread carefully around international complications. Unfortunately, his race, various intrigues, and his Communist Chinese mistress all manage to gum up the works for him.

2818. ___ and Herbert Burkholz. *The Death Freak.* New York: Summit, 1978. Coincidentally, the top assassins of the KGB and CIA are planning to retire; first, however, they must eliminate their sectional colleagues, knowing that if they do not, they will not survive.

2819. Irving, Clive. *Axis.* New York: Atheneum, 1980. Just before World War II a group of Nazi sympathizers, noblemen and aristocrats, meet in Lady Astor's castle to settle upon Britain's fate in the event of conflict.

2820. Irwin, Robert. *The Mysteries of Algiers.* Harmondsworth, Eng.: Viking, 1988. Phillipe Roussel's job in 1959 North Africa is to interrogate resistance fighters, but when cohort and lover Chantal denounces him as a double agent to authorities, he has to make a run for his life. An early novel:

2821. ___. *The Arabian Nightmare*. London: Daedalus, 1983.

2822. Isaacs, Susan. *Shining Through*. New York: Ballantine, 1989. Follows the path of a woman from secretary to boss's wife to spy in Nazi Germany.

2823. Ison, Graham. *Confirm or Deny*. New York: St. Martin's, 1990. Penned by a retired detective chief superintendent of Scotland Yard; Special Branch detective John Gaffney is given the assignment to track the mole in MI-5 when two highly sensitive operations fail. Another:

2824. ___. *The Home Secretary Will See You Now*. New York: St. Martin's, 1990.

J

2825. Jackman, Stuart. *Sandcatcher*. New York: Atheneum, 1980. Four SAS commandos are sent to Saudi Arabia in 1944 to determine whether a marauding band of bedouins are the prelude to a Moslem Holy War—sponsored by the Germans—against the Allies.

Jacks, Oliver, pseud. *See* Gandley, Kenneth Royce

2826. Jackson, Blyden. *Operation Burning Candle*. New York: Viking, 1973. A Black ex-Army officer builds a street gang into an elite corps which will be employed to sabotage a presidential convention in New York City and kill a group of racist Southern senators.

2827. Jackson, James. *Dzerzhinsky Square*. London: Severn, 1986. Grigory Nikolayevich Malmudov is captured by the Germans during WW II; at his release, fearful of being executed as a collaborator if he returns to Russia, he accepts an offer of a new identity and papers from the Americans if he will be their spy.

2828. Jackson, Jon J. *The Blind Pig*. New York: Random, 1979. The hijacking of arms from a train wreck involves Detective Sergeant Mulheisen with the FBI and Cuban revolutionaries.

2829. Jacobs, Joseph. *Blood and Water*. By Charles Humana, pseud. New York: Random, 1960. To keep outsiders out of the Promised Land, Jewish terrorists threaten the life of an engineer they are holding hostage in Israel.

Jacobs, T. C. H., pseud. *See* Pendower, Jacques

2830. Jahn, Michael. *The Six Million Dollar Man: Wine, Women, and War.* New York: Warner, 1975. Tied into the popular TV series, which was in turned based on the "Cyborg" titles of Martin Caidin. Steve Austin is sent to the Bahamas to uncover a cache of stolen missiles. *P*

2831. James, Colin. *Sleepers Can Kill.* By Simon Jay, pseud. Garden City, NY: Doubleday, 1968. Mike Conners of the undercover New Zealand intelligence agency known as "the Fisheries" must recover a stolen secret laser weapon before the Communists can employ it.

2832. James, Donald. *The Fall of the Russian Empire.* New York: Putnam's, 1982. Concatenation of events leading to the collapse of the Soviet Union.

2833. James, John. *Seventeen of Leyden: A Frolic through This Vale of Tears.* New York: St. Martin's, 1972. An historical romp through the court of James II from the viewpoint of Dr. Richard Oliver Wormset, physician and spy. One more:

2834. ___. *Talleyman.* London: Gollancz, 1986.

2835. James, Leigh. *The Capitol Hill Affair.* New York: Weybright & Talley, 1969. Ernie Sessens of the CIA must employ the services of reporter Tony Baylor to find out how and why important secrets are oozing out of the US Congress.

2836. ___. *The Chameleon File.* New York: Weybright & Talley, 1969. A deadly chase through the Cuban underworld involves smalltime adventurer Jack Wilson in a network of espionage and murder.

2837. ___. *The Push-Button Spy.* Englewood Cliffs, NJ: Prentice-Hall, 1970. A CIA operative is deliberately "brainwashed" by his superiors to believe he is operating for the Russians, but fights to prevent his becoming an automaton—or push-button spy.

2838. ___. *Triple Mirror.* New York: Mason & Lipscomb, 1973. CIA agents must untangle a case of exchanged identities between a Texas scientist bent on selling a super secret and a Soviet diplomat planning to defect.

2839. Jameson, Storm. *Before the Crossing.* New York: Macmillan, 1947. Writer-agent David Penn seeks the murderer of his friend in 1939 London—a nasty who turns out to be a spy seeking to assist Hitler's projected invasion of Great Britain. *

2840. Jamieson, Ian R. *Triple "O" Seven.* New York: Mysterious, 1990. OO7's boy is a flop at espionage, but the lad gets another opportunity to follow in his famous father's footsteps when the inventor of a secret gas insists that he'll pass the gas to one person only: 0007.

Jardine, Warwick, pseud. *See* Warwick, Francis A.

Jay, Charlotte, pseud. *See* Jay, Geraldine

2841. Jay, Geraldine. *Arms for Adonis.* By Charlotte Jay, pseud. New York: Harper, 1961. A story of espionage-intrigue in the Arab world as Sarah, who witnesses a bomb exploding on a Beirut street, is immediately picked up by a handsome stranger who leads her through various thrilling episodes of derring-do.

Jay, Simon, pseud. *See* James, Colin

2842. Jeffries, Graham M. *The "D" Notice.* By Bruce Graeme, pseud. London: Hutchinson, 1974. Detective Sergeant Roger Mather becomes involved with a security fiasco and the efforts of the British intelligence services to keep it out of the newspapers through the process known in Britain as "the D Notice."
   Jeffries wrote a number of espionage-related detective yarns both before and after World War II (see Part 1). Two other tales of interest here, neither of which were published in America, are:

2843. ___. *Holiday for a Spy.* By Bruce Graeme, pseud. London: Hutchinson, 1963.

2844. ___. *Much Ado about Something.* By Bruce Graeme, pseud. London: Hutchinson, 1967.

2845. Jeffries, Roderic. *A Man Condemned.* By Peter Alding, pseud. Inspector Fusil juggles various interlocking assignments, including guarding an irascible Iranian, investigating a murder-robbery, and hunting for a terrorist.

2846. Jenkins, Geoffrey. *A Grue of Ice.* New York: Putnam's, 1962. A naval officer is kidnapped because he alone knows the location of an important secret island.

2847. ___. *Hunter-Killer.* New York: Putnam's, 1967. An astronaut turned American Vice President and an agent of British Naval Intelligence collaborate to launch an Anglo-American missile, despite opposition from a hunter-killer task force of the US Seventh Fleet.

2848. ___. *The River of Diamonds.* New York: Viking, 1964. In South Africa, a mining company surveyor escapes plotters seeking large diamond holdings. Three others:

2849. ___. *In Harm's Way.* London: Collins, 1986.

2850. ___. *A Twist of Sand.* New York: Viking, 1960.

2851. ___. *The Watering Place of Good Peace.* London: Collins, 1960.

2852. Jepson, Selwyn. *The Assassin.* Philadelphia: Lippincott, 1957. Ex-Major John Farr is in the top secret British Secret Service. His tranquility as a broker (his cover) is broken by murder, espionage, embezzlement, stock-manipulation, and adultery all related to one important, but difficult intelligence caper.

2853. ___. *A Noise in the Night.* Philadelphia: Lippincott, 1957. A mild-mannered Suffolk England bank manager sets out merely to save his daughter from marrying "the wrong man" and ends up saving civilization from World War III as plotted by Arab extremists.

2854. John, Hendrix. *The Carnellian Circle.* New York: Atheneum, 1975. A high-powered Los Angeles law firm fronting for the CIA sends tough ex-Marine John Hammond to investigate the causes behind the "accidental deaths" of right-wing political figures, thus allowing him to become the prime target of a KGB hit team.

2855. John, Owen. *Dead on Time.* New York: Dutton, 1969. What happens when aging Israeli leader Yehuda ben David sets out to sign a peace treaty with the Arabs—a signature not wanted by or profitable to all?

2856. ___. *The Disinformer.* New York: Dutton, 1967. CIA agent Charles Mason and SIS operative Haggai Golan must combine forces to stop the Department of Disinformatsiya from making its final thrust at "the Company"—a thrust which could humiliate America before the entire world.

2857. ___. *Sabotage.* New York: Dutton, 1973. A Communist saboteur, passing as a contractor's technician, infiltrates the defenses of a nuclear power plant in Wales and plants a bomb in a tank of fuel on the conveyor that feeds the reactor. In London, MI-5 learns this fellow is on the loose and sends some people to collar him.

2858. ___. *The Shadow in the Sea.* New York: Dutton, 1972. An unidentified submarine is lurking off the British coast awaiting a shipment to Israel scheduled to be made aboard the freighter *Nijmegen.* A half-Russian secret agent is sent to the Soviet Union to find out what's up—or rather, what is going down.

2859. ___. *Thirty Days Hath September.* New York: Dutton, 1967. Haggai Godin is the spy hero of this series of seven novels, which went into paperback editions in England (NEL) and America (Paperback).

2860. Johnson, James L. *A Piece of the Moon Is Missing.* Philadelphia: Lippincott, 1974. Operator Sebastian is pitted against ruthless enemy agents and the Arctic perils of wolves, frostbite, and snow blindness in an effort to recover a vital package. Earlier spy thrillers featuring the cloak-and-dagger spy with the collar:

2861. ___. *Code Name Sebastian.* Philadelphia: Lippincott, 1967.

2862. ___. *A Handful of Dominoes.* Philadelphia: Lippincott, 1970.

2863. ___. *The Nine Lives of Alphonse.* Philadelphia: Lippincott, 1970.

2864. Johnson, Stanley. *The Doomsday Deposit.* New York: Dutton, 1980. When a US spy satellite shows a big plutonium deposit in a river on the Russo-Chinese border, plans are laid to explode an A-bomb which will rechannel the tributary into Chinese territory and thus, conceivably, into American hands.

2865. ___. *Presidential Plot.* New York: Paperback, 1969. A fantastic scheme is engineered by the CIA and a Black Power group to remove the President of the United States from the scene during a crucial period of peace negotiations. *P*

2866. Johnson, Uwe. *Speculations About Jakob.* Trans. from the German. New York: Grove, 1963. An East German railway worker falls in love with a NATO agent. The Intelligence bosses of the People's Republic are (naturally) upset about this and suspecting him of wanting to defect and her of some odious mission, order their men out to keep a close watch.

2867. Johnson, William. *The Zero Factor.* New York: Pocket, 1980. A group of Cuban expatriates hire professional assassin LeBombardier to murder a US President who has instigated a crack-down on their anti-Castro activities. *P*

2868. Johnston, Ronald. *The Stowaway.* New York: Harcourt, 1966. A stowaway may be a missing Soviet scientist whose secret weapon can destroy the world.

2869. Johnston, William. *Get Smart.* New York: Signet, 1965. The bumbling agent Maxwell Smart and his female helper, No. 99, were a comedy stalwart of American TV during the James Bond era. Smart's apology, "Sorry About That, Chief," became almost as popular as the series. In this outing, Smart and No. 99 are assigned to keep a special robot out of enemy hands. Additional titles by this author based on the series are: *PHy*

2870. ___. *Get Smart: And Loving It.* New York: Signet, 1967. *PHy*

2871. ___. *Get Smart: Max Smart and the Perilous Pellets.* New York: Signet, 1966. *y*

2872. ___. *Get Smart: Max Smart Loses Control.* New York: Signet, 1968. *PHy*

2873. ___. *Get Smart: Max Smart, the Spy Who Went Out to the Cold.* New York: Signet, 1968. *PHy*

2874. ___. *Get Smart: Missed by That Much!* New York: Signet, 1967. *PHy*

2875. ___. *Get Smart: Once Again.* New York: Signet, 1966. *PHy*

2876. ___. *Get Smart: Sorry Chief!* New York: Signet, 1966. *PHy*

2877. Jones, Bradford. *Layers of Deceit.* Indianapolis: Bobbs-Merrill, 1970. Planning his retirement, MI-5 agent Andrew Ferguson is sent on one last case—to check out Britain's neo-Nazi group, the National Democratic Party.

Jones, Bradshaw, pseud. *See* Bradshaw-Jones, Malcolm H.

2878. Jones, Dennis. *Barbarossa Red*. Boston: Little, 1985. Just as a new Soviet-American arms limitation treaty is about to be signed in Vienna in 1989, West Germany's chancellor spurns it and precipitates a Soviet invasion of Europe. The scene shifts between Moscow, the two Germanys, and the corridors of power in Washington as war escalates.

2879. ___. *Concerto*. New York: St. Martin's, 1990. Mikhail Gorbachev is kidnapped by Polish nationalists while visiting the US to make a UN speech. CIA's Sean Brennan has orders to find him, fast, before a nuclear war erupts.

2880. ___. *Winter Palace*. Boston: Little, 1988. In the final decade of this century, Soviet leadership announces that all Russian Jews will be permitted to leave the country; however, Sam Cole, ex-CIA agent, has discovered what this really means: "Winter Palace" is code for a new Holocaust—this time, in the Middle East. Two others:

2881. ___. *Rubicon One*. New York: Beaufort, 1983.

2882. ___. *Russian Spring*. New York: Beaufort, 1984.

2883. Jones, J. Sydney. *Time of the Wolf*. New York: Signet, 1990. A police detective and his lover, a concert pianist in 1942 Vienna, acquire stolen documents from Berlin revealing Hitler's plans; their goal is to get these top-secret papers to Switzerland before Wolf Hartmann, Nazi killer, tracks them down and eliminates them. *P*

2884. Jones, Peter. *Delivery*. New York: Crown, 1990. Terrorists hijack seven bombs from a nuclear convoy and plan to detonate them in different locations throughout the US.

2885. Jones, Philip. *The Fifth Defector*. London: Heinemann, 1967. A series of important scientists are leaving Britain and an intrepid agent of MI-5 is called upon to find out why.

2886. ___. *The Month of the Pearl*. New York: Holt, 1965. A battle of wits is described between a professional assassin and an SIS agent in Rome.

2887. Jones, Robert F. *Blood Tide*. Boston: Atlantic Monthly, 1990. A father and daughter sail to the Philippines in a complicated search for revenge for his ruined naval career.

2888. Jones, Tristan. *Dutch Treat.* Kansas City, MO: Sheed, Andrews & McMeel, 1979. Five British Commandos enter Amsterdam early in World War II and steal the Dutch crown jewels out from under the noses of their German captors.

2889. Jordan, David. *Nile Green.* Briarcliff Manor, NY: Stein & Day, 1974. Essentially a spy story, this tale concerns the twisting turns growing out of commercial rivalries between the British and the Russians over their development schemes in Egypt.

2890. Jordan, Len. *Operation Perfidia.* New York: Warner, 1975. Who is setting up an ex-CIA man fresh out of prison? *P*

2891. Joseph, Mark. *Typhoon.* New York: Simon & Schuster, 1991. *Typhoon* is one of six Typhoon-class supersubmarines built by the Soviets. A fanatic Soviet admiral, enraged that his country has dissolved, concocts a plot to blackmail the Russian government with the Typhoons offshore and threatening to use them, beginning with Tbilisi. Vice Admiral Stefan Zenko, a brilliant sub skipper, learns of the plot and takes one out to see to combat the rest of the Typhoons, if necessary. His first submarine technothriller:

2892. ___ . *To Kill the Potemkin.* New York: Fine, 1986. *P*

2893. Judd, Alan. *Tango.* New York: Summit, 1990. This farcical but incisively written novel centers around the dictatorship of a South American country in the hands of three baddies. An Englishman is drawn into the action because of his love for the figurehead-only dictator's mistress. *H* More:

2894. ___ . *A Breed of Heroes.* New York: Coward, 1981.

2895. ___ . *The Devil's Own Work.* Glasgow, Scotland: HarperCollins, 1991.

2896. ___ . *The Noonday Devil.* London: Hutchinson, 1987.

2897. ___ . *Short of Glory.* New York: Viking, 1985.

2898. Julitte, Pierre. *Block 26: Sabotage at Buchenwald.* Trans. from the French. Garden City, NY: Doubleday, 1971. Outside the infamous death camp where a number of French Resistance workers are housed, the Germans have a secret plant where several are employed. When they discover that the project is building components for the V-2 rocket, they plot to blow up "the factory." *

2899. Just, Ward. *Stringer.* Boston: Little, 1974. The last mission of a US civilian guerrilla is to destroy a North Vietnamese convoy in the mountains.

2900. Jute, André. *Eight Days in Washington.* London: Hale, 1986. Readers will be interested in the author's *Writing a Thriller* (New York: St. Martin's, 1987); it is his pronouncement on the techniques of the thriller/espionage craft. (See Mr. Jute's commentary in CRAFT NOTES.)

2901. ___. *Reverse Negative.* New York: Norton, 1975. An elderly Cambridge don is implicated as the Fourth Man; pretty soon, agents from American, British, Israeli, and Soviet intelligence services are trying to kill or capture him in a wild, escapade through half a dozen countries. Three others:

2902. ___. *Festival.* London: Hale, 1986.

2903. ___. *Sinkhole.* London: Secker & Warburg, 1982.

2904. ___. *The Zaharoff Commission.* New York: David & Charles, 1983.

K

2905. Kagley, Rudolf. *The Imposter.* By Kurt Steel, pseud. New York: Harcourt, 1942. Appointed director of US warplane production after Pearl Harbor, James Morgan must contend with Nazi agents and imitators out to close down his vital operation. *y

2906. Kalb, Marvin and Ted Koppel. *In the National Interest.* New York: Simon & Schuster, 1977. To withhold his story in the national interest or break it, thus endangering the life of a major political figure as well as the Middle East peace, is the quandary facing ace TV correspondent Darius Kane. The authors are both well-known to the newscasting industry.

2907. Kalme, Egils. *In the Shadow of Freedom.* New York: Manor, 1979. Latvian Legionnaires fight the Russians as guerrillas on the Eastern Front during World War II, but are forced to flee into the arms of the Americans in April 1945. *P*

2908. Kalish, Robert. *Bloodmoon.* New York: Avon, 1985. Series hero "Skipper" Gould uses his Vietnam fighting skills to combat domestic terrorism. *P*

2909. Kaminsky, Stuart M. *Black Knight in Red Square*. New York: Charter, 1984.   Porfiry Petrovich Rostnikov is a Moscow chief inspector whose assignment is to stop a terrorist organization called World Liberation led by a "dark-eyed woman," whose plans include blowing up crowded theaters and bombing Lenin's tomb.

2910. ___. *A Cold Red Sunrise*. New York: Scribner's, 1988. Inspector Porfiry Rostnikov has been ordered by Moscow to find out who killed a child and a high-ranking commissar.

2911. ___. *Death of a Russian Priest*. New York: Fawcett, 1992. A saintly priest is murdered, and an Arab oil minister's daughter disappears in Moscow—another assignment for MVD's "Washtub" (Inspector Rostnikov, senior weightlifting champ) and sidekicks Emil Karpo ("the Vampire"), "handsome" Sasha Tkach and new member of the team Elena Timofeyeva.

2912. ___. *The Howard Hughes Affair*. New York: St. Martin's, 1979. When in 1941 Howard Hughes, the nervous millionaire, discovers a spy at his dinner party, he hires a Los Angeles private eye to investigate the subject.

2913. ___. *The Man Who Walked Like a Bear*. New York: Scribner's, 1990. Moscow police Inspector Rostnikov and assistants Sasha Tkach and Emil Karpo are beset by incredible coincidences involving a huge, naked man muttering a tale of a "devil" in the factory, a mother who informs on her son's intent to kidnap a Politburo member, and the mysterious disappearance of Bus 43 from the streets of Moscow.

2914. ___. *Red Chameleon*. New York: Scribner's, 1985. Inspector Rostnikov is assigned a murder investigation of an old man who was killed in his bathtub by two men who take a brass candlestick after the murder. More Inspector Rostnikov mysteries:

2915. ___. *Death of a Dissident*. New York: Ivy, 1981. [*Rostnikov's Corpse*. London: Macmillan, 1981.]

2916. ___. *The Devil Met a Lady*. New York: Mysterious, 1993.

2917. ___. *A Fine Red Rain*. New York: Scribner's, 1987.

2918. ___. *Rostnikov's Vacation*. New York: Scribner's, 1991.

2919. Kane, Henry. *Conceal and Disguise.* By Anthony McCall, pseud. New York: Macmillan, 1967. Inspector McGregor is hired back by his old firm, the CIA, to evaluate a potential assassin.

2920. ___. *Holocaust.* By Anthony McCall, pseud. New York: Macmillan, 1967. The "Company" asks McGregor to do his utmost to prevent a mad scientist from starting mankind's last war.

2921. ___. *Laughter in the Alehouse.* By Anthony McCall, pseud. New York: Macmillan, 1968. A beautiful Israeli agent entices McGregor into a deadly Manhattan manhunt for a Nazi war criminal-at-large.

2922. ___. *Operation Delta.* By Anthony McCall, pseud. New York: Simon & Schuster, 1967. Tragedy strikes the four men responsible for a new missile project. Chris Adams, head of his own Adams Associates, must find the faceless enemy responsible for mucking up his firm's enterprise.

2923. ___. *The Tripoli Documents.* By Anthony McCall, pseud. New York: Simon & Schuster, 1976. The Mossad employs an Irish-American to eliminate a PLO "sleeper" posing as a psychology professor at Columbia University.

2924. Kanfer, Stefan. *Fear Itself.* New York: Putnam's, 1981. In 1943, OSS agent Carl Beirin must halt a plan by a crazed Jewish actor to assassinate FDR for his indifference to the plight of Holocaust victims.

2925. Kaplan, Andrew. *Dragonfire.* New York: Warner, 1988. In the dangerous Golden Triangle of Southeast Asia, lone American agent Sawyer's mission is to prevent another Vietnam. *P*

2926. ___. *Hour of the Assassins.* New York: Dell, 1980. A retired CIA agent in South America is called upon to stop Nazi war criminal Joseph Mengele's creation of a Fourth Reich. *P*

2927. ___. *War of the Raven.* New York: Simon & Schuster, 1989. Argentina in 1939 is a hotbed of political and sexual intrigue. The American intelligence community is as yet stillborn under FDR, but "Wild Bill" Donovan knows that someone with special skills is required to go down there or America could lose South America in the coming years to the Nazis. Another:

2928. ___. *Scorpion.* New York: Macmillan, 1985.

2929. Kaplan, Howard. *Bullets of Palestine*. Toronto: Worldwide, 1987. An Israeli agent and a former Palestinian terrorist team up to kill the world's most hated and feared assassin, Abu Nidal.

2930. ___. *The Chopin Express*. New York: Dutton, 1978. A California student caught smuggling Hebrew books into Russia becomes a pawn in a dangerous game between the KGB and the Israeli Mossad.

2931. ___. *The Damascus Affair*. New York: Dutton, 1977. To learn how much information a young agent spilled under torture to the Syrians, the Mossad sends veteran agent Ari ben-Sion on a dangerous mission into the enemy's capital.

2932. Karman, Max. *The Foxbat Spiral*. New York: Dell, 1980. Ex-CIA man Jay Hiller, given only a blurred photo of five men and the key word "foxbat," must locate and rescue the kidnapped US President. *P*

2933. Karp, Marvin A., ed. *The Spy in the Shadows*. New York: Popular, 1965. Two collections each containing eighteen short stories by such famous practitioners of the spy thriller genre as E. Phillips Oppenheim, W. Somerset Maugham, Manning Coles, pseud., and Geoffrey Household. *P* Another Karp work:

2934. ___. *Catch a Spy*. New York: Popular, 1965. *P*

2935. Kartun, Derek. *Beaver to Fox*. New York: St. Martin's, 1986. Series character Alfred Baum is introduced in Kartun's first espionage novel; he is a high-ranking official in French counterintelligence whose assignment here is to stop a terrorist campaign of random bombings in Paris.

2936. ___. *Flittermouse*. London: Century, 1984. When a French politician commits suicide in a London hotel, British Intelligence sends an agent to France to investigate; however, the deeper he goes into the politician's shady past, the greater the stonewalling he meets with in official quarters. Three others:

2937. ___. *The Courier*. New York: St. Martin's, 1985.

2938. ___. *The Defector*. London: Century, 1989.

2939. ___. *Megiddo*. New York: Walker, 1987.

2940. Katcher, Leo. *The Blind Cave*. New York: Viking, 1966. American agent Richard Landon leads his colleagues from various other intelligence agencies on a search for stolen plutonium; all the clues lead them to a little Adriatic island.

2941. ___. *Hot Pursuit*. New York: Atheneum, 1971. Seven mercenaries attack a Communist rebel camp on the Greco-Albanian border during the Greek Civil War of the late 1940s, in order to root out the terrorists who have been kidnapping children.

2942. Katkov, Norman. *The Judas Kiss*. New York: Signet, 1992. A woman in 1937 Vienna marries a Prussian aristocrat so that the man she loves can be given an exit visa from Hitler's terror against Jews; however, her husband betrays her, completely unaware that his wife is also a member of the Resistance. *P*

2943. Katz, Robert. *The Spoils of Ararat*. Boston: Houghton, 1978. Agent Tony McIntyre seeks to discover the reason behind a mysterious bulge on a tall mountain in the Middle East; his mission almost collapses when his long climb results in a chilling surprise.

2944. ___. *Ziggurat*. Boston: Houghton, 1977. Assisted by his secretary and a friendly CIA agent, Zack Roberts works to halt a terrorist plot which would have a homemade atomic bomb detonated at the North Pole.

2945. Katz, William. *Ghostflight*. New York: Dell, 1980. Fifty-five years after her disappearance, Amelia Earhart returns with the warning that Hitler is also alive and planning a comeback. *P*

2946. ___. *North Star Crusade*. New York: Putnam's, 1976. Several officers and crewmen aboard the US submarine *John Hay*, members of the right-wing North Star Society, take over the ship and sink a Soviet destroyer as their first step in a plan to cause a nuclear war that will rid the world of Communism.

2947. Kaufelt, David A. *Souvenir*. New York: Signet, 1983. In 1942 Paris Floy Devon is an American film actress who must flee the Nazis; unfortunately, her only hope of escaping to the Spanish border is to trust a Nazi collaborator, a man with his own agenda who once lusted for her. *P*

2948. Kauffman, Ray F. *Coconut Wireless*. New York: Macmillan, 1948. American mining engineer Bob Graydon is the hero of this spy thriller set in Malaya during the closing days of the World War II Japanese occupation. *

2949. Kearey, Charles. *The Last Plane from Uli.* New York: Holt, 1972. An English pilot runs a mercenary air force for a Texas oil millionaire who is trying to win concessions from Nigeria at the time of the Biafran succession.

2950. Keating, Henry R. F. *Inspector Ghote Caught in Meshes.* London: Collins, 1967. An astute Bombay detective is assigned to a mythical intelligence branch of the Indian government and is asked to look into an apparently routine murder, which turns out to have national security implications.

2951. Keeble, John. *Broken Ground.* New York: Harper & Row, 1988. A sinister multinational corporation recruits an engineer to build a prison in an isolated part of Oregon. One other:

2952. ___. *Yellowfish.* New York: Harper & Row, 1980.

2953. Keeley, Edmund. *The Imposter.* Garden City, NY: Doubleday, 1970. CIA agent Sam Kean leaves his love, goes to Greece where he is involved with Cypriot spies, reunites with his first girl after dallying with a second, and returns to America and an uncertain fate.

2954. Keene, Tom and Brian Haynes. *Spyship.* New York: Marek, 1980. Martin Taylor investigates the loss of an English fishing vessel off the coast of Norway and learns that the ship has been employed as a Soviet electronics snooper.

2955. Kelleher, Brian. *Storm Birds #3: The Gathering Storm.* New York: Signet, 1989. Technothriller set in the days of the Korean war when America's top test pilots take the F-86 Sabre into combat against the deadly MiG fighters. *P* Another in the "Storm Birds" series:

2956. ___. *Storm Birds #2: Thunder from Heaven.* New York: Signet, 1988. Test pilot and war hero Gil "Hurricane" Hughes tests the XF-86 Sabre, America's latest post-WW II jet fighter, over the New Mexico desert. *P*

2957. Keller, Beverly. *The Baghdad Defections.* Indianapolis: Bobbs-Merrill, 1973. A German scientist has devised the ultimate in biochemical warfare and the Arabs, having captured him, plan to use his knowledge to build a strong alliance of all the Moslem countries against Israel.

2958. Kelly, John. *The Wooden Wolf.* New York: Dutton, 1976. The Allies in November 1944 want to change the course of history in a single, final act:

the means is John Croft, an American pilot flying a British Mosquito who will track and bomb Reichsmarschall Göring's private train—with Hitler aboard.

2959. Kelly, Judith. *Diplomatic Incident.* Boston: Houghton, 1949. When a Russian peace party mission arrives in Washington, an American State Department agent falls in love with one of their important delegates. When America rejects the Soviet offer, she is returned to Russia for "processing." An excellent example of early Cold War intrigues in which not a kind thought can be spared for the Soviets. *y

2960. Kelly, Michael. *Assault.* New York: Harcourt, 1967. Four members of the British Special Operations Executive are parachuted into a field near Copenhagen with orders to assist the Danish resistance in destroying a nearby Nazi factory codenamed "Knightsbridge." *

Kelly, Patrick, pseud. *See* Allbeury, Ted

2961. Kemelman, Harry. *One Fine Day the Rabbi Bought a Cross.* New York: Morrow, 1987. Kemelman's David Small, rabbi and sleuth, takes an espionage thriller turn in this one when the rabbi, visiting Jerusalem, gets involved in the murder investigation of an American professor who was duped into delivering a letter to Druse freedom fighters containing information about a PLO arms cache.

2962. Kempley, Walter. *The Invaders.* New York: Saturday Review, 1976. Deserter Eddie Palmer's North Vietnamese captor plots attacks on American urban centers in retaliation for US air raids on Hanoi.

2963. Kendrick, Baynard. *Flight From a Firing Wall.* New York: Simon & Schuster, 1966. A Cuban refugee in Miami elects to make his way back into Castro's Cuba to rescue his wife from the secret police.

2964. ___. *The Odor of Violets.* Boston: Little, 1941. Detective Captain Duncan Maclain pursues Nazi agents bent on sabotage in the New York City area on the eve of America's entry into World War II. *

2965. Keneally, Thomas. *A Season in Purgatory.* New York: Harcourt, 1977. An English surgeon is parachuted into wartime Yugoslavia to treat wounded Partisans.

2966. Kenmore, Frank J. *The Jasmine Sloop.* New York: Pinnacle, 1988. Colin Smallpiece is an ex-intelligence man of rare skills, though only twenty-seven years of age, who must locate a missing US Senator who has vanished. *P* Two more:

2967. ___. *The Frankincense Trail*. New York: Pinnacle, 1989. *P*

2968. ___. *Southeast of Mandalay*. New York: Pinnacle, 1990. *P*

2969. Kennedy, Adam. *The Domino Principle*. By John Redgate, pseud. New York: Viking, 1975. An unnamed intelligence agency employs an ex-con as a political assassin in the United States to "liquidate" people embarrassing to the Federal government.

2970. ___. *The Domino Vendetta*. New York: Beaufort, 1984. A resourceful con is recruited while in prison by a mystery man for a hush-hush government agency to do an assassination job, and then he finds himself the hunted.

2971. ___. *The Killing Season*. By John Redgate, pseud. New York: Simon & Schuster, 1967. Examines the relationship between three US agents operating in East Berlin after one defects thinking that he has successfully eliminated the other two. Others:

2972. ___. *Debt of Honor*. New York: Delacorte, 1981.

2973. ___. *Somebody's Fool*. New York: Severn, 1992.

2974. Kennedy, William P. *The Himmler Equation*. New York: St. Martin's, 1989. Karl Anders is part of Germany's desperate team of scientists in 1944 working to perfect an atomic bomb; he also happens to be an American plant that Himmler has come to suspect.

Kenny, Stan, pseud. *See* Gigga, Kenneth

2975. Kenrick, Tony. *The Eighty-First*. New York: Signet, 1980. In the decades after World War II, a loyal Nazi soldier searches for a secret V-2 rocket launching site as agent Jimmy Pelham attempts to thwart his crazed plan to destroy London. *P*

2976. ___. *The Nighttime Guy*. New York: Morrow, 1979. Unable to see by day, Max Ellis is asked to participate in a CIA experiment in night vision and ends up finding himself pursued by enemy agents who want him dead or alive.

2977. ___. *Stealing Lillian*. New York: McKay, 1975. Employing a fake family made up of agents, US Immigration Service operatives plan to induce four terrorists into kidnapping and then apprehend the perpetrators as they pick up the ransom.

2978. ___. *A Tough One to Lose*. Indianapolis: Bobbs-Merrill, 1972. A poverty-stricken young lawyer races to find the secret landing place of a 747 airliner which was hijacked by a band of terrorists over San Francisco.

2979. Kenyon, Michael. *The Elgar Variation*. New York: Coward-McCann, 1981. An aristocratic murder suspect, who has threatened to release vital secrets to the press, becomes the target of an intensive manhunt by agents of the CIA and SIS.

2980. ___. *May You Die in Ireland*. New York: Morrow, 1965. Willie Foley is off to claim an ancestral home in the land of shamrocks, but unknown to him, his travel agency manages to sneak secret microdots into his luggage.

2981. Kenyon, Paul. *The Baroness: Black Gold*. New York: Pocket, 1975. While posing as an international model and head of a multimillion dollar cosmetic firm, the American-born Baroness, Penelope St. John-Orsini, is, in fact, a supersecret superagent ally known only to a few in the US government. Like Modesty Blaise, she responds to intelligence requests for that kind of last-ditch assistance which the boys and girls in the organized bureaus cannot provide. In this outing, she takes on the mysterious "Spoiler" organization, a firm devoted to turning the world's most precious commodity into an all-devouring instrument of death. *P*

2982. ___. *The Baroness: Diamonds Are for Dying*. New York: Pocket, 1974. The heroine of this single-year series gives the appearance of being simply another international playgirl. Those in the know appreciate, however, that she is a top adventurer-agent. In this outing, she becomes involved in a monstrous plot to divert diamonds from jewelers into the hands of a big-time nasty bent to destroying international peace. *P*

2983. ___. *The Baroness: The Ecstasy Connection*. New York: Pocket, 1974. The Baroness investigates the relationship between a national security problem and a ring of very beautiful women. *P*

2984. ___. *The Baroness: Flicker of Doom*. New York: Pocket, 1974. Don Alejandro, descendent of the original Spanish Inquisitor, along with computer genius Dr. Otto Funke, has a surefire plan for world domination using nothing more than a sophisticated camera. Can the Baroness thwart her deadly adversaries in the ultimate battle or is the world doomed to suffer blinding and horrible obliteration? *P*

2985. ___. *The Baroness: Hard-Core Murder*. New York: Pocket, 1974. A particularly evil villain is employing the porno business as a cover for murder and espionage and must be stopped by the Baroness. Three other titles are: *P*

2986. ___. *The Baroness: Death is a Ruby Light*. New York: Pocket 1974. *P*

2987. ___. *The Baroness: Operation Doomsday*. New York: Pocket, 1974. *P*

2988. ___. *The Baroness: Sonic Slave*. New York: Pocket, 1974. *P*

2989. Kern, John. *The Falstaff Cross*. New York: Lynx, 1988. Based on the covert CIA program that went by the acronym *Mknaomi*, which involved the stockpiling of toxins and which were ordered destroyed by President Nixon in 1970. A KGB-backed terrorist known as Falstaff is after a biochemical bomb of concentrated anthrax at the bottom of the Irish Sea. *P*

2990. Kessel, Joseph. *The Army of Shadows*. Trans. from the French. New York: Knopf, 1944. Another wartime view of the heroism displayed by resistance fighters of the French Maquis against the German oppressor. *

2991. Kiefer, Warren. *The Kidnappers*. New York: Harper & Row, 1977. An old tailor tries to sell his knowledge of Argentine political kidnappings and revolutionary movements to agents of both the CIA and ODESSA.

2992. ___. *The Lingala Code*. New York: Random, 1972. Michael Vernon, the CIA's resident trouble-shooter in Leopoldville, the Congo, in the 1960s, was a busy man, but never more active than when he tried to solve the murder of his ex-Air Force buddy.

2993. ___. *The Perpignon Exchange*. New York: Fine, 1990. A black-humored *tour de force* about an Arab who is mistaken for a terrorist and befriended by a truly evil terrorist leader. The quick-witted protagonist comes up with a scheme that will extricate him from his problems.

2994. Kielland, Axel. *Dangerous Honeymoon.* Boston: Brown, 1946. A Swedish industrialist marries an American OSS agent in order to help her get the secrets of the V-2 rocket out of wartime Berlin. *

2995. Kiker, Douglas. *Death at the Cut.* New York: Random, 1988. NBC News correspondent Kiker's second novel returns hero "Mac" McFarland to action when he finds a senator's car on Cape Cod with a dead young woman inside; the rest is Chappaquiddick history. Two Kiker mysteries:

2996. ___. *Death below Deck.* New York: Random, 1991.

2997. ___. *Murder on Clam Pond.* New York: Random, 1986.

2998. Kilgore, Axel. *They Call Me the Mercenary: The Slaughter Run.* New York: Zebra, 1980. One-eyed "merc" captain Hank Erest battles a Communist terrorist army out to assassinate the President of a Latin nation. *P*

2999. Kilian, Michael. *By Order of the President.* New York: St. Martin's, 1986. The President has been shot and immediately whisked off to Camp David—no one knows whether he's dead or alive; reporter Charley Dresden thinks he's dead and that there's a cover-up, and when he tries to prove it, he finds himself a hunted man "by order of the President." Others:

3000. ___. *The Big Score.* New York: St. Martin's, 1993.

3001. ___. *Blood of the Czars.* New York: St. Martin's, 1984.

3002. ___. *Dance of the Sinking Ship.* New York: Bantam, 1989. *P*

3003. ___. *Looker.* New York: St. Martin's, 1991.

3004. King, Charles. *Mama's Boy.* New York: Pocket, 1992. Julian Lamb is an academic with a dangerous secret: he was once a highly trained member of a hush-hush group known as Red Queen, a CIA hit squad. He's also a psychotic butcher who has lately begun a rampage of the wholesale slaughter of families.

3005. King, Clifford. *The Paint-Stained Flannels.* By Peter Fry, pseud. New York: Roy, 1966. In England a private eye and his client become involved in a plot to assassinate high government officials.

3006. ___. *The Red Stockings.* By Peter Fry, pseud. New York: Roy, 1962. What happens following the mysterious death of a British Foreign Office official who has been working for the Department of Psychological Warfare?

3007. ___. *The Thick Blue Sweater.* By Peter Fry, pseud. New York: Roy, 1964. A man must join with a woman, known to be a pawn of secret agents, in a perilous clandestine meeting.

3008. King, David. *The Brave and the Damned.* New York: Paperback, 1966. Sergeant Bailey leads a unit of Merrill's Marauders on a dangerous mission deep behind Japanese lines in Burma. **P*

3009. King, Graham. *Killtest.* New York: St. Martin's, 1978. SIS agents take on Killtest, Inc., a conglomerate run by ruthless men who stage diabolical forms of gladiatorial combat for a price.

3010. King, Harold. *Closing Ceremonies.* New York: Coward-McCann, 1979. A team of Nazi-hunters in Paraguay raids an underground memorial and steals the urn containing Hitler's ashes; the act draws the attention of various groups, including the remaining Nazi leaders-in-exile who want the urn back.

3011. ___ and Lawrence Block. *Code of Arms.* New York: Coward-McCann, 1981. An American flyer who wants to prevent a Nazi invasion of Britain in 1940 must contact sympathetic members of the German hierarchy led by Rudolf Hess.

3012. ___. *The Taskmaster.* New York: Coward, 1977. "Taskmaster" is the codename of an ex-Cuban agent who is murdering CIA men, all retired now, who were involved in the Bay of Pigs fiasco. Alec Gunther, out of favor with his superiors for a failed operation in Germany, is given the assignment to find and stop him. Five more:

3013. ___. *The Contenders.* By William Haroldson, pseud. New York: Pocket, 1980. *P*

3014. ___. *Four Days.* Indianapolis: Bobbs-Merrill, 1976.

3015. ___. *The Hahnemann Sequela.* New York: Windsor, 1984. *P*

3016. ___. *Paradigm Red.* By Brian Harris, pseud. Indianapolis: Bobbs-Merrill, 1975.

3017. ___. *World War III.* By Brian Harris, pseud. New York: Pocket, 1982.

3018. King, Stephen. *The Dead Zone.* New York: Viking, 1979. Recovering from a coma and discovering his clairvoyant power, Johnny Smith is drawn into a violent confrontation with a would-be American Hitler.

3019. ___. *The Firestarter.* New York: Viking, 1980. A mysterious government intelligence agency plans to make use of the mysterious fire-starting talent of 8-year-old Charlie McGee.

3020. Kinsley, Peter. *Pimpernel 60.* New York: Dutton, 1968. Father Ben Lomax is assigned by the Columbia Group to penetrate Albania and employ his considerable talent as an escape co-ordinator to engineer the defection of an important Soviet nuclear physicist.

3021. Kirk, Lydia. *The Man on the Raffles Verandah.* Garden City, NY: Doubleday, 1969. A rather poor ex-British agent has retired to Singapore where he has just enough cash to allow himself one gin each day on his hotel's verandah, but one day a letter arrives from his former chief . . .

Kirk, Philip, pseud. *See* Levinson, Leonard

3022. Kirsch, Steven J. *Oath of Office.* New York: Fawcett, 1988. A Constitutional crisis erupts when the President-elect, the nation's first Jewish President, is kidnapped the day after his election. *P*

3023. Kirschner, Fritz. *SS.* London: Brown, 1959. After running afoul of the SS, a World War II German Wehrmacht conscript defects to assist the French Maquis underground. *

3024. Kirst, Hans H. *Hero in the Tower.* Trans. from the German. New York: Coward-McCann, 1972. A crack German anti-aircraft unit is constantly besieged by mysterious "accidents." * Kirst is the author of the popular series featuring the war antics of Gunner Asch.

3025. ___. *The Seventh Day.* Garden City, NY: Doubleday, 1959. [*Keiner Kommt Davon.* Trans. George Weidenfeld. Munich: Desch, 1957]. An early tale of nuclear annihilation between the Soviets and Americans when "atomic" bombs are unleashed against the US.

3026. Klainer, Albert and Jo-Ann. *The Judas Gene.* New York: Marek, 1980. A Nazi doctor at Dachau in 1939 experiments with a "slow" virus fatal to Jews and, in America under an assumed name, perfects his discovery thirty years later. *P*

3027. Klawans, Harold L. *The Jerusalem Code.* New York: Signet, 1988. An American neurosurgeon visiting Jerusalem gets caught up in a murder investigation which connects to a terrorist threat by extremists hoping to galvanize the Jewish people against the Arabs occupying the site of Temple Mount. *P*

3028. Klein, Edward. *The Parachutists.* New York: Ballantine, 1981. An OSS agent is recruited for a mission that will save 250,000 Hungarian Jews from Nazi death camps if he achieves one objective: kill Adolph Eichmann.

3029. Klose, Kevin and Philip A. McCombs. *The Typhoon Shipments.* New York: Norton, 1974. Two federal agents are sent to Saigon to stop a heroin ring and discover a conspiracy so dangerous that Washington, DC may prove a deadlier place than the Saigon underworld or the guerilla-infested mountains.

3030. Knapp, Gregory C. *Stranglehold.* Boston: Little, 1973. A US military intelligence agent is put on the trail of a young lieutenant who has disappeared from his Korean base. Soon the fellow is found in Japan, being fought over by a couple of fanatical groups who want him for anti-American purposes.

3031. Knebel, Fletcher. *Crossing in Berlin.* Garden City, NY: Doubleday, 1981. While attempting to assist a West Berlin woman, an American, on assignment in East Berlin, becomes a pawn in a fearsome plot engineered by the East German secret police.

3032. ___. *Trespass.* Garden City, NY: Doubleday, 1969. Four Black militants occupy the home of Tim Crawford and his family during the early stages of a national revolution.

3033. ___. *Vanished.* Garden City, NY: Doubleday, 1968. When a prominent Washington attorney disappears, the President forbids CIA involvement.

3034. ___. *The Zinzin Road.* Garden City, NY: Doubleday, 1966. A Peace Corps worker is drawn into the leadership of a battle against the establishment in a West African nation.

3035. Knight, Kathleen M. *Intrigue for Empire.* Garden City, NY: Doubleday, 1944. Recently released from a North African POW camp, a young Mexican returns home just in time to help foil an Axis plot to set up a Latin American empire. *

Knight, Mallory T., pseud. *See* Hurwood, Bernhardt J.

3036. Knipscheer, James M. *No Dark Crusade.* By James M. Fox, pseud. Boston: Little, 1954. Agents chase atomic spies against a backdrop of Paris, Rotterdam, Cologne, and New York.

3037. Knopp, Jerome M. *The Eternal Reich.* New York: Tower, 1981. Conspirators inside the West German government intend to restore the Nazis to power. *P*

3038. Knott, Will C. *Mission Code #4: Granite Island.* By Bryan Swift, house pseud. New York: Jove, 1981. Mac Wingate is a demolitions expert and scourge of the Nazis in this paperback series (*see* Wise, Arthur for other Wingate adventures). *P* Two more from Knott's word processor:

3039. ___. *Mission Code #10: Scorpion.* By Bryan Swift, house pseud. New York: Jove, 1982. *P*

3040. ___. *Mission Code #11: Survival.* By Bryan Swift, house pseud. New York: Jove, 1982. *P*

3041. Knowles, William. *Our Man from SADISTO.* By Allison Clyde, pseud. Brixham, Devonshire, Eng.: Ember, 1965. This paperback spy-spoof series spawned a dozen adventures of Agent 008 in the mid-1960's. Other titles:

3042. ___. *For Your Sighs Only.* By Allison Clyde, pseud. Brixham, Devonshire, Eng.: Ember, 1966. *PH*

3043. ___. *Gamefinger.* By Allison Clyde, pseud. Brixham, Devonshire, Eng.: Ember, 1966. *PH*

3044. ___. *Our Girl from MEPHISTO.* By Allison Clyde, pseud. Brixham, Devonshire, Eng.: Ember, 1965. *PH*

3045. ___. *SADISTO Royale.* By Allison Clyde, pseud. Brixham, Devonshire, Eng.: Ember, 1966. *PH*

3046. Knox, Bill. *Cave of Bats.* By Robert MacLeod, pseud. New York: Holt, 1966. U.N. "peacemaker" Cord, in Burma to settle a labor dispute involving the building of a dam, soon learns that Red China is attempting to halt the facility's construction.

3047. ___. *The Drum of Ungara.* By Robert MacLeod, pseud. Garden City, NY: Doubleday, 1963. Mercenary Robert Hartford searches for a drum wanted by both the dictator and his opponent in a new East African state.

3048. ___. *The Iron Sanctuary.* By Robert MacLeod, pseud. New York: Holt, 1967. This novel, like its series, all paperback, stars Talos Cord, a United Nations troubleshooter. *P*

3049. ___. *Place of Mists.* By Robert MacLeod, pseud. New York: McCall, 1970. After an assassination in New York City, Cord is ordered to Morocco to protect a visiting dignitary and the action takes him on to the Atlas Mountains, where a strange mist always rises in the morning.

3050. ___. *The Scavengers.* Garden City, NY: Doubleday, 1964. Halted by the Scottish Fishery Protection Service, a trawler is found to have the body of a dead British nuclear scientist in its nets. Three other Cord stories not published in America are:

3051. ___. *Isle of Dragons.* By Robert MacLeod, pseud. London: Long, 1967.

3052. ___. *Nest of Vultures.* By Robert MacLeod, pseud. London: Long, 1973.

3053. ___. *Path of Ghosts.* By Robert MacLeod, pseud. London: Long, 1971.

3054. Koenig, Joseph. *Brides of Blood.* New York: Grove, 1993. A police procedural about a murdered prostitute in present-day Iran.

3055. Kolpacoff, Victor. *The Raid.* New York: Atheneum, 1971. Follows Al Fatah guerrilla chief Faisal and his people during an attack on an Israeli power station.

3056. Konsalik, Heinz G. *Strike Force 10.* New York: Putnam's, 1981. Just after D-Day, the Germans dispatch ten Russian-speaking commandos deep into the USSR with the suicidal mission of assassinating the Russian leader, Joseph Stalin.

3057. Koontz, Dean R. *Hanging On.* New York: Evans, 1973. A company of GI misfits is air-dropped into France by a slightly crackpot general to carry out a demented secret mission. Sort of a clandestine M*A*S*H. *H*

3058. Kosinski, Jerzy. *Cockpit.* New York: Bantam, 1978. Depicts the debriefing of a former government agent, Taiden, following a particularly long and tortuous mission. *P*

3059. Kozhevnikov, Vadim. *Shield and Sword.* Trans. from the Russian. London: Mayflower, 1973. A Soviet Communist named Belov travels from Latvia to infiltrate Germany and assumes a new identity and friends in the process; during World War II, Belov establishes a spy network which penetrates into the highest level of the Nazi military machine. *
    One of a number of volumes undertaken to show the Soviet people the wisdom, courage, and daring of their agents during and after World War II—rather a public relations job for the KGB.

3060. Kruse, John. *The Hour of the Lily.* New York: St. Martin's, 1987. Mike McCabe parachutes into Afghanistan on a CIA-backed mission to prove that Soviets are using toxic weapons; his contact inside is codenamed Lily, a woman operating a network of agents in Kabul which has penetrated Soviet military intelligence.

3061. ___. *Red Omega.* New York: Random, 1981. Two agents, one a Russian survivor of the Soviet deathcamps, are ordered to kill Stalin before he discovers the identity of "Omega," a Soviet leader—and a critically important mole for US Intelligence.

3062. Kuhlken, Ken. *The Loud Adios.* New York: St. Martin's, 1990. Border guard Tom Hickey is an ex-p.i. who agrees to help a young soldier free his sister from a Tijuana dive and encounters a fanatical band of Nazis.

3063. Kuhn, Edward, Jr. *The American Princess.* New York: Simon & Schuster, 1971. When an American girl marries the prince of a little Asian country on China's border, she finds her ex-boyfriend, a CIA agent, has come along too.

3064. Kunetka, James W. *Shadow Man.* New York: Warner, 1988. A "Star Wars" scientist is found murdered in a cave near Los Alamos, but the evidence points away from a ritual killing toward the theft of weapons data from a computer. One more:

3065. ___. *Parting Shot.* New York: St. Martin's, 1991.

3066. Kuniczak, W. S. *The Sempinski Affair.* Garden City, NY: Doubleday, 1970. In Central Europe to examine some ancient documents relative to the trial and execution of Christ, O. H. Shippe uncovers a plot by a splinter group to assassinate the Soviet premier and place the blame on the United States.

3067. Kurland, Michael. *Plague of Spies.* New York: Pyramid, 1969. Agent Peter Carthage of the private espionage firm War, Inc. is sent to infiltrate and destroy a combine of international assassins gathered in a monastery on the sunny shores of Elba. *P*

   Kurland is the author of *The Spymaster's Handbook* (New York: Facts on File, 1988). A collection of annecdotal humor about espionage.

3068. ___ and Bart Whaley. *The Last President.* New York: Morrow, 1980. A young CIA agent and a retired OSS man risk a coup d'etat against Richard Nixon, who remained in office after Watergate, gradually blackmailed his opponents into silence, and was attempting to take over all the top posts of the government including the military.

   The following novels are collaborations Kurland wrote under his Jennifer Plum pseudonym or are, mainly, collaborations with Chester Anderson:

3069. ___. *Button Bright.* New York: Jove, 1990. *P*

3070. ___ and H. Beam Piper. *Death by Gaslight.* By Jennifer Plum, pseud. New York: Signet, 1980. *P*

3071. ___. *The Infernal Device.* By Jennifer Plum, pseud. New York: Signet, 1978. *P*

3072. ___ and Chester Anderson. *Mission: Tank War.* New York: Pyramid, 1968.

3073. ___ and Chester Anderson. *Mission: Third Force.* New York: Pyramid, 1967.

3074. ___. *Perchance.* New York: Signet, 1989. *P*

3075. ___. *Pluribus*. By Jennifer Plum, pseud. Garden City, NY: Doubleday, 1975.

3076. ___. *The Princes of Earth*. By Jennifer Plum, pseud. Nashville, TN: Nelson, 1978.

3077. ___. *The Secret of Benjamin Square*. By Jennifer Plum, pseud. New York: Lancer, 1972.

3078. ___ and Chester Anderson. *Ten Years to Doomsday*. New York: Pyramid, 1964.

3079. ___. *Tomorrow Knight*. By Jennifer Plum, pseud. New York: DAW, 1976.

3080. ___ and Chester Anderson. *Transmission Error*. New York: Pyramid, 1971.

3081. ___ and Chester Anderson. *The Unicorn Girl*. New York: Pyramid, 1969. The second in a trilogy written by different authors. (Chester Anderson wrote the first, *The Butterfly Kid*, and T.A. Waters wrote the third: *The Probability Pad*.)

3082. ___. *The Whenabouts of Burr*. By Jennifer Plum, pseud. New York: DAW, 1975.

Kyle, Duncan, pseud. *See* Broxholme, John F.

L

3083. Lafferty, Perry. *The Downing of Flight <u>Six Heavy</u>*. New York: Fine, 1990. The CIA wants to test a new gizmo designed to knock out an enemy's missile guidance system, so it concocts a scheme to have its own device "hijacked," then taken to a hand-picked site on foreign soil; naturally, things go very wrong from the start.

3084. Lait, Robert. *Massacre at Tangini*. New York: Random, 1963. Mercenaries participate in the violence which is rampant in the birthpangs of a new African nation.

3085. Lamb, Max and Harry Sanford. *The Last Nazi.* New York: Belmont-Tower, 1980. Red Baxter-Harrow tries to get through a murderous screen of guards and assassins in order to get at Martin Bormann, who is hiding in Spain. **P**

3086. Lambert, Derek. *Angels in the Snow.* By Richard Falkirk, pseud. New York: Coward-McCann, 1969. This critically acclaimed spy thriller established Lambert's reputation in the genre. Compares well—in its brooding, oppressive atmosphere of Moscow—with the novels of Martin Cruz Smith and Anthony Olcott.

   Lambert began writing police procedurals with the historical setting of early nineteenth-century London; widely translated, these novels featured the detective exemplar Edmund Blackstone (see *The Twisted Wire* below for a partial listing). A young British diplomat on his first assignment in Moscow becomes involved with three people of various backgrounds: his beautiful Russian language teacher, an experienced, blasé CIA agent, and a British defector who still has a dream of once more seeing his homeland.

3087. ___. *The Chill Factor.* By Richard Falkirk, pseud. Garden City, NY: Doubleday, 1971. An SIS agent is ordered to assist the Americans in uncovering a Russian spy ring in Iceland.

3088. ___. *The Man Who Was Saturday.* New York: Stein & Day, 1985. Calder is an American defector with information so explosive that it keeps him alive until KGB boss Spandarian in the Kremlin can seal his fate quietly, and he intends to—with a ruthless killer named Tokarev.

3089. ___. *The Red Dove.* Briarcliff Manor, NY: Stein & Day, 1983. The US and USSR launch separate space missions that may culminate in global destruction. **P**

3090. ___. *The Red House.* New York: Coward, 1972. A Soviet diplomat assigned to Washington during the 1968 Czech crisis must consider not only his daughter's disaffection, but his own loyalty as well.

3091. ___. *The Yermakov Transfer.* New York: Saturday Review, 1974. A Russian computer expert heads a Zionist plot to kidnap Premier Yermakov and hold him hostage in order to force the KGB to allow Jewish physicists to leave the Soviet Union for Israel. Several more Lambert thrillers:

3092. ___. *For Infamous Conduct.* New York: Coward-McCann, 1970.

3093. ___. *The Golden Express*. London: Hamilton, 1984.

3094. ___. *The Great Land*. Fort Wayne, IN: Arlington, 1977.

3095. ___. *I, Said the Spy*. Fort Wayne, IN: Arlington, 1980.

3096. ___. *The Judas Code*. New York: Stein & Day, 1984.

3097. ___. *The Kites of War*. New York: Coward-McCann, 1969.

3098. ___. *The Lottery*. London: Piatkus, 1983.

3099. ___. *The Memory Man*. Fort Wayne, IN: Arlington, 1979.

3100. ___. *The Saint Peter's Plot*. London: Corgi, 1982.

3101. ___. *Touch the Lion's Paw*. New York: Saturday Review, 1976.

3102. ___. *Trance*. Fort Wayne, IN: Arlington, 1981.

3103. ___. *Triad*. New York: Walker, 1991.

3104. ___. *The Twisted Wire*. By Richard Falkirk, pseud. Garden City, NY: Doubleday, 1971.

3105. ___. *Vendetta*. New York: Walker, 1990. Lambert novels featuring Blackstone include:

3106. ___. *Beau Blackstone*. By Richard Falkirk, pseud. Briarcliff Manor, NY: Stein & Day, 1974. Lambert is the author of several historical espionage tales written in the seventies under the *nom de plume* Richard Falkirk; his hero is Edmund Blackstone, an detective-agent to Queen Victoria. More in the series:

3107. ___. *Blackstone*. By Richard Falkirk, pseud. New York: Stein & Day, 1973. *H*

3108. ___. *Blackstone and the Scourge of Europe*. By Richard Falkirk, pseud. Briarcliff Manor, NY: Stein & Day, 1974. *H*

3109. ___. *Blackstone's Fancy*. By Richard Falkirk, pseud. New York: Stein & Day, 1973. *H*

3110. ___. *Blackstone on Broadway.* By Richard Falkirk, pseud. London: Methuen, 1977. *H*

Lancaster, David, pseud. *See* Heald, Timothy V.

3111. Lancaster, Graham. *The Nuclear Letters.* New York: Atheneum, 1979. The CIA and SIS recruit a high-living London dentist to assist in breaking a terrorist group's nuclear blackmail of England.

3112. Land, Jon. *The Alpha Deception.* New York: Ballantine, 1988. Blaine McCracken and his former KGB nemesis, the beautiful Natalya Tomachenko, are reunited in this tale about an ancient gemstone which can power a laser-like weapon capable of obliterating entire towns from the face of the earth. *P*

3113. ___. *The Doomsday Spiral.* New York: Zebra, 1990. "Alabaster" is the codename of an agent and trained assassin who occasionally works for Mossad; this time, his mission is to stop a plot, originating from the hideous days of Auschwitz's bizarre genetic experiments, before it destroys America. *P*

3114. ___. *Labyrinth.* New York: Ballantine, 1986. Christopher Locke is a college professor who uncovers a plot known as Tantalus, brainchild of an Austrian-based secret organization known as "The Committee," which is out to control the world by becoming the world's largest crop producer and insinuating its members into parliaments and senates all over the globe. *P*

3115. ___. *The Lucifer Directive.* New York: Zebra, 1984. America is held hostage again—this time by terrorists who shock the nation at the Hollywood Oscar ceremony and then threaten the free world when they hijack three nuclear fighter bombers. *P*

3116. ___. *The Ninth Dominion.* New York: Fawcett, 1991. Eighty-four criminally insane inmates have been sprung by a serial killer called the Candy Man from their maximum-security facility. Agent Jared Kimberlain has to stop them before they wipe out the population of the US. *P*

3117. ___. *The Omega Command.* New York: Ballantine, 1986. Rogue agent Blaine McCracken is sent out to investigate a sinister conspiracy that links a murdered agent in a New York massage parlor to a billionaire's corporate empire and a Middle Eastern terrorist. *P*

3118. ___. *The Omicron Legion*. New York: Fawcett, 1991. A team of "serial" assassins, "the Legion," has been assembled for a diabolical conspiracy of mass exterminations in America—unless Blaine McCracken and sidekick John Wareagle can stop it. *P*

3119. ___. *Vortex*. New York: Zebra, 1990. The US President and the Soviet Premier are at the mercy of three vindictive men who have manipulated nuclear strikes against the two superpowers. *P* More by Land:

3120. ___. *The Council of Ten*. New York: Ballantine, 1987. *P*

3121. ___. *Day of the Delphi*. New York: TOR, 1993. *P*

3122. ___. *The Eighth Trumpet*. New York: Ballantine, 1989. *P*

3123. ___. *The Gamma Option*. New York: Ballantine, 1989. *P*

3124. ___. *The Valhalla Testament*. New York: Ballantine, 1991. *P*

3125. ___. *The Vengeance of the Tau*. New York: Fawcett, 1993. *P*

3126. Landau, Mark A. *Nightmare and Dawn*. By Mark Aldanov, pseud. New York: Duell, Sloan & Pearce, 1957. While the American and Soviet espionage establishments are concerned primarily with tricking each other, their operatives on the scene in Berlin, Venice, and Paris are more worried about their personal problems. Foreshadows early John le Carré.

3127. Landon, Christopher. *Flag in the City*. New York: Macmillan, 1954. The bold hero, a sympathetic intelligence agent, a beautiful woman and an elusive villain all cross paths in World War II Iran.

3128. Lange, John. *Binary*. New York: Knopf, 1972. A State Department agent attempts to foil the plot of a right-wing millionaire to loose poison gas over San Diego during a 1972 Republican National Convention.

3129. Langley, Bob. *Autumn Tiger*. New York: Walker, 1986. An OSS man impersonates a German POW to elicit from him a secret that could change the course of the war.

3130. ___. *Traverse of the Gods*. New York: Morrow, 1980. In the summer of 1941 an elite German commando squad scales Eiger Mountain in the Swiss

Alps in order to abduct an OSS-guarded scientist who is working on a formula for an atomic bomb.

3131. ___. *The War of the Running Fox.* New York: Scribner's, 1978. In a final effort to save white Rhodesia, a group of mercenaries find themselves betrayed by friends and trapped by enemies as they fight a battle across England's Lake District in an effort to escape after having botched a plutonium theft.

3132. ___. *Warlords.* New York: Morrow, 1981. When the British economy collapses, the CIA must manipulate the ensuing chaos to protect critical American military installations throughout the British Isles. Several more:

3133. ___. *Avenge the Belgrano.* New York: Walker, 1988. [*Conqueror Down!* New York: Bantam, 1991. *P*]

3134. ___. *The Churchill Diamonds.* New York: Walker, 1987.

3135. ___. *East of Everest.* New York: Walker, 1987.

3136. ___. *Falklands Gambit.* New York: Walker, 1985. [*Conquistadores.* Leicester, Eng.: Thorpe, 1987.]

3137. ___. *Hour of the Argentine.* New York: Walker, 1987.

3138. ___. *Precipice.* New York: Bantam, 1991. *P*

3139. Lantigua, John. *Burn Season.* New York: Putnam's, 1989. The plot seems lifted right out of *Casablanca*: a cynical nightclub owner, shady characters including a fat man and a whimpering type who is to be snuffed, but this one is set in Costa Rica—and the beautiful woman is a spy. All the action swirls about an attempt tumble Costa Rica from neutrality while Sandanistas battle it out with Contras.

LaPierre, Dominique. *See* Collins, Larry for a list of his collaborations in spy fiction.

3140. Larauy, David. *The Big Red Sun.* Englewood Cliffs, NJ: Prentice-Hall, 1971. George Benachen, an amateur revolutionary, is sent by the French Intelligence chief to Peking to arrange for the defection of a high Communist official.

3141. Lartéguy, Jean. *The Bronze Drums.* Trans. from the French. New York: Knopf, 1968. Francois Ricq is air dropped into 1944 Laos to form a native resistance group to battle the Japanese.

3142. ___. *The Hounds of Hell.* Trans. from the French. New York: Dutton, 1966. Follows the personal and political activities of three European mercenaries in the Congolese civil war of the early 1960s.

3143. Latham, Aaron. *Orchids for Mother.* Boston: Little, 1977. "Mother" is Francis Xavier Kimball, director of counterintelligence and head of the Israeli desk. His rivalry with the head of covert operations begets a series of "incredible" maneuverings that threaten to bring down the entire government around the ears of the thinly disguised Kissinger and Nixon.

Lathen, Emma, pseud. *See* Latsis, Mary J. and Martha Hennissart

3144. Latsis, Mary J. and Martha Hennissart. *Murder Against the Grain.* By Emma Lathen, pseud. New York: Macmillan, 1967. When someone steals almost a million dollars from the Sloan Guaranty Trust, a Russian-American trade treaty is endangered. John P. Thatcher, hero of a number of other outright mysteries by this author, must get the money back and keep the deal on track.

3145. Latter, Simon. *The Girl from UNCLE: The Global Globules Affair.* London: Souvenir, 1967. April Dancer is mixed up in a THRUSH plot to spread a particularly nasty and incapacitating form of flu. *P* One other by this writer is:

3146. ___. *The Girl from UNCLE: The Golden Boats of Taradata Affair.* London: Souvenir, 1967. *P*

3147. Lauder, Peter. *Noble Lord.* Briarcliff Manor, NY: Stein & Day, 1986. About a million-dollar racehorse at the center of a plot to assassinate the Queen at Epsom Downs.

3148. Lauer, Pierre. *The Suns of Badarane.* Trans. from the French. New York: Morrow, 1972. Thirteen mercenaries are sent to capture and hold an outpost in the oil rich kingdom of Ramador.

3149. Laumer, Keith. *The Avengers: The Gold Bomb.* New York: Berkley, 1968. Steed and Emma are assigned to look into a projected bombing of gold reserves in the Bank of England. *P* Two others are:

3150. ___. *The Avengers: The Afrit Affair.* New York: Berkley, 1968. *P*

3151. ___. *The Avengers: The Drowned Queen.* New York: Berkley, 1968.
P

3152. Lawrence, Marjorie K. *Intruder.* Mitcham, Eng: Maiden & Bridge,
1961. Aircraft and espionage are intermingled in Moscow and the Middle East.

     Layne, Marion Margery, pseud. *See* Woolf, Marion, Margery W.
Papich and Layne Torkelson

3153. Leasor, James. *Frozen Assets.* New York: St. Martin's, 1989. Dr.
Jason Love accepts an assignment from British Intelligence to go to Pakistan.

3154. ___. *Host of Extras.* London: Pan, 1975. A used car salesman is sent
to Coventry to examine two Rolls-Royces needed for a film being made in
Corsica, but which are, in fact, required in an international criminal plan he
must eventually foil. *P*

3155. ___. *Passport for a Pilgrim.* Garden City, NY: Doubleday, 1969. Dr.
Jason Love, an admirer of judo and Cord motor cars, and agent McGillivray of
MI-6 seek missing persons in the Monastery of the Sacred Flame in Maloula.

3156. ___. *Passport to Oblivion.* Philadelphia: Lippincott, 1965. [*Where the
Spies Are.* London: Pan, 1964]. SIS agent "K" has disappeared in Iran and
Dr. Jason Love is asked to go in and find him.

3157. ___. *Spylight.* Philadelphia: Lippincott, 1966. [*Passport to Peril.*
London: Heinemann, 1966]. Dr. Jason Love travels to India to help out a
prince whose son is being held hostage by Red Chinese operatives in Pakistan.

3158. ___. *A Week of Love.* London: Heinemann, 1969. A collection of 21
espionage stories featuring Jason Love.

3159. ___. *The Yang Meridian.* Philadelphia: Lippincott, 1967. [*Passport
in Suspense.* London: Heinemann, 1967]. In the Bahamas and Mexico, Dr.
Jason Love faces an archvillain who does not mind killing in order to further his
fiendish plot to capture a NATO missile submarine for use against England and
America. A final Dr. Love:

3160. ___. *Code Name Nimrod.* Boston: Houghton, 1981. [*The Unknown
Warrior.* Long Preston, Eng.: Magna, 1982.]

3161. ___. *Love and the Land Beyond.* London: Heinemann, 1979.

3162. ___. *Ship of Gold.* London: Collins, 1984.

3163. ___. *Tank of Serpents.* London: Collins, 1986.

3164. Leather, Edwin. *The Vienna Elephant.* New York: Dodd, 1977. A fabulous carving thought lost in World War II resurfaces and eventually involves Rupert Conway on a dangerous mission behind the Iron Curtain.

3165. Leather, Stephen. *The Chinaman.* New York: Pocket, 1992. Nguyen Ngoc Minh's family is killed in a department store terrorist bombing, and Minh is ignored by government officials when he presses for answers. But this small, slight "Chinaman" fought with the Special Forces until the fall of Saigon and begins his own campaign of terror against a suspected Irish terrorist leader who may be in a position to reveal the identities of the bombers.

3166. ___. *The Vets.* New York: Pocket, 1993. A former Vietnam colonel brings together a team of five vets, each with a specialty, for a "mission" in Hong Kong. Two others:

3167. ___. *Hungry Ghost.* New York: Pocket, 1993.

3168. ___. *Pay Off.* New York: St. Martin's, 1987.

Le Carré, John, pseud. *See* Cornwell, David J. M.

3169. Lederer, William J. and Eugene Burdick. *The Ugly American.* New York: Norton, 1958. The authors of *A Connoisseur's Guide* cite a source as stating that this novel "is believe to be based on that remarkable CIA covert operations agent, Air Force Colonel Edward Landsale, whose exploits in the Philippines in the 1950s and later in Vietnam, were so publicized that he was made the model for the heroes of at least two books" [Graham Greene's *The Quiet American* being the other] (158). The film featured Marlon Brando (US, 1962) who reprised the role of the thoughtful diplomat at ideological odds with his former comrade in arms, now the guerilla leader of a Marxist-backed movement to liberate his country from an oppressive regime and undue Yankee influence.

Lee, Elsie, pseud. *See* Sheridan, Elsie L.

3170. Lee, John. *Assignment in Algeria.* New York: Walker, 1971. Brian Douglas gets mixed up with the OAS terrorist group which wishes to keep Algeria as a province of France.

3171. ___. *Lago.* Garden City, NY: Doubleday, 1980. As Mussolini moves north for a last stand, OSS agent James Landry joins an Italian partisan group to stop Il Duce and take possession of vital documents still in the dictator's hands.

3172. ___. *Lake of the Diamond.* Garden City, NY: Doubleday, 1979. At the close of World War II, Mussolini embarks on a dangerous mission to northern Europe, accompanied by his mistress, his close associates, and $90 million in treasure.

3173. ___. *The Ninth Man.* Garden City, NY: Doubleday, 1976. Captain Andy Blaszek foils a Nazi raid off the US coast, but one man escaped and his mission is to kill FDR.

3174. ___. *The Thirteenth Hour.* Garden City, NY: Doubleday, 1978. As the Russians advance on Berlin, OSS agent Henry Bascom finds himself a fugitive trapped by both the Soviets and the Germans in a doomed city. Two more:

3175. ___. *The Unicorn Piece.* New York: TOR, 1993. *P*

3176. ___. *The Unicorn Solution.* New York: TOR, 1991. *P*

3177. Lee, Norman. *Bullets and Brown Eyes.* By Mark Corrigan, pseud. London: Laurie, 1948. Between 1948 and 1964, Lee wrote over 30 tales of US Intelligence Agent Mark Corrigan. This novel is the first in the series. The last:

3178. ___. *The Riddle of the Spanish Circus.* By Mark Corrigan, pseud. Sydney: Angus & Robertson, 1964.

3179. Lee, Stan. *Dunn's Conundrum.* New York: Harper & Row, 1985. Harry Dunn works in the Intelligence Library—a collection and storage agency where all the information that used to be classified Need to Know is nowadays Need to Know Everything—and thanks to all the gee-whiz technology—it's possible to know everything about everybody. But someone is leaking vital information, and Harry's fellow librarian, Walter Coolidge, is on a mission to ferret the traitor out. *H*

3180. ___. *The GOD Project.* London: Weidenfeld, 1990. Richard "Doc" Halliday is the new, liberal US President who vows to achieve disarmament despite a CIA project that guarantees US soldiers can be sent anywhere without public resistance in this black-humored look at power in America.

3181. Leffingwell, Albert. *Court of Shadows.* New York: Dial, 1943. New York reporter and secret agent Niles Boyd goes into action after finding a friend who lives near the waterfront has been murdered by Nazi operatives.

3182. ___. *Nine Against New York.* By Dana Chambers, pseud. New York: Holt, 1941. Nazi agents and American fifth columnists will engineer an attack on New York City unless they can be stopped by intrepid FBI agent Pope.

3183. Le Grand, Leon. *The Von Kessel Dossier.* New York: Lorevan, 1987. The Von Kessel dossier exposes the true identity of a vicious ex-Nazi corporate billionaire who plots to bring the world's governments to their knees once he has ruined them financially. Michael Berresford, head of an oil exploration company in Australia, comes into possession of this dangerous document, and bad things begin happening all around him. *P* Another:

3184. ___. *The 210 Conspiracy.* New York: Lorevan, 1988. *P*

3185. Lehman, Ernest. *The French Atlantic Affair.* New York: Atheneum, 1977. Terrorist threaten to destroy 3,000 passengers on an ocean liner unless a huge ransom is paid within 48 hours.

3186. Lehrer, Jim. *The Sooner Spy.* New York: Putnam's, 1990. The author is co-host of the acclaimed "MacNeil/Lehrer Newshour." A young graduate of an Oklahoma college wants the state's governor to help him get aboard the CIA; the solution to the young man's problem, after he is rejected, is to prove his worth—by capturing a retired Russian spy living in the Sooner State. *H*

3187. Leib, Franklin A. *Fire Arrow.* Novato, CA: Presidio, 1988. About a rescue attempt to save American military personnel hijacked and taken to Libya. Two more for Leib:

3188. ___. *Sea Lion.* New York: Signet, 1990. *P*

3189. ___. *Valley of the Shadow.* Novato, CA: Presidio, 1991.

3190. Leigh, James. *The Caliph Intrigue.* New York: Dodd, 1979. A politically ambitious senator holds hearings on weather the powerful Caliph of

Islam is preparing to wage economic warfare on the US, an investigation which triggers violence and murder.

3191. ___. *The Ludi Victor.* New York: Coward-McCann, 1980. While investigating a gigantic fraud behind the deaths of policyholders, the consultant to a European insurance firm encounters a sinister global cult of secret warriors.

3192. Leighton, Tom. *The Phoenix Formula.* New York: Dell, 1980. A female OSS officer and a renegade German officer oppose the quest of a surviving Hitler to find a secret weapon with which to end the Second World War in a Nazi triumph. *P*

3193. Lemieux, Kenneth. *The Doomsday List.* By Kenneth Orvis, pseud. London: Hale, 1974. CIA agent Adam Beck must halt a nasty who is knocking off prominent people whose names appear on a mysterious hit list.

3194. ___. *Night without Darkness.* By Kenneth Orvis, pseud. New York: Coward-McCann, 1966. Agent Beck must either kill or free Dr. Beldon, inventor of a paralysis mist more deadly than an H-bomb, who is being held captive by Communist operatives who want his secret formula.

Leonard, Charles L., pseud. *See* Heberden, Mary V.

3195. Leonard, Elmore. *Bandits.* New York: Warner, 1988. The incomparable "Dutch" Leonard, master of realistic crime fiction, offers brutal portraits of Contras and Sandinistas in a plot about a Nicaraguan woman held in a leper colony in Louisiana.

3196. Leopold, Christopher. *Blood-and-Guts Is Going Nuts.* Garden City, NY: Doubleday, 1977. Relieved of his command of the US Army's 3rd Army in Europe shortly after V-E Day, General George Patton hatches a plan for an attack on Russia.

3197. Leslie, Peter. *The Bastard Brigade.* New York: Pyramid, 1969. After parachuting into France to contact the French Maquis, SOE agent Barton finds he must empty a prison train in order to recruit a "dirty-dozen" type commando brigade with which he must thwart a German panzer thrust that could change the outcome of World War II. *P*

3198. ___. *The Gay Deceiver.* New York: Stein & Day, 1967. A humorous British spy chase involving the winner of a TV quiz program given a map to find his 500-quid prize and agents of MI-6 engaged in a plot to discredit an Arab leader and bring down the price of Middle East crude oil. *H*

3199. ___. *The Girl from UNCLE: The Cornish Pixie Affair.* New York: Ace, 1967. April Dancer is assigned to look into a series of THRUSH-backed crimes apparently committed by "little people." *P*

3200. ___. *The Man from UNCLE: The Finger in the Sky Affair.* New York: Ace, 1971. Illya and Napoleon uncover a fantastic THRUSH plan to rule the world's air lanes. *P* Five other Man from UNCLE titles are:

3201. ___. *The Man from UNCLE: The Diving Dames Affair.* New York: Ace, 1967. *P*

3202. ___. *The Man from UNCLE: The Radioactive Camel Affair.* New York: Ace, 1966. *P*

3203. ___. *The Man from UNCLE: The Splintered Sunglasses Affair.* New York: Ace, 1968. *P*

3204. ___. *The Man from UNCLE: The Stone-Cold Dead in the Market Affair.* New York: Ace, 1970. *P*

3205. ___. *The Man from UNCLE: The Unfair Fare Affair.* New York: Ace, 1968. *P* One more Leslie:

3206. ___. *Secret Agent: Hell for Tomorrow.* New York: Macfadden-Bartells, 1965. British secret agent John Drake must uncover a seemingly innocent plot with international ramifications for the future. *P*

3207. Lesser, Milton A. *Come Over Red Rover.* By Stephen Marlowe, pseud. New York: Macmillan, 1968. Agent Chester Drum must stop a double agent's plan to use a USIA official's kidnapped daughter to convince the commentator to defect.

3208. ___. *Danger Is My Line.* By Stephen Marlowe, pseud. New York: Macmillan, 1960. A lethal blonde is Chester Drum's only lead to three assassinations and an espionage ring in Iceland.

3209. ___. *Death Is My Comrade.* By Stephen Marlowe, pseud. Greenwich, CT: Fawcett, 1960. Agent Drum travels to Moscow to learn why a Russian turned down the Nobel Prize for Literature. *P*

3210. ___. *Drum Beat—Berlin*. By Stephen Marlowe, pseud. Greenwich, CT: Fawcett, 1964. Chester Drum is a p.i. in the nation's capital who often takes on cases of international intrigue in this paperback series which ran from the mid-fifties to the late-sixties. *P*

3211. ___. *Francesca*. By Stephen Marlowe, pseud. Greenwich, CT: Fawcett, 1963. Agent Drum is on mission in Italy and gets mixed up with a tempestuous actress. *P*

3212. ___. *Manhunt Is My Mission*. By Stephen Marlowe, pseud. Greenwich, CT: Fawcett, 1961. A revolution in an Arab nation hinders Chester Drum's hunt for a surgeon who disappeared there. *P*

3213. ___. *Nineteen Fifty-Six*. By Stephen Marlowe, pseud. New York: Arbor, 1981. While seeking to avert a third world war and moving back and forth between the Suez Crisis and the Hungarian Revolution, two intelligence agents—a man and a woman—from opposing sides fall in love.

3214. ___. *Peril Is My Pay*. By Stephen Marlowe, pseud. New York: Macmillan, 1960. In Rome for the Olympics, Chester Drum finds himself wanted by the police of three nations, as well as the story's evildoers.

3215. ___. *The Search for Bruno Heidler*. By Stephen Marlowe, pseud. New York: Macmillan, 1966. Ted Dunbar, working for the US Army War Graves Investigation Division, is asked to help find Nazi war criminal Bruno Heidler.

3216. ___. *The Summit*. By Stephen Marlowe, pseud. Cleveland, OH: World, 1970. When Soviet troops mass on the Yugoslav border and America prepares for action, a meeting between the President and the Premier is arranged for Geneva, complete with spies, kidnappings, and violence.

3217. ___. *The Valkyrie Encounter*. By Stephen Marlowe, pseud. New York: Putnam's, 1977. Two spies, one from the East and one from the West, are sent to Berlin to abort an assassination plot against Hitler; there their paths cross, leading to a vicious confrontation that only one can survive. During the James Bond era, the author produced a large number of his Chester Drum parodies on the 007 theme. Additional of these include:

3218. ___. *Drum Beat—Dominique*. By Stephen Marlowe, pseud. Greenwich, CT: Fawcett, 1965. *P*

3219. ___. *Drum Beat—Erica.* By Stephen Marlowe, pseud. Greenwich, CT: Fawcett, 1967. *P*

3220. ___. *Drum Beat—Madrid.* By Stephen Marlowe, pseud. Greenwich, CT: Fawcett, 1966. *P*

3221. ___. *Drum Beat—Marianne.* By Stephen Marlowe, pseud. Greenwich, CT: Fawcett, 1968. *P*

3222. ___. *Homicide Is My Game.* By Stephen Marlowe, pseud. Greenwich, CT: Fawcett, 1959. *P*

3223. ___. *Mecca for Murder.* By Stephen Marlowe, pseud. Greenwich, CT: Fawcett, 1956. *P*

3224. ___. *Model for Murder.* By Stephen Marlowe, pseud. New York: Berkley, 1960. *P*

3225. ___. *Murder Is My Death.* By Stephen Marlowe, pseud. Greenwich, CT: Fawcett, 1957. *P*

3226. ___. *Terror Is My Trade.* By Stephen Marlowe, pseud. New York: Macmillan, 1958.

3227. ___. *Trouble Is My Name.* By Stephen Marlowe, pseud. New York: Macmillan, 1956.

3228. ___. *Violence Is My Business.* By Stephen Marlowe, pseud. New York: Macmillan, 1958.

3229. Lestienne, Voldemar. *Furioso.* New York: St. Martin's, 1973. A French best seller, this yarn details the Bondian adventures of four French Resistance commandos during World War II. The quartet has all sorts of activities that involve pretty women, the springing of a stranger from the inner area of Dartmoor Prison, the commandeering of Churchill's car—complete with the PM—and the obtaining of a propaganda folio from Heydrich the Merciless.

3230. Leuci, Bob. *Odessa Beach.* New York: Signet, 1986. A Russian black marketeer flees the KGB and comes to Brooklyn, where he immediately begins to horn in on the Mafia's action. *P*

3231. Levi, Peter. *Knit One, Drop One.* New York: Walker, 1987. Ben Jonson, a British archeologist is asked by the Russians to visit Leningrad and give a demonstration of a new supercomputer capable of "reading" through many levels of a document. The invitation, however, has been issued by the KGB, which has a more practical aim in mind for so valuable a machine. One more by Levi:

3232. ___. *Grave Witness.* London: Quartet, 1985.

3233. Levin, Ira. *The Boys from Brazil.* New York: Random, 1976. Only old Nazi hunter Yakov Liebermann can stop the mad plot of the infamous former SS doctor to clone exact doubles of Adolf Hitler.

3234. Levine, Larry. *Snowbird.* Greenwich CT: Fawcett, 1977. A power-mad CIA Director attempts to create a police state in America. *P*

3235. Levine, Paul. *False Dawn.* New York: Bantam, 1993. Series character Jake Lassiter, ex-pro football player and now Miami lawyer, gets involved with stolen art and CIA derring-do in this tale of a missing Fabergé egg and a murder victim. Two more:

3236. ___. *Night Vision.* New York: Bantam, 1991. *P*

3237. ___. *To Speak for the Dead.* New York: Bantam, 1990. *P*

3238. Levinson, Leonard. *Butler: The Hydra Conspiracy.* New York: Leisure, 1979. Butler was a CIA man who criticized the Agency too much—at least that is what they told him before, suddenly, he became the prime suspect in a sensational murder case; escaping to Mexico, he must return to learn if he was framed or whether a foreign power is trying to get him rattled enough to reveal state secrets. *P* Other Butler tales are:

3239. ___. *Butler: Chinese Roulette.* By Philip Kirk, pseud. New York: Leisure, 1979. *P*

3240. ___. *Butler: Dead Fall.* By Philip Kirk, pseud. New York: Leisure, 1980. *P*

3241. ___. *Butler: Killer Satellites.* By Philip Kirk, pseud. New York: Leisure, 1980. *P*

3242. ___. *Butler: Love Me to Death.* By Philip Kirk, pseud. New York: Leisure, 1980. *P*

3243. ___. *Butler: The Midas Factor.* By Philip Kirk, pseud. New York: Leisure, 1984. *P*

3244. ___. *Butler: The Q Factor.* By Philip Kirk, pseud. New York: Leisure, 1984. *P*

3245. ___. *Butler: The Slayboys.* By Philip Kirk, pseud. New York: Leisure, 1979. *P*

3246. ___. *Butler: The Smart Bombs.* By Philip Kirk, pseud. New York: Leisure, 1979. *P* Levinson also wrote a military action series featuring Sgt. C.J. Mahoney, whose codename is Parrot and who has a sidekick named Cranepool:

3247. ___. *The Liberation of Paris.* By Gordon Davis, pseud. New York: Bantam, 1981. *P* Levinson has also written (under the pen name John Mackie) about some WW II heroes, a motley crew calling itself the "Rat Bastards." One such:

3248. ___. *Hit the Beach!* By John Mackie, pseud. New York: Jove, 1983. *P*

3249. Lewellen, T. C. *The Billiken Courier.* New York: Random, 1968. Drinking to forget his Vietnam service, Robert Chessick is shadowed by the mysterious Alpine Hat, who seeks a secret of the soldier's past.

3250. Lewis, David. *The Andromeda Assignment.* New York: Pyramid, 1976. Agent Steve Savage is ordered to recover $100 million in gold bullion from a U-boat lying on the harbor floor of a quiet Norwegian village. *P*

3251. Lewis, Norman. *Flight from a Dark Equator.* New York: Putnam's, 1972. An American agent is sent to investigate a totalitarian South American nation on the verge of revolution.

3252. ___. *The Sicilian Specialist.* New York: Random, 1975. Mafia godfather Don Vicente dispatches hitman Marco Richards into the employ of the CIA, which in turn sends him down to Texas on a very tough assignment.

3253. ___. *A Small War Made to Order.* New York: Harcourt, 1966. An Englishman is hired to pose as a leftist reporter, visit Cuba, and make the final reconnaissance necessary for a proposed US invasion.

3254. Lewis, Roy H. *Where Agents Fear to Tread.* New York: St. Martin's, 1984. A mild librarian with a specialty in Arab manuscripts goes to Pakistan for SIS and finds himself in James Bond situations.

3255. Liddy, G. Gordon. *The Monkey Handlers.* New York: St. Martin's, 1990. Michael Stone is a real-estate lawyer in Rhinekill, NY who used to be a Navy Seal commando. He gets involved with the sister of a Vietnam buddy who has problems with a big, sinister pharmaceutical company in town with links to Arab terrorists and trafficking in illegal aliens.

3256. ___. *Out of Control.* New York: St. Martin's, 1979. When the CIA attempts to confirm rumors that the head or the largest US multinational company is a Soviet agent, maverick former agent Richard Rand, who left "the Company" under ambiguous circumstances, is called in for the assignment.

3257. Lieberman, Herbert. *The Climate of Hell.* New York: Simon & Schuster, 1978. An ex-Auschwitz doctor who is wanted by the intelligence services of West Germany, the wartime Allies, and Israel, continues to practice his cruel craft in Paraguay.

3258. Lilley, Peter and Anthony Stansfeld. *Boiled Alive.* By Bruce Beckingham, pseud. London: Joseph, 1957. A Mexican detective seeks a murdering foreign agent who is after mercury deposits near the resort of Tuxpan.

3259. Lilley, Tom. *The "K" Section.* London: Macmillan, 1972. Sequel to the next title. Carter, head of the SIS Special Branch in a British Southeast Asian colony, fights Russian and Chinese attempts to take over the country; Soviet reaction leads to the bombing of a cathedral and the deaths of several royal guests and all of the colony's leading administrators.

3260. ___. *The Officer from Special Branch.* Garden City, NY: Doubleday, 1971. Published in Britain the previous year as *The Projects Section.* When the Reds began a guerrilla revolution in Malaya in 1948, the British established a counterterrorist group, Projects Section, to offset the Communist influence. Based on actual events.

3261. Limón, Martin. *Jade Lady Burning.* New York: Soho, 1992. Two Army investigators probe the death of a Seoul prostitute who was the lover of an American soldier.

3262. Linaweaver, Brad. *Moon of Ice.* New York: TOR, 1988. A "what-if" tale in which the Nazis gain the atomic bomb, Hitler dies in 1965, and Joseph Goebbels' daughter Hilda becomes a revolutionary leader against the Nazis. *P*

3263. Lindquist, Donald. *Berlin Tunnel 21.* New York: Avon, 1978. Sandy Mueller, an ex-US Army officer, enlists fellow freedom fighters in a bold attempt to liberate their East German relatives and his own lover. The plan: dig a 70-meter tunnel under the border. The obstacles: bad weather, adverse geologic conditions, and a deepening climate of fear and suspicion. The TV movie version starred Richard Thomas and Horst Buchholz. *P*

3264. ___. *The Red Gods.* New York: Delacorte, 1981. The United States is ordered to surrender in light of the development of a new Soviet nuclear weapons system.

3265. Lindsey, David L. *Black Gold, Red Death.* New York: Ballantine, 1983. Like his contemporary Thomas Harris who turned from espionage to psycho-sexual thrillers, David Lindsey's first novel invokes espionage themes and his later books feature series character Stuart Haydon in stories of detection. Here, Martin Gallagher, newspaperman, becomes involved in revolutionary intrigue; it centers around a briefcase of documents, an assassin named Tony Sleep, FBI, CIA, and Federales—all of whom want the documents.

3266. Linebarger, Paul M. A. *Atomsk.* New York: Duell, Sloan & Pearce, 1949. A US Army G-2 agent penetrates the Iron Curtain, purposefully leaves evidence of his visit, and returns to the United States to await developments. *

3267. Lippincott, David. *E Pluribus Bang!* New York: Viking, 1971. One day in the future, the 39th US President finds his bed compromised and shoots his wife. The CIA is called in to dispose of the evidence, but a few in the know commence blackmail proceedings. Soon, important bodies are lying all over Washington, DC.

3268. ___. *Salt Mine.* New York: Viking, 1977. A credibly detailed narrative of the days preceding, during, and after the takeover of parts of the Kremlin—including Lenin's body!—by a dedicated group of Russian dissidents.

3269. ___. *Voice of Armageddon.* New York: Putnam's, 1974. A criminal assassin has given the US government pictures of himself, a timetable of planned killings, and 48 hours to stop him; a special group of agents is established to deal with the problem, but then the madman changes the rules.

3270. Littell, Blaine. *The Dolorosa Deal.* New York: Saturday Review, 1974. Samuel Webster, a Black operative for the highly secret US "Projects Bureau," is ordered to Israel to defuse a dangerous plot.

3271. Littell, Robert. *The Amateur.* New York: Simon & Schuster, 1981. A CIA cryptologist, busy trying to prove who really wrote the Shakespeare plays, is grief-stricken when German terrorists kill his fiancée; seeking revenge, he blackmails his superiors into training him as a killer and sending him to Czechoslovakia for the ultimate showdown.   Not to be trifled with, this "amateur's" bosses secretly dispatch an agent to liquidate the upstart once his self-imposed mission is completed. According to *Contemporary Authors*, Littell edited a translation of *Sedm prazskych dnu [The Czech Black Book.* New York: Praeger, 1969], which detailed the infamous days between August 21 and 28, 1968 when Soviet tanks invaded Czechoslovakia (Vol. 112. 310).

3272. ___. *An Agent in Place.* New York: Bantam, 1991. A hush-hush bureau in Washington, DC evolves a complex scheme that requires putting an agent in place—Moscow—and manipulating him without his knowledge; the problem is that the agent falls in love with a Russian feminist poet.

3273. ___. *The Debriefing.* New York: Harper & Row, 1979. American agent Stone, an expert in sophisticated debriefing methods, must learn every detail concerning the life of a highly placed Soviet courier.

3274. ___. *The Defection of A. J. Lewinter.* Boston: Houghton, 1973. Lewinter is the inventor of a super garbage disposal system and a defector to the USSR. While he settles into life in Moscow, agents of the KGB are still trying to decide what they've got—while the CIA wonders what, if anything, it may have lost. *H*

3275. ___. *The October Circle.* Boston: Houghton, 1976. A group of friends, who were celebrated partisans during the Second World War, reunite in Bulgaria to protest and take action against the 1968 Soviet invasion of Czechoslovakia.

3276. ___. *The Once and Future Spy.* New York: Bantam, 1990. A rogue operation within CIA known as Stufftingle intends a nuclear "accident" that will wipe out Tehran. Silas Sibley, known as "the Weeder" and as crafty a spy as his ancestor Nathan Hale, intends to thwart the conspirators by using a piece of American Revolutionary history against them.

3277. ___ . *The Revolutionist*. New York: Bantam, 1989. The saga of the man who forever altered Russia and her people in the October Revolution of 1917.

3278. ___ . *The Sisters*. New York: Bantam, 1986. Two aging spymasters within the CIA battle it out for supremacy oblivious to the money, time, and lives spent.
     Notes *A Connoisseur's Guide*: "*The Sisters* is another example of one of the novels that offers an explanation of events that led up to the assassination of President Kennedy" (164).

3279. ___ . *Sweet Reason*. Boston: Houghton, 1974. Littel is attempting a black comedy about Vietnam in the way that Joseph Heller did for WW II in his classic *Catch 22*. It's a mixed bag of characters aboard a destroyer off the coast of a small Asian country. The captain, J. P. Horatio Jones, and crew are busy sinking junks, torpedoing a pod of whales and shelling harmless villages. *H* An early Littell:

3280. ___ . *Mother Russia*. New York: Harcourt, 1978.

3281. Little, Lloyd. *Among the Demons*. New York: Viking, 1978. Sent into Laos to check the opium trade, CIA agent Martin Borzek joins a local sorcerer to battle spirits threatening the village of Sop Hao.

3282. Litvinoff, Emmanuel. *A Death Out of Season*. New York: Stein & Day, 1973. Litvinoff was born in the East End of London, served in the British Army during WW II and has much first-hand knowledge of Russia. He has authored short stories, poems, and plays and a documentary on Soviet antisemitism. This novel compares favorably with Ken Follett's *The Man from St. Petersburg*. The notorious Sidney Street Massacre, a shootout between police and anarchists in 1910 in East London, is the setting of this fascinating account of the relationships among pre-Lenin revolutionaries and Tsarist police including the beautiful Lydia, the enigmatic Schtern, and the unlucky Murontzoff. (See Mr. Litvinoff's commentary in CRAFT NOTES.)

3283. ___ . *The Face of Terror*. New York: Morrow, 1978. Lydia Alexandrova's loyalty to Stalin's Soviet system is shaken by the excesses of her husband, an NKVD commissar and sometimes double agent in Berlin.

3284. ___. *Falls the Shadow.* Briarcliff Manor, NY: Stein & Day, 1983. Amos Sharon is an Israeli version of *Gorky Park*'s Renko, and he has a similar problem: when a prominent Israeli businessman is gunned down in the streets of Tel Aviv, his killer demands a trial so that he may tell why he assassinated his victim, but a public trial is the last thing Shomron's superiors want. Litvinoff has produced other novels which bear upon the lives of Jewish survivors:

3285. ___. *The Lost Europeans.* New York: Vanguard, 1959. Acclaimed portrait of the lives of Jews in Germany after the Holocaust. Two more:

3286. ___. *The Man Next Door.* London: Hodder & Stoughton, 1968.

3287. Litzinger, Boyd. *Watch It, Dr. Adrian.* New York: Putnam's, 1977. The CIA employs a disgruntled professor to smuggle a microdot into Britain where the scholar is pursued by KGB agents who know the document is a forgery designed to discredit the Soviet Union in the eyes of the Arabs.

3288. Llewellyn, Richard. *But We Didn't Get the Fox.* Garden City, NY: Doubleday, 1969. Llewellyn's saga of growing up in a Welsh town established him as one of the most widely read authors in the world (*How Green Was My Valley.* New York: Macmillan, 1940. The first volume of the tetralogy.) His espionage fiction presents Edmund Trothe, an agent for British SIS in a series of four novels.

3289. ___. *The End of the Rug.* Garden City, NY: Doubleday, 1968. A career diplomat is an expert on international trade; he is also one of MI-5's most valuable troubleshooters, with emphasis on the second part of the word. Others:

3290. ___. *The Night Is a Child.* Garden City, NY: Doubleday, 1972.

3291. ___. *White Horse to Banbury Cross.* Garden City, NY: Doubleday, 1970.

3292. Llewellyn, Sam. *Blood Knot.* New York: Pocket, 1992. Bill Tyrrell is skipper of the *Vixen* and is about to lose it because his watch got herself drunk and failed to avert an accident with a small boat. There's a dead Russian involved too, but the girl insists that somebody must have planted the body and scuttled the boat.

3293. Lockhart, Robin Bruce. *Reilly: Ace of Spies*. New York: Stein & Day, 1967. Mostly historical and biographical account of the real-life derring-do of the famous Sidney Reilly. The sequel inspired a TV series:

3294. ___. *Reilly: The First Man*. New York: Penguin, 1987.

3295. Lockridge, Richard and George H. Estabrooks. *Death in the Mind*. New York: Dutton, 1945. An agent must discover who is committing a series of treasonable acts inside the inner circles of the British military establishment. *

3296. Lodwick, John. *Aegean Adventure*. New York: Dodd, 1946. British commandos raid a German-held island off the coast of Greece during World War II. *

3297. ___. *Man Dormant*. New York: Duell, Sloan & Pearce, 1950. First published in England as *First Steps Inside a Zoo*. A British spy works out of the home of a wealthy, eccentric American on the French Riviera in the summer of 1949. *

3298. Loewengard, Heidi H. *After Midnight*. By Martha Albrand, pseud. New York: Random, 1948. An American veteran returns to Italy to relive his wartime experiences and discover who betrayed him to the Germans. *y
    Born Heidi Huberta Freybe, "Albrand" was a respected European journalist before her immigration to the United States in 1937. She published her first work in German under the pseudonym Katrin Holland at the age of seventeen. Possessed of strong religious faith, her view is international and many of her serialized stories, often published as novels, have been widely translated. Many of her tales involve no espionage theme and she is as noteworthy as an author of "straight" detection as for her tales of spies and operatives. After the war and until her death in 1981 she replaced Nazis and resistance fighters with neo-nazis or Communists and protagonists who opposed their kind of modern evil.

3299. ___. *A Call from Austria*. By Martha Albrand, pseud. New York: Random, 1963. An American newsman comes to Vienna to find his missing brother and finds a pretty girl who bears him an old grudge. *y
    Readers of Albrand appreciate her mixture of romance, mystery, and espionage.

3300. ___. *A Door Fell Shut*. By Martha Albrand, pseud. New York: Signet, 1966. When famed violinist Bronsky returns to his home town of East

Berlin to give a concert, he is drawn into a CIA effort to get a Russian named Cassan over the Wall. **yP*

3301. ___. *Endure No Longer.* By Martha Albrand, pseud. Boston: Little, 1944. Frederica von Storm, proud daughter of a Prussian military family, comes of age in a Germany preparing for another great war.

3302. ___. *Hunted Woman.* By Martha Albrand, pseud. New York: Random, 1952. A beautiful Czech woman attempting to flee to Switzerland with her child is chased by Communist agents and aided by a shy American student. **y*

3303. ___. *The Linden Affair.* By Martha Albrand, pseud. New York: Random, 1957. A German, long a Russian prisoner, returns to his wife and family and is given an important post in the US Security Department. A reporter and a CIA agent are suspicious of the man and pursue their doubts. **y*

3304. ___. *Manhattan North.* By Martha Albrand, pseud. New York: Coward-McCann, 1975. When a Supreme Court justice is assassinated, a young corporation lawyer is appointed to work with a Presidential Commission looking into the effects of terrorist tactics on the judicial system. ***

3305. ___. *The Mask of Alexander.* By Martha Albrand, pseud. New York: Random, 1955. The heroine is caught up with Italian Communists and neo-Nazis who are battling one another for power in postwar Venice and Paris. **y*

3306. ___. *Meet Me Tonight.* By Martha Albrand, pseud. New York: Random, 1960. In Brussels to meet her husband, a lady meets instead one Farkas, reputedly responsible for the imprisonment and deaths of many of her friends and relatives in Hungary. Soon it becomes apparent that this is wrong . . . **y*

3307. ___. *Nightmare in Copenhagen.* By Martha Albrand, pseud. New York: Random, 1954. A Danish fisherman recovers secret explosives from a wrecked German U-boat and is hounded by Soviet agents; then, a young American scientist mixes into the affair. **y*

3308. ___. *No Surrender.* By Martha Albrand, pseud. Boston: Little, 1952. A young Dutch lawyer, secretly working for the underground, accepts a government position under the eyes of the Gestapo and to the contempt of his friends and neighbors. First published, as were many of her stories, in the *Saturday Evening Post.* **y*

3309. ___. *None Shall Know.* By Martha Albrand, pseud. Boston: Little, 1945. Two young citizens of Occupied France busy themselves smuggling children into neutral Switzerland. Captured by the Gestapo, the children of a border town contrive to obtain the boys' freedom. **y*

3310. ___. *Remembered Anger.* By Martha Albrand, pseud. Boston: Little, 1946. American intelligence officer Chester Burton returns to Paris from a German prison camp with one burning question: who told the SS he was parachuting into France on a special mission the night of his capture?

3311. ___. *Rhine Replica.* By Martha Albrand, pseud. New York: Random, 1969. Up from Rome for the carnival in Cologne, the hero finds the only room available to be in an old castle out of town; there he meets a beautiful girl and is drawn into one of those sinister neo-Nazi plots against world peace. **y*

3312. ___. *Without Orders.* By Martha Albrand, pseud. Boston: Little, 1943. Lt. Charles Barrett awakens in an Italian insane asylum, where doctors tell him he's been their patient, a nobleman, for twenty-four years. He "accepts" his identity and joins the Italian resistance movement against the Germans. **y*

3313. ___. *Zurich/AZ 900.* By Martha Albrand, pseud. New York: Holt, 1974. A doctor with an as yet incompletely tested formula for the cure of atherosclerosis is kidnapped by one of several competing and conflicting interests and must be rescued by an intrepid agent. ***

3314. Longstreet, Stephen. *Ambassador.* New York: Avon, 1978. A major security breach and the secret arrival of the Vice President thrust the American ambassador in Rome into a controversy which can mean disaster for his government—as well as his own death. *P*

Loraine, Philip, pseud. *See* Estridge, Robin

3315. Lord, Graham. *Marshmallow Pie.* New York: Coward-McCann, 1970. A British newspaperman is sent to see how the hippie movement functions. Undercover, he finds that its bearded leader has come up with a dangerous drug wanted by the agents of various unfriendly governments.

3316. ___. *The Spider and the Fly.* New York: Viking, 1974. A spy thriller reminiscent of the real-life Profumo scandal involves a British member of Parliament and a "liberated" American divorcée.

3317. Loring, Emilie. *Love Came Laughing By.* Boston: Little, 1950. A girl returns to Washington from South American carrying important secret papers and meets a Congressman with a dangerous political opponent. *

3318. Lorraine, John. *Men of Career.* New York: Crown, 1961. Drastic changes in State Department functions and loyalty questions plague diplomats who are negotiating with the Russians in 1953 Vienna.

3319. Lottman, Eileen. *The Bionic Woman.* By Maude Willis, pseud. New York: Berkley, 1977. Based on the ABC network series which ran from 1976 through 1977 and a spinoff of the *Six-Million Dollar Man.* Jaime Sommers is outfitted with bionic parts after an accident and goes to work for Oscar Goldman of OSI. *P* Two more:

3320. ___. *Welcome Home, Jaime.* By Maude Willis, pseud. New York: Berkley, 1977. *P*

3321. ___. *Extracurricular Activities.* By Maude Willis, pseud. New York: Berkley, 1977. *P*

3322. Lourie, Richard. *First Loyalty.* New York: Harcourt, 1985. A prolific Russian and Polish translator, including Andrei Sakharov's *Memoirs* (New York: Knopf, 1990), Lourie has also written a *Miami Vice* screenplay. His second novel is about a Soviet agent who assumes the cover of a dissenting poet and "defects" to the West.

3323. ___. *Sagittarius in Warsaw.* New York: Vanguard, 1973. An American has a series of incredible adventures aboard a train travelling across Poland. *H*

3324. ___. *Zero Gravity: A Novel.* New York: Harcourt, 1985. The US and USSR compete to see which country can send a poet to the moon first. *H*

3325. Louvish, Simon. *The Silencer.* Brooklyn, NY: Interlink, 1993. Joe Dekel is an Israeli journalist in this surrealistic caper about an anti-hero who refuses to give in when confronted by the "Silencer," a mystery figure whose job is to prevent the captious Dekel, critical toward Jew and Arab equally, from being published outside the US.

3326. Lovejoy, William H. *Alpha Kat.* New York: Zebra, 1992. The President orders the CIA to shut down Burmese drug lord Lon Pot's operation. The means: America's high-tech stealth fighter known as Alpha Kat. *P*

3327. ___. *Delta Green.* New York: Zebra, 1993. Colonel Kevin ("Snake Eyes") McKenna leads his elite team of Stealth skyfighters against hardliners in the Soviet Union who call themselves the New World Order. *P*

Lovell, Marc, pseud. *See* McShane, Mark

3328. Lowden, Desmond. *Bandersnatch.* New York: Holt, 1969. Retired Royal Navy Commander Alec Sheldon and his aging wartime crew plan to extract a cool 2 million pounds sterling from a Greek shipping mogul they have kidnapped.

3329. Luard, Nicholas. *The Orion Line.* New York: Harcourt, 1977. A British SIS agent and the daughter of a French Maquis heroine work together in the Basque territory of Spain to discover the connection between their past and the murderous events in the Separatist present.

Proficient in languages, a skilled athlete, a satirist of the first order, and co-owner of a journal called *Private Eye*, Luard was educated in both Great Britain and the United States. During his time in the British Army, he was assigned as an intelligence agent-saboteur to work with NATO long-range patrols. Well-travelled, Luard has emphasized locale and close connections with real events in his spy thrillers; indeed, as we will note below, some scenarios were so realistic as to cause genuine concern by certain agencies that trade secrets had leaked out. For the record, it was Luard's *Private Eye* which broke, for the first time, the identity of the SIS chief, naming Sir Dick Goldsmith-White (accurately) in 1963. The series of scandals swirling about the government during these years (the Vassall Scandal, Profumo Scandal, the Blake Affair—not to mention Philby's slipping through the net to safety in Russia) may have kept *Private Eye* off the court dockets because HMG was very reluctant to air more dirty linen in public.

3330. ___. *The Robespierre Serial.* New York: Harcourt, 1975. An SIS agent named Carswell, unaware that his service is to carry out a "fake" hit on a defecting Arab leader in order to throw the CIA off the scent, pursues his target intent on an actual murder and after moving through the Pyrenees, almost succeeds despite the efforts of his own superiors, the Americans, and local police to stop him.

In the wake of the Church Committee Hearings, the CIA was, putting it mildly, quite concerned with what it understood would be a most revealing Vincent Marchetti-like tale. In fact, agents of its Q Section attempted to obtain an advance look at the proof, justifying the action by claiming that a foreign firm was seeking translation rights.

3331. ___. *The Shadow Spy.* New York: Harcourt, 1979. [*The Dirty Area.* London: Hamilton, 1979]. SIS agent Steele is dispatched to Lisbon to deal with a psychotic ex-operative who wants to kill the man he thinks ruined his life and threatens to blow the cover of every spy he has ever known. The problem is that the target never existed.

3332. ___. *Travelling Horseman.* New York: Harcourt, 1975. A British agent is ordered to penetrate the inner circle of that small group which runs the PLO's Black September terrorist squad. Coming in the wake of the author's *The Robespierre Serial,* which saw the CIA buying more copies than any other American purchaser, this yarn also worried critics at the Agency, who believed that the plot an events in this novel were not only based on real-life events, but were documented by leaks from within the Langely headquarters itself.

3333. ___. *The Warm and Golden War.* New York: Harcourt, 1967. A multimillionaire hires a band of mercenaries to open part of the Austrian-Hungarian border to allow a thousand refugees to flee to the West. The author's first novel, it was based on his experiences just outside Hungary during the 1956 revolt.

3334. Lucas, Ruth. *Who Dare to Live.* Boston: Houghton, 1966. An Englishwoman trapped inside Germany by the outbreak of war in 1939 loses her daughter to the authorities and her husband to the Gestapo. When the underground rescues her child, she agrees to work with them in what becomes a seven-year struggle against terror. *

3335. Luddecke, Werner J. *Morituri.* Trans. from the German. Greenwich, CN: Fawcett, 1965. The SIS contacts an anti-Nazi German demolitions expert in 1942 India and asks him to pose as an SS agent aboard a ship bound from Tokyo to Bordeaux—a vessel which must be scuttled in order to destroy its vital cargo. *P*

3336. Ludlum, Robert. *The Bourne Identity.* New York: Richard Marek, 1980. Suffering from amnesia, a shooting victim finds a Swiss bank account which identifies him as a professional assassin who is being manipulated by a top secret US government bureau into killing the dreaded terrorist leader Carlos the Jackal.

   According to a recent interview, Ludlum turned to writing after tiring of a career as a voice-over announcer for US television commercials. Preferring the den of his Connecticut home to exotic locales, this author finds it necessary to work early in the morning to avoid the constant interruptions of the telephone. An astute student of intelligence matters who never had any formal connection with any government agency, Ludlum frequents the reference room of the New York Public Library to do research before undertaking each new title. In his travels over the years, one of his favorite tricks has been to take hundreds of photographs of the scenery around him—photos which can later provide the intricate place details for story climaxes. Critic Thomas R. Edwards, writing in the *New York Review of Books*, has coined the term *ludlums* to describe the sameness of these novels that, despite their vast popularity, are characterized by improbabilities and sheer bad writing (qtd. *Contemporary Authors*. New Ser. Vol. 25: 294).

3337. ___. *The Aquitaine Progression*. New York: Random, 1984. The dying words of a CIA man begin Joel Converse's involvement in a world-shattering secret, one that explains how the world's most dangerous terrorist organizations are provided arms and explosives: "Aquitaine" is the name given to this mad scheme to resurrect the Fourth Reich and a new order of rulers (*Sonnenkinder*, "Children of the Sun") who will step to power on a day of worldwide mass demonstrations ending in chaos and anarchy.

3338. ___. *The Bourne Supremacy*. New York: Random, 1986. The Vice Premier of China's own blood was used to scrawl the name "Jason Bourne," infamous assassin, next to him. But the CIA alone is supposed to know the secret of Jason Bourne—a man who never existed except in the persona of covert operative David Webb, now living in seclusion with the woman who saved him.

3339. ___. *The Bourne Ultimatum*. New York: Random, 1990. The sequel of *The Bourne Identity* pits the amnesiac with the double identity (Jason Bourne) against the international terrorist Carlos the Jackal, who intends to wipe him and his family out.

3340. ___. *The Chancellor Manuscript*. New York: Dial, 1977. Researcher Peter Chancellor discovers that FBI chief J. Edgar Hoover may have been assassinated an is plunged into an inter-agency war between rival US intelligence organizations.

3341. ___. *The Cry of the Halidon*. By Jonathan Ryder, pseud. New York: Delacorte, 1974. An American geologist doing a secret survey of the island of Jamaica finds himself the pawn of British Intelligence and even his own team members.

3342. ___. *The Gemini Contenders*. New York: Dial, 1976. The twin sons of a former Italian government official search for a mysterious document he was forced to leave behind when fleeing his fascist-dominated homeland in 1939.

3343. ___. *The Holcroft Covenant.* New York: Dial, 1978. Noel Holcroft seeks an old document drawn up thirty years before by his father and other Nazi leaders which, upon his signature, will release $800 million to descendants of Holocaust victims.

3344. ___. *The Icarus Agenda.* New York: Random, 1988. Congressman Evan Kendrick once saved American embassy hostages from Arab terrorists and had felt himself safe from unwanted publicity for that act of valor; now, however, his secret is out and those whom he defied have vowed to kill him.

3345. ___. *The Matarese Circle.* New York: Richard Marek, 1979. The world's two best secret agents, Brando Scofield of the CIA and Vasili Taleniekov of the KGB, are forced to set aside their personal vendetta to halt the financing of terrorist organizations by the Matarese Corporation.

3346. ___. *The Osterman Weekend.* Cleveland, OH: World, 1972. A TV news executive is recruited by the CIA to help break up a Soviet espionage ring which has been codenamed "Omega."

3347. ___. *The Parsifal Mosaic.* New York: Random, 1982. Mikhail Havlîcek is a native Czech who has become a protégé of Anton Matthias, fellow Czech and Secretary of State. Known as Michael Havelock, he has been for sixteen years a brilliant deep-cover operative; then sinister forces dupe him into believing that the woman he intends to marry—Jenna Karas, a Czech national—is a double agent and member of the Voyennaya, a KGB terrorist group. He witnesses her termination, and after learning the truth, begins a desperate search for the conspirators.

3348. ___. *The Rhineman Exchange.* New York: Dial, 1974. An OSS agent travels to Buenos Aires in 1943 to meet a Gestapo agent and make arrangements for an obscene deal between the US and Germany, the exchange of industrial diamonds for gyroscopes.

3349. ___. *The Road to Gandolfo.* By Michael Shepherd, pseud. New York: Bantam, 1982. First published in 1975, this is a nonespionage comic novel rpt. in 1982 by Bantam under the author's own name. *H*

3350. ___. *The Road to Omaha.* New York: Random, 1992. General MacKenzie Hawkins, retired, convinces lawyer Sam Devereaux to represent Indian claims that certain lands, including the site of SAC, in Nebraska belong to the tribe. *H*

3351. ___. *The Scarlatti Inheritance.* Cleveland, OH: World, 1971. An American agent becomes concerned about the decline is his family's fortune and looking into the matter finds that his relative, Ulster Scarlatti, is using the money to bankroll Hitler's World War II effort.

3352. ___. *The Scorpio Illusion.* New York: Bantam, 1993. Ty Hawthorne is an ex-naval intelligence officer on the trail of the Scorpios, a group of conspirators led by Amaya Bajaratt, a Basque terrorist, whom he knew as Dominique, his lover.

3353. ___. *Trevayne.* New York: Bantam, 1989. First published in 1973 by Bantam under the pseudonym Jonathan Ryder. An aide to the President stumbles upon a secret and corrupt enclave within the government. An early Ludlum:

3354. ___. *The Matlock Paper.* New York: Dial, 1973.

3355. Lyall, Gavin. *Blame the Dead.* New York: Viking, 1973. Failing to protect his employer from death, a bodyguard who was once an intelligence agent enters into the tricky world of marine insurance as his investigation of the killing unfolds.

Lyall flew in the RAF before taking his degree at Cambridge, and he produced an acclaimed account of the RAF during the war years (*The War in the Air.* New York: Morrow, 1968). Additionally, he was an outstanding journalist and directed films for the BBC. He has scored two Silver Daggers from the British Crime Writers Association, including one for *Midnight Plus One.* Today he is considered the equal of Allbeury and Deighton.

3356. ___. *The Conduct of Major Maxim.* New York: Viking, 1983. Deals with the characteristic Lyall theme of loyalty to one's friends and country and the often paradoxical conflict that such loyalty begets. The situation is the interminable conflict between rival secret services in British Intelligence over another byzantine East German conspiracy to undermine the West.

3357. ___. *The Crocus List.* London: Hodder & Stoughton, 1985. In this third Harry Maxim spy-adventure, an explosion of gunfire in Westminster Abbey begins Major Maxim's quest for the perpetrators and the secret behind the Crocus List, an organization bent on sabotaging East-West detente. (See Mr. Lyall's commentary in CRAFT NOTES.)

3358. ___. *Judas Country.* New York: Viking, 1975. An Eastern Mediterranean morass of espionage and terrorists, and Greco-Turkish tension, compound the efforts of a group to locate the fabled sword of Richard the Lion-Hearted.

3359. ___. *Midnight Plus One.* New York: Scribner's, 1965. Lewis Cane, who still dreams of his glory days as the French Maquis leader "Caneton," agrees to an SIS assignment put to him by his one-time Resistance paymaster, Henry the Lawyer: to guard and infiltrate an international financier's transit of the East European frontiers.

3360. ___. *The Most Dangerous Game.* New York: Scribner's, 1963. A free-lance pilot's mission to a northern Finnish town is beset by murder and an effort by the KGB to bring him down.

3361. ___. *The Secret Servant.* New York: Viking, 1980. Major Harry Maxim, assigned to 10 Downing Street, is involved with a Cambridge scientist who harbors a secret he is desperate to keep from discovery.

3362. ___. *Uncle Target.* New York: Viking, 1988. The MBT90 is a new supertank that exists in prototype and is being tested in the Jordanian desert; while he and his team are in the desert, a Soviet-backed coup erupts within the Jordanian army, and Maxim must use the tank to escape, or its capture could result in its becoming a Soviet possession. Two early adventure-thrillers, before he moved into the espionage genre, are:

3363. ___. *Shooting Script.* New York: Scribner's, 1966.

3364. ___. *Venus with Pistol.* New York: Scribner's, 1969.

3365. Lyandres, Yulian Semenovich. *TASS Is Authorized to Announce—* By Julian Semenov, pseud. Trans. Charles Buxton. New York: Riverrun, 1987. [*TASS Upolnomochen Zayavit—* Moscow: Druzhba Narodov, 1979; trans. and rpt. under this title by John Calder of London, 1987]. Julian Semenov, whose name includes other transliterations from the cyrillic alphabet, such as Julian Semyonov or Yulian Semyonov, is referred to by the 1988 Avon blurb reprint as "Russia's bestselling author with 35 million books in print," Semyonov's contacts in high Soviet circles gave him access to information from KGB files in the decade before the Soviet Union's collapse. In addition, he is a prolific writer of screenplays with over 65 to his credit. This espionage novel, with its cast of dozens, is based on then-KGB chief Yuri Andropov's remark to Semyonov that the US had a very important covert operation running in the Soviet Union. This tale is set during the Carter Administration about a Pentagon plot known as Operation Torch and action that moves between

Moscow, Africa ("Nagonia"), and the US; the good guys, however, are in the KGB and their opponents are CIA, Pentagon, and various powerful, rich capitalists of the military-industrial complex with the odd neo-Nazis and corrupt CIA official tossed in.

3366. ___. *The Himmler Ploy*. By Julian Semenov, pseud. Trans. H. W. Chalsma. New York: Arrow, 1979. [*Semnadtsat' Mgnovenii Vesny*. Moscow: Voenizdat, 1970; pub. by Progress in 1973 as *Seventeen Moments of Spring* and translated by Katherine Judelson]. As the Reich crumbles under Allied attack, only double agent von Stirlitz, known to the Russians as their most trusted agent and to the Germans as their spy-chief, could thwart the ultimate last-minute Nazi masterstroke. *P

3367. ___. *Petrovka 38*. By Julian Semenov, pseud. Trans. Michael Scammell. Briarcliff Manor, NY: Stein & Day, 1965. This was the first James Bond era spy thriller from the Soviet Union to be translated for Western readers. Three KGB operatives seek a gang of capitalist agents who are organizing robbery and murder throughout Russia. * Other Lyandres stories:

3368. ___. *Diplomaticheskii Agent* [*Diplomatic Agent*]. By Julian Semenov, pseud. Moscow: Molodaya Gvardia, 1958.

3369. ___. *Intercontinental Knot*. By Julian Semenov, pseud. Trans. from the Russian. New York: Riverrun, 1994.

3370. ___. *Tainaya voina Maksima Maksimovicha: Dokum* [*The Secret War of Isaev*]. By Julian Semenov, pseud. Moscow: Sovetskaya Rossiya, 1974.

3371. Lyle-Smythe, Alan. *Assault on Loveless*. By Alan Caillou, pseud. New York: Avon, 1971. Interpol agent Cabot Cain and a freelance troubleshooter are in Portugal to destroy a ruthless mercenary named "Loveless." *P*

3372. ___. *Marseilles*. By Alan Caillou, pseud. New York: Pocket, 1965. Mike Benasque is living on borrowed time as he seeks to expose a notorious French terrorist organization. *P*

3373. ___. *Mindanao Pearl*. By Alan Caillou, pseud. New York: Pinnacle, 1973. First published in London in 1959. In the jungles of the Philippines, soldier-of-fortune Caleb and a beautiful native girl seek a fellow Englishman and a fabulous black diamond. *P*

3374. ___. *The Plotters.* By Alan Caillou, pseud. New York: Harper & Row, 1960. A former OSS officer, now a newsman, is asked by the CIA to undertake a dangerous mission deep into the South American jungles. There he discovers left-over Nazis plotting a comeback.

3375. ___. *The Private Army of Colonel Tobin: Afghan Assault.* By Alan Caillou, pseud. New York: Pinnacle, 1973. Colonel Tobin's private army is the deadliest force in the world; these mercenaries will fight wars anywhere. In this outing, they are asked to move into Afghanistan to stop a projected Communist takeover. *P*

3376. ___. *The Private Army of Colonel Tobin: Congo War Cry.* By Alan Caillou, pseud. New York: Pinnacle, 1972. Tobin's men are sent to the mercenary-rich former Belgian colony to stamp out a plot designed to break the U.N.-sponsored peace. *P*

3377. ___. *The Private Army of Colonel Tobin: The Dead Sea Submarine.* By Alan Caillou, pseud. New York: Pinnacle, 1970. Tobin and his men are sent on a deadly mission—to stop a submarine operating in the Sinai Desert! *P*

3378. ___. *The Private Army of Colonel Tobin: Death Charge.* By Alan Caillou, pseud. New York: Pinnacle, 1973. Tobin and his people go to Mexico where political kidnappings of American businessmen have been on the rise; the terrorist involved are believed to be hiding in the Sierra Madres and the mercenaries must ferret them out. *P*

3379. ___. *The Private Army of Colonel Tobin: Terror in Rio.* By Alan Caillou, pseud. New York: Pinnacle, 1971. When the Brazilian Army cannot handle the guerrillas and outlaws and poison-arrow-throwing Indians in the fanatical revolutionary force, Colonel Tobin and his hand-picked mercenaries are brought in from England to do the job. *P* Among the following tales are the other "Assault" novels that feature Cabot Cain, agent of Dept. B-7 of Interpol:

3380. ___. *Assault on Aimata.* By Alan Caillou, pseud. New York: Avon, 1975. *P*

3381. ___. *Assault on Agathon.* By Alan Caillou, pseud. New York: Avon, 1972. *P*

3382. ___. *Assault on Fellawi.* By Alan Caillou, pseud. New York: Avon, 1972. *P*

3383. ___. *Assault on Kolchak.* By Alan Caillou, pseud. New York: Avon, 1969. *P*

3384. ___. *Assault on Ming.* By Alan Caillou, pseud. New York: Avon, 1969. *P*

3385. ___. *Diamonds Wild.* By Alan Caillou, pseud. New York: Pocket, 1966. *P*

3386. ___. *The Private Army of Colonel Tobin: Swamp War.* By Alan Caillou, pseud. New York: Pocket, 1973. *P*

3387. ___. *Who'll Buy My Evil.* By Alan Caillou, pseud. New York: Pocket, 1966. *P* Lyle-Smythe, as Caillou, also wrote about a devil-may-care group of resistance fighters (Josh Dekker, "Wild Bill" Donovan, and Jill Magran) in a paperback series set during WW II in France. Two from this series:

3388. ___. *Blood Run.* By Alan Caillou, pseud. New York: Pinnacle, 1985. *P*

3389. ___. *Dekker's Demons.* By Alan Caillou, pseud. New York: Pinnacle, 1985. *P* Caillou has returned to espionage-intrigue thrillers in recent years with agent-hero Ian Quayle. Two of these:

3390. ___. *A League of Hawks.* By Alan Caillou, pseud. New York: Lorevan, 1986. *P*

3391. ___. *The Swords of God.* By Alan Caillou, pseud. New York: Lorevan, 1987. *P* Two other thrillers:

3392. ___. *The House on Curzon Street.* By Alan Caillou, pseud. New York: Morrow, 1983. [*A Woman of Quality.* New York: Zebra, 1984. *P*]

3393. ___. *Joshua's People.* By Alan Caillou, pseud. New York: Pinnacle, 1982. *P*

Lynn, Margaret, pseud. *See* Battye, Gladys S.

3394. Lyon, Bentley. *White Crow.* New York: St. Martin's, 1990. Arnold Kent is en route to an international forestry conference in Spain when he is asked to deliver a message, a message that will result in dead KGB agents and himself as the object of a manhunt by his own embassy, the CIA, and the Spanish police.

3395. Lyons, Nan and Ivan. *The President Is Coming to Lunch.* New York: Doubleday, 1988. Libby's is Manhattan's elite place to be seen at a power lunch. Now the President is coming to lunch and Libby has to keep her and the President's twenty-year-old secret a secret from the Secret Service. *H*

3396. Lypsyte, Robert. *Liberty Two.* New York: Simon & Schuster, 1974. Former astronaut Charles Rice and his seemingly fantastic crusade to awaken the American people to sundry dangers is "helped" by an agent provocateur from a semi-governmental group.

M

3397. MacAlister, Ian. *Driscoll's Diamonds.* Greenwich, CT: Fawcett, 1973. Somewhere off the African coast tough mercenary Driscoll matches wits with Royan, his teacher in terror, for possession of a fortune in stolen diamonds. *P*

3398. ___. *The Skylark Mission.* Greenwich, CT: Fawcett, 1973. In early 1942, a small group of British Commandos must hold open a vital strait near New Guinea to allow the survivors of the Singapore fiasco to escape capture by the advancing Japanese. *P*

3399. ___. *Strike Force 7.* Greenwich, CT: Fawcett, 1974. A band of mercenaries lead by a cynical ex-army officer is sent to rescue two women from a terrorist stronghold. *P*

3400. ___. *Valley of the Assassins.* Greenwich, CT: Fawcett, 1976. When adventurer Eric Larson discovers a treasure map in Iraq, he is pursued by Kurdish guerrillas and the Iraqi secret police. *P*

McBain, Ed, pseud. *See* Hunter, Evan

3401. MacBeth, George. *The Samurai.* New York: Harcourt, 1975. SIS agent Cadbury matches her allure and martial skills against the unscrupulous perversities of a ruthless Samurai society.

3402. McBriarty, Douglas. *Snowshot.* New York: Walker, 1988. Sheriff Peter McPhee has big-time murder on his hands when Pentagon officials and arms manufacturers meet at a luxury ski resort and one of their number gets killed.

arms manufacturers meet at a luxury ski resort and one of their number gets killed.

McCall, Anthony, pseud. *See* Kane, Henry

3403. McCammon, Robert R. *The Wolf's Hour*. New York: Pocket, 1989. Michael Gallatin is a spy with a ludicrous difference: he can change himself into a werewolf. He parachutes into Occupied France en route to Berlin to unravel the secret of—and destroy—the Nazi plot known as Iron Fist.

3404. McCarry, Charles. *The Miernik Dossier*. New York: Saturday Review, 1973. A drunken Polish official on overseas duty is recalled. Fearing his reception, he elects to defect and various intelligence agencies, Western and Soviet, attempt to determine if his decision is true or if he is a double agent.

A former journalist and speech writer for President Eisenhower, McCarry joined the CIA in the late 1950s, seeing service at various stations in Asia and Africa. This, his first effort, was widely praised for its technical construction and realism, pleasing even Eric Ambler. Following this success, McCarry has turned out a number of spy thrillers, all very authentic as to mood, locale, character, and plotting.

3405. ___. *The Better Angels*. New York: Dutton, 1979. A Washington political novel with espionage overtones. President Lockwood is seeking re-election against a sinisterly charismatic foe; on his side is a small group of men and women of various talents but single-minded loyalty.

3406. ___. *The Last Supper*. New York: Dutton, 1983. In his most ambitiously plotted novel, McCarry opens with Paul Christopher as a captive of the Chinese with half his twenty-year sentence served; the events that betrayed him begin with family history when Christopher's father courted his mother in Germany and extend through his secret life in the Outfit right up to his betrayal by a close member of his own intelligence service.

3407. ___. *Second Sight*. New York: Dutton, 1991. The continuing saga of Paul Christopher, former poet, CIA agent—now with a daughter whom he has not seen in ten years.

3408. ___. *The Secret Lovers*. Greenwich, CT: Fawcett, 1978. A CIA officer must find the killer of an exiled Russian dissident whose latest novel has just been delivered to the West with a request that it not be published until after the author's death. *P*

3409. ___. *The Tears of Autumn.* New York: Saturday Review, 1975. Agent Paul Christopher believes he knows who in the year 1963 arranged for the killing of President Kennedy and why, but his theory that friends of South Vietnamese President Diem ordered it in retaliation for their leader's death, proves so destructive that he is ordered to give it up. Fortunately for the reader, the agent is thoroughly dedicated to it and pursues a crusade for the truth which takes him through Europe and Asia.

This volume caused a stir throughout official Washington at a time when the Agency was under intense fire from the Church Committee. It also provided additional grist for the mills of those who have always held JFK's murder to have been the result of a conspiracy. "Maybe the Vietnamese did kill Kennedy," McCarry once said, "but they sure didn't tell me." (Donald McCormick, *Who's Who in Spy Fiction* [New York: Taplinger, 1977], 122).

3410. McCarthy, John [Shaun] L. *Dead Man Alive.* By Desmond Cory, pseud. New York: Walker, 1969. Posing as a Nazi while leading a party of five men and a feisty blonde, secret agent Johnny Fedora endures a mission which has become a bloody nightmare as he seeks a man in a part of the Congo where no one has survived before.

3411. ___. *Even If You Run.* By Desmond Cory, pseud. Garden City, NY: Doubleday, 1972. More character than action is displayed in this account of how a young and naive SIS agent is sent out to Spain to help three hardened British agents thwart a coup against the Franco government.

3412. ___. *Feramontov.* By Desmond Cory, pseud. New York: Walker 1966. SIS operative Johnny Fedora is ordered to a vacation spot on the English coast to investigate a man named Ortiz.

3413. ___. *The Gestapo File.* By Desmond Cory, pseud. New York: Award, 1971. Fedora gets mixed up with a plot by left-over Nazis against the government of West Germany. *P*

3414. ___. *High Requiem.* By Desmond Cory, pseud. New York: Walker, 1965. Fedora is dispatched to a super-secret base in the North African desert where a saboteur is loose and the ultimate weapon is at stake.

3415. ___. *The Hitler Diamonds.* By Desmond Cory, pseud. New York: Award, 1969. A fabulous treasure left over from the closing days of the Third Reich becomes the prize sought by both Fedora and assorted scum. *P*

3416. ___. *Johnny Goes West.* By Desmond Cory, pseud. New York: Walker, 1958. The prize of a rich lode of uranium-bearing carbotite is enough to have the SIS send Fedora to South America.

3417. ___. *Mountainhead.* By Desmond Cory, pseud. New York: Walker, 1968. The survivors of a plane crash in Chinese-occupied Tibet must be rescued by secret agent Johnny Fedora.

3418. ___. *The Nazi Assassins.* By Desmond Cory, pseud. New York: Award, 1970. Fedora is asked to look into the matter of high government officials who are being killed by men who look mysteriously like hit-men from the old Third Reich. *P*

3419. ___. *Shockwave.* By Desmond Cory, pseud. New York: Walker, 1964. A Soviet plot to overthrow the Spanish government is quashed by the quick actions of operative Fedora.

3420. ___. *Sunburst.* By Desmond Cory, pseud. New York: Walker, 1972. Agent Fedora is sent to end nuclear blackmail by the Spanish military against other European governments.

3421. ___. *Timelock.* By Desmond Cory, pseud. New York: Walker, 1964. Fedora is held in a leaden vice—trapped by a Spanish torturer and his own amnesia.

3422. ___. *Trieste.* By Desmond Cory, pseud. New York: Award, 1968. A Soviet plot against the government of this Yugoslav city must be crushed by agent Fedora. *P*

3423. ___. *Undertow.* By Desmond Cory, pseud. New York: Walker, 1963. Fedora races Soviet agents for vital records aboard a sunken U-boat off the Spanish coast. Three other Fedora tales are:

3424. ___. *Johnny Goes South.* By Desmond Cory, pseud. New York: Walker, 1964.

3425. ___. *Lucky Ham.* By Desmond Cory, pseud. London: Macmillan, 1977.

3426. ___. *Swastika Hunt.* By Desmond Cory, pseud. New York: Award, 1969. *P*

3427. McCarthy, Mary. *Cannibals and Missionaries.* New York: Harcourt, 1979. A hijacked Iranian airliner carries a committee of liberal US politicians who have been sent to investigate claims of human rights violations and SAVAK torture in Iran.

3428. McCarthy, Wilson. *The Detail.* London: Hutchinson, 1973. In the plot of this one, the author, an ex-secret service agent who was responsible for the Presidential Advance Team, emphasizes the other role of the service: to protect US currency from counterfeiters as the action moves from the Customs at LAX to Washington, DC and London and back to the US on the trail of currency forgers.

3429. ___. *The Fourth Man.* London: Hutchinson, 1972. Psychopaths, right-wing extremists, and the Mafia conspire to assassinate the President of the United States and agents of the US Secret Service seem powerless to prevent the tragedy.

3430. McClure, James. *The Blood of an Englishman.* New York: Harper & Row, 1980. Lieutenant Tromp Kramer and his Bantu sidekick Detective Mickey Zondi of the Trekkersburg Murder and Robbery Squad investigate two violent crimes, including the execution of a man found in the trunk of a society matron's elephant car, that seem to have a single source dating back to WW II.

3431. ___. *Rogue Eagle.* New York: Harper & Row, 1977. In South Africa SIS agent Finbar Buchanan and CIA operative Nancy Kitson attempt to foil the plans of a white terrorist band which is committed to keeping apartheid at any cost.

3432. McCormick, Donald. *Zita: A Do-It-Yourself Romance.* By Richard Deacon, pseud. London: Muller, 1983. An agent on leave from SIS notices the signature of a man's name above his in the exact calligraphy of his immediate superior, but his boss claims otherwise, and when it's alibied by a powerful government figure, the agent is focred to "go private"—almost losing his life in the process to KGB killers.

   A prolific and versatile author on many subjects, McCormick's expertise ranges from the Cambridge Apostles, one of the most elite of English secret societies, through biographies of spies (*John Dee.* By Richard Deacon, pseud. London: Muller, 1968), to numerous books on the great intelligence services of the world and several excellent reference sources on espionage fiction and fact, such as *Who's Who in Spy Fiction, Spy Fiction: A Connoisseur's Guide (with Katy Fletcher),* and *Spyclopaedia (see the* BIBLIOGRAPHY and CRAFT NOTES sections of this text).

3433. McCrum, Robert. *In the Secret State*. New York: Avon, 1981. One of those wheels-within-wheels capers in which the man who used to direct an elite and highly secret department within British Intelligence conducts his own investigation into the demise of the man who forced him out. *P*

3434. McCurtin, Peter. *Soldier-of-Fortune: Bloodbath*. New York: Leisure, 1985. Jim Rainey is a soldier-of-fortune mixed up in various intrigues in this action paperback series. *P*

3435. ___. *Soldier-of-Fortune: Body Count*. New York: Belmont-Tower, 1978. Mercenary Jim Rainey leads his men into action in the wilds of New Guinea where a Dutch traitor named Kuyker has been selling arms to bloodthirsty Kiwai tribesmen. *P*

3436. ___. *Soldier-of-Fortune: Spoils of War*. New York: Belmont-Tower, 1976. Employing exotic weapons, mercenary Jim Rainey goes to Lebanon to fight for the government, but finds only chaos and in-fighting. *P* Others in his series include:

3437. ___. *Soldier-of-Fortune: Ambush at Derali Wells*. New York: Belmont-Tower, 1978. *P*

3438. ___. *Soldier-of-Fortune: The Guns of Palembang*. New York: Belmont-Tower, 1977. *P*

3439. ___. *Soldier-of-Fortune: Operation Hong Kong*. New York: Belmont-Tower, 1977. *P*

3440. ___. *Soldier-of-Fortune: Somali Smashout*. New York: Leisure, 1985. *P*

3441. McCutchan, Philip. *Blood Run East*. London: Severn, 1976. Detective Chief Superintendent Simon Shard is asked to remove IRA bomber Katie Farrell from England, but loses her; then word is received of a plot to blow up the Chemical Defense Establishment.

3442. ___. *The Bright Red Businessmen*. New York: Day, 1969. Commander Shaw and the boys of MAX and D-2 must solve the mystery of the elastic water, a creeping natural disturbance that occurs in isolated areas.

3443. ___. *Call for Simon Shard.* London: Harrap, 1975. Simon Shard of MI-5 makes his first appearance and immediately becomes involved in smashing a plot against the security of Great Britain.

3444. ___. *Cameron's Chase.* New York: St. Martin's, 1986. Cameron is in command of HM *Glenshiel*, a destroyer part of a fleet in search of Hitler's most powerful battleship, which is seeking a vital convoy homeward bound from Halifax.

3445. ___. *Coach North.* New York: Walker, 1975. Shard and his fellows must recover a tour bus with 31 passengers aboard which was hijacked somewhere between London and Scotland.

3446. ___. *The Convoy Commodore.* New York: St. Martin's, 1986. John Mason Kemp is a convoy commander mobilized for service with the Royal Navy during the early days of the Battle of the Atlantic, when urgently needed supplies and troops are being brought back to England from Canada.

3447. ___. *Convoy of Fear.* New York: St. Martin's, 1990. During WW II a British convoy tries to make it from Gibraltar through the Suez Canal against odds that include a German battleship, a bout of cholera aboard ship, and a typhoon.

3448. ___. *The Day of the Coastwatch.* London: Harrap, 1968. In this grim, futuristic tale of a Britain called the New Socialist State, important persons are prevented from leaving the country. John Slade is Surgical Officer aboard a vessel of the Coastwatch when a friend dies attempting to escape; Slade adopts the man's children, but falls under the suspicion of the Bureau of Statistical Research, which decides to take him in for "treatment."

3449. ___. *The Man from Moscow.* New York: Day, 1965. A group of Russian extremists, backed by the MVD, plans a coup in the Kremlin during a foreign minister's conference and simultaneously an "accidental" nuclear strike at Britain. Learning of this scheme, the SIS dispatches Shaw to deal with it.

3450. ___. *Moscow Coach.* New York: Day, 1966. Shaw is sent on a bus trip to Moscow with orders to eliminate a fanatical British Communist who plans to assassinate the Russian leadership, thereby allowing an extremist regime to take over and bring on an explosive war.

3451. ___. *The Mullah from Kashmir.* By Duncan MacNeil, pseud. New York: St. Martin's, 1976. Captain James Ogilvie of the 114th Queen's Own

Strathspeys is the series of hero of these tales of a British regiment in nineteenth-century India. In this one, Ogilvie assumes native disguise and scouts the alleys of Peshawar for a Mullah from Kashmir who is stirring up religious hatred between Muslim and Hindu at the very moment Czar Nicholas is massing troops on the Afghanistan border.

3452. ___. *A Very Big Bang.* London: Severn, 1975. Shard must prevent a terrorist group from detonating a huge bomb in the London subway.

3453. ___. *Warmaster.* New York: John Day, 1964. Commander Shaw travels the globe seeking to destroy those behind an international crime organization bent on causing a Third World War. A few other Commander Shaw tales are:

3454. ___. *The All-Purpose Bodies.* New York: John Day, 1970.

3455. ___. *Bluebolt One.* New York: John Day, 1962.

3456. ___. *The Dead Line.* New York: John Day, 1966.

3457. ___. *Gibraltar Road.* New York: John Day, 1960.

3458. ___. *Hartinger's Mouse.* London: Harrap, 1970.

3459. ___. *Poulter's Passage.* New York: John Day, 1967.

3460. ___. *Skyprobe.* New York: John Day, 1968. Some early and late McCutchan suspense novels over the course of his prolific career, in addition to a few in the Shaw or Shard canon, include tales of a fighting British regiment in India and seafaring adventure tales of series characters Lieutenant St. Vincent Halfhyde and Donald Cameron (See Mr. McCutchan's commentary in CRAFT NOTES):

3461. ___. *Blackmail North.* London: Hodder & Stoughton, 1978.

3462. ___. *The Boy Who Liked Monsters.* London: Hodder & Stoughton, 1989.

3463. ___. *Cameron Comes Through.* London: Barker, 1980.

3464. ___. *Cameron: Ordinary Seaman.* London: Barker, 1980.

3465. ___. *Cameron's Convoy*. London: Barker, 1982.

3466. ___. *Cameron's Troop Lift*. London: Weidenfeld & Nicholson, 1987.

3467. ___. *Corpse*. London: Hodder & Stoughton, 1980.

3468. ___. *The Eros Affair*. London: Hodder & Stoughton, 1977.

3469. ___. *The Executioners*. London: Hodder & Stoughton, 1986.

3470. ___. *Greenfly*. London: Hodder & Stoughton, 1987.

3471. ___. *The Guns of Arrest*. New York: St. Martin's, 1976.

3472. ___. *Halfhyde and the Chain Gangs*. London: Weidenfeld & Nicholson, 1985.

3473. ___. *Halfhyde Goes to War*. New York: St. Martin's, 1987.

3474. ___. *Halfhyde's Island*. New York: St. Martin's, 1976.

3475. ___. *Halfhyde to the Narrows*. New York: St. Martin's, 1977.

3476. ___. *The Hoof*. London: Hodder & Stoughton, 1983.

3477. ___. *Kidnap*. London: Hodder & Stoughton, 1993.

3478. ___. *The Last Farewell*. New York: St. Martin's, 1991.

3479. ___. *Redcap*. London: Harrap, 1961.

3480. ___. *The Restless Frontier*. New York: St. Martin's, 1980.

3481. ___. *Rollerball*. London: Hodder & Stoughton, 1984.

3482. ___. *Shard at Bay*. London: Hodder & Stoughton, 1985.

3483. ___. *Shard Calls the Tune*. London: Hodder & Stoughton, 1981.

3484. ___. *Sunstrike*. London: Hodder & Stoughton, 1979.

3485. ___. *This Drakotny*. London: Harrap, 1971.

3486. ___. *Werewolf.* London: Hodder & Stoughton, 1982. McCutchan's regimental novels under the Duncan MacNeil alias:

3487. ___. *Charge of Cowardice.* By Duncan MacNeil, pseud. New York: St. Martin's, 1978.

3488. ___. *Drums along the Khyber.* By Duncan MacNeil, pseud. London: Hodder & Stoughton, 1969.

3489. ___. *A Matter for the Regiment.* By Duncan MacNeil, pseud. London: Hodder & Stoughton, 1982.

3490. ___. *The Red Daniel.* By Duncan MacNeil, pseud. New York: St. Martin's, 1974.

3491. ___. *The Screaming Dead Balloons.* New York: Day, 1968.

3492. ___. *Subaltern's Choice.* By Duncan MacNeil, pseud. New York: St. Martin's, 1974.

3493. ___. *The Train at Bundabar.* By Duncan MacNeil, pseud. New York: Walker, 1986. McCutchan also wrote a series of espionage adventures about James Packard between the early sixties to the early seventies under another pseudonym. A few of these:

3494. ___. *Assignment Andalusia.* By Robert Conington Galway, pseud. London: Hale, 1965.

3495. ___. *Assignment New York.* By Robert Conington Galway, pseud. London: Hale, 1963.

3496. ___. *Assignment Sydney.* By Robert Conington Galway, pseud. London: Hale, 1970.

3497. ___. *The Negative Man.* By Robert Conington Galway, pseud. London: Hale, 1971.

3498. ___. *The Timeless Sleep.* By Robert Conington Galway, London: Hale, 1963.

3499. McDaniel, David. *The Man from UNCLE: The Rainbow Affair.* New York: Ace, 1967. Napoleon Solo and his sidekick Illya Kuryakin battle a THRUSH plot to change the world's weather patterns. *P*

3500. ___. *The Man from UNCLE: The Vampire Affair.* New York: Ace, 1966. People are dying from apparent vampire attacks and Solo is called in to investigate. Four other UNCLE titles by this author are: *P*

3501. ___. *The Man from UNCLE: The Dagger Affair.* New York: Ace, 1965. *P*

3502. ___. *The Man from UNCLE: The Hollow Crown Affair.* New York: Ace 1969. *P*

3503. ___. *The Man from UNCLE: The Monster Wheel Affair.* New York: Ace 1967. *P*

3504. ___. *The Man from UNCLE: The Utopia Affair.* New York: Ace, 1968. *P*

3505. McDonnel, Gordon. *Crew of the "Anaconda."* Boston: Little, 1940. A merchantman's chief officer becomes involved with Nazi espionage afloat. **y*

3506. ___. *Intruder from the Sea.* Boston: Little, 1953. An American veteran vacationing in California helps to smash a Communist spy ring. A good McCarthy-era tale. **y*

3507. MacEoin, Denis. *Brotherhood of the Tomb.* By Daniel Easterman, pseud. New York: Doubleday, 1990. The remains of Jesus, James, and the Virgin Mary are discovered by an Israeli archeologist and a Catholic bishop in a tomb in 1968; the bishop murders the Israeli to prevent the foundation of the Church from cracking; jump cut to the present and an ex-CIA man, Patrick Canavan, who is following his own investigation of sacrificial killings—until a KGB man's murder links him to this vast conspiracy of silence and murder.

3508. ___. *The Last Assassin.* By Daniel Easterman, pseud. Garden City, NY: Doubleday, 1984. Peter Randall, CIA field agent, must stop fanatical Shi'ites from killing President Carter, Premier Breshnev, and Anwar al-Sadat.

3509. ___. *The Ninth Buddha.* By Daniel Easterman, pseud. New York: Doubleday, 1989. Christopher Wylam, British agent, leaves India to find his kidnapped son whom the Tibetans believe to be the reincarnation of a Buddhist holy man. Three more:

3510. ___. *The Name of the Beast.* New York: HarperCollins, 1992.

3511. ___. *Night of the Seventh Darkness.* New York: HarperCollins, 1991.

3512. ___. *The Seventh Sanctuary.* By Daniel Easterman, pseud. Garden City, NY: Doubleday, 1987.

3513. McEwan, Ian. *The Innocent.* New York: Doubleday, 1990. A psychological thriller with an espionage plot set in Berlin in 1955 and based on Operation Gold, a joint CIA-MI-6 operation in 1956. The British and Americans are cooperating on a 500-yard tunnel from the American sector to tap a cluster of communication cables from the Russian side, and a nondescript, young post office employee named Leonard Marnham is the "innocent" who will be a part of this enterprise—and get more than he bargained for.

3514. McGarrity, Mark. *The Passing Advantage.* New York: Wade, 1980. During a winter storm, an American general near the Russian border seizes the chance to turn two strong nearby Soviet forces against themselves in a short war fought on his terms.

3515. McGarvey, Robert. *The Battle in Botswana.* By Steve White, pseud. New York: Warner, 1981. Tough-guy merc adventures of a unit called Strategic Commandos, or S-Com. *P*

3516. ___. *Stars and Swastikas. S-Com, No. 2.* By Steve White, pseud. New York: Warner, 1981. An elite group of American commandos must take out a Nazi base which is flying the American flag and appears to be the property of the US Army.

3517. ___. *Terror in Turin. S-Com, No. 1.* By Steve White, pseud. New York: Warner, 1981. The S-Com unit of Strategic Commandos finds that time is running out on their efforts to recover a hostage who is being held for a $50 million ransom. One more from this Men of Action series:

3518. ___. *Sierra Death Dealers.* By Steve White, pseud. New York: Warner, 1982. *P*

3519. McGerr, Patricia. *Is There a Traitor in the House?* Garden City, NY: Doubleday, 1965. Section Q of the CIA wants Selena Mead to trace the connection between the near fatal fall of a party girl and a Congressman seeking to become Vice President.

3520. ___. *Legacy of Danger.* New York: McKay, 1971. Miss Mead is a Washington-based combination of Modesty Blaise and the Baroness who, in this adventure, examines a present danger which has grown out of some old, almost-forgotten documents.

3521. McGill, Gordon. *War Story.* New York: Delacorte, 1980. Under the guise of national security, British commando-agents are sent to besieged Berlin in April 1945 to eliminate General Gerhard Bergner, who is being held prisoner by Hitler.

3522. McGivern, William P. *Caper of the Golden Bulls.* New York: Dodd, 1966. British agents are sent to Spain to foil a plot against the government of aging dictator Franco.

3523. ___. *Caprifoil.* New York: Dodd, 1972. Caprifoil is the codename of a top French minister who once operated in espionage with an American and a British agent. Now he is missing and the other two are detailed to find him.

3524. ___. *A Choice of Assassins.* New York: Dodd, 1963. An American derelict in Spain offers to exchange his life for a drink—booze which is offered to him by agents if he will undertake a suicidal mission.

3525. ___. *Margin of Terror.* New York: Dodd, 1954. A young American engineer in Rome is drawn into a counter-espionage caper against the Soviets.

3526. ___. *A Matter of Honor.* New York: Arbor, 1984. Couched within a tale of a smuggling ring operating between Germany and Chicago and a homicide investigation into the murders of several servicemen is the story of a father-son conflict.

3527. ___. *Seven Lies South.* New York: Dodd, 1960. An American expatriate in Spain finds himself involved in an international plot against world peace.

3528. McGovern, James. *The Berlin Couriers.* New York: Abelard-Schuman, 1961. An aeronautical engineer is trained as a spy, is sent to East Berlin, captured, and is put on public trial. Sentenced to death, he is saved by patriots during the 1953 uprising. **y*

3529. MacInnes, Helen. *Above Suspicion*. New York: Harcourt, 1954. First issued in 1941, this was the first in a long line of spy thriller-romances written by this author. An Oxford don and his pretty wife are chosen to perform a secret mission to Germany in late 1939. While using their vacation as a cover, they are to locate the whereabouts of an anti-Nazi agent. The plan seems foolproof—until someone betrays it and them. **y*

Well-travelled, she has employed her vast talent to create smooth, well-constructed tales featuring "ordinary people" drawn into espionage situations as in Eric Ambler. None of her tales are based on any intelligence experience (she has none), but are pure invention, suspenseful, but not as sadistic or bloody as those penned by many of her male contemporaries. Her tasteful handling of sex would seem to make her the Barbara Cartland of spy fiction.

3530. ___. *Agent in Place*. New York: Harcourt, 1976. A US newsman and his wife and an English wine merchant are mixed up in a KGB effort in New York to obtain a top secret NATO memorandum. **y*

3531. ___. *Assignment in Brittany*. Boston: Little, 1942. A young British officer is sent to Occupied France in the guise of a wounded French soldier to learn what the Germans planned to do about coastal defenses. Almost too late, he discovers important gaps in his information. **y*

3532. ___. *Cloak of Darkness*. New York: Harcourt, 1982. MacInness' twentieth novel resumes Bob Renwick's secret career within his NATO posting; now, as head of the counterterrorist agency, Interintell, Renwick learns that an American export firm has switched from farm machinery to sophisticated weaponry exports and that its clients include subversives and terrorists—worse, he has discovered their "Minus List" of individuals to be executed—and he occupies the number three position.

3533. ___. *Decision at Delphi*. New York: Harcourt, 1960. Strang and his Greek-American friend Kladas are to meet in Athens on a magazine assignment, but the reporter disappears, leaving some clues. His newspaper sends a resourceful young woman to take his place and soon she and Strang are involved in a web of intrigue stretching back to World War II. **y*

3534. ___. *The Double Image*. New York: Harcourt, 1966. An American encounters a favorite former professor on a Paris street one day, which leads him to a Nazi-Soviet spy caper and to the Greek island of Mykonos. **y*

3535. ___. *The Hidden Target*. New York: Harcourt, 1980. Nina O'Connell meets Bob Renwick in Amsterdam after six years' hiatus and tells him she is on an expense-free trip with other students, but she does not realize that terrorists are leading the tour and that she has a part to play in their sinister designs.

3536. ___. *The Hidden Terror.* New York: Harcourt, 1980. A young American girl on a world tour is unwittingly entangled in a terrorist plot which sends her into the suspense-filled world of secret agents, terrorists, and counter-terrorists. *y

3537. ___. *I and My True Love.* New York: Harcourt, 1953. Against the backdrop of diplomatic intrigue and political maneuverings in Washington, DC, two lovers are caught between Red spies and the American government's then-current fear of Communists in government. An excellent portrayal of the fears and suspense of the McCarthy era. *y

3538. ___. *Message from Malaga.* New York: Harcourt, 1973. Hopping about Spain from one espionage caper to another it seems that Russian agents are always ahead of their American counterparts. Why? *y

3539. ___. *Neither Five nor Three.* New York: Harcourt, 1951. A publisher discovers his magazine is being subtly employed to disparage and undermine faith in America. *y

3540. ___. *Pray for a Brave Heart.* New York: Harcourt, 1955. Two agents are embroiled in an effort to recover the Hertz diamonds, which a Communist espionage ring has earmarked to fight democracy. *y

3541. ___. *Prelude to Terror.* New York: Harcourt, 1978. Commissioned to purchase a painting for an eccentric millionaire, a New York City art consultant becomes involved in a web of terrorism, secret agents, and laundered cash. *y

3542. ___. *Ride a Pale Horse.* New York: Harcourt, 1984. A staff reporter covering a peace convention for a news magazine is about to leave Prague when a high-ranking Czech official approaches her with documents proving his identity and value as defector, but can she be sure that this is not a Soviet disinformation plot?

3543. ___. *The Salzburg Connection.* New York: Harcourt, 1968. A hardheaded Yankee did not know that his Austrian business trip would draw him into a suspenseful chase for a chest hidden in an Alpine lake or that death and a beautiful woman awaited him in the shadows. *y

3544. ___. *The Snare of the Hunter*. New York: Harcourt, 1974. Political intrigue revolves around Irinia Kusak's flight from Czechoslovakia in search of her Nobel Prize-winning father. *y

3545. ___. *The Venetian Affair*. New York: Harcourt, 1963. A raincoat switch suckers an American reporter on vacation in Paris into a Red plot to blame the anticipated assassination of President de Gaulle on the United States. *y

3546. ___. *While Still We Live*. Boston: Little, 1944. After waving goodbye to friends departing with the last group of escaping Englishmen in September 1939, Sheila Matthews stays behind to help the Polish resistance in Warsaw. *y One other MacInnes novel is:

3547. ___. *North from Rome*. New York: Harcourt, 1958.

3548. McKay, Alistair M. *The Third Conspiracy*. New York: Bantam, 1978. Unless it can be stopped by an intrepid agent, the powerful TRIAD group plans to take over all crime in the West. *P*

3549. McKay, Lewis H. *The Third Force*. By Hugh Matheson, pseud. New York: Washburn, 1961. An English inventor produces a secret weapon and then gets mixed up in the many plots of various spy groups to grab it. *

3550. McKelway, St. Clair. *The Edinburgh Caper*. New York: Holt, 1963. A New York City crime fighter on vacation in Scotland discovers a Red plot to kill President Eisenhower, Premier Khrushchev, and Prince Philip when they arrive for a visit. Based on a shorter version first appearing in *The New Yorker*.

3551. McKenna, Marthe. *Arms and the Spy*. London: Jarrolds, 1942. An agent of MI-5 is ordered to halt a fifth column group which is stashing away weapons in anticipation of a Nazi invasion of England. *
    McKenna was a noted pre-war author of British spy thrillers, the plotting of which were largely based on her own experiences in World War I (see Part 1). With the coming of the Second World War, she was able to make the transition of theme from the Great War to the Big War with little difficulty.

3552. ___. *Nightfighter Spy*. London: Jarrolds, 1943. MI-5 must look into the matter of German saboteurs who are attempting to destroy the RAF's capability to disrupt Luftwaffe night bombing attacks. *

3553. ___. *Spy in Khaki.* London: Jarrolds, 1941. An agent must enlist in the British Army in order to find a traitor. *

3554. ___. *Watch Across the Channel.* London: Jarrolds, 1944. British Intelligence and the French Resistance co-ordinate the gathering of information for the pending Allied invasion of the Continent. * The author's last two works dealt with the Cold War and are:

3555. ___. *Three Spies for Glory.* London: Jarrolds, 1950. *

3556. ___. *What's Past Is Prologue.* London: Jarrolds, 1951. *

3557. MacKenzie, Compton. *Whiskey Galore.* London: Cassell, 1947. A humorous portrait of Great Britain during World War II which includes a number of satirical jabs at MI-5. *H*
       MacKenzie was once an active agent who, before the Second World War, found himself in difficulty over his reminiscences in *Greek Memories*, which book was withdrawn under the Official Secrets Act in 1932 and not reissued until 1940. The author was tried in 1933 and fined £100. A ludicrous fact of that episode, and perhaps an explanation for his inveterate sarcasm toward MI-5 and MI-6, is revealed in *Spy Fiction*'s assessment of the cause of his arrest: "This officer was so tediously attentive to detail that he obtained samples of various types of coal used in that part of Turkey in order to choose a few pieces, to be forwarded to England, to serve as models for the casings of the bombs." (See Part 1).

3558. MacKenzie, Donald. *Double Exposure.* Boston: Houghton, 1963. A professional thief is released from prison in exchange for his agreement to visit Düsseldorf and pull off a delicate safe-rifling job for British Intelligence.

3559. ___. *Night Boat from Puerto Verde.* Boston: Houghton, 1970. In the Caribbean dictatorship of Montoro, Canadian journalist Douglas MacNeill has accidentally photographed a mysterious stranger at the race track and is now wanted by Colonel Weber, a former Nazi and head of the local secret police.

3560. ___. *The Quiet Killer.* Boston: Houghton, 1968. Canadian journalist Hamish Hunter, in Poland on assignment, comes to follow a dangerous lead which is based on a faded photo of himself and a Polish lad which was taken at a Swiss school before World War II.

3561. ___. *The Raven and the Kamikaze.* Boston: Houghton, 1977. A Polish emigré attempts to stop a deranged British agent bent on blowing up the Soviet Embassy in London.

3562. ___. *Salute from a Dead Man.* Boston: Houghton, 1966. Released from a British jail, a Canadian journalist goes straight until waitress Linda Swan passes him a roll of secret microfilm one day in his lunch.

3563. ___. *The Spreewald Collection.* Boston: Houghton, 1975. A Canadian journalist agrees to an impossible mission for British Intelligence: travel to Portugal and remove the jewels of sinister neo-Nazi Baron Szily from his impregnable mansion.

MacKenzie, Steve, pseud. *See* Randle, Kevin D.

3564. McKeon, John J. *The Serpent's Crown.* New York: Walker, 1991. A US Presidential election is sabotaged at the highest levels.

3565. MacKinnon, Alan. *Assignment in Iraq.* Garden City, NY: Doubleday, 1961. A young Scottish tutor named Don Kendrick gets mixed up in an SIS scam against the Soviets in Iraq.

3566. ___. *Cormorant's Isle.* Garden City, NY: Doubleday, 1962. Kendrick, now working for the SIS, is mixed up in a Scottish kidnapping related to a caper then going down in Turkey.

3567. ___. *Report from Argyll.* Garden City, NY: Doubleday, 1964. Middle East security is threatened by the presence of a top Soviet agent in Scotland; the murder of a British reporter who had unmasked the KGB-man sets off a chase by MI-5 and a fellow journalist.

3568. ___. *Summons from Baghdad.* Garden City, NY: Doubleday, 1958. Kendrick must travel to the fabled city of flying carpets in order to rescue a colleague who has become involved in an espionage caper.

3569. MacKinnon, Colin. *Finding Hoseyn.* London: Hutchinson, 1987. In the final days of the Shah's reign in 1977, journalist Jim Morgan investigates what appears to be a random terrorist murder of an Israeli in Tehran; however, his investigation of the assassin Hoseyn leads him onto a trail that takes him from Paris to Beirut.

3570. MacKintosh, Ian. *The Sandbaggers*. London: Corgi, 1978. According to the London *Daily Telegraph* (12 July 1977), MacKintosh received an MBE: "No reason for the honour was given in the official lists, but colleagues believed that for many years he had been connected with secret work and that the award was for his job in Whitehall" (3). Tragically, that issue also reported his death; MacKintosh, along with the pilot and Ms. Susan Insole, went down in the frigid waters of the Gulf of Alaska. The paper reported that he was checking scenes for a forthcoming *Sandbaggers* series. Much of MacKintosh's thriller fiction wound up on television: BBC produced *Warship*, a mid-1970's drama about the Royal Navy; *Wilde Alliance* was a Yorkshire comedy-thriller in 1978; *Thundercloud*, also by Yorkshire TV, was a naval comedy produced in 1979. However, he will be remembered by spy fans most for *The Sandbaggers* (Yorkshire, 1978 - 1980), one of the most meticulously detailed and interesting accounts of the Game ever produced on television—despite the fact that he has not been published in the US (once in Canada). Its novelization here represents a part of the series. First issued in paperback, Severn House of London brought out a new edition in April of 1979. There is one other out-of-print novelization, written by William Marshall called *The Sandbaggers: Think of a Number* (London: Corgi, 1980).

3571. ___. *The Brave Cannot Yield*. London: Hale, 1970.

3572. ___. *Count Not the Cost*. London: Hale, 1976.

3573. ___. *A Drug Called Power*. London: Hale, 1968.

3574. ___. *H.M.S. Hero*. London: Barker, 1976.

3575. ___. *Holt RN*. London: Barker, 1977.

3576. ___. *The Man from Destiny*. London: Hale, 1969.

3577. ___. *A Slaying in September*. London: Hale, 1967.

3578. ___. *Warship*. London: Hutchinson, 1973.

3579. ___. *Wilde Alliance*. London: Severn, 1978.

3580. McLachlan, Ian. *The Seventh Hexagram*. New York: Bantam, 1978. SIS agent Donald Winn is in Hong Kong to halt a revolution being plotted by a half English-half Chinese madman named Jordan King. *P*

3581. McLartz, Nancy. *Chain of Death.* Garden City, NY: Doubleday, 1962. An American girl on holiday in Guatemala is tangled up with a US Army officer who, himself, is involved in a complicated plot involving murder and treason. *

3582. Maclean, Alistair. *Athabasca.* Garden City, NY: Doubleday, 1980. A group of ruthless men arrive on the Alaskan coast with a complicated plot to hold the entire oil-producing industry hostage to their terroristic demands. *

Alistair Maclean was a product of the World War II Royal Navy who years later turned his attention to the writing of nautical stories which would allow him to employ the knowledge and background picked up during those years at sea. Maclean found a ready-made audience for his brand of action which, after the *Guns of Navarone* and *H.M.S. Ulysses*, took his readers further and further inland with only occasional trips back, for instance, *Ice Station Zebra.*

The "filmable" quality of his fiction is one reason why many of his novels have been successfully adapted to film, including *The Guns of Navarone*, *Force 10 from Navarone*, and *Where Eagles Dare*; another reason is that MacLean has been his own best screenplay writer.

3583. ___. *Bear Island.* Garden City, NY: Doubleday, 1971. A Hollywood film crew sets up on location in the Arctic, but soon it is revealed that one of its members is a mass-murderer using the cover for some nasty business while another is the British agent sent to look into the affair. *

3584. ___. *The Black Shrike.* By Ian Stuart, pseud. New York: Scribner's, 1965. British agent John Bentall is assigned to find eight scientists and their wives who have disappeared enroute to Australia. His search leads him to an island in the far Pacific where a deadly new super-missile, "the Black Shrike," is being tested. *

3585. ___. *Caravan to Vaccares.* Garden City, NY: Doubleday, 1970. Every year for centuries the gypsies have gathered in a small French tourist town to honor their patron saint. This time, however, the pilgrimage is not so innocent: the caravan is a cover for a sinister conspiracy. Only a few know the group's secret is its hiding of Russian rocket fuel experts and discovery may cost them their lives. *

3586. ___. *Circus.* Garden City, NY: Doubleday, 1975. Three East German refugee trapeze artists accept a CIA job offer: to join with an agent in removing a secret scientific formula from an assault-proof East European fortress. *

3587. ___. *The Dark Crusader.* By Ian Stuart, pseud. New York: Collins, 1961. [rpt. under author's name. New York: Collins, 1963]. A brave but dimwitted agent finds himself on an island in the South Pacific where a new rocket is being tested.

3588. ___. *Fear Is the Key.* Garden City, NY: Doubleday, 1961. A British agent being tried for illegal entry shoots his way out of a Florida courtroom, kidnaps a girl, and escapes. Never fear, it is only the hero's cover for the investigation of a gang operating a mysterious salvage operation from an offshore oil rig in the Gulf of Mexico. *

3589. ___. *Floodgate.* Garden City, NY: Doubleday, 1984. Terrorists threaten to submerge major sections of Holland under sea water by blowing up the country's dykes unless three daring operatives working inside the terrorist organization can foil the plot.

3590. ___. *Force 10 from Navarone.* Garden City, NY: Doubleday, 1969. Three members of the team that destroyed the famous guns are parachuted into wartime Yugoslavia to rescue the leaders of previous missions gone awry there and, incidentally, to destroy an important enemy-held bridge in the mountains. *

3591. ___. *The Golden Gate.* Garden City, NY: Doubleday, 1976. Terrorists hold the President of the United States, two oil dignitaries from Arabia, and a busload of reporters hostage on San Francisco's Golden Gate Bridge as they await the delivery of a half billion dollar ransom. Only an intrepid maverick FBI agent stands between them and success. *

3592. ___. *The Golden Rendezvous.* Garden City, NY: Doubleday, 1962. A tactical nuclear weapon and its creator are missing in the Caribbean and must be recovered at all costs. *

3593. ___. *Goodbye California.* Garden City, NY: Doubleday, 1978. A highway patrolman confronts Moro, a mad religious terrorist who has threatened to unleash an atomic earthquake through destruction of a hostage nuclear power plant. *

3594. ___. *The Guns of Navarone.* Garden City, NY: Doubleday, 1957. In what has to be ranked as one of the most successful clandestine action stories at all time, a small band of British commandos set out to destroy a pair of huge cannon covering a Grecian strait. *

3595. ___. *Ice Station Zebra*. Garden City, NY: Doubleday, 1964. When a capsule containing satellite reconnaissance photos lands near the British Arctic meteorological station "Zebra," a worker locates it and begins sending out signals. The American nuclear submarine Dolphine races to the site, carrying aboard an SIS agent and a Russian defector. When after an almost fatal crash dive, the sub emerges near the station and nearly succeeds in recovering the capsule, a contingent of Soviet paratroops drop in with the same idea in mind. In the movie version, Patrick McGoohan of "Secret Agent" TV fame portrayed the SIS man. *

3596. ___. *The Lonely Sea*. Garden City, NY: Doubleday, 1986. Collection of short stories of sea adventures.

3597. ___. *Night without End*. Garden City, NY: Doubleday, 1960. An airliner crashes near an Arctic IGY camp and one murder follows another. *

3598. ___. *Partisans*. Garden City, NY: Doubleday, 1983. Major Peter Petersen draws a dangerous assignment: he and his commandos must deliver a message from Italian Fascists, who are switching loyalties, to Yugoslavian partisans behind the lines in their Balkan stronghold.

3599. ___. *The Peking Payoff*. By Ian Stuart, pseud. New York: Macmillan, 1975. Hong Kong's leading businessman travels to China for an audience with the Red premier and becomes involved with Politburo fanatics who want to assassinate their leader. *

3600. ___. *Puppet on a Chain*. Garden City, NY: Doubleday, 1969. An Interpol agent is sent to get the goods on a nasty narcotics gang operating out of Holland. The book opens and closes with scenes of a huge crane overlooking an urban renewal project, thereby reflecting the title. *

3601. ___. *River of Death*. Garden City, NY: Doubleday, 1981. About an expedition to the Brazilian rain forest in search of the Lost City of the Amazon.

3602. ___. <u>San Andreas</u>. Garden City, NY: Doubleday, 1985. The *San Andreas* is a hospital ship crossing the Atlantic when a saboteur knocks out her power system, and thus her lights identifying her as a red Cross medical ship. Bosun Archie McKinnon assumes command of the crippled ship as warplanes and U-Boats attack.

3603. ___. *Santorini*. Garden City, NY: Doubleday, 1987. Commander Talbot of HMS *Ariadne*, a NATO spy ship, is patrolling the Aegean when a yacht blows up in his vicinity; then a bomber with a nuclear payload mysteriously crashes.

3604. ___. *The Satan Bug.* By Ian Stuart, pseud. New York: Scribner's, 1962. Someone has swiped a dangerous germ from the Mordon Microbiological Research Establishment and Pierre Caval must find it before its new owners can use it against the world. *

3605. ___. *Seawitch.* Garden City, NY: Doubleday, 1977. Agents of various top oil men plot to destroy a highly sophisticated drilling rig being employed by one ruthless tycoon to undercut world petroleum prices. *

3606. ___. *The Secret Ways.* Garden City, NY: Doubleday, 1959. [*The Last Frontier.* London: Collins, 1959]. A cynical American adventurer is paid $60,000 by British Intelligence to induce an aging underground leader and professor to leave Budapest. Posing as a newsman, Reynolds gets into Hungary easily enough and finds his mark at a Communist-sponsored conference. It takes the entire resources of the Hungarian freedom movement and Reynolds' own courage to get them over the frontier to the West. *

3607. ___. *The Way to Dusty Death.* Garden City, NY: Doubleday, 1973. Johnny Harlow, "golden boy of the Grand Prix circuits," is secretly working for the British in their efforts to bag some ruthless heroin smugglers who have penetrated the auto racing world. *

3608. ___. *When Eight Bells Toll.* Garden City, NY: Doubleday, 1966. SIS operative Philip Calvert is called upon to stop a gang of modern-day pirates operating in the islands off the west coast of Scotland. *

3609. ___. *Where Eagles Dare.* Garden City, NY: Doubleday, 1968. Eight Allied agents led by Major John Smith of MI-6 are inserted into the Bavarian Alps by air to rescue an American general from an isolated cliffside castle, the Schloss Adler. Shortly after landing, one of these magnificent seven is killed and Smith figures there is a traitor in their midst. Nevertheless, the survivors move to a village near the cliff, take on two female agents, and prepare for their gamble. After considerable difficulty, Smith and an American Ranger are the only team members left alive and in position to act. After several bad moments inside, they complete their mission, return to the village atop a cable car, and are left with the question of identifying the traitor who had been causing them so much difficulty. Richard Burton and Clint Eastwood had the movie leads. * Two more adventures by the author:

3610. ___. *H.M.S. Ulysses.* New York: Collins, 1955.

3611. ___. *The Snow on the Ben.* By Ian Stuart, pseud. London: Lock, 1961.

3612. McLean, Robinson. *Baited Blond.* New York: Mills, 1948. An American intelligence officer attempts to locate three missing parts of a diagram from his country's new strategic bombing mechanism; the chase takes him from Djibouti to Port Said and on to Beirut. *

3613. McLeave, Hugh. *A Borderline Case.* New York: Scribner's, 1978. When a mysterious outbreak of disease coincides with earthquake activity in Central Asia, SIS agent Paul Brodie, working in the Himalayas under cover of the World Health Organization, moves into China to investigate, is captured, and later makes a daring escape with the answers to his questions.

3614. ___. *Double Exposure.* New York: Scribner's, 1979. Retired agent Paul Brodie seeks to rescue a colleague from a KGB-run Siberian camp where dissidents are being used as victims in radiation and other medical experiments.

3615. ___. *Only Gentlemen Can Play.* New York: Harcourt, 1974. The title is based on a quote from real-life masterspy Reinhard Gehlen. An SIS operative must perform a mission for both Whitehall and the KGB knowing that he will be a dead man if he is apprehended by either.

3616. ___. *Vodka on Ice.* New York: Harcourt, 1969. Enroute to a scientific conference in Sofia, Bob McIllhenney is watched by Soviet agent Karen, who loves to show off that native Russian product, Vodka.

3617. MacLeish, Rod. *Crossing at Ivalo.* Boston: Little, 1990. A Jewish scientist is the brain behind Russia's own "Star Wars" program. An enterprising KGB major kidnaps him so that he can ransom him to the higher bidder between the US and the USSR.

MacLeod, Robert, pseud. *See* Knox, Bill

3618. McNamara, Michael. *The Dancing Floor.* London: Allen, 1979. Brothers Brendan and Colum Donnelly are IRA men but opposites: Brendan wields a gun, but Colum uses a pen in the cause of freedom; however, both brothers are dupes in a ruthless power struggle that may destroy them.

3619. ___. *The Sovereign Solution.* New York: Crown, 1979. In Northern Ireland to familiarize himself with British methods, FBI antiterrorist expert Dennis Hegarty becomes involved in stopping an IRA plot to assassinate the Queen of England.

3620. Macnee, Patrick and Peter Leslie. *The Avengers: The Dead Duck.* London: Hodder and Stoughton, 1966. When a nasty captures Emma and incapacitates Steed, it looks as though the British may lose two of their most unique agents. Author MacNee portrayed Steed in the noteworthy television series.

3621. ___ and Peter Leslie. *The Avengers: The Deadline.* London: Hodder & Stoughton, 1965. The first tale spawned from the popular television series featuring the impeccable John Steed and his lovely, resourceful sidekick Emma Peel (succeeded by Tara King). The spinoff TV series *New Avengers* featured Mike Gambit and Purdey in the late 70's. Authors who contributed to the series after Leslie and Macnee include John Garforth, Keith Laumer, and Norman Daniels.

MacNeil, Duncan, pseud. *See* McCutchan, Philip

MacNeil, Neil, pseud. *See* Ballard, Willis T.

3622. McNeilly, Wilfred. *Secret Agent: No Way Out.* New York: Macfadden, 1966. British agent John Drake is captured by "the other side" and try as he might to escape it looks as though his career may be over.

3623. MacPherson, Malcolm. *Protégé.* New York: Dutton, 1980. Forty years after their mentor's death, protégés of Abwehr boss Admiral Wilhelm Canaris move to establish a slave-labor estate in South Africa.

3624. ___. *The Lucifer Key.* New York: Dutton, 1981. A computer-caper yarn in which the US and Soviet Union are brought to the brink of nuclear war.

3625. McQuay, Mike. *Escape from New York.* New York: Bantam, 1981. Screenplay for the John Carpenter film starring Kurt Russell, Lee Van Cleef, Ernest Borgnine, and Donald Pleasance. In 1997, the island of Manhattan is a vast penal colony. Flying over it one day, Air Force One is forced down and the President is taken prisoner by the "inmates." American intelligence agencies recruit an ex-con to infiltrate the prison and rescue him before the convicts execute the US leader for "high crimes." *P*

3626. McQuinn, Donald E. *Shadow of Lies*. New York: TOR, 1985. Two agents face each other in the Pacific Northwest: an American whose career in counterintelligence was ruined by the other, a Soviet agent who is cultivating a man in the defense-intelligence industry who can has access to codes that can turn American missiles against American cities. *P*

3627. ___. *Targets*. New York: Macmillan, 1980. USMC Major Charles Taylor has been detailed to that infamous Vietnam War counterespionage operation known as "Operation Phoenix." His orders are to find and liquidate a legendary Viet Cong leader but as the officer seeks his quarry, he is unaware that he is a target not only of the VC but of the CIA as well.

3628. McShane, Mark. *Apple Spy in the Sky*. By Marc Lovell, pseud. Garden City, NY: Doubleday, 1983. The 6' 7" agent is sent to Ibiza because British Intelligence believes that drugs are being smuggled to British military bases from there. *H*

3629. ___. *Apple to the Core*. By Marc Lovell, pseud. Garden City, NY: Doubleday, 1983. British Intelligence orders Appleton to kidnap four old men in their nineties who are visiting London as part of a singing quartet. *H*

3630. ___. *Comfort Me with Spies*. By Marc Lovell, pseud. New York: Doubleday, 1990. Britain's worst covert operations agent is sent to an Ontario wrestling tournament as a contestant to discredit three popular wrestlers who support a Canadian subversive. *H*

3631. ___. *Ethel and the Naked Spy*. By Marc Lovell, pseud. New York: Doubleday, 1989. Appleton Porter is worried about his fellow member in the British Old Vehicles Association because, at the next annual rally, that member is going to defect to the Soviet Union. *H*

3632. ___. *Good Spies Don't Grow on Trees*. Garden City, NY: Doubleday, 1986. Appleton's linguistic fluency earns him a choice assignment: he is to engage the beautiful but reclusive Alicia Suvov, Soviet chess champion, in conversation for fifteen minutes. *H*

3633. ___. *The Hostage Game*. New York: Zebra, 1979. What happens when the terrorist opposition to Member of Parliament Harold Vale kidnaps the popular government official—only to learn that they have captured a two-bit music hall impersonator named Edgar Carlton? *P*

3634. ___. *How Green Was My Apple*. By Marc Lovell, pseud. Garden City, NY: Doubleday, 1984. Appleton teams up with a tall woman to bungle another case involving a Soviet emissary—and his most prized possession: a London taxi named Ethel. *H*

3635. ___. *The Only Good Apple in a Barrel of Spies*. By Marc Lovell, pseud. Garden City, NY: Doubleday, 1984. Cunning linguist Porter falls for a pickpocket named Sylvia on assignment; he is supposed to discover what happened to a Soviet agent, last seen in the underground station in Piccadilly getting his pocket picked. *H*

3636. ___. *The Spy Game*. By Marc Lovell, pseud. Garden City, NY: Doubleday, 1980. Appleton is supposed to assist in the defection of visiting Russians from the ballet—and a mind-reading team. *H*

3637. ___. *Spy on the Run*. By Marc Lovell, pseud. Garden City, NY: Doubleday, 1982. Appleton is sent to compete at an international track meet in Paris, where he is supposed to memorize formulas from a Soviet gold medalist working for the CIA. *H*

3638. ___. *The Spy Who Got His Feet Wet*. By Marc Lovell, pseud. Garden City, NY: Doubleday, 1985. The blushing, oversized agent is sent to Dublin to compete in an international basketball tournament. *H*

3639. ___. *The Spy with His Head in the Clouds*. By Marc Lovell, pseud. Garden City, NY: Doubleday, 1982. Angus Watkin, Apple's "cold fish" of a superior, dupes him with some practice tradecraft and then dopes him with Soma-2, a new Soviet truth serum; finally, he sends him to a circus run by the KGB to procure the brilliant chemist who designed it. *H* Three more Apples:

3640. ___. *The Great Big Trenchcoat in the Sky*. By Marc Lovell, pseud. New York: Doubleday, 1988.

3641. ___. *The Spy Who Barked in the Night*. By Marc Lovell, pseud. Garden City, NY: Doubleday, 1986. *H*

3642. ___. *The Spy Who Fell Off the Back of the Bus*. By Marc Lovell, pseud. New York: Doubleday, 1988.

3643. McVean, James. *Bloodspoor*. New York: Dial, 1978. Guide Jerry Haston agrees to lead a handful of agents into the Kalahari Desert to rescue a world-famous naturalist who is being held by terrorists demanding sophisticated weapons as ransom.

3644. Mace, David K. *Demon-4.* New York: Berkley, 1986. In a world ravaged by nuclear annihilation, the US and USSR must cooperate to contain the damage; one special problem arises when a robot weapon runs amok in the waters of Antarctica.

3645. ___. *The Highest Ground.* London: NEL, 1989. The moon becomes the site for a showdown between the US and USSR in the fight over the "Star Wars" initiative: the US has it, the Russians want it, and a pair of idealists want it for peace. Two more sci-fi/spy thrillers by Mace:

3646. ___. *Fire Lance.* London: Grafton, 1986.

3647. ___. *Frankenstein's Children.* Sevenoaks: NEL, 1989.

Mackie, John, pseud. *See* Levinson, Leonard

3648. Maddock, Larry. *The Flying Saucer Gambit.* New York: Ace, 1966. This late-1960's sci-fi paperback series featured Hannibal Fortune, agent of TERRA, in various espionage escapades with nemesis EMPIRE. *P* Other titles:

3649. ___. *The Emerald Elephant Gambit.* New York: Ace, 1967. *P*

3650. ___. *The Time Trap Gambit.* New York: Ace, 1969. *P*

Maddock, Stephen, pseud. *See* Walsh, J. M.

3651. Madsen, David. *U.S.S.A.* New York: Morrow, 1989. Moscow is a city teeming with vice, exploitation, and displaced persons in the era after the US has defeated the Soviet Union in WW III. Private investigator, ex-CIA man Dean Joplin gets an assignment that takes him through the innermost corruption when a murder victim turns up in the Kosmos Hotel.

3652. Maeston, Edward. *The Queen's Head.* New York: St. Martin's, 1988. Drawing upon lore surrounding the Elizabethan School of Night and Kit Marlowe's infamous death in a tavern brawl, Marston explores the intrigues of Elizabeth's court in the days before the invasion of the Spanish Armada. *HI*

3653. Maggio, Joe. *The Company of Man.* New York: Putnam's, 1972. A yarn of modern espionage designed to expose the inner workings of the CIA. Although classified as fiction, the tale is a thinly disguised recitation of the author's real-life covert action adventures from the Bay of Pigs to the Congo and Laos. The author lived dangerously as a field agent dangerous between 1965 and 1966 in Cuba, Laos, and Vietnam. Others:

3654. ___. *Days of Glory and Grieving*. New York: Viking, 1981.

3655. ___. *Scam*. New York: Viking, 1980.

3656. Magowan, Ronald. *Funeral for a Commissar*. New York: Roy, 1970. MI-5's most ruthless killer is ordered to uncover Russian infiltration into the top echelons of British industry.

3657. Mailer, Norman. *Harlot's Ghost*. New York: Random, 1991. "Harlot" is legendary agent Hugh Tremont Montague's codename; "Ghost" is his protégé Harry Hubbard, himself the son of an OSS hero, in this Mailer opus (over 1,000+ pages) that mingles history and politics of names famous and infamous in recent US history, although technically it is about a covert operation against Cuba. The real story is how Hubbard, a master manipulator, almost loses his soul—America's too—through the mundane world of intelligence machinations. The book's power owes less to its exciting story than it does to the dynamic sweep and evocative power of one of America's great novelists; the author went to Russia in 1993 to work on a sequel. (See Mr. Mailer's commentary in CRAFT NOTES.)

3658. Mair, George B. *The Day Khrushchev Panicked*. New York: Random, 1962. Learning about "antimatter" at a 1958 embassy party in Moscow, SIS agent David Grant launches an investigation that eventually involves agents from both sides of the Cold War in a Russian plot for world domination.

3659. ___. *Death's Foot Forward*. New York: Random, 1964. Dr. David Grant, now working as NATO's head security agent, is ordered to capture the Russian scientist who developed "space sickness" and introduced it to the West.

3660. ___. *The Girl from Peking*. New York: Random, 1967. Grant must smash a conspiracy designed to guarantee Red China a seat in the United Nations.

3661. ___. *Miss Turquoise*. New York: Random, 1965. NATO agent Grant must battle a Chinese faction and the strange man called Zero to gain control of a rare metal found only in the Spanish Sahara. Other titles in the Grant series, four of which were not published in America, include:

3662. ___. *Black Champagne.* New York: Random, 1968.

3663. ___. *Crimson Jade.* London: Jarrolds, 1971.

3664. ___. *Goddesses Never Die.* London: Jarrolds, 1969.

3665. ___. *Kisses from Satan.* New York: Random, 1965.

3666. ___. *Live, Love and Cry.* New York: Random, 1966.

3667. ___. *Paradise Spells Danger.* London: Jarrolds, 1973.

3668. ___. *A Wreath of Camellias.* London: Jarrolds, 1970.

3669. Malashenko, Aleksai. *The Last Red August.* Trans. Anthony Olcott. New York: Scribner's, 1993. Malashenko is a Russian journalist (*see* Olcott, Anthony for a list of his novels) who describes the dying of the Soviet Union; the action begins with a murder investigation of a high-ranking bureaucrat's secretary right after she finds evidence of a coup in her boss's compter files.

3670. Malleson, Lucy B. *Ring for a Noose.* By Anthony Gilbert, pseud. New York: Random, 1960. The murder of an imposter in London's Bohemia section sets off a search for a real Hungarian refugee. *

Mallory, Drew, pseud. *See* Garfield, Brian

3671. Maloney, Mark. *The Circle War.* New York: Zebra, 1987. Series adventures about "America's last hope," Hawk ("Wingman") Hunter. *P* Two more:

3672. ___. *The Lucifer Crusade.* New York: Zebra, 1987. *P*

3673. ___. *Wingman.* New York: Zebra, 1987. *P*

3674. Manchester, William R. *Beard the Lion.* New York: Mill, 1959. An American pharmacologist involuntarily finds himself bearing a document which proves a conspiracy between the Cypriotes and a faction of Egypt's Nasser government. In real life, the author is a distinguished American historian and teacher.

3675. Mandell, Mark. *Nazi Hunter #1.* New York: Pinnacle, 1981. Capt. Curt Jaeger of the US Army Special Forces tracks Nazi criminals, including his own father, an engineer who perfected the design of the gas chamber. *P* Two others:

3676. ___. *Nazi Hunter #4: Butcher Block*. New York: Pinnacle, 1982. *P*

3677. ___. *Nazi Hunter #5: Hell Nest*. New York: Pinnacle, 1983. *P*

3678. Mann, Jessica. *Death beyond the Nile*. New York: St. Martin's, 1989. Mystery novelist Mann is a Cambridge-educated archeologist whose heroine Tamara Hoyland shares her professional interest and doubles as a secret agent for an anonymous agency in British Intelligence. In this adventure, Hoyland is on a dig in Egypt but is also keeping tabs on a scientist under suspicion.

3679. ___. *Grave Goods*. Garden City, NY: Doubleday, 1985. The East German government plans to exhibit Charlemagne's crown jewels; however, Tamara's friend Margot Ellice is about to publish a paper that will provoke an international incident when she asserts that these jewels are a fake.

3680. ___. *No Man's Island*. Garden City, NY: Doubleday, 1984. Tamara Hoyland, working on Forway, an island off the English coast that is brewing controversy because of a quest for independence, exacts revenge against terrorists for a dead lover. Two recent ones:

3681. ___. *Faith, Hope, and Homicide*. New York: St. Martin's, 1991.

3682. ___. *Telling Only Lies*. New York: Carroll & Graf, 1993.

3683. Mann, Patrick. *Steal Big*. New York: St. Martin's, 1981. In London author Max Patrick wonders about the connection between the US embassy and a neighboring bank and uncovers a strange alliance between the CIA and the Mafia.

3684. Mann, Paul J. *The Britannia Contract*. New York: Carroll & Graf, 1993. Queen Elizabeth and Prince Philip are kidnapped by IRA terrorists aboard the royal yacht off Saudi Arabia.

3685. ___. *The Traitor's Contract*. New York: Knightsbridge, 1990. Two trained killers (one works for the IRA; the other for an American billionaire with his own spy network) go toe-to-toe.

3686. Mannin, Ethel E. *The Road to Beersheba*. Chicago: Regnery, 1964. Examines what happens to a single family of Palestinian Arabs which was driven out of Israel in 1948.

3687. Manning, Adelaide F. O. and C. Henry Coles. *Alias Uncle Hugo*. By Manning Coles, pseud. Garden City, NY: Doubleday, 1952. Secret agent Hambledon of British Intelligence is sent behind the Iron Curtain to rescue a small boy from a Russian school, a lad destined one day to be king of a little European mini-state. *

In the realm of romance fiction, it is not unheard of for former spies to meet and attract beautiful girls to themselves through recitation of tales concerning personal valor. That such an event may actually have occurred in real life seems somewhat fanciful, but on at least one occasion relative to this compilation, it was true.

Sometime around 1936, or so the story goes, an ex-Major of British Army Intelligence named Cyril Henry Coles sat down for a spot of reminiscing with his neighbor Adelaide Frances Manning at her home in their Hampshire, England village. She, an author, was fascinated with his tales of derring-do behind German lines in World War I. Out of this meeting grew the most famous collaboration in the history of the spy thriller and the *nom de plume* Manning Coles.

The Coles stories mostly featured a schoolmaster named Thomas Elphinstone Hambledon, who was not only irrepressible, but also almost ageless and so it seems, on semi-permanent loan to British Intelligence. For twenty years between 1940 and 1960, he was engaged in what Allen Dulles has called, a running "game of imaginary hare-and-hounds against the changing German background of the last forty years or so: the Kaiser's empire of World War I (*Drink to Yesterday*), the rise of Hitler's Reich (*Toast to Tomorrow*), right up to the divided Germany of the Iron Curtain epoch (*No Entry*)" (*Great Spy Stories from Fiction* [New York: Harper & Row, 1969], 153). These workmanlike tales all closely resemble the pre-war works of Buchan, Creasey, and others of the Pre-Ambler school of realism.

3688. ___. *All That Glitters*. By Manning Coles, pseud. Garden City, NY: Doubleday, 1954. Hambledon becomes involved in a high-powered plot counter-plot against world peace which features the Russian MVD, the Bonn Security Police, assorted Berlin crooks, and a couple of Polish fanatics. *

3689. ___. *Among Those Absent*. By Manning Coles, pseud. Garden City, NY: Doubleday, 1948. Hambledon is asked to look into a matter concerning some British gangsters with sinister German ties. *

3690. ___. *Basle Express.* By Manning Coles, pseud. Garden City, NY: Doubleday, 1956. Off on vacation to the Tyrol, Tommy Hambledon must halt his holiday when a fellow passenger aboard his train is murdered and a mysterious gang comes to suspect the British agent of having "the Papers." *

3691. ___. *The Concrete Crime.* By Manning Coles, pseud. Garden City, NY: Doubleday, 1960. In this final collaboration of Manning and Coles, Hambledon pursues an odious mastermind of crime in France—a man who has stolen some secret papers and whose history dates back to World War II. *

3692. ___. *Dangerous by Nature.* By Manning Coles, pseud. Garden City, NY: Doubleday, 1950. When the Soviets try to take over the Central American republic of Esmeralda and destroy the Panama Canal with atomic missiles, Tommy Hambledon is called upon to save the day. *

3693. ___. *Death of an Ambassador.* By Manning Coles, pseud. Garden City, NY: Doubleday, 1957. SIS operative Hambledon and his friend Letord of the Sûreté move through Paris seeking the dark past of an ambassador murdered in London, as well as the identity of the mysterious assassin. *

3694. ___. *Diamonds to Amsterdam.* By Manning Coles, pseud. Garden City, NY: Doubleday, 1949. While attempting to solve the mystery behind the death of a scientist and the disappearance of three men, Tommy Hambledon is led to a fabulous cache of diamonds in Amsterdam. *

3695. ___. *Drink to Yesterday.* By Manning Coles, pseud. New York: Knopf, 1941. A lad with a gift for languages joins the British Army in 1914 against the wishes of his family and is immediately tapped for espionage work behind German lines. Based very loosely on C. H. Coles' own Great War experiences. *

3696. ___. *The Fifth Man.* By Manning Coles, pseud. Garden City, NY: Doubleday, 1946. One day off Britain's southern coast, a U-boat surfaces and sends ashore a party of five Englishmen who are being traded; Agent Hambledon and an aide come to suspect the fifth man in the group and go on to ferret out the mastermind behind a Nazi sabotage ring. *

3697. ___. *Green Hazard.* By Manning Coles, pseud. Garden City, NY: Doubleday, 1945. Hambledon is smuggled into Nazi Germany under the guise of being a top chemist; while there, he works to undermine the Reich. *

3698. ___. *A Knife for the Juggler.* By Manning Coles, pseud. Garden City, NY: Doubleday, 1965. After Manning's death in 1959, Henry Coles continued the use of the pseudonym. Tommy Hambledon attempts to rescue a kidnapped Russian diplomat in France while simultaneously proving himself innocent of a homicide. *

3699. ___. *Let the Tiger Die.* By Manning Coles, pseud. Garden City, NY: Doubleday, 1947. Hambledon is both the pursuer and the pursued as he traces a missing agent from Stockholm to Holland, France, Spain, and finally on to the Canary Islands. *

3700. ___. *The Man in the Green Hat.* By Manning Coles, pseud. Garden City, NY: Doubleday, 1955. While looking for a missing British diplomat, Tommy Hambledon is plunged into the vicious double-dealing of the Italian underworld. *

3701. ___. *Night Train to Paris.* By Manning Coles, pseud. Garden City, NY: Doubleday, 1952. Hambledon joins forces with Bagshott of Scotland Yard to pursue some lost German plans coveted by clever Soviet agents who do not mind murder. *

3702. ___. *No Entry.* By Manning Coles, pseud. Garden City, NY: Doubleday, 1958. A wandering Oxford University student who just happens to be the son of the British Foreign Minister, disappears into East Germany and operative Hambledon is ordered to fetch him out. *

3703. ___. *Not Negotiable.* By Manning Coles, pseud. Garden City, NY: Doubleday, 1949. Tommy Hambledon's unique espionage talents are required by friendly police powers, and so he is assigned to smash an international band of counterfeiters operating out of Brussels and Paris. *

3704. ___. *Nothing to Declare.* By Manning Coles, pseud. Garden City, NY: Doubleday, 1961. In twelve short stories, Tommy Hambledon and his colleagues face a variety of criminals and foreign agents. *

3705. ___. *Now or Never.* By Manning Coles, pseud. Garden City, NY: Doubleday, 1951. Following the deaths of three men in Munich, Hambledon is sent in to unravel the mystery of the Silver Ghosts, a new Nazi party which is conspiring to take over West Germany by bringing to power Hitler's young son by Eva Braun. *

3706. ___. *Search for a Sultan.* By Manning Coles, pseud. Garden City, NY: Doubleday, 1961. Written by Coles alone. Hambledon scours England, France, and Tunisia looking for a possible heir to an Arab kingdom. *

3707. ___. *They Tell No Tales.* By Manning Coles, pseud. Garden City, NY: Doubleday, 1942. The mysterious sinking of British battleships exiting Portsmouth harbor brings secret agent Tommy Hambledon into a desperate search for Nazi saboteurs. *

3708. ___. *This Fortress.* By Manning Coles, pseud. Garden City, NY: Doubleday, 1941. Follows the adventures of Tom Langrish from his World War I stay in Schloss Rensburg through his insertion as an Abwehr agent into the quiet English village of Westerly. *

3709. ___. *A Toast to Tomorrow.* By Manning Coles, pseud. Garden City, NY: Doubleday, 1941. Sequel to *Drink to Yesterday* above. Suffering from amnesia, a young man enters the Nazi party after years of aimless wandering. Following the 1933 Reichstag fire, he becomes Chief of the Nazi Police—and then regains his memory! This tale, together with *Alias Uncle Hugo* and *Drink to Yesterday*, are contained in the omnibus *The Exploits of Tommy Hambledon*, which was published by Doubleday in 1959. *

3710. ___. *With Intent to Deceive.* By Manning Coles, pseud. Garden City, NY: Doubleday, 1947. Assisted by Scotland Yard sleuths, Hambledon investigates the theft of some cash which was originally secreted away in South America by the Nazis, stolen, and brought to England by the thieves. *

3711. ___. *Without Lawful Authority.* By Manning Coles, pseud. Garden City, NY: Doubleday, 1943. An English officer who was unjustly discharged from the Royal Tank Corps enlists Hambledon's aid in uncovering the Nazi spy who had him framed. *

3712. Marcus, Martin. *The Brezhnev Memo.* New York: Dell, 1980. A CIA agent has five days in which to undo a new and recently tested Soviet weapon which can cause terrible earthquakes. *P*

3713. Marchetti, Victor. *The Rope Dancer.* New York: Grosset & Dunlap, 1973. The special assistant to the Deputy Director of the national Intelligence Agency goes over to the Russians and reveals much about the inner workings of his former organization.
   In publishing this novel, Marchetti ran into the same sort of response which had bothered Compton MacKenzie years earlier: the active unhappiness

of a major intelligence agency. In Marchetti's case, the CIA believed that his work went too far in its revelations concerning "the Company," and although it took no active legal position concerning this work, it was not so lenient the next time it crossed swords with this author.

Marchetti, like MacKenzie, was an active duty intelligence officer. After joining the CIA in 1955, Marchetti worked his way up to the position of executive assistant to the Deputy Director, Admiral Rufus Taylor, in 1966-1969. Having become disillusioned with his employer, he resigned late in 1969 and began to prepare, with John D. Marks, a volume which would become unique in American publishing history, *The CIA and the Cult of Intelligence*. As is normal practice, Marchetti submitted the text for routine approval (required by law to make certain that no secrets are inadvertently disclosed), but before it was all over, the Agency and the courts ruled that 168 passages had to be deleted. The publishers went ahead and printed the book with big gaps where the deletions occurred in an effort to show the Agency's heavy hand. The book, coming as it did just before the Church Committee investigations, was very successful and Marchetti went on to become one of CIA's most vocal opponents.

A footnote. Unlike E. Howard Hunt and other active duty people involved with intelligence work, Marchetti published *The Rope Dancer* under his real name.

3714. Marcinko, Richard and John Weisman. *Rogue Warrior II: Red Cell.* New York: Pocket, 1994. Marcinko spent a year in a federal prison in Petersburg, Virginia on one count of conspiracy to defraud the government, a result, he claims of doing his job too well. During this time he wrote his autobiography, *Rogue Warrior*, and it proved a bestseller. Marcinko is the creator of the US Navy's elite counter-terrorist SEAL Team Six and its own "dirty dozen" unit: Red Cell, which was given the mission of testing the Navy's readiness at its most secure missions. Based on the same kind of infiltration operation as its predecessor, the novel incorporates the same kind of Ramboesque-cum-technothriller approach; the plot concerns smugglers, assisted by powerful traitors in America, who are providing North Korea and Japan with nuclear material.

Marin, A. C., pseud. *See* Coppel, Alfred

Mariner, David, pseud. *See* Smith, David M.

Mark, Ted, pseud. *See* Gottfried, Theodore M.

Markham, Robert, pseud. *See* Amis, Kingsley

3715. Markstein, George. *Chance Awakening*. New York: Ballantine, 1977. One man becomes a pawn in a treacherous game of secret warfare and deadly pursuit. *P*

　　Before his death in 1987, Markstein's credits included his five thrillers, screenplays *Special Branch* and one for Forsyth's *The Odessa File*, but he is widely known in the US for creating the popular TV series *The Prisoner*, starring Patrick McGoohan; interestingly, the late actor Steve McQueen asked Markstein to devise a car-chase sequence for his film *Bullitt* on the strength of his award-winning screenplay *Robbery*.

3716. ___. *The Cooler*. Garden City, NY: Doubleday, 1974. British agents unhinged by their kill-training, are sent to the rest camp of Inverlock in Scotland, a spot complete with all the amenities except freedom to leave.

3717. ___. *The Goering Testament*. New York: Ballantine, 1979. Discredited crime reporter Harry Heron vies with the world's foremost intelligence agencies to retrieve the Reich Marshal's final written statement. *P*

3718. ___. *Traitor*. New York: Ballantine, 1981. First published in England under the title *Traitor for a Cause*. Nikolai Galov, a KGB defector, is everything he seems to be—except to one man: head of CIA counterintelligence, Carl Bishop, wants to know why three defectors hidden by the agency years ago across the US were all systematically executed.

3719. ___. *Ultimate Issue*. New York: Ballantine, 1981. When an Air Force captain from a bomber base in England is being tried on the flimsy charge of adultery, the attorney defending him is soon drawn into global political intrigue in the frenetic months before the Berlin Wall. Also by the author:

3720. ___. *The Man from Yesterday*. London: Souvenir, 1976.

3721. ___. *Soul Hunters*. New York: Watts, 1987.

　　Marlin, Henry, pseud. *See* Gigga, Kenneth

3722. Marlowe, Dan J. *Death Deep Down*. Greenwich, CT: Fawcett, 1965. A naval intelligence officer becomes involved with murder in a scuba-diving party. *P*

3723. ___. *Earl Drake: Operation Breakthrough*. Greenwich, CT: Fawcett, 1972. Earl Drake, "the man with nobody's face," and his beautiful girlfriend

Hazel always seem to get the cases special agent Euhson's US intelligence department cannot handle. *P*

3724. ___. *Earl Drake: Operation Drumfire.* Greenwich, CT: Fawcett, 1972. Drake and Hazel must quash a fantastic plot on San Francisco which is being bankrolled by someone high in the Department of Defense. *P*

3725. ___. *Earl Drake: Operation Fireball.* Greenwich, CT: Fawcett, 1972. Drake poses as a ranking member of a Mafia squad and is sent to recover a $2 million cache hidden in the heart of Castro's Cuba. *P*

3726. ___. *Earl Drake: Operation Hammerlock.* Greenwich, CT: Fawcett, 1974. Drake and Hazel are mixed up with a brutal Mexican detective who seeks revenge against corrupt politicians. *P*

3727. ___. *Earl Drake: Operation Whiplash.* Greenwich, CT: Fawcett, 1973. When the maverick Mafioso Bolts Colisimo kidnaps Hazel, Drake must employ all of his resources to save her. Others in the Earl Drake series include: *P*

3728. ___. *Earl Drake: Operation Deathmaker.* Greenwich, CT: Fawcett 1973. *P*

3729. ___. *Earl Drake: Operation Endless Hours.* Greenwich, CT: Fawcett 1975. *P*

3730. ___. *Earl Drake: Operation Flashpoint.* Greenwich, CT: Fawcett 1972. *P*

3731. ___. *Earl Drake: Operation Overkill.* Greenwich, CT: Fawcett 1972. *P*

3732. ___. *Earl Drake: Operation Stranglehold.* Greenwich, CT: Fawcett 1974. *P*

3733. Marlowe, Derek. *A Dandy in Aspic.* New York: Putnam's, 1966. Russian assassin Alexander Eberlin has devoted his life to cracking into the British Intelligence apparatus, where as a double agent he takes out various of his Limey colleagues from time to time. One day, his English employers order him to seek out and destroy whoever is doing these terrible things; or, in other words, to assassinate himself!

Marlowe, Hugh, pseud. *See* Patterson, Harry

Marlowe, Stephen, pseud. *See* Lesser, Milton A.

3734. Marquand, John P. *Last Laugh, Mr. Moto.* Boston: Little, 1942. American Bob Bolles, stripped to his last sailboat on a West Indian island, overcomes the intrigues of Japanese agent Moto. The Moto series (see Part 1) was virtually killed off by Pearl Harbor, despite its great popularity in previous decades. *

3735. ___. *Stopover: Tokyo.* Boston: Little, 1957. An unsuccessful effort to rehabilitate the author's popular pre-World War II Japanese agent, Mr. Moto. Two American agents are sent to break up a Communist espionage and terrorist ring operating in Tokyo and known to be planning anti-American riots. Moto lends a helping hand. *

3736. Marsh, James J. *The Peking Switch.* New York: McKay, 1972. An American spy plane pilot, captured and brainwashed by the Communist Chinese, is sent to the US to destroy Russo-American disarmament talks.

3737. Marshall, Bruce. *The Month of the Falling Leaves.* Garden City, NY: Doubleday, 1963. A British professor of philosophy lecturing in Warsaw is mistaken by the Reds for a secret agent.

3738. Marshall, Joseph R. *Carla.* Greenwich, CT: Fawcett, 1961. A special US agent is ordered to find a missing secret American Army cannon. *P*

3739. Martin, Dwight. *The Triad Imperative.* New York: Congdon & Lattes, 1980. To appease Triad, an Asian group threatening to take over Thailand, American agent Michael Hudson is ordered to retrieve and turn over to it a large cache of opium.

3740. Martin, Ian K. *Billions.* New York: Atheneum, 1979. Ex-cop John Ross is mixed up as an intermediary in Howard Hughes' last scheme—to buy Nicaragua for $3 billion.

3741. ___. *The Manhattan File.* New York: Holt, 1976. An English detective in New York City must confront the FBI in his search for missing British military hardware.

3742. ___. *Rekill.* New York: Putnam's, 1977. A Viet Cong officer seeks those Americans responsible for the massacre of an entire Vietnamese village.

3743. Martin, Robert B. *Illegal Entry.* By Robert Bernard, pseud. New York: Norton, 1972. An American chemist in England disappears and it looks like he has defected. To solve the mystery, his brother must enter Great Britain illegally.

3744. ___. *The Ullman Code.* By Robert Bernard, pseud. New York: Putnam's, 1974. A Jewish scholar is employed to decode a secret manuscript which may contain the names of those who betrayed freedom-fighting partisans in the German concentration camps.

3745. Martin, Trevor. *The Terminal Transfer.* New York: Avon, 1984. A computer whiz, burning for revenge because of his family's humiliation by the government, concocts a program that enables him to "transfer" huge amounts of money to his own Swiss account and bring the US corporate defense system close to ruin. *P*

3746. Marton, George and Michael Burren. *The Obelisk Conspiracy.* New York: Citadel, 1976. A French policeman must halt an insane Korean War veteran who is killing all who can testify against a group of collaborators at trial of returned SS Major Kurt Hoffner, who was taken by commandos in Chile.

3747. ___ and Tibor Meray. *Catch Me a Spy.* New York: Harper & Row, 1970. On the first night of her honeymoon in Sofia, the police burst in and arrest Jessica Fenton's husband John. Shopping around, she learns that the only way to get him back is to catch a Russian spy and offer him in exchange.

3748. Mason, Colin. *Hostage.* New York: Walker, 1973. A shaky peace in the Middle East is shattered when a right-wing gang of Israelis steal some American A-bombs stockpiled in Tel Aviv and use them to blow up Cairo. The Russians respond by sending a missile submarine to Australian waters and holding the city of Sydney hostage until the US and Britain surrender their allegiance to Israel.

3749. Mason, Francis Van Wyck. *Dardanelles Derelict.* Garden City, NY: Doubleday, 1949. Major Hugh North pretends to be a traitor, obtains an important Soviet microfilm, and makes a hazardous mad dash from behind the Iron Curtain to the "safety" of Turkey. *

Mason began his North series in the 1930s (see Part 1) and through the years his character was promoted in rank from captain through colonel.

3750. ___. *The Deadly Orbit Mission.* Garden City, NY: Doubleday, 1968. Promoted to colonel, North is sent to Tangier to learn who has caused a Soviet nuclear-warhead missile to leave Russian control and enter an orbit over America. *

3751. ___. *The Gracious Lily Affair*. Garden City, NY: Doubleday, 1957. In Bermuda on vacation, Colonel North discovers a dead man with a briefcase locked to his wrist and is subsequently drawn into a case involving arson, murder, an Oriental seductress, and Soviet attempts to sell submarines to the Red Chinese. *

3752. ___. *A Himalayan Assignment*. Garden City, NY: Doubleday, 1952. North is sent to trap enemy agents who are up to no good in Tibet. *

3753. ___. *Maracaibo Mission*. Garden City, NY: Doubleday, 1966. North is ordered to the shores of Lake Maracaibo with instructions to prevent sabotage to the oil refineries there. *

3754. ___. *Rio Casino Intrigue*. New York: Reynal, 1941. Major North is instructed to break up a Nazi conspiracy in Brazil. *

3755. ___. *Saigon Singer*. Garden City, NY: Doubleday, 1946. North searches for the Black Chrysanthemum, key to the dossier of the infamous Baron Tenno—a list which contains the names of British and American traitors in the wartime intelligence services. *

3756. ___. *Secret Mission to Bangkok*. Garden City, NY: Doubleday, 1960. North is ordered to prevent the rumored kidnapping of a famous American space scientist who is pursuing his errant child through Thailand. *

3757. ___. *Trouble in Burma*. Garden City, NY: Doubleday, 1962. In an effort to prevent a Chinese interception, North must race through the steamy hell of the Burmese jungle to destroy a vital US rocket capsule which has crashed there off-course. *

3758. ___. *Two Tickets for Tangier*. Garden City, NY: Doubleday, 1955. North must reach Tangier to procure the formula for Thulium-X before it falls into the hands of the nasties. *

3759. ___. *Zanzibar Intrigue*. Garden City, NY: Doubleday, 1964. A CIA agent has apparently defected to the Soviet Union and Colonel North is charged with looking into the matter and "rescuing" the man if possible. *

3760. Mason, Michael. *71 Hours.* New York: Coward-McCann, 1972. Seventy-one hours before Soviet leaders are due to arrive in America to conclude a disarmament treaty, US agents learn that someone is plotting against the life of one of the negotiators. Whether the Soviet premier or the American president they do not know.

3761. Mason, Richard. *The Fever Tree.* Cleveland, OH: World, 1962. An English author must prevent a Communist agent from assassinating the King of Nepal.

3762. Mason, Robert. *Weapon.* New York: Putnam's, 1989. A brilliant American designer creates Solo—a $2 billion robot with artificial intelligence designed for the Army and destined to be the ultimate combat soldier—and prepares him for his first assignment to Nicaragua on a killing mission. The ever-percipient Newgate Callendar calls *Weapon* a "parable," Solo a "Christ figure" and the book a "serious one."

3763. Mason, William. *Dagger.* New York: Zebra, 1984. Soldier-for-hire "Dagger" has a tough assignment: someone, perhaps even one of the agents of the Secret Service, is going to assassinate the US President very soon. *P*

3764. Masterman, John. *The Case of the Four Friends: A Diversion in Pre-Detection.* London: Hodder & Stoughton, 1956. Portrays an international center which takes in secrets and other data and resells them to the highest bidder. As several participatory purchasers learn to their harm, much of the information obtained is false. *

Sir John was an Oxford don before World War II who went on to play a very important role in that conflict. As chairman of the XX Committee, that group which caught and turned all German agents entering Britain, he so controlled the Abwehr espionage apparatus in England that it could be used to provide the Germans with large quantities of misinformation. His 1946 report on the process was released in 1972 under the commercial title, *The Double-Cross System in the War of 1939-45.* His interesting memoirs, *On the Chariot Wheel*, were published three years later.

3765. Masters, John. *The Breaking Strain.* New York: Dial, 1967. A lady Russian scientist who plans defection to America must overcome assorted difficulties, not the least of which are the KGB and the CIA.

3766. ___. *The Himalayan Concerto.* Garden City, NY: Doubleday, 1976. As he travels the Asian concert circuit, British composer-spy Rodney Bateman is in peril from deadly assaults by a woman he suspects of being a KGB agent.

3767. ___. *Thunder at Sunset.* Garden City, NY: Doubleday, 1974. The British are about to quit the mystical mythical Southeast Asian country of Mingora, but the new army commander and the resident SIS chief clash over a Communist terror group's attempt to take over the government.

Masterson, Whit, pseud. *See* Wade, Robert and Bill Miller

3768. Masterton, Graham. *The Burning.* New York: TOR, 1991. Horror writer Masterton mixes the occult with espionage thriller in this tale of mysterious cultists who become "Salamanders," bursting into flame and whose leader, Otto Mander, is preparing them for a Fourth Reich. *P*

3769. Mather, Arthur. *The Mind Breaker.* New York: Delacorte, 1980. An Arab terrorist kidnaps a psychic's wife and orders him to blackmail the US government via the President, whose mind the psychic can probe at will.

3770. ___. *The Tarantula Hawk.* New York: Bantam, 1989. Agent Matt Hegarty is working with Mossad to investigate an Australian, who may well be a vicious Nazi war criminal. Three more by Mather:

3771. ___. *Deep Gold.* New York: Bantam, 1986. *P*

3772. ___. *The Raid.* New York: Bantam, 1986. *P*

3773. ___. *The Los Alamos Contract.* New York: Bantam, 1988. *P*

Mather, Berkeley, pseud. *See* Davies, John E. W.

Matheson, Hugh, pseud. *See* MacKay, Lewis H.

3774. Maugham, Robert C. R. *The Man with Two Shadows.* New York: Harper, 1959. A British agent finds himself handicapped by a personality dissociation resulting from injuries received during World War II. *

3775. Maugham, W. Somerset. *Hour before Dawn.* Garden City, NY: Doubleday, 1942. Pictures the difficulty of an English family during the first months of the Second World War. The eldest son is a member of British Intelligence while the wife of one of the members is suspected of being a German spy. *
Maugham was the "godfather," if you will, of the realistic spy story (see Part 1), but aside from the single entry here, wrote no additional espionage-related tales after 1940.

3776. Maxfield, Henry. *Legacy of a Spy.* New York: Harper, 1958. A leak at the American embassy in Zurich sends CIA man Slater to the Austrian Tyrol where he finds Communist and West German emissaries entangled with hotel-keeping, skiing, and the escape of an important Hungarian.

3777. Maxim, John R. *Bannerman's Law.* New York: Bantam, 1991. Film student Lisa Benedict discovers the secret of the insane asylum called Sur La Mer: it's a training facility for some of the world's most dangerous people.

3778. ___. *The Bannerman Effect.* New York: Bantam, 1990. Paul Bannerman's group of elite contract agents is the target of a Department of Defense experiment generated by a computer program that targets subversive groups. *P* Several more:

3779. ___. *Abel/Baker/Charley.* Boston: Houghton, 1983.

3780. ___. *The Bannerman Solution.* New York: Bantam, 1989.

3781. ___. *A Matter of Honor.* New York: Bantam, 1993.

3782. Maxwell, A. E. *The Frog and the Scorpion.* Garden City, NY: Doubleday, 1986. Fiddler is a p.i. who helps a man being blkackmailed by an Arab terrorist.

3783. Maxwell, Kurt. *Equinox.* New York: Arbor, 1987. When terrorists capture his oldest friend, pacifist Dieter Helm, the Agency's Paul Fontana risks his career to save him despite orders; it seems that Helm is in possession of a dossier called the Equinox File, which could accelerate the nuclear arms race.

3784. May, Peter. *The Noble Path.* New York: St. Martin's, 1993. A British mercenary is hired to get a family out of Cambodia.

3785. Mayer, Rob. *Dragon SIM-13.* Novato, CA: Presidio, 1992. A Chinese defector working at the Pentagon has devised a computerized war game that involves simulated attacks against China. Unknown to the Defense Department, the "game" is real and the attack begins.

3786. ___. *Eyes of the Hammer.* Novato, CA: Presidio, 1991. Green berets invade Columbia to smash the drug trade.

Mayo, James, pseud. *See* Coulter, Stephen

3787. Meade, Everard. *The President's Team.* New York: Major, 1976. Big time ad man Byran Dexter undertakes a special and private intelligence mission for the President of the United States. **P**

3788. Meigs, Henry, pseud. *Gate of the Tigers.* New York: Viking, 1992. A Japanese police inspector, who hates Americans, must team up with an American agent to investigate the murder of a computer expert working in Tokyo.

3789. Meiring, Desmond. *The Brinkman.* Boston: Houghton, 1965. The "brinkman" pursues his officially secret life of murder and intimidation in Laos and Vietnam only to be opposed by a sophisticated French newsman.

3790. ___. *The Wildcatter.* New York: St. Martin's, 1987. Born in Kenya and a former police inspector of that country, Meiring joined the 6th South African Armoured Division and fought in the Italian Campaign. Author of eight previous novels, Meiring, former oil executive, is fluent in Arabic. This novel revolves about two men, one a "wildcatter" who goes to work for a Gulf Coast Arab nation and his former boss, at the moment that OPEC holds the world's economies in its grasp over the price of oil during the seventies.

3791. Meissner, Hans. *Duel in the Snow.* Trans. from the German. New York: Morrow, 1942. Following the Japanese invasion of the Aleutians in 1942, the Imperial High Command sends a group of Japanese meteorologists and scouts to the Alaskan Range to radio weather reports. Learning of this, the Americans send in their own team of commandos to capture or eliminate the "Nips." *

3792. Melchior, Ib. *The Haigerlock Project.* New York: Harper & Row, 1977. In a Black Forest cave during the last months of World War II, Nazi leaders and scientists feverishly labor to create an A-bomb; tipped off, the OSS sends two of its best agents to halt "the Haigerlock Project."
     Melchior's novels derive from his World War II experience as Military Intelligence Investigator for the Counter Intelligence Corps in the European Theatre of Operations. (See Mr. Melchior's comment in CRAFT NOTES.)

3793. ___. *Code Name: Grand Guignol.* New York: Dodd, 1987. A feckless band of civilians must stave off Nazi plans to sabotage the imminent D-Day invasion with their secret weapon.

3794. ___. *Eva.* New York: Dodd, 1984. A "what-if?" tale: Eva Braun doesn't perish in the Bunker but must escape with Bormann, at the *Führer*'s insistence, because she's carrying the seed of the Fourth Reich in her womb.

3795. ___. *The Marcus Device.* New York: Harper & Row, 1980. US officials and East German agents mount a desperate manhunt in Death Valley for a test pilot who, having crashed, has wandered off with amnesia and the subconscious knowledge of the whereabouts of a homing device for secret missiles.

3796. ___. *Order of Battle.* New York: Harper & Row, 1972. American agents must discover and destroy the Nazis fabled Werewolf Corps before it can complete its only mission—the assassination of Supreme Allied Commander Dwight D. Eisenhower. *

3797. ___. *Sleeper Agent.* New York: Harper & Row, 1975. American counterintelligence agent Jaeger, himself of German extraction, discovers a Nazi plan to open underground escape routes which will allow top German leaders to emigrate to the US and must battle a mysterious Abwehr "sleeper agent" to the death in order to halt it.

3798. ___. *The Watchdogs of Abaddon.* New York: Harper & Row, 1979. A retired Los Angeles policeman joins forces with the son of a prominent psychologist to destroy the surviving son of Adolf Hitler, who is planning to set up a Fourth Reich. Somewhat reminiscent of the Manning Coles (pseud.) title *Now or Never.* More Melchior novels:

3799. ___. *The Tombstone Cipher.* New York: Bantam, 1983.

3800. ___. *V-3.* New York: Dodd, 1985.

Meldrum, James, pseud. *See* Broxholme, John F.

3801. Mercer, Charles E. *Promise Morning.* New York: Putnam's, 1966. Mercenaries help an American woman missionary doctor and six Europeans to flee Congolese revolutionaries.

3802. Merek, Jack. *Blackbird.* New York: Contemporary, 1990. Right-wing Russians want to start a war in the Middle East by knocking out a US spy satellite.

3803. ___. *Target Stealth.* New York: Warner, 1990. This technothriller offers the STB-1 Stealth bomber—the latest item in America's defense arsenal that an elite team of Iranian pilots, commandos, and assorted terrorists are out to rip off.

3804. Merrick, Gordon. *Hot Season.* New York: Morrow, 1958. David Spofford is an intelligence agent assigned to one of America's unnamed Mediterranean embassies. During one five-day period, he attempts to get the People's Choice elected in the host country's first, but rigged, election. *

3805. ___. *The Strumpet Wind.* New York: Morrow, 1947. An OSS officer is assigned to assist a resistance cell of the French Maquis in its battle against the Nazis. *

3806. Merrick, William. *No One of That Name.* New York: Holt, 1965. An American minister is in an African nation where civil war threatens. There he finds an apparent Communist plot to take over the place, but when he attempts to get a mystical leader to step in and quash it, he is opposed by the cynical chief of the local CIA detachment. *

3807. ___. *The Packard Case.* New York: Random, 1961. Set in Paris, this is the story of Agent Bradock's attempt to prevent Packard's defection to the Russians. In the process, we are treated to many flashbacks as Bradock reviews his career and his links to the escape-minded Packard. *

Merrill, P. J., pseud. *See* Roth, Holly

3808. Messman, Jon. *The Handyman: The Game of Terror.* New York: Pyramid, 1973. Jefferson Boone is a literate, cultured agent as good with a book or painting as with a gun or a doll—so versatile is he that he wears the codename "Handyman." In this tale, the cancer of terrorism is spreading, but before he can stop the carnage, Boone has to learn the rules and identify the players. *P*

3809. ___. *The Handyman: The Inheritors.* New York: Pyramid, 1975. Investigating the brutal murder of an American consul in Spain, Jefferson Boone encounters a beautiful heiress who is, in fact, the leader of a cruel band of revolutionaries. *P*

3810. ___. *The Handyman: The Moneta Papers.* New York: Pyramid, 1973. Boone travels to Venice to accomplish a mission failed by two others: to deliver certain documents to the richest heiress in the world before she marries her Italian lover. *P*

3811. ___. *The Handyman: Ransom.* New York: Pyramid, 1975. In the jungles of South America, Boone smashes a million-dollar double cross involving the mysterious kidnapping of American citizens. Others in "the Handyman" series include: *P*

3812. ___. *The Handyman: City for Sale.* New York: Pyramid, 1975. *P*

3813. ___. *The Handyman: Fire in the Streets.* New York: Pyramid, 1974. *P*

3814. ___. *The Handyman: Murder Today, Money Tomorrow.* New York: Pyramid, 1973. *P*

3815. ___. *The Handyman: A Promise of Death.* New York: Pyramid, 1975. *P*

3816. ___. *The Handyman: The Revenger.* New York: Pyramid, 1973. *P*

3817. ___. *The Handyman: The Stiletto Signature.* New York: Pyramid 1974. *P*

3818. ___. *The Handyman: The Swiss Secret.* New York: Pyramid, 1974. *P*

3819. ___. *The Handyman: The Vendetta Contract.* New York: Pyramid 1975. *P*

3820. Meyers, Martin. *Spy and Die.* New York: Paperback, 1976. Patrick Hardy runs an agency called Trouble Limited and is occasionally involved in espionage as well as sleuthing in this mid-1970's series. *P*

Michaels, Philip, pseud. *See* van Rjndt, Philippe

3821. Michener, James A. *Poland.* New York: Random, 1983. Covers eight important periods of Polish history, from the twelfth century to the present of Nazi and Soviet Occupations, and interweaves the saga of three families. *HI*

3822. Miehe, Ulf. *Puma.* Trans. from the German. New York: St. Martin's, 1979. Terrorists kidnap the volatile teenage daughter of Germany's richest armaments manufacturer and the ransom plan seems to be going well—until the girl elects to join in with her captors. Reminiscent of the Patricia Hearst case. Another:

3823. ___. *A Dead One in Berlin*. Trans. Sophie Wilkins. New York: Bantam, 1976.

3824. Mikes, George. *The Spy That Died of Boredom*. New York: Harper & Row, 1974. The KGB is slipping up by flooding the West with a horde of half-trained agents. One of these, whose story we follow here, is sent to England to woo secrets from susceptible young secretaries working in defense agencies.

3825. Miles, John. *Operation Nightfall*. New York: Berkley, 1976. Atlanta International Airport is threatened with aerial bombardments by three deranged pilots seeking a $3 million ransom. *P*

3826. Miller, Beulah M. *The Fires of Heaven*. Los Angeles: Douglas-West, 1974. Only three people knew the Arabian mission Weber was to undertake for the American government and only one man could prepare him for that assignment in time!

3827. Miller, Helen T. *Sheridan Road*. New York: Appleton-Century, 1942. Mistaken for somebody else, a young American girl executive must be rescued from a gang of Nazi saboteurs by a daring news photographer. *

3828. Miller, Rex. *Profane Men*. New York: Signet, 1989. A Vietnam saga about a platoon on a secret mission in the jungle to destroy an outlaw radio station broadcasting coded enemy messages. *P*

3829. Mills, James. *The Power*. New York: Warner, 1990. A scientist is drawn into the development of mind technology—the use of psychic weapons for intelligence and military objectives.

3830. ___. *The Seventh Power*. New York: Dutton, 1976. A Princeton graduate and two friends plan to become the world's seventh nuclear power by building an A-bomb with which they will black mail the government into redistributing the world's wealth by holding New York City hostage.

3831. ___. *The Truth about Peter Harley*. New York: Dutton, 1979. Reporter Tony Denisert follows Agent Harley into the jungles of Thailand where the latter is attempting to smash a drug smuggling operation.

3832. Mills, Osmington. *Traitor Betrayed.* New York: Roy, 1966. A superintendent at Scotland Yard who also works for that police agency's Special Branch is sent to a scientific meeting disguised as a historian with orders to prevent one Mervyn Marshland's defection to the Soviets with a hat full of vital documents.

3833. Milne, John. *Daddy's Girl.* New York: St. Martin's, 1990. London p.i. Jimmy Jenner gets mixed up with terrorists.

3834. Milton, David. *The Hyte Maneuver.* New York: Dutton, 1988. Lieutenant Raymond Hyte of the NYPD engineers the rescue of passengers from a hijacked Tangier flight, but someone—perhaps a passenger—is now methodically killing the first-class passengers.

3835. Milton, Joseph. *Bart Gould: Assignment—Assassination.* New York: Lancer, 1964. Believed to have died a war hero in 1945, a man reappears again as a Communist agent and must be caught by the President's own agent, Bart Gould. *P*

3836. ___. *Bart Gould: Baron Sinister.* New York: Lancer, 1965. Bart Gould, the suave free-lance spy, trails five government employees reported missing in Europe to a menacing castle and a cabal of evil, warped-minded plotters. *P*

3837. ___. *Bart Gould: The Death Makers.* New York: Lancer, 1966. One renegade American could ensure a Communist victory in Vietnam unless operative Bart Gould could stop him. *P*

3838. ___. *Bart Gould: The President's Agent.* New York: Lancer, 1967. The President of the United States personally orders Bart Gould to stop at nothing to destroy a group of loonies who are out to destroy the Panama Canal. Bernard Drew's *Action Series & Sequels* notes that the author's name on this title was spelled as Hilton (119). *P*

3839. ___. *Bart Gould: The Worldbreaker.* New York: Lancer, 1964. Seeking a defector, Bart Gould stumbles upon a new and deadly weapon under development by the enemy. *P* Other Gould stories are:

3840. ___. *Bart Gould: Big Blue Death.* New York: Lancer, 1965. *P*

3841. ___. *Bart Gould: The Man Who Bombed the World.* New York: Lancer 1966. *P*

3842. ___. *Bart Gould: Operation—World War Three.* New York: Lancer, 1966. *P*

3843. Milton, Nancy. *The China Option.* New York: Random, 1982. Author Milton taught at the Peking First Foreign Languages Institute in the early 1960's. Rookie reporter Anne Campbell arrives in China and stumbles over a story that could make her career—if it doesn't make her dead first: the US is arming China with nuclear weapons.

3844. Minick, Michael. *The Kung Fu Avengers.* New York: Bantam, 1975. A brother-sister team of martial arts experts smash an international band of evildoers. *P*

3845. Mitchell, James. *Death and Bright Water.* New York: Morrow, 1974. SIS agent Callan must run interference from Russian and British Intelligence to rescue a young woman under house arrest in Crete.

3846. ___. *Die Rich, Die Happy.* By James Munro, pseud. New York: Knopf, 1966. James Craig, top dog in Britain's hush-hush "K Department," is assigned to protect a shipping tycoon about to fall into the hands of the Red Chinese. Published first in *Cosmopolitan* installments.

3847. ___. *Innocent Bystanders.* By James Munro, pseud. New York: Knopf, 1970. The boss sends Craig on a desperate mission from which he is not expected to return with orders to find a missing scientist of immense importance.

3848. ___. *The Man Who Sold Death.* By James Munro, pseud. New York: Knopf, 1965. Black Belt expert Craig did not plan on becoming a professional killer, but in this first in a series, he is recruited by "Department K" of MI-6 to liquidate one St. Briac, the head of a radical group planning to draw England into the Algerian mess.

3849. ___. *The Money that Money Can't Buy.* By James Munro, pseud. New York: Knopf, 1968. Craig and the KGB are in complete agreement in their search for the murderer of a Chinese waiter in a Lake District eatery who was found with a phony $20 bill in his pocket.

3850. ___. *A Red File for Callan.* New York: Simon & Schuster, 1971. [*A Magnum for Schneider.* London: Jenkins, 1969]. After sixteen exciting years with MI-6, Callan began having such horrible nightmares that he had to retire.

Then after six months at a dreary accountant's job, he decides he is recovered enough to come back for one last assignment.

3851. ___. *Russian Roulette*. New York: Morrow, 1973. One day Callan received word that he is being deliberately sacrificed to the Russians for the exchange of a more important spy.

3852. ___. *Smear Job*. New York: Putnam's, 1977. To embarrass an East German leader, Callan must steal a trivial book from an English nobleman and arrange disastrous gambling losses for an impoverished East German.

3853. ___. *A Way Back*. New York: Morrow, 1960. Henry Walker, a British foundry worker, relives his part in a Red bomb plot and finds to his dismay that this knowledge is held by others who want him to pick up where he left off years before. Five early Mitchell novels:

3854. ___. *Among African Sands*. London: Davis, 1963.

3855. ___. *Here's a Villain*. New York: Morrow, 1958.

3856. ___. *Ilion like a Mist*. London: Cassell, 1969.

3857. ___. *Soldier in the Snow*. London: Faber & Faber, 1961.

3858. ___. *Steady Boys, Steady*. London: Davis, 1961.

3859. Mochan, Ben. *The Assassin Code*. New York: Jove, 1985. About a mad assassin calling himself Achilles who knocks off one of the Queen's relatives and threatens to kill her majesty unless she comes up with £100,000 in ten days. *P*

3860. Moffat, James. *Justice for a Dead Spy*. New York: Signet, 1971. Agent Silar Manners is called upon to review the circumstances surrounding the death of an operative later discredited. *P*

3861. ___. *The Girl from HARD*. London: NEL, 1973. Virginia Box is the heroine of this spoof, an obvious, if racy, spinoff of the UNCLE series. *P* One more:

3862. ___. *Perfect Assignment*. New York: Signet, 1975. *P*

3863. Molloy, Michael J. *The Kid from Riga.* London: Hodder & Stoughton, 1987. The "kid from Riga" has graduated from the rubble of Berlin to become a top mole in British SIS. Lewis Horne, intelligence officer and academic, must find him fast. Two others:

3864. ___. *The Black Dwarf.* London: Hodder & Stoughton, 1986.

3865. ___. *The Harlot of Jericho.* London: Macdonald, 1989.

3866. Monsarrat, Nicholas. *Smith and Jones.* New York: Sloane, 1963. A pair of British diplomats defect to the other side. A security officer, known as the "Drill Pig," who has charge of their files and is blamed for their walk-out, is sent to keep them under surveillance. *

3867. Monteleleone, Thomas F. *Blood of the Lamb.* New York: TOR, 1993. A mix of sci-fi and thriller from this veteran of twenty novels who gives us Christ's return in the form of a charismatic Brooklyn priest who discovers he can perform miracles but doesn't know he is the Vatican's creature (literally, through miraculous recombinant DNA research).

3868. ___. *Night Train.* New York: Pocket, 1984. *P*

3869. ___ and David Bischoff. *Day of the Dragon Star.* New York: Berkely, 1983. *P*

3870. Montelheit, Hubert. *Return from the Ashes.* Trans. Richard Howard. New York: Simon & Schuster, 1963. [*Le Retour des Cendres.* Paris: Éditions Denoël, 1961]. Told in diary form by a woman named Elizabeth Wolf, believed killed by the Nazis, who returns to Paris so altered by her experiences that she is not recognized by her own family; they enlist her in a scheme—to impersonate herself!—so that they can obtain her fortune. More Montelheit tales:

3871. ___. *The Cupedevil.* New York: Simon & Schuster, 1970.

3872. ___. *Cupid's Executioners.* New York: Simon & Schuster, 1967.

3873. ___. *Murder at the Frankfort Book Fair.* Garden City, NY: Doubleday, 1976.

3874. ___. *The Praying Mantises.* New York: Simon & Schuster, 1982.

3875. ___. *The Prisoner of Love*. New York: Simon & Schuster, 1965.

3876. ___. *The Road to Hell*. New York: Simon & Schuster, 1964.

Montross, David, pseud. *See* Backus, Jean L.

3877. Moody, John. *Moscow Magician*. New York: St. Martin's, 1992. A small-time operator in Moscow runs afoul of the KGB and must flee to the West.

3878. Moody, Susan. *Mosaic*. New York: Dell, 1991. Romance mingles with intrigue in Istanbul as a reporter seeking answers to her father's murder meets a hazel-eyed stranger. *P*

3879. Moorcock, Michael. *The Chinese Agent*. New York: Macmillan, 1970. British agent Jerry Cornell is assigned to find Kung Fu Tsu, the local Red Chinese spy-in-residence, whose people have stolen and mislaid vital secret plans. *H* Two other Cornell yarns are:

3880. ___. *A Cure for Cancer*. New York: Holt, 1971. *H*

3881. ___. *The English Assassin*. New York: Harper & Row, 1974. *H*

3882. Moore, Brian. *The Color of Blood*. New York: Dutton, 1987. Catholic novelist Moore presents the inner conflict of a man divided within the structure of an espionage tale. Cardinal Bem serves an unnamed Eastern European country and must walk a tightrope between his duty to the Church and this totalitarian regime. Suddenly, he is the victim of an assassination plot and is whisked away by security police—from whom he escapes.

3883. Moore, Robert L., Jr. *The Country Team*. By Robin Moore, pseud. New York: Crown, 1967. The situation in a mythical Asian country (Vietnam?) deteriorates so badly that the local CIA team must enlist the services of an American adventurer who owns a rubber plantation in the nation.

3884. ___. *Court Martial*. By Robin Moore, pseud. Garden City, NY: Doubleday, 1971. A Vietnamese counterspy is alleged to have been murdered and a vindictive general orders five US Army Green Berets to stand trail for "the crime."

3885. ___. *The Green Berets*. By Robin Moore, pseud. New York: Crown, 1965. The controversial story of US Army Special Forces in Vietnam that John

Wayne made into a hawkish movie; several sections deal with espionage and clandestine operations.

3886. ___. *The London Switch.* By Robin Moore, pseud. New York: Pinnacle, 1974. Devoted to the world of electronic surveillance and pushbutton destruction, this yarn concerns a man framed for murder and on the run. As much a detective story as a spy thriller, it incorporates elements of both genres. *P*

Moore, Robin, pseud. *See* Moore, Robert L., Jr.

3887. Morgan, Allan. *The Essential Man.* New York: Playboy, 1977. In the White House Cabinet Room a Presidential advisor takes the Secretary of State, First Lady, and other top government officials hostage in a bizarre terrorist plot.

3888. ___. *The Spandau Warrant.* New York: Award, 1973. Secret US assassin Mark Blood stalks Hitler's most sadistic executioner thirty years after the end of World War II. *P*

3889. Morgan, Brian S. *The Business of Blanche Capel.* Boston: Little, 1954. At a virus research station in Essex, England, the good doctor and his beautiful assistant are working on an agent (germ) of bacterial warfare. When the flask containing the virus is taken, the two scientists set out to pursue the thief across Europe. Like Alistair Maclean's *The Satan Bug* above. *

3890. Morgenstern, Joseph. *World Champion.* New York: Simon & Schuster, 1968. An unlikely peace negotiator tries to save his island homeland from total destruction by a civil war which is supported on one side by the Red Chinese and on the other by the Americans.

3891. Morgulas, Jerrold. *Scorpion East.* New York: Seaview, 1981. During World War II a disgruntled Soviet general agrees to form a large renegade Russian army to assist in the German war effort against Stalin.

3892. ___. *The Torquemada Principle.* New York: Wade, 1980. An SS officer is sent to hunt down correspondents who are sending a series of letters between Germany and London containing information which could topple Hitler.

3893. Morrell, David. *Assumed Identity.* New York: Warner, 1993. An agent whose specialty is impersonating others so well that he barely knows himself now finds himself unmasked and abandoned by his agency.

3894. ___. *The Brotherhood of the Rose.* New York: St. Martin's, 1984. Two brothers raised in an orphanage are trained as intelligence operatives and assassins by their foster father.

3895. ___. *The Covenant of the Flame.* New York: Warner, 1991. Investigative reporter Tess Drake meets a mysterious gray-eyed man, one of the "Keepers of the Flame" and before she can learn more of this secret group devoted to protecting the earth from despoilers, he is killed; soon gray-eyed killers are stalking her.

3896. ___. *The Fifth Profession.* New York: Warner, 1990. Savage is the hero of this tale of "executive protectors," or members of the "fifth profession," whose task is to protect wealthy clients; Savage joins with a modern samurai master to save a woman from her billionaire husband's wrath.

3897. ___. *The Fraternity of the Stone.* New York: Marek, 1985. Drew MacLane, for years a government-sanctioned assassin until he sickened of killing, is now himself the target of a mysterious assassin working for "Scalpel."

3898. ___. *The League of Night and Fog.* New York: Dutton, 1987. This time Saul and Drew are opposed by a team of assassins named Seth and Icicle, who are themselves sons of Nazi assassins, called into action when Mossad operatives and survivors of Nazi death camps begin exterminating former SS fugitives all over the world. Recent thrillers from the creator of Rambo:

3899. ___. *Rambo (First Blood Part II).* New York: Jove, 1985. *P*

3900. ___. *Rambo III.* New York: Jove, 1988. Based on a screenplay written by Sylvester Stallone and Sheldon Lettich. *P*

3901. Morris, Jean. *Sleeping Dogs Lying.* By Kenneth O'Hara, pseud. New York: Macmillan, 1962. Checking up on the record of a scientist's girlfriend, an agent uncovers a four-year-old murder, security problems, and espionage.

3902. ___. *Underhandover.* By Kenneth O'Hara, pseud. New York: Macmillan, 1963. Agent Bron Armine, technical advisor to a Central European state, is caught in a web being spun around the country's three policing forces.

Morris, John, pseud. *See* Hearne, John and Morris Cargill

3903. Morris, M. E. *The Last Kamikaze.* New York: Random, 1990. A Japanese pilot during WW II had his kamikaze mission canceled; now an old man, he intends to carry it out at last—unless a young Japanese-American in the State Department can stop him.

3904. ___. *Sword of the Shaheeni.* Novato, CA: Presidio, 1990. Russian nuclear armaments fall into the hands of Arab terrorists, forcing the Soviets to work alongside the US to stop them from triggering WW III. More tales:

3905. ___. *The Icemen.* New York: Pocket, 1989. *P*

3906. ___. *Alpha Bug.* Novato, CA: Presidio, 1986. *P*

3907. Morrows, Susan. *A Season of Evil.* Garden City, NY: Doubleday, 1970. Midge is in St. Croix because Quinn of the CIA is worried about a potential Black Power struggle on the little island. **y*

Morton, Anthony, pseud. *See* Creasey, John

3908. Mosley, Nicholas. *Assassins.* New York: Coward-McCann, 1967. Mysterious agents attempt to halt the apparently successful talks between the British Foreign Secretary and Korin, head of an important but unnamed East European satellite country.

3909. Moss, Robert. *Carnival of Spies.* New York: Villard, 1987. Young Johnny is in Rio for the Carnival of 1936—but not to celebrate; as one who has devoted his life to international Communism, he has become disillusioned with its ruthless principles and decides to play double agent against the system.
    Moss began editing *Foreign Report* in 1974 (the *Economist*'s weekly) and is an expert on terrorism.

3910. ___. *Death Beam.* New York: Crown, 1981. The Soviets have it and the Americans want it: the Death Beam is a super-laser that may not burn a hole through the moon, but it can surely melt a fighter pilot in his warplane as easily as a hot knife through a stick of butter.

3911. ___. *Mexico Way.* New York: Simon & Schuster, 1991. An oil billionaire plots to take over the vast northern Mexican oil fields unless CIA agent Jim Kreeger can stop him.

3912. ___. *Moscow Rules.* New York: Villard, 1985. A young man whose father has been liquidated and fiance arrested by the KGB, sent to the camps, and brutalized until she committed suicide vows revenge on his government and bides his time as he marries into power and becomes the youngest Soviet military general.

3913. ___ and Arnaud de Borchgrave. *Monimbó*. New York: Simon & Schuster, 1983. "Monimbó" is Castro's plot, financed with tons of South Florida narcodollars, to destroy US society by sending hundreds of agents and terrorists along with boatloads of criminal scum to synchronize race riots, blackouts, and murder across the nation.

3914. ___ and Arnaud de Borchgrave. *The Spike*. New York: Crown, 1980. Former Director of the CIA Richard Helms praised this collaboration by Moss and Chief Foreign Correspondent of *Newsweek* de Borchgrave. Robert Hockney, liberal journalist, becomes a pariah for his efforts to expose a brilliant, global disinformation plot by the KGB's Directorate A—one that is assisted by a mole in the ultrasecret NSA and that, if successful, will enable the Soviet Union to conquer the world without firing a shot.

3915. Moyes, Patricia. *Death and the Dutch Uncle*. New York: Holt, 1969. In this combination detective-spy story, Inspector Tibbett of Scotland Yard searches from England to the Netherlands for the answer to the question: "How does the killing of a small-time British pub owner affect an international dispute between two new African nations?"

3916. Muir, Douglas. *American Reich*. New York: Berkley, 1985. An it-can't-happen-here novel in which fascist troops are ready to take over a crumbling democracy—unless one hero can prevent the President's imminent assassination. *P*

3917. ___. *Red Star Run*. New York: Charter, 1988. A Bolshoi ballet star's defection to Southern California causes more than usual embarrassment this time because the positions of Chair and Premier of the Politburo and Presidium happen to be held by the young man's father. It is now bodyguard Jon Saart's job to protect him and his actress lover from the KGB's contract hit man. *P*

3918. ___. *Tides of War*. New York: Berkley, 1987. The U-boat facilities in Brittany must be crippled on the eve of the invasion; an American sub commander and a seductive Norwegian spy team up to do the job. Another:

3919. ___. *Midnight Admiral*. New York: Charter, 1989. *P*

3920. Mullane, Mike. *Red Sky: A Novel of Love, Space & War*. Salt Lake City: Northwest, 1993. Former astronaut Mullane's novel concerns the lives and loves of five astronauts toward Cold War's end and a Soviet plot.

3921. Mullin, Christopher J. *The Last Man out of Saigon*. New York: Bantam, 1989. CIA operative MacShane is ordered to set up a network in the fall of Saigon that will undermine the new regime; however, his cover is blown, he is captured and then sent by his captors into the country for brainwashing.

3922. ___. *A Very British Coup*. London: Hodder & Stoughton, 1982. HMG disapproves of it; therefore, SIS attempts to overthrow an elected foreign government (serialized on British television in 1988).

3923. ___. *The Year of the Fire Monkey*. London: Trafalgar Square, 1992. A young, innocent village boy gets involved with the CIA and an assassination plot in Maoist China.

3924. Mullally, Frederick. *The Assassins*. New York: Walker, 1966. A *Washington Post* reporter in London falls in love with a Russian correspondent for TASS. Both are in town for the end of the Cold War, due to be brought about by the formal reunification of Germany. It turns out, however, that she is the niece of the Soviet premier and a member of a right-wing Soviet splinter group that plans to break up the festivities by killing her uncle.

Munro, James, pseud. *See* Mitchell, James

3925. Murakami, Haruki. *Hard-Boiled Wonderland and the End of the World*. Trans. Alfred Birnbaum. New York: Vintage, 1991. [*Sekai no owari to hādo-boirudo wandārando*. Tokyo: Shinchosha, 1991]. Although the plot can be paraphrased as an espionage tale in which a man launders data for national security from "an office building with a river chasm at the bottom" in the middle of Tokyo, there is more fable than espionage—narrated in the wacky "new fictioneer" style of T. Coraghessan Boyle and Thomas Pynchon.

3926. Mure, David W. *The Last Temptation: A Novel of Treason*. London: Buchan & Enright, 1984. Once much admired for his nonfictional work on tradecraft and espionage (Mure once ran five major networks) by head of MI-6, Sir Maurice Oldfield himself, Mure's only novel is an erudite work that borrows its title from T. S. Eliot's *Murder in the Cathedral* and exposes "real" characters fictionally, such as Kim Philby ("Red Knight"), Guy Burgess ("Duchess"), Sir Anthony Blunt ("Red Queen") etc.

3927. Murphy, Christopher. *The Jericho Rumble.* New York: Walker, 1987. A British freelance agent smuggles a sonic device which can scramble brains and buildings alike into a tiny African country to rescue a woman's husband and father.

3928. Murphy, James. *Cedar.* London: Malvern, 1986. Joseph Mercer, head of Russia section, is a casualty of political fallout in the Secret Service, but the treachery within combines with the treachery without when a Soviet politburo source, codename Cedar, begins feeding utmost secret information to HMG. When Mercer's own network falls inside Russia, it begins to look as though *he* is the mole that Cedar claims is about to surface in the wake of his own defection.

Murphy, John, pseud. *See* Grady, Ronan C., Jr.

3929. Murphy, Walter F. *The Roman Enigma.* New York: Macmillan, 1981. Toward the close of World War II in Europe, an OSS agent is dispatched to Rome in a desperate effort to prevent the Germans from learning that the British have broken a top secret code.

3930. Murphy, Warren. *The Ceiling of Hell.* New York: Fawcett, 1984. Ex-Secret Service agent Steve Hooks is a freelance bodyguard who takes an assignment to track down a woman for an anti-Nazi author, but the investigation leads him to a worldwide conspiracy fueled by old Nazi money. Another series collaboration:

3931. ___ and Molly Cochran. *The Grandmaster.* New York: Pinnacle, 1984. *P*

Murphy, Warren, co-author. *See* Sapir, Richard

3932. Murray, William H. *Dark Rose the Phoenix.* New York: McKay, 1965. Three retired secret agents open their own international organization to handle special cases.

3933. Myers, Paul. *Deadly Cadenza.* New York: Vanguard, 1986. Mark Holland investigates the murder of a promising violinist.

3934. ___. *Deadly Crescendo.* New York: Doubleday, 1990. Mystery-espionage series character Mark Holland stars in this tale about murder and the music business; he used to work for British SIS but is now an international concert manager for highbrow artists.

3935. ___. *Deadly Score.* New York: Doubleday, 1989. Mark Holland goes to East Berlin in search of lost Mahler scores and discovers intrigue.

3936. ___. *Deadly Sonata.* New York: Doubleday, 1990. Mark Holland wants to help a brilliant Russian pianist defect, and the pianist wants Holland to get his sister, a Bolshoi ballerina, out too when she appears in London; the KGB has different plans for all three.

3937. ___. *Deadly Variations.* New York: Vanguard, 1986. The first Mark Holland caper introduces a German refugee scientist working in Switzerland who creates a deadly virus that attracts the wrong kind of interest, and Holland, now a concert manager living in Geneva, is pressed back into intelligence work. Another "Deadly" title:

3938. ___. *Deadly Aria.* New York: Vanguard, 1987.

3939. Mykel, A. W. *The Windchime Legacy.* New York: St. Martin's, 1980. An American computer scientist jeopardizes top secret "Project Sentinal" while two CIA agents try to stop the KGB from obtaining the program's schematics. Two more tales:

3940. ___. *The Luxus.* New York: St. Martin's, 1991.

3941. ___. *The Salamandra Glass.* New York: St. Martin's, 1983.

N

3942. Nabarro, Derrick. *Rod of Anger.* New York: Sloane, 1954. Five years after the war, Englishman John Granger returns to Europe to pick up Anna, his love left behind in the underground. Another old friend, Anton, is now a fugitive from the party controlling Anna's nation and Granger attempts to help him escape from the secret police chief Brud.

3943. Nance, John J. *Final Approach.* New York: Crown, 1990. A tipster tells an investigator for the National Transportation Safety Board that an airliner's crash is sabotage that can be linked to a racist, right-wing politician.

3944. Napier, Geoffrey. *Very Special Agent.* Greenwich, CT: Fawcett, 1968. Was Stefan Gerhardi simply a lowly Hungarian UN Delegate in love with an American female scholar or was he a professional spy trained in the art of seduction? *P*

3945. Nash, N. Richard. *Aphrodite's Cave*. Garden City, NY: Doubleday, 1980. On Cyprus, two Yanks are drawn into a plot by a fanatical revolutionary group to destroy a government monastery-fortress.

3946. Nason, Leonard H. *Contact Mercury*. Garden City, NY: Doubleday, 1946. American tank officer Colonel Eadie is sent on a secret mission to Paris, from which he later escapes with information vital to the Allies' Manhattan Project. *

3947. Nathan, Robert Stuart. *The White Tiger*. New York: Simon & Schuster, 1987. Dr. Peter Ostrander is an American psychiatrist invited to China after the bloody days of the Cultural Revolution; investigator Lu Hong believes there is an insidious purpose to his invitation that belies China's "open door" policy.

3948. Nathanson, E. M. *A Dirty Distant War*. New York: Viking, 1987. In this sequel to *The Dirty Dozen*, Major John Reisman's new OSS mission is to drop behind enemy lines in French Indochina.

3949. ___. *The Dirty Dozen*. New York: Bantam, 1965. "Project Amnesty" called for the training of a dozen condemned criminals as super-secret commandos and the dropping of same behind enemy lines in France to take out a German headquarters just before D-Day. *

3950. Nazarian, Barry. *The Circe Factor*. New York: Playboy, 1981. A beautiful, politically ambitious woman compromises her scruples and sleeps with the President unaware until now that she has been manipulated to her position by a man with assassination as his purpose.

3951. Neely, Richard. *The Smith Conspiracy*. New York: Signet, 1972. Employing mind control techniques, billionaire political manipulator V. R. Smith forces assassin Ridge Collins to murder a Black leader in a plot designed to create bloody riots which would put "his man" in the White House. *P*

3952. Nelson, Walter. *Bloody Christmas*. Boston: Little, 1980. Obsessed by PLO revolutionary dialogue, five terrorists enter Buckingham Palace and kidnap the Queen, threatening to murder her unless their colleagues are released from jails in West Germany, Britain, and Israel.

3953. ___. *The Siege of Buckingham Palace*. Boston: Little, 1979. A fanatical Iraqi chieftan intends to unite the Arab world in a daring move against the West by assembling an international team of terrorists from the German and

Japanese Rad Army factions, as well as the IRA, and take Queen Elizabeth II hostage inside Buckingham Palace.

3954. Nessen, Ron. *The First Lady.* New York: Playboy, 1980. Libby Blair, the most celebrated First Lady since Jackie Kennedy, is kidnapped by maniacal terrorists.

3955. Newman, Bernard. *The Balkan Spy.* By Don Betteridge, pseud. London: Jenkins, 1942. Secret agent Papa Pontivy is sent to ascertain German activities in wartime Yugoslavia. *

  Newman, who served in the British Ministry of Information during World War II, had begun penning spy thrillers in the years before the outbreak of conflict. (see Part 1). From 1934 on, Newman made espionage his special interest and combined that interest with his ardent hobby of cycling in order to check his research and locale. His books, which also included travel and straight detective yarns, numbered 125 by the time of his death in 1968 and his spy thrillers were noted for their detail and accuracy.

3956. ___. *Black Market.* London: Gollancz, 1942. War profiteers and shady civilians alike are becoming rich as the result of a massive black market deal and Papa Pontivy is assigned by British Intelligence to break up the ring. *

3957. ___. *The Case of the Berlin Spy.* By Don Betteridge, pseud. London: Hale, 1954. At the close of the Berlin airlift, a British SIS man is sent to Berlin to see who has been selling Western secrets to the Soviets. *

3958. ___. *Death to the Fifth Column.* London: Gollancz, 1941. Agents of MI-5 close in on a Nazi-supported group of English traitors devoted to the success of a proposed German invasion of England. *

3959. ___. *The Escape of General Gerard.* By Don Betteridge, pseud. London: Jenkins, 1943. Agents of Great Britain assist the French general in breaking out of a German trap. *

3960. ___. *The Gibraltar Conspiracy.* By Don Betteridge, pseud. London: Hale, 1955. During World War II British agents work to keep the Spanish from taking "the Rock" and turning it over to Hitler. *

3961. ___. *Moscow Murder.* London: Gollancz, 1948. Papa Pontivy is in the Russian capital city to solve the mysterious death of a diplomat from the British embassy. *

3962. ___. *Operation Barbarossa.* London: Hale, 1956. Papa Pontivy is sent by British Intelligence to warn Stalin about a forthcoming Nazi invasion of Russia—but the Soviet dictator chooses not to believe. *

3963. ___. *The Potsdam Murder Plot.* By Don Betteridge, pseud. London: Jenkins, 1947. While Truman, Atlee, and Stalin confer in the German city late in 1945, British agents stalk an assassin bent on disrupting the proceedings. *

3964. ___. *Second Front—First Spy.* London: Gollancz, 1944. British agents team up with members of the French Resistance to clear the way for D-Day, the Allied invasion of France. *

3965. ___. *Secret Weapon.* London: Gollancz, 1942. An intrepid British agent working in Germany uncovers information about a new German secret weapon. Interestingly enough, Newman ran across evidence of German work on a rocket later called the V-2 while cycling around Peenemunde in 1938. When he told the SIS about it, the agency ignored his report! *

3966. ___. *Spy-Counter Spy.* By Don Betteridge, pseud. London: Hale, 1953. A series of short stories concerning covert action and counterespionage. *

3967. ___. *The Spy at No. 10.* London: Hale, 1965. The author's last tale. A Soviet spy is known to be among the Prime Minister's advisors and Papa Pontivy is called in to ferret him/her out. *

3968. ___. *Spy Catchers.* By Don Betteridge, pseud. London: Gollancz, 1945. A collection of thirty-three short stories, four of which feature ace counterespionage agent Papa Pontivy and many of which feature the author's interest in codes and ciphers. *

3969. ___. *The Spies of Peenemunde.* By Don Betteridge, pseud. London: Hale, 1958. A couple of SIS agents are relaying information concerning German rocket testing home to England and eventually the RAF visits the Baltic coast establishment and flattens it. *

3970. ___. *The Travelling Executioners.* By Don Betteridge, pseud. London: Hale, 1954. British agents must halt a group of dedicated Soviet agents who are afoot liquidating opposing politicians and others in West Germany. Shades of SMERSH. * Other Newman spy tales are:

3971. ___. *The Centre Court Murder.* London: Gollancz, 1951.

3972. ___. *Contact Man.* By Don Betteridge, pseud. London: Hale, 1960.
*

3973. ___. *The Dead Man Murder.* London: Gollancz, 1946.

3974. ___. *The Death at Lord's.* London: Gollancz, 1952.

3975. ___. *Dictator's Destiny.* By Don Betteridge, pseud. London: Jenkins, 1945. *

3976. ___. *The Double Menace.* London: Hale, 1954.

3977. ___. *Draw the Dragon's Teeth.* London: Hale, 1967.

3978. ___. *The Evil Phoenix.* London: Hale, 1966.

3979. ___. *The Flying Saucer.* New York: Macmillan, 1950.

3980. ___. *Not Single Spies.* By Don Betteridge, pseud. London: Hale, 1951. *

3981. ___. *The Otan Plot.* London: Hale, 1957.

3982. ___. *The Package Holiday Spy Case.* By Don Betteridge, pseud. London: Hale, 1962. *

3983. ___. *Shoot!* London: Gollancz, 1949.

3984. ___. *The Silver Greyhound.* London: Hale, 1960.

3985. ___. *Spies Left!* By Don Betteridge, pseud. London: Hale, 1956. *

3986. ___. *The Spy in the Brown Derby.* By Don Betteridge, pseud. London: Gollancz, 1945. A Papa Pontivy tale. *

3987. ___. *Taken at the Flood.* London: Hale, 1958.

3988. ___. *This Is Your Life.* London: Brown, Watson, 1964.

3989. ___. *The Wishful Think.* London: Hale, 1954.

3990. Nichols, Peter. *Patchwork of Death.* New York: Holt, 1965. Hunted by a mysterious pursuer, a London shopkeeper flees to Argentina only to be confronted by the Nazi past he had tried so hard to bury.

3991. Nicolaysen, Bruce. *Perilous Passage.* New York: Playboy, 1976. A Basque mountain guide unhappily agrees to help the French Resistance smuggle a Jewish professor and his family to safety during World War II.

3992. Nicole, Christopher. *Operation Destruct.* New York: Holt, Rinehart, 1969. This tale, *Operation Manhunt* (New York: Holt, Rinehart, 1970) and *Operation Neptune* (New York: Holt, Rinehart, 1972) are young-adult spy stories featuring Jonathan Anders, agent for British SIS. *Py*
    In 1966, Nicole published the first of his Jonas Wilde stories. Coming at the height of the James Bond mania, these tales of a careful official assassin for British Intelligence were immensely successful in aping Bond and certainly were not intended to display the humor of John Gardner's "Boysie Oakes."

3993. ___. *The Captivator.* By Andrew York, pseud. Garden City, NY: Doubleday, 1974. Jonas Wilde, code-named "The Eliminator," an assassin for a special branch of British Intelligence, sets off in his catamaran to deliver the ransom for a kidnapped West European princess. At sea, he meets both the kidnappers and a mighty storm.

3994. ___. *The Co-Ordinator.* By Andrew York, pseud. Philadelphia: Lippincott, 1967. In this sequel to *The Eliminator* cited below, Wilde is assigned to take out a man known to the British as "The Swedish Falcon"—a fellow about to betray Great Britain.

3995. ___. *The Deviator.* By Andrew York, pseud. Philadelphia: Lippincott, 1970. Unbeknownst to him, Wilde's cover has been unmasked by the KGB and his upcoming mission to the Soviet Union may be fatal.

3996. ___. *The Eliminator.* By Andrew York, pseud. Philadelphia: Lippincott, 1967. The first Wilde tale. One of our assassin's superiors has defected to Russia and so "the Eliminator" is sent forth to kill a sufficient number of Soviet villains until he can take out the turncoat. Filmed as *Danger Route* (US, 1967).

3997. ___. *The Expurgator.* By Andrew York, pseud. Garden City, NY: Doubleday, 1973. Someone is knocking off important Americans visiting Britain. Agent Wilde's chief learns the killer is named O'Dowd and lives in the village of Dort in the Medoc region of France. Wilde is sent over with orders to eliminate—and runs into a whole clan of O'Dowds.

3998. ___. *The Fascinator.* By Andrew York, pseud. Garden City, NY: Doubleday, 1975. The last Wilde tale. Tiring of the assassination game, even if it is officially licensed, Wilde retires to the island of Ibiza to lose himself in wine and song—mostly wine. But old government killers never go to pasture and his former superiors call him back to seek the would-be assassins of the oil-prince of Xanda, a man whose relationship with the West is vital to the world's peace and economy.

3999. ___. *The Infiltrator.* By Andrew York, pseud. Garden City, NY: Doubleday, 1971. Wilde infiltrates a gang causing all sorts of mischief in and around the British Isles.

4000. ___. *Operation Manhunt.* New York: Dell, 1974. Agent Jonathan Anders dodges KGB and CIA operatives as he seeks a missing Polish general on the basis of one clue—the photo of a luxury yacht that shows a steward with a remarkable resemblance to the Communist military man. *P*

4001. ___. *The Predator.* By Andrew York, pseud. Philadelphia: Lippincott, 1968. Wilde is fired when his Five Star Photographic Agency (an "Eliminator" section cover) is raided and three of its people are killed. Jonas wants to avenge this setback, but his only lead is the disappearance in Rome of a CIA man who knew the company's address. Other Nicole novels are:

4002. ___. *The Combination.* Garden City, NY: Doubleday, 1983.

4003. ___. *The Crimson Pagoda.* New York: Signet, 1983. *P*

4004. ___. *Days of Wine and Roses?* New York: Severn, 1991.

4005. ___. *December Passion.* New York: Signet, 1979. *P* Originally published under the title *Brumaire.*

4006. ___. *The Dominator.* London: Hutchinson, 1969.

4007. ___. *Haggard.* London: Joseph, 1980.

4008. ___. *Last Battle.* New York: Severn, 1993.

4009. ___. *Operation Neptune.* New York: Holt, 1971.

4010. ___. *The Passion and the Glory: The Story of the McGann Family and the War against Japan.* New York: Severn, 1990.

4011. ___. *Seeds of Rebellion.* London: Severn, 1984.

4012. ___. *The Regiment.* New York: St. Martin's, 1989.

4013. ___. *Resumption.* New York: Severn, 1993.

4014. ___. *The Sea & the Sand.* London: Severn, 1987.

4015. ___. *The Ship with No Name.* London: Severn, 1987.

4016. ___. *Sunset.* New York: St. Martin's 1978.

4017. ___. *The Titans.* New York: Severn, 1992.

4018. ___. *Wind of Destiny.* London: Severn, 1988.

4019. Nichols, Leigh. *The Key to Midnight.* New York: Pocket, 1979. When an attorney begins to investigate his girlfriend's mysterious past, which has been erased from her memory, he attracts the attention of the Central Intelligence Agency. *P*

4020. Nicholson, Michael. *The Partridge Kite.* New York: Holt, 1978. Tom McCullin is asked by MI-5 to head off a right-wing coup, but is given only twelve days in which to find and neutralize the leaders of the plot.

4021. Niesewand, Peter. *Fall Back.* New York: Morrow, 1982. David Cane from Defense Intelligence trains a think-tank professor with top-security clearance amd Russian fluency for a dangerous mission in Moscow, but when the mission is aborted, a fall-back plan is activated, one that will fuse these two men's lives and destinies in a single operation.

4022. ___. *Scimitar.* Briarcliff Manor, NY: Stein & Day, 1983. Niesewand was a foreign correspondent who covered conflicts in Africa, the Middle east, and Afghanistan. He was a much-decorated journalist who was kept in solitary confinement for seventy-three days for his coverage of the guerilla war in Rhodesia in 1973. He lost his life as a correspondent covering the Russian invasion of Afghanistan. In this novel, the Kremlin's disinformation machine is preparing for the next decade's laser technology by discrediting America with its neutron bomb research; however, a Jewish Soviet scientist's defection will result in a mission into Afghanistan by two American agents to seek evidence of poison gassing.

4023. ___. *The Word of a Gentleman.* New York: Stein & Day, 1985. St. David's is an island in the Atlantic, a post-colonial British possession, with its strategic value alone as the reason for international interest, especially among rival intelligence communities, and particularly among three men: the police chief responsible for island security, the head of the army, and a CIA man. One other:

4024. ___. *The Underground Connection.* New York: Stein & Day, 1985.

4025. Nixon, Alan. *The Attack on Vienna.* New York: St. Martin's, 1972. After raiding secret bank accounts in Switzerland, Mossad agents battle old Nazi leaders in South America and an international crime organization called the Rilke Crime Syndicate.

4026. Nixon, William. *Strategic Compromise.* Secaucus, NJ: Carol, 1990. A reporter uncovers a triple murder in an elegant hotel in Rome and discovers facts that connect it to the ongoing power struggle between proponents of the Strategic Defense Initiative ("Star Wars") and its opposition. He may have the story of a lifetime—or he may be launching WW III.

4027. Noel, Sterling. *Few Die Well.* New York: Farrar, 1953. Sold as a "hard-hitting-hard-kissing" tale of international intrigue in the post-war atomic age.

4028. ___. *I Killed Stalin.* New York: Farrar, 1951. In a daring episode of a future war, an American agent is sent to liquidate the Soviet dictator. As Stalin died in 1953, readers may have to substitute a different name for the Russian leader.

4029. Nolan, Frederick W. *The Algonquin Project.* New York: Morrow, 1974. The title refers to an OSS plot, apparently approved by Supreme Commander Eisenhower, to kill a loud-mouthed US Army Air Force general (modeled on Patton) with a hit-man supplied by exiled Mafia boss Lucky Luciano. *

4030. ___. *The Mittenwald Syndicate.* New York: Morrow, 1976. While seeking a missing SS officer, a British agent uncovers a cabal of US Army officers who are plotting to steal millions in Nazi booty. *

4031. ___. *Red Center.* New York: St. Martin's, 1987. An American and a British agent discover a plot by a GRU officer to destroy "Star Wars."

4032. ___. *The Ritter Double-Cross.* New York: Morrow, 1975. The British Ministry of Defense in 1941 puts together a do-or-die Maclean-style band to drop behind German lines to blow up a German nerve-gas factory. In a twist, the group's leader turns out to be a top Nazi agent who has set the participants up for Gestapo capture. In a double-cross, the British know all along, have sent another leader (named Smith) along, dispose of the traitor, and carry out an entirely different mission from which not all return. *

4033. ___. *Wolf Trap.* New York: St. Martin's, 1984. "Wolf Trap" is the codename behind a British plot to assassinate Adolph Hitler. One more:

4034. ___. *White Nights, Red Dawn.* New York: Macmillan, 1980. *P*

4035. Nordhoff, James. *Eastward/Westward.* New York: Morrow, 1980. In a six-day, life-and-death race, a historian must circumvent a terrorist's demand on the American President: reposition US subs to launch a missile strike on Russia or San Francisco dies.

4036. North, Anthony. *Strike Deep.* New York: Dial, 1974. The codes to Pentagon computers containing ultra-classified data are in the hands of persons-or-person unknown but bent on America's destruction.

4037. Null, Gary. *The Cuban Expedition.* New York: Pyramid, 1974. An international underground organization known as the "Secret Circle" works to right a monstrous plot involving America's security and Castro's Cuba. *P* One other "Secret Circle" story is:

4038. ___. *Operation Royal Family.* New York: Pyramid, 1975. Agents of the "Secret Circle" must prevent a terrorist plot against the British Royal Family. *P*

O

4039. O'Brian, Patrick. *The Letter of Marque.* New York: Norton, 1990. A series modeled on the Horatio Hornblower sea tales of C. S. Forester; O'Brian's tales are set in the early 1800's of the Napoleonic Wars and concern the adventures of Captain Jack Aubrey who, in this one, receives a royal "letter of marque," sanctioning his vessel a privateer in the British Navy. *HI* Three more Aubrey tales:

4040. ___. *The Fortune of War*. New York: Norton, 1991. *HI*

4041. ___. *H.M.S.* Surprise. New York: Norton, 1991. *HI*

4042. ___. *The Ionian Mission*. New York: Norton, 1992. *HI*

4043. O'Brien, Frank J. *Stealth Strike*. Blue Ridge Summit, PA: Aero, 1990. Mikhail Gorbachev has been succeeded by a hard-line faction who knock out the US "Star Wars" defense with a powerful laser. Two pilots in Stealth planes are sent to destroy the laser in this technothriller.

O'Brien, Robert C., pseud. *See* Conly, Robert L.

4044. O'Brine, Padraic Manning. *Mills*. New York: Delacorte, 1969. MI-6 and KGB agents vie for an old Nazi's secret formula for an improved mind-bending drug, LSD-25.

4045. ___. *No Earth for Foxes*. New York: Delacorte, 1975. Two tough-minded British operatives are sent to cooperate with their Russian and American counterparts in finding and destroying an ex-Gestapo agent wanted for war crimes; in the swine's Alpine lair, they encounter ghosts of the Nazi past who are plotting to take over Europe in order to build a new Reich.

4046. ___. *Pale Moon Rising*. New York: St. Martin's, 1978. SOE agent Patrice Mourgot seeks vengeance against the Nazi butchers who had imprisoned him with other members of the French Resistance cell he belonged to and who caused the death of his wife and unborn child.

4047. Obstfeld, Raymond. *The Centaur Conspiracy*. By Carl Stevens, house pseud. Toronto: Worldwide, 1983. Christian Daguerre, a.k.a. Dagger, is a war correspondent whose adventures cross over into espionage. *P* Another:

4048. ___. *Ride of the Razorback*. Toronto: Worldwide, 1984. *P*

4049. O'Connor, Brian. *One-Shot War*. New York: Time, 1980. FBI and SIS agents pool their efforts to prevent an unknown terrorist from assassinating the British Prime Minister during his state visit to Washington DC.

4050. O'Connor, Richard. *Double Defector.* By Patrick Wayland, pseud. Garden City, NY: Doubleday, 1965. Counterstroke agent Lloyd Nicolson searches for an old friend and fellow agent who has defected to the Russians.

4051. ___. *The Waiting Game.* By Patrick Wayland, pseud. Garden City, NY: Doubleday, 1965. Following the disappearance of a beautiful Soviet ballerina at Kennedy airport, Nicolson tails his leads from Vermont to Chicago. One other Lloyd Nicolson adventure is:

4052. ___. *Counterstroke.* By Patrick Wayland, pseud. Garden City, NY: Doubleday, 1964.

4053. Odell, William C. *Doubled and Vulnerable.* New York: Apollo, 1972. Pete ("Magnum") Foster is a secret agent in this tale.

4054. O'Donnell, Peter. *I, Lucifer.* Garden City, NY: Doubleday, 1967. This, the third of the Modesty Blaise series, involves a young man named Lucifer, who can predict with 80% accuracy who is to die within a six month period. Modesty and her faithful friend Willie Garvin are asked to look into the matter.
  Author O'Donnell began this female superagent's adventures as a 1962 cartoon strip for the London *Evening Standard*. She and Garvin were expressly designed as "high camp" counterparts to James Bond and as such enjoyed a successful run both in print and the comics.

4055. ___. *The Impossible Virgin.* Garden City, NY: Doubleday, 1971. Dr. Brunel and his friend Lisa draw Modesty and Willie to the site of their East German goldmine, there to do them in. Even after such sundry trials as imprisonment in a cage with a belligerent gorilla, attacks by savages, and a death-struggle with the villains, they must somehow manage to escape the wasp-filled jungles of Ruanda.

4056. ___. *Modesty Blaise.* Garden City, NY: Doubleday, 1965. The first in a series devoted to the gorgeous ex-mobstress and her faithful knife-toting companion, Willie Garvin. Having received all the benefits of a successful career in big-time crime, Modesty had "retired." Fit as a fiddle, but bored, she turns a willing hand when British Intelligence asks her to help with a crisis in the Middle East created by arch-villain Gabriel. In addition, Gabriel has swiped about £10 worth of diamonds which need to be returned to their rightful owners. Calling up Garvin, now a successful pub owner, the two set out for the Mediterranean, where they are promptly captured by Gabriel.

4057. ___. *Pieces of Modesty*. London: Pan, 1972. A collection of Modesty Blaise short stories, some of which appeared in American magazines like *Playboy*. P

4058. ___. *Sabre-Tooth*. Garden City, NY: Doubleday, 1966. Deep in a secret valley of the Hindu Kush, a lethal army of international desperadoes from a dozen countries is training in a diabolical plot to capture the oil-rich country of Kuwait. Modesty and Willie are asked by British Intelligence to break up these terrible proceedings.

4059. ___. *A Taste for Danger*. Garden City, NY: Doubleday, 1969. Modesty and Willie set out to rescue an archaeological expedition from an arch-fiend and end up "sailing" across the Algerian desert in a desperate race against a cruel death. O'Donnell continued Modesty's adventures throughout the seventies with more tales, many of which were reprinted in paperback by Mysterious Press in the mid-1980's:

4060. ___. *Dead Man's Handle*. London: Souvenir, 1985.

4061. ___. *Dragon's Claw*. London: Souvenir, 1976.

4062. ___. *Last Day in Limbo*. London: Souvenir, 1976.

4063. ___. *The Night of Morningstar*. London: Souvenir, 1982.

4064. ___. *The Silver Mistress*. London: Souvenir, 1973.

4065. ___. *The Xanadu Talisman*. London: Souvenir, 1981.

4066. Offutt, Andrew. *Operation Super Ms*. New York: Warner, 1974. Superspy Eve Smith is sent to check into a drug-smuggling caper in France. Sort of a cross between Modesty Blaise and The Baroness. P

4067. Ogilvie, Charlton, Jr. *The Marauders*. Greenwich, CT: Fawcett, 1964. A fictionalized account of some of the adventures of Merrill's Marauders in 1944 Burma. P

4068. Ognall, Leopold H. *Department "K."* By Hartley Howard, pseud. London: Collins, 1970. Philip Scott is a British toymaker who employs his frequent merchandizing trips to Germany as a cover for his espionage activities on behalf of the SIS. Basis of the movie "Assignment K."

O'Hara, Kenneth, pseud. *See* Morris, Jean

4069. O'Keefe, Bernard J. *Trapdoor*. Boston: Houghton, 1988. The former Chair of the International Task force on Nuclear terrorism presents a technothriller with a twist: The PLO steals a nuclear warhead—and the computer programmer who has rigged the system to ignore all commands except hers.

4070. Olcott, Anthony. *May Day in Magadan*. New York: Bantam, 1983. This sequel to *Red October* picks up Duvakin four years later in the permafrost of Magadan, where he has been sent into exile by his superiors. This time he stumbles upon an old cleaning woman at the airport and discovers valuable state property in her possession—furs. Duvakin is again led into the thick of a conspiracy of murder, theft, and personal danger among the elite of Brezhnev's regime.

4071. ___. *Murder at the Red October*. Chicago: Academy, 1981. The murder of a rich American in room 852 of the hotel Red October sends Duvakin into a dangerous investigation. Olcott's novel compares favorably to *Gorky Park* in its everyday, grimy atmosphere of Moscow and one man's attempt to keep from getting crushed in a spiraling atmosphere of corruption. The first title below is Olcott's first novel and the second is another Ivan Duvakin tale:

4072. ___. *Chevengur*. New York: Ardis, 1978.

4073. ___. *Rough Beast*. New York: Scribner's, 1992.

4074. Olson, Selma. *Ana Mistral*. North Hollywood, CA: Domina, 1975. A liberated woman is a maverick secret agent who battles Russian agents on behalf of an unnamed US government intelligence agency. *P*

4075. O'Malley, Mary D. *The Dangerous Islands*. By Ann Bridge, pseud. New York: McGraw-Hill, 1964. Julia Probyn joins forces with Colon Philip Jamieson of MI-5 to locate clandestine Soviet satellite tracking stations in the Hebrides. **y*
   Mary O'Malley was the wife of a British diplomat with experience in living around the globe. Her stories have proven especially appealing to teen-aged girls who seek a little romance with their derring-do.

4076. ___. *Emergency in the Pyrenees*. By Ann Bridge, pseud. New York: McGraw-Hill, 1965. That dazzling, anything-but-dumb blonde Julia Probyn has now married Col. Jamieson and when he is sent off to the Middle East for MI-

6, she elects to stay behind at his boyhood home in the Pyrenees to have their child. The baby is born prematurely and Julia becomes involved in a sabotage plot with international complications before hubby can return. *y

4077. ___. *The Episode at Toledo.* By Ann Bridge, pseud. New York: McGraw-Hill, 1966. Julia sits out this story while her friend Hetta, wife of a British diplomat in Spain, has her hands full with two cases of Communist conspiracy aimed against VIPs from America. *y

4078. ___. *The Lighthearted Quest.* By Ann Bridge, pseud. New York: Macmillan, 1956. Julia Probyn goes off to the deserts of North Africa to find a missing cousin and becomes involved with the Moroccan freedom movement and the Communist effort to take it over. *y

4079. ___. *The Malady in Madeira.* By Ann Bridge, pseud. New York: McGraw-Hill, 1970. Recently widowed, Julia Probyn visits the lush island of Madeira and finds a clue to her husband's disappearance while on a top-level SIS mission to somewhere in Central Asia. Armed with this data, she takes over his job and discovers that the Russians are experimenting with nerve gas. *y

4080. ___. *Numbered Account.* By Ann Bridge, pseud. New York: McGraw-Hill, 1960. Funds left in a Swiss bank by a dead Greek shipping magnate prove a pot of honey which draws not only Julia Probyn, there to protect it, but an extremely thorough and artistic set of thieves, a phony "Heiress," and an MI-6 agent seeking to solve the Soviet theft of blueprints for nuclear submarine tankers. *y

4081. ___. *The Portuguese Escape.* By Ann Bridge, pseud. New York: Macmillan, 1958. Julia arrives in Portugal to cover a wedding and becomes involved in the escape of a Hungarian priest, his Red pursuers, and a Hungarian countess recently released from prison behind the Iron Curtain. *y

4082. O'Malley, Patrick. *The Affair of Chief Strongheart.* New York: Morrow, 1964. Comical secret agents Harrigan and Hoeffler are assigned to uncover a free-lance American Indian group's fool-proof information center—near an ICBM base—with which, through the use of electronic snooping, it plans to learn all and tell all to the Soviets. *H*

4083. ___. *The Affair of John Donne.* New York: Morrow, 1964. Harrigan and Hoeffler are assigned to infiltrate an ultra far-right organization and prove that it really is linked to the Communists. *H*

4084. ___. *The Affair of Jolie Madame*. New York: Morrow, 1964. Only a beautiful blonde knows the fate of a missing computer scientist and Harrigan and Hoeffler must convince her to reveal it. *H*

4085. ___. *The Affair of Swan Lake*. New York: Mill, 1962. In the counterespionage role, Harrigan and Hoeffler move into the Minnesota lakes region to smell out suspected hostile agents threatening America's missile defenses. *H*

4086. ___. *The Affair of the Blue Pig*. New York: Morrow, 1965. Harrigan and Hoeffler stop off to help a detective friend solve a murder. More a detective yarn than a spy thriller. *H*

4087. ___. *The Affair of the Bumbling Briton*. New York: Morrow, 1965. When England's foremost counterespionage agent (James Bond?) comes to America and promptly disappears, Harrigan and Hoeffler move to save him from a femme fatale holding him captive in northern California. *H*

4088. ___. *The Affair of the Red Mosaic*. New York: Morrow, 1961. In which the author introduces those two zany American counterintelligence agents, Harrigan and Hoeffler—the Abbott and Costello of espionage; in this outing, they are sent to investigate Communist activities at a New Mexico atomic research establishment. *H*

4089. O'Neil, Kerry. *Death at Dakar*. Garden City, NY: Doubleday, 1943. An American war correspondent traces and helps eliminate a Nazi spymaster who has fled Rio for Dakar in West Africa. *

4090. O'Neill, Edward A. *The Rotterdam Delivery*. New York: Coward-McCann, 1975. In a time of an Arab oil embargo, a multinational group of five terrorists hijack a Dutch supertanker and demand a ransom of $25 million.

4091. O'Neill, Frank, pseud. *Agents of Sympathy*. New York: Putnam's, 1985. An international amateur sportsman, whose research into the background of his second spy novel found him interesting enough to the East German police to warrant an investigation.

4092. ___. *Roman Circus*. New York: Simon & Schuster, 1990. A CIA man resumes his romantic relationship with an Italian princess in the midst of Arab terrorism in Italy, but there's much more in this stylish novel, including a satirical look at the American presence in Italy, the hopelessly insurmountable problems of Italian bureaucracy of a police investigation, the Red Brigades running amok, and a brilliant intellectual who has brought in a viperish assassin to fulfill his terrorist campaign of anarchy.

4093. ___. *The Secret Country*. New York: Crown, 1987. Like the early le Carré, O'Neill evokes a moody atmosphere; here, a trio of characters works at cross purposes to exfiltrate an East German officer from the cold. Dr. Krel runs an escape organization; Giovanni "Wop" Stears is a banker and fledgling CIA officer; and Renata Segla, herself an escapee, returns to East Germany to assist Dr. Krel, unaware that she has been betrayed.

4094. O'Neill, Will. *The Libyan Kill*. New York: Norton, 1980. CIA agent Allenford and a French female spy are assigned to halt the masterplan of Colonel Qadafi to devastate Israel with a terrible disease.

4095. Oppenheim, E. Phillips. *Milan Grill Room*. Boston: Little, 1941. Ten short stories of wartime intrigue featuring Major Lyson of British Intelligence are related from the restaurant of London's Milan Hotel. *
    Oppenheim was a major figure in the pre-war history of the spy thriller (see Part 1). Chased out of his homes in France and on the island of Guernsey in 1940, he published this final tale before his death in 1945:

4096. ___. *Mr. Mirakel*. Boston: Little, 1943.

4097. Oram, John. *The Man from UNCLE: The Copenhagen Affair*. New York: Ace, 1965. Illya and Napoleon are sent to Denmark to thwart a THRUSH plan involving the pleasures of that pleasurable city-capital. *P*

4098. Oran, Dan and Lon Hoklin. *The Z Warning*. New York: Ballantine, 1979. Kelly Gilliam must warn the President of the United States about a plot by terrorists to steal plutonium from a Connecticut nuclear power plant. *P*

4099. Orde, Lewis. *Munich 10*. New York: Zebra, 1982. An internationally famous actress is swept into the world of terrorism when her lover and young son are murdered. *P*

4100. ___ and Bill Michaels. *The Night They Stole Manhattan*. New York: Putnam's, 1980. When his wife is killed during a bank robbery despite his pleas to the police for caution, a former US Army general promises revenge. Teaming up with a South African mercenary and terrorists, he plots to capture Manhattan and hold it for a billion dollar ransom.

4101. Ordway, Peter. *Face in the Shadows.* New York: Wyn, 1953. A newsman pegged as a Communist trails a Red agent all around the country and into Canada until he can capture him and prove himself a good security risk after all. *

4102. O'Reilly, Victor. *Games of the Hangman.* London: Weidenfeld, 1991. Hugo Fitzduane is an ex-soldier and combat photographer who discovers a corpse hanging from a tree on his estate in Ireland. Soon he is off on an international investigation to prove that the victim was anything but the suicide the authorities ruled.

4103. Orgill, Douglas. *The Cautious Assassin.* New York: Morrow, 1964. First published in England the previous year under the title, *Ride a Tiger.* A British journalist searches for a colleague lost on assignment to a Caribbean island which is controlled by a ruthless dictator.

Orvis, Kenneth, pseud. *See* Lemieux, Kenneth

4104. Orwell, George. *Nineteen Eighty Four.* New York: Harcourt, 1949. A literary classic often required as reading by college students. A depiction of a future police state where people are controlled by a "Big Brother" government and a secret "Thought Police." *See also* Blair, Eric. *

4105. Osborn, David. *Love and Treason.* New York: Signet, 1982. Harold Volker is a foreign-born Secretary of State with enormous political clout—and a wife who begins to suspect he may be a traitor. *P* Another:

4106. ___. *The French Decision.* Garden City, NY: Doubleday, 1980.

4107. Osmond, Andrew. *Saladin.* New York: Doubleday: 1975. Based on the infamous murder of eleven Israeli athletes on September 5, 1972. Anis Kubayin, codename Saladin, and Stephen Roscoe, ex-SAS officer, head two groups opposed to an Israeli-Arab peace accord and want an independent Palestinian state. Their bizarre solution: an act of violence so great that it will rupture relationships between Arabs and Israelis forever. (For Osmond's collaborations with another espionage writer, see *Hurd, Douglas.*)

4108. Ostrovsky, Victor. *Lion of Judah.* New York: St. Martin's, 1993. A Stasi colonel flees to Syria when the Wall comes down and works with terrorists to undermine Mossad by means of a disinformation plot that there is a mole in Israeli Intelligence.

4109. O'Toole, George. *An Agent on the Other Side.* New York: McKay, 1973. An expert in cryptography, O'Toole worked for the CIA for three years and rose to the rank of chief of the Problem Analysis Branch. Messages by a medium conveying the reports of double-agent Oleg Penkovsky (a real-life person) warning of the 1968 invasion of Czechoslovakia, are what our hero, John Sorel, maker of documentary films and unwilling dupe of the CIA, finds himself up against. Two more:

4110. ___. *The Cosgrave Report.* New York: Wade, 1979.

4111. ___. *Poor Richard's Game.* New York: Delacorte, 1982. *HI*

4112. Ovalov, Lev S. *Comrade Spy.* Trans. from the Russian. New York: Award, 1965. Another KGB-inspired spy thriller designed to give the Russian and East European peoples their own James Bond. In this outing, an intrepid KGB agent traps and catches a CIA spy, who is put on public trial in Moscow to confess his crimes. *P*

4113. Overguard, William. *The Divide.* New York: Jove, 1980. Thirty years after America *loses* World War II, Hitler and Tojo meet in a summit on the continental divide, unaware that members of the American Resistance are about to strike. *P*

4114. Owen, Richard. *Nightmare.* New York: St. Martin's, 1979. A journalist discovers a group of teen-aged terrorist-assassins who are operating under the protection of the newly elected President of Costa Verde.

P

4115. Pace, Eric. *Any War Will Do.* New York: Random, 1972. "The Firm" was a very private, all-powerful arms trading organization run with ruthless efficiency with profits from the Paris demi-monde, the Sicilian underworld, and a labyrinth of Arab politics and African violence. Agent Harker was ordered in to break it up and put an end to its motto (the title).

4116. ___. *Nightingale.* New York: Random, 1979. A small-time con's skills are put to work by agents of a terrorist group which has kidnapped his daughter in hopes of forcing him to help them steal Iran's crown jewels.

4117. ___. *Saberlegs.* Cleveland, OH: World, 1970. A German chemist who developed a poison gas during World War II plans to sell it to an Egyptian commando outfit unless a Jewish Nazi-hunting group can find "Saberlegs" first.

4118. Page, Martin. *The Pilate Plot.* New York: Coward-McCann, 1978. A retired agent comes across a startling document concerning the death of Christ which upsets the Vatican and raises hopes of the Jews.

4119. Palmer, John L. and Hiliary Aiden St. George Saunders. *Eleven Were Brave.* By Francis Beeding, pseud. New York: Harper, 1941. Focuses on the British Intelligence reaction to French resistance, German espionage, and other operations in France following the French collapse on the Meuse River in May 1940.

   The Beeding team continued to function into early World War II when it split up, with author Saunders going to work for the Ministry of Information. Prior to the war, Palmer and Saunders were in top form turning out quite a few spy thrillers (see Part I). Following the war, Saunders was Librarian of the British House of Commons.

4120. ___. *The Secret Weapon.* By Francis Beeding, pseud. New York: Harper, 1940. Published in England as *Not a Bad Show.* SIS agent Roger Marples escapes a torpedoed ship, is taken to Germany aboard a U-boat where he meets Hitler and Goering, participates in covert action in Poland against Nazi installations, and flees back home with the formula for a hush-hush German weapons system. *

4121. ___. *The Twelve Disguises.* By Francis Beeding, pseud. New York: Harper, 1942. In order to search for Propaganda Minister General Creighton who is missing in Occupied France, Colonel Granby must employ all of his expertise at disguise after being spotted by the Gestapo. Another Colonel Granby tale during the war years:

4122. ___. *There Are Thirteen.* By Francis Beeding, pseud. New York: Harper, 1946.

4123. Pape, Gordon and Tony Aspler. *The Music Wars.* New York: Vanguard, 1985. A Jewish violinist attracts the KGB's interest in Moscow when he enters the Tchaikovsky Competition, and his sensibilities are directed toward the plight of dissidents and, in particular, a fellow musician who wants out of Russia.

4124. ___ and Tony Aspler. *The Scorpion Sanction.* New York: Viking, 1980. An extremist cult smuggles two small A-bombs into Egypt and threatens devastation unless that nation turns to fundamental Islam.

4125. Parker, Lee. *The Assassination Is Set for July 4.* New York: Award, 1974. Capt. James L. Donovan leads "Donovan's Devils" against the world's terrorist groups in this paperback series. *P* Two more:

4126. ___. *Blueprint for Execution.* New York: Award, 1974. *P*

4127. ___. *The Guns of Mazatlan.* New York: Award, 1975. *P*

4128. Parker, Maude. *Invisible Red.* New York: Rinehart, 1953. After a seven-year stay in Russia, a young American woman returns home only to be met at the airport with a warrant for her arrest as a Communist spy. A lawyer who loved her years before risks his career to prove her innocent. A good McCarthy era piece. *

4129. ___. *Ticket to Oblivion.* New York: Rinehart, 1950. With help from a beautiful redheaded counter-spy and a group of Maquis, an American agent in France succeeds in preventing the Russians from hijacking a shipment of French gold.

4130. Parker, Robert B. *The Judas Goat.* Boston: Houghton, 1978. Parker is the popular author of the Boston-based private eye Spenser. Spenser pursues to the Montreal Olympics a group of terrorists who have killed his client's wife.

4131. Parry, David and Patrick Withrow. *The Jacamar Nest.* New York: St. Martin's, 1992. A New Hampshire insurance investigator is pulled off a case involving an Arab couple by his boss, but the ex-CIA man investigates on his own and uncovers a terrorist plot involving the blackmail of American businesses.

4132. Parry, Hugh J. *Dark Road.* By James Cross, pseud. New York: Messner, 1959. An American lawyer in West Germany is trapped by circumstances into becoming an undercover agent across the mid-German border. *

4133. Patrick, William. *Blood Winter.* New York: Viking, 1990. Berlin in 1917 is in dire straits: the British have the city blockaded, and it is slowly caving in to the vice and corruption of black marketeers, spies, and police; the one way out is germ warfare.

4134. Patterson, Harry [Henry]. *Bloody Passage.* By James Graham, pseud. New York: Macmillan, 1974. A former SAS major is coerced into rescuing a political prison from a Libyan prison. The dust jacket of the latest Higgins novel (*On Dangerous Ground.* New York: Putnam's, 1994) notes that Patterson has, from his earliest days in Belfast, experienced real-life escapades with bombs and bullets. (See Mr. Patterson's commentary in CRAFT NOTES for his own synopsis of the dangers he routinely experienced as a boy.) He has served in the Royal Horse Guards, been a circus roustabout, and truck driver. He holds advanced degrees in three disciplines, including economics, from the University of London. Mr. Patterson currently lives on Jersey in the Channel Islands. His most recent novels, including *On Dangerous Ground*, show a preference for the dashing ex-terrorist Sean Dillon, who must combine with Brigadier Charles Ferguson's personal action force to locate and suppress a secret document signed by Mao and Lord Mountbatten in 1944 China. This secret paper could destroy the delicate balance of power as Hong Kong prepares to be ceded back to China.

4135. ___. *Brought in Dead.* London: Long, 1967. Det. Sgt. Nick Miller returns in this novel about a young girl murdered and dumped in the canal.

4136. ___. *A Candle for the Dead.* By Hugh Marlowe, pseud. New York: Abelard-Schulman, 1966. Later retitled *The Violent Enemy*, this tale features IRA gunman Sean Rogan just sprung from prison and now being hunted by both Scotland Yard and his former cronies.

4137. ___. *Cold Harbour.* By Jack Higgins, pseud. New York: Simon & Schuster, 1990. Just before D-Day, OSS agent Craig Osbourne is picked up by a German U-Boat as he floats helplessly off the coast of Brittany; the skipper turns out to be a former Harvard classmate.

4138. ___. *Comes the Dark Stranger.* London: Long, 1962. Martin Shane tracks down the men who betrayed him to the Chinese Communists.

4139. ___. *Confessional.* By Jack Higgins, pseud. London: Collins, 1985. Liam Devlin's fourth appearance; this time he's hired by SIS to find "Cuchulain," a merciless KGB assassin operating in Ireland.

4140. ___. *Cry of the Hunter.* London: Long, 1960. Patterson's second novel concerns the ex-IRA gunman Martin Fallon, who—though killed in this novel—returns nine years later in *A Fine Night for Dying*. Fallon's job is to free Patrick Rogan, IRA chief, from his prison.

4141. ___. *The Dark Side of the Island*. London: Long, 1963. Hugh Lomax returns to Krystos intent to find the traitor who betrayed him and his partisan fighters to the Nazis—only to discover that everyone believes he was the traitor.

4142. ___. *The Dark Side of the Street*. By Martin Fallon, pseud. London: Long, 1967. Paul Chavasse in a tale that has him befriending a thief named Harry Youngblood in the hope of tracking an arch-criminal known as the "Baron."

4143. ___. *Day of Judgment*. By Jack Higgins, pseud. The Russians are trying to turn a Jesuit priest into their agent in 1963 Berlin. Simon Vaughan, now a major, returns in this tale to rescue him from his fortress prison.

4144. ___. *The Eagle Has Flown*. By Jack Higgins, pseud. New York: Simon & Schuster, 1991. This sequel to *The Eagle Has Landed* involves another bold and brazen German scheme; whereas the first book (which, incidentally, was reissued in 1992 with new material) attempted to capture Churchill and bring him to Germany, this one is designed to free the intrepid Colonel Steiner from his Tower of London prison and return him as a hero to Germany before the war is lost.

4145. ___. *The Eagle Has Landed*. By Jack Higgins, pseud. New York: Harper & Row, 1975. The author's most famous tale. A crack German commando team lands in England during World War II with the task of finding and killing Prime Minister Winston Churchill. This, his most popular novel, was also a popular film (GB, 1976). The 1982 edition, "The Special Edition," brought out by Pan of London contains revisions and deletions from the original. Col. Steiner, IRA gunman-poet Liam Devlin and the rest of Steiner's commando team parachute into 1943 England to capture Churchill.*

4146. ___. *East of Desolation*. By Jack Higgins, pseud. London: Hodder & Stoughton, 1968. Pilot Joe Martin is hired by an insurance agency to investigate missing diamonds in Greenland.

4147. ___. *Exocet*. By Jack Higgins, pseud. Briarcliff Manor, NY: Stein & Day, 1983. SAS Major Tony Villiers tries to stop a shipment of Exocet missiles from reaching Argentinians during the Falklands War.

4148. ___. *The Eye of the Storm*. by Jack Higgins, pseud. New York: Simon & Schuster, 1992. Sean Dillon is an ex-IRA gunman plying his trade for the Iraqis during the Gulf War; another mercenary from Ireland, on the side of the angles now, is hunting him.

4149. ___. *A Fine Night for Dying*. By Martin Fallon, pseud. London: Long, 1969. Paul Chavasse is on the track of criminals smuggling immigrants into Great Britain.

4150. ___. *A Game for Heroes*. New York: Macmillan, 1970. Col. Owen Morgan and his commando team are sent to St. Pierre in the Channel Islands to gather intelligence on the Nazis.

4151. ___. *The Graveyard Shift*. London: Long, 1965. Det. Sgt. Nick Miller is assigned the case of a murdered ex-con.

4152. ___. *Hell Is Always Today*. London: Long, 1968. A serial killer known as the "Rainlover" is loose and Det. Sgt. Nick Miller is in charge of the case.

4153. ___. *Hell Is Too Crowded*. London: Long, 1962. Matt Brady is framed for a murder he didn't commit.

4154. ___. *In the Hour before Midnight*. By Jack Higgins, pseud. Garden City, NY: Doubleday, 1969. [Rpt. as *The Sicilian Heritage*. New York: Lancer, 1970]. A Sicilian millionaire hires ex-paratrooper Stacey Wyatt to rescue his daughter from a kidnapper.

4155. ___. *The Iron Tiger*. London: Long, 1966. Jack Drummond is a gun smuggler to the Tibetans against their Chinese invaders.

4156. ___. *The Keys of Hell*. By Martin Fallon, pseud. New York: Abelard-Schulman, 1965. Another Paul Chavasse adventure; this time he goes into Communist Albania seeking a religious object called the Black Madonna, which will rally the anti-Communist partisans.

4157. ___. *The Khufra Run*. By James Graham, pseud. Garden City, NY: Doubleday, 1973. The Algerian secret police attempts to stop a determined nun and an Australian bush pilot from finding and removing a fabulous treasure. *

4158. ___. *The Last Place God Made*. By Jack Higgins, pseud. New York: Holt, Rinehart, 1972. Neil Mallory, freelance pilot, is hired to fly mail to a dangerous stretch of river in Brazil.

4159. ___. *Luciano's Luck*. By Jack Higgins, pseud. London: Collins, 1981. A British Army major and the infamous gangster Charles "Lucky" Luciano conspire in 1943 against the Nazis in Sicily.

4160. ___. *Memoirs of a Dance Hall Romeo*. By Jack Higgins, pseud. London: Collins, 1989. A mainstream novel about Oliver Shaw, recently demobbed, who returns as an aspiring writer to Yorkshire and finds love and romance in the local dance halls.

4161. ___. *Midnight Never Comes*. By Martin Fallon, pseud. London: Long, 1966. Paul Chavasse is in the Western Islands on the trail of a Soviet agent who intends to hijack the new NATO missile being tested currently under test there.

4162. ___. *Night Judgment at Sinos*. By Jack Higgins, pseud. London: Hodder & Stoughton, 1970. Off the Greek island of Sinos lies a Nazi freighter with documents important enough to send Capt. Jack Savage to locate and salvage it.

4163. ___. *Night of the Fox*. By Jack Higgins, pseud. London: Collins, 1986. During WW II, a philosophy professor and a young beauty named Sarah Draxton, both SOE members, are given a mission to rescue a British officer held in Jersey.

4164. ___. *Passage by Night*. By Hugh Marlowe, pseud. New York: Abelard-Schulman, 1964. Harry Manning goes after Cuban terrorists who have accidentally killed his woman.

4165. ___. *Pay the Devil*. London: Barrie & Rockliff, 1963. Confederate officer Clay Fitzgerald returns to Ireland to start a new life. *H*

4166. ___. *A Phoenix in the Blood*. London: Barrie & Rockliff, 1964. A story of interracial love between a West Indian student doing military service in Yorkshire and a fifteen-year-old girl.

4167. ___. *A Prayer for the Dying*. By Jack Higgins, pseud. New York: Holt, Rinehart, 1974. An ex-IRA gunman and a gun-toting priest team up to go after a gangster named Dandy Jack Meehan.

4168. ___. *The Run to Morning*. By James Graham, pseud. Briarcliff Manor, NY: Stein & Day, 1974. Adventurer Grant is blackmailed into breaking a gangster's grandson from an almost impregnable Libyan fortress where he has been imprisoned. *

4169. ___. *Sad Wind from the Sea*. London: Long, 1959. Harry Patterson's first novel, an adventure thriller, has Mark Hagen rescuing a young woman from a Chinese gang in Macao.

4170. ___. *The Savage Day*. By Jack Higgins, pseud. New York: Holt, Rinehart, 1972. Simon Vaughan is an ex-British Army major freed from a prison in Greece by SIS and hired to infiltrate the IRA.

4171. ___. *A Season in Hell*. By Jack Higgins, pseud. New York: Pocket, 1989. The daughter of a Boston millionaire enlists the aid of ex-SAS mercenary Sean Egan after her murdered stepson's body arrives in England stuffed to the gills with pure heroin.

4172. ___. *Seven Pillars to Hell*. By Hugh Marlowe, pseud. New York: Abelard-Schulman, 1963. According to Phil Stephensen-Payne in his annotated checklist on Jack Higgins, this Patterson book is "one of the four books never reprinted in paperback" (40).

4173. ___. *Solo*. By Jack Higgins, pseud. Asa Morgan of the SAS is trying to track his daughter's killer, a man who also happens to be a worl-renowned concert pianist from Crete.

4174. ___. *Storm Warning*. By Jack Higgins, pseud. New York: Holt, Rinehart, 1976. Twenty Germans stranded in Brazil at the end of WW II hijack a vessel and—with a cluster of nuns aboard—set sail across the Atlantic to return to Germany.

4175. ___. *The Testament of Caspar Schultz*. By Martin Fallon, pseud. New York: Abelard-Schulman, 1962. Paul Chevasse returns in this tale as the man who hunts one Caspar Schultz, top-ranking former Nazi, about to publish his memoirs, revealing Nazi sympathizers—who are also looking for him.

4176. ___. *The Thousand Faces of Night*. London: Long, 1961. Hugh Marlowe tries to retrieve £20,000 in stolen swag before his enemies settle up with him.

4177. ___. *Thunder at Noon*. London: Long, 1964. Writes Phil Stevensen-Payne of this one: it's very much "an oddity in the Higgins canon"; this Western set in Mexico in 1930 "was later revised and published as *Dillinger* (London: Hutchinson, 1983) with the eponymous gangster translated, for no apparent reason, into the role of main protagonist" (39).

4178. ___. *Thunder Point.* By Jack Higgins, pseud. New York: Putnam's, 1993. This Sean Dillon adventure links Martin Bormann's escape to a shipwrecked German U-Boat in the Caribbean that HMG and a ruthless billionaire are contending for because of the deadly secret it contains.

4179. ___. *To Catch a King.* London: Hutchinson, 1979. In 1940 General Walter Schellenberg plots to capture the Duke and Duchess of Windsor from Lisbon and persuade them to side with Hitler; for their support, after Germany's conquest of England, they will be allowed to rule the country.

4180. ___. *Toll for the Brave.* London: Long, 1971. Ellis Jackson awakes to discover his mistress and best friend dead and wonders whether his Vietnam experiences have made him psychotic.

4181. ___. *Touch the Devil.* By Jack Higgins, pseud. Briarcliff Manor, NY: Stein & Day, 1982. Liam Devlin of the *Eagle* novels returns here on the trail of terrorist Frank Berry, who is out to trade missile secrets with the Soviets.

4182. ___. *The Valhalla Exchange.* London: Hutchinson, 1977. General Hamilton Canning tries to track Martin Bormann, top Nazi, after his escape from the rubble of Berlin.

4183. ___. *The Wrath of God.* New York: Macmillan, 1971. In 1922 Mexico an Irish gunman and a priest hunt a vicious Mexican bandit named Tómas de la Plata.

4184. ___. *Wrath of the Lion.* London: Long, 1964. Members of the OAS are fighting their enemies with a U-boat; ex-SAS colonel Neil Mallory is hired to kill them.

4185. ___. *Year of the Tiger.* New York: Abelard-Schulman, 1963. Paul Chavasse goes to Tibet to rescue a missionary from the Chinese Communists, a man who happens to be a leading rocket scientist. One more:

4186. ___. *The Cretan Lover.* By Jack Higggins, pseud. New York: Holt, 1980.

4187. Patterson, James. *Black Market.* New York: Simon & Schuster, 1986. Crazed Vietnam vets form a terrorist band and begin their mayhem by a firebombing on Wall Street.

4188. ___. *The Jericho Commandment.* New York: Crown, 1979. A revenge plot first hatched in Nazi death camps germinates at the 1980 Olympics when a terrorist group delivers a horrifying ultimatum. A recent one:

4189. ___. *Along Came a Spider.* Boston: Little, 1993.

4190. Pattinson, James. *The Petronov Plan.* New York: Zebra, 1974. When a hostage plan against a Brazilian dictator backfires, one of the perpetrators is captured and sent to an island prison where a mercenary has been secretly sent to free him and thus learn the location of a vital document. *

4191. Paul, Celeste. *The Berlin Covenant.* New York: Signet, 1992. Almost half a century after Nazi Germany had abandoned Operation Brimstone, and with it the chance of victory, its diabolical evil is resurrected in America. P

Paul, F. W., pseud. *See* Fairman, Paul W.

4192. Paul, William. *Seasons of Revenge.* London: Severn, 1985. An ex-SAS man with a shameful secret, his IRA antagonist, and a revengeful loner collide destinies in this tale of an IRA plot against the Royals.

Paull, Jessyca, pseud. *See* Perceval, Julia and Roseaylmer Burger

4193. Paulsen, Gary. *The Death Specialists.* New York: Major, 1977. To insure its insurance, an American oil conglomerate hires a half dozen specialists to destroy its Venezuelan refinery before it can be nationalized. P

4194. Payne, Donald G. *Flight of the Bat.* By Donald Gordon, pseud. New York: Morrow, 1964. British agents are sent to the Gulf of Finland to guard a super-secret bomber which has been dispatched to pick up a message from the Soviet premier.

4195. Payne, Laurence R. *Spy for Sale.* Garden City, NY: Doubleday, 1971. An underskilled petty thief, upon release from jail, is immediately recruited by "the Brotherhood" to hand out religious tracts all over London. One day on a corner he is picked up by a glamorous girl in a white Aston Martin who insists that somebody named Colonel Carruthers needs his assistance.

4196. ___. *Vienna Blood.* New York: Garden City, NY: Doubleday, 1986. Mark Savage returns in a caper that has him in Austria investigating the sudden appearance of his great aunt's long-lost son, a man being tracked by Nazi hunters.

4197. Payne, Ronald and John Garrod. *The Seventh Fury.* By John Castle, pseud. New York: Walker, 1963. In the best James Bond fashion, British Intelligence pries Dr. Boland away from his London practice and dispatches him deep into the Turkish desert to recover a toxic horror.

4198. Pearce, Michael. *The Mamur Zapt and the Donkey-Vous.* New York: Mysterious, 1992. Captain Owen investigates a Frenchman who has disappeared from the Shepheard's Hotel in Cairo.

4199. ___. *The Mamur Zapt and the Men Behind.* New York: Mysterious, 1993. The fourth novel in the series about Captain Cadwallader Owen in the Egypt of British rule. This time, Cairo is teeming with revolution and murder because the Khedive is about to appoint a new Prime Minister, and many aspire to the position.

4200. ___. *The Mamur Zapt and the Night of the Dog.* New York: Doubleday, 1991. In this sequel, Captain Owen has a civil war between Copts and Muslims brewing on his hands when someone leaves the worst possible insult, a dead dog, in front of a Coptic crypt.

4201. ___. *The Mamur Zapt and the Return of the Carpet.* New York: Doubleday, 1990. *Mamur Zapt* is the title of the head of Egypt's secret police, and in 1908 it's not an easy job for Cadwallader Owen; he has just learned that anarchists have stolen a crate of grenades from the British Army and intend to use them on the upcoming religious holiday, the Return of the Holy Carpet.

4202. Pearl, Jack. *Our Man Flint.* New York: Pinnacle, 1965. One day a report comes into the Zonal Organization of World Intelligence and Espionage (ZOWIE for short) that three mad scientists, heading up their own group called GALAXY, plan to take over the world by controlling its weather conditions. Chief Dramden of ZOWIE decides that his ace agent Derek Flint is the best man to assign on the job of halting this dastardly scheme. Armed only with his wits and a wonderous cigarette lighter which secretly contains 83 weapons, Flint trots off on a trail that leads him to Rome and then on to a small rocky island in the Mediterranean. This clever take-off on James Bond proved a successful motion picture. *PH*

4203. ___. *The Plot to Kill the President.* New York: Pinnacle, 1970. Flint is assigned by Chief Dramden of ZOWIE to look in on a nasty's plan to liquidate the American leader.

4204. Pearson, John. *James Bond: The Authorized Biography of 007.* New York: Morrow, 1973. Following a fit of depression, Bond is ordered by "M" to seek a rest on the island of Bermuda. Because of some apparent discrepancies in Mr. Fleming's novels, Mr. Pearson is ordered to interview the noted secret agent at his Caribbean hide-away and 007 proceeds to set the record straight. Pearson also wrote a biography of Ian Fleming (*The Life of Ian Fleming.* New York: Bantam, 1967).

4205. Pearson, Ridley. *Blood of the Albatross.* New York: St. Martin's, 1986. A mystery revolving around a woman who asks a Seattle man to teach her to sail; soon, however, the FBI and CIA are hovering about the pair.

4206. ___. *Never Look Back.* New York: St. Martin's, 1985. A KGB agent, codenamed "Dragonfly," possesses a deadly briefcase of bacteria he will release if his mission fails; agent Andrew Clayton has a personal reason besides a professional one for ensuring Dragonfly does fail—without triggering wholesale toxic devastation: Dragonfly had killed his own brother.

4207. Pearson, Ryne Douglas. *Cloudburst.* New York: Morrow, 1993. Libyan terrorists kill the US President and hijack a jumbo jet as the first step in a plot to detonate a nuclear device over New York or the nation's capital.

4208. Peart, Robert. *Angels of Death.* London: Collins, 1984. Nat Morgan, known as The Dragon, must penetrate a top Nazi mansion in France where his sworn enemy, SS Col. Ulrich, collects military secrets from the women hostages who serve Nazi officers there.

4209. Pedler, John B. F. *Diplomatic Cover.* By Dominic Torr, pseud. New York: Harcourt, 1967. In Paris during a diplomatic crisis, an American security official and a Soviet agent duel for the success of their nation's maneuvering.

4210. ___. *The Treason Line.* By Dominic Torr, pseud. New York: Stein & Day, 1970. In Geneva during a disarmament conference, the Red Chinese spy chief persuades his American counterpart to let the Reds have America's nuclear fail-safe missile device.

4211. Peel, Colin D. *Atoll.* New York: St. Martin's, 1992. The French government has promised to cease underwater nuclear testing, but British geologist John Carlisle and two friends have proof that the French government is covering up the fact that radioactive poisons are seeping into the Pacific near an island in French Polynesia.

4212. ___. *Covenant of the Poppies.* New York: St. Martin's, 1993. Mike McConnel is a British arms dealer in Afghanistan who falls afoul of a powerful organization, ostensibly a relief organization, but one that McConnel knows is dirty in drugs and conspiracies, and he sets out to get the goods on them after they kill his wife and child.

4213. ___. *Firestorm.* Garden City, NY: Doubleday, 1984. A British explosives expert and an American woman tackle international terrorists when a bomb-induced firestorm destroys a West German oil depot.

4214. ___. *Flameout.* New York: St. Martin's, 1978. In Canada's Pacific woodland, Englishman Steven Marsh finds himself in the middle of a struggle over vital oil reserves which is being fought out by agents of the Mossad, CIA, and the PLO.

4215. ___. *Nightdive.* New York: St. Martin's, 1977. Extraordinary information from World War II leads a small group of two men and a woman to try to recover a fortune still lying at the bottom of the sea.

4216. ___. *Snowtrap.* Garden City, NY: Doubleday, 1984. A squadron leader is duped into carrying out a bombing mission for NATO that will keep Iran from acquiring uranium.

Pendleton, Don, house pseud. *See* Garside, Jack and Don Pendleton

4217. Pendleton, Don and Laurence R. Payne. *The Tower of Terror.* By Dick Stivers, house pseud. Toronto: Gold Eagle, 1982. This action series features three mercenaries (Carl Lyons, Pol Blancanales, and "Gadgets" Schwarz) known as "Mack Bolan's Able Team." Beginning with book #60, "Mack Bolan" became the series imprint, and the adventures continued to stream forth under various authors' hands.

Pendleton coauthored the first three with Laurence R. Payne and Norman Winski; other authors of the dozens of soldier-of-fortune episodes in this paperback series include Tom Arnett, Alan Bomack, G. H. Frost, Paul Hofrichter, Patrick Neary, Ray Obstfeld, Steven Krauser, Larry Powell, and C. J. Shiao. This series reached its 100th issue in 1987 with *Blood Testament* (Don Mills, Ont.: Gold Eagle, 1987). Other Pendleton novels in his "Executioner" series, of which he authored over 30, include these:

4218. ___. *The Executioner: Canadian Crisis.* New York: Pinnacle, 1975. P

4219. ___. *The Executioner: Command Strike.* New York: Pinnacle, 1975.
P

4220. ___. *The Executioner: Cleveland Pipeline.* New York: Pinnacle, 1977. P

4221. ___. *The Executioner: The Executioner's War Book.* New York: Pinnacle, 1977. P Another series under the Don Pendleton name began in the late 1980's and featured a former naval officer and spy in the James Bond mold named Ashton Ford. One of his adventures scripted by house writers:

4222. ___. *Mind to Mind.* By Don Pendleton, pseud. New York: Popular, 1987. P

4223. Pendower, Jacques. *Traitor's Island.* London: Hale, 1967. For almost three decades, between the late thirties to the mid-seventies, Jacques Pendower cranked out a tremendous number of novels in many genres, including espionage fiction; under his most famous pseudonym (T.C.H. Jacobs) he tended to write novels of detection. His single series character, Slade McGinty, is featured in a very few, however, of the following list of novels, including this one, in which he makes his last appearance (Pendower died in 1976). Like many others, Pendower produced adventure novels that combined detection and espionage. Such as:

4224. ___. *Betrayed.* New York: Paperback, 1967. [*The Widow from Spain.* London: Hale, 1961].

4225. ___. *The Black Devil.* By T.C.H. Jacobs, pseud. London: Hale, 1969.

4226. ___. *Brother Spy.* By T.C.H. Jacobs, pseud. London: Paul, 1941.

4227. ___. *Cause for Alarm.* London: Hale, 1971.

4228. ___. *The Dark Avenue.* London: Lock, 1955.

4229. ___. *Date with Fear.* London: Hale, 1974.

4230. ___. *Death on the Moor.* London: Hale, 1962.

4231. ___. *Diamonds for Danger.* London: Hale, 1970.

4232. ___. *Double Diamond*. London: Hale, 1959.

4233. ___. *The Elusive Monsieur Drago*. By T.C.H. Jacobs, pseud. London: Hale, 1964.

4234. ___. *The Golden Statuette*. London: Hale, 1969.

4235. ___. *The Hunted Woman*. London: Lock, 1955.

4236. ___. *The Long Shadow*. London: Hale, 1959.

4237. ___. *Master Spy*. London: Hale, 1964. Another McGinty tale.

4238. ___. *Mission in Tunis*. London: Hale, 1958. [Rpt. New York: Paperback, 1967].

4239. ___. *Operation Carlo*. London: Hale, 1963.

4240. ___. *The Perfect Wife*. London: Hale, 1962. The first Slade McGinty tale.

4241. ___. *Reward for Treason*. By T.C.H. Jacobs, pseud. London: Paul, 1944.

4242. ___. *The Secret Power*. By T.C.H. Jacobs, pseud. London: Hale, 1963.

4243. ___. *Security Risk*. By T.C.H. Jacobs, pseud. London: Hale, 1972.

4244. ___. *She Came by Night*. London: Hale, 1971.

4245. ___. *Sinister Talent*. London: Hale, 1964. A McGinty novel.

4246. ___. *Spy Business*. By T.C.H. Jacobs, pseud. London: Hale, 1965.

4247. ___. *Target for Terror*. By T.C.H. Jacobs, pseud. London: Hale, 1961.

4248. ___. *Traitor Spy*. By T.C.H. Jacobs, pseud. London: Paul, 1939.

4249. ___. *A Trap for Fools*. London: Hale, 1968.

4250. ___. *Try Anything Once.* London: Hale, 1967.

Pentecost, Hugh, pseud. *See* Philips, Judson P.

4251. Pepper, Dan. *The Enemy General.* New York: Monarch, 1960. French Maquis troops battle the Germans near Paris in World War II; book-length treatment of a Van Johnson movie screenplay. *P*

4252. Perakh, Mark. *Man in a Wire Cage.* New York: Lorevan, 1988. When a colleague's head is smashed in by an impact tester, physics teacher Boris Tarutin of Kalinin State University in Moscow must find the killer to save a brilliant Jewish physicist from becoming the KGB's scapegoat—especially when it turns out that Boris has fallen in love with the man's daughter. *P*

4253. Perceval, Julia and Roseaylmer Burger. *Destination Terror.* By Jessyca Paull, pseud. New York: Award, 1968. Tracy Larrimore and Mike Thompson become involved with a gang of dangerous terrorists. Two others by this team are: *P*

4254. ___. *Passport to Danger.* By Jessyca Paull, pseud. New York: Award, 1968. *P*

4255. ___. *Rendezvous with Death.* By Jessyca Paull, pseud. New York: Award, 1969. *P*

4256. Perdue, Lewis. *The Tesla Bequest.* New York: Pinnacle, 1984. A secret society of conspirators intend to use the stolen papers of the brilliant physicist Nikola Tesla to create a superweapon that will conquer the world.

4257. Perry, Ritchie. *Bishop's Pawn.* New York: Pantheon, 1979. British SIS agent Philis rescues a bishop from East Germany, only to learn that the man's past included experiments in mass murder and links with terrorists.

4258. ___. *The Fall Guy.* Boston: Houghton, 1972. The head of SR(2) has the unhappy job of finding the source of cocaine being smuggled into England from South America. Similar in vein to Mclean's *Puppet on a Chain.*

4259. ___. *Fool's Mate.* New York: Pantheon, 1981. SIS agent Philis is ordered to escort a former mistress of Ugandan dictator Idi Amin across France to the safety of England while beating off attacks of Marseilles mobsters, African fanatics, and agents of Amin's secret police.

4260. ___. *Foul Up.* Garden City, NY: Doubleday, 1982. Philis rescues the staff of the British Embassy of a small Caribbean island from terrorists, who turn out to be highly trained locals; Philis' assignment is to infiltrate the group and find out what is behind this training school for terrorists.

4261. ___. *Grand Slam.* New York: Random, 1980. While searching for the lost daughter of an oil millionaire, SIS agent Philis finds himself in the midst of a Manson-like terrorist cult group.

4262. ___. *A Hard Man to Kill.* Boston: Houghton, 1973. [*Nowhere Man.* London: Collins, 1973]. An English SR(2) agent is involved in a joint effort with the KGB to track down a free-lance agent once usefully employed by several countries.

4263. ___. *Holiday with a Vengeance.* Boston: Houghton, 1975. Operative Philis is diverted to the Santa Monica Republic from Nassau in an effort to rescue a kidnapped British consul from a gang of rebel guerrillas.

4264. ___. *Kolwezi.* Garden City, NY: Doubleday, 1985. Philis is sent to Oslo to trap a Carlos-like terrorist, and he baits the trap for the playboy-killer with a beautiful porno actress accompanying him.

4265. ___. *MacAllister.* Garden City, NY: Doubleday, 1984. Frank MacAllister's best friend from Lisbon, Robert Latimer, is killed while visiting MacAllister at his home.

4266. ___. *One Good Death Deserves Another.* Boston: Houghton, 1977. A Greek assassin hired to kill the West German chancellor during his visit to Brazil must be liquidated by Agent Philis.

4267. ___. *Ticket to Ride.* Boston: Houghton, 1974. Philis is assigned to guard a pretty widow against the boys of the Mafia and then finds out that she is linked to one of their more fantastic schemes.

4268. ___. *Your Money and Your Wife.* Boston: Houghton, 1976. While honeymooning in Norway, Agent Philis has his wife snatched by the KGB and is told by them that the only way he can get her back is to defect and do a job for the Soviet Union—which he eventually does with the full knowledge of his chief. More Ritchie Perry novels:

4269. ___. *Comeback.* New York: Doubleday, 1991.

4270. ___. *Dead End*. London: Collins, 1977.

4271. ___. *Dutch Courage*. New York: Ballantine, 1982.

4272. ___. *Presumed Dead*. Garden City, NY: Doubleday, 1987.

4273. Perry, Will. *The Kremlin Watcher*. New York: Dodd, 1978. A New York City Kremlinologist correctly predicts a Polish workers' strike and the subsequent Soviet military intervention.

4274. Persico, Joseph E. *The Spiderweb*. New York: Crown, 1979. Corrupt American immigration officials, a skilled Jewish printer, and agents of the Soviet NKVD conspire to keep Nazism alive after V-E Day and to finance the escape of German leaders from the defeated Reich.
     A naval officer during the Korean War, Persico later became a USIA officer in South America and was for eleven years the chief speechwriter for Nelson A. Rockefeller. In 1979, he published one of the most interesting of all true espionage epics to date, *Piercing the Reich: The Penetration of Nazi Germany by American Secret Agents During World War II*.

     Peters, Brian, pseud. *See* George, Peter B.

4275. Peters, Elizabeth. *The Dead Sea Cipher*. New York: Dodd, 1970. Opera singer Dinah Van der Lyn becomes the target of various secret agents after she overhears a violent argument in the room next to hers in a Cairo hotel.

4276. Peters, Ellis. *The Piper on the Mountain*. New York: Morrow, 1966. Did British agent Terrell die by accident or was he "eliminated" for getting too close to the trail of a defector, who had stolen some hush-hush plane secrets. His stepdaughter Tossa elects to find out and borrowing the cape of Modesty Blaise, grimly sets off for Czechoslovakia. *y

     Peters, Ludovic, pseud. *See* Brent, Peter

4277. Peters, Ralph. *Flames of Heaven: A Novel of the End of the Soviet Union*. New York: Pocket, 1993. A saga of Russia in collapse—a mix of romance and intrigue among the characters, one of whom is a KGB colonel who, in bringing down a powerful Muslim clan ruler, may destroy his own brother.

4278. ___. *Bravo Romeo*. New York: Marek, 1981. Idealistic Vietnam veteran Major Jack Thorne is drawn into a German terrorist plot to assassinate a NATO commander who looks and sounds a lot like real-life former NATO boss and former U. S. Secretary of State Alexander Haig. Haig, by the way, was the target of a terrorist bomb attack during the time he was the NATO chief.

4279. ___. *Red Army.* New York: Pocket, 1989. A high-tech portrait of the intersecting Soviet points of view in their blueprint for war in the days before the collapse of the mighty Soviet Union.

4280. ___. *The War in 2020.* New York: Bantam, 1991. The US and USSR combine to defeat a Muslim invasion, but the Japanese bring their ultimate weapon to the clash.

4281. Peters, Stephen. *The Park Is Mine.* Garden City, NY: Doubleday, 1981. Armed with VC weapons, a crazed Vietnam veteran "captures" Central Park in New York City, encloses it with mines and wire, and initiates a guerrilla-style "campaign."

4282. Peterson, Bernard. *The Peripheral Spy.* New York: Coward-McCann, 1980. KGB agents descend on an American reporter in Paris when a secret package in his possession is linked to the theft of cash intended for the French Communist Party by the Kremlin.

4283. Peterson, Michael. *A Time of War.* New York: Pocket, 1990. Former marine lieutenant during the Tet Offensive of 1967, Peterson focuses on that critical time in US involvement in Vietnam when LBJ sends Bradley Marshall, JFK protégé, to Saigon. Marshall wants to abort the war effort, but the CIA wants to lure him into a trap him that will prevent him from bringing back the truth about Vietnam's sordid political and military situation.

4284. Peterson, Paul. *The Smugglers.* New York: Pocket, 1974. These are the adventures of Eric Saveman, who, together with his highly trained superfriends "the Smugglers," goes about busting up the schemes of various criminal and diabolical types. In this outing, Saveman and company knock out an enemy's underground spy headquarters. Three others in this series are: *P*

4285. ___. *The Smugglers: Mother Luck.* New York: Pocket, 1974. *P*

4286. ___. *The Smugglers: Murder in Blue.* New York: Pocket, 1974. *P*

4287. ___. *The Smugglers: Tools of the Trade.* New York: Pocket, 1974. *P*

4288. Petievich, Gerald. *Paramour.* New York: Dutton, 1991. A suicide in the White House's top-secret file room points a finger at the President's mistress, who may be an agent working for the Arabs. Secret Service agent Jack Powers is given the case.

4289. Pettit, Mike. *The Axmann Agenda.* New York: Dell, 1980. A sinister Nazi scheme to swell the ranks of the "master race" underlies the grass-roots patriotism of a present-day American organization which is causing agents law-enforcement fits. *P*

4290. Philips, Judson P. *Birthday, Deathday.* By Hugh Pentecost, pseud. New York: Dodd, 1972. How can a luxury hotel manager, even with the help of the CIA and the FBI, foil the assassin who has sworn to kill a guest, General Ho Chang of the People's Liberation Army?

4291. ___. *The Deadly Friend.* By Hugh Pentecost, pseud. New York: Dodd, 1961. A newsman and a famous scientist are drawn into a plot to destroy the state of Israel.

4292. Phillifent, John T. *The Man from UNCLE: The Corfu Affair.* New York: Ace, 1970. Napoleon Solo's newest assignment is to find out what role a French countess is playing in a deadly THRUSH plot. Two others by this author are: *P*

4293. ___. *The Man from UNCLE: The Mad Scientist Affair.* New York: Ace 1966. *P*

4294. ___. *The Man from UNCLE: The Power Cube Affair.* New York: Ace 1968. *P*

4295. Phillips, David Atlee. *The Carlos Contract.* New York: Macmillan, 1978. A self-proclaimed terrorist is systematically liquidating American petroleum company executives and CIA station chiefs overseas.
  David Atlee Phillips rose through the ranks of the CIA's covert action divisions during some of the Agency's more interesting years of the 1950s and 1960s. Before he died in 1988, David Atlee Phillips had written one of the most widely read CIA memoirs (*The Night Watch: Twenty-Five Years of Peculiar Service.* New York: Atheneum, 1977), founded the Association of Former Intelligence Officers, served as editor in 1986 of *International Journal of Intelligence and Counterintelligence* (*see* INTELLIGENCE JOURNALS in the BIBLIOGRAPHY section of this text), edited *Periscope* (under the pseudonym George Spelvin), and founded Stone Trail Press. Significant also is the fact

that, as head of CIA covert operations during the Kennedy years, Phillips was nearly indicted for perjury by the 1978 House Select Committee probing the JFK assassination because of a Cuban exile witness's testimony that Phillips, posing as a CIA operative named Maurice Bishop, had contact with Oswald before the killing.

4296. Phillips, James A. *Joe Gall: The Black Venus Contract.* By Philip Atlee, pseud. Greenwich, CT: Fawcett, 1975. Free-lance superspy of "the agency," Joe Gall, top-secret nullifier, America's ace hit man, accepts contracts from American intelligence to bounce around the world liquidating difficult problems before they become acute embarrassments to the US government. In this outing, he agrees to go to Brazil to rescue a top CIA official who is being held hostage by terrorists. *P*

This Joe Gall series compares favorably with the Jonas Wilde "Eliminator" tales of Christopher Nicole (Andrew York, pseud.) and is a step above Joseph Rosenberger's "The Death Merchant." Undertaken during the height of the James Bond mania, this series reflects all of the positive attributes and many more negative points than does Fleming's man.

4297. ___. *Joe Gall: The Canadian Bomber Contract.* By Philip Atlee, pseud. Greenwich, CT: Fawcett, 1971. Gall travels to Canada to chase a team of Quebec terrorists with long-range Separatist plans and a very short fuse. *P*

4298. ___. *Joe Gall: The Death Bird Contract.* By Philip Atlee, pseud. Greenwich, CT: Fawcett, 1966. "The Nullifier" is sent to Mexico to locate a shady US diplomat who has been reported missing. *P*

4299. ___. *Joe Gall: The Fer-de-Lance Contract.* By Philip Atlee, pseud. Greenwich, CT: Fawcett, 1970. Joe Gall travels on a lethal hunt through various Caribbean islands in pursuit of a lethal underground army of assassins which is dedicated to the proposition that only a few men are created equal. *P*

4300. ___. *Joe Gall: The Green Wound.* By Philip Atlee, pseud. Greenwich, CT: Fawcett, 1963. Joe Gall comes to believe that he is fighting for the wrong side and is forced to take action to overcome a dangerous misperception. *P*

4301. ___. *Joe Gall: The Ill-Wind Contract.* By Philip Atlee, pseud. Greenwich, CT: Fawcett, 1969. In Indonesia Joe Gall must grab five tons of gold from the heart of an enemy camp and deliver it to its rightful owners. *P*

4302. ___. *Joe Gall: The Irish Beauty Contract.* By Philip Atlee, pseud. Greenwich, CT: Fawcett, 1966. In South America, Joe Gall encounters a sadistic Irish beauty while his contract calls for him to defuse a human time bomb in the Andes. *P*

4303. ___. *Joe Gall: The Judah Lion Contract.* By Philip Atlee, pseud. Greenwich, CT: Fawcett, 1972. Gall shows up in Ethiopia to smuggle a deposed president out of the country and must run the gauntlet of mercenaries and paid assassins committed to blocking his mission. *P*

4304. ___. *Joe Gall: The Kiwi Contract.* By Philip Atlee, pseud. Greenwich, CT: Fawcett, 1972. Joe Gall plays decoy for oil billionaire Michael Donoghue, whose new explorations are top secret. *P*

4305. ___. *Joe Gall: The Kowloon Contract.* By Philip Atlee, pseud. Greenwich, CT: Fawcett, 1974. In Hong Kong Joe Gall seeks to learn who is terrorizing the women of that city. *P*

4306. ___. *Joe Gall: The Last Domino Contract.* By Philip Atlee, pseud. Greenwich, CT: Fawcett, 1976. Gall is sent to Korea to take on extreme elements in the South Korean secret police (KCIA) and a trigger-happy American general about to light the fuse for World War III. *P*

4307. ___. *Joe Gall: The Makassar Strait Contract.* By Philip Atlee, pseud. Greenwich, CT: Fawcett, 1976. Together with his beautiful assistant, Joe Gall gets mixed up with the recovery of manganese nodules mined from the waters off Indonesia. *P*

4308. ___. *Joe Gall: The Rockabye Contract.* By Philip Atlee, pseud. Greenwich, CT: Fawcett, 1970. Gall pursues a cuddly toy koala bear, loaded with high explosives—a pawn in a brilliant scheme to overthrow a Latin American dictatorship. *P*

4309. ___. *Joe Gall: The Shankill Road Contract.* By Philip Atlee, pseud. Greenwich, CT: Fawcett, 1973. An American in Northern Ireland is suspected of mounting his own mass-murder campaign and Joe Gall is contracted to stop him. *P*

4310. ___. *Joe Gall: The Spice Route Contract.* By Philip Atlee, pseud. Greenwich, CT: Fawcett, 1973. Joe Gall travels to Yemen to flush out a turned agent named Richards who, with his gang—an Arab version of Murder, Inc.—is systematically killing off people friendly to the US. *P*

4311. ___. *Joe Gall: The Star Ruby Contract.* By Philip Atlee, pseud. Greenwich, CT: Fawcett, 1967. Joe Gall faces the task of removing a force of Chinese marauders from Burma—and ends up with the assistance of an entire Gurkha regiment. *P*

4312. ___. *Joe Gall: The Trembling Earth Contract.* By Philip Atlee, pseud. Greenwich, CT: Fawcett, 1969. Aided by injections which change his color, Joe Gall infiltrates a guerrilla group terrorizing the American South, masquerades as a "brother," and sets the band's leaders up for an ambush. *P*

4313. ___. *Joe Gall: The Underground Cities Contract.* By Philip Atlee, pseud. Greenwich, CT: Fawcett, 1974. Joe Gall inherits the dangerous job of liberating three American agents who have been taken prisoner by Turkish terrorists. Others in the Joe Gall Contract series include: *P*

4314. ___. *Joe Gall: The Paper Pistol Contract.* By Philip Atlee, pseud. Greenwich, CT: Fawcett, 1968. *P*

4315. ___. *Joe Gall: The Silkon Baroness Contract.* By Philip Atlee, pseud. Greenwich, CT: Fawcett, 1967. *P*

4316. ___. *Joe Gall: The Skeleton Coast Contract.* By Philip Atlee, pseud. Greenwich, CT: Fawcett, 1968. *P*

4317. ___. *Joe Gall: The White Wolverine Contract.* By Philip Atlee, pseud. Greenwich, CT: Fawcett, 1971. *P*

4318. Phillips, Mark. *Brain Twister.* New York: Pyramid, 1962. An agent has a special advantage over his opponents—he can read their minds. *P*

4319. Picard, Sam. *Notebook No. 1: Mission Number One.* New York: Award, 1969. These three citations tell of the adventures of a secret agent group and hero John Scott supposedly based on items taken from a notebook, hence "the Notebook Series." In this first outing, only operative Scott can explode a world-shattering conspiracy—and he is a hunted target. *P*

4320. ___. *Notebook No. 2: The Man Who Never Was.* New York: Award, 1971. Framed for murdering a Soviet spy, John Scott is hunted by both the CIA and the real killer, now posing as the Russian. *P*

4321. ___. *Notebook No. 3: Dead Man Running.* New York: Award, 1971. The closer he comes to an important rendezvous, the harder Soviet agents try to kill Agent Scott. *P*

4322. Pickering, Paul. *The Blue Gate of Babylon.* New York: Random, 1989. Black-humored tale of a young Britisher, a career diplomat, in West Berlin whose job is to run a bordello to get information from East German officers in the days before the Berlin Wall. "Superior," extols Newgate Callendar: "Highly literate, brooding and sad, *The Blue Gate of Babylon* is much more than a spy story." Also by Pickering:

4323. ___. *Charlie Peace.* New York: Random, 1991.

4324. Pickering, R. E. *The Uncommitted Man.* New York: Farrar, Straus & Giroux, 1967. Dick Philip is one of that mid-1960s le Carré school of disillusioned agents; while representing a British business firm in Central Europe, he is caught up with espionage and intrigue in Vienna. First published in England as *Himself Again.*

4325. Pierce, Noel. *Messenger from Munich.* New York: Coward-McCann, 1973. Baron von Gottfried is on a New York mission that involves him in private revenge and political assassination on behalf of a neo-Nazi organization based in Munich.
4326. Pierson, Eleanor. *The Good Neighbor Murder.* New York: Howell, 1941. A US official on a good will trip to Brazil is drawn into a Nazi plot against that huge South American country. *

4327. Pietrkiewicz, Jerzy. *Isolation.* New York: Holt, 1961. A free-lance spy uses all of the techniques of his espionage training to ensure the success of his affair with the wife of a South American diplomat.

4328. Pincher, Chapman. *Dirty Tricks.* Briarcliff Manor, NY: Stein & Day, 1981. Nearly ready to retire, John Falconer, chief of the CIA's covert action group, learns of a Soviet plan to invade Western Europe and, in "Operation Cliffhanger," undertakes a single-handed mission to block the Russian adventure and end his career in a spectacular fashion.

Pincher is a veteran British journalist who has long been interested in espionage affairs at home and abroad. Early in 1981, he leveled charges that the former head of MI-5 was an agent of the KGB, an idea dismissed in Parliament by Prime Minister Margaret Thatcher.

4329. ___. *The Eye of the Tornado.* Briarcliff Manor, NY: Stein & Day, 1976. A traitorous British Cabinet minister working with foreign power is involved in an IRA plot to hijack Polaris missiles with which to back a coup against the English government. Four more Pincher novels:

4330. ___. *The Four Horses.* London: Joseph, 1978.

4331. ___. *Not with a Bang.* New York: Signet, 1965. *P*

4332. ___. *The Penthouse Conspirators.* London: Joseph, 1970.

4333. ___. *The Skeleton at the Villa Wolkonsky.* London: Joseph, 1975.

4334. Pineiro, R. J. *Siege of Lightning.* New York: Berkley, 1993. A foolproof, fail-safe space shuttle, *Lightning*, has been sabotaged by an unseen enemy. *P*

4335. Pitts, Denis. *The Predator.* New York: Mason-Charter, 1977. The richest and most powerful industrialist in Europe decides to employ his private army to take over an entire continent.

4336. ___. *This City is Ours.* New York: Mason-Charter, 1975. Plotters maneuver an oil tanker into New York harbor and will blow up Manhattan unless a $130 billion ransom is paid.

Plum, Jennifer, pseud. *See* Kurland, Michael

4337. Pogue, David. *Hard Drive.* New York: Berkley, 1993. A doomsday thriller that opens with a new computer about to be unveiled in Silicon Valley. *P*

4338. Pohl, Frederick. *The Cool War.* New York: Random, 1981. A cross between science fiction and spy thriller. In the near future, the Rev. H. Hornswell Hake is swept into a spying mission for a US intelligence agency and becomes involved in international dirty tricks the nature of which make no sense.

4339. Pollard, Alfred O. *A.R.P. Spy.* London: Hutchinson, 1940. Agents of British Intelligence dupe the Nazis regarding a vital secret early in World War II.

Pollard penned a large number of spy thrillers between 1940 and 1956, none of which were published in the United States. His tales were like those being written about the same time by Peter Cheney, pseud.

4340. ___. *The Counterfeit Spy*. London: Hutchinson, 1952. An Englishman on the Continent is not really a spy—but agents of the Soviet MVD believe him to be one and pursue him accordingly.

4341. ___. *The Criminal Airman*. London: Hutchinson, 1953. MI-5 must prevent a traitorous RAF pilot from turning an advanced jet fighter over to the Russians.

4342. ___. *Secret Weapon*. London: Hutchinson, 1941. The Nazis want to snitch a new development in British warfare hardware and agents of MI-5 must prevent their doing so.

4343. ___. *Wanted by the Gestapo*. London: Hutchinson, 1941. On a highly dangerous mission to Occupied France, a British agent must elude agents of the German secret police who are hot on his trail. Other spy thrillers by this author include:

4344. ___. *Blood Hunt*. London: Hutchinson, 1946.

4345. ___. *Dead Man's Secret*. London: Hutchinson, 1949.

4346. ___. *Death Intervened*. London: Hutchinson, 1951.

4347. ___. *The Death Parade*. London: Hutchinson, 1951.

4348. ___. *The Death Squadron*. London: Hutchinson, 1943.

4349. ___. *Double Cross*. London: Hutchinson, 1946.

4350. ___. *The Fifth Freedom*. London: Hutchinson, 1945.

4351. ___. *Gestapo Fugitive*. London: Hutchinson, 1944.

4352. ___. *Homicidal Spy*. London: Hutchinson, 1954.

4353. ___. *Invitation to Death*. London: Hutchinson, 1944.

4354. ___. *The Iron Curtain*. London: Hutchinson, 1947.

4355. ___. *Red Hazard*. London: Hutchinson, 1950.

4356. ___. *The Secret Vendetta*. London: Hutchinson, 1949.

4357. ___. *Sinister Secret*. London: Hutchinson, 1956.

4358. Pollitz, Edward A. *The Forty-First Thief*. New York: Delacorte, 1975. Western agents must halt an attempt by oil suppliers to blackmail the Western consuming nations.

4359. Pollock, Daniel. *Duel of the Assassins*. New York: Pocket, 1991. An American defecter to the KGB becomes one of its top killers—and is ordered to hit the Soviet premier in a right-wing coup attempt; a Russian defector to the CIA, now one of its specialists in dirty work, is ordered to hit the American assassin.

4360. ___. *Lair of the Fox*. New York: Walker, 1989. Kurdish terrorists grab canisters from a Soviet poison gas arsenal and then take over a sailing vessel with a film crew aboard.

4361. Pollock, J. C. *Centrifuge*. New York: Crown, 1984. Ex-Green Beret Mike Slater is invited to his former Vietnam unit commander's home in Maine, who happens to be head of a top-security CIA installation, and before he can learn why he—and two other surviving members of his team—are in danger, his host is murdered before his eyes.

4362. ___. *Crossfire*. New York: Crown, 1985. There's a manhunt on for a missing Soviet scientist with the key to a revolutionary missile guidance system along the West German-Czechoslovakian border; caught up in it are two innocents, a Czech skater and her lover, and a canny, tough Special Forces sergeant.

4363. ___. *Payback*. New York: Delacorte, 1989. A man with Delta Force training goes up against a KGB agent with a specialty in wet operations after the man's wife is murdered, and he is told by the State Department, FBI, and CIA to lay off.

4364. ___. *Threat Case*. New York: Delacorte, 1991. Jack Gannon, the hero of *Payback*, returns in this tale of a contract killer working for the drug cartel who intends to assassinate the President. Gannon joins forces with Special Agent Mike McGuire of the Secret Service to launch a plan to catch the killer before the President's UN speech in eleven days.

4365. Ponthier, François. *Assignment Basra.* New York: McKay, 1969. German spy Lt. Richter, right-hand man of Admiral Canaris, head of the Abwehr, selects Max Wolf, a Jew from Dachau, for "rehabilitation" and sends him off to Palestine to spy for the Reich.

4366. Porter, Joyce. *Only with a Bargepole.* New York: McKay, 1974. Eddie Brown, the world's most reluctant spy and just about the worst operative ever turned loose by British Intelligence, despite his ability to louse up almost every assignment he is given, nevertheless somehow seems able to accomplish his ends. In this outing, he bumbles his way to victory over a top Soviet agent up to mischief in Venice. *H* Three other Brown tales are:

4367. ___. *The Chinks in the Curtain.* New York: McKay, 1967. *H*

4368. ___. *Neither a Candle nor a Pitchfork.* New York: McKay, 1970. *H*

4369. ___. *Sour Cream with Everything.* New York: McKay, 1966. *H* Porter had been fluent in Russian and served in the WRAF [Women's Royal Air Force]. Prior to her death in 1990, she completed several "Dover" mysteries. Among which are:

4370. ___. *Dead Easy for Dover.* London: Weidenfeld & Nicholson, 1978.

4371. ___. *Dover and the Unkindest Cut of All.* New York: Scribner's, 1967.

4372. ___. *Dover Beats the Band.* London: Weidenfeld & Nicholson, 1980.

4373. ___. *Dover Goes to Pott.* Woodstock, VT: Countryman, 1990.

4374. ___. *Dover One.* New York: Scribner's, 1964.

4375. ___. *Dover Strikes Again.* London: Weidenfeld & Nicholson, 1971.

4376. ___. *Dover Three.* London: Cape, 1965.

4377. ___. *Dover Two.* New York: Scribner's, 1965.

4378. Portway, Christopher. *All Exits Barred.* New York: Pinnacle, 1974. Betrayed by British Intelligence and hounded by Communist pursuers, plucky Tabard and his Czech fiancée race across Europe to safety in West Berlin. One other Tabard story is: *P*

4379. ___. *The Tirana Assignment.* New York: Pinnacle, 1975. *P*

4380. Posey, Carl A. *Bushmaster Fall.* New York: Fine, 1991. The CIA, science and skulduggery in the Bolivian Rain Forest.

4381. ___. *Kiev Footprint.* New York: Dodd, 1983. Space shuttle *Excalibur* has been sabotaged, and the crew lie dead as the ship drifts helplessly in gravity's pull—worse, the onboard nuclear power station is going critical, transforming the spacecraft into a nuclear bomb on a target that will aim it at the USSR. *P* Two others by Posey:

4382. ___. *Prospero Drill.* Toronto: Worldwide, 1988. *P*

4383. ___. *Red Danube.* New York: St. Martin's, 1985.

4384. Posner, Gerald L. *The Bio-Assassins.* New York: McGraw-Hill, 1989. Posner, along with John ware, wrote an outstanding biography of the infamous Dr. Josef Mengele of Auschwitz (McGraw-Hill, 1986). This novel concerns a vaccine developed by CIA technicians that attacks the central nervous system and stolen by the KGB. Maverick CIA agent Richard McGinnis is put on the case.

4385. Powell, Richard P. *All Over But the Shooting.* New York: Simon & Schuster, 1944. An Arab lady points out German spies in wartime Washington. *

4386. Poyer, D. C. *The White Continent.* New York: Jove, 1980. In an energy-starved world, a crack international team is sent to secure the resources of Antarctica; a traitor, working from within the tight little band, must be found and exposed before he can ruin the mission. *P*

4387. Poyer, David. *The Circle.* New York: St. Martin's, 1992. Sea thriller about an ensign on his first voyage with a sadistic captain and an old rust bucket en route to NATO exercises in the North Atlantic.

4388. ___. *The Gulf.* New York: St. Martin's, 1990. A technothriller centering on naval action during the Gulf War.

4389. ___. *The Med.* New York: St. Martin's, 1988. The US Sixth Fleet, with thousands of Marines and sailors, is steaming toward Syria, where a hundred US Embassy hostages have been taken.

4390. ___. *Winter in the Heart.* New York: TOR, 1993. This novel belongs to his "Hemlock County" cycle begun with *The Dead of Winter* (New York: TOR, 1988) concerning big oil, greed, corruption and the railroading of an innocent man in a scandal involving toxic waste in Northwestern Pennsylvania.

4391. Poyer, Joe. *The Balkan Assignment.* Garden City, NY: Doubleday, 1971. A group of neo-Nazis attempt to finance their current operations from a cache of gold stolen from the SS at the close of World War II. A motley crew of agents, including a former U-boat commander, a Yugoslav partisan, and an American air force veteran is assembled to stop them. *

Poyer's novels are marked by realism and authenticity based upon solid research. A communications graduate of the University of Michigan, he is currently an executive with a California pharmaceutical company.

4392. ___. *The Chinese Agenda.* Garden City, NY: Doubleday, 1972. A joint team made up of six agents from the USA and USSR, complete with a traitor in their midst, parachutes into the treacherous snow-capped peaks of the Tien Shan Mountains on the Russo-Chinese border. Once down, they must proceed to a hush-hush installation which is threatening world peace and in a suicidal assault which leads to slaughter, take it out. *

4393. ___. *The Contract.* New York: Atheneum, 1978. An Interpol agent and his friend attempt to foil a group of international terrorists who finance their activities through the work of professional robbers and drug dealers. *

4394. ___. *North Cape.* Garden City, NY: Doubleday, 1969. A lone pilot is returning from a flight in a supersonic spy plane over the Russo-Chinese border when he discovers that the Soviets are out to get him at all costs. *

4395. ___. *Operation Malacca.* Garden City, NY: Doubleday, 1968. A tense Colin Forbes-type adventure set in the area around Malaya. *

Before turning to full-time writing, Joe Poyer was Senior Project Manager and Research Administrator at Allergan Pharmaceuticals in Irvine, CA. Other Joe Poyer novels:

4396. ___. *Day of Reckoning.* London: Weidenfeld & Nicholson, 1976.

4397. ___. *Devoted Friends.* New York: Atheneum, 1982.

4398. ___. *The Shooting of the Green.* Garden City, NY: Doubleday, 1973.

4399. ___. *Tunnel War.* New York: Atheneum, 1979.

4400. ___. *Vengeance 10.* New York: Atheneum, 1980.

4401. Praeger, J. Simon. *The Newman Factor.* New York: Dell, 1973. A political spy thriller set in Washington DC, involving a Russian warhead, the bungled kidnapping of American scientist Newman, and a cast of agents and socialites from all over town. *P*

4402. Price, Anthony. *The Alamut Ambush.* Garden City, NY: Doubleday, 1972. Two British agents must foil the plot of Hassan, head of a fanatical Arab group, who wants no part in a prospective Arab-Israeli agreement and is working to thwart it. *

A graduate of Oxford University, Anthony Price entered the world of journalism in the early 1950s and became editor of the *Oxford Times.* Price's tales have won several awards and are considered by critics to be way above the average due to their wit and plotting. Many of this writer's yarns reflect his intense interest in archaeology and military history and often provide the reader with detailed descriptions of events long ago. The authors of *Spy Fiction: A Connoisseur's Guide* quote Anthony Price: "I think I once wrote 'the past lies in wait to ambush the present' and that I suppose is my favourite theme: the excavation of an event in the fairly recent past to establish the truth about a present mystery or problem, the action often being set against some more distant historical event" (217). (See Mr. Price's commentary in CRAFT NOTES.)

4403. ___. *The Alamut Bomb.* Garden City, NY: Doubleday, 1972. A bomb planted in a car kills a British agent. A case of mistaken identity some wonder. Dr. David Audley, cool, intellectual, and deadly agent of British Intelligence, searches for the answer and is drawn deep into the activities of various Palestinian terrorist groups. *

4404. ___. *Colonel Butler's Wolf.* Garden City, NY: Doubleday, 1972. When a Soviet agent for some unknown reason infiltrates Oxford University, Dr. Audley assigns his associate, military man Colonel Jack Butler to find out why. *

4405. ___. *For the Good of the State.* New York: Mysterious, 1987. Two aged secret agents—one a Russian archeologist, the other a British medievalist—meet in England to reminisce, but the Russian also has some important news to impart to his worthy antagonist.

4406. ___. *The '44 Vintage.* Garden City, NY: Doubleday, 1978. During World War II, young British corporal Jack Butler is transferred from his unit to the elite Chandos Force, which has orders to capture an important castle from the Germans. *

4407. ___. *Gunner Kelly*. Garden City, NY: Doubleday, 1984. What brings so many KGB agents to this quiet stretch of British countryside? Dr. David Audley must find out.

4408. ___. *The Labyrinth Makers*. Garden City, NY: Doubleday, 1971. The author's first novel. Dr. Audley is ordered to discover why the Russians are so interested in an RAF Dakota (DC-3) that crashed in 1945 and was not discovered until a certain lake was recently drained. Soon the agent is involved in a scramble for the fabulous Schliemann Treasure, lost during one of Stalin's purges. *

4409. ___. *A New Kind of War*. New York: Mysterious, 1988. David Audley at the end of WW II is intrigued by the new kind of war that replaces tanks and guns.

4410. ___. *The October Men*. Garden City, NY: Doubleday, 1974. While visiting Italy, Dr. Audley is suspected by his superiors of defecting to the other side; actually, he is attempting to plug a leak in Western security. *

4411. ___. *Other Paths to Glory*. Garden City, NY: Doubleday, 1975. Audley must learn how an obscure World War I battle threatens the peace of today's world. *

4412. ___. *Our Man in Camelot*. Garden City, NY: Doubleday, 1976. The CIA is convinced that the KGB has hatched a plot concerning the site of the sixth-century Battle of Badon and dispatches Agent Mosley to contact Dr. Audley who is just then writing a piece on the life of an obscure medieval knight. Posing as an historian researching the Arthurian legend, Mosley draws Audley into the chase, which does, in fact, involve Russian interest in a US military aircraft which disappeared while on a routine flight. *

4413. ___. *A Prospect of Vengeance*. London: Gollancz, 1988. Dr. Audley becomes the victim of a vicious smear campaign by journalists who blame him for the death of Jack Butler's rival, a death which catapulted Butler into the top spot in British Intelligence's Research & Development.

4414. ___. *Soldier No More*. Garden City, NY: Doubleday, 1982. The Soviets in 1957 France take an interest in recruiting David Audley to their side.

4415. ___. *War Game.* Garden City, NY: Doubleday, 1977. Dr. Audley and Colonel Butler are called upon to investigate a mysterious series of deaths surrounding an English Civil War reenactment near Standingham Castle. * More by Price:

4416. ___. *Here Be Monsters.* New York: Mysterious, 1986.

4417. ___. *The Hour of the Donkey.* London: Gollancz, 1980.

4418. ___. *The Memory Trap.* New York: Armchair, 1991.

4419. ___. *The Old Vengeful.* Garden City, NY: Doubleday, 1983.

4420. ___. *Sion Crossing.* New York: Mysterious, 1985.

4421. ___. *Tomorrow's Ghost.* Garden City, NY: Doubleday, 1979.

4422. Price, John-Allen. *The Pursuit of the Phoenix.* New York: Zebra, 1990. Commander Ed Cochran is ordered to abandon his mission to go to the rescue of three Soviet cosmonauts trapped in their damaged Soyuz capsule; however, his orders are countermanded after the Soviets decline help and he learns that he is forbidden to assist the marooned men—or risk starting WW III. P More by John-Allen Price:

4423. ___. *Extinction Cruise.* New York: Zebra, 1987. P

4424. ___. *A Mission for Eagles.* New York: Zebra, 1988. P

4425. ___. *Phoenix Caged.* New York: Zebra, 1993. P

4426. ___. *The Siege of Ocean Valkyrie.* New York: Zebra, 1992. P

4427. Priestley, John B. *Black-Out in Gretley.* New York: Harper, 1952. Humphrey Neyland, British counterespionage ace, tells how he came to be assigned to the little town of Gretley to plug a damaging leak and was immediately involved with a bizarre group of fifth columnists and Nazi agents stealing secrets from 1942 Britain. *

4428. ___. *Saturn over the Water.* Garden City, NY: Doubleday, 1962. As he searches for the husband of his dying cousin, a painter uncovers a conspiracy aimed at world domination which exists under the cover of a science institute. *

4429. ___. *The Shapes of Sleep*. Garden City, NY: Doubleday, 1962. A British free-lance reporter searches for the story behind the theft of an innocent-looking piece of green paper. *

4430. Proffitt, Nicholas. *The Embassy House*. New York: Bantam, 1986. Award-winning journalist and former infantry sergeant Proffitt received much critical acclaim for his *Gardens of Stone* (New York: Carroll & Graf, 1983; rev. 1987) (the film starred James Caan and James Earl Jones). His second novel is about a Special Forces officer, Jake Gulliver, in Vietnam, who is assigned to whip Vietnamese soldiers into shape for Operation Phoenix. Gulliver acquires a Vietnamese mistress and becomes romantically involved with Sally Teacher, a CIA officer and tangles with a superior officer over the dubious criminal actions he is also partly responsible for in the Army's program to wipe out the Vietcong from the Mekong delta. Another novel is:

4431. ___. *Edge of Eden*. New York: Bantam, 1990. Proffitt turns his experience as *Newsweek*'s bureau chief to service in this tale of power politics and poaching in Kenya.

4432. Prokosch, Frederic. *The Conspirators*. New York: Harper, 1943. In wartime Lisbon, a Dutch girl, married to an official of the German embassy, falls for a heroic Dutch partisan recently released from prison and assists him in obtaining secrets for British Intelligence from her husband's files. *

4433. Pronzini, Bill. *Acts of Mercy*. New York: Putnam's, 1977. An American President, under pressure from the media and the intricacies of partisan politics, must contend with a mysterious assassin at work within his inner circle.

4434. Proud, Franklin M. *The Golden Triangle*. New York: St. Martin's, 1978. Assigned to head an operation in Southeast Asia's opium-rich Golden Triangle, agent Joe Stanford finds himself a target of both the KGB and the CIA.

4435. Puccetti, Roland. *Death of the Fuehrer*. New York: St. Martin's, 1973. Examines a mad assassination attempt on Adolf Hitler.

4436. Purdue, Lewis. *Queen's Gate Reckoning*. New York: Pinnacle, 1982. A wounded CIA agent and a defecting Russian ballerina team up to prevent a Soviet conspiracy of mammoth proportions. *P*

4437. ___. *The Linz Testament*. New York: Fine, 1985.

Q

Q., John, pseud. *See* Quirk, John E.

4438. Quammen, David. *The Soul of Viktor Tronko.* Garden City, NY: Doubleday, 1987. Versatile author Quammen has written science and nature essays, a collection of stories and a short novel about fathers and sons (*Blood Line.* St. Paul: Graywolf, 1988). Quammen uses a le Carréan technique in threading narratives together; each retired agent has a convoluted story to tell a CIA investigator, who is searching for an elusive mole within the Company.

4439. ___. *The Zolta Configuration.* Garden City, NY: Doubleday, 1983. A political thriller involving the beginnings of the hydrogen bomb research and the personalities brought together.

4440. Quayle, Anthony. *Eight Hours from England.* London: Heinemann, 1946. Major Overton, a British Army officer working for the SOE, is landed on the Albanian coast to safeguard the delivery of an arms shipment to the partisans and in this fictional memoir, describes the dangers and frustrations involved in his effort. *
  This novel by the noted English actor is, in fact, a transparent reminiscence of his actual World War II service and is, despite its presentation as a work of fiction, an important assessment of what a spy-operative's life is like in enemy-occupied territory. The name of the central character, Overton, is Quayle's mother's family name.

4441. ___. *On Such a Night.* Boston: Little, 1948. A look at the fictional espionage events taking place on the British-governed island of Palleria in the Mediterranean on the single evening of July 1, 1942. *

4442. Quayle, Marilyn T. and Nancy Northcott. *Embrace the Serpent.* New York: Crown, 1992. Castro's death precipitates a Soviet move to install a lackey and regain influence in the Western Hemisphere; opposing that move is *La Causa*, a pro-Western movement with its own man, and a US president more concerned with public relations than policy.

4443. Quigley, John. *The Last Checkpoint.* New York: McCall, 1972. Walter Eisler, Premier of East Germany, offers a proposal to the West which includes removal of the Berlin Wall. Before proposing this deal, however, he had failed to check with Moscow and soon finds out he has created an international crisis which may lead to World War III.

4444. ___. *The Secret Soldier.* New York: Signet, 1966. A whiskey drummer on Formosa finds himself caught up in the smuggling and intrigues of a half-caste Chinese friend. *P*

4445. Quinn, Derry. *The Solstice Man.* New York: St. Martin's, 1978. An SIS man with a tarnished reputation, Archive Snow walks into a dangerous scenario as the US, Europe, and Japan battle against the threat posed by Arab terrorists.

4446. Quinn, Jake. *The Mindbenders.* New York: Leisure, 1975. Writer Patrick Shannon creates espionage capers for Kelly O'Bannion, but his own are as exciting. *P* Two more Shannon-O'Bannions:

4447. ___. *The Shallow Grave.* New York: Leisure, 1974. *P*

4448. ___. *The Undertaker.* New York: Leisure, 1974. *P*

Quinn, John, pseud. *See* Rodriguez, Dennis

Quinn, Simon, pseud. *See* Smith, Martin C.

4449. Quinnell, A. J., pseud. *In the Name of the Father.* New York: Signet, 1987. Moscow's attempted assassination of the pontiff in 1981 begets another assassination attempt of equal audacity: this time, a secret papal envoy is the triggerman off to see the Soviet premier. *P*
Mr. Quinnell was born in Great Britain in 1941, and he keeps his life very private.

4450. ___. *Man on Fire.* New York: Morrow, 1980. Creasy, a drifter and soldier-of-fortune with a drinking problem, is persuaded by a comrade to become the bodyguard of little Pinta Balletto, daughter of a rich Italian family, which like so many in modern Italy fears kidnapping; the child regenerates the man, and he reciprocates with a love for her, and when she is kidnapped, he takes merciless vengeance on the kidnappers—systematically executing them one at a time.

4451. ___. *Siege of Silence.* New York: Dutton, 1986. The US President has an awful choice to make when pro-Cuban guerrillas undermine a Central American nation vital to American interests: send our best antiterrorist team to free him or, as CIA analysts urge, treat him as a security risk—and have him hit to keep him quiet. Other Quinnells:

4452. ___. *Blood Ties*. London: Hodder & Stoughton, 1984.

4453. ___. *The Mahdi*. New York: Morrow, 1982.

4454. ___. *Papa's Envoy*. New York: Dutton, 1988.

4455. ___. *Snap Shot*. New York: Morrow, 1983. [*The Snap*. London: Macmillan, 1982].

4456. Quirk, John E. *The Bunnies*. By John Q., pseud. New York: Avon, 1965. Peter Trees is a spy hero in this paperback series. *P* Two others:

4457. ___. *The Survivor*. By John Q., pseud. New York: Avon, 1965. *P*

4458. ___. *The Tournament*. By John Q., pseud. New York: Avon, 1966. *P*

R

4459. Rabe, Peter. *Code Name Gadget*. Greenwich, CT: Fawcett, 1967. An unjustly neglected writer, Rabe began publishing at a prolific pace in the 1950s—mostly hard-boiled detective fiction, such as *Dig My Grave Deep* (New York: Fawcett, 1956. *P*) and *Time Enough to Die* (Greenwich, CT: Fawcett, 1959. *P*) in which the hero, Daniel Port, has dropped out of the Mafia; occasionally international intrigue intersects with gangsters and espionage, and series character Manny DeWitt is involved. Other Rabe novels with an espionage theme are:

4460. ___. *Blood on the Desert*. Greenwich, CT: Fawcett, 1958.

4461. ___. *Girl in a Big Brass Bed*. Greenwich, CT: Fawcett, 1965.

4462. ___. *Kill the Boss Good-Bye*. New York: Vintage, 1993.

4463. ___. *A Shroud for Jesso*. Greenwich, CT: Fawcett, 1958.

4464. ___. *The Spy Who Was Three Feet Tall*. Greenwich, CT: Fawcett, 1966.

4465. Rae, Hugh C. *Sullivan*. New York: Playboy, 1978. A beautiful young assassin, her mind turned to Jell-O by drugs, is being brutally and systematically taught to kill while a smug, fanatical doctor, obsessed with his discoveries, conducts sick experiments at the expense of US taxpayers; both become revenge targets for an embittered CIA agent, his mind eroded by torture and betrayal. *P*

Raine, Richard, pseud. *See* Sawkins, Raymond H.

Rame, David, pseud. *See* Divine, Arthur D.

4466. Ramrus, Al and John Shaner. *The Ludendorff Pirates.* Garden City, NY: Doubleday, 1978. Twelve British commandos and a "neutral" American playboy hijack a huge German battleship early in World War II. *

Ramsey, Eric, pseud. *See* Hagberg, David

4467. Randall, John D. *The Jihad Ultimatum.* New York: Pinnacle, 1989. Three Islamic fanatics with a crude nuclear device are loose somewhere in the US; on their trail are KGB operatives Alexander Rostov and Katrina Tambov—not to stop them but to lend silent support. *P*

4468. ___. *The Tojo Virus.* New York: Zebra, 1991. A sales rep for the most important computer company in the world is sexually blackmailed with a porno tape of his antics at a convention; what he doesn't know is that a Japanese consortium is behind it and the goal is to infect the his company's internal network with a virus so deadly that its effects will be tantamount to a second Pearl Harbor—only far more devastating in consequence. *P*

4469. Randle, Kevin D. *Ambush!* By Steve MacKenzie, pseud. New York: Avon, 1987. One of four tales published by Avon in 1987 of derring-do about the Navy's famous commando unit—SEALS. *P*

4470. Rankin, Ian James. *Watchman.* London: Bodley Head, 1988. His third novel presents Miles Flint, a surveillance specialist, finds himself on the run in a complicated mission in Northern Ireland.

4471. Raphael, Rick. *The Defector.* Garden City, NY: Doubleday, 1980. Vowing revenge for the death of his Finnish parents at the hands of Soviet agents, Andrei Barsukov betrays a KGB attempt to snatch a secret Canadian weapons system and defects to the US with his former colleagues hot on his trail.

4472. Rascovich, Mark. *The Bedford Incident.* New York: Atheneum, 1963. Comparable to Gallery's *The Brink*, this nautical intrigue reveals how the American destroyer *Bedford* cornered a Russian sub in the Arctic and the tragedy which ensued for both. *

4473. Rathbone, Julian. *Base Case.* New York: Pantheon, 1981. Jan Argand, that complex Commissioner of the Brabt police, is working with the security force of a nuclear installation off the coast of Spain and tangles with ideologues opposed to the base, drug dealers, gem thieves, and a murderer.

Writes Newgate Callendar in the *New York Times* (17 May 1981, sec. 7): "Argand is as much a specialist in his field as the literary scholars are in theirs. But he is also not in the best of health, and prone to nearly hysterical fits of black dejection . . . *Base Case* is unusually literate and a joy to read. Its characters and their milieu come vividly to life—even though Mr. Rathbone is utterly dispassionate in his clinical dissection of people and their motives" (125).

Rathbone writes political thrillers which critics have described as having a leftist slant, although Argand himself is a very conservative man. (Indeed, he characterizes his politics as "unaffiliated Marxist.") His evocations of time and place and vivid characterization have been compared to the best of espionage writers, such as Allbeury and Deighton, and like them, he knows the European political scene, with its shifting loyalties and byzantine politics. He has long been declared one of the best writers of espionage fiction in his own country, frequently singled out by reviewers in the London *Times*, its *Literary Supplement*, and *Spectator*. In the US no less a critic of spy fiction than Newgate Callendar has frequently singled his works out for high praise, particularly *Carnival!* Notes reviewer Jean M. White of the *Washington Post Book World* of *The Euro-Killers*, the first of the Argand series tales: "[It is] an unusual thriller which combine[s] suspense with serious commentary on today's international political unrest." She concludes, "Rathbone is as complex as his hero, a suspense writer who makes intelligent observations on European social and economic problems" (qtd. in *Contemporary Authors*. New Ser. Vol. 34: 374).

4474. ___. *Diamonds Bid.* New York: Walker, 1967. An enormous bribe changes hands in a Turkish police station and a man named Smollett has the misfortune to witness this first step in a vicious secret agent power game.

4475. ___. *Greenfinger.* New York: Viking, 1987. [*ZDT.* London: Grafton, 1988.] The story of how a huge agribusiness uses the CIA and other agencies to wipe out a strain of perennial maize cultivated by land-squatters in Costa Rica.

4476. ___. *Hand Out.* New York: Walker, 1968. A British agent stops by Ankara enroute to a secret assignment on the Turkish frontier. At an embassy party, an old friend casually boasts about his espionage coups and when he leaves town, our hero is not sure whether his cover is still intact.

4477. ___. *Kill Cure.* New York: St. Martin's, 1975. After Claire Mundham signs on as cook to a Bangladesh relief expedition, she realizes that not only isn't it a mercy mission, but that she is a pawn aimed at discrediting a Turkish guerrilla movement.

4478. ___. *King Fisher Lives.* New York: St. Martin's, 1976. It is in these make-believe journals of Mark Southan that readers will learn if radical American thinker Lewis Fisher was gunned down in Spain on orders of the CIA.

4479. ___. *Lying in State.* New York: Putnam's, 1986. Using a narrative that mixes flashback and the tape-recorded diary entries, Rathbone's central character is an old man in possession of incriminating tapes of Juan and Eva Peron (his Nazi affiliations, her sexual antics), which tapes are an object of interest to opposing factions.

4480. ___. *The Pandora Option.* London: Heinemann, 1990. The central theme is a US plot to poison grain silos in Iran and the manipulation of history by US agencies to ensure Bush's election in 1988.

4481. ___. *Sand Blind.* London: Serpent's Tail, 1993. Explains how the Pentagon and the CIA convinced Saddam Hussein that his advanced air defence systems could take out bombers protected by Stealth technology, thus luring him into a war he could not possibly win.

4482. ___. *A Spy of the Old School.* New York: Pantheon, 1982. Based on the Cambridge spies of the thirties and centered on Richard Austen, an academic and archeologist, who is exposed as a spy.

4483. ___. *With My Knives I Know I'm Good.* New York: Putnam's, 1970. Milyutin defects while visiting Lebanon and is immediately drawn into the world of espionage, where agents drop one another with regularity and some even try to liquidate him. Other Rathbone political thrillers and mysteries:

4484. ___. *Bloody Marvelous.* New York: St. Martin's, 1976.

4485. ___. *Carnival!* New York: St. Martin's, 1976.

4486. ___. *Crystal Contract.* London: Heinemann, 1988.

4487. ___. *The Euro-Killers.* New York: Pantheon, 1980.

4488. ___. *A Raving Monarchist.* New York: St. Martin's, 1978.

4489. ___. *Trip Trap.* New York: St. Martin's, 1972.

4490. ___. *Watching the Detectives.* New York: Pantheon, 1983.

4491. Raven, Simon. *The Sabre Squadron.* New York: Harper & Row, 1967. In 1952 Daniel Mond, a Cambridge mathematician, finds the answers to some secret ciphers. Pursued, he retires to the anonymity of a tradition-ridden British regiment. *

4492. Ray, Robert J. *The Cage of Mirrors.* Philadelphia: Lippincott, 1980. International sleuth Clayton Yankee Taggart, working from a clue in *Playboy*, tracks the killer of an ex-Army buddy to the mega-organization "La Matrice Economique."

4493. Raymond, René B. *This Is for Real.* By James H. Chase, pseud. New York: Walker, 1967. Mark Girland is the only SIS agent left to send to Senegal to search for a colleague known to be playing for the other side. Published in Britain simultaneously as *Have This One on Me*.

4494. ___. *You Have Yourself a Deal.* By James H. Chase, pseud. New York: Walker, 1968. Girland is sent to Paris to find out why a girl found along the Seine with amnesia had the initials of a top Chinese agent stenciled across her anatomy. Published in England simultaneously as *Believed Violent*. Another Raymond tale:

4495. ___. *The Whiff of Money.* By James H. Chase, pseud. London: Hale, 1969.

4496. Rayner, William. *The Interface Assignment.* New York: Atheneum, 1977. An American scientist in London to receive a prize becomes the kidnap victim of three Mossad agents out to pressure the US government.

Redgate, John, pseud. *See* Kennedy, Adam

Reed, Eliot, pseud. *See* Ambler, Eric and Charles Rodda

4497. Reeman, Douglas. *The Deep Silence.* New York: Putnam's, 1968. The British nuclear submarine *Termeraire* is sent to find a damaged American sub and in the process runs afoul of the Chinese Communists. *

4498. Reid, James. *The Offering.* New York: Putnam's, 1977. A Boston priest, who has refused to supply money for violence, joins forces with the FBI in its search for some local IRA terrorists.

4499. Reiffel, Leonard. *The Contaminant.* New York: Harper & Row, 1978. Too late a US President learns that a shipment of wheat with a cancer-causing substance has been shipped to the USSR.

4500. Reiss, Bob. *The Casco Deception.* Boston: Little, 1983. In 1942 the Gestapo concocts a brilliant scheme to siphon off men from the European war effort: a convoy of raiders will invade Casco Bay near Portland, Maine and send America into panic. The first step begins when American misfit and mercenary John Ryker is sent to Captain's Island to prepare the way.

4501. ___. *The Last Spy.* New York: Simon & Schuster, 1993. Three sleeper agents have been working their way up the ladders of success in America for so long that they have become the people they play; now, it is fifteen years later and the Soviet Union is gone, and they want to know why their assignments are changing and who is calling the shots back home.

4502. ___. *Summer Fires.* New York: Simon & Schuster, 1980. The US President faces the ultimate decision of his office—to push or not to push the button. More by Reiss:

4503. ___. *Divine Assassin.* Boston: Little, 1985.

4504. ___. *Flamingo.* New York: St. Martin's, 1990.

4505. ___. *The Road to Extrema.* New York: Summit, 1992.

4506. ___. *Salt Maker.* New York: Viking, 1988.

4507. Reiss, Curt. *High Stakes.* New York: Putnam's, 1942. Looking through the eyes of the FBI, the reader watches a Nazi spy ring working in pre-war New York under the cover of a German news agency. *

4508. Renfroe, Martha K. *Curiosity Didn't Kill the Cat.* By M. K. Wren, pseud. Garden City, NY: Doubleday, 1973. When a Navy captain is found dead in Oregon, the grieving wife calls in a secret agent friend to find out "who done it." As much a detective story as a spy caper.

4509. Revere, Justin D. *Born to Kill.* New York: Pinnacle, 1984. Justin Perry is a CIA hitman. Others:

4510. ___. *Death's Running Mate.* New York: Pinnacle, 1985. *P*

4511. ___. *Stud Service.* New York: Pinnacle, 1985. *P*

4512. ___. *Vatican Kill.* New York: Pinnacle, 1984. *P*

4513. Reynolds, Howard. *The Defector.* New York: Viking, 1987. A Soviet physicist takes the secret of his design for a sonar surveillance device with him to a California research center.

4514. Reynolds, Philip. *When and If.* Trans. from the French. New York: Duell, Sloan & Pearce, 1952. An RAF intelligence officer sets up a spy network during a fictional future war between the West and Soviet Russia. *

4515. Rhodes, Russell. *The Herod Conspiracy.* New York: Dodd, 1980. Irgun terrorists steal many weapons, some sophisticated, from Free World arsenals and demand a ranson for them to be paid with the lost wealth of the Great Temple of Jerusalem. The hitch is that the location of the treasure is known only to one man and he does not want to reveal it.

Richards, Clay, pseud. *See* Crossen, Kendell F.

4516. Richards, David. *The Double Game: He Played Both Ends against the Middle.* London: Brown, 1958. Examines the operations of a double agent who secretly worked for the British within the hierarchy of Nazi Germany. *

4517. ___. *Four Men.* London: Brown, Watson, 1960. Follows the special exploits of four British commandos against various German World War II targets. *

Richards, Paul, house pseud. *See* Streib, Dan

4518. Richmond, Donald. *The Dunkirk Directive.* Briarcliff Manor, NY: Stein & Day, 1980. The events leading up to the Dunkirk evacuation.

4519. Rico, Don. *The Man from PANSY.* New York: Lancer, 1967. Features Burgess ("Buzz") Cardigan in a spy spoof. *PH* A second:

4520. ___. *The Daisy Dilemma.* New York: Lancer, 1967. *PH*

4521. Rider, Rick. *Dyed for Death.* New York: Belmont-Tower, 1980. In revolutionary Iran, Eric Wainhurst is rescued from a mob by a female US embassy official; when the mob's unnamed instigator elects to strike again, he sends a band of killers recruited from an army of local terrorist. *P*

4522. Ritner, Peter. *Red Carpet for the Shah.* New York: Morrow, 1975. A power mad ruler of Iran sets out to make his country a super power by attacking Russia with American-supplied nuclear missiles; as the USSR prepares for a counterstrike, US President George Arnold attempts to prevent a world-encompassing holocaust.

4523. Rivers, Gayle and James Hudson. *The Five Fingers.* Garden City, NY: Doubleday, 1978. Seven American agents are assigned to infiltrate Red China in April 1969 and "eliminate" eleven high-ranking Chinese and North Vietnamese leaders meeting in a conference.

4524. ___. *Hunter's Run.* New York: Putnam's, 1989. Major Bob Yardley has to rescue the US embassy hostages in Iran, but first he has to steal the Peacock Throne from the Royal Palace in Tehran. One more by the former specialist in covert operations:

4525. ___. *The Teheran Contract.* Garden City, NY: Doubleday, 1981.

4526. Robbins, Harold. *The Pirate.* New York: Simon & Schuster, 1974. When his family is captured by PLO terrorists, an Arab financier is forced to turn to Israeli Intelligence for help in saving them.

Roberts, James H., pseud. *See* Duncan, Robert L.

4527. Roberts, Jan. *The Judas Sheep.* New York: Saturday Review, 1975. CIA agent MacDonald asks an art dealer to check out artist Stavros, a former colleague in the Greek Resistance; arriving at the scene of bitter fighting during World War II, the dealer is immediately mixed up with various agents seeking a lost treasure.

4528. Roberts, Katherine E. *Center of the Web.* Garden City, NY: Doubleday, 1942. A trained but amateur British spy is sent to the House on

Harmony Street, in occupied Antwerp, to break up the web of agents headed by the Fraulein Doktor. First serialized in *Liberty Magazine*. *

4529. ___. *Private Report*. Garden City, NY: Doubleday, 1943. On the 1940 night of Belgium's surrender to the Nazis, Major Paul Denyn goes underground to help build the resistance into a cohesive, smooth-working group of guerrilla fighters. *

4530. Roberts, Thomas A. *The Heart of the Dog*. New York: Random, 1972. A former CIA linguist accepts a Middle East courier job from "the Company" and runs into a maelstrom of problems.

4531. Robertson, Charles. *Directive 16*. New York: Pocket, 1980. "Directive 16" is Hitler's order to invade England, and during the Blitz of 1940 seems everyday more imminent, but the tale really concerns the political machinations of two important figures of the time who want to move in opposite directions: FDR, if elected to a third term, wants to join the fight; Joseph Kennedy, Ambassador to Great Britain, is avidly pro-German. *P*

4532. ___. *The Elijah Conspiracy*. New York: Bantam, 1980. An ex-CIA agent races against time to halt a band of PLO and Neo-Nazi terrorists who are plotting to assassinate a world leader at an upcoming Geneva Peace Conference. *P*

4533. ___. *The Omega Deception*. New York: Bantam, 1983. When Danish physicist Niels Bohr fled a Nazi detention order, he may have left behind the secrets of the atom bomb in his briefcase—and salvation for the crumbling Nazi regime. *P*

4534. ___. *Red Chameleon*. New York: Bantam, 1985. At a top-secret defense facility in the Silicon Valley, ex-CIA agent Gordie Hardwick is in charge of security; when he is killed by someone on the inside, whose codename is Red Chameleon, his own brother is brought in to find the killer and plug the leak before the US's new defense system, Prometheus II, is compromised. *P*
One more:

4535. ___. *Culebra Cut*. New York: Pocket, 1989.

4536. Robertson, Colin. *The Judas Spies*. London: Hale, 1966. MI-6 agent Alan Steel must run to ground a vicious band of double agents whom others considered to be SIS colleagues.

4537. ___. *Soho Spy*. London: Ward, Lock, 1940. Inspector Robert Strong of Scotland Yard seeks Nazi agents in London's wartime working class district. Two other tales about Agent Steel, which were also never published in America, are:

4538. ___. *Clash of Steel*. London: Hale, 1965.

4539. ___. *Project X*. London: Hale, 1968.

4540. Robinson, Derek. *The Eldorado Network*. New York: Norton, 1980. After an initial loss of confidence, the Abwehr is surprised by the quality of intelligence coming from a young Spaniard inserted into England as a Nazi spy in 1941—never guessing that he was a plant fostered by the famed British XX Committee.

4541. ___. *Rotten with Honour*. New York: Viking, 1973. A young British banker who does a bit of moonlighting as a spy must beat an old Russian master agent to the recovery of a nuclear scientist who has discovered a new kind of weapon. A couple of others:

4542. ___. *Kramer's War*. New York: Viking, 1977.

4543. ___. *War Story*. New York: Knopf, 1988.

Robson, Dirk, pseud. *See* Robinson, Derek

4544. Roderick, Robert. *The Greek Position*. New York: Wyndham, 1981. An early tale of schemers and the underside of high finance; here, Eric Schotten, a Swiss private banker, knows that huge money results from knowing where and when the next war occurs—in this case, the Six Day War a full two years before it erupts.

4545. Rodriguez, Dennis. *Chameleon Kill*. By John Quinn, pseud. New York: Pinnacle, 1984. Rod Gavin is a CIA hitman in this paperback series. P One more:

4546. ___. *The Checkmate Kill*. By John Quinn, pseud. New York: Pinnacle, 1984. P

4547. Rogers, Barbara. *Project Webb*. New York: Dodd, 1980. Scientist Howard Shaw is drawn into an undercover race between America and Russia to be the first superpower to contact extraterrestrial beings.

4548. Rogers, Ray M. *The Negotiator.* New York: McKay, 1975. Lowly US State Department official Stuart Leland tries to prove that a very successful Secretary of State is, in fact, a double agent in the pay of the Kremlin.

Rohmer, Sax, pseud. *See* Ward, Arthur Sarsfield

4549. Rohrbach, Peter T. *A French Killing.* By James P. Cody, pseud. New York: Berkley, 1975. Brian Peterson, known as the D.C. Man, is a self-appointed guardian of justice who works out of the nation's capital in this paperback series. *P* One more in the series:

4550. ___. *Search and Destroy.* New York: Berkley, 1974. *P*

4551. Roman, Eric. *A Year as a Lion.* Briarcliff Manor, NY: Stein & Day, 1978. A college professor agrees to go to Hungary to act as a CIA spy on a one-year contract.

4552. Romano, Deane. *Flight From Time One.* New York: Walker, 1972. In which another potential nightmare is appropriately handled by the boys from Britain's MI-6.

4553. Roos, Audrey and William. *A Few Days in Madrid.* New York: Scribner's, 1965. Chosen to escort a 12-year-old boy to Spain, a legal secretary finds herself enmeshed in espionage, an assassination plot, and problems caused by a series of grisly characters.

4554. Roosevelt, Elliott. *Murder and the First Lady.* New York: St. Martin's, 1984. Roosevelt, son of FDR and Eleanor Roosevelt, portrays his parents as coming to the aid of a secretary arrested for the murder of a White House staff member in his first novel.

4555. ___. *A First Class Murder.* New York: St. Martin's, 1991. First Lady and amateur sleuth Eleanor Roosevelt attempts to fathom which of the passengers aboard an ocean liner in the Atlantic knocked off the Russian ambassador.

4556. ___. *The Hyde Park Murder.* New York: St. Martin's, 1985. The First Lady smells a rat in two dubious coincidences involving her Hyde Park neighbors: first, Alfred Doolittle Hannah is accused of a stock swindle and then Adriana van der Meer, nineteen-year-old debutante, commits suicide on the eve of her wedding.

4557. ___. *Murder at the Palace*. New York: St. Martin's, 1987. First Lady is visiting the Queen in 1942 at Buckingham Palace and is on the scene to investigate the murder of Sir Anthony Brooke-Hardinge.

4558. ___. *Murder in the Oval Office*. New York: St. Martin's, 1989. A locked-room mystery in which the room is the Oval Office itself and the victim an Alabama congressman with the pistol lying next to him.

4559. ___. *Murder in the Rose Garden*. New York: St. Martin's, 1989. A blueblooded society matron—and a blackmailer in high-society circles—turns up dead in the Rose Garden.

4560. ___. *The President's Man*. New York: St. Martin's, 1991. "Blackjack" Endicott is FDR's boarding school chum who comes to his aid in 1932 as FDR announces for the Presidency; as New York Governor, Roosevelt has made many underworld enemies through his stance on Prohibition, and Endicott works to foil an assassination plot.

4561. ___. *The White House Pantry Murder*. New York: St. Martin's, 1987. It's a bleak Christmas in 1941 with the Nazis overrunning Europe, and Churchill is about to visit the Roosevelts, so security measures are stepped up a notch—especially after Eleanor's maid finds a man frozen stiff during a morning inspection of the pantry. One more mystery featuring his famous parents:

4562. ___. *Murder at Hobcaw Barony*. New York: St. Martin's, 1986.

4563. Rooth, Anne R. and James P. White. *The Ninth Car*. New York: Putnam's, 1978. The Mossad, KGB, ODESSA, and agents of various international bankers vie for the key to the mystery of a boxcar filled with old Nazi gold.

4564. Rosenberg, Robert. *Crimes of the City*. New York: Simon & Schuster, 1991. Jerusalem police detective Avram Cohen is assigned a case that involves two murdered nuns in a Russian Orthodox convent.

4565. Rosenberger, Joseph. *Death Merchant: The Castro File*. New York: Pinnacle, 1974. Master of disguise, deception, and destruction, Richard Camellion is called in whenever the local authorities and the CIA are stumped. Well does he deserve his codename, "the Death Merchant."

In this outing, he must prevent a battle for power between the Cubans and the Russians in a plot which includes the elimination of Castro and his replacement with a look-alike Russian stooge. *P*

4566. ___. *Death Merchant: The Enigma Project.* New York: Pinnacle, 1977. Camellion goes undercover as a member of the Grundy Bible Institute party which is climbing Mt. Ararat in Turkey to examine the reported ruins of Noah's Ark. His mission: Bring back photos of secret Soviet border installations. His problem: a Russian expedition has been allowed by the wily Turks to climb at the same time. *P*

4567. ___. *Death Merchant: The Kronos Plot.* New York: Pinnacle, 1977. The "DM" is ordered to quash a plot by the KGB and Castro's secret service, the DGI, to assist the ultra-nationalist Panamanian National Department in blowing up the Panama Canal. *P*

4568. ___. *Death Merchant: Nipponese Nightmare.* New York: Pinnacle, 1978. Camellion is tipped off by the Japanese Kompei concerning a United Red Army terrorist plot to assassinate the President of the Philippines and the Emperor of Japan, blaming their deaths on the CIA. He must quash the scheme and its conspirators to save the US—and the world—from ultimate disaster. *P*

4569. ___. *Death Merchant: The Pole Star Secret.* New York: Pinnacle, 1977. Without starting World War III, the "DM" must destroy a secret Soviet weather base which has been set up at the North Pole to study and control world weather patterns. *P*

4570. ___. *Death Merchant: The Zemlya Expedition.* New York: Pinnacle, 1976. Camellion must infiltrate Zemlya One, an experimental Soviet undersea city in the Arctic Ocean, which is guarded by the infamous KGB security boss Colonel Vershensky, obtain information on its construction, and escape, taking with him the Russian-born CIA contact in the place. Others in this rather lengthy paperback series include: *P*

4571. ___. *Death Merchant: Afghanistan Crashout.* New York: Pinnacle, 1983. *P*

4572. ___. *Death Merchant: Alaska Conspiracy.* New York: Pinnacle 1979. *P*

4573. ___. *Death Merchant: Albanian Connection.* New York: Pinnacle 1973. *P*

4574. ___. *Death Merchant: Apocalypse, U.S.A.* New York: Pinnacle, 1983. *P*

4575. ___. *Death Merchant: Armageddon, U.S.A.* New York: Pinnacle 1976. *P*

4576. ___. *Death Merchant: The Atlantean Horror.* New York: Pinnacle, 1985. *P*

4577. ___. *Death Merchant: The Bermuda Triangle Action.* New York: Pinnacle, 1980. *P*

4578. ___. *Death Merchant: The Billionaire Mission.* New York: Pinnacle, 1974. *P*

4579. ___. *Death Merchant: Blood Bath.* New York: Pinnacle, 1981. *P*

4580. ___. *Death Merchant: Blueprint Invisibility.* New York: Pinnacle 1980. *P*

4581. ___. *Death Merchant: The Budapest Action.* New York: Pinnacle 1977. *P*

4582. ___. *Death Merchant: The Bulgarian Termination.* New York: Pinnacle, 1985. *P*

4583. ___. *Death Merchant: The Burma Probe.* New York: Pinnacle, 1984. *P*

4584. ___. *Death Merchant: The Burning Blue Death.* New York: Pinnacle 1980. *P*

4585. ___. *Death Merchant: The Chinese Conspiracy.* New York: Pinnacle 1973. *P*

4586. ___. *Death Merchant: The Cobra Chase.* New York: Dell, 1986. *P*

4587. ___. *Death Merchant: The Cosmic Reality Kill.* New York: Pinnacle 1979. *P*

4588. ___. *Death Merchant: The Death Merchant.* New York: Pinnacle 1972. *P*

4589. ___. *Death Merchant: The Devil's Trashcan.* New York: Pinnacle 1981. *P*

4590. ___. *Death Merchant: Escape from Gulag Taria.* New York: Dell, 1986. *P*

4591. ___. *Death Merchant: Fatal Formula.* New York: Pinnacle, 1978. *P*

4592. ___. *Death Merchant: The Flight of the Phoenix.* New York: Pinnacle, 1982. *P*

4593. ___. *Death Merchant: The Fourth Reich.* New York: Pinnacle, 1980. *P*

4594. ___. *Death Merchant: The Greenland Mystery.* New York: Dell, 1988. *P*

4595. ___. *Death Merchant: Hell in Hindu Land.* New York: Pinnacle 1977. *P*

4596. ___. *Death Merchant: High Command Murder.* New York: Pinnacle 1980. *P*

4597. ___. *Death Merchant: The Hindu Trinity Caper.* New York: Dell, 1987. *P*

4598. ___. *Death Merchant: The Inca File.* New York: Pinnacle, 1982. *P*

4599. ___. *Death Merchant: Invasion of the Clones.* New York: Pinnacle 1976. *P*

4600. ___. *Death Merchant: The Iron Swastika Plot.* New York: Pinnacle 1976. *P*

4601. ___. *Death Merchant: The Judas Scrolls.* New York: Pinnacle, 1982. *P*

4602. ___. *Death Merchant: The KGB Frame.* New York: Pinnacle, 1975. *P*

4603. ___. *Death Merchant: The Kondrashev Chase.* New York: Pinnacle 1977. *P*

4604. ___. *Death Merchant: The Laser War.* New York: Pinnacle, 1974. *P*

4605. ___. *Death Merchant: The Mainline Plot.* New York: Pinnacle 1974. *P*

4606. ___. *Death Merchant: Manhattan Wipeout.* New York: Pinnacle 1975. *P*

4607. ___. *Death Merchant: Massacre in Rome.* New York: Pinnacle, 1979. *P*

4608. ___. *Death Merchant: The Mato Grosso Horror.* New York: Pinnacle 1975. *P*

4609. ___. *Death Merchant: The Methuselah Factor.* New York: Pinnacle, 1984. *P*

4610. ___. *Death Merchant: The Mexican Hit.* New York: Pinnacle, 1978. *P*

4611. ___. *Death Merchant: The Miracle Mission.* New York: Dell, 1987. *P*

4612. ___. *Death Merchant: Nightmare in Algeria.* New York: Pinnacle 1976. *P*

4613. ___. *Death Merchant: Operation Mindmurder.* New York: Pinnacle 1979. *P*

4614. ___. *Death Merchant: Operation Overkill.* New York: Pinnacle 1972. *P*

4615. ___. *Death Merchant: Operation Skyhook.* New York: Pinnacle, 1981. *P*

4616. ___. *Death Merchant: Operation Thunderbolt.* New York: Pinnacle 1978. *P*

4617. ___. *Death Merchant: The Pakistan Mission.* New York: Pinnacle, 1985. *P*

4618. ___. *Death Merchant: The Psionics War.* New York: Pinnacle, 1982. *P*

4619. ___. *Death Merchant: The Psychotran Plot.* New York: Pinnacle 1972. *P*

4620. ___. *Death Merchant: The Romanian Operation.* New York: Pinnacle, 1984. *P*

4621. ___. *Death Merchant: Satan Strike.* New York: Pinnacle, 1973. *P*

4622. ___. *Death Merchant: The Shambhala Strike.* New York: Pinnacle 1978. *P*

4623. ___. *Death Merchant: The Shamrock Smash.* New York: Pinnacle 1980. *P*

4624. ___. *Death Merchant: Slaughter in El Salvador.* New York: Pinnacle, 1983. *P*

4625. ___. *Death Merchant: The Soul Search Project.* New York: Pinnacle, 1985. *P*

4626. ___. *Death Merchant: The Surinam Affair.* New York: Pinnacle 1978. *P*

4627. ___. *Death Merchant: Vengeance of the Golden Hawk.* New York: Pinnacle, 1976. *P* A final entry:

4628. ___. *Murder Master: The Caribbean Caper.* New York: Manor, 1974. Lou King, the Murder Master, travels to a Caribbean island seeking to block heroin shipments into the US and becomes involved with Mossad agents who are trying to run down a Nazi band headed by Dr. Mengele. *P*

4629. Rosenblum, Robert. *The Mushroom Cave.* Garden City, NY: Doubleday, 1973. A student radical attempting to smuggle a revolutionary manuscript out of Russia is caught and when the news breaks in the West, he becomes a pawn in a ruthless game between the KGB and the CIA.

4630. Rosenhaupt, Hans. *The True Deceivers*. New York: Dodd, 1954. A German-born OSS officer works for the American Army interrogating Nazi POWs during World War II. *

4631. Rosner, Joseph. *Public Faces in Private Places*. New York: Delacorte, 1966. An agent is detailed to keep the indiscreet son of a US President from giving either the opposition party or the KGB a convenient scandal.

Ross, Angus, pseud. *See* Gigga, Kenneth

4632. Ross, Frank, pseud. *A Conspiracy of Angels*. New York: Atheneum, 1987. Complex story about a troubled genius and defector who, in a depressed state of premature old age, wants to return to the US. The man who would bring him in is himself a byzantine character, a retired CIA agent, with a dubious past.

4633. ___. *Dead Runner*. New York: Atheneum, 1977. Arab terrorists have a plutonium bomb on board an aircraft at London's Heathrow airport which must be carefully handled by agents of the Mossad and MI-5.

4634. ___. *The Shining Day*. New York: Atheneum, 1981. Hoping that he will be valuable for later invasion plans as a source of "disinformation," the Germans send their own man, an amateur, to England to impersonate a British professor who has just died.

4635. ___. *The Sixty-Fifth Tape*. New York: Atheneum, 1979. Lucas Garfield battles to prevent a secret Matrix organization plot from succeeding in the complete takeover of the US government.

4636. ___. *Sleeping Dogs*. New York: Atheneum, 1978. When someone begins knocking off members of an underground radical network in New England, the lone survivor runs to CIA agent Sam Hanlon for help.

4637. Ross, Hal. *The Fleur-de-Lys Affair*. Garden City, NY: Doubleday, 1975. An RCMP agent tracks FLQ terrorists who have kidnapped a young family and plan to snatch a fortune in diamonds.

Ross, Ian, pseud. *See* Rossman, John F.

4638. Ross, Philip. *Hovey's Deception*. New York: St. Martin's, 1986. When an American professor cracks under duress and confesses to working for the CIA—the Agency doesn't know him—an operative goes in to rescue him from his Czechoslovakian prison.

4639. ___. *True Lies.* New York: TOR, 1988. David Bowen, CIA operative, has assumed the identity of a mild-mannered investment counselor from New York, when he arranges to meet a German woman working as a translator at a concert in London. He has a difficult time explaining himself after they become lovers because people are following them, and someone is trying hard to kill him. The 1994 film, loosely based on the novel, stars Arnold Schwarzenegger and Jamie Lee Curtis. Some others:

4640. ___. *Choice of Evils.* New York: TOR, 1987.

4641. ___. *A Good Death.* New York: Dodd, 1983.

4642. ___. *Talley's Truth.* New York: TOR, 1987.

4643. ___. *White Flower.* New York: TOR, 1989.

4644. Ross, Regina. *Falls the Shadow.* New York: Delacorte: 1974. An SIS agent has been kidnapped by a French Communist underground gang and is being tortured to reveal the whereabouts of a priceless Holy Crown. In the background are two KGB agents waiting to snatch both the agent and the Crown to embarrass Britain at a forthcoming peace conference.

4645. Rossiter, John. *The Deadly Gold.* New York: Walker, 1975. British agent Roger Tallis infiltrates a gang planning to steal a priceless gold statue from Spain.

4646. ___. *The Deadly Green.* New York: Walker, 1971. A now-and-then agent for the Directorate of Special Services, Roger Tallis must locate a man from the Foreign Office who has vanished with one million pounds sterling.

4647. Rossman, John F. *Amazons.* By Ian Ross, pseud. New York: Signet, 1976. The fourth tale in a series of paperback espionage capers about a secret organization known as Mero and the Pentagon's search for scientist Britt St. Vincent. *P* The first:

4648. ___. *The Mind Masters.* New York: Signet, 1974. *P*

Rostand, Robert, pseud. *See* Hopkins, Robert S.

4649. Rosten, Leo. *A Most Private Intrigue.* New York: Atheneum, 1967. Galton goes to Istanbul to help obtain three Western scientists from behind the Iron Curtain.

4650. Roth, Holly. *The Content Assignment.* New York: Random, 1954. When an American agent with whom he has fallen in love disappears in Berlin, an English journalist picks up her trail to the United States. *

4651. ___. *The Van Dreisen Affair.* New York: Random, 1960. Elena van Dreisen effects the escape of a professed Communist, is distrusted upon her return to America, and produces an overall action designed to protect US citizens. *

4652. ___. *Gauge of Deception.* By K. G. Ballard, pseud. Garden City, NY: Doubleday, 1963. A CIA agent must halt the surreptitious export of a special instrument manufactured in West Germany and sanctioned by Bonn for shipment to East Germany. Other Holly Roth novels, the first below of which features Lieutenant Kelly in a second espionage caper:

4653. ___. *Button, Button.* New York: Harcourt, 1966.

4654. ___. *The Coast of Fear.* By K. G. Ballard, pseud. New York: Doubleday, 1957.

4655. ___. *The Crimson in the Purple.* New York: Simon & Schuster, 1957.

4656. ___. *The Mask of Glass.* New York: Vanguard, 1954.

4657. ___. *Shadow of a Lady.* New York: Simon & Schuster, 1956.

4658. ___. *The Sleeper.* New York: Simon & Schuster, 1955.

4659. ___. *The Slender Thread.* By P. J. Merrill, pseud. New York: Harcourt, 1959.

4660. Roth, Philip. *Operation Shylock: A Confession.* New York: Simon & Schuster, 1993. Roth's twentieth work is described in the advance reader's copy: "By turns a spy story, political thriller, a meditation on identity, and a confession." Roth notes in his Preface: "I've drawn *Operation Shylock* from notebook journals. The book is as accurate an account as I am able to give of actual occurrences that I lived through . . . culminated, early in 1988, in my agreeing to undertake an intelligence-gathering operation for Israel's foreign intelligence service, the Mossad" (13).

4661. Rothberg, Abraham. *The Great Waltz.* New York: Putnam's, 1977. As the US and Soviet presidents negotiate at an ultimate summit meeting, Soviet dissidents and American right-wingers plan a strike which will lead their leaderless nations to the brink of nuclear war.

4662. ___. *The Heirs of Cain.* New York: Putnam's, 1967. Via flashbacks in which he recounts his mission to liquidate a pair of ex-Nazi scientists working in Switzerland for Egypt, Nissim reveals how he became the "Sword" of the Mossad and the "Heir of Cain."

4663. ___. *The Stalking Horse.* New York: Saturday Review, 1972. Years ago at the American embassy in Moscow, Chapman knew a Russian playwright-KGB agent named Federov. Now after his retirement to a farm, the CIA asks him to hide a Russian defector who turns out to be his old acquaintance. The peace is broken when the remote farm hideout is discovered by Soviet operatives bent on homicide.

4664. Rothwell, Henry T. *Duet for Three Spies.* New York: Roy, 1967. Michael Brooks is sent by "the Company" to rescue a secret geological survey team in the Congo, under attack by guerrillas and with a Belgian spy in its midst.

4665. ___. *No Honor amongst Spies.* New York: Roy, 1969. [*No Honour Amongst Spies.* London: Hale, 1969]. Agent Brooks is hustled off to Rhodesia to rescue Deidre Page from the horrors of a Russian exchange. With both his own people and the KGB after him, Brooks has the certain knowledge that success will end his career—if a bullet doesn't first. Three other Brooks thrillers are:

4666. ___. *Dive Deep for Danger.* New York: Roy, 1966.

4667. ___. *Exit of a Spy.* New York: Roy, 1969.

4668. ___. *No Kisses from the Kremlin.* New York: Roy, 1969.

4669. Rouch, James. *Blind Fire.* New York: Zebra, 1985. Two NATO soldiers, Major Revell and British Sergeant Hyde, combine to keep the peace in a war-torn section of Europe known as "The Zone." *P* Two more from this paperback series:

4670. ___. *Plague Bomb*. New York: Zebra, 1986. *P*

4671. ___. *Sky Strike*. New York: Zebra, 1986. *P*

4672. Rovin, Jeff and Sander Diamond. *Staꓤik*. New York: Pinnacle, 1988. There is an imminent confrontation with the Soviets who have a fanatical Premier with his band of thugs called *Lenin Ultra* unless—Lenin's corpse, symbol of this repressive regime, can be stolen from its resting place. *P*

4673. Rowan, Hester. *Alpine Encounter*. New York: Scribner's, 1979. Kate Paterson, visiting the grave of her beloved mountain climber, is informed by mysterious men that his death was not an accident but the result of a KGB-CIA clash.

4674. Rowe, James N. *The Judas Squad*. Boston: Little, 1975. Revolutionaries and ex-US soldiers take over a Pennsylvania nuclear reactor and hold it for ransom. *

4675. Rowe, John. *The Aswan Solution*. Garden City, NY: Doubleday, 1979. An American electronics genius aids Israeli commandos, armed with a nuclear bomb, seize control of Egypt's Aswan Dam, which is to be held hostage against the cessation of Arab atomic bomb testing.

4676. ___. *Long Live the King*. Briarcliff Manor, NY: Stein & Day, 1984. Prince George—soldier, playboy—has a girlfriend with a Catholic, rebel past made even less acceptable to the rest of the Royals, and their myriad protectors, when his own brother is killed at the coronation ceremony at Westminster Abbey. Another one:

4677. ___. *Count Your Dead*. Sydney, Australia: Angus & Robertson, 1968.

Royce, Kenneth, pseud. *See* Gandley, Kenneth Royce

4678. Rumanes, George N. *The Man with the Black Worrybeads*. New York: Dutton, 1973. A group of underground fighters in wartime Athens are called upon by British Intelligence to keep a convoy of ships from reaching Rommel's forces in North Africa.

4679. Rumbold-Gibbs, Henry St. John Clair. *Assassin's Road*. By Simon Harvester, pseud. New York: Walker, 1966. Secret agent Dorian Silk is in Jerusalem to discover the identity of "the Prophet" and to prevent his revival of the ancient sect known as "the Assassins." If he fails, this gang will stir up so much mischief in the Israeli countryside as to start a *jihad* or Holy War.

Rumbold-Gibbs was one of the most prolific and little-known writers of the spy thriller, there being a paucity of biographical material about him. His works are noted for their attention to detail on locale (something he could have taught to Fleming) and political mood. Following World War II, the author visited nearly every country in what is now called the Third World, gathering background information which gave him much insight into world affairs and allowed him to spice his spy thrillers with a certain amount of "prophecy," some of which has come to pass. Rumbold-Gibbs also labored to make his lead character, Dorian Silk, as realistic as story lines would allow—no James Bond here. In short, his tales were highly authentic and in their heyday offered his readers not only adventure but information of an educational nature as well. Donald McCormick, in his biographical register of spy thriller writers, tells of the Soviet reaction to Rumbold-Gibbs: "The Russians regarded him as serious and compulsory reading for the KGB and when the latter had their No. 1 listening post at Kuala Lumpur, they surprised a local book importer one day by sending a dozen different people to order six copies each of certain Harvester books! (*Who's Who in Spy Fiction* [New York: Taplinger, 1977], 96).

4680. ___. *The Bamboo Screen* By Simon Harvester, pseud. New York: Walker, 1969. Dorian Silk assists a British hydroelectric expert who has become mixed up with American and Chinese spies in Taiwan.

4681. ___. *The Chinese Hammer.* By Simon Harvester, pseud. New York: Walker, 1961. Silk is sent to rescue an English astronaut who, in returning from space, has crash-landed in Chinese-occupied Tibet.

4682. ___. *The Copper Butterfly.* By Simon Harvester, pseud. New York: Walker, 1957. Dorian Silk is rushed to Japan to thwart a KGB plot against that nation's government.

4683. ___. *Dragon Road.* By Simon Harvester, pseud. New York: Walker, 1956. Silk battles a gang of ruthless Chinese-backed guerrillas operating in Thailand and Burma.

4684. ___. *Epitaph for Lemmings.* By Simon Harvester, pseud. New York: Walker, 1945. Former Commando Stephen Murray is transferred to the MI-5 group led by Roger Fleming, whose task it is to ferret out the Nazis responsible for destroying English food dumps. *

4685. ___. *Flight in Darkness.* By Simon Harvester, pseud. New York: Walker, 1964. Brainwashed and unaware of his identity, Lewis Grant flees his Red Chinese captors and escapes to the mountains where friendly locals nurse his recovery.

4686. ___. *The Flying Horse.* By Simon Harvester, pseud. New York: Walker, 1964. First published in England as *Troika.* British agent Dorian Silk is sent to North Korea to recover an important defector.

4687. ___. *Forgotten Road.* By Simon Harvester, pseud. New York: Walker, 1974. Silk turns up with amnesia at a village on the Indo-Afghani border.

4688. ___. *An Hour before Zero.* By Simon Harvester, pseud. New York: Walker, 1960. Silk is in South Vietnam to look into a Viet Cong ring operating against the Saigon government.

4689. ___. *Moonstone Jungle.* By Simon Harvester, pseud. New York: Walker, 1961. Dorian Silk in the Far East.

4690. ___. *Moscow Road.* By Simon Harvester, pseud. New York: Walker, 1971. With a crash course in computer salesmanship as a cover, Silk is rushed off to the Soviet capital.

4691. ___. *Nameless Road.* By Simon Harvester, pseud. New York: Walker, 1970. Silk is sent to Inner Mongolia to eliminate the threat emanating from COMPACIN.

4692. ___. *Paradise Men.* By Simon Harvester, pseud. New York: Walker, 1956. A Communist-backed guerrilla group fermenting trouble in New Guinea becomes a target for Dorian Silk's many talents.

4693. ___. *Red Road.* By Simon Harvester, pseud. New York: Walker, 1964. His mission completed, Silk must make a desperate escape across the Soviet frontier from Samarkand.

4694. ___. *Sahara Road.* By Simon Harvester, pseud. New York: Walker, 1972. Disguised as an archaeologist, Silk is sent to Algeria to rescue a defecting KGB agent.

4695. ___. *Shadows in a Hidden Land.* By Simon Harvester, pseud. New York: Walker, 1966. An ex-British agent accepts a dangerous assignment which involves traversing the Sinkiang mountains in China.

4696. ___. *Siberian Road.* By Simon Harvester, pseud. New York: Walker, 1976. The final Dorian Silk adventure. Posing as an anthropologist, the ace agent is dispatched to the disputed Russo-Chinese border area to gather data on a KGB plot.

4697. ___. *Silk Road.* By Simon Harvester, pseud. New York: Walker, 1964. In China on a delicate mission, Silk finds that his identity has been betrayed.

4698. ___. *Tiger in the North.* By Simon Harvester, pseud. New York: Walker, 1963. In Rajpul, a (fictitious) border kingdom of India, Silk must assist some British oil prospectors caught up in Red Chinese intrigue.

4699. ___. *Treacherous Road.* By Simon Harvester, pseud. New York: Walker, 1967. Can Dorian Silk persuade a fellow spy not to defect?

4700. ___. *Unsung Road.* By Simon Harvester, pseud. New York: Walker, 1961. Silk is involved with a pair of fellow British agents who, hating each other, are forced to work together on a mission in Iran.

4701. ___. *Yesterday Walkers.* London: Jarrolds, 1958. Attempting to stir up the insurgency of the late 1940s, Communist guerrillas in Malaya become a target of Dorian Silk.

4702. ___. *Zion Road.* By Simon Harvester, pseud. New York: Walker, 1968. Dorian Silk in the Middle East conflict. Other of Rumbold-Gibbs' spy thrillers include:

4703. ___. *Arrival in Suspicion.* By Simon Harvester, pseud. New York: Walker, 1953. *

4704. ___. *Battle Road.* By Simon Harvester, pseud. New York: Walker, 1967.

4705. ___. *Breastplate for Aaron.* By Simon Harvester, pseud. New York: Walker, 1949.

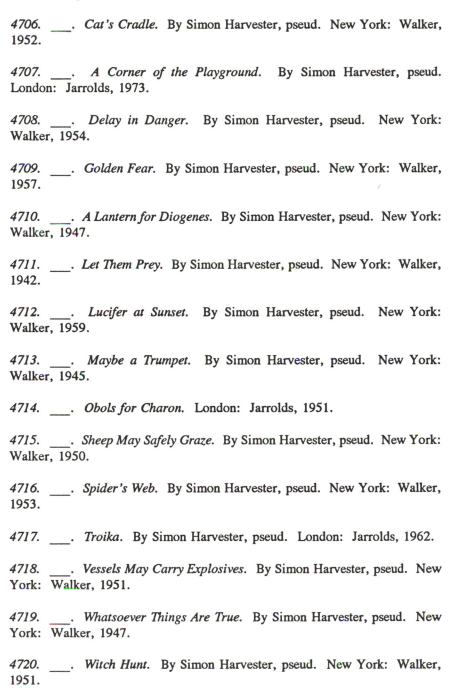

4706. ___. *Cat's Cradle.* By Simon Harvester, pseud. New York: Walker, 1952.

4707. ___. *A Corner of the Playground.* By Simon Harvester, pseud. London: Jarrolds, 1973.

4708. ___. *Delay in Danger.* By Simon Harvester, pseud. New York: Walker, 1954.

4709. ___. *Golden Fear.* By Simon Harvester, pseud. New York: Walker, 1957.

4710. ___. *A Lantern for Diogenes.* By Simon Harvester, pseud. New York: Walker, 1947.

4711. ___. *Let Them Prey.* By Simon Harvester, pseud. New York: Walker, 1942.

4712. ___. *Lucifer at Sunset.* By Simon Harvester, pseud. New York: Walker, 1959.

4713. ___. *Maybe a Trumpet.* By Simon Harvester, pseud. New York: Walker, 1945.

4714. ___. *Obols for Charon.* London: Jarrolds, 1951.

4715. ___. *Sheep May Safely Graze.* By Simon Harvester, pseud. New York: Walker, 1950.

4716. ___. *Spider's Web.* By Simon Harvester, pseud. New York: Walker, 1953.

4717. ___. *Troika.* By Simon Harvester, pseud. London: Jarrolds, 1962.

4718. ___. *Vessels May Carry Explosives.* By Simon Harvester, pseud. New York: Walker, 1951.

4719. ___. *Whatsoever Things Are True.* By Simon Harvester, pseud. New York: Walker, 1947.

4720. ___. *Witch Hunt.* By Simon Harvester, pseud. New York: Walker, 1951.

4721. Runyon, Poke. *Night Jump—Cuba.* New York: Pyramid, 1965. In an effort to avert World War III, four US airborne commandos are inserted into Cuba to recover a missing document. *P* One other by this author is:

4722. ___. *Commando X.* New York: Pyramid, 1967. *P*

4723. Ruse, Gary A. *A Game of Titans.* Englewood Cliffs, NJ: Prentice-Hall, 1977. An American nuclear dirigible and a Soviet carrier enter combat near an island where a dying scientist holds vital missile secrets.

4724. Russell, A. J. *Pour the Hemlock.* New York: Random, 1977. Agreeing to an espionage assignment, a US State Department China expert finds himself hunted by three separate groups operating within and without the government.

4725. Russell, Martin. *Death Fuse.* New York: St. Martin's, 1981. Chief Inspector Harry Cullen and his crack team hunt a mad terrorist bomber who has put London into a state of panic.

4726. Ryan, Charles. *The Capricorn Quadrant.* New York: Signet, 1990. The Russians have a stealth plane far superior to the West; however, an enterprising Swedish hacker plants a virus into the system's brain; it ejects its pilots, heads for the South Pacific where it begins destroying everything within reach, including passenger planes. *P*

4727. ___. *The Panjang Incident.* New York: Signet, 1989. A US Navy cargo ship with a nuclear weapon that will trigger global destruction is timed to explode as it floats beneath the surface of the South Pacific. *P*

4728. Ryck, Francis. *Green Light, Red Catch.* Trans. from the French. New York: Stein & Day, 1973. Russian space scientist Kazienko, vacationing at a Crimean beach resort, is snatched by SIS agents on behalf of Israel. It then becomes the turn of KGB operatives to try to get him back.

4729. ___. *Loaded Gun.* Trans. from the French. New York: Stein & Day, 1972. Yako, a Soviet spy, is captured by the British, but is later released. Unknown to him, the SIS has attached a tracking device on him, which leads to a chase through the French and Spanish countrysides.

4730. ___. *Woman Hunt.* Trans. from the French. New York: Stein & Day, 1972. Dominique has no idea that her husband is a spy. When she catches him in bed with another beauty, the gun in her hand goes off and he is dead. Not knowing that he was actually "on business," she runs—pursued by French and Russian agents who want to silence her for what they believe she knows of her ex's espionage past.

4731. Rydberg, Louis and Ernie. *The Shadow Army*. New York: Nelson, 1976. When the Germans invade Crete in 1941, young Demetrios, vowing to help the underground, joins his comrades in the mountains to continue the fight. *y

Ryder, Jonathan, pseud. *See* Ludlum, Robert

S

4732. Saberhagen, Fred. *A Century of Progress*. New York: TOR, 1983. Fantasy and espionage mix in this tale of a man named Norlund who has it in his power to shape the future—or, more precisely, to prevent the future descending from Nazi Germany from becoming the present. *P*

4733. Sachar, Howard. *The Man on the Camel*. New York: Times, 1980. An American professor-Mossad agent locks horns with a former Nazi collaborator bent on wreaking social and political havoc in Israel.

4734. Sadler, Barry. *The Eternal Mercenary*. New York: Charter, 1979. Creator of *CASCA: The Eternal Mercenary* series featuring a soldier-of-fortune hero condemned to wander the earth (see Barabbas in the SERIES CHARACTERS section of this text). Sadler has authored more than 25 novels of soldiering and mercenary heroics; the former Green Beret composed the popular hit *The Ballad of the Green Beret* in 1966. Senior editor of *Soldier of Fortune* magazine, John Coleman, is quoted in a Cleveland *Plain Dealer* article in 1992 as stating that Sadler had shot himself "accidentally" while waving a handgun around during a taxi ride in Guatemala City; he was left mentally incapacitated as a result. *P* A Sadler sampler:

4735. ___. *The Sentinel*. New York: Charter, 1983. *P*

4736. ___. *The Warrior*. New York: Charter, 1987. *P*

4737. Sager, Gordon. *The Formula*. Philadelphia: Lippincott, 1952. A secret plan is hidden somewhere among the art treasures of Venice and agents from everywhere want to get their hands on it. *

4738. Sagola, Mario. *The Naked Bishop.* New York: Coward-McCann, 1980. During the early 1960s, J. Edgar Hoover recruits three commandos to wage a secret, FBI-sponsored war on the Mafia.

4739. St. George, Geoffrey. *The Proteus Pact.* Boston: Little, 1975. A German scientist, revolted by the Nazis, works secretly for MI-6 on a new super alloy.

St. Germain, Gregory, pseud. *See* Wallman, Jeffrey M.

4740. St. James, Ian. *The Balfour Conspiracy.* New York: Atheneum, 1981. The illegitimate daughter of a Palestinian refugee becomes a pawn in an explosive terrorist plot involving a shipment of stolen plutonium.

St. John, David, pseud. *See* Hunt, E. Howard

4741. St. John, Robert. *The Man Who Played God.* Garden City, NY: Doubleday, 1963. A man struggles to rescue over 1,600 Jews trapped in wartime Hungary. *

4742. Sale, Richard. *For the President's Eyes Only.* New York: Simon & Schuster, 1985. "Keyhole" is a worldwide secret organization that specializes in blackmailing important people through electronic high-tech electronic surveillance. The President orders NSA to put a stop to it, and one Navy man is chosen: Simon Kincade, a part-Soshoni, part-Irish hellraiser, who leaves the Antarctic ice for Nairobi to track the conspirators.

4743. Salinger, Pierre. *The Lollipop Republic.* Garden City, NY: Doubleday, 1971. During a Latin American revolution in the 1980s, America sits by until it is too late.

President Kennedy's press secretary and later a US senator from California, Salinger has returned to journalism and works for ABC-News in Paris. His most recent non-fiction is *Secret Dossier: The Hidden Agenda behind the Gulf War* (New York: Penguin, 1991). See Mr. Salinger's commentary in CRAFT NOTES.

4744. ___. *On Instructions of My Government.* Garden City, NY: Doubleday, 1971. A Chinese-led revolutionary army topples the South American republic of Santa Clara despite the best efforts of the US diplomats and agents on the scene.

4745. ___ and Leonard Gross. *The Dossier.* Garden City, NY: Doubleday, 1984. Camille Laurent may become the next President of France; the problem: he could have been a Nazi collaborator; TV news reporter André Kohl joins the daughter of the "top professional in the CIA" to find the truth in a missing dossier.

4746. ___ and Leonard Gross. *Mortal Games.* New York: Doubleday, 1988. André Kohl is back and in serious trouble when he digs up a secret network of rogue agents, KGB and CIA, who are trying to destroy the balance of power for their own ends. Kohl must fake his own death to pursue his investigation.

4747. Salisbury, Harrison E. *The Gates of Hell.* New York: Random, 1975. The distinguished American journalist and Russian authority here shows how the Soviet secret police, through its various name and leadership changes, harried a writer from the time of Cheka to his exile by the KGB to Siberia.

Sandberg, Berent, pseud. *See* Sandberg, Peter Lars

4748. Sandberg, Peter Lars. *Brass Diamonds.* By Berent Sandberg, pseud. New York: Signet, 1980. Matt Eberhart is a CIA agent in this paperback series. *P* Two more:

4749. ___. *The Chinese Spur.* By Berent Sandberg, pseud. New York: Signet, 1983. *P*

4750. ___. *The Honeycomb Bid.* By Berent Sandberg, pseud. New York: Signet, 1981. *P*

4751. Sanders, Bruce. *The Secret Dragnet.* New York: Roy, 1957. MI-5 agent Howard Digburn seeks a missing document and a nefarious Soviet agent in Cold War Britain. Two other Digburn tales, neither of which was published in America, are: *

4752. ___. *Feminine for Spy.* London: Jenkins, 1967.

4753. ___. *To Catch a Spy.* London: Jenkins, 1958.

Sanders, Buck, pseud. *See* Frentzen, Jeffrey

4754. Sanders, Lawrence. *Capital Crimes.* New York: Putnam's, 1990. A mesmerizing, sex-crazed faith healer calling himself Brother Kristos gets an emotionally unstable President under his spell after he—shades of Rasputin—heals the President's son of hemophilia.

4755. ___. *The Tangent Objective.* New York: Putnam's, 1976. With help from the CIA, a wheeler-dealer undercover agent for a US oil company organizes the fight against the oil-rich dictator of the little country of Asante. Three more:

4756. ___. *McNally's Lunch.* New York: Putnam's, 1992.

4757. ___. *The Timothy Files.* New York: Putnam's, 1987.

4758. ___. *Timothy's Game.* New York: Putnam's, 1988.

4759. Sanders, Leonard. *The Hamlet Warning.* New York: Scribner's, 1976. [rpt. *The Hamlet Ultimatum.* New York: Scribner's, 1979]. A disaffected former CIA agent must help "the Company" by stopping the Santo Domingo terrorist group's scheme to capture an A-bomb and use it, together with stolen computer data, to gain control of the world. Another:

4760. ___. *Act of War: A Novel of Love and Treason.* New York: Simon & Schuster, 1982.

4761. Sandulescu, Jacques and Annie Gottlieb. *The Carpathian Caper.* New York: Putnam's, 1975. To avenge his father's death at the hands of the secret police, a man organizes a colorful band of adventurers in Transylvania dedicated to the heist of a $5-million art treasure hidden in a monastery high in the forbidding Carpathian mountains.

4762. Sangster, James ("Jimmy"). *Foreign Exchange.* New York: Norton, 1972. Secret agent John Smith is sent to Russia posing as a tractor salesman to carry off an ultra secret caper. *H*

4763. ___. *Private I.* New York: Norton, 1967. John Smith crisscrosses several continents secure in his belief that he has finally escaped the usual fate of MAX agents who desert "the Firm." Unfortunately, his conscience suckers him into stopping off to help his ex-wife divorce her current husband—and BANG! *H*

4764. ___. *Touchfeather.* New York: Norton, 1969. Katy Touchfeather is an airline hostess with a difference—she is a Modesty Blaise-style secret agent who bops around the globe carrying out the assignments of her employer,

Whitehall's mysterious Mr. Blaser. This installment tells how she was recruited into the dirty but spirited world of super-agentry.

4765. ___. *Touchfeather, Too.* New York: Norton, 1970. Her cover as a "stew" intact, Katy seeks information as to the source of the gold bullion which a Greek industrial magnate is smuggling. Other Sangster mystery novels:

4766. ___. *Blackball.* New York: Holt, 1987.

4767. ___. *Hardball.* New York: Holt, 1988.

4768. ___. *Snowball.* New York: Holt, 1986.

4769. Santesson, Hans S., ed. *The Award Espionage Reader.* New York: Award, 1965. A collection of short stories, drawn from various sources, which glamorize the derring-do of fictional secret agents. *P*

4770. Saperstein, David. *Red Devil.* New York: Berkley, 1989. A demonic manipulator in the Kremlin is about to seize absolute power and wreak havoc on the world. *P*

4771. Sapir, Richard and Warren Murphy. *The Destroyer: Bay City Blast.* New York: Pinnacle, 1979. Written by Murphy alone. CURE, the world's most secret crime and spying organization, created the perfect weapon—Remo Williams—a man programmed to become a cold calculating death machine and codenamed "the Destroyer." In this outing, it had to happen—the Mafia finally got smart enough and rich enough to own an American city—until CURE sends Remo and the artillery to scotch the caper. *P*

4772. ___. *The Destroyer: Bottom Line.* New York: Pinnacle, 1979. The US dollar is saved when Remo, his friend Chiun, and their sexy CIA friend Ruby Gonzales, discover a deadly conspiracy involving America's wealthiest family. *P*

4773. ___. *The Destroyer: Dangerous Games.* New York: Pinnacle, 1980. Written by Murphy alone. Terrorist threats grip the athletes arriving for the Moscow Olympics—until Remo and Chiun make sport of the deadliest of games. *P*

4774. ___. *The Destroyer: Dark Horse.* New York: Signet, 1992. The eighty-ninth volume in this famous paperback series featuring Remo and his karate-chopping sidekick Chiun. The California gubernatorial election is up for grabs when the governor and his lieutenant-governor slam into Mt. Whitney with the rest of the airliner's passengers and crew. But things heat up even more quickly when someone targets the candidates for murder while Remo and Chiun are hamstrung—Remo by official orders and Chiun by a mesmerizing love for newsreporter Cheeta Ching. *P*

4775. ___. *The Destroyer: Dr. Quake*. New York: Pinnacle, 1972. Remo Williams is asked to halt the mad scheme of Forben, called "Dr. Quake," who has invented an incredible machine which accelerates or starts earthquakes. *P*

4776. ___. *The Destroyer: Firing Line*. New York: Pinnacle, 1980. Written by Murphy alone. When New York City's firemen go on strike a gang of professional arsonists threaten to torch the city unless their ransom demand is met. *P*

4777. ___. *The Destroyer: The Head Man*. New York: Pinnacle, 1977. Remo and Chiun are at the US capital to fight some assassins' plans for a capital crime against the US President. *P*

4778. ___. *The Destroyer: Killer Chromosomes*. New York: Pinnacle, 1978. A mad scientist discovers how to manipulate genetic patterns that keep different creatures from intermingling and turns a woman into a man-eating tiger. *P*

4779. ___. *The Destroyer: King's Curse*. New York: Pinnacle, 1976. When a stone idol on display in a New York museum is despoiled, an ancient, diabolical Mexican Indian tribe demands revenge in human sacrifice against American citizens; CURE dispatches Remo Williams and his friend Chiun to eliminate the eliminators—without having their hearts cut out first! *P*

4780. ___. *The Destroyer: The Last War Dance*. New York: Pinnacle, 1974. Williams must deliver a monument, which the Revolutionary Indian Party wishes destroyed and which masks the Cassandra, an atomic doomsday machine. *P*

4781. ___. *The Destroyer: Power Play*. New York: Pinnacle, 1979. Williams and Chiun are hired to protect America's raunchiest publisher—and wind up in a maelstrom of oil-inspired mysticism and murder. *P*

4782. ___. *The Destroyer: Summit Chase*. New York: Pinnacle, 1973. Williams and Chiun fly the Atlantic to attend a top-level meeting of world mob leaders and make a killing—in more ways than one! *P*

4783. ___. *The Destroyer: Terror Squad.* New York: Pinnacle, 1973. CURE's top agent is ordered to break up an international network of terrorists whose nasty deeds have created a wildly chaotic crisis involving the White House, Moscow, and Red China. *P*

4784. ___. *The Destroyer: Timber Line.* New York: Pinnacle, 1980. Written by Murphy alone. An unknown killer is murdering all of those connected with the development of a new oil-producing tree and Williams must get to the root of the matter. *P*

4785. ___. *The Destroyer: Voodoo Die.* New York: Pinnacle, 1978. The pro-Communist leader of the Caribbean island of Baqia obtains a new "happy drug" called Mung which, when mixed with radiation, turns people into puddles. Suddenly, the world is beating a path to the dictator's door wanting his Mung-making machine and when the Russians and Chinese agree to place nuclear missiles on the island, Williams and Chiun enter the picture—running smack into a voodoo plot to keep America out of the picture. Other titles in this rapidly expanding series include: *P*

4786. ___. *The Destroyer: Acid Rock.* New York: Pinnacle, 1973. *P*

4787. ___. *The Destroyer: Arabian Nightmare.* New York: Signet, 1991. *P*

4788. ___. *The Destroyer: Assassin's Play Off.* New York: Pinnacle 1975. *P*

4789. ___. *The Destroyer: Blood Lust.* New York: Signet, 1991. *P*

4790. ___. *The Destroyer: Brain Drain.* New York: Pinnacle, 1989. *P*

4791. ___. *The Destroyer: Chained Reaction.* New York: Pinnacle, 1978. *P*

4792. ___. *The Destroyer: Child's Play.* New York: Pinnacle, 1976. *P*

4793. ___. *The Destroyer: Chinese Puzzle.* New York: Pinnacle, 1972. *P*

4794. ___. *The Destroyer: Created, The Destroyer.* New York: Pinnacle 1971. *P*

4795. ___. *The Destroyer: Deadly Seeds.* New York: Pinnacle, 1975. *P*

4796. ___. *The Destroyer: Death Check.* New York: Pinnacle, 1977. *P*

4797. ___. *The Destroyer: Death Therapy.* New York: Pinnacle, 1972. *P*

4798. ___. *The Destroyer: The Final Death.* New York: Pinnacle, 1977. *P*

4799. ___. *The Destroyer: Funny Money.* New York: Pinnacle, 1975. *P*

4800. ___. *The Destroyer: Holy Terror.* New York: Pinnacle, 1975. *P*

4801. ___. *The Destroyer: In Enemy Hands.* New York: Pinnacle, 1977. *P*

4802. ___. *The Destroyer: Judgment Day.* New York: Pinnacle, 1974. *P*

4803. ___. *The Destroyer: Kill or Cure.* New York: Pinnacle, 1974. *P*

4804. ___. *The Destroyer: Last Call.* New York: Pinnacle, 1978. *P*

4805. ___. *The Destroyer: The Last Temple.* New York: Pinnacle, 1977. *P*

4806. ___. *The Destroyer: Mafia Fix.* New York: Pinnacle, 1980. Written by Murphy alone. *P*

4807. ___. *The Destroyer: Missing Link.* New York: Pinnacle, 1980. Written by Murphy alone. *P*

4808. ___. *The Destroyer: Mugger's Blood.* New York: Pinnacle, 1977. *P*

4809. ___. *The Destroyer: Murder Ward.* New York: Pinnacle, 1974. *P*

4810. ___. *The Destroyer: Murder's Shield.* New York: Pinnacle, 1973. *P*

4811. ___. *The Destroyer: Oil Slick.* New York: Pinnacle, 1974. *P*

4812. ___. *The Destroyer: Ship of Death.* New York: Pinnacle, 1977. *P*

4813. ___. *The Destroyer: Slave Safari.* New York: Pinnacle, 1974. *P*

4814. ___. *The Destroyer: Sweet Dreams*. New York: Pinnacle, 1976. *P*

4815. ___. *The Destroyer: Union Bust*. New York: Pinnacle, 1973. *P*

4816. Sargent, Patricia. *Mortal Encounter*. New York: Avon, 1979. Judith Weber, a beautiful young pianist, escaped the horror of Auschwitz long ago determined to seek revenge; vowing to kill the once-dreaded former SS Doktor, Kurt Wallner, whom she has recently identified, she pursues him across two continents, while trying to stay ahead of his ODESSA colleagues. *P*

4817. Sariola, Mauri. *The Helsinki Affair*. Trans. from the Finnish. New York: Walker, 1971. Finland is a country, like Switzerland, which remains extremely "neutral" in all aspects of the post-1940 secret wars; her top operative Osmo Kilpi, must walk a delicate tightrope while trying to deal with agents of both the CIA and KGB who are fighting over a secret in his nation's capital city. One other by this author is:

4818. ___. *The Torvich Affair*. Trans. from the Finnish. New York: Walker, 1972.

4819. *Saturday Evening Post*, Editors of. *Danger: Great Stories of Mystery and Suspense*. Garden City, NY: Doubleday, 1967. Contains several reprinted spy thriller short novels by, among others, Ian Fleming.

4820. Saul, John R. *The Birds of Prey*. New York: McGraw-Hill, 1977. A French journalist uncovers old hatreds between Vichy French and Gaullists as the root cause of an airliner crash that kills the French Army's Chief of Staff and eighteen others.

4821. Sauter, Eric. *Hunter*. New York: Avon, 1983. This is the fourth series of Hunter paperbacks, the first three of which by authors Norman Conway, Ralph Hayes, and Mike Newton concerned intrigue and sleuthing among heroes Adam Hunter, John Yard, and Det. Jon Steel. Sauter's version of Hunter concerns Robert Hunter, a man who lives on an island in the Delaware River and who takes on the KGB or similar thug-killers in these paperback tales. *P* Two more:

4822. ___. *Hunter and Raven*. New York: Avon, 1984. *P*

4823. ___. *Hunter and the Ikon*. New York: Avon, 1984. *P*

4824. ___. *Skeletons*. New York: Dutton, 1990.

Savage, Ian, pseud. *See* Gigga, Kenneth

4825. Savarin, Julian Jay. *Gunship.* New York: St. Martin's, 1985. David Pross is a Royal Air Force helicopter pilot who is coerced by a shadowy government agency to go on a dangerous mission.

4826. ___. *Hammerhead.* New York: St. Martin's, 1987. Spies and counterspies in a tale about a new high-tech helicopter.

4827. ___. *Lynx.* New York: Walker, 1986. A British pilot tries to free a man held captive in Communist China.

4828. ___. *Naja.* New York: St. Martin's, 1990. Gallagher comes out of retirement from British SIS to take on a cunning assassin.

4829. ___. *Trophy.* New York: HarperCollins, 1990. Technothriller about a NATO superplane and two rival pilots in a secret mission called the November Project. Others:

4830. ___. *Villiger.* New York: St. Martin's, 1991.

4831. ___. *Water Hole.* New York: St. Martin's, 1982.

4832. ___. *Wolf Run.* New York: Walker, 1991.

4833. Savchenko, Vladimir. *Self-Discovery.* Trans. from the Russian. New York: Macmillan, 1979. A young Soviet research student must outwit the KGB and his fellow scientists in order to prevent their discovery of his astounding invention—a computer that can duplicate and biologically modify humans. Reminiscent of Martin Caidin's *Cyborg.* *

4834. Sawkins, Raymond H. *Avalanche Express.* By Colin Forbes, pseud. New York: Dutton, 1977. CIA and SIS agents on the Transalpine Atlantic Express work to save a high-level Russian defector from KGB killers and to avert a Soviet invasion of Western Europe. *y

4835. ___. *Bombshell.* By Richard Raine, pseud. New York: Harcourt, 1969. The fourteenth explosion of its kind in Europe claims the scientific friend of a British lawyer and industrialist, David Martini, who then publicly announces his intention to find whoever is responsible and draws the appropriate response from the nasties.

4836. ___. *The Burning Fuse.* By Jay Bernard, pseud. New York: Harcourt, 1970. While protecting a former Nazi during a trip from Dusseldorf to London, SIS agent Carter must contend with both the ODESSA and the Israeli intelligence team codenamed Verona.

4837. ___. *The Corder Index.* By Richard Raine, pseud. New York: Harcourt, 1968. Martini attempts to find his old acquaintance Dick Raine, thriller-writer and compiler of the Corder Index, a file containing the scoop on the industrial espionage system of the GILA Corporation.

4838. ___. *The Heights of Zervos.* By Colin Forbes, pseud. New York: Dutton, 1970. A British agent and three patriots must prevent the crack German Alpenkorps from taking the monastery atop Mount Zervos in 1940 Greece. *y

4839. ___. *The Janus Man.* By Colin Forbes, pseud. New York: Harcourt, 1988. Spymaster Tweed must discover the connection between the rape-strangulation young women to a high-ranking mole in the Secret Service; he and his journalist friend Newman follow the connecting thread from murder to East Germany to Scandinavia in search of the mole's identity.

4840. ___. *Night of the Hawk.* By Richard Raine, pseud. New York: Harcourt, 1968. A Swiss banker-diplomat has in his possession some highly sensitive evidence which threatens to compromise Swiss neutrality. Martini must find the man and negotiate a deal enabling the little democracy to keep its centuries-old independence.

4841. ___. *The Palermo Affair.* By Colin Forbes, pseud. New York: Dutton, 1972. [*The Palermo Ambush.* London: Collins, 1972]. Two Allied saboteurs employing local Mafia strongmen are involved in a race to sink a huge train-ferry between Sicily and the Italian mainland before the Germans can get their panzer divisions across. *y

4842. ___. *The Stone Leopard.* By Colin Forbes, pseud. New York: Dutton, 1976. With the French president in Moscow, a former famous Resistance leader, codenamed "Leopard," plots a coup which only the perfect Marc Grelle can halt. *y

4843. ___. *Target Five.* By Colin Forbes, pseud. New York: Dutton, 1973. A Russian scientist with vital data makes a run for freedom across the Arctic icepack. US and Soviet agents employing everything from helicopters to icebreakers race to secure his person. *y

4844. ___. *Year of the Golden Ape.* By Colin Forbes, pseud. New York: Dutton, 1974. Sheik Tafak plans to steal a British oil tanker, put a nuclear bomb aboard, and blow up San Francisco with it. The anti-Arab outcry sure to follow can then be used as an excuse to cut off all oil to the West until Israel is abandoned by her capitalist allies. Pitted against this mad caper is a lone British SIS agent. **y* Other Forbes tales:

4845. ___. *Cover Story.* By Colin Forbes, pseud. New York: Atheneum, 1986.

4846. ___. *The Leader of the Damned.* By Colin Forbes, pseud. New York: Atheneum, 1984.

4847. ___. *Snow on High Ground.* By Colin Forbes, pseud. New York: Harcourt, 1967.

4848. ___. *Snow in Paradise.* By Colin Forbes, pseud. New York: Harcourt, 1967.

4849. ___. *The Stockholm Syndicate.* By Colin Forbes, pseud. New York: Dutton, 1982.

4850. ___. *Terminal.* By Colin Forbes, pseud. New York: Atheneum, 1985.

4851. ___. *Tramp in Armour.* By Colin Forbes, pseud. New York: Dutton, 1970. [*Tramp in Armour.* London: Collins, 1969].

4852. Schaill, William S. *Cabot Station.* New York: Walker, 1990. An American sub commander picks up signals from a mysterious underwater craft, presumed to be a Soviet vessel, lying on the bottom of the North Atlantic.

4853. Schiff, Barry and Hal Fishman. *The Vatican Target.* New York: St. Martin's, 1979. Black September takes the Pope hostage aboard his plane enroute to San Francisco and demands the complete withdrawal of the Israelis from the Left Bank in exchange for his life.

4854. Scholefield, Alan. *Berlin Blind.* New York: Morrow, 1980. Reacting to the murder of his wife by West German terrorists, John Spencer seeks and eventually confronts the evil Bruno, who was last seen amid the rubble of dying Berlin in 1945.

4855. ___. *Point of Honor.* New York: Morrow, 1979. Forty years after his father was awarded the Victoria Cross for his gallantry at Dunkirk, Turner learns that his "old man" was actually shot in the back, and thus sets out on a quest through history to find the killer and the reason for his action.

4856. Schurmacher, Emile C., ed. *Assignment X: Top Secret.* New York: Paperback, 1965. A collection of fifteen espionage adventures drawn from the writings of the genre's most respectable practitioners. *P*

4857. Schutz, Benjamin M. *A Tax in Blood.* New York: Bantam, 1989. Washington, DC detective Leo Haggarty follows a case that leads to terrorist bombings and assassinations.

4858. Schwartz, Alan. *No Country for Old Men.* New York: Signet, 1980. A professor, a CIA agent, and a female French reporter follow clues which lead them to a mind-reading machine and a former top Nazi thought long dead. *P*

4859. Scortia, Thomas N. and Frank M. Robinson. *The Gold Crew.* New York: Warner, 1980. Something has gone wrong when the US missile submarine *Alaska*, out on a training mission, is ordered to fire her "dummy" missiles at the Soviet Union. *P*

4860. ___. *The Nightmare Factor.* New York: Bantam, 1979. Is a fatal plague which breaks out in San Francisco a carefully planned experiment in biological warfare? *P*

4861. Scott, Chris. *To Catch a Spy.* New York: Viking, 1977. Ten years after Kim Philby defects, George Stevens, his successor at MI-5, also shows up in Moscow—prompting speculation about his status, whether spymaster or spy.

4862. Scott, Don. *Tijuana Traffic.* New York: Pinnacle, 1982. Raker is a Dirty Harry-type who works for "the Company." *P*

4863. Scott, Douglas. *Chains.* London: Secker & Warburg, 1984. Captain Hector Chisholm escapes his Nazi tormentors to safety across the Channel, but he discovers that his debriefing is really an interrogation, for other escapees have convinced his own superiors that he is a traitor and collaborator.

4864. ___. *Operation Artemis.* Indianapolis: Bobbs-Merrill, 1979. A group of World War II Allied agents sent into Greece to unify the underground movement becomes involved with a deadly enemy and some ambiguous guerrillas.

4865. Scott, Gavin. *A Flight of Lies.* New York: St. Martin's, 1981. A London shopkeeper assists MI-5 in the investigation of a mysterious archaeological theft and a madman's power plot.

4866. ___. *Hot Pursuit.* New York: St. Martin's, 1978. In New Zealand to look into the mystery of a missing English business executive, a newsman is, for some unknown reason, pursued by agents of both the KGB and the CIA.

4867. Scott, Hardiman. *No Exit.* New York: Vanguard, 1985. A British journalist working in Moscow is tipped to a newsbreaking story and must deliver an envelope to the Prime Minister before the KGB stops him.

4868. ___. *Operation 10.* New York: Harper & Row, 1982. A crack IRA team intends to kidnap Margaret Thatcher. A few more:

4869. ___. *Bait of Lies.* New York: Vanguard, 1986.

4870. ___. *Blueprint for a Terrorist.* New York: Vanguard, 1986.

4871. ___. *Deadly Nature.* London: Bodley Head, 1985.

4872. Scott, John D. *The Sea File.* New York: McGraw-Hill, 1981. When a scientist who learns the answer to the world's sudden climatic changes disappears, a tough CIA agent is sent to find him.

4873. Scott, Justin. *Normandie Triangle.* New York: Arbor, 1981. In the months before America enters World War II, agent Steven Gates seeks the Nazi saboteur who engineered the sinking of the liner *Normandie.*

4874. ___. *The Shipkiller.* New York: Dial, 1978. When his wife is killed in the collision of her small boat with a supertanker, the bereaved husband, Peter Hardin, pursues the vessel around the world in an effort to sink it.

4875. Scott, Leonard B. *The Iron Men.* New York: Ballantine, 1993. Silver star winner Col. Scott writes of the fates of three soldiers in the aftermath of Berlin's collapse the years ahead: two German paratroopers with the Knight's Cross and an American, a washed-up lieutenant colonel whose "iron" comes in the form of a DSO for valor in Vietnam.

4876. Scott, Robert L. *Look of the Eagle.* New York: Dodd, 1956. A transport pilot and a former Flying Tiger ace conspire to steal a Russian jet out of North Korea.   Readers may want to compare this post-Korean War thriller with Craig Thomas' *Firefox.*   *

4877.   Scott, Virgil and Dominic Koski.   *The Kreutzman Formula.*   New York: Simon & Schuster, 1974.   Professor Kregg is sent off to Jamaica with an important formula in his notes in a desperate ploy by MI-5 to catch a spy known only as Aristotle.

4878.   ___.   *The Walk-in.*   New York: Simon & Schuster, 1976. A CIA agent must keep a top defector from the Red Chinese intelligence service alive while his premier—and vengeful escorting agents—are visiting the United States.

4879.   Seaman, Donald.   *The Bomb That Could Lip Read.*   Briarcliff Manor, NY: Stein & Day, 1974.   Kelly, the world's highest paid mercenary, must create and plant a bomb that conveys to its detonator the best time for the blast. British SAS Major Welbourne is determined to stop both Kelly and his plaything.

A former merchant sailor and journalist much travelled through world trouble-spots, Seaman first became interested in espionage when he covered the Burgess-Maclean spy scandal in the early 1950s from which came his co-authored (with John S. Mather) *The Great Spy Scandal.*   His spy thrillers have been widely acclaimed on both sides of the Atlantic for their plots and characters, to say nothing of excellent local treatment gleaned from years of foreign correspondent duty.

4880.   ___.   *The Chameleon Course.*   New York: Coward-McCann, 1976. [*The Defector.* London: Hamilton, 1975]. A defecting Soviet scientist is torn between returning home to visit an ill child and remaining in Great Britain where he faces murder charges.   The publicity gained in England puts KGB killers on his trail.   Published in Britain as *The Defector.*

4881.   ___.   *The Duel.*   Garden City, NY: Doubleday, 1979.   An international terrorist-bomber is taken on by one of the world's leading experts in bomb disposal in a deadly contest with hundreds of innocent lives hanging in the balance.

4882.   ___.   *The Terror Syndicate.*   New York: Coward-McCann, 1976.   SIS agent Sydenham finds himself in Moscow seeking a terrorist group which has bombed a top-security London-Dusseldorf flight.   One more Seaman novel is:

4883.   ___.   *Chase Royal.*   London: Hamilton, 1980.

4884. Searls, Hank. *Altitude Zero.* New York: Norton, 1991. A hijacking results in a crippled plane that the pilot must get down to safety.

4885. ___. *Pentagon.* New York: Geis, 1972. Colonel Lee Frost of the Counterintelligence Corps is assigned to see who took a pot-shot at the window of the Chief of the officially abolished Chemico-Biological Warfare Division of the Pentagon. Enroute to solving that mystery, he encounters three more.

4886. Sebastian, Tim. *The Spy in Question.* New York: Delacorte, 1988. As a BBC Moscow correspondent, Sebastian was expelled from the Soviet Union on charges of spying. Dimitry Kalyagin has been serving in the Politburo for twenty years—and serving the British as its highest-placed mole; now his cover is collapsing, the KGB are in hot pursuit, and he desperately wants out of the cold, but the British want to keep him in place just a little longer.

4887. ___. *Spy Shadow.* New York: Delacorte, 1990. The General Secretary is en route to Poland, but an uprising seems imminent despite the age of *glasnost.* James Tristram, whose own father was murdered after being betrayed by a mole, must abort the uprising or the Soviets will retake Poland and exterminate the rebels. Three recent ones:

4888. ___. *Last Rights.* New York: Morrow, 1994.

4889. ___. *The Memory Church.* New York: Morrow, 1993.

4890. ___. *Saviour's Gate.* New York: Delacorte, 1991.

4891. Sela, Owen. *The Bearer Plot.* New York: Pantheon, 1973. A young pilot-spy is involved with the infamous ODESSA in a deal concerning the sale of some valuable stamps to a Spanish nobleman who is fronting for the group.

Little is known about the shy, reclusive Sela except that he is an accountant and naturalized British citizen. His spy thrillers have often been compared to those of Len Deighton.

4892. ___. *An Exchange of Eagles.* New York: Pantheon, 1977. In an effort to encounter the active SIS campaign aimed at bringing America into World War II in 1939-1940, agents of US Army G-2 team up with Abwehr operatives to keep the US neutral.

4893. ___. *The Kiriov Tapes.* London: Hodder & Stoughton, 1973. While investigating the disappearance of some tapes, MI-5 officer Quimper, who is nearing retirement age and really doesn't need the bother, uncovers the KGB's best-kept secret since the defection of Kim Philby.

4894. ___. *The Portuguese Fragment.* New York: Pantheon, 1973. Agreeing to visit Asia for a bit of "harmless smuggling," Maaston ends up battling evildoers for a treasure off the coast of Ceylon. Two more Sela mysteries:

4895. ___. *The Bengali Inheritance.* New York: Pantheon, 1975.

4896. ___. *The Petrograd Consignment.* New York: Dial, 1979.

4897. Sellers, Connie L., Jr. *Operation Vengeance.* By Robert Crane, pseud. New York: Pyramid, 1965. An American agent must smash a Communist heroin ring which is slipping drugs to American troops in Korea. *P*

4898. ___. *Tongue of Treason.* By Robert Crane, pseud. New York: Pyramid, 1967. This paperback action series features a special agent named Sgt. Ben Corbin. *P*

Semenov, Julian S., pseud. *See* Lyandres, Yulian Semenovich

4899. Semprun, Jorgé. *The Second Death of Ramon Mercader.* Trans. from the French. New York: Grove, 1973. A mysterious agent of some unknown government arrives in Amsterdam and soon runs afoul of the Dutch, Soviet, East German, and American intelligence stations.

4900. ___. *Prayer for an Assassin.* Trans. from the French. Garden City, NY: Doubleday, 1960. Mark Vargas is in the post-war city of Budapest with orders to kill a high Communist official.

4901. Sentjurc, Igor. *The Torrents of War.* Trans. Eric Mosbacher. New York: McKay, 1962. World War II fiction by the author whose real name may be Igor von Percha; the US edition contains minor additions and restorations by Elsie Stern of certain passages omitted from the basic translation.

4902. Serling, Robert. *Air Force One Is Haunted.* New York: St. Martin's, 1984. A President contemplates pushing the button at a time when the US is staggering under the worst depression since the 1930's and the Soviets have signed a nonaggression pact with the Chinese. Suddenly, the ghost of FDR appears aboard Air Force One's flight to offer the beleagured President needed counsel.

4903. Seth, Ronald. *In the Nude.* New York: John Day, 1962. [*Spy in the Nude.* London: Hale, 1962]. SIS agent Alex Marceau is known to his neighbors as a mild-mannered writer of spy fiction; his problem is that he seems unable to keep from confusing the main points in his fictional and real-life capers.

Seth's wartime experiences are the stuff of fiction. He was a volunteer for the SOE, dropped into Estonia, betrayed by a Nazi sympathizer, tortured and sent to Berlin, where he experienced more torture. Sentenced to death, the merest accident—a malfunctioning scaffold—saved his life at the last moment; he was returned to prison and again tortured. Finally, he bluffed the Germans into using him as an agent (a bluff that nearly cost him his life by his own side in a POW camp in Paris); at last, back in Frankfurt toward the end of the war, Himmler himself attempted to use him in Switzerland on a spy mission.

This adventure is set forth in his fascinating memoir, *A Spy Has No Friends.* After World War II, Seth turned to the production of many volumes on the history and workings of espionage, some of which remain the finest on their particular subjects. His 1971 *Encyclopedia of Espionage*, despite its British and World War II bias, remains essential for any student of the spy, real-life or fictional.

4904. ___. *Operation Getaway.* New York: John Day, 1954. [*Patriot.* London: Owen, 1954]. A British agent is parachuted behind the Iron Curtain to rescue the young son of an important Communist scientist. Two more "Spy" tales:

4905. ___. *The Spy in Silk Breeches.* London: Frewin, 1968.

4906. ___. *The Spy Who Wasn't Caught.* London: Hale, 1966.

4907. Setlowe, Frank. *The Brink.* New York: Fields, 1976. Based on the Quemoy-Matsu conflict during the Eisenhower Administration in the late 1950's; the war between the US and China erupts over these tiny islands when a pilot and his attack squadron are ordered into combat.

4908. Seward, Jack. *The Cave of the Chinese Skeletons.* Rutland, VT: Tuttle, 1964. British agent Curt Stone, a James Bond type, battles Red Chinese operatives in the Far East as he searches for the vital Izu cache. Three other Curt Stone adventures are:

4909. ___. *Assignment: Find Cherry.* New York: Belmont-Tower, 1969. Curt Stone works for Army counterintelligence in this paperback series completed by 1969 in 5 novels. *P*

4910. ___. *Eurasian Virgins*. Rutland, VT: Tuttle, 1968.

4911. ___. *Frogman Assassination*. Rutland, VT: Tuttle, 1968.

4912. Seymour, Gerald. *Archangel*. New York: Dutton, 1982. When a covert operation goes awry in Moscow, agent Michael Holly discovers that he will be imprisoned in one of the most brutal camps in the Siberian gulag; refusing to yield, Holly's personal revolt leads to a camp revolt by all the inmates. (See Mr. Seymour's commentary in CRAFT NOTES.)

4913. ___. *The Contract*. New York: Holt, Rhinehart, 1980. Johnny Donoghue ended his Intelligence Corps career on a bitter day in Northern Ireland when his troops on a stakeout killed a fifteen-year-old girl. Now SIS wants Johnny back in the game by having him bring an aging defector over the wires of the "chopping field" in East Germany to freedom.

4914. ___. *An Eye for an Eye*. New York: Morrow, 1988. Young Peter Holt witnesses his fiancée murdered alongside the British Ambassador to the Soviet Union, whom she has accompanied to Yalta. Holt seeks revenge against the Arab terrorist assassin and is trained for a dangerous mission into Lebanon—right into the terrorist haven of the Bekaa Valley itself.

4915. ___. *The Glory Boys*. New York: Random, 1976. PLO and IRA terrorists scheme to assassinate an Israeli atomic scientist attending a London conference and it falls to the boys and girls from MI-5 and the Mossad to safeguard him.

4916. ___. *The Harrison Affair*. New York: Summit, 1980. [*Red Fox*. London: Collins, 1979]. An employee of a multinational corporation is kidnapped in Italy, and the abductors demand the release of their leader as a condition for freeing the victim, but the Italian government refuses to revoke its policy of not dealing with terrorists.

4917. ___. *Harry's Game*. New York: Random, 1975. In Ulster, British Army agent Harry Brown must infiltrate and destroy a militant group of IRA terrorists, not knowing that his cover has been blown and that he is a target of an expert assassin.

4918. ___. *In Honor Bound*. New York: Norton, 1984. The Hind is the name of the Soviet's finest attack helicopter, the Mi-24, used with ruthless efficiency against Afghani resistance. It is Barney Crispin's job to bring one down with a Redeye missile, and return to SIS, but it is Major Medev's job to use every Soviet gunship at his disposal to prevent that from occurring.

4919. ___. *The Journeyman Tailor.* New York: HarperCollins, 1992. Seymour returns to the basic plot of *Harry's Game* by presenting a young man who is inserted by his MI-5 desk chief into one of the most dangerous strongholds of the IRA in Ireland in the isolated village of Tyrone. Although Gary Brennard is handled by the expert Cathy Parker, the duplicity and backstabbing treachery of espionage, where "touts" are immediately executed, makes Brennard vulnerable from both sides.

4920. ___. *Kingfisher.* New York: Summit, 1978. When a hijacked Russian airliner arrives in England, the authorities must decide how to rescue the passengers and handle the three Jewish refugee dissidents who have taken the plane over.

4921. ___. *The Running Target.* New York: Morrow, 1990. The chinless wonder of a new head of British SIS breaks a golden rule: never, ever send a deskman into the field because he knows too much, and if he's captured, too many agents will die and networks crumble, which is exactly what happens when a top deskman is sent out and is captured by Iranians. The question becomes: How long can he hold out? Four other Seymour narratives:

4922. ___. *At Close Quarters.* London: Collins, 1987.

4923. ___. *Field of Blood.* London: Collins, 1985.

4924. ___. *Home Run.* London: Harvill, 1989.

4925. ___. *A Song in the Morning.* New York: Norton, 1987. [*Shadow on the Sun.* New York: Jove, 1990. *P*]

4926. Shabtai, Sabi H. *Five Minutes to Midnight.* New York: Delacorte, 1980. A novelist who has just written on nuclear terrorism, Sam Sartain confronts in real life a terrorist group which has obtained an A-bomb and is holding the United States hostage.

4927. Shagan, Steve. *The Circle.* New York: Morrow, 1982. President Park of South Korea is betrayed and murdered by his lifelong friend and head of Korean Intelligence in a brothel; this man is then betrayed by a General Chung and, as the circle of conspiracy widens, a US Deputy Attorney General must negotiate between an alliance of international drug criminals and political conspirators.

4928. ___. *The Formula.* New York: Morrow, 1979. Investigator Barney Caine is drawn into the search for the elusive Genesis Formula for the synthetic fuel which kept the German Reich's war machine running even unto the eve of defeat. The movie version starred George C. Scott.

4929. ___. *Pillars of Fire.* New York: Pocket, 1989. Ex-Nazi rocket scientists are on the verge of presenting Qaddafi with an ICBM capable of delivering a warhead that will snuff Israel. Tom Lawford, journalist and former CIA agent, combines forces with Mossad to locate the missile silo before Pakistan can deliver the nuclear warhead. Three more:

4930. ___. *The Discovery.* New York: Morrow, 1984.

4931. ___. *Vendetta.* New York: Morrow, 1986.

4932. Shakar, David. *His Majesty's Agent.* New York: Harcourt, 1980. Traces the fictional espionage career of Reinhold, a mysterious German-born Jew who first appeared in Jerusalem in 1945, through the four decades of Israel's growth.

4933. Shakespeare, L. M. [L. Marguerite]. *Utmost Good Faith.* New York: St. Martin's, 1987. Arab terrorists plot against Lloyd's of London by bringing shipping to a halt in the Persian Gulf. Others:

4934. ___. *Poisoning the Angels.* New York: St. Martin's, 1993.

4935. ___. *A Question of Risk.* New York: St. Martin's, 1987.

4936. Shapiro, Lionel. *Torch for a Dark Journey.* Garden City, NY: Doubleday, 1950. The lives of an American oil tycoon, a Hungarian adventurer, an American reporter, a Czech scientist, and a Czech Communist all interweave in this tale of post-war intrigue. *

4937. Sharp, Marilyn. *Sunflower.* New York: Marek, 1979. CIA agent Richard Owen is ordered by the President to kidnap the Chief Executive's four-year-old daughter without letting the operative know when, where, how, or why. Two more by Sharp:

4938. ___. *Falseface.* New York: Marek, 1984.

4939. ___. *Masterstroke.* New York: Marek, 1981.

4940. Shaw, Bynum. *Days of Power, Nights of Fear.* New York: St. Martin's, 1980. The aide to a powerful senator in Washington, DC, during the McCarthy period must choose between helping or hindering a scheming terrorist.

4941. ___. *The Nazi Hunter.* New York: Norton, 1968. An American agent and an aging Jewish victim of Hitler's concentration camps pursue an evil SS officer who has surfaced after many years of hiding.

4942. ___. *The Sound of Small Hammers.* New York: Morrow, 1962. Examines one man's attempt to privately subsidize a propaganda operation in East Germany.

4943. Shaw, Irwin. *An Evening in Byzantium.* New York: Delacorte, 1973. Film director Jesse Craig becomes involved in a terrorist plot to destroy American cities with A-bombs aboard civil aircraft.

4944. Sheckley, Robert. *Dead Run.* New York: Dial, 1961. A gang snatches a briefcase of secret documents in Berlin, only to be relieved of it by a petty pickpocket, who is subsequently chased by secret agents who do not want him to discover or sell the contents.

4945. ___. *The Game of X.* New York: Dial, 1966. William Nye is invited by a "friend" to help trap a Russian spy.

4946. ___. *Hunter/Victim.* New York: Signet, 1988. Mostly spoofing on right-wing politics and CIA antics in central America. *PH*

4947. Shedley, Ethan I. *The Medusa Conspiracy.* New York: Viking, 1980. When the elaborate computer network controlling US military-intelligence agencies goes awry, war is threatened in the Middle East.

4948. Sheehan, Edward R. F. *The Kingdom of Illusion.* New York: Random, 1964. The sleepy Arab nation of Al Khadra becomes a strategic Cold War pawn between Russia and America. *

4949. Sheers, James C. *The Counterfeit Courier.* New York: Dell, 1961. A man given the important task of transporting vital documents turns out to be a "plant" and a crack agent must track him down to ensure the papers' return. *P*

4950. Sheffield, Charles. *Cold as Ice*. New York: TOR, 1992. A sci-fi thriller that extrapolates a contemporary theme: the interplanetary war is long over, but thousands of weapons are still orbiting the sun, and factionalist rivalries have resurfaced to threaten the world in 2067. *P*

4951. Sheldon, Sidney. *The Doomsday Conspiracy*. New York: Morrow, 1992. A naval officer investigating an "accident" in the Alps encounters more mystery.

Shepherd, Michael, pseud. *See* Ludlum, Robert

4952. Sheridan, Elsie L. *The Spy at the Villa Miranda*. By Elsie Lee, pseud. New York: Delacorte, 1967. Siri Quain accepts the companionship of a sophisticated older woman visiting Greece. Soon the lady reveals herself as more than just a fellow tourist. **y*

4953. Sherlock, John. *The Ordeal of Major Grigsby*. New York: Morrow, 1964. A retired British guerrilla leader is asked to return to Malaya and destroy Chen Tak, a young Chinese insurgent he had trained to fight against the Japanese. ***

4954. Sherman, Dan[iel] M. *Dynasty of Spies*. New York: Arbor, 1980. A terrible family stigma is passed down from OSS agent John Dancer to his son Allen, who taps the Kremlin for secrets, and to his grandson, Jessie, a CIA veteran of Vietnam who becomes a victim of the "secret wars."

4955. ___. *King Jaguar*. New York: Arbor, 1979. In South America a former French resistance fighter trails a fugitive ex-Nazi, while a seductive CIA agent falls for her colleague, who is also her target.

4956. ___. *The Mole*. New York: Arbor, 1977. Peter ("Poet") Jaeger is an unorthodox agent who investigates a friend's execution in a dual murder that puts him on the track of a deep-penetration agent inside the CIA.

4957. ___. *The Prince of Berlin*. New York: Arbor, 1983. Twenty-five-year CIA veteran Harry Rose ran Berlin his way and earned the title "prince of Berlin"; however, when an operation goes awry in East Berlin, and he's demoted, he disappears—and takes his secrets with him.

4958. ___. *Swann*. New York: Arbor, 1978. Agent Josey Swann joins forces with a grain company meteorologist to prevent a CIA plot which could cause a world famine. Three more Sherman novels:

4959. ___. *The Glory Trap*. New York: Walker, 1977.

4960. ___. *Riddle*. New York: Arbor, 1977.

4961. ___. *The White Mandarin*. New York: Arbor, 1982.

4962. Sherwood, John. *Ambush for Anatol*. Garden City, NY: Doubleday, 1953. An unwholesome figure known only as Anatol, who seems to be able to get the goods on all sorts of important people and drive them into helping him in a currency exchange racket, gets knocked off; the British agent on his trail is now forced to change gears and pursue the mysterious figure who has taken over the business. *

4963. ___. *Mr. Blessington's Imperialist Plot*. Garden City, NY: Doubleday, 1951. [*Mr. Blessington's Plot*. London: Hodder & Stoughton, 1951]. Mild-mannered Mr. Blessington of the British Treasury journeys to a Balkan country and manages to get himself kidnapped. An SIS agent is then sent in to rescue him from his Soviet abductors. *H

4964. ___. *Two Die in Singapore*. Garden City, NY: Doubleday, 1954. Another twisting spy story in which both the hero and the villain "buy it" in the end. Three other tales by Sherwood:

4965. ___. *Dr. Bruderstein Vanishes*. Garden City, NY: Doubleday, 1949. [*The Disappearance of Dr. Bruderstein*. London: Hodder & Stoughton, 1949].

4966. ___. *Murder of a Mistress*. London: Mercury, 1954. [noted as abridged edition by Bernard Drew's *Action Series & Sequels*].

4967. ___. *Vote against Poison*. London: Hodder & Stoughton, 1954.

4968. Shreve, L. G. [Levin Gale]. *The Phoenix with Oily Feathers*. New York: Moore, 1980. A retired CIA agent in Nantucket spots a Nazi war criminal whom he trails to a band of no-goods interested in the impending attempt to raise the *Andrea Doria*. Compare with Clive Cussler's *Raise the Titanic*. *

4969. Shub, Joyce L. *Moscow by Nightmare*. New York: Coward-McCann, 1973. An American female tourist, a product of suburbia, runs afoul of the KGB when she shows too much interest in dissident paintings.

4970. Siegrist, Robert R. *Rotunda.* New York: Condor, 1977. The President, Vice President, and the House Speaker all die on national television in a fusillade of bullets. The new President launches an investigation into their murders. *P*

4971. Sigel, Efrem. *The Kermanschah Transfer.* New York: Macmillan, 1973. Harold Kiels, an American engineering officer in Iran, is recruited by the Mossad to see that a shipment of arms is delivered to the Kurds, who are fighting the Iraqi Army. *

4972. Silone, Ignazio. *The Fox and the Camellias.* Trans. from the Italian. New York: Harper & Row, 1961. At a Swiss farm near Brissago, a heroine maintains a secret outpost for the wartime Italian resistance.

4973. Simmel, Johannes Mario. *I Confess.* Trans. Catherine Hutter. New York: Popular, 1977. [*Ich Gestehe Alles.* Hamburg: Zsolnay, 1968]. A Hollywood screenwriter, dying of a brain tumor, puts pen to paper to confess to his secret life as an embezzler and dupe of a Nazi plot in Germany and Austria before the war. *P*

4974. ___. *The Caesar Code.* Trans. from the German. New York: Popular, 1976. A young man searching for his father's killers encounters a mysterious code and an ODESSA plot. *P*

4975. ___. *The Cain Conspiracy.* Trans. from the German. New York: Popular, 1976. The neo-Nazi Spider Organization seeks a reporter's tapes, which tell of the group's infiltration high into the Egyptian government. *P*

4976. ___. *Dear Fatherland.* Trans. from the German. New York: Random, 1969. Set in the Berlin of the recent past, this German spy thriller concerns a sometime burglar who is involved in a plot to kidnap a man who bankrolls freedom tunnels from the East.

4977. ___. *Double Agent—Triple Cross.* Trans. from the German. New York: Popular, 1977. A ruthless master criminal who had made a devil's bargain for his freedom, the two beautiful prostitutes he used, and a pair of rival intelligence chiefs face each other in divided Berlin. *P*

4978. ___. *It Can't Always be Caviar: The Fabulously Daring Adventures of an Involuntary Secret Agent.* Trans. from the German. Garden City, NY: Doubleday, 1965. Examines the quarter-century espionage service of French agent Thomas Lieven who made friends, swapped information, and never missed a chance to increase the size of his savings account! *

4979. ___. *The Secret Protocol.* Trans. Ivanka Roberts. New York: Warner, 1987. [*Die in Dunkeln Sieht Man Nicht.* Hamburg: Droemer Knaur, 1985.] A reporter, an ex-Nazi, and an idealistic politician are the only three men in the world who know of a secret 1943 agreement between Stalin's Soviet regime and FDR's USA to divide the postwar world between them. *P*

4980. Simmons, Diane. *Let the Bastards Freeze in the Dark.* New York: Wyndham, 1980. Unless their demands are met, terrorists who have taken over the electric company in the dead of winter, threaten to freeze the city of Fairbanks, Alaska.

4981. Simmons, Geoffrey. *The Z-Papers.* New York: Arbor, 1975. Doctors must save the life of the Secretary of State, whose health is in jeopardy from a wound received while shaking hands in Chicago.

4982. Simmons, Mary K. *The Year of the Rooster.* New York: Delacorte, 1971. While visiting Tokyo, Eliot is impressed into CIA service to find a stolen list of enemy operatives obtained by his predecessor—who was killed while trying to hang onto it!

4983. Simon, Roger L. *California Roll.* New York: Villard, 1985. Private investigator Moses Wine was created in the mid-seventies and enters the world of espionage in this one; he is sent to the Silicon Valley as a security agent where one of the computer whiz kids is murdered for a special program on a floppy disk that both the Soviets and the Japanese would kill for.

4984. Simpson, George E. and Neal R. Burger. *Blackbone.* New York: Dell, 1985. A twenty-five-hundred-year-old demon is alive and well in a German POW prison camp in Montana in December of 1944. *P*

4985. ___. *Fair Warning.* New York: Delacorte, 1980. US Army G-2 officer Patrick T. Snyder is sent to Japan on a secret mission—secret even from President Harry S. Truman—to warn Japanese leaders of the potential devastation which will be caused if America must A-bomb Hiroshima.

4986. ___. *The Ghost Boat.* New York: Dell, 1976. A US submarine, which has resurfaced after being lost in the Devil's Triangle for thirty years, becomes the 1974 beat of a navel intelligence officer. *P*

4987. Simpson, Howard R. *Assignment for a Mercenary.* New York: Harper & Row, 1965. US soldier-of-fortune Michael Craig goes undercover to help overthrow an African dictatorship.

4988. ___. *The Three-Day Alliance.* Garden City, NY: Doubleday, 1971. Soviet and British intelligence operatives team up in a three-day effort to block a Chinese attempt at establishing a power base somewhere in continental Europe.

4989. Sinclair, Michael. *The Dollar Covenant.* New York: Norton, 1973. When the government of Scotland goes bankrupt, an agency known as "The Federation of American Caledonian Societies" literally takes over the country and turns it into a totalitarian state. This leaves Mockinham no choice but to plot its overthrow.

4990. ___. *Folio Forty One.* New York: Putnam's, 1972. MI-5 agent MacCraig is assigned to investigate a Scots organization called "the Norsemen," which is conspiring to set up a new nation made up of Scandinavia and Scotland.

4991. ___. *A Long Time Sleeping.* New York: Norton, 1976. Prominent US and British officials have their past pro-Nazi activities brought to light by a recovered diary, which shows that Adolf Hitler did not die in a Berlin bunker in 1945, but in a Philadelphia clinic in 1967.

4992. ___. *Sonntag.* New York: Putnam's, 1971. British operative Sonntag comes unexpectedly to public view with the discovery of some bodies in the western border area of Berlin.

4993. Sinclair, Upton B. *Dragon Harvest.* New York: Viking, 1945. Presidential secret agent Lanny Budd gathers intelligence in Vichy France and Germany from the likes of Goering and Hitler themselves. Sequel to *Presidential Agent*, below.
     A noted American "muckraker," Sinclair first made his mark on the literary scene in 1906 with the publication of *The Jungle*, which exposed evils in the meat-packing industry. Thereafter, his aim was to expose social and political evils in both his fiction and non-fiction. The series under consideration here was written to reflect the author's concern with Communism and Fascism.
*

4994. ___. *O Shepherd, Speak.* New York: Viking, 1949. Lanny Budd's adventures are chronicled through the end of the war and take him to

Nuremburg for the war crimes trials and on to Russia as President Truman's personal agent to Stalin. Sequel to *One Clear Call*, cited next. *

4995. ___. *One Clear Call.* New York: Viking, 1948. As President Roosevelt's personal agent, Budd operates in Italy, France, Germany, and Spain. In Germany he poses as a friend of top Nazis and in France, as an advisor to the forces defending Norway. Sequel to *Presidential Mission*, cited below. *

4996. ___. *Presidential Agent.* New York: Viking, 1944. Because of his life-time intimacy with men in the news, FDR chooses Lanny Budd to be his personal secret agent. In this first outing, Budd looks into the plots and counterplots undertaken in the period between Munich and Pearl Harbor. *

4997. ___. *Presidential Mission.* New York: Viking, 1947. Budd is sent to North Africa to talk with the French before the 1942 invasion and then moves on to Germany gathering all kinds of information useful to the Allies. Sequel to *The World to Win*, cited below. *

4998. ___. *The Return of Lanny Budd.* New York: Viking, 1953. In this final installment to his series, Budd is called out of retirement to become involved in the various crises of 1946-1949, involving the spy trial of his sister. *

4999. ___. *The World to Win.* New York: Viking, 1946. In this sequel to *Dragon Harvest*, cited above, agent Budd continues his espionage work for FDR, visiting Vichy France for a visit with Pierre Laval and Russia for a conversation with Stalin. *

5000. Singer, Sally M. *For Dying You Always Have Time.* New York: Putnam's, 1971. Sydelle abandons the regular tour of Italy to deliver a corpse as a favor for her lover—which gets her mixed up in the Middle East crisis and the hunt for an unknown secret weapon.

5001. Siodmak, Curt. *Hauser's Memory.* New York: Putnam's, 1968. A young doctor agrees to a CIA request to have the brain fluid of a dying scientist transferred into his own head to retain the man's secrets.

5002. Skeggs, Douglas. *The Estuary Pilgrim.* New York: St. Martin's, 1990. John Napier, art expert, discovers a Monet thought destroyed in the war; in so doing, he uncovers an international conspiracy brewing these last four decades. Two recent works by Skeggs:

5003. ___. *The Talinin Madonna*. New York: St. Martin's, 1992.

5004. ___. *The Triumph of Bacchus*. New York: St. Martin's, 1993.

5005. Slager, Nigel. *Crossfire*. New York: Atheneum, 1978. Mercenaries tackle a military dictatorship in an African nation much like Idi Amin's Uganda. Compare with Forsyth's *The Dogs of War*.

5006. Slappey, Sterling. *Exodus of the Damned*. New York: Signet, 1968. A look at how a group of ex-Nazis bribed a Jew to smuggle 500 war criminals from Germany to an enclave in South America. *P*

5007. Slater, Humphrey. *The Conspirator*. New York: Harcourt, 1948. A naive British woman marries an Army officer, little suspecting that her suave husband is actually a Red agent who is passing vital military secrets to Russia.

5008. Slater, Ian. *Air Glow Red*. New York: Doubleday, 1981. In the future, the President proposes to alleviate the terrible energy shortage by building a solar-energy station, although his scientific advisor opposes the plan as dangerous and ill-conceived; soon, opponents of the project begin dying.

5009. Slater, Nigel. *Falcon*. New York: Berkley, 1981. The CIA is ordered by the President to thwart a British-Italian venture to develop a high-tech attack plane. *P*

5010. Slattery, Jesse. *The Juliet Effect*. New York: St. Martin's, 1988. A manufactured, virulent disease hits a small New England town, and people die within three days as government agencies vie for the cause and cure.

5011. Slaughter, Frank G. *Devil's Harvest*. New York: Pocket, 1970. In a Laotian valley, two scientist discover a new formula; one wants to use it to save lives, the other desires to give it to the Red Chinese for use as a new weapon. *P*

5012. Smith, Colin. *The Cut-Out*. New York: Viking, 1981. A school teacher hunts the German terrorist whose bomb, by chance, killed his wife when it exploded.

5013. Smith, David M. *Countdown 1000*. By David Mariner, pseud. New York: Pinnacle, 1974. A civilian pilot stumbles into a scheme by nasties to assassinate the participants in a summit conference. *P*

5014. ___. *Operation Scorpio.* By David Mariner, pseud. New York: Pinnacle, 1975. MI-6 must locate a secret high-power Nazi bomb located somewhere in the Adriatic during World War II. *P*

5015. Smith, Don. *Secret Mission: Angola.* New York: Award, 1971. In this Nick Carter-Sam Durell style action series, the hero agent Phil Sherman, is called upon to smash sundry enemies in the name of American freedom, independence, and liberty. In this outing, Sherman, with a price on his head for a murder he didn't commit, tries to save a man he never met, for the future of a country that isn't his. *P*

5016. ___. *Secret Mission: Athens.* New York: Award, 1973. Bone-chilling danger and deadly treachery are the name of the game as Phil Sherman races to quash a neo-Nazi group's plans for a coup against the Greek government. *P*

5017. ___. *Secret Mission: Cairo.* New York: Award, 1974. A stolen atomic bomb hair-triggered to explode on touch is buried somewhere in Egypt and Agent Sherman must find and disarm it. *P*

5018. ___. *Secret Mission: Corsica.* New York: Award, 1973. A million Americans are doomed to die unless Phil Sherman can untangle the secret of a Chinese-controlled narcotics jungle. *P*

5019. ___. *Secret Mission: Corsican Takeover.* New York: Award, 1974. Sherman races against time to halt a Mafia plot against the unstable government on the unhappy Mediterranean island. *P*

5020. ___. *Secret Mission: Death Stalk in Spain.* New York: Award, 1972. A sunken treasure holds the key to a terrifying conspiracy and Sherman must find that key and solve the mystery. *P*

5021. ___. *Secret Mission: Haitian Vendetta.* New York: Award, 1973. Agent Sherman tracks a lethal conspiracy to that impoverished Caribbean nation. *P*

5022. ___. *Secret Mission: Istanbul.* New York: Award, 1972. If Sherman can rescue his young nymphomaniac wife from a top security prison, a Soviet masterspy promises to defect to the US. *P*

5023. ___. *Secret Mission: The Kremlin Plot.* New York: Award, 1971. Sherman becomes a moving target as agents of four powers move in for the kill in a plot involving a vital Soviet secret and a dead Russian skyjacker. *P*

5024. ___. *Secret Mission: The Libyan Contract.* New York: Award, 1974. Unless Sherman can successfully step in, conspirators will achieve their aims of assassinating a Middle East dictator and triggering a bloody international conflict. *P*

5025. ___. *Secret Mission: The Marseilles Enforcer.* New York: Award, 1974. Powerful crime lords of an international drug syndicate prove to be Agent Sherman's deadliest enemies. *P*

5026. ___. *Secret Mission: Morocco.* New York: Award, 1974. A bizarre duplicate of Ian Fleming's Goldfinger—one who has already robbed Fort Knox—is behind a world-wide plan to murder US intelligence agents. Sherman is called upon to put him out of business. *P*

5027. ___. *Secret Mission: Munich.* New York: Award, 1970. Phil Sherman travels to Europe to discover why that continent has been flooded with millions of counterfeit American dollars and runs into a neo-Nazi group, headed by former SS officers who are determined to pick up where Hitler left off. *P*

5028. ___. *Secret Mission: The Night of the Assassin.* New York: Award, 1973. Sherman walks into a trap in Albania where he has been sent to check on rumors of Chinese missile installations; in fact, he becomes involved in a plot to murder top Russians with the blame placed on the United States. *P*

5029. ___. *Secret Mission: North Korea.* New York: Award, 1970. Sherman is ordered to command a crew of thieves, perverts, and murderers on a lethal mission of reprisal. They must blow up a North Korean harbor—if Sherman can keep his men from killing each other first. *P*

5030. ___. *Secret Mission: Peking.* New York: Award, 1968. A faulty black-market computer, sold to Red China, may trigger World War III unless Sherman can do something about it. *P*

5031. ___. *Secret Mission: The Peking Connection.* New York: Award, 1974. Agent Sherman takes on Chinese death merchants in a race to stop an international doomsday plot. *P*

5032. ___. *Secret Mission: Prague.* New York: Award, 1974. Fueled with secret deliveries of Czech arms, American Black Power revolutionaries are employed as pawns in a plot to seize control of the US government. *P*

5033. ___. *Secret Mission: The Strausser Transfer.* New York: Charter, 1978. Phil Sherman must battle both a fanatical fellow operative and the KGB to recover the kidnapped daughter of scientist Herman Strausser before the latter defects to the Russians with US secrets. *P*

5034. ___. *Secret Mission: Tibet.* New York: Award, 1969. Sherman must destroy a Chinese death ray which is wrecking US and Russian space ships. His only ally—the American traitor who built the weapon for Red China in the first place! Two other Secret Mission adventures are: *P*

5035. ___. *Secret Mission: The Padrone.* New York: Award, 1971. *P*

5036. ___. *Secret Mission: The Payoff.* New York: Award, 1973. *P*

5037. Smith, Graham N. and Donna Smith. *The Nicodemus Code.* New York: Pinnacle, 1988. An ancient parchment holds the secret of a vast conspiracy that will destroy the Pope and all Christianity with it. *P*

5038. Smith, Kate Nolte. *Country of the Heart.* New York: Villard, 1988. A daughter who, with her mother, left the Soviet Union twenty years ago flies to Finland to meet her father who remained behind when it is announced that he will be conducting his own music at a festival there.

5039. Smith, Lou. *Master Plot.* New York: St. Martin's, 1977. A female SS agent is infiltrated into the KGB where, as the Chairman's mistress, she uncovers a daring plot to change the face of the earth.

5040. ___. *Primrose, the Fourth Man.* New York: St. Martin's, 1976. The heads of Britain's SIS and Scotland Yard CID Division identify a crack KGB agent within their midst, but lack the proof of his misdeeds necessary to make an arrest.

5041. ___. *The Secret of MI-6.* New York: St. Martin's, 1978. Examines the unforeseen present consequences of secrets passed to the Germans by an MI-6 agent during World War II.

5042. Smith, Martin Cruz. *Gorky Park.* New York: Random, 1981. Moscow Police Chief Arkady Renko attempts to solve a triple murder despite the constant and uncooperative presence and interference of the KGB. (Mr. Smith comments in CRAFT NOTES.)

5043. ___. *The Inquisitor: The Devil in Kansas.* By Simon Quinn, pseud. New York: Dell, 1974. This has got to be just about the most preposterous of all the postwar paperback secret agent-adventurer series yet conceived. Ex-CIA agent Frank Kelly is an Inquisitor, a member of the Vatican's espionage agency. As the Pope's hired gun, he is the only spy in the genre required to do fifteen days penance after each killing! In this outing, he travels to mid-America to investigate the human connection to reports of Satanic possessions. Others in the Inquisitor series include: *P*

5044. ___. *The Inquisitor: His Eminence Death.* By Simon Quinn, pseud. New York: Dell, 1974. *P*

5045. ___. *The Inquisitor: Last Rites for the Vulture.* By Simon Quinn, pseud. New York: Dell, 1975. *P*

5046. ___. *The Inquisitor: The Last Time I Saw Hell.* By Simon Quinn, pseud. New York: Dell, 1974. *P*

5047. ___. *The Inquisitor: The Midas Coffin.* By Simon Quinn, pseud. New York: Dell, 1975. *P*

5048. ___. *The Inquisitor: Nuplex Red.* By Simon Quinn, pseud. New York: Dell, 1974. *P*

5049. ___. *Polar Star.* New York: Random. 1989. In this sequel to *Gorky Park*, Former Moscow investigator Arkady Renko has been fleeing his KGB enemies two years, working on the "slime line" of the fish-factory ship *Polar Star*. When the body of a woman turns up in the net of an American trawler working the Bering Sea waters behind the factory ship, it becomes Renko's responsibility to discover how she got there, and homicide soon leads to espionage as Renko discovers what the real purpose of this joint Soviet-American venture really is.

5050. ___. *Red Square.* New York: St. Martin's, 1992. Renko is back in Moscow, but it's a city with new rules and rulers: greedy entrepreneurs, Mafia chieftans, black marketeers, and ex-Party commissars—all of whom are trying to get their snouts into the public trough. Arkady gets mixed up with them, and reunited with his *Gorky Park* lover, Irina Asanova, when he undertakes an investigation of an underworld banker's violent death.

5051. ___. *Stallion Gate.* New York: Random, 1986. Cruz Smith's novel blends fact and fiction in this tale of the scientists and soldiers of the Los

Alamos A-Bomb at Stallion's Gate. Among whom is tough-guy Sgt. Joe Peña, friend of Robert Oppenheimer and lover of Anna Weiss, mathematician and Oppenheimer prótegé—and quite possibly the traitor in the midst.

5052. Smith, Murray. *Devil's Juggler.* New York: Pocket, 1993. Three men for different reasons—London's head of Secret Service operations in South America, a New York detective, and a Dublin politician-terrorist—follow a path to the same destination—Bogotá.

5053. Smith, Robert A. *The Kramer Project.* Garden City, NY: Doubleday, 1976. US scientists working on a secret project in Canada are called upon to counter a new Russian computer technique for the deciphering of North American Air Defense codes.

5054. Smith, Robert C. *The Counter-Terror Mission Trilogy.* By Robert Charles, pseud. 3 vols. New York: Pinnacle, 1975. Three previously published titles (*The Hour of the Wolf, The Flight of the Raven,* and *The Scream of the Dove,* all 1975) in which Mossad agents battle PLO terrorists who threaten to blow up cities, destroy the world's supertankers, and assassinate pro-Israeli leaders. *P*

5055. ___. *Stamboul Intrigue.* By Robert Charles, pseud. New York: Roy, 1968. During the 1964 Cyprus crisis, British agents are sent to Istanbul to look into reported Soviet schemes to provoke open warfare between Greece and Turkey.

5056. Smith, Terence L. *The Money War.* New York: Atheneum, 1978. In an effort to halt a US—Israel trade deal, a band of mercenary-terrorists have sacked St. Louis, killing 1,300 people; a man whose son was killed during the atrocity vows revenge and seeks the African soldier-of-fortune who was in charge.

5057. Smith, Wilbur A. *The Delta Decision.* Garden City, NY: Doubleday, 1979. Peter Stride, commando extraordinaire, is set on a collision course with Caliph—head of the combined forces of international terrorism.

5058. ___. *Power of the Sword.* Boston: Little, 1986. Saga of two half-brothers during the turbulent thirties, who find themselves adversaries during Hitler's sweep to power.

5059. ___. *The Train from Katanga*. New York: Viking, 1965. Four white mercenaries discover their individual destinies as they take a native task force by train into the Congo interior during the 1960s civil war.

5060. Smolonsky, Marc. *Dirty Laundry*. New York: Walker, 1991. Very important officials, acting at the behest of the Oval Office, attempt to stop Carney Fitzgerald's Senate investigation of the connection between mobsters and the truckers' union.

5061. Snelling, Laurence. *The Heresy*. New York: Norton, 1973. When a film company decides to record the true-life adventures of a French Resistance outfit, its efforts are sabotaged by veterans still in the business of knocking out excessively repressive governments on the left and the right.

5062. ___. *Long Shadows*. New York: Norton, 1976. An American writer and former Germany Army officer in newly liberated Paris learn of an SS plot to kill Hitler and execute thousands of Allied POWs.

5063. Snow, C. P. *A Coat of Varnish*. New York: Scribner's, 1981. Like his contemporaries Greene and Waugh, Snow is esteemed outside the purview of espionage fiction; the author, who died in 1980, established himself as a force in the British novel with a cycle of autobiographical novels known as *Strangers and Brothers* (1940 - 1970) about a scientist and civil servant named Lewis Eliot. In this, his last novel, Snow takes a weary look at a moribund civilization through the eyes of Humphrey Leigh, a semi-retired intelligence agent investigating Lady Ashbrook's murder in Belgravia.

5064. Snyder, Gene. *Crimson Comes the Dawn*. New York: Golden Apple, 1985. About a family saga of a wealthy Prussian industrialist family at the beginning of the Nazi era. *P* One other by Snyder:

5065. ___. *The Sigma Project*. New York: Jove, 1988. *P*

5066. Sohmer, Steve. *Favorite Son*. New York: Bantam, 1987. A Washington political thriller in which a young Texas Senator is thrust into a power struggle amidst several forces who want to use him to get a President re-elected and maintain a dirty war in Central America. Another:

5067. ___. *Patriots*. New York: Random, 1991.

5068. Solzhenitsyn, Aleksandr I. *One Day in the Life of Ivan Denisovich*. Trans. from the Russian. New York: Dutton, 1963. Solzhenitsyn's breakthrough novel which examines the hardships and brutality suffered by a single prisoner in a Soviet forced labor camp administered by the secret police in Stalin's time.

5069. Southcott, Audley. *The Black General.* New York: Morrow, 1969. In London to sign a treaty which many in his African country of Dhania do not want, Oba the Protector must be guarded by British free-lance agent Fletcher Todd, who uncovers a vicious plot against the old man's life.

5070. Southwell, Samuel. *If All the Rebels Die.* Garden City, NY: Doubleday, 1966. When the US surrenders to Russia after the latter's first strike, the people of the town of Travan band together to resist the Soviet occupation.

5071. Spain, Peter. *Blood Scenario.* New York: Coward-McCann, 1980. IRA terrorists plot to take over the US by kidnapping the President and forcing the remaining government officials to do their bidding or see their leader "executed."

5072. Spang, Michael Grundt. *The Spy Who Longed for Home.* Trans. J. Basil Cowlishaw. New York: St. Martin's, 1989. [*Spionen Som Lengtet Hjem.* Oslo: Aschehoug, 1986.] Norwegian agent Peter Nordheim is trying to get to a defecting diplomat before the KGB gets to him.

5073. Spark, Muriel. *The Mandelbaum Gate.* New York: Knopf, 1965. A young Englishwoman causes difficulties when she insists on crossing the Israeli border into Jordan. *

5074. Spencer, D. J. *The Jing Affair.* New York: Funk and Wagnalls, 1965. On Taiwan, a handful of men and women attempt to thwart the plans of a powerful general for a war with Red China.

5075. Spencer, Ross H. *The Devereaux File.* New York: Fine, 1990. Author of over a dozen well-received mysteries, "Spence" Spencer occasionally forays into espionage, as in this novel. A bronze star medalist for action at Guadalcanal, Spencer's hard-boiled but dopey detective tales are frequently leavened with humor and sly self-mockery, especially in the earlier Chance Purdue novels; his latest hero is an ex-Chicago cop, Lacey Lockington, p.i., was introduced in *The Fifth Script* and returns here for action and spoofing. It seems a CIA buddy is killed just when he and Lacey plan to meet; enter a KGB vamp and a mysterious killer named Copperhead—and pretty soon, Lacey is neck-deep in trouble. Says Spencer, who writes a book a year on or about

October 15, the date he joined the service: "None of my detectives are terribly brilliant . . . They get there, but they don't get there like Sherlock Holmes did. They stumble onto it or stumble over it or fall over it and then they finally see it, sometimes with the help of a lady or a friend" (*The Vindicator* [Youngstown, OH] 9 Sept. 1990: A1). *H*

5076. ___. *Kirby's Last Circus*. New York: Fine, 1987. Birch Kirby, a loser as a private eye, winds up serving his country (CIA) by performing undercover as a catcher for the Grizzly Gulch, Illinois No Sox. *H*

5077. ___. *The Fedorovich File*. New York: Fine, 1991. Another wacky Lacey Lockington caper (along with his woman from *The Devereaux File*—the beautiful, Polish ex-KGB Natasha); this time, the ex-Chicago cop is looking for a Soviet defector in Youngstown, Ohio. *H* Other Spencer tales:

5078. ___. *Death Wore Gloves*. New York: Fine, 1988. *H*

5079. ___. *Echoes of Zero*. New York: St. Martin's, 1981. *H*

5080. ___. *The Fifth Script*. New York: Fine, 1989. *H*

5081. ___. *The Missing Bishop*. New York: Mysterious, 1985. *H*

5082. ___. *Monastery Nightmare*. New York: Mysterious, 1986. *H*

5083. ___. *The Stranger City Caper*. New York: Avon, 1980. *P*

5084. Spetz, Steven. *Yellow Rain*. Don Mills, Ont.: Worldwide, 1989. US Intelligence orders Lt. Col. Mark Schad and his three-man team into the mountains of Afghanistan to retrieve an unexploded cylinder of the Soviet's deadly new nerve gas.

5085. Spicer, William Michael. *Cotswold Manners*. New York: St. Martin's, 1989. This is the first of a tetralogy involving Lady Jane Hildreth, rich and glamorous agent for British Intelligence, Patricia Huntington, her capable, 70-year-old assistant and vintage car fanatic, and the Chief who is, according to the author, her "super intelligent and languid boss." The action moves from ancient and rural villages of the British Cotswold hills to sundry jet-setting spots in the world—Hong Kong, Western Australia, Monte Carlo, and West Palm beach. Their opponents are the IRA, the Triads (Chinese heroin gang), and Muslim fundamentalists of various stripes. In addition to the action, there is a love interest as Lady Jane moves through various romances toward the ultimate goal—the bachelor Chief.

Michael Spicer, according to *Spy Fiction*, entered Parliament as MP for Worcester South in 1974, later became Vice-Chair of the Conservative Party in 1981 and Deputy Chair in 1983 before becoming Minister for Aviation in 1984. The others in this English-countryside murder series:

5086. ___. *Cotswold Mistress.* New York: St. Martin's, 1992.

5087. ___. *Cotswold Moles.* New York: St. Martin's, 1993.

5088. ___. *Cotswold Murders.* New York: St. Martin's, 1991.

5089. ___. *Final Act.* London: Severn, 1981. Britain in the year 2005, controlled by the Soviet Union.

5090. ___. *Prime Minister Spy.* London: Severn, 1987. Hitler has a fling with a cook in the bunker in the final days; the child is born of Konstanze Monzially and placed after the war, by the colonel in Soviet Intelligence, with a couple in London; although the British know who sired him, Rupert Higginson grows up to become a popular Prime Minister, who refuses to be used by either side.

5091. Spies and More Spies. Ed. Robert Arthur. New York: Random, 1967. Although classed a young-adult collection, this anthology of twelve espionage tales contains some excellent pieces, such as Edward D. Hoch's *The People of the Peacock* & *The Spy Who Did Nothing*, Julian Symons' *The Case of XX-2*, Patricia McGerr's *Ladies with a Past*, and Eric Ambler's *Belgrade 1926*, excerpted from *A Coffin for Dimitrios.* *y

5092. Spike, Paul. *The Night Letter.* New York: Putnam's, 1978. In 1940 American agent John Jackson is ordered to stop a ruthless Nazi spymaster from delivering negatives showing FDR's romantic indiscretions into the hands of traitor's who are ready to launch a savage blackmail campaign against the President designed to halt US aid to Great Britain.

5093. Spillane, Frank M. *The Delta Factor.* By Mickey Spillane, pseud. New York: Dutton, 1965. Recaptured after his attempt to flee a maximum security prison, Morgan is offered a deal: return to jail or take on a little special mission for the CIA in the Caribbean.

5094. ___. *The Girl Hunters.* By Mickey Spillane, pseud. New York: Dutton, 1963. To avenge the death of a girlfriend, private eye Mike Hammer must take on a Communist spy ring and a master assassin known only as "the Dragon."

5095. ___. *The Killing Man.* By Mickey Spillane, pseud. New York: Dutton, 1989. Mike Hammer tangles with a drug ring, two gorgeous babes, and the CIA.

5096. ___. *Tiger Mann: Bloody Sunrise.* By Mickey Spillane, pseud. New York: Signet, 1965. While fighting his way through Iron Curtain intrigue and murder, ace secret agent Tiger Mann almost meets his master in the undressed and underhanded enemy operative, Sonia. *P*

5097. ___. *Tiger Mann: The By-Pass Control.* By Mickey Spillane, pseud. New York: Dutton, 1966. Working for the secret Martin Grady Organization, Mann must save the world from nuclear holocaust by finding a missing scientist who specializes in the miniaturization of equipment and thus has found a way to by-pass presidential control of America's doomsday arsenal.

5098. ___. *Tiger Mann: Day of the Guns.* By Mickey Spillane, pseud. New York: Dutton, 1965. Agent Mann discovers an old flame who had shot him, leaving him for dead in Austria just before the end of the war. Promising to "take care" of her, he finds a major Communist conspiracy is more pressing and thus he must "take care" of it first; or, as the old adage goes, "business before pleasure."

5099. ___. *Tiger Mann: The Death Dealers.* By Mickey Spillane, pseud. New York: Dutton, 1965. American superspy Tiger Mann outwits an ace KGB agent, deals with a plot to assassinate a Saudi Arabian oil king, and recovers a ruby from the navel of a restless bellydancer. A recent collection of the hard-nosed private eye's adventures.

5100. ___. *Mickey Spillane: Five Complete Mike Hammer Novels.* New York: Avenel, 1987.

Spillane, Mickey, pseud. *See* Spillane, Frank M.

5101. Spinelli, Marcos. *Assignment without Glory.* Philadelphia: Lippincott, 1945. Nazi spies plotting in Brazil are pursued and finally put out of business by a Brazilian-born American OSS officer. *

5102. Spinrad, Norman. *Russian Spring.* New York: Bantam, 1991. Author of a biography of Hitler banned in Germany for seven years, screenplays and novels, Spinrad chronicles the relationship of an American working for the newly created European Space Agency and a beautiful, talented Russian woman in the chaotic but promising days after Gorbachev/Yeltsin.

5103. Stackleborg, Gene. *Double Agent.* New York: Popular, 1959. Discredited CIA agent Bill Maclean joins a friend in a plot to capture a Soviet spy, turn him over to the Intelligence boys, and take a big reward. The only problem is that the Russian in question doesn't want to play along. *P*

5104. Stackman, Arthur. *Hit.* New York: Bantam, 1973. A Black CIA agent and a crack assassination team are sent to liquidate a powerful French cartel running the international heroin traffic. *P*

5105. Stacy, Ryder. *Doomsday Warrior.* New York: Zebra, 1984. Ted Rockson leads a macho band of soldiers against the Russians in this apocalyptic paperback series. *P* Two more:

5106. ___. *American Nightmare.* New York: Zebra, 1987. *P*

5107. ___. *Red America.* New York: Zebra, 1984. *P*

5108. Stagg, Delano. *The Glory Jumpers.* New York: Monarch, 1959. A group of US paratroopers are sent on a dangerous mission behind German lines during the 1944 Normandy invasion. *P*

5109. Stahl, Norman. *The Assault on Marvis A.* New York: Random, 1978. Intent on bankrupting England, IRA terrorists capture a supertanker and steer it directly at a huge British-owned North Sea oil rig.

5110. Stanford, Alfred. *The Mission in Sparrow Bush Lane.* New York: Morrow, 1963. In 1943 London, Abwehr agents are trying to penetrate the secrets of the "Mulberry" artificial harbors which will be employed to support the 1944 D-Day landings at Normandy. *

5111. Stanley, Michael. *The Swiss Conspiracy.* New York: Avon, 1976. A p.i. takes on a mission in Zurich to protect five wealthy depositors from blackmail. *P*

5112. Stanley, William. *Mr. Holroyd Takes a Holiday*. New York: Abelard-Schumann, 1966. When a cowardly former agent is asked to find a defector of his acquaintance, he finds the mission very distasteful—and dangerous. *H

Stanton, Ken, pseud. *See* Stokes, Manning Lee

5113. Stanwood, Donald. *The Seventh Royale*. The Bugatti Royale is a priceless French-made car—only six were believed made. But two men who meet in the North African desert of WW II—a race car driver and an American filmmaker—vie each other for the seventh.

5114. Stapp, Robert. *A More Perfect Union*. New York: Harper & Row, 1970. Growing up in a divided America, a Southerner finds that he is the man tapped to assassinate the President of the Confederate States of America. Shades of George Orwell, James Bond, and "Mission Impossible."

Stark, Richard, pseud. *See* Westlake, Donald E.

5115. Starrett, Vincent, ed. *The World's Great Spy Stories*. Cleveland, OH: World, 1944. Twenty tales make up this, the first American anthology of spy thriller stories; authors included are such as Eric Ambler, W. Somerset Maugham, and E. Phillips Oppenheim. *

Steel, Kurt, pseud. *See* Kagley, Rudolf

5116. Stein, Aaron, M. *The Finger*. Garden City, NY: Doubleday, 1973. The dangerous game of smuggling scientific "brains" from behind the Iron Curtain engulfs Matt Erridge, a "visitor" to Karlsbad, Czechoslovakia.

5117. Stein, Benjamin J. *The Croesus Conspiracy*. New York: Ballantine, 1977. With the general election approaching, a vast hidden network of neo-Nazis tightens its grip on an unsuspecting America. (See Mr. Stein's comments in CRAFT NOTES.) P

5118. ___. *The Manhattan Gambit*. Garden City, NY: Doubleday, 1983. In April of 1943 *Obersturmbannführer* Joachim Trattner is in a prison camp in Monterey, California when he is ordered to travel across the country to kill the one man who can tip the balance of the war—Albert Einstein.

5119. Stein, Sol. *A Deniable Man*. New York: McGraw-Hill, 1989. A trial lawyer's lover is slated to die by terrorists after her father, a US Army general, is murdered; she, however, falls in love with her mysterious bodyguard.

5120. ___. *The Touch of Treason.* New York: St. Martin's, 1985. When Soviet expert Martin fuller explodes in a ball of flame because someone put gas in a kerosene heater, suspicion falls on a brilliant young scholar who worshiped at his feet. George Thomassy, star defense attorney, finds himself defending the accused killer.

5121. Stella, Charles. *Blue Lightning.* New York: Warner, 1990. Stella, flight instructor, taught Stephen Coonts, and now follows him into the technothriller trade with a story of fighter pilots over the skies of North Vietnam.

5122. Stephens, Edward. *The Submariner.* Garden City, NY: Doubleday, 1973. A semi-derelict US diesel submarine is sent to destroy an enemy which has been mysteriously snatching American nuclear missile boats. Shades of the movie version of Ian Fleming's James Bond thriller, "The Spy Who Loved Me."
*

5123. Stern, Richard M. *I Hide, We Seek.* New York: Scribner's 1966. Before leaving America to turn over an invention which the government will not allow him to make public, a scientist, intent upon defection to a more "understanding" nation, falls in love with an American female agent.

5124. ___. *In Any Case.* New York: McGraw-Hill, 1963. A father fights to clear his son of treason charges emanating from his failure in working with an underground group in Europe during World War II.

5125. ___. *The Kessler Legacy.* New York: Scribner's, 1967. An American professor travels to Austria where he learns that a German officer whom he admires was, in fact, a dreaded SS officer responsible for thousands of deaths during the war.

5126. ___. *The Search for Tabatha Carr.* New York: Scribner's, 1960. Willard Robbins searches across Europe for a girl who stands to gain a cool one million dollars if she can be found in time.

Stevens, Carl, pseud. *See* Obstfeld, Raymond

5127. Stevens, David. *White for Danger.* Briarcliff Manor, NY: Stein & Day, 1979. A geologist finds a "lost valley civilization" in the frozen Arctic landscape, which turns out to be a top-secret Soviet installation.

5128. Stevenson, Anne. *Mask of Treason*. New York: Putnam's, 1979. Enroute to her parents' Scotland home, Fiona Grant meets a naval intelligence officer and is drawn into a ruthless espionage operation.

5129. ___. *A Relative Stranger*. New York: Putnam's, 1970. When a convicted spy is returned to England from Russia on exchange, his sister finds him a much changed man. Is he, she wonders, a plant?

5130. Stevenson, Dorothy E. *Crooked Adam*. New York: Rinehart, 1942. A crippled British schoolmaster helps break a Nazi ring attempting to circumvent all inventions of value to Britain's war effort. *

5131. Stevenson, John. *Beyond the Prize*. By Mark Denning, pseud. New York: Jove, 1978. With the assistance of a beautiful girl, spy John Marshall must unmask the unknown enemy who has baited a hellish trap for them in Northern Ireland. *P*

5132. ___. *Die Fast, Die Happy*. By Mark Denning, pseud. New York: Pyramid, 1976. John Marshall is the agent-hero of this and two other paperback adventures by Stevenson. *P*

5133. Stevenson, William. *Booby Trap*. Garden City, NY: Doubleday, 1987. Stevenson is a WW II fighter pilot whose reputation in nonfiction espionage was established by the immediate success of *A Man Called Intrepid* (followed by *Intrepid's Last Case*)—Agent "Intrepid" was to WW II espionage what Sidney Reilly was to WW I. This novel concerns a ruthless Arab leader who has acquired the best brains money can buy and plans to gain control of the Windfall Islands in the Caribbean.

5134. ___. *Eclipse*. Garden City, NY: Doubleday, 1986. A "what-if" novel about that famous prisoner in Spandau. This time, a television journalist, during an interview with Hess, discovers an alarming truth: the wacky Deputy Führer was not alone during his famous flight and that particular individual has plans for a Fourth Reich.

5135. ___. *The Ghosts of Africa*. New York: Harcourt, 1980. Paul von Lettow is a German commander of a small garrison in East Africa during WW I who flouts his orders to remain neutral and leads a small "guerilla" army against the might of the British Army.

5136. Stewart, Edward. *They've Shot the President's Daughter*. Garden City, NY: Doubleday, 1973. When the President visits his home town to lay a wreath at the grave of his parents, someone kills his daughter. Why? Was the assassin just a poor shot or was the girl really the target?

5137. Stewart, John I. M. [Innes Mackintosh]. *The Man from the Sea.* By Michael Innes, pseud. New York: Dodd, 1955. A man of deep mystery possessing scientific knowledge which can endanger world peace is the principal quarry in a chase-filled novel which employs almost every sort of vehicle known in the United Kingdom, from helicopter to ambulance.

5138. ___. *The Secret Vanguard.* By Michael Innes, pseud. New York: Dodd, 1941. In seeking to solve the death of a minor poet, Scotland Yard detective John Appleby travels to the Scottish Highlands where he receives directions conveyed through an invented stanza added to Swinburne's "Forsaken Garden" and becomes involved with Nazi spies and the recovery of a missing mathematician and a secret formula. Generally regarded as a highly literate contribution to the genre. *

5139. Stewart, Kerry. *The Concorde: Airport '79.* New York: Jove, 1979. US and Soviet athletes flying to the Moscow Olympics on the Anglo-French SST are unaware it carries a device which could destroy them all. Paperback novelization of the movie screenplay. *P

5140. Stimson, Robert G. and James Bellah. *The Avenger Tapes.* New York: Pinnacle, 1971. Agent Case must find a set of stolen tapes which show the trajectory patterns for the experimental Avenger missile. P

5141. Stine, Hank. *The Prisoner.* New York: Ace, 1970. Although the inhabitants were allowed physical comforts, they were never allowed to leave a Disneylandish village for people who knew too much about critical government projects; another from the TV series which starred Patrick McGoohan. *P

Stivers, Dick, pseud. *See* Pendleton, Don and Laurence R. Payne

5142. Stokes, Donald H. *Captive in the Night.* New York: Coward-McCann, 1951. An ex-American soldier finds himself wrapped up in a tale of Cold War intrigue in the Algeria still occupied by France. *

5143. Stokes, Manning Lee. *The Aquanauts: Cold Blue Death.* By Ken Stanton, pseud. New York: Macfadden-Bartell, 1970. In this nautical spy series, a secret organization known as the Aquanauts operates out of the Navy Department under the leadership of a crusty old admiral responsible only to the

Chief of Naval Operations and the President. Its chief agent is Lt. Cmdr. William Martin, a superior diver known as "the Tiger Shark," who can usually be found either chasing the girls or boating about in the ultra-secret mini-submarine in which he performs all of his missions. In this outing, the Aquanauts are pitted against the Russians and dive into espionage and murder in the mysterious waters of the Bermuda Triangle. *P*

5144. ___. *The Aquanauts: Evil Cargo.* By Ken Stanton, pseud. New York: Macfadden-Bartell, 1973. Bill Martin is ordered to stop the Mafia from using a stolen Cuban submarine to run drugs in the Caribbean. *P*

5145. ___. *The Aquanauts: Operation Sargasso Secret.* By Ken Stanton, pseud. New York: Macfadden-Bartell, 1971. What is really causing all of those mysterious disappearances in the Devil's Triangle? That is the question handed to Bill Martin and the Aquanauts. *P*

5146. ___. *The Aquanauts: Operation Sea Monster.* By Ken Stanton, pseud. New York: Macfadden-Bartell, 1974. A mysterious sea creature seems to be doing nasty things to innocent seafarers, and the Tiger Shark is called in to "dispose" of the problem. *P*

5147. ___. *The Aquanauts: Seek, Strike and Destroy.* By Ken Stanton, pseud. New York: Macfadden-Bartell, 1971. The Tiger Shark must put a stop to underwater Chinese espionage off the west coast of the United States. *P*

5148. ___. *The Aquanauts: Stalkers of the Sea.* By Ken Stanton, pseud. New York: Macfadden-Bartell, 1972. Bill Martin must take on the James Bond of the KGB in a series of titanic land and sea encounters. *P*

5149. ___. *The Aquanauts: Ten Seconds to Zero.* By Ken Stanton, pseud. New York: Macfadden-Bartell, 1970. The Aquanauts must locate the deadly new Russian underwater missile being deployed against American nuclear submarines. *P*

5150. ___. *The Aquanauts: Whirlwind beneath the Sea.* By Ken Stanton, pseud. New York: Macfadden-Bartell, 1972. Who is behind the unnatural eruption that rose from the seabed of the Indian Ocean and killed a half million Bengalis? Others in this series include: *P*

5151. ___. *The Aquanauts: Operation Deep Six.* By Ken Stanton, pseud. New York: Macfadden-Bartell, 1972. *P*

5152. ___. *The Aquanauts: Operation Mermaid.* By Ken Stanton, pseud. New York: Macfadden-Bartell, 1974. *P*

5153. ___. *The Aquanauts: Operation Steelfish.* By Ken Stanton, pseud. New York: Macfadden-Bartell, 1972. *P* Stokes also authored, under house pseudonym Paul Edwards, a series of action thrillers involving John Eagle, "The Expeditor"; one of these:

5154. ___. *Operation Weatherkill.* By Paul Edwards, pseud. New York: Pyramid, 1975. *P*

5155. Stone, David. *The Tired Spy.* New York: Putnam's, 1962. Paul Porlock, agent 776H of MI-13 British Counterintelligence, has gone on vacation to Italy to escape his harried home life—nagging wife, kids, dogs, debts, etc. The only problem is that his colleagues do not believe that he is simply off on holiday. *H*

5156. Stone, Robert. *A Flag for Sunrise.* New York: Knopf, 1981. Tecan is a miserable banana republic sweltering under revolutionary discontent and a dictator. Frank Holliwell, anthropologist, is gently coerced by the CIA to go there and monitor the situation. Bruce Weber, in "An Eye for Danger," in the *New York Times*, writes of Stone's life and work, saying that "it's fitting that he reveres Samuel Beckett above all writers. 'For his humor,' Stone says, 'in the primal situation in which we all find ourselves.' . . . [It is best set out] in *A Flag for Sunrise*, a dense, detailed, hardly Beckett-like book that is nonetheless infused with the buzz of sinister fate" (19 Jan. 1992: 20).

5157. Stone, Scott. *Spies.* New York: St. Martin's, 1980. Agents converge at the Bangkok mountaintop refuge of a conman-turned-guru in search of a precious object hidden by a desperate thief.

5158. Stone, Todd. *Kriegspiel: A Novel of Tomorrow's Europe.* Novato, CA: Presidio, 1992. In the Germany of the near-future, a neo-Nazi group takes over, led by a charismatic general who fancies himself another hitler; opposing him is a small group of American forces.

5159. Stovall, Walter. *Presidential Emergency.* New York: Dutton, 1978. An aide is caught in the middle when he learns that the US President may be about to defect to Red China.

Stratton, Thomas, pseud. *See* DeWeese, Thomas G. and Robert S. Coulson

5160. Street, Bradford. *In Like Flint.* New York: Dell, 1966. Employing his wonderful cigaret lighter, Agent Flint seeks to destroy a nasty plot to change the world's weather, thereby controlling the world. Paperback version of the movie screenplay. *P*

5161. Streib, Dan. *Counter Force.* Greenwich, CT: Fawcett, 1983. A paperback original series starring Counter Force Agent Steve Crown. *P*

5162. ___. *Hotline: Moscow at Noon Is the Target.* By Paul Richards, house pseud. New York: Award, 1973. This "hotline espionage" series features "détente" between Soviet and American agents. In this episode, the operatives of the two sides work to head off a madman who has this title in mind. *P*
     Streib, along with George Snyder and Chet Cunningham, coauthored this and two other paperback adventures of undercover agent Grant Fowler, who works for the President:

5163. ___. *Hotline: One of Our Spacecraft Is Missing.* By Paul Richards, house pseud. New York: Award 1973. *P*

5164. ___. *Hotline: The President Has Been Kidnapped.* By Paul Richards, house pseud. New York: Award 1974. *P*

5165. Streiber, Whitley and James W. Kunetka. *Warday.* New York: Holt, 1984. Post-apocalyptic tale of the aftermath of a nuclear confrontation on 28 October 1988 that took the lives of seven millions of Americans in thirty-six minutes.

5166. Strong, Michael. *The Wolves Come Down from the Mountain.* New York: Walker, 1979. A brutal terrorist group—"the Wolves"—in the French Alps kidnaps the mistress of an SIS agent, forcing him to mount a daring rescue.

5167. Stuart, Anthony, pseud. *Force Play.* New York: Arbor, 1979. Russian defector and U.N. interpreter Vladimir Gull heads to Chile to free his former love—only to discover that she has disappeared as the result of an espionage plot.

5168. ___. *The London Affair.* New York: Arbor, 1981. In London, Gull is drawn into a romantic liaison with the pretty editor of a radical magazine, but becomes enmeshed in murder and espionage against the Crown.

5169. ___. *That Man Gull.* New York: Arbor, 1979. [*Snap Judgment.* London: Macdonald, 1977]. Vladimir Alexandrovich Chaikov has adjusted to the West quite well since leaving the Russian Army, unofficially, after the Hungarian invasion of 1956. But someone forces him at gunpoint to write an inflammatory interpretation of a UN speech, and he pursues the conspirators to Romania for the answer why. More tales of Gull, that Russian defector, ladies' man, UN interpreter, and *bon vivant*, are:

5170. ___. *Midwinter Madness*. New York: Arbor, 1979.

5171. ___. *Russian Leave*. New York: Arbor, 1981.

5172. ___. *Vicious Circles*. New York: Arbor, 1979.

Stuart, Ian, pseud. *See* Maclean, Alistair

5173. Stuart, Warren. *The Sword and the Net*. New York: Morrow, 1941. Love for an American girl causes a Nazi spy to change sides. *

5174. Sugar, Andrew. *Israeli Commandos: The Alps Assignment*. New York: Manor, 1975. Crack Mossad and Israeli Army agents pursue a group of dangerous PLO terrorists to a mountain hideout in the Alps, from where they plan a series of lightning raids into Europe. *P* Others in this short, blood-soaked series include:

5175. ___. *Israeli Commandos: The Aswan Assignment*. New York: Manor 1974. *P*

5176. ___. *Israeli Commandos: The Fireball Assignment*. New York: Manor 1974. *P*

5177. ___. *Israeli Commandos: The Kamikaze Plot*. New York: Manor 1975. *P*

5178. Suhl, Yuri. *Uncle Misha's Partisans*. New York: Four Winds, 1974. A Jewish youth joins a Russian partisan band in fighting the Germans on the Eastern Front early in World War II. **y*

5179. Sullivan, Tim. *Glitter Street*. New York: Wade, 1979. FBI agent Hugh McBride tracks down IRA terrorists who have escaped a siege in the New York diamond district with a billion dollars worth of jewels.

5180. Sulzberger, C. L. *The Tooth Merchant.* Chicago: Quadrangle, 1973. Starting out ugly, this tale portrays an Armenian crook who uncovers an astonishing secret and attempts to sell it to world leaders in 1953. *P*

Swift, Bryan, house pseud. *See* Knott, Will C. and Arthur Wise

5181. Swiggett, Howard. *The Hidden and the Hunted.* New York: Morrow, 1951. An American spy battles a Russian agent for the recovery and possession of the papers of a Czech economist. *

5182. ___. *Most Secret, Most Immediate.* Boston: Houghton, 1944. In 1941 France to contact the underground, Garret Maynard, G-2 chief of an Allied supply mission, barely escapes with his life from an encounter with the Gestapo. *

5183. Symons, Julian. *The Broken Penny.* London: Carroll & Graf, 1953. A British agent is brought out of retirement to smuggle a leader back into a country to bring about a revolution. A recent mystery:

5184. ___. *Something like a Love Affair.* New York: Mysterious, 1992.

5185. Szulc, Tad. *Diplomatic Immunity.* New York: Simon & Schuster, 1981. With wide experience as an author and lecturer on the CIA and foreign policy affairs, especially in Latin America, Szulc's novel deals with a woman ambassador to a South American dictatorship who tries to steer between policy extremes: the CIA wants the current government to remain in power; the White House and State Department want to end it.

T

5186. Tack, Alfred. *The Spy Who Wasn't Exchanged.* Garden City, NY: Doubleday, 1969. In Moscow, James Mason and Anne Blane find out they have to play both sides of the espionage game knowing that if caught, it will be a long time before they ever see home again.

"Taffrail," pseud. *See* Dorling, Henry T.

5187. Talmy, Shel. *The Web.* New York: Dell, 1981. [*Hunter Killer.* London: Pan, 1981]. Four SS officers have been set up with new identities and Swiss bank accounts in preparation for the Fourth Reich. On their trail is the man who as a four-year-old saw her raped and then both parents killed. *P*

5188. Tanenbaum, Robert K. *Depraved Indifference.* New York: Signet, 1989. Courtroom-thriller author and former New York District Attorney Tanenbaum turns to espionage in this tale of Croatian terrorists who have hijacked a plane and demand to be flown to then-Yugoslavia; to make their point, a bomb placed in a locker at Grand Central Terminal kills a police officer trying to disarm it; more perplexing yet is the stonewalling of the case by higher-ups: it seems there is an ex-Nazi in the woodpile pulling strings. *P* A recent Butch Karp mystery:

5189. ___. *Reversible Error.* New York: Dutton, 1992.

5190. Tanner, Mack. *Target: Subic Bay.* New York: Zebra, 1992. A sub commander must fight to save the US Naval Base in the Philippines against terrorists.

5191. Tanous, Peter. *The Earhart Legacy.* New York: Simon & Schuster, 1979. Half a billion dollars in gold is at stake as the result of a complicated series of events surrounding an old woman's claim that she is the famous aviatrix and that she has detailed knowledge of the hush-hush "Project Bluejay."

5192. ___ and Paul Rubinstein. *The Petrodollar Takeover.* New York: Putnam's, 1975. Oil-rich Arabs scheme to take over General Motors.

5193. Tapply, William G. *Death at Charity Point.* New York: Scribner's, 1984. Detective fiction writer Tapply's first novel involves a Boston lawyer's rich client, one missing and one dead son, and a link to a neo-Nazi group.

Tarrant, John, pseud. *See* Egleton, Clive

5194. Tasker, Peter. *Silent Thunder.* New York: Kodansha, 1992. Financial thriller involving right-wingers in the US and Japan who plot to take over the world.

5195. Taylor, Anthony. *Hour of the Scorpion.* New York: Jove, 1982. One hundred thousand fans are packed into the stadium in Madrid awaiting the World Cup soccer matches; a terrorist calling himself the Scorpion, however, has other plans for them: a stolen crate of ultra-secret Cobor nerve gas is going to be released in their midst. *P*

5196. Taylor, Charles D. *Boomer.* New York: Pocket, 1990. Captain Wayne Newell is a commander of a nuclear attack sub patrolling beneath the Pacific; he is also a traitor who has convinced the crew of the USS *Pasadena* that America is at war and must destroy "enemy" subs disguising their sounds to resemble the Americans. *P*

5197. ___. *Shadow Wars*. New York: Pocket, 1992. Two of the world's most elite fighting units, the US Navy SEALS Team Six (*see* Richard Marcinko) and the KGB's Hostage Rescue Unit, join forces to fight a shadow army organized by the embittered Communist elite in the aftermath of the Soviet Union's collapse. Pitted against them is the new strike force headed by two former enemies: Capt. Bernie Ryng and Spetsnaz Col. Paul Voronov. *P* Others:

5198. ___. *Choke Point*. New York: Charter, 1986. *P*

5199. ___. *Counterstrike*. New York: Jove, 1988. *P*

5200. ___. *Deep Sting*. New York: Pocket, 1991. *P*

5201. ___. *First Salvo*. New York: Jove, 1985. *P*

5202. ___. *Show of Force*. New York: St. Martin's, 1980.

5203. ___. *Silent Hunter*. New York: Jove, 1987. *P*

5204. ___. *The Sunset Patriots*. New York: Jove, 1989. *P*

5205. ___. *War Ship*. New York: Jove, 1989. *P*

5206. Taylor, Ray W. *The Doomsday Square*. New York: Dutton, 1966. An international crisis results when American plans for a new secret weapon are leaked to the Soviets.

5207. Taylor, Thomas. *A-18*. New York: Crown, 1967. A US Army Special Forces team is sent into North Vietnam to ambush a group of Red Chinese officials who are taking over the Hanoi government of Ho Chi-minh.

5208. Taylor, Walker. *The Admiral's a Spy*. London: Hodder & Stoughton, 1941. An intrepid British counterintelligence officer must examine a case of an admiral who is suspected of leaking vital defense secrets to the Germans. *

5209. Teilhet, Darwin L. *The Big Runaround*. New York: Coward-McCann, 1947. At a California space-rocket research lab, an industrial spy is forced to swallow a microfilm capsule containing top secret moonshot intelligence—a capsule that will kill him if it is not removed within 15 hours.

Darwin Teilhet was a successful exponent of the spy thriller alone as well as with his wife Hildegarde, who also wrote separately on occasion. Their heyday was World War II and the immediate post-war years.

5210. ___ and Hildegarde Teilhet. *The Assassins*. New York: Coward-McCann, 1946. An effort is made to establish a rug factory in the Communist section of China which can be employed as a cover for the espionage work of SIS agent Sam Hook. *

5211. ___. *The Double Agent*. New York: Coward-McCann, 1945. Agent Hook must ferret out an enemy "mole" deep within the folds of the OSS cloak. *

5212. ___. *Odd Man Plays*. Boston: Little, 1944. In London during the war, MI-5 saves an American airman who has innocently been drawn into an Abwehr espionage plot. *

5213. ___. *The Rim of Terror*. New York: Coward-McCann, 1950. Enroute to Seattle, Elizabeth Whitehill picks up a man and gets mixed up with a group of alien agents attempting to capture her rider for a mock trial which is to be held in an unnamed totalitarian country. * One more by Darwin Teilhet:

5214. ___. *Russian Flag over Hawaii: The Mission of Jefferey Tolamy*. Honolulu, HI: Mutual, 1986.

5215. Teilhet, Hildegarde. *Private Undertaking*. New York: Coward-McCann, 1952. A young poet travelling from Nice to Belgrade becomes involved with Communist agents, three beautiful women and a cigaret lighter which emits poison gas. *

5216. Telfair, Richard. *The Bloody Medallion*. New York: Fawcett, 1959. Wryly humorous espionage adventures of Monty Nash beginning with this novel. P Telfair, along with Peter Leslie, W. A. Ballinger and others, also contributed to the John Drake character ("Secret Agent") books which became the television series; Telfair's first book, below, belongs to the "Danger Man" series:

5217. ___. *Good Luck, Sucker*. New York: Fawcett, 1961. Agent Nash cleans up an espionage ring operating out of Rome and San Juan and which is dedicated to obtaining US defense data. P

5218. ___. *Scream Bloody Murder.* New York: Fawcett, 1960. Monty Nash loses yet another partner and must once again track down the assassins, breaking an espionage plot in the process. *P*

5219. ___. *The Slavers.* New York: Fawcett, 1961. Nash must save an Arab princess from slave traders. *P*

5220. ___. *Target for Tonight.* New York: Dell, 1962. *P*

5221. Templeton, Charles. *The Kidnapping of the President.* New York: Simon & Schuster, 1975. A CIA operative must rescue the US President, who has been captured by a band of Latin American revolutionaries.

5222. Terlouw, Jan. *Winter in Wartime.* Trans. from the Dutch. New York: McGraw-Hill, 1976. Michael and his fellow villagers join the Dutch resistance to battle the German occupiers during World War II. *

5223. Terman, Douglas. *First Strike.* New York: Scribner's, 1979. This novel was first published in 1978 by Vermont crossroads press as *The Three Megathon Gamble.* An ambitious US senator hires as his personal pilot an ex-combat pilot named Brian Loss, who is drawn into a dangerous espionage game.
    Pilot, military intelligence officer, and launch crew commander for the first ICBMs, Terman, besides being a writer of technothrillers, skippers yachts and flies sailplanes. (See Mr. Terman's commentary in CRAFT NOTES.)

5224. ___. *Enemy Territory.* New York: Bantam, 1991. A captured Vietnam pilot breaks down under ruthless interrogation by a KGB officer; years later the KGB officer is a general selected to destroy America's space program with a scheme that will spread nuclear contamination across the US, but the man who opposes him is the pilot he once broke down.

5225. ___. *Shell Game.* New York: Simon & Schuster, 1985. Like *Topaz*, Terman's novel mixes political intrigue, romantic lust, and global intrigue with a Cuban setting; the focus of world attention will soon be on the surface missiles in the aftermath of Castro's revolution—what matters to the Kremlin is the underground silo complex that will call President Kennedy's bluff. One more:

5226. ___. *Free Flight.* New York: Scribner's, 1980.

5227. Thayer, Charles W. *Checkpoint.* New York: Harper & Row, 1964. Harry Harding, deputy to US Representative Schuyler, becomes involved in Soviet-American military intrigue and a German underground activity which blows up into a crisis at the Berlin Wall.

5228. ___. *Moscow Interlude*. New York: Harper & Row, 1962. A tale of espionage and intrigue centering around an American attaché and his Russian wife, whose brother has met a strange death for reasons not revealed by Soviet authorities.

5229. Thayer, James Stewart. *The Earhart Betrayal*. New York: Putnam's, 1980. Nine years after aviatrix Earhart disappears, OSS agent Joe Snow traces her route and discovers the truth behind her loss. *

5230. ___. *The Hess Cross*. New York: Putnam's, 1977. Considered a defector from Hitler's inner circle, Rudolph Hess has actually flown to England in 1941 as the first step in an elaborate Abwehr plot to capture Allied atomic genius Enrico Fermi. *

5231. ___. *Pursuit*. New York: Crown, 1986. As the bombs fall, Berlin intelligence tries one final measure to turn the tide: veteran Afrika Korps soldier Kurt Monck is a lone-wolf killer now a POW in America. The plan: stalk and kill FDR. Monck holds his own to Forsyth's "Jackal."

5232. ___. *The Stettin Secret*. Putnam's, 1979. The *Graf Zeppelin*, Hitler's lone air carrier and pride of the Reich Navy, is a derelict hulk in a Polish harbor in 1947; now Stalin wants it for the Soviet Navy, but CIA agent Andrew Jay's job is to sink it before it gets to Leningrad. Another:

5233. ___. *Ringer*. New York: Crown, 1988.

5234. ___. *S-Day: A Memoir of the Invasion of England*. New York: St. Martin's, 1990.

5235. Theroux, Paul. *The Family Arsenal*. Boston: Houghton, 1976. A discredited ex-American consul becomes involved with four apprentice IRA terrorists operating in London.

5236. Thomas, Craig. *Emerald Decision*. By David Grant, pseud. Rev. ed. New York: Harper & Row, 1987. First published in 1980 in England under the pseudonym David Grant, Thomas's novel is about Operation Emerald, Churchill's own plan to forestall a German invasion of Britain via Ireland—a secret plan buried deep but which an American researcher uncovers after forty years.
     Robin W. Winks (see BIBLIOGRAPHY) says that Thomas is a better novelist than Robert Ludlum. Thomas is quoted in McCormick & Fletcher's *Spy Fiction* as saying that he writes "'espionage adventures' rather than spy

novels" (241). His novels, tending toward the technothriller—in fact, he may rightly claim to share the distinction of initiating the subgenre along with Tom Clancy—have been widely popular ever since *Firefox*—the film tie-in starring Clint Eastwood enhanced this (US, 1982). Amazingly, Thomas has no technical or military training; he taught English after graduating from University College, Cardiff, Wales, in 1967. (See Mr. Thomas' commentary in CRAFT NOTES.)

5237. ___. *Firefox*. New York: Holt, 1977. The Soviets have a secret fighter plane, the MIG-31, certain to alter the balance of power because it uses a sophisticated mind-technology so that the pilot's brain waves actually activate and guide the weapons system. The US sends a fighter pilot, now a burnout from his Vietnam days, to Russia to steal the plane.

5238. ___. *A Hooded Crow*. New York: HarperCollins, 1992. Patrick Hyde crosses swords with ruthless businessmen, mercenaries, smugglers, and double agents in this tale of high-tech smuggling in the world after Desert Storm.

5239. ___. *Jade Tiger*. New York: Viking, 1982. When a defecting senior Chinese official is plucked out of Hong Kong harbor, he tells the British that the man next to the West German Premier in importance is actually the key to a Soviet plot to discredit the West German government, veteran British agent Kenneth Aubrey is ordered to find out the truth about Zimmermann.

5240. ___. *The Last Raven*. New York: Harper & Row, 1990. The crash of a military transport plane during the Soviet withdrawal from Afghanistan coupled with an eye-witness report from Patrick Hyde, Britain's top operative, exposes one thread of a vast conspiracy of powerful men who do not want to see the world moving toward peace.

5241. ___. *Moscow 5000*. By David Grant, pseud. New York: Holt, 1980. A terrorist bomb threat at the 1980 Moscow Olympics baffles both the CIA and the KGB.

5242. ___. *Playing with Cobras*. New York: HarperCollins, 1993. Agent Patrick Hyde is beguiled out of retirement by his former superior, Peter Shelley, to go to India to assist the agent who had saved his life—now being held by authorities for the murder of his mistress, a woman who also happens to be the wife of the Indian Prime Minister.

5243. ___. *Rat Trap*. New York: Bantam, 1976. A hijacking at Heathrow results in a massive manhunt for an escaped Arab terrorist who is to be bartered for the passengers' freedom.

5244. ___. *Wildcat.* New York: Putnam's, 1988. [*All the Grey Cats.* London: Collins, 1988]. A sequel to *Lion's Run,* this novel begins with Sir Kenneth Aubrey's career at its nadir; distrusted by his superiors, he is given all the mickeymouse assignments until he accepts an assignment to exfiltrate the son of his worst enemy—General Brigitte Winterbach of East German Intelligence. More thrillers by Thomas:

5245. ___. *Firefox Down.* New York: Bantam, 1983.

5246. ___. *Lion's Run.* New York: Bantam, 1985. [*The Bear's Tears.* London: Joseph, 1985].

5247. ___. *Sea Leopard.* New York: Viking, 1981.

5248. ___. *Snow Falcon.* New York: Holt, 1980.

5249. ___. *Winter Hawk.* New York: Morrow, 1987.

5250. ___. *Wolfsbane.* New York: Holt, 1978.

5251. Thomas, Gordon. *Deadly Perfume.* New York: HarperCollins, 1992. The deadly "perfume" is a lethal poison held by an insane terrorist who, in the aftermath of the Gulf War, demonstrates its effectiveness by killing everyone in a Small South African town. David Morton, brilliant Mossad agent, must stop him from holding the world hostage, but he has only seven days to do it.

5252. Thomas, Leslie. *Orange Wednesday.* New York: Delacorte, 1968. When US, British, French, German, and Russian leaders plan to meet and sign a treaty unifying both Germanies, certain conspirators try to prevent the agreement.

5253. Thomas, Michael M. *Green Monday.* New York: Wyndham, 1980. An Arab minister and a financial genius manipulate world oil prices to a point where Western economies are threatened with collapse.

5254. ___. *The Ropespinner Conspiracy.* New York: Warner, 1987. Codenamed "Ropespinner" from Lenin's dictum that capitalism will sell the rope with which it will be hanged, the Soviets commence a vast conspiracy to destroy America through its financial heart that begins with a devastating banking revolution on Wall Street.

5255. Thomas, Paul. *The Spy*. New York: Tower, 1965. In order to receive further government grants, an American science professor agrees to turn an upcoming private visit to East Germany into a mission during which he will help a Russian physicist to defect. *P*

5256. Thomas, Ross. *The Backup Men*. New York: Morrow, 1971. [rpt. *The Backup Men: A McCorkle and Padillo Novel*. New York: Harper, 1986]. The further adventures of Padillo and McCorkle, who act as "backup men" for a pair of famous British secret agents. *H*

5257. ___. *The Brass Go-Between*. By Oliver Bleeck, pseud. New York: Morrow, 1969. Professional mediator Philip St. Ives is not the only party interested in recovering a brass shield—the prize possession of the new African state of Jandola—stolen while on loan to a Washington, DC museum.

5258. ___. *Briarpatch*. New York: Simon & Schuster, 1984. A government agent investigates his sister's murder in a car bombing and learns of a conspiracy.

5259. ___. *Cast a Yellow Shadow*. New York: Morrow, 1967. While Agent McCorkle tends a wounded Agent Padillo, the latter's wife is kidnapped by a group of men who want to turn Padillo into their own private assassin. *H*

5260. ___. *Chinaman's Chance*. New York: Simon & Schuster, 1978. Artie Wu and Quincy Durant are assisted by colorful friends in their challenge to a powerful Mafia boss, late of the CIA, and pretender to the throne of China involved in a southern California murder.

5261. ___. *The Cold War Swap*. New York: Morrow, 1966. [*Spy in the Vodka*. London: Hodder & Stoughton, 1967; also rpt. *The Cold War Swap: A McCorkle and Padillo Novel*. New York: Harper, 1986]. Mac McCorkle, barkeep in West Berlin, has a partner named Michael Padillo, who uses the job as a cover for his espionage activities. When Washington decides to sacrifice Padillo to recover a pair of defectors, McCorkle must go to his friend's aid. *H*

5262. ___. *The Eighth Dwarf*. New York: Simon & Schuster, 1979. Assisted by a beautiful woman and a Rumanian dwarf, ex-OSS agent Minor Jackson vies with Soviet, British, and other American agents in a contest to locate assassin Kurt Oppenheimer.

5263. ___. *The Fools in Town Are on Our Side*. New York: Morrow, 1971. The director of US intelligence in the Far East retires and upon returning home, becomes involved in a municipal election. *H*

5264. ___. *If You Can't Be Good*. New York: Morrow, 1973. An historian seeks the answer to a Senator's mysterious resignation.

5265. ___. *The Money Harvest*. New York: Morrow, 1975. About a conspiracy of criminals and government figures.

5266. ___. *The Mordida Man*. New York: Simon & Schuster, 1981. While CIA man Chubb Dundee seeks the kidnappers of the President's brother, who believe "the Company" has abducted their leader, the real culprit, a convicted computer genius, is waiting his chance to bargain his way back into America.

5267. ___. *No Questions Asked*. By Oliver Bleeck, pseud. New York: Harper & Row, 1976. Philip St. Ives is on a case involving a book held ransom for $250,000.

5268. ___. *Out on the Rim*. New York: Mysterious, 1987. Terrorism expert Booth Stallings is supposed to bribe a Communist Filipino guerrilla leader with a cool $5 million.

5269. ___. *Protocol for a Kidnapping*. By Oliver Bleeck, pseud. New York: Warner, 1971. Another St. Ives caper involving the ransoming of the US Ambassador in Yugoslavia.

5270. ___. *The Singapore Wink*. New York: Morrow, 1969. A one-time movie stunt man and a retired SIS agent go to Singapore to find a man the former has dreamed was dead.

5271. ___. *Twilight at Mac's Place*. New York: Mysterious, 1989. Steadfast "Steady" Haynes, agency freelancer, dies at 57 and leaves behind four people to mourn him—not counting whoever blackmailed the agency into burying Steady at Arlington National Cemetery. Three of the four are immediately killed, and suddenly there's a scramble on to find out whether it all has to do with Steady's memoirs—a 400+ page ms., totally blank. Other Thomas novels that combine the mystery of detection with the "political thriller" are:

5272. ___. *The Fourth Durango*. New York: Mysterious, 1989.

5273. ___. *Missionary Stew*. New York: Simon & Schuster, 1983.

5274. ___. *The Porkchoppers*. New York: Morrow, 1972.

5275. ___. *The Seersucker Whipsaw*. New York: Morrow, 1967. A recent Artie Wu & Quincy Durant suspense novel concerning a billionaire's murder, his frame-up, and two dead hypnotists:

5276. ___. *Voodoo, Ltd*. New York: Mysterious, 1993.

5277. Thomey, Tedd. *The Prodigy Plot*. New York: Warner, 1987. President Reagan's newest advisor is a child prodigy codenamed Chicken Little, who can absorb vast quantities of military, political, and intelligence data and produce near-perfect recommendations; however, a handful of top executives known as Secret team target her for assassination when she proves that recent American foreign-policy blunders could have been avoided. *P*

5278. Thompson, Anne A. *Message from Absalom*. New York: Pocket, 1976. Agent Susannah is pursued by the KGB as she attempts to get a message out of Russia to the President of the United States. *P*

5279. ___. *The Romanov Ransom*. New York: Simon & Schuster, 1978. Racing against time and the KGB in an effort to effect the release of a colleague, a CIA agent and his beautiful assistant attempt to contact various Russian exile groups to obtain a collection which consists of a dozen Faberge-made Easter eggs, the lost treasure of the last Czar, Nicholas II.

5280. Thompson, Arthur L. B. *All Men Are Lonely Now*. By Francis Clifford, pseud. New York: Coward-McCann, 1967. An East German discloses a secret laser-guided missile and the revelation is investigated by British security.
  Thompson was in the industrial business before World War II, serving as a rice merchant and later as a trade journalist. His career as a writer of spy thrillers began rather late in life, but having won prizes and big sales on both sides of the Atlantic, this career remained his new line of work until his death in mid-1975. Thompson's stories were noted for their realistic characterization. *

5281. ___. *Amigo, Amigo*. By Francis Clifford, pseud. New York: Coward-McCann, 1973. A free lance British writer follows up a tip and travels to the interior of Guatemala in search of an ex-SS officer who once ran the Auschwitz concentration camp.

5282. ___. *Another Way of Dying.* By Francis Clifford, pseud. New York: Coward-McCann, 1964. Kidnapped by terrorists on Sicily, British demolitions expert Neal Forrester is forced to take part in the planning and execution of a rescue of another member of the band held in prison.

5283. ___. *The Blind Side.* By Francis Clifford, pseud. New York: Coward-McCann, 1971. A priest out of favor with the church for his Biafra activities, Richard Laurence gets mixed up with his brother Howard's hidden activities on behalf of MI-5.

5284. ___. *Drummer in the Dark.* By Francis Clifford, pseud. New York: Harcourt, 1976. This author's final work. For a stiff price, a greedy trucker agrees to transport detonators for the IRA.

5285. ___. *The Hunting Ground.* By Francis Clifford, pseud. New York: Coward-McCann, 1964. A photographer is the sole witness to a plane crash shrouded in official silence.

5286. ___. *The Naked Runner.* By Francis Clifford, pseud. New York: Coward-McCann, 1966. Successful British businessman Sam Laker reluctantly agrees to act as an unpaid agent for the West while on a visit to East Germany; taken together with his son, he is forced upon death of the youngster, to become a coldblooded Communist assassin. Frank Sinatra starred in the movie version of this, the author's most successful work. *

5287. ___. *A Wild Justice.* By Francis Clifford, pseud. New York: Coward-McCann, 1972. In Northern Ireland, a group of IRA terrorists attempt to hold out against advancing British troops as their colleagues escape; two members of the band are picked up for questioning and one, a girl named Clodagh, manages to escape. Two more Thompson novels are:

5288. ___. *Act of Mercy.* By Francis Clifford, pseud. New York: Coward-McCann, 1960.

5289. ___. *Goodbye and Amen.* By Francis Clifford, pseud. New York: Coward-McCann, 1974. [*The Grosvenor Square Goodbye.* London: Hodder & Stoughton, 1974].

5290. Thompson, David. *Broken English.* New York: Holt, 1987. Veteran IRA killer Martin Burke wants out of the Troubles, out of Northern Ireland, but he has one small job to do first; little does he know that this one job will put him in the center of a plot to assassinate Prince Charles and son, due in Belfast in a week.

5291. Thompson, Stephen. *Recovery.* New York: Warner, 1980. Racing agents of three other nations, a specialized and secret US rescue team is sent to recover a plane which has been downed in an unacknowledged war zone. *P

5292. Thompson, Steven L. *Bismarck Cross.* New York: TOR, 1985. Two German officers have their own reunification plot: it's codenamed Operation Blood & Iron, and it will be up to agent Max Moss to stop them from taking over 18 nuclear warhead sites and firing their payloads at Warsaw Pact and NATO cities unless, that is, the superpowers agree to leave Germany within twenty-four hours. *P* Two others by this author:

5293. ___. *Airburst.* Toronto: Worldwide, 1988. *P*

5294. ___. *Top End.* Toronto: Worldwide, 1989. *P*

5295. Thomson, June. *The Long Revenge.* Garden City, NY: Doubleday, 1975. An anonymously written letter to a retiring SIS agent sets forth a desperate hunt for a threatening killer.

5296. Thornbury, Ethel M. *We've Been Waiting for You.* Indianapolis: Bobbs-Merrill, 1947. The FBI assists a former AAF flyer to solve a friend's death and the mystery of its connection to a group of four pursuers, one of whom is recognized as an ex-Nazi. *

5297. Thorne, E. P. *The Bengal Spider Plan.* London: Wright, 1961. Major ("Brains") Cunningham works for Department S as an agent; his foe, Koi San, figures prominently in several adventures. Some others:

5298. ___. *Chinese Poker.* London: Wright, 1964.

5299. ___. *The Caribbean Affair.* London: Wright, 1966.

5300. ___. *Codeword "Proton."* London: Wright, 1968.

5301. ___. *The Moscow File* London: Wright, 1967.

5302. ___. *Operation Dragnet.* London: Wright, 1966.

5303. ___. *Red Bamboo.* London: Wright, 1954.

5304. ___. *The Shadow of Dr. Ferrari.* London: Wright, 1950.

5305. ___. *Sinister Sanctuary.* London: Wright, 1949.

5306. ___. *The Smile of Cheng Su.* London: Wright, 1946.

5307. ___. *Zero Minus Nine.* London: Wright, 1964.

5308. Thorp, Duncan. *Over the Wall.* New York: Pinnacle, 1973. Five men and a woman fight among themselves and plot a Caribbean revolution against a brutal dictator whose rule has been absolute for years. *P*

5309. Thorp, Roderick. *Nothing Lasts Forever.* New York: Norton, 1979. At the height of the Christmas rush, Los Angeles cop Joe Leland finds himself in a deadly fight with German terrorists who have taken over the Klaxon Oil Building.

5310. Thurburn, Rose. *The Wilderness Is Yours.* New York: Morrow, 1950. Slade, a ruthless, self-seeking government official, encounters the mysterious Patkov during a war between two minor unnamed European nations. *

5311. Thurman, Steve. *Night after Night.* New York: Monarch, 1959. A naval intelligence officer seeks an assassin aboard a ship bound for Java. *P*

5312. Tickell, Jerrard. *High Water at Four.* Garden City, NY: Doubleday, 1966. Court-martialed and cashiered, Commander Millerton is given a berth aboard the yacht of a Greek millionaire and is led into a tight chase when he enters an Iron Curtain port where women are used to ensnare foreigners. *

5313. ___. *Island Rescue.* Garden City, NY: Doubleday, 1952. A satire in which a little-occupied SIS in 1940 engineers the removal of a cow from one of the Channel islands occupied by the Germans.

5314. ___. *The Villa Mimosa.* Garden City, NY: Doubleday, 1961. British agent Major Charles Addison in the months just before D-Day arranges a daring plan to spirit anti-Hitler German officers and their "friends" out of a French brothel they have been employing as a meeting place.

Tiger, John, pseud. *See* Wager, Walter

5315. Tillman, Barrett. *Warriors.* New York: Bantam, 1990. A US Navy pilot is commissioned by the Saudis to train an elite corps of fighter pilots, but is not told the object is to attack Israel. *P* Two more by Tillman:

5316. ___. *Dauntless: A Novel of Midway and Guadalcanal.* New York: Bantam, 1992. *P*

5317. ___. *The Sixth Battle: A Novel of the Next War.* New York: Bantam, 1992. *P*

5318. Tine, Robert. *State of Grace.* New York: Viking, 1980. A corrupt cardinal who administers the Vatican finances plots the newly elected Pope's murder.

5319. Tippette, Giles. *The Mercenaries.* New York: Delacorte, 1976. An elite mercenary force from Rhodesia raids rebel bases in nearby Zambia.

5320. Tobino, Mario. *The Underground.* Trans. from the Italian. Garden City, NY: Doubleday, 1966. This story concerns "one segment" of the Italian resistance movement during World War II.

5321. Tonkin, Peter. *The Coffin Ship.* New York: Crown, 1990. A saboteur kills the captain and crew of the supertanker *Prometheus* with an arranged "accident"; now the new captain must find him and the bomb hidden belowdecks or 250,000 tons of crude oil will spill.

5322. ___. *The Fire Ship.* New York: Crown, 1992. A husband and wife aboard a high-tech sailing vessel in the Indian Ocean encounter a derelict freighter with crew and armaments cargo missing and shortly after learn of the hijacking of the flagship of a tanker fleet in the Persian Gulf.

5323. Topol, Allan. *A Woman of Valor.* New York: Morrow, 1980. Mossad agent Leora Baruch pursues a nasty Arab terrorist who has assassinated her colleague, Dan Yaacobi.

5324. Topol, Edward. *Red Snow.* New York: Dutton, 1987. *Gorky Park*-influenced tale of a murder investigation of three sexually-mutilated Russians above the Arctic Circle; here, however, Renko's part is played by Militia Lieutenant Anna Kovina, who follows the corpses' trail backwards to its source, and discovers, as does Renko, the Kremlin has access to more than one corrupt American millionaire along with its other dirty secrets of sex scandals and payola.

5325. ___. *Russkaia Semerka.* Moscow: Molodaia, 1992. As yet an untranslated fiction about the Soviet occupation in Afghanistan, the title of which translates as *Russian Seventh.* Topol's collaboration:

5326. ___ and Fridrikh Neznanskii. *Red Square.* New York: Berkely, 1984.

Torr, Dominic, pseud. *See* Pedler, John B. F.

5327. Toulmin, June. *Courier to Peking.* New York: Farrar, 1972. Without his knowing it, the scientist-leader of a US delegation to a Peking meeting is being used by the CIA to smuggle a secret message to China's leaders.

5328. Tracy, Don. *Naked She Died.* New York: Pocket, 1962. A routine security investigation at a US military base turns up murder and subversion. *P*

5329. Tralins, Bob. *The Chic Chic Spy.* New York: Belmont-Tower, 1966. A sexy and dangerous British female spy, who must have studied under Modesty Blaise, is ordered to find a nasty who is masquerading as an important figure in the garment business. *P* One other by this author is:

5330. ___. *The Miss from SIS.* New York: Belmont-Tower, 1966. *P*

Tranter, Nigel, pseud. *See* Tredgold, Nye

5331. Tredgold, Nye. *Cable from Kabul.* By Nigel Tranter, pseud. London: Hodder & Stoughton, 1967. A pro-Western intelligence group attempts to spirit a defecting Soviet scientist out of China via Afghanistan.

5332. ___. *The Man behind the Iron Curtain.* By Nigel Tranter, pseud. London: Hodder & Stoughton, 1959. A reserve Royal Navy officer is sent into the Baltic with orders to rescue a defecting Polish scientist off the Pomeranian coast. *

5333. Tregaskis, Richard. *China Bomb.* New York: Washburn, 1967. The famed combat correspondent and author of *Guadalcanal Diary* tells of activities of a small group of American agents assigned to destroy Red China's first H-bomb, which the "Commies" are planning to drop on the US Seventh Fleet off Vietnam. *

5334. Trenhaile, John. *Blood Rules.* New York: HarperCollins, 1992. Colin Raleigh and his fourteen-year-old son are aboard a flight to Sydney when it is hijacked by a beautiful Muslim woman, Leila Hanif, and a band of Shiite terrorists demanding that Iranian prisoners be released in exchange for the plane and its hostages; she also happens to be the boy's own estranged mother. (See Mr. Trenhaile's commentary in CRAFT NOTES.)

5335. ___. *Kyril*. London: Severn House, 1981. [rpt. *The Man Called Kyril*. London: Congdon & Weed, 1983; serialized on British TV as *Codename Kyril* in 1988]. This novel began Trenhaile's career in spy fiction, the first of his first trilogy (the second concerns the Chinese secret service), and one that features the remarkable General Povin, a Christian and a homosexual, who passes KGB material to Sir Richard Bryant in British SIS.

5336. ___. *The Gates of Exquisite View*. New York: Signet, 1989. Saga of English capitalist Simon Young, his Hong Kong enterprise, and the secrets in his supercomputer. *P*

5337. ___. *The Mah-Jongg Spies*. New York: Dutton, 1986. Simon Young must keep his corporation thriving and intact amidst the powerplays of China and the USSR as the countdown to 1997 looms—the date China will receive its vastly important financial center in Hong Kong—because the Russians would like to see China inherit financial ruins rather than a dynasty which can upset the balance of power, a plot which the Mah-Jongg Brigade, Chinese Central Intelligence's elite unit headed by Qui Quianwei, must thwart.

5338. ___. *Nocturne for the General*. London: Bodley Head, 1985. The third part of General Povin's trilogy. The General's betrayal by ambitious Colonel General Boris Frolov, his subordinate from Dzerzhinsky Square, lands him in a gulag where he experiences more torture and interrogation while the British scheme to save him, or kill him, before he finally breaks down and confesses all he knows.

5339. ___. *The Scroll of Benevolence*. London: Collins, 1988. The "Club of Twenty" is the most powerful of Hong Kong's trading companies and financial empires, and the "Scroll of Benevolence" is their mutual scheme for removing their vast fortunes when the Chinese armies roll in to take back Hong Kong before the end of the nineties.

5340. ___. *A View from the Square*. London: Bodley Head, 1983. The second part of the trilogy concerning General Povin. Frolov, never having believed that a man named Michaelov was the traitor, tries to expose Povin and is confronted by the dreaded KGB head himself, Kazin, who tells his cringing subordinate that he knows of Povin's treachery: "I've known it for years." More terrorist fiction:

5341. ___. *Acts of Betrayal.* New York: HarperCollins, 1991.

5342. ___. *Krysalis.* New York: Harper & Row, 1990.

Trevanian, pseud. *See* Whitaker, Rodney

5343. Trevor, Elleston. *The Freebooters.* Garden City, NY: Doubleday, 1967. With only their weapons, skill, and snarling pride to keep them alive, eight hard-bitten angry professional mercenaries fight in a half-savage new African nation on behalf of the established order.

5344. ___. *The Kobra Manifesto.* By Adam Hall, pseud. Garden City, NY: Doubleday, 1976. British secret agent Harry Quiller, working out of his London bureau, races across Europe attempting to infiltrate a group of international terrorists, known as KOBRA, in order to learn where and when it is planning a summit meeting.

5345. ___. *The 9th Directive.* By Adam Hall, pseud. New York: Simon & Schuster, 1967. Agent Quiller is assigned to protect a British big-shot who is scheduled to visit Bangkok.

5346. ___. *The Peking Target.* New York: Playboy, 1983. [*Pekin Target.* London: Collins, 1981]. Quiller comes face to face with killers of a Korean organization that is trying to louse up the Sino-American friendship. *P*

5347. ___. *Quiller Bamboo.* New York: Morrow, 1991. Quiller in Hong Kong is assigned to secure a Chinese dissident's safety, but the dissident wants to go to Tibet, not London.

5348. ___. *Quiller Barracuda.* By Adam Hall, pseud. New York: Morrow, 1990. Agent Quiller is in Florida on a mission that invokes elements of *The Manchurian Candidate*; here, someone is using mind-control technology to plant ideas in the minds of key aides in the Presidential race that could swing the balance of power between East and West.

5349. ___. *Quiller KGB.* By Adam Hall, pseud. London: Allen, 1989. Agent Quiller in Berlin is brought into the post-Cold War era when he is assigned to help Colonel Yasolev of the KGB prevent an assassination plot against Premier Gorbachev.

5350. ___. *The Quiller Memorandum.* By Adam Hall, pseud. New York: Simon & Schuster, 1965. Like le Carré, Trevor [born Trevor Dudley-Smith] attempts to depict realistically in his Quiller series the mundane existence of real-life spies. In this famous tale, published in Great Britain as *The Berlin Memorandum*, Agent Quiller is assigned to ferret out the headquarters of a neo-Nazi group running amuck in Berlin. Quiller does not care for his automaton assignments in the big intelligence apparatus, but carries them out anyway, knowing in this case that the ODESSA-like group will grow stronger in the future even if he succeeds in taking it down a few pegs during this outing.

5351. ___. *Quiller Meridian.* By Adam Hall, pseud. New York: Morrow, 1993. In this post-Cold War tale, Quiller boards the Trans-Siberian Express on the heels of an agent whose plot, unless foiled, will result in the end of democracy as we know it.

5352. ___. *Quiller's Run.* By Adam Hall, pseud. London: Allen, 1981. Quiller, once more fed up, quits the agency and goes freelance to the Far East. where he is supposed to foil a dragon lady's evil plot.

5353. ___. *Quiller Solitaire.* By Adam Hall, pseud. New York: Morrow, 1992. Quiller must penetrate a Red Army faction in Germany and foil their plot.

5354. ___. *The Scorpion Signal.* By Adam Hall, pseud. Garden City, NY: Doubleday, 1980. Quiller's ninth mission is to rescue an ally who has escaped from the torture of the infamous Lubyanka prison in Moscow.

5355. ___. *The Sinkiang Executive.* By Adam Hall, pseud. Garden City, NY: Doubleday, 1978. Having been fired for paying off a personal debt, Quiller is soon back on board for a final mission against huge odds—one which takes him into the very center of political intrigue in Russia.

5356. ___. *The Striker Portfolio.* By Adam Hall, pseud. New York: Simon & Schuster, 1969. Quiller must learn why three dozen supersonic Striker aircraft have all crashed, killing their pilots and destroying any evidence of sabotage.

5357. ___. *The Tango Briefing.* By Adam Hall, pseud. Garden City, NY: Doubleday, 1973. Quiller races enemy agents to find the mystery cargo of a plane which has crashed in the Sahara; unfortunately, he does not know exactly what he is seeking.

5358. ___. *The Warsaw Document.* By Adam Hall, pseud. Garden City, NY: Doubleday, 1971. Quiller arrives in Warsaw in the midst of an important conference and while the underground is planning a revolt. While he seeks contact with that unhappy group, he is shadowed by the KGB. More Quiller tales from the pen of Trevor:

5359. ___. *The Mandarin Cypher.* By Adam Hall, pseud. Garden City, NY: Doubleday, 1975.

5360. ___. *Northlight: A Quiller Mission.* By Adam Hall, pseud. London: Allen, 1985. [*Quiller.* New York: TOR, 1985. *P*].

5361. ___. *The Sibling.* By Adam Hall, pseud. New York: Playboy, 1979.

5362. Trevor, James. *The Savage Game.* New York: Award, 1967. One-eyed killer-hero John Savage is a primitive Charlie Muffin but one British Intelligence can count on. *P* Two more:

5363. ___. *The Savage Height.* New York: Award, 1969. *P*

5364. ___. *The Volcanoes of San Domingo.* London: Inner Circle, 1984.

5365. Trew, Antony. *The Antonov Project.* New York: St. Martin's, 1979. To probe its mysteries, British naval intelligence infiltrates two agents aboard a new Soviet aircraft carrier. *

5366. ___. *The Chalk Circle.* New York: St. Martin's, 1989. Three people against guerillas and wild animals in the Mozambique wilds create the plot in this adventure thriller.

5367. ___. *Two Hours to Darkness.* New York: Random, 1963. Unless he can be stopped the mad Captain Shadde of H.M. nuclear submarine *Retaliate* will launch sixteen missiles deep into the USSR. *

5368. ___. *Ultimatum.* New York: St. Martin's, 1978. Scotland Yard Special Branch and Mossad agents work against a seventy-two-hour deadline set by terrorists, who have placed an A-bomb somewhere in London and are threatening to detonate it unless Palestine is made an independent state under PLO control. *

5369. ___. *The Zhukov Briefing.* New York: St. Martin's, 1976. Agents from around the globe are drawn to a new Russian nuclear submarine which has beached itself on the Norwegian coast. *

5370. Trotter, William R. *Winter Fire.* New York: Dutton, 1993. Trotter has authored a history on the year of war between Finland and Germany between 1939—1940 and uses his knowledge for a backdrop in a tale about a youthful Nazi officer, a brilliant symphonic conductor, who embarks for Finland with a mission to convert the Fins to allies of the Reich.

5371. Truman, Margaret. *Murder at the Kennedy Center.* New York: Random, 1989. Truman is the daughter of President Harry Truman, founder of the CIA; ironically, his daughter takes a sharp view of the CIA's contemporary policies. A writer of mostly murder mysteries, she usually chooses Washington locales of power as settings; this one concerns the mysterious death of a Presidential candidate's aide.

5372. ___. *Murder in the CIA.* New York: Random, 1987. When her best friend—a CIA courier and literary agent—is murdered, Collette Cahill is assigned to investigate; the trail leads to a double agent working inside the agency.

5373. ___. *Murder at the National Cathedral.* New York: Ballantine, 1990. A newlywed couple is pursued by someone who leaves bodies in churches on two continents.

5374. ___. *Murder in the Supreme Court.* New York: Arbor, 1982. The chief clerk of the court is found sitting in the chair of the Chief Justice of the US—with a hole in his head.

5375. ___. *Murder on Embassy Row.* New York: Arbor, 1984. A captain of detectives in the nation's capital wants to know why there's a cover-up occurring when high government officials try to scuttle his investigation of the British Ambassador's poison-murder. Other Truman "Murder" books:

5376. ___. *Murder at the FBI.* New York: Arbor, 1985.

5377. ___. *Murder in Georgetown.* New York: Arbor, 1986.

5378. ___. *Murder at the Pentagon.* New York: Arbor, 1992.

5379. Tuccile, Jerome and Philip Sayetta Jacobs. *The Mission.* New York: Fine, 1991. Deputy Führer Rudolph Hess's clandestine mission is the plot element in this tale of a journalist who gets too close to the secret behind a downed German pilot's crash in the Scottish countryside and subsequent spiriting away to the Tower of London.

5380. Tucker, Alan J. *Alias Man.* By David Craig, pseud. New York: Popular, 1969. When a British agent assumes Ray Rickman's identity and is subsequently murdered, Rickman becomes involved in an intricate web of murder and espionage. *P*

5381. ___. *Contact Lost.* By David Craig, pseud. New York: Stein & Day, 1970. In a future where the US is isolated from world politics, Agent Rickman of the Soviet-Bonn Group must prevent a Bay of Pigs type invasion by the Free Britain Group.

5382. ___. *Message Ends.* By David Craig, pseud. New York: Stein & Day, 1969. "Negotiate Now" propaganda demanding that Britain capitulate to the Soviet-Bonn Bloc threatens her economy and military independence.

5383. ___. *A Walk at Night.* By David Craig, pseud. New York: Stein & Day, 1971. SIS agents Stephen Bellecroix and Sheila Roath outwit the KGB and succeed in smuggling two dissident Soviet writers out of their homeland.

5384. ___. *Young Men May Die.* By David Craig, pseud. New York: Stein & Day, 1970. An adventurer pops up here and there recruiting other mercenaries for an unspecified operation. British agents Bellecroix and Roath are ordered to track him down and learn what is coming off.

5385. Tucker, John Bartholomew. *The Man Who Looked Like Howard Cosell.* New York: St. Martin's, 1989. Spy spoof in which a television agent, who used to work for military intelligence, is coerced into helping out after he witnesses a murder. *H*

5386. Tucker, Wilson. *A Procession of the Damned.* Garden City, NY: Doubleday, 1964. A decade after a vital theft from an Army depot in Germany, "Boatman" Ross is offered $1 million for a quick trip across the US and the use of his vessel in the Caribbean.

5387. ___. *The Warlock.* Garden City, NY: Doubleday, 1968. A story of electronic espionage in which an American agent/radio specialist is dropped into his native Poland to set up a secret transmitter which will advise the US of the spy satellites Russia is orbiting.

5388. Tute, Warren. *The Cairo Sleeper.* London: Constable, 1976. Mado is in Beirut assigned to protect a wealthy naturalized citizen of England, when he gets himself involved with the KGB, a Kim Philby-like traitor from the old days, and an ongoing plot to overthrow the government of Egypt.

5389. ___. *A Matter of Diplomacy.* New York: Coward-McCann, 1970. The wife of a British defector comes to Athens as the guest of a big shipping tycoon and there contacts the head of her husband's former "department," who has been demoted over the affair.

5390. ___. *The Powder Train.* London: Dent, 1972. Introduces series character George Mado, who is sent behind the Iron Curtain to destabilize governments. Other Tute tales:

5391. ___. *Next Saturday in Milan.* London: Constable, 1975.

5392. ___. *The Resident.* London: Constable, 1974.

5393. ___. *The Tarnham Connection.* London: Dent, 1973.

5394. Tyler, Alison. *Chase the Storm.* New York: Dell, 1987. A series featuring Jennifer Heath in tales that mix romance and espionage. *P* Two more "Chase" tales:

5395. ___. *Chase the Sun.* New York: Dell, 1987. *P*

5396. ___. *Chase the Wind.* New York: Dell, 1987. *P*

Tyler, W. T., pseud. *See* Hamrick, Samuel J.

U

Underwood, Michael, pseud. *See* Evelyn, John M.

5397. Unkeefer, Duane. *Gray Eagles.* New York: Morrow, 1986. At a California air show in 1976 a formation of Messerschmitts out of the clear blue sky attacks the P-51 Mustangs below!

5398. Upton, Robert. *The Golden Fleecing.* New York: St. Martin's, 1979. A reporter falls into the bad graces of the CIA when he probes a Swiss financial concern called "Off Shore Mutual."

5399. Uris, Leon. *Topaz.* New York: McGraw-Hill, 1967. The head of the KGB's anti-NATO bureau defects to the West and reveals the existence of a Russian espionage network in Paris, codenamed "Topaz," which included in its membership a senior French official and a close advisor to the French President, Charles de Gaulle.

If one were searching the product of spy writers for a novel based on fact and realism which had an impact far beyond its own merits as a novel, one could stop right here. *Topaz* made an extremely big splash in intelligence circles when published because it was based on a series of actual incidents involving the actual "Sapphire" spy ring which did, in fact, operate in France along lines suggested in the story. When SDECE head Philippe Thyraud de Vosjoli was ordered back to Paris after a liaison with CIA, he resigned and accused the French government of being riddled by the KGB. The resulting hubbub caused intense embarrassment to the French, who upon investigation found a spy in Georges Paques, disruption of CIA-SDECE cooperation, and intense glee at Lubianka KGB headquarters.

5400. ___. *The Angry Hills.* New York: Random, 1956. While attempting to smuggle out vital papers, an American adventurer is caught in wartorn Greece between the retreating Allies and the advancing Germans.

5401. ___. *The Haj.* Garden City, NY: Doubleday, 1984. This sequel to *The Exodus* features Haj ("leader") Ibrahim of Tabah, a man who must take his family on a dangerous odyssey from their homeland to a Jericho refugee camp festering with terrorism and violence.

5402. ___. *Mitla Pass.* New York: Bantam, 1989. A writer's conflicts with his two loves and his heritage during the 1956 Sinai War.

5403. Usher, Frank H. *The KGB Is Here.* By Charles Franklin, pseud. London: Hale, 1972. A romance between his wife and a writer causes the Soviet secret service to hustle an embassy official out of Britain—not out of any fear that the diplomat will discover the liaison but because the woman has turned the author into an effective KGB "sleeper" agent.

5404. Ustinov, Peter. *The Disinformer.* New York: Arcade, 1989. Noted actor Ustinov's novella consists of two tales: *The Disinformer,* about a retired British spy who, out of boredom, concocts a game for his colleagues involving Arab terrorists and is hoist by his own petard; the other, *A Nose by Any Other Name,* is about a girl whose operation to reduce her enormous nose leads her to an epiphany about her heritage.

V

5405. Vacha, Robert. *Phantoms over Potsdam.* London: Everest, 1975. British journalist Robert Craig uncovers a Foreign Office conspiracy designed to reunite the two Germanies, but which could more easily bring on World War III. *P*

5406. ___. *A Spy for Churchill.* London: Everest, 1974. While in the guise of a captured officer given the freedom of the German camp, a British intelligence officer manages to smuggle out a steady flow of information of use to Churchill and the British Army in their need for insight into the strategy of Field Marshal Erwin Rommel. *P*

5407. Vailland, Roger. *Playing for Keeps.* Trans. from the French. Boston: Houghton, 1948. Follows the activities of five Free French Maquis irregulars who took part in the 1944 struggle for the liberation of Paris. *

Valentine, Douglas, pseud. *See* Williams, Valentine

5408. Valin, Jonathan. *Dead Letter.* New York: Dodd, 1981. Private eye Harry Stoner gets mixed up with missing top-secret documents.

5409. Vallance, Douglas. *The Man in the Lubianka.* London: Hale, 1971. SIS agents race to free an important personage held in Moscow's KGB headquarters.

5410. Vance, Charles C. *A Grave for a Russian.* New York: Avon, 1985. The CIA's top agent, born in the Ukraine, is on his way to Russia to get information from a colonel, who also happens to be the man who tortured and imprisoned his parents. *P*

5411. Van der Post, Laurens. *Flamingo Feather.* New York: Morrow, 1955. Pierre de Beauvillers searches Africa for a friend and ends up in a Communist-inspired plot to make the Black natives rise against their white rulers.

5412. Van Greenway, Peter. *Take the War to Washington.* New York: St. Martin's 1975. The US aircraft carrier *Carolina* has been hijacked by a tough band of battle-weary veterans in the Far East, who shape a course for America and a showdown with the President's war policy.

5413. Vanhee, Gregory G. *The Shooter*. New York: Richardson, 1988. In 1954 the CIA recruits a sniper from the ranks of the Marine Corps to assassinate a North Korean general. Another by Vanhee:

5414. ___. *Night Strike*. New York: Avon, 1990. *P*

5415. Van Lustbader, Eric. *Zero*. New York: Random, 1988. Philip Doss, agency man and trained killer, is murdered in Japan; his son is recruited by the agency to investigate and discovers a mysterious assassin named "Zero," warring clans, and forty-year-old conspiracies.

Two of those below, *Miko* and *The Kaisho*, feature series character Nicholas Linnear, half-Caucasian, half-Oriental hero; *Jian* and *Zero* feature another cycle and character, China Maroc:

5416. ___. *Angel Eyes*. New York: Fawcett, 1991. *P*

5417. ___. *Black Blade*. New York: Fawcett, 1993. *P*

5418. ___. *Miko*. New York: Villard, 1984.

5419. ___. *Jian*. New York: Villard, 1985.

5420. ___. *The Kaisho*. New York: Pocket, 1993.

5421. Van Oradell, John. *Ragland*. Cleveland, OH: World, 1972. When the CIA discovers the Chinese may be trying to sneak nuclear devices into America, President Jeffrey Ragland comes disastrously close to starting a war on what eventually proves to be misinformation.

5422. Van Rjndt, Philippe. *The Tetramachus Collection*. New York: Putnam's, 1976. The author mixes stereotype of espionage/thriller fiction between one set of book covers: a secret organization, a Nazi hunter, a dying Pope, a millionaire Marxist publisher, a crooked financier, a crack undercover agent, a beautiful woman assassin, and, of course, the whole alphabet soup of the world's government intelligence agencies—all here competing for the Tetramachus Collection.

5423. ___. *Blueprint*. New York: Putnam's 1977. The head of the GRU defects to the West in an effort to get at a plot and to learn why one Soviet spy after another is mysteriously dying. Others:

5424. ___. *Come, Follow Me.* By Philip Michaels, pseud. New York: Avon, 1983.

5425. ___. *Grail.* By Philip Michaels, pseud. New York: Avon, 1982.

5426. ___. *Samaritan.* New York: Dial, 1983.

5427. ___. *The Trial of Adolph Hitler.* New York: Summit, 1978.

5428. Veraldi, Gabriel. *Spies of Good Intent.* Trans. from the French. New York: Atheneum, 1969. A secret international body of scientists sends out an agent who, in cooperation with the SDECE, disrupts an American plan to insert instruments into the heads of various people and thereby control whole populations.

5429. Vicas, Victor and Victor Haim. *The Impromptu Inspector.* New York: Abelard-Schuman, 1971. After accidentally killing a French policeman, an American escapes to Israel *sans* passport. There he is blackmailed into helping ODESSA in their game of killing off top Jewish officials.

5430. Vidal, Gore. *Burr.* New York: Random, 1973. Reconstructs the intriguing life of America's third Vice-President along the lines of a political thriller. *HI*
    In the early 50's, Vidal wrote three mysteries under the alias Edgar Box, which have been recently reprinted:

5431. ___. *Death before Bedtime.* New York: Armchair, 1991.

5432. ___. *Death in the Fifth Position.* New York: Armchair, 1991.

5433. ___. *Death Likes It Hot.* New York: Vintage, 1979.

5434. Von Elsner, Don. *Countdown for a Spy.* New York: Signet, 1966. A carefree vacationer in exotic Hawaii, CIA agent David Denning is suddenly ordered back on duty and is charged with finding a super-secret weapon which is being developed somewhere on the island. *P* Denning also troubleshoots in the corporate spying arena; some adventures:

5435. ___. *Don't Just Stand There, Do Something.* New York: Signet, 1962. *P*

5436. ___. *Just Not Making Them like They Used to.* New York: Signet, 1961. *P*

5437. ___. *Pour a Swindle through a Loophole.* New York: Belmont, 1964. *P*

5438. ___. *You Can't Do Business with Murder.* New York: Signet, 1962. *P*

5439. ___. *Who Says a Corpse Has to Be Dull.* New York: Signet, 1963. *P*

5440. Vonnegut, Kurt. *Mother Night.* New York: Harper & Row, 1966. One of America's most respected writers, Vonnegut's novels touch upon espionage, as they do science fiction, but his are novels of ideas that use elements of espionage to make their points. Howard W. Campbell, Jr. is an American playwright living in Germany before the outbreak of World War II. He is persuaded to remain in Germany and pose as a radio propagandist—a cover he maintains after the war in obscurity until Israeli agents kidnap him for his war crime. Two other Vonnegut novels that use certain elements of espionage fiction are:

5441. ___. *Slaughterhouse Five, or the Children's Crusade.* New York: Delacorte, 1969.

5442. ___. *Deadeye-Dick.* New York: Delacorte, 1982.

5443. Vorhies, John R. *Pre-Empt.* Chicago: Regnery, 1967. The captain of a US submarine offers the world an ultimatum: form an international council and surrender all nuclear weapons to the wreckers or he will loose his eighteen Poseidon missiles. *

W

5444. Wacht, Leo. *Mission to Warsaw.* London: Brown, Watson, 1960. During World War II, a pair of British SOE officers are sent to Warsaw to find a brilliant Polish scientist who is hiding from the SS. *

5445. Waddell, Martin. *Otley.* New York: Stein & Day, 1966. From the moment when Gerald Otley, a British thief, steals a figurine, he is drawn into a hectic series of adventures involving assassination and espionage. *H*

5446. ___. *Otley Forever.* New York: Stein & Day, 1968. Trouble finds Otley again as, working for the SIS, he seeks to locate a nuclear device lost by the United States. *H*

5447. ___. *Otley Pursued.* New York: Stein & Day, 1967. Together with his female counterpart, Grace, Agent Otley is sent across the Channel to look in on neo-Nazi stirrings and mysterious cults which threaten the peace. *H*

5448. ___. *Otley Victorious.* New York: Stein & Day, 1969. Released from prison, Gerald is just in time to crash his way into the "New Day Operation," which leads to a strange fight between his colleague, Grace, and one Bandy Alice. *H*

5449. Wade, Jonathan. *Running Sand.* New York: Random, 1963. The daughter of an important American journalist is kidnapped by the Russians to keep her father from printing articles which would embarrass them at an upcoming summit meeting.

5450. Wade, Robert and Bill Miller. *Hunter of the Blood.* By Whit Masterson, pseud. New York: Dodd, 1977. Security pro Gus Gamble must prevent a religious fanatic from blowing up the Vatican with a homemade A-bomb.

5451. ___. *The Man with Two Clocks.* By Whit Masterson, pseud. New York: Dodd, 1974. A California professor is conned into a spy caper which involves the use of his knowledge to fool Soviet reconnaissance satellites.

5452. Wager, Walter. *Blue Leader.* New York: Arbor, 1978. Employing surplus World War II B-17s and led by an ex-CIA agent, a group of former wartime American airmen attack a heroin convoy in modern Burma.

American Wager has enjoyed a varied career as an aviation lawyer, United Nations editor, magazine writer, and screenwriter for TV documentaries. His novels are a mixture of Maclean and Deighton with emphasis on action. (See Mr. Wager's commentary in CRAFT NOTES.)

5453. ___. *58 Minutes.* New York: Macmillan, 1987. Captain Frank Malone, head of the New York Police department's antiterrorist squad is at Kennedy Airport to meet his wife and daughter when terrorists take over the electronic systems of New York's airports. Filmed as the sequel to *Die Hard*, also starred Bruce Willis.

5454. ___. *Blue Murder.* New York: Arbor, 1981. While seeking the missing brother of a movie star, private detective Alison Gordon uncovers a kidnap plot against the President of the United States and a plan for an attack on America.

5455. ___. *Death Hits the Jackpot.* New York: Popular, 1954. A CIA agent tries to solve the mystery of how money stolen from the OSS in 1944 Madrid has shown up in a Chicago gambling club nine years later.

5456. ___. *I Spy.* By John Tiger, pseud. New York: Popular, 1965. Two American agents posing as tennis stars are sent on an impossible assignment to stop the scheme of a madman. This original story became the pilot for the TV series starring Bill Cosby-Robert Culp. Others in the "I Spy" series: *P*

5457. ___. *I Spy: Countertrap.* By John Tiger, pseud. New York: Popular, 1967. *P*

5458. ___. *I Spy: Death-Twist.* By John Tiger, pseud. New York: Popular, 1968. *P*

5459. ___. *I Spy: Doomdate.* By John Tiger, pseud. New York: Popular, 1967. *P*

5460. ___. *I Spy: Masterstroke.* By John Tiger, pseud. New York: Popular, 1966. *P*

5461. ___. *I Spy: Superkill.* By John Tiger, pseud. New York: Popular, 1967. *P*

5462. ___. *I Spy: Wipeout.* By John Tiger, pseud. New York: Popular, 1967. *P*

5463. ___. *Mission Impossible.* By John Tiger, pseud. New York: Popular, 1967. Dan Briggs' IM force is asked by "the Secretary" to liquidate two Nazi masters of evil still plotting twenty years after the end of World War II. *P*

5464. ___. *Mission Impossible: Code Name, Little Ivan.* By John Tiger, pseud. New York: Popular, 1969. The IM force sets out to kidnap a huge tank, which might be the Communists' greatest defense weapon. *P*

5465. ___. *Otto's Boy.* New York: Macmillan, 1985. Otto's "boy" is a deranged ex-US Army vet who uses stolen nerve gas from a chemical munitions depot in Utah to kill 117 subway riders in New York and blackmail the rest of the city; detective Bloom is assigned to catch the killer.

5466. ___. *Sledgehammer*. New York: Macmillan, 1970. An elite group of World War II-trained OSS agents take over a town in order to track down the killer of an old buddy.

5467. ___. *The Swap*. New York: Macmillan, 1972. An ex-Green Beret, Captain Garrison works for a dying US Jewish tycoon to get the old man's niece out of the USSR.

5468. ___. *Telefon*. New York: Macmillan, 1976. The KGB must halt an old plan, now activated, that will send 430 sleeper agents against their American targets. Charles Bronson played the agent sent to stop them.

5469. ___. *Time of Reckoning*. New York: Playboy, 1977. A wise-cracking but ferocious CIA specialist in violence, codenamed "Merlin," must battle a conscientious doctor who is wreaking a merciless personal vengeance on Nazi war criminals.

5470. ___. *Viper Three*. New York: Macmillan, 1971. Five death-row convicts seize a missile base and threaten to trigger World War III. Another thriller by Wager:

5471. ___. *Designated Hitter*. New York: Arbor, 1982.

5472. Wagner, Geoffrey A. *A Passionate Land*. New York: Simon & Schuster, 1953. In Mexico, the British ambassador is killed by a fanatical society everyone believes to be the creature of English cement tycoon Edward Dodds. *

5473. Wahloo, Per. *The Steel Spring*. By Peter Wahloo. Trans. Joan Tate. New York: Delacorte, 1970. [*Stalsprånget*. Stockholm: Norstedt & Sönners, 1968]. A man returns to find his homeland devastated and the streets littered with corpses in this early Kafkaesque novel by the renowned detective-fiction writer.

5474. ___ and Maj Sjowall. *The Fire Engine That Disappeared*. Trans. Joan Tate. New York: Pantheon, 1970. [*Brandbilen som Forsvann*. Stockholm: Norstedt, 1963.] Agent Martin Beck is involved in several weird occurrences: a suicide leaves a note with two words, "Martin Beck"; an incendiary device blows the roof off an old apartment building in Stockholm; and a local crime seems to lead off in a number of trails to the heart of Europe.

5475. ___ and Maj Sjowall. *The Man Who Went Up in Smoke.* New York: Pantheon, 1969. Beck is ordered to Stockholm to find a hard-drinking Swedish reporter who knows something the intelligence boys also want to learn.

Wahloo, Peter, pseud. *See* Wahloo, Per

5476. Wakeman, Frederick. *A Free Agent.* New York: Simon & Schuster, 1963. After marrying a Greek girl, a US agent learns some unpleasant truths about his work as he seeks to block the Russians and Chinese from controlling a new African country.

5477. Walker, David Esdaile. *C.A.B.—Intersec.* By David Esdaile, pseud. Boston: Houghton, 1968. Approached by Intersec, a top-level powerful secret agency, Harry Ambler is given a mission and must decide if he can betray the person with whom he broke out of a German POW camp years earlier.

5478. ___. *Diamonds for Danger.* By David Esdaile, pseud. New York: Harper, 1954. An American banker, mistaken as a CIA agent upon his arrival in Lisbon for trade talks, becomes engulfed in a conspiracy to swipe industrial diamonds and negotiable bonds.

5479. Walker, Martin. *The Infiltrator.* New York: Dial, 1978. Unaware of KGB-CIA collaboration, David Maddox is assigned to oversee a Portuguese revolution and prevent a Communist takeover.

5480. Walker, Max. *Mission Impossible: Codename Judas.* New York: Popular, 1968. The IM force must ferret out a dangerous traitor. *P*

5481. ___. *Mission Impossible: Codename Rapier.* New York: Popular, 1968. On a sunny Caribbean island, Jim Phelps' agents begin to disappear and soon the IM force finds itself with a nightmare assignment: kill itself. *P*

5482. Wallace, Irving. *The Pigeon Project.* New York: Simon & Schuster, 1979. Fleeing the Soviet Union, an expatriate British scientist arrives in Venice with the formula for a substance which could extend human life by 150 years.

5483. ___. *The Plot.* New York: Simon & Schuster, 1967. The four main characters attempt to refurbish their tarnished reputations in the shadow of a Paris disarmament conference. As they interweave one with another, a plot transcending their own problems and threatening the future of mankind is uncovered.

5484. ___. *The R Document.* New York: Simon & Schuster, 1976. The Attorney General discovers that the FBI is harassing citizens and, under the new 35th Amendment to the US Constitution, has plans to open a concentration camp in the Arizona desert.

5485. ___. *The Second Lady.* New York: Signet, 1980. The Russians substitute an actress for the American First Lady and only journalist Gay Parker notices a few tiny inconsistencies in this KGB plant. *P*

5486. ___. *The Seventh Secret.* New York: Dutton, 1986. Another one of those "what-if" Eva-Braun-is-still-alive tales, which begs the question: Can Hitler be far behind?

5487. Walkins, Leslie. *The Unexplored Man.* New York: Morrow, 1978. An English publisher is kidnapped by a Soviet agent, who wants to destroy key British government officials with information tortured out of the captive.

5488. Wallis, Arthur J. and Charles F. Blair. *Thunder Above.* New York: Holt, 1957. An American aviator bound for Berlin is forced down behind the Iron Curtain, but is helped to escape by a pretty girl. Once across, alone, our hero decides to return and rescue her.

5489. Wallman, Jeffrey M. *Magyar Massacre.* By Gregory St. Germain, pseud. New York: Signet, 1983. WW II military action series featuring international soldiers against the Nazis. *P* Others:

5490. ___. *Night and Fog.* By Gregory St. Germain, pseud. New York: Signet, 1983. *P*

5491. ___. *Shadows of Death.* By Gregory St. Germain, pseud. New York: Signet, 1983. *P*

5492. ___. *Target: Sahara.* By Gregory St. Germain, pseud. New York: Signet, 1983. *P*

5493. Walsh, J. M. [James Morgan]. *Danger Zone.* London: Collins, 1942. These post-1939 novels feature heroic Oliver Keene (*see* Part 1). Others:

5494. ___. *Death at His Elbow.* London: Collins, 1941.

5495. ___. *Face Value.* London: Collins, 1943.

5496. ___. *Island Alert.* London: Collins, 1943.

5497. ___. *Whispers in the Dark.* London: Collins, 1945. Some post-1940 adventures of Timothy Terrel (*see* Walsh's entry in Part 1):

5498. ___. *East of Piccadilly.* By Stephen Maddock, pseud. London: Collins, 1948.

5499. ___. *I'll Never Like Friday Again.* By Stephen Maddock, pseud. London: Collins, 1945.

5500. ___. *Something on the Stairs.* By Stephen Maddock, pseud. London: Collins, 1944.

5501. ___. *Spades at Midnight.* By Stephen Maddock, pseud. London: Collins, 1940.

5502. ___. *Overture to Trouble.* By Stephen Maddock, pseud. London: Collins, 1946.

5503. Walsh, Thomas F. M. *A Thief in the Night.* New York: Simon & Schuster, 1962. A man concocts a scheme to free his brother, who is in jail as a spy in an Iron Curtain country.

5504. Ward, Arthur Sarsfield. *Bimbashi Baruk of Egypt.* By Sax Rohmer, pseud. New York: McBride, 1944. Ten tales involving the intelligence activities of British Major Brian Baruk, whose command of ten languages gets him admitted to all sorts of North American native intrigues. *
    Ward was a major practitioner of the adventurer school of spy fiction in the pre-war years and creator of the Fu Manchu (see Part I for the pre-1940 novels).

5505. ___. *The Daughter of Fu Manchu.* By Sax Rohmer, pseud. New York: Avon, 1949. *y

5506. ___. *The Emperor Fu Manchu.* By Sax Rohmer, pseud. Greenwich, CT: Fawcett, 1959. *y

5507. ___. *The Fire Goddess.* By Sax Rohmer, pseud. New York: Fawcett, 1952. *y

5508. ___. *The Island of Fu Manchu*. By Sax Rohmer, pseud. Garden City, NY: Doubleday, 1941. **y*

5509. ___. *Re-Enter Dr. Fu Manchu*. By Sax Rohmer, pseud. Greenwich, CT: Fawcett, 1957. **y*

5510. ___. *The Secret of Holm Peel and Other Strange Stories*. By Sax Rohmer, pseud. New York: Ace, 1970. Contains one Fu Manchu tale. **y*

5511. ___. *The Seven Sins*. By Sax Rohmer, pseud. New York: McBride, 1943. A French detective, a Scotland Yard sleuth, an Egyptologist, and the beautiful owner of a secret roulette wheel work to block Nazi agents from spiriting war secrets out of England *

5512. ___. *The Shadow of Fu Manchu*. By Sax Rohmer, pseud. Garden City, NY: Doubleday, 1948. **y*

5513. ___. *The Wrath of Fu Manchu and Other Stories*. New York: Daw, 1976. Includes four Fu Manchu tales. **Py*

5514. Ward-Thomas, Evelyn B. P. *The Defector*. By Evelyn Anthony, pseud. New York: Putnam's, 1981. A top KGB agent, who holds the key to Soviet strategy in the oil-rich nations of the Middle East, has defected to the SIS and fallen in love with the beautiful agent assigned to debrief him; as the attachment becomes mutual, both struggle to maintain their love in the face of treachery and counter-treachery.
    Daughter of a British naval officer and inventor, Anthony began her writing career in 1949 with the publication of her first short story. Since that time, she has turned her attention to the production of historical novels and spy thrillers. Although she has never worked for any intelligence agency, she has, like other practitioners, known a number of "spooks" who have provided her with information. She shares with Helen MacInnes an emphasis on strong female characters and authenticity of locale and with le Carré, a thematic interest in betrayal and duty's conflicts.

5515. ___. *The Janus Imperative*. By Evelyn Anthony, pseud. New York: Coward-McCann, 1980. After witnessing two political murders thirty-five years apart, a former member of the Hitler Youth is caught up in a mad plot originally conceived by Der Fuehrer himself. [Published the previous year in Great Britain as *The Grave of Truth*. London: Hutchinson, 1979]. *

5516. ___. *The Legend.* By Evelyn Anthony, pseud. New York: Coward-McCann, 1969. A retired British agent attends a weekend party where he meets a beautiful divorcée and before he can say "James Bond," finds himself back in "the game." *

5517. ___. *Mission to Malaspiga.* By Evelyn Anthony, pseud. New York: Coward-McCann, 1974. Italian relatives are suspected of smuggling heroin into American via their export trade. *

5518. ___. *The Persian Price.* By Evelyn Anthony, pseud. New York: Coward-McCann, 1975. Arab terrorists hold a woman hostage to force her husband's oil company out of negotiations with the Shah of Iran. *

5519. ___. *The Poellenberg Inheritance.* New York: Coward-McCann, 1972. Paula Stanley's father, an ex-SS general long thought dead, informs her through an intermediary that a priceless Cellini "stolen" from him is available. Others, willing to murder, want it again. *

5520. ___. *The Rendezvous.* By Evelyn Anthony, pseud. New York: Coward-McCann, 1967. An ex-Nazi war criminal and a beautiful Resistance agent are bound together by an overwhelming passion which threatens to destroy them twenty years after the end of World War II. *

5521. ___. *The Return.* By Evelyn Anthony, pseud. New York: Coward-McCann, 1978. The daughter of an American industrialist is linked to a mysterious man who may be a fanatical anti-Soviet agitator out to obtain revenge for the Polish victims of Yalta. *

5522. ___. *Stranger at the Gate.* By Evelyn Anthony, pseud. New York: Coward-McCann, 1973. A banker on business from Switzerland in German-occupied France during the war is, in fact, an American OSS officer. *

5523. ___. *The Tamarind Seed.* By Evelyn Anthony, pseud. New York: Coward-McCann, 1971. American Judith Farrow flies to Barbados and romance with a Soviet UN diplomat who is actually a KGB operative. An international crisis develops as each is suspected of defecting. * One more:

5524. ___. *Voices on the Wind.* By Evelyn Anthony, pseud. New York: Putnam's, 1985.

5525. Ware, Wallace. *Charka Memorial.* Garden City, NY: Doubleday, 1955. The representative of a Central European government is summoned home from Washington to what he knows is certain doom.

5526. Warfield, Gallatin. *State v. Justice.* New York: Warner, 1992. Courtroom mystery with political intrigue as two lawyers lock horns over a case involving a Russian diplomat's murdered six-year-old son by a psychotic drifter.

5527. Warren, Christopher. *The Allah Conspiracy.* New York: Scribner's, 1981. As the President prepares to implement the Camp David Accords, he becomes the target of a bitter terrorist named Jamil Rashid.

5528. Warwick, Francis A. *A Case for MI-5.* By Warwick Jardine, pseud. London: Amalgamated, 1950. British private eye and Nick Carter type Sexton Blake gets mixed up in a security case which has him working for the British security service against a pack of Russky agents.

5529. Washburn, Mark. *The Armageddon Game.* New York: Putnam's, 1977. Sam Boggs constructs a special bomb for a US agency and thus becomes involved in a life-and-death race between terrorists and the CIA for its possession.

5530. ___. *The Omega Threat.* New York: Dell, 1980. Ex-CIA agent Sam Boggs must defuse a terrorist plot to place a bomb aboard the space shuttle *Discovery.* P

5531. Watkins, Leslie. *The Killing of Idi Amin.* New York: Avon, 1977. A team of mercenaries and assassins attempt to kill the former unpopular ruler of Uganda. P

5532. Watson, Colin. *Hopjoy was Here.* New York: Walker, 1963. A Bond-spoof in which an agent named Ross seeks a secret operative who has vanished into thin air. H

5533. Watson, Geoffrey. *The Nooriabad File.* New York: Scribner's, 1979. Looking into an elaborate fraud at a UN agency in Central Asia, investigator Mike Ellis is kidnapped by West German terrorists who force him to mastermind a coverup of the scandal.

5534. Watson, Ian. *The Jonah Kit.* New York: Scribner's, 1976. The Soviets telepathically program the intelligence of a whale for evil doings.

5535. Waugh, Alec. *The Mule on the Minaret.* New York: Farrar, 1966. During World War II, Professor Noel Reid is assigned an espionage mission which takes him to Beirut and Baghdad for British Intelligence. Twenty years later, he relives the job and recalls the old Arab proverb: "a man who takes his mule to the top of a minaret must bring it down himself."

5536. Waugh, Evelyn. *The End of the Battle.* Boston: Little, 1962. British novelist Evelyn Arthur St. John Waugh's trilogy—this is the finale of the series—concerns the military career of young Guy Crouchback, who begins his military service in the Royal Corps of Halberdiers in 1939 when he hears news of the Molotov-Ribbentrop Treaty. The others:

5537. ___. *Men-at-Arms.* Boston: Little, 1952.

5538. ___. *Officers and Gentlemen.* Boston: Little, 1955.

Wayland, Patrick, pseud. *See* O'Connor, Richard

5539. Weaver, Graham. *Count on the Saint.* Garden City, NY: Doubleday, 1980. Leslie Charteris's durable Simon Templar lives on for further escapades in this, one of many others, adventures by various authors after his original creator. (See Yin, Leslie C.B.) One more by Weaver:

5540. ___. *The Saint and the Templar Treasure.* Garden City, NY: Doubleday, 1979.

5541. Webb, Sharon. *Pestis 18.* New York: TOR, 1987. Terrorists steal two vials of a deadly toxin developed by the US and threaten to detonate a "plague" bomb unless one-half billion dollars extortion is paid.

5542. Weber, Janice. *Frost the Fiddler.* New York: St. Martin's, 1992. Features a female James Bond, a violinist, who doubles as a spy for a hush-hush government agency.

5543. Weber, Joe. *Defcon One.* Novato, CA: Presidio, 1989. When *perestroika* and *glasnost* fail, the US and USSR lock horns in this technothriller. His other tales include:

5544. ___. *Rules of Engagement.* Novato, CA: Presidio, 1991.

5545. ___. *Shadow Flight.* Novato, CA: Presidio, 1990.

5546. ___. *Targets of Opportunity*. New York: Putnam's, 1993.

5547. Weber, Ron. *Company Spook*. New York: St. Martin's, 1986. Inspired by Watergate's "Deep Throat," Weber's tale concerns a high government informer called "Deep Well" who tells secrets to two reporters responsible for removing a President and sending his staff to prison. One other:

5548. ___. *Troubleshooter*. New York: St. Martin's, 1988.

5549. Weeks, William R. *Knock and Wait Awhile*. Boston: Houghton, 1957. An American agent is sent to stop a reporter from visiting the Soviet Union.

5550. Weil, Barry. *Dossier IX*. Indianapolis: Bobbs-Merrill, 1969. Bitter Mossad agent Jacob Asher is sent on a year's training mission with the British SIS. Working out of London with SIS and SDECE assistance, he hunts down an escaped master spy, breaks up an espionage ring, and stops a nuclear holocaust.

5551. Weinstein, Sol. *Loxfinger: A Thrilling Adventure of Hebrew Secret Agent Oy-Oy-7, Israel Bond*. New York: Pocket, 1965. A Bond-spoof featuring Jewish agent Oy-Oy-7. *PH*

5552. ___. *Matzohball: A New Adventure of Hebrew Secret Agent Oy-Oy-7, Israel Bond*. New York: Pocket, 1966. In which the hero is assigned to recover valuable objects. *PH*

5553. ___. *On the Secret Service of His Majesty, the Queen: A Thrilling Adventure of Oy-Oy-7 Israel Bond*. New York: Pocket, 1966. The Jewish superspy is asked to guard an Arab Queen. One other, not published in America, is: *PH*

5554. ___. *You Only Live Until You Die: The Last Adventure of Oy-Oy-7 Israel Bond*. London: Trident, 1968. *PH*

5555. Weisman, John. *Blood Cries*. New York: Viking, 1987. An American journalist discovers his Jewish identity in the crisis over Israel's invasion of Lebanon.

5556. Weismiller, Edward. *The Serpent Sleeping*. New York: Putnam's, 1963. In Cherbourg just after its capture by the Allies, a French girl is arrested as a Nazi spy and wrongly prosecuted. An American private believes her innocent and works to prove that in the face of stern opposition from a superior.

The author's only spy tale, it is one of the most important in the history of the genre, described by Norman Holmes Pearson as "one of the few accounts of the handling and psychology of a turned agent, in this case after the invasion of France, when German agents attempted to operate behind the American lines." (McCormick & Fletcher, *Spy Fiction*, New York: Facts on File, 1990: 254). The work is based, to a large extent, on the author's first-hand experience with Britain's Double Cross system.

Welcome, John, pseud. *See* Brennan, John

5557. Wentworth, Patricia. *Dead or Alive*. New York: Warner, 1990. Meg O'Hara wants to divorce her husband, a charming Irish rogue and spy; the problem: the Foreign Office insists he is dead.

5558. West, Elliot. *The Night Is a Time for Listening*. New York: Random, 1966. Daross would strike a bargain with Satan himself for the privilege of killing the SS agent who had tortured his wife to death.

5559. ___. *These Lonely Victories*. New York: Putnam's, 1972. East German defector Adele Webber is due to be exchanged for a much-needed American spy. CIA agent Brian Colman doubts the wisdom of the deal—so he runs off with Adele!

5560. West, Morris L. *The Clowns of God*. New York: Berkley, 1982. Before the Pope can pronounce his terrible prophecy of doom, his own Vatican Cardinals imprison him.

5561. ___. *Harlequin*. New York: Morrow, 1974. Sophisticated computers program human beings to acts of assassination, kidnapping, and revolution.

5562. ___. *Lazarus*. New York: St. Martin's, 1990. This volume completes the trilogy of *The Shoes of the Fisherman* and *The Clowns of God*. Pope Leo XIV faces death from heart disease as the novel opens and is targeted for assassination by a fundamentalist group, but he realizes a need for tolerance and begins to undo the very policies that have made him a reactionary.

5563. ___. *Proteus*. New York: Morrow, 1979. John Spada is Proteus, a powerful New York capitalist and head of a secret organization, one that he springs into action the moment his daughter is tortured and violated by professional interrogators acting under the orders of the President of Argentina.

5564. ___. *The Salamander.* New York: Morrow, 1973. An Italian Colonel, seeking to preserve his life and find out who killed a general plotting against the government, has one clue: a card with a crowned salamander codename signifying survival. *

5565. ___. *The Shoes of the Fisherman.* New York: Morrow, 1963. A newly elected Pope, who spent years as a political prisoner of the KGB in the Ukraine, has the support of the Russians and the Americans as he uses the Church's resources to feed a warlike but starving Asian land remarkably like Red China. *

5566. ___. *The Tower of Babel.* New York: Morrow, 1968. The lives of numbers of Jews in Israel just before the Six-Day War of 1967. One of those placed under the microscope is Jakov Baratz, Director of Israeli Intelligence. *

5567. West-Watson, Keith Campbell. *Born Beautiful.* By Keith Campbell, pseud. New York: Macdonald, 1951. Mike Brett is a hardnosed p.i. who occasionally dabbles in matters of espionage on his capers. Others:

5568. ___. *Darling, Don't.* By Keith Campbell, pseud. New York: Macdonald, 1950.

5569. ___. *Goodbye, Gorgeous.* By Keith Campbell, pseud. New York: Macdonald, 1947.

5570. ___. *Listen, Lovely.* By Keith Campbell, pseud. New York: Macdonald, 1949.

5571. ___. *Pardon My Gun.* By Keith Campbell, pseud. New york: Macdonald, 1954.

5572. ___. *That Was No Lady.* By Keith Cambell, pseud. New York: Macdonald, 1942.

5573. Westbrook, Robert. *Lady Left.* New York: Crown, 1991. Radical chic in Hollywood when celebrities mingle with Sandinistas.

5574. Westheimer, David. *Lighter Than a Feather.* Boston: Little, 1971. What would have happened if the US Joint Chiefs of Staff had not permitted the A-bomb to be dropped on Hiroshima, but instead ordered up an invasion of Japan known as "Operation Olympic?" *

5575. ___. *Von Ryan's Express.* Garden City, NY: Doubleday, 1964. A group of Allied POWs, led by US martinet Colonel Joseph Ryan, capture a German train and attempt to flee 1943 Italy; the movie version starred Frank Sinatra and Trevor Howard. *

5576. ___. *Von Ryan's Return.* New York: Coward-McCann, 1980. Colonel Joseph "Von" Ryan takes on an OSS mission to find an Abwehr agent who has infiltrated a partisan band in northern Italy. *

5577. Westlake, Donald E. *The Blackbird.* By Richard Stark, pseud. New York: Macmillan, 1969. Alan Grofield, actor, thief, and agent for the secret government agency called "Brand X," is sent off to a conference in Quebec, where he tangles with the beautiful and menacing spy, Vivian Kamdela from Undurwa.

5578. ___. *The Spy in the Ointment.* By Richard Stark, pseud. New York: Random, 1966. The FBI persuades pacifist Gene Raxford to infiltrate a terrorist group which is run by his girlfriend's Communist brother. Additional tales involving Agent Grofield include:

5579. ___. *The Butcher's Moon.* By Richard Stark, pseud. New York: Random, 1974.

5580. ___. *The Dame.* By Richard Stark, pseud. New York: Macmillan, 1969.

5581. ___. *The Damsel.* By Richard Stark, pseud. New York: Macmillan, 1967.

5582. ___. *The Handle.* By Richard Stark, pseud. New York: Pocket 1966. P

5583. ___. *Lemons Never Die.* By Richard Stark, pseud. Cleveland, OH: World, 1971.

5584. ___. *The Score.* By Richard Stark, pseud. New York: Pocket, 1966. P

5585. Weston, Garnett. *The Man with the Monocle.* Garden City, NY: Doubleday, 1943. When an archaeologist receives a mysterious script, he sets off in search of a newspaper friend who is being held by Nazi conspirators in a Mayan ruin. *

5586. Weverka, Robert. *One Minute to Eternity*. New York: Morrow, 1969. A Pentagon agent is sent to Mexico to find a Cuban explosives expert.

5587. Wheatley, Dennis. *The Black Baroness*. New York: Macmillan, 1942. SIS agent Gregory Sallust trails a fanatical pro-Hitler French woman from Oslo to Rome during the time between the invasion of Norway and the fall of France, 1940.

      After selling his father's business in 1931, Wheatley took up writing full time, devoting his energies to creating a realistic-type of detective story based on the printing of police dossiers. (See Wheatley in Part 1 for a list of his pre-1940 fiction.) At the outbreak of war in 1939, he turned his talent to the production of spy thrillers before becoming involved in the British war effort as the only civilian member of the Joint Planning Staff in Churchill's warroom. Here he had input into the Major Martin scam employed as a cover for the invasion of Sicily ("The Man Who Never Was") and the creation of a double for Field Marshal Sir Bernard L. Montgomery. His reminiscences of wartime planning were published in 1959 as *Stronger Than Fiction*. *

5588. ___. *Come into My Parlour*. London: Hutchinson, 1946. Agent Sallust must contend with the difficulties raised by his old-fashioned and over-aged chief, Sir Pellinore Gwaine-Cust. The tale is meant to be a parody on the SIS as it was before and during the Second World War.

5589. ___. *Faked Passports*. New York: Macmillan, 1943. SIS Agent Gregory Sallust gets mixed up in the intrigues surrounding the Russo-Finnish War of 1939-1940 and the Allied desire to send assistance to the heroic Finns. *

5590. ___. *Gateway to Hell*. London: Hutchinson, 1978. A millionaire steals $1 million from his own Buenos Aires bank on behalf of Satanists who are planning to bring open race-war to every city in the world.

5591. ___. *The Scarlet Imposter*. London: Hutchinson, 1940. Gregory Sallust becomes a lone-wolf SIS agent and is involved in an attempt to blow up Hitler in a Munich beer hall. *

5592. ___. *The Strange Conflict*. London: Hutchinson, 1978. While bombs fall on London in 1940, the Duke of Richleau moves to discover the source of a security leak. His findings are supernatural.

5593. ___. *Sword of Fate.* London: Hutchinson, 1944. A British Army officer and a girl become involved with a Nazi spy ring in Greece during the time of the ill-fated 1940 British relief expedition. *

5594. ___. *They Used Dark Forces.* London: Hutchinson, 1978. Sent to penetrate the secrets of a German V-weapons establishment, Gregory Sallust finds himself employing occult forces in an attempt to destroy Hitler. Three more tales featuring Gregory Sallust:

5595. ___. *The Island Where Time Stands Still.* London: Hutchinson, 1954.

5596. ___. *Traitors' Gate.* London: Hutchinson, 1958.

5597. ___. *The White Witch of the South Seas.* London: Hutchinson, 1968.

5598. ___. *"V" for Vengeance.* London: Hutchinson, 1942. Together with his friend Kuporovitch and the girl Madeleine, Sallust gets mixed up in resistance work in France in the period between the fall of France in 1940 and Hitler's invasion of Russia in 1941. *
   Following the war, Wheatley turned his attention to creating a series of espionage yarns set in the Napoleonic period and which feature series character Roger Brook:

5599. ___. *The Dark Secret of Josephine.* London: Hutchinson, 1955. *HI*

5600. ___. *Desperate Measures.* London: Hutchinson, 1974. *HI*

5601. ___. *Evil in a Mask.* London: Hutchinson, 1969. *HI*

5602. ___. *The Irish Witch.* London: Hutchinson, 1973. *HI*

5603. ___. *The Launching of Roger Brook.* London: Hutchinson, 1947. *HI*

5604. ___. *The Man Who Killed the King.* New York: Putnam's, 1965. *HI*

5605. ___. *The Rape of Venice.* London: Hutchinson, 1959. *HI*

5606. ___. *The Ravishing of Lady Mary Ware.* London: Hutchinson, 1971. *HI*

5607. ___. *The Rising Storm.* London: Hutchinson, 1949. *HI*

5608. ___. *The Shadow of Tyburn Tree*. New York: Ballantine, 1973. *HI*

5609. ___. *The Sultan's Daughter*. London: Hutchinson, 1963. *HI*

5610. ___. *The Wanton Princess*. London: Hutchinson, 1966. *HI*

5611. Wheeler, Keith. *The Last Mayday*. Garden City, NY: Doubleday, 1969. When the ex-First Secretary of the Communist Party decides to defect with the assistance of a CIA contract agent, the Americans send a nuclear submarine into the Black Sea to pick him up; then the Soviet Navy sinks the US vessel and the problem of salvaging the personnel while avoiding World War III falls upon the shoulders of the President and Chief of Naval Operations.

5612. Wheeler, Paul. *And the Bullets Were Made of Lead*. Garden City, NY: Doubleday, 1969. A freelance writer is in Paris attempting to prevent a political assassination and clear up the tragedy of an old friend.

5613. Whitaker, Rodney. *The Eiger Sanction*. By Trevanian, pseud. New York: Crown, 1972. American art professor-mountain climber Dr. Jonathan Hemlock moonlights as an assassin in the employ of the Search and Sanction Division of the mythical counter-assassination bureau known as C-11. In his last mission before retirement, he is sent along on a top-flight mountain climbing expedition in Switzerland with orders to liquidate one of three companions known to have killed an unlucky C-11 agent in Montreal. Not knowing the identity of the assassin Hemlock ruthlessly plans to bump off all three. Clint Eastwood starred in the movie version, remarkable for its mountaineering stunts and photography.
    One of the most intriguing of *noms de plume* was finally cracked by Donald McCormick and Katy Fletcher, the authors of *Spy Fiction: A Connoisseur's Guide*. Whitaker is a speech & communications theorist, who headed the Division of Communications at the University of Texas-Austin in the mid-sixties, acted as consultant to McGraw-Hill for books on film, and has authored a text on the cinema under the pseudonym Nicholas Searle.

5614. ___. *The Loo Sanction*. By Trevanian, pseud. New York: Crown, 1973. Dr. Hemlock is sent to England by his employer to liaise with the Loo Section of British Intelligence, which provides protection to MI-5 and MI-6 agents through "counter-assassination." As the result, he becomes involved in a plan to infiltrate a vicious gang that specializes in sex and incriminating photos of British VIPs.

5615. ___. *Shibumi.* By Trevanian, pseud. New York: Crown, 1979. Nicholai Hel, possessed of super-human strength and mental ability, destroys political terrorism in the world and then takes on a supermonolith of espionage and economic monopoly known as "the Mother Company."

5616. White, Alan. *Dark Finds the Day.* New York: Harcourt, 1965. A tale which probes the emotions and motivations of three soldiers who have volunteered for a dangerous Allied Mission in World War II. *

5617. ___. *The Long Drop.* New York: Harcourt, 1970. British Commando Group 404 is trained and sent to on a near-suicidal secret wartime operation in Belgium. *

5618. ___. *The Long Fuse.* New York: Harcourt, 1974. In "Operation Rundfunk," Captain Colson and his British Commandos jump into France, establish contact with the Resistance, and capture a German radio station for use in broadcasting Allied propaganda. *

5619. ___. *The Long Midnight.* New York: Harcourt, 1974. Colson and his sergeant land in German-occupied Norway with the twin missions of killing a quisling and destroying a titanium mine being worked by starving Lithuanian prisoners. *

5620. ___. *The Long Night's Walk.* New York: Harcourt, 1969. Colson and three Commandos are parachuted behind German lines in Holland to take out an important Nazi communications headquarters. *

5621. ___. *The Long Silence.* New York: Ace-Charter, 1977. Colson and his fellows are dropped into France to destroy an important rail center on the eve of D-Day. *P

5622. ___. *The Long Watch.* New York: Harcourt, 1971. In late 1943, Colson leads a Commando drop into France with orders to find and extract a French scientist who is being held captive by the Nazis. *

5623. White, James D. *The Brandenburg Affair.* London: Hutchinson, 1979. Retiring SIS agent Sebastian Kettle is talked into one more job—join a certain Colonel Petrov of the GRU in learning why two spies disappeared in East Germany.

5624. White, John M. *The Garden Game.* Indianapolis: Bobbs-Merrill, 1974. Sent to jail for "security reasons," intelligence chief Colonel Richman is later released, but can find no trace of his old team.

5625. ___. *The Moscow Papers.* New York: Major, 1978. CIA agent Brock Banner is sent to Greece to rescue an SIS agent—an old flame—trapped with top secret Russian documents. *P*

5626. White, Lionel. *The House on K Street.* New York: Dutton, 1965. The scene of a plot by the Sons of Columbia to get the next world war on and over while the US is still strong enough to win it.

5627. White, Osmar. *Silent Reach.* New York: Scribner's, 1978. George Galbraith is a former undercover agent hired by a rich man to protect his ranching and mining operation in the Australian Outback from the sabotaging of terrorists.

5628. White, Robin A. *Angle of Attack.* New York: Crown, 1992. Technothriller about pilots in the Persian Gulf War.

5629. ___. *The Flight from Winter's Shadow.* New York: Fawcett, 1990. Aviation techothriller in which two men must avert apocalypse when Russian hardliners conspire with US fanatics. *P* One more:

5630. ___. *Sword of Orion.* New York: Crown, 1993.

White, Steve, pseud. *See* McGarvey, Robert

5631. White, Stuart. *Operation Raven.* New York: McGraw-Hill, 1985. Heydrich sends a psychotic agent to kidnap Princesses Margaret and Elizabeth in 1940, but the scheme takes a twist when the operation is canceled; the Germans now have to send a man to stop him, and he teams up with Scotland Yard to follow the murderous trail before princesses become a blood sacrifice to the glory of the Reich.

5632. Whiting, Charles. *Operation Fox Hunt.* New York: Pinnacle, 1974. One of three paperback novels featuring one-eyed hero Mark Crook, who leads his team of daredevils against the Nazis. *P*

5633. Whittington, Henry. *The Man From UNCLE: The Doomsday Affair.* New York: Ace, 1965. Napoleon Solo and his colleague Illya must combat a THRUSH secret weapon which, if unleashed, will destroy the world. *P*

5634. Wilcox, Harry. *Afraid in the Dark.* By Mark Derby, pseud. New York: Viking, 1952. An insecure ex-British army officer accepts a dangerous mission in Malaya, where he finds himself and saves the woman he loves.

5635. ___. *The Bad Step.* By Mark Derby, pseud. New York: Viking, 1954. SIS agent Largo battles Communist-backed insurgents in the remote island of Indonesia. *

5636. ___. *The Big Water.* By Mark Derby, pseud. New York: Viking, 1953. In the fierce jungles of Borneo, tribesmen led by a Chinese Communist cross swords with a British agent-hero of World War II, a former island princess, and an Estonian who has survived two Nazi concentration camps.

5637. ___. *Echo of a Bomb.* By Mark Derby, pseud. New York: Viking, 1957. In the Far East a young English photographer and a Chinese girl get mixed up in a Red Chinese plot against the peace.

5638. ___. *Element of Risk.* By Mark Derby, pseud. New York: Viking, 1952. A young English commando-turned-actor goes to the countryside for a rest and meets a beautiful woman recently acquitted of murdering her husband.

5639. ___. *Ghost Blonde.* By Mark Derby, pseud. New York: Viking, 1960. Agent Nicko Strang is involved with murder and Red Chinese-inspired violence in Singapore.

5640. ___. *Sun in the Hunter's Eye.* By Mark Derby, pseud. New York: Viking, 1958. Near Singapore, Robert Avery searches for his lost cousin Andrew and runs smack into a mysterious and dangerous conspiracy.

5641. ___. *Woman Hunt.* By Mark Derby, pseud. New York: Viking, 1960. SIS agent Dickson is ordered to investigate a college on the west coast of Malaya which is suspected of being a cover for Communist activities; in the process, he is forced to hunt down a man-eating tiger. One other by this writer is:

5642. ___. *Sunlit Ambush.* By Mark Derby, pseud. New York: Viking, 1955.

5643. Wijkmark, Carl-Henning. *The Hunters of Karinhall.* Trans. Georg Bisset. New York: Avon, 1976. [*Jägarna på Karinhall.* n.p.: n.p., 1972]. Karinhall is Göring's infamous hunting lodge where powerful figures of the Reich and special visitors indulge their sexual fantasies and sometimes reveal state secrets to his hand-picked whores so that the tubby Reichsmarschall can tighten his hold on power.

5644. Wilden, Theodore. *Exchange of Clowns*. Boston: Little, 1981. The "clowns" are captured agents, pawns of their governments. The British, West German, and Russian governments negotiate a complex spy-swap deal—into the midst of which arrive two opposing agents, an American freelancer and a Soviet.

5645. ___. *To Die Elsewhere*. New York: Harcourt, 1976. When Garianian decides to retire on money he will obtain from selling secret US documents, he becomes the subject of a manhunt by agents from various East-West intelligence agencies.

5646. Wilhelm, Kate. *The Nervous Affair*. Garden City, NY: Doubleday, 1966. A group of American scientists held captive in a remote valley of the Rocky Mountains are forced to participate in a madman's diabolical project.

5647. Wilkinson, Burke. *Night of the Short Knives*. New York: Scribner's, 1965. A tale of espionage and counterespionage set in SHAPE, the present-day Supreme Headquarters Allied Powers Europe.

5648. Williams, Alan. *The Beria Papers*. New York: Simon & Schuster, 1973. A pair of American writers forge and publish the supposed diaries of Soviet secret police chief Lavrenti Beria.
　　Williams once worked for the CIA-sponsored Radio Free Europe. His spy tales are exceedingly realistic and depend for their success on his ability to take an actual historical event and embellish it with believable fictional sub-plots and characters.

5649. ___. *Gentleman Traitor*. New York: Harcourt, 1974. British journalist Barry Cayle interviews Kim Philby in Moscow and helps that unhappy traitor to decide to return to "the game" as an active agent, working on behalf of the SIS in war-torn Rhodesia.

5650. ___. *Shah-Mak*. New York: Coward-McCann, 1976. A group of mercenaries are paid to carry out an intricately plotted assassination of the Shah of Iran.

5651. ___. *The Tale of the Lazy Dog*. New York: Simon & Schuster, 1971. Could Murray Wilde's rag-tag gang of adventurers succeed in stealing $1 million out from under the nose of the American Army? *

5652. ___. *The Widow's War.* New York: Rawson Wade, 1980. To help her gain control of the country once ruled by her husband, a widow hires retired CIA agent Hugh Ryan.

5653. Williams, Eric. *The Borders of Barbarism.* New York: Coward-McCann, 1963. The Startes return to the Balkans once more to engage in amateur espionage. Sequel to the next entry. *

5654. ___. *Dragoman Pass.* New York: Coward-McCann, 1960. Writer Roger Starte and his wife Kate are touring the Balkans by jeep and get mixed up in smuggling an English anthropologist and former Communist out of Rumania. *

5655. Williams, Gilbert M. *The Chinese Fire Drill.* By Michael Wolfe, pseud. New York: Harper & Row, 1976. A journalist is sent back to Vietnam with covert orders to rescue the supposedly captive son-in-law of a US senator.

5656. ___. *Man on a String.* By Michael Wolfe, pseud. New York: Harper & Row, 1973. The sinister Colonel Xe of the ARVN lures an American officer into an ingenious scheme to retrieve a huge US payroll "lost" years before in the mountains north of Saigon.

5657. ___. *The Panama Paradox.* By Michael Wolfe, pseud. New York: Harper & Row, 1977. By breeding a lethal form of yellow fever, Michael Keefe assist the US Army command in the Canal Zone in resisting a nationalist takeover of the strategic waterway.

5658. Williams, Jay. *The China Expert.* By Michael Delving, pseud. New York: Scribner's, 1977. An American Jew assists MI-5 in recovering a vase stolen just before the opening of an important London art exhibition.

5659. Williams, Valentine. *Courier to Marrakesh: A Clubfoot Story.* By Douglas Valentine, pseud. Boston: Houghton, 1946. During the North African and Italian campaigns, a USO girl befriends an Italian countess, who gets her mixed up with the evil Nazi spy Clubfoot, from whom she must be rescued by two intrepid Allied agents, one each from SIS and OSS. The last in a series of Clubfoot tales begun in the pre-war years. (see Part 1). *

5660. Williamson, Tony. *The Connector.* Briarcliff Manor, NY: Stein & Day, 1976. CIA agent Lee Corey tries to help a girl from whom an international criminal seeks a special kind of entertainment by hiring the Baader-

Meinhof terrorist gang to hijack a fabulous gold shipment from an airport at Rome.

5661. ___. *The Doomsday Contract.* Briarcliff Manor, NY: Stein & Day, 1978. An American, a Lebanese, and an Israeli woman band together to obtain a number of nuclear bombs to destroy the Arab world.

5662. ___. *The Samson Strike.* New York: Atheneum, 1980. Two former agent-colleagues, now adversaries, compete when one plans to destroy a North Sea oil platform worth $4 million.

5663. ___. *Technicians of Death.* New York: Atheneum, 1978. CIA agent Lee Corey is sent to stop a PLO plan for the takeover of Asia's heroin production, funds from which would underwrite their atrocities.

5664. Willis, Anthony A. *Room at the Hotel Ambre.* By Anthony Armstrong, pseud. Garden City, NY: Doubleday, 1956. Jane, an English girl, wants to look at French life and checks into a Paris hotel. By coincidence, she has picked the very establishment used by a Communist spy ring as its headquarters. Noticing that something is amiss, she spills her thoughts to another young Britisher she meets, who just happens to be an SIS man there to look into the situation.

5665. Willis, Edward [Ted] Henry. *The Left-Handed Sleeper.* New York: Putnam's, 1976. While investigating her case, an SIS officer falls in love with the wife of a British Parliament member who has fled after being accused of being KGB mole and a traitor to England.

5666. ___. *The Lion of Judah.* New York: Holt, 1980. Captured in a failed attempt at assassination, a young Jew and his companions are offered a vicious bargain by Hermann Goering—one that will require a terrible payment.

5667. ___. *Westminster One.* New York: Putnam's, 1975. When the abduction of the Prime Minister plunges Britain into social and political turmoil, MI-5, the SIS, and Scotland Yard's Special Branch are left to ferret out the truth of the affair.

Willis, Maude, pseud. *See* Lottman, Eileen

5668. Wills, Maralys. *Scatterpath.* Novato, CA: Presidio, 1993. A federal aircraft-accident investigator seeks a psychopathic hacker who is destroying an airlines by causing mysterious crashes.

5669. Wilson, John A. B. *Honey for the Bears.* By Anthony Burgess, pseud. New York: Norton, 1964. The KGB tracks a British antiques dealer and his wife, who have travelled to Leningrad to engage in an illegal economic venture.

5670. ___. *Tremor of Intent.* By Anthony Burgess, pseud. New York: Norton, 1966.

5671. Wilson, Mitchell A. *Stalk the Hunter.* New York: Simon & Schuster, 1953. Harassed in Manhattan by Nazi agents, a young Czech girl is saved by an American chemist. *

5672. Wiltse, David. *Home Again.* New York: St. Martin's, 1986. An FBI man kills a female terrorist and returns home to Nebraska to take up his law practice.

5673. Winch, Arden. *Blood Royal.* New York: Viking, 1982. Terrorists capture and hold for ransom a young British prince of the blood.

5674. Winchester, Jack. *The Solitary Man.* New York: Coward-McCann, 1980. By staging his own death, double agent Hugo Hartmann hopes to escape his KGB-CIA connections and eradicate a memory of his own Nazi collaboration during World War II.

5675. Winder, Robert. *No Admission.* New York: Viking, 1989. A computer hacker robs millions for terrorists.

5676. Wingate, John. *Avalanche.* New York: St. Martin's, 1977. Fleeing Beirut with a secret code, an England bank manager desperately tries to reach British authorities and requires the assistance of an able agent. *

5677. ___. *Fireplay.* New York: Coward-McCann, 1977. With unlimited cash and permission, the director of a special CIA team will stop at nothing to raise a sunken Russian nuclear submarine. Shades of the Howard Hughes-CIA "Glomar Explorer" effort to raise a similar vessel in the Pacific during the 1970s. *

5678. ___. *Oil Strike.* New York: St. Martin's, 1976. International criminals with their own atomic submarine stalk a North Sea oil rig. *

5679. ___. *Red Mutiny.* New York: St. Martin's, 1978. Alex Stepak is ordered to restore morale and efficiency aboard a Soviet spy ship whose captain

is unstable and whose political officer is a ruthless schemer tied to the KGB.
*

5680. Winner, Percy. *Scene in the Ice-Blue Eyes.* New York: Harcourt, 1947. An American journalist puts his knowledge of Italy and the Italians to work for the SIS in Portugal and France. *

5681. Winsor, Diana. *The Death of Convention.* London: Macmillan, 1974. Tavy Martin travels to Amsterdam to attend a conservation convention and becomes involved with the secret service intrigues surrounding the defection of a Soviet physicist.

5682. ___. *Red on Wight.* London: Macmillan, 1972. The KGB plots to immobilize the fleets of NATO when the Russian Army invades Africa, but does not reckon with Tavy Martin, an astute Royal Navy typist.

5683. Winspear, Violet. *Time of the Temptress.* London: Mills and Boon, 1977. In Africa, a tough mercenary saves Eve Tarrant from possible death in the revolution-torn jungles. Published in America as a number in the "Harlequin Romance" series of paperbacks.

5684. Winston, Peter. *The Adjusters: The ABC Affair.* New York: Award, 1967. Here is another of those Nick Carter-type action-espionage series which have appeared so abundantly in an exclusively paperback format. In this one, our hero-narrator works for a secret organization known as "the Adjusters" and battles a ruthless warmonger whose plans may yet destroy the world. *P*

5685. ___. *The Adjusters: Assignment to Bahrein.* New York: Award, 1968. Adjusters' agent Peter Winston foils assassination attempts and torture, Arab style, in a powderkeg sheikdom. *P*

5686. ___. *The Adjusters: Doomsday Vendetta.* New York: Award, 1969. Winston must seduce a beautiful enemy spy—whose lovers always end up dead. *P*

5687. ___. *The Adjusters: The Glass Cipher.* New York: Award, 1968. An ominous message arrives from a scientist in China warning of a monstrous new weapon that could destroy America's missiles; Winston hunts for the mysterious Red spy, who has already murdered the key man in the betrayal of this weird, kill-America plot. One other by this author is: *P*

5688. ___. *The Adjusters: The Temple at Ilumquh.* New York: Award 1969. *P*

Winters, Jon, pseud. *See* Cross, Gilbert B.

5689. Winterton, Paul. *The Ascent of D-13.* By Andrew Garve, pseud. New York: Harper & Row, 1969. A Russian agent attempts to hijack a plane carrying a new detection device, but succeeds only in cracking it up on the summit of D-13, a nasty peak on the Soviet-Turkish border. The Soviets send a recovery team as do the British, led by one of their best mountain climbers.

5690. ___. *The Ashes of Loda.* By Andrew Garve, pseud. New York: Harper & Row, 1965. A correspondent begins asking why the Soviets accused his girlfriend's father of war crimes.

5691. ___. *Counterstroke.* By Andrew Garve, pseud. New York: Crowell, 1978. A terrorist held in prison is to be released as ransom for the hostage daughter of a British Member of Parliament; an unemployed actor volunteers to impersonate the criminal in hopes of leading authorities to the perpetrators after the girl has been saved.

5692. ___. *The Fifth Passenger.* By Andrew Garve, pseud. New York: Harper & Row, 1963. A young lawyer and an attractive widow become involved in an MI-5 search for a security risk which ends up aboard a submarine.

5693. ___. *A Hero for Leanda.* By Andrew Garve, pseud. New York: Harper, 1959. Mike is offered a deal by millionaire Metavas: sail to Heureuse, a thousand miles from any land, and rescue Kastella, the political leader of Spyros, who is being held by the British.

5694. ___. *A Hole in the Ground.* By Andrew Garve, pseud. New York: Harper, 1952. A mad British Parliament member with Communist leanings plans to blow up a nuclear reactor with a device planted in a cave under the power plant.

5695. ___. *Murder in Moscow.* New York: Harper, 1951. [*Murder through the Looking Glass.* London: Collins, 1951]. When the Reverend Andrew Mullet is murdered in Moscow, British reporter Verney begins his own investigation when the authorities offer up an obvious scapegoat to mask the real reasons why the Soviets deemed it necessary to take out the leader of a peace delegation in their midst.

5696. ___. *Two If by Sea*. By Roger Bax, pseud. New York: Harper, 1949. Two Englishmen seek to remove their Russian wives from behind the Iron Curtain by means of a small boat raid. Of the three pseudonyms Winterton used, most of his thriller/adventure novels were written under the name of Andrew Garve; others include:

5697. ___. *Boomerang*. By Andrew Garve, pseud. New York: Harper, 1970.

5698. ___. *By-Line for Murder*. By Andrew Garve, pseud. New York: Harper, 1951. [*A Press of Suspects*. By Andrew Garve, pseud. London: Collins, 1951].

5699. ___. *The Case of Robert Quarry*. By Andrew Garve, pseud. New York: Harper, 1972.

5700. ___. *The Cuckoo Line Affair*. By Andrew Garve, pseud. New York: Harper, 1953.

5701. ___. *Death and the Sky Above*. By Andrew Garve, pseud. New York: Harper, 1954.

5702. ___. *The End of the Track*. By Andrew Garve, pseud. New York: Harper, 1956.

5703. ___. *The Far Sands*. By Andrew Garve, pseud. New York: Harper, 1960.

5704. ___. *Fontego's Folly*. By Andrew Garve, pseud. New York: Harper, 1950. [*No Mask for Murder*. By Andrew Garve, pseud. London: Collins, 1950].

5705. ___. *Frame-Up*. By Andrew Garve, pseud. New York: Harper, 1964.

5706. ___. *The Galloway Case*. By Andrew Garve, pseud. New York: Harper, 1958.

5707. ___. *The Golden Deed*. By Andrew Garve, pseud. New York: Harper, 1960.

5708. ___. *Hide and Go Seek*. By Andrew Garve, pseud. New York: Harper, 1966. [*Murderer's Fen*. By Andrew Garve, pseud. London: Collins, 1966].

5709. ___. *Home to Roost*. By Andrew Garve, pseud. New York: Crowell, 1976.

5710. ___. *The House of Soldiers*. By Andrew Garve, pseud. New York: Harper, 1961.

5711. ___. *The Late Bill Smith*. By Andrew Garve, pseud. New York: Harper, 1971.

5712. ___. *The Lester Affair*. By Andrew Garve, pseud. New York: Harper, 1974. [*The File on Lester*. By Andrew Garve, pseud. London: Collins, 1974].

5713. ___. *The Long Short Cut*. By Andrew Garve, pseud. New York: Harper, 1968.

5714. ___. *The Megstone Plot*. By Andrew Garve, pseud. New York: Harper, 1957.

5715. ___. *The Narrow Search*. By Andrew Garve, pseud. New York: Harper, 1958.

5716. ___. *No Tears for Hilda*. By Andrew Garve, pseud. New York: Harper, 1950.

5717. ___. *Prisoner's Friend*. By Andrew Garve, pseud. New York: Harper, 1962.

5718. ___. *The Riddle of Samson*. By Andrew Garve, pseud. New York: Harper, 1955.

5719. ___. *The Sea Monks*. By Andrew Garve, pseud. New York: Harper, 1963.

5720. ___. *A Very Quiet Place*. By Andrew Garve, pseud. New York: Harper, 1967.

5721. Winton, John. *The Fighting Temeraire.* New York: Coward-McCann, 1971. In the silent war between Russia and the West, a nuclear submarine enters the Black Sea on a secret mission which becomes an international incident. Compare with Keith Wheeler's *The Last Mayday.*

5722. Winward, Walter. *Fives Wild.* New York: Atheneum, 1976. To assure nonalignment of their nation through possession of the latest weapons, a gang, led by master criminal Carl Carlson, attempts to knock over a CIA armored truck transporting $3 million over some of Europe's roughest terrain.

5723. ___ . *Hammerstrike.* New York: Simon & Schuster, 1979. In the fall of 1942, Goering devises a plan to confuse the Allied war effort which calls for the simultaneous escape of all German POWs being held in Great Britain.

5724. ___ . *Seven Minutes past Midnight.* New York: Simon & Schuster, 1980. In 1945, a top Nazi betrays the Reich to save himself and is rescued by the SOE at a midnight rendezvous near dying Berlin. One other by Winward:

5725. ___ . *Circle of Deceit.* New York: Charter, 1985. [*The Last and Greater Art.* London: Hamilton, 1983.]

5726. Winwood, John, ed. *The Mammoth Book of Spy Thrillers.* New York: Carroll & Graf, 1989. This collection contains Oppenheim's *Wrath to Come*, Household's *Rogue Male*, and Clifford's *Naked Runner.*

5727. Wise, Arthur. *Mission Code #7: Acropolis.* By Bryan Swift, house pseud. New York: Jove, 1982. Mac Wingate is a hero skilled in demolitions and a terror to the Nazis. *P* One more tale:

5728. ___ . *Mission Code #1: Symbol.* By Bryan Swift, house pseud. New York: Jove, 1982. (See Knott, Will C. for more Wingate tales.)

5729. Wise, David. *Spectrum.* New York: Viking, 1981. Knowing that the exposure of a 1965 theft of uranium will damage further the reputation of "the Company," CIA Director Towny Black battles three separate investigations in an effort to cover up the truth.

Author Wise, together with Thomas B. Ross, was one of the first reporters to look into the matter of so-called CIA abuses. Their *The Invisible Government* was published by Random House in 1964. Since then, Wise and Ross, separately and together, have written a number of books and articles on that theme. Wise's most recent non-fiction book on espionage is *Molehunt: The Secret Search for Traitors that Shattered the CIA* (New York: Random, 1992).

5730. ___ . *Children's Game.* New York: St. Martin's, 1983. Ex-CIA agent William Danner is coerced back into service by his former bosses. Danner discovers that Special Operations plans to insert an agent as a clown in the Moscow Circus with an assignment to "neutralize" the Soviet premier in attendance.

5731. Wiseman, Thomas. *The Day before Sunrise.* New York: Holt, 1976. OSS agent Howard Elliott is sent to ensure that a surrender of Italian troops in Northern Italy, negotiated between Allen W. Dulles and the SS General commanding, is carried though.

5732. ___ . *A Game of Secrets.* New York: Delacorte, 1979. In 1947 a presidential advisor on intelligence matters, ex-OSS man Bill Hardtmann is sent to New York to investigate the mysterious death of a doctor, who fell off a skyscraper as the result of a possible drug experiment, and gets mixed up with an unseen "mole," codenamed "Homer," the most highly placed Soviet spy in history.

5733. Wittman, George. *A Matter of Intelligence.* New York: Macmillan, 1975. A KGB agent, posing as a loyal American, fumbles his mission to steal US missile secrets.

5734. Wohl, Burton. *The Ten-Tola Bars.* New York: Delacorte, 1975. Arab terrorists and agents of the KGB, SIS, and Mossad all pursue a financial writer as he seeks $20 million in tiny stolen gold bars.

5735. Wohl, James P. *The Nervana Contracts.* Indianapolis: Bobbs-Merrill, 1977. A Paris-bound jetliner carrying a variety of agents is blown up by one of the passengers when it reaches a point two hours from Kennedy International.

5736. Wolf, S. K. [Sarah]. *The Harbinger Effect.* New York: Simon & Schuster, 1989. When a Soviet photo-journalist attempts seeks asylum at the US embassy in a small African nation, agents of the two superpowers try to retrieve the photos he took of military intervention in that country. (See Ms. Wolf's comment in CRAFT NOTES.)

5737. ___ . *MacKinnon's Machine.* New York: Simon & Schuster, 1991. Sgt. Major MacKinnon comes out of his New Zealand retirement to lead a combat team against Muammar el-Qaddafi; however, after one of his own team leaders tries to kill him, he begins to wonder who is sending him on this mission—and why?

Wolfe, Michael, pseud. *See* Williams, Gilbert M.

5738. Wolk, George. *The Leopard Contract.* New York: Random, 1969. An American operative works to liquidate an enemy spy while posing as the bodyguard to a US scientist.

5739. Wood, Christopher. *North to Rabaul.* New York: Dutton, 1979. In 1943, Allied commandos attempt to assist a predicted eruption of Mount Matupi with explosives, thereby sealing off the tunnel network in the Japanese fortress of Rabaul on New Britain island.

5740. Wood, James. *Fire Rock.* New York: Vanguard, 1966. In the Arctic, Jim Fraser becomes involved in dirty tricks being played on fishermen by a looney British naval officer.

5741. ___. *The Friday Run.* London: Hutchinson, 1967. James Fraser is a Scots fisherman who takes on the Nazis in this and seven other novels, all written between 1954 and 1969. The last:

5742. ___. *The Lisa Bastian.* New York: Vanguard, 1961. Fraser, a Scots shepherd and fisherman on the payroll of British Intelligence, gets mixed up in a dangerous expedition to raise a sunken ship.

5743. ___. *The Sealer.* New York: Vanguard, 1961. Fraser relates his mission to ferret out a secret Nazi raider in the waters of Tierra del Fuego. Another:

5744. ___. *Three Blind Mice.* New York: Vanguard, 1969. *P*

5745. Woodhouse, Martin. *Blue Bone.* New York: Coward-McCann, 1973. Having uncovered a cryptic message in a shipment of toys from Czechoslovakia, Kate Seaton aids Giles Yeoman of the Department of Scientific Security as he seeks to free her uncle from a prison in East Germany.

5746. ___. *Bush Baby.* New York: Coward-McCann, 1969. [*Rock Baby.* London: Heinemann, 1968]. Someone has tampered with an automatic seismograph and Agent Yeoman, sent to locate it, uncovers a dangerous laser crystal which certain Albanian operatives want.

5747. ___. *Mama Doll.* New York: Coward-McCann, 1972. Having recovered from a surgery performed as the result of an attack in Scotland,

Yeoman emerges filled with the fires of vengeance and proceeds to hack down a powerful arms dealer's large hidden store of weapons.

5748. ___. *Phil and Me.* New York: Coward-McCann, 1970. Employing his Commando training, Michael Keyes battles for the hidden cargo in Phillipa Conway's missing Bahamian sailboat.

5749. ___. *Rock Baby.* New York: Coward-McCann, 1968. Giles Yeoman must locate a faulty automatic-spy seismograph, which went off course when launched and landed in a remote section of Yugoslavia.

5750. ___. *Tree Frog.* New York: Coward-McCann, 1966. Agent Yeoman is doped and whisked off to a Polish hideout in the Tyrolean Alps, where his captors torture him for data concerning a new pilotless reconnaissance plane codenamed "Tree Frog."

5751. Woods, Stuart. *Deep Lie.* New York: Norton, 1986. A CIA disinformation operation designed to convince the Soviets that the Swedes are going to join NATO works too well—the Soviets plan an invasion operation against Sweden. His latest mystery thriller:

5752. ___. *Dead Eyes.* New York: HarperCollins, 1994.

5753. Woods, William H. *Edge of Darkness.* Philadelphia: Lippincott, 1942. Norwegian resistance fighters struggle to free their captive people from Nazi tyranny. *

5754. Woolf, Marion, Margery W. Papich, and Layne Torkelson. *The Balloon Affair.* By Marion Margery Layne, pseud. New York: Dodd, 1981. A solar engineer plans to kidnap the governor of New Mexico as a publicity stunt when he announces a state tax on solar energy.

5755. Wormser, Richard. *Operation Crossbow.* New York: Dell, 1965. Three men are sent on a suicidal mission to destroy German V-2 launching sites in France. *P*

Wren, M. K., pseud. *See* Renfroe, Martha K.

5756. Wright, Glover. *Blood Enemies.* New York: Arbor, 1987. The Soviets run a brilliant "False Flag" operation against the British and Americans when a patriot is recruited to assassinate four intelligence officers who are, he thinks, Russian moles.

5757. ___. *The Hound of Heaven*. New York: Arbor, 1986. A mix of supernatural and espionage in this thriller about a soldier who saves a priest about to be crucified by the Viet Cong; years later the officer becomes a priest who is commissioned by a sinister reactionary in the Church hierarchy to eliminate the very priest he once saved—now a living "saint" leading a mass movement antithetical to the Church's teachings.

5758. ___. *The Torch*. New York: Putnam's, 1980. A British colonel plots to take over the KGB communications center in London and reveal vital military secrets unless a Russian-backed African nation agrees to release its imprisoned white mercenaries.

5759. Wright, William Talboy. *Churchill's Gold*. New York: Tudor, 1988. Churchill orders a salvaging expedition to the Pacific to recover gold bullion so that England can avoid collapse in her darkest hour. *P*

5760. Wuorio, Eva-Lis. *The Woman with the Portuguese Basket*. New York: Holt, 1964. Adelaide, a middle-aged art teacher on sabbatical in Europe, is plunged into a whirlpool of espionage and danger when she accepts a Portuguese basket as a gift from a counterintelligence agent. *

5761. ___. *Z for Zaborra*. New York: Holt, 1966. Toria Walden, an ex-agent, carries on a deadly masquerade for British Intelligence in a hospital where a courier from a neo-Nazi organization is supposed to deliver information dangerous to the whole world. *

5762. Wylie, James. *The Sign of Dawn*. New York: Viking, 1981. Mercenary Jordan Mallory leads a small group of free-lance soldiers and a new president through the revolution-torn jungles of Brazil in hopes of placing the politician in power against the will of the Communists running the country's oppressive government.

5763. Wylie, Philip. *The Smuggled Atom Bomb*. Garden City, NY: Doubleday, 1965. Bad men have come into the possession of an A-bomb and plan to use it for blackmail purposes.

5764. ___. *The Spy Who Spoke Porpoise*. Garden City, NY: Doubleday, 1970. A retired American intelligence agent is secretly commissioned by the President to sneak information out of the CIA and with the help of a porpoise, halt a Communist plot against Hawaii.

5765. Wynd, Oswald. *The Bitter Tea.* By Gavin Black, pseud. New York: Harper & Row, 1972. Malaysian businessman Paul Harris becomes involved in the kidnapping of a high Chinese official.

5766. ___. *The Cold Jungle.* By Gavin Black, pseud. New York: Harper & Row, 1969. Harris returns to England from Malaysia to have a ship built for his company by an old friend. Pressure is put upon him, the friend is murdered, and our hero is threatened in various ways by an unknown power for apparently unknown reasons.

5767. ___. *Death, the Red Flower.* By Gavin Black, pseud. New York: Harcourt, 1961. The captain of a British freighter is the unknowing dupe in a Communist plot to start World War III.

5768. ___. *A Dragon for Christmas.* By Gavin Black, pseud. New York: Harper & Row, 1963. Harris gets mixed up in foreign intrigue while attempting to peddle his wares in Peking.

5769. ___. *The Eyes around Me.* By Gavin Black, pseud. New York: Harper & Row, 1964. In Hong Kong, a lovely girl is found dead in her bed and a Scot is wrongly singled out as chief suspect in an unhappy scheme.

5770. ___. *The Golden Cockatrice.* By Gavin Black, pseud. New York: Harper & Row, 1975. Harris is caught in the middle of a Chinese-Russian shipping rivalry.

5771. ___. *Sumatra Seven Zero.* By Gavin Black, pseud. New York: Harcourt, 1968. A retired SIS officer named McFay is recalled to help his old agency find the missing daughter of a murdered Burmese ruby mine owner.

5772. ___. *A Time of Pirates.* By Gavin Black, pseud. New York: Harper & Row, 1971. Harris is involved with a group of murderous modern-day buccaneers operating off the coast of Malaysia.

5773. ___. *Walk Softly, Men Praying.* By Gavin Black, pseud. New York: Harcourt, 1967. Ian Douglas meets CIA agent Calcotl, who needs information about some strange exports from Japan to China.

5774. ___. *You Want to Die, Johnny?* By Gavin Black, pseud. New York: Harper & Row, 1966. Paul Harris, in Borneo to help his old friend the British resident, must contend with teenager Lil and Chinese infiltrators.

Y

5775. Yates, Alan Geoffrey. *And the Undead Sing.* By Carter Brown, pseud. New York: Signet, 1974. Private investigator and occasional secret agent Mavis Seidlitz is the product of this Australian writer, who began publishing her adventures in 1955. *P*

5776. ___. *The Hong Kong Caper.* By Carter Brown, pseud. New York: Signet, 1962. An American soldier-of-fortune undertakes a dangerous mission against the Red Chinese espionage apparatus located in the British Crown colony. *P* Two others:

5777. ___. *Murder Is So Nostalgic.* By Carter Brown, pseud. New York: Signet, 1972. *P*

5778. ___. *Seidlitz and the Super-Spy.* By Carter Brown, pseud. New York: Signet, 1967. [*The Super-Spy.* By Carter Brown, pseud. Sevenoaks: NEL, 1968.] *P*

5779. Yates, Brock W. *Dead in the Water.* New York: Farrar, 1975. Canadian agents must foil a French Separatist plot to kidnap the Prime Minister.

5780. Yates, Margaret T. *Murder by the Yard.* New York: Macmillan, 1942. A prying woman outwits Japanese agents, led by a German spymaster, in Honolulu in the days just before Pearl Harbor. *

5781. Yerby, Frank. *The Voyage Unplanned.* New York: Dial, 1974. Searching for a comrade-in-arms twenty years after the end of the Second World War, a French Resistance fighter is drawn into a bloody angle of the Arab-Israeli conflict.

5782. Yin, Leslie C. B. *The Saint in Pursuit.* By Leslie Charteris, pseud. London: Hodder & Stoughton, 1972. The Saint unravels the mystery of an American OSS agent who disappeared in Lisbon in 1944.

Yin began his tales of the freelance detective Simon Templar in the 1930s (see Part I) and has occasionally had him involved in security and espionage matters. The Saint's adventures are continued into the present and Leslie Charteris has become a house pseudonym.

5783. ___. *The Saint in Trouble.* By Leslie Charteris, pseud. Garden City, NY: Doubleday, 1979. Two Simon Templar tales. In *The Red Sabbath*, the

Saint ends a terrorist assassination spree, while in *The Imprudent Professor*, he keeps a brilliant professor from defecting to the Soviet Union.

5784. ___. *The Saint on Guard*. By Leslie Charteris, pseud. Garden City, NY: Doubleday, 1944. Cooperating with the FBI, Templar smashes the iridium black market and a Nazi saboteur ring in wartime Galveston. *

5785. ___. *The Saint Returns*. By Leslie Charteris, pseud. London: Hodder & Stoughton, 1969. Simon Templar gets mixed up with a girl who claims to be Hitler's daughter.

5786. ___. *The Saint Steps In*. By Leslie Charteris, pseud. Garden City, NY: Doubleday, 1943. The Saint again cooperates with the FBI to smash an Axis spy ring operating in North America during the Second World War. * The Saint has proved durable through the past decade; his further adventures have been published under the aegises of Doubleday and the Detective Book Club in the US and Hodder & Stoughton in Great Britain. Both houses published *The Fantastic Saint*, edited by Martin H. Greenberg and Charles G. Waugh (Garden City, NY: Doubleday, 1982; London: Hodder & Stoughton, 1983). Most recently *Leslie Charteris' Salvage for the Saint* by John Kruse and Peter Bloxson (Garden City, NY: Doubleday, 1983) and *The Saint and the Templar Treasure* by Charles King and Graham Weaver (Garden City, NY: Doubleday, 1979). Also:

5787. ___. *The Saint: Five Complete Novels*. New York: Avenel, 1983. Contains: *The Man Who Was Clever*, *The Lawless Lady*, *The Saint Closed the Case*, *The Avenging Saint*, and *The Saint vs. Scotland Yard*.

5788. Yorch, Ruth L. *Sixty to Go*. New York: Messner, 1944. A group of what we would now call "beautiful people" at play on the French Riviera actually constitute an underground cell which is working to smuggle people into neutral Spain where they will be safe from the Gestapo. *

York, Andrew, pseud. *See* Nicole, Christopher

5789. Young, Edward P. *The Fifth Passenger*. New York: Harper & Row, 1963. A London solicitor is on the spot when a defecting naval officer, who saved his life years before, seeks his aid. The great chase scene takes place through the stacks of the London Public Library.

5790. Yurick, Sol. *Richard A.* New York: Arbor, 1981. During the Cuban Missile Crisis of 1962, a gifted young man serves as a special liaison between President Kennedy and Premier Khrushchev.

Z

5791. Zachary, Hugh. *The Adlon Link.* By Zachery Hughes, pseud. New York: Jove, 1981. This series concerns Nazi intrigue on the threshold of World War II. *P*

5792. ___. *The Venus Venture.* New York: Vanguard, 1986. A gang of mostly Americans conspires to steal the *Venus de Milo* on exhibit in Moscow. Others:

5793. ___. *Deep Freeze.* New York: DAW, 1992. *P*

5794. ___. *The Fires of Paris.* By Zachery Hughes, pseud. New York: Jove, 1981. *P*

5795. ___. *Fortress London.* By Zachery Hughes, pseud. New York: Jove, 1981. *P*

5796. ___. *Tower of Treason.* By Zachery Hughes, pseud. New York: Jove, 1982. *P*

5797. Zarubica, Mladin. *Scutari.* New York: Farrar, 1968. American businessman Urosh Gore becomes an unwitting cog in a plan which sends him to Albania to penetrate a Red Chinese missile base.

5798. ___. *The Year of the Rat.* New York: Harcourt, 1965. A hunting guide in the Alps tells of a hoax in which Allied Intelligence substituted their own agent for his double, a German courier general, to get false plans for "Operation Overlord" (D-Day) into Nazi hands. *

5799. Zeno, pseud. *The Four Sergeants.* New York: Atheneum, 1977. Four platoon sergeants lead British paratroops in a desperate effort to blow a bridge which, if destroyed, will prevent the escape of a German division on Sicily in 1943.
      A British First Airborne Division sergeant, the man who uses the pseudonym Zeno has won high praise from discerning military historians for his meticulous accuracy. He fought in North Africa and was wounded at Arnheim.

The dust jacket blurb of *The Four Sergeants* quotes Zeno as saying that since the war he has led a "fairly eventful life." Some of his "eventful" life is recorded in *Life*, which autobiography (New York: Stein & Day, 1968) is set in London's infamous Wormwood Scrubs Prison.

5800. ___. *The Cauldron.* New York: Stein & Day, 1966. Notes the dust jacket: "The author of this extraordinary novel is now serving a life sentence for homicide."

5801. ___. *Grab.* New York: Stein & Day, 1971. A mercenary agrees to a job escorting a certain Arab out of Libya.

5802. Zerwick, Chloë and Harrison Brown. *The Cassiopeia Affair.* Garden City, NY: Doubleday, 1968. Dr. Max Gaby, a presidential assistant, receives a special signal from Cassiopeia and dies of a stroke. Later, in China, another scientist receives a similar message. This is a different type of spy thriller, a cross between intrigue, espionage, and science fiction. *

5803. Zezza, Carlo. *Paris 2005.* New York: Ivy, 1991. In this futuristic thriller, Russia and Germany have combined forces, the Japanese have used their technological dominance to shift the balance of power from the US. One man, a former computer whiz, leads an underground (literally) battle for freedom beneath the catacombs of the Arc de Triomphe.

5804. Zilinsky, Ursula. *Before the Glory Ended.* Philadelphia: Lippincott, 1967. The decline of the aristocracy and the changes which rocked Europe between 1919 and 1957 are viewed through the eyes of two men, a French SDECE agent and a Hungarian spy.

5805. Zimmerman, R. D. [Robert Dingwall]. *The Cross and the Sickle.* New York: Zebra, 1983. An American is enlisted in a scheme to smuggle historical documents important to the underground church movement throughout the Ukraine to the West. *P* Two more:

5806. ___. *Dead Fall in Berlin.* New York: Fine, 1990. *P*

5807. ___. *Mindscream.* New York: Zebra, 1990. *P*

Appendix A: Craft Notes

There was a good Nazi proverb you should remember, "Der Zweck heiligt die Mittel"—the end justifies the means . . . It was not true then and it's not true now . . . So let us be quite clear that what we must do has no platform of morality. We are not heroes—we are just different thugs, different scum.
                —Col. Munsel of the Abwehr in Ted Allbeury's
                Mission Berlin [*The Only Good German*], 119

I DIDN'T START writing until I was fifty-five. I had never thought about being a writer nor particularly wanted to be one. My start didn't come out of sudden inspiration but out of an entirely negative situation. Something happened in my private life that depressed me deeply. Enough to end up taking those green pills to get through the day and the purple ones to get through the night. I gave up work and the world and retreated into the lethargy and despair that goes with depression. For some unknown reason I wrote four chapters of a book. Its central thrust was based on my experiences as an intelligence officer in occupied Germany. The four chapters were shown by somebody to a literary agent who phoned me a few days later to say that he had sold my book to St. Martin's Press in New York and was selling it to a British publisher the next day. Would I get a move on and finish it? As all would-be writers know, it's not this easy to get published—but that's how it happened. It sure was a cure for my depression because the pretty Polish girl from the typing agency who came to type the manuscript is still around. We got married.

Since then I've written thirty-one novels, some short stories and a number of radio plays and serials for the BBC. And, naturally, you learn a few things in the course of all that writing. When I first started writing I worked out a plot and bolted on the characters, but by about book number seven I realized that what I liked writing about most was the people. Their problems and their relationships. It also dawned on me that nobody was stopping me from writing any way I wanted to. So I start now with the people and the plot allows them to work out their destinies. I think that I now write novels that just happen to have espionage as their setting.

I am often asked what makes a writer, and how to set about being one. The second question is the easier to answer. Buy yourself a W. H. Smith jumbo pad and a pencil—and start writing. There are books on how to write. Some good, some not so good. Then read a lot, especially the kind of books you would like to write. But when it comes to what makes a writer I don't know the answer. It's like playing the piano by ear. You don't know how you do it.

However I can tell you what doesn't make a writer. It's not formal education. My headmaster told my Grandma that I was on the dustheap of the school and would be on the dustheap of life. I was pleased to be guest of honour a few years back at the school's bicentenary. More importantly it's obviously never too late to start. If I can start from scratch at age fifty-five so can anyone else. I strongly recommend that you write while you still have a full-time job. I did, and this meant writing until two in the morning and all day Saturdays and Sundays. I'm a strong believer that anyone can do anything if they want to do it enough. And it's the last part that is the test. Do you really want to do it enough?

Obviously I get asked if it helps that I was an intelligence officer myself. It does help in some ways, but just knowing what happens doesn't mean that you can write about it well enough to interest readers. Authenticity doesn't come from knowing which way the safety catch goes on a Walther PPK. It comes from the everyday feelings of what it was like when you were being trained and what it felt like on your first job.

Perhaps the most important thing that you learn from doing the job is that whether you are SIS, CIA, or KGB you are all men, recruited in much the same way and trained much the same way. And doing the same kind of work. This means that you end up with more in common with your opposite numbers than you have with your own civilian population.

There is a kind of hypocrisy, particularly in this country, that surrounds the security and intelligence services. Even when they catch a spy or a traitor the shout goes up—"Why didn't they catch him sooner?" Every country has its own intelligence services and certainly ours and the Americans' do a good job of work. Sometimes things have to be done that are not "kosher" but if the nation wants protection from foreigners' interference these things have to be done. The men who work in these services are admittedly specially trained to do their jobs. But they are perfectly ordinary men with mortgages, families, and responsibilities. Like the rest of us they can be lonely and perhaps cynical, but on the whole they behave like you and I would behave doing their job. And what I have said about men applies equally to the women in the services.

It seems a terrible thing to say, but for young men like me from the less posh suburbs of Birmingham, the war was our university. A broadening of our vision and the exercise of our minds and imaginations far beyond what would have happened if we had not been involved. Irrational though it may be I still feel an affinity with those men and women who were in the services rather than those who were not. Shakespeare's *Henry V* speech at Agincourt about "gentlemen in England now a-bed" is still valid for me. And that means that I have little sympathy for those, mainly Brits, who write non-fiction books purporting to prove that our intelligence services are being run by traitors and double-agents. And even less sympathy for those who publish the names of serving officers so that their lives are endangered.

Ted Allbeury

My favorite authors are Christie, Carr, Dickens, and Maugham. [About today's mystery writers] Dick Francis, for me, after 1970, didn't have a single new thing to say—I'm all "raced" out—and to this day I don't know how a seasoned pro can get by with so many I-Said and He-Saids on one page. Le Carré and Francis are prime examples of The Emperor's Clothes School of Criticism. No more about that.

I love—and loved—writing spy-espionage novels. They are first-class entertainments when they are fashioned for entertainment and not totally too deep or too lecturish in delivery—nobody ever topped the great Graham Greene or Eric Ambler for the serious side in this select area—and still haven't—and I've yet to read one that really beats *The Great Impersonation* and that's E. Phillips Oppenheim. I expressed my own feelings for espionage in *The Man* and *Girl Uncle* books, the *Hawaii Five-O*'s and the Intrex Series while never forgetting what Ian Fleming knew from the start: they should be larks and entertainments, full-rigged from the start, and anything after that is pure bonus and gravy . . .

The private eye of fiction is really a fantasy figure; le Carré's mean little men aren't. Nations still employ "spy labor" as Victor Francen said in the great *The Mask of Dimitrios* (Warner Brothers, 1944).

[About the *Uncle* TV series] The show soared, the world went Uncle crazy and my book stayed in print five years, sold in the millions and would end up in something like sixty foreign editions. There is no telling the royalty money I lost but on the good side, the book was always a great showcase for my talents, got me a lot of writing jobs and made me known abroad. To this day I meet people who still recall *The Thousand Coffins Affair* as one of their memorable "escape reading" experiences.

Michael Avallone

As to my choice of subjects for spy fiction? In each instance I elected to deal with bureaucratic cultures true to form, and with this disinterest, ambition that characterizes them. Le Carré did the same. My own concern—other than an exciting story line which meant exciting places—was with the sadness of which must be a consequence of living lives where bureaucracies, by reasons of being intelligence agencies, were even further removed from accountability. *The Mexican Assassin* deals with life in Mexico very much as I saw it: cruel and corrupt. The named assassin who the reader may see as an enemy is, in fact, a thoughtful man. A dear friend of mine was such an assassin. Barbour, the ostensible hero—and here again as with the author's pseudonym itself I use genuine family names to indicate no full flight from self identification—is, upon examination, also assassin. It has troubled me that no reader who has talked to me about the book has understood the identity of the two. Barbour is less the hero for he works for the government. Whilst betrayed by his superiors in many ways, Barbour at least enjoys sanctioned killing, moral stuff, and such protections as being an employee provide. The Mexican who is also assassin has none, and is the braver man. Many of the events are genuine, although gathered from around the western hemisphere's Latin parts, as is the priest who is modeled on Camillo Torres of Columbia, a man whom I knew and liked, and sought to counsel to abandon the machine gun which was so incompatible with the collar. He too would be an assassin, although he considered himself a fighter for whatever hopeless revolution the "good" could seek in that savage land. He died a few months after our last visit (ambushed, but expected). And look at Columbia now—more savage than during *La Violencia*. Assassins do not make for social improvement. As for Mexico, my picture of it is not of guitars, nor should it be. Combine Conquistadors and Aztecs and the outcome is hardly in doubt, not yesterday or tomorrow. Ask our current drug enforcement people if that is not so.

Whisper of Treason was based on my genuine affection for Yugoslavs, but my dismay at the behavior of their intelligence people in foreign assassinations. The Nazi-like partisans and regional nationalists whom they hunted and sought to forfend were by no means good folks. Hardly. But I happened to be troubled by governments of people I like (whether Western European, US, Yugoslavs) using the dagger. But the book is really about the treachery of the bureaucrat; in this instance the American embassy variety. It is not a political treachery which is at the heart of my concern—that is rare—but rather the hypocrisy and selfish ambition whose consequences are so destructive to effective, task oriented action whatever the mandate of an agency, bureau, may be.

An important theme in *Whisper* was mostly deleted by the publisher—publishers always push to reduce pages and keep to TV style scene hopping—had to do with the nature of an high-level Soviet defector. Most of that material—his introspection, his philosophical base—was lost. But I did wish sympathetically to show the wrenching it is for a many of decency and knowledge to leave his homeland, and the why of it—at that level almost always it was ideological. The contrast is with the typical NATO defector—alcohol, greed,—the Eastern bloc recruits from NATO, an inferior breed. Not that their information need be less valuable—as we have seen recently.

Codename Starlight is a bit more lighthearted, but concerns itself equally with the pointlessly ugly environments in which people on either side of the Iron Curtain work. The rest is but exciting story line.

And so, in sum, my effort is to present the spy novel within the context of actual cultures, including the bureaucratic, with sensitivity to the Janus nature of the heroes/villains on both sides. One may question the heroes, give pause before defaming enemies, insofar as both partake of similar backgrounds and intentions. The humanities of those involved is not to be ignored.

Well, I trust this is enough commentary. I may soon be embarked, well, a year or so, in another spy novel, this one with a former colleague. Tentatively entitled The Last Literate Spy, it will deal with the growth of mediocrity, computers, the debasing of typical educational backgrounds, the movement of mainstream (Nixon, Reagan, Bush) short-term thinking, materialism, into thematic primacy in government and national life. The setting ought to be the Middle East, if for no other reason than that venality there is so common. But now we are beginning to catch up, unaware even of that. Naturally one will have heroes but I am not sure that any alien spy would be the enemy, for with the changes in China (never really an enemy but to herself) and the [former] USSR, one will have to look more within the common boundaries to find treachery—not the "he lied" sort, but the selfish kind, which eats away at kindness and generosity as Western world commitments.

Hartshorne
[Richard H. A. Blum]

If you think of intelligence officers as well trained, highly motivated white-collar criminals (and after all, if their activities were legal they wouldn't need to be covert) and the counterespionage people as cops (which they are for the most part), then you have the basis for figuring out how they do what they do.

One's job is to outsmart other people who are performing investigative police work, though not always with Miranda Rules to hold them back. The advantage of the intelligence officer is the same as that of the criminal—anonymity. The "crook" has the thrill of yanking the system's beard and the stress of knowing that he may be caught. Spies historically come to very bad ends; the lucky ones are executed by civilized means.

The job of the counterintelligence officer is twofold: first to determine whether or not a crime has been actually committed (the hard part), and second to discover who did it (the easy part). His advantage is the human fallibility of his prey. The "cop" feels that he "only catches the dumb ones," and never escapes the frustration of not knowing how many he's missing. In this the counterintelligence officer always overrates his enemy—if brain surgeons and airline pilots can make mistakes, so can the best of spies. Everyone's a little dumb once in a while, but few are willing to admit it.

All in all, it's quite a game. *The only one in which nobody, not even the players, can ever know who's ahead.*

Tom Clancy

Are we thriller/espionage writers to be consigned to the dustbins of history now that *détente* is here? Should we lie awake at night worrying about our conversion to some other fruitful form of endeavor—selling insurance, for example?

On balance, I think not. I'm ready to stick with Winston Churchill's observation that the reports of his demise had been greatly exaggerated. There are other, neighboring vineyards in which to labor, those of our friends in the Middle East, for example, which can replace the Evil Empire. Or, an idea which fascinates me, going back into the past and taking a close look at a disinformation or espionage operation of the Cold War from the perspective of *both* sides to see how things really played out.

Larry Collins

After a lifetime of reading spy thrillers, a real fan will try to write one sooner or later. Before you do you should cogitate a few moments on just what it is about the genre that has always intrigued you. This is the magic that you are going to try to capture on paper.

Like everyone else, I have my own theory. These books are fantasies for the bored, mind candy for us powerless moderns trapped by the laws and mores of civilized society. Those spy thrillers that seem to work best are those with a hero that the reader can subconsciously identify with who acts boldly, using intelligence, guile, and if necessary, violence, to outwit the villains' foul plots. The hero moves in a world of gray half-lights where nothing is ever quite what is seems, which every reader will recognize as a pretty fair portrait of modern reality. Our hero is on his own, out on the edge, with little but his own resources to combat the evil confronting him.

One of the ever-present themes in modern society is that of the conspiracy—the front pages are full of it every day. We see threads of conspiracies in reports of crime, foreign affairs, finance, news from the courts, Hollywood, and so on. The vague "they" who rule our lives for good and ill are the real stars of the spy thriller, the menace our fantasy hero is going to act against in a decisive way. He will triumph over the faceless ones as we, the readers, quietly rejoice.

The story needs sufficient plot twists so the reader can't figure out the whole thing in the first four chapters. Here the craft of fiction writing comes into full play: one must write good characters, good dialogue, and good action, all carefully erected upon a solid, devious plot.

Mistakes to avoid—making the hero an anti-hero, killing off your hero, letting the hero figure out which door hides the tiger too early in the tale, letting the bad guys win. Now you can do any one or all of these things, but if you do you no longer have a spy thriller: you have written a serious novel that can be sold only to intellectuals, a small, miserable, nitpicking, poverty-stricken audience that you will starve to death trying to please.

Stephen Coonts

The espionage novel will never be the same. Once America became the only superpower, the threat of sudden annihilation disappeared. Spy novelists are probably drifting toward the terrorist novel or the high-tech adventure story. There will always be books dealing with more personal betrayals and the aging spy remembering past triumphs. However they lack a sense of urgency.

I expect there will be an attempt to write about new villains, but without the "Evil Empire," such books will be relatively tame. Industrial espionage is a possible topic to be developed, but it is hard to make such spying earth-shaking. Of course, World War II spies and the Nazis are not going to disappear, but they are getting a bit long in the tooth.

Jon Winters
[Gilbert Cross]

Are we witness to the *decline* and *fall* of the spy thriller? Spy stories at which our British friends excel since their countrymen were so good at the real stuff? Writers tend to write of their times. It's easier. This is specifically true of writers in the thriller-form. Readers, all through the 40s, 50s, 60s were onslaughted by the news, by TV, by *Time, Newsweek,* by a hundred other things that told them they lived in nasty times. Luckily, very luckily, writers could find believable bogeymen in every other paragraph. You carved yourself a handy KGB agent, or cut yourself a Russian lady with Kremlin persuasions, or a modern Manchu fanatic from Beijing.

Easy pickings.

When it came to Cold War spy stories, the media set the genre up. They wrote the characters in their everyday dispatches and didn't charge for the service. Much of recent spy fiction was built from the hard bricks of reality.

The media, the politicians, the cold-warriors had made a wondrous present to the writer. For they had lit the stage for the reading public, making the plots, the places, and the characters of fiction at once more understandable and thus more acceptable.

It was a gift. Empires of the written page were created.

But what now?

Who will the new ogres be? From Moscow blows a wind with fewer and warmer teeth. Kiss them off in time. China, the same. No western pol worth her or his salt can raise real campaign money till they're photoed walking the Wall. They made the golden egg, now they're breaking it, and don't know it.

From where will come the new enemies?

Seriously. We may see a slacking off of the thriller-types we've become used to over the past twenty-five years. That's a loss, if it happens, a true loss. Most every espionage-thriller is tailored of political or military cloth that shapes, styles, and cloaks the body of the story. And those bodies saw some of the best writing of the twentieth century.

To keep the garden in color and high-dress, we need a new breed of belladonna. In the form of mass inspiration, and some new writers, or new writing, that thwarts the mind as it freezes the blood.

That's the quandary facing us. Help!

David R. Cudlip

Jacques Barzun once wrote, "The soul of the spy is somehow the model for us all." In all my writings, as in all of life, the element of spying, or more delicately put, information gathering, is central to the human condition.

Human beings are infinitely curious about the world around them and the people with whom they interact.

Spying falls into several categories: personal, military, political, diplomatic, industrial, and so forth, and we've created organizations and institutions to accomplish all of these aspects, from the private eye, to the police, the CIA, FBI, State Department of Intelligence, and on and on.

So, even if the Cold War is over, the spy, by whatever name he or she goes by, is still with us and still survives in reality and fiction.

Nelson DeMille

One of the primary problems of writing convincingly about espionage or indeed about all forms of international skulduggery, is that the tradecraft and the technology is constantly changing. To remain convincing one has to be constantly up with the game and this requires a high level of accurate research.

The historical writer, setting his novel in the American Civil War, may be assured that the uniforms and insignia of the forces involved, once researched, are unlikely to change by next year. The poor spy writer has no such comfort—while writing my latest book, *The Negotiator*, during September of this year [1990], I set a scene in July 1991 in which Mr. Gorbachev fired the chairman of the KGB, General Chebrikov. Hardly had my typewriter ceased to chatter, than the amiable Mikhail did exactly that, on October 2nd! The entire passage then had to be re-written.

Sometimes this intensive research can pay off by giving an impression of prophecy. In *The Devil's Alternative*, also set three years after its actual writing, I "invented" the Condor satellites which could give live photographic coverage of any sport on the world's surface right back to Fort Mead simultaneously. By the time the book was two years old, these satellites (not called Condor) were proudly announced by the US as their latest electronic surveillance aces. The point is, I had already been told of the existence of the prototype four years before they went into service.

So for me at any rate, it is the business of keeping up with the Joneses, or the Gorbachevs. In all the little things such as new technology, fresh spy chief appointments, changes of address, and so on, that prove the most onerous and yet sometimes the most fascinating task.

Frederick Forsyth

A good many years ago, St. Johns College in Annapolis asked me to conduct an evening class in Creative Writing.

The first night, I told my students that while I'd be happy to talk to them, there really wasn't much about writing that could be taught, and they'd be a lot better off if they took their money across the hall and enrolled in a class on touch typing.

Substitute word processors for typewriters, and I feel that my opinion is still valid.

Donald Hamilton

I can't remember ever reading an American spy novel. I rarely read suspense or mystery novels because few interest me. When someone asks my opinion of a popular writer he or she is reading, as they sometimes do, I usually say I haven't read the writer, a polite way of saying I probably tried to read him or her once but found the book unreadable. But my opinion isn't that of most readers.

If I finish a novel at all, it's because it's held my interest beyond the first twenty pages or so. Few do. But even then fifty or even one hundred pages is no guarantee: many skillful writers can convincingly begin a novel, few are gifted enough to convincingly end it. In any case if the novel proves to be readable, at some point I'll be drawn in, a moment roughly equivalent to the moment of rotation or lift-off for a pilot. If that happens, the genre is as irrelevant as the make of the aircraft to its passengers.

A good novel makes genre irrelevant. Critics nevertheless insist in saying a novel has "transcended the genre," a sniffing-down-the-nose patronization which gives readers of so-called serious novels a reason for dipping into it. This is literary hypocrisy, no more. The early le Carré was also writing of the hypocrisy and rot of the English class system and its disastrous consequences. Espionage or rather its agencies were his instrument, not his true subject; yet he was characterized as a spy novelist by those too blindly self-absorbed to recognize his purpose, typical of the society he was dissecting. This makes it a half-truth at best. Not surprisingly the quality of his work fell off when he began to take himself too seriously and imagined himself a political prophet, substituting pronouncement for entertainment, but by then he'd become an institution. British society isn't American society and it's preposterous to speak of an American le Carré, as some do.

So I find it difficult and even meaningless to talk about genre fiction. There are only three kinds of novels, great novels, good novels, and bad novels. George Orwell once made a claim for good *bad* novels, and I suppose the same claim could be made for bad *good* novels. I doubt it. Book publishers and critics write about popular as opposed to literary novels, as if the latter were so serious in intent they must be admired, never mind their poor sales; or the former so slight they must be dismissed, never mind their popular success. This is nonsense. Few great novels are written in any century, few fine novels are written in any decade, and in their absence literary rubbish is as common as popular rubbish. Both flourish in different ways and for different reasons.

So what makes a good novel? I have no idea. But a basic rule is that it must entertain and entertain convincingly. For me, three elements are essential to create that self-sustaining world essential to any novel that holds my interest: the integrity of the characters, the integrity of the prose, and the integrity of the tale. The people must be interesting and believable. If they are, the prose has done its work. In a good novel, however, it's almost impossible to separate one from the other. If effective prose helps make a good novel, some prose styles, including a highly literate or self-conscious one, can also kill off character, which makes so many serious novels so dismal. If strong characters and strong prose are in command, the story will almost inevitably follow. Novelists who insist they're simply telling a story are conceding the irrelevance of their pasteboard characters and awful style.

My difficulty with suspense novels in general is that both are so weak, primitively drawn clichés croaking in boglike prose. Since both lack integrity, the plot is just as laughable. With all so stupidly unconvincing, how can I be entertained?

I have another problem with suspense fiction quite beyond its characters, prose, and derring-do. The Washington world is very much a mystery to those beyond the Beltway. Yet the public in general and novelists in particular invent it as they see fit (the Vietnam MIA issue is a recent example of popular ignorance and fantasy run amok). Writers of suspense novels constantly run amok in inventing Washington and its agencies, whether the White House, the NSC, the Pentagon, the State, or the CIA. Washington is preposterous enough in reality without having to add additional fantasy. Far better to dramatize what exists. Few do (I don't read SciFi or vampire tales for the same reason).

The fact is the Washington world, including its diplomatic and intelligence agencies here and abroad, simply doesn't work the way most suspense writers tell us. Yet ignorance of a particular milieu isn't a disadvantage to an imaginative novelist, who creates a world as authentic as our own. But ignorance quickly betrays the bad novelist, for whom story is more important than people or prose. In any case, having been a diplomat for over twenty years, both in Washington and abroad, I'm somewhat difficult to convince, which makes me a poor or unideal popular reader.

I have a novel coming out in January [*Last Train from Berlin*. New York: Holt, 1994]. I leave it to you to decide whether espionage is its subject or its instrument.

W. T. Tyler
[*Samuel J. Hamrick*]

I'm afraid I don't have a lot to say on the subject. My own novels and short stories sometimes contain an element of espionage but it's nearly always dealt with in a light, mildly satirical way as in "the Rigby File" which you may or may not have seen. This was a sort of linked anthology about one of the great British spies of the century, Dorothy Rigby. In my episode I had Rigby impersonating Mrs. Thatcher on a visit to Buckingham Palace during the 1979 election campaign. I reckoned this was good stuff as socio-political satire but not quite so hot as serious espionage. And it's fairly typical of my approach.

As a reviewer of thrillers, mainly for *The Times*, over a number of years, I'm extremely jaded about the spy in fiction. Very few writers, of whom Deighton and le Carré strike me as much the best now in business, do it at all well. Most people are stale and derivative and deal entirely in stereotypes with the Oval Office in the White House and dangerous ladies with "high cheekbones and generous mouths," as the prime offenders.

Post-Cold War politics clearly means change but I don't see that as a problem. There will always be international tension and conflict and espionage will always be a part of that. A more volatile and complex situation may mean that thriller writers have to be more imaginative and well informed about contemporary affairs, but that's no bad thing. Gerald Seymour and Tim Sebastian are both good at this and I guess that a background in TV or newspapers, as a foreign correspondent, probably helps!

Tim Heald

I suppose the main point I'd make, where the craft of thriller writing is concerned, is the ironic one that only three or four years ago we were being told that now the Berlin Wall was down the spy thriller would be in deep trouble. I took part in a number of BBC TV shows discussing this with the likes of le Carré, Follet, Craig Thomas, and so forth. Needless to say the whole thing proved to be nonsense as novels by Clancy and myself, *Eye of the Storm* and *Thunder Point*, have indicated.

We are all a collage of our own cutups. Watching a reprise of Dennis Potter plays on late night TV spanning many years surprised one because only watching night after night did one realize the common themes and obsessions. Same applies to me. There is always God poking around in the background of a Higgins thriller someone once said. Quite true. Priests, nuns, churches, the smell of incense, and the holy water. Back to an Irish childhood when a Protestant boy was looked after by a very Catholic aunt in a *very* IRA country town, Crossmaglen. That imagery stayed with me all my life plus the obsession with Irish politics and the IRA. I ran from my first bomb at seven and can smell it now. My mother lay on top of me in a tram at ten with rifle fire crackling across the square. Relatives heavily involved on both sides. My Orange uncle gave us tea on Sundays and always opened the secret drawer under the stairs and showed us the hand guns.

So I have an abiding obsession with the Irish who, after all, invented urban guerilla warfare. As regards methodology in writing, I think it proper to recognize that we can only create an illusion of reality. Even James Joyce failed to actually picture life in its totality. We cut out the boring bits if you like, jump from one important scene to another just like a movie, cross cutting. I agree with Checkov that if the pistol is mentioned in the first act it must be discharged in the third whereas in real life it might have no actual purpose. I agree with Poe who said every word must contribute to the whole. I agree with Fitzgerald that action is character. In other words the plot, the thrust, is derived from how people act and behave. A fine lesson for thriller writers who make the mistake of mapping out a plot then creating characters to act that plot out. Result, cardboard characters.

I also believe with the Ancient Greeks that it is good to have some sort of important theme in the work, however much it is intended simply to entertain. I believe popular art as good a way of educating as any. *Savage Day* which dealt with an English/Irish major penetrating the IRA and which many of my fans hold to be their favourite actually does make five or six important points about the nature of the Irish Troubles; that it is a kind of theatre of the street and that many of its actors do not envisage it finishing. Who wants to go back to being a bricklayer or clerk or schoolmaster after being a gallant Provo gunman?

Finally, my characters. Some critics may say they don't exist, that I'm no great shakes. Fine. I'm the first to agree that I'm not Tolstoy but then I never said I was. When they review people like me I often feel they use false standards. They compare us with the greats of literature and find us wanting. I could say that we are still closer to the greats than the average critic will ever be, but that is simply an opinion.

I think it a shame that we are often maligned simply because of large sales. This is a bad reflection on the average reader who is perhaps better informed and more intelligent than many critics in spite of wearing a hard hat and dropping in at the local bar for a beer after work. I always say you get more sense talked about politics in the local pub than at Westminster.

Enough rambling. The only thing left is the Higgins hero. Always an anti-hero, usually burned out case. The spoiled army officer who does the dirty work and is thrown to the wolves afterward by an ungrateful establishment, the IRA man who believed and then, usually because of terrible carnage happening, the slaughter of the innocents, reforms, but it is too late. These men are what they are. Heidegger said: "Life is action and passion and a man fails to take part in the action and passion of his times at peril of being judged not to have lived." Oliver Wendell Holmes said: "Between two groups of men that want to make inconsistent kinds of worlds I see no remedy except force." It seems to me that every society rests on the death of men. In the centre between those two statements rests, for me, the Higgins novel. Some critics christen it Higgins Country. Maybe they are right.

Jack Higgins
[*Harry Patterson*]

I can say only that I began the [Agent] Rand series more as puzzle stories involving codes and ciphers than as a full-bodied espionage series. It did evolve into that, and has continued long after Rand's retirement from British Intelligence in the thirty-second story. Rand's future, and the future of spy fiction in general, has very little to do with the collapse of communism and the Soviet Union. Some of our greatest intrigue novels—Graham Greene's *This Gun for Hire*, Eric Ambler's *A Coffin for Dimitrios*, John le Carré's *The Little Drummer Girl*, for example—have virtually nothing to do with the East-West conflict or with formal Cold War espionage.

Ed Hoch

It seems to me that cloak and dagger fiction, as well as other genre writing, must be judged first as fiction—that is, on the strength of the story, the quality of the writing, the depth of characterization, and the author's realization of the locale.

For me, genre substance comes second. Is the story essentially plausible? Is the book just another thriller tarted up and ostensibly authenticated as a spy book by staging it in a glamorous locale, and adding a few buzz words—*safehouse, workname, honeytrap, cutout*—usually filched from other novels? (Two of the above expressions were created by le Carré, and were previously unknown within the racket.)

Granted that for the sake of their readers, most cloak and dagger authors need to compress the time usually involved in boring operational routines, eliminate the layers of supervision and control inherent in real life espionage, and even intensify existing conflicts by adding bits of violence—I still must ask, if the story might really have happened? If the story does not meet this standard, then as far as I am concerned it has lost all interest as a genre piece.

To pass this test, an author must have some grasp of espionage dynamics and the motives of its practitioners. For an outsider, this may involve a very selective reading of the literature and perhaps some relatively sophisticated research.

There is relatively little involved in police work that is deliberately kept secret. Any outsider embarking on a detective novel can easily bone up on police procedure, consult friendly cops, and even solicit intensive briefings by police public relations departments. By definition, the details of secret intelligence operations have to the degree possible always been cloaked from outsiders.

Sometime ago I picked up a cloak and dagger novel which an established reviewer declared confidently to have been written by an "authority on espionage." After reading a few chapters, I began to feel like a carpenter who, after some years at his trade, had come upon a well-recommended book on how to build a house. He learned that one begins by constructing the roof, the attic, thence second-floor bedrooms, and on until the cellar is dug and the family room put in order. That is not the way to build a house, and all too much espionage fiction is just as far wide of the mark.

William Hood

The espionage fiction genre has been taken over largely by writers who lack any background in espionage. Their products, accordingly, lack verisimilitude for which they compensate by creating sensational plots echoing "Amazing Stories" of bygone years. I was a published author long before I became an intelligence officer, and while twenty-five years experience quite naturally provided me with plot ideas that same experience limited me to writing about things that were within the realm of possibility. I have also had to reject the usual theme of moral equivalency—that the KGB and CIA are equally bad. From personal experience I know it just is not so. It is important to me that former and present intelligence colleagues—whether CIA or SIS—find no flaws or absurdities in my books. They, not editors and publishers are, after all, the experts.

E. Howard Hunt

I write spy novels in the tradition that begins with John Buchan and Somerset Maugham, continues with Eric Ambler and Graham Greene, and carries into the present through Len Deighton and John le Carré—to mention just the representative names.

The first piece of advice given to young writers is to "write about what you know." I have never done so. On the contrary, I always write about what I don't know—but what I want to know. Writing, for me, is always discovering, finding out, *seeing*. I do a lot of research, and love it; and some of this even gets into my books. But the research is even more important than that, for it gives me a way of living through the story. The novel, when I write it, then becomes *my* story, and I try to bring the reader along with me, letting him or her find out too. So, when I start a novel, I always know the beginning—where I am—and something about the ending—where I want to go—but I like to keep the middle part hazy, so that the reader and I can keep discovering new things as we go forward.

For me, there are two especially important aspects to any book, *time* and *place*.

I don't know why place is so important to me, but it is. Characters and plot never really mean anything to me until I can put them in a setting. And the location always seems to have both a large, thematic role but also a much more particular one (though naturally I only see this in retrospect). In *The Red Fox*, for example, I'm showing how we're involved with history, whether we like it or not—an old, crucial, Amblerish theme. So the book is about some of the most important history of this century—the fate of communism—but everything happens on the periphery, in places like Halifax, Detroit, Karelia. Every place, I'm saying, even the most unlikely, was touched by those events. At the same time, I always get my characters involved with place in a more intimate way; I want to see them acting in the natural world, in the bush, in the desert. I want them to experience physical realities, to be out of breath, too hot, exhausted; to define themselves in terms of the lay of the land. I suppose that's the Buchan in me. (I was born, and have lived most of my life, in Ottawa; and of course Buchan died here.)

Time is the other great factor. Officially, I'm a spy novelist, but inside me is a historical novelist trying to get out. Of course, history defines a good deal of what I don't know—and, therefore, of what I want to know. History, above all, is what we have to discover. Half the time it's hidden from us; the other half, we hide it from ourselves. So finding out what really happened, and truly remembering, takes up a lot of my books. I'm sure there's even an autobiographical side to this.   *China Lake* takes place in the American southwest, and is about scientists working at a research station, places and activities which couldn't be more remote from my own life and experience. But, in another sense, the book is very much about my childhood, because I'm trying to capture the feel of the 1950s, the period when I was growing up.

I suppose these concerns—obsessions, to tell the truth—are why I write spy novels.   No other kind of novel is so well adapted to explore them.   On the one hand, we have the strange, shadowy world in which our characters dwell—a dream-world more extreme, more lurid, than anything the Surrealists could imagine.   And then we have the real world, the world of fact, journalism, brand-names, chronology; which is equally ours.   We can go back and forth so easily, narrating the dream of history, and the history of the dream, as we choose.

Anthony Hyde

The death of the thriller, as a result of a shortfall of Cold War tension, has been prematurely pronounced.   The thriller was also announced dead after Conan Doyle, E. Phillips Oppenheim, Erskine Childers, Bulldog Drummond, Leslie Charteris, the two World Wars, the foundation of the League of Nations, the founding of the United Nations, and various lesser events.   Innovative writers will find the window of opportunity.   What used to be the Russian Empire will offer all the opportunities that the Balkans once gave earlier writers. The thriller is in permanent resurrection.

André Jute

Falls the Shadow is not strictly cloak and dagger stuff.   It's a holocaust novel which examines the effect on the psychology of Israel.   Sometime in the mid-1950s *Commentary* magazine carried an article speculating that Eichmann (then still at large and something of a mystery) had grown up in the German Colony of Jerusalem and knew something of Hebrew and the Jewish religion. This idea germinated slowly and provided the ambiguous ideality of the assassinated victim with whom the novel opens.   I did not need to carry out detailed research; my knowledge of Israel and the Holocaust was fairly extensive.   Certain points of Israeli law were checked with a lawyer friend in Israel and the novel's local Israeli background was vetted by another friend.

Emanuel Litvinoff

The (apparent?) end of the Cold War prompted me to tackle a project I'd long had in mind: espionage in the days before the World War I.   This was the period when a few far-sighted men realized that collecting purely military intelligence would not be enough.   Armies and navies were only the end products of nations' political ambitions, scientific skills, and industrial capacity (among other factors) and that these needed investigating as well. This is a commonplace nowadays: then, the idea of a "broad front" secret service was revolutionary and, of course, strongly opposed by entrenched interests.

This is just background. What interests me is exploring the characters who might have been recruited to the fledgling service, who must find or invent the rules of modern espionage—along with overcoming a distaste for the whole dirty business (unless they're the sort of romantic fruitcakes whom espionage will always attract but would rather do without).

Time-travelling the period with eighty-year-old Baedekers has been a fascinating experience, throwing up some real-life characters who appear to be a great deal larger than life (and I don't think this is just the magnifying glass of legend). Disguised thinly or not at all, I've added many of these to my cast. But most of all, I think, it's been a chance to look at not only the techniques of espionage in their most basic form, but the whole ethos of it.

My central characters are a British Army officer saved from bankruptcy and resignation by the new Secret Service Bureau which is anxious to get its hands on *anybody* who knows which fork to use at the high table, aided by a Fenian on the run from his own compatriots and who knows the etiquette of the darker alleys. Give them a ticket on the Orient Express and (in those days of less than instant communication) leave them to get on with it.

Gavin Lyall

Over the last seven years, whenever I would mention working on a novel about the CIA, nearly everyone, and I think this is a compliment to the Agency rather than to the author, would say, "I can hardly wait." The next reaction, particularly among people who were not familiar with how a novel gets written day by day, would appear in the following polite form: "Do you know someone in the CIA very well?" which is, I expect, a substitute for saying, "How do you understand enough to write about *them*?"

I would generally answer that, yes, I knew a few people in the organization although, of course, I could not say much more than that. While this was not without its truth, the general assumption that to know a couple of intelligence officers will prepare the solid ground for writing about a good many of them, is as innocent, when you get down to it, as asking a professional football coach whether he has stolen the secrets of the team to be played next week.

So, I could have answered that I wrote this book with the part of my mind that has lived in the CIA for forty years. *Harlot's Ghost*, after all, is the product of a veteran imagination that has pondered the ambiguous and fascinating moral presence of the Agency in our national life for the last four decades; I did not have to be in the organization, nor know its officers intimately to feel the confidence that I had come to understand the tone of its inner workings.

I am obviously suggesting that some good novels can stray far from one's immediate life and derive instead from one's cultural experience and one's ongoing imaginative faculty. Over the years, that faculty can build nests of context onto themes that attract it.

Now, the process, of course, is not always so magical. In the case of a novel like *Harlot's Ghost*, one does a great deal of research. If I have not absorbed one hundred books on the CIA, then I must have come near, and I had the great good fortune that, as I wrote, new works on the subject of Intelligence kept coming out, and some of them were very good.

Nonetheless, *Harlot's Ghost* is a work of fiction, and most of its main characters and the majority of its accompanying cast are imaginary.

If I have succeeded, *Harlot's Ghost* will offer an imaginary CIA that will move in parallel orbit to the real one, and will be neither an over- nor underestimation of its real powers.

Norman Mailer

The future of the spy novel presents a number of problems, not merely because of the end of the Cold War, but because the techniques of espionage have changed so much in recent years. To succeed, most spy novels of the future will need to be closer to real life and actual facts than has been the case in the past. Real life characters may need to be used in fiction, possibly one or two characters who have only recently passed on. What, however, is crying out to be tackled as spy fiction is the story of who and how manipulated events so that the Cold War ended. This requires a great deal of research, but while the full story (if at this stage anyone could get it) of this affair would make a best-seller, a skillfully done fictional version of it could also be a great success, provided some documentary real-life facts were worked into it.

The computer virus scares certainly offer scope for some writers, and I have often thought that an original theme could be that of the radio and computer buff who set himself up on some small island to create his own private worldwide intelligence service.

Somebody might pay attention to the theme of a spy who uses astrology—not all that far fetched when one considers that the Chinese have frequently used I CHING for this purpose.

I personally should like to see an American author writing a spy novel which set out to show how the KGB decided that if one couldn't beat the western world, one should join 'em. There was, of course, no hope of "joining" the United States but every possibility of infiltrating the European community. The book would then show how the KGB created a communist-style bureaucracy within the Community. In fact what is happening now is in one way along those lines: the extent of the bureaucracy and interference with national laws and habits is almost unbelievable.

Donald McCormick

Fiction writing is a fraud, and that includes writing "Cloak and Dagger Fiction" or "Spy Fiction"; it is not really writing *fiction*. When a "fiction" writer sits down to stare at the pristine, white paper in his typewriter, or at the empty, waiting screen of his computer, what ultimately will cover it, is what already exists within the writer's mind; his experiences, his observations, his discoveries, and his interpretations. All of this factual material forms a pool of knowledge, which his imagination and sense of form, fashion into a cohesive story—a story of facts, simply used in a different sequence of events, in a different manner or in a different context. The accomplished, certainly the most successful "spy-thriller" writer, likely as not has had some personal experience with the subject matter of his craft in one form or another, and he will draw upon that pool of intelligence to flesh out his story.

In all my own dozen or so "spy thrillers" I have used my personal experiences drawn from four years of service as a U.S. Counter Intelligence Agent during World War II, simply altered to fit the situation or plot I had in mind. It is my firm belief that the author who has a thorough, first-hand knowledge of the subject matter he wants to write about will create the most accurate, the most authentic and believable "fiction" story, largely because of that first-hand knowledge, however acquired, and that most assuredly holds true for the genre called Cloak and Dagger or Spy Fiction.

Ib Melchior

These are some of the things I try to bear in mind once I have switched on the word processing.

My first duty is to entertain—it's a waste of trees if I do not entertain: but also I must recall that entertainment is not the only thing on the agenda of thrill-packed narratives like the *Odyssey* and the *Iliad*, *The Secret Agent*, and *The Quiet American*.

Action and a strong narrative keep the pages turning, but they also reveal more about reality than any amount of analysis and description. How do you know a man is evil? By presenting his thought processes? By describing his satanic appearance in minute detail? Or by presenting him in evil action? This matters in presenting minutiae, as well as on the grand scale. In *Sand Blind*, my most recently published book, the hero's father is introduced in his apartment on the Costa del Sol making a Spanish omelette, ticking off his son for abandoning his marriage and his father's grandchildren, and generally moving about and talking. In less than two pages, with almost no description, we know about his innate honesty, his neatness and orderliness, his willingness to adapt to his surroundings and master new techniques, that he comes from the artisan end of the British working class, that he adored his dead wife but has little time for other women, that he does not suffer fools gladly, and that he is sensitive enough not to want to jeopardize his relationship with his son by having a purposeless quarrel with him. And we know all this by what he does and how he does it.

Sex 'n violence. Of course they should never be gratuitous or there because the publisher thinks the public expects a good dollop of both. Nevertheless both take place in time, they are powerful moments in a narrative, and the how and why of both reveal the protagonists in action. I would go further. The presentation of sexual and violent acts can be justified for their own sake: there is usefulness, for want of a better word, in showing these elemental forces stripped of social context, of seeing Thanatos and Eros as stark realities unencumbered by guilt or motive. Blood or semen spill and the world shakes and that is enough reason for inviting them into the book. But done without prurience, voyeurism, not seen through the keyhole but striding across the pages. Thriller writing is perhaps the only literary genre where this elemental nature of sex 'n violence can be presented without awkwardness.

But finally all writing is moral in effect and it is well to know where one stands and stand there firmly and openly. Of course positions of doubt and questioning are as valid as firm commitment, though there is to me a hint of laziness in the Don't Know, Can't Know attitude—world-weary cynicism can cloak the fireproof: let things stay the bloody awful way they are, Jack, I'm all right.

Which is why the accolade bestowed on me by a reviewer that I most cherish, also for *Sand Blind*, is "Rathbone is an ideologically correct Frederick Forsyth."

Julian Rathbone

Knowing I was in the middle of writing a book, a friend asked me if I knew how it was going to end. I told him I had no idea. A few months later, halfway through the last chapter, I was still not sure. But there were several options open to me.

This, I find, is one of the main differences between suspense stories/adventure/spy/thrillers, and "who dunnits." Most suspense writers I know work within a loose framework of plot and see where their characters lead them. Of necessity, a "who dunnit" has to be pre-planned; contrived if you like. The end must be known in advance and the red herrings laid. This is, of course, a personal view and not designed to take away the skill of the genre.

To me, one of the many pleasures of thriller writing is its unpredictability. A really good thriller is storytelling at its best. And there is rarely any cheating as characters do not act out of character. A top thriller is the present day novel. Research is hard and sometimes painful but mostly enjoyable and always informative.

I went down the London sewers for one of the old Spider Scott books. Unpleasant? Not at all. The main sewers are the old London rivers like the Fleet and the Tyburn. The medieval bridges are still down there.

The real pleasure is getting the book to hang together and the feel of it taking shape, and to be lucky enough to have those alternative endings.

It's time I got down to another.

Kenneth Royce

In the period when I wrote two spy books with Leonard Gross, we were still heavily involved in the Cold War. What I enjoyed most was to use Soviet and U.S. spies I had known well and transfer them into fiction. The Soviet spy who dies in *The Dossier* is still alive and he very much enjoyed our book.

But with the Cold War crumble, it will be more and more difficult to write this kind of book. The only author who has really done a good job in writing a post-Cold War spy novel was John le Carré in his book *The Russia House*.

When I write my next novel, it will probably not be about spy, but terrorist.

Pierre Salinger

Amongst the "literati" there is too often the sneer at the craft of the suspense novel—and that is an attitude that gets me more annoyed than almost anything else. The suspense story is most certainly not merely an escapist exercise to while away a boring plane flight. The genre has the capability of informing an audience, giving them more insight into the problems we are all talking about, than a forest of newspapers and a cloud of TV newscasts. I would expect to tell my readership more about the real and human situation in Northern Ireland or the Middle East or Afghanistan than they can ever obtain from the dried up river courses of non-fiction. This is the medium for getting into the skulls of *people*, of discovering attitudes, for pecking out the motivation of the few men and women who will make the headlines across our breakfast tables. To me, as a writer, it is critical that I research my characters sufficiently well so that I can comprehend the psychology of the proxy bomber, the master sniper, the anti-terrorist chief of operations. They are real individuals, not just the cardboard cut-outs of my imagination. I want to know what drives them forward when the going gets hard, when most of us would quit and run. If you want to know what is really happening in our world, today, then cancel the newspapers, unplug the TV, and head down to the bookshop.

Gerald Seymour

I still read espionage fiction, and I'm a sucker for a well-written, evocative spy novel such as le Carré's *The Spy Who Came in from the Cold*—which is insanely, beautifully written—or Len Deighton's *Funeral in Berlin*. A real golden age of the spy novel. But I have a hard time with Tom Clancy and some current spy fiction; it seems poorly written, thin.

The sixties was the summit of the craft, as far as I'm concerned. Writers are less well educated nowadays. Then, we all took espionage seriously; now it's all flash, cash, and trash. It's become more and more brand names and less and less characterization.

Benjamin Stein

Although I hate to give the plot of my next thriller away, I thought I'd share it with your readers just to give them an insight into the underlying motives that compel authors to write about certain subjects.

I once lived near Ashtabula [Ohio] and as you will see, the experience figured large in my formative years and explains my preoccupation with Soviet skullduggery.

When I was still in knickers, my Mom died and Dad, who was working in Pittsburgh, had to place me with my aunt and uncle who lived outside Ashtabula.

Jimmy Fisher, a mature lad of my age—both of us pushing a world-weary six--was my closest peacetime friend and neighbor. He was also my fiercest foe in the Great Tomato War of 1939, waged in the fields of Uncle Chap's and Aunt Eva's garden.

As I recall, it was just about this time of year. The tomatoes were ripe, making very suitable grenades that left a bloodlike spatter when they connected with the foe. (*Glancers* did not count for although they produced a satisfying mess when they struck the ground, they didn't figure in the body count.)

For forts, we had orange crates thatched over with impenetrable stalks of rhubarb. Cucumbers (they really smarted if you took one in the head!) were held in reserve as a retaliatory weapon and hurled only if the enemy was stupid enough to charge.

Peace negotiations had broken off, our emissaries recalled, and war was imminent. We had both been stockpiling tomatoes and each of us had an ungodly number in our inventory, far exceeding those limitations agreed to in our own version of *SALT*.

The day came—hot winds from the west with building cumulus—a good day for killing. Waiting until Uncle Chap and Aunt Eva headed off in the Nash for choir practice—he was a preacher and Aunt Eva led the choir—Jimmy and I concluded that our differences could not be resolved by an further palaver, declared unconditional and total war, then proceeded to walk and in a couple of rounds until we had each other's positions straddled. Nanoseconds later with both range and elevation zeroed, we both let go with the main barrage. (A military glossary is [to be] included in the front matter for readers unfamiliar with techno-thriller vocabulary.)

Unfortunately, Aunt Eva had forgotten her baton and directed Uncle Chap to return to the farm. Jimmy and I were caught—literally—red-handed, red-faced and red-everythinged. Jimmy rapidly withdrew from the field of conflict (the rotten little bastard), leaving me holding the bag. Believing that the wasting of food was an abomination to the Lord, Aunt Eva forced me eat the remaining tomatoes, both those that were whole and those that could be salvaged from the walls of the forts and the mire of the trenches. Fried, stewed, baked, raw, mushed, juiced, and mashed (naturally and otherwise) tomatoes were my only food intake for a week. I argued vainly that I wasn't receiving enough animal protein, and that the early settlers, in their wisdom, believed tomatoes to be a poison fruit. I even tried the one about how I would get fat like the daughter of the creamery manager (who was great with illegitimate child) but whose condition had been foisted off on me by Uncle Chap as having been caused by ". . . swallowing tomato seeds." Aunt Eva (her wet mustache quivering at the thought of Uncle Chap giving me a man to man on the dirty little secrets of sex) allowed as how he had it wrong again and the condition had actually been brought on by ". . . *that* woman eating punkin' seeds and not spitting out the shells and that even a City-bred fool like me should know that."

After six days, my sub-systems revolted and I could not force down another tomato. (As I recall, I barfed in the bath tub, not having enough time or strength to make it to the head.) In all fairness, I must admit that Aunt Eva relieved my diet with occasional slices of cucumbers and a rhubarb pie or two, but other than that, nothing else graced my lips except water from the well and a Baby Ruth that Jimmy sent me, hidden inside a rolled-up copy of *Boy's Life*. (Jimmy always was good on spook tradecraft.)

Ten years ago, I finally was able to swallow tomato sauce on spaghetti. Bloody Mary's don't bother me (actually, never did), and I have been toying with trying a *very* thin wedge of slimy tomato buried between two massive all-beef patties, smothered in secret goop, and swaddled in a sesame seed bun. On second, third, and fourth thoughts, hold the tomato and substitute an order of fries.

I still can't stand rhubarb, cucumbers, or the dreaded T-word stuff (at least in recognizable form) and if you've been to the CIS (at least back when it was the good old bad old USSR) you'll understand that a man could starve over there because that's *exactly* what they give you for a salad, along with the Chicken Kiev (which, from its diminutive size and muscular nature, was undoubtedly forced to run to Moscow rather than being shipped from Kiev in the normal manner.) Which fits in perfectly with my theory as to how the Commies kept the masses from revolting. The poor bloody sods were too weak and nauseous to revolt. Until, you will note, burgers came to Moscow. All it took was for a cadre of counter-revolutionaries to chow down on a couple of bags of Double Whoppers. With their beef-induced vigor revitalized, this brave band was able, against all nutritional odds, to finally blow the commissars out of power. Simple as that.

So there you have the plot of my next thriller, *STICKMAN*. Well, sort of.

The moral of this very true tale is that *everything* has an explanation, regardless of how flimsy.

Doug Terman

There are two traditions in the genre that have become known as the thriller—that of the espionage novel, a close relation of the detective story, and the adventure novel which descends from Rider Haggard and John Buchan. There has always been a great deal of cross-fertilization and hybridity between the two strains, but my books almost always belong to the tradition of what I call "political adventure," even when their surface appears to be that of the Cold War espionage novel.

In the political adventure, the scale is perhaps greater, the prize larger and more abstract, the dangers probably more physical than moral. There is less ambiguity but a more pronounced ethical stance—not necessarily either imperialist or right-wing—than in the espionage "mystery" tale. Indeed, it has been the political adventure story, much more than the espionage novel, which has always sought to make the Cold War an ethical conflict between democracy and totalitarianism, represented in the individuals who are in conflict. There is no real parity of greyness between the characters.

It is this stand of political adventure that, in the uncertainties and danger of the coming decade, is more likely than the "spy story" to move the genre toward "fresh fields" and pastures new." I intend to be one of the shepherds moving the flock!"

Craig Thomas

People sometimes ask whence comes my apparent fascination with trilogies. The answer is simpler than they usually expect: a "big" character takes over the writing at some stage and demands more space than a single book will allow. But trilogies are fraught with danger. If the reading public goes along with your own assessment of the "big" character, fine. But if readers take against him/her, it's going to be a long, desolate road to the final word of that third novel.

At the heart of every thriller there is a paradox. Readers of the genre expect, first and foremost, a good *story*, with many ingenious twists and turns, hardware, politics, perhaps sex and gratuitous violence, certainly a death or two.

These ingredients, irrespective of the precise mix, will usually be present. But every good *story* ever written has been, first and foremost, character-driven. And since a really first-class story will trump a so-called "mere" thriller every time, this explains why the best "thrillers" are actually serious novels about real characters who fortuitously live out their lives against backgrounds more exotic than our own. Putting it another way, all the best thrillers aren't!

So you want to write a thriller but can't see how to break into the market? Go and read your favourite spy novel. Then ask yourself: "What's the opposite of that?"

J. S. Trenhaile

We're emerging from a period in which many people have avoided the life and death realities of the cloak and dagger world by seeing it as a fantasy of giddy pranks. This view has been exemplified by many silly satires of James Bond and what happened to Bond himself in latter films.

This pseudo-sophisticated "let's pretend" attitude to espionage thrillers has alternately irked and embarrassed me, so I infrequently find it amusing. I used to have more ironic banter in my books, but reduced that when I wanted to focus and maintain tension and urgency. A spy can have a splendid sense of humor, but espionage is dangerous—not comical.

I aim at a realistic tone in both human character and in technology and situation. My satires are often "what if" rooted, with a fair amount of research to contribute authenticity. Unlike some of my talented colleagues, I don't believe in giving lectures on archaeology or nuclear physics or stamp collecting. In fiction, I sometimes enjoy the way they do it, but often it seems to slow down the forward thrust of the story.

I'm delighted that the explosion of junk spy books and movies appear to have subsided. What they've left behind is a real challenge to be creative—to do something fresh and gripping. A number of excellent U.S. and British writers are contributing highly original stories with compelling characters—a whole range of them. That's why the nineties could be a golden era for cloak and dagger fiction.

I must acknowledge that it is a pleasure to do the research and travel and to write espionage fiction. I think that I'm very lucky—and so does my wife who helps with research. It is never boring or routine, not for an instant. Neither is the process—no, the *experience*—of writing.

Walter Wager

With the apparent breakup of the Soviet Union, people wonder what spy-fiction writers will find to write about. Don't worry; we're as devious and innovative as the folks we write about.

Some of humankind's earliest stories might be considered spy stories. Think of the *Iliad*: the wife of a high government official is kidnapped and a strike force is mounted to get her back—and the world's most famous operation of deception takes place. Think of Moses—a clandestine Israelite growing up in the court of the pharaoh—maybe history's earliest mole. And Shakespeare is full of spies and secret plots and devious dealings.

It's true that we're going to have to be more inventive. The Soviets as an automatic enemy are no longer available to us, so we'll see espionage in other areas of the world. We'll see more terrorists, more drug cartels, and probably more corporate dirty dealing. We're also seeing more historical spy stories—World War II continues to be a favorite among espionage writers because we're all so clear who the good guys and the bad guys were. But my guess is that historical espionage stories will begin to stretch as far back as the imagination.

People love reading about secrets, about clandestine operations, about plots and counterplots and conspiracies; and as long as there are people who want to read about those things, there will be people who will write about them.

S. K. Wolf

Appendix B: Guide to Pseudonyms

"We betray to be loyal. Betrayal is like imagining when the reality isn't good enough."

—Magnus Pym's journal entry in John le Carré's *A Perfect Spy*, 121

A PSEUDONYM IS to an author what a disguise is to a spy: protective covering designed to hide a true identity. A number of writers of spy thrillers have chosen pen names for different reasons that may range from fear of exposing active intelligence agents or operations to foreign intelligence services—perhaps even their own superiors—to the desire to put one over on their own readers—and even publishers. Consider what must surely be the greatest mystery in English letters: the authorship of the plays of William Shakespeare. Internal evidence from the plays points conclusively in the direction of the Earl of Oxford, Edward de Vere, rather than the image of the well-known bust that today adorns the abbey where the remains of the man known as William Shak-speare[sic] lie. Aside from a forged line in the will connecting Shakespeare to the actors-biographers of the First Folio, virtually no evidence exists to suggest that this glovemaker's son without formal education could possibly have been privy to the intrigues of Elizabeth's energetic court and the personalities that inspired the world's greatest literature.

The pseudonyms listed below are cross-referenced to their real names (where known) both in this guide and within the text of this bibliography.

Abbot, John, pseud. = Unknown
Abro, Ben, pseud. = Unknown
Albrand, Martha, pseud. = Heidi H. Loewengard
Aldanov, Mark, pseud. = Mark A. Landau

Alding, Peter, pseud. = Roderic Jeffries
Allan, John, pseud. = Ritchie Perry
Andreyev, Vladimir, pseud. = Unknown
Anthony, Evelyn, pseud. = Evelyn B. P. Ward-Thomas
Arden, William, pseud. = Dennis Lynds
Armstrong, Anthony, pseud. = Anthony A. Willis
Ashe, Gordon, pseud. = John Creasey
Atlee, Philip, pseud. = James Atlee Phillips
August, John, pseud. = Bernard A. DeVoto
Ayres, Paul, pseud. = Edward S. Aarons
Baldwin, Alex, pseud. = W. E. [William Edmund] Butterworth III
Ballard, K. G., pseud. = Holly Roth
Ballinger, W. A., pseud. = W. Howard Baker and Wilfrid G. McNeilly
Bannerman, David, pseud. = David Hagberg
Barak, Michael, pseud. = Michael Bar-Zohar
Barrington, Maurice, pseud. = Denis W. Brogan
Bax, Roger, pseud. = Paul Winterton
Baxter, John, pseud. = E. Howard Hunt
Beckingham, Bruce, pseud. = Peter Lilley and Anthony Stasfield
Beech, Webb, pseud. = W. E. [William Edmund] Butterworth III
Beechcroft, William, pseud. = William Finn III Hallstead
Beeding, Francis, pseud. = John Leslie Palmer and Hilary Aiden St. George
    Saunders
Bernard, Jay, pseud. = Raymond H. Sawkins
Bernard, Robert, pseud. = Robert B. Martin
Betteridge, Don, pseud. = Bernard Newman
Black, Gavin, pseud. = Oswald Wynd
Black, Lionel, pseud. = Dudley Barker
Blake, Nicholas, pseud. = Cecil Day-Lewis
Blake, Patrick, pseud. = Clive Egleton
Bleeck, Oliver, pseud. = Ross Thomas
Booth, Irwin, pseud. = Edward D. Hoch
Bridge, Ann, pseud. = Mary D. O'Malley
Bruce, Jean, pseud. = Jean A. Brochet
Brown, Carter, pseud. = Alan Geoffrey Yates
Brust, Harold, pseud. = Reginald Southouse Cheyney
Bullogh, Paul, pseud. = Reginald John Gadney
Burgess, Anthony, pseud. = John A. B. Wilson
Burke, Jonathan, pseud. = John F. Burke and George Theiner
Butler, Richard, pseud. = Ted Allbeury
Caillou, Alan, pseud. = Alan Lyle-Smythe
Campbell, Keith, pseud. = Keith Campbell West-Watson

Carter, Nick (or Nicholas), house pseud. = (1880s - 1930s) John Russell Coryell (originator), Frederick van Rensselaer Dey (wrote most of the early stories); Frederick William Davis; Eugene T. Sawyer; (various modern authors) Michael Angelo Avallone, Jr.; Robert Clurman, Richard Condon, Valerie Moolman, Manning Lee Stokes and Martin Cruz Smith

Castle, John, pseud. = Ronald Payne and John Garrod

Cavendish, Peter, pseud. = Sydney Horler

Chaber, M. E., pseud. = Kendell F. Crossen

Chambers, Dana, pseud. = Albert Leffingwell

Charles, Robert, pseud. = Robert Charles Smith

Charteris, Leslie, pseud. = Leslie C. B. Yin

Chase, Glen, pseud. = Gardner Fox

Chase, James Hadley, pseud. = René B. Raymond

Chase, Nicholas, joint pseudonym = Anthony Hyde

Chase, Philip, pseud. = Philip Freedman

Cheyney, Peter, pseud. = Reginald Southouse Cheyney

Circus, Anthony, pseud. = Edward D. Hoch

Clifford, Francis, pseud. = Arthur L. B. Thompson

Clifford, James, pseud. = Reginald John Gadney

Clinton, Jeff, pseud. = Jack M. Bickham

Clouston, Joseph Storer, pseud. = Francis Mandell-Essington

Clyde, Allison, pseud. = William Knowles

Cody, James P., pseud. = Peter Thomas Rohrbach

Coffin, Geoffrey, pseud. = Francis Van Wyck Mason and Helen Brawner

Coles, Manning, pseud. = Adelaide F. O. Manning and Cyril Henry Coles

Coltrane, James, pseud. = James P. Wohl

Conway, Troy, house pseud. = Michael Avallone and various authors

Copplestone, Bennet, pseud. = Frederick Kitchin

Cordell, Alexander, pseud. = George A. Graber

Corrigan, Mark, pseud. = Lee Norman

Cory, Desmond, pseud. = John [Shaun] L. McCarthy

Craig, David, pseud. = Allan J. Tucker

Crane, Robert, pseud. = Connie Leslie Sellers, Jr.

Cross, James, pseud. = Hugh J. Parry

Cunningham, E. V., pseud. = Howard Fast

Dark, James, pseud. = James Edmond McDonald

Davies, Frederic, pseud. = Ron Ellik and Frederic Langley

Davis, Gordon, pseud. = E. Howard Hunt and Leonard Levinson

Deacon, Richard, pseud. = Donald McCormick

Deane, Norman, pseud. = John Creasey

Delving, Michael, pseud. = Jay Williams

Denning, Mark, pseud. = John Stevenson

Dentinger, Stephen, pseud. = Edward D. Hoch
Derby, Mark, pseud. = Harry Wilcox
Dietrich, Robert, pseud. = E. Howard Hunt
Diplomat, pseud. = John Franklin Carter
Dugan, Jack, pseud. = W. E. [William Edmund] Butterworth III
E-7, pseud. = Unknown
East, Michael, pseud. = Morris L. West
Easterman, Daniel, pseud. = Denis MacEoin
Edwards, Paul, house pseud. = Manning Lee Stokes
Esdaile, David, pseud. = David Esdaile Walker
Evans, Jonathan, pseud. = Brian Freemantle
Falkirk, Richard, pseud. = Derek Lambert
Fallon, Martin, pseud. = Henry Patterson
Fitch, Clarke, pseud. = Upton Sinclair
Flannery, Sean, pseud. = David Hagberg
Fleming, Ian, pseud. = Bennet Cerf and Michael K. Frith
Forbes, Colin, pseud. = Raymond H. Sawkins
Forrest, David, pseud. = Robert Forrest-Webb
Fox, James M., pseud. = James M. Knipscheer
Franklin, Charles, pseud. = Frank H. Usher
Frede, Richard, pseud. = Macdowell Frederics
Freyer, Frederick, pseud. = William S. Ballinger
Frost, Frederick, pseud. = Frederick Shiller Faust
Fry, Peter, pseud. = Clifford King
Gainham, Sarah, pseud. = Rachel Ames
Galway, Robert Conington, pseud. = Philip McCutchan
Gant, Richard, pseud. = Brian Freemantle
Garrison, Frederick, pseud. = Upton Sinclair
Garve, Andrew, pseud. = Paul Winterton
Gascar, Pierre, pseud. = Pierre Fournier
George, Jonathan, pseud. = John F. Burke and George Theiner
George, Peter, pseud. = Peter Bryant
Gilbert, Anthony, pseud. = Lucy B. Malleson
Gilman, Dorothy, pseud. = Dorothy Gilman Butters
Gilman, Robert Cham, pseud. = Alfred Coppel
Godey, John, pseud. = Morton Freedgood
Gordon, Alexander, pseud. = Gordon Cotler
Gordon, Donald, pseud. = Donald G. Payne
Gould, Alan, pseud. = Victor Canning
Graeme, Bruce, pseud. = Graham M. Jeffries
Graham, James, pseud. = Henry Patterson
Grant, David, pseud. = Craig Thomas

Griffin, W. E. B., pseud. = W. E. [William Edmund] Butterworth III
Griffith, Bill, pseud. = Bill Granger
Griswold, George, pseud. = Robert G. Dean
Guenter, C. H. = Unknown
Habe, Hans, pseud. = Jean Bekessy
Haggard, William, pseud. = Richard H. M. Clayton
Hall, Adam, pseud. = Elleston Trevor (originally Trevor Dudley-Smith)
Hamilton, Adam, pseud. = Marilyn Granbeck and Allen Moore
Hardt, Michael, pseud. = Gwen L. Davenport and Gustav J. Breuer
Haroldson, William, pseud. = Harold King
Harper, David, pseud. = Edwin Corley
Harris, Brian, pseud. = Harold King
Hartshorne, pseud. = Richard H. A. Blum
Harvester, Simon, pseud. = Henry St. John Clair Rumbold-Gibbs
Hastings, Michael, pseud. = Michael Bar-Zohar
Hebden, Mark, pseud. = John Harris
Heritage, Martin, pseud. = Sydney Horler
Higgins, Jack, pseud. = Henry Patterson
Hild, Jack, pseud. = Jack Garside
Holland, Katrin, pseud. = Martha Albrand
Holly, J. Hunter, pseud. = Joan C. Holly
Homewood, Harry, pseud. = Charles H. Homewood
Howard, Hartley, pseud. = Leopold H. Ognall
Hughes, Zachary, pseud. = Hugh Zachary
Humana, Charles, pseud. = Joseph Jacobs
Innes, Hammond, pseud. = Ralph Hammond-Innes
Innes, Michael, pseud. = John I. M. Stewart
Jacks, Oliver, pseud. = Kenneth Royce Gandley
Jacobs, T.C.H., pseud. = Jacques Pendower
Jardine, Warwick, pseud. = Francis A. Warwick
Jay, Charlotte, pseud. = Geraldine Jay
Jay, Simon, pseud. = Colin James
Jones, Bradshaw, pseud. = Malcolm H. Bradshaw-Jones
Kelly, Patrick, pseud. = Ted Allbeury
Kilgore, Axel, pseud. = Jerry Ahern
Kirk, Philip, pseud. = Leonard Levinson
Kirton, James, pseud. = Kenneth C. Benton
Knight, Mallory T., pseud. = Bernhardt J. Hurwood
Krauss, Bruno, pseud. = Kenneth Bulmer
Kyle, Duncan, pseud. = John F. Broxholme
Ladner, Kurt, pseud. = Nelson DeMille
Lambert, Christine, pseud. = Martha Albrand

Lancaster, David, pseud. = Tim[othy] V. Heald
Lancaster, Donald, pseud. = William Marshall
Lathen, Emma, pseud. = Mary J. Latsis and Martha Hennissart
Layne, Marion Margery, pseud. = Marion Woolf, Margery W. Papich, and
    Layne Torkelson
le Carré, John, pseud. = David J. M. Cornwell
Lee, Elsie, pseud. = Elsie L. Sheridan
Leonard, Charles L., pseud. = Mary V. Heberden
Loraine, Philip, pseud. = Robin Estridge
Lovell, Marc, pseud. = Mark McShane
Luckless, John, pseud. = Herbert Burkholtz
Lynn, Margaret, pseud. = Gladys S. Battye
McBain, Ed, pseud. = Evan Hunter
McCall, Anthony, pseud. = Henry Kane
MacKenzie, Steve, pseud. = Kevin D. Randle
MacLeod, Robert, pseud. = Bill Knox
McMahon, Pat, pseud. = Edward D. Hoch
MacNeil, Duncan, pseud. = Philip McCutchan
MacNeil, Neil, pseud. = Willis T. Ballard
McVean, James, pseud. = Nicholas Luard
Maddock, Stephen, pseud. = J. M. Walsh
Mallory, Drew, pseud. = Brian Garfield
Marin, A. C., pseud. = Alfred Coppel
Mariner, David, pseud. = David M. Smith
Mark, Ted, pseud. = Theodore Mark Gottfried
Markham, Robert, pseud. = Kingsley Amis
Marlowe, Hugh, pseud. = Henry Patterson
Marlowe, Stephen, pseud. = Milton A. Lesser
Mason, Frank W., pseud. = Francis Van Wyck Mason
Masterson, Whit, pseud. = Robert Wade and Bill Miller
Mather, Berkely, pseud. = John E. W. Davies
Matheson, Hugh, pseud. = Lewis H. MacKay
Maxwell, John, pseud. = Brain Freemantle
Mayo, James, pseud. = Stephen Coulter
Meldrum, James, pseud. = John F. Broxholme
Merrill, P. J., pseud. = Holly Roth
Michaels, Philip, pseud. = Philippe van Rjndt
Miles, John, pseud. = Jack M. Bickham
Montross, David, pseud. = Jean L. Backus
Moore, Robin, pseud. = Robert L. Moore, Jr.
Morris, John, pseud. = John Hearne and Morris Cargill
Morris, Julian, pseud. = Morris L. West

Morton, Anthony, pseud. = John Creasey
Mr. X, pseud. = Edward D. Hoch
Mundy, Talbot, pseud. = William L. Gribbon
Munro, James, pseud. = James W. Mitchell
Murphy, John, pseud. = Ronan C. Grady, Jr.
Myles, Simon, pseud. = Ken Follett
Nord, Pierre, pseud. = André Léon Brouillard
O'Brian, Frank, pseud. = Brian Garfield
O'Brien, Robert C., pseud. = Robert L. Conly
O'Hara, Kenneth, pseud. = Jean Morris
Operator 1384, pseud. = John H. Harvey
Orvis, Kenneth, pseud. = Kenneth Lemieux
Orwell, George, pseud. = Eric Blair
Paul, F. W., pseud. = Paul W. Fairman
Paull, Jessyca, pseud. = Julia Perceval and Roseaylmer Burger
Pendleton, Don, house pseud. = Jack Garside
Penn, John, joint pseud. = Palma Harcourt
Pentecost, Hugh, pseud. = Judson P. Philips
Peters, Brian, pseud. = George B. Peter
Peters, Ludovic, pseud. = Peter Ludwig Brent
Pilgrim, David, pseud. = John Leslie Palmer and Hilary Aidan St. George
     Saunders
Plum, Jennifer, pseud. = Michael Kurland
Porter, R. E., pseud. = Edward D. Hoch
Q., John, pseud. = John E. Quirk
Queen, Ellery, pseud. = Edward D. Hoch
Quinn, John, pseud. = Dennis Rodriguez
Quinn, Simon, pseud. = Martin Cruz Smith
Quinnell, A. J., pseud. = Unknown
Raine, Richard, pseud. = Raymond H. Sawkins
Rame, David, pseud. = Arthur D. Divine
Ramsey, Eric, pseud. = David Hagberg
Redgate, John, pseud. = Adam Kennedy
Reed, Eliot, pseud. = Eric Ambler and Charles Rodda
Richards, Clay, pseud. = Kendell F. Crossen
Richards, Paul, house pseud. = Chet Cunningham; Jon Messman; George
     Snyder; Dan Streib
Roberts, James H., pseud. = Robert L. Duncan
Robson, Dirk, pseud. = Derek Robinson
Rohmer, Sax, pseud. = Arthur Sarsfield Ward
Ronns, Edward, pseud. = Edward S. Aarons
Ross, Angus, pseud. = Kenneth Gigga

Ross, Ian, pseud. = John F. Rossman
Rostand, Robert, pseud. = Robert S. Hopkins
Royce, Kenneth, pseud. = Kenneth Royce Gandley
Ryder, Jonathan, pseud. = Robert Ludlum
St. Germain, Gregory, pseud. = Jeffrey M. Wallman
St. John, David, pseud. = E. Howard Hunt
Sanborn, B. X., pseud. = William S. Ballinger
Sandberg, Berent, pseud. = Peter Lars Sandberg
Sanders, Buck, pseud. = Jeffrey Frentzen
Sapper, pseud. = Herman C. McNeile
Seare, Nicholas, pseud. = Rodney Whitaker
Semenov, Julian = Yulian Semenovich Lyandres
Seton, Graham, pseud. = Graham Seton Hutchison
Shaw, George, pseud. = Jack M. Bickham
Shepherd, Michael, pseud. = Robert Ludlum
Spillane, Mickey, pseud. = Frank Morrison Spillane
Stanton, Ken, pseud. = Manning Lee Stokes
Stark, Richard, pseud. = Donald E. Westlake
Steel, Kurt, pseud. = Rudolf Kagley
Steele, Curtis, pseud. = Emile Tepperman and Frederick C. Davis
Stevens, Carl, pseud. = Raymond Obstfeld
Stevens, R. L., pseud. = Edward D. Hoch
Stirling, Arthur, pseud. = Upton Sinclair
Stivers, Dick, pseud. = Don Pendleton and Laurence R. Payne
Stratton, Thomas, pseud. = Thomas DeWeese and Robert Coulson
Stuart, Anthony, pseud. = Julian Anthony Stuart Hale
Stuart, Ian, pseud. = Alistair Maclean
Swift, Bryan, house pseud. = Will C. Knott and Arthur Wise
Taffrail, pseud. = Henry T. Dorling
Tarrant, John, pseud. = Clive Egleton
Tiger, John, pseud. = Walter Wager
Torr, Dominic, pseud. = John B. F. Pedler
Tranter, Nigel, pseud. = Nye Tredgold
Trevanian, pseud. = Rodney Whitaker
Tyler, W. T., pseud. = Samuel J. Hamrick
Underwood, Michael, pseud. = John M. Evelyn
Valentine, Douglas, pseud. = Valentine Williams
Wahloo, Peter, pseud. = Per Wahloo
Ward, Jonas, pseud. = Brian Garfield
Wayland, Patrick, pseud. = Richard O'Connor
Weaver, Ward, pseud. = Francis Van Wyck Mason
Webb, Alex, pseud. = Alan Lyle-Smythe

Welcome, John, pseud. = John Brennan
White, Adam, pseud. = Reginald John Gadney
White, Steve, pseud. = Robert McGarvey
Willis, Maude, pseud. = Eileen Lottman
Winchester, Jack, pseud. = Brian Freemantle
Winters, Jon, pseud. = Gilbert B. Cross
Wolfe, Michael, pseud. = Gilbert M. Williams
Wren, M. K., pseud. = Martha K. Renfroe
Wynne, Brian, pseud. = Brian Garfield
Wynne, Frank, pseud. = Brian Garfield
York, Andrew, pseud. = Christopher Nicole
Zeno, pseud. = Unknown

Appendix C:
Guide to Characters in Series

> What enables the wise sovereign and the good general to strike and conquer, and achieve things beyond the reach of ordinary men is *foreknowledge*.
>
> —Sun Tzu, *The Art of War*, 78

IN THE SPY-THRILLER genre, as in others, some authors have created characters whom they continue from one title to the next. It is rarely problematical for the series fan who will follow his/her character's exploits regardless of genre label. "Escapist/Action Series," "Foreign Intrigue," "Headline or Current-Affairs thrillers," "Soldier-of-Fortune/Mercenary tales," "War Adventures," "Terrorist thrillers" or, most recently, "Technothrillers"—these are a few of many ways to describe this subclass of espionage which, all too often, lends itself toward a kind of potboiled, borderline espionage fiction at its worst. At its best, it becomes literature. But the vast numbers of these works being cranked out by single and series authors requires its own reference text, one destined never to be definitive, because of the great numbers of paperbacks produced in the U.S. monthly.

Consider only the talented and prolific Mr. Michael Avallone, self-styled "Fastest Typewriter in the East," who in his amazing thirty-plus-year career as a professional writer (under a dozen pseudonyms male and female) has spawned almost two hundred novels, of which forty million are still in print.[1] In a 1992 interview for *P.I.* magazine, he noted that *The Man from Uncle: The Thousand Coffins Affair #1* was written in December of 1964 in a single day,[2] and in one year he completed a mind-boggling twenty-seven books (*CA* 33).

It is always, we believe, a reader's prerogative to decide what is "best." You should note, however, that much of the negative criticism directed against the earliest of espionage literature—of Oppenheim, Sapper [Gerald MacNeile], and Buchan—to name only three prominent writers of this early group—for racism and sadistic nastiness has its corollary in this kind of mass-market fiction. Although humor and purely adventurous escapades can often be the main thrust, this kind of fiction can be appallingly bad—enough, that is, to remind the reader of what George Orwell said about *No Orchids for Miss Blandish*—namely, that some fiction is bad for a country's health.[3] One critic's review of John G. Cawelti and Bruce A. Rosenberg's *The Spy Story* (Chicago: U of Chicago P, 1987) finds an "ineradicable nastiness at the genre's core" (10ᴜ₁). A view we spurn. However, there is frequently found in pulp fiction of this caliber a rash of juvenile, mindless violence, and super-patriotic, Ramboesque action that discerning readers would reject in the same way that Eric Ambler and Graham Greene turned from the jingoistic rodomontade and blatant racism of early spy heroes and gave us great fiction with genuine characters and true-to-life themes. One wishes for the good health and lengthened days of writers of such style and class as Mr. Anthony Price, whose Dr. David Audley and Jack Butler, continue to weave a spell of excitement in novel after novel. The same to Mr. Ted Allbeury, one of the finest living writers, and his series of agents—be they called Tad Anders or Ted Bailey.

Even so, hordes of hard-hitting, hard-kissing heroes of pulp fiction continue to perpetuate stereotypes of masculinity and femininity in prose that is best described in Graham Greene's coinage: entertainments. We cite here such types as Aarons' Sam Durell, Fleming's Bond, and Don Pendleton's Mack Bolan, for their durability and popularity in the public imagination.

The purpose of this short guide is to provide the user with quick access to particular authors noted within the text of the two parts by way of their characters. To that end, the name of the character appears first followed by the name or names of the various writers who have chronicled his or her exploits. All references to authors are to the names as they appear in the bibliographic sections. Cross-references are made between codenames of series characters—for example, "The Death Merchant," and their operational names—in this instance, "Camellion, Richard." Certain organizations are cross-referenced to the characters whom they affect, such as UNCLE *see* Napoleon Solo; April Dancer.

Lastly, we include within this guide a small number of series characters (here defined as occurring in at least two works) an assortment of military-adventure types being churned out monthly under series titles like Able Team, Phoenix Force, the Survivalist series, the Butler series, and Barry Sadler's Casca series—featuring that most literal soldier-of-fortune Casca Longinus. For a comprehensive listing of this latter category, we recommend Bernard A. Drew's *Action Series and Sequels: A Bibliography of Espionage, Vigilante, and Soldier-of-Fortune Novels* (New York: Garland, 1988).

We include the following notations for the reader's convenience: *F* (futuristic/apocalyptic adventure); *H* (humor/spoof); *HI* (historical intrigue); *MA* (military adventure); *SOF* (soldiers-of-fortune/special forces/Vietnam); *TV* (television series/made-for-TV movie), and *YA* (young adult).

NOTES

1. *Contemporary Authors*, NR Series, vol. 4: 33-38.
2. Letter to the authors, October 15, 1992. The excerpt cited from Mr. Avallone's interview is found between pp. 48-49 of *P.I. Magazine* in the Fall 1992 issue and is quoted with author's permission.
3. John Sutherland, "Taxonomy of the Clandestine," rev. of *The Spy Story*, by John G. Cawelti and Bruce A. Rosenberg (Chicago: Chicago U P, 1987), *Times Literary Supplement* September 11-17: 1001+. Further citation is in the text.

ABLE Team = Dick Stivers, house pseud. (first three of this 1982-83 series co-written by Don Pendleton) (*SOF*)
"The Ace" *see* Justin Marsh
"The Adjusters" *see* Peter Winston
Agency Zero *see* Colin Garrett
Agent 86 *see* Maxwell Smart
Agent Nine = Graham Dean (*YA*)
Agent 6-X *see* Rand Stannard
Agent of TERRA *see* Hannibal Fortune (*F*)
Agent 008 = Allison Clyde, pseud. (William Knowles) (*H*)
Agent 13 = Flint Dille and David Marconi
"Alpha Triad" *see* Blade
Anders, Jonathan = Christopher Nicole (*YA*)
Anders, Tad = Ted Allbeury
APE [American Policy Executive] *see* John Keith
"The Aquanauts" *see* William Martin
Argand, Jan = Julian Rathbone
Asch, Gunner = Hans Hellmut Kirst (*MA/H*)
Ashenden = W. Somerset Maugham
"The Assassin" *see* Justin Perry
"The A-Team" = Charles Heath, pseud. (Ron Renauld) (*TV*)
Aubrey, Sir Kenneth = Craig Thomas
Audley, Dr. David = Anthony Price
Austin, Steve = Martin Caidin; Michael Jahn; Evan Richards; Jay Barbree (*TV*)

"The Avengers" *see* John Steed
AXE *see* Nick Carter
Barrabas [The Eternal Mercenary] = Barry Sadler
"The Baron" = Anthony Morton, pseud. (John Creasey) (*TV*)
Baron, Bruce = Norman Daniels
"The Baroness" = Paul Kenyon
Barzilia, Papa = Olga Hesley
Baum, Alfred = Derek Kartun
Beck, Adam = Kenneth Lemieux
Beck, Martin = Per Wahloo
Bellecroix, Stephen = Allen J. Tucker
Benasque, Mike = Alan Caillou, pseud. (Alan Lyle-Smythe)
Bentley, Steve = Robert Dietrich, pseud. (E. Howard Hunt)
Beresford, Tommy and Tuppence = Agatha Christie
"The Bionic Woman" *see* Jaime Sommers
"The Black Berets" = Mike McCray (*MA*)
Blackstone, Edmund = Richard Falkirk, pseud. (Derek Lambert) (*HI*)
Blade = David Robbins (*F*)
Blaise, Modesty = Peter O'Donnell (*TV*)
Blake, Sexton = Walter W. Sayer; Francis A. Warwick
Blakeney, Sir Percy = Emma Magdalena Rosalia Maria Josefa Barbara Orczy
    (Baroness Orczy)
Blessington, Charles = John Sherwood
Blofeld, Ernst Stavro *see* James Bond
Blonde, Jane = Inge Carnell (*H*)
"Blue Mask" *see* John Mannering
Boggs, Sam = Mark Washburn
Bognor, Investigator Simon = Tim[othy] V. Heald
Bond, Israel = Sol Weinstein (*H*)
Bond, James = Ian Fleming; Robert Markham, pseud. (Kingsley Amis);
    Bennett Cerf; Cyril Connolly; John Pearson; Christopher Wood (*TV*);
    John Gardner; Barbara and Scott Siegel; Jean M. Favors; R. L. Stine
Boone, Jefferson = Jon Messman
Bourne, Jason *see* David Webb
Box, Virginia = James Moffat (*H*)
Boxer, Commander Jack = Irving A. Greenfield (*MA*)
Brandeis, Kyle = William Ash
Brandon, Anthony = Peter B. George
Brett, Mike = Keith Campbell, pseud. (Keith Campbell West-Watson)
Brewer, Charlie = William H. Hallahan
Bristow, Superintendent *see* John Mannering
Brock = John M. W. Bingham (Lord Clanmorris)

Brodie, Paul = Hugh McLeave
Brook, Roger = Dennis Wheatley (*HI*)
Brooks, Michael = Henry T. Rothwell
Brown, Eddie = Joyce Porter
Budd, Lanny = Upton Sinclair
Bulman, Inspector *see* Willie "Spider" Scott
"The Bureau" *see* Harry Quiller
Butler = Philip Kirk, pseud. (Leonard Levinson)
Butler, Jack = Anthony Price
Cable, Sarah = Michael Hartland
Cain, Cabot = Alan Caillou, pseud. (Alan Lyle-Smythe)
Cajun *see* Sam Durell
Callan, David = James W. Mitchell
Camellion, Richard = Joseph Rosenberger
Campion, Albert = Margery Allingham; Youngman Carter
Cardigan, Burgess ("Buzz") = Don Rico (*H*)
Carstairs, "Apples" = Symon Myles, pseud. (Ken Follett)
Carstairs, Brett = Sydney Horler
Carter = Thomas W. Lilley
Carter, Nick = Nick Carter (house pseudonym: John Coryell; Frederick van
    Rensselaer Dey; Frederick William Davis; Eugene T. Sawyer; Michael
    Avallone; Robert Clurman; Valerie Moolman; Manning Lee Stokes;
    Martin Cruz Smith)
Carver, Rex = Victor Canning
CASCA = Barry Sadler
Castle, Major Peter = Gilderoy Davison
CAT (Crisis Aversion Team) = Spike Andrews (*MA*)
Caution, Lemmy = Peter Cheyney, pseud. (Reginald Southouse Cheyney)
Charlie M *see* Charlie Muffin
Chavasse, Paul = Jack Higgins, pseud. (British byline: Martin Fallon,
    pseud. = Henry Patterson)
Chayne, Alexander = Ralph Hayes
"The Check Force" *see* Alexander Chayne; Vladimir Karlov
Chipstead, Buncombe ("Bunny") = Sydney Horler
Christopher, Jimmy = Curtis Steele, pseud. (Emile Tepperman and Frederick
    C. Davis)
Christopher, Paul = Charles McCarry
CII *see* Jonathan Hemlock
"Clubfoot" *see* Adolph Grundt
COBRA *see* Skul; Debbie Miles
Cody = David Brierly
Cody, John = Jim Case (*MA*)

Colson, Captain = Allan White
"Cominsec" *see* Taggart
"The Condor" *see* Ronald Malcolm
CONTROL *see* Maxwell Smart
"Counter Force" *see* Steve Crown
Corbett, Kyle = Dean Ing
Corbin, Ben = Robert Crane, pseud. (Connie Leslie Sellers, Jr.)
Cord, Talos = Robert MacLeod, pseud. (Bill Knox)
Cornell, Jerry = Michael Moorcock
"The Corps" = W.E.B. Griffin (*MA*)
Corrigan, Mark = Mark Corrigan, pseud. (Norman Lee)
Cotton, Gunston ("Gun") = Rupert Grayston
Counterpol *see* Kim Smith
"The Coxeman" *see* Rod Damon
Crader, Carl and Earl Jazine = Edward D. Hoch
Craig, John = James Munro, pseud. (James W. Mitchell)
Craig, Peter = Kenneth Benton
Craigie, Gordon = John Creasey
Crèvecoeur *see* Cody
Crook, Mark = Charles Whiting (*MA*)
Crosley, Lee = Robert Tralins
Crown, Steve = Dan Streib
Crouchback, Guy = Evelyn Waugh
Cunningham, Major ("Brains") = E. P. Thorne
CURE *see* Remo Williams
"Dagger" *see* Christian Daguerre
Daguerre, Christian = Carl Stevens, pseud. (Raymond Obstfeld)
Damon, Rod = Troy Conway, house pseud. (Michael Avallone and various
     authors) *H*
Dancer, April = Michael Avallone; Simon Latter; Peter Leslie (*TV*)
Danning, David = Don Von Elsner
"The D.C. Man" *see* Brian Peterson
"The Danger Man" *see* John Drake
"The Dark Series" *see* Everard Peter Quayle
Da Silva, José = Robert L. Fish
Dawlish *see* Harry Palmer
Dawlish, Patrick = Gordon Ashe, pseud. (John Creasey)
Deacon, Lieutenant and Sergeant Campbell = James Albany (*MA*)
"The Death Dealer" *see* Jim Rainey
"The Death Merchant" *see* Richard Camellion
Dell, Mary = Norman Deane, pseud. (John Creasey)
"Dekker's Demons" = Alex Webb, pseud. (Alan Lyle-Smythe) (*MA*)

Delight, Cherry = Glenn Chase, pseud. (Gardner Fox) (*H*)
Denson, John = Richard Hoyt
"Department B-7" *see* Cabot Cain
"Department S" *see* Major "Brains" Cunningham
"Department 6" *see* Philip McAlpine
"Department Z" *see* Gordon Craigie; Dr. Stanislaus Alexander Palfrey
"The Destroyer" *see* Remo Williams
"The Destroyer I" = Warren Murphy and Richard Sapir (other authors include
    Richard S. Meyers; Robert Randisi; Molly Cochran; Will Murray)
Devereaux = Bill Granger
Devlin, Liam = Jack Higgins, pseud. (Harry Patterson)
DeWitt, Manny = Peter Rabe
Dexter, Charles = John Fredman
Digburn, Howard = Bruce Sanders
Dixon, Scott (Lt. Col.) = Harold Coyle
Donovan, Capt. James L. = Lee Parker (*MA*)
Doomschen, the = E. Phillips Oppenheim
Dragon *see* Jonathan Hemlock
Drake, Earl = Dan J. Marlowe
Drake, John = W. Howard Baker; W. A. Ballinger, pseud. (W. Howard Baker
    and Wilfrid G. McNeilly); Peter Leslie; Wilfred McNeilly: "The Secret
    Agent" (*TV*) and Richard Telfair: "The Danger Man" (*TV*)
Driscoll, Clifford = William L. DeAndrea
Drum, Chester = Stephen Marlowe, pseud. (Milton A. Lesser)
Drum, Eve = Rod Gray (*H*)
Drummond, Captain Hugh ("Bulldog") = Gerald Fairlie; Herman C. McNeile
Ducane = John M. W. Bingham (Lord Clanmorris)
Dupin, C. Auguste = Edgar Allan Poe
Durell, Sam = Edward S. Aarons; Will B. Aarons
Duvakin = Anthony Olcott
Eagle, John = Paul Edwards, house pseud. (Manning Lee Stokes)
Eberhart, Matt = Berent Sandberg, pseud. (Peter Lars Sandberg and Mark
    Berent)
Eisenberg, Ron = Philip Chase, pseud. (Philip Freedman)
"The Eliminator" *see* Jonas Wilde
EMPIRE *see* Hannibal Fortune
"The Eternal Mercenary" *see* Casca Longinus
"The Expeditor" *see* John Eagle
Farrow, Marcus Aurelius ("Mike") = Angus Ross
Fedora, Johnny = Desmond Cory, pseud. (John L. [Shaun] MacCarthy)
Feltham, Peter = Berkeley Mather, pseud. (John E. W. Davies)
Fenton, Lawrie = Michael Annesley

Feramontov *see* Johnny Fedora
Fields, Jan = Harold Coyle
Firth, Ian = Peter Brent
Fleming, Roger = Simon Harvester, pseud. (Henry St. John Clair Rumbold-
       Gibbs)
Flint, Derek = Jack Pearl; Bradford Street
"The Force" *see* Steve Sinclair
Ford, Ashton = Don Pendleton
Fordinghame, Sir Brian = Sydney Horler
Fortune, Hannibal = Larry Maddock
Fortune, Temple = T.C.H. Jacobs, pseud. (Jacques Pendower)
Foster, Pete = William C. Odell
Fowler, Grant = Paul Richards, house pseud. (Jon Messman; George Snyder;
       Dan Strieb; Chet Cunningham)
Fraser, James = James Wood
Frost, Gerald ("Nighthawk") = Sydney Horler
Frost, Hank = Axel Kilgore, pseud. (Jerry Ahern) (*SOF*)
Fu Manchu (Dr.) = Sax Rohmer, pseud. (Arthur Sarsfield Ward)
Fusil, Inspector = Peter Alding, pseud. (Roderic Jeffries)
Gail, John = Stephen Frances
Galan, Max = C. H. Guenther, pseud. (C. H. Gunther)
Gall, Joe = Philip Atlee, pseud. (James Atlee Phillips)
Gambit, Mike and Purdey *see* "The New Avengers"
Gannon, Jack = J. C. Pollock
Gant, Mitchell = Craig Thomas
Gantian, Colonel Peter = Carlton Dawe
Garfield, Lucas = Frank Ross
Garnett, David = Clive Egleton
Garrett, Colin = Gary Bradner
Garrison, Captain = Walter Wager
Garvin, Willie *see* Modesty Blaise
Gavin, Rod = John Quinn, pseud. (Dennis Rodriguez)
"Genops" [General Operations] = Irwin R. Blacker
"The Gentleman" *see* John George Norman Hyde
Gideon, Scott; Jomar Viten and Sven Dahle = Gregory St. Germain, pseud.
       (Jeffrey M. Wallman)
Gilead, Justin = Warren Murphy and Molly Cochran
Gillard, Patrick = Margaret Duffy
Giordino, Al *see* Dirk Pitt
The Girl from BUST *see* Jane Blonde
The Girl from HARD *see* Virginia Box
The Girl from PUSSYCAT = Ted Mark, pseud. (Theodore Mark Gottfried)

The Girl from UNCLE *see* April Dancer

Girland, Mark = James Hadley Chase, pseud. (René B. Raymond)

"The Glasshouse Gang Commando Unit" = Gordon Lansborough (*MA*)

Glenne, Al = M. G. Brown

Godin, Haggai = Owen John

Gould, Bart = Joseph Milton [Lancer's 1963 edition of *President's Agent* spells
    author's surname as *H*ilton]

Gould, Skipper = Robert Kalish

Grafton, Jake = Stephen Coonts

Graham, Davina = Evelyn Anthony, pseud.

Graham, Richard = John Welcome

Granby, Colonel Alistair ("Toby") = Francis Beeding, pseud. (John L. Palmer
    and Hilary Aiden St. George Saunders)

"The Grandmaster" *see* Justin Gilead

Grant, Colonel Duncan = Graham Seton, pseud. (Graham Seton Hutchison)

Grant, Dr. David = George B. Mair

Grim, James Schuyler ("Jimgrim") = Talbot Mundy, pseud. (William L.
    Gribbon)

Gringo, Captain = Ramsay Thorne (*HI/SOF*)

Grisman, Saul = David Morrell

Grofield, Alan = Donald E. Westlake

Grundt, Dr. Adolph ("Clubfoot") = Valentine Williams

"The Guardians" = Richard Austin (*F*)

Gull, Vladimir = Anthony Stuart, pseud. (Julian Anthony Stuart Hale)

Hambledon, Thomas Elphinstone ("Tommy") = Adelaide F. O. Manning and
    Cyril Henry Coles

Hamilton, Anthony = Frederick Frost, pseud. (Frederick Shiller Faust)

Hammer, Mike = Frank M. Spillane

"The Handyman" *see* Jefferson Boone

Hannay, Richard = John Buchan

Harden, Mark = Lionel Derrick

Hardy, Patrick = Martin Meyers

Harrigan and Hoeffler = Patrick O'Malley

Harris, Paul = Gavin Black, pseud. (Oswald Wynd)

Hawk, Michael = Dan Streib

Hawk, Sergeant James = Patrick Clay (*MA*)

Hawks, Joaquin = Bill S. Ballinger

Heald, Max = Harry Hossent

Heath, Jennifer = Alison Tyler

Helm, Matt = Donald Hamilton

Hemlock, Jonathan = Trevanian, pseud. (Rodney Whitaker)

Hewes-Bradford, Barrington = Marilyn Granbeck and Arthur Moore

Hiller, Gregory = Jack Laflin
Hillsden, Alec = Alan Furst
Holmes, Sherlock and Dr. Watson = Arthur Conan Doyle
Holland, Mark =   Paul Myers
Hood, Charles = James Mayo, pseud. (Stephen Coulter)
Hood, Mark Kingsley = James Dark, pseud. (James Edmond McDonald)
Hook, Sam = Darwin and Hildegarde Teilhet
"The Hotline" = Paul Richards
Hunter, Robert = Eric Sauter
Hunter, Sir Robert = Geoffrey Household
Hyde, John George Norman = John Boland
Hyde, Patrick = Craig Thomas
"I Spy" = John Tiger, pseud. (Walter Wager) (*TV*)
"The Inquisitor" *see* Frank Kelly
"Israeli Commandos" = Andrew Sugar
ITRB [International Trade Research Bureau] *see* Lloyd Nicolson
Jackson, Kane = William Arden, pseud. (Dennis Lynds)
Jaeger, Curt = Mark Mandell
Jagger, Mike = William Gardner
Jamieson, Colonel Philip *see* Julia Probyn
Jenner, Jimmy = John Milne
Jonson, Ben = Peter Levi
"K Section" *see* Sam Durell
Karla = John le Carré, pseud. (David J. M. Cornwell)
Karlov, Vladimir = Ralph Hayes
Keene, Oliver ("O.K.") = J. M. Walsh
Keith, John = Norman Daniels
Kelly, Frank = Martin Cruz Smith
Kelly, Lieutenant = Holly Roth
Kemp, John Mason = Philip McCutchan
Kendell, Bill = Philip Chase, pseud. (Philip Freedman)
Kendrick, Don = Alan MacKinnon
Kilgerrin, Paul = Charles L. Leonard, pseud. (Mary V. Heberden)
"Killmaster" *see* Nick Carter
King, Dakota = Jake MacKenzie (*YA*)
King, Lou = Joseph Rosenberger
King, Reefe = Albert Barker
Kirk, General Charles = John F. Blackburn
Kuryakin, Illya *see* Napoleon Solo
Kruger, Herbie = John Gardner
The **Lady** from LUST *see* Eve Drum
Lance, Peter = Hunter Adams (*H*)

Langley Ingrid = Margaret Duffy
Larren, Simon = Robert Charles, pseud. (Robert Charles Smith)
Latimer, Charles = Eric Ambler
Laver, Richard = William Haggard, pseud. (Richard H. M. Clayton)
Lawson, Peter = Melvin Bolton
"Leathermouth" *see* Colonel Peter Gantian
Lohmann, Ernst = Jack Gerson
Lester, "Tiger" = Don Betteridge, pseud. (Bernard Newman)
Levin, Roger = Alan Furst
Lincoln, John A. = David Lodge
Linge, Prince Malko = Gerard De Villiers
Lissendale, Gerald = Sydney Horler
Locke, Kim = Kendell Foster Crossen
Locken, Mike = Robert Rostand, pseud. (Robert S. Hopkins)
Lockington, Lacey = Ross H. Spencer
Longinus, Casca = Barry Sadler (*HI/SOF*)
Love, Dr. Jason = James Leasor
"The Lunatic" = Joseph Storer Clouston, pseud. (Francis Mandell-Essington)
M. *see* James Bond
Maasten, Nick = Owen Sela
"Mack Bolan's ABLE Team" *see* ABLE Team
"The Manhunter" *see* Max Galan
Mannering, John = Anthony Morton, pseud. (John Creasey)
McAlpine, Philip = Adam Diment
McCorkle, Mac = Ross Thomas
McCracken, Blaine = Jon Land
McCunn, Dickson = John Buchan
McGarret, Steve = Michael Avallone
McGee, Travis = John D. MacDonald
McGinty, Slade = Jacques Pendower
McGowan, Charles *see* Marcus Aurelius ("Mike") Farrow
McGregor, Inspector = Henry Kane
McHugh = Jay Flynn
MacLane, Drew = David Morrell
"McLeane's Rangers" = John Darby (*MA*)
McVeigh, Mike = Robert Emmett
Mado, George = Warren Tute
"The Magic Man" = David Bannerman, pseud. (David Hagberg)
Magnum *see* Pete Foster
Mahoney, Sergeant C. J. ("Parrot") = Gordon Davis, pseud. (Leonard Levinson) (*MA*)
Mahoney, Wallace and John = Sean Flannery, pseud. (David Hagberg)

Malcolm, Ronald = James Grady
Malko, Linge = Gerald DeVilliers
Mallory, Captain = Alistair Maclean
The Man from APE *see* John Keith
The Man from CHARISMA = Ted Mark, pseud. (Theodore Mark Gottfried) (*H*)
The Man from ORGY *see* Steve Victor
The Man from STUD = F. W. Paul, pseud. (Paul W. Fairman) (*H*)
The Man from TOMCAT *see* Timothy O'Shane
The Man from UNCLE *see* Napoleon Solo
Mann, Tiger = Frank M. Spillane
Mansel, Jonathan = Dornford Yates, pseud. (Maj. Cecil William Mercer)
"Marc Dean Mercenary" = Peter Buck (*MA*)
March, Milo = M. E. Chaber, pseud. (Kendell F. Crossen)
Marlow, Peter = Joseph Hone
Marsh, Justin = Sydney Horler
Marshall, John = Mark Denning, pseud. (John Stevenson)
Marshall, Sergeant/Inspector = Bernard Newman
Martin, Octavia ("Tavy") = Diana Winsor
Martin, William = Ken Stanton
Martini, David = Richard Raine, pseud. (Raymond H. Sawkins)
Mastrovin *see* Dickson McCunn
Maxim, Harry = Gavin Lyall
Mead, Selena = Patricia McGerr
"Men at War" = Alex Baldwin (*MA*)
Merlin = Walter Wager
Mero *see* Britt St. Vincent
"M.I.A. Hunter" = Jack Buchanan
Miles, Debbie = Joseph R. Rosenberger
Miro = Shaun Herron
"Mission Impossible" = Walter Wager; Max Walker (*TV*)
Mr. Moto = John P. Marquand
Mr. Sabin [Duc de Souspenier] = E. Phillips Oppenheim
Mohume, Peter = Pelham Groom
Morgan, "Railway" Joe = John R. Howlett
Morrison, Nigel = Norman Fisher
Muffin, Charlie = Brian Freemantle
Munday, Alexander = Gil Brewer
Murdock, Bruce = Norman Deane, pseud. (John Creasey)
N-3 *see* Nick Carter
Nairn, David = Michael Hartland
Nash, Montgomery ("Monty") = Richard Telfair

"The New Avengers" = John Carter; Justin Cartwright; Peter Cave; Walter Harris (*TV*)

Nicolson, Lloyd = Patrick Wayland, pseud. (Richard O'Connor)

Noon, Ed = Michael Avallone

Norrington, Lady Jennifer; Count Alessandro di Ganzarello; and Coleridge Tucker III = Ivor Drummond

North, Hugh = Francis Van Wyck Mason

"The Notebooks" = Sam Picard

"The November Man" *see* Devereaux

"The Nullifier" *see* Joe Gall

NUMA [National Underwater and Marine Agency] *see* Dirk Pitt

NYMPHO [New York Mafia Prosecution and Harassment Organization] *see* Cherry Delight

ORGY *see* Steve Victor

007 *see* James Bond

OSS 117 = Jean A. Brochet

Oakes, Blackford = William F. Buckley, Jr.

Oakes, Boysie = John Gardner

Okewood, Desmond = Valentine Williams

Operator 5 *see* Jimmy Christopher

Ormiston, Colonel = J. M. Walsh

O'Shane, Timothy = Mallory T. Knight, pseud. (Bernhardt J. Hurwood)

Otley, Gerald Arthur = Martin Waddell

Owen, Captain Cadwallader = Michael Pearce

Oy-Oy-7 = Sol Weinstein

Packard, James = Robert Connington, pseud. (Philip McCutchan)

Padillo, Michael = Ross Thomas

Pagan, Inspector = Campbell Armstrong

Palfrey, Dr. Stanislaus Alexander = John Creasey

Palmer, Harry = Len Deighton

PANSY *see* Burgess "Buzz" Cardigan

"The Peacemaker" *see* Barrington Hewes-Bradford

Peel, Emma *see* John Steed

Pemberty, Dick = Phillip Conde

"The Penetrator" *see* Mark Harden

Perry, Justin = John D. Revere

Peterson, Brian = James P. Cody, pseud. (Peter Thomas Rohrbach)

Peterson, Carl *see* "Bulldog" Drummond

Philip, Dick = Ritchie Perry

Philis = Ritchie Perry

"The Phoenix Force" = Gar Wilson (*MA*)

Pitt, Dirk = Clive Cussler

Poirot, Hercule = Agatha Christie
Pollifax, Emily = Dorothy Gilman
Pontivy, Papa = Bernard Newman
Porter, Appleton = Marc Lovell, pseud. (Mark McShane)
Povin, Stepan = John Trenhaile
"The Prisoner" = George Markstein; Hank Stine (*TV*)
Probyn, Julia = Ann Bridge, pseud. (Mary D. O'Malley)
Purdue, Chance = Ross H. Spencer
Quayle, Everard Peter = Peter Cheyney, pseud. (Reginald Southouse Cheyney)
Quayle, Ian = Alan Caillou, pseud. (Alan Lyle-Smythe)
Quiller, Harry = Adam Hall, pseud. (Elleston Trevor)
Quinn = Franklin M. Davis, Jr.
Quintain, Richard = W. Howard Baker
Rainey, Jim = Peter McCurtain (*SOF*)
Rambo, John = David Morrell
Rand, Jeffrey = Edward D. Hoch
"The Rat Patrol" = Norman Daniels; David King (*MA/TV*)
Raven, Richard = John Griffin
Rees, Idwhal = Berkely Mather, pseud. (John E. W. Davies)
Regina = Dagmar, pseud. (Dagmar and Lou Cameron) (*H*)
Rehmy, Etienne and Gaston de Blanchegarde = Francis Beeding, pseud. (John
     Leslie Palmer and Hilary Aidan St. George Saunders)
Reilly, Sydney = Robin Bruce Lockhart (*TV*)
Renwick, Nina and Bob = Helen MacInnes
Revell, Major and Sergeant Hyde = James Rouch
Rickman, Ray = Allan J. Tucker
Roath, Sheila = Allan J. Tucker
Rockson, Ted = Ryder Stacy (*MA/F*)
Rollinson, Richard = John Creasey
Roper, Piers = Ken Follett (*H*)
Ross, Jeff and Willie Caine = Ian MacKintosh (*TV*)
Rostnikov, Inspector Porfiry = Stuart M. Kaminsky
Roth, Max = Henry Arvay (*MA*)
Rourke, John Thomas = Jerry Ahern (*F*)
Royce, Rupert = James Aldridge
Russell, Colonel Charles = William Haggard, pseud. (Richard H. M. Clayton)
Ryan, John ("Jack") Patrick = Tom Clancy
Ryan, Sean = Brian T. Cleeve
Ryder, Harry = Robert Footman
S-COM [Strategic Commandoes] = Steve White, pseud. (Robert McGarvey)
     (*SOF*)
"The Saint" *see* Simon Templar

St. John-Orsini, Baroness Penelope = Paul Kenyon

St. Vincent, Britt = John F. Rossman (part of series issued as by Ian Ross)

SATAN *see* Dr. David Grant

Sallust, Gregory = Dennis Wheatley

Samson, Bernard = Len Deighton

"The Sandbaggers" = Ian MacKintosh (*TV*); Donald Lancaster *aka* William Marshall published *The Sandbaggers: Think of a Number* in 1980; the Yorkshire television series ran from 1978 to 1980)

Savage, John = James Trevor

Savage, Mark = Matthew Eden

Saveman, Eric = Paul Peterson

"The Scarlet Pimpernel" = Baroness Orczy (*HI*)

Scott, Willie ("Spider") = Kenneth Royce, pseud. (Kenneth Royce Gandley)

Search and Sanction Division *see* Jonathan Hemlock

Sebastian = James L. Johnson

"Secret Agent" *see* John Drake

"The Secret Circle" = Gary Null

"Secret Mission" = Don Smith

"Section Q" *see* Selena Mead

Security Executive *see* Col. Charles Russell

Seidlitz, Mavis = Carter Brown, pseud. (Alan Geoffrey Yates)

"The Sexecutioner" *see* Cherry Delight

Shannon, Patrick = Jake Quinn

Shard, Detective Chief Superintendent Simon = Philip McCutchan

"Shaun O'Mara Thrillers" = Peter Cheyney, pseud. (Reginald Southouse Cheyney)

Shaw, Commander Esmonde = Philip McCutchan

Sherman, Phil = Don Smith

Silk, Dorian = Simon Harvester, pseud.

Simpson, Arthur Abdel = Eric Ambler

Sinclair, Steve = Jake Decker

6D2-Ministry of Defence *see* Commander Esmonde Shaw

"The Six Million Dollar Man" *see* Steve Austin

Skul = Joseph R. Rosenberger

Slade = Desmond Bagley

Slayton, Ben = Buck Sanders, pseud. (Thomas L. Adcock; Jeffrey Frentzen)

Smart, Maxwell = William Johnston (*HI/TV*)

SMERSH *see* James Bond

Smiley, George = John le Carré, pseud. (David J. M. Cornwell)

Smith, Aurelius = R.T.M. Scott

Smith, Brad = Jack M. Bickham

Smith, John = James (Jimmy) Sangster

Smith, Kim = John Boland

Smith, Nayland = Sax Rohmer, pseud. (Arthur Henry Sarsfield Ward)

"The Smugglers" *see* Eric Saveman

SOBS [Soldiers of Barrabas] = Jack Hild (*SOF*)

Solo, Napoleon = Michael Avallone; Joel Bernard; Frederic Davies; Thomas
    G. DeWeese; George S. Elrich; Ron Ellik; John Hill; Joan C. Holly; J.
    Hunter Holly; Brandon Keith; Peter Leslie; David McDaniel; John Oram;
    John T. Phillifent; Thomas Stratton, pseud. (Thomas DeWeese and
    Robert Coulson); Henry Whittington (*TV*)

Sommers, Jaime = Maude Willis, pseud. (Eileen Lottman) (*TV*)

Sparrow, Charlie = Tom Ardies

"Special Intelligence" *see* Charles Hood

"The Special Unit" *see* Bill Kendall; Ron Eisenberg

SPECTRE *see* James Bond

Standish, John = Klaus Nettson (*MA*)

Standish, "Tiger" = Sydney Horler

Stannard, Rand = Richard L. Hershatter

Stears, Giovanni Sidgewick = Frank O'Neill

Steed, John = Norman Daniels; John Garforth; Keith Laumer; Peter Leslie;
    Patrick McNee (*TV*)

Steel, Alan = Colin Robertson

Steiner, Colonel Kurt = Jack Higgins, pseud. (Harry Patterson)

Stok, Colonel *see* Bernard Samson

Stone, Curt = Jack Seward

Stoner, Mark = Ralph Hayes (*SOF*)

Strong, John = Marc Acres

Sumuru = Sax Rohmer, pseud. (Arthur Henry Sarsfield Ward)

"The Survivalist" *see* John Thomas Rourke

Swain, Ape = Daniel da Cruz

Sylvester *see* Brad Smith

"T-Force" = Charles Whiting (*MA*)

Tabard = Christopher Portway

Taggart = Ralph Hayes

Taine, Roger = Geoffrey Household

Tallis, Roger = John Rossiter

Tanner, Evan = Lawrence Block

Tarrant, Sir Gerald *see* Modesty Blaise

Templar, Simon = Leslie Charteris, pseud. (Leslie C. B. Yin) (*TV*)

Terrel, Timothy = Stephen Maddock, pseud. (J. M. Walsh)

THRUSH [Technological Hierarchy for the Removal of Undesirables and the
    Subjugation of Humanity] *see* April Dancer; Napoleon Solo

"Tiger Shark" *see* William Martin

Tobin, Colonel Matthew = Alan Caillou, pseud. (Alan Lyle-Smythe)

Todd = Kenneth Royce, pseud. (Kenneth Royce Gandley)

"The Toff" *see* Richard Rollinson

Tomachenko, Natalya = Jon Land

TOMCAT [Tactical Operations Master Counterintelligence Assault Team] *see* Tim O'Shane

Touchfeather, Katherine ("Katy") = James (Jimmy) Sangster

Trees, Peter = John Q., pseud. (John Edward Quirk)

Tremayne, Tommy *see* Mark Hood

Trosper, Alan = William Hood

Troth, Edmund = Richard Llewellyn

Troy, David = Alan Gardner

Tyler, Dennis = Diplomat, pseud. (John Franklin Carter)

Urban, Robert = C. H. Guenther, pseud. (G. H. Gunther)

UNCLE [United Network Command for Law and Enforcement] *see* Napoleon Solo; April Dancer

Valeshoff, and Tamara = Eric Ambler

Vallon, Johnny = Peter Cheyney, pseud. (Reginald Southouse Cheyney)

Velvet, Nick = Edward D. Hoch

Veseloffsky, Baron Serge = Sydney Horler

Victor, Steve = Ted Mark, pseud. (Theodore Mark Gottfried)

Von Hegnitz, Otto = William LeQueux

Von Romain, Kurt = John Creasey

Von Ryan, Joseph = David Westheimer

Wainwright, James = Berkely Mather, pseud. (John E. W. Davies)

Wallace, Sir Leonard = Alexander Wilson

Ward, Peter = E. Howard Hunt

Wareagle, John = Jon Land

Watson, Angus *see* Appleton Porter

Webb, David = Robert Ludlum

Wilde, Jonas = Andrew York, pseud. (Christopher Nicole)

Williams, Remo = Richard Sapir and Warren Murphy

Wingate, Mac = Bryan Swift

Winkman, Jake = Don Von Elsner

Winslow, Don = Frank V. Martinak (*YA*)

Winston, Peter = Peter Winston, pseud.

"The Withered Man" *see* Kurt Von Romain

Woiz, Baldur = Bruno Krauss, pseud. (Kenneth Bulmer) (*MA*)

Wolfram, Hugo = Richard L. Graves

Woodhead, Alister = E. H. Clements

"World Strike Force" = Frank Garrett

Wu, Artie and Quincy Durant = Ross Thomas

Wyman, Michael = Bob Cook
Yeoman, Giles = Martin Woodhouse
Z-5 *see* Dr. Stanislaus Alexander Palfrey
ZED *see* Eric Saveman
Zharkov, Alexander *see* Justin Gilead
"The Zone" *see* Major Revell and Sergeant Hyde
Zordan, Anna = James Eastwood
ZOWIE *see* Derek Flint

Appendix D:
Guide to Intelligence and Terrorist Organizations

In making tactical dispositions, the highest pitch you can attain is to conceal them; conceal your dispositions, and you will be safe from the prying of the subtlest spies, from the machinations of the wisest brains.

—Sun Tzu, *The Art of War*, 28

READERS OF THE spy thriller and the annotations within this guide will find references made to large numbers of factual espionage, covert action, commando, and terrorist organizations. A few were swept away or dismantled in the political upheaval in eastern Europe triggered by Solidarity and *glasnost* between the fall of the infamous Berlin Wall and the Soviet Union's dismantling between 1989 and 1992—including the mighty KGB, the most emulated and feared of all. Consider that the U.S. State Department recorded sixty-three terrorist incidents in the Middle East in 1990 alone (down from three hundred *per annum* since 1985) and you have an idea of the seething cauldron of secret intelligence organizations in countries like Iraq, Syria, and Libya known as *mokhabarats*. Often these references will be to initials or to groups whose identity is not of the English language, so we have alphabetically arranged and cross-indexed the most important here. (We gratefully acknowledge Donald R. Morris for the SmerSh anecdote; see our introduction to Appendix E.)

Abu Nidal Organization - The bloodiest of the Arab terrorist groups; now Libyan-backed, Nidal's thugs have killed or maimed hundreds since splitting from the **PLO** in 1974; other Nidal organizations include Palestine Secret Organization and Black June (named for the month when Syrian troops entered Lebanon); like Carlos and the Argentine Montoneros, Nidal works for personal profit.

Abwehr - Intelligence Service, Nazi Germany Armed Forces; Admiral Wilhelm
    Canaris, its chief, was a bitter enemy of the Nazis and betrayed them for
    years. He was uncovered as a conspirator in the July 20, 1944 plot to
    assassinate Hitler and was tortured, hanged, revived, and hanged again.

Action Directe - French terrorists.

Akali Dal - Sikh political party in the Punjab region.

April 19 Movement - The **Medellín Cartel's** hired gun, a revolutionary group
    also known as **M-19**; formed in Columbia in 1970 as a populist
    movement.

ASALA - Armenian Secret Army for the Liberation of Armenia.

ASIO - Australian Secret Intelligence Organization.

AVB - see **AVH.**

AVH - *(Allamvedelmi Osztaly)* State Security Section, Hungary.

Bandera Roja - Marxist group, Venezuela.

Baader-Meinhoff Group - German terrorist organization begun by student
    radicals in West Berlin the late 1960s; similar to the American Weather
    Underground and Symbionese Liberation Front; named for its two
    principal figures, Ulrike Meinhoff and Andreas Baader, found hanging in
    their cells; also known as the **Red Army Faction.**

BfV - *(Bundesamt für Verfassungsschutz)* West German Federal Internal
    Security.

Black September - Secret commando wing of Arafat's *Fatah*; responsible for the
    abduction and slaughter of Israeli athletes at the Olympics in Munich
    1972.

BND - *(Bundesnachrichtendienst)* Intelligence Service, Federal Republic of
    Germany.

BOSS - Bureau of State Security, Republic of South Africa.

CCP - Central Committee Military Commission. China's ruling body overseeing the People's Liberation Army, consisting of a dozen revolutionary organizations in 1967, such as the Shanghai Workers' Rebellion-Making Headquarters, all of which comprised China's sweeping Cultural Revolution; it governed both military and ideological activities during the late sixties and the establishment of the Red Guard.

CESID - *(Centro Superior para la Información de la Defensa)* Secret Service, Spain.

Cheka - *(Chrezuvychayna Komissiya po Borbe s Kontrrevolutisnei i Sabottazahem)* Extraordinary Commission for the Struggle Against Counterrevolution and Sabotage; Bolshevik secret police organization headed by the notorious Feliks Dzerzhinsky under Lenin; responsible for intelligence, counterintelligence, trials and punishments.

Cheng Pao K'o - Counterespionage Service, China.

CIA - Central Intelligence Agency, USA. Located in Langley, VA, this vast intelligence complex still trains agents at "The Farm" nearby; its request of an operating budget of $30 billion for 1992, a sum many times greater than most nations' GNPs, shows that the shifting alignments and problems of the world—especially the $200 billion drug "industry" stretching from Central and South America to America's streets—have not diminished its power or purview.

CIC - Counterintelligence Corps, United States Army.

CID - Criminal Investigation Division, Scotland Yard, Great Britain.

DGI - *(Dirección General de Intelligencia)* Secret Service, Cuba.

DGSI - *(Direction Général de Sécurité Extérieure)* See **SDECE**.

DI5 - See **MI5**.

DI6 - See **MI6**.

DIA - Defense Intelligence Agency, Department of Defense, USA.

DS - *(Darjavna Sugarnost)* Secret Service, Bulgaria.

DST - *(Direction de la Surveillance du Territoire)* Internal Security Service, France.

Etsivakeskus - Secret Police, Finland.

ETA - *(Euzkadi Ta Askatasuna)* Translation: Basque Homeland and Liberty; fights for the creation of an independent Basque Marxist state.

FALN - Puerto Rican Marxist guerrilla group; fights for an independent Puerto Rico. Chief suspect in the December 29, 1975 La Guardia Airport bombing of the TWA terminal that killed eleven.

FARC - Columbian Revolutionary Armed Forces, a leftist group.

El Fatah - Yasser Arafat's guerrilla group.

FBI - Federal Bureau of Investigation, USA.

FDR - *Frente Democratico Revolucionario*, El Salvador.

FLNP - Marxist-affiliated terrorist organization to free Puerto Rico.

FMLN - *Frente Farabundo Marti para la Liberación Nacional*, El Salvador.

FSLN - *Frente Sandinista de Libaración Nacional*, Nicaragua.

G-2 - Intelligence Staff, US Army.

GCHQ - Government Communications Headquarters, Cheltenham, England.

General Investigation Directorate - Libya's intelligence and counterintelligence bureau which reports to the Secretariat for External Security, formed in 1984 by order of the General People's Congress.

Gong An Ju (in pinyin system) - Chinese Intelligence Service, HQ is in Tiananmen Square.

Gray Wolves - (Turkey's symbol is the wolf) Fascist extremists, outlawed by Turkish authorities.

GRU - *(Glavnoye Razvedyvatelnoye Upravlenie)* Intelligence Service of the General Staff, USSR Armed Forces; the KGB's archrival.

Gestapo - *(Geheime Staatspolizei)* State Police and Internal Security Service, Nazi Germany, under the direction of Heinrich Himmler; Reinhard Heydrich, known as The Hangman, was chief of the Security Police of the Gestapo until May 1942 when he was assassinated by Czech patriots at Prague.

GSG9 - *Grenzschutzgruppe 9.*

Hamas - Extremist Palestinian group opposed to Middle East peace talks of which four hundred were expelled by Israel to the no-man's land between Israel and Lebanon.

Hauptverwaltung Aufklarung - Intelligence Service, East Germany.

Hepp-Hexel Group - Neo-Nazi German movement founded in 1982 by Walter Hexel and Odfried Hepp.

Hezbollah ("Party of God") - Pro-Iranian Shiite fundamentalist; directs Islamic *Jihad*.

IRA - Irish Republican Army.

Islamic Jihad - Iranian terrorists, fanatical Muslims of the Shiite sect and holder of most Western and all the American hostages.

JIC - Joint Intelligence Committee, Great Britain.

Justice Commandos for Armenian Genocide - Anti-Turkish terrorist group.

KGB - *(Komitet Gosudarstvennoy Bezopasnosti)* Committee on State Security (Intelligence, Counterespionage, and Internal Security Service), Communist Party, USSR; each directorate or division of the KGB is signaled by a prefix number and a specific responsibility—for instance, assassinations or *mokryye dela* against its enemies (not Westerners, contrary to popular opinion) were the special province of the Thirteenth (Executive Action) Department of the First Chief Directorate of the KGB. Renamed in 1991 as the Agency for Federal Security.

Liberation Army Fifth Battalion - Moslim fundamentalist group based in the New York-New Jersey area which claimed responsibility for the bombing of the World Trade Center building on March 5, 1993 that killed seven people and wounded one thousand.

M-19 - Columbian revolutionary movement.

Macheteros - Puerto Rican terrorists.

Maximilian Hernández Anti-Communist Brigade - El Salvadoran right-wing party.

MNLF - Marti National Liberation Front, rebels opposed to U.S.-backed Salvadoran government.

Medellín Cartel - Multibillion-dollar drug cartel of five "families" operating out of Columbia.

MI-5 - Internal Security Service, Great Britain.

MI-6 - Intelligence Service, Great Britain (also known as Secret Intelligence Service or SIS).

MfS - *(Ministerium für Sicherheit)* The East German ministry responsible for counterespionage activity.

Montoneros - ("Bushwhackers") Argentine terrorists opposed to "economic imperialism" of multinational corporations.

Moro National Liberation Front - Extremist faction in the Philippines.

Mossad - *(ha-Mossad le-Modiin ule-Tafkidim Meyuhadim)* Institute for Intelligence and Special Tasks, Israel; formed in 1951 and considered the most fearless, some say ruthless, intelligence organization in the West today.

MPLA - *Movimento Popular para a Libertacao de Angola.*

MVD - *(Ministerstvo Vnutrennikh Del)* Soviet Ministry of Internal Affairs.

NRO - National Reconnaissance Office, USA. The most secret government spy agency in the United States until 1992, when threats to its multibillion-dollar budget forced director and spy-satellite expert Martin C. Faga to brief the press about this ultra-secret agency responsible for America's spy technology.

NSA - National Security Agency, USA. The second-most secret agency in America's intelligence community. Although President Truman created it by executive order on October 24, 1952, it was not officially acknowledged until 1957; its predecessor was the Armed Forces Security Agency. NSA is part of the Fort Meade military reservation, technically responsible for the security of US communications and code-breaking, but it also "directs" intelligence agencies, including CIA, via its NSCID or NEE-SIDS (National Security Council Intelligence Directives).

Nokorbal - Cambodian secret police under Pol Pot; responsible for the deaths of a million people in the 1970s.

NKVD - Red Army, Stalinist-era spy apparatus consisting of a vast network of informants and agents, *agents provocateurs* throughout Russia and Europe.

OAS - (*Organisation Armée Secrète*) Antinationalist, later anti-French terrorist organization, Algeria.

OKH - *(Ober-Kommando des Heeres)* Supreme Command of the Army, Germany World War II.

Okhrana - Tsarist, pre-Revolutionary ancestor of the Cheka.

OKW - *(Ober-Kommando der Wehrmacht)* Supreme Command of the Armed Forces, Germany, World War II.

Ordine Nero - Libyan-backed, neo-Nazi organization.

OSS - Office of Strategic Services, USA; the progenitor of CIA, established in June 1942 and headed by Gen. William "Wild Bill" Donovan, organized commando and intelligence operations against Germany in World War II.

Patani Liberation Organization - Terrorist organization, Thailand.

PFIAB - President's Foreign Intelligence and Advisory Board, USA.

PLO - Palestine Liberation Organization, the most widely known of the dozen factions of Palestinian groups; led by Yasser Arafat.

PKK - Kurdistan Workers' Party led by Abdullah Ocalan who demand an end to military repression against their people in southeastern Turkey, home to six million Kurds.

PLF - Palestine Liberation Front, led by Abu Abbas in Baghdad, considered the most radical of the PLO's factional leaders; grabbed world headlines in 1985 with the capture of the *Achille Lauro* cruise ship.

Popular Front for the Liberation of Palestine-General Command - led by Ahmed Jibril, former Syrian army officer; his group destroyed Pan Am Flight 103 over Scotland in 1988.

PZPR - State Police and Intelligence Agency, Poland.

RAF - Red Army Faction, successor to the **Baader-Meinhoff** group.

Red Army (Japanese) - left-extremist terrorists who are known to link up with other terrorist groups such as the African organization Polisario and the Italian **Red Brigade.**

Red Brigade - *(Il Rosso Brigatto)* Italian terrorist organization.

Red Orchestra - *(Rote Kapelle)* One of the most brilliant agent networks of Soviet intelligence; established in 1939 in France and Belgium by the **NKVD** and nicknamed by the Germans.

RUCB - Royal Ulster Constabular Branch.

RZ - Revolutionary Cells, anti-Zionist terrorists, Germany.

SÄPO - Intelligence Service, Sweden.

SAS - Special Air Service; the elite anti-terrorist branch of British Army.

SB - *(Sluzba Bezpleczentstwa)* State Police and Intelligence, Poland; see also **PZPR.**

SD - *(Sicherheitsdienst)* Intelligence Service, Nazi Party.

SDECE - *(Service du Documentation Exterieure et de Contre-Espionage)* now is called DGSE *Direction Générale de la Securite Exterieure* (noted in

Allbeury's *Seeds of Treason*). Intelligence and Counterespionage Service, France.

Serbian Liberation Front - One of the Balkan factions opposed to Croatian militants and Bosnian Muslims; so-called "freedom fighters," these virulent nationalists have been described by Balkans expert Xavier Raufer as extremely dangerous: "These guys make Abu Nidal look like Mother Teresa" (qtd. in *Time* March 8, 1993: 33).

SHAEF - Supreme Headquarters, Allied Expeditionary Forces.

Shining Path, The - *(Sendero Luminosa)* Maoist, auto-genocidal movement of guerrilla forces in Peru. *Senderistas* have slaughtered over twenty-three thousand people in the 1990s equivalent of Pol Pot's *Khmer Rouge*'s infamous "Year Zero" of the 1970s, but the capture of ideologue Abimael Guzmán Reynoso in 1992 may signal Sendero's eclipse.

Siguranta - Romanian political police under the Ministry of Internal Affairs.

Sinn Fein ("Ourselves Alone") - Political arm of the IRA.

SIS - See **MI6** above.

SmerSh - Ian Fleming's network of enemies, obsolete at the time of the James Bond novels, is Stalin's pre-KGB military police who went out to execute partisans fighting for Germany behind Russian lines in 1943. Never a secret police, SmerSh (*Sh* is one letter in Russian) was created by fiat (an eyewitness defecting officer from the Guards Directorate said in the 1950s) when Stalin issued the GUKR NKO order ("Chief Counterintelligence Directorate of the People's Commissariat of the Armed Forces") with its original acronym SmerInSh: *Smert Inostrannikh Shpionam* ["Death to **Foreign** Spies"] reduced by Stalin himself to SmerSh, wolfishly grinning as he crossed out *Foreign*: "No, no, death to **all** spies!"

SOE - Special Operations Executive, Great Britain.

SSD - *(Staatsicherheitsdienst)* Ministry for State Security, East Germany, known as the *Stasi*.

SSU - Strategic Services Unit (operated between 1946 and 1949, roughly the period between the termination of the OSS and the inception of the CIA).

Stasi - Slang for East Germany's secret police apparatus.

STB - *(Statni Tajna Bezpecnosti)* State Secret Security Forces, Czechoslovakia.

Sûreté - French Intelligence Service.

Tupamaros - Uruguayan terrorist movement.

UDBA - Former-Yugoslavian Secret Police.

UNITA - (National Union for the Total Independence of Angola) [*Uniao Nacional para a Independencia Total de Angola*]) Angolan extremists.

USFA - US Forces in Austria (American military command headquartered in Vienna between 1945-1955).

Wadi Haddad Group - Palestinian Arabs who hijacked Air France 139 from Tel Aviv to Paris in June 1976.

WEB - West European Bureau of the Comintern, Soviet Union.

White Hand - Name given to the real or apocryphal alliance of rogue right-wing CIA agents and organized crime figures believed responsible for the deaths of the Kennedys along with members of the Giancana-Marcello-Trafficante crime syndicates; plotted Castro's assassination before the Bay of Pigs, organized Operation Mongoose, and mutually assisted each other's interests in Central and South America.

WSW - *(Wojskowa Sluzba Wewnetrzna)* Internal Military Service, Poland.

XX Committee - The Twenty Committee, a pun on double cross; set up by British Intelligence (OSS) to turn and run double agents during World War II. The American Office of Strategic Services in London was headed by Prof. Norman Holmes Pearson of Yale (Pearson was CIA counterintelligence chief James Jesus Angleton's mentor).

Zapatista National Liberation Army - Rebel movement of Chiapas (Mexico) Indians against the government; their January 1994 uprising led to captured towns in the southernmost region of Mexico and hundreds killed in a protest against living conditions.

ZE-2 - Military Intelligence, Poland.

Appendix E:
Guide to the Jargon of Espionage
(Spookspeak)

The CIA: Our business is knowing the world's business.
—*The CIA's new recruiting motto*

THE JARGON OF spies—**Spookspeak** or **Spyspeak**—is a natural result of the fact that so many writers of espionage fiction are themselves former practitioners of tradecraft. Both British and American intelligence is amply represented by such writers as William F. Buckley, Jr., E. Howard Hunt, David John Moore Cornwell, Nicholas Luard, and Ted Allbeury—some of whom, in fact, prefer using spookonyms to their real names for a number of reasons. They follow in the footsteps of predecessors as noteworthy as Somerset Maugham and Grahame Greene in bringing to their art the speech habits of the men and women of espionage at levels that range from bureaucrat through field agent to wartime undercover agent. Rich in jargon, slang, and euphemisms, the language of spies, Soviet and Western, evokes in miniature the themes of espionage itself, a covert world of conviction and betrayal, heroism and cowardice, treachery and faith, truth and lies.

Needless to say, the reader must understand that a good many terms, which pass muster as the everyday talk of agents in the field or at the desk, is purely made up for literary effect. Le Carré's novels bristle with a lively language that has never been seen in the communications of actual professional intelligence. Donald R. Morris, an intelligence officer of seventeen-years experience in Soviet counterespionage operations with CIA, claims that much of what passes for intelligence jargon in le Carré's fiction is merely "arch colloquial expressions" used "for dramatic impact," such as *baby-sitter, gorilla, hood, bloodhound, reptile fund, leash dog, scalphunter, duck dive, hard-man* because le Carré "introduces into his fiction violence and potential violence which simply don't exist in real life" (4). There are, Morris asserts, many concepts that do exist but which le Carré and other writers must find racy substitutes because of the layperson's ignorance of the official vocabulary.

We recommend the following sources: Henry S. A. Becket's *The Dictionary of Espionage: Spookspeak into English* (New York: Stein and Day, 1986); Ronald Kessler's *Spy vs. Spy* (New York: Scribner's, 1988). An excellent article is Victor Lasseter's "John le Carré's Spy Jargon: An Introduction and Lexicon," *Verbatim: The Language Quarterly* 8.4 (1982): 1-2. See also Mr. Morris's excellent commentary and response to Lasseter in his letter to *Verbatim* 9.2 (Autumn 1982): 3-5. (Permission to use copyrighted material received from Simon & Schuster; copyright © 1994 by Richard Marcenko and John Weisman. Reprinted by permission of Pocket Books, a division of Simon & Schuster, Inc. Permission to quote from the above issues of *Verbatim: The Language Quarterly* is gratefully acknowledged.)

Accommodation address - Mail drop or live-letter box (LLB) for intelligence purposes.

Active measures - The Soviet expression *aktivnye meropriyatiya* once referred to operations designed to influence a nation's policy—specifically, to insinuate Soviet policy into that nation's; it is CIA jargon for its own influencing operations, whether overt or covert.

Ag & Fish - British Ministry of Agriculture and Fisheries; became 1950s slang for agents needing a cover address between assignments.

Agent - Like **spy**, a term that lends itself to confusion: CIA operatives are "officers"; the people they handle are **agents**. Professionals disdain the term among themselves. The FBI, in its own glossary of foreign intelligence terms, uses terms such as **illegal agent** (agent who operates out of a residency) and **principal agent** (agent who controls an operation); it refers to "turned" agents as **redoubled agents** and even **triple agents** as a **double agent** servicing three agencies and who "wittingly or unwittingly withholds significant information from two services at the instigation of the third!"

Agent 86 - Maxwell Smart of the TV spy spoof of the 1960s, "Get Smart." *Eighty-six* is restaurant shoptalk for having run out of something.

Agent of influence - Any agent whose task is to influence policy in the country of his/her assignment.

Agent potential - Assessment of an agent's access to information.

Agent provocateur - An agent whose job is to worsen situations, ripen them for a possible takeover by his/her own side.

Alimony - Le Carréism for payment owed an agent who operates in dangerous territory and therefore cannot receive funds for services without drawing attention.

Alternate meet - Back-up meeting site in case the first is called off.

Apparatchik - Loosely synonymous for Soviet spies; mainly refers to Soviet bureaucrats with clout.

Appetizer - Le Carré uses this to mean any morsel of information designed to draw interest.

Asset - Any resource, human or technical, available for an agent's use.

Audition - The place where a source produces his or her **appetizer**.

Backstop - The steps taken to ensure credibility of a **cover story** (FBI jargon).

Bazaar intelligence - Rumors.

Bear leader - Instructor at the **Nursery**.

Bigot list - Names of those classified "need to know"—those privy to sensitive information; originated as an anagram from World War II days when Operation Overlord planners borrowed from officers' orders stamped TO GIB[RALTAR] in preparation for the invasion of North Africa.

Biographic leverage - Blackmail.

Black-bag job - Originally, an FBI term before passing into SIS/CIA jargon, it used to mean "surreptitious entry," and such entries were wartime procedure (known as SEs); now it refers to a kind of criminal entry or other illegal work for espionage purposes. It is not a term used in professional intelligence communities.

Black operations - Illegal or criminal tasks, which may include murder, performed by "special tasks" agents.

Black propaganda - Opposite of white propaganda: **disinformation.**

Black trainees - Foreign agents, mostly mercenaries, trained in weaponry and undercover work on the CIA's "Farm" in Virginia.

Blown - Infiltrated, exposed; said of agents and networks.

Body talk - An agent's specialized safety signals.

Box - Polygraph machine. See **Vetting.**

Boyeva gruppa - KGB hit squads.

Bugging - Electronic surveillance, whether a sophisticated device or a telephone tap.

Burn notice - Warning circulated to friendly intelligence services advising them to have no contact with an unreliable agent.

Burnt - Said of useless or compromised agents.

Burrower - Le Carré's reference to a **Circus** researcher.

Brush contact - Also known in FBI jargon as a "brief encounter," this refers to the momentary contact between agents in passing information.

C - The initial that denotes the head of British Secret Service.

Cache - **Dead drop.**

Cacklebladder - A blood-smeared dummy-corpse which is "killed" by an enemy agent; the agent is then ripe for blackmail.

Cannon - A professional thief on the payroll of an intelligence agency whose skills are used to "steal" back items, objects, or money paid to informants or enemy agents.

Case officer - American and British intelligence-gathering services use the term identically to refer to a principal officer with responsibility for an operation.   A **case officer** may also be further classified as **headquarters** or **field case officer**.

CASMS - Computer-Controlled Area Sterilization Multisensor Systems. Vietnam-tested bugging devices dropped from planes to detect the ground movement of troops.

CAT - Civil Air Transport. CIA's Taiwan-based air support system for **covert operations.**

CELD - Central External Liaison Department. Chinese Secret Service unit responsible for foreign intelligence.

Cell - A term that reaches back through nineteenth-century Russian history and refers to a cluster of **agents.** Lenin envisioned **cells** as self-contained; exposure destroys only the individual **cell.** Loosely synonymous with **network.**

Centre - The KGB's Moscow headquarters. Not to be confused with ordinary usage of **Center** as an intelligence service's headquarters.

Charlie India Alpha - SIS slang for CIA (also **Charlie's Indians**) according to Gavin Lyall's *The Crocus List*.

Chekist - From **Cheka**; offhand reference to KGB.

Chickenfeed - What British intelligence allowed **doubled** agents to feed back to Berlin.

Chief of Outpost (COO) - CIA officer in charge of a field outpost.

CI - Counterintelligence.

CI-3 - FBI's counterintelligence division. From Ronald Kessler's *Spy vs. Spy* (Scribner's, 1988): "Arrayed against them [foreign undercover spies] are the FBI's counterintelligence agents—more than half the five hundred agents assigned to the Washington field office, plus thousands of other agents assigned to each of the FBI's fifty-nine field offices and four hundred resident agencies."

Cipher - One of several methods of concealing the contents of a message—for example, **a substitute cipher** replaces letters or numbers in predetermined sequences; **a transposition cipher** changes the order of the letters or numbers in a pattern known to the communicating individuals. A **cipher pad** or **one-time pad** is a machine-printed, thin pad of paper sheets with a nonrepeating key for use in sending code.

Circus - Le Carré's coinage for British **SIS**.

Clandestine operation - **Covert action/operation.** Any action conducted in secrecy is, technically speaking, clandestine. But **covert actions** or CA programs are not to be confused with paramilitary operations; intelligence services are administrative, not military. As one expert noted: "This is hard to get across to a public raised on James Bond novels and the 'Mission Impossible' series; people are willing to believe absolutely anything about an intelligence service.... the intelligence services are used for administration and logistic support, because they don't clank as loudly as the military when they have to lay something on."

Clean - Term for an **agent, legend,** or **safe house** never before used.

Cobbler - Forger of false passports and documents.

Code word - A pre-arranged word used in communicating between agents or in conversation to convey the real intent behind what may seem ordinary in meaning.

COINTELPRO - The FBI's "counterintelligence program" between 1956 and 1971 used against student anti-war movements and radicals.

Come over - Said of a **turned** or **doubled** agent, whether or not force accompanies the conversion.

COMINT - Communications Intelligence of the U.S. Intercepts and processes scrambled or encrypted wire and electromagnetic transmissions throughout the world.

Company - Slang for CIA.

COMSEC - Communications Security. Provision of codes and ciphers to the armed forces and any branch of the government requiring them.

Condemned spy - A term from the Chinese Secret Service which involves a calculated form of **disinformation**—that is, setting up one's own agent for betrayal so that the agent will unwittingly disclose false information to the enemy. The Soviets call a similar situation a *screen operation*, in which a **double agent** is allowed to continue. Sun Tzu notes in *The Art of War*: "Having *doomed spies* means doing certain things openly for purposes of deception, and allowing our own spies to know of them and, when betrayed, report them to the enemy" (80). Sun Tzu notes casually that these spies are then put to death.

CONUS - FBI acronym for "continental United States."

Controller - A field agent or desk-bound intelligence officer who handles an agent in place or a defecting agent.

Control questions - Moscow **Centre**'s system of verifying agent identities abroad; refers to prepared questions known only to an agent and the **Resident Director** of the embassy.

Co-opted agent - A citizen, official, tourist, student, and so on, who assists a foreign-intelligence agency. **Also called** co-opted worker or **co-optee**.

Counterintelligence - Actions undertaken to oppose espionage, sabotage, or intelligence operations of a foreign government.

Counterspy - An agent infiltrated solely to betray another agent or network.

Cousins - British slang for American counterparts in CIA.

Cover - May refer to an individual's, organization's, or even an installation's guise to prevent discovery of a true purpose.

Cover story - Fabricated story for any intelligence purpose. Used with terms like **Build-up material** or **Feed material** (FBI).

Covert action - CIA euphemism for its riskier, disruptive foreign programs; also known as *CA programs*.

Crash meeting - Clandestine meeting, emergency (le Carré).

Creative intelligence - As defined by Miles Copeland in *Without Cloak or Dagger*, **creative intelligence** is ordinary researchers "working quietly in their offices" who can infer secret information. Example: "changes in the geographical disposition of scientists with known specialities ... might suggest important new policies" (315).

Cryptology - The science of secret communications.

Cultivation - Inducement to get control over an individual.

Customer - Official or department to receive intelligence information (le Carré).

Cut-out - An agent-handler whose job is to act as go-between for a spy and the **field agent controlling** him or her, especially when oral or written contact threatens exposure. **Cut-outs** may be *block* (the contact knows every member of the **network** or **cell**) or *chain* (the contact knows only one agent).

D-Notice - Defense-Notice. Issued by **MI5** or **MI6** whenever it feels imminent disclosure by the mass media would affect national security. **D-Notices** are "voluntary" censorship.

DCI/DDCI - Director of Central Intelligence. Deputy Director of Central Intelligence.

DDO - Deputy Director for Operations (CIA).

Dead drop - A location where materials or documents can be left by one **agent** to be retrieved later by a second. Also known as a **dead-letter box** (**DLB**) or a "drop." May also refer to a hiding place; in FBI jargon, a long-term drop is called a **black cache**.

Debriefing - The formal but friendly interview conducted by a supervising agent of one who has completed an assignment or of anyone who knows something important to an operation.

Defector - A national of one country who defects to, or seeks political asylum from, another **country**. **Defectors** are rarely ordinary citizens; they must have special propaganda, political, or intelligence significance to warrant attention.

Demote maximally - CIA euphemism—not, however, of the Orwellian variety which "makes murder respectable," as Trevanian uses it (and variations of this phrase) in *The Eiger Sanction* and *The Loo Sanction*.

DIA - Defense Intelligence Agency of the US's Department of Defense.

Dirty tricks - A gentler CIA euphemism for **black operations**, usually breaking and entering with an aim toward theft or installing bugging devices.

Disinformation - Manufactured, false information to discredit an enemy; originally ascribed to the KGB's notorious Department D of the First Chief Directorate (from Russian *desinformatsiya*) but is in reality a practice of all intelligence services and their governments.

DITSA - Defense Technical Security Administration. The agency responsible for keeping dual-use technology out of reach of America's enemies. "They are often stymied by State Department diplo-dinks and Commerce Department apparatchiki" (Marcinko's *Rogue Warrior II: Red Cell*).

Doctor - Civil authorities, the police.

Double agent - An agent who works for both sides has **doubled** or **turned**; generally it means that one side is being betrayed; **fictional** intelligences agencies use **doubles** frequently—a contract agent who serves two masters, neither side deceived about the agent's "loyalties." No intelligence service, veteran CIA officer Donald R. Morris asserts, would ever consider using a **triple** agent or spy for any reason.

Double-cross system - Refers to **turning** an agent—that is, "converting" an agent via money, coercion, or ideology to work against that planted him or her in the enemy's country.

Drop Simple communication system between agents and handlers or controllers: using hiding places for messages; can also refer to drop sites in covert operations.

Dry cleaning - Any technique used to detect surveillance.

DS&T - Directorate of Science and Technology (CIA).

Dubok - KGB term for the **drop** or hiding places for messages used by its agents.

Duck dive - Quick exit (le Carré).

Ears - The antenna of a radio.

Earwig - Bugging device.

ECM - Electronic Counter Measures. Devices used to evade submarine detection or special (spy) satellite devices for similar purpose.

E&E - Escape and evasion.

EEI - Essential Elements of Information. Refers to critical assessment information on an enemy or **target**.

Elicitation - An **agent**'s subtle interrogation technique by which important information is casually **elicited** from outsiders or tourists without their being aware of the true nature of what they are revealing to the **agent**.

ELINT - Electronic Intelligence. A portmanteau word of **National Security** coinage that refers to the collation, processing, and analysis of electronic data from any electromagnetic source of communication.

Equity - As in "Soviet equity": a spy. (Hampton Howard's *Friends, Russians, and Countrymen.*)

Espionage - Intelligence activity intended to acquire the opposition's classified or secret information. *For the organization of a modern intelligence agency see Miles Copeland's *Without Cloak or Dagger* (New York: Simon & Schuster, 1974).

Executive action - CIA jargon for assassination orders; see **ZR/Rifle**.

Exfiltration - Originally a military term, it is the opposite of *infiltration* and means bringing an agent out of hostile territory.

Fallback - Alternative meeting between **agents** and handlers when contact is too risky or one of them fails to show up.

False confirmation - Giving credibility to a deception or **disinformation** operation by "confirming" an item of information being passed to the other side.

False-flag recruitment - Co-opting an individual to believe that he or she is assisting one country's intelligence service against another's. All the while, of course, the individual is cooperating with the "enemy's" service.

Farm, The - CIA's version of le Carré's **Nursery**—except that **"The Farm"** is "official" slang for the American in-house training school located close to CIA headquarters in Langley, VA.

Feed smoke - Lie.

Field - An agent on assignment is "in the field" as opposed to an administrator or *deskman*.

Firm - British colloquial reference to their own Secret Service.

Fix - Gambler's argot borrowed by CIA for potentially troubling situations or people that require **fixing** by blackmail or coercion.

Fluttered - CIA's and SIS's term for examining via lie-detector an agent's loyalty but may also refer weeding out unsuitable recruits.

Friends, The - MI-6.

Fumigating - Cleaning out the bugs (electronic eavesdropping devices).

Gaijin - (Japanese) Foreigner. Conveys an overtone of contempt.

Game, The - Espionage, the profession of intelligencegathering.

Gas gun - The KGB's sinister device used to kill anti-Communist editor Lev Rebet in 1957 and Stephan Bandera, a Ukrainian nationalist, in 1959. The gun resembled a tube that fired a burst of hydrocyanide into its victim's face.

GCHQ - Government Communications Headquarters. Great Britain's major **listening post**, located at Cheltenham, responsible for monitoring worldwide intercepted radio messages.

Going private - Leaving **the game** for private life.

Gold seam - In le Carré, the route laundered payments to Soviet agents take.

HAHO - High-Altitude High-Opening parachute jump.

HALO - High-Altitude Low-Opening parachute jump.

Handling agent - FBI term for the **agent** who "handles" an informant; not CIA jargon.

Handwriting - An **agent**'s "style" or **signature**.

Hard man - In le Carré's world, a tough guy, a strongarm specialist.

Harmonica bug - Transistorized transmitter placed inside the mouthpiece of a telephone.

HMCC - Her Majesty's Government Communications Centre.

Honey trap - Sexual bait to trap or blackmail a male agent.

Hospital - Prison.

Housekeeper - Le Carréism for London headquarters internal security officer. Other terms: a senior secretary would be a *mother*; a conference room is a *rumpus room*.

HUMINT - Human Intelligence. Information gathered by agents as opposed to **ELINT**.

Identifier - A Soviet term used by Stalin's KGB for informants who **identified** persons who were ideologically unsound or suspicious; its blandness masks the multitudes exterminated in the purges on the word of these informants who were often themselves victims of another **identifier**.

Illegals - Soviet agents operating in foreign countries on false passports. An **illegal net** would refer to the intelligence-gathering agency operating under the residency's control. **Legal operations** refer to intelligence work under the control of a legal residency.

Inquisitor - Interrogator (le Carré).

IO - Intelligence officer.

Janitor - Circus guard.

Joe - World War II slang for agent, probably OSS in origin for its own spies; Le Carré resurrects the term in *A Perfect Spy*.

Joe-house - OSS lingo, or perhaps a le Carré coinage frequent in *The Russia House*, for accommodations for agents awaiting overseas assignment.

JSOC - Joint Special Operations Command.

L-pill - The cyanide capsule concealed in a false tooth and carried by American/British operatives during World War II.

Lacrosse - Latest ,in US spy-in-the-sky satellite development with upgraded capabilities along with the KH-11 and KH-12 series satellites (Marcinko's *Red Cell*).

Lamplighters - Le Carré coinage from *Tinker, Tailor, Soldier, Spy* for a special team of agents whose talents range from domestic surveillance to black-bag jobs.

Lapanka - Polish term used during World War II to describe the German round-ups of people for execution or shipping off to labor camps.

Leak - Exposure of classified information, whether intentional or accidental.

Legend - An operative's fake but meticulously detailed biography supported by false documents.

Lightning bolt - (*Blyskawica* in Polish) Originally a term Polish code clerks used for top-priority messages, especially from their Soviet masters.

Linecrossers - Army intelligence term for low-level agents sent behind enemy lines or, as in Deighton, agents who assist other agents in crossing dangerous borders such as the former East Germany's.

Lion-tamer - A le Carréan operative sent around to keep a rogue agent submissive through threats and coercion.

Lippman - A high-resolution emulsion used in preparing **microdots** and **mikrats**.

Listener - Bugging expert.

Loose cannon - An old metaphor resurrected and applied to maverick operators like Col. Oliver North. A **singleton** who causes havoc. See also **sheep dipping**.

LP - Listening post, either fixed or mobile.

Magpie board - An agent's escape kit containing tools, maps, and so on.

Measles - A contract hit made to seem natural.

Microdot - Photographic reduction of documents to 3 x 6 millimeters.

Mikrat - Smaller than a microdot's size.

Milk run - Field agent's slang for an easy assignment.

Minders - Official "chaperones" of an agent or defector.

Misinformation - Planting false information.

Mokryye dela - Russian criminal argot for "wet affairs": KGB jargon for murder. No official term exists in the West for this concept, although such thuggery may be referred to in Western lingo as *cowboying* or *cowboy stuff*.

Mole - A le Carréism now in wide use in counterintelligence for an agent who has infiltrated a sensitive agency or government branch with access to secret information. **Moles** are never **double agents** because they have not been **turned**; instead they are **penetration** agents.

Mongoose - Operational codename to destabilize Castro's Cuba before the Bay of Pigs.

Mother - Flippant reference to legendary CIA figure James Jesus Angleton.

Mozhno girls - Girls recruited by the KGB who are "allowed" to sleep with Westerners for their information.

Mukhabarat - Middle Eastern intelligence service.

Music box - A spy's wireless radio.

Musician - A transmitting spy.

Nacht und Nebel - ("Night and Fog") Said of Himmler's SS for its middle-of-the-night secrecy and terrorism.

Naked - Said of an agent who operates alone.

Neighbor - Soviet reference to a Communist sympathizer; a Westerner's term for a "fellow traveler."

Neighbors - Warsaw Pact nations.

Network - A unit of agents usually arranged in a hierarchy. See the diagram of Alan Furst's Opal Network after this section.

NFAC - National Foreign Assessment Center (CIA). Analyzes, collates, and assesses information; briefs the President and high government officials cleared to receive sensitive data.

NRO - National Reconnaissance Office. Agency responsible for coordinating satellite operations for US Intelligence.

NSA - National Security Agency (US).

NSCID - Formal orders from the National Security Council directing CIA assignments; an "en-skid" is formally known as a **National Security Council Intelligence Directive.**

Nursery - Le Carré colloquially defines the British tradecraft school as a "charm school for outward bound penetration agents"; George Smiley and senior agents pass on their wisdom in tradecraft to the young. See **The Farm.**

Orchestra - Lenin's term for a loosely knit spy network composed of people of high social background (or vulnerability to blackmail) with access to information; also said of a network of agents.

OTP - One-time pad; see **Cipher.**

OTS - Office of Technical Services (CIA); see **DS&T**.

Overt activities - Activities openly attributed to the government responsible for them.

OWRL - One-Way Radio Link.

Parole - Pre-arranged verbal exchange between **agents**.

Pavement artists - Another le Carréism for surveillance teams.

Peep - Agent who specializes in photographic surveillance.

Perimeter surveillance - Surveillance that surrounds a **target**; also known as **picket surveillance**.

PHOTINT - Photographic Intelligence.

Piano concerto - Secret message.

Piano study - Secret radio transmissions.

Place of conspiracy - Ponderous KGB lingo for an agent's foreign hideout.

Playback - A captured agent's special radio signal or code to his home base that alerts his side to his capture and forced **turning**.

Plumbers - **Black operatives** responsible for casing a building for surveillance purposes or planting **bugs**.

PNG - *Persona non grata*.

Positive intelligence - Intelligence confirmed or interpreted.

Principal Agent - According to Harris Green's *Inference of Guilt*, a senior agent, "usually non-American, with supervisory authority over other agents." **Principal agents are not** CIA staff officers and are usually directed by such staffers.

Product - Intelligence.

Pseudonym - False name.

Pudding Club - Contemptuous reference to the gossip-ridden United Nations.

Puzzle Palace - National Security headquarters in Fort Meade, MD—so named for its encrypting and decoding facilities.

Queen Anne's Gate - Refers to the early days of organized intelligence in Britain when the Intelligence Branch was founded at Queen Anne's Gate in 1871. DI6, as it is known today, used to be found at 21 Queen Anne's Gate and was listed in the phonebook under the Ministry of Land & Natural Resources.

Questors - Investigators of Section Q of CIA.

Quick trip around the Horn - Radio operator's check for signals activity.

R-12 - Known as the Buzby **bug** and codenamed **R-12**, this gadget can eavesdrop on conversations from anywhere in the world.

RABCOR - From Russian *rabcor*, a "worker-correspondent"; an early system of industrial espionage set up in France prior to World War II.

Radar button - A locating device for pinpointing an agent's whereabouts.

Ratissage - "Rat hunt," a closing down of enemy agents/networks in a sweep (Alan Furst's *Dark Star*).

Raven - A male used to seduce men or women.

Recognition signals - Pre-arranged visual signals.

Recruitment - The process of enlisting individuals to work for an intelligence agency.

Recruitment in place - A foreign official who remains in his government's service while yet providing intelligence against his or her own government.

Red line - Secure CIA internal telephone circuit.

Referentura - Soviet term for rooms "swept clean of bugs" that contain classified files, ciphering and radio transmission facilities.

Resident Director - Soviet "diplomat" who frequently runs a network in a country separate from the one of residence.

Residentura - The **Resident Director's** spy network.

RIF - Reduction in Force; refers to the occasional house-cleaning or mass reductions of personnel in government.

R&R - Rest and Recuperation; in agent lingo, it refers to the vacation, out of country, given to personnel serving in hardship posts.

SAC - Special Agent in Charge (FBI).

SACPG - ("Sackpig") Senior Arms Control Policy Group consisting of Joint Chiefs, senior members of NSC, Defense Department and State.

Safe house - An agent's hideout; also a secure residence for interrogations of agents and informers.

Sanctification - Blackmail for political favors rather than money.

Sanction - Trevanian's term of choice for murdering an opponent with an agency's approval.

Sandman, The - George Smiley's archrival, Karla, in Soviet counterespionage.

Scalphunters - Le Carré's term for those professional agents who spot a defector and analyze his or her genuineness. The Wild West metaphor is beguiling; **scalphunters** do not engage in strongarm tactics in their own kind of **elicitations**; nor do they murder.

Setting-up - Framing, trapping.

Shavki - ("Trash-eating dogs") Russian term of contempt for outsiders and low-level agents.

Sheep dipping - Two principal uses: placing an agent in a situation where his or her credentials will be accepted by the organization or terrorist group being penetrated; secondly, using civilian cover to disguise paramilitary operations, such as the CIA's **sheep dipping** of military hardware to the *Contras* in the 1980s.

Shoe - Fake passport.

Shopped - Betrayed, sold out; sometimes it means assassinated.

SIGINT - Signals Intelligence.

Signature - The precise way an **agent** handles his radio transmissions, his characteristic touch and speed that enable another radioman to tell his **signature**.

Sign-of-life signal - A periodic signal from an agent to signal he or she is still operational.

Silent school - A KGB term for special operatives who receive individual instruction for deep cover work.

Singleton - An agent who operates alone (cf. Charles McCarry's Paul Christopher and, of course, Fleming's James Bond).

Sisters - Women, usually prostitutes on contract, employed by an agency for sexual seductions.

Sleeper - An agent whose residency and background keep him or her under such deep cover that decades may pass before, in reserve, the need arises to "awaken" such an agent to begin operating.

Soap - Sodium pentathol (truth drug).

Soft film - Special film from which the gelatin has been removed so that it can be rolled and secreted in a small place.

Son et lumiere - (*"Sound and light"*). Obtaining evidence via a camera-recorded seduction.

Source - An individual (never refers to an **agent**) who furnishes information to an intelligence agency.

Special Forces Club - Although Special Forces is the British elite commando unit, this is the drinking establishment, which Ted Allbeury locates at 8 Herbert Crescent in London, for members of espionage organizations from World War II to the present.

Special projects/tasks - CIA lingo for its **covert operations.**

Spitzl - German slang for an informer.

Spike - To tap a telephone.

Spoofing - Prior to American U-2 operations in the mid-1950s, aerial reconnaissance involved flying across Soviet borders to collect radar intelligence.

Spook - **Spy** or **agent.**

Spookonym - *Nom de plum* of an espionage-fiction writer—for example, E. Howard Hunt, former CIA officer of Watergate fame, has written dozens of books under such pseudonyms as Robert Dietrich, John Baxter, Gordon Davis, and David St. John. Some spookonyms have recently been penetrated, such as Trevanian (Rodney Whitaker); others, like Zeno, released from a British prison in 1968 for murder continue to write—and intrigue.

Spookspeak - Espionage jargon whether fictional or official.

Spotter - An individual engaged in **recruitment** in behalf of an intelligence agency. Also called a **talent spotter.**

Spy - The term most obvious yet crucial to the differences between real spies and literary agents.

SSCI Stable - Senate Select Committee for Intelligence. The list of women, sometimes men also, kept for seduction and blackmail operations.

Staging - Sending an **agent** to an area for training before an operation. See **The Farm.**

Station chief - CIA's chief officer in its resident embassy.

Stepped on - Before it became underworld narcotics slang, it meant signal and radio interference.

Sterile funds - Money used in intelligence operations that cannot be traced.

Sterilize/Sanitize - To remove incriminating devices, equipment, or documents from an area that can be traced back to an agency. In fiction, either term may refer to individuals or corpses that need to be removed from an area.

Stroller - Agent operating a walkie-talkie.

Svoi - Russian for "one of us."

Svyana - Russian for **cut-out.**

Svyazniye - Russian for "go-between," an official who contacts agents and KGB agents operating from their embassy.

SW or S/W - Secret writing.

Swallow - Women used by the KGB for seductions. Contrary to popular belief, not sexual athletes but prostitutes with minimal intelligence training.

Swallow's nest - The house, appropriately bugged for audio and video, to record the seduction of a **target.**

Sweetener - A gift to assist bribery.

Swim - Sending a KGB officer abroad—going for a **swim.**

Talent spotting - Locating potential agents or defectors (le Carré).

Target - A "mark" or human object of an operation.

TELINT - Telemetry Intelligence, a subdivision of **ELINT.**

To terminate - To assassinate; a **sanctioned** killing. Of course, Trevanian and other spy-fiction writers have usurped business euphemisms for more colorful and sinister purposes. **To terminate** means to sever contact with an agent on friendly terms; **to terminate with prejudice** means that a note will be filed warning others not to deal with an unreliable or recalcitrant agent; **to terminate with extreme [maximum] prejudice** is formally known as a **burn notice** and has nothing to do with murder, for it circulates to friendly intelligence services and warns them to have no contact with a troublesome agent.

Thermal detector - Body-heat detector.

Thirty-threes - Crisis, emergency.

Tradecraft - The mechanics of espionage in all its forms: operations, security, and practices.

Tradesmen - These are contacts and civilian collaborators in le Carré who, if called upon, are pledged "to drop everything and, asking no questions, put their skills at the service's disposal."

Traveling salesman - Spy (le Carré).

Triple agent - In the real world of intelligence-gathering, there is no such thing. Writes one experienced professional of counterintelligence: "No intelligence service in its right mind plays such games: the agent is dropped."

Turned - An agent who has been **doubled**.

Twisted balls - Originally a Russian expression for torturing an agent by giving him electric shocks in the genitals. Loosely, an easy subject to interrogate.

Unpack - Confess (le Carré).

Vetted - To be given a polygraph (said of one's own intelligence agency).

Walk-in - Someone who volunteers his or her services for spying.

War of diversion - Soviet term for the sabotage activities within Western facilities, factories, and so forth under the control of the 9th Section of Terror and Diversion of Soviet Intelligence.

What's your twenty? - Radio jargon query for giving a location.

White crow - Any agent who is too noticeable in appearance to take an assignment involving surveillance. (cf. Bentley Lyon's *White Crow*)

Witchhunt - A most dreaded event in le Carré: a purge of an intelligence service—usually in search of a **mole**.

Wrangler - Code breaker (le Carré).

Y Service - False radio transmissions.

Zeta man - A graduate of St. Antony's, Oxford, working in Intelligence.

Za chto? - As noted in Alan Furst's *Dark Star*, *Za chto?* was the expression repeatedly asked and scrawled on the Lubyanka walls during the Stalin purges of the faithful; it means "But why? Why?"

Zoo - Police station.

ZR/Rifle - CIA argot: assassinate (cf. Norman Mailer's *Harlot's Ghost*).

The OPAL Network, Brussels/Paris/Berlin (1938)

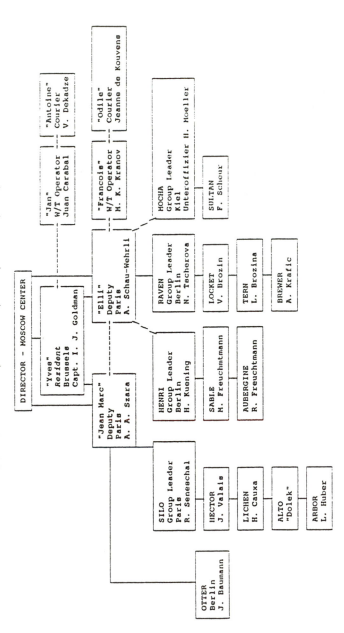

Author Index

THE CITATIONS TO authors and joint-authors in this index are keyed to the entry numbers within both Parts of the guide. Cross references are provided between pseudonyms and real names.

Aaron, David, 377-378
Aarons, Edward S., 379-426
Aarons, Will B., 427-432
Aasheim, Ashley, 433
Abbott, John, pseud., 434
Abrahams, Peter, 435
Abro, Ben, pseud., 436
Adams, Cleve F., 437
Adams, Eustace L., 438
Adams, Nathan M., 439
Addeo, Edmond G., 2149-2150
Adler, Warren, 440-445
Aellen, Richard, 446-449
Agel, Jerome, 450
Alan, Ray, 451
Albert, Marvin H., 452-453
Albertazzie, Ralph, 1859-1865
Albrand, Martha, pseud. *See*
    Loewengard, Heidi H.
Aldanov, Mark, pseud. *See*
    Landau, Mark A.

Alding, Peter, pseud. *See*
    Jeffries, Roderic
Aldridge, James, 454-456
Alexander, David, 457-458
Alexander, David M., 459
Alexander, Patrick, 460-461
Aline, Countess of Romanones, 462
Allbeury, Ted, 463-494
Allen, Ralph, 495
Allingham, Margery, 496-498
Ambler, Eric, 1-4, 499-517
Ames, Rachel, 518-524
Amis, Kingsley, 525-526
Andersch, Alfred, 527
Anderson, Chester, 3072-3073, 3078, 3080-3081
Anderson, Jack, 528
Anderson, James, 529-531
Anderson, John R. L., 532
Anderson, Patrick, 533

Andrews, Shelly, 534
Andreyev, Vladimir, pseud., 535
Andric, Ivo, 536
Angus, Sylvia, 537
Annesley, Michael, 5-7, 538-546
Anthony, Evelyn, pseud. *See*
    Ward-Thomas, Evelyn B. P.
Appel, Benjamin, 547
Appleby, John, 548
Archer, Charles S., 549
Archer, Jeffrey, 550
Arden, William, 551
Ardies, Tom, 552-557
Ardman, Harvey, 558
Arent, Arthur, 559-560
Aricha, Amos, 561-563
Armstrong, Anthony, pseud. *See*
    Willis, Anthony A.
Armstrong, Campbell, 564-568
Arnold, Elliott, 569-572
Arnothy, Christine, 573
Arvay, Harry, 574-578
Ash, William, 579-580
Ashe, Gordon, pseud. *See*
    Creasey, John
Ashford, Jeffrey, 581-582
Aspler, Tony, 4123-4124
Asprey, Robert B., 583
Astrup, Helen, 584
Atkinson, Hugh, 585
Atlee, Philip, pseud. *See* Phillips
    James Atlee
Atwater, James D., 586
August, John, pseud. *See*
    DeVoto, Bernard A.
Avallone, Michael A., Jr., 587-
    617
Ayer, Frederick, 618-619

Bachmann, Lawrence P., 620
Backus, Jean L., 621-623

Baddock, James, 624-627
Bagley, Desmond, 628-639
Bahr, Jerome, 640
Bailey, Anthony, 641
Baker, Charlotte, 642
Baker, Elliott, 643
Baker, Ivon, 644
Baker, Peter, 645
Baker, W. Howard, 646-656
Baker, William A. H., 657
Baldwin, Alex, pseud. *See*
    Butterworth, W. E. [William
    Edmund III]
Ballard, K. G., pseud. *See* Roth,
    Holly
Ballard, Willis T., 658
Ballinger, Bill S., 659-665
Bamford, James, 666
Banks, Carolyn, 667
Bannerman, David, pseud. *See*
    Hagberg, David
Bar-Zohar, Michael, 668-678
Barak, Michael, pseud. *See* Bar-
    Zohar, Michael
Barber, Rowland, 679
Bark, Conrad Voss, 680-681
Barker, Albert, 682-683
Barker, Dudley, 684-685
Barker, Joseph, 686
Barlay, Stephen, 687
Barley, Rex, 688
Baron, Stanley W., 689
Barrington, Maurice, pseud. *See*
    Brogan, Denis W.
Barron, Donald G., 690-691
Bartholomew, Cecilia, 692
Barton, Donald R., 693
Bartram, George, 694-696
Barwick, James, 697-698
Basile, Gloria Vitanza, 699
Bass, Ronald, 700
Battye, Gladys S., 701

Bax, Roger, pseud. *See*
    Winterton, Paul
Bayne, Spencer, 702
Beach, Edward L., 703
Beare, George, 704-705
Beatty, Elizabeth, 706
Becher, Ulrich, 707
Beck, K. K., 708
Becker, Stephen W., 709-710
Beckingham, Bruce, pseud. *See*
    Lilley, Peter and Anthony
    Stansfeld
Beech, Webb. *See* Butterworth,
    W. E. [William Edmund III]
Beechcroft, William, pseud. *See*
    Hallstead, William Finn III
Beecher, William, 711
Beeding, Francis, pseud. *See*
    Palmer, John Leslie and
    Hiliary Aiden St. George
    Saunders
Beevor, Antony, 712-713
Behn, Noel, 714-715
Behr, Edward, 716
Beinhart, Larry, 717-718
Bekessy, Jean, 719
Belhancourt, T. Ernesto, 720
Bellah, James, 5140
Bellow, Saul, 721
Benchley, Nathaniel, 722
Bennett, Dorothea, 723
Bennett, Jack, 724
Bennett, Ken, 725-726
Benson, Eugene P., 727
Benton, Kenneth, 728-737
Berent, Mark, 738-741
Bergamini, David, 742
Bernard, Jay, pseud. *See*
    Sawkins, Raymond H.
Bernard, Joel, 743
Bernard, Robert, pseud. *See*
    Martin, Robert B.

Bernhardsen, Christian, 744
Bernau, George, 745
Bernstein, Ken, 746-747
Berrassi, Mark, 748
Beste, R. Vernon, 749-751
Betteridge, Don, pseud. *See*
    Newman, Bernard
Bickers, Richard T., 752
Bickham, Jack M., 753-758
Bindloss, Harold, 8
Bingham, John M. W. (Lord
    Clanmorris), 759-762
Bingham, Roger, 2521
Binyon, T. J. [Timothy John],
    763
Bischoff, David, 764, 3869
Black, Campbell, 765-770
Black, Gavin, pseud. *See* Wynd,
    Oswald
Black, Ian S., 771-772
Black, Lionel, pseud. *See* Barker,
    Dudley
Blackburn, John, 773-779
Blacker, Irwin R., 780-781
Blagowidow, George, 782
Blair, Charles F., 5488
Blair, Eric. *See* Orwell, George,
    pseud.
Blake, Nicholas, pseud. *See* Day-
    Lewis, Cecil
Blake, Patrick, pseud. *See*
    Egleton, Clive
Blakenship, William, 783
Blankfort, Michael, 9, 784
Blasco-Ibanez, Vincente, 10
Bleeck, Oliver, pseud. *See*
    Thomas, Ross
Block, Lawrence, 3011
Block, Thomas H., 785-789
Blum, Richard H. A. [Hosmer
    Adams], 790-792
Bobker, Lee R., 793-794

Bocca, Geoffrey, 795
Boe, Eugene, 450
Boland, John, 796-798
Bolton, Alexander, 799
Bolton, Melvin, 800-802
Bond, Larry, 803-805
Bond, Raymond T., ed., 806
Bonfiglioli, Kyril, 807
Bonnecarrère, Paul, 808-811
Bonner, Paul, 812
Bontly, Thomas, 813-814
Borden, Mary, 815
Bornemark, Kjell-Olof, 816
Bosse, M. J., 817
Bottome, Phyllis, 11, 818
Boulle, Pierre, 819-821
Bova, Ben, 822
Bowen, Elizabeth, 823
Boyer, Bruce H., 824
Boyington, Gregory "Pappy," 825
Boyle, Kay, 826
Boyne, Walter J., 827
Braddon, Russell, 828-829
Bradshaw-Jones, Malcolm H.,
    830-838
Brady, Michael, 839
Brain, Leonard, 840
Braine, John, 841
Branon, Bill, 842
Brelis, Dean, 843
Brennan, Frederick H., 844
Brennan, John, ed., 845-847
Brent, Peter, 848-858
Breslin, Patrick, 859
Breuer, Gustav J., 1537
Bridge, Ann, pseud. *See*
    O'Malley, Mary D.
Brierley, David, 860-867
Briley, John, 868
Brinkley, Joel, 869
Brochet, Jean A., 870-876
Brodeur, Paul, 877

Brogan, Denis W., 878
Brome, Vincent, 879
Bronson-Howard, George, 12
Brook-Shepherd, Gordon, 880
Brothers, Jay, 881
Brown, Carter, pseud. *See* Yates,
    Alan Geoffrey
Brown, Dale, 882-888
Brown, Dee A., 889
Brown, Harrison, 5802
Browne, Gerald, 890
Broxholme, John F., 891-902
Bruce, Jean, pseud. *See* Brochet,
    Jean A.
Brust, Harold, pseud. *See*
    Cheyney, Reginald Southouse
Bryant, Peter, 903-904
Bryers, Paul, 905
Buchan, John, 13-19, 906
Buchan, William, 907
Buchanan, James D., 908
Buchard, Robert, 909
Buckley, Christopher, 910-911
Buckley, William F., Jr., 912-921
Buckmaster, Henrietta, 922
Bulliet, Richard, 923-924
Burdick, Eugene, 925, 3169
Burger, Neal R., 4984-4986
Burger, Roseaylmer, 4253-4255
Burgess, Anthony, pseud. *See*
    Wilson, John A. B.
Burke, John F., 926-927
Burke, Jonathan, pseud. *See*
    Burke, John F. and George
    Theiner
Burkhardt, Robert F. and Eve,
    928
Burkholz, Herbert, 929-932
Burmeister, Jon, 933-934
Burnett, Hallie, 935
Burren, Michael, 3746
Burt, Katharine, 936

Burton, Anthony, 937-938

Busch, Nivan, 939

Butler, Jimmie H., 940-941

Butler, Richard, pseud. *See*
Allbeury, Ted

Butters, Dorothy Gilman, 942-950

Butterworth, Michael, 951

Butterworth, W. E. [William
Edmund III], 952-984

Byrd, Max, 985

Byrne, Robert, 986

Caidin, Martin, 987-994

Caillou, Alan, pseud. *See* Lyle-
Smythe, Alan

Cairns, Robert, 995

Calder-Marshall, Arthur, 996

Calin, Harold, 997-998

Callas, Theo, 999

Callison, Brian, 1000-1003

Calmer, Ned, 1004

Cameron, Lou, 1005-1007

Campbell, Alice, 1008

Campbell, Keith, pseud. *See*
West-Watson, Keith Campbell

Campbell, R. Wright, 1009-1010

Canning, Victor, 1011-1031

Cannon, John, 1032

Cape, Tony, 1033-1034

Caputo, Philip, 1035

Carey, Constance, 1036

Cargill, Morris, 2545

Carney, Daniel, 1037

Carpenter, Scott, 1038

Carroll, Gerry, 1039

Carroll, James, 1040-1045

Carter, John F., 20-26

Carter, Lin, 1046

Carter, Nick, house pseud. *See*
Nick Carter, pseud.; Michael
A. Avallone, Jr.; W. T.
Ballard; Marilyn Granbeck;
Ralph E. Hayes; Jeffrey M.
Wallman & a hundred others.

Carter, Nick, pseud., 1047-1175

Carter, Youngman, 1176

Cartwright, Justin, 1177

Cassell, Stephen, 1178-1180

Cassidy, John, 1181

Cassill, R. V., 1182

Castle, John, pseud. *See* Payne,
Ronald and John Garrod

Catano, James V., 1183

Catto, Max, 1184

Cave, Peter, 1185

Cerf, Bennett, comp., 1186-1187

Chaber, M. E., pseud. *See*
Crossen, Kendell F.

Chacko, David, 1188-1190

Chamales, Thomas, 1191

Chamberlain, William, 1192

Chambers, Dana, pseud. *See*
Leffingwell, Albert

Chandler, David, 1193

Channing, Mark, 27

Chantler, David T., 1194

Charbonneau, Louis, 1195-1199

Charles, Martin, 1200

Charles, Robert, pseud. *See*
Smith, Robert C.

Charteris, Leslie, pseud. *See* Yin,
Leslie C. B.

Chase, Glen, pseud. *See* Fox,
Gardner

Chase, James H., pseud. *See*
Raymond, René B.

Chase, Philip, pseud. *See*
Friedman, Philip

Chesbro, George C., 1201-1203

Chesterton, Gilbert K., 28

Cheyney, Peter, pseud. *See*
Cheyney, Reginald Southouse

Cheyney, Reginald Southouse, 1204-1213

Chevalier, Paul, 1214

Childers, Erskine, 29

Childers, James S., 1215

Childs, Marquis, 1216-1217

Christian, John, 1218

Christie, Agatha, 30-31, 1219-1225

Christie, William, 1226

Clancy, Leo, 1227

Clancy, Tom, 1228-1234

Clark, Eric, 1235-1237

Clark, William, 1238-1239

Clavell, James, 1240

Clayton, Richard, 1241-1263

Cleary, Jon, 1264-1269

Cleeve, Brian T., 1270-1274

Clements, Eileen H., 1275-1276

Clewes, Howard, 1277

Clifford, Francis, pseud. See Thompson, Arthur L. B.

Clive, John, 1278-1279, 2203

Clouston, Joseph S., 32

Clyde, Allison, pseud. See Knowles, William

Cobb, Humphrey, 33

Cochran, Molly, 3931

Cody, James P., pseud. See Rohrbach, Peter T.

Coen, Franklin, 1280

Cohen, Arthur A., 1282

Cohen, Stanley, 1283

Cohen, Stephen Paul, 2122

Cohen, William S., 2504-2505

Coles, C. Henry, 3687-3711

Coles, Manning, pseud. See Manning, Adelaide F.O. and C. Henry Coles

Collin, Richard O., 1284

Collingwood, Charles, 1285

Collins, Larry, 1286-1293

Collins, Norman, 1294

Coltrane, James, 1295-1297

Conde, Phillip, 34-40

Condon, Richard, 1298-1304

Conly, Robert L., 1305

Connable, Alfred, 1306

Conners, Bernard F., 1307

Connolly, Cyril, 1308

Connolly, Ray, 1309

Conrad, Brenda, 1310

Conrad, Joseph, 41-42

Cook, Bob, 1311-1315

Cook, Nick, 1316-1317

Cook, Sly, 1318

Cooke, David C., 1319

Cooney, Michael, 1320

Coonts, Stephen, 1321-1325

Cooper, Alfred Duff, 1326

Cooper, Brian, 1327-1328

Cooper, James Fenimore, 43

Cooper, Tom, 1329

Copeland, William, 1330

Copp, DeWitt, 1331

Coppel, Alfred, 1332-1343

Copplestone, Bennet, pseud. See Kitchin, Frederick

Corley, Edwin, 1344-1351

Cormier, Robert, 1352

Cornford, Philip, 1353

Cornwell, Bernard, 1354

Cornwell, David J. M., 1355-1368

Corrigan, Mark, pseud. See Norman, Lee

Cort, Ned, 1369-1370

Cory, Desmond, pseud. See McCarthy, John L.

Cotler, Gordon, 1371

Couch, Dick, 1372-1374

Coulson, Robert S., 1640-1641

Coulter, Stephen, 1375-1387

Courter, Gay, 1388

Cox, Richard, 1389-1394
Coxe, George H., 1395-1396
Coyle, Harold, 1397-1401
Coyne, Joseph E., 1402
Craig, David, pseud. *See* Tucker,
    Allan J.
Craig, John, 1403
Craig, M. S., 1404
Craig, William, 1405-1406
Craik, Roger, 1407
Crane, Robert, pseud. *See*
    Sellers, Connie L., Jr.
Creasey, John, 44-62, 1408-1460
Creighton, Christopher, 2114,
    2796
Crichton, Michael, 1461-1462
Crisp, N. J. [Norman James],
    1463-1470
Crook, William, 1471
Crosby, John, 1472-1476
Cross, Gilbert B., 1477-1479
Cross, James, pseud. *See* Parry,
    Hugh J.
Crossen, Kendell F., 1480-1483
Crowder, Herbert, 1484-1486
Cudlip, David R., 1487-1488
Cullen, Robert, 1489
Cunningham, E. V., pseud. *See*
    Fast, Howard
Cunningham, Richard, 1490
Curtis, Jack, 1491
Cussler, Clive, 1492-1503
Cutler, Roland, 1504

Da Cruz, Daniel, 1505-1507
Dan, Uri, 1508-1509
Daniel, David, 1510-1511
Daniels, J. R., 1512
Daniels, Max, 1513
Daniels, Norman, 1514-1524
Dark, James, 1525-1536

Davenport, Gwen L., 1537
Davey, Jocelyn, 1538
Davidsen, Leif, 1539-1540
Davidson, Lionel, 1541
Davies, Frederic, pseud. *See*
    Ellik, Ron and Frederic
    Langley
Davies, John E. W., 1542-1548
Davis, Bart, 1549-1555
Davis, Clyde B., 1556
Davis, Dorothy S., 1557-1560
Davis, Franklin M., Jr., 1561-
    1562
Davis, Gordon, pseud. *See* Hunt,
    E. Howard and Leonard
    Levinson
Davis, J. Madison, 1563
Davis, Maggie, 1564
Davison, Gilderoy, 63-67
Dawe, William Carlton Lanyon,
    68-73
Dawson, James, 1565
Day, Gina, 1566
Day-Lewis, Cecil, 74, 1567
Deacon, richard, pseud. *See*
    McCormick, Donald
Dean, Elizabeth, 1568
Dean, Robert G., 1569-1570
DeAndrea, William L., 1571-
    1576
Deane, Norman, pseud. *See*
    Creasey, John
DeBorchgrave, Arnaud, 3913-
    3914
DeFelice, Jim, 1577
Deford, Frank, 1578
DeGramont, Sanche, 1579
Deighton, Len, 1580-1599
Dekker, Anthony, 1600
Delaney, Laurence, 1601
DeLillo, Don, 1602-1603
Delman, David, 1604

Delving, Michael, pseud. *See*
  Williams, Jay
Dembo, Samuel, 1605
DeMille, Nelson, 1606-1612
Dempsey, Al, 1613-1614
Denning, Mark, pseud. *See*
  Stevenson, John
Dennis, Ralph, 1615
Denny, Robert, 1616-1617
Derby, Mark, pseud. *See*
  Wilcox, Harry
Derrick, Lionel, 1618
De St. Jerre, John, 1619
DeStefano, Anthony, 1620
Deutermann, P. T., 1621
Deverell, William, 1622
DeVilliers, Catherine, 1623
DeVilliers, Gerard, 1624-1637
DeVoto, Bernard A., 1638-1639
DeWeese, Thomas G., 1640-1641
Diamond, Sander, 4672
Dickey, Fred, 1642-1643
Diehl, William, 1644-1646
Dietrich, Robert, pseud. *See*
  Hunt, E. Howard
Diment, Adam, 1647-1650
DiMercurio, 1651
DiMona, Joseph, 1652-1654
Dinallo, Greg, 1655-1657
"Diplomat," pseud. *See* Carter,
  John F.
Dipper, Alan, 1658-1659
Disney, Doris C., 1660
Divine, Arthur D., 1661
Dixon, H. Vernor, 1662
Dixon, Mark, 1663-1665
Doctorow, E. L., 1666
Dodge, David, 1667-1669
Dodson, Daniel B., 1670
Doherty, Kevin, 1671
Doherty, P. C., 1672-1675
Dolinger, Roy, 1676-1679

Donald, Miles, 1680-1681
Donner, Kyle, 1682
Donoghue, P. S., 1683
Donoso, José, 1684
Dorling, Henry T., 75-77, 1685
Douglas, Richard, 1686
Downes, Donald C., 1687-1688
Downes, Hundon, 1689-1690
Doyle, Arthur Conan, 78-80
Doyle, David W., 1691
Driggs, Laurence, L. T., 81
Driscoll, Peter, 1692-1697
Drummond, Ivor, 1698-1703
Drury, Allen, 1704-1714
Dryer, Bernard V., 1715
Duane, Allan, 1716
Duffy, Margaret, 1717-1722
Dugan, Jack, pseud. *See*
  Butterworth, W. E. [William
  Edmund III]
Duggan, Ervin S., 1723
Duke, Madelaine, 1724-1725
Dulles, Allen, ed., 1726
Duncan, Lee, 1727
Duncan, Robert L., 1728-1736
Dunham, Donald, 1737
Dunmore, Spencer, 1738
Dunne, Lee, 1739
Dunne, Thomas L., 1740
Dunnett, Dorothy, 1741
Durand, Loup, 1742-1743
Durham, Guy, 1744-1745
Durrell, Lawrence, 1746
Dwiggins, Toni, 1747
Dwyer, K. R., 1748
Dye, Dale, 1749-1750

"E-7," pseud., 1751
Eachus, Irving, 1752
Easterman, Daniel, pseud. *See*
  MacEoin, Denis

Eastwood, James, 1753-1755
Ebert, Virginia, 1756
Eckert, Allan W., 1757
Edelman, Maurice, 1758-1760
Eden, Matthew, 1761-1765
Edwards, Anne, 1766
Edwards, Paul, 1767-1772
Egleton, Clive, 1773-1799
Ehrlichman, John, 1800-1803
Eisenberg, Hershey, 1804
Elder, Mark, 1805
Elegant, Robert S, 1806
Ellik, Ron, 1807
Ellis, Scott, 1808
Elman, Richard, 1809
Elon, Amos, 1810
Elwood, Roger, 1811
Emmett, Robert, 1812-1815
Engel, Alan, 1816
Engstrand, Stuard D., 1817
Epstein, Edward Jay, 1818
Erdman, Paul E., 1819-1823
Esdaile, David, pseud. *See*
    Walker, David Esdaile
Estabrooks, George H., 3295
Estey, Dale, 1824
Estridge, Robin, 1825
Evans, Jonathan, pseud. *See*
    Freemantle, Brian
Evans, Kenneth, 1826
Evelyn, John M., 1827-1829
Everett, Peter, 1830

Fairbairn, Douglas, 1831
Fairlie, Gerald, 82-83, 1832-1838
Fairman, Paul W., 1839
Falkirk, Richard, pseud. *See*
    Lambert, Derek
Fallon, Martin, pseud. *See*
    Patterson, Harry
Farr, Finis, 1840

Fast, Charles, 1841
Fast, Howard, 1842
Faur, Michael P., Jr., 1843
Faust, Frederick S., 84-86
Faust, Ron, 1844
Feakes, G. J., 1845
Feegel, John R., 1846
Fennell, George, 1847
Fenner, Phyllis, ed., 1848
Fergusson, Bernard E., 1849
Ferris, Paul, 1850
Fick, Carl, 1851
Fickling, G. G., 1852
Finch, Phillip, 1853
Finder, Joseph, 1854
Fish, Robert L., 1855-1858
Fisher, David E., 1859-1865
Fisher, Norman, 1866-1868
Fishman, Hal, 4853
Fitzmaurice, Eugene, 1869
Fitzsimons, Christopher, 1870-
    1871
Flannery, Sean, pseud. *See*
    Hagberg, David
Fleischman, A. S., 1872
Fleming, Ian, pseud. *See* Cerf,
    Bennett and Michael K. Frith
Fleming, Ian, 1873-1890
Fleming, Joan, 1891
Fleming, Nichol, 1892
Fletcher, Lucille, 1893
Flynn, Jay, 1894-1895
Follett, James, 1896-1906
Follett, Ken, 1907-1916
Footman, Robert, 1917-1918
Forbes, Bryan, 1919-1920
Forbes, Colin, pseud. *See*
    Sawkins, Raymond H.
Forbes, Stephen, 1921-1922
Ford, John M., 1923
Forrest, David, pseud. *See*
    Forrest-Webb, Robert

Forrest-Webb, Robert, 1924-1925
Forrester, Larry, 1926
Forsyth, Frederick, 1927-1935
Forvé, Guy, 1936
Fournier, Pierre, 1937
Fowlkes, Frank, 1938-1939
Fox, Anthony, 1940
Fox, Gardner, 1941-1945
Fox, James M., pseud. *See*
    Knipscheer, James M.
Fox, Victor J., 1946
Frabutt, Paul, 1947
Frances, Stephen, 1948-1952
Francis, Clare, 1953-1954
Francis, Dick, 1955
Frank, Patrick, 1956
Frankau, Gilbert, 87
Frankel, Sandor, 1957
Franklin, Charles, pseud. *See*
    Usher, Frank H.
Franklin, Max, 1958
Franklin, Steve, 1959
Fraser, Antonia, 1960
Frayn, Michael, 1961-1962
Frazer, Steve, 1963
Freadhoff, Chuck, 1964
Frede, Richard, pseud. *See*
    Frederics, Macdowell
Frederics, Macdowell, 1965-1966
Freed, Donald, 1967-1968
Freedgood, Morton, 1969
Freedman, John, 1970-1971
Freeling, Nicholas, 1972
Freemantle, Brian, 1973-2001
French, Richard P., 2002
Frentzen, Jeffrey, 2003
Freshman, Bruce J., 2004
Freund, Philip, ed., 2005
Frey, James N., 2006-2007
Friedman, Phillip, 2008-2011
Frizell, Bernard, 2012-2013

Frost, Frederick, pseud. *See*
    Faust, Frederick S.
Frost, Mark, 2014
Fry, Peter, pseud. *See* King,
    Clifford
Fuentes, Carlos, 2015
Fuller, Jack, 2016
Furst, Alan, 2017-2022

Gadney, Reginald, 2023-2029
Gaines, Robert, 2030
Gainham, Sarah, pseud. *See*
    Ames, Rachel
Gallagher, Stephen, 2031-2034
Gallery, Daniel J., 2035
Gallico, Paul, 2036-2038
Galway, Robert Conington,
    pseud. *See* McCutchan,
    Philip
Gandley, Kenneth Royce, 2039-
    2069
Garbo, Norman, 2070-2072
Gardiner, Wayne J., 2073
Gardner, Alan, 2074-2077
Gardner, John, 2078-2108
Garfield, Brian, 2109-2117
Garforth, John, 2118-2121
Garn, Jake, 2122
Garner, William, 2123-2130
Garrett, George, 2131
Garrett, Robert, 2132
Garrison, Jim, 2133
Garrod, John, 4197
Garside, Jack, 2134-2144
Garth, David, 88, 2145-2148
Garve, Andrew, pseud. *See*
    Winterton, Paul
Garvin, Richard M., 2149-2150
Gascar, Pierre, pseud. *See*
    Fournier, Pierre
Gash, Jonathan, 2151

Gaskin, Catherine, 2152
Gates, Natalie, 2153
Gavin, Catherine, 2154
Gazzaniga, Donald A., 2155
Geddes, Paul, 2156-2159
Geller, Stephen, 2160
George, Jonathan, pseud. *See*
    Burke, John F. and George
    Theiner
George, Peter B., 2161-2162
Gerrard, R. J., 164
Gerson, Jack, 2163-2167
Gerson, Noel B., 2168
Gethin, David, 2169
Gibbs, George, 89
Gibbs, Henry, pseud. *See*
    Rumbold-Gibbs, Henry St.
    John Clair
Gibbs, Tony, 2170-2172
Gibson, Frank E., 2173
Gifford, Thomas, 2174-2177
Gigga, Kenneth, 2178-2197
Gilbert, Anthony, pseud. *See*
    Malleson, Lucy B.
Gilbert, Harriett, 2198
Gilbert, Michael, 2199-2201
Gill, Bartholomew, 2202
Gilman, Dorothy, pseud. *See*
    Butters, Dorothy Gilman
Gilman, J. D., 2203
Gilroy, Dan, 2204
Gimpel, Erich, 2205
Giovannetti, Alberto, 2206
Gladilin, Anatoly, 2207
Glaskin, G. M., 2208
Goble, Neil, 2209
Goddard, Harry, 2210
Goddard, Ken, 2211-2213
Godey, John, pseud. *See*
    Freedgood, Morton
Golan, Matti, 2214
Goldberg, Marshall, 2215

Goldman, James, 2216
Goldman, William, 2217
Goodfield, June, 2218
Goodkind, Howard, 2072
Goodman, George J. W., 2219
Gordon, Alexander, pseud. *See*
    Cotler, Gordon
Gordon, Donald, pseud. *See*
    Payne, Donald G.
Gordon, Mildred and Gordon,
    2220-2221
Gottfried, Theodore M., 2222-
    2228
Gottlieb, Annie, 4761
Gough, Laurence, 2229
Gould, Heywood, 2230
Gowing, Nik, 2231
Grace, Alexander M., 2232
Grady, James, 2233-2235
Grady, Ronan C., Jr., 2236
Graeme, Bruce, pseud. *See*
    Jeffries, Graham M.
Graham, James, pseud. *See*
    Patterson, Harry
Graham, Mark, 2237-2238
Graham, Winston, 2239
Granbeck, Marilyn, 2240-2243
Granger, Bill, 2244-2259
Grant, David, pseud. *See* Thomas
    Craig
Grant, Edward, 2260
Grant, James, 2261
Grant, Pete, pseud., 2262
Graves, Richard L., 2263-2267
Gray, Rod, 2268-2276
Grayson, Rupert, 90-93
Greatorex, Wilfred, 2277-2281
Green, Frederick L., 2282
Green, Stagg, 2283-2284
Green, William M., 2285-2288
Greene, Graham, 94-95, 2289-
    2300

Greene, Harris, 2301-2306
Greener, William O., 96
Greenfield, Irving, 2307-2309
Greenland, Francis, 2310
Greenlee, Sam, 2311
Grey, Anthony, 2312-2317
Gribbon, William L., 97-109
Griffin, John, 2318-2323
Griffin, W. E. B., pseud. *See*
    Butterworth, W. E. [William
    Edmund III]
Griffiths, John, 2324-2328
Griswold, George, pseud. *See*
    Dean, Robert G.
Groom, A. J. Pelham, 2329
Gross, Leonard, 4745-4746
Gross, Martin L., 2330-2332
Gross, Sheldon, 2333
Gruber, Frank, 2334
Guenter, C. H., pseud., 2335-
    2337
Guerard, Albert, 2338
Guild, Nicholas, 2339-2345
Guillou, Jan, 2346
Gulyashki, Andrei, 2347-2350
Gunther, John, 2351
Gurewich, David, 2352
Gurr, David, 2353-2354
Gutteridge, Lindsay, 2355-2356

Habe, Hans, pseud. *See* Bekessy,
    Jean
Hackforth-Jones, Gilbert, 2357-
    2359
Haddad, C. A., 2360-2362
Hagberg, David, 2363-2383
Haggard, William, pseud. *See*
    Clayton, Richard
Haig, Alec, 2384
Hailey, Arthur, 2385
Haim, Victor, 5429

Hale, John, 2386
Halkin, John, 2387-2388
Hall, Adam, pseud. *See* Trevor,
    Elleston
Hall, Andrew, 2389
Hall, Patrick, 2390
Hall, Roger, 2391
Hall, Warner, 2392
Hallahan, William H., 2393-2398
Halliday, Brett, 2399
Hallstead, William Finn III, 2400-
    2406
Hamill, Pete, 2407
Hamilton, Adam, pseud. *See*
    Granbeck, Marilyn and Allen
    Moore
Hamilton, Bruce, 110
Hamilton, Donald, 2408-2436
Hammon, Henry, 2437
Hammond-Innes, Ralph, 2438-
    2442
Hamrick, Samuel J. Jr., 2443-
    2448
Hanlon, Sean, 2449-2450
Hanson, Dirk, 2451
Harcourt, Palma, 2452-2469
Hardt, Michael, pseud. *See*
    Davenport, Gwen L. and
    Gustav J. Breuer
Hardy, Jocelyn L., 111
Hardy, Ronald, 2470
Harling, Robert, 2471-2472
Haroldson, William, pseud. *See*
    King, Harold
Harper, David, pseud. *See*
    Corley, Edwin
Harper, Richard J., 2473
Harrington, Denis J., 2474
Harrington, Kent, 2475-2476
Harrington, R. E., 2477-2478
Harrington, William, 2479-2488

Harris, Brian, pseud. *See* King, Harold

Harris, Harry, 2489-2490

Harris, John, 2491-2493

Harris, Leonard, 2494

Harris, MacDonald, 2495

Harris, Richard, 2496

Harris, Robert, 2497

Harris, Thomas, 2498

Harrison, Harry, 2499

Harrison, Payne, 2500-2501

Harrison, William, 2502-2503

Hart, Gary, 2504-2505

Hart, Roy, 2506

Hart-Davis, Duff, 2507

Hartenfels, Jerome, 2508

Hartland, Michael, 2509-2512

Hartley, Norman, 2513-2515

Hartmann, Michael, 2516-2517

Hartov, Steven, 2518

Hartshorne, pseud. *See* Blum, Richard H. A. [Hosmer Adams]

Harvester, Simon, pseud. *See* Rumbold-Gibbs, Henry St. John Clair

Harvey, John H., 112-119

Hastings, Michael, pseud. *See* Bar-Zohar, Michael

Hauser, Thomas, 2519-2520

Hawkey, Raymond, 2521

Hawkins, John and Ward, 2522

Haycraft, Howard, ed., 2523

Hayes, Ralph, 2524-2531

Hayes, Roy, 2532

Haynes, Brian, 2954

Heald, Timothy V., 2533-2544

Hearne, John, 2545

Heath, Layne, 2546

Heatter, Basil, 2547-2548

Hebden, Mark, pseud. *See* Harris, John

Heberden, Mary V., 2549-2557

Heckstall-Smith, Anthony, 2558

Heffernan, William, 2559-2560

Heim, Michael, 2561

Heinrich, Willi, 2562

Helitzer, Florence, 2563

Helwig, David, 2564

Hemingway, John, 813-816

Hempstone, Smith, 2565

Henaghan, Jim, 2566

Henderson, James, 2567

Henderson, Laurence, 2568-2569

Henissart, Paul, 2570-2572

Hennissart, Martha, 3144

Henrick, Richard P., 2573-2584

Henriques, Robert D. Q., 2585

Herbert, James, 2586

Herlin, Hans, 2587

Herman, Richard, Jr., 2588-2592

Hernandez, Arnaldo, 2593-2594

Herrick, William, 2595

Herron, Shaun, 2596-2600

Hershatter, Richard L., 2601-2603

Herst, Roger E., 2604

Hesky, Olga, 2605-2607

Hewitt, Kathleen D., 2608

Heydenau, Friedrich, 2609

Heym, Stefan, 2610

Heywood, Joseph, 2611-2612

Hiatt, Fred, 2613

Higgins, Jack, pseud. *See* Patterson, Harry

Highet, Helen *See* MacInnes, Helen

Highsmith, Patricia, 2614

Hild, Jack, house pseud. *See* Garside, Jack

Hill, John, 2615

Hill, Peter, 2616

Hill, R. Lance, 2617

Hill, Reginald, 2618

Hilton, James, 120
Himmel, Richard, 2619-2620
Hirschfeld, Burt, 2621
Hirschhorn, Richard C., 2622
Hitchcock, Raymond, 2623
Hoch, Edward D., 2624-2627
Hoffenberg, Jack, 2628-2629
Hogan, James P., 2630-2632
Hogstrand, Olle, 2633-2634
Hoklin, Lon, 4098
Holland, William E., 2635-2636
Holbrook, Marion, 2637
Holles, Robert, 2638
Holt, Robert L., 2639-2640
Holly, J. Hunter, pseud. *See*
    Holly, Joan C.
Holly, Joan C., 2641
Holzer, Erika, 2642
Home, Michael, 2643-2644
Homewood, Charles H., 2645
Homewood, Harry, pseud. *See*
    Charles H. Homewood
Hone, Joseph, 2646-2650
Hood, William, 2651-2653
Hoover, Thomas, 2654-2657
Hopkins, Robert S., 2658-2662
Horler, Sydney, 121-129, 2663-
    2664
Hornig, Doug, 2665-2666
Horton, Forest W., Jr., 2667
Hossent, Harry, 2668-2675
Hostovsky, Egon, 2676
Household, Geoffrey, 130, 2677-
    2691
Houston, Robert, 2692-2694
Hoving, Thomas, 2695
Howard, Clark, 2696-2697
Howard, Hampton, 2698-2699
Howard, Hartley, pseud. *See*
    Ognall, Leopold H.
Howe, George, 2700
Howlett, John, 2701-2702

Howley, Brendan, 2703
Hoyt, Richard, 2704-2714
Hubler, Richard G., 2715
Hudson, James, 4523-4525
Hughes, Dorothy B., 2716-2718
Hughes, Zachery, pseud. *See*
    Zachary, Hugh
Hugo, Richard, 2719-2721
Huie, William B., 2722
Humana, Charles, pseud. *See*
    Jacobs, Joseph
Humes, H. L., 2723
Hunt, E. [Everette] Howard,
    2724-2754
Hunter, Evan, 2755
Hunter, Jack D, 2756-2764
Hunter, Robin, 2765-2767
Hunter, Stephen, 2768-2773
Hurd, Douglas, 2774-2780
Hurwood, Bernhardt J., 2781-
    2786
Hutchison, Graham S., 131
Hyde, Anthony, 2787-2788
Hyde, Christopher, 2789
Hyland, Henry S., 2790-2791
Hyman, Tom, 2792-2793
Hyman, Vernon T., 2794
Hynd, Noel, 2795-2801

Iams, Jack, 2802
Ignatius, David, 2803-2804
Iles, Greg, 2805
Ing, Dean, 2806-2816
Innes, Hammond, pseud. *See*
    Hammond-Innes, Ralph
Innes, Michael, pseud. *See*
    Stewart, John I. M.
Irving, Clifford, 2817-2818
Irving, Clive, 2819
Irwin, Robert, 2820-2821
Isaacs, Susan, 2822

Ison, Graham, 2823-2824

Jackman, Stuart, 2825
Jacks, Oliver, pseud. *See*
    Gandley, Kenneth Royce
Jackson, Blyden, 2826
Jackson, James, 2827
Jackson, Jon J., 2828
Jacobs, Joseph, 2829
Jacobs, Philip Sayetta, 5379
Jacobs, T. C. H., pseud. *See*
    Pendower, Jacques
Jacot, B. L., 588
Jahn, Michael, 2830
James, Colin, 2831
James, Donald, 2832
James, John, 2833-2834
James, Leigh, 2835-2838
Jameson, Storm, 2839
Jamieson, Ian R., 2840
Jardine, Warwick, pseud. *See*
    Warwick, Francis A.
Jay, Charlotte, pseud. *See* Jay,
    Geraldine
Jay, Geraldine, 2841
Jay, Simon, pseud. *See* James,
    Colin
Jeffries, Graham M., 132, 2842-
    2844
Jeffries, Roderic, 2845
Jenkins, Geoffrey, 2846-2851
Jepson, Selwyn, 2852-2853
John, Hendrix, 2854
John, Owen, 2855-2859
Johnson, James L., 2860-2863
Johnson, Stanley, 2864-2865
Johnson, Uwe, 2866
Johnson, William, 2867
Johnston, Ronald, 2868
Johnston, William, 2869-2876
Jones, Bradford, 2877

Jones, Bradshaw, pseud. *See*
    Bradshaw-Jones, Malcolm H.
Jones, Dennis, 2878-2882
Jones, J. Sydney, 2883
Jones, Peter, 2884
Jones, Philip, 2885-2886
Jones, Robert F., 2887
Jones, Tristan, 2888
Jordan, David, 2889
Jordan, Len, 2890
Joseph, Mark, 2891-2892
Judd, Alan, 2893-2897
Julitte, Pierre, 2898
Just, Ward, 2899
Jute, André, 2900-2904

Kagley, Rudolf, 2905
Kalb, Marvin, 2906
Kalme, Egils, 2907
Kalish, Robert, 2908
Kaminsky, Stuart M., 2909-2918
Kane, Henry, 2919-2923
Kanfer, Stefan, 2924
Kaplan, Andrew, 2925-2928
Kaplan, Howard, 2929-2931
Karman, Max, 2932
Karp, Marvin A., ed., 2933-2934
Kartun, Derek, 2935-2939
Katcher, Leo, 2940-2941
Katkov, Norman, 2942
Katz, Robert, 2943-2944
Katz, William, 2945-2946
Kaufelt, David A., 2947
Kauffman, Ray F., 2948
Kearey, Charles, 2949
Keating, Henry R. F., 2950
Keeble, John, 2951-2952
Keeley, Edmund, 2953
Keene, Tom, 2954
Kelleher, Brian, 2955-2956
Keller, Beverly, 2957

Kelly, John, 2958
Kelly, Judith, 2959
Kelly, Michael, 2960
Kelly, Patrick, pseud. *See*
    Allbeury, Ted
Kemelman, Harry, 2961
Kempley, Walter, 2962
Kendrick, Baynard, 2963-2964
Keneally, Thomas, 2965
Kenmore, Frank J., 2966-2968
Kennedy, Adam, 2969-2973
Kennedy, William P., 2974
Kenny, Stan, pseud. *See* Gigga,
    Kenneth
Kenrick, Tony, 2975-2978
Kenyon, Michael, 2979-2980
Kenyon, Paul, 2981-2988
Kern, John, 2989
Kessel, Joseph, 2990
Kiefer, Warren, 2991-2993
Kielland, Axel, 2994
Kiker, Douglas, 2995-2997
Kilgore, Axel, 2998
Kilian, Michael, 2999-3003
King, Charles, 3004
King, Clifford, 3005-3007
King, David, 3008
King, Graham, 3009
King, Harold, 3010-3017
King, Stephen, 3018-3019
Kinsley, Peter, 3020
Kipling, Rudyard, 133
Kirk, Lydia, 3021
Kirk, Philip, pseud. *See*
    Levinson, Leonard
Kirsch, Steven J., 3022
Kirschner, Fritz, 3023
Kirst, Hans H., 3024-3025
Kitchin, Frederick, 134
Klainer, Albert and Jo-Ann, 3026
Klawans, Harold L., 3027
Klein, Edward, 3028

Klose, Kevin, 3029
Knapp, Gregory C., 3030
Knebel, Fletcher, 3031-3034
Knight, Kathleen M., 3035
Knight, Mallory T., pseud. *See*
    Hurwood, Bernhardt J.
Knipscheer, James M., 3036
Knopp, Jerome M., 3037
Knott, Will C., 3838-3040
Knowles, William, 3041-3045
Knowlton, Winthrop, 2219
Knox, Bill, 3046-3053
Koenig, Joseph, 3054
Kolpacoff, Victor, 3055
Konsalik, Heinz G., 3056
Koontz, Dean R., 3057
Koppel, Ted, 2906
Kosinski, Jerzy, 3058
Koski, Dominic, 4877-4878
Kozhevnikov, Vadim, 3059
Kruse, John, 3060-3061
Kuhlken, Ken, 3062
Kuhn, Edward, Jr., 3063
Kunetka, James W., 3064-3065,
    5165
Kuniczak, W. S., 3066
Kurland, Michael, 3067-3082
Kyle, Duncan, pseud. *See*
    Broxholme, John F.

Lafferty, Perry, 3083
Lait, Robert, 3084
Lamb, Max, 3085
Lambert, Derek, 3086-3110
Lamport, Stephen, 2777
Land, Jon, 3152-3165
Lancaster, David, pseud. *See*
    Heald, Timothy V.
Lancaster, Graham, 3111
Land, Jon, 3112-3125
Landau, Mark A., 3126

Landon, Christopher, 3127
Lange, John, 3128
Langley, Bob, 3129-3138
Langely, Frederic, 1807
Lantigua, John, 3139
LaPierre, Dominique. *See*
    Collins, Larry for a list of his
    collaborations in spy fiction.
Larauy, David, 3140
Lartéguy, Jean, 3141-3142
Latham, Aaron, 3143
Lathen, Emma, pseud. *See*
    Latsis, Mary J. and Martha
    Hennissart
Latsis, Mary J., 3144
Latter, Simon, 3145-3146
Lauder, Peter, 3147
Lauer, Pierre, 3148
Laumer, Keith, 3149-3151
Lawrence, Marjorie K., 3152
Layne, Marion Margery, pseud.
    See Woolf, Marion, Margery
    W. Papich and Layne
    Torkelson
Leasor, James, 3153-3163
Leather, Edwin, 3164
Leather, Stephen, 3165-3168
Le Carré, John, pseud. *See*
    Cornwell, David J. M.
Lederer, William J., 3169
Lee, Elsie, pseud. *See* Sheridan,
    Elsie L.
Lee, John, 3170-3176
Lee, Norman, 3177-3178
Lee, Stan, 3179-3180
Leffingwell, Albert, 3181-3182
Le Grand, Leon, 3183-3184
Lehman, Ernest, 3185
Lehrer, Jim, 3186
Leib, Franklin A., 3187-3189
Leigh, James, 3190-3191
Leighton, Tom, 3192

Lemieux, Kenneth, 3193-3194
Leonard, Charles L., pseud. *See*
    Heberden, Mary V.
Leonard, Elmore, 3195
Leopold, Christopher, 3196
LeQueux, William T., 135-161
Leslie, Peter, 3197-3206, 3620-
    3621
Lesser, Milton A., 3207-3228
Lestienne, Voldemar, 3229
Leuci, Bob, 3230
Levi, Peter, 3231-3232
Levin, Ira, 3233
Levine, Larry, 3234
Levine, Paul, 3235-3237
Levinson, Leonard, 3238-3248
Lewellen, T. C., 3249
Lewis, David, 3250
Lewis, Norman, 3251-3153
Lewis, Roy H., 3254
Liddy, G. Gordon, 3255-3256
Lieberman, Herbert, 3257
Lilley, Peter, 3258
Lilley, Tom, 3259-3260
Limón, Martin, 3261
Linaweaver, Brad, 3262
Lindquist, Donald, 3263-3264
Lindsey, David L., 3265
Linebarger, Paul M. A., 3266
Lippincott, David, 3267-3269
Littell, Blaine, 3270
Littell, Robert, 3271-3280
Little, Lloyd, 3281
Litvinoff, Emmanuel, 3282-3286
Litzinger, Boyd, 3287
Llewellyn, Richard, 3288-3291
Llewellyn, Sam, 3292
Lockhart, Robin Bruce, 3293-
    3294
Lockridge, Richard, 3295
Lodwick, John, 3296-3297
Loewengard, Heidi H., 3298-3313

Longstreet, Stephen, 3314
Loraine, Philip, pseud. *See*
    Estridge, Robin
Lord, Graham, 3315-3316
Loring, Emilie, 3317
Lorraine, John, 3318
Lottman, Eileen, 3319-3321
Lourie, Richard, 3322-3324
Louvish, Simon, 3325
Lovejoy, William H., 3326-3327
Lovell, Marc, pseud. *See*
    McShane, Mark
Lowden, Desmond, 3328
Luard, Nicholas, 3329-3333
Lucas, Ruth, 3334
Luddecke, Werner J., 3335
Ludlum, Robert, 3336-3354
Lyall, Gavin, 3355-3364
Lyandres, Yulian Semenovich,
    3365-3370
Lyle-Smythe, Alan, 3371-3393
Lynn, Margaret, pseud. *See*
    Battye, Gladys S.
Lyon, Bentley, 3394
Lyons, Nan and Ivan, 3395
Lypsyte, Robert, 3396

MacAlister, Ian, 3397-3400
McBain, Ed, pseud. *See* Hunter,
    Evan
MacBeth, George, 3401
McBriarty, Douglas, 3402
McCall, Anthony, pseud. *See*
    Kane, Henry
McCammon, Robert R., 3403
McCarry, Charles, 3404-3409
McCarthy, John [Shaun] L.,
    3410-3426
McCarthy, Mary, 3427
McCarthy, Wilson, 3428-3429
McClure, James, 3430-3431

McCombs, Philip A., 3029
McCormick, Donald, 3432
McCrum, Robert, 3433
McCulley, Johnston, 162
McCurtin, Peter, 3434-3440
McCutchan, Philip, 3441-3498
McDaniel, David, 3499-3504
McDonnel, Gordon, 3505-3506
MacEoin, Denis, 3507-3512
McEwan, Ian, 3513
McGarrity, Mark, 3514
McGarvey, Robert, 3515-3518
McGerr, Patricia, 3519-3520
McGill, Gordon, 3521
McGivern, William P., 3522-3527
McGovern, James, 3528
MacInnes, Helen, 3529-3547
MacIntyre, John T., 163
McKay, Alistair M., 3548
McKay, Lewis H., 3549
McKay, Randle, 164
McKelway, St. Clair, 3550
McKenna, Marthe, 165-172,
    3551-3556
MacKenzie, Compton, 173, 3557
MacKenzie, Donald, 3558-3563
McKeon, John J., 3564
MacKinnon, Alan, 3565-3568
MacKinnon, Colin, 3569
MacKintosh, Ian, 3570-3579
McLachlan, Ian, 3580
McLartz, Nancy, 3581
Maclean, Alistair, 3582-3611
McLean, Robinson, 3612
McLeave, Hugh, 3613-3616
MacLeish, Rod, 3617
MacLeod, Robert, pseud. *See*
    Knox, Bill
McNamara, Michael, 3618-3619
Macnee, Patrick, 3620-3621
MacNeil, Duncan, pseud. *See*
    McCutchan, Philip

MacNeil, Neil, pseud. *See*
　Ballard, Willis T.
McNeile, Herman C., 174-186
McNeilly, Wilfred, 3622
MacPherson, Malcolm, 3623-3624
McQuay, Mike, 3625
McQuinn, Donald E., 3626-3627
McShane, Mark, 3628-3642
McVean, James, 3643
Mace, David K., 3644-3647
Mackie, John, pseud. *See*
　Levinson, Leonard
Maddock, Larry, 3648-3650
Maddock, Stephen, pseud. *See*
　Walsh, J.M.
Madsen, David, 3651
Maeston, Edward, 3652
Maggio, Joe, 3653-3655
Magowan, Ronald, 3656
Mailer, Norman, 3657
Mair, George B., 3658-3668
Malashenko, Aleksai, 3669
Malleson, Lucy B., 3670
Mallory, Drew, pseud. *See*
　Garfield, Brian
Maloney, Mark, 3671-3673
Manchester, William R., 3674
Mandell, Mark, 3675-3677
Mandell-Essington, Francis, 187-
　190
Mann, Jessica, 3678-3682
Mann, Patrick, 3683
Mann, Paul J., 3684-3685
Mannin, Ethel E., 3686
Manning, Adelaide F. O., 3687-
　3711
Manor, Peter, 1508-1509
Marcus, Martin, 3712
Marchetti, Victor, 3713
Marcinko, Richard, 3714
Marin, A. C., pseud. *See*
　Coppel, Alfred

Mariner, David, pseud. *See*
　Smith, David M.
Mark, Ted, pseud. *See* Gottfried,
　Theodore M.
Markham, Robert, pseud. *See*
　Amis, Kingsley
Markstein, George, 3715-3721
Marlin, Henry, pseud. *See*
　Gigga, Kenneth
Marlowe, Dan J., 3722-3732
Marlowe, Derek, 3733
Marlowe, Hugh, pseud. *See*
　Patterson, Harry
Marlowe, Stephen, pseud. *See*
　Lesser, Milton A.
Marquand, John P., 191-194,
　3734-3735
Marsh, James J., 3736
Marshall, Bruce, 3737
Marshall, Joseph R., 3738
Martin, Dwight, 3739
Martin, Ian K., 3740-3742
Martin, Robert B., 3743-3744
Martin, Trevor, 3745
Marton, George, 3746-3747
Mason, Alfred E. W., 195-196
Mason, Colin, 3748
Mason, Francis Van Wyck, 197-
　212, 3749-3759
Mason, Michael, 3760
Mason, Richard, 3761
Mason, Robert, 3762
Mason, William, 3763
Masterman, John, 213-214, 3764
Masters, John, 3765-3767
Masterson, Whit, pseud. *See*
　Wade, Robert and Bill Miller
Masterton, Graham, 3768
Mather, Arthur, 3769-3773
Mather, Berkeley, pseud. *See*
　Davies, John E. W.

Matheson, Hugh, pseud. *See*
    MacKay, Lewis H.
Maugham, Robert C. R., 3774
Maugham, W. Somerset, 215,
    3775
Maxfield, Henry, 3776
Maxim, John R., 3777-3781
Maxwell, A. E., 3782
Maxwell, Kurt, 3783
May, Peter, 3784
Mayer, Rob, 3785-3786
Mayo, James, pseud. *See*
    Coulter, Stephen
Meade, Everard, 3787
Meigs, Henry, pseud., 3788
Meiring, Desmond, 3789-3790
Meissner, Hans, 3791
Melchior, Ib, 3792-3800
Meldrum, James, pseud. *See*
    Broxholme, John F.
Meray, Tibor, 3747
Mercer, Charles E., 3801
Merek, Jack, 3802-3803
Merrick, Gordon, 3804-3805
Merrick, William, 3806-3807
Merrill, P. J., pseud. *See* Roth,
    Holly
Messman, Jon, 3808-3819
Meyers, Martin, 3820
Michaels, Bill, 4100
Michaels, Philip, pseud. *See* van
    Rjndt, Philippe
Michener, James A., 3821
Miehe, Ulf, 3822-3823
Mikes, George, 3824
Miles, John, 3825
Miller, Beulah M., 3826
Miller, Bill, 5450-5451
Miller, Helen T., 3827
Miller, Rex, 3828
Mills, James, 3829-3831
Mills, Osmington, 3832

Milne, John, 3833
Milton, David, 3834
Milton, Joseph, 3835-3842
Milton, Nancy, 3843
Minick, Michael, 3844
Minsky, Marvin, 2499
Mitchell, James, 3845-3858
Mochan, Ben, 3859
Moffat, James, 3860-3862
Molloy, Michael J., 3863-3865
Monsarrat, Nicholas, 3866
Monteleleone, Thomas F., 3867-
    3869
Montelheit, Hubert, 3870-3876
Montross, David, pseud. *See*
    Backus, Jean L.
Moody, John, 3877
Moody, Susan, 3878
Moorcock, Michael, 3879-3881
Moore, Allen, 2240-2243
Moore, Brian, 3882
Moore, Robert L., Jr., 3883-3886
Moore, Robin, pseud. *See*
    Moore, Robert L., Jr.
Morgan, Allan, 3887-3888
Morgan, Brian S., 3889
Morgenstern, Joseph, 3890
Morgulas, Jerrold, 3891-3892
Morrell, David, 3893-3900
Morris, Jean, 3901-3902
Morris, John, pseud. *See* Hearne,
    John and Morris Cargill
Morris, M. E., 3903-3906
Morrows, Susan, 3907
Morton, Anthony, pseud. *See*
    Creasey, John
Moskowitz, Sam, ed., 1811
Mosley, Nicholas, 3908
Moss, Robert, 1592-1593, 3909-
    3914
Moyes, Patricia, 3915
Muir, Douglas, 3916-3919

Mullane, Mike, 3920
Mullin, Christopher J., 3921-3923
Mullally, Frederick, 3924
Mundy, Talbot, pseud. *See*
  Gribbon, William L.
Munro, James, pseud. *See*
  Mitchell, James
Murakami, Haruki, 3925
Mure, David W., 3926
Murphy, Christopher, 3927
Murphy, James, 3928
Murphy, John, pseud. *See*
  Grady, Ronan C., Jr.
Murphy, Walter F., 3929
Murphy, Warren, 3930-3931,
  4771-4815
Murphy, Warren, co-author. *See*
  Sapir, Richard
Murray, William H., 3932
Myers, Paul, 3933-3938
Mykel, A. W., 3939-3941

Nabarro, Derrick, 3942
Nance, John J., 3943
Napier, Geoffrey, 3944
Nash, N. Richard, 3945
Nason, Leonard H., 3946
Nathan, Robert Stuart, 3947
Nathanson, E. M., 3948-3949
Nazarian, Barry, 3950
Neely, Richard, 3951
Nelson, Walter, 3952-3953
Nessen, Ron, 3954
Nevins, Francis M., 2625
New, Clarence H., 216
Newman, Bernard, 217-230,
  3955-3989
Neznanskii, Fridrikh, 5326
Nichols, Peter, 3990
Nicolaysen, Bruce, 3991
Nicole, Christopher, 3992-4018

Nichols, Leigh, 4019
Nicholson, Michael, 4020
Niesewand, Peter, 4021-4024
Nixon, Alan, 4025
Nixon, William, 4026
Noel, Sterling, 4027-4028
Nolan, Frederick W., 4029-4034
Nordhoff, James, 4035
North, Anthony, 4036
Northcott, Nancy, 4442
Null, Gary, 4037-4038

O'Brian, Patrick, 4039-4042
O'Brien, Frank J., 4043
O'Brien, Robert C., pseud. *See*
  Conly, Robert L.
O'Brine, Padraic Manning, 4044-
  4046
Obstfeld, Raymond, 4047-4048
O'Connor, Brian, 4049
O'Connor, Richard, 4050-4052
Odell, William C., 4053
O'Donnell, Peter, 4054-4065
Offutt, Andrew, 4066
Ogilvie, Charlton, Jr., 4067
Ognall, Leopold H., 4068
O'Hara, Kenneth, pseud. *See*
  Morris, Jean
O'Keefe, Bernard J., 4069
Olcott, Anthony, 4070-4073
Olson, Selma, 4074
O'Malley, Mary D., 4075-4081
O'Malley, Patrick, 4082-4088
O'Neil, Kerry, 4089
O'Neill, Edward A., 4090
O'Neill, Frank, pseud., 4091-
  4093
O'Neill, Will, 4094
"Operator 1384," pseud. *See*
  Harvey, John H.

Oppenheim, E. Phillips, 231-282,
    4095-4096
Oram, John, 4097
Oran, Dan, 4098
Orczy, Emmuska Baroness, 283-
    294
Orde, Lewis, 4099-4100
Ordway, Peter, 4101
O'Reilly, Victor, 4102
Orgill, Douglas, 4103
Orvis, Kenneth, pseud. *See*
    Lemieux, Kenneth
Orwell, George, 4104
Osborn, David, 4105-4106
Osmond, Andrew, 2775, 2778,
    4107
Ostrovsky, Victor, 4108
O'Toole, George. 4109-4111
Ovalov, Lev S., 4112
Overguard, William, 4113
Owen, Richard, 4114

Pace, Eric, 4115-4117
Page, Martin, 4118
Palmer, John Leslie, 295-310,
    4119-4122
Pape, Gordon, 4123-4124
Papich, Margery W., 5754
Parker, Lee, 4125-4127
Parker, Maude, 4128-4129
Parker, Robert B., 4130
Parry, David, 4131
Parry, Hugh J., 4132
Patrick, William, 4133
Patterson, Harry [Henry], 4134-
    4186
Patterson, James, 4187-4189
Pattinson, James, 4190
Paul, Celeste, 4191
Paul, F. W., pseud. *See*
    Fairman, Paul W.

Paul, William, 4192
Paull, Jessyca, pseud. *See*
    Perceval, Julia and
    Roseaylmer Burger
Paulsen, Gary, 4193
Payne, Donald G., 4194
Payne, Laurence R., 4195-4196,
    4217
Payne, Ronald, 4197
Pearce, Michael, 4198-4201
Pearl, Jack, 4202-4203
Pearson, John, 4204
Pearson, Ridley, 4205-4206
Pearson, Ryne Douglas, 4207
Peart, Robert, 4208
Pedler, John B. F., 4209-4210
Peel, Colin D., 4211-4216
Pendleton, Don, house pseud.
    See Garside, Jack and Don
    Pendleton
Pendleton, Don, 4217-4222
Pendower, Jacques, 4223-4250
Pentecost, Hugh, pseud. *See*
    Philips, Judson P.
Pepper, Dan, 4251
Perakh, Mark, 4252
Perceval, Julia, 4253-4255
Perdue, Lewis, 4256
Perry, Ritchie, 4257-4272
Perry, Will, 4273
Persico, Joseph E., 4274
Peters, Brian, pseud. *See* George,
    Peter B.
Peters, Elizabeth, 4275
Peters, Ellis, 4276
Peters, Ludovic, pseud. *See*
    Brent, Peter
Peters, Ralph, 4277-4280
Peters, Stephen, 4281
Peterson, Bernard, 4282
Peterson, Michael, 4283
Peterson, Paul, 4284-4287

Petievich, Gerald, 4288
Pettit, Mike, 4289
Philips, Judson P., 4290-4291
Phillifent, John T., 4292-4294
Phillips, David Atlee, 4295
Phillips, James A., 4296-4317
Phillips, Mark, 4318
Picard, Sam, 4319-4321
Pickering, Paul, 4322-4323
Pickering, R. E., 4324
Pierce, Noel, 4325
Pierson, Eleanor, 4326
Pietrkiewicz, Jerzy, 4327
Pincher, Chapman, 4328-4333
Pineiro, R. J., 4334
Piper, H. Beam, 3070
Pitts, Denis, 4335-4336
Plum, Jennifer, pseud. *See*
　　Kurland, Michael
Poe, Edgar Allan, 311
Pogue, Bill, 827
Pogue, David, 4337
Pohl, Frederick, 4338
Pollard, Alfred O., 4339-4357
Pollitz, Edward A., 4358
Pollock, Daniel, 4359-4360
Pollock, J. C., 4361-4364
Ponthier, François, 4365
Porter, Joyce, 4366-4377
Portway, Christopher, 4378-4379
Posey, Carl A., 4380-4383
Posner, Gerald L., 4384
Post, Melville D., 312
Powell, Edward A., 313
Powell, Richard P., 4385
Poyer, D. C., 4386
Poyer, David, 4387-4390
Poyer, Joe, 4391-4400
Praeger, J. Simon, 4401
Price, Anthony, 4402-4421
Price, John-Allen, 4422-4426
Priestley, John B., 4427-4429

Proffitt, Nicholas, 4430-4431
Prokosch, Frederic, 4432
Pronzini, Bill, 4433
Proud, Franklin M., 4434
Puccetti, Roland, 4435
Purdue, Lewis, 4436-4437

Q., John, pseud. *See* Quirk, John
　　E.
Quammen, David, 4438-4439
Quayle, Anthony, 4440-4441
Quayle, Marilyn T., 4442
Quigley, John, 4443-4444
Quinn, Derry, 4445
Quinn, Jake, 4446-4448
Quinn, John, pseud. *See*
　　Rodriguez, Dennis
Quinn, Simon, pseud. *See* Smith,
　　Martin C.
Quinnell, A. J., pseud., 4449-
　　4455
Quirk, John E., 4456-4458

Rabe, Peter, 4459-4464
Rae, Hugh C., 4465
Raine, Richard, pseud. *See*
　　Sawkins, Raymond H.
Rame, David, pseud. *See* Divine,
　　Arthur D.
Ramrus, Al, 4466
Ramsey, Eric, pseud. *See*
　　Hagberg, David
Randall, John D., 4467-4468
Randle, Kevin D., 4469
Rankin, Ian James, 4470
Raphael, Rick, 4471
Rascovich, Mark, 4472
Rathbone, Julian, 4473-4490
Raven, Simon, 4491
Ray, Robert J., 4492

Raymond, René B., 4493-4495

Rayner, William, 4496

Redgate, John, pseud. *See*
    Kennedy, Adam

Reed, Eliot, pseud. *See* Ambler,
    Eric and Charles Rodda

Reeman, Douglas, 4497

Reeve, Arthur B., 314-315

Reid, James, 4498

Reiffel, Leonard, 4499

Reiss, Bob, 4500-4506

Reiss, Curt, 4507

Renfroe, Martha K., 4508

Revere, Justin D., 4509-4512

Reynolds, Howard, 4513

Reynolds, Philip, 4514

Rhodes, Russell, 4515

Richards, Clay, pseud. *See*
    Crossen, Kendell F.

Richards, David, 4516-4517

Richards, Paul, house pseud. *See*
    Streib, Dan

Richmond, Donald, 4518

Rico, Don, 4519-4520

Rider, Rick, 4521

Ritner, Peter, 4522

Rivers, Gayle, 4523-4525

Robbins, Harold, 4526

Roberts, James H., pseud. *See*
    Duncan, Robert L.

Roberts, Jan, 4527

Roberts, Katherine E., 4528-4529

Roberts, Thomas A., 4530

Robertson, Charles, 4531-4535

Robertson, Colin, 4536-4539

Robinson, Derek, 4540-4543

Robinson, Frank M., 4859-4860

Robson, Dirk, pseud. *See*
    Robinson, Derek

Roderick, Robert, 4544

Rodriguez, Dennis, 4545-4546

Rogers, Barbara, 4547

Rogers, Ray M., 4548

Rohmer, Sax, pseud. *See* Ward,
    Arthur Sarsfield

Rohrbach, Peter T., 4549-4550

Roman, Eric, 4551

Romano, Deane, 4552

Roos, Audrey and William, 4553

Roosevelt, Elliott, 4554-4562

Rooth, Anne R., 4563

Rosenberg, Robert, 4564

Rosenberger, Joseph, 4565-4628

Rosenblum, Robert, 4629

Rosenhaupt, Hans, 4630

Rosner, Joseph, 4631

Ross, Angus, pseud. *See* Gigga,
    Kenneth

Ross, Frank, pseud., 4632-4636

Ross, Hal, 4637

Ross, Ian, pseud. *See* Rossman,
    John F.

Ross, Philip, 4638-4643

Ross, Regina, 4644

Rossiter, John, 4645-4646

Rossman, John F., 4647-4648

Rostand, Robert, pseud. *See*
    Hopkins, Robert S.

Rosten, Leo, 4649

Roth, Holly, 4650-4659

Roth, Philip, 4660

Rothberg, Abraham, 4661-4663

Rothwell, Henry T., 4664-4668

Rouch, James, 4669-4671

Rovin, Jeff, 4672

Rowan, Hester, 4673

Rowe, James N., 4674

Rowe, John, 4675-4677

Royce, Kenneth, pseud. *See*
    Gandley, Kenneth Royce

Rubinstein, Paul, 5192

Rumanes, George N., 4678

Rumbold-Gibbs, Henry St. John
    Clair, 4679-4720

Runyon, Poke, 4721-4722
Ruse, Gary A., 4723
Russell, A. J., 4724
Russell, Martin, 4725
Ryan, Charles, 4726-4727
Ryck, Francis, 4728-4730
Rydberg, Louis and Ernie, 4731
Ryder, Jonathan, pseud. *See*
    Ludlum, Robert

Sabatini, Rafael, 316
Saberhagen, Fred, 4732
Sachar, Howard, 4733
Sadler, Barry, 4734-4736
Sager, Gordon, 4737
Sagola, Mario, 4738
St. George, Geoffrey, 4739
St. Germain, Gregory, pseud.
    See Wallman, Jeffrey M.
St. James, Ian, 4740
St. John, David, pseud. *See*
    Hunt, E. Howard
St. John, Robert, 4741
Sale, Richard, 4742
Salinger, Pierre, 4743-4746
Salisbury, Harrison E., 4747
Sandberg, Berent, pseud. *See*
    Sandberg, Peter Lars
Sandberg, Peter Lars, 4748-4750
Sanders, Bruce, 4751-4753
Sanders, Buck, pseud. *See*
    Frentzen, Jeffrey
Sanders, Lawrence, 4754-4758
Sanders, Leonard, 4759-4760
Sandulescu, Jacques, 4761
Sanford, Harry, 3126
Sangster, James ("Jimmy"), 4762-
    4768
Santesson, Hans S., ed., 4769
Saperstein, David, 4770
Sapir, Richard, 4771-4815

"Sapper," pseud. *See* McNeile,
    Herman C.
Sargent, Patricia, 4816
Sariola, Mauri, 4817-4818
Saul, John R., 4820
Saunders, Hiliary Aiden St.
    George, 295-310, 4119-4122
Sauter, Eric, 4821-4824
Savage, Ian, pseud. *See* Gigga,
    Kenneth
Savarin, Julian Jay, 4825-4832
Savchenko, Vladimir, 4833
Sawkins, Raymond H., 4834-4851
Sayer, Walter W., 317-322
Schaill, William S., 4852
Schiff, Barry, 4853
Scholefield, Alan, 4854-4855
Schurmacher, Emile C., ed., 4856
Schutz, Benjamin M., 4857
Schwartz, Alan, 4858
Scortia, Thomas N., 4859-4860
Scott, Chris, 4861
Scott, Don, 4862
Scott, Douglas, 4863-4864
Scott, Gavin, 4865-4866
Scott, Hardiman, 4867-4871
Scott, John D., 4872
Scott, John R., 323
Scott, Justin, 4873-4874
Scott, Leonard B., 4875
Scott, Reginald T. M., 324-326
Scott, Robert L., 4876
Scott, Virgil, 4877-4878
Seaman, Donald, 4879-4883
Searls, Hank, 4884-4885
Sebastian, Tim, 4886-4890
Sela, Owen, 4891-4896
Sellers, Connie L., Jr., 4897-4898
Semenov, Julian S., pseud. *See*
    Lyandres, Yulian Semenovich
Semprun, Jorgé, 4899-4900
Sentjurc, Igor, 4901

Serling, Robert, 4902
Seth, Ronald, 4903-4906
Setlowe, Frank, 4907
Seton, Graham, pseud. *See*
    Hutchinson, Graham S.
Seward, Jack, 4908-4911
Seymour, Gerald, 4912-4925
Shabtai, Sabi H., 4926
Shagan, Steve, 4927-4931
Shakar, David, 4932
Shakespeare, Brian, 1637
Shakespeare, L. M. [L.
    Marguerite], 4933-4935
Shaner, John, 4466
Shapiro, Lionel, 4936
Sharp, Marilyn, 4937-4939
Shaw, Bynum, 4940-4942
Shaw, Irwin, 4943
Sheckley, Robert, 4944-4946
Shedley, Ethan I., 4947
Sheehan, Edward R. F., 4948
Sheers, James C., 4949
Sheffield, Charles, 4950
Sheldon, Sidney, 4951
Shepherd, Michael, pseud. *See*
    Ludlum, Robert
Sheridan, Elsie L., 4952
Sherlock, John, 4953
Sherman, Dan[iel] M., 4954-4961
Sherwood, John, 4962-4967
Shreve, L. G. [Levin Gale], 4968
Shub, Joyce L., 4969
Siegrist, Robert R., 4970
Sigel, Efrem, 4971
Silone, Ignazio, 4972
Simmel, Johannes Mario, 4973-
    4979
Simmons, Diane, 4980
Simmons, Geoffrey, 4981
Simmons, Mary K., 4982
Simon, Roger L., 4983
Simpson, George E., 4984-4986

Simpson, Howard R., 4987-4988
Sinclair, Michael, 4989-4992
Sinclair, Upton B., 4993-4999
Singer, Sally M., 5000
Siodmak, Curt, 5001
Sjowall, Maj, 5474-5475
Skeggs, Douglas, 5002-5004
Slager, Nigel, 5005
Slappey, Sterling, 5006
Slater, Humphrey, 5007
Slater, Ian, 5008
Slater, Nigel, 5009
Slattery, Jesse, 5010
Slaughter, Frank G., 5011
Smith, Colin, 5012
Smith, David M., 5013-5014
Smith, Don, 5015-5036
Smith, Donna, 5037
Smith, Graham N., 5037
Smith, Kate Nolte, 5038
Smith, Lou, 5039-5041
Smith, Martin Cruz, 5042-5051
Smith, Murray, 5052
Smith, Robert A., 5053
Smith, Robert C., 5054-5055
Smith, Terence L., 5056
Smith, Wilbur A., 5057-5059
Smolonsky, Marc, 5060
Snelling, Laurence, 5061-5062
Snow, C. P., 5063
Snyder, Gene, 5064-5065
Sohmer, Steve, 5066-5067
Solzhenitsyn, Aleksandr I., 5068
Southcott, Audley, 5069
Southwell, Samuel, 5070
Spain, Peter, 5071
Spang, Michael Grundt, 5072
Spark, Muriel, 5073
Spencer, D. J., 5074
Spencer, Ross H., 5075-5083
Spetz, Steven, 5084

Spicer, William Michael, 5085-5090

Spike, Paul, 5092

Spillane, Frank M., 5093-5100

Spillane, Mickey, pseud. *See* Spillane, Frank M.

Spinelli, Marcos, 5101

Spinrad, Norman, 5102

Stackleborg, Gene, 5103

Stackman, Arthur, 5104

Stacy, Ryder, 5105-5107

Stagg, Delano, 5108

Stahl, Norman, 5109

Stanford, Alfred, 5110

Stanley, Michael, 5111

Stanley, William, 5112

Stansfeld, Anthony, 3258

Stanton, Ken, pseud. *See* Stokes, Manning Lee

Stanwood, Donald, 5113

Stapp, Robert, 5114

Stark, Richard, pseud. *See* Westlake, Donald E.

Starrett, Vincent, ed., 5115

Steel, Kurt, pseud. *See* Kagley, Rudolf

Stein, Aaron, M., 5116

Stein, Benjamin J., 5117-5118

Stein, Sol, 5119-5120

Stella, Charles, 5121

Stephens, Edward, 5122

Stern, Richard M., 5123-5126

Stevens, Carl, pseud. *See* Obstfeld, Raymond

Stevens, David, 5127

Stevenson, Anne, 5128-5129

Stevenson, Dorothy E., 5130

Stevenson, John, 5131-5132

Stevenson, William, 5133-5135

Stewart, Edward, 5136

Stewart, John I. M. [Innes Mackintosh], 5137-5138

Stewart, Kerry, 5139

Stimson, Robert G., 5140

Stine, Hank, 5141

Stivers, pseud. *See* Pendleton, Don and Laurence R. Payne

Stokes, Donald H., 5142

Stokes, Manning Lee, 5143-5154

Stone, David, 5155

Stone, Robert, 5156

Stone, Scott, 5157

Stone, Todd, 5158

Stovall, Walter, 5159

Stratton, Thomas, pseud. *See* DeWeese, Thomas G. and Robert S. Coulson

Street, Bradford, 5160

Streib, Dan, 5161-5164

Streiber, Whitley, 5165

Stringer, Arthur J. A., 327

Strong, Michael, 5166

Stuart, Anthony, pseud., 5167-5172

Stuart, Ian, pseud. *See* Maclean, Alistair

Stuart, Warren, 5173

Sugar, Andrew, 5174-5177

Suhl, Yuri, 5178

Sullivan, Tim, 5179

Sulzberger, C. L., 5180

Swift, Bryan, house pseud. *See* Knott, Will C. and Arthur Wise

Swiggett, Howard, 5181-5182

Symons, Julian, 5183-5184

Szulc, Tad, 5185

Tack, Alfred, 5186

"Taffrail," pseud. *See* Dorling, Henry T.

Talmy, Shel, 5187

Tanenbaum, Robert K., 5188-
5189
Tanner, Mack, 5190
Tanous, Peter, 5191-5192
Tapply, William G., 5193
Tarrant, John, pseud. *See*
Egleton, Clive
Tasker, Peter, 5194
Taylor, Anthony, 5195
Taylor, Charles D., 5196-5205
Taylor, Ray W., 5206
Taylor, Thomas, 5207
Taylor, Walker, 5208
Teilhet, Darwin L., 328, 5209-
5214
Teilhet, Hildegarde, 5210, 5215
Telfair, Richard, 5216-5220
Templeton, Charles, 5221
Terlouw, Jan, 5222
Terman, Douglas, 5223-5226
Thayer, Charles W., 5227-5228
Thayer, James Stewart, 5229-5234
Theiner, George, 933-934
Theroux, Paul, 5235
Thomas, Craig, 5236-5250
Thomas, Gordon, 5251
Thomas, Leslie, 5252
Thomas, Michael M., 5253-5254
Thomas, Paul, 5255
Thomas, Ross, 5256-5276
Thomey, Tedd, 5277
Thompson, Anne A., 5278-5279
Thompson, Arthur L. B., 5280-
5289
Thompson, David, 5290
Thompson, Stephen, 5291
Thompson, Steven L., 832, 5292-
5294
Thomson, June, 5295
Thornbury, Ethel M., 5296
Thorne, E. P., 5297-5307
Thorp, Duncan, 5308

Thorp, Roderick, 5309
Thurburn, Rose, 5310
Thurman, Steve, 5311
Thurston, Temple, 329
Tickell, Jerrard, 5312-5314
Tiger, John, pseud. *See* Wager,
Walter
Tillman, Barrett, 5315-5317
Tine, Robert, 5318
Tippette, Giles, 5319
Tobino, Mario, 5320
Tonkin, Peter, 5321-5322
Topol, Allan, 5323
Topol, Edward, 5324-5326
Torkelson, Layne, 5754
Torr, Dominic, pseud. *See*
Pedler, John B. F.
Toulmin, June, 5327
Tracy, Don, 5328
Tralins, Bob, 5329-5330
Tranter, Nigel, pseud. *See*
Tredgold, Nye
Tredgold, Nye, 5331-5332
Tregaskis, Richard, 5333
Trenhaile, John, 5334-5342
Trevanian, pseud. *See* Whitaker,
Rodney
Trevor, Elleston, 5343-5361
Trevor, James, 5362-5364
Trew, Antony, 5365-5369
Trotter, William R., 5370
Truman, Margaret, 5371-5378
Tuccile, Jerome, 5379
Tucker, Alan J., 5380-5384
Tucker, John Bartholomew, 5385
Tucker, Wilson, 5386-5387
Tute, Warren, 5388-5393
Tyler, Alison, 5394-5396
Tyler, W. T., pseud. *See*
Hamrick, Samuel J.
Tyson, John A., 330

Underwood, Michael, pseud. *See* Evelyn, John M.
Unkeefer, Duane, 5397
Upton, Robert, 5398
Upward, Allen, 331-332
Uris, Leon, 5399-5402
Usher, Frank H., 5403
Ustinov, Peter, 5404

Vacha, Robert, 5405-5406
Vailland, Roger, 5407
Valentine, Douglas, pseud. *See* Williams, Valentine
Valin, Jonathan, 5408
Vallance, Douglas, 5409
Vance, Charles C., 5410
Vance, Louis J., 333
Van der Post, Laurens, 5411
Van Greenway, Peter, 5412
Vanhee, Gregory G., 5413-5414
Van Lustbader, Eric, 5415-5420
Van Oradell, John, 5421
Van Rjndt, Philippe, 5422-5427
Veraldi, Gabriel, 5428
Vicas, Victor, 5429
Vidal, Gore, 5430-5433
Von Elsner, Don, 5434-5439
Vonnegut, Kurt, 5440-5442
Vorhies, John R., 5443

Wacht, Leo, 5444
Waddell, Martin, 5445-5448
Wade, Jonathan, 5449
Wade, Robert, 5450-5451
Wager, Walter, 5452-5471
Wagner, Geoffrey A., 5472
Wahloo, Per, 5473-5475
Wahloo, Peter, pseud. *See* Wahloo, Per
Wakeman, Frederick, 5476

Walker, David Esdaile, 5477-5478
Walker, Martin, 5479
Walker, Max, 5480-5481
Wallace, Edgar, 334-336
Wallace, Irving, 5482-5486
Walkins, Leslie, 5487
Wallis, Arthur J., 5488
Wallman, Jeffrey M., 5489-5492
Walsh, J. M. [James Morgan], 337-345, 5493-5502
Walsh, Thomas F. M., 5503
Ward, Arthur Sarsfield, 346-359, 5504-5513
Ward-Thomas, Evelyn B.P., 5514-5524
Ware, Wallace, 5525
Warfield, Gallatin, 5526
Warren, Christopher, 5527
Warwick, Francis A., 5528
Washburn, Mark, 5529-5530
Watkins, Leslie, 5531
Watson, Colin, 5532
Watson, Geoffrey, 5533
Watson, Ian, 5534
Waugh, Alec, 5535
Waugh, Evelyn, 5536-5538
Wayland, Patrick, pseud. *See* O'Connor, Richard
Weaver, Graham, 5539-5540
Webb, Sharon, 5541
Weber, Janice, 5542
Weber, Joe, 5543-5546
Weber, Ron, 5547-5548
Weeks, William R., 5549
Weil, Barry, 5550
Weinstein, Sol, 5551-5554
Weisman, John, 3714, 5555
Weismiller, Edward, 5556
Welcome, John, pseud. *See* Brennan, John
Wentworth, Patricia, 5557

West, Elliot, 5558-5559
West, Morris L., 5560-5566
West-Watson, Keith Campbell,
    5567-5572
Westbrook, Robert, 5573
Westheimer, David, 5574-5576
Westlake, Donald E., 5577-5584
Weston, Garnett, 5585
Weverka, Robert, 5586
Whaley, Bart, 3068
Wheatley, Dennis, 360-362, 5587-
    5610
Wheeler, Harvey, 932
Wheeler, Keith, 5611
Wheeler, Paul, 5612
Whitaker, Rodney, 5613-5615
White, Alan, 5616-5622
White, Ethel L., 363
White, James D., 5623
White, James P., 4563
White, John M., 5624-5625
White, Lionel, 5626
White, Osmar, 5627
White, Robin A., 5628-5630
White, Steve, pseud. *See*
    McGarvey, Robert
White, Stewart E., 364
White, Stuart, 5631
Whiting, Charles, 5632
Whittington, Henry, 5633
Wilcox, Harry, 5634-5642
Wijkmark, Carl-Henning, 5643
Wilden, Theodore, 5644-5645
Wilhelm, Kate, 5646
Wilkinson, Burke, 5647
Williams, Alan, 5648-5652
Williams, Eric, 5653-5654
Williams, Gilbert M., 5655-5657
Williams, Jay, 5658
Williams, Valentine, 365-375,
    5659
Williamson, Tony, 5660-5663

Willis, Anthony A., 5664
Willis, Edward [Ted] Henry,
    5665-5667
Willis, Maude, pseud. *See*
    Lottman, Eileen
Wills, Maralys, 5668
Wilson, John A. B., 5669-5670
Wilson, Mitchell A., 5671
Wiltse, David, 5672
Winch, Arden, 5673
Winchester, Jack, 5674
Winder, Robert, 5675
Wingate, John, 5676-5679
Winner, Percy, 5680
Winsor, Diana, 5681-5682
Winspear, Violet, 5683
Winston, Peter, 5684-5688
Winters, Jon, pseud. *See* Cross,
    Gilbert B.
Winterton, Paul, 5689-5720
Winton, John, 5721
Winward, Walter, 5722-5725
Winwood, John, ed., 5726
Wise, Arthur, 5727-5728
Wise, David, 5729-5730
Wiseman, Thomas, 5731-5732
Withrow, Patrick, 4131
Wittman, George, 5733
Wohl, Burton, 5734
Wohl, James P., 5735
Wolf, S. K. [Sarah], 5736-5737
Wolfe, Michael, pseud. *See*
    Williams, Gilbert M.
Wolk, George, 5738
Wood, Christopher, 5739
Wood, James, 5740-5744
Woodhouse, Martin, 5745-5750
Woods, Stuart, 5751-5752
Woods, William H., 5753
Woolf, Marion, 5754
Wormser, Richard, 5755

Wren, M. K., pseud. *See*
 Renfroe, Martha K.
Wright, Glover, 5756-5758
Wright, William Talboy, 5759
Wuorio, Eva-Lis, 5760-5761
Wylie, James, 5762
Wylie, Philip, 5763-5764
Wynd, Oswald, 5765-5774

Yates, Alan Geoffrey, 5775-5778
Yates, Brock W., 5779
Yates, Margaret T., 5780
Yerby, Frank, 5781
Yin, Leslie C. B., 376, 5782-
 5787
Yorch, Ruth L., 5788
York, Andrew, pseud. *See*
 Nicole, Christopher
Young, Edward P., 5789
Yurick, Sol, 5790

Zachary, Hugh, 5791-5796
Zarubica, Mladin, 5797-5798
Zeno, pseud., 5799-5801
Zerwick, Chloë, 5802
Zezza, Carlo, 5803
Zilinsky, Ursula, 5804
Zimmerman, R. D. [Robert
 Dingwall], 5805-5807

Title Index

THE CITATIONS IN this index are keyed by entry numbers to the references in both Parts of the guide. In those cases where titles are identical, they are arranged in order by author.

The 9th Directive, 5345
17 Ben Gurion, 2628
17th Letter, 1660
19, 2391
27, 1646
30 for Harry, 2705
The '44 Vintage, 4406
58 Minutes, 5453
71 Hours, 3760
The 210 Conspiracy, 3184
330 Park, 1283
10,000 Days, 2050

A-18, 5207
A.R.P. Spy, 4339
Abel/Baker/Charley, 3779
The Aberdeen Conundrum, 2182
The Abolition of Death, 529
Above Suspicion, 3529
Academic Factor, 2360

An Account to Render, 1380
An Accurate Watch, 1691
Aces, 1616
The Achilles Affair, 1542
Act of Mercy, 5288
An Act of War, 1000
Act of War: A Novel of Love and Treason, 4760
Acts of Betrayal, 5341
Acts of Mercy, 4433
The Adjusters: The ABC Affair, 5684
The Adjusters: Assignment to Bahrein, 5685
The Adjusters: Doomsday Vendetta, 5686
The Adjusters: The Glass Cipher, 5687
The Adjusters: The Temple at Ilumquh, 5688
The Adlon Link, 5791

The Admiral's a Spy, 5208
Advance Agent, 1638
*The Adventures of Major Haynes
    (of the Counter Espionage
    Bureau) with Some Additional
    Stories*, 334
*The Adventures of the Albanian
    Avenger*, 317
Advice Limited, 231
Aegean Adventure, 3296
The Aelian Fragment, 694
Affair for the Baron, 1458
The Affair of the Blue Pig, 4086
The Affair of the Bumbling Briton,
    4087
The Affair of Chief Strongheart,
    4082
The Affair of John Donne, 4083
The Affair of Jolie Madame, 4084
The Affair of the Red Mosaic,
    4088
An Affair of Strangers, 1472
The Affair of Swan Lake, 4085
Afghan Intercept, 2136
Afraid in the Dark, 5634
Africana, 2502
After Midnight, 3298
After the Fine Weather, 2199
After the First Death, 1352
After You with the Pistol, 807
Against All Enemies, 1723
Agent Double-Agent, 1047
Agent Extraordinary, 702
*Agent for COMINSEC: The
    Bloody Monday Conspiracy*,
    2524
An Agent in Place (Littell), 3272
Agent in Place (MacInnes), 3530
An Agent Intervenes, 538
Agent of Evil, 2401
Agent of Influence, 377
An Agent on the Other Side, 4109

Agents of Darkness, 564
Agents of Influence, 2454
Agents of Innocence, 2803
Agents of Sympathy, 4091
Aggressor, 1317
Air Apparent, 2078
Air Force One, 1346
Air Force One Is Haunted, 4902
Air Glow Red, 5008
Airburst, 5293
Airship Nine, 785
The Alamut Ambush, 4402
The Alamut Bomb, 4403
The Alarming Clock, 598
Alaska Deception, 2137
The Alchemist, 2212
The Aleph Solution, 1957
The Algonquin Project, 4029
Alias Man, 5380
Alias the Lone Wolf, 333
Alias Uncle Hugo, 3687
All Exits Barred, 4378
All Men Are Lonely Now, 5280
All My Enemies, 689
All Our Tomorrows, 463
All Over But the Shooting, 4385
All Stations to Malta, 2359
All That Glitters, 3688
The All-Purpose Bodies, 3454
The Allah Conspiracy, 5527
Alligator, 1187
Almost Midnight, 987
Along Came a Spider, 4189
Alpha Bug, 3906
The Alpha Deception, 3112
Alpha Kat, 3326
The Alpha List (Allbeury), 464
The Alpha List (Anderson), 530
Alpine Encounter, 4673
Alpine Gambit, 1369
Altitude Zero, 4884
Always a Spy, 1917

Always Kill a Stranger, 1855

The Amateur, 3271

The Amazing Mrs. Pollifax, 942

Amazon, 1048

Amazons, 4647

Ambassador, 3314

The Ambassador and the Spy, 879

The Ambassador's Plot, 1948

Amber Nine, 2079

Ambrose Lavendale, Diplomat, 261

Ambush!, 4469

Ambush at Osirak, 1484

Ambush for a Hunter, 2282

Ambush for Anatol, 4962

The Ambushers, 2408

American Hero, 717

American Nightmare, 5106

The American Princess, 3063

American Reich, 3916

American Sextet, 440

American Surrender, 839

An Amiable Charlatan, 262

Amigo, Amigo, 5281

Among African Sands, 3854

Among the Demons, 3281

Among Those Absent, 3689

The Ampurias Exchange, 2178

Amsterdam, 1049

The Amsterdam Diversion, 2183

Ana Mistral, 4074

Anasazi, 2810

And Next the King, 1050

And the Bullets Were Made of Lead, 5612

And the Undead Sing, 5775

And to My Nephew Albert I Leave the Island What I Won Off Fatty Hagan in a Poker Game, 1924

The Andromeda Assignment, 3250

Angel, Archangel, 1316

Angel Eyes, 5416

Angels in the Snow, 3086

Angels of Death, 4208

Angle of Attack, 5628

The Angry Hills, 5400

The Angry Island, 2051

Ann's Crime--Still Another Adventure of "Secret Service Smith," 324

Anna the Adventuress, 263

The Annihilators, 2432

Another Way of Dying, 5282

The Antagonists, 1241

The Anti-Death League, 525

The Antonov Project, 5365

The Ants of God, 2443

Any War Will Do, 4115

Aphrodite's Cave, 3945

The Apocalypse Brigade, 1332

The Apollo Legacy, 682

Apple Spy in the Sky, 3628

Apple to the Core, 3629

Appointment in Vienna, 518

The Aquanauts: Cold Blue Death, 5143

The Aquanauts: Evil Cargo, 5144

The Aquanauts: Operation Deep Six, 5151

The Aquanauts: Operation Mermaid, 5152

The Aquanauts: Operation Sargasso Secret, 5145

The Aquanauts: Operation Sea Monster, 5146

The Aquanauts: Operation Steelfish, 5153

The Aquanauts: Seek, Strike and Destroy, 5147

The Aquanauts: Stalkers of the Sea, 5148

The Aquanauts: Ten Seconds to Zero, 5149

The Aquanauts: Whirlwind beneath the Sea, 5150
The Aquitaine Progression, 3337
The Arab Plague, 1051
Arabesque, 2677
The Arabian Nightmare, 2821
Arafat Is Next!, 684
Ararat, 2693
Archangel, 4912
The Arena, 1242
Ariel, 757
Ark, 1510
The Armageddon Game (Frey), 2006
The Armageddon Game (Washburn), 5529
Armoured Doves, a Peace Book, 222
Arms and the Spy, 3551
Arms for Adonis, 2841
The Army of Shadows, 2990
Arrival in Suspicion, 4703
Arrows of Desire, 2691
Article 92: Murder-Rape, 960
The Ascent of D-13, 5689
Ashenden: or, The British Agent, 215
The Ashes of Loda, 5690
Ashton Kirk: Secret Agent, 163
The Asian Mantrap, 1052
Ask the Name of the Lion, 495
Asking for It, 1381
Assassin (Anderson), 531
The Assassin (Butterworth), 952
The Assassin (Jepson), 2852
The Assassin Code, 3859
The Assassin Who Gave Up His Gun, 1842
Assassin: Code Name Vulture, 1053
Assassin's Road, 4679
Assassination, 436

The Assassination Brigade, 1054
Assassination Day, 2039
The Assassination Is Set for July 4, 4125
The Assassini, 2174
Assassins (Mosley), 3908
The Assassins (Mullally), 3924
The Assassins (Teilhet), 5210
Assassins and Victims, 768
Assassins Don't Die in Bed, 587
Assault, 2960
Assault on Agathon, 3381
Assault on Aimata, 3380
Assault on England, 1055
Assault on Fellawi, 3382
Assault on Kolchak, 3383
Assault on Loveless, 3371
The Assault on Marvis A., 5109
Assault on Ming, 3384
Assignment Andalusia, 3494
Assignment Basra, 4365
Assignment for a Mercenary, 4987
Assignment Hong Kong, 1530
Assignment in Algeria, 3170
Assignment in Brittany, 3531
Assignment in Guiana, 1395
Assignment in Iraq, 3565
Assignment New York, 3495
Assignment Sydney, 3496
Assignment Tokyo, 1525
Assignment without Glory, 5101
Assignment: Afghan Dragon, 379
Assignment: Amazon Queen, 380
Assignment: Angelina, 381
Assignment: Ankara, 382
Assignment: Argentina, 411
Assignment: Bangkok, 383
Assignment: Black Gold, 384
Assignment: Black Viking, 412
Assignment: Budapest, 385
Assignment: Burma Girl, 386

Assignment: The Cairo Dancers, 387

Assignment: Carlotta Cortez, 388

Assignment: Ceylon, 389

Assignment: Cong Hai Kill, 390

Assignment: Death Ship, 427

Assignment: Find Cherry, 4909

Assignment: The Girl in the Gondola, 391

Assignment: Golden Girl, 392

Assignment: Helene, 393

Assignment: Intercept, 1056

Assignment: Israel, 1057

Assignment: Karachi, 394

Assignment: Lili Lamaris, 413

Assignment: London, 414

Assignment: Lowlands 395

Assignment: Madeleine, 415

Assignment: Malta, 416

Assignment: Maltese Maiden, 417

Assignment: Manchurian Doll, 396

Assignment: Mara Tirana, 418

Assignment: Mermaid, 428

Assignment: Moon Girl, 419

Assignment: New York, 420

Assignment: Nuclear Nude, 397

Assignment: Palermo, 421

Assignment: Peking, 398

Assignment: Quayle Question, 399

Assignment: School for Spies, 422

Assignment: Sea Bird, 423

Assignment: Sheba, 429

Assignment: Silver Scorpion, 400

Assignment: Sorrento Siren, 424

Assignment: Star Stealers, 401

Assignment: Stella Marni, 402

Assignment: Suicide, 403

Assignment: Sulu Sea, 404

Assignment: Sumatra, 405

Assignment: Tahiti, 2075

Assignment: Thirteenth Princess, 431

Assignment: Tiger Devil, 432

Assignment: To Disaster, 406

Assignment: Tokyo, 425

Assignment: Treason, 407

Assignment: Tyrant's Bride, 430

Assignment: Unicorn, 408

Assignment: White Rajah, 409

Assignment: Zoraya, 426

Assignment X: Top Secret, 4856

Assumed Identity, 3893

The Assyrian, 2343

Asterisk Destiny, 765

Aswan, 2561

The Aswan Solution, 4675

At Close Quarters, 4922

At High Risk, 2455

At the Sign of the Sword, 135

Athabasca, 3582

Atlantic Run, 1550

Atoll, 4211

Atomsk, 3266

Atropos, 1571

Attack Alarm, 2438

Attack in the Desert, 2643

The Attack on Vienna, 4025

Australia, 1169

Autumn Heroes, 2040

Autumn Tiger, 3129

Avalanche, 5676

Avalanche Express, 4834

Avenge the Belgrano, 3133

The Avenger, 264

The Avenger Tapes, 5140

The Avengers: The Afrit Affair, 3150

The Avengers: The Dead Duck, 3620

The Avengers: The Deadline, 3621

The Avengers: The Drowned Queen, 3151

The Avengers: The Floating Game, 2119

The Avengers: The Gold Bomb, 3149

The Avengers: Heil Harris, 2120

The Avengers: The Laugh was on Lazarus, 2121

The Avengers: The Magnetic Man, 1515

The Avengers: Moon Express, 1514

The Avengers: · The Passing of Gloria Munday, 2118

Avenging Saint, 376

The Aviators, 981

The Award Espionage Reader, 4769

Axis, 2819

The Axmann Agenda, 4289

Azor, 2566

Azrael, 1572

The Aztec Avenger, 1058

The Back of the Tiger, 2164

Backfire, 1773

Background to Danger, 1

The Backup Men, 5256

A Bad April, 2184

The Bad Step, 5635

The Baghdad Defections, 2957

Bait of Lies, 4869

Baited Blond, 3612

Balefire, 2213

The Balfour Conspiracy, 4740

The Balkan Assignment, 4391

The Balkan Spy, 3955

The Balloon Affair, 5754

The Bamboo Bomb, 1526

The Bamboo Screen, 4680

The Bamboo Whistle, 84

The Banana Men, 1184

Bandersnatch, 3328

Bandits, 3195

The Bang, Bang Birds, 1647

The Bannerman Effect, 3778

The Bannerman Solution, 3780

Bannerman's Law, 3777

Barbarossa Red, 2878

The Barboza Credentials, 1692

The Baron and the Chinese Puzzle, 1459

The Baron and the Mogul Swords, 1460

The Baron of Hong Kong, 1518

The Baroness: Black Gold, 2981

The Baroness: Death is a Ruby Light, 2986

The Baroness: Diamonds Are for Dying, 2982

The Baroness: The Ecstasy Connection, 2983

The Baroness: Flicker of Doom, 2984

The Baroness: Hard-Core Murder, 2985

The Baroness: Operation Doomsday, 2987

The Baroness: Sonic Slave, 2988

Barossa, 1278

The Barrabas Sweep, 2134

Barracuda, 2307

Bart Gould: Assignment-- Assassination, 3835

Bart Gould: Baron Sinister, 3836

Bart Gould: Big Blue Death, 3840

Bart Gould: The Death Makers, 3837

Bart Gould: The Man Who Bombed the World, 3841

Bart Gould: Operation--World War Three, 3842

Bart Gould: The President's Agent, 3838

Bart Gould: The Worldbreaker, 3839

Base Case, 4473

Basle Express, 3690

The Bastard Brigade, 3197

The Bat That Flits, 1294

The Battle in Botswana, 3515

Battle Road, 4704

Battle Zone, 1664

Battleground, 971

Bay of Lions, 1004

Beacon in the Night, 659

The Beam, 1899

Bear Island, 3583

The Bear Raid, 1908

Beard the Lion, 3674

The Bearer Plot, 4891

The Bearpit, 1986

Beat a Distant Drum, 1812

Beau Blackstone, 3106

Beaver to Fox, 2935

The Bedford Incident, 4472

The Bedroom Bolero, 599

The Bee Sting Deal, 704

The Beethoven Conspiracy, 2519

Before It's Too Late, 1005

Before the Crossing, 2839

Before the Glory Ended, 5804

Behind the Throne, 154

Beirut Incident, 1059

The Beirut Pipeline, 451

The Bellarosa Connection, 721

Beneath the Silent Seas, 2574

Benedict Arnold Connection, 1652

The Bengal Spider Plan, 5297

The Bengali Inheritance, 4895

The Bent Hostage, 1200

The Berets, 965

The Beria Papers, 5648

The Berkut, 2611

Berlin, 1060

Berlin Blind, 4854

The Berlin Couriers, 3528

The Berlin Covenant, 4191

The Berlin Ending, 2724

Berlin Fugue, 1477

Berlin Game, 1580

Berlin Tunnel 21, 3263

The Berlin Warning, 2344

Bermuda Calling, 2145

Best Secret Service Stories, 845

The Betrayal, 265

Betrayal in Eden, 2009

Betrayals, 1974

Betrayed, 4224

The Betrayers, 2409

The Better Angels, 3405

Between the Thunder and the Sun, 1333

Beware of Midnight, 846

Beyond the Prize, 5131

Big Bear, Little Bear, 862

The Big Dark, 2449

The Big Enough Wreath, 2127

The Big H, 2161

Big Lifters, 2811

The Big Red Sun, 3140

The Big Runaround, 5209

The Big Score, 3000

The Big Snatch, 2274

The Big Water, 5636

Bigfoot, 2706

The Billiken Courier, 3249

The Billion Dollar Brain, 1581

The Billion Dollar Sure Thing, 1819

Billions, 3740

Bimbashi Baruk of Egypt, 5504

Binary, 3128

The Bio-Assassins, 4384

The Bionic Woman, 3319

The Bird in Last Year's Nest, 2599

Birdcage, 1011

The Birds of Prey, 4820

Birthday, Deathday, 4290

Bishop's Pawn, 4257

Bismarck Cross, 5292

The Bitter Lake, 620

The Bitter Tea, 5765

The Black Arab, 112

The Black Arrows, 295

Black August, 361

The Black Baroness, 5587

Black Blade, 5417

The Black Box, 266

Black Camelot, 891

The Black Chamber, 1189

Black Champagne, 3662

The Black Death, 1061

The Black Devil, 4225

Black Dragon, 337

The Black Dwarf, 3864

Black Flamingo, 1012

Black Gambit, 1235

The Black Gang, 181

The Black General, 5069

The Black Gold of Malaverde, 2263

Black Gold, Red Death, 3265

Black Knight in Red Square, 2909

The Black Magician--Another Adventure of "Secret Service Smith," 326

Black Market (Newman), 3956

Black Market (Patterson), 4187

Black Sheet, White Lamb, 1560

The Black Shrike, 3584

The Black Spiders, 1408

Black Sunday, 2498

The Black Tide, 2442

Black Work, 1965

The Black Yacht, 2744

Black-Out in Gretley, 4427

Blackball, 4766

Blackbird (Merek), 3802

The Blackbird (Westlake), 5577

The Blackbirder, 2716

Blackbone, 4984

Blackmail North, 3461

Blackstone, 3107

Blackstone and the Scourge of Europe, 3108

Blackstone on Broadway, 3110

Blackstone's Fancy, 3109

Blame the Dead, 3355

A Blast of Trumpets, 1409

The Blight, 1423

The Blind Cave, 2940

Blind Conspiracy, 2593

Blind Fire, 4669

The Blind Pig, 2828

Blind Prophet, 1551

The Blind Run, 1975

The Blind Side, 5283

The Blind Trust Kills, 1296

Blindfold, 1893

Block 26: Sabotage at Buchenwald, 2898

Blood and Water, 2829

Blood Cries, 5555

Blood Enemies, 5756

Blood Group O, 861

Blood Hunt, 4344

Blood Knot, 3292

The Blood of an Englishman, 3430

Blood of Eagles, 2812

Blood of the Albatross, 4205

Blood of the Czars, 3001

Blood of the Eagle, 1643

Blood of the Lamb, 3867

Blood on the Desert, 4460

Blood Rose, 2560

Blood Royal, 5673

Blood Rules, 5334

Blood Run, 3388

Blood Run East, 3441

Blood Scenario, 5071

Blood Sport, 1955

The Blood Star, 2345

Blood Tango, 2694

Blood Tide, 2887

Blood Ties, 4452

Blood Winter, 4133

Blood-and-Guts Is Going Nuts,
3196

Bloodmoon, 2908

Bloodspoor, 3643

Bloody Bastogne, 2745

Bloody Christmas, 3952

Bloody Marko, 1563

Bloody Marvelous, 4484

The Bloody Medallion. 5216

The Bloody Monday Conspiracy,
2525

Bloody Passage, 4134

Bloody September, 2361

The Bloody Sun at Noon, 705

Blue Blood Will Out, 2537

Blue Bone, 5745

Blue Deep, 2546

The Blue Gate of Babylon, 4322

Blue Ice, 2439

Blue Leader, 5452

Blue Lightning, 5121

Blue Murder, 5454

Bluebolt One, 3455

Blueprint, 5423

Blueprint for a Terrorist, 4870

Blueprint for Execution, 4126

Boast, 1680

Body Count, 2746

A Body for McHugh, 1894

Boiled Alive, 3258

*Bolo, the Super Spy: An Amazing
Exposure of the Traitor's
Secret Adventures as a Spy in
Britain and France Disclosed
from Official Documents by
Armand Mejan, ex-Inspector
of the Paris Sureté Generale,*
155

The Bomb That Could Lip Read,
4879

Bombshell, 4835

The Bond of Black, 156

"Bond Strikes Camp," 1308

Bonded Fleming, 1873

Bones in the Sand, 2052

Booby Trap, 5133

The Book of Daniel, 1666

Boomer, 5196

Boomerang, 5697

A Borderline Case, 3613

The Borders of Barbarism, 5653

Bormann Brief, 1774

The Bormann Receipt, 1724

The Bormann Report, 1725

Born Beautiful, 5567

Born to Kill, 4509

The Borzoi Control, 1808

The Bourne Identity, 3336

The Bourne Supremacy, 3338

The Bourne Ultimatum, 3339

The Box with Broken Seals, 232

The Boy on Platform One, 1030

The Boy Who Liked Monsters,
3462

Boys from Brazil, 3233

The Bradford Business, 2185

The Brain Trust Murder, 22

Brain Twister, 4318

Brainfire, 766

The Branded Spy Murders, 202

The Brandenburg Affair, 5623

Brandon of the Engineers, 8

Brass Diamonds, 4748

Brass Eagle, 1722

The Brass Go-Between, 5257

The Brave and the Damned, 3008

The Brave Cannot Yield, 3571

Bravo Romeo, 4278

The Brea File, 1199

The Breadfruit Lotteries, 1809

The Break, 1543

Breakfast at Wimbledon, 753

The Breaking Strain, 3765

Breastplate for Aaron, 4705

A Breed of Heroes, 2894

The Brezhnev Memo, 3712

Briarpatch, 5258

Brick Alley, 1190

Brides of Blood, 3054

Bridge on the Drina, 536

The Bright Red Businessmen,
    3442

Bright Star, 1397

Brimstone, 1728

The Brink (Crisp), 1465

The Brink (Gallery), 2035

The Brink (Setlowe), 4907

The Brinkman, 3789

The Britannia Contract, 3684

The British Cross, 2244

Brock, 760

Brock and the Defector, 761

Broken Boy, 773

Broken English, 5290

Broken Ground, 2951

Broken Idols, 2363

Broken Image, 1756

The Broken Penny, 5183

Brokenclaw, 2080

The Bronze Drums, 3141

Brother Spy, 4226

A Brother to Dragons, 2476

The Brotherhood of the Rose,
    3894

Brotherhood of the Tomb, 3507

Brothers, 673

Brought in Dead, 4135

Brought to Book, 2538

"The Bruce-Partington Plans," 78

The Bucharest Ballerina Murders,
    203

The Budapest Parade Murders,
    204

The Bulgarian Exclusive, 2313

Bulldog Drummond, 174

Bulldog Drummond at Bay, 175

Bulldog Drummond at War, 1832

Bulldog Drummond Attacks, 83

*Bulldog Drummond
    Doubleheader, Including
    Third Round and Final
    Count,* 182

Bulldog Drummond on Dartmoor,
    82

Bulldog Drummond Returns, 176

Bulldog Drummond Stands Fast,
    1834

Bulldog Drummond Strikes Back,
    183

*Bulldog Drummond's Third
    Round,* 184

A Bullet for Fidel, 1062

Bullets and Brown Eyes, 3177

Bullets for Breakfast, 338

Bullets of Palestine, 2929

The Bulls of Ronda, 727

The Bunnies, 4456

The Burgos Contract, 2186

Burial in Moscow, 1642

Burn Season, 3139

The Burning, 3768

The Burning Fuse, 4836

*The Burning Mountain: A Novel
    of the Invasion of Japan,*
    1334

Burning the Apostle, 2245

Burr, 5430
Bush Baby, 5746
Bushmaster Fall, 4380
Business as Usual, 2539
The Business of Blanche Capel, 3889
Bustillo, 2041
But We Didn't Get the Fox, 3288
Butcher Bird, 2806
The Butcher of Belgrade, 1063
The Butcher's Moon, 5579
Butler: Chinese Roulette, 3239
Butler: Dead Fall, 3240
Butler: The Hydra Conspiracy, 3238
Butler: Killer Satellites, 3241
Butler: Love Me to Death, 3242
Butler: The Midas Factor, 3243
Butler: The Q Factor, 3244
Butler: The Slayboys, 3245
Butler: The Smart Bombs, 3246
Button Bright, 3069
Button, Button, 4653
The Button Man, 1976
Button Zone, 2277
By Order of the President, 2999
By the Rivers of Babylon, 1606
By-Line for Murder, 5698

C.A.B.--Intersec, 5477
C.L.A.W., 2264
Cab of the Sleeping Horse, 323
Cabal, 2070
Cable from Kabul, 5331
Cabot Station, 4852
The Caesar Code, 4974
The Cage, 2023
A Cage of Ice, 892
The Cage of Mirrors, 4492
The Cain Conspiracy, 4975
The Cain Conversion, 446

The Cairo Garden Murders, 197
The Cairo Mafia, 1064
The Cairo Sleeper, 5388
California Roll, 4983
The Caliph Intrigue, 3190
Call for Simon Shard, 3443
Call for the Dead, 1355
A Call from Austria, 3299
Call It Treason, 2700
A Call on Kuprin, 1758
Call to Arms, 972
Call to Duty, 2588
Calling Bulldog Drummond, 1835
Cambodia, 1065
The Cambridge Theorem, 1033
The Camelot Conundrum, 2318
Cameron Comes Through, 3463
Cameron: Ordinary Seaman, 3464
Cameron's Chase, 3444
Cameron's Convoy, 3465
Cameron's Troop Lift, 3466
Canadian Sanction, 2138
The Canaris Legacy, 2623
Cancelled Accounts, 2303
A Candle for the Dead, 4136
Cannibals and Missionaries, 3427
The Cape, 988
Caper of the Golden Bulls, 3522
Capital Crimes, 4754
The Capitol Hill Affair, 2835
The Capricorn Quadrant, 4726
Caprifoil, 3523
The Captain and the Enemy, 2290
Captain Bulldog Drummond, 1836
Captain Millett's Island, 936
The Captains, 966
The Captivator, 3993
The Captive Cardinal, 573
The Captive City, 1505
A Captive in the Land, 454
Captive in the Night, 5142

Caravan to Vaccares, 3585

The Cardinal of the Kremlin,
   1229

Care of American Embassy, 1319

The Care of Time, 499

The Caress of Conquest, 1949

Cargo of Eagles, 496

The Caribbean Account, 2018

The Caribbean Affair, 5299

Carla, 3738

The Carlos Contract, 4295

Carlos Must Die, 1508

The Carnellian Circle, 2854

Carnival!, 4485

Carnival for Killing, 1066

Carnival of Spies, 3909

Caroline R., 2540

The Carpathian Caper, 4761

Carriers of Death, 45

The Carrion Eaters, 660

Cartel, 1818

The Casablanca Opening, 1194

The Casanova Embrace, 441

Casbah Killers, 1067

The Casco Deception, 4500

A Case for MI-5, 5528

The Case of the Berlin Spy, 3957

The Case of the Bouncing Betty,
   600

The Case of the Crazy Pilot, 34

*The Case of the Four Friends: A
   Diversion in Pre-Detection*,
   3764

The Case of the King's Spy, 318

The Case of Robert Quarry, 5699

The Case of the Violent Virgin,
   601

Casino Royale, 1874

The Cassiopeia Affair, 5802

Cast a Yellow Shadow, 5259

Cast Iron Alibi, 223

The Castle Island Case, 205

Cat's Cradle, 4706

The Catacombs of Death, 113

Catalyst, 1353

Catch a Falling Spy (Benchley),
   722

Catch a Falling Spy (Deighton),
   1582

Catch a Spy, 2934

Catch Me a Spy, 3747

Catch Me, Kill Me, 2393

The Catenary Exchange, 1478

Cathedral, 1607

Cathouse, 2813

Catspaw, 815

Cauldron (Bond), 803

The Cauldron (Zeno), 5800

Cause for Alarm (Ambler), 2

Cause for Alarm (Pendower),
   4227

The Cautious Assassin, 4103

The Cavalry Goes Through, 224

Cave of Bats, 3046

*The Cave of the Chinese
   Skeletons*, 4908

Cedar, 3928

The Ceiling of Hell, 3930

Celestial Chess, 814

The Centaur Conspiracy, 4047

Center of the Web, 4528

The Centre Court Murder, 3971

Centrifuge, 4361

A Century of Progress, 4732

*A Ceremony in the Lincoln
   Tunnel*, 1490

Chain of Death, 3581

Chain of Vengeance, 2402

Chain Reaction, 2339

Chains, 4863

Chains of Command, 882

Chairman of the Board, 1987

The Chalk Circle, 5366

Challenge: A Bulldog Drummond Novel, 177
Chameleon, 1644
The Chameleon Course, 4880
The Chameleon File, 2836
Chameleon Kill, 4545
Chance Awakening, 3715
The Chancellor Manuscript, 3340
Channel Assault, 2053
Charge of Cowardice, 3487
Charka Memorial, 5525
Charlie Chan and the Curse of the Dragon Queen, 602
Charlie M, 1973
Charlie Muffin and Russian Rose, 1988
Charlie Muffin U.S.A., 1977
Charlie Peace, 4323
The Charm School, 1608
The Chase, 2715
Chase Royal, 4883
Chase the Storm, 5394
Chase the Sun, 5395
Chase the Wind, 5396
Check Force, 2527
Check Force: 100 Megaton Kill, 2528
Check Force: Clouds of War, 2529
Check Force: Peking Plot (the), 2530
Check Force: Seeds of Doom, 2531
Check Point Charlie, 2117
Checkmate in Rio, 1068
The Checkmate Kill, 4546
Checkpoint, 5227
The Chekhov Proposal, 1036
Cherry Harvest, 1275
Chevengur, 4072
The Chic Chic Spy, 5329
The Child and the Serpent, 1318

Children of Tender Years, 465
Children's Game, 5730
The Chill Factor, 3087
Chimera, 2032
China Bomb, 5333
The China Card (Ehrlichman), 1801
The China Card (Freed), 1967
China Dawn, 1729
The China Doll, 615
The China Expert, 5658
China Gold, 1791
China Lake, 2787
The China Option, 3843
The Chinaman, 3165
Chinaman's Chance, 5260
The Chinese Agenda, 4392
The Chinese Agent, 3879
The Chinese Assassin, 2312
The Chinese Bandit, 709
The Chinese Fire Drill, 5655
The Chinese Hammer, 4681
The Chinese Mask, 661
The Chinese Paymaster, 1069
Chinese Poison, 2358
Chinese Poker, 5298
Chinese Red, 2725
The Chinese Spur, 4749
The Chinese Visitor, 1753
The Chinks in the Curtain, 4367
The Chocolate Spy, 459
The Choice, 466
A Choice of Assassins, 3524
A Choice of Enemies, 467
Choice of Evils, 4640
Choke Point, 5198
The Chopin Express, 2930
The Christmas Spy, 2701
Chuck You, Farley!, 1943
The Churchill Diamonds, 3134
Churchill's Gold (Follett), 1896
Churchill's Gold (Wright), 5759

The Cipher, 1371
Cipher Six, 136
The Circe Factor, 3950
The Circle (Poyer), 4387
The Circle (Shagan), 4927
Circle of Deceit, 5725
The Circle War, 3671
Circus, 3586
Circus Couronne, 1010
The Circus Maker's Mission, 869
City of Gold, 1583
The City of Kites, 999
The Clash of Distant Thunder,
    1341
Clash of Loyalties, 2452
Clash of Steel, 4538
Class Distinctions, 2541
The Clauberg Trigger, 1775
Clear and Present Danger, 1230
Climate for Conspiracy, 2456
The Climate of Hell, 3257
Cloak of Darkness, 3532
Cloak-and-Dagger: Ten Thrilling
    Stories of Espionage, 1280
Cloak-and-Doctor, 2173
Close Combat, 964
Closed Circuit, 1243
Closing Ceremonies, 3010
A Cloud of Doves, 2457
Cloudburst, 4207
The Clowns of God, 5560
Clubfoot the Avenger Being Some
    Further Adventures of
    Desmond Okewood of the
    British Secret Service, 365
The Co-Ordinator, 3994
Coach North, 3445
The Coast of Fear, 4654
A Coat of Varnish, 5063
Cobalt 60, 2265
Cobra Kill, 1070
Cockpit, 3058

Coconut Wireless, 2948
The Code, 1071
Code Ezra, 1388
Code Name Gadget, 4459
Code Name Nimrod, 3160
Code Name Sebastian, 2861
Code Name Werewolf, 1072
Code Name: Grand Guignol,
    3793
Code Name: Woodcutter, 2042
Code of Arms, 3011
Code of Conduct, 569
Codename Starlight, 791
Codename: Cipher, 1964
Codeword Cromwell, 468
Codeword "Proton," 5300
A Coffin for Dimitrios, 3
The Coffin Ship, 5321
Cold as Ice, 4950
The Cold, Dark Night, 519
The Cold Front, 2450
Cold Harbour, 4137
Cold is the Sea, 703
The Cold Jungle, 5766
A Cold Red Sunrise, 2910
The Cold Smell of Sacred Stone,
    1201
Cold War, 860
Cold War in a Country Garden,
    2355
The Cold War Swap, 5261
Colonel Butler's Wolf, 4404
Colonel Sun, 526
The Colonels, 967
The Color of Blood, 3882
The Colossus of Arcadia, 267
Columbo: The Grassy Knoll,
    2482
The Combination, 4002
Come Die With Me, 1527
Come, Follow Me, 5424
Come into My Parlour, 5588

Come Ninevah, Come Tyre: The Presidency of Edward M. Jason, 1708
Come Over Red Rover, 3207
Comeback, 4269
The Comedians, 2289
Comes the Dark Stranger, 4138
Comfort Me with Spies, 3630
The Coming Out Party, 1966
The Commander, 2585
Commando Escape, 2283
Commando X, 4722
The Commandos, 570
The Company, 1800
The Company of Friends, 1473
The Company of Man, 3653
Company Spook, 5547
The Compassionate Tiger, 1689
Comprador, 1487
Comrade Charlie, 1978
Comrade Spy, 4112
Conceal and Disguise, 2919
Concert of Ghosts, 567
Concerto, 2879
The Concorde: Airport '79, 5139
Concrete Boot, 2043
The Concrete Crime, 3691
Condition Green: Tokyo, 2209
The Conduct of Major Maxim, 3356
Conduct Unbecoming, 1750
Confessional, 4139
The Confidential Agent, 94
Confirm or Deny, 2823
A Conflict of Interest, 581
A Conflict of Interests, 1776
Confrontation, 2072
The Congleton Lark, 2187
Congo, 1461
The Connector, 5660
Conquest before Autumn, 1761
Consequence of Fear, 469

A Conspiracy of Angels, 4632
A Conspiracy of Eagles, 1549
The Conspirator, 5007
The Conspirators (Clayton), 1244
The Conspirators (Prokosch), 4432
Conspirators in Capri, 342
Contact Lost, 5381
Contact Man, 3972
Contact Mercury, 3946
The Contaminant, 4499
The Contenders, 3013
The Content Assignment, 4650
Contraband, 362
The Contract (Poyer), 4393
The Contract (Seymour), 4913
Contract on the President, 1474
Convergence, 2016
The Convoy Commodore, 3446
Convoy of Fear, 3447
A Cool Day for Killing, 1245
Cool Runnings, 2707
The Cool War, 4338
The Cooler, 3716
The Copper Butterfly, 4682
Copperhead, 2567
The Corder Index, 4837
Cormorant's Isle, 3566
A Corner of the Playground, 4707
The Corps, 973
Corpse, 3467
The Corpse on the White House Lawn, 23
Corsican Honor, 2559
The Cosgrave Report, 4110
Cotswold Manners, 5085
Cotswold Mistress, 5086
Cotswold Moles, 5087
Cotswold Murders, 5088
The Council of Ten, 3120
Count Backwards to Zero, 2399
Count Not the Cost, 3572

Count on the Saint, 5539

Count Your Dead, 4677

Countdown 1000, 5013

Countdown, 2364

Countdown for a Spy, 5434

Countdown to Crisis, 1764

Counter Force, 5161

Counter Paradise, 1892

The Counter-Terror Mission Trilogy, 5054

Counterattack, 974

Counterfeit Agent, 1073

The Counterfeit Courier, 4949

The Counterfeit Kill, 2747

The Counterfeit Spy, 4340

Counterforce, 2575

Counterpol in Paris, 796

Counterspy Express, 1872

The Counterspy Murders, 1212

Counterstrike (Hagberg), 2365

Counterstrike (Taylor), 5199

Counterstroke (O'Connor), 4052

Counterstroke (Winterton), 5691

Country of the Heart, 5038

The Country Team, 3883

Coup!, 2232

The Courier, 2937

Courier to Marrakesh: A Clubfoot Story, 5659

Courier to Peking (Goodfield), 2218

Courier to Peking (Toulman), 5327

Court Martial, 3884

Court of Shadows, 3181

The Courts of the Morning, 13

The Coven, 2748

The Covenant of the Flame, 3895

Covenant of the Poppies, 4212

The Coventry Option, 937

Cover for a Traitor, 2458

Cover Story, 4845

Coyote Bird, 1577

The Coyote Connection, 1074

Cozumel, 2749

The Crack of Doom, 2562

Crackdown, 1354

Craig and the Jaguar, 731

Craig and the Living Dead, 732

Craig and the Midas Touch, 733

Craig and the Tunisian Tangle, 734

The Crash of '79, 1820

The Crazy Mixed-Up Corpse, 603

The Cretan Lover, 4186

Crew of the "Anaconda," 3505

Crime Code, 137

The Crime Haters, 1443

Crime Wind, 2637

Crimes of the City, 4564

The Criminal Airman, 4341

Crimson Comes the Dawn, 5064

The Crimson in the Purple, 4655

Crimson Jade, 3663

The Crimson Pagoda, 4003

Crinkled Crown, 138

Crisis, 1861

Critical Mass, 2366

The Crocus List, 3357

The Croesus Conspiracy, 5117

The Cromwell File, 2483

Cronus, 1573

Crooked Adam, 5130

The Crooked Phoenix, 830

The Cross and the Sickle, 5805

Cross to Bear Proudly, 688

Crossed Swords, 2367

Crossfire (Hagberg), 2368

Crossfire (Pollock), 4362

Crossfire (Slager), 5005

The Crossing, 488

Crossing at Ivalo, 3617

Crossing in Berlin, 3031

The Crouching Beast: A Clubfoot Story, 366

Crown Court, 1900

Crows' Parliament, 1491

Crux, 447

Cry of the Deep, 2580

The Cry of the Halidon, 3341

Cry of the Hunter, 4140

Cry Spy, 2651

Cry Vengeance, 848

Crypto Man, 2054

Crystal Contract, 4486

The Cuban Expedition, 4037

The Cuckoo Line Affair, 5700

Culebra Cut, 4535

The Cupedevil, 3871

Cupid's Executioners, 3872

A Cure for Cancer, 3880

Curfew, 1684

Curiosity Didn't Kill the Cat, 4508

The Curse of Doone, 126

The Cut-Out, 5012

Cyborg, 989

Cyborg IV, 990

Cyclops, 1499

Czar's Spy: The Mystery of a Silent Love, 139

Czechmate, 863

The "D" Notice, 2842

The D'Artagnan Signature, 2658

Dachau Treasure, 1620

Daddy, 1742

Daddy's Girl, 3833

Dagger, 3763

The Daisy Dilemma, 4520

The Daleth Effect, 2489

The Damascus Affair, 2931

The Dame, 5580

The Damsel, 5581

The Dance Card, 1846

Dance for Diplomats, 2459

Dance of the Sinking Ship, 3002

The Dancing Dodo, 2081

The Dancing Floor, 3618

The Dancing Men, 900

A Dandy in Aspic, 3733

Danger is the Password: Stories of Wartime Spies, 1848

Danger Is My Line, 3208

Danger Key, 1075

The Danger Within, 2200

Danger Zone, 5493

Danger: Great Stories of Mystery and Suspense, 4819

Dangerous by Nature, 3692

Dangerous Exchange, 1765

A Dangerous Fortune, 1909

The Dangerous Game, 140

Dangerous Honeymoon, 2994

The Dangerous Islands, 4075

Dangerous Journey, 58

Dangerous Quest, 1410

The Danziger Transcript, 1851

Dardanelles Derelict, 3749

The Dark Avenue, 4228

Dark Blood, Dark Terror, 1270

The Dark Crusader, 3587

Dark Finds the Day, 5616

The Dark Frontier, 4

The Dark Goddess, 452

The Dark Harvest, 1424

Dark Hero, 1204

Dark Interlude, 1205

Dark Omnibus, 1206

Dark Peril, 1413

Dark Road, 4132

Dark Rose the Phoenix, 3932

The Dark Secret of Josephine, 5599

The Dark Side of the Island, 4141

The Dark Side of the Street, 4142

Dark Star, 2017
Dark Street, 1207
The Darkroom, 667
Darling, Don't, 5568
The Darlington Jaunt, 2188
Date with Fear, 4229
Date With Darkness, 2410
The Daughter of Fu Manchu, 5505
Dauntless: A Novel of Midway and Guadalcanal, 5316
The Davidian Report, 2717
Dawn Attack, 1001
Dawn of Darkness, 1435
The Day before Sunrise, 5731
The Day Before Midnight, 2768
The Day Khrushchev Panicked, 3658
The Day of Disaster, 1414
Day of Judgment, 4143
Day of Reckoning, 4396
Day of the Cheetah, 883
The Day of the Coastwatch, 3448
Day of the Delphi, 3121
The Day of the Dingo, 1076
Day of the Dragon Star, 3869
The Day of the Jackal, 1927
The Day the Sun Fell, 1730
Day the Wind Dropped, 2055
The Day the World Ended, 346
Days of Danger, 46
Days of Glory and Grieving, 3654
Days of Power, Nights of Fear, 4940
Days of Thunder, 2516
Days of Wine and Roses?, 4004
Dead Easy for Dover, 4370
Dead End, 4270
Dead Eyes, 5752
Dead Fall in Berlin, 5806
Dead Game, 604
Dead in the Water, 5779

Dead Letter, 5408
The Dead Line, 3456
Dead Man Alive, 3410
The Dead Man Murder, 3973
Dead Man Running, 774
Dead Man's Handle, 4060
Dead Man's Secret, 4345
The Dead of Winter, 2397
Dead on Time, 2855
A Dead One in Berlin, 3823
Dead or Alive (Creasey), 1411
Dead or Alive (Wentworth), 5557
Dead Run (Gibbs), 2171
Dead Run (Sheckley), 4944
Dead Runner, 4633
The Dead Sea Cipher, 4275
The Dead Zone, 3018
Deadeye-Dick, 5442
Deadline, 2542
Deadline for Destruction, 2552
Deadly Aria, 3938
Deadly Cadenza, 3933
Deadly Crescendo, 3934
The Deadly Document, 669
Deadly Force, 1663
The Deadly Friend, 4291
The Deadly Gold, 4645
The Deadly Green, 4646
Deadly Legacy, 551
Deadly Nature, 4871
The Deadly Orbit Mission, 3750
Deadly Perfume, 5251
The Deadly Piece, 2407
Deadly Reunion, 582
Deadly Score, 3935
Deadly Sonata, 3936
The Deadly Trade, 831
Deadly Variations, 3937
Deadpoint, 1179
Dear Fatherland, 4976
Death and Bright Water, 3845
Death and the Dutch Uncle, 3915

Death and the Sky Above, 5701
Death at Charity Point, 5193
Death at Dakar, 4089
Death at His Elbow, 5494
The Death at Lord's, 3974
Death at the Cut, 2995
Death Beam, 3910
Death before Bedtime, 5431
Death below Deck, 2996
Death beyond the Nile, 3678
Death by Gaslight, 3070
Death by Night, 47
Death Charter, 438
Death Deep Down, 3722
The Death Freak, 2818
Death from the Air, 35
Death Fuse, 4725
Death Hits the Jackpot, 5455
Death in Aqaba, 2335
Death in Flames, 1444
Death in High Places, 1445
A Death in Ireland, 1830
Death in the Desert, 532
Death in the Fifth Position, 5432
Death in the Mind, 3295
Death in the Rising Sun, 1436
Death in the Senate, 24
Death Intervened, 4346
Death Is Forever, 2082
Death Is My Comrade, 3209
Death Laughs Aloft, 36
Death Likes It Hot, 5433
Death Merchant: Afghanistan Crashout, 4571
Death Merchant: Alaska Conspiracy, 4572
Death Merchant: Albanian Connection, 4573
Death Merchant: Apocalypse, U.S.A., 4574
Death Merchant: Armageddon, U.S.A., 4575

Death Merchant: The Atlantean Horror, 4576
Death Merchant: The Bermuda Triangle Action, 4577
Death Merchant: The Billionaire Mission, 4578
Death Merchant: Blood Bath, 4579
Death Merchant: Blueprint Invisibility, 4580
Death Merchant: The Budapest Action, 4581
Death Merchant: The Bulgarian Termination, 4582
Death Merchant: The Burma Probe, 4583
Death Merchant: The Burning Blue Death, 4584
Death Merchant: The Castro File, 4565
Death Merchant: The Chinese Conspiracy, 4585
Death Merchant: The Cobra Chase, 4586
Death Merchant: The Cosmic Reality Kill, 4587
Death Merchant: The Death Merchant, 4588
Death Merchant: The Devil's Trashcan, 4589
Death Merchant: The Enigma Project, 4566
Death Merchant: Escape from Gulag Taria, 4590
Death Merchant: Fatal Formula, 4591
Death Merchant: The Flight of the Phoenix, 4592
Death Merchant: The Fourth Reich, 4593
Death Merchant: The Greenland Mystery, 4594

Death Merchant: Hell in Hindu
Land, 4595
Death Merchant: High Command
Murder, 4596
Death Merchant: The Hindu
Trinity Caper, 4597
Death Merchant: The Inca File,
4598
Death Merchant: Invasion of the
Clones, 4599
Death Merchant: The Iron
Swastika Plot, 4600
Death Merchant: The Judas
Scrolls, 4601
Death Merchant: The KGB
Frame, 4602
Death Merchant: The Kondrashev
Chase, 4603
Death Merchant: The Kronos
Plot, 4567
Death Merchant: The Laser War,
4604
Death Merchant: The Mainline
Plot, 4605
Death Merchant: Manhattan
Wipeout, 4606
Death Merchant: Massacre in
Rome, 4607
Death Merchant: The Mato
Grosso Horror, 4608
Death Merchant: The Methuselah
Factor, 4609
Death Merchant: The Mexican
Hit, 4610
Death Merchant: The Miracle
Mission, 4611
Death Merchant: Nightmare in
Algeria, 4612
Death Merchant: Nipponese
Nightmare, 4568
Death Merchant: Operation
Mindmurder, 4613

Death Merchant: Operation
Overkill, 4614
Death Merchant: Operation
Skyhook, 4615
Death Merchant: Operation
Thunderbolt, 4616
Death Merchant: The Pakistan
Mission, 4617
Death Merchant: The Pole Star
Secret, 4569
Death Merchant: The Psionics
War, 4618
Death Merchant: The Psychotran
Plot, 4619
Death Merchant: The Romanian
Operation, 4620
Death Merchant: Satan Strike,
4621
Death Merchant: The Shambhala
Strike, 4622
Death Merchant: The Shamrock
Smash, 4623
Death Merchant: Slaughter in El
Salvador, 4624
Death Merchant: The Soul Search
Project, 4625
Death Merchant: The Surinam
Affair, 4626
Death Merchant: Vengeance of
the Golden Hawk, 4627
Death Merchant: The Zemlya
Expedition, 4570
Death Message: Oil 74-2, 1077
Death Mission: Havana, 1170
The Death Mizer, 44
Death of an Ambassador, 3693
Death of a Bitter Englishman,
1271
Death of a Citizen, 2411
Death of a Dissident, 2915
Death of a Harlot, 225
Death of a Hittite, 537

Death of a Patriot, 2477
Death of a Raven, 1717
Death of a Russian Priest, 2911
Death of a Sahib, 1792
Death of a Thin-Skinned Animal, 460
The Death of Convention, 5681
Death of the Falcon, 1078
Death of the Fuehrer, 4435
Death on a Pale Horse, 832
Death on Demand, 59
Death on the Appian Way, 735
Death on the Moor, 4230
A Death Out of Season, 3282
The Death Parade, 4347
Death Round the Corner, 60
The Death Specialists, 4193
Death Squad, London, 2163
The Death Squadron, 4348
Death Stands By, 48
Death Strain, 1080
Death, the Red Flower, 5767
Death to the Fifth Column, 3958
Death to the Spy, 226
Death under Gibraltar, 227
Death Wore Gloves, 5078
Death's Foot Forward, 3659
Death's Head, 767
Death's Head, Berlin, 2165
Death's Head Conspiracy, 1079
Death's Running Mate, 4510
Death-Makers Conspiracy, 2526
Deathwatch '39, 2166
The Debriefing, 3273
The Debt, 2633
Debt of Honor, 2972
The Deceiver, 1928
December Passion, 4005
Decision, 1709
Decision at Delphi, 3533
Decoys, 2708
Deep Cover, 2109

The Deep, Deep Freeze, 2123
Deep Freeze, 5793
Deep Gold, 3771
Deep Kill, 984
Deep Lie, 5751
Deep Purple, 470
The Deep Silence, 4497
Deep Six, 1500
Deep Sting, 5200
Defame and Destroy, 2010
Defcon One, 5543
The Defection of A. J. Lewinter, 3274
The Defector (Carter), 1081
The Defector (Collingwood), 1285
The Defector (Kartun), 2938
The Defector (Raphael), 4471
The Defector (Reynolds), 4513
The Defector (Ward-Thomas), 5514
Dekker's Demons, 3389
Delay in Danger, 4708
Deliverance in Shanghai, 450
Delivery, 2884
The Delta Decision, 5057
The Delta Factor, 5093
Delta Green, 3327
Demon-4, 3644
A Den of Savage Men, 833
A Deniable Man, 5119
Department "K," 4068
The Department of Death, 1415
Depraved Indifference, 5188
Desert Fire, 2369
Desert Strike, 2135
Designated Hitter, 5471
Desperate Measures, 5600
Destination Dieppe, 647
Destination Terror, 4253
Destroy the Kentucky, 1552
The Destroyer: Acid Rock, 4786

The Destroyer: Arabian Nightmare, 4787

The Destroyer: Assassin's Play Off, 4788

The Destroyer: Bay City Blast, 4771

The Destroyer: Blood Lust, 4789

The Destroyer: Bottom Line, 4772

The Destroyer: Brain Drain, 4790

The Destroyer: Chained Reaction, 4791

The Destroyer: Child's Play, 4792

The Destroyer: Chinese Puzzle, 4793

The Destroyer: Created, The Destroyer, 4794

The Destroyer: Dangerous Games, 4773

The Destroyer: Dark Horse, 4774

The Destroyer: Deadly Seeds, 4795

The Destroyer: Death Check, 4796

The Destroyer: Death Therapy, 4797

The Destroyer: Dr. Quake, 4775

The Destroyer: The Final Death, 4798

The Destroyer: Firing Line, 4776

The Destroyer: Funny Money, 4799

The Destroyer: The Head Man, 4777

The Destroyer: Holy Terror, 4800

The Destroyer: In Enemy Hands, 4801

The Destroyer: Judgment Day, 4802

The Destroyer: Kill or Cure, 4803

The Destroyer: Killer Chromosomes, 4778

The Destroyer: King's Curse, 4779

The Destroyer: Last Call, 4804

The Destroyer: The Last Temple, 4805

The Destroyer: The Last War Dance, 4780

The Destroyer: Mafia Fix, 4806

The Destroyer: Missing Link, 4807

The Destroyer: Mugger's Blood, 4808

The Destroyer: Murder Ward, 4809

The Destroyer: Murder's Shield, 4810

The Destroyer: Oil Slick, 4811

The Destroyer: Power Play, 4781

The Destroyer: Ship of Death, 4812

The Destroyer: Slave Safari, 4813

The Destroyer: Summit Chase, 4782

The Destroyer: Sweet Dreams, 4814

The Destroyer: Terror Squad, 4783

The Destroyer: Timber Line, 4784

The Destroyer: Union Bust, 4815

The Destroyer: Voodoo Die, 4785

The Detail, 3428

The Detonators, 2433

The Devastators, 2412

The Devereaux File, 5075

The Deviator, 3995

The Devil Has Wings, 37

The Devil Met a Lady, 2916
Devil's Agent, 719
The Devil's Alternative, 1929
The Devil's Chaplain, 12
The Devil's Cockpit, 1082
Devil's Current, 725
The Devil's Diplomats, 114
The Devil's Dozen, 1083
The Devil's Finger, 1813
Devil's Guard, 97
Devil's Harvest, 5011
Devil's Juggler, 5052
The Devil's Own Work, 2895
The Devil's Paw, 233
The Devil's Spy, 671
Devoted Friends, 4397
Diabolus, 2726
Dial 999, 339
The Diamond Bubble, 1856
The Diamond Smugglers, 1876
Diamonds Are Deadly, 1754
Diamonds Are Forever, 1875
Diamonds Bid, 4474
Diamonds for Danger (Pendower), 4231
Diamonds for Danger (Walker), 5478
Diamonds to Amsterdam, 3694
Diamonds Wild, 3385
Dictator's Destiny, 3975
Die Fast, Die Happy, 5132
Die Rich, Die Happy, 3846
A Different Drummer, 1777
A Different Night, 2605
The Dinner Club Stories, 185
Diplomacy, 1681
Diplomatic Cover, 4209
Diplomatic Immunity, 5185
Diplomatic Incident, 2959
Diplomaticheskii Agent [*Diplomatic Agent*], 3368
Directive 16, 4531

A Dirty Distant War, 3948
The Dirty Dozen, 3949
Dirty Laundry, 5060
Dirty Story, 500
Dirty Tricks, 4328
Discovery, 4930
The Disinformer (John), 2856
The Disinformer (Ustinov), 5404
Disorderly Elements, 1311
The Distant Stranger, 2460
Ditto, Brother Rat, 2128
Dive Deep for Danger, 4666
Dive to Oblivion, 2576
The Divide, 4113
Divine Assassin, 4503
The Doctor, 2617
Doctor Death, 2508
Doctor Frigo, 501
Doctor of Pimlico, 141
A Dog Fight with Death, 64
The Dogs of War, 1930
Dollar Covenant, 4989
The Dolly, Dolly Spy, 1648
The Dolorosa Deal, 3270
Dominator (Follett), 1897
The Dominator (Nicole), 4006
The Domino Conspiracy, 2612
The Domino Principle, 2969
The Domino Vendetta, 2970
Don't Embarrass the Bureau, 1307
Don't Just Stand There, Do Something, 5435
Doom River, 2750
Doom's Caravan, 2678
The Doomsday Bag, 588
The Doomsday Carrier, 1013
The Doomsday Conspiracy, 4951
The Doomsday Contract, 5661
The Doomsday Deposit, 2864
Doomsday England, 1320
The Doomsday Exercise, 1553

The Doomsday Formula, 1084
The Doomsday List, 3193
The Doomsday Spiral, 3113
The Doomsday Spore, 1085
The Doomsday Squad, 2696
The Doomsday Square, 5206
The Doomsday Ultimatum, 1901
Doomsday Warrior, 5105
A Door Fell Shut, 3300
*Door of Dread: A Secret Service
    Romance*, 327
Doris Fein: Superspy, 720
Dorothy Rigby, 1802
The Dossier, 4745
Dossier IX, 5550
The Double Agent (Bingham), 759
Double Agent (Stackleborg), 5103
The Double Agent (Teilhet), 5211
Double Agent--Triple Cross, 4977
Double Cross (Bar-Zohar), 670
Double Cross (Pollard), 4349
Double Crossing, 2642
Double Deceit, 2461
A Double Deception, 1778
Double Defector, 4050
Double Diamond, 4232
Double Exposure (MacKenzie),
    3558
Double Exposure (McLeave),
    3614
*The Double Game: He Played
    Both Ends against the
    Middle*, 4516
Double Griffin, 1793
Double Identity, 1086
Double Image, 3534
*The Double Life of Mr. Alfred
    Burton*, 268
The Double Man, 2504
The Double Menace, 3976
*Double Nought; in Which Lionel
    Hipwell of His Majesty's*

*Foreign Office Recounts His
    Exciting Adventures Following
    His Follies and Discloses the
    Truth Concerning the Most
    Amazing and Desperate
    Conspiracy, with World-Wide
    Ramifications*, 157
Double Spy, 168
Double Take, 852
The Double Traitor, 269
Doubled and Vulnerable, 4053
Doubled in Diamonds, 1014
The Doubtful Disciple, 1260
*Dover and the Unkindest Cut of
    All*, 4371
Dover Beats the Band, 4372
Dover Goes to Pott, 4373
Dover One, 4374
Dover Strikes Again, 4375
Dover Three, 4376
Dover Two, 4377
Down among the Dead Men, 2509
Down River, 2033
The Downing of Flight Six Heavy,
    3083
Dr. Bruderstein Vanishes, 4965
Dr. Cobb's Game, 1182
Dr. No, 1877
Dr. Strangelove, 903
Dragoman Pass, 5654
The Dragon (Coppel), 1335
Dragon (Cussler), 1492
Dragon Flame, 1087
A Dragon for Christmas, 5768
Dragon Harvest, 4993
The Dragon Portfolio, 2709
Dragon Road, 4683
Dragon SIM-13, 3785
The Dragon Tree, 1015
Dragon's Claw, 4061
Dragonfire, 2925
Dragonfly, 1748

The Dragonhead Deal, 2473
Dragons at the Gate, 1731
The Drakov Memoranda, 1479
Draw the Dragon's Teeth, 3977
Drawn Blanc, 2024
A Dream of Treason, 1759
The Dresden Green, 1972
Drink to Yesterday, 3695
Driscoll's Diamonds, 3397
Dropshot, 754
Drover, 2254
A Drug Called Power, 3573
Drum Beat--Berlin, 3210
Drum Beat--Dominique, 3218
Drum Beat--Erica, 3219
Drum Beat--Madrid, 3220
Drum Beat--Marianne, 3221
The Drum of Ungara, 3047
Drummer in the Dark, 5284
Drums along the Khyber, 3488
Drums Never Beat, 169
The Drums of Fu Manchu, 353
Drums of the Dark Gods, 648
The Dublin Affair, 1683
The Duel, 4881
Duel in the Snow, 3791
Duel of the Assassins, 4359
Duet for Three Spies, 4664
The Dunfermline Affair. 2189
The Dunkirk Directive, 4518
Dunn's Conundrum, 3179
The Dutch Caper, 624
Dutch Courage, 4271
Dutch Treat, 2888
Dyed for Death, 4521
Dynasty of Spies, 4954
Dzerzhinsky Square, 2827

E Pluribus Bang!, 3267
The Eagle Has Flown, 4144
The Eagle Has Landed, 4145

Eagle Station, 738
Eagles Fly, 2375
The Earhart Betrayal, 5229
The Earhart Legacy, 5191
Earl Drake: Operation Breakthrough, 3723
Earl Drake: Operation Deathmaker, 3728
Earl Drake: Operation Drumfire, 3724
Earl Drake: Operation Endless Hours, 3729
Earl Drake: Operation Fireball, 3725
Earl Drake: Operation Flashpoint, 3730
Earl Drake: Operation Hammerlock, 3726
Earl Drake: Operation Overkill, 3731
Earl Drake: Operation Stranglehold, 3732
Earl Drake: Operation Whiplash, 3727
Early Warning, 1870
Ears of the Jungle, 819
East and West, 98
East of Desolation, 4146
East of Everest, 3135
East of Hell, 2139
East of Piccadilly, 5498
The Easter Dinner, 1687
Eastward in Eden, 88
Eastward/Westward, 4035
The Ebony Cross, 1088
Echo of a Bomb, 5637
Echo of Treason, 926
Echoes of Zero, 5079
Eclipse, 5134
Edge of Darkness, 5753
Edge of Eden, 4431
The Edinburgh Caper, 3550

The Edinburgh Exercise, 2190

The Eferding Diaries, 880

The Eiger Sanction, 5613

Eight Card Stud, 1089

The Eight Crooked Trenches, 308

Eight Days in Washington, 2900

Eight Hours from England, 4440

The Eighth Dwarf, 5262

The Eighth Trumpet, 3122

The Eighty-First, 2975

Einstein Plot, 2547

The Eisenhower Deception, 1779

The El Murders, 2255

The Eldorado Network, 4540

Eldorado: A Story of the Scarlet Pimpernel, 286

Element of Risk, 5638

The Elephant Valley, 1840

Eleven Bullets for Mohammed, 576

Eleven Were Brave, 4119

The Elgar Variation, 2979

The Elijah Conspiracy, 4532

The Eliminator, 3996

The Elusive Monsieur Drago, 4233

The Elusive Mrs. Pollifax, 943

The Elusive Pimpernel, 287

Embassy, 1375

The Embassy House, 4430

The Embers of Hate, 835

Embrace of the Butcher, 938

Embrace the Serpent, 4442

Emerald, 627

Emerald Decision, 5236

The Emerald Elephant Gambit, 3649

The Emerald Illusion, 700

Emergency in the Pyrenees, 4076

The Emperor Fu Manchu, 5506

Emperor of America (Condon), 1299

The Emperor of America (Ward), 347

The End of the Battle, 5536

The End of the Rug, 3289

The End of the Track, 5702

Endgame, 558

Endgame Enigma, 2631

Endgame in Berlin, 2479

Endless Colonnade, 2471

The Endless Game, 1919

Endure No Longer, 3301

Enemies, 2496

The Enemy, 628

Enemy and Brother, 1557

The Enemy General, 4251

Enemy Outpost, 1215

Enemy Territory, 5224

The Enemy Within, 1416

Enemy's Enemy, 2346

England's Peril, 142

The English Assassin, 3881

The English Lady, 2480

Enigma, 674

The Enormous Shadow, 2472

Entered from the Sun, 2131

Envoy Extraordinary, 234

The Episode at Toledo, 4077

Epitaph for a Spy, 502

Epitaph for Lemmings, 4684

Epitaph for Love, 1277

Equinox, 3783

The Eros Affair, 3468

The Escalator, 2076

Escape from New York, 3625

Escape from Prague, 1274

The Escape of General Gerard, 3959

Escape to Athens, 1780

The Essential Man, 3887

The Estuary Pilgrim, 5002

The Eternal Mercenary, 4734

The Eternal Reich, 3037

Ethel and the Naked Spy, 3631
Eurasian Virgins, 4910
The Euro-Killers, 4487
Eva, 3794
Even If You Run, 3411
Even Jericho, 2392
An Evening in Byzantium, 4943
Evil in a Mask, 5601
The Evil Phoenix, 3978
Exchange of Clowns, 5644
Exchange of Doves, 2056
An Exchange of Eagles, 4892
*The Executioner: Canadian
    Crisis*, 4218
*The Executioner: Cleveland
    Pipeline*, 4220
*The Executioner: Command
    Strike*, 4219
*The Executioner: The
    Executioner's War Book*,
    4221
The Executioners (Carter), 1090
The Executioners (McCutchan),
    3469
Exit a Dictator, 235
Exit Mr. Brent, 65
Exit of a Spy, 4667
Exocet, 4147
Exodus of the Damned, 5006
Expeditor: The Brain Scavengers,
    1768
Expeditor: The Fist of Fatima,
    1769
Expeditor: The Glyphs of Gold,
    1767
Expeditor: The Laughing Death,
    1770
Expeditor: Needles of Death,
    1771
Expeditor: Valley of Vultures,
    1772
The Expendable Spy, 2756

An Expensive Place to Die, 1584
Expiation, 270
The Expurgator, 3997
Extinction Cruise, 4423
Extracurricular Activities, 3321
Extreme Prejudice, 1744
Eye for an Eye (Hutchison), 131
An Eye for an Eye (Seymour),
    4914
Eye of the Needle, 1907
The Eye of the Storm. 4148
The Eye of the Tornado, 4329
The Eyes around Me, 5769
Eyes of the Hammer, 3786
The Eyes of the Tiger, 1091

Face in the Shadows, 4101
Face Me When You Walk Away,
    1979
The Face of Jalanath, 2470
The Face of Terror, 3283
Face Value, 5495
Faceless Mortals, 1315
Fail-Safe, 925
A Fair Exchange, 2453
Fair Warning, 4985
Faith, Hope, and Homicide, 3681
Faked Passports, 5589
Falcon, 5009
A Falcon for the Hawks, 1794
Falklands Gambit, 3136
Fall Back, 4021
Fall from Grace, 1286
The Fall Guy, 4258
Fall of Terror, 853
The Fall of the Russian Empire,
    2832
Fall-Out, 2057
The Fallen Sparrow, 2718
Fallout for a Spy, 2601

Falls the Shadow (Litvinoff),
  3284
Falls the Shadow (Ross), 4644
False Cross, 1921
False Dawn, 3235
False Flags, 2795
The False Joanna, 1970
False Prophets, 2370
False-Face, 122
Falseface, 4938
The Falstaff Cross, 2989
A Family Affair, 1466
The Family Arsenal, 5235
Family Trade, 1044
The Famine, 1425
*Famous Stories of Code and
  Cipher*, 806
Fanatic of Fez, 2549
The Fanatics, 2616
The Fanatics of Al Asad, 1092
The Far Sands, 5703
Farewell to Russia, 2719
The Fascinator, 3998
The Fat Death, 605
Fatal Odds, 2388
Fate Cannot Harm Me, 213
Fatherland, 2497
The Faust Conspiracy, 625
The Faustian Pact, 712
The Favor, 2340
Favorite Son, 5066
Fear Is the Key, 3588
Fear Itself, 2924
A Fearful Symmetry, 1862
The February Doll Murders, 589
The February Plan, 1732
The Fedorovich File, 5077
Fellow Passenger, 2679
Fellow Traveler, 621
The Female of the Species, 178
Feminine for Spy, 4752
Fenton of the Foreign Service, 5

Feramontov, 3412
Festival, 2902
Festival for Spies, 2727
Fever Grass, 2545
The Fever Tree, 3761
A Few Days in Madrid, 4553
Few Die Well, 4027
A Few Good Men, 2155
Fidel Castro Assassinate, 1727
Field of Blood, 4923
Fifteen Keys, 69
The Fifth Defector, 2885
The Fifth Freedom, 4350
The Fifth Horseman (Adams), 439
The Fifth Horseman (Collins),
  1288
The Fifth Man, 3696
The Fifth Passenger (Winterton),
  5692
The Fifth Passenger (Young),
  5789
The Fifth Profession, 3896
The Fifth Script, 5080
The Fight in the Mountains, 744
The Fighting Agents, 956
The Fighting Temeraire, 5721
The File on Devlin, 2152
The Filthy Five, 1093
Final Act, 5089
Final Answers, 1655
Final Approach, 3943
The Final Count, 179
Final Countdown, 991
Final Flight, 1321
The Final Glass, 2568
*The Final Voyage of the S.S.N.
  Skate*, 1178
The Finalist, 828
Finding Hoseyn, 3569
A Fine Night for Dying, 4149
A Fine Red Rain, 2917
The Finger, 5116

The Finger of Saturn, 1016
Fire and Forget, 1312
Fire Arrow, 3187
The Fire Engine That Disappeared, 5474
The Fire Goddess, 5507
Fire in the Hole, 1944
Fire Lance, 3646
Fire Rock, 5740
The Fire Ship, 5322
The Fire Theft, 2238
Fire Tongue, 348
Firebird, 1040
Firebreak, 2589
Firecrest, 1017
Firefight 2000, 2814
Firefox, 5237
Firefox Down, 5245
Firegold, 1512
Fireplay, 5677
The Fires of Heaven, 3826
The Fires of Paris, 5794
The Firestarter, 3019
Firestorm, 4213
First Blood, 1006
First Came a Murder, 49
A First Class Murder, 4555
The First Lady, 3954
First Loyalty, 3322
First Salvo, 5201
The First Sir Percy: An Adventure of the Laughing Cavalier, 288
First Strike, 5223
Fish Out of Water, 2357
Fish Story, 2710
The Five Fingers, 4523
Five Flamboys, 296
Five Gates to Armageddon, 1218
Five Great Spy Novels, 2523
Five Hours from Isfahan, 1330
Five Minutes to Midnight, 4926
Fives Wild, 5722

Fix, 1227
A Flag for Sunrise, 5156
Flag in the City, 3127
The Flags at Doney, 2305
A Flame from Persepolis, 2319
Flameout, 4214
Flames of Heaven: A Novel of the End of the Soviet Union, 4277
Flamingo, 4504
Flamingo Feather, 5411
Flash Point, 448
The Fleet in the Window, 742
The Fleur-de-Lys Affair, 4637
Flight from a Dark Equator, 3251
The Flight from Winter's Shadow, 5629
Flight From a Firing Wall, 2963
Flight From Time One, 4552
Flight in Darkness, 4685
Flight into Fear, 893
Flight of a Dragon, 793
Flight of Hawks, 1762
A Flight of Lies, 4865
Flight of the Bat, 4194
Flight of the Condor, 2581
Flight of the Intruder, 1322
Flight of the Old Dog, 887
Flittermouse, 2936
Floodgate, 3589
The Florentine Madonna, 2320
Florida Is Closed Today, 2757
The Flower-Covered Corpse, 590
Flowers from Berlin, 2800
The Flying Camel, 561
The Flying Horse, 4686
The Flying Saucer, 3979
The Flying Saucer Gambit, 3648
Folio Forty One, 4990
Fontego's Folly, 5704
Fool's Mate, 4259

The Fools in Town Are on Our
    Side, 5263
For Dying You Always Have
    Time, 5000
For Infamous Conduct, 3092
For Reasons of State, 713
For Special Services, 2083
For the Good of the State, 4405
For the President's Eyes Only,
    4742
For the Queen, 271
For Your Eyes Only, 1878
For Your Sighs Only, 3042
Forbidden Area, 1956
The idden Frontiers, 343
The idden Territory, 360
Force 10 from Navarone, 3590
Force of Eagles, 2590
Force Play, 5167
Forced Landing, 786
Foreign Exchange (Beinhart), 718
Foreign Exchange (Sangster),
    4762
Forest of Eyes, 1018
Forgotten Road, 4687
The Formula (Sager), 4737
The Formula (Shagan), 4928
Forsyth's Three, 1931
The Fort Terror Murders, 206
The Fortec Conspiracy, 2149
Fortress in the Rice, 547
Fortress London, 5795
Fortress of the Marquis, 2284
The Fortune of War, 4040
The Forty-First Thief, 4358
Foul Up, 4260
Founder Member, 2084
The Four Armourers, 297
Four Days (Crook), 1471
Four Days (King), 3014
The Four Horses, 4330
The Four Just Men, 335

Four Men, 4517
Four Rounds of Bulldog
    Drummond, 186
The Four Sergeants, 5799
Fourteen Seconds to Hell, 1094
The Fourth Agency, 1971
The Fourth Angel, 2765
Fourth at Junction, 686
The Fourth Codex, 2692
The Fourth Durango, 5272
The Fourth Funeral, 2553
The Fourth Horseman, 795
The Fourth Man, 3429
The Fourth Plague, 336
The Fourth Protocol, 1932
The Fox and the Camellias, 4972
The Fox Prowls, 367
Foxbat, 1185
The Foxbat Spiral, 2932
Foxcatcher, 2394
Frame-Up, 5705
Francesca, 3211
Frankenstein's Children, 3647
The Frankincense Trail, 2967
The Fraternity of the Stone, 3897
The Fratricides, 1760
Fraulein Spy, 1095
A Free Agent, 5476
Free Flight, 5226
The Freebooters, 5343
Freedom at Midnight, 1289
The Freedom Trap, 629
The Freelancers, 2280
The French Atlantic Affair, 3185
The French Decision, 4106
French Entrapment, 1370
A French Killing, 4549
A Frenchman Must Die, 826
The Friday Run, 5741
A Friendly Place to Die, 1843
Friends, Russians, and
    Countrymen, 2698

The Frighteners, 2434

The Frog and the Scorpion, 3782

The Frog in the Moonflower, 1699

Frogman Assassination, 4911

From Russia with Love, 1879

Frontier of Fear, 2511

Frost, 2389

Frost the Fiddler, 5542

Frozen Assets, 3153

FSO-1, 2304

Fu Manchu's Bride, 354

Full Fathom Five, 1554

Funeral for a Commissar, 3656

Funeral in Berlin, 1585

Furioso, 3229

Gabriel Samara, Peacemaker, 236

Gabrielle, 2338

Gad, 2160

Gage, 1188

The Galloway Case, 5706

Gamailes, and Other Tales from Stalin's Russia, 535

A Game for Heroes, 4150

A Game of Secrets, 5732

A Game of Titans, 4723

The Game of X, 4945

Game, Set, & Match, 1586

Game without Rules, 2201

Gamefinger, 3043

Games of the Hangman, 4102

The Gamma Option, 3123

The Gamov Factor, 2376

Gangster Movies, 2669

The Garden Game, 5624

The Garden of Weapons, 2085

The Gargoyle Conspiracy, 453

Gate of the Tigers, 3788

The Gates of Exquisite View, 5336

The Gates of Hell, 4747

The Gates of Sagittarius, 1504

Gateway to Hell, 5590

Gauge of Deception, 4652

The Gaunt Woman, 775

The Gay Deceiver, 3198

The Gaza Intercept, 2728

The Gemini Contenders, 3342

The General's Daughter, 1609

The Generals, 968

Genesis in the Desert, 997

The Genesis Rock, 1347

The Geneva Crisis, 2214

The Gentle Assassin, 1480

The Gentleman at Large, 797

The Gentleman Reform, 798

Gentleman Traitor, 5649

German Spy, 217

The Gestapo File, 3413

Gestapo Fugitive, 4351

Get Smart, 2869

Get Smart: And Loving It, 2870

Get Smart: Max Smart and the Perilous Pellets, 2871

Get Smart: Max Smart Loses Control, 2872

Get Smart: Max Smart, the Spy Who Went Out to the Cold, 2873

Get Smart: Missed by That Much!, 2874

Get Smart: Once Again, 2875

Get Smart: Sorry Chief!, 2876

Getting Even, 716

Ghost Blonde, 5639

The Ghost Boat, 4986

Ghostflight, 2945

Ghostrider One, 1039

The Ghosts of Africa, 5135

Giant Killer, 2794

The Giant's Shadow, 813

The Gibraltar Conspiracy, 3960

Gibraltar Road, 3457

The Gift from Berlin, 683
The Gift of a Falcon, 2475
Gilt-Edged Bonds, 1880
The Gilt-Edged Traitor, 1763
A Girl Called Fathom, 1926
The Girl from Addis, 489
The Girl from HARD, 3861
The Girl from Peking, 3660
The Girl from PUSSYCAT, 2226
The Girl from UNCLE: The Birds of a Feather Affair, 591
The Girl from UNCLE: A Blazing Affair, 592
The Girl from UNCLE: The Cornish Pixie Affair, 3199
The Girl from UNCLE: The Global Globules Affair, 3145
The Girl from UNCLE: The Golden Boats of Taradata Affair, 3146
The Girl Hunters, 5094
Girl in a Big Brass Bed, 4461
Give Us This Day, 2729
Given the Ammunition, 2198
The Glendower Legacy, 2175
Glitter Street, 5179
Glitterburn, 2230
Global 2000: Eye of the Eagle, 699
The Glory Boys, 4915
The Glory Jumpers, 5108
The Glory Trap, 4959
Go Away Death, 1417
God against the Gods, 1710
The God Machine, 992
The GOD Project, 3180
Goddesses Never Die, 3664
The Goering Testament, 3717
The Goering Treasure, 2730
The Gold Coast, 1612
The Gold Crew, 4859
The Gold of Troy, 1857

The Golden Cockatrice, 5770
The Golden Deed, 5707
The Golden Express, 3093
Golden Fear, 4709
The Golden Fleecing, 5398
The Golden Gate, 3591
The Golden Keel, 630
The Golden Rendezvous, 3592
The Golden Salamander, 1019
The Golden Scorpion, 355
The Golden Serpent, 1096
The Golden Statuette, 4234
The Golden Triangle (Bonnecarrère), 809
The Golden Triangle (Proud), 4434
The Golden U-Boat, 2577
The Golden Virgin, 1658
Goldfinger, 1881
Goliath, 2156
A Good Death, 4641
Good Friday, 2639
Good Guys Wear Black, 1958
Good Luck, Sucker, 5217
The Good Neighbor Murder, 4326
Good Spies Don't Grow on Trees, 3632
Good Spy, 2324
Goodbye and Amen, 5289
Goodbye California, 3593
Goodbye, Gorgeous, 5569
Goodbye to an Old Friend, 1980
The Gorbachev Version, 2721
Gorky Park, 5042
The Gotland Deal, 1467
Grab, 5801
The Gracious Lily Affair, 3751
Grail, 5425
The Grand Defiance, 2012
Grand Slam, 4261
The Grandmaster, 3931
Grave Doubt, 644

A Grave for a Russian, 5410
Grave Goods, 3679
Grave Witness, 3232
Gravedigger's Funeral, 559
The Graveyard Shift, 4151
Gray Eagles, 5397
The Great Affair, 1020
The Great Big Trenchcoat in the Sky, 3640
The Great Impersonation, 237
The Great Land, 3094
The Great Plot, 158
The Great Prince Shan, 272
The Great Secret, 238
Great Spectators, 2670
Great Spy Novels and Stories, 1811
The Great Spy Race, 1649
Great Spy Stories from Fiction, 1726
The Great Waltz, 4661
The Great War in England in 1897, 143
The Greek Position, 4544
The Green Berets, 3885
Green Grow the Tresses-O, 2790
Green Hazard, 3697
Green Light, Red Catch, 4728
Green Monday, 5253
Green River High, 901
The Green Wolf Connection, 1097
Greenfinger, 4475
Greenfly, 3470
The Greenham Plot, 2179
Greenmantle, 14
Grishin, 2587
Ground Zero, 1391
Group Seven, 534
The Grudge, 1214
A Grue of Ice, 2846
Guadalajara, 2751
Guerrilla, 1662

Guilty Bonds, 144
The Gulf, 4388
A Gun for Sale, 95
Gunner Kelly, 4407
The Guns of Arrest, 3471
The Guns of Mazatlan, 4127
The Guns of Navarone, 3594
Gunship, 4825
Gunston Cotton: A Romance of the Secret Service, 90
Gunston Cotton: Secret Agent, 91
Gunston Cotton: Secret Airman, 92

H.M.S. Hero, 3574
H.M.S. Surprise, 4041
H.M.S. Ulysses, 3610
The Hab Theory, 1757
The Habit of Fear, 1558
The Hadrian Ransom, 1716
Haggard, 4007
The Hahnemann Sequela, 3015
The Haigerlock Project, 3792
Haiti, 1098
The Haj, 5401
Halfhyde and the Chain Gangs, 3472
Halfhyde Goes to War, 3473
Halfhyde to the Narrows, 3475
Halfhyde's Island, 3474
The Hamburg Switch, 2180
The Hamlet Problem, 834
The Hamlet Warning, 4759
Hammerhead (Coulter), 1376
Hammerhead (Hunt), 2752
Hammerhead (Savarin), 4826
Hammerheads, 884
Hammerstrike, 5723
The Hand of Fu Manchu, 349
Hand of Mary Constable, 2036
Hand Out, 4476

A Handful of Dominoes, 2862
A Handful of Silver, 1021
The Handle, 5582
Hands Off Bulldog Drummond, 1833
The Handyman: City for Sale, 3812
The Handyman: Fire in the Streets, 3813
The Handyman: The Game of Terror, 3808
The Handyman: The Inheritors, 3809
The Handyman: The Moneta Papers, 3810
The Handyman: Murder Today, Money Tomorrow, 3814
The Handyman: A Promise of Death, 3815
The Handyman: Ransom, 3811
The Handyman: The Revenger, 3816
The Handyman: The Stiletto Signature, 3817
The Handyman: The Swiss Secret, 3818
The Handyman: The Vendetta Contract, 3819
The Hanged Men, 1344
Hanging On, 3057
Hangman, 2157
The Hangman's Crusade, 697
Hankow Return, 549
Hanoi, 1099
Hans, Who Goes There?, 2563
Hantu, 2387
The Harbinger, 2237
The Harbinger Effect, 5736
Hard Drive, 4337
A Hard Man to Kill, 4262
The Hard Men, 933
The Hard Sell, 1246

Hard Target, 2789
Hard-Boiled Wonderland and the End of the World, 3925
Hardball, 4767
The Hardliners, 1247
The Hargrave Deception, 2731
Harlequin, 5561
The Harlot of Jericho, 3865
Harlot's Ghost, 3657
The Harrison Affair, 4916
Harry's Game, 4917
Hartinger's Mouse, 3458
Hartman's Game, 1389
The Hastings Conspiracy, 1336
Hate Is for the Hunted, 1950
Hauser's Memory, 5001
Havana Heat, 2640
Havana X, 2333
Havoc, 273
Hawaii, 1100
Hawaii Five-O, 593
Hawaii Five-O: Terror in the Sun, 594
Hawkeland Cache, 1869
The Hawthorne Group, 2520
Hazard, 890
Head of State, 2711
The Heart of the Dog, 4530
Heartland, 2371
The Heat of Ramadan, 2518
Heat of the Day, 823
The Heights of Rimring, 2507
The Heights of Zervos, 4838
The Heirs of Cain, 4662
Helen All Alone, 907
Hell Gate, 1565
Hell Is Always Today, 4152
Hell Is Too Crowded, 4153
Hell Let Loose, 298
The Helsinki Affair, 4817
Hemingway's Notebook, 2256
Henry McGee Is Not Dead, 2246

Here Be Monsters, 4416
Here Comes Charlie M, 1981
Here's a Villain, 3855
The Heresy, 5061
A Hero for Leanda, 5693
A Hero in His Time, 1282
Hero in the Tower, 3024
The Herod Conspiracy, 4515
The Hess Cross, 5230
The Hidden and the Hunted, 5181
The Hidden Kingdom, 299
The Hidden Target, 3535
The Hidden Terror, 3536
Hide and Go Seek, 5708
High Citadel, 631
The High Commissioner, 1264
High Crystal, 993
High Jinx, 919
The High Place, 2680
High Requiem, 3414
High Stakes, 4507
High Stand, 2440
High Terror, 2308
High Water at Four, 5312
The High Wire, 1248
The Highest Ground, 3645
Hijacked, 1345
The Hill of Summer: A Novel of the Soviet Conquest, 1704
A Himalayan Assignment, 3752
The Himalayan Concerto, 3766
The Himmler Equation, 2974
The Himmler Ploy, 3366
His Majesty's Agent, 4932
Hit, 5104
Hit the Beach!, 3248
The Hitler Diamonds, 3415
The Holcroft Covenant, 3343
A Hole in the Ground, 5694
Holes in the Wall, 640
Holiday for a Spy, 2843
Holiday with a Vengeance, 4263

The Hollow Men, 2377
Holocaust, 2920
Holt RN, 3575
Home Again, 5672
Home Run, 4924
The Home Secretary Will See You Now, 2824
Home to Roost, 5709
Homicidal Spy, 4352
Homicide Is My Game, 3222
The Honey Ant, 894
Honey for the Bears, 5669
Honey on Her Tail, 1852
The Honeycomb Bid, 4750
The Hong Kong Airbase Murders, 207
The Hong Kong Caper, 5776
Hong Kong Kill, 2162
Honor among Thieves, 550
Honor Bound, 982
The Honorary Consul, 2291
The Honourable Schoolboy, 1356
Hood of Death, 1101
A Hooded Crow, 5238
The Hoof, 3476
Hooligan, 1667
Hopjoy was Here, 5532
Hopscotch, 2110
Horn of Africa, 1035
The Horse of Darius, 1177
Horse under Water, 1587
Host of Extras, 3154
Hostage, 3748
Hostage Game, 3633
Hostage in Peking, 2314
Hostage One, 1859
Hostage-London: The Diary of Julian Despard, 2681
Hostages, 2610
Hostile Intent, 1781
Hot Pursuit (Katcher), 2941
Hot Pursuit (Scott), 4866

Hot Season, 3804

Hotline: Moscow at Noon Is the Target, 5162

Hotline: One of Our Spacecraft Is Missing, 5163

Hotline: The President Has Been Kidnapped, 5164

The Hound and the Fox and the Harper, 2596

The Hound of Heaven, 5757

The Hounds of Hell, 3142

Hour before Dawn, 3775

An Hour before Zero, 4688

Hour of the Argehtine, 3137

Hour of the Assassins, 2926

Hour of the Clown, 562

The Hour of the Donkey, 4417

The Hour of the Lily, 3060

Hour of the Scorpion, 5195

Hour of the Wolf, 1102

House of Exile, 1402

House of Shade, 2644

The House of Soldiers, 5710

House of the Roses, 642

The House of Whispers, 159

The House on Curzon Street, 3392

The House on K Street, 5626

Hovey's Deception, 4638

How Green Was My Apple, 3634

The Howard Hughes Affair, 2912

The Huddersfield Job, 2191

The Human Factor, 2292

Human Time-Bomb, 1103

The Hungarian Game, 2532

Hungry Ghost, 3167

The Hunt Club, 1519

The Hunt for <u>*Red October*</u>, 1228

Hunt the Spy, 170

Hunted Woman (Loewengard), 3302

The Hunted Woman (Pendower), 4235

Hunter, 4821

Hunter and Raven, 4822

Hunter and the Ikon, 4823

Hunter of the Blood, 5450

Hunter/Victim, 4946

Hunter's Run, 4524

Hunter-Killer, 2847

The Hunters of Karinhall, 5643

The Hunting Ground, 5285

Huntingtower, 15

Hush, Hush Johnson, 2153

The Hyde Park Murder, 4556

The Hydra Head, 2015

The Hyte Maneuver, 3834

I Am the Withered Man, 1454

I and My True Love, 3537

I Confess, 4973

I Hide, We Seek, 5123

I Killed Stalin, 4028

I, Lucifer, 4054

I Met a Man, 9

I, Said the Spy, 3095

I Spy, 5456

I Spy: Countertrap, 5457

I Spy: Death-Twist, 5458

I Spy: Doomdate, 5459

I Spy: Masterstroke, 5460

I Spy: Superkill, 5461

I Spy: Wipeout, 5462

I Will Repay, 289

I'll Never Like Friday Again, 5499

I'll Say She Does, 1208

The Icarus Agenda, 3344

The Ice (Charbonneau), 1198

Ice (Follett), 1902

The Ice Raid, 1392

Ice Station Zebra, 3595

Ice Trap Terror, 1171

Ice-Bomb Zero, 1104

Iceberg, 1493
Icebreaker, 2086
The Icemen, 3905
If All the Rebels Die, 5070
If You Can't Be Good, 5264
Ilion like a Mist, 3856
Illegal Entry, 3743
The Illustrious Prince, 239
Image Makers, 1715
Image of Evil, 2403
Imbroglio, 1284
Immaculate Deception, 444
The Impossible Virgin, 4055
The Imposter (Kagley), 2905
The Imposter (Keeley), 2953
The Impromptu Inspector, 5429
In a Lady's Service, 553
In Any Case, 5124
In Connection with Kilshaw, 1693
In Council Rooms Apart, 1403
In Harm's Way, 2849
In High Places, 2385
In Honor Bound, 4918
In Like Flint, 5160
In the Company of Spies, 687
In the Forest of the Night, 1844
In the Hour before Midnight, 4154
In the House of Night, 2722
In the House of Secret Enemies, 1203
In the Long Run, 1463
In the Name of the Father, 4449
In the National Interest, 2906
In the Nude, 4903
In the Red, 1782
In the Secret State, 3433
In the Shadow of Freedom, 2907
Inca Death Squad, 1105
An Incident at Bloodtide, 1202
The Incident at Naha, 817

The Incongruous Spy: Two Novels of Suspense, 1357
The Incursion, 2451
The Infant of Prague, 2247
Inference of Guilt, 2301
The Infernal Device, 3071
The Inferno, 1437
The Infiltrator (Nicole), 3999
The Infiltrator (Walker), 5479
The Infiltrators, 2435
An Infinity of Mirrors, 1300
The Innocent, 3513
Innocent Bystanders, 3847
The Inquisitor: The Devil in Kansas, 5043
The Inquisitor: His Eminence Death, 5044
The Inquisitor: Last Rites for the Vulture, 5045
The Inquisitor: The Last Time I Saw Hell, 5046
The Inquisitor: The Midas Coffin, 5047
The Inquisitor: Nuplex Red, 5048
The Inscrutable Charlie Muffin, 1989
The Insidious Dr. Fu Manchu, 350
Inspector Ghote Caught in Meshes, 2950
The "Intelligence" Game of Secret Service Cases and Problems, 164
Intercept, 746
The Intercom Conspiracy, 503
Intercontinental Knot, 3369
The Interface Assignment, 4496
The Interlopers, 2413
The International Spy, 331
Interrupt, 1747
Intersect File: Death Cruise, 1032

Interventions, 859
The Intimidators, 2414
Into Thin Air, 2802
Intrigue for Empire, 3035
Intrigue: Four Great Spy Novels, 504
Intriguers (LeQueux), 145
The Intriguers (Hamilton), 2415
The Intriguers: Four Superb Novels of Suspense, 505
Intruder, 3152
Intruder from the Sea, 3506
The Invaders, 2962
The Invasion of 1910, 146
The Invisible Evil, 2030
Invisible Red, 4128
The Invisibles, 1531
Invitation to Death, 4353
The Ionian Mission, 4042
The Ipcress File, 1588
The Irish Witch, 5602
The Iron Curtain, 4354
The Iron Men, 4875
The Iron Sanctuary, 3048
The Iron Tiger, 4155
Is Paris Burning?, 1290
Is There a Traitor in the House?, 3519
The Iskra Incident, 940
Island Alert, 5496
The Island of Fu Manchu, 5508
Island of Gold, 2261
The Island of Peril, 50
The Island of Sheep, 906
Island of Spies, 340
Island Rescue, 5313
The Island Where Time Stands Still, 5595
Isle of Dragons, 3051
Isolation, 4327
Israeli Commandos: The Alps Assignment, 5174

Israeli Commandos: The Aswan Assignment, 5175
Israeli Commandos: The Fireball Assignment, 5176
Israeli Commandos: The Kamikaze Plot, 5177
Istanbul, 1106
Isvik, 2441
It Can't Always be Caviar: The Fabulously Daring Adventures of an Involuntary Secret Agent, 4978
It's a Free Country, 840
Italian Assets, 490

The Jacamar Nest, 4131
Jackals of the Secret Service, 115
Jade Lady Burning, 3261
The Jade Lizard, 1685
Jade Tiger, 5239
Jade Woman, 2151
Jaguar, 1743
James Bond: The Authorized Biography of 007, 4204
The Janus Imperative, 5515
The Janus Man, 4839
The Jasmine Sloop, 2966
The Jaws of the Watchdog, 1700
The Jericho Commandment, 4188
The Jericho Rumble, 3927
The Jerusalem Code, 3027
The Jerusalem File, 1107
Jewel of Doom, 1108
Jian, 5419
Jig, 565
The Jigsaw Man, 723
The Jihad Ultimatum, 4467
Jimgrim, 99
Jimgrim and Allah's Peace, 100
The Jing Affair, 5074
A Job Abroad, 695

Joe Gall: The Black Venus Contract, 4296

Joe Gall: The Canadian Bomber Contract, 4297

Joe Gall: The Death Bird Contract, 4298

Joe Gall: The Fer-de-Lance Contract, 4299

Joe Gall: The Green Wound, 4300

Joe Gall: The Ill-Wind Contract, 4301

Joe Gall: The Irish Beauty Contract, 4302

Joe Gall: The Judah Lion Contract, 4303

Joe Gall: The Kiwi Contract, 4304

Joe Gall: The Kowloon Contract, 4305

Joe Gall: The Last Domino Contract, 4306

Joe Gall: The Makassar Strait Contract, 4307

Joe Gall: The Paper Pistol Contract, 4314

Joe Gall: The Rockabye Contract, 4308

Joe Gall: The Shankill Road Contract, 4309

Joe Gall: The Silkon Baroness Contract, 4315

Joe Gall: The Skeleton Coast Contract, 4316

Joe Gall: The Spice Route Contract, 4310

Joe Gall: The Star Ruby Contract, 4311

Joe Gall: The Trembling Earth Contract, 4312

Joe Gall: The Underground Cities Contract, 4313

Joe Gall: The White Wolverine Contract, 4317

Johnny Goes South, 3424

Johnny Goes West, 3416

The Jonah Kit, 5534

Joshua's People, 3393

Journey into Fear, 506

Journey to a Safe Place, 771

The Journeyman Tailor, 4919

The Judas Code, 3096

Judas Country, 3358

The Judas Diary, 649

The Judas Factor, 471

The Judas Gene, 3026

The Judas Goat, 4129

The Judas Hour, 2732

The Judas Kiss, 2942

Judas Mandate, 1783

The Judas Sheep, 4527

The Judas Spies, 4536

Judas Spy, 1109

The Judas Squad, 4674

Judgment on Deltchev, 507

The Juliet Effect, 5010

Jungle Jest, 101

The Jupiter Crisis, 2481

The Jupiter Missile Mystery, 706

Just Desserts, 2543

Just Not Making Them Like They Used to, 5436

Justice for a Dead Spy, 3860

The "K" Section, 3259

The Kaisho, 5420

Kalahari Kill, 1605

Karamanov Equations, 2215

Katie's Terror, 1863

The Katmandu Contract, 1110

The Kermanschah Transfer, 4971

The Kessler Legacy, 5125

The Key to Midnight, 4019

The Key to Rebecca, 1910

The Keys of Hell, 4156

KG-200, 2203

The KGB Directive, 1393

The KGB Is Here, 5403

The Khufra Run, 4157

The Kid from Riga, 3863

Kidnap, 3477

The Kidnappers, 2991

The Kidnapping of the President, 5221

Kiev Footprint, 4381

Kill Cure, 4477

The Kill Dog, 927

Kill Her with Love, 2275

Kill the Boss Good-Bye, 4462

Killed on the Ice, 1574

The Killer Elite, 2659

A Killer for a Song, 2087

A Killer for the Chairman, 2491

Killer Patrol, 1847

Killer Pine, 2356

A Killing Affair, 645

The Killing Game (Brent), 854

The Killing Game (Cheyney), 1213

A Killing in Rome, 2660

A Killing in the Market, 2219

The Killing Man, 5095

The Killing of Idi Amin, 5531

The Killing Season, 2971

The Killing Winds, 1954

Killtest, 3009

The Kilroy Gambit, 780

Kim, 133

A Kind of Anger, 508

A Kind of Prisoner, 1418

A Kind of Treason, 1806

King, Bishop, Knight, 1814

King Fisher Lives, 4478

King in Check, 102

King Jaguar, 4955

The King's Commisssar, 895

King's Enemies, 341

King--of the Khyber Rifles, 103

The Kingdom of Illusion, 4948

The Kingdom of the Blind, 240

Kingfisher, 4920

Kingfisher Scream, 1940

Kirby's Last Circus, 5076

The Kiriov Tapes, 4893

Kiss the Tiger, 1561

Kisses from Satan, 3665

The Kites of War, 3097

The Knife behind the Curtain: Tales of Crime and the Secret Service, 368

A Knife for the Juggler, 3698

Knit One, Drop One, 3231

Knock and Wait Awhile, 5549

The Kobra Manifesto, 5344

Kolchak's Gold, 2111

Kolwezi, 4264

Korean Tiger, 1111

Kosygin Is Coming, 552

The Kramer Project, 5053

Kramer's War, 4542

The Kremlin Connection, 1990

The Kremlin Conspiracy (Hagberg), 2372

The Kremlin Conspiracy (Hunt), 2753

The Kremlin File, 1112

The Kremlin Kiss, 1991

The Kremlin Letter, 714

The Kremlin Watcher, 4273

The Kreutzman Formula, 4877

Kriegspiel: A Novel of Tomorrow's Europe, 5158

The Kruschev Objective, 2796

Krysalis, 5342

The Kummersdorf Connection, 2378

The Kung Fu Avengers, 3844

Kyril, 5335

Labyrinth, 3114
The Labyrinth Makers, 4408
*Ladies of the Dark: The Lives,
    Loves, and Daring Exploits of
    Famous Female Spies*, 799
Lady Doctor-Woman Spy, 228
*The Lady from LUST: The 69
    Pleasures*, 2273
*The Lady from LUST: Five Beds
    to Mecca*, 2268
*The Lady from LUST: Kiss My
    Assassin*, 2269
*The Lady from LUST: Lay Me
    Odds*, 2270
*The Lady from LUST: Lust Be a
    Lady Tonight*, 2271
*The Lady from LUST: Skin Game
    Dame*, 2272
Lady Left, 5573
Lago, 3171
The Lair, 1195
Lair of the Fox, 4360
Lake of the Diamond, 3172
Lambs of Fire, 1937
Lamp-Post 592, 344
Lancer Spy, 165
A Land of Mirrors, 1339
Landfall, 2170
A Landing of the Sun, 1961
Landslide, 637
A Lantern for Diogenes, 4710
The Lantern Network, 472
Lapis, 2437
The Last Act, 1795
The Last Assassin, 3508
The Last Assignment, 1867
Last Battle, 4008
The Last Bridge, 2112
The Last Checkpoint, 4443

Last Day in Limbo, 4062
The Last Defector, 1034
The Last Exile, 455
The Last Farewell, 3478
The Last Flying Tiger, 1864
The Last Gambit, 1604
The Last Good German, 2248
The Last Heroes, 957
Last Judgment, 2720
The Last Kamikaze, 3903
Last Laugh, Mr. Moto, 3734
The Last Liberator, 1279
Last Man at Arlington, 1653
The Last Man out of Saigon, 3921
The Last Mandarin, 710
The Last Mayday, 5611
The Last Nazi, 3085
The Last Place God Made, 4158
The Last Plane from Uli, 2949
Last Post for a Partisan, 1784
The Last President, 3068
The Last Raven, 5240
The Last Red August, 3669
Last Rights, 4888
The Last Spy (Griffiths), 2326
The Last Spy (Reiss), 4501
The Last Supper, 3406
*The Last Temptation: A Novel of
    Treason*, 3926
Last Train from Berlin
    (Blagowidow), 782
Last Train from Berlin (Hamrick),
    2447
The Last Train Out, 241
The Last Trump, 2088
Last Two Weeks of Georges Rivac,
    2682
The Last Word, 2293
The Late Bill Smith, 5711
Laughter in the Alehouse, 2921
The Launching of Roger Brook,
    5603

Layers of Deceit, 2877
The Laying on of Hands, 560
Lazarus, 5562
The Leader of the Damned, 4846
The League of Dark Men, 1412
The League of Discontent, 300
A League of Hawks, 3390
The League of Light, 1438
The League of Night and Fog, 3898
League of Terror, 2249
Leap for the Sun, 2517
Leathermouth, 68
Leathermouth's Luck, 70
The Leeds Fiasco, 2192
The Left-Handed Sleeper, 5665
Legacy of a Spy, 3776
Legacy of Danger, 3520
The Legend, 5516
Legion of the Lost, 1426
The Leipzig Manuscript, 2193
Lemons Never Die, 5583
The Leopard Contract, 5738
The Leopard Woman, 364
The Lester Affair, 5712
Let a Soldier Die, 2636
Let Him Die, 1276
Let Sleeping Dogs Lie, 2544
Let Sleeping Girls Lie, 1382
Let the Bastards Freeze in the Dark, 4980
Let the Tiger Die, 3699
Let Them Prey, 4711
Let Us Prey, 842
The Letter of Marque, 4039
Letters from the Dead, 769
The Levanter, 509
The Liberation of Paris, 3247
Liberty Two, 3396
Libra, 1602
The Libyan Kill, 4094
License Renewed, 2089

License to Kill, 2090
Lie Down with Lions, 1911
Lieutenant Katia, 1623
The Lieutenants, 969
The Life and Death of Peter Wade, 685
Life Line, 818
The Light Beyond, 242
A Light in the Window, 701
The Light of Day, 510
Lighter Than a Feather, 5574
The Lighthearted Quest, 4078
Lights of Sharo, 1668
The Limbo Line, 1022
Limited Options, 2462
The Linden Affair, 3303
Line of Fire (Butterworth), 975
Line of Fire (Hamilton), 2416
Line of Succession, 2113
The Lingala Code, 2992
The Linz Tattoo, 2341
The Linz Testament, 4437
The Lion and the Jackal, 2448
The Lion in the Stone, 922
Lion of Judah (Ostrovsky), 4108
The Lion of Judah (Willis), 5666
Lion of Petra, 104
Lion's Run, 5246
Lions at Night, 2619
The Liquidator (Carter), 1113
The Liquidator (Gardner), 2091
The Lisa Bastian, 5742
The List, 1114
The List of 7, 2014
Listen, Lovely, 5570
Little Dragon from Peking, 1755
The Little Drummer Girl, 1358
Little Grey Mice, 1992
Little Hercules, 2334
Live and Let Die, 1882
Live, Love and Cry, 3666

Lives and Times of Bernardo Brown, 2683
Lives to Give, 1579
The Living Bomb, 595
Living Death, 1115
Loaded Gun, 4729
The Lollipop Republic, 4743
London Affair, 5168
The London Assignment, 2194
London, Bloody London, 606
The London Connection, 2766
The London Deal, 1468
London Match, 1589
The London Switch, 3886
Lonely Man, 87
The Lonely Margins, 491
The Lonely Sea, 3596
The Long Arm of Mannister, 274
The Long Corridor, 2058
A Long Day's Dying, 1671
The Long Drop, 5617
The Long Fuse, 5618
Long Live the King, 4676
The Long Midnight, 5619
The Long Night's Walk, 5620
The Long Pursuit, 1265
The Long Revenge, 5295
The Long Shadow, 4236
Long Shadows, 5062
The Long Short Cut, 5713
Long Shots, 1348
The Long Silence, 5621
A Long Time Sleeping, 4991
The Long Watch, 5622
The Longely Bungalow, 75
The Loo Sanction, 5614
Look of the Eagle, 4876
Looker, 3003
The Looking Glass War, 1359
Lord Tony's Wife: An Adventure of the Scarlet Pimpernel, 290
The Los Alamos Contract, 3773

The Lost Ambassador; or, The Search for the Missing Delora, 243
The Lost Europeans, 3285
A Lost Leader, 275
The Lost Naval Papers, 134
A Lost Tale, 1824
The Lost Victory, 810
The Lottery, 3098
The Loud Adios, 3062
Love and Terror, 2595
Love and the Land Beyond, 3161
Love and Treason, 4105
Love Came Laughing By, 3317
Love Comes Flying, 928
The Loved Enemy, 1383
Loxfinger: A Thrilling Adventure of Hebrew Secret Agent Oy-Oy-7, Israel Bond, 5551
A Loyal and Dedicated Servant, 2325
Luciano's Luck, 4159
Lucifer at Sunset, 4712
The Lucifer Crusade, 3672
The Lucifer Directive, 3115
The Lucifer Key, 3624
The Luck of the Secret Service, 147
Lucky Ham, 3425
The Ludendorff Pirates, 4466
The Ludi Victor, 3191
The Lunatic at Large, 187
The Lunatic at Large Again, 189
The Lunatic Fringe: A Novel Wherein Theodore Roosevelt Meets the Pink Angel, 1575
The Lunatic Still at Large, 190
Lust Is No Lady, 607
The Luxembourg Run, 2195
The Luxus, 3940
Lying in State, 4479
Lynx, 4827

M*A*S*H Goes to Moscow, 953

M*A*S*H Goes to Paris, 954

M*A*S*H Goes to Vienna, 955

MacAllister, 4265

McGarr at the Dublin Horse Show, 2202

McNally's Lunch, 4756

Macao, 1116

MacKinnon's Machine, 5737

MacTaggart's War, 1615

Maculan's Daughter, 520

Madame Spy, 132

Madonna Red, 1041

Madrigal, 2092

Madrigal for Charlie Muffin, 1993

Maestro, 2093

The Magic Man, 2379

The Magnificent Hoax, 276

Magyar Massacre, 5489

The Mah-Jongg Spies, 5337

The Mahdi, 4453

Majendie's Cat, 1938

The Majors, 970

Make War in Madness, 961

The Maker of History, 244

Making Progress, 641

The Malady in Madeira, 4079

The Malcontents, 1959

The Malefactor, 277

Malko: Angel of Vengeance, 1624

Malko: The Belfast Connection, 1625

Malko: Checkpoint Charlie, 1626

Malko: The Countess and the Spy, 1627

Malko: Death in Santiago, 1628

Malko: Death on the River Kwai, 1629

Malko: Hostage in Tokyo, 1630

Malko: Kill Kissinger, 1631

Malko: Man From Kabul, 1632

Malko: Operation New York, 1633

Malko: The Portuguese Defection, 1634

Malko: Que Viva Guevara, 1635

Malko: Versus the CIA, 1636

Malko: West of Jerusalem, 1637

Mam'zelle Guillotine: An Adventure of the Scarlet Pimpernel, 291

Mama Doll, 5747

Mama's Boy, 3004

Mambo, 566

MAMista, 1590

The Mammoth Book of Spy Thrillers, 5726

The Mamur Zapt and the Donkey-Vous, 4198

The Mamur Zapt and the Men Behind, 4199

The Mamur Zapt and the Night of the Dog, 4200

The Mamur Zapt and the Return of the Carpet, 4201

The Man above Suspicion, 1384

The Man behind the Iron Curtain, 5332

A Man Condemned, 2845

Man Dormant, 3297

Man from Barbarossa, 2094

The Man from CHARISMA, 2228

The Man from Destiny, 3576

The Man from Moscow, 3449

The Man from ORGY, 2222

The Man from ORGY: The Nine-Month Caper, 2223

The Man from ORGY: The Real-Gone Girls, 2224

The Man from PANSY, 4519

The Man from St. Petersburg, 1912

The Man from STUD in the Solid Gold Screw, 1839

The Man from the Sea, 5137

The Man from TOMCAT: The Dirty Rotten Depriving Ray, 2781

The Man from TOMCAT: The Dozen Deadly Dragons of Joy, 2782

The Man fron TOMCAT: The Malignant Metaphysical Menace, 2786

The Man from TOMCAT: The Million Missing Maidens, 2783

The Man from TOMCAT: The Terrible Ten, 2784

The Man from TOMCAT: Tsimmis in Tangier, 2785

The Man from UNCLE, 596

The Man from UNCLE: The Assassination Affair, 2641

The Man from UNCLE: The Copenhagen Affair, 4097

The Man from UNCLE: The Corfu Affair, 4292

The Man from UNCLE: The Cross of Gold Affair, 1807

The Man from UNCLE: The Dagger Affair, 3501

The Man from UNCLE: The Diving Dames Affair, 3201

The Man from UNCLE: The Doomsday Affair, 5633

The Man from UNCLE: The Finger in the Sky Affair, 3200

The Man from UNCLE: The Hollow Crown Affair, 3502

The Man from UNCLE: The Invisibility Affair, 1640

The Man from UNCLE: The Mad Scientist Affair, 4293

The Man from UNCLE: The Mind-Twisters Affair, 1641

The Man from UNCLE: The Monster Wheel Affair, 3503

The Man from UNCLE: The Power Cube Affair, 4294

The Man from UNCLE: The Radioactive Camel Affair, 3202

The Man from UNCLE: The Rainbow Affair, 3499

The Man from UNCLE: The Splintered Sunglasses Affair, 3203

The Man from UNCLE: The Stone-Cold Dead in the Market Affair, 3204

The Man from UNCLE: The Thinking Machine Affair, 743

The Man from UNCLE: The Thousand Coffins Affair, 608

The Man from UNCLE: The Unfair Fare Affair, 3205

The Man from UNCLE: The Utopia Affair, 3504

The Man from UNCLE: The Vampire Affair, 3500

The Man from UNCLE's ABC of Espionage, 2615

The Man from Yesterday, 3720

Man in a Wire Cage, 4252

Man in Question, 1969

The Man in the Green Hat, 3700

The Man in the Lubianka, 5409

The Man in the Middle, 585

The Man in the Mirror, 618

The Man Next Door, 3286

Man of Blood, 1718

Man on a Short Leash, 2044

Man on a String, 5656

Man on Fire, 4450

The Man on the Bridge, 772

The Man on the Camel, 4733

The Man on the Left, 2073

The Man on the Raffles Verandah, 3021

The Man Who Called Himself Devlin, 2285

The Man Who Didn't Count, 2208

The Man Who Heard Too Much, 2250

The Man Who Killed the King, 5604

The Man Who Knew Too Much, 657

The Man Who Looked Like Howard Cosell, 5385

The Man Who Lost the War, 2444

The Man Who Played God, 4741

The Man Who Ran Away, 1670

The Man Who Shook the World, 1439

The Man Who Sold Death (Carter), 1117

The Man Who Sold Death (Mitchell), 3848

The Man Who Used Perfume, 2663

The Man Who Walked Like a Bear, 2913

The Man Who Wanted Tomorrow, 1982

The Man Who Was Saturday, 3088

The Man Who Was There, 690

The Man Who Was Thursday: A Nightmare, 28

The Man Who Was Too Much, 2077

The Man Who Went Up in Smoke, 5475

The Man with Half a Face, 66

The Man with the Black Worrybeads, 4678

The Man with the Clubfoot, 369

The Man with the Golden Gun, 1883

The Man with the Monocle, 5585

The Man with the President's Mind, 473

The Man with the Twisted Face, 63

The Man with Two Clocks, 5451

The Man with Two Shadows, 3774

The Man with Yellow Shoes, 2558

The Manchester Thing, 2181

The Manchurian Candidate, 1298

The Mandarin Cypher, 5359

The Mandelbaum Gate, 5073

The Manhattan File, 3741

The Manhattan Gambit, 5118

Manhattan North, 3304

Manhunt Is My Mission, 3212

The Manipulators, 2129

The Manna Enzyme, 2712

Mao II, 1603

Maracaibo Mission, 3753

Marathon Man, 2217

The Marauders, 4067

March of Violence, 2492

Marco Polo, If You Can, 913

The Marcus Device, 3795

Mardi Gras Massacre, 1618

Mare Nostrum, 10

Margin of Error, 2570

Margin of Terror, 3525

Mark Coffin, U.S.S.: A Novel of Capitol Hill, 1711

The Mark of Cosa Nostra, 1118

The Mark of the Crescent, 51

The Mark of Zorro, 162

Marseilles, 3372

Marshmallow Pie, 3315

The Masada Plan, 2494

The Mask of Alexander, 3305

The Mask of Fu Manchu, 356

The Mask of Glass, 4656

The Mask of Memory, 1023

Mask of Treason, 5128

The Masked Man, 1672

Massacre at Tangini, 3084

Massacre in Milan, 1119

The Master Plan, 2004

Master Plot, 5039

The Master Sniper, 2769

Master Spy, 4237

Masterpiece, 2695

The Masterpiece Affair, 2059

The Masters Affair, 2621

The Masters Connection, 1193

Masterstroke, 4939

The Matarese Circle, 3345

The Matlock Paper, 3354

Matorni's Vineyard, 245

A Matter for the Regiment, 3489

A Matter of Conscience, 2463

A Matter of Diplomacy, 5389

A Matter of Honor (Maxim), 3781

A Matter of Honor (McGivern), 3526

A Matter of Intelligence, 5733

A Matter of Priority, 2645

Matzohball: A New Adventure of Hebrew Secret Agent Oy-Oy-7, Israel Bond, 5552

Max Galan: Hunter of Men, 2336

May Day in Magadan, 4070

May You Die in Ireland, 2980

Maybe a Trumpet, 4713

Mayday (Block), 787

Mayday! (Cussler), 1501

Mayday Man, 711

Mazatlan, 2754

Maze, 1287

Means of Escape, 1738

Meanwhile Back at the Morgue, 609

Mecca for Murder, 3223

The Med, 4389

The Median Line, 1261

The Mediterranean Caper, 1494

The Medusa Conspiracy, 4947

Meet Me Tonight, 3306

Megiddo, 2939

The Megstone Plot, 5714

Meirovitz Plan, 577

Memo to a Firing Squad, 844

Memoirs of a Dance Hall Romeo, 4160

Memorial Bridge, 1045

The Memory Church, 4889

The Memory Man (Griffiths), 2327

The Memory Man (Lambert), 3099

Memory of Treason, 2668

The Memory Trap, 4418

Men in Blue, 977

Men of Career, 3318

Men-at-Arms, 5537

Menace, 52

The Menacers, 2417

The Menwith Tangle, 2196

The Mercenaries, 5319

Mercenary, 998

Merchants of Death, 2011

Message Ends, 5382

Message from Absalom, 5278

Message from Malaga, 3538

Messenger from Munich, 4325

The Messenger Must Die, 816

The Mexican Assassin, 790

Mexican Standoff, 1945

Mexico Set, 1591

Mexico Way, 3911

Mice Are Not Amused, 2608

Mickey Spillane: Five Complete Mike Hammer Novels, 5100

The Midas Men, 1994

The Midas Operation, 2321
Midnight Admiral, 3919
Midnight Never Comes, 4161
The Midnight Patient, 2676
Midnight Plus One, 3359
The Midnighters, 679
Midwinter Madness, 5170
The Miernik Dossier, 3404
Miklos Alexandrovitch Is Missing,
    1766
Miko, 5418
Milan Grill Room, 4095
*Military Intelligence-8: Captain
    North's Most Celebrated
    Intrigues*, 198
Mills, 4044
The Mills Bomb, 1785
The Mind Breaker, 3769
The Mind Killers, 1120
The Mind Masters, 4648
The Mind Poisoners, 1121
Mind to Mind, 4222
Mindanao Pearl, 3373
The Mindbenders, 4446
Mindfield, 1622
Mindscream, 5807
The Miniatures Frame, 2060
Ministry of Fear, 2294
The Minotaur, 1323
Mirage, 1903
Miro, 2597
The Mirror Maze, 2632
The Mischiefmaker, 246
The Misericordia Drop, 2310
Misfire, 1995
Miss Brown of the X.Y.O., 278
The Miss from SIS, 5330
Miss Mystery, 121
Miss Turquoise, 3661
Missing, 597
The Missing Bishop, 5081
Missing from the Record, 1786

The Mission (Brelis), 843
The Mission (Tuccile), 5379
Mission Berlin, 474
Mission Code #1: Symbol, 5728
Mission Code #4: Granite Island,
    3038
Mission Code #7: Acropolis,
    5727
Mission Code #10: Scorpion,
    3039
Mission Code #11: Survival,
    3040
A Mission for Eagles, 4424
Mission Impossible, 5463
*Mission Impossible: Code Name,
    Little Ivan*, 5464
*Mission Impossible: Codename
    Judas*, 5480
*Mission Impossible: Codename
    Rapier*, 5481
*The Mission in Sparrow Bush
    Lane*, 5110
Mission in Tunis, 4238
Mission to Malaspiga, 5517
Mission to Venice, 1122
Mission to Warsaw, 5444
Mission: Tank War, 3072
Mission: Third Force, 3073
Missionary Stew, 5273
Mister Target, 2484
The Mists of Fear, 1427
Mitla Pass, 5402
Mittenwald Syndicate, 4030
Mixed Doubles, 1507
The Mobius Trap, 2124
Model for Murder, 3224
Modesty Blaise, 4056
The Moghul, 2654
Mohune's Nine Lives, 2329
Mole (Hood), 2652
The Mole (Sherman), 4956
The Mona Intercept, 2418

Monastery Nightmare, 5082

The Money Harvest, 5265

The Money that Money Can't Buy, 3849

The Money War, 5056

The Mongol Mask, 2733

Mongoose R.I.P., 914

Monimbó, 3913

The Monkey Handlers, 3255

Monopoly, 1996

The Month of the Falling Leaves, 3737

The Month of the Pearl, 2886

Moon of Ice, 3262

Moon of Madness, 351

The Moonbeams, 749

Moonraker, 1884

Moonrakers and Mischief, 1845

Moonstone Jungle, 4689

The Mordida Man, 5266

More Gilt-Edged Bonds, 1885

A More Perfect Union, 5114

Morituri, 3335

Moroccan, 2362

Mortal Encounter, 4816

Mortal Friends, 1042

Mortal Games, 4746

The Mortal Storm, 11

Mosaic, 3878

Moscow, 1123

Moscow 5000, 5241

Moscow by Nightmare, 4969

The Moscow Club, 1854

Moscow Coach, 3450

Moscow Crossing, 2373

The Moscow File, 5301

The Moscow Intercept, 578

Moscow Interlude, 5228

Moscow Magician, 3877

Moscow Murder, 3961

The Moscow Papers, 5625

Moscow Quadrille, 475

Moscow Racetrack, 2207

Moscow Road, 4690

Moscow Rules, 3912

The Moscow Sacrament, 2594

Moscow Twilight, 2635

Mosley Receipt, 2045

Mosquito Run, 2591

The Most Dangerous Game, 3360

A Most Private Intrigue, 4649

Most Secret, Most Immediate, 5182

Mother Night, 5440

Mother Russia, 3280

Mountainhead, 3417

Mountbatten and the Partition of India, 1291

Moving Targets, 2380

The Mozart Leaves at Nine, 2306

Mr. Billingham, the Marquis, and Madelon, 247

Mr. Blessington's Imperialist Plot, 4963

Mr. Campion's Farthing, 1176

Mr. Essington in Love, 188

Mr. Grex of Monte Carlo, 248

Mr. Holroyd Takes a Holiday, 5112

Mr. Marx's Secret, 279

Mr. Mirakel, 4096

Mr. Moto Is So Sorry, 191

Mr. Ramosi, 375

Mr. Standfast, 16

Mrs. Pollifax and the Golden Triangle, 944

Mrs. Pollifax and the Second Thief, 946

Mrs. Pollifax and the Whirling Dervish, 950

Mrs. Pollifax on Safari, 945

Mrs. Pollifax: Three Complete Mysteries, 947

Much Ado about Something, 2844

The Mule on the Minaret, 5535
The Mullah from Kashmir, 3451
Munich 10, 4099
Murder a Mile High, 1568
Murder Against the Grain, 3144
Murder and the First Lady, 4554
Murder at Hobcaw Barony, 4562
Murder at Moose Jaw, 2534
Murder at the FBI, 5376
*Murder at the Frankfort Book
    Fair*, 3873
Murder at the Kennedy Center,
    5371
Murder at the National Cathedral,
    5373
Murder at the Palace, 4557
Murder at the Pentagon, 5378
Murder at the Red October, 4071
Murder by the Yard, 5780
Murder in Focus, 1741
Murder in Georgetown, 5377
Murder in Havana, 1396
Murder in Moscow, 5695
Murder in State, 2734
Murder in the CIA, 5372
Murder in the Embassy, 20
Murder in the Oval Office, 4558
Murder in the Rose Garden, 4559
Murder in the State Department,
    21
Murder in the Supreme Court,
    5374
Murder Is My Death, 3225
Murder Is So Nostalgic, 5777
*Murder Master: The Caribbean
    Caper*, 4628
Murder Most Foul, 1447
Murder Must Wait, 53
Murder of a Mistress, 4966
Murder of a Moderate Man, 2702
A Murder of Crows, 1719
A Murder of Quality, 1360

Murder on Clam Pond, 2997
Murder on Embassy Row, 5375
Murder on Her Mind, 2735
Murder Wears a Cowl, 1674
Murderers' Row, 2419
The Mushroom Cave, 4629
The Music Wars, 4123
The Mussolini Murder Plot, 218
Mutilators, 2548
My Master Spy, 171
My Turn to Die, 2047
The Mysteries of Algiers, 2820
The Mysterious Mr. Sabin, 249
Mystery of Khufu's Tomb, 105
The Mystery of the Gold Box, 370
The Mystery of the Green Ray,
    148
*The Mystery of the Lost
    Battleship*, 319
The Mystery of the Motor Car,
    149
*The Mystery of the Vanishing
    Aerodrome*, 38

N or M?, 1219
The N-3 Conspiracy, 1124
Naja, 4828
The Naked Bishop, 4738
The Naked Runner, 5286
Naked She Died, 5328
The Name of the Beast, 3510
Nameless Road, 4691
Narrow Exit, 2571
The Narrow Search, 5715
"*The Naval Treaty*," 79
The Nazi Assassins, 3418
The Nazi Hunter, 4941
Nazi Hunter #1, 3675
Nazi Hunter #4: Butcher Block,
    3676
Nazi Hunter #5: Hell Nest, 3677

The Necklace of Skulls, 1698
The Negative Man, 3497
The Negotiator (Forsyth), 1933
The Negotiator (Rogers), 4548
Neither a Candle nor a Pitchfork, 4368
Neither Five nor Three, 3539
The Nemesis Mission, 2807
The Nemesis of Evil, 1046
Nepal, 1125
Neptune, 2168
Neptune's Lance, 1922
The Nervana Contracts, 5735
The Nervous Affair, 5646
Nest of Vultures, 3052
Never Look Back, 4206
Never Send Flowers, 2095
Never So Few, 1191
The New Breed, 983
A New Kind of War, 4409
The Newman Factor, 4401
Newsdeath, 1309
Next Saturday in Milan, 5391
Next Time I'll Pay My Own Fare, 750
The Nicodemus Code, 5037
Night after Night, 5311
Night and Fog, 5490
Night Boat from Puerto Verde, 3559
Night Falls on the City, 521
Night Flying Avenger, 2262
The Night Is a Child, 3290
The Night Is a Time for Listening, 5558
Night Journey, 2239
Night Judgment at Sinos, 4162
Night Jump--Cuba, 4721
Night Launch, 2122
The Night Letter, 5092
The Night, My Friend: Stories of Crime and Suspense, 2625

The Night of Morningstar, 4063
Night of the Avenger, 1126
Night of the Fox, 4163
Night of the Hawk (Brown), 885
Night of the Hawk (Sawkins), 4840
Night of the Seventh Darkness, 3511
Night of the Short Knives, 5647
Night of the Wolf, 650
A Night of Watching, 571
Night of Wenceslas, 1541
Night over Water, 1913
Night Probe, 1495
Night Run, 1617
The Night Seekers, 2061
Night Soldiers, 2019
Night Strike, 5414
The Night They Stole Manhattan, 4100
Night Train, 3868
Night Train to Paris, 3701
Night Vision, 3236
Night without Darkness, 3194
Night without End, 3597
Nightdive, 4215
Nightfall, 1476
Nightfighter Spy, 3552
Nightingale, 4116
Nightmare, 4114
Nightmare and Dawn, 3126
The Nightmare Factor, 4860
Nightmare in Copenhagen, 3307
Nightmare with Angel, 2034
Nightshade, 2025
The Nighttime Guy, 2976
Nile Green, 2889
Nine Against New York, 3182
The Nine Lives of Alphonse, 2863
Nine Unknown, 106
The Nine Waxed Faces, 301
Nineteen Eighty Four, 4104

Nineteen Fifty-Six, 3213
The Ninth Buddha, 3509
The Ninth Car, 4563
The Ninth Circle, 1469
The Ninth Dominion, 3116
The Ninth Man, 3173
The Nirvana Contracts, 1297
No Admission, 5675
No Comebacks, 1934
No Country for Old Men, 4858
No Dark Crusade, 3036
No Darker Crime, 1419
No Deals, Mr. Bond, 2096
No Earth for Foxes, 4045
No End to Fear, 2671
No Entry, 3702
No Exit, 4867
No French Leave, 962
No Hero, 192
No Honor amongst Spies, 4665
No Kisses from the Kremlin, 4668
No Man's Island, 3680
No One of That Name, 3806
No Place for Strangers, 651
No Place to Hide, 476
No Questions Asked, 5267
No Surrender, 3308
No Tears for Hilda, 5716
No Way Back, 2062
No Way Back from Prague, 855
Noble House, 1240
Noble Lord, 3147
The Noble Path, 3784
A Noble Profession, 820
Nobody Lives Forever, 2097
Nocturne for the General, 5338
A Noise in the Night, 2853
None Dare Call It Treason, 2154
None Shall Know, 3309
The Noonday Devil, 2896
The Nooriabad File, 5533
Normandie Triangle, 4873

North Cape, 4394
North from Rome, 3547
North Star Crusade, 2946
North to Rabaul, 5739
Northlight: A Quiller Mission,
  5360
The Nostradamus Traitor, 2098
Not Negotiable, 3703
Not Single Spies, 3980
Not the Glory, 821
Not with a Bang, 4331
Notch on the Knife, 1249
*Notebook No. 1: Mission Number
  One*, 4319
*Notebook No. 2: The Man Who
  Never Was*, 4320
*Notebook No. 3: Dead Man
  Running*, 4321
Nothing Lasts Forever, 5309
Nothing to Declare, 3704
The November Man (Freemantle),
  1997
The November Man (Granbeck),
  2251
Now or Never, 3705
The Nuclear Letters, 3111
Number Ten, 1238
No. 70 Berlin, 160
Numbered Account, 4080

O Jerusalem!, 1292
O Shepherd, Speak, 4994
O'Farrell's Law, 1983
Oasis of Fear, 1826
Oath of Office, 3022
The Obelisk Conspiracy, 3746
Oberst, 2485
Obols for Charon, 4714
Ocean Road, 724
The October Circle, 3275
The October Men, 4410

Octopussy, 1886

Odd Man Plays, 5212

The Odd-Job Man, 1464

Odessa Beach, 3230

The ODESSA File, 1935

The Odor of Violets, 2964

Ofanu, 1936

The Offering (Bolton), 801

The Offering (Reid), 4498

The Officer from Special Branch, 3260

Officers and Gentlemen, 5538

Offshore!, 1385

Oil Strike, 5678

Oktober, 2031

Old Ugly Face, 107

The Old Vengeful, 4419

Old Wars, 2564

Olura, 2684

The Omega Command, 3117

The Omega Deception, 4533

Omega Minus, 477

The Omega Terror, 1127

The Omega Threat, 5530

The Omicron Legion, 3118

On Hazardous Duty, 2736

On Her Majesty's Secret Service, 1887

On Her Majesty's Service, 332

On Instructions of My Government, 4744

On Secret Air Service, 81

On Such a Night, 4441

On the Edge, 1676

On the Prime Minister's Account, 2634

On the Secret Service of His Majesty, the Queen: A Thrilling Adventure of Oy-Oy-7 Israel Bond, 5553

Once a Spy, 1918

The Once and Future Spy, 3276

Once in a Lifetime, 1386

Once in Aleppo, 693

One Clear Call, 4995

One Day in the Life of Ivan Denisovich, 5068

One Fine Day the Rabbi Bought a Cross, 2961

One Good Death Deserves Another, 4266

One Lives, One Dies, 864

One Minute to Eternity, 5586

One of Our Agents Is Missing, 2737

One of Our Dinosaurs Is Missing, 1925

One of Us Works for Them, 2758

The One Sane Man, 302

One-Shot War, 4049

Only Gentlemen Can Play, 3615

The Only Good Apple in a Barrel of Spies, 3635

Only with a Bargepole, 4366

Operation 10, 4868

Operation Artemis, 4864

Operation Barbarossa, 3962

Operation Burning Candle, 2826

Operation Carlo, 4239

Operation Che Guevara, 1128

Operation Crossbow, 5755

Operation Delta, 2922

Operation Destruct, 3992

Operation Dragnet, 5302

Operation Fox Hunt, 5632

Operation Getaway, 4904

Operation Heartbreak, 1326

Operation Hi-Jack, 1129

Operation Ice Cap, 1532

Operation "K," 1516

Operation Kuwait, 574

Operation Malacca, 4395

Operation Manhunt, 4000

Operation MO, 76

Operation Moon Rocket, 1130

Operation "N," 1520

Operation Neptune, 4009

Operation Nightfall, 3825

Operation Nuke, 994

Operation Octopus, 1533

Operation Perfidia, 2890

Operation Prophet, 583

Operation Raven, 5631

Operation Royal Family, 4038

Operation Scorpio, 5014

Operation Scuba, 1534

Operation Sea Lion, 1394

Operation Shylock: A Confession,
    4660

Operation "SL," 1517

Operation Snake, 1131

Operation Starvation, 1132

Operation Super Ms., 4066

Operation "T," 1521

Operation "VC," 1522

Operation Vengeance, 4897

Operation Weatherkill, 5154

The Opium Strategem, 1690

Or I'll Dress You in Mourning,
    1293

The Orange Air, 1677

Orange Wednesday, 5252

Orbit, 788

Orchids for Mother, 3143

The Ordeal of Major Grigsby,
    4953

Order of Battle, 3796

*Oriental Division G-2: Captain
    North's Three Famous
    Intrigues of the Far East*, 199

The Orion Line, 3329

Oslo Intrigue, 584

The Osterman Weekend, 3346

The Ostrekoff Jewels, 250

The Otan Plot, 3981

Other Paths to Glory, 4411

The Other Side of Silence, 478

Otley, 5445

Otley Forever, 5446

Otley Pursued, 5447

Otley Victorious, 5448

The Ottawa Allegation, 2158

Otto's Boy, 5465

Our Agent in Rome is Missing,
    1133

Our Girl from MEPHISTO, 3044

Our Man Flint, 4202

Our Man from SADISTO, 3041

Our Man in Camelot, 4412

Our Man in Havana, 2295

Out by the River, 856

Out of Control, 3256

Out on the Rim, 5268

The Outlaws of Yugo-Slavia, 320

Outrage, 1749

Over the Wall, 5308

Overhead, 755

Overkill (Daniels), 1523

Overkill (Garner), 2125

Overture to Trouble, 5502

Ox, 881

The Oxford Gambit, 2646

An Oxford Tragedy, 214

Pacific Outcry, 2140

Pacific Vortex!, 1502

The Package Holiday Spy Case,
    3982

Packard Case, 3807

Packed for Murder, 776

The Paint-Stained Flannels, 3005

Palace of Enchantments, 2777

The Paladin, 2114

The Pale Betrayer, 1559

Pale Moon Rising, 4046

The Palermo Affair, 4841

A Palm for Mrs. Pollifax, 948

Palm Springs, 554
The Panama Paradox, 5657
The Panama Plot, 314
Pandemic, 555
The Pandora Option, 4480
Pangolin, 1694
Panic, 54
The Panic of '89, 1821
The Panjang Incident, 4727
Panther's Moon, 1024
Papa Pontivy and the Maginot Murder, 219
Papa's Envoy, 4454
Paper Chase, 1313
The Parachutists, 3028
Paradigm Red, 3016
The Paradise Formula, 1659
Paradise Men, 4692
Paradise Spells Danger, 3667
Paramour, 4288
Pardon My Gun, 5571
Paris, 1172
Paris 2005, 5803
The Paris Drop, 2020
The Paris Trap, 2649
The Park Is Mine, 4281
The Parsifal Mosaic, 3347
Parting Shot, 3065
Partisans, 3598
The Partridge Kite, 4020
Party of the Year, 1475
The Pass Beyond Kashmir, 1544
Passage by Night, 4164
Passage of Arms, 511
Passenger to Frankfurt, 1220
The Passing Advantage, 3514
The Passion and the Glory: The Story of the McGann Family and the War against Japan, 4010
A Passionate Land, 5472
Passport for a Pilgrim, 3155

Passport for a Renegade, 726
Passport to Danger, 4254
Passport to Oblivion, 3156
Passport to Terror, 1513
Patchwork of Death, 3990
Path of Ghosts, 3053
Paths of Glory, 33
The Patriot Game, 1619
Patriot Games, 1231
The Patriotic Murders, 1221
Patriots (Gandley), 2046
Patriots (Sohmer), 5067
The Pawns Count, 251
Pay Any Price, 479
Pay Off, 3168
Pay on the Way Out, 2236
Pay the Devil, 4165
Payback, 4363
The Peacemaker: The Wyss Pursuit, 2240
The Peacemaker: The Xander Pursuit, 2242
The Peacemaker: The Yashar Pursuit, 2241
The Peacemaker: The Zaharan Pursuit, 2243
The Peacemakers, 1216
Pearls Before Swine, 497
A Peck of Salt, 2063
Peking, 2315
Peking and the Tulip Affair, 1173
The Peking Dossier, 1134
The Peking Payoff, 3599
The Peking Switch, 3736
The Peking Target, 5346
Pentagon (Drury), 1712
Pentagon (Searls), 4885
The Pentagon Case, 1946
The Penthouse Conspirators, 4332
Perchance, 3074
Perfect Assignment, 3862
A Perfect Spy, 1361

The Perfect Wife, 4240

The Peril Ahead, 1420

Peril Is My Pay, 3214

Perilous Passage, 3991

The Peripheral Spy, 4282

The Perpignon Exchange, 2993

The Persian Price, 5518

Peruvian Contracts, 1939

Pestis 18, 5541

Peter's Pence, 1266

The Petrodollar Takeover, 5192

The Petrograd Consignment, 4896

The Petronov Plan, 4190

Petrovka 38, 3367

The Phantom Conspiracy, 675

Phantom Leader, 739

The Phantom of the Pacific, 321

Phantoms over Potsdam, 5405

Phil and Me, 5748

The Phoenix, 563

Phoenix #1: Dark Messiah, 457

Phoenix #2: Ground Zero, 458

Phoenix Caged, 4425

The Phoenix Formula, 3192

A Phoenix in the Blood, 4166

The Phoenix Odyssey, 2578

The Phoenix with Oily Feathers, 4968

Photo Finish, 871

Piccolo, 626

Picture of the Year, 1796

A Piece of Resistance, 1787

A Piece of the Moon Is Missing, 2860

Pieces of Modesty, 4057

The Pigeon Project, 5482

Pika Don, 1614

The Pilate Plot, 4118

Pilebuck, 2522

Pillars of Fire, 4929

The Pillars of the Earth, 1914

Pimpernel 60, 3020

Pimpernel and Rosemary, 284

Pinned Man, 1569

The Pious Agent, 841

Pipeline from Hell, 2381

The Piper on the Mountain, 4276

The Piraeus Plot, 575

The Pirate, 4526

Place of Mists, 3049

Plague Bomb, 4670

A Plague of Sailors, 1002

The Plague of Silence, 1428

Plague of Spies, 3067

Platinum Bullet, 2266

Playing for Keeps, 5407

Playing with Cobras, 5242

Playtime Is Over, 1556

The Plot, 5483

The Plot to Kill the President, 4203

The Plotters, 3374

The Plunderers, 1281

Pluribus, 3075

Pocock & Pitt, 643

The Poellenberg Inheritance, 5519

Point of Honor, 4855

Point of Impact, 2770

The Poison People, 1262

Poison Shadows, 161

The Poisoned Mountain, 27

The Poisoned Pussy, 2276

The Poisoners, 2420

Poisoning the Angels, 4934

Poland, 3821

Polar Day 9, 1682

Polar Star, 5049

Pole Reaction, 872

Poor Richard's Game, 4111

The Porkchoppers, 5274

Portrait of a Spy, 329

The Portuguese Escape, 4081

The Portuguese Fragment, 4894

A Position of Trust, 2506

Position of Ultimate Trust, 2400
The Postern of Fate, 1222
The Potsdam Bluff, 2762
The Potsdam Murder Plot, 3963
Poulter's Passage, 3459
*Pour a Swindle through a
   Loophole*, 5437
Pour the Hemlock, 4724
The Powder Barrel, 1250
The Powder Train, 5390
The Power, 3829
The Power Game, 2279
The Power House, 1251
The Power of the Bug, 1701
Power of the Sword, 5058
Power Play, 2220
The Power Sellers, 2390
Praetorian, 2176
Pray for a Brave Heart, 3540
Prayer for an Assassin, 4900
A Prayer for the Dying, 4167
The Praying Mantises, 3874
Pre-Empt, 5443
Precipice, 3138
The Predator (Nicole), 4001
The Predator (Pitts), 4335
Prelude to Terror, 3541
Prepare for Action, 1421
Preserve and Protect, 1713
President Fu Manchu, 357
*The President Is Coming to
   Lunch*, 3395
The President's Man, 4560
The President's Mistress, 533
The President's Team, 3787
Presidential Agent, 4996
*Presidential Agent: Ride the
   Golden Tiger*, 1841
Presidential Emergency, 5159
Presidential Mission, 4997
Presidential Plot, 2865
Pressure Point (Couch), 1372

Pressure Point (Garside), 2141
Presumed Dead, 4272
Pretty Sinister, 303
Prey, 2211
A Pride of Dolphins, 2493
Prime Minister Spy, 5090
The Prime Minister Was a Spy,
   2316
Primrose, the Fourth Man, 5040
The Prince of Berlin, 4957
The Prince of Darkness, 1675
The Prince of Spies, 67
A Prince of the Captivity, 17
The Princes of Earth, 3076
The Prisoner, 5141
The Prisoner of Love, 3875
Prisoner's Friend, 5717
*The Private Army of Colonel
   Tobin: Afghan Assault*, 3375
*The Private Army of Colonel
   Tobin: Congo War Cry*,
   3376
*The Private Army of Colonel
   Tobin: The Dead Sea
   Submarine*, 3377
*The Private Army of Colonel
   Tobin: Death Charge*, 3378
*The Private Army of Colonel
   Tobin: Swamp War*, 3386
*The Private Army of Colonel
   Tobin: Terror in Rio*, 3379
Private I, 4763
Private Report, 4529
The Private Sector, 2647
Private Undertaking, 5215
Private Vendetta, 836
A Procession of the Damned,
   5386
The Prodigy Plot, 5277
Profane Men, 3828
The Professional, 908
The Profiteers, 252

Project Cyclops, 2655
Project Daedalus, 2656
Project Webb, 4547
Project X, 4539
The Prometheus Operation, 1805
Promise Morning, 3801
*The Promise of Joy: The
    Presidency of Orrin Knox*,
    1705
Promises to Keep, 745
The Prophet of Fire, 1440
A Prospect of Vengeance, 4413
Prospero Drill, 4382
The Protectors, 1252
Protégé, 3623
Proteus, 5563
The Proteus Operation, 2630
The Proteus Pact, 4739
Protocol for a Kidnapping, 5269
Proving Ground, 572
Prussian Blue, 2792
Psychedelic-40, 1196
Public Faces in Private Places,
    4631
The Pulse of Danger, 1267
Puma, 3822
Puppet on a Chain, 3600
The Purloined Letter, 311
Purpose of Evasion, 1657
Pursuit, 5231
Pursuit in Peru, 2554
The Pursuit of Agent M, 1331
*The Pursuit of Benjamin
    Grossman: A Novel about a
    Nazi War Criminal Who
    Posed as a Jew*, 1858
Pursuit of Fear, 2404
The Pursuit of the Phoenix, 4422
The Push-Button Spy, 2837
Pussycat Transplant, 2227

*The Puzzle Palace: A Report on
    America's Most Secret
    Agency*, 666
The Python Project, 1025

The Q Document, 1733
Quarry's Contract, 2767
Queen of the Riffs, 116
Queen Victoria's Revenge, 2490
Queen's Crossing, 2257
Queen's Gate Reckoning, 4436
The Queen's Head, 3652
The Queen's Messenger, 1734
Queen's Pawn, 1026
The Quest for Karla, 1362
A Question of Risk, 4935
Questions of Identity, 1314
The Quests of Simon Ark, 2626
Quick Silver, 2267
Quicksand, 2281
Quicksilver, 2514
The Quiet American, 2296
The Quiet Dogs, 2108
The Quiet Killer, 3560
Quiller Bamboo, 5347
Quiller Barracuda, 5348
Quiller KGB, 5349
Quiller Memorandum, 5350
Quiller Meridian, 5351
Quiller Solitaire, 5353
Quiller's Run, 5352
Quintain, 2478

The R Document, 5484
The Rabelais Ms., 1407
Ragland, 5421
The Raid (Kolpacoff), 3055
The Raid (Mather), 3772
Raid on the <u>Bremerton</u>, 1752
The Raid on Villa Joyosa, 2662

Raiders of the Lost Ark, 770
Rain Before Seven, 1639
The Rainbow Pattern, 1027
Raise the Red Dawn, 1555
Raise the Titanic, 1496
Rambo (First Blood Part II), 3899
Rambo III, 3900
The Ransom of Black Stealth One, 2808
The Rape of Berlin, 646
The Rape of Venice, 5605
Rare Adventure, 1849
Rat Trap, 5243
The Ravagers, 2421
The Raven and the Kamikaze, 3561
A Raving Monarchist, 4488
The Ravishing of Lady Mary Ware, 5606
Re-Enter Dr. Fu Manchu, 5509
The Reaper, 492
The Rebuilt Man, 2405
Recoil, 111
Recovery, 5291
Red Alert, 904
Red America, 5107
Red Anger, 2685
Red Army, 4279
Red Bamboo, 5303
Red Carpet for the Shah, 4522
Red Center, 4031
Red Chameleon (Kaminsky), 2914
Red Chameleon (Robertson), 4534
The Red Daniel, 3490
Red Danube, 4383
The Red Defector, 2332
Red Devil, 4770
The Red Dove, 3089
Red Drums, 313
Red Eye, 449
A Red File for Callan, 3850
The Red Fox, 2788

The Red Gods, 3264
The Red Guard, 1135
Red Hazard, 4355
The Red Hen Conspiracy, 736
Red Herrings, 2535
The Red Horseman, 1324
The Red House, 3090
Red January, 1192
Red Lightning--Black Thunder, 941
The Red Mass, 374
Red Message, 435
Red Mutiny, 5679
Red Omega, 3061
Red on Wight, 5682
Red Pawns, 1570
Red Phoenix, 804
The Red President, 2331
Red Rays, 1136
Red Rebellion, 1137
Red Road, 4693
Red Rose for Maria, 1688
Red Sky: A Novel of Love, Space & War, 3920
Red Snow, 5324
Red Square (Smith), 5050
Red Square (Topol), 5326
Red Star Run, 3917
The Red Stockings, 3006
Red Storm Rising, 1232
The Red Swastika, 2330
Redcap, 3479
The Redhead (Andersch), 527
The Redhead (Creasey), 55
Redolmo Affair, 1138
Reflex Action, 1871
The Regensburg Legacy, 756
The Regiment, 4012
Reich Four, 1139
Reilly: Ace of Spies, 3293
Reilly: The First Man, 3294
The Reinhard Action, 1804

Rekill, 3742

A Relative Stranger, 5129

The Reluctant Defector, 2464

Remains to Be Seen, 951

Remembered Anger, 3310

The Removers, 2422

The Rendezvous, 5520

Rendezvous with Death, 4255

Repeat the Instructions, 751

Report from Argyll, 3567

Report From Group 17, 1305

Requiem for a Spy, 2206

The Resident, 5392

The Restless Frontier, 3480

Resumption, 4013

The Retaliators, 2423

The Return, 5521

Return from the Ashes, 3870

Return from Vorkuta, 2738

The Return of Fu Manchu, 352

The Return of Lanny Budd, 4998

The Return of the Black Gang,
   1837

Revenge, 2797

The Revengers, 2436

Reverse Negative, 2901

Reversible Error, 5189

The Revolutionist, 3277

Reward for a Defector, 1827

Reward for Treason, 4241

Rhine Replica, 3311

The Rhineman Exchange, 3348

Rhodesia, 1140

Richard A., 5790

Riddle, 4960

The Riddle of Samson, 5718

*The Riddle of the Sands: A
   Record of Secret Service*, 29

The Riddle of the Spanish Circus,
   3178

Ride a Pale Horse, 3542

Ride a Paper Tiger, 579

Ride of the Razorback, 4048

The Rig, 1686

The Rim of Terror, 5213

Ring for a Noose, 3670

A Ring of Roses, 777

Ringed with Fire, 1008

Ringer, 5233

The Ringmaster, 1739

Rio Casino Intrigue, 3754

Riot '71, 849

Ripley's Game, 2614

Rise at Dawn, 1868

Rise with the Wind, 1342

The Rising Storm, 5607

The Risk, 692

Ritter Double-Cross, 4032

River of Darkness, 2233

River of Death, 3601

The River of Diamonds, 2848

The Road to Beersheba, 3686

The Road to Extrema, 4505

The Road to Gandolfo, 3349

The Road to Glenfairlie, 2146

The Road to Hell, 3876

The Road to Omaha, 3350

Roads of Earth, 1714

The Robespierre Serial, 3330

Rock Baby, 5749

Rockets' Red Glare, 1656

Rod of Anger, 3942

Rogue Eagle, 3431

Rogue Justice, 2686

Rogue Male (Man Hunt), 130

Rogue Warrior II: Red Cell,
   3714

Rogue's March, 2445

Role of Honor, 2099

Rollerball, 3481

Roman Circus, 4092

The Roman Enigma, 3929

Romance of a Spy, 1751

The Romanov Connection, 2286

The Romanov Ransom, 5279

The Romanov Succession, 2115

The Rommel Plot, 1788

Rommel's Gold, 1564

Rook-Shoot, 1720

Room at the Hotel Ambre, 5664

The Rope Dancer, 3713

The Ropespinner Conspiracy, 5254

Rosebud, 808

The Ross Forgery, 2398

Rostnikov's Vacation, 2918

Rotten with Honour, 4541

The Rotterdam Delivery, 4090

Rotunda, 4970

Rouges Rampant, 1448

Rough Beast, 4073

A Rough Shoot, 2687

A Royal Alliance, 71

Rubicon One, 2881

Rules of Engagement, 5544

The Run Around, 1984

Run for Cover, 847

Run for Your Death, 2672

Run, Spy, Run, 617

The Run to Morning, 4168

Running Blind, 632

Running Sand, 5449

Running Scared, 934

The Running Target, 4921

The Russia House, 1363

The Russian Enigma, 1797

Russian Flag over Hawaii: The Mission of Jefferey Tolamy, 5214

The Russian Interpreter, 1962

Russian Leave, 5171

Russian Roulette, 3851

The Russian Singer, 1539

Russian Spring (Jones), 2882

Russian Spring (Spinrad), 5102

Russkaia Semerka, 5325

S-Day: A Memoir of the Invasion of England, 5234

SPQR, 812

SS, 3023

SS-GB: Nazi-Occupied Britain, 1941, 1596

Saberlegs, 4117

Sabotage (Adams), 437

Sabotage (Creasey), 1422

Sabotage (John), 2857

The Sabre Squadron, 4491

Sabre-Tooth, 4058

Sad Variety, 1567

Sad Wind from the Sea, 4169

SADISTO Royale, 3045

Safari for Spies, 1141

Sagittarius in Warsaw, 3323

The Sagomi Gambit, 1998

Sahara, 1497

Sahara Road, 4694

Saigon (Avallone), 616

Saigon (Grey), 2317

Saigon Singer, 3755

The Saint and the Templar Treasure, 5540

The Saint in Pursuit, 5782

The Saint in Trouble, 5783

The Saint on Guard, 5784

The Saint Peter's Plot, 3100

The Saint Returns, 5785

The Saint Steps In, 5786

The Saint: Five Complete Novels, 5787

St. Catherine's Wheel, 2322

Sakhalin Breakout, 2142

Saladin, 4107

The Salamander, 5564

The Salamandra Glass, 3941

The Salisbury Manuscript, 2288

Salt Maker, 4506

Salt Mine, 3268

Salute from a Dead Man, 3562
The Salzburg Connection, 3543
SAM-7, 1390
Samaritan, 5426
The Samson Strike, 5662
Samurai, 3401
The Samurai Strategy, 2657
San Andreas, 3602
Sand Blind, 4481
The Sandbaggers, 3570
Sandcatcher, 2825
Sandler Inquiry, 2798
Sandra Rifkin's Jewels, 1678
Sandstorm, 2229
*Sant of the Secret Service: Some
    Revelations of Spies and
    Spying*, 150
Santorini, 3603
The Sardine Deception, 1540
Sargasso, 1349
The Satan Bug, 3604
The Satan Touch, 2064
Saturn over the Water, 4428
The Savage Day, 4170
The Savage Game, 5362
The Savage Height, 5363
Savannah Blue, 2503
Saving the Queen, 912
Saviour's Gate, 4890
Scam, 3655
"A Scandal in Bohemia," 80
Scandal in the Chancery, 25
Scaramouche, 316
The Scarlatti Inheritance, 3351
The Scarlet Imposter, 5591
The Scarlet Pimpernel, 283
Scarlet Tanager, 330
Scatterpath, 5668
The Scavengers, 3050
Scene in the Ice-Blue Eyes, 5680
A Scent of New Mown Hay, 778
The Schirmer Inheritance, 512

Schism, 2258
The Scholars of Night, 1923
Scimitar (Abbott), 434
Scimitar (Crowder), 1485
Scimitar (Niesewand), 4022
The Score, 5584
Scorpio 5, 2486
The Scorpio Illusion, 3352
The Scorpio Letters, 1028
Scorpion, 2928
Scorpion East, 3891
*Scorpion in the Sea: The
    Goldsborough Incident*, 1621
The Scorpion Sanction, 4124
The Scorpion Signal, 5354
The Scorpion's Tail, 1263
Scorpius, 2100
Scotch on the Rocks, 2775
The Scotland Yard Alibi, 229
The Scourge, 1740
The Scourge of the Desert, 117
Scream Bloody Murder, 5218
The Screaming Dead Balloons,
    3491
The Scroll of Benevolence, 5339
Scutari, 5797
The Sea & the Sand, 4014
Sea Devil, 2582
The Sea File, 4872
Sea Leopard, 5247
Sea Lion, 3188
The Sea Monks, 5719
Sea of Death, 2573
Sea Scape, 1528
Sea Trap, 1142
Seal Team One, 1373
Seal Team Two, 1374
The Sealer, 5743
Search and Destroy (Blacker), 781
Search and Destroy (Rohrbach),
    4550
Search for a Sultan, 3706

The Search for Bruno Heidler,
3215
The Search for Tabatha Carr,
5126
A Season in Hell, 4171
A Season in Purgatory, 2965
Season of Doubt, 1268
A Season of Evil, 3907
Seasons of Revenge, 4192
Seawitch, 3605
The Second Death of Ramon
Mercader, 4899
Second Front--First Spy, 3964
The Second Lady, 5485
The Second Saladin, 2772
Second Sight, 3407
Secret Adversary, 30
The Secret Agent (Conrad), 41
The Secret Agent (Horler), 123
Secret Agent in Africa, 93
A Secret Agent in Port Arthur, 96
Secret Agent Number One, 85
Secret Agent: Departure
Deferred, 654
Secret Agent: The Exterminator,
655
Secret Agent: Hell for Tomorrow,
3206
Secret Agent: No Way Out, 3622
Secret Agent: Storm Over
Rockall, 656
The Secret Country, 4093
The Secret Dragnet, 4751
Secret Errand, 61
The Secret Families, 2101
The Secret Generations, 2102
The Secret Hand: Some Further
Adventures of Desmond
Okewood of the British Secret
Service, 371
The Secret Houses, 2103
Secret Kills, 2406

The Secret List of Heinrich
Roehm, 668
The Secret Lovers, 3408
Secret Mission to Bangkok, 3756
Secret Mission: Angola, 5015
Secret Mission: Athens, 5016
Secret Mission: Cairo, 5017
Secret Mission: Corsica, 5018
Secret Mission: Corsican
Takeover, 5019
Secret Mission: Death Stalk in
Spain, 5020
Secret Mission: Haitian Vendetta,
5021
Secret Mission: Istanbul, 5022
Secret Mission: The Kremlin
Plot, 5023
Secret Mission: The Libyan
Contract, 5024
Secret Mission: The Marseilles
Enforcer, 5025
Secret Mission: Morocco, 5026
Secret Mission: Munich, 5027
Secret Mission: The Night of the
Assassin, 5028
Secret Mission: North Korea,
5029
Secret Mission: The Padrone,
5035
Secret Mission: The Payoff, 5036
Secret Mission: Peking, 5030
Secret Mission: The Peking
Connection, 5031
Secret Mission: Prague, 5032
Secret Mission: The Strausser
Transfer, 5033
Secret Mission: Tibet, 5034
Secret Mountains, 548
The Secret Murder, 1449
The Secret of Benjamin Square,
3077

The Secret of Holm Peel and Other Strange Stories, 5510

The Secret of MI-6, 5041

The Secret of the Frozen North, 322

The Secret of the Scarlet Bomber, 39

The Secret of the Spa, 2555

The Secret Pilgrim, 1364

The Secret Power, 4242

The Secret Protocol, 4979

Secret Servant (Newman), 220

The Secret Servant (Lyall), 3361

Secret Service, 152

The Secret Service Man, 124

Secret Service Omnibus, Number One, 253

"Secret Service Smith"--the Wanderings of an American Detective, 325

The Secret Soldier, 4444

The Secret Sun, 2613

The Secret Vanguard, 5138

The Secret Vendetta, 4356

The Secret Warriors, 958

The Secret Ways, 3606

Secret Weapon (Newman), 3965

The Secret Weapon (Palmer), 4120

Secret Weapon (Pollard), 4342

The Secret Whispers, 480

Secret: Hong Kong, 1562

Secrets for Sale, 2550

Secrets of the Foreign Office, 151

Security Risk, 4243

Sedemte Dni Na Nashiia Zhivot, 2348

Seduction of a Tall Man, 2026

See Charlie Run, 1985

See How They Run, 2287

See the Living Crocodiles, 680

See You Later Alligator, 920

Seeds of Destruction, 2323

Seeds of Rebellion, 4011

The Seeds of Treason, 481

The Seersucker Whipsaw, 5275

Seidlitz and the Super-Spy, 5778

Self-Discovery, 4833

The Semenov Impulse, 896

Semper Fi, 976

The Sempinski Affair, 3066

Senator Love, 445

The Senator's Ransom, 747

Send Him Victorious, 2778

Send in the Lions, 1236

The Sensitives, 929

The Sentinel, 4735

The Sentries, 2755

The Serpent Sleeping, 5556

The Serpent's Crown, 3564

The Serpent's Mark, 1736

The Serpent's Smile, 2606

Set a Spy, 172

Seven Against Greece, 1143

The Seven Conundrums, 254

Seven Days to a Killing, 1789

Seven Days to Petrograd, 2793

The Seven Dials Mystery, 31

Seven Lies South, 3527

Seven Minutes past Midnight, 5724

Seven Pillars to Hell, 4172

Seven Seas Murders, 200

The Seven Sins, 5511

The Seven Sleepers, 304

Seven Steps to Treason, 2510

Seventeen of Leyden: A Frolic through This Vale of Tears, 2833

Seventh Day, 3025

The Seventh Fury, 4197

The Seventh Hexagram, 3580

The Seventh Power, 3830

The Seventh Royale, 5113

The Seventh Sanctuary, 3512

The Seventh Secret, 5486

The Sexecutioner: Silverfinger, 1942

The Sexecutioner: Tong in Cheek, 1941

A Shade of Difference, 1706

The Shadow Army, 4731

The Shadow Cabinet, 2446

Shadow Flight, 5545

The Shadow Game, 1828

Shadow in the Sea, 2858

Shadow Man, 3064

Shadow of a Lady, 4657

The Shadow of Dr. Ferrari, 5304

The Shadow of Fu Manchu, 5512

Shadow of Lies, 3626

Shadow of Shadows, 482

Shadow of the Condor, 2234

Shadow of the Wolf, 698

The Shadow of Tyburn Tree, 5608

Shadow Queen, 2172

The Shadow Spy, 3331

Shadow Trade, 2021

Shadow Wars, 5197

The Shadowboxer, 715

The Shadowers, 2424

Shadowplay, 2515

Shadows, 1350

Shadows in a Hidden Land, 4695

Shadows of Death, 5491

Shadows of Doubt, 2465

Shah-Mak, 5650

The Shakeout, 1915

The Shallow Grave, 4447

Shamelady, 1377

The Shanghai Bund Murders, 208

The Shapes of Sleep, 4429

Shard at Bay, 3482

Shard Calls the Tune, 3483

The Shattered Eye, 2252

She Came by Night, 4244

Sheep May Safely Graze, 4715

Shell Game, 5225

The Shepherd File, 681

Sheridan Road, 3827

The Shetland Plan, 77

Shibumi, 5615

Shield and Sword, 3059

The Shining Day, 4634

Shining Through, 2822

Ship of Gold, 3162

The Ship with No Name, 4015

The Shipkiller, 4874

Shockwave, 3419

The Shoes of the Fisherman, 5565

Shoot!, 3983

The Shooter, 5413

The Shooting of the Green, 4398

Shooting Script, 3363

Shooting Star, 865

Short of Glory, 2897

Short Wave, 873

Show Me a Hero (Alexander), 461

Show Me a Hero (Coppel), 1337

Show of Force, 5202

A Shroud for Jesso, 4463

Siberian Road, 4696

The Sibling, 5361

The Sicilian Specialist, 3252

The Sick Fox, 877

Siege, 1351

The Siege of Buckingham Palace, 3953

Siege of Lightning, 4334

The Siege of Ocean Valkyrie, 4426

Siege of Silence, 4451

The Siege of the Villa Lipp, 513

The Siegfried Spy, 230

Sierra Death Dealers, 3518

Sight Unseen, 2204

The Sigma Project, 5065

The Sign of Dawn, 5762

Sign of the Cobra, 1144
The Sign of the Prayer Shawl,
    1145
Sign on for Tokyo, 2384
The Silencer, 3325
The Silencers, 2425
The Silent Force, 2210
The Silent Hostage, 522
Silent Hunter, 5203
The Silent Pursuits, 2474
Silent Reach, 5627
Silent Thunder, 5194
Silent Warriors, 2579
Silk Road, 4697
The Silver Greyhound, 3984
The Silver Mistress, 4064
Silver Tower, 888
The Singapore Exile Murders, 209
Singapore Sling, 2143
The Singapore Wink, 5270
Single Combat, 2815
A Single Monstrous Act, 728
Single to Hong Kong, 2065
Sinister Errand, 1209
Sinister Sanctuary, 5305
Sinister Secret, 4357
Sinister Shelter, 2556
Sinister Talent, 4245
Sinkhole, 2903
The Sinkiang Executive, 5355
Sion Crossing, 4420
*Sir Percy Hits Back: An
    Adventure of the Scarlet
    Pimpernel*, 292
Siro, 2804
The Siskiyou Two-Step, 2713
The Sisters, 3278
Sitting Target, 2569
Six Bloody Summer Days, 1146
Six Days of the Condor, 2235

*The Six Million Dollar Man:
    Wine, Women, and War*,
    2830
The Six Proud Walkers, 305
Six-Day Week, 2074
*The Sixth Battle: A Novel of the
    Next War*, 5317
The Sixth Directorate, 2648
Sixty to Go, 5788
The Sixty-Fifth Tape, 4635
*The Skeleton at the Villa
    Wolkonsky*, 4333
Skeletons, 4824
Skin Deep, 2487
Skirmish, 1790
Skorpion's Death, 866
The Sky Block, 1963
Sky Masters, 886
Sky Riders, 1007
Sky Strike, 4671
Skyfall, 789
The Skylark Mission, 3398
Skyprobe, 3460
*Slaughterhouse Five, or the
    Children's Crusade*, 5441
The Slavers, 5219
A Slaying in September, 3577
Sledgehammer, 5466
The Sleep, 1429
A Sleep of Spies, 2466
The Sleeper (Clark), 1237
The Sleeper (Roth), 4658
Sleeper Agent, 3797
Sleepers Can Kill, 2831
Sleeping Dogs, 4636
Sleeping Dogs Lying, 3901
The Slender Thread, 4659
Slow Burner, 1253
Slow Death in Geneva, 26
A Small Masterpiece, 2536
A Small Town in Germany, 1365

A Small War Made to Order, 3253

Smear Job, 3852

The Smile of Cheng Su, 5306

The Smile on the Face of the Tiger, 2776

The Smiler with the Knife, 74

Smiley's People, 1366

Smith and Jones, 3866

The Smith Conspiracy, 3951

The Smuggled Atom Bomb, 5763

The Smugglers, 4284

The Smugglers: Mother Luck, 4285

The Smugglers: Murder in Blue, 4286

The Smugglers: Tools of the Trade, 4287

Snake Charmer, 2328

The Snake Flag Conspiracy, 1147

Snap Shot, 4455

The Snare of the Hunter, 3544

Snark, 1576

A Snatch of Music, 857

Snow Falcon, 5248

The Snow Gods, 931

Snow in Paradise, 4848

Snow on High Ground, 4847

The Snow on the Ben, 3611

The Snow Tiger, 639

Snowball (Allbeury), 483

Snowball (Sangster), 4768

Snowbird, 3234

Snowline (Brierley), 867

Snowline (Davies), 1545

Snowshot, 3402

Snowtrap, 4216

So Many Steps to Death, 1223

Soft Sell, 874

Soft Targets, 2809

The Soft-Footed Moor, 2066

The Softener, 800

Soho Spy, 4537

Soldier in the Snow, 3857

Soldier No More, 4414

The Soldier Spies, 959

Soldier-of-Fortune: Ambush at Derali Wells, 3437

Soldier-of-Fortune: Bloodbath, 3434

Soldier-of-Fortune: Body Count, 3435

Soldier-of-Fortune: The Guns of Palembang, 3438

Soldier-of-Fortune: Operation Hong Kong, 3439

Soldier-of-Fortune: Somali Smashout, 3440

Soldier-of-Fortune: Spoils of War, 3436

Sole Agent, 729

The Solitary Man (Freemantle), 1999

The Solitary Man (Winchester), 5674

Solo, 4173

The Solstice Caper, 824

The Solstice Man, 4445

Somebody's Fool, 2973

Something like a Love Affair, 5184

Something on the Stairs, 5500

Something Worth Fighting For, 2027

Somewhere in England, 2028

A Song in the Morning, 4925

Sonntag, 4992

The Sooner Spy, 3186

The Sorcerers, 2739

Soul Hunters, 3721

The Soul of Viktor Tronko, 4438

The Sound of Small Hammers, 4942

A Sour Apple Tree, 779

Sour Cream with Everything,
    4369
Southeast of Mandalay, 2968
Souvenir, 2947
The Sovereign Solution, 3619
Soviet Sources, 1489
The Soyuz Affair, 1387
Spades at Midnight, 5501
Spandau Phoenix, 2805
The Spandau Warrant, 3888
The Spanish Connection, 1148
The Spanish Gambit, 2771
The Spanish Soldier, 932
Spawn, 2638
Spawn of the Hawk, 40
The Speaker, 62
Spear, 2586
Spearhead, 1695
The Special Collection, 484
Special Delivery, 1665
A Special Kind of Nightmare,
    2159
Special Operations, 978
Special Relationship, 1239
Spectrum, 5729
Speculations About Jakob, 2866
The Spider and the Fly, 3316
The Spider's Touch, 372
Spider's Web, 4716
The Spiderweb, 4274
Spies, 5157
Spies Abounding, 539
Spies against the Reich, 540
Spies along the Severn, 345
Spies among Us, 1224
*Spies and Intrigues: The
    Oppenheim Secret Service
    Omnibus*, 255
Spies and More Spies, 5091
Spies and Rebels, 118
Spies Die at Dawn, 2673
Spies Have No Friends, 2674

Spies in Action, 6
Spies in the Web, 7
Spies, Inc., 2759
Spies Left!, 3985
Spies of Good Intent, 5428
The Spies of Peenemunde, 3969
*Spies of the Kaiser Plotting the
    Downfall of England*, 153
The Spike, 3914
Spiral, 2132
The Spitting Image, 610
The Splintered Man, 1481
The Spoilers, 633
The Spoils of Ararat, 2943
The Spook Who Sat by the Door,
    2311
The Spreewald Collection, 3563
Spring 1940, 1817
Spy (Garbo), 2071
Spy (Newman), 221
The Spy (Horler), 127
The Spy (Thomas), 5255
Spy and Die, 3820
The Spy and the Thief, 2624
The Spy at Angkor Wat, 662
The Spy at No. 10, 3967
The Spy at the Villa Miranda,
    4952
A Spy at Twilight, 1920
Spy Business, 4246
Spy Castle, 1149
The Spy Catchers (Ballard), 658
Spy Catchers (Newman), 3968
Spy Corner, 541
Spy Counter-Spy, 542
A Spy for a Spy, 1546
A Spy for Churchill, 5406
Spy for Germany, 2205
Spy for Sale, 4195
The Spy Game, 3636
The Spy Ghost, 1524
Spy Hook, 1592

The Spy in Bangkok, 663
Spy in Black, 32
Spy in Chancery (Benton), 730
Spy in Chancery (Doherty), 1673
Spy in Khaki, 3553
The Spy in Question, 4886
The Spy in Silk Breeches, 4905
The Spy in the Brown Derby, 3986
The Spy in the Deuce Court, 1578
The Spy in the Java Sea, 664
The Spy in the Jungle, 665
The Spy in the Ointment, 5578
The Spy in the Shadows, 2933
A Spy in Winter, 677
A Spy Is Forever, 2002
Spy Island, 543
Spy Meets Spy, 86
A Spy of Napoleon, 285
A Spy of the Old School, 4482
Spy on the Run, 3637
The Spy Paramount, 280
Spy Shadow, 4887
Spy Sinker, 1593
Spy Story, 1594
The Spy That Died of Boredom, 3824
A Spy was Born, 166
Spy Wednesday, 2653
The Spy Who Barked in the Night, 3641
The Spy Who Came in from the Cold, 1367
The Spy Who Died Twice, 676
The Spy Who Fell Off the Back of the Bus, 3642
The Spy Who Got His Feet Wet, 3638
The Spy Who Got Off at Las Vegas, 2675
The Spy Who Hated Fudge, 2602

The Spy Who Hated Licorice, 2603
The Spy Who Longed for Home, 5072
The Spy Who Loved Married Blood, 1947
The Spy Who Loved Me, 1888
The Spy Who Sat and Waited, 1009
The Spy Who Spoke Porpoise, 5764
The Spy Who Was Three Feet Tall, 4464
The Spy Who Was Vertically Challenged, 1183
The Spy Who Wasn't Caught, 4906
The Spy Who Wasn't Exchanged, 5186
The Spy with His Head in the Clouds, 3639
The Spy Wore Silk, 462
The Spy: A Tale of the Neutral Ground, 43
The Spy's Bedside Book, 2297
The Spy's Wife, 2618
Spy-Counter Spy, 3966
Spying Blind (Dark), 1529
Spying Blind (McKenna), 167
Spylight, 3157
Spyline, 1595
The Spymaster (Freed), 1968
The Spymaster (Freund), 2005
The Spymaster (Oppenheim), 256
Spyship, 2954
Stained Glass, 915
The Stalin Account, 2067
Stalk, 1197
Stalk the Hunter, 5671
The Stalking Angel, 485
The Stalking Horse, 4663
Stalking Point, 902

Stallion Gate, 5051

Stamboul Intrigue, 5055

Star of Egypt, 2003

The Star-Spangled Contract, 2133

The Star-Spangled Crunch, 1301

Stars and Swastikas. S-Com, No. 2, 3516

Stars Are Dark, 1210

The Stars Give Warning, 1310

The State Department Murders, 410

State of Grace, 5318

State of Siege, 514

State Scarlet, 378

State v. Justice, 5526

State Visit, 1798

The Statesman's Game, 456

A Station in the Delta, 1181

Status 1 S.Q., 2604

StaＴik, 4672

Steady Boys, Steady, 3858

Steal Big, 3683

Stealing Lillian, 2977

Stealth, 1745

Stealth Strike, 4043

The Steel Albatross, 1038

The Steel Mirror, 2426

The Steel Spring, 5473

Steel Tiger, 740

A Stench of Poppies, 1702

The Stendhal Raid, 1613

The Stettin Secret, 5232

Stinger, 2665

The Stockholm Syndicate, 4849

The Stolen Squadron, 2557

The Stone Leopard, 4842

The Stone Roses, 523

Stop on the Green Light, 878

Stopover: Tokyo, 3735

Storm Birds #2: Thunder from Heaven, 2956

Storm Birds #3: The Gathering Storm, 2955

Storm Flight, 741

A Storm of Spears, 1343

Storm Warning, 4174

Storming Intrepid, 2500

The Story of Henri Tod, 921

The Stowaway, 2868

Strange Bedfellows, 930

The Strange Conflict, 5592

Stranger and Afraid, 1537

Stranger at the Gate, 5522

A Stranger Called the Blues, 1378

The Stranger City Caper, 5083

Strangers in Blood, 1488

Stranglehold, 3030

The Strasbourg Legacy, 1405

Strategic Compromise, 4026

The Strategies of Zeus, 2505

Street 8, 1831

Strike Deep, 4036

Strike Force 10, 3056

Strike Force 7, 3399

Strike Force Terror, 1150

Strike North, 652

Strike of the China Falcon, 1180

Strike of the Hawk, 1151

The Striker Portfolio, 5356

Stringer, 2899

Strip Jack Naked, 2130

Strip Tease, 875

The Strumpet Wind, 3805

Stud Service, 4511

Subaltern's Choice, 3492

The Submariner, 5122

The Sufi Fiddle, 923

Sugarland, 1853

The Suicide Seat, 1174

Suicide Spies, 544

Sukhumi Destruction, 2144

Sullivan, 4465

The Sultan's Daughter, 5609

The Sulu Sea Murders, 210
The Sum of All Fears, 1233
Sumatra Seven Zero, 5771
Summer Fires, 4502
The Summer Soldier, 2342
The Summit, 3216
Summit Kill, 2697
The Summons, 195
Summons from Baghdad, 3568
Sun in the Hunter's Eye, 5640
Sunburst, 3420
Sunflower, 4937
Sunlit Ambush, 5642
The Suns of Badarane, 3148
Sunset, 4016
The Sunset Patriots, 5204
Sunstrike, 3484
Supply of Heros, 1043
The Survivor, 4457
The Suvarov Adventure, 897
Swan Song, 763
Swann, 4958
The Swap, 5467
Swastika Hunt, 3426
Sweeney's Run, 2763
Sweet Reason, 3279
Swift, 1898
A Swinger Named Zefano, 2337
The Swiss Account, 1822
Swiss Conspiracy, 5111
The Sword and the Net, 5173
Sword of Fate, 5593
Sword of Genghis Khan, 1535
Sword of Orion, 5630
Sword of the Shaheeni, 3904
Sword Point, 1398
The Swords of God, 3391

Tagget, 2309

*Tainaya voina Maksima
    Maksimovicha: Dokum* [*The
    Secret War of Isaev*], 3370
Taint of Innocence, 1217
Take It Crooked, 306
Take the War to Washington,
    5412
Take-Off, 580
Taken at the Flood, 3987
Takeover, 2000
The Talbot Odyssey, 1610
The Talbott Agreement, 2150
The Tale of the Lazy Dog, 5651
Tales of Adventure, 2688
Tales of Chinatown, 358
Talespin, 2764
The Talinin Madonna, 5003
Talk to Me About England, 1850
The Talking Sparrow Murders,
    328
The Tall Dolores, 611
Talley's Truth, 4642
Talleyman, 2834
Talon, 1295
The Tamarind Seed, 5523
The Tangent Objective, 4755
Tango, 2893
The Tango Briefing, 5357
The Tank of Sacred Eels, 1703
Tank of Serpents, 3163
Tarakian, 850
The Tarantula Hawk, 3770
Tarantula Strike, 1152
Target, 2773
Target Five, 4843
Target for Terror, 4247
Target for Tonight, 5220
Target Manhattan, 2116
Target Mayflower, 2622
Target of Opportunity, 985
Target Stealth, 3803
Target: Doomsday Island, 1153

Target: Plutex, 905
Target: Sahara, 5492
Target: Subic Bay, 5190
Targets, 3627
Targets of Opportunity, 5546
The Tarnham Connection, 5393
The Tashkent Crisis, 1406
The Taskmaster, 3012
TASS Is Authorized to Announce--,
  3365
A Taste for Danger, 4059
A Tax in Blood, 4857
Team Yankee, 1399
The Tears of Autumn, 3409
Technicians of Death, 5663
The Technocrats, 2667
The Teheran Contract, 4525
Telefon, 5468
The Telemann Touch, 1254
Tell No Tales, 1566
Telling Only Lies, 3682
Temple Dogs, 1735
Temple of Fear, 1154
Temple Tower, 180
Temptation in a Private Zoo, 1600
Ten Days in August, 2013
The Ten Holy Terrors, 307
Ten Thousand, 1401
Ten Years to Doomsday, 3078
The Ten-Tola Bars, 5734
Tender to Danger, 516
The Tenth Man, 2298
Terminal, 4850
The Terminal Man, 1462
The Terminal Transfer, 3745
Termination Order, 2008
The Terminators (Davies), 1547
The Terminators (Hamilton), 2427
The Terrible Ones, 1155
The Terror, 1430
The Terror Alliance, 2760
Terror by Day, 1450

Terror in Turin. S-Com, No. 1,
  3517
Terror Is My Trade, 3226
Terror on Tiptoe, 128
The Terror Syndicate, 4882
The Terror Trap, 56
Terror's Cradle, 898
The Terrorizers, 2428
The Tesla Bequest, 4256
The Testament of Caspar Schultz,
  4175
Testament of Evil, 837
The Testing, 802
The Tetramachus Collection, 5422
Thai Horse, 1645
Thank You, Mr. Moto, 193
That Man Gull, 5169
That Was No Lady, 5572
The Thefts of Nick Velvet, 2627
Their Man in the White House,
  556
There Are No Spies, 2253
There Are Thirteen, 4122
There Goes Death, 1451
*There Is Something about a
  Dame*, 612
These Lonely Victories, 5559
*They Call Me the Mercenary: The
  Slaughter Run*, 2998
They Came to Baghdad, 1225
They Found Each Other, 1838
They Tell No Tales, 3707
They Thought He Was Dead, 2664
They Used Dark Forces, 5594
They Went Thataway, 889
They Won't Lie Down, 545
*They've Shot the President's
  Daughter*, 5136
The Thick Blue Sweater, 3007
A Thief in the Night, 5503
The Thieves of Tumbutu, 2302
Thin Line, 1679

Think Fast, Mr. Moto, 194
Think, Inc., 1650
The Third Arm, 2048
The Third Betrayal, 2512
The Third Circle, 2703
The Third Conspiracy, 3548
The Third Force, 3549
The Third Man, 2299
The Third Truth, 678
The Thirteenth Hour, 3174
The Thirteenth Spy, 1156
Thirty Days Hath September, 2859
The Thirty Nine Steps, 18
Thirty Seconds over New York, 909
The Thirty-Eighth Floor, 2817
Thirty-Four East, 1338
This City is Ours, 4336
This Drakotny, 3485
This Fortress, 3708
This Is for Real, 4493
This Is Your Life, 3988
This Suitcase is Going to Explode, 557
This Woman Is Death, 1952
The Thor Option, 748
The Thousand Faces of Night, 4176
Threat Case, 4364
The Threateners, 2429
Three Blind Mice, 5744
Three Famous Spy Novels, 1186
The Three Fishers, 309
The Three Hostages, 19
The Three of Clubs, 373
Three Potato, Four, 2278
Three Spies for Glory, 3555
The Three-Day Alliance, 4988
Threshold, 1379
Throne of Saturn, 1536
The Throne of Saturn: A Novel of Space and Politics, 1707

Through the Dark and Hairy Wood, 2598
Thunder Above, 5488
A Thunder at Dawn, 2629
Thunder at Noon, 4177
Thunder at Sunset, 3767
The Thunder Dragon Gate, 108
Thunder in Europe, 57
Thunder of Erebus, 2501
Thunder Point, 4178
Thunderball, 1889
Thunderstrike in Syria, 1157
Ticket to Oblivion, 4130
Ticket to Ride, 4267
Tides of War, 3918
Tiebreaker, 758
Tiger from the Shadows, 838
Tiger in the North, 4698
Tiger Mann: Bloody Sunrise, 5096
Tiger Mann: The By-Pass Control, 5097
Tiger Mann: Day of the Guns, 5098
Tiger Mann: The Death Dealers, 5099
Tiger on my Back, 2221
Tiger Standist Steps on It, 125
Tiger Ten, 783
The Tightrope Men, 634
Tijuana Traffic, 4862
Time Bomb, 586
Time Clock of Death, 1158
Time for Treason, 2607
A Time of Pirates, 5772
Time of Reckoning, 5469
Time of the Temptress, 5683
Time of the Wolf, 2883
A Time of War, 4283
Time Right Deadly, 524
A Time to Kill, 2689
The Time Trap Gambit, 3650

A Time without Shadows, 486
The Timeless Sleep, 3498
Timelock, 3421
Timetable, 1810
The Timothy Files, 4757
Timothy's Game, 4758
The Tin Cravat, 2761
Tinker, Tailor, Soldier, Spy, 1368
The Tiptoe Boys, 1904
The Tirana Assignment, 4379
The Tired Spy, 5155
The Titan Game, 939
The Titans, 4017
To Catch a King, 4179
To Catch a Spy (Sanders), 4753
To Catch a Spy (Scott), 4861
*To Catch a Spy: An Anthology of
    Favourite Spy Stories*, 515
To Die Elsewhere, 5645
To Kill the <u>Potemkin</u>, 2892
To Love and Yet to Die, 1951
To Play the Fox, 1404
To Speak for the Dead, 3237
To the Eagle's Nest, 1654
A Toast to Tomorrow, 3709
The Tojo Virus, 4468
Toll for the Brave, 4180
The Tomb of the Twelfth Imam,
    924
The Tombstone Cipher, 3799
Tomorrow Knight, 3079
Tomorrow's Ghost, 4421
Tomorrow's Treason, 2467
Tongue of Treason, 4898
Tonya, 825
Too Many Enemies, 1255
The Tooth Merchant, 5180
Top Bloody Secret, 2791
Top End, 5294
Top Secret, 876
Topaz, 5399
The Torch, 5758

Torch for a Dark Journey, 4936
The Torquemada Principle, 3892
The Torrents of War, 4901
Tortured Angel, 2147
The Torvich Affair, 4818
The Touch of Death, 1431
A Touch of Thunder, 1327
The Touch of Treason, 5120
Touch the Devil, 4181
Touch the Lion's Paw, 3101
The Touchables, 2001
Touchfeather, 4764
Touchfeather, Too, 4765
Tough Company, 72
A Tough One to Lose, 2978
The Tournament, 4458
The Tower of Babel, 5566
The Tower of Terror, 4217
Tower of Treason, 5796
The Towers of Silence, 2740
A Tract of Time, 2565
The Trade, 2395
The Trail of Fu Manchu, 359
The Train at Bundabar, 3493
The Train from Katanga, 5059
The Traitor (Horler), 129
Traitor (Markstein), 3718
Traitor Betrayed, 3832
Traitor Spy, 4248
The Traitor's Contract, 3685
Traitor's Doom, 1441
Traitor's Exit, 2104
Traitor's Island, 4223
Traitor's Purse, 498
Traitor's Way, 110
Traitor's Wife, 622
The Traitors (Briley), 868
The Traitors (Oppenheim), 281
Traitors' Gate, 5596
Tramp in Armour, 4851
Trance, 3102
Trans-Siberian Express, 442

Transmission Error, 3080

A Trap for Fools, 4249

Trapdoor, 4069

Trapp's War, 1003

Trapspider, 2068

The Travelling Executioners, 3970

Travelling Horseman, 3332

Travels with Dubinsky and Clive, 2352

Travels with My Aunt, 2300

Traverse of the Gods, 3130

Treacherous Road, 4699

Treachery in Trieste, 2551

The Treason Line, 4210

Treasure, 1503

Treasury Alarm, 1538

Tree Frog, 5750

Tremor of Intent, 5670

Trespass, 3032

Trevayne, 3353

Triad, 3103

The Triad Imperative, 3739

Trial by Fire, 1400

Trial by Terror, 2037

The Trial of Adolph Hitler, 5427

Trieste, 3422

The Trikon Deception, 822

The Trinity Factor, 2382

Trip Trap, 4489

Triple "O" Seven, 2840

Triple, 1916

Triple Cross, 1159

Triple Mirror, 2838

Tripletrap, 2396

The Tripoli Documents, 2923

The Triton Ultimatum, 1601

The Triumph of Bacchus, 5004

The Triumph of the Scarlet Pimpernel, 293

Troika (Backus), 623

Troika (Egleton), 1799

Troika (Gurr), 2353

Troika (Rumbold-Gibbs), 4717

Trojan Horses, 1815

Trophy, 4829

Trotsky's Run, 2704

Trouble in Burma, 3757

Trouble in Tokyo Bay, 870

Trouble Is My Name, 3227

Troubled Midnight, 2351

Troubleshooter (Dodge), 1669

Troubleshooter (Weber), 5548

The True Deceivers, 4630

True Lies, 4639

Truman's Spy, 2799

The Truth about Peter Harley, 3831

Truth Game, 2779

Try Anything Once, 4250

Tucker's Last Stand, 916

The Tuesday Man, 1511

The Tunnel, 986

Tunnel from Calais, 1661

Tunnel War, 4399

The Turing Option, 2499

The Turkish Bloodbath, 1160

A Turn of Traitors, 2468

The Turncoat, 1161

The Twelve Disguises, 4121

Twelve Trains to Babylon, 1306

The Twentieth Day of January, 493

The Twenty-Fourth Level, 737

The Twenty-Third Web, 2620

Twilight at Mac's Place, 5271

A Twist of Sand, 2850

The Twisted Tree, 2469

The Twisted Wire, 3104

Two After Malic, 851

Two Die in Singapore, 4964

Two Hours to Darkness, 5367

Two If by Sea, 5696

Two Men Missing, 1452

The Two O'Clock Sun, 995

Two Sets to Murder, 858
Two Tickets for Tangier, 3758
The Two Undertakers, 310
The Tyneside Ultimatum, 2197
Typhoon, 2891
Typhoon Ray, 1175
The Typhoon Shipments, 3029

U.S.S.A., 3651
U700, 1905
The Ugly American, 3169
The Ullman Code, 3744
The Ultimate Code, 1162
Ultimate Issue, 3719
*The Ultimate Weapon: From the
    Log of the U.S.S. Devilfish*,
    2260
Ultimatum (Bonnecarrère), 811
Ultimatum (Trew), 5368
Ultimatum: PU 94, 1509
Unbecoming Habits, 2533
The Unbegotten, 1432
Uncle Misha's Partisans, 5178
Uncle Target, 3362
The Uncommitted Man, 4324
Under Siege, 1325
Under the Freeze, 696
Under the Ice, 2583
Under Western Eyes, 42
*Undercover: Memoirs of an
    American Secret Agent*, 2741
The Underground, 5320
The Underground City, 2723
The Underground Connection,
    4024
Underhandover, 3902
Understrike, 2105
The Undertaker, 4448
Undertow, 3423
The Unexpected Mrs. Pollifax,
    949

The Unexplored Man, 5487
Unfriendly Persuasion, 653
The Unicorn Girl, 3081
The Unicorn Group, 794
The Unicorn Piece, 3175
The Unicorn Solution, 3176
Unknown Agent, 546
The Unknown Mission, 1457
The Unknown Soldier, 672
The Unprofessional Spy, 1829
The Unquiet Sleep, 1256
*The Unseen Hand: Adventures of
    a Diplomatic Free-Lance*, 216
Unsung Road, 4700
The Us or Them War, 2126
Utmost Good Faith, 4933

"V" for Vengeance, 5598
V-3, 3800
The Valhalla Exchange, 4182
The Valhalla Testament, 3124
The Valkyrie Encounter, 3217
The Valley of Fear, 1442
Valley of the Assassins, 3400
The Valley of the Fox, 2650
Valley of the Shadow, 3189
The Van Dreisen Affair, 4651
The Van Langeren Girl, 1328
Vanished, 3033
The Vanished Messenger, 257
The Vanishers, 2430
Vanishing Point, 1031
Variant, 1816
Variation on a Theme, 1865
Vatican Kill, 4512
The Vatican Target, 4853
The Vatican Vendetta, 1163
Vedrovo, 2349
Vendetta (Lambert), 3105
Vendetta (Shagan), 4931
The Venerable Bead, 1302

The Venetian Affair, 3545

Venetian Blind, 1257

Vengeance 10, 4400

The Vengeance of the Tau, 3125

The Venus Probe, 2742

The Venus Venture, 5792

Venus with Pistol, 3364

A Very Big Bang, 3452

A Very British Coup, 3922

A Very Private Affair, 917

A Very Private War, 1269

A Very Quiet Place, 5720

Very Special Agent, 3944

The Vesper Service Murders, 211

Vessels May Carry Explosives,
    4718

The Vets, 3166

Vice Isn't Private, 1272

Vicious Circles, 5172

The Victim, 979

Victoria, 2029

Vienna Blood, 4196

The Vienna Elephant, 3164

A View from the Square, 5340

The Viking Process, 2513

The Villa Mimosa, 5314

Villiger, 4830

Violence in Velvet, 613

Violence Is My Business, 3228

Viper Three, 5470

The Viper's Game, 2661

Virus, 2488

Visa to Limbo, 1258

Viva McHugh, 1895

The Vivero Letter, 638

Vixen 03, 1498

Vodka on Ice, 3616

Voice of Armageddon, 3269

The Voiceless Ones, 1433

Voices on the Wind, 5524

The Volcanoes of San Domingo,
    5364

Volunteers for Danger, 752

The Von Kessel Dossier, 3183

Von Ryan's Express, 5575

Von Ryan's Return, 5576

Voodoo, Ltd, 5276

The Voodoo Murders, 614

Vortex (Bond), 805

Vortex (Land), 3119

Vote against Poison, 4967

Vote to Kill, 2774

Vote X for Treason, 1273

Voyage of the Devilfish, 1651

The Voyage Unplanned, 5781

The Vulcan Disaster, 1164

Vulcan Rising, 433

Vulcan's Hammer, 1506

Vulture in the Sun, 762

W.I.L. One to Curtis, 1825

Waiting for Orders, 517

The Waiting Game, 4051

Waldorf, 2216

Walk at a Steady Pace, 1866

A Walk at Night, 5383

Walk Softly, Men Praying, 5773

The Walk-in, 4878

Walker of the Secret Service, 312

Wanted by the Gestapo, 4343

Wanted: Dead Men, 1482

The Wanton Princess, 5610

War From the Clouds, 1165

War Game, 4415

The War in 2020, 4280

War of the Raven, 2927

The War of the Running Fox,
    3131

War Ship, 5205

War Story (McGill), 3521

War Story (Robinson), 4543

The War Terror, 315

War Toys, 2699

War without Frontiers, 2780
War*Moon, 1329
The Warbirds, 2592
Warday, 5165
'Ware Danger, 1453
WarGames, 764
The Warlock, 5387
Warlords, 3132
The Warm and Golden War, 3333
Warmaster, 3453
The Warrior, 4736
Warrior's Way, 963
Warriors, 5315
The Warriors of God, 1226
Wars and Winters, 1340
The Warsaw Document, 5358
Warship, 3578
Washington Legation Murders,
    201
Waste Lands, 73
Watch Across the Channel, 3554
Watch It, Dr. Adrian, 3287
The Watch on the Bridge, 2148
Watch on the Wall, 935
The Watchdogs of Abaddon, 3798
Watcher in the Shadows, 2690
Watching the Detectives, 4490
Watchman, 4470
Water Hole, 4831
Water on the Brain, 173
*The Watering Place of Good
    Peace*, 2851
Waterman, 2666
A Way Back, 3853
The Way of the Scarlet Pimpernel,
    294
The Way to Dusty Death, 3607
Way to Santiago, 996
*We Are Holding the President
    Hostage*, 443
We've Been Waiting for You,
    5296

Weapon, 3762
The Weapon of Night, 1166
Weatherhawk, 1486
The Web, 5187
Web of Spies, 1167
A Week of Love, 3158
Welcome Home, Jaime, 3320
Werewolf, 3486
Werewolf Trace, 2106
Westminster One, 5667
Wet Work, 910
What's Past Is Prologue, 3556
Whatsoever Things Are True,
    4719
The Wheel Spins, 363
When and If, 4514
When Duty Calls, 2584
When Eight Bells Toll, 3608
When I Grow Rich, 1891
The Whenabouts of Burr, 3082
Where Agents Fear to Tread, 3254
Where All the Girls Are Sweeter,
    494
Where Eagles Dare, 3609
Where Is the Withered Man, 1455
Where No Flags Fly, 619
Where's Your ORGY?, 2225
The Whiff of Money, 4495
While Still We Live, 3546
The Whip Hand, 1029
Whiskey Galore, 3557
Whisper Her Name, 2743
The Whisper of the Axe, 1303
Whisper of Treason, 792
Whispers in the Dark, 5497
The Whistle Blower, 2386
The White Continent, 4386
White Crow, 3394
White Eagles Over Serbia, 1746
White Flower, 4643
White for Danger, 5127

White Horse to Banbury Cross, 3291

The White House Mess, 911

The White House Pantry Murder, 4561

The White Lie Assignment, 1696

White Light, 568

The White Mandarin, 4961

The White Mouse, 829

White Nights, Red Dawn, 4034

The White Tiger, 3947

The White Tuareg, 119

The White Witch of the South Seas, 5597

Whitehall Sanction, 2167

Whiteout!, 899

Who Dare to Live, 3334

Who Killed Cock Robin?, 1721

Who Says a Corpse Has to Be Dull, 5439

Who Was the Jester?, 1446

Who'll Buy My Evil, 3387

Who's on First, 918

The Whole Truth, 1803

Whoo?, 2714

The Whore-Mother, 2600

The Widow's War, 5652

The Widow-Makers, 784

The Wilby Conspiracy, 1697

The Wild Blue, 827

Wild Card, 2521

Wild Country, 2816

The Wild Geese, 1037

A Wild Justice (Gandley), 2069

A Wild Justice (Thompson), 5287

Wild Midnight Falls, 1483

Wildcat, 5244

The Wildcatter, 3790

Wilde Alliance, 3579

The Wilderness Is Yours, 5310

A Wilderness of Mirrors, 487

Win, Lose or Die, 2107

The Wind Chill Factor, 2177

Wind of Destiny, 4018

The Windchime Legacy, 3939

Windfall, 635

The Winding Stair, 196

Wingman, 3673

Wings of Peace, 1434

Winter Fire, 5370

Winter Hawk, 5249

Winter in the Heart, 4390

Winter in Wartime, 5222

Winter Kills, 1304

Winter of the Wolves, 2007

Winter Palace, 2880

The Winter Spy, 2572

Winter: A Novel of a Berlin Family, 1597

The Wire, 2231

The Wishful Think, 3989

Witch Hunt, 4720

With Extreme Prejudice, 1548

With Intent to Deceive, 3710

With My Knives I Know I'm Good, 4483

The Withered Man, 1456

Without a Trace, 708

Without Armor, 120

Without Honor, 2383

Without Lawful Authority, 3711

Without Orders, 3312

Without Remorse, 1234

The Witness, 980

Wolf Run, 4832

Wolf Trap, 4033

Wolf Winter, 1953

The Wolf's Hour, 3403

Wolfsbane, 5250

The Wolves Come Down from the Mountain, 5166

The Woman Ayisha, 109

A Woman Called Scylla, 2354

Woman Hunt (Ryck), 4730

Woman Hunt (Wilcox), 5641
A Woman of Valor, 5323
*The Woman with the Portuguese
    Basket*, 5760
The Woodchuck Hunt, 707
The Wooden Wolf, 2958
The Word of a Gentleman, 4023
Word of Honor, 1611
World Champion, 3890
The World to Win, 4999
World War III, 3017
The World's Great Snare, 282
The World's Great Spy Stories,
    5115
The Wotan Warhead, 1906
Wrath of Eagles, 2609
*The Wrath of Fu Manchu and
    Other Stories*, 5513
The Wrath of God, 4183
Wrath of the Lion, 4184
The Wrath to Come, 258
A Wreath of Camellias, 3668
The Wrecking Crew, 2431
The Wrong Man, 1860
Wyatt and the Moresby Legacy,
    2169
Wyatt's Hurricane, 636
The Xanadu Talisman, 4065

XPD, 1598
The XYY Man, 2049

The Yang Meridian, 3159
A Year as a Lion, 4551
The Year of the Fire Monkey,
    3923
Year of the Golden Ape, 4844
The Year of the Rat, 5798
The Year of the Rooster, 4982
Year of the Tiger, 4185

The Yellow Arrow Murders, 212
The Yellow Crayon, 259
The Yellow Dove, 89
Yellow Rain, 5084
Yellowfish, 2952
The Yermakov Transfer, 3091
Yesterday Walkers, 4701
Yesterday's Enemy, 1259
Yesterday's Gone, 1470
Yesterday's Spy, 1599
*You Can't Do Business with
    Murder*, 5438
You Have Yourself a Deal, 4494
You Only Live Twice, 1890
*You Only Live Until You Die:
    The Last Adventure of Oy-Oy-
    7 Israel Bond*, 5554
You Want to Die, Johnny?, 5774
Young Men May Die, 5384
Your Day in the Barrel, 2022
Your Deal, My Lovely, 1211
Your Money and Your Wife, 4268
Your Royal Hostage, 1960
Yukiko, 2495

The Z Document, 1168
Z for Zaborra, 5761
The Z Warning, 4098
The Z-Papers, 4981
The Zaharoff Commission, 2904
The Zakhov Mission, 2347
Zanzibar Intrigue, 3759
The Zebra Network, 2374
The Zeppelin's Passenger, 260
Zero, 5415
Zero Coupon, 1823
The Zero Factor, 2867
Zero Gravity: A Novel, 3324
Zero Minus Nine, 5307
Zero Time, 528
The Zhukov Briefing, 5369

Ziggurat, 2944

Zigzag, 2801

The Zilov Bombs, 691

The Zinzin Road, 3034

Zion Road, 4702

Zita: A Do-It-Yourself Romance,
     3432

Zlatnata Zhena, 2350

The Zolta Configuration, 4439

Zone of Violence, 1737

Zoo Gang, 2038

Zurich/AZ 900, 3313

The Zurich Numbers, 2259

About the Authors

MYRON J. SMITH, JR., is a Library Director and Professor of History at Tusculum College as well as a longtime bibliographer in numerous subject areas.

TERRY WHITE is an Assistant Professor of English at Kent State University, Ashtabula Campus, and a scholar of modern fiction.